Jordan
An Archaeological Reader

Jordan
An Archaeological Reader

edited by

Russell B. Adams

equinox

LONDON   OAKVILLE

Published by

Equinox Pubishing Ltd., Unit 6, The Village, 101 Amies St., London SW11 2JW

DBBC, 28 Main Street, Oakville, CT 06779

www.equinoxpub.com

First published 2008

A catalogue record for this book is available from the British Library.

Library of Congress Cataloguing in Publication Data

Jordan: an archaeological reader / edited by Russell B. Adams.
  p. cm.
  Includes bibliographical references and index.
  ISBN-13: 978-1-84553-037-2 (pbk.)
  ISBN-10: 1-84553-037-3 (pbk.)
1. Jordan—Antiquities. 2. Archaeology—Jordan. I. Adams, Russell B., 1957-
  DS153.3.J675 2005
  933—dc22
                    2005026253

ISBN-10 (Paperback) 1845530373
ISBN-13 (Paperback) 9781845530372

Chapter site maps produced by Don Shewan, City Cartographic.
Typeset and edited by Queenston Publishing, Hamilton, Canada
Printed and bound in Great Britain by Antony Rowe Ltd.

In Memory of Emile Massadeh

Contents

List of Figures

List of Tables

Contributors

Russell Adams specializes in the archaeology of the Ancient Near East and has research interests in the origin and development of early complex societies; the impact of innovation and technological change upon the emergence of these societies; and the interdisciplinary analysis of archaeological ceramics. His PhD research pioneered investigation of Early Bronze Age copper producing communities of southern Jordan, which is also the focus of his ongoing research. The author of numerous contributions to books and journals, he is currently a research associate in the Department of Anthropology at McMaster University.

Phillip Macumber has a PhD in hydrogeology with strong research interests in geohydrology and geomorphology focusing on the relationship between man and the environment—salinity, lakes, wetlands etc. He has been involved with Australian prehistory in the study of several Pleistocene archaeological lake and swamp sites. He worked for several decades in Jordan with the Department Archaeology of Sydney University locating and describing Palaeolithic sites mostly at Tabaqat Fahl. He has also worked extensively in Oman, where he lived for seven years, working on groundwater resource assessment. He is an honorary fellow in Earth Sciences at Melbourne University, Australia.

Deborah I. Olszewski specializes in Middle Eastern and North African Upper Paleolithic and Epipaleolithic. She has worked extensively in Jordan, Egypt, and Morocco, and wrote her PhD on Abu Hurayra, Syria. Her interests center on interpretation of stone tool assemblages, adaptations of prehistoric hunter-gatherers, and the origins of agriculture. She is a Senior Research Scientist at Penn Museum and Adjunct Associate Professor in the Department of Anthropology at the University of Pennsylvania.

Gary Rollefson has conducted research in the Near East for more than 35 years, 30 of them investigating prehistoric archaeology in Jordan. His excavations have centered on Lower and Middle Paleolithic as well as a long-term project at Neolithic Ayn Ghazal. Recently he has turned his attention to the ritual aspects of pastoral nomads in the Wadi Ramm area and in the Badiyat ash-Sham east of Azraq. He has also recently begun a long term project in southern Saudi Arabia. Rollefson is Professor of Anthropology at Whitman College.

Stephen Bourke has research interests which span the Neolithic through Iron Ages, and centre on Levantine pre-state societies, the rise of complex urban civilization, trade and international relations, religion and cult practice, ceramic analysis and bioarchaeology. After a PhD on the Second Millennium BC materials from ancient Qadesh on the Orontes in Syria, he led four seasons of renewed fieldwork at Tulaylat Ghassul in Jordan, and now directs excavations at multi-period Pella in Jordan. Stephen has written or contributed to more than 70 archaeological publications, and is currently a Research Associate in Archaeology at the University of Sydney.

Graham Philip has research interests in landscape archaeology, artefact studies, and the nature of early complex societies, themes explored in the context of the later Prehistory and Bronze Ages of the Middle East. He has published two monographs, and edits the journal *Levant*. He directs a joint Syrian-British landscape project in the Orontes Valley near Homs, and is co-investigator on *The Fragile Crescent Project*, a comparative analysis of Bronze Age settlement data from the "Fertile Crescent". He is Professor of Archaeology at Durham University.

Gaetano Palumbo received his PhD from the Università di Roma "La Sapienza" and is author of *The Early Bronze Age IV in the Southern Levant: Settlement Patterns, Economy, and Material Culture of a "Dark Age"* (1991). He has previously held positions at the Getty Conservation Institute (USA), the Institute of Archaeology, University College London (UK), and the American Center for Oriental Research (Jordan). Palumbo is currently Director of archaeological conservation: Africa, Europe, the Middle East and Central Asia at the World Monuments Fund.

Steven Falconer specializes in the prehistory and history of Southwestern Asia and the Mediterranean Basin, focusing on the growth and dissolution of complex societies. His current research concentrates on villages and household economies in early urbanized societies and the impacts of agrarian systems on ancient landscapes. Falconer has served as a Mellon Postdoctoral Fellow at New York University, Research Fellow at La Trobe University (Melbourne) and the Australia National University (Canberra) and Visiting Scholar at the Cyprus American Archaeological Research Institute (Nicosia). He has directed multidisciplinary research projects at a series of Bronze Age villages in Jordan and is currently involved in new field research on Bronze Age village life on Cyprus.

John Strange studied theology and later Near Eastern Archaeology; his doctoral dissertation was on the Caphtor/Keftiu problem. He has participated in excavations in Israel and Jordan and was director of the excavations at Tall Fukhar, Jordan. He is currently preparing the final report on the Tall Fukhar excavations. Other research interests include the archaeology and history of Jerusalem, which is the subject of a short book published in 2007. A contributor of numerous papers to books and journals, he plans to write a short history of the Middle East.

Larry Herr has research interests in the stratigraphy and pottery of Ancient Jordan during the Bronze and Iron Ages, as well as the scripts of Iron Age inscriptions. His PhD research under Frank Cross examined the national scripts of Iron Age inscribed seals from the southern Levant. The author of numerous contributions to books and journals, he is currently Professor of Religious Studies at Canadian University College in Lacombe, Alberta.

Mohammed Najjar is formerly the Director of Excavations for the Department of Antiquities of Jordan. He received his BA and PhD from the Institute of Archaeology, Russian Academy of Sciences, Moscow. One of the most prolific archeologists working in Jordan, Mohammed Najjar has worked with numerous international research teams, in virtually all periods and regions of the country.

Piotr Bienkowski is Deputy Director of Manchester Museum, and Professor of Archaeology and Museology at the University of Manchester. He has directed excavations in Jordan and published widely, particularly on the Iron Age of southern Jordan. His research interests are the Iron Age of the southern Levant, phenomenological approaches to landscape archaeology, and the ethics of the excavation, retention and treatment of human remains in archaeology and museums.

Stephan G. Schmid is professor of classical archaeology at the Humboldt-Universität zu Berlin (Germany). Awarded his PhD from Basel University (Switzerland) and a Habilitaton from Paris I–Sorbonne (France), he has previously held a professorship at the University Paul Valéry–Montpellier 3 (France) and was scientific secretary of the Swiss School of Archaeology in Greece. His research interests focus on the art and archaeology of the eastern Mediterranean in Hellenistic and Roman times, and he directs the International Wadi Farasa Project (www.auac.ch/iwfp) at Petra, exploring one of the most prominent funerary complexes of the Nabataean aristocracy.

Philip Freeman is lecturer in Roman archaeology in the School of Archaeology, Classics and Egyptology at the University of Liverpool. He has surveyed and excavated extensively in Britain, Jordan, Turkey and Crimea, mainly on Roman military sites. His original research has focused on the process of annexation of provinces to the Roman Empire but has more recently moved to the analysis of the phenomenon known as the 'romanization' of the western provinces of the Roman Empire. Most recently this has been complimented by his publications on the historiography of the study of Roman Britain.

Pamela Watson has worked extensively as an historical archaeologist and project director in Australia and the Middle East. A specialist in Roman and Byzantine archaeology in the Levant, she was Assistant Director of the British Institute at Amman for Archaeology and History (Jordan), where she was involved in field projects as well as management, communication, strategic planning and policy in heritage areas.

Donald Whitcomb is an archaeologist at the Oriental Institute of the University of Chicago specialized in Islamic Archaeology. His research began in Iran, with the sites of Istakhr and Qasr-i Abu Nasr. He has directed excavations at Quseir al-Qadim, on the Egyptian coast of the Red Sea, on the medieval mound at Luxor, and the port of Aqaba in Jordan. Most recently he has begun excavations at Hadir Qinnasrin, near Aleppo. He is interested in the origins of the Islamic city and, by extension, urban planning and social organization. More generally he works toward the development of the field of Islamic Archaeology.

Alan Walmsley is an archaeologist whose research focus is the East Mediterranean during the first millennium AD, with a particular emphasis upon social and economic conditions in Syria-Palestine. He began his career in New Zealand (MA Hons. University of Auckland), and received his PhD in 1988 from the University of Sydney where his research focused upon the urban history of early Islamic Syria-Palestine. He is currently Associate Professor of Islamic Archaeology and Art at the University of Copenhagen. He has worked in the Middle East for over 30 years, directing four field projects including the Danish-Jordanian Islamic Jarash Project. Walmsley has organized many conferences and workshops, presented papers at numerous meetings, lectured widely, and published over 60 titles including four books.

Alison McQuitty has research interests centred on the investigation of the rural settlement of Jordan from the sixth century A.D. onwards, particularly the later periods. Her fieldwork projects have included archaeological excavation, ethnographic survey and the recording of vernacular architecture. She is also involved in heritage management: recent projects have included the refurbishment of the Salt Archaeological Museum, a brochure for the King's Highway (Ministry of Tourism) and contribution to the Umm Qays Management Plan. She currently works for the Association of Heritage Interpretation (UK) and is Research Associate at the Centre of Tourism and Culture Change, Leeds Metropolitan University (UK).

Preface and Acknowledgements

For those scholars engaged in teaching Levantine archaeology, the lack of a single volume dedicated to the rich archaeological heritage of Jordan has been a major lacuna. For many years students of the archaeology of Israel have been able to choose amongst several volumes which provide good overviews of the archaeology of Israel. Three of these in particular standout: A. Mazar's *The Archaeology of the Land of the Bible 10,000–586 BCE* (Doubleday, 1990); A. Ben Tor (ed.) *The Archaeology of Ancient Israel* (Open University of Israel, 1992); and T.E. Levy (ed.) *The Archaeology of Society in the Holy Land* (Leicester University Press, 1995). Although these volumes vary widely in terms of the periods reviewed and occasionally in the quality of some individual summaries, they each provide a useful synopsis of the state of knowledge in the archaeology of Israel suitable for students and non-specialists. More recently these volumes have been joined by a very fine volume by M.M.G. Akkermans and G. Schwartz on *The Archaeology of Syria* (Cambridge University Press, 2003). Until now, there has been no similar overview or introduction to archaeology in Jordan available as a single and affordable volume.

Realizing that there was a rather obvious void in the coverage of the archaeology of the Levant, I first raised the idea of such a volume in 1994 with Jean Allen, the Managing Director of Sheffield Academic Press (SAP). At that time I was writing my PhD at Sheffield University and had been involved in archaeological research in Jordan for some years but also had a foot in the world of publishing. After lengthy discussion, we agreed to proceed with the production of a single volume overview of archaeology in Jordan, to which we would invite leading scholars to contribute overviews of chronological periods as well as shorter topical summaries (pottery technology, archaeological survey, etc.). After some rather lengthy delays—almost inevitable in such a commissioned book—this volume was published in 2001 as *The Archaeology of Jordan*. However, the book which developed from my early discussions with Jean Allen was not at all what I had first envisaged. In the process of producing the book, I had gained two editorial colleagues and the volume had evolved into a very expensive 700 page hardback book with limited distribution. The end result was a book which almost completely defeated my original purpose, making it neither reasonably priced nor widely available. To make matters worse, within a few years the volume was no longer in print.

Undeterred, in 2004 I set out again to see if it might be possible to produce a volume on Jordanian archaeology of both high quality and one which students and non-specialists alike might actually be able to afford. By this time Sheffield Academic Press had been taken over by Continuum Books, which shortly thereafter decided to stop publishing archaeology altogether. Quite by chance, I spoke with Janet Joyce, a former director at Continuum Books who was in the process of creating Equinox Publishing, and after a brief discussion Janet expressed her interest in publishing this overview of archaeology in Jordan. Without Janet's vision and interest in archaeology this book would never have been published.

This volume is composed of fifteen summaries of chronological periods which range from the Palaeolithic through to the Ottoman, and thus provides a full chronological overview of the entirety of the archaeology of Jordan. These summaries are introduced by a brief history of the development of archaeology in Jordan as well as by an overview of the evolving landscape and environment of the country. The resulting book is therefore—as much as is possible—an up-to-date overview of the current state of knowledge of the archaeology of Jordan.

The contributions to this volume have been updated from the period summaries originally published in *The Archaeology of Jordan*. The decision not to re-publish the shorter topical summaries from that volume, should in no way be construed as a reflection on either the importance of the subjects covered or the quality of the contributions. The redaction to the current coverage was simply necessary to reduce the size of the volume in order to provide an affordable single volume overview of archaeology in Jordan—which had been my intension from the beginning.

I would like to acknowledge Continuum Books/T&T Clark International for very kindly agreeing to revert the publishing rights to *The Archaeology of Jordan* to the individual authors. I am grateful to Don Shewan at City Cartographic for producing the splendid site maps for each chapter, which as usual, are to a very high standard. My sincere thanks to all of the contributors for agreeing to be part of this volume. In a number of cases contributors have not only revised but completely re-written or vastly expanded their summaries, which was a huge imposition on their academic schedules, and I thank them for doing so. Finally, I would like to thank the contributors for enduring the rather slow progress made on this volume since its inception, which has been unavoidable as a result of the editor's itinerate academic wanderings.

Russell Adams
Hamilton, Canada
April 2008

1. Archaeology in Jordan: A Brief History

Russell B. Adams

The area known today as Jordan (formerly Transjordan) lies between Palestine (Cisjordan or modern Israel and the Palestinian Territories) and Mesopotamia, and is intimately connected to these surrounding regions of ancient Western Asia, in both geography and history. This survey of the development of archaeology in Jordan will outline the major phases of exploration in this region and highlight briefly some of the important developments in archaeology in Jordan.

The Earliest Phase of Exploration (1805–1918)

> Who that has ever travelled in Palestine has not longed to cross the Jordan-valley to those mysterious hills which close ever eastward view with their long horizontal outline, their overshadowing height, their deep purple shade?

With these words from his 1856 travel log, Arthur Stanley (1856), the Dean of Westminster summed up the relationship between Palestine and Transjordan for the earliest explorers of the Levant. At the time of his visit Transjordan was a place less travelled, largely unknown, and poorly explored, yet it remained of great interest largely due to the connections between the two regions from both historical and biblical accounts. By the mid-nineteenth century, interest in Transjordan was growing, and discoveries in both Palestine (Dever 2001a, 2001b); and Mesopotamia (Potts 2001) were leading scholars to explore the history of the region in the contexts of both the Biblical and classical texts.

Unlike Cisjordan or Palestine however, the exploration of Transjordan started somewhat late and received only the occasional interest of scholars and travellers during the earliest part of the nineteenth century. The earliest explorations in Transjordan were largely by antiquarians and biblical scholars intent upon recording sites of historical or biblical interest. Explorers such as the German, Ulrich Jasper Seetzen, who visited between 1805 and 1807, and the Swiss explorer Johann Ludwig Burckhardt, who visited between 1810 and 1812, were amongst the first to record some the great sites of classical antiquity in Transjordan. Seetzen visited the sites of Jarash (Gerasa) and Amman (Philadelphia), while Burckhardt "rediscovered" Petra. Others followed, including brief visits by the Biblical scholar Edward Robinson and his missionary travelling companion Eli Smith, who are considered to be the fathers of historical geography in the Levant.

Their extensive work in Palestine (1837–38, 1851–52) identified many ancient sites and was published as *Biblical Researches in Palestine, Mount Sinai and Arabia Petrea* (1841) and *Biblical Researches in Palestine and Adjacent Regions* (1853). Although Robinson and Smith made brief visits to Petra and Pella, their important work in Palestine was unfortunately not duplicated on the same scale east of the Jordan River.

In 1847 Lt. William Francis Lynch received orders from the U.S. Department of the Navy to lead an expedition to complete a survey and exploration of the Dead Sea. In orders to Lynch, the Secretary of the Navy gives the objectives of the expedition "to promote the cause of Science, and advance the character of the Naval Service" (Mason 1847), making this perhaps the first largely "scientific" exploration in the Levant. In reality commercial concerns were perhaps just as important, as the Navy was interested in the possibility of opening up an inland water route for trade. Lynch and his small team used three boats to sail down the Jordan River from its source to the Dead Sea, where they spent three weeks sketching, collecting specimens, taking soundings of the Dead Sea and looking for biblical evidence. In 1852, Lynch's report entitled, *The Official Report of the US Expedition to Explore the Dead Sea and River Jordan* was published by the U.S. Navy (see also Rook 1998).

One of the reasons that comparatively little exploration was undertaken in Transjordan at this time, was due to the political instability of the region. Although under Ottoman Turkish rule, this meant very little outside the more densely populated areas. The region was populated with a combination of small settled villages and semi-nomadic Bedouin tribes with only a few larger towns. The activities of the Bedouin tribes, who were occasionally aggressive towards both villages and travellers made exploration difficult and often unpredictable and dangerous. In general the visits of these early explorers and travellers to Transjordan were therefore sporadic, and usually directed to specific known sites, since their primary interest remained the "Holy Land" (Cisjordan or Palestine), its historical geography and the classical sites of late antiquity.

By the mid-nineteenth century Ottoman control of Transjordan began to increase with eventual control of various regions with governors appointed at Irbid to oversee the district of Ajlun (1851) and at Salt to oversee the central district of Balqa (1868). One of the primary reasons for this increasing control of Transjordan by the

Ottoman Empire was due to the need to control the Haj pilgrimage route between Damascus and the Hijaz. One of the outcomes of this control was increased exploration of the region by western scholars.

There was considerable academic interest in the Levant developing in the latter half of the nineteenth century. Following the founding of the Palestine Exploration Fund in 1865, a survey of western Palestine was undertaken between 1872–1878, under the direction of Lt. Claude R. Condor and assisted by Horatio H. Kitchener. The work by Condor and Kitchener west of the Jordan produced the first modern maps of the Levant and were published in 1884 as *The Survey of Western Palestine*. An attempt to continue this work east of the Jordan in the Hauran and Golan in 1881 was halted after only a 1000 square kms had been surveyed due to political difficultues between the English and Turkish governments.

In 1870, The American Palestine Exploration Society was formed as a privately funded society for archaeological and geographic exploration of the Holy Land. Its first expedition in 1873, led by E.Z. Steever was only moderately successful as they were only able to survey a small area of the Moab region of Transjordan, south of Hisban. In 1874, however, the American Palestine Exploration Society appointed Selah Merrill a clergyman and archaeologist to lead its second expedition. During three excursions through Palestine and Transjordan Merrill collected numerous archaeological, ethnological and geographical specimens. He also produced maps of ancient sites in Ammon and Moab, and published the results in *East of the Jordan* in 1881. Unfortunately the American Palestine Exploration Society was disbanded in 1884 largely due to infighting and lack of funding.

Following the abrupt end to Condor's explorations for the Palestine Exploration Fund in Transjordan, archaeological survey there were continued by the American born engineer Gottlieb Schumacher. Schumacher became interested in the ancient sites of the region while conducting a geographic survey of the Golan in preparation to build a railway line from Damascus to Haifa. Schumachers' pioneering work in the region, undertaken independently of a sponsoring organization, was prolific. In addition to drawing the map of Transjordan (in 10 sheets), he also published a number of monographs on the archaeology of the region in quick succession which include: *Across the Jordan: Being an Exlploration and Survey of Part of the Hauran and Jaulan* (1886); *The Jaulan* (1888); *Pella* (1888); *Abila of the Decapolis* (1889); and *Northern 'Ajlun, "within the Decapolis"* (1890).

Schumacher also published numerous articles in the journal of the newly formed (1877) Der Deutsche Verein zur Erforschung Pälestinas (German Society for the Exploration of Palestine). At this time numerous other foreign societies were also being formed in the region, including the French École Biblique et Archéologique

(1892) and the American Schools of Oriental Research (1900). American Schools of Oriental Research was the successor to the American Palestine Exploration Soceity, but instead of being privately funded, it was founded as a consortiuum of institutions of higher education, each of which paid an annual subscription. The expansion of these new institutes paralleled the competition between colonial powers for a stake in the exploration of the Levant and wider Near East.

The closing years of the nineteenth and early twentieth centuries saw an expansion of expeditions sponsored by these national schools. In Transjordan the École Biblique sponsored the expeditions of Rudolf Ernst Brünnow and Alfred von Domaszewski which documented the Nabataean and Roman ruins of Central Moab, the Roman road system and associated fortifications, as well as the rock-cut tombs of Petra (1904–9). Following his success at Tell Hesi, the American Frederick Jones Bliss continued the work of the Palestine Exploration Fund excavating at Jerusalem from 1894–1897. While there Bliss made a brief exploratory trip to explore Central Transjordan where he was able to chart the upper branches of the Wadi Mujib (Bliss 1895).

Representatives of National schools were not the only active explorers of the region. Independent travelers also made important contributions to the exploration of Transjordan. The independent Czech scholar Alois Musil made several excursions in the region during the years 1896–1902. One of his key discoveries was the Umayyad site of Qusayr Amra and its famous frescoes in 1898. Musil was not just an explorer but an early ethnographer and his work *The Manners and Customs of the Rwala Bedouins* (1928) was an important contribution to early anthropology and Oriental Studies. He published the results of his travels in the region as *Arabia Petraea* (1907–8).

The Development of Jordanian Archaeology During the British Mandate (1918–1946)

In 1918, following the First World War, the defeat of the Ottoman Empire and the subsequent Sykes-Picot agreement, a British Mandate was established for the region of Palestine and Transjordan which came under the control of the British Empire. The British authorities established a Department of Antiquities in Palestine in 1920 under John Garstang, and subsequently a Department of Antiquities was established in Amman in 1923 to oversee the region of Transjordan.

As a result of the establishment of British control, archaeologists found the region increasingly accessible (and safe) and during this period established some of the major groundwork for understanding the archaeology and history of the region. Research was not however restricted to British interests, but rather several international schools, including the French, German and American, carried out significant research in the southern Levant during this period.

A great deal of this work was concentrated in Palestine, but some work was carried out at major sites of classical antiquity in Transjordan, including Amman, Gerasa (Jarash), and Petra. At Petra the first systematic excavations were undertaken in 1929 by George Horsfield, the first chief officer (curator) of the Transjordan Department of Antiquities. Horsfield, a student of John Garstang, carried out work on several of the major tombs of Petra, including the Palace tomb, al-Kazneh, the Urn Tomb, and the Tomb of the Roman Soldier. In 1924, Horsfield also initiated the first work at Gerasa (Jarash), where he directed considerable energy to the clearing and reconstruction of several of the major monuments at the site, including the south and north theatres, the propylaeum of the Temple of Artemis and the Nymphaeum. He was later joined in 1928 by an Anglo-American expedition from the British School of Archaeology in Jerusalem and Yale University led by John Crowfoot, and later in 1930 by a team from the American Schools of Oriental Research (ASOR) initially under the direction of Clarence Fisher and later by Nelson Glueck (1933–34). At Amman work on the citadel was carried out by the Italian Archaeological Mission beginning in 1927 and concluding in the 1930s, and from 1936 in other parts of the city by the then Director of the Transjordan Department of Antiquities, Gerald Lancaster Harding. The overall result of these excavations was the revelation of the exceptional state of preservation of many of these sites of classical antiquity, and an attempt to begin to preserve them from both destruction and development threatened by the expanding populations in the region.

Other notable work during this period included the discovery of the site of Tulaylat Ghassul, one of the key sites of the Chalcolithic period in the southern Levant, near the shores of the Dead Sea. Work at this site by Mallon, Koeppel and Neuville of the Pontifical Biblical Institute (PBI) in Jerusalem between 1929–38 revealed, perhaps for the first time, the extent of the richness of the prehistoric archaeology of Jordan.

Last of all, the work of Nelson Glueck during his periods as Director of American Schools of Oriental Research Institute in Jerusalem (1932–33, 1936–40, 1942–47), were to have a lasting impact upon Transjordan. Glueck, a student of W.F. Albright, was one of the pioneers of archaeological survey in Transjordan, and in the period between 1932 and 1947 surveyed more than a thousand sites, including many previously unknown. In particular, Glueck, as a student of Biblical history, focused upon the Biblical kingdoms of Ammon, Moab and Edom. Glueck's extensive survey work included mapping, photography and site collections, and set the precedent for all subsequent archaeological survey work in the region. His four volume report, *Explorations in Eastern Palestine* (1934–51) and *The Other Side of Jordan* (1940) are still consulted extensively by those working in Jordan, and al-

though some errors were made, Glueck's work has proven to be remarkably accurate. Glueck also undertook two excavations in Transjordan, first (1937–38) at Khirbat Tannur a Nabatean temple site in the Wadi Hasa, and later (1938–40) at the site of Tall Khalayfi which he believed to be King Solomon's seaport Ezion Geber. These two periods of the Iron Age and the Nabateans were to be the main focus of Glueck's career, which was inspirational to a generation of archaeologists who followed.

Archaeology in the Hashemite Kingdom of Jordan (1946–67)

During the period from 1946, when the region of Transjordan became an independent Kingdom under the rule of the Hashemites, the area underwent a period of steady growth in development of a national archaeology. The retreat of British sovereignty in the region, did not mean an immediate withdrawl of British interests or support, and G.L. Harding continued on as Director of the now Department of Antiquities of Jordan until 1956. In total Harding served as director of the Department of Antiquities for twenty years (1936–56) and was instrumental in the formation of archaeological policies which helped to form the national school of archaeology in Jordan. In 1951 he founded the *Annual of the Department of Antiquities of Jordan* which reported on the yearly archaeological work in the country, and later he wrote the first major popularisation of the archaeology of Jordan in his volume *The Antiquities of Jordan* (1959).

During this period, and following the partition of Palestine and the formation of the State of Israel (1948), The Department of Antiquities of Jordan found itself also responsible for the archaeology of a portion of Palestine which came to be known as the West Bank. This region included many of the major Biblical sites including Jerusalem, and in this period many of the international schools preferred to continue to work in this region, and major excavations in the former Transjordan were not as frequent as one might expect.

Some of the best known include the excavations of Kathleen Kenyon, who carried out a series of excavations first at Jericho (1952–58) as Director of the British School of Archaeology in Jerusalem (BSAJ), and later in Jerusalem at the "City of David" (Ophel), with a multi-national team under the auspices of the Palestine Exploration Fund (1961–68). American fieldwork (1956–68) under the direction of G.E. Wright at Tall Balatah (ancient Shechem) sponsored by Drew University and McCormick Theological Seminary (also later Harvard University) and affiliated with ASOR was the principal American excavation during this period. The École Biblique et Archéologique Français excavated the site of Tall Farah North (thought to be Biblical Tirzah) under the direction of Roland De Vaux from 1946–1960, and later at Qumran (see below).

Outside of the West Bank and in Jordan proper, excavations began at the site of ancient Dhiban/Dibon, under F. Winnett, W. Reed and D. Tushingham (1950–56), and at Tall Dayr Alla under H.J. Franken, who led a Dutch team from Leiden University (1960–67). The German Evangelical Institute also began work at Umm Qays, the Decapolis city of Gadara in 1966. Other notable work included British (Peter Parr) and American (Philip Hammond) led teams at Petra between 1954 and 1968, as well as renewed work at Tulaylat Ghassul by R. North on behalf of the Pontifical Biblical Institute (1960), and later Basil Hennessey under the auspices of the British School of Archaeology in Jerusalem (1967). American work under ASOR affiliation was also undertaken at Iraq al-Amir (1961–62) and later Bab adh-Dhra (1965–67) under Paul Lapp, then Director of the American School in Jerusalem.

Perhaps the most spectacular archaeological discovery in this period was the finding of the "Dead Sea Scrolls." This group of Biblical and extra-Biblical texts dating to the first and second centuries AD, were discovered by local Bedouin in caves along the north-western shore of the Dead Sea. The finding of these scrolls, led to a series of concentrated excavations of the various caves, and later at Khirbat Qumran under the Jordanian Department of Antiquities, the Palestine Archaeological Museum and The École Biblique et Archéologique Français under the direction of Roland De Vaux (1951, 1953–56). The finds from both the caves and also the nearby site at Qumran (thought to be the complex associated with the writers of many of the scrolls, the Essenes) have been critical to modern Biblical research, allowing a glimpse into the early biblical communities in the region.

In general this period of archaeological research in Jordan, both in the West Bank and in Jordan itself, established a pattern of archaeological fieldwork by "schools" of most of the major western powers, and which produced (to that time) the longest period of uninterrupted and continuous research in the region. The effect of this period are still being felt, with many of the principal researchers (only now retiring) in the field of Levantine archaeology having "cut their teeth" in this period on many of these projects, and who in turn have been instrumental in establishing the study of Levantine Archaeology in many countries. This period also established the practice of the Department of Antiquities of Jordan as the partner of these international schools in the documentation, publication and preservation of the rich archaeological heritage of Jordan.

Archaeology in Jordan 1967 to the present

After Jordan's loss of the West Bank following the Six-Day War in 1967, the focus of Jordanian archaeology was once again focused upon lands east of the Jordan River. Many of the International Schools (British, American, German) set up "temporary" offices in Jordan (Amman) at this time, so as to continue archaeological research but to avoid ex-

cavation in the occupied territories which was in breach of United Nations rules. The American Schools of Oriental Research in Jerusalem was the first to set up a branch office in support of research in Jordan in 1968 and was soon followed by the British. Within a few years the American Center for Oriental Research (ACOR) was founded (1971) and somewhat later the establishment of the British Institute at Amman for Archaeology and History (now the Council for British Research in the Levant) under the direction of Crystal Bennett (1978) formalized the shift from Jerusalem to Amman for British researchers.

The establishment of headquarters in Amman for many of the international schools at this time marks a transition or break in archaeological research and direction in Jordan and in Israel/West Bank. From this period forward, archaeological work in Israel and and Jordan developed along independent lines, with increasingly little contact between scholars working in both countries. This situation was true of both the indigenous archaeologists (Israeli and Jordanian), as well as the international schools. In particular, many of those formally working in Jordan were reluctant to jeopardise this situation by contacts and active research west of the Jordan Rift. In this situation archaeology in Israel developed on an independent trajectory, and along specific national lines (see Dever 2001) in a way which was quite distinctly different from archaeology in Jordan.

Unlike the development of the national school in Israel, which sought its roots in the archaeology of Ancient Israel and Judah and Jewish history in general, archaeology in Jordan was less politicized. The populations in Jordan being largely Bedouin and Palestinain were not particularly interested in developing a history of occupation for the region along the lines of Israeli "Biblical archaeologists," and claimed no distinctly historical links with either the Nabataeans or the Iron Age Kingdoms of Ammon, Moab and Edom. As a result, archaeological research in Jordan has to some degree been more diverse, and one in which a number of specific sub-fields of archaeology were free to develop without the constraints of ideology.

There were still those researchers who were interested in "Biblical Archaeology" and tended towards research in the Bronze and Iron Age, such as the excavations of Cyrstal Bennett in Edom at sites such as Tawilan and the ancient Edomite capital at Busayrah (1968–74, 1980). There were, however, just as many scholars who focused upon the world of Classical and late Antiquity up to and including the Islamic periods. The wealth of extremely well preserved and important sites from these periods in Jordan (often due to lack of continuous occupation at the site in modern times) was no doubt a contributor to this tendency. Sites such as Petra, Jarash, Gadara and Philadelphia (Amman) were an obvious attraction to researchers, but there were also smaller sites which were also of great appeal, such as Umm Jimal a Roman-Byzantine city on the desert fringe (excavated since 1973 by Calvin College) and the Roman Legionary Fort at Lajjun a spectacularly preserved fortress of the Roman *limes* or frontier (excavated by S. Thomas Parker), both of which have contributed to our understanding of life on the fringes of the Roman and Byzantine empires.

Perhaps the least expected direction of archaeological work in Jordan since 1967 has come with the advances of the "New Archaeology" in the 1970s and early 1980s, which saw the expansion of anthropological archaeology in Jordan, and in particular an expansion in research on the earliest prehistory of the region from the Palaeolithic up to the end of the Neolithic period. As rich as Jordan is in its many well preserved sites of Classical Antiquity and the Bronze and Iron Ages, no one could have predicted the wealth of prehistoric sites in Jordan, nor that they would be so spectacularly well preserved. The expansion of a scientific and specific anthropological approach to prehistoric archaeology in Jordan has been one of the most significant advances over the last twenty years. This has also often been undertaken with a distinctly environmental approach which has sought to understand the development of the region in the late Pleistocene and Holocene, the adaptation of early modern humans to the region and the development of Neolithic societies and the transition to settled life and agricultural societies.

Projects which have contributed to this research are numerous, but a few of the key projects are worthy of special mention. These include work of Diana Kirkbride-Helbaek at Bayda and more recently the pioneering work of Andrew Garrard while Assistant and then Director of the British Institute at Amman at sites in the Azraq Basin and at Wadi Jilat (1982–89) which trained a generation of British prehistorians and environmental archaeologists. Also the work of Gary Rollefson and others at the now famous site at Ayn Ghazal, perhaps one of the most spectacular (and largest) Neolithic sites in the Levant, which has produced such spectacular finds including two groups of near life-size anthropomorphic figurines. Still further sites in the vicinity of Petra such as Basta excavated by Hans Nissan, Nans Georg Gebel and Zeidan Kafafi, and in the Black Desert investigated by Alison Betts, have shown the wealth and extent of prehistoric occupation of Jordan in virtually every environmental and geographic zone, from the Mediterranean to the steppe and desert.

Complimentary to the part that excavation has played in revealing the archaeology of Jordan, has been the extensive role of survey in recent years. Extensive surveys have now covered many of the regions of Jordan, including the Black Desert, the Kerak Plateau, the Wadi Hasa, and Wadi Arabah and many, many others. All of these surveys have been instrumental in helping to piece together the many thousands of archaeological sites in Jordan from all periods, which are in turn recorded in JADIS: Jordanian Antiquities Database and Information System—which

is a compiled database of all archaeological sites in Jordan. This cultural resource management tool allows for the preservation and conservation of Jordan's rich cultural heritage.

One of the most significant aspects of contemporary Jordanian archaeology is the diversity of researchers who have taken an interest in the history, archaeology, geography and environment of Jordan. These researchers come from a wide variety of academic disciplines and traditions and from many different countires, only a few of which are represented in this volume. The extensive number of foreign research teams working in Jordan also pays testimony to the generosity of both the government and people of Jordan in hosting and supporting this research.

Last of all, a significant part in the development of archaeology in Jordan has been played by Jordanians in both the Jordan Department of Antiquities and Departments of Archaeology at Jordan's universities. The hospitality and partnership of Jordanians in the ongoing development of archaeology and cultural resource management of archaeological sites in the country has been one of the keys to the vast amount of archaeology undertaken since 1946. In this regard the Department of Antiquities has been fortunate to have had directors of both vision and energy who carried on the work of Horsfield and Harding, including Adnan Hadidi, Ghazi Bisheh, Safwan Tell and Fawaz al-Khrayshah.

The future of archaeology in Jordan is a bright one, with many Jordanians taking an active interest in the history and archaeology of their country, as evidenced by the thriving departments of archaeology at the University of Jordan (Amman), Yarmuk University (Irbid) and Mutah University (near Karak). Many of the graduates of these departments are employed in the Department of Antiquities and other aspects of Jordanian heritage and in partnership with international research are now creating a distinctive Jordanian archaeology.

Bibliography

Adams, R.B.

2001 Jordan. In Tim Murray (ed.), *Encyclopedia of Archaeology: Histories and Discoveries*, 3 vols., 747–754. Santa Barbara, CA: ABC CLIO.

Bliss, Frederick Jones

1895 Narrative of an expedition to Moab and Gilead in March 1895. *Palestine Exploration Fund Quarterly Statement* (July): 203–235. London: Palestine Exploration Fund.

Brünnow, Rudolf Ernst and Alfred von Domaszewski

1904–9 *Die Provincia Arabia auf Grund Zweier in den Jahren 1897 und 1898 unternommenen Reisen und der Berichte früherer Reisender*, 3 vols. Strassburg: Karl J. Trübner.

Dever, W.G.

2001a Syro-Palestinian and Biblical Archaeology. In Tim Murray (ed.), *Encyclopedia of Archaeology: Histories and Discoveries*, 3 vols., 1244–1253. Santa Barbara, CA: ABC CLIO.

2001b Israel. In Tim Murray (ed.), *Encyclopedia of Archaeology: Histories and Discoveries*, 3 vols., 715–721. Santa Barbara, CA: ABC CLIO.

Glueck, Nelson

1934 *Explorations in Eastern Palestine I.* Annual of the American Schools of Oriental Research 14.

1935 *Explorations in Eastern Palestine II.* Annual of the American Schools of Oriental Research 15.

1937 *Explorations in Eastern Palestine III.* Annual of the American Schools of Oriental Research 18-19.

1940 *The Other Side of Jordan. New Haven.* Revised edition 1971. Cambridge, MA: American Schools of Oriental Research.

1951 *Explorations in Eastern Palestine IV.* Annual of the American Schools of Oriental Research 25-28.

Harding, G.L.

1959 *The Antiquities of Jordan.* London: Lutterworth Press.

Lynch, William F.

1852 *The Official Report of the US Expedition to Explore the Dead Sea and River Jordan.* Baltimore, MD: John Murphy and Co.

MacDonald, B., R.B. Adams and P. Bienkowski (eds.)

2001 *The Archaeology of Jordan.* Sheffield: Sheffield Academic Press.

Mason, J.Y.

1847 *Captain William Francis Lynch, "Orders to Proceed on Expedition."* Washington DC: Navy Department Library. http://www.history.navy.mil/library/manuscript/lynch_orders.htm.

Merrill, Selah

1881 *East of the Jordan: A Record of Travel and Observation in the countries of Moab Gilead and Bashan during the years 1875–1877.* London: Ricard Bentley and Son.

Musil, Alois

1907–8 *Arabia Petraea.* Kaiserliche Akademie der Wissenschaften, 2 vols. Wien: Alfred Holder.

1928 *The Manners and Customs of the Rwala Bedouins.* American Geographical Society Oriental Explorations and Studies 6.

Potts, T.

2001b Mesopotamia. In Tim Murray (ed.), *Encyclopedia of Archaeology: Histories and Discoveries*, 3 vols., 871–828. Santa Barbara, CA: ABC CLIO.

Robinson, Edward

1841 *Biblical Researches in Palestine, Mount Sinai and Arabia Petrea*, 3 Vols. Boston.

1853 *Biblical Researches in Palestine and Adjacent Regions.* Boston.

Rook, Robert E.

1998 *The 150th Anniversary of the United States' Expedition to Explore the Dead Sea and the River Jordan.* Amman: American Center for Oriental Research.

Schumacher, Gottlieb

1886 *Across the Jordan: Being and Exlporation and Survey of Part of the Hauran and Jaulan.* New York.

1888 *The Jaulan.* London.

1888 *Pella.* London.

1889 *Abila of the Decapolis.* London.

1890 *Northern 'Ajlun, "within the Decapolis.* London.

Stanley, A.P.

1856 *Sinai and Palestine in Connection with Their History.* London: John Murray.

2. Evolving Landscape and Environment in Jordan

Phillip G. Macumber

Introduction

The following contribution examines aspects of the physiography of Jordan as a basis for understanding processes and events that influence population distribution and occupational environment, both at present and in the past. When attempting to examine landscape alone, it becomes clear that in any archaeological context, landscape cannot be removed from the broader physical setting and must be considered alongside hydrological and climatic factors. Of special significance is the role of (palaeo) hydrology, since the availability of water is the one essential element without which ongoing occupation cannot exist, and which strongly influences the nature of that occupation, where it does exist (Figure 2.1).

This chapter provides a description of the physiography of Jordan based largely on the physiographic provinces initially erected by Bender (1968, 1974, 1975), but with some modifications. For each province it examines and compares events from a small selection of well-documented sites, where the nature of long-term occupation reflects strongly on the physical evolution of Jordan through time. In dealing with palaeoenvironmental reconstructions there are many difficulties in comparing the palaeohydrology and palaeoclimatology from different areas, and this is especially the case using archaeological evidence. One reason for this is that Palaeolithic man did not live in an average geographic setting, but instead chose those areas where he could best survive. Attempts at landscape and environmental reconstruction for a region based largely on geoarchaeological data are thus strongly biased by the favourable hydrological settings of the long-term occupation sites from which the most complete records come.

Landscape, Palaeoenvironmental Interpretation and Regional Correlation

Throughout much of Jordan, landscape evolution has been highly dynamic, the region having undergone numerous physiographic and climatic changes during the period of human occupation. From the hominid occurrences at Ubaydiya in the northern Rift Valley, this is known to have lasted for almost 1.5 million years (Tchernov 1988). Much of our understanding of palaeoenvironmental change over this time stems from environment-related investigations during archaeological studies. However, one factor that strongly complicates landscape and climatic interpretations arising from studies of Levantine prehistory is the degree of geographic and climatic diversity occurring throughout what is essentially a rather small region. In addition, for much of the region, archaeological sites are located in thin surficial sequences where aeolian, alluvial and colluvial sediments rapidly interchange, both vertically and horizontally, reflecting fine-scale temporal instability.

The theoretical and disciplinary bases for palaeoenvironmental interpretations are of a diverse nature; they include pollen curves, faunal analyses, geomorphic and sedimentological studies, hydrological studies including lake level changes, etc. Ideally, for best results, such studies should contain elements of all these approaches. However, this is not normally the case, and in many instances, given limited site objectives, they cannot be justified or afforded. For instance, while detailed pollen analyses have been carried out on a number of sites, insufficient sequences have adequate absolute dating. This is especially the case in the Middle and Lower Palaeolithic. Where little or no absolute dating exists, the erection of a local temporal framework is made using stone tool industries, stratigraphic interpretation, pollen curves, etc. This framework is then related to similar but better documented/dated and understood sequences elsewhere. Where absolute chronologies are not available, these types of analyses remain the only effective way of determining and comparing evolving palaeogeographic settings for prehistoric occupation.

This is not always simple, however. Problems of local interpretation in the first instance, followed by regional correlation, are very real and cannot be expediently discounted: for example, how to interpret regionally the occurrence of erosion or sedimentation at a site within a drainage basin, given that erosion in one part of the catchment implies sedimentation in another part. The difficulties inherent in broader sequence matching are obvious, and, while there may be strong similarities in overall character, the precise correlation of the various events often remains problematical. Therefore, there must often be concern about how really representative a specific site is to the regional synthesis.

The problems of erecting regional syntheses in the light of the individuality of specific sites are obvious. However, where insufficient well-documented and dated sequences exist, it may inevitably result in the gradual reinforcement of a few better-established sequences into one or occasionally two, often opposing, structures. In many respects, the proposed reconstructions may be valid, but there may

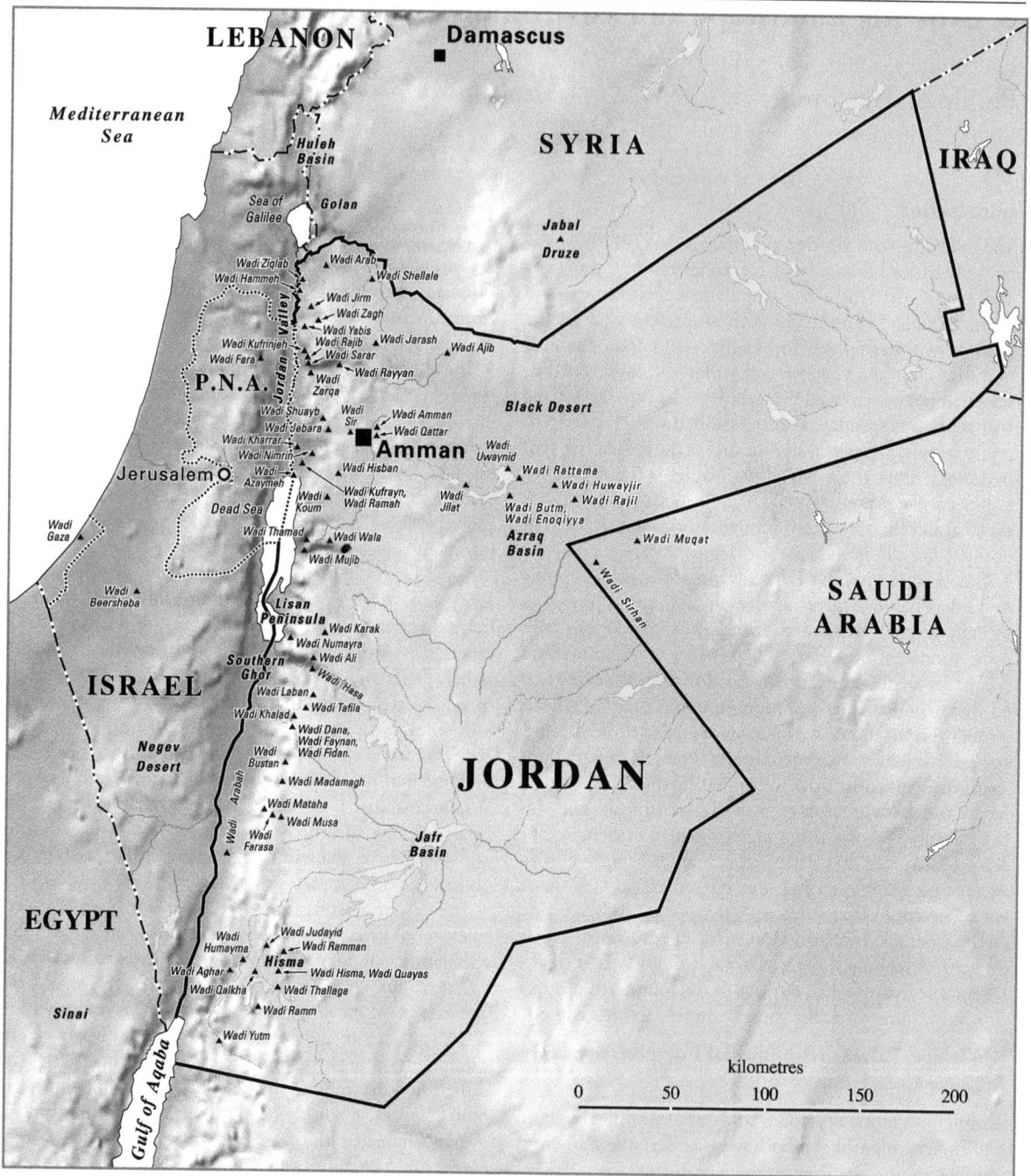

Figure 2.1   The location of principal wadi systems mentioned in the volume.

equally be times when the final monolithic presentation is far removed from reality, relying on an underpinning of many inadequate interpretations, themselves mirroring the supposed broader understanding.

Whatever the case, landscape and palaeoenvironmental interpretations must be regarded as evolving inductive hypotheses, which gain strength when subjected to rigor-

ous examination and the accumulation of more information. One test of the worth of the monolith is its ability to encompass not simply the large number of fragmentary records, which may be inadvertently distorted to fit the hypothesis, but the fewer more complete sequences that may occasionally arise.

Water, Landscape and Occupation

In arid and semiarid regions, such as large parts of Jordan today, occupation is synonymous with water. Without water there is no occupation. However, surface water supplies, both fluvial and lacustrine, are at the mercy of seasonality and drought. It is the groundwater-based spring-fed sites that provide the best short-and long-term buffers to aridity. Through time, the ongoing presence of man and animals is commonly associated with major spring systems. This is the case where extended periods of occupation occur at Pella (Pottery Neolithic to present-day occupation) in the Jordan Valley. It has been the case in the surrounding region of Tabaqat Fahl/Wadi Hammeh for at least the last 0.5 million years, and also in the otherwise arid Azraq Basin since Lower Palaeolithic times. Both areas, one in eastern and one in western Jordan, are associated with regional groundwater discharge, with large-scale continuous spring outflow through long periods of time.

This account examines three different landscapes where occupation is closely linked to spring activity—the Azraq Basin, Tabaqat Fahl and the Wadi Hasa. These well-documented settings are also compared and contrasted with sites from several other areas having significant input into an understanding of the basis and relevance of palaeoenvironmental and palaeoclimatic reconstructions in Jordan. Additional sites are the upper Wadi Zarqa region, the Wadi Hisma of southwestern Jordan and the Badia of northeastern Jordan.

Physiographic Framework of Jordan

The Hashemite Kingdom of Jordan covers an area of 96,500 km² at the eastern end of the Arabian Peninsula. The geology and physiography have been previously detailed in the work of Bender (1968, 1974, 1975). Given the widespread acceptance of Bender's *Geology of Jordan* as the principal authority on the underlying structural and stratigraphic framework on which the geomorphology is overlain, this paper follows closely, with some minor modification, his geomorphologic subdivisions. Accordingly, Jordan is divided into five principal geomorphologic provinces (Figure 2.2):

1. The Rift Valley (includes the Jordan Valley (north of the Dead Sea), the Wadi Arabah (south of the Dead Sea, and the Dead Sea *graben*).
2. Central Plateau (includes the Jafr Basin and Azraq/Wadi Sirhan Basins).
3. Northern Basalt Plateau and Northeastern Limestone Plateau.
4. Southern Mountain Desert.
5. Western Highlands (Bender's highlands east of the Rift).

The following discussion examines the physiographic framework of Jordan using examples from major geo-archaeological studies carried out in each geomorphologic province. The history of landscape evolution at the sites is compared and contrasted to provide a broad understanding of the relationship existing between physiography and occupation across Jordan.

The Rift Valley Province

Jordan lies at the western edge of the Arabian plate, which extends eastwards across Saudi Arabia to Oman. Undoubtedly, the most striking physiographic feature of Jordan is the Rift Valley at the western extremity of the country (Figure 2.2). The Rift Valley is a northward extension of the Great Rift Valley system, which extends northwards from East Africa, and includes the Red Sea, the Gulf of Aden, Gulf of Suez and Gulf of Aqaba. The Jordan's Rift Valley marks the boundary between the Arabian and African plates with a suggested 106 km lateral strike slip movement between the plates of 0.4-0.9 cm/yr (Quennel 1958). The valley reaches a width of about 32 km near Jericho but narrows to less than 10 km farther north. It is bounded on either side by steep fault-controlled edges. Close to the Dead Sea, the floor of the Jordan Valley is some 400 m below sea level, but the landscape rises precipitously to the east on to the Western Mountain Province. Southwards, between the Dead Sea and the Gulf of Aqaba, the Wadi Arabah consists of a series of shallow interconnected basins.

In Jordan, the Rift Valley may be divided into three sub-provinces (Figure 2.3):

1. The Dead Sea and adjacent plain containing the Lisan Peninsula that extends southwards to the Khanazir Fault that is expressed as a 50 m high escarpment.
2. The Wadi Arabah extends from the Gulf of Aqaba northwards to the Khanazir Fault.
3. The Jordan Valley/Jordan River north of the Dead Sea.

The rifting in western Jordan commenced about 25–30 million years ago in the late Oligocene or early to middle Miocene period. The resulting sedimentary pile in the Dead Sea Basin is up to 10 km deep, with subsidence probably commencing in the Pliocene accompanied by the accumulation of thick deposits of evaporites and some marine sequences (Ginzberg and Kashai 1981). Subsidence is still continuing today. Much of the later fill reflects a number of cycles of lacustrine and fluvial sedimentation when alternating lake and river systems occupied the depression. The Late Pleistocene Lake Lisan and its precursor Lake Samra were the last megalakes occupying the Rift Valley.

With continued subsidence in the centre, concomitant

Figure 2.2   Principal physiographic provinces in Jordan (modified from Bender 1975).

uplifting and arching of the edges of the Rift Valley created the high mountainous regions lying lateral to the rift graben. The mountainous area in Jordan was termed by Bender (1968, 1974) "the Mountain Ridge and Northern Highlands East of the Rift." For simplicity, it is here referred to as the Western Mountain Province. The accumulation of thick sedimentary deposits in the graben accelerated during the Pleistocene with the deposition of alternating continental fluvial and lacustrine sequences as large volumes of sediment eroded from the steep valley flanks poured into the Rift Valley.

Tectonic activity during Rift Valley development occurred over the period of human occupation, for which the earliest evidence is about 1.4 million years old (Tchernov 1988). This is from Ubaydiya, to the south of Lake Tiberias, where steeply dipping conglomerates and clays representing former fluvial and lacustrine sequences, now overturned, contain human and animal faunal remains and Oldowan and early Acheulean stone tool industries (Stekelis *et al.* 1969). Wadis, such as the Wadi Hasa and the Wadi Hisma, which were important areas of Pleistocene occupation, are associated with major lateral faults, one of which led to the development of the Late Pleistocene Lake Hasa. Farther north in the Rift Valley, zones of spring outflow in the Tabaqat Fahl region are tectonically controlled, and neo-tectonic activity has had a significant impact upon the landscape (Macumber and Head 1991). Early phases of uplift of the Rift Valley sides led to landscape incision and the development of large ancestral wadis. These ancestral valleys underwent a phase of extensive alluviation in Late Pleistocene times in response to the filling of Lake Lisan.

Volcanic activity is associated with rifting. It began in the early Miocene period and continued to early recent times with phases of activity dated from about 18.9 million years to less than 10 million years ago. The basalts were commonly extruded along major fault zones; examples occur in the area of Dhra west of Karak, the Wadi Hisma and at Ghor Katar.

The development of the Rift Valley resulted in the capture of regional groundwater systems that previously passed eastwards to the Mediterranean and westwards to the inland depressions of the Central Plateau (Salameh 1985). Groundwater from inland Jordan now flows eastwards into the Rift Valley where it emerges as springs. The importance of the Rift Valley groundwater outflow zone to continuing occupation in the Jordan Valley cannot be overstated. The springs are conduits for the naturally regulated release of regional groundwater that is fed from large recharge catchments, refilled over millennia and

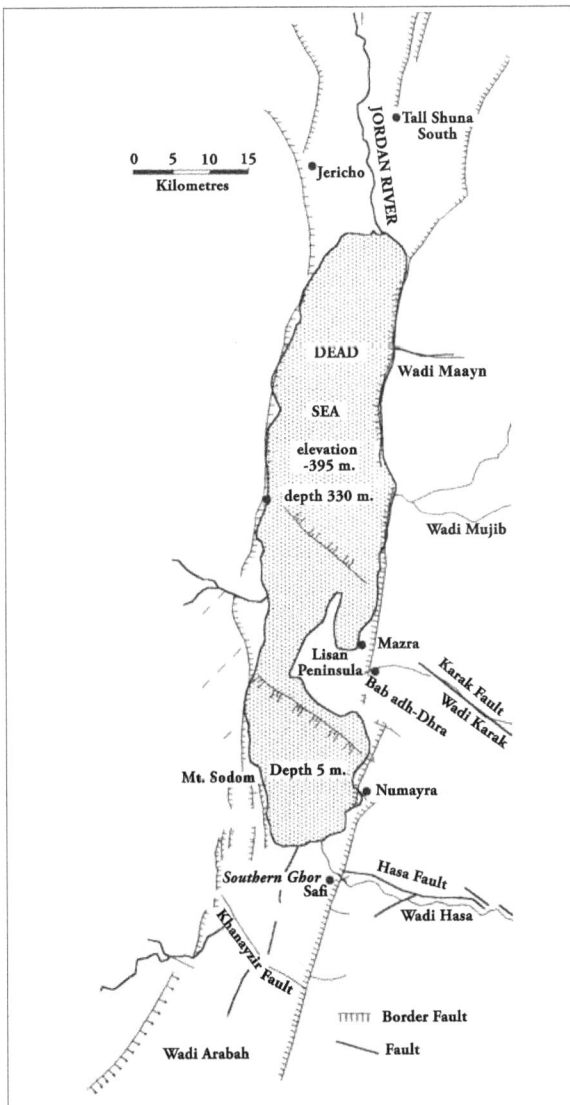

Figure 2.3   Central Jordan Valley and Dead Sea.

extending over thousands of square kilometres as far eastwards as the Azraq Basin. Flow times for water infiltrating within the highland catchments as far away as Azraq and discharging into the Rift Valley are put at about 3,500 years (Salameh and Udluft 1985). Unlike the rivers and streams, the springs and their associated discharge zones are strongly buffered against seasonality and short term to long term periods of aridity that are known to have affected the region since Early Pleistocene times. As a consequence, the well-watered Jordan Valley has been a corridor for migration between Africa and Europe for more than 1.5 million years.

Lake Lisan

Throughout Quaternary times the Jordan Rift Valley was aggraded by cycles of fluvial and lacustrine deposition, such as those that contain the Early Pleistocene occupation sequences at Ubaydiya (Stekelis *et al.* 1969). During the Late Pleistocene period the Jordan Valley from the Dead Sea to Lake Tiberias (Sea of Galilee) was occupied by Lake Lisan (Neev and Emery 1967; Begin *et al.* 1974, 1985), in which were deposited thick sequences of chemical and detrital calcareous sediments. An earlier lake, Lake Samra, for which the ages are less certain, preceded Lake Lisan. Lake Lisan existed for a considerable time ranging from 80,000–60,000 bp up to 18,000–15,000 bp (Neev and Emery 1967), or up to 13,000–11,000 bp (Neev and Hall 1976; Macumber and Head 1991). It reached an uppermost level of about minus 180 m before finally drying up at about 11,000 bp.

A large number of archaeological sites occur on the floor of the Rift Valley (e.g. Bab adh-Dhra to the east of the Lisan Peninsula [Figure 2.3]). These sites postdate the drying of Lake Lisan and reflect environmental changes occurring only over the Holocene period, a very small albeit important part of the time in which humans occupied the Rift Valley. A broader understanding of long-term landscape evolution affecting human occupation can be obtained by examining areas marginal to the Jordan Valley that have undergone considerable modification through time, and exhibit a long record of environmental change. These well-watered riftside landscapes are associated with intense human occupation, and geoarchaeological studies of such areas have permitted the reconstruction of palaeoenvironmental changes over long periods of time.

Four well-documented case histories covering different physiographic provinces where occupation spans the lifetime of Lake Lisan are discussed and compared with respect to landscape evolution in the north, central and southern parts of the Rift Valley. A feature of three of the areas is the strong influence of tectonics, which clearly plays an important part in the geomorphic and, hence, environmental history of archaeological sites occurring adjacent to the Rift Valley. While all four regions have recorded histories spanning the existence of Lake Lisan, the Tabaqat Fahl region has the thickest and most complete sedimentary sequences (spanning 170 m over two contiguous vertical sequences) representing perhaps 0.5 million years of occupation. The areas chosen, passing from north to south, are Tabaqat Fahl/Pella, Upper Wadi Zarqa, Wadi Hasa and the Quwayra Depression/Wadi Hisma. These areas represent the Rift Valley, the Western Mountain and the Southern Mountain Desert provinces respectively.

Example: Landscape and Occupation at Tabaqat Fahl and Wadi Hammeh

While not directly situated on the Rift Valley floor, the Tabaqat Fahl region protrudes westwards into the Jordan Valley, and geomorphic and sedimentary processes reflect events occurring in the abutting Rift Valley environment. The Tabaqat Fahl/Wadi Hammeh area lies opposite the junction of the Jezreel Valley and the Jordan Valley about 30 km south of the Lake Tiberias (Sea of Galilee). The 10 km² of the Tabaqat Fahl region and its two bounding wadis, the Wadi Hammeh and the Wadi Jirm al-Moz, provides one of the longest recorded histories of semi-continuous occupation anywhere in the Middle East, going back perhaps 500,000 years (Macumber 1992a; Edwards and Macumber 1995). This area contains the Lower Palaeolithic Masharia sites, the Middle Palaeolithic to Epipalaeolithic Wadi Hammeh sites, and the Pella tell sites on the Wadi Jirm, where occupation was from Pottery Neolithic virtually up to the present (Figure 2.4). The intense occupation in the Tabaqat Fahl region is associated with the tectonically uplifted Tabaqah Block composed largely of tufaceous limestone, deposited within a major zone of regional groundwater discharge at the edge of the Rift Valley (Macumber 1992b). The presence of thick tufaceous deposits (Tabaqat Fahl Formation, 100 m.; Knob Limestone, 35 m) is attributed to structural control, linked to Jezreel and Jordan Valley rifting, which through time has focused regional groundwater discharge into the area. The present active major springs feeding the Wadi Jirm and the Wadi Hammeh represent a continuation of this process.

The long geomorphic, sedimentologic and archaeological record from the Tabaqat Fahl region is undoubtedly the clearest obtained from any continental open-air sequence spanning the Lower, Middle, Upper and Epipalaeolithic periods in Jordan. While a number of *in situ* Lower Palaeolithic sites have been recorded in the 120 m thick Middle Pleistocene Tabaqat Fahl Formation, the work here is just beginning (Macumber and Edwards 1997). The 60 m thick Late Pleistocene Wadi Hammeh deposits are continuous, clearly visible sequences, showing ongoing sedimentation covering a number of discrete geologic settings with equally clear stratigraphic relationships (Figure 2.5). These observations are supported by an exhaustive

Figure 2.4   Topography and Palaeolithic site distribution at Tabaqat Fahl (from Macumber 1992b).

suite of radiocarbon dates and by a very large number of excavated *in situ* Middle, Upper and Epipalaeolithic sites occurring both vertically within the sequences and laterally down the wadi system (Figure 2.6). The radiocarbon dates from the sites are consistent with their accompanying stone tool industries.

Physical Setting

Near the Rift Valley, the Middle Pleistocene Tabaqat Fahl Formation overlies the steeply dipping Plio-Pleistocene Ghor Katar Formation. The lower-most unit in the Tabaqat Fahl Formation sequence is a conglomerate, which is, in turn, overlain by thick sequences of tufaceous silt and limestone. The conglomeratic unit thickens on passing eastward away from the Rift Valley, at the expense of the tufaceous sediments. At the Rift Valley edge, the conglomerate merges with and is replaced by dense white uniform paludolacustrine limestone. The overall pattern of facies variation on approaching the Rift Valley represents a change from a fluvial setting (represented by the conglomerate) to a zone of massive spring deposition in a zone of groundwater outflow (tufaceous limestone) adjacent to a large lake (dense uniform limestone) occurring within the Rift Valley.

A similar sedimentary sequence, containing a comparable lateral facies change from conglomerate to tufaceous limestone, occurs in the Late Pleistocene Wadi Hammeh sequence, indicating essentially the same physical setting (Figure 2.6). The Wadi Hammeh sequence occupies an ancestral valley carved into the Tabaqat Fahl Formation. Infilling of the ancestral valley by fluvial and tufaceous sequences was in response to rising levels of Lake Lisan from c. 65,000 (80,000?) bp to 11,100 bp. Unbroken sedimentation continued throughout the upper Middle, Upper and Epipalaeolithic times. The resulting 60 m thick valley-fill sediments are the terrestrial lateral time equivalents of the lacustrine Lisan Formation.

In the Wadi Hammeh sequence, a basal conglomerate containing red clay bands (Wadi Hammeh Conglomerate) is overlain by tufaceous limestone (Knob Limestone) with an intervening black humic clay (Black Clay) varyingly present. The conglomerate represents a fluvial wadi fill deposit; the tufaceous limestones are derived from spring outflow in a zone of regional groundwater discharge in the lower parts of the wadi, and the black clay is a fluviopaludal deposit. All three units contain bands of the fluviatile freshwater snail *Melanopsis praemorsa*, which is only found in fresh perennial streams like the Wadi Jirm. The presence of travertine horizons and *Melanopsis praemorsa* throughout the calcareous sequences indicates permanent spring-fed fresh water in the lower Wadi Hammeh during the period of deposition of the Knob Limestone. Archaeological sites occur scattered through all sedimentary units, and their common association with *Melanopsis* bands is seen as reflecting occupation alongside flowing streams.

The boundary between the conglomerate and tufaceous limestone units is diachronous as coarse clastic wadi-type sedimentation is gradually replaced by low-energy flood plain organic-rich paludal and spring-derived chemical deposits (Figure 2.6). The diachroneity is due to the gradual up-wadi migration of the springhead in response to rising base levels as Lake Lisan filled. The highest level reached by wadi aggradation occurred at 11,100 bp, when the uppermost sediments were deposited. It is equated with the time of highest Lake Lisan levels. Drying of Lake Lisan at about 11,000 bp was quickly followed by 30–60 m incision of the wadi-fill sequence, to form the present day topography, thereby exposing numerous *in situ* archaeological sites in the sediments of the valley walls.

A similar, albeit thinner record comes from the Wadi Hisban at the northern end of the Dead Sea. Here the extensive silt terraces of Wadi Hisban contain Epipalaeolithic sites towards the top of the sequence.

The final sedimentation on the terrace was dated to 11,100 bp and this is underlain by the *in situ* Natufian site Wadi Hammeh 27 dated to c. 12,000 bp.

Archaeological Sites at Tabaqat Fahl

Three major cycles of sedimentation and occupation

Figure 2.5 Scematic cross-section through Wadi Hammeh, showing the stratigraphic relationship between the Masharia and Wadi Hammeh Palaeolithic sites (from Macumber1992b).

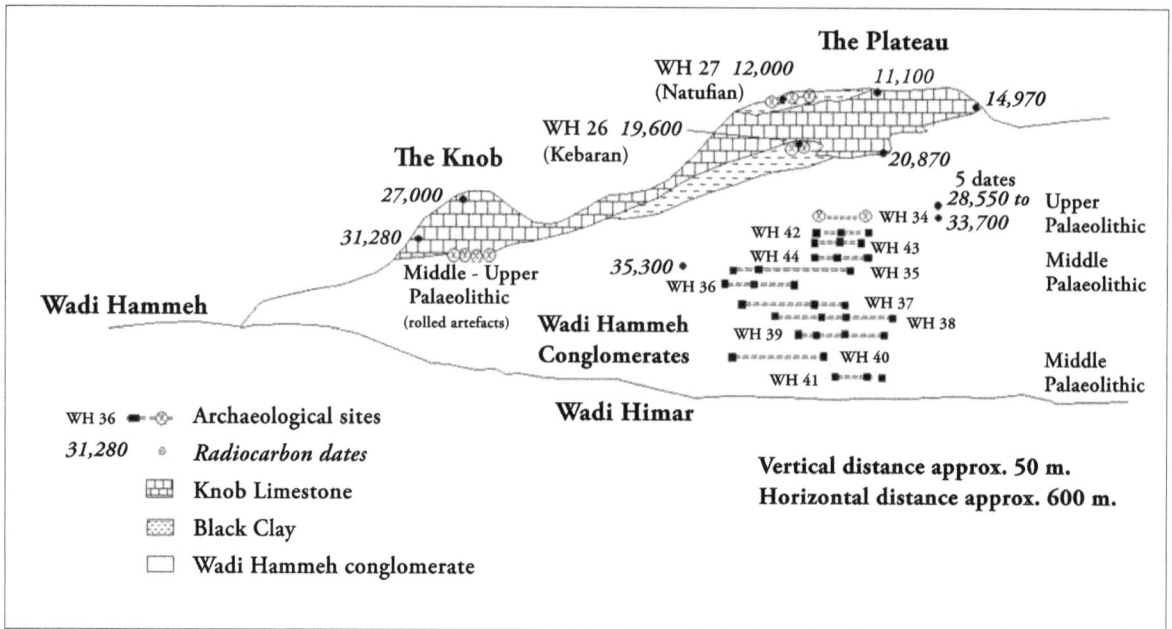

Figure 2.6   Stratigraphic section beneath the plateau showing the vertical distribtution of Palaeolithic sites.

are recognized at Tabaqat Fahl: a Lower Palaeolithic (Acheulean) phase; a Middle Palaeolithic to Epipalaeolithic (Natufian) phase; and the final ongoing Holocene phase. The latter period saw the long-term occupation of the Pella *tall*, from Pottery Neolithic times up to the present (Edwards and Macumber 1995). Five Lower Palaeolithic sites (Masharia sites, Figure 2.4) containing bifaces occur on the Tabaqat Fahl Plateau. Of these, two sites (Masharia 1 and 3) are situated in the upper limestone member of the Tabaqat Fahl Formation towards the western end of the Tabaqat Fahl Plateau (Macumber 1992b). The most extensive site (Masharia 1) occurs within tufaceous limestone some 30 m below the top of the Tabaqat and extends for perhaps 400 m around the cliff face. These artefacts are Upper Acheulean with an age range of between 200,000 and 250,000 bp and are archaeologically *in situ*. A further three sites occur in the lower conglomeratic member, in the north-central and eastern areas of the plateau (Masharia 2, 4 and 5). It is likely that certain of these sites were *in situ*, especially in the case of Masharia 4 and Masharia 2 where in both instances two hand axes were found together, in the latter case, at the base of Tabaqat Fahl conglomerate (Macumber 1992).

Locality

Locality	U–Th Age
Jafr limestone	83,000 ± 8,000 bp
Azraq-limestone below Azraq 31	220,000 ± 30,000 bp
Azraq–Umayri	146,000 ± 15,000 bp
Azraq–Ayn Bayda	44,000 ± 5,000 bp

Table 2.1 U–Th dates from the Central Plateau Region.

Sites in the conglomerate are stratigraphically lower in the sequence and older than those in the limestone. Given their position deep within the Tabaquat Fahl conglomerate, it is possible that the Masharia 4 and Masharia 2 sites may be as old as 0.5 million years. Copeland (1998) observes that the two bifaces from the Masharia 4 site would be "quite at home within the Latamne Middle Acheulean of Latamne in the Orontes Valley of Syria dated to a minimum of 560 Kya."

A large number of *in situ* Middle Palaeolithic to Epipalaeolithic (Kebaran and Natufian) sites occur within well-exposed valley fill sediments along the Wadi Hammeh for more than 3 km upstream from the Rift Valley (Edwards and Macumber 1995; Edwards *et al.* 1996). In a single 60 m thick vertical sequence beneath the "Plateau" are many *in situ* sites spanning the period from the upper Middle Palaeolithic to the Natufian period (Figure 2.6). At the top of the sequence is the very extensive 12,000 year-old Wadi Hammeh 27 Natufian site. Vertically beneath the Natufian site are the Kebaran sites Wadi Hammeh 33 and 26 (19,500 bp), which have an extensive stone tool industry and faunal remains. Below Wadi Hammeh 26 is the extensive *in situ* Upper Palaeolithic Wadi Hammeh 34 site, which extends for 50 m along the cliff face. Radiocarbon dates from a dense band of *Melanopsis* shells immediately above the Wadi Hammeh 34 site gave an average age of 30,000 bp. Farther down the sequence, a second dense shell band, situated above the *in situ* Middle Palaeolithic Wadi Hammeh 35 site, gave an age of c. 35,300 bp. Spot excavations on three intervening clay bands between the Wadi Hammeh 34 and 35 sites demonstrated a verti-

Figure 2.7 Geology of Azraq Basin, eastern Jordan (from Garrard *et al.* 1985).

cal continuity of occupation in the Wadi Hammeh 42, 43 and 44 sites. Below Wadi Hammeh 35, a further six Middle Palaeolithic sites (WH 36–41) have been excavated spanning the section to the base of the sequence.

Occupational Environment at Tabaqat Fahl/Wadi Hammeh

During Quaternary times, upwelling carbonate-rich groundwater emerged as outseepage in the lower parts of the wadi system(s) and around the margins of Lake Lisan and an earlier lake that occupied the Jordan Valley at the time of deposition of the Tabaqat Fahl Formation. Thick tufaceous sedimentary sequences accumulated in an actively aggrading, fluvio-paludal embayment(s) across which the sluggish spring-fed water flowed gradually to build the Tabaqat Fahl Formation and, later, the 60 m thick Wadi Hammeh sequences. The main occupation occurred on spring-fed river flats in the lower reaches of the wadis and around the margins of ancient lakes into which they flowed. The prime factor for long-term occupation has been the existence of a highly supportive microenvironment developed around large permanent

springs, which provide a buffer against seasonal, short-term, and even long-term aridity.

The Central Plateau

In eastern Jordan there are four major physiographic features: the Sirhan Depression, including the Azraq Basin; the Jafr Basin; the Black Desert; and the Limestone Desert (Figure 2.2). Of the four, the Sirhan Depression, Azraq Basin and Jafr Basin are part of the Central Plateau Province, while the Black Desert and Limestone Deserts of the Jordan "panhandle" form the Northern Basalt Plateau and Northeastern Limestone Plateau Province. The Central Plateau is the largest physiographic province and occupies much of central Jordan. It extends from the catchment of the broad Azraq/Wadi Sirhan depressions on the east and north, to the Western Highlands Province in the west. The southern boundary is the Ras al-Naqab escarpment and the rising ground of the Tubayq Highlands. It includes the Azraq Basin with its spring-fed Azraq Marshes, and the depression of the Jafr Basin, a broad tectonically formed basin of internal drainage about 100 km wide and 150 km long, developed at the foot of the elongated leeward slope of the upwarped Western Highlands. The Azraq Basin (Figure 2.7) contains a long record of occupation from Lower Palaeolithic times.

The floor of the Central Plateau is cut across Upper Cretaceous to early Tertiary marine sequences of limestone, marl, phosphorites and chert. Shallow dipping to flat-lying, more resistant beds result in a landscape that in places consists of tableland scarps, mesas and cuestas surrounded by weathering debris. The elevation at times reaches 1000 m above sea level, falling to about 850 m in the south. The lowest part of the Central Plateau occurs in the Jafr Basin. Chert fragments derived from the underlying marine sequences are scattered across the landscape often covering hundreds of square kilometres and forming the familiar *hammad* desert.

Drainage of the Central Plateau is eastwards towards the Jafr Basin in the south, while in the northeast it is towards the Azraq–Sirhan Depression. In the west of the Central Plateau, headward erosion from the deeply incised wadis of the Wadi Karak, Wadi Hasa and Wadi Mujib has captured much of the drainage that previously flowed eastwards, and it now passes towards the Rift Valley. In wadis like the Wadi Hasa there is a 1200 m drop from the plateau to the Rift Valley floor. In a similar setting, at the boundary between the Central Plateau and Western Highlands Province is the very large late Acheulean site at Fjaje near Shawbak castle overlooking the Wadi Bustan that drains towards the Wadi Arabah. Advantage was taken by Acheulean hunters of the view from the plateau rim across the wadi system to intercept herds of animals migrating between the Rift Valley and grasslands of the Central Plateau (Rollefson 1985).

The Jafr and Azraq Basins, lying within deserts of limestone, chalk and flint, owe their origin to subsidence, commencing in Cretaceous times. In the Jafr Basin a Pleistocene lake covered 1000–1800 km² at its maximum (Huckriede and Wiesemann 1968) resulting in the deposition of a 25 m thick limestone and marl unit. During the Quaternary period, there were alternating wet and dry phases, leading to the present situation represented by a mud flat, the Qa Jafr. Middle and Upper Palaeolithic artefacts overlie the lacustrine limestone.

The central part of the Azraq Basin contains perennial springs and pools, the Azraq springs being an important source of water for cities of western Jordan. The Azraq region has the most complete archaeological record so far obtained in eastern Jordan, with sites ranging from the Acheulean to the present. The basin, which covers 13,000 km², is an irregularly shaped depression with an elevation ranging from 1800 m along its northern boundary with Jabal Druze to about 500 m at its centre in Qa Azraq. Its eastern and western flanks rise to about 600–900 m The southern portion of the basin is underlain by Cretaceous and Tertiary limestone, chalk and marl capped by a flint

hammad, while the northern part is covered by Miocene to Pleistocene basalt and tuff. Azraq Basin is an extension of, albeit tectonically separated from, the Wadi Sirhan Depression, which passes into Saudi Arabia.

Central to the Azraq Depression is the largely fault-controlled Qa Azraq. It is bounded on the northeast and southwest by the Bayda Fault and Sirhan Fault respectively, and to the southeast and northwest by the Baqawiyya and Qaisiyeh Faults. To the north lies the Basalt Plateau with a 5–15 m scarp rising from the limestone plain. On the plateau the scoria cone Tall Hassan marks one of the many eruption points for basalt flows.

From late Tertiary times, lakes and marshes have been a feature of the Azraq region. The earliest recognized lacustrine sequence in the Azraq Basin is the Late Miocene calcareous sandstone of the Qirma Formation (Ministry of Energy and Mineral Resources 1993), which outcrops alongside the Wadi Rajil in the eastern parts of the region. The Azraq Depression contains a thick Quaternary suite, which includes the Plio-Pleistocene Azraq Formation, thick Pleistocene alluvial sequences, and the Dashsha Silt—a widespread largely aeolian silt, observed during archaeological surveys and excavations in the area. The Azraq Formation reaches a maximum exposed thickness of 15 m, and consists of evaporites, claystone and marl. Gastropods and diatoms show it to be lacustrine. This is clearly seen at Faydhat Dihikiya on the Saudi Arabian border at the margins of the Azraq Basin. Here, a gorge-like depression, with cliffed 30–50 m high wadi sides incised into Cretaceous–Lower Tertiary limestone and marl, has eroded back from Wadi Sirhan into the Azraq Basin. The sediments consist of a 55 m thick marly sequence of brackish to saline lacustrine deposits that contain gypsum and halite evaporites. The sequence includes a 5 m thick layer of brackish water molluscs—*Cardium edule paladosa*.

In the mid-1980s, Andrew Garrard and I collected a number of limestone and shell samples from the Jafr and Azraq Basins for Uranium–Thorium (U–Th) dating. These came from a range of lacustrine settings, which reflect wetter periods within the Azraq and Jafr Basins and provide a few initial dates on eastern Jordan's Pleistocene lacustrine sequences. For instance, a single U–Th date on a lacustrine limestone sample from the Jafr Basin gave an age of 83,000±8000 bp. In the Azraq Basin, limestone samples were collected 100 m south of the Azraq Playa at Ayn Bayda, from dense limestone beneath the Neolithic site at Azraq 31, and from a brackish lacustrine sequence containing a band of *Cardium edule* north of Umayri. The samples, dated at the Australian National University in Canberra are listed in Table 2.1.

In both the Jafr and Azraq Basins, lacustrine influences have been active for a considerable time. The earliest age obtained is from dense limestone or travertine beneath Azraq 31, which was dated on U–Th at 220,000±30,000 bp. The dense travertine horizon passes northwestward and occurs along the canals near Crab Spring and at C-Spring (Besançon *et al.* 1989), where Lower Palaeolithic artefacts occur towards the base of a 3.5 m sequence. If, as it seems, it is younger than this sequence, it provides a minimal date of 220,000±30,000 bp for the site.

Example: the Azraq Basin

The central area of the Azraq Oasis, lying at an elevation of 506 m above sea level, is a 6–8 km² area of essentially permanent wetlands, marshes and pools, fed by permanent springs in two major areas of regional groundwater outflow. A number of large and small freshwater springs and seeps emerge from the base of the low scarp at the periphery of the basalt flow where it peters out along the northern and western edge of the basin. Near their outlets, the larger springs form shallow pools and marshes. Estimates of the pre-development spring flow rates range from 14–20 MCM (million m³/year), with approximately 3–4 MCM from Druze Springs, 10–12 MCM from Shishan Springs and 3–4 MCM from other springs and seepages (e.g. Lion Spring and the "canal"). The central area is surrounded by a larger seasonally wet *sabkha* or playa lake, the Qa Azraq, covering an area of about 50–90 km². During wetter years, the Qa Azraq can flood to a depth of over 2 m, with the floodwater sitting on shallow saline groundwater occurring normally at a depth of 1–2 m beneath the otherwise dry *sabkha* surface.

The present-day climate of the Azraq Basin is essentially arid, with rainfall in the western areas ranging from between 100 and 200 mm/year, while that in the east is bordering on hyper-arid with precipitation less than 50 mm. A number of normally dry wadis with associated terraces feed into the central Azraq region. They only flow after storms and the water either infiltrates or is lost by evaporation from small playas.

Silt dunes surround the marshy area and outcrop within it. Similar silts contain and also underlie a number of archaeological sites. Their probable source is deflation of the playa/lake floor or from the periphery of the permanently wet area. Deflation occurs wherever water tables are within capillary distance of the groundsurface, permitting salt efflorescence and break-up of the fine-grained surface sediments into sand and silt-sized aggregates prior to deflation as loess (Macumber 1970). This is likely to have been an ongoing process through time, given that saline water tables are within 1–2 m of the surface beneath much of the Azraq *sabkha*. Indeed, silt is the major component of the shallow sedimentary sequences beneath the lake/marsh (Gilbertson *et al.* 1985; Garrard and Betts *et al.* 1988).

Both the wadi systems and the central playa/lake/spring area have a long history of occupation. For instance, Copeland and Hours (1988) have shown that Wadi Rattama, Wadi Butm and the Qasr Kharrana wadi complex was rich in Lower Palaeolithic (Desert Acheulean) and, to a lesser degree, Middle Palaeolithic material. Other Acheulean occurrences are found within the swamp deposits of the main Azraq marsh areas at C-Spring and Lion Spring (Rollefson 1982).

As Copeland (1988) noted, the Azraq Basin is in a climatically transitional zone with small changes in climate capable of having large impacts upon the physical environment. However, while this applies to the basin as a whole, it is less applicable to the spring-fed marsh region that receives regional groundwater flow, recharged on Jabal Druze. With a long flow path, the regional groundwater may be fossil to subfossil with origins reflecting wetter periods in the past, as may have been the case in the early Holocene. The groundwater emerging as springs around the perimeter of the basalt is largely buffered against adverse climatic change and provides a hydrologically stable setting in a region of otherwise environmental instability. In addition to the spring flow, locally recharged groundwater allows ephemeral base flow in certain of the lower wadis (Wadi Rattama, lower Wadi Butm and Wadi Enoqiyya) that permits them to maintain flow longer than would otherwise be the case.

Overall, the Azraq region provides a wide range of environmentally different settings, in which in some instances the full impact of deteriorating physical conditions through time would be felt, while elsewhere micro-environmental regimes provide well-watered asylum conditions largely immune to seasonal and longer term regional aridity.

Palaeoenvironment

The sediments of the Azraq Basin have a long stratigraphic, biological and archaeological record, ranging from Acheulean times up to the present, that permits the construction of its environmental and climatic history from Middle to Late Pleistocene times. For instance, a detailed geomorphological study of the Azraq Basin, together with palaeoclimatic interpretation, has been carried out by Besançon *et al.* (1989) who note the stratigraphic complexity of the region, which, together with the thinness and discontinuity of the deposits, leads to "its interpretation being unfortunately problematic." This is a common feature of many inland arid regions, especially where aeolian processes continue to be strongly active and the sedimentary sequences condensed. Despite this limitation, Besançon *et al.* (1989) divide the events into a number of "morphoclimatic" cycles. Garrard and Colledge *et al.* (1988), with a more restricted archaeological perspective, recognize that five terraces are present along the wadis, perhaps representing wet and dry phases.

Given the clear complexity of the region, the intention here is to address only certain of the processes and events occurring during the latter part of the period in late Glacial and early Holocene times, covered by the more recent archaeological studies. This covers only the last 4 of the 17 episodes recorded by Besançon *et al.* (1989). A feature of this period is the presence of the very extensive *in situ* sites, such as Kharrana 4 and Jilat 6. While there is some uncertainty about why these sites were favoured (Garrard and Byrd 1992), it is difficult to see how they could have existed without permanent water, probably fed from active springs.

Despite a common practice of splitting the palaeoenvironmental record into a plethora of wets, dries, hots and colds, this has not been done by Garrard and Betts *et al.* (1988). Instead, recognizing the difficulties of interpretation, they limit the division of Late Pleistocene palaeoclimate into two phases, 23,000–15,000 bp, when it was deemed wetter (reflected by zones of soil formation within silt sequences), and post 15,000 bp when it was drier (reflected by aeolian silts without palaeosols). Garrard and Betts *et al.* (1988) note that there is much work still to be done in the Azraq Basin before a detailed statement about the palaeoenvironment can be made. However, even for their simplified climatic interpretation, much rests on the origins of the silt.

From an environmental perspective, perhaps the most important feature of the Late Pleistocene and Holocene landscape are the ubiquitous silt deposits found throughout the region. Many excavated and dated archaeological sites in the wadis occur within aeolian silt that sometimes contains palaeosols. This is best seen in the Wadi Jilat study (Garrard and Colledge *et al.* 1988). For instance, at the Wadi Jilat 6 site, aeolian silts underlay a sequence containing two palaeosols with archaeological sites dated at 19,000 bp and >14,500 bp respectively. The palaeosols are deemed to be short-term humid interruptions to an otherwise uniform phase of silt accumulation (Garrard and Colledge *et al.* 1988). Similarly, at Wadi Jilat 9, a palaeosol developed on aeolian silt beneath fluvial deposits of "aggradation unit B" was interpreted as indicating a more humid event interrupting an otherwise arid setting. Two additional soils occur within the aggradational unit B sequence, the upper being dated at 21,250±400 bp. Finally, at the Wadi Jilat 10 site (dated at 14,790–12,700 bp and also situated in aeolian silts), silty marsh deposits recorded from the base of the aeolian sequence are tentatively correlated to the humid event corresponding to the palaeosol between the aeolian silt and fluvial sediments in Wadi Jilat 9 (above).

At sites Wadi Jilat 8, 10 and 6, Late Epipalaeolithic assemblages younger than 14,500 bp are contained within unmodified aeolian silts. This was also the case for Late Epipalaeolithic, Natufian and Neolithic sites at the central playa where a series of copious springs occur around the sides of the playa. Here, the mid–late Natufian Azraq 18 and PPNB Azraq 31 sites are in aeolian silts, and silts are still being deposited.

A similar record to that of Wadi Jilat comes from sites at Wadi Uwaynid. At Wadi Uwaynid 18, silts occur throughout the sequence with humic silts at the base overlain by aeolian silt containing a hearth dated at 23,200 bp. The silts contain a number of poor soil horizons prior to a hiatus at c. 19,800–19,500 bp, during which there was strong pedogenesis. In a similar sedimentary setting is the nearby Uwaynid 14 site with dates of 18,900–18,400 bp. The industry is similar to that from the lower parts of Jilat 6, also contained within a palaeosol. More silts accumulated, before a final fluvial sequence was deposited containing a further palaeosol. The sequence was then incised and remains as a terrace.

Discussion

The correlation between the palaeosols in different silt sequences remains tentative. The sequences overall suggest that the period from well before 21,250 bp up to the present was one of an otherwise uniform silty depositional environment containing a number of occupation sites, which in the earlier part of the record sometimes related to periods of pedogenesis. It is clear from this data that aeolian activity was not restricted to the latter part of the Epipalaeolithic and the Holocene period but was semicontinuous back into Upper Palaeolithic times, beyond the limits of the dated archaeological sequences.

While aeolian activity is so prevalent, despite the long history of lacustrine activity in the Azraq Basin, there is no unequivocal record of a late Pleistocene phase of expanded lake levels commensurate with the significantly wetter conditions reported from western Jordan (Tabaqat Fahl, the Wadi Hasa and the Wadi Hisma) at the time. Earlier, Garrard and Harvey *et al.* (1985) considered that a caliche layer in the silt occurring at a level above that of the Wadi Uwaynid 18 and 14 horizons and found within the 530 m contour, represented a lacustrine deposit following lake expansion. This interpretation was later abandoned and the caliche deemed to be non-lacustrine and due to capillary emplacement by high water tables, or of aeolian origin (Garrard and Betts *et al.* 1988). These alternative origins are not mutually exclusive, but instead may simply reflect different source areas undergoing essentially the same processes. If formed at the site (as a $CaSO_4/CaCO_3$ capillarity-induced evaporite), it indicates higher water tables and, therefore, wetter conditions than at present.

If the caliche is aeolian, it is probably deflated from a nearby source having high water tables where capillarity permits the break-up of surface crusts by salts into deflatable components (cf. the formation of copi deposits and clay/gypsum lunettes in Australia, Macumber 1970, 1991). The most likely ongoing source of silt is deflation from the Azraq Playa and others such as Qa Umayri. If this is the case, the presence of silt throughout much of the recorded history from Upper Palaeolithic times indicates that, while water tables at Azraq may have undergone fluctuations, they were always close to the surface. Silt deflation occurs under a range of climatic conditions from semi-arid to hyper-arid.

During the periods of aeolian activity, whatever the climatic situation, the local hydrological setting around the Azraq Oasis cannot have been significantly different than at present. It follows that the one essential reason for the lack of strong evidence for more clearly defined climatic fluctuations in a region, shown by Copeland (1988) as being climatically in a state of disequilibrium, is the hydrological buffering provided by the Azraq Oasis throughout the Late Pleistocene. This dampens the climatic extremes and locally limits the impacts of physiographic and climatic processes, which continue to affect the surrounding landscape. Given that the silts reflect not increased regional aridity but deflation from nearby areas underlain by high water tables, the association of archaeological sites with the silt sequences at the Azraq underpins the notion that in arid settings humans live in (micro) climatically favourable sites not necessarily representative of the region as a whole.

Yet the period from Late Glacial times to the present is a time when major climatic change was under way. It is clearly seen in changing occupation patterns in deserts across the Middle East and North Africa. Of special significance, across much of this broad region, has been the period of increased temperatures and monsoonal activity from 10,000 to 6000 bp. This followed the cold of the Glacial Maximum and the aridity of the Younger Drias from 11,000 to 10,000 bp, a period represented by the drying of the megalake Lake Lisan. The very dry/cold phase of the Younger Drias would have obliged populations to seek refuge in such areas as the Azraq Oasis and Tabaqat Fahl region where the groundwater-fed systems provide buffering from the climatic extremes. After the aridity of the Younger Drias, there followed an amelioration of climate in early to mid Holocene times in North Africa and parts of Arabia extending from the Nile River to Oman, during which many presently dry lake systems were full.

While there are no major environmental fluctuations observed in the Holocene Azraq record, where groundwater buffering limits or even overrides the effects of climatic change, a clearer indication of regional environmental/climatic change as reflected in its impact on occupation would be expected from areas peripheral to the basin. Such a situation exists in the nearby northeastern basalt and limestone steppe deserts of the Badia.

Northern Basalt Plateau and Northeastern Limestone Plateau

The area referred to by Bender (1968, 1974, 1975) as the Northeastern Deserts of Jordan, or more commonly, the Badia, with its basalt (*harra*) and limestone (*hammad*) deserts, lies to the northeast of the Azraq Basin–Wadi Sirhan Depression. The deserts comprise two distinct geomorphological units: the Northern Basalt Plateau (often referred to as the Black Desert); and the Northeastern Limestone Plateau farther to the east. Both units are treated here together.

The Basalt Plateau/Black Desert is a southwards extension of the Jabal Druze Basalts, and covers about 11,000 km² in Jordan or about 25% of the total basalt plateau (Shammah Plateau) most of which lies in Syria. It is an extensive and rather inaccessible undulating plateau, a lava plain covered in places with a surface of basalt cobbles and boulders, forming the upper surface of lava flows that issue from basaltic and scoriaceous volcanic cones that now dot the landscape. The cones form linear patterns suggestive of fissure eruptions. Volcanic activity occurred from late Eocene to Pleistocene times and the most recent eruptions may have continued into historical times. Six different phases of volcanic activity have been recognized and the overall thickness in places reaches 270 m The fissure eruptions are thought to correlate with the sixth stage of activity and are believed to be Pleistocene in age. The flows continue into Saudi Arabia forming an eastern limit to the Wadi Sirhan–Azraq Basin.

Eastward of the Black Desert is the Northeastern Limestone Plateau, consisting of a flat stony surface formed across early Tertiary marine siliceous and calcareous sequences. Resistant limestone beds form low scarps. Features on the Limestone Plateau are subdued, but include a number of northwest–southeast-trending depressions filled with Quaternary sediments, their shape being dictated by structural patterns in the limestone. In places, the depressions appear to suggest remnants of palaeodrainage patterns. The direction of the depressions is dictated by the principal direction of structural deformation in eastern Jordan.

The present-day climate of the eastern Badia is arid with 50–150 mm rainfall. A feature of such arid regions is great rainfall variability in which there may be months without rainfall, yet when it rains it may be intense with a single storm producing as much as the mean annual precipitation. The presence of mudflats shows that there is at times sufficient local runoff and perhaps groundwater outflow to permit occasional visits by pastoralists and in places limited occupation. The only reliable surface water is the distant Azraq Oasis but rain-pools and limited groundwater outflow provide a number of other temporary potential water sources. Such is the case with Ibn al-Ghazzi situated on the periphery of the Azraq Basin some 75 km from Azraq (Betts and Helms 1989).

Occupation of the Black Desert

Despite the present inhospitable environment, occupation in the Black Desert has gone on, perhaps sporadically, for a considerable time. Little is known about the history prior to the twelfth millennium bp, other than for small scatters of Middle Palaeolithic and Epipalaeolithic artefacts. Betts (1992, 1993) notes that sites representing the first part of the early Neolithic (PPNA) are rare. By the second half of the ninth millennium bp, occupation and knapping sites are common, and hunters extensively used the Badia and especially the *harra*. Betts (1993) considers this expansion in terms of similar expansions elsewhere in Syria and the Negev. This, however, is not an explanation but a comparison, and the expansion probably reflects a more generally hospitable environment than previously existed (or followed).

Example: Neolithic Settlements in the Black Desert

Helms (1982) similarly notes that, while humans probably lived in the Black Desert as early as 12,000 bp, the bulk of the physical evidence comes later. The abundance of manmade structures in the desert, principally stone hut circles and desert "kites," implies a once intensive occupation with suggestions of relatively dense semi-permanent settlements and a highly organized system of hunting technology. Stone tool assemblages associated with the structures represent the PPNB and Late Neolithic periods dating from the early sixth (or perhaps seventh) to late fifth millennium bc. A large "palaeo-Bedouin" population is hypothesized as existing up to the Late Neolithic period followed by a decline in which, until the late fourth millennium bc, there was no artefactual, datable evidence of occupation. The explanation postulated by Helms is that migration occurred to more verdant areas to the east, north and west, and apart from a relatively short-lived period represented by the Jawa occupation (Helms 1977), there is no archaeological evidence for significant occupation of the Black Desert up to the third millennium bc. The reason for the migration is unclear.

The number of Neolithic sites dated between 8350 and 6900 bp (Betts 1993), and their subsequent absence, raises the question of the extent of climatic influence on the landscape and occupation in eastern Jordan during the early Holocene. The early–mid-Holocene phase of occupation in the Badia desert coincides with the time when higher rainfalls resulting from increased monsoonal activities were strongly affecting nearby areas of Arabia and North Africa—areas that today have arid or even hyper-arid climates (McClure 1976, 1978). Strongest flooding occurred along the Nile River from 9000 to 6000 bp, a period seen as being one of climatic optimum throughout the Eastern Mediterranean region by Rossignol-Strick (1993). Cores from the Arabian Sea show that strong monsoonal conditions were present, and in what is now arid eastern Oman, the interdune corridors in the Wahiba Sands had seasonal ponds; nearer the coast, silts with thick zones of rhyzoconcretions were deposited (Gardner 1988). There was occupation of the Wahiba Sands during this early–mid-Holocene moist period, but this ceased once aridity returned, and has only recommenced in relatively recent times (Eden 1988).

In the Levant, increased monsoonal activity resulting in higher rainfall in the more arid southern regions has previously been suggested by a number of authors (Gat and Carmi 1987; Goldberg and Rosen 1987). However, while wetter conditions are recorded in the southern Levant during this period, they contradict drier conditions recorded in the more northern areas of the Rift Valley (Weinstein-Evron 1989) and perhaps southwestern areas at the same time. The explanation provided is that palaeoclimatic difference across the Levant may reflect different rain sources, with the southern and eastern areas being influenced by the monsoonal activity, while the more northerly areas receive rains during glacial periods from an Atlantic source.

Whatever the case, there is a clear indication that conditions were significantly wetter for much of the Middle East and North Africa than today in early–mid-Holocene times. In these latter areas there is a widespread appearance of Neolithic sites across the landscape attesting to a significant expansion of occupation lasting until mid-Holocene times. While the timing of the early–mid-Holocene moist period seems to be slightly different for different areas, it is likely that this same impact was also experienced in eastern Jordan and recorded in the events in the eastern deserts up to the onset of a more arid phase that has continued up to the present.

Finally, Rollefson (1992) has noted that major increases in population in Jordan and Palestine between 9600 and 8500 bp can be attributed to the growth of agriculture and goatherding. This is undoubtedly true, but this argument does not explain the expansion of populations into the more arid areas, nor their retreat following the demise of the early–mid-Holocene moist phase, which caused a reversion to a more poorly watered setting. Clearly both climatic and cultural factors influenced occupation in different ways.

Southern Mountain Desert Province

At its southern edge, the Central Plateau terminates against the fault-controlled Ras al-Naqab scarp that marks the boundary between the Central Plateau and the Southern Mountain Desert provinces (Figures 2.2, 2.8). The geomorphic boundary roughly follows the lithologic boundary between Mesozoic–early Tertiary limestone/marl and Palaeozoic (Ordovician–Silurian) sandstone and shale, which give the province much of its physical character. The sandstone-shale sequences overlie an acid igneous basement of granites, granodiorites, quartz porphyry and diorites, which outcrop in the southwest to form mountainous regions at the southern limit of the adjacent Western Highland Province. The highest points of the escarpment reach 1700 m above sea level. To the southeast are the Tubayq Highlands, separated from the Southern Mountain Desert Province by outcropping Cretaceous sediments, forming an extension of the

Central Plateau. South of Ras al-Naqab the topography falls abruptly almost 600 m and slopes towards the Wadi Hisma–Quwayra Depression developed at the western end of Wadi Hisma. Three steps or levels (pediments, Figure 2.9) have been recognized on the Ras al-Naqab escarpment, at 1600 m, 1400 m and about 1200 m, each representing erosional

cycles in the development of the scarp (Hassan 1995).

The sandstone landscapes of the Southern Mountain Desert Province are deeply incised especially along the scarps. As in the case of the limestone Central Plateau, more resistant beds strongly influence the landscape, with the development of inselbergs, mesas and buttes (table

Legend:

- Recent terrestrial, fluvial and lacustrine sediments
- Recent mudflat sediments
- Pleistocene gravel, lacustrine limestone and gypsum
- **B** Pleistocene basalt and basalt-tuff undifferentiated
- Tertiary limestone with chert layers
- Cretaceous limestone, chalk, dolomite, phosphorite-chert, shale and sandstone
- Ordovician to Silurian sandstone and shale
- Cambrian sandstone, basal conglomerate, continental deposits, limestone and shale
- Pre-Cambrian granite, diorite gabbro, gneiss and schist
- Fault

Figure 2.8 Geology of southwestern Jordan showing Quwayra-WadiHisma region (Geology after Bender 1975).

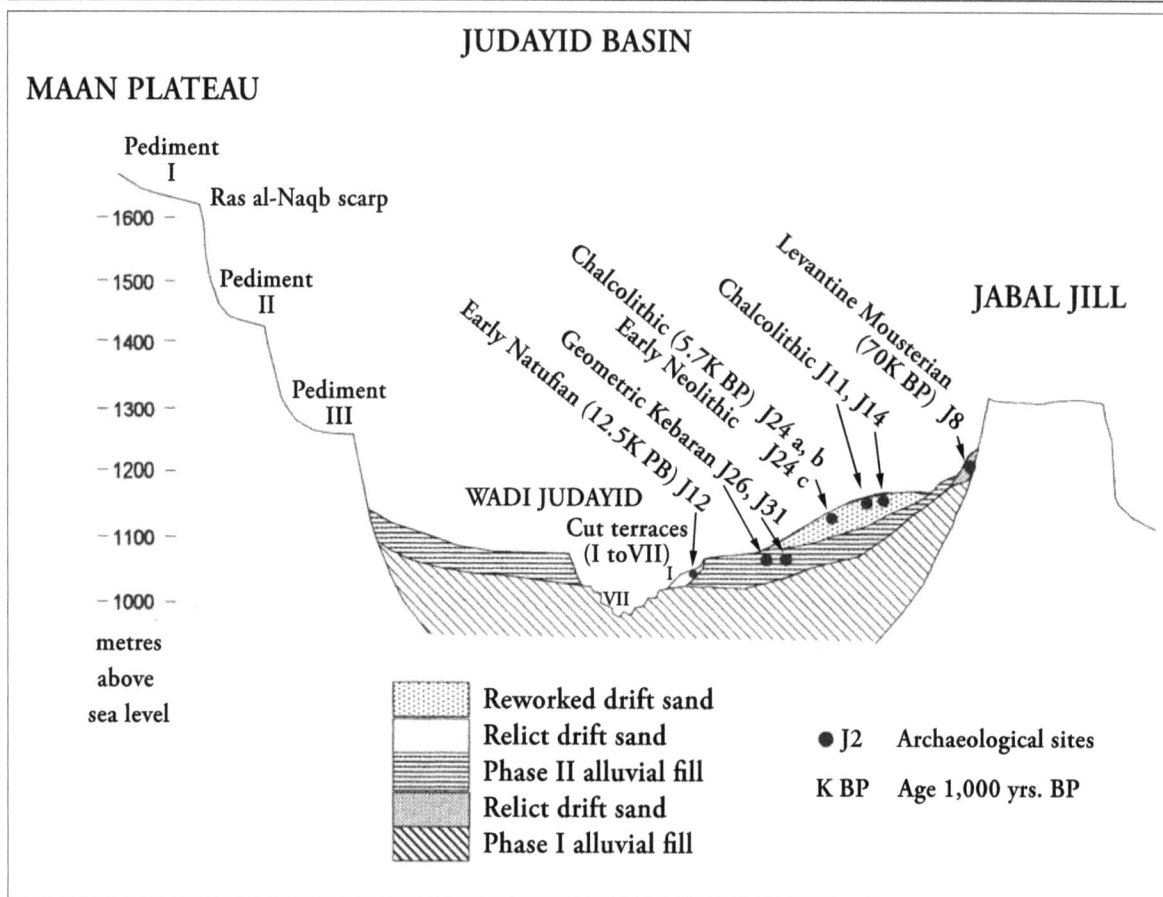

Figure 2.9 Geological section through the Judayid Basin, southwestern Jordan (from Hassan 1995).

mountains), and cuestas. In the Tubayq area, a tabletop landscape of inselbergs interspersed with large flat depressions predominates, with extensive mudflats developed over thick alluvial deposits, representing deposition during fluvial phases during the Quaternary period.

The strong influence of tectonics on drainage systems bordering the Rift Valley (also evident in the case of the Wadi Hasa) is visible in the southern Wadi Arabah. Faults paralleling the northwest–southeast-trending Hasa Fault mark the edge of the Ras al-Naqab Scarp. Faulting determines the course of the Wadi Hisma, which follows a fracture zone created by tension fissures, along which basalt dykes have intruded (marked as "B" in Figure 2.8).

Faulting has formed the Wadi Hisma–Quwayra Depression into which ephemeral wadis, such as Wadi Judayid, Wadi Qalkha and Wadi Thallaga, drain from the north, and Wadi Ramman and Wadi Ramm from the south. Lying less than 20 km from the Rift Valley, the western edge of the Quwayra Depression is bounded by a north–south-trending fault passing a little to the west of Quwayra where the Precambrian basement out-crops. This fault has in the past dammed Wadi Yutm, which

drains westward towards the Gulf of Aqaba. Eastwards of the fault there has been extensive alluviation and playa development with a line of mudflats occurring along the Wadi Hisma between Quwayra and Mudawwara. In the uppermost parts of the region near Mudawwara, lacustrine sequences of the Halat Ammar Formation contain a brackish to saline molluscan fauna. It is uncertain whether this lacustrine sequence relates to similar deposits from Umayri near Azraq dated at 146,000 bp or whether it represents a more recent event, such as that recorded across North Africa, eastern Arabia and perhaps in the Badia of northeastern Jordan. Terrace evidence at the lower Wadi Hisma, however, suggests that incision predominated during the Holocene, and it is more likely to equate with earlier wet phases.

Poking up through alluvium are Ordovician sandstone buttes and inselbergs, with Jabal Ram and Jabal Sahm occurring to the south. The Wadi Hisma region, from the edge of the Ras al-Naqab scarp southwards to the lowland area of inselbergs and sand plains/mud flats, has been extensively studied (Henry 1979, 1995). Over 100 archaeological sites, ranging in age from Lower Palaeolithic to Chalcolithic, were observed scattered across the deeply incised sandstone landscape of wadis and inselbergs. Detailed investigations carried out in the Judayid Basin and at Jabal Qalkha, Jabal Muaysi and Jabal Hamra recorded sites from a number of settings, namely alluvial fans, river terraces and rock shelters.

Example: The Wadi Hisma Region of Southwestern Jordan

A feature of the Wadi Hisma area is the number of sites spanning a range of different wadi and jabal settings that provide detailed accounts of environmental changes during the Middle–Late Pleistocene period. Many of the sites are, however, in stratigraphic isolation, for instance, in rock shelters with very few radiocarbon dates. While providing data on localized climatic conditions via pollen, fauna, etc., they are less useful in the reconstruction of a more general environmental framework, as would be the case if they occurred in more readily related landscapes, such as terraces, lake shorelines, etc. Nevertheless a detailed account of landscape evolution has been established (Hassan 1995), best seen in the Judayid Basin immediately south of Ras al-Naqab.

Two phases of fan-alluviation are present in the Judayid Basin (Figure 2.9). The main phase (Phase I) was aggraded prior to the Middle Palaeolithic period. The earliest artefacts obtained from the region are an assemblage containing Late Acheulean bifaces (Henry 1995) coming from near the top of a 30 m thick section of early alluvial fill (Qalkha Formation of Hassan) in a deeply incised wadi draining Jabal Qalkha. The Phase I alluviation was followed by a period of downcutting and dune development (Hassan 1995). Remnants of dune sand overlying Phase I alluviation contain the c. 69,000-year-old Tor Sabiha Mousterian site (Henry 1982, 1995), the date being one of two obtained by amino acid racemization on ostrich shell (Henry and Miller 1992). While conditions were generally cold and arid, pollen and faunal evidence from Layer C at Tor Sabiha, and a similarly dated Mousterian deposit at Tor Faraj, suggest that conditions may have been moister than today.

The next significant period of occupation is represented by six Upper Palaeolithic sites, found at shallow depth in rock shelters in the vicinity of Jabal Qalkha, at elevations of 940–980 m above sea level. They occur in pinkish silt similar to that occurring at the nearby Mousterian site of Tor Faraj. However, their location makes it difficult to place the sites with any certainty into any local geostratigraphic framework or regional stratigraphic context (Coinman and Henry 1995).

A second phase of fan-alluviation (Phase II) commenced under warm and moister conditions. The age of commencement is unclear. Its termination, however, was put at c. 14,000–13,000 bp based on the presence of Geometric Kebaran (Middle Hamran) sites J26 and J31 eroding from alluvial fans comprising the upper units of the alluvium. There are no absolute dates, but instead the age was determined by comparison of the tool assemblages with dated Geometric Kebaran sequences elsewhere in the Levant. The period covering Phase II alluviation incorporates the early Epipalaeolithic "Qalkhan" period represented by sites older than 14,000–15,000 bp occurring along Wadi Qalkha tributaries in the vicinity of the Jabal Qalkha (Henry 1995). Here again, dates are scarce and a suggested age for the Qalkhan of 20,000–15,500 bp is based on similarities of the material with stratified assemblages from the Wadi Uwaynid 14 and 18 sites at Azraq radiocarbon dated at 19,800–15,500 bp (Garrard and Betts *et al.* 1988).

The second period of alluviation was in turn followed by further erosion, during which phases of wadi incision produced minor terracing along the Wadi Judayid. As downcutting of the wadi proceeded, dune drift sand accumulated on the Phase II fan-alluvium sequence (Figure 2.9). The uppermost terrace (Terrace I) is the largest, and contains an early Natufian site (Wadi Judayid J2) radiocarbon dated to c. 12,500 bp. This indicates that the initial stage of wadi incision occurred prior to 12,500 bp. The Natufian date from the terrace is similar to the two dates (c. 12,680 and 12,320 bp) from upper Layer C in the Tor Hamar rock shelter (Wadi Judayid site J431) covering the period of introduction of Helwan lunates. In the shelter, Layers B, C and D contain Epipalaeolithic (Mushabian) artefacts, while rubble Layer E contained a Qalkhan industry.

Elsewhere, dune sequences occur overlying Phase II alluvium. These contain early Neolithic and Chalcolithic sites, showing that aeolian processes were active during early to mid-Holocene times.

The 12,500 bp radiocarbon age for the Wadi Judayid J2 Natufian site, and the 12,680 and 12,320 bp dates for the Tor Hamar site, are the next oldest absolute dates in the Judayid sequence after that of the amino acid racemization dates from the Mousterian sites at c. 70,000 bp (Figure 2.9). The lack of absolute dates over this intervening period emphasizes the uncertainties inherent in relating local chronologies of rock shelter and scattered open-air stratigraphies to any more general regional geomorphic/stratigraphic framework. This is especially the case when fine subdivisions are adopted and then dated by reference to broad regional understandings or distant sites, many of which have their own uncertainties.

Wadi Hisma Summary

The Wadi Hisma region has a long history of landscape evolution and human occupation. For the former, a broad relative sequence of erosional and depositional events can be constructed and tentatively compared with similar major events elsewhere in Jordan. However, at a more detailed level, correlations within the local sequences and with other regional systems are made difficult by the dis-

Figure 2.10 Terraces of the Upper Wadi Zarqa region (from Besançon *et al.* 1984).

continuous nature of the sequences and lack of datable material, even though there is a surfeit of archaeological sites. The most complete stratigraphic sections come from isolated rock shelters, such as site J431 at Tor Hamar, where Natufian/Geometric Kebaran sequences overlie Kebaran sequences, which in turn overlie Upper Palaeolithic horizons. Yet even here only two dates exist (12,680 and 12,320 bp), from upper Layer C. As a consequence, the localized stratigraphies are largely artefact-based and their absolute ages obtained by comparison with similar sequences elsewhere. Because of the richness of artefactual material, the sequences are finely divided, and where fine subdivisions are erected there is always the problem of typological diachroneity. Perhaps this explains an apparent rapid climatic shift from the "marked humid phase" from 13,000–12,500 bp from Qa Salab to "very cold and dry conditions" at Wadi Judayid J2 site from 12,780 to 12,090 bp (Emery-Barbier 1995). Whatever the case, it is clear that detailed climatic syntheses based on diversely erected chronologies from widely different physical settings (in this case, a rock shelter and a river terrace) must always be regarded as tentative.

Western Highlands/Western Mountain Province

The Western Highlands/Western Mountain Province border the eastern side of the Jordan Rift Valley and extend for about 370 km from Lake Tiberias to the Gulf of Aqaba (Figure 2.2). In the north, the Western Mountain Province is largely composed of Cretaceous and Early Tertiary limestone, sandstone and shale sequences deposited in the Tethys Ocean, which in Mesozoic and Cenozoic times covered large areas of northeast and eastern Jordan, extending westwards across the Arabian Peninsula. In the southwest, however, the Western Mountain Province consists essentially of pre-Cambrian crystalline rocks overlain in part by red Palaeozoic sandstone (Figure 2.8). The crystalline basement forms part of the Nubo-Arabian shield that was an important source of sediment supply for the Cambrian and Ordovician sandstone landscapes of southern Jordan, and is well known from Wadi Ramm in the Wadi Hisma Region. Extensive work in this latter area at Jabal Qalkha, Judayid Basin, Jabal Muaysi and Jabal Hamra (Henry 1995) shows occupation ranged from the Lower Palaeolithic up to the Chalcolithic period.

Uplift of the Western Mountains has different expressions in the north and south of the country. In the north, tilting and arching dominate, producing such features as the broad flat upwarp of the Ajlun Region. To the south, block faulting is more prominent (Bender 1975). Here the courses of major river valleys, such as the Wadi Karak, Wadi Hasa (downthrown to the south) and Wadi Hisma between Quwayra and Mudawwara are strongly influenced by northwest–southeast-trending lateral faults, a trend that is also parallel to that of the Red Sea Rift.

The Western Highlands reflect many of the attributes of mountainous landscapes bordering rift valleys, with long gentle slopes away from the rift towards the depressions of the Central Plateau, and a steep sharp fall into the Rift Valley graben. The highest areas in Jordan are in the southern mountains to the west of Maan where the elevation reaches over 1800 m Drainage is to the west to the Jordan Valley and Wadi Arabah, and to the southwest to the Gulf of Aqaba. Farther east, drainage is inland, towards the Jafr and Azraq Basins and Wadi Sirhan.

As a consequence of rifting and lowered base levels, the Western Highlands are deeply incised by wadis, such as the Yarmuk River, Zarqa River, Wadi Karak, Wadi Hasa and Wadi Mujib. Many of the deeply incised wadis intersect the saturated zones of Upper Cretaceous limestone aquifers, such as those of the Ajlun and Belqa group, and receive water as base flow and from springs, sufficient to permit perennial flow and provide water for many small settlements. Parker (1970) records a high permeability zone that occurs along the course of Wadi Hasa, arising from secondary porosity caused by intense jointing. He estimates that the base flow and spring flow to Wadi Hasa as being about 25 million m³/year.

The wadis are variously terraced, reflecting periods of incision, backfilling and further incision in response to changes in base level brought about by tectonism and by lake level changes in the adjacent Rift Valley to which they are graded. Upstream of their junction with the Rift Valley, thick sequences of Late Pleistocene Lisan Formation or its time-equivalent alluvium commonly infill canyons previously cut by ancestral wadis, such as the Wadi Hasa, Wadi Mujib, Wadi Hammeh and Wadi Jirm. In some cases, tectonics has resulted in localized blocking of major wadis, resulting in the development of temporary lake systems until further downcutting has re-established the previous fluvial landscape, leaving a suite of terraces to record the various stages in the development of the lake/wadi. Such was the case in the Wadi Yutm/Wadi Hisma (Osborn 1985; Hassan 1995), Wadi Hasa (Clark *et al.* 1987; Schuldenrein and Clark 1994) and at Gharandal (Bender 1974).

Example 1: Upper Zarqa/Khirbat Samra Region of West-Central Jordan

One important geoarchaeological study was that carried out in the upper Wadi Zarqa catchment, north of Amman (Besançon *et al.* 1984). The area includes Wadi Dhulail, a tributary of upper Wadi Zarqa, the zone of its confluence with Wadi Zarqa, and the area 5 km downstream from the junction (Figure 2.10).

The Wadi Zarqa sequence is one of the better terrace sequences in Jordan where a stratigraphical framework has been clearly related to middle Pleistocene archaeological

content. Besançon *et al.* (1984) compare the terraces with terrace sequences in Syria. This assumes, however, a more generalized and uniform evolution of the landscape than has yet been firmly established, especially given the role of tectonics as well as climate in erosion/deposition cycles. The Wadi Zarqa system tectonics have been varyingly active, and an early downcutting phase is linked to deepening of the Ghor. Similarly, tectonics have been suggested as being responsible for significant differences in the terrace system above and below Hashimiya, clearly shown in Figure 2.10.

The upper Wadi Zarqa region was strongly influenced by basalt flows, with an early phase, which now caps the surrounding hills, dated at c. 7–5 million years bp. Following deep incision by the wadis, a second phase of basalt flows dated at 2.92–3.35 million years bp flowed along the wadis. Four (or in some instances five) alluvial or colluvial terraces were recognized, the oldest overlying the younger basalts (Figure 2.10). These terraces were termed:

Qf3   Dauqara Formation
Qf2   Bire Formation
Qf2-1 Bire-Samra
Qf1   Khirbat Samra Formation, last Glacial/Pluvial
Qf0   Sukhna Formation

The high terrace Qf3 (Dauqara Formation) backfills and overtops a trench carved into the basalt. It now occurs at 70–80 m above the Zarqa valley floor. It is composed largely of cemented conglomerates and contains traces of likely Middle Acheulean occupation. The next oldest terrace, the Bire Formation, containing large amounts of weathered basalt cobbles and pebbles, overlies the Dauqara Formation. It contains rolled Late Acheulean assemblages of bifaces, cores and flakes, with a suggested age of about 200,000 years bp (Besançon *et al.* 1984; Copeland and Hours 1988). The third terrace (Qf1), the Khirbat Samra Formation (together with an intermediate Bire-Samra unit, which may be a different facies containing reworked deposits), consists more of colluvium than alluvium but includes aeolian material. It is a low terrace consisting of gravels with a silty matrix and contains Middle Palaeolithic Levallois flakes and cores. It has a suggested age of "Last Glacial/Pluvial, the early Wurm." Following a further phase of incision of the earlier terraces, the Final Wurm to Holocene Qf0 terrace (Sukhna Formation) was deposited. It contains Epipalaeolithic to Bronze Age material. For instance, at Site 27 (Figure 2.10) there is multi-period occupation with a Kebaran site overlain by a possible Neolithic site. Copeland and Hours (1988) consider that the terrace is Holocene and that the Kebaran material may be reworked.

The two earliest documented phases of incision along the Wadi Zarqa occur prior to and following the 3.35 million years bp basalt flow, the latter preceding the deposition of the Qf3 (Middle Acheulean) sequence.

These events are much earlier and cannot be readily correlated with most other sites under discussion. However, they may have equivalents in the Ras al-Naqab escarpment facing the Wadi Hisma catchment where three steps (pediments) at 1600 m, 1400 m and c. 1200 m respectively represent erosional cycles in the development of the scarp (Hassan 1995). Subsequently, a number of phases of downcutting and backfilling are represented by the terrace system, reflecting major base level changes affecting the Wadi Zarqa system. From Middle Pleistocene times, the evolution of the terraces has been interpreted in terms of climatic change, with aggradation linked to colder or drier phases (Besançon *et al.* 1984).

Artefact assemblages were associated with the different terraces and four age groups for the artefacts were determined based on the geomorphologic data, but patina was also an important consideration:

a. Those geologically *in situ* within the Dauqara Formation (considered Middle Pleistocene).
b. Those of the Bire Formation: Qf2 (equated with the Late Acheulean of the Levant and considered to represent the end of the Middle Pleistocene c. 200,000 bp and the penultimate Glacial/Pluvial).
c. Those in the Bire-Samra and Khirbat Samra Formations. The Qf1 terrace contains Levallois flakes; it is seen as representing Last Glacial (early Wurm).
d. The most recent terraces, such as the Sukhna Formation contain Epipalaeolithic to Bronze Age material and even pottery. There may be several phases present.

Example 2: The Wadi Hasa Region of Southwestern Jordan

In the southwestern area of Jordan, there is a steep rise from the Dead Sea (elevation c. 400 metres below sea level) to the Western Highlands and then on to the Central Plateau (at 1200 m). The Western Highlands are deeply incised by a number of major wadis draining westwards to the Jordan Valley. Drainage on the Central Plateau in most instances slopes gently to the east, with an important exception being Wadi Hasa. Occupation in westwards-flowing valleys has occurred since Lower Palaeolithic times and the well-documented Wadi Hasa sequence demonstrates the close relationship between landscape evolution and archaeology in these areas.

Wadi Hasa drains to the Southern Ghor, a part of the JordanRift Valley near the southern end of the Dead Sea. It is the only perennial stream between the Dead Sea and the Gulf of Aqaba to rise in the Central Plateau and pass westwards across the Western Highlands to enter the Rift Valley. The catchment area is 1740 km² and the rainfall lies between 100 and 200 mm/year. In its upper catchment region, Wadi Hasa receives perennial base flow from the Upper Cretaceous limestone aquifer. Like Wadi Hammeh, the course of Wadi Hasa has been varyingly influenced by base level changes caused by tectonism associated with Rift Valley development, and by cyclic lacustrine and fluvial activity. The Wadi Hasa lies to the southern (downthrown) side of the east–west-trending Hasa Fault, which has diverted the course of the wadi from a former northwards flow, westwards into the Rift Valley (Clark *et al.* 1987).

As a consequence of the ongoing subsidence of the Dead Sea graben, the lower tract of Wadi Hasa is very deeply incised (as much as 1200 m) into Cretaceous and late Pre-Cambrian sandstone and limestone. Upstream, the gradient flattens, and the course of the wadi traverses a landscape that consists of a remnant plain formed across a dissected former lake bed situated at an elevation of c. 815 m The incised valleys range from 0.2–1.0 km in width. The boundary between the upper (lake-plain) and lower (gorge) tract is seen as being where the wadi passes across the Wadi Hasa Fault that created the barred Wadi Hasa upper basin.

Hasa Wadi Terraces–Upper Wadi Hasa

At Wadi Hasa a well-developed set of terraces spans a period ranging from Middle Palaeolithic times to Late Holocene. Terraces occur both upstream and downstream from a fault that was responsible for the damming of the wadi in late Pleistocene times.

Vita-Finzi (1964) recognized three terraces in the upper Wadi Hasa. The highest is a 10–15 m high fluvial terrace consisting of a white calcareous silt with zones of grey, green and khaki, which on the basis of Kebaran artefacts was regarded as having formed by 16,000 bp (Copeland and Vita-Finzi 1978). This terrace is the same as the one that Schuldenrein and Clark (1994) later interpreted as a lake-plain sequence developed across lacustrine marl. A second terrace (and alluvial fill) of silty gravel is also present. Distribution of the alluvial fill is somewhat localized. It was dated to 11,000–8,000 bp (Vita-Finzi 1964, 1966).

A 4–6 m high third terrace that forms the high valley floor of the upper Wadi Hasa is very extensive. It consists of two discrete units. At the base of the sequence is 2–3 m of silts and fine sands overlain by a 1–2 m thick layer of cross-bedded and banded silts and fine sands (Schuldenrein and Clark 1994). Artefacts from near the base of the sequence led Vita-Finzi to conclude that aggradation commenced about 10,000 bp. Dates of 3950±150 bp (Vita-Finzi 1966; Copeland and Vita-Finzi 1978) and 990±120 bp (Schuldenrein and Clark 1994) have been obtained from the interval between the two sequences, suggesting a significant Middle to Late Holocene hiatus. This terrace probably corresponds with the low terrace (LT) of Wadi Ali (see below).

Remnants of a fourth terrace were also recognized by

Vita-Finzi and he identified this as a late Roman phase of wadi aggradation. A similar phase of alluviation is present elsewhere in the Jordan Valley, for instance, in the upper Wadi Hammeh and in upper Wadi Jirm of the Tabaqat Fahl region.

In the lower Wadi Hasa and along the Wadi Ali tributary, a three-tiered cut and fill terrace system has also been identified. The uppermost terrace is some 12–30 m above the present wadi floor, the intermediate terrace lies 5–6 m above the channel floor, and a lowermost terrace (modern flood plain) is only 0.5–1.5 m above the channel. The uppermost (high) terrace consists mainly of fluvial coarse sand and gravel but locally contains tufa, representing palaeospring deposits. At the Wadi Hasa Survey 634 site, situated some 11 km downstream of the western limit of the Hasa palaeolake, the high terrace surface passes laterally into a rock shelter, with the sequence containing Middle Palaeolithic occupation. An age of 105,000 bp ±1500 years was obtained for near the top of the high terrace.

Lake Hasa

Clark *et al.* (1987) and Schuldenrein and Clark (1994) indicate that the upper part of the Wadi Hasa was occupied during Late Pleistocene times by a lake (Lake Hasa) that reached a maximum level of 815 m (Figure 2.11). Lake Hasa was, therefore, at an elevation almost 1000 m above the highest level reached by the Late Pleistocene Lake Lisan (minus 180 m). Sediments from Lake Hasa consist of lacustrine marly sequences interdigitated with fluvial deposits, across which a number of terraces have developed.

Archaeological sites ranging in age from the Lower Palaeolithic are scattered along Wadi Hasa; a number of these are associated with the shoreline(s) of the lake. A lake-plain in the upper Wadi Hasa was eroded across a suite of marly lacustrine/fluvial sediments, at times capped with spring tufa. The palaeolake had an area of about 18 km long by 4 km wide and reached a maxi-

Figure 2.11 The maximum extent of Late Pleistocene Lake Hasa (from Clark *et al.* 1988).

Figure 2.12 Upper Wadi Hasa: Schematic stratigraphic section and archaeological sites (from Schuldenrein and Clark 1994).

mum altitude of 815 m (Clark 1984). The western limit of the lake is about 40 km from the edge of the Dead Sea graben. Most archaeological sites occur nearer the western end of the lake.

The marly deposits consist of two distinct lacustrine facies. Finely laminated chemically deposited gypseous and calcareous marls abutting the outer flanks of the lake basin at elevations of 810–815 m represent the highest levels reached by the lake. They are in isolated instances capped by thin (<2 m thick) spring-derived tufa deposits, which represent deposition during the high lake stand. At slightly lower levels (<810 m) the lake sediments consist of blocky to laminar sandy silts that grade laterally into the contemporary Hasa terraces. They are considered to represent a paludal or ponded facies. The picture is one of an evolving environment in which the former lake represented by the highly calcareous and gypseous suite gives way to a marshy landscape of pools and swamps in which marly sandy silts accumulate. Occupation occurred around the margins of the lake and in tributaries entering the lake.

Middle Palaeolithic lithic sites occur in both the upper and lower regions of Wadi Hasa. For instance, the Wadi

Hasa Survey 621 site in the upper Hasa region (Figure 2.12) is linked to an early phase of Lake Hasa. Site Wadi Hasa Survey 634, situated 10 km to the west, is Wadi Ali, in an entirely fluvial section well below the limits of the lake. At Wadi Hasa Survey 621, artefacts cluster around an oval of calcreted rubble, which may be the remains of a former spring. Middle Palaeolithic artefacts also occur in adjacent lacustrine marls causing Clark *et al.* (1987) to note that they are not *in situ* but instead were washed into the lake. Therefore, their origin either predates the lake or at the latest was contemporaneous with it. On this basis, Clark *et al.* (1987) and Schuldenrein and Clark (1994) suggest that the earliest phase of lake activity may date to the Middle Palaeolithic period, and estimate an age of 70,000 years.

Much clearer evidence for the former existence of a lake is seen in the Upper Palaeolithic site Wadi Hasa Survey 618 with radiocarbon dates that range in age from c. 26,000–19,000 bp. Nearby, Epipalaeolithic sites Wadi Hasa Survey 1065 and Wadi Hasa Survey 618 occupy high spurs of the dissected lake plain. At Wadi Hasa Survey 618, calcite-rich lacustrine sequences grade laterally into wadi alluvium and colluvium emanating from adjacent wadi systems. In the western locus of the site, tufaceous spring deposits and organic rich marshy deposits containing large numbers of microliths unconformably overlie laminated lacustrine marls. Northwards, the organic sediments are, in turn, overlain by alluvium. The spring activity is deemed to have occurred at peak lake levels with groundwater discharge outseeping around the margins of the lake. The high organic content of the sediments probably reflects vegetation growing within the spring zone. A date on spring tufa gave an age of 20,300±600 bp.

At Wadi Hasa Survey 1065, situated only 200 m from Wadi Hasa Survey 618, stratified marly sandy silts and clays, which contain extensive silicified root casts, overlie the lacustrine marls. They are seen as being marshy paludal deposits that developed after 20,000 bp, following the demise of Lake Hasa. Six dates on the occupation complex cluster between 16,900 bp and 15,600 bp, which agrees well with Kebaran stone tool industries present. Occupation in the paludal (at least seasonally) settings may have lasted until later than 12,000 bp as additional dates occur younger than 12,000 bp, which may represent a Natufian component. Pollen from the site suggested a Mediterranean open woodland/steppe environment, moister than that occurring at the older Wadi Hasa Survey 618.

Schuldenrein and Clark (1994) comment that the dated sequences of Wadi Hasa neither represent all time periods, nor cover the full extent of occupation. Instead, the clustering of dates, for example, in intervals of between 26,000 and 19,000 bp and 16,900 and 15,600 bp, is seen as representing phases of landscape stability, while the absence of dates during the intervening period is deemed as indicating landscape instability and erosion. Here the long interval prior to the Upper Palaeolithic date (26,000 bp) would imply erosion, at a time when it has been suggested that Lake Hasa was full. Indeed, it has been suggested that the lake may have been initiated as long as 70,000 years ago and lasted until about 20,000 bp (Schuldenrein and Clark 1994). However, the actual time when it originated is still problematical, as the Middle Palaeolithic stone tools in lake marl sequences at site Wadi Hasa Survey 621 are not *in situ* but instead were derived from adjacent areas prior to being deposited within the marls. Therefore, dating of the lake marls by the tools depends upon firstly clearly demonstrating that the lake and the tools were contemporaneous.

Whatever the case, it seems unlikely that with the limited catchment area (1740 km^2) there would have been sufficient runoff, other than during exceptionally wet periods, to maintain a permanent lake high in the landscape for 50,000 years, during which time there were a number of climatic oscillations. Furthermore the lake is tectonically initiated and does not occupy a closed terminal lake basin, as is the case with other long-enduring palaeolake systems, such as Lake Lisan/Dead Sea, Azraq Basin, Jafr Basin, etc. Instead it occurs within the upper reaches of a deeply incised wadi system, lying 1000 m above the nearby Rift Valley. Its presence in this position is unusual and is due to the fault barrier separating the upper and lower Hasa regions. The lake's survival and its history will therefore be closely linked to the history of the downstream barrier. In this setting, it is most unlikely that closure of the lake could be maintained over extremely long time periods given recurrent tectonic effects and the relatively short period for which the lake basin could remain unsilted. Silting, leading in turn to over-topping, would quickly destroy the barrier and hence the lake. A lake lasting from Upper Palaeolithic times (26,000 bp) into the Epipalaeolithic period is more easily accepted.

Palaeoenvironmental Summary for Wadi Hasa

The archaeological sites occurring along Wadi Hasa and Wadi Ali range from the Middle Palaeolithic (with an age greater than 105,000 bp) up to the Chalcolithic. However, from an environmental perspective, the most significant aspect of the Wadi Hasa record is the presence during the Late Pleistocene of Lake Hasa. While now forming a wadi terrace, the marly lacustrine sequences associated with tufaceous and organic-rich sediments suggest a lake/spring-zone setting from about 26,000 to c. 19,000 bp. The moist conditions prevailed into Kebaran times and possibly into Natufian times when pools and swamps replaced the lake.

It is likely that the favourable occupation environment ended with the onset of the Younger Drias cold/dry phase, which was followed by postglacial warming. This period saw the drying of Lake Lisan, at about 11,000 bp. This would have led to a further phase of incision of the Wadi Hasa, causing the breaching of any remaining barriers and the opening of the upper wadi to the lower wadi and hence to the Jordan Valley. By 9000–8000 bp, extensive dissection had cut tributaries down to bedrock.

Conclusion

Landscape evolution in a region as physically diverse as Jordan is not a uniform process. On the one hand, there is a tectonically active rift valley in the west, which provides the basis for large changes in base level, resulting in accelerated erosion and sedimentation both in the valley and on adjacent catchments. By contrast, in the east are the large shallow Azraq and Jafr Basins of internal drainage where base levels are relatively static. Erosion is commonly by deflation, resulting in condensed sedimentary sequences.

Any discussion on landscape evolution will therefore reveal as many differences as similarities, and no single monolithic pattern can be expected. Furthermore, while climate plays an important role in many of the evolutionary processes, other factors, such as groundwater and tectonics, will at times be locally dominant and act independently and varyingly across the region. Given that

Site	Landform	*	Time (yr bp)	Occupation and examples of Sites
Wadi Zarqa	Qf3 Terrace-Dauqara Formation	A	> 600,000 to >?250,000	Middle Acheulean
Tabaqat Fahl	Lower Tabaqat Fahl Formation	A	?400,000 to ~250,000	?Middle Acheulean: Sites M2, and M4
Wadi Zarqa	Qf3–Qf2 interval	E	>250,000 to ~200,000	
Azraq	Lacustrine carbonate	A	220000 ± 30,000	Travertine overlies C-Spring Lower Palaeolithic site
Wadi Zarqa	Qf2 Bire Formation	A	200,000	Late Acheulean
Tabaqat Fahl	Upper Tabaqat Fahl Formation	A	250,000–150,000	Late Acheulean. Sites M1 and M3
Hisma	Phase 1 alluvium (Qalkha Formation)	A	> 150,000	Late Acheulean, from near top of 30 m section of Phase 1 fill
Azraq	Edule lacustrine deposits	A	146.000 ± 15,000	
Tabaqat Fahl	Wadi Hammeh palaeovalley cut	E	~150,000 to 80/65,000	
Wadi Hasa	Wadi Ali, near top of high terrace	A	105,000 ± 15,000	Middle Palaeolithic WHS 634 (rock shelter) Middle Palaeolithic
Wadi Hasa	Calcreted rubble-spring tufa?			
Wadi Hisma	Dune sands in Phase 1 and 2 hiatus	E	> 70,000 to > 20,000	Tor Faraj and Tor Sabiha Mousterian sites
Wadi Zarqa	Qf2–1/Qf-1 terraces. Bire-Samra and Khirbat Samra Formation	A	"Early Wurm"	Levallois flakes in Qf1 terrace
Tabaqat Fahl	Wadi Hammeh fill of palaeovalleys	A	80/65,000–11,100	Middle Palaeolithic to Natufian sites
Wadi Hisban	Wadi Hisban terrace	A	?80/65,000–11,000	Near top, Epipalaeolithic–Geom. Kebaran/Natufian
Wadi Hisma	Phase 2 fill/rock shelters	A	> 20,000–12,300	Upper Palaeolithic and Epipalaeolithic, including Qalkhan, Madamaghan, and Hamran sites
Azraq Basin	Wadi Jilat: soils in aeolian silt	A	21,250 to >14,790	Upper Palaeolithic and Epipalaeolithic. Jilat 9, Jilat 6
Azraq Basin	Wadi Jilat: aeolian silts	A	14,790–present	Late Epipalaeolithic, Jilat 6, 8 and 10; Natufian, Azraq 18; PPNB, Azraq 31
Azraq Basin	Wadi Uwaynid: aeolian silt with palaesols	A	23,200–15,500	Uwaynid 14, 18
Wadi Hasa	Lake edge = part Terrace 1 Vita-Finzi (1964)	A	c. 26,000–19,000	Upper Palaeolithic WHS 618
Wadi Hasa	Swamp/marsh deposits postdate lake = part = Terrace 1 Vita-Finzi	A	16,900– 15,600	Kebaran: WHS 1065
Wadi Hasa	Data hiatus between Terrace 1 and 2	E	15,600–11,280	
Wadi Hasa	Marsh setting = Terrace 2 Vita-Finzi	?A	11,280–9,010	Natufian
Wadi Hisma	Incision of Phase 2 fill, terraces formed	E	>12,500–present	Natufian J2 site in terrace sediments
Tabaqat Fahl	Incision of Wadi Hammeh/Wadi Jirm terraces	E	<11,100–	
Wadi Hisban	Incision of Hisban terraces	E	11,000–	
Wadi Hisma	Dune accretion	A	11,000–9,000	

Table 2.2   Summary of major Pleistocene events from selected sites. * Aggradation (A) or erosion (E).

the basis for this analysis is geoarchaeological data, then aggradational features will have more relevance than erosional features. This is born out in Table 2.2, which is a résumé of Pleistocene events from the various sites.

The earliest landscape features discussed above are Pliocene, and predate human occupation. They include the development of the Jordan Rift Valley, the three erosive levels or pediments along the Ras al-Naqab scarp, and the Pliocene basalt flows that now cap the hills and infill ancient valleys in the upper Wadi Zarqa region. However,

the main focus in this paper is the time range spanned by occupation, from the Middle Pleistocene period to the present. Of the examples chosen, there are broad similarities in the evolution of the Jordanian landscape between some of the sites, especially during Early Palaeolithic times. For instance, the time span for the aggradation of the Qf2 Bire Formation at Wadi Zarqa, the Phase I fill at Wadi Hisma and the upper Tabaqat Fahl Formation. From Middle Palaeolithic times to the present, a number of broad cycles of incision and deposition are recorded across these sites, all the catchments of which border the Jordan Valley.

However, while there are many additional similarities and coincidences of events, there are also many major differences, resulting in no clearly defined ongoing uniformity in the pattern of geomorphic evolution across the country. The problem stems partially from the lack of dating and partially because of the great diversity between the sites. For instance, the nature of the Azraq sites is dominated by the position of the area at the lower extremes of a basin of internal drainage, and the presence of the Azraq (and other) playas through time. The resulting strong aeolian influences reflecting deflationary processes, coupled with the thin discontinuous sedimentary sequences, make it difficult to slot landscape evolution into a regional (countrywide) framework. External climatic influences, although having real and identifiable impacts, are to a large extent muted by the hydrological and geomorphologic influence of the playas.

Similarly, Lake Hasa, while an important centre of occupation throughout its history, is a fault-controlled landform lying high up on the side of the Jordan Valley. The history of the creation and destruction of the barrier behind which the lake formed therefore largely determines the landscape history of the lake. Its base level is determined by the fault and not by the level of the Dead Sea. The wadi is deeply incised and a base flow system. Any barrier could lead to temporary lake formation, lasting until the barrier was breached, either through further tectonic activity or to overtopping during times of very high lake levels, or maybe headward erosion of the truncated Wadi Hasa. There is no requirement that the evolution of this system should bear any close relationship to the regional changes affecting other areas under discussion.

Of the sites examined, the Wadi Zarqa, Tabaqat Fahl and Wadi Hisma sites are best suited to reflect major regional trends in geomorphic evolution. Erosion and deposition in their catchments are strongly influenced by Rift Valley lake levels, which in turn are influenced by climate and tectonics. Of all the sites discussed, the Badia sites in the Eastern Basalt Desert Province, although limited in time, best reflect purely climatic influences.

Finally, when examining the archaeological/geomorphologic record, it seems there is an unintentional interplay between a relatively small number of environmental specialists, who commonly overlap on sites and carry with them to new sites understandings that greatly influence their interpretations, especially where limited data is present. This is brought out clearly in the large amount of site cross-referencing used to support interpretations in cases where there is otherwise too little data on which to base a conclusion. Despite this cross-pollination of ideas, there have still arisen significantly different interpretations on the nature of palaeohydrologic events occurring

across Jordan since Middle Pleistocene times.

The environmental reconstructions discussed here seem to be inherently valid within the limits of their data, yet separately they have many differences. It follows that in the case of a number of the better-documented sites, attempts to reach consensus on a broad regional syntheses are not easy. It is even less appropriate, therefore, to carry out detailed regional reconstructions and correlations on the basis of less well-documented, more fragmentary sites, in widely different geographic and climatic settings. Perhaps then, before trying to tie in with any broader framework, it must be asked how appropriate is a site to meet such objectives? Clearly there will often be a stand-alone story, with or without a requirement that it be regionalized. Indeed where regionalization occurs, originality can be lost for the dubious gain of appearing to conform and by doing so add legitimacy. The absence of such questioning raises the spectre that the "science" or "art" of regional synthesis may at times survive simply because the fragmentary nature of the evidence lends itself to the construction of discrete schools whose doctrines prosper as much by the lack of evidence as by its availability.

Bibliography

Begin, Z.B., A. Ehrlich and Y. Nathan

1974 Lake Lisan: The Pleistocene Precursor of the Dead Sea. *Geological Survey of Israel Bulletin* 63: 1–30.

Begin, Z.B., W. Broecker, B. Buchbinder, Y. Druckman, A. Kaufman, M. Margaritz and D. Neev

1985 Lake Lisan Levels in the Last 30,000 Years: A Preliminary Report. *Geological Survey of Israel Report* 29/85. Jerusalem: Geological Survey of Israel.

Bender, F.

1968 *Geologie von Jordanie*. Berlin: Borntraeger.

1974 *Geology of Jordan*. Berlin: Borntraeger.

1975 Geology of the Arabian Peninsula–Jordan. *United States Geological Survey Professional Papers* 56: I.

Besançon, J., B. Gayer and P. Sanlaville

1989 Contribution to the Study of the Geomorphology of the Azraq Basin, Jordan. In L. Copeland and F. Hours (eds.), *The Hammer on the Rock*, 7–63. British Archaeological Reports International Series 540. Oxford: British Archaeological Reports.

Besançon, J., L. Copeland, F. Hours, J.-J. Macaire and P. Sanlaville

1984 The Lower and Middle Palaeolithic in the Upper Zarqa/Khirbet Samra Area of Northern Jordan: 1982–83 Survey Results. *Annual of the Department of Antiquities of Jordan* 28: 91–142.

Betts, A.V.G.

1985 Black Desert Survey, Jordan: Third Preliminary Report. *Levant* 17: 29–35.

1988 The Black Desert Survey: Prehistoric Sites and Subsistence Strategies in Eastern Jordan. In A.N. Garrard and

H.G. Gebel (eds.), *The Prehistory of Jordan: The State of Research in 1986*, 369–391. British Archaeological Reports International Series 396. Oxford: British Archaeological Reports.

1992 Eastern Jordan: Economic Choices and Site Locations in the Neolithic Periods. In S. Tell, G. Bisheh, F. Zayadine, K. 'Amr, and M. Zaghloul (eds.), *Studies in the History and Archaeology of Jordan IV,* 111–114. Amman: Department of Antiquities.

1993 The Neolithic Sequence in the East Jordan Badia: A Preliminary Overview. *Paléorient* 19(1): 43–53.

Betts, A.V.G. and S.W. Helms

1989 A Water Harvesting and Storage System at Ibn El-Ghazzi in Eastern Jordan: A Preliminary Report. *Levant* 21: 3–11.

Clark, G.A.

1984 The Negev Model for Palaeoclimatic Change and Human Adaption in the Levant. *Annual of the Department of Antiquities of Jordan* 28: 225–248.

Clark, G.A., N. Coinman and J. Lindly

1986 Palaeolithic Site Placement in the Wadi Hasa, West-Central Jordan. *Annual of the Department of Antiquities of Jordan* 30: 23–29.

Clark, G.A., J.H. Lindly, M. Donaldson, A. Garrard, N. Coinman, J. Schuldenrein, S. Fish and D. Olszewski

1987 Palaeolithic Archaeology in the Southern Levant: A Preliminary Report of Excavations at Middle, Upper and Epipalaeolithic Sites in Wadi el-Hasa, West-Central Jordan. *Annual of the Department of Antiquities of Jordan* 31: 19–77.

1988 Excavations at Middle, Upper and Epipalaeolithic Sites in the Wadi Hasa, West-Central Jordan. In A.N. Garrard and H.G. Gebel (eds.), *The Prehistory of Jordan: The State of Research in 1986*, 209–285. British Archaeological Reports International Series 396(i). Oxford: British Archaeological Reports.

Clark, G.A., M.P. Neeley, B. MacDonald, J. Schuldenrein and K. 'Amr

1992 Wadi Hasa Palaeolithic Project, 1992: A Preliminary Report. *Annual of the Department of Antiquities of Jordan* 36: 13–23.

Coinman, N. and D.O. Henry

1995 The Upper Palaeolithic Sites. In D.O. Henry, *Prehistoric Cultural Ecology and Evolution: Insights from Southern Jordan*, 123–213. New York: Plenum.

Copeland, L.

1988 Environment, Chronology, and Lower-Middle Palaeolithic Occupations of the Azraq Basin, Jordan. *Paléorient* 14: 66–75

1998 The Lower Palaeolithic of Jordan. In D.O. Henry (ed.), *The Prehistoric Archaeology of Jordan*, 5–22. British Archaeological reports International Series 705. Oxford: British Archaeological Reports.

Copeland, L. and F. Hours

1988 The Palaeolithic in North Central Jordan: An Overview of Survey Results from the Upper Zarqa and Azraq 1982–1986. In A.N. Garrard and H.G. Gebel (eds.), *The Prehistory of Jordan: The State of Research in 1986*, 287–309. British Archaeological Reports International Series 396. Oxford: British Archaeological Reports.

Copeland, L. and C. Vita-Finzi

1978 Archaeological Dating of Geological Deposits in Jordan. *Levant* 10: 10–25.

Eden, C.

1988 Archaeology of the Sands and Adjacent Portions of the Sharqiyah. In The Scientific Results of the Royal Geographic Society's Oman Wahiba Sands Project 1985–1987. *Journal of Oman Studies Special Report* 3: 113–130.

Edwards, P. C. and P. G. Macumber

1995 The Last Half Million Years at Pella. In S. Bourke and J.-P. Descoeudres (eds.), *Trade, Contact and Movement of Peoples in the Eastern Mediterranean*. Mediterranean Archaeological Supplement 3: 1–14. Sydney: Meditarch.

Edwards, P.C., P.G. Macumber and M.J. Head

1996 The Early Epipalaeolithic of Wadi Hammeh. *Levant* 28: 115–130.

Emery-Barber, A.

1995 Pollen Analysis: Environmental and Climatic Implications. In D.O. Henry, *Prehistoric Cultural Ecology and Evolution: Insights from Southern Jordan*, 375–384. New York: Plenum.

Gardner, R.A.M.

1988 Aeolianite and Marine Deposits of the Wahiba Sands: Character and Palaeoenvironments. *Journal of Oman Studies Special Report 3*: 75–95.

Garrard, A.N. and B. Byrd

1992 New Dimensions to the Epipalaeolithic of the Wadi El Jilat in Central Jordan. *Paléorient* 18(1): 47–62.

Garrard, A.N., B. Byrd, P. Harvey and F. Hivernel

1985 Prehistoric Environment and Settlement in the Azraq Basin: A Report on the 1982 Survey Season. *Levant* 17: 1–52

Garrard, A.N., P. Harvey, F. Hivernel and B. Byrd

1985 The Environmental History of the Azraq Basin. In A. Hadidi (ed.), *Studies in the History and Archaeology of Jordan II*, 109–115. Amman: Department of Antiquities.

Garrard, A.N., A. Betts, B. Byrd and C. Hunt

1988 Summary of Palaeoenvironmental and Prehistoric Investigations in the Azraq Basin. In A.N. Garrard and H.G. Gebel (eds.), *The Prehistory of Jordan: The State of Research in 1986*, 311–337. British Archaeological Reports International Series 396(i). Oxford: British Archaeological Reports.

Garrard, A.N., S. Colledge, C. Hunt and R. Montague

1988 Environment and Subsistence during the Late Pleistocene and Early Holocene in the Azraq Basin. *Paléorient* 14: 40–49.

Gat, J.R. and I. Carmi

1987 Effect of Climatic Change on the Precipitation Patterns and Isotopic Composition of Water in a Climate Transition Zone: Case of the East Mediterranean Sea Area. *IAHS Publication* 168: 513–523.

Gilbertson, D.D., C.O. Hunt and S. Bradley

1985 Micropalaeontological and Palaeoecological Studies of Recent Sediments from the Azraq Marshes in the Jordanian Desert. In A. Hadidi (ed.), *Studies in the History and Archaeology of Jordan II*, 347–352. Amman: Department of Antiquities.

Ginzberg, A. and E. Kashai

1981 Seismic Measurements in the Southern Dead Sea. In R. Freund and Z. Garfunkel (eds.), *The Dead Sea Rift: Tectonophysics* 80: 67–80.

Goldberg, P. and A.M. Rosen

1987 Early Holocene Palaeoenvironments of Israel. In T.E. Levy (ed.), *Shiqmim I: Studies Concerning Chalcolithic Sites in the Northern Negev Desert, Israel*, 23–32. British Archaeological Reports International Series 356. Oxford: British Archaeological Reports.

Goodfriend, G.A., M. Magaritz and I. Carmi

1986 A High Stand of the Dead Sea at the End of the Neolithic Period: Palaeoclimatic and Archaeological Implications. *Climatic Change* 9: 349–356.

Goren-Inbar, N.

1988 The Lower Palaeolithic-Synthesis. *Paléorient* 13(2): 109–111.

Hassan, F.A.

1995 Late Quaternary Geology and Geomorphology of the Area in the Vicinity of Ras en Naqb. In D.O. Henry, *Prehistoric Cultural Ecology and Evolution: Insights from Southern Jordan*, 23–31. New York: Plenum.

Helms, S.W.

1977 Jawa Excavations 1975: Third Preliminary Report. *Levant* 9: 21.

1982 Paleo-Bedouin and Transmigrant Urbanism. In A. Hadidi (ed.), *Studies in the History and Archaeology of Jordan* I, 97–112. Amman: Department of Antiquities.

Helms, S.W. and A.V.G. Betts

1987 The Desert 'Kites' of the Badiyat esh-Sham and North Arabia. *Paléorient* 12(1): 41–67.

Henry, D.O.

1979 Palaeolithic Sites in the Ras en Naqb Basin, Southern Jordan. *Palestine Exploration Quarterly* 111: 79–85.

1982 The Prehistory of Southern Jordan and Relationships with the Levant. *Paléorient* 2(2): 389–393.

1995 *Prehistoric Cultural Ecology and Evolution: Insights from Southern Jordan*. New York: Plenum.

Henry, D.O. and G.H. Miller

1992 The Implications of Amino Acid Racemization Dates of Levantine Mousterian Deposits in Southern Jordan. *Paléorient* 18(2): 45–52.

Huckriede, R.

1966 Das Quartar des Arabischen Jordan-Thales und Beobachtungen über 'Pebble Culture' und 'Prae-Aurignac'. *Eizeitalter Genenwart* 17: 211–212.

Huckriede, R. and G. Wiesemann

1968 Der Jungpleistozane Pluvial-Von Al Jafr und Weitere Daten zum Quartar Jordaniens. *Geologica et Palaeontologica* 2: 73–79.

MacDonald, B.

1992 Settlement Patterns along the Southern Flank of Wadi al-Hasa: Evidence from 'the Wadi al-Hasa Archaeological Survey'. In M. Zaghloul, K. Amr, F. Zayadine, R. Nabeel and N. Rida Tawfiq (eds.), *Studies in the History and Archaeology of Jordan IV*, 73–76. Amman: Department of Antiquities.

MacDonald, B., G. Rollefson, E. Banning, B. Byrd and C. d'Annibale

1983 The Wadi el Hasa Archaeological Survey 1982. *Annual of the Department of Antiquities of Jordan* 27: 31–34.

MacDonald, B. (ed.)

1988 *The Wadi el-Hasa Archaeological Survey 1979–1983, West-Central Jordan*. Waterloo, ON: Wilfrid Laurier University.

McClure, H.A.

1976 Radiocarbon Chronology of Late Quaternary Lakes in the Arabian Desert. *Nature* 263: 755–756.

1978 Ar Rub Al Khali. In S.S. al-Sayari and J.G. Zotl (eds.), *Quaternary of Saudi Arabia* 1: 252–263. New York: Springer.

Macumber, P.G.

1970 Lunette Initiation in the Kerang District. *Victorian Mining and Geological Journal* 6: 16–18.

1984 Geology and Geomorphology of the Lower Wadi Hammeh Sites. In A.W. McNicholl, W. Ball, S. Basset, P. Edwards, D. Petves, T. Potts, L. Randle, L. Villiers and P. Watson. Preliminary Report on the University of Sydney's Fifth Season of Excavation at Pella. *Annual of the Department of Antiquities of Jordan* 28: 81–86.

1986 Environmental Reconstruction of the Wadi Hammeh Region in the Late Pleistocene. In A.W. McNicholl, P. Edwards, J. Hosking, P.G. Macumber, A.G. Walmsley and P.M. Watson. Preliminary Report on the University of Sydney's Seventh Season of Excavation at Pella (Tabaqat Fahl) in 1985. *Annual of the Department of Antiquities of Jordan* 30: 156–157.

1991 *Interaction between Groundwater and Surface Systems in Northern Victoria, Australia*. Melbourne: Ministry of Environment

1992a The Geology and Geomorphology of the Wadi Hammeh-Wadi Jirm Region, Northwestern Jordan. In A.

McNicholl, J.B. Hennessy, T.F. Potts and R.H. Smith (eds.), *Pella in Jordan* 2, 205–214. Canberra: Australian National Gallery.

1992b The Geological Setting of Palaeolithic Sites at Tabaqat Fahl, Jordan. *Paléorient* 18(2): 31–44.

Macumber, P.G. and P.C. Edwards

1997 Preliminary results from the Acheulian site of Masharia 1, and a new stratigraphic framework for the Lower Palaeolithic of the east Joprdan Valley. In H.G.K. Gebel, Z. Kafafi and G.O. Rollefson (eds.), *The Prehistory of Jordan II. Perspectives from 1997.* Studies in Near Eastern production, subsidence and environment 4. Berlin: *ex oriente.*

Macumber, P.G. and H.J. Head

1991 Implications of the Wadi al-Hammeh Sequences for the Terminal Drying of Lake Lisan, Jordan. *Palaeogeography, Palaeoclimatology, Palaeoecology* 84: 163–173.

Ministry of Energy and Mineral Resources

1993 *Al 'Azraq 1:50000.* Amman, Jordan.

Neev, D. and K.O. Emery

1967 The Dead Sea, Depositional Processes and Environments of Evaporites. *Geological Survey of Israel Bulletin* 41.

Neev, D. and J.K. Hall

1976 Dead Sea Geophysical Survey 19 July–Aug. 1974. *Proceedings of the Annual Meeting of the Geological Survey of Israel, Ashqelon,* 8–10.

Nelson, B.

1973 *Azraq, Desert Oasis.* London: Lane.

Osborn, G.

1985 Evolution of Late Cenozoic Inselberg Landscape of Southwestern Jordan. *Palaeogeography, Palaeoclimatology, Palaeoecology* 49: 1–23.

Parker, D.H.

1970 *The Hydrogeology of the Mesozoic–Cainozoic Aquifers of the Western Highlands and Plateau of Eastern Jordan.* UNDP/FAO, Ag 2: SF/JOR 9, Technical Report No. 2, 424pp. Rome.

Quennel, A.M.

1958 The Structural and Geomorphic Evolution of the Dead Sea Rift. *Quarterly Journal of the Geological Society of London* 114: 1–24.

Rollefson, G.O.

1982 Late Acheulian Artefacts from Ain el-Assad (Lion's Spring), near Azraq, Eastern Jordan. *Bulletin of the American Schools of Oriental Research* 240: 1–20.

1985 Late Pleistocene Environments and Seasonal Hunting Strategies: A Case Study from Fjaje, near Shobak, Southern Jordan. In A. Hadidi (ed.), *Studies in the History and Archaeology of Jordan II,* 103–108. Amman: Department of Antiquities.

1992 Neolithic Settlement Pattern in Northern Jordan and Palestine. In M. Zaghloul, K. Amr, F. Zayadine, R. Nabeel and N. Rida Tawfiq (eds.), *Studies in the History and Archaeology of Jordan IV,* 123–127. Amman: Department of Antiquities.

Rollefson, G.O. and A.H. Simmons

1988 The Neolithic Settlement at 'Ain Ghazzal. In A.N. Garrard and H.G. Gebel (eds.), *The Prehistory of Jordan: The State of Research in 1986,* 393–405. British Archaeological Reports International Series 396. Oxford: British Archaeological Reports.

Rossingnol-Strick, M.

1993 Late Quaternary Climate in the Eastern Mediterranean Region. *Paléorient* 19(1): 135–152.

Salameh, E.

1985 The Development of the Hydrodynamic System in Connection with the Formation of the Jordan Graben and its Effects on the Generation of Oil. *Beiträge zur Hydrologie* 5(1): 49–66.

Salameh, E. and P. Udluft

1985 The Hydrodynamic Pattern of the Central Part of Jordan. *Geologie Jahrbuch* 38: 39–53.

Schuldenrein, J. and G.A. Clark

1994 Landscape and Prehistoric Chronology of West-Central Jordan. *Geoarchaeology* 9(1): 31–35.

Stekelis, M., O. Bar-Yosef and T. Schick

1969 *Archaeological Excavations at 'Ubeidiya, 1964–1966.* Jerusalem: Israel Academy of Sciences and Humanities.

Tchernov, E.

1988 The Age of 'Ubeidiya Formation (Jordan Valley, Israel) and the Earliest Hominids in the Levant. *Paléorient* 14(2): 63–65.

Vita-Finzi, C.

1964 Observations on the Late Quaternary of Jordan. *Palestine Exploration Quarterly* 95: 19–31.

1966 The Hasa Formation: An Alluvial Deposition in Jordan. *Man* 1: 386–390.

1982 The Prehistory and History of the Jordanian Landscape. In A. Hadidi (ed.), *Studies in the History and Archaeology of Jordan I,* 23–27. Amman: Department of Antiquities.

Weinstein, M.

1976 The Late Pleistocene Vegetation and Climate of the Northern Golan. *Pollen et Spores* 17(4): 553–562.

Weinstein-Evron, M.

1989 Palynological History of the Last Peniglacial in the Levant. Les Industries 'Pointes Foliacá ees du Paléolithique Superior Européen, Krakow 1989. Ètudes et Recherches Archéologiques de l'Université de Liège No. 42. Liège: Université de Liège.

3. The Palaeolithic Period, including the Epipalaeolithic

Deborah Olszewski

Introduction

The modern country of Jordan is within the eastern or inland Levant, a region that has undergone striking climatic and ecological change during the course of the approximately 450,000 years of its Palaeolithic prehistory. Its story of ancient humans is one told largely through the stone tools they discarded, their campsites, the remains of their food, and the reconstruction of the landscapes they inhabited. More rarely, this story also includes evidence from burials and of artistic expression. The study of these Palaeolithic groups and their lifeways is part of a research tradition with a lengthy history, one which has accelerated at a dramatic pace since the 1970s.

Prior to the 1970s, only a few researchers had recorded and excavated Palaeolithic sites in Jordan. Notable among these early efforts are surveys by Rees (1929), Rhotert (1938), Zeuner *et al.* (1957) and Field (1960), and excavations by Waechter *et al.* (1938) and Kirkbride (1958, 1966). These studies documented the existence of a substantial Palaeolithic presence in Jordan, but pursuit of Palaeolithic research was limited, as most researchers focused their work on the sites of later time periods. In the 1970s, however, several individuals began extensive archaeological research programmes that were centered both on resurvey of areas explored in earlier decades or on vast tracts of land for which little archaeological documentation existed. Many of these programmes carried over into the 1980s and 1990s, and have been augmented by additional projects.

Palaeolithic research has concentrated on four regions explored by these projects. These are the Azraq Basin (Garrard *et al.* 1977, 1985, 1986, 1987; Rollefson *et al.* 2001), the Wadi Hasa (MacDonald *et al.* 1980, 1982, 1983; Clark *et al.* 1988, 1992, 1994; Coinman *et al.* 1999; Olszewski *et al.* 1998, 2001), the Ras al-Naqab region (Henry 1995; Kerry 1997; Olson 1997; Williams 1997), and the Tabaqat Fahl area (Edwards *et al.* 1988, 1999; Macumber and Edwards 1997). Surveys and excavations in the Petra area (Johnson *et al.* 1999; Schyle and Gebel 1997; Schyle and Uerpmann 1988), the Black Desert (Betts 1998), the Wadi Ziqlab (Maher *et al.* 2001), the Jafr Basin (Quintero and Wilke 1998), the Jurf Darawish area (MacDonald *et al.* 2000, 2001), the Khanasyra region (Bartl *et al.* 2001), and the Wadi Koum (Bisson *et al.* in press) have also added sites to the Palaeolithic roster, as have dozens of smaller surveys and single site excavations. This research on the Palaeolithic landscape

of Jordan has resulted in a significant transformation of our understanding of ancient lifeways, not only because there are now hundreds of documented sites, but, more importantly, because the archaeological record of the eastern Levant has shown that the adaptations of these hunter-gatherer groups were much more varied, flexible and dynamic than predicted by archaeological models developed in the western Levant.

Terminology

The Palaeolithic is a period of time commonly known as the "Old Stone Age." The use of the term Palaeolithic refers to the tradition of manufacturing tools from stone, a tradition that began with the ancestors of modern human groups and continued well-beyond the end of the Palaeolithic era. Human groups during the Palaeolithic were hunter-gatherers, most of whom were highly mobile. The majority of the Palaeolithic time period coincides with the Pleistocene, although the first stone tools are earlier and date to the Pliocene. During the latter part of the Pleistocene, glaciers across the northern and southern latitudes advanced and retreated numerous times. These advances (stadials) and retreats (interstadials), as well as many smaller oscillations within stadials and interstadials, had a significant effect on world-wide climate and environment. Although glaciers were not present in the Middle East, except at the tops of some mountain peaks, there were notable long-term changes in temperature, the amount of rainfall, and the seasonal distribution of rainfall. These types of changes meant that the geographic extent of vegetation communities and the diversity of plant species that characterized them were subject to fluctuations over time. In turn, both the types and the abundance of animal species that depended on particular vegetation communities were also influenced, as were the human groups who hunted these animals and made use of plant foods.

Stone tools were an important adaptive technology for ancient peoples. Early groups developed methods to remove effectively sharp edged pieces of stone from larger blocks of stone. These could be used as they were or modified into special forms of tools. Removing pieces of stone is a process known as knapping (flint knapping) in which a core, such as a nodule or cobble, is struck with a stone hammerstone, a hard piece of wood or an antler segment (percussion technique). Pieces of stone are sometimes pressed off a core using pressure technique. With proper control and practice, a flintknapper can remove blades (long, parallel edged pieces) or bladelets (small versions of blades) or flakes (wide, non-parallel edged pieces). Blades and flakes serve as blanks that can be modified into tools such as endscrapers, sidescrapers and burins. Bladelets are often retouched or backed, becoming a tool form known as a microlith. There are also special forms of core tools such as bifaces, that are retouched on both sides; those known as handaxes can vary in shape from pointed to oval, while cleavers have a flat edge at one end. Early flintknappers also developed specialized core techniques such as Levallois technology, where cores were carefully prepared so that particular shapes and sizes of blanks could be removed (Figure 3.1).

The earliest archaeological evidence of Palaeolithic groups is from eastern Africa during the Pliocene, about 2.6 million years bp. It was not until somewhat before 1 million years bp, during the Pleistocene, however, that ancient humans of the Palaeolithic began to migrate from Africa into the Middle East. Archaeological work in Jordan appears to have documented sites as early as 0.9 to 1.0 million years bp (Parenti *et al.* 1997). The majority of the earliest sites in the archaeological record of Jordan, however, appear to date to about 450,000 years bp.

The Palaeolithic has been subdivided by archaeologists working in Western Eurasia (Europe and the Middle East) into four major periods based on chronology and the technology and typology of stone artefact assemblages. These periods are the Lower, Middle, and Upper Palaeolithic, and the Epipalaeolithic. Although this classification system was designed to provide a set of distinct analytical units, many decades of research have now shown that there is considerable technological overlap between the Lower and Middle Palaeolithic, and substantial chronological overlap between the late Upper and the Early Epipalaeolithic. Additional difficulties are raised by the lack of dates from many of the relevant sites and the advent of newer dating methodologies, for example, electron spin resonance (ESR) and thermoluminescence (TL), that have yielded dates for sites that are considerably older than expected. These are key issues that have not always been satisfactorily resolved, and which can have an important bearing on how Palaeolithic behaviors are interpreted.

Stone artefact assemblages form the primary basis of the delineation of the Palaeolithic periods. In the discussions that follow, lithic assemblages are grouped into phases, industries, and complexes, following Henry (1995: 35–36). Briefly, an assemblage is a set of lithic artefacts recovered from a specific context within an archaeological site, generally from a particular layer or level. When assemblages share specific technological and typological characteristics, they are grouped into a phase designation, such as "Early" or "Late." An industry consists of one or more phases that are similar in technology and in typology at the level of tool classes and tool types; this is an intermediate category of classification, for example, the "Early Natufian." A complex is composed of one or more industries that share a general technological pattern, but which have less overall similarity in specific tool types. The Early and Late Natufian, for example, contain different forms of lunate microliths; both phases/industries are components of the "Natufian Complex."

The Lower Palaeolithic is the oldest period (beginning in Africa about 2.6 million years bp). In Jordan, the oldest sites of this period are about 0.9–1.0 million years bp; this period continues until about 150,000 years bp. The stone artefact assemblages of the Lower Palaeolithic in Jordan are usually classified into the Acheulean Complex. The most distinctive Acheulean stone tools are bifaces—sometimes referred to as handaxes—and cleavers; other tools include scrapers, notches, and retouched flakes. A prominent technological attribute of some Acheulean assemblages is the use of the proto-Levallois and Levallois techniques of core reduction. The Acheulean is subdivided into four phases: Early, Middle, Late and Final. Of these, it is the Middle, Late and Final phases that are found most often in Jordan. Other distinctions noted are differences between the "Desert Wadi Acheulean" and the "Acheulean of Azraq" phases (Copeland 1988; Copeland

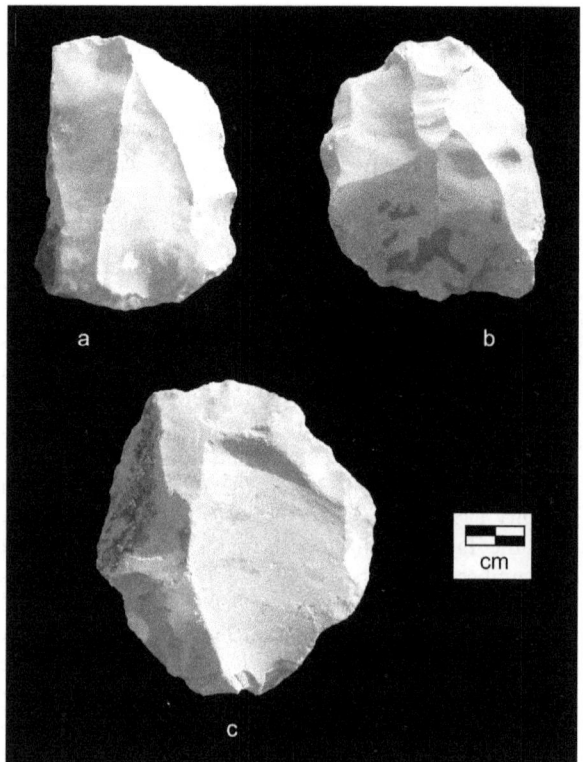

Figure 3.1 Examples of Levallois cores from a surface site near Amman. a: Levallois point core; b: Levallois blade core; c: Levallois flake core.

and Hours 1988). These are further discussed later.

Sites of the Middle Palaeolithic span the interval from about 150,000 to 45,000 years bp, although recent dates from the northern Levant are as late as 33,300 years bp (Richter *et al.* 2001). Stone artefact assemblages of this period are representative of the Levantine Mousterian Complex. The industries of this complex are named for the sequence discovered at the site of Tabun in the western Levant (Mount Carmel area). At that site, the earliest industry is classified as Tabun D-type; this is followed by Tabun C-type, and then by Tabun B-type. Although these types of industries have been identified elsewhere in the Levant, they do not appear to delineate chronologically distinct entities except at the site of Tabun. Many researchers believe that the differences between the industries are more likely related to the exploitation of the resources of differing local ecologies. (The sequence at Tabun may therefore represent changes in local ecology over time.) For example, steppic and desert zones characterize many areas of Jordan; assemblages here are primarily of the Tabun D-type (Clark *et al.* 1997; Henry 1995: 37). Typical features of these assemblages are the use of the Levallois technique to produce laminar blanks, such as blades and points. In most assemblages, these points are elongated in size; they are the primary tool type, along with tools on blades, such as burins. There are, however, also rare examples of Tabun C/B-type assemblages, characterized by the use of Levallois technique to produce Levallois flakes and other blanks that are used to manufacture various sidescrapers (Clark *et al.* 1988: 214–225; 1997; Bisson *et al.* in press). The distinctions between Tabun D and Tabun C/B assemblages are explored in further detail in the Middle Palaeolithic section below.

The Upper Palaeolithic period lasts from approximately 45,000 to 20,000 years bp in the eastern Levant and possibly as late as 16,000 years bp in the western Levant. Two major complexes of this period, found in the Middle East, are the Ahmarian and the Levantine Aurignacian. Ahmarian assemblages are characterized by blade and bladelet technology, with many of the bladelets modified into microlithic tools such as Ouchtata bladelets and al-Wad points. There are also many endscrapers on blades and burins (Coinman 1998; Henry 1995: 38). Currently, the evidence from Jordan indicates that sites of the Ahmarian complex are present, but the Levantine Aurignacian has not been found. Instead, there are stone artefact assemblages that occasionally include characteristic Levantine Aurignacian tools, such as endscrapers and burins on thick blades, but these are technologically more similar to the Ahmarian (Coinman 1998). Although researchers in Jordan have used the term Levantine Aurignacian to describe these assemblages, it is possible that they simply represent variability within the Ahmarian complex itself. These issues are further discussed below in the Upper Palaeolithic section.

The final period is the Epipalaeolithic, which begins about 22,500 years bp and terminates at the end of the Pleistocene, about 10,300 years bp. This portion of the Palaeolithic is the most complicated with respect to complexes of stone artefact assemblages, reflecting the large amount of technological and typological variability found within these assemblages. The major complexes include the Qalkhan, Kebaran, Geometric Kebaran, Mushabian, and Natufian (Henry 1995: 36), although some researchers have preferred to use terminology that is more generic, that is, the "Non-Natufian Microlithic" (Byrd 1994: 210–211). Each complex has been further subdivided into industries (Qalkhan in the Qalkhan Complex; Madamaghan in the Mushabian Complex; Early Hamran in the Kebaran Complex; Middle, Late and Final Hamran in the Geometric Kebaran Complex; Natufian in the Natufian Complex) and phases (Early, Middle, Late, and Final) within particular industries. The major lithic assemblage characteristics of these complexes are blade and bladelet technology, with bladelets fashioned into a variety of retouched and/or backed microliths. There is a trend for microliths to be nongeometric in form during the early part of the Epipalaeolithic and geometric in morphology during the later portion of this period. Aside from the documentation of extensive assemblage variability, one of the most interesting developments revealed by research on Jordanian Epipalaeolithic lithic assemblages has been the recognition of the early occurrence of the microburin technique, a specialized method to segment bladelets to manufacture various types of microliths. This occurs earlier than 20,000 years bp (Byrd 1988: 260; Olszewski 2003: 232–236). The Epipalaeolithic section below examines the complexity of this period of the Palaeolithic in more detail.

Although the majority of the discussion in this chapter focuses on the Palaeolithic and Epipalaeolithic of Jordan, it is important to remember that the research themes that characterize it are common to the research programmes in many regions of the Levant and the greater Middle East. It is virtually impossible in some instances to discuss these themes without reference to areas such as the western Levant, where the archaeological record has been intensively studied for many decades and various scholars have generated important models of Palaeolithic settlement, subsistence and other adaptive strategies. Research in Jordan, in fact, has often used these western Levantine models as initial approximations of past lifeways that can then be modified and refined using the data from archaeological sites in Jordan.

Chronology

The temporal framework of the Palaeolithic period in Jordan has been developed from both relative and chronometric sources. The relative sequence of complexes and industries resulted from the excavation of sites with stratigraphically separated assemblages. In general, materials from the lower levels of sites are older than those from upper levels. In some cases, chronometric dates have been obtained for some of these levels, allowing archaeologists to assign particular assemblages to certain ranges of time. Numerous sites, especially those which are surface lithic scatters, are relatively placed within the Palaeolithic framework on the basis of the techno-typological characteristics of their assemblages and other attributes. For example, heavily patinated surface assemblages that include numerous bifaces are likely to be attributed to the Lower Palaeolithic, while more lightly patinated surface assemblages yielding various forms of microliths usually are either Upper or Epipalaeolithic in age, depending on the specific morphologies of the microliths. Because suitable samples for chronometric dating are not always recovered from all levels of excavated sites, many of the assemblages from *in situ* contexts are also relatively dated using the characteristics of the lithic assemblages.

Until recently, the major chronometric technique used for sites in Jordan and many other areas of the Levant was radiocarbon. This method requires organic samples such as wood charcoal, burnt animal bone or burnt seeds; it can be used to date materials from approximately the past 45,000 years. Materials that are older than this are recorded as "greater than" dates, for example >45,000 years bp. In the Palaeolithic framework, radiocarbon is thus most useful for Upper and Epipalaeolithic sites, and is not very informative for the earlier ranges of Palaeolithic time. Middle Palaeolithic sites are often dated using one or more of several relatively new dating methodologies. These include thermoluminescence (TL), carried out on burnt lithic artefacts, electron spin resonance (ESR) used on animal teeth, uranium series (Th/U) determinations on samples of travertine, and amino acid racemization on materials such as ostrich egg shell. The application of these techniques to sites from both the western and eastern Levant has yielded dates in the range from about 245,000 to 40,000 years bp. No Lower Palaeolithic sites from Jordan have yet been dated using chronometric techniques; potential methods include potassium-argon (K/Ar) and other types of uranium series. Both of these techniques require finding sites that are stratigraphically positioned either immediately above or below volcanic rock layers, such as tuff or lava.

Although chronometric dates provide an absolute determination of age, they are not infallible methodologies. Great care must be taken to collect noncontaminated samples or to remove contaminants that affect the accuracy of the dates. All chronometric dates are cited with a standard deviation (±), for instance, 58,400±4,000 years bp. This reflects the fact that the true age of the sample dated has a 68% probability of being within one standard deviation of the mean age (e.g., 54,400–62,400 years bp) and a 95% probability of lying within two standard deviations of the mean age (e.g., 50,400–66,400 years bp). Because standard deviations can be large, the range of dates for any given level of a site often can overlap with the range for layers below and above it. Chronometric tables for Middle, Upper, and Epipalaeolithic sites can be found in Byrd (1994), Clark *et al.* (1997), and Phillips (1994).

Research Themes

The main research themes of the Palaeolithic and Epipalaeolithic concern settlement patterning and settlement systems, subsistence, and technology, primarily because the archaeological remains of these remote periods of time best lend themselves to these issues. In order to examine settlement patterning and settlement systems, for example, archaeologists recover information about the geographic and topographic location of sites, past global and local environments (from oxygen isotope ratios in deep sea cores, palynology and geoarchaeology), and aspects of lithic technology that can be used to infer the level of mobility of past groups. They also consider how landscapes have changed over time, usually to obtain a rough idea about the degree to which sites have disappeared due to erosional processes or destruction from later cultural modification of regions. Archaeological assemblages of animal bones (vertebrate fauna) and shellfish (invertebrate fauna), which are primarily found in late sites (Epipalaeolithic), as well as plant remains, which preserve only rarely, are used to reconstruct the subsistence of ancient groups. Because animal bones are the most commonly found subsistence item, much of this research has focused on hunting patterns, although, based on analogy to remnant modern hunter-gatherer groups, archaeologists hypothesize that most ancient groups probably had a diet composed principally of plant foods.

One controversial research theme that is temporally restricted to the Middle Palaeolithic involves the origin of modern humans. The Middle Eastern region has yielded fossil humans of the modern type (*Homo sapiens sapiens*) and an ancient type (*Homo sapiens neanderthalensis*), both of which are associated with Middle Palaeolithic stone tool industries. Currently, however, none of the sites of this time period in Jordan have produced human remains, thus this research theme has been only indirectly pursued here.

Archaeological sites that date to the late Upper Palaeolithic and Epipalaeolithic can contain a more diverse array of artefacts and structures than sites of the earlier Palaeolithic, including occupation floors, stone-walled or semi-subterranean dwellings, hearths, ornaments, art, and human burials. Burials and their grave goods, ornaments and art can sometimes be used to infer social status, levels of inequality within human groups, and identity as a social grouping. There have also been attempts to isolate attributes of lithic tools that may serve as indicators of social group identity or of cultural traditions of manufacturing particular types of stone tools. One reason that the Epipalaeolithic period in particular has been the centre of these research themes is because many archaeologists believe that environmental and ecological conditions during the latter part of the Epipalaeolithic resulted in conditions favorable to the development of less mobile hunter-gatherer societies. Some of these groups apparently began to rely more heavily on cereal grasses as a food item, which eventually resulted in the deliberate cultivation of cereal grasses. Ultimately a reliance on cultivation sparked the development of settled agricultural societies with complex social organizations in the Neolithic period that followed (see Chapter 4).

The research themes briefly outlined in this section are discussed more fully within the divisions of the Palaeolithic and Epipalaeolithic periods that follow below.

The Lower Palaeolithic: 900,000 ± c.150,000 years bp

There are numerous sites and isolated finds of the Lower Palaeolithic recorded in Jordan. The majority of these are derived rather than *in situ* surface scatters of lithic artefacts. A small number of *in situ* sites, however, have been located and several have undergone test excavations, yielding not only lithics but also fossil animal bones. Sites discussed in this section include examples from the upper Zarqa Valley, the Wadi Sirhan, the Azraq Basin, the Wadi Bustan (near Shawbak), the Tabaqat Fahl area of the east Jordan Valley, and the Ras al-Naqab region of southern Jordan. All known sites of this period in Jordan are open-air rather than cave or rockshelter sites (Figure 3.2).

Although the Lower Palaeolithic spans a chronologically lengthy period of time, the understanding of its archaeological record is limited for several reasons. Principal among these are the destruction of sites over time through erosional processes, the transport of artefacts from *in situ* contexts to their current derived locations either on deflated land surfaces or in wadi deposits, poor chronology, and the limited number of associated assemblages, such as faunal remains. Reconstructing ancient settlement systems has thus proven difficult, although there are a few examples of efforts to predict why some localities appear to have been favored for repeated visits.

Environment

The environment of the Middle East during this period was considerably different from today. Climatic conditions fluctuated between cool and moist to cool and dry. Many areas of Jordan experienced a higher water table, which resulted in numerous springs throughout many regions of the upland plateau (Transjordanian Plateau) and in Pleistocene lakes and marshes, such as those found in the Azraq Basin and near Lake Lisan, the precursor to the Dead Sea (Copeland and Hours 1988: 296–299; Macumber and Edwards 1997). Some of these areas

would have been heavily vegetated with riparian species such as reeds (*Phragmites*) and willow (*Salix*). Areas away from the springs and lakes may have been somewhat less hospitable, but it is likely that vegetation zones like the Mediterranean forest and the steppe grasslands were much greater in geographic extent than they are today (e.g., Rollefson 1985: 105).

Research Themes

Because lithic artefacts are durable and have survived in a variety of contexts, the most developed research theme for this period of Palaeolithic time has been the intensive study of the technology and typology of lithic artefacts. This has produced a relative chronology of Early, Middle, Late and Final Acheulean industries, which can also be separated into spatial contexts, such as the Desert Wadi Acheulean (DWA) and the Late Acheulean of Azraq phases (e.g., Copeland 1988; Copeland and Hours 1988). The major distinguishing typological and technological criteria for the division of assemblages into chronological periods within the Acheulean are the classes and types of bifaces, and the average length of bifaces (Gilead 1970; Macumber and Edwards 1997; Rollefson 1981, 1984). In general, ovate-shaped and Abbevillian types of bifaces typify earlier assemblages, while later assemblages contain more numerous cordiform- and lanceolate-shaped types. Average biface length appears to decrease over time. Typology and technology are also used to separate relatively contemporary assemblages from various geographic locales. For example, cleavers are particularly abundant in assemblages that lack Levallois technology; these are found in mesic settings, that is, in areas characterized by lakes and marshes that were highly productive resource locales. Other assemblages are characterized by use of Levallois technology and biface types other than cleavers; these are found in xeric contexts, that is, in areas away from lakes or marshes or when these were much reduced in extent or absent. It is difficult to assess the degree to which this variability is due to chronology, over which there is relatively poor control for the Acheulean period, or to other factors, such as different sets of activities in differing ecological contexts.

Sites

The earliest lithic assemblages from Jordan are from the Dauqara Formation in the upper Zarqa Valley north of Amman (Parenti *et al.* 1997). These are classified as Early Acheulean, and are dated to about 0.9–1.0 million years bp on the basis of biostratigraphy, which uses the known dates of extinct types of animals to provide an age range for the associated lithic assemblages. There are no bifaces present, and only one chopper. Most of the assemblage is flakes. Perhaps this is not surprising because the context for the lithics and associated fauna is derived, and not all materials were likely transported from the original site(s).

Figure 3.2 Sites of the Lower and Middle Palaeolithic mentioned in the text.

Another set of Early, as well as Middle, Acheulean sites is in the Wadi Sirhan Basin, near the border with Saudi Arabia (Whalen and Kolly 2001). All of these sites are located at escarpment bases or on small mountain slopes, and all are in derived context. They are attributed to the early part of the Lower Palaeolithic on the basis of their technology, as well as the degree to which they are weathered and patinated. The assemblages include many chop-

pers and scrapers, as well as a few bifaces. This research is intriguing because Whalen and Kolly (2001: 17–18) suggest that the Wadi Sirhan may have been one of the major travel routes for early groups of human ancestors who, after leaving Africa, arrived in Yemen, and then moved north-northwest into the Levant.

Another Middle Acheulean occurrence is a surface scatter from the Wadi Uwaynid in the Azraq Basin (Rollefson 1984). The assemblage is derived rather than *in situ* because the artefacts are heavily abraded and rolled, and there are few small to medium-sized flakes present. The scatter occurs along an approximately 2 km length of the wadi, with the majority of the bifaces from a 750m long stretch near the center of the distribution (Rollefson 1984: 128). The high frequency of the class of ovate bifaces and Abbevillian types are the distinguishing trait that favors a designation of this assemblage as Middle Acheulean. Because the assemblage has been transported from an unknown location to its present place, knowledge of the geographic location of this Wadi Uwaynid site is informative only as an indicator that Middle Acheulean groups were present in this area of Jordan sometime earlier than about 450,000 years bp.

Other probable Middle Acheulean sites include Masharia 2, 4 and 5 in the Tabaqat Fahl area of the east Jordan Valley. They are designated Middle Acheulean based on a small number of metrically large bifaces and on their stratigraphic context, which underlies deposits containing sites that are Late Acheulean in age (Macumber 1992; Macumber and Edwards 1997).

In the Azraq Basin, the next groups to exploit the area are those identified as the Desert Wadi Acheulean (DWA), associated with the Late Acheulean. These finds are all derived, being heavily patinated and rolled; they consist of numerous bifaces, some cleavers, large sized cores, and use of a proto-Levallois technique of core reduction (Copeland 1988: 68–71; Copeland and Hours 1988: 294–296). These materials may date to the interval between about 500,000 to 300,000 years bp (Copeland 1988: 69). Although all of these materials were transported from their original locations, it is thought that these assemblages represent exploitation of the steppe grassland areas characteristic of many portions of the Azraq Basin and its perimeters.

Marshes, lakes and springs were also present during certain intervals in the Azraq Basin. These were attractive resource areas that served as focal points for both animals and the human groups who preyed upon them. Rapid burial of archaeological remains by water deposited sediments resulted in good preservation of artefacts and fauna *in situ*. Many of the sites were found during periods of lowered water levels at the springs that exposed deposits otherwise inaccessible. The best-known sites are Ayn Assad (Copeland 1989a, 1989b; Rollefson 1982, 1983), Ayn Soda (Rollefson *et al.* 1997) and C-Spring (Copeland 1991). Unusually dense concentrations of lithic artefacts have been recovered from these sites— thousands of lithics, of which hundreds are classified as bifaces (Figure 3.3). Cleavers comprise close to a third of the biface assemblage in some levels of the sites, with the majority of the other bifaces classified as ovate or discoid forms. Other lithics are cores, various flake tools and the debris from knapping; there is no use of the Levallois

technique of core reduction. The high concentrations of bifaces, particularly the cleavers, are thought to be associated with butchering activities; fossil bone representative of prey species includes camel (*Camelus*), hartebeest (*Alcelaphus*), wild boar (*Sus scrofa*), rhinoceros (*Dicerorhinus hemitoechus*), aurochs (*Bos primigenius*), equid (*Equus*), and elephant (*Elephas*) (Clutton-Brock 1970; Rollefson *et al.* 1997). Copeland (1988: 71–73; Copeland and Hours 1988: 296–299, 303) has classified these lithic assemblages as the Late Acheulean of Azraq phase because of the high number of cleavers present in the assemblages, and suggests that they may date to about 250,000 to 200,000 years bp.

Another region of Jordan characterized by freshwater marsh and spring conditions during the Late Acheulean period is the Tabaqat Fahl region of the east Jordan Valley (Macumber and Edwards 1997). The *in situ* site of Masharia 1 is associated with these deposits. Recent excavations here yielded a large lithic assemblage characteristic of a biface reduction site—numerous biface thinning flakes and small flakes, shatter and debris. The recovery of very few bifaces suggests that most bifaces were curated to other locations. There are, however, many notched flakes, invasively retouched flakes and other tools, indicating that Masharia 1 was used for more activities than just biface manufacture and reduction.

Surface scatters of Late Acheulean artefacts have also been found in the highland plateau areas away from marsh and lake locales. Like the DWA, these are derived assemblages and their information potential is somewhat limited compared to *in situ* sites. One example of a highland plateau site is Fjaje in the Wadi Bustan, near Shawbak. The assemblage is from a deflated land surface and thus represents a palimpsest of numerous occupations (Rollefson 1981: 6–7). Unlike the DWA, where assemblages have been transported over unknown distances, the assemblage from Fjaje is in its approximate original locale on the landscape because its artefacts have been deflated rather than transported. The topographic position of the Fjaje assemblage can thus be used to address the question of why early groups returned repeatedly over time to this locale. Rollefson (1985) hypothesizes that hunters favored this spot because it lay along a seasonal migration route for herd animals. Animals traveling through the Wadi Bustan from the low areas of the Wadi Arabah to the highlands during the spring could be relatively easily ambushed by hunters waiting along the rim at Fjaje. Prevailing winds from the west and northwest during the spring placed hunters in a downwind position, and the long climb from the Wadi Arabah up to the highlands may have tired the animals. Both of these factors increased the success rate of hunters at Fjaje and led to their repeated use of this site area.

Another highland site is Wadi Qalkha in the Ras al-Naqab area of southern Jordan. The artefacts are light-

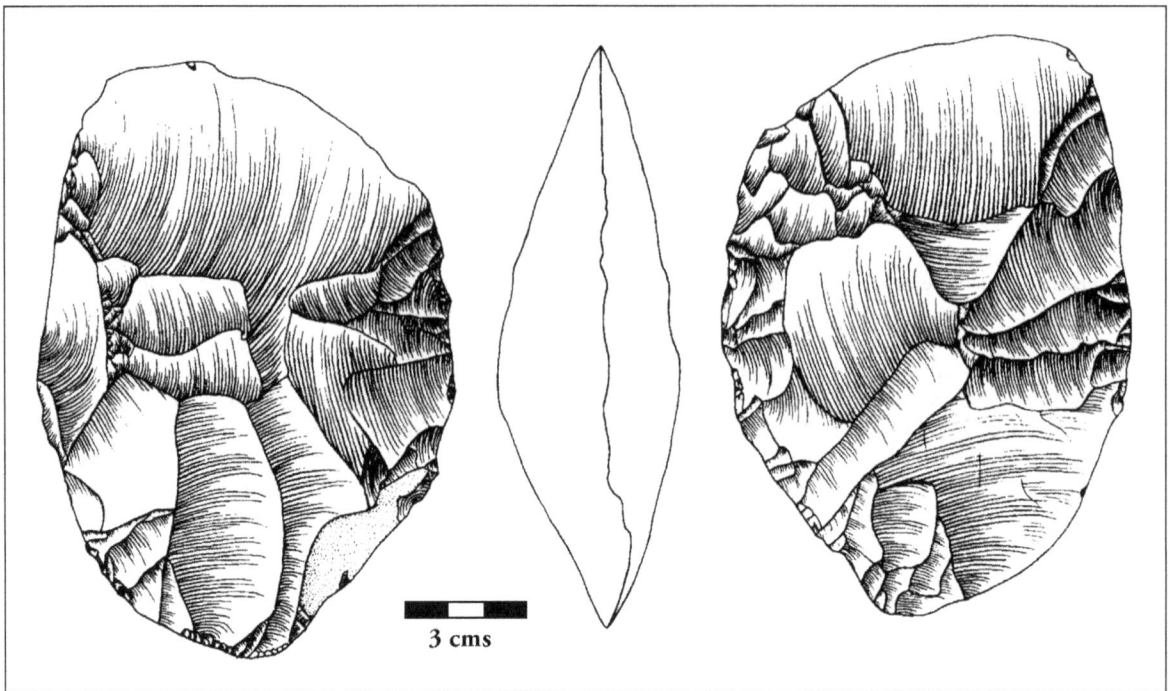

Figure 3.3 Late Acheulian bifacial cleaver from Ayn Assad ("Lion Spring"), Azraq Oasis, eastern Jordan (Drawing by Brian Byrd, courtesy of Gary Rollefson).

ly patinated and have sharp edges, indicating that they have not been transported very far nor been exposed for long periods of time (Henry 1995: 43). The assemblage includes examples of bifaces, sidescrapers and retouched pieces, as well as flakes and blades; use of Levallois technology is documented. This assemblage is similar to that from Fjaje. Henry (1995: 47) suggests this industry represents a Late Acheulean adaptive strategy common throughout steppe and light woodlands environments that were situated near plains and plateaus.

The Middle Palaeolithic: c. 150,000–45,000 years bp

Sites of the Middle Palaeolithic in Jordan, like those of the Lower Palaeolithic, have been most frequently recorded in derived contexts, primarily as deflated surface scatters of lithic artefacts. Unlike the Lower Palaeolithic, however, there are examples of *in situ* Middle Palaeolithic sites from rockshelters and open-air contexts, some of which have been test excavated. Discussed in this section are sites from the Wadi Hasa region, the Wadi Zagh in northwestern Jordan, the Jafr Basin, and the Ras al-Naqab area (see Figure 3.2). All assemblages identified to date are attributed to the Levantine Mousterian Complex that is characterized by the use of Levallois technology. New dates that extend the lower boundary of the Middle Palaeolithic much farther back into the past, as well as shared techno-typological characteristics with the Lower Palaeolithic, have prompted a number of researchers to regard a strict boundary between the Lower and Middle

Palaeolithic as no longer tenable (e.g., Clark *et al.* 1997).

Environment

Environmental conditions during the 100,000 or more years of the Middle Palaeolithic were subject to considerable short and long-term fluctuations, as well as regional variation. Pollen from lake cores, and pollen and phytoliths from archaeological sites across the Levant, indicate that north–south and west–east climatic clines existed (Clark *et al.* 1997). In general, vegetation zones like the Mediterranean forest and open steppe extended farther to the south, for example, into the Negev highlands, and to the east, for example, the Wadi Hasa area, during certain intervals. Lakes and marshes or seasonal ponds, resulting in small patches of trees including oak (*Quercus*) and riparian vegetation such as rushes (*Cyperus*) also characterized many locales. The early part of the Middle Palaeolithic, based on pollen evidence from Ayn Difla in the Wadi Hasa, appears to have been relatively cool and dry, although more moist than modern conditions in this region (Clark *et al.* 1997). This area was primarily an open steppe or desert/steppe grassland with scattered trees along the wadi. Later in the Middle Palaeolithic, pollen and phytolith evidence from Tor Sabiha and Tor Faraj in the Ras al-Naqab region indicate a warm, dry interval, ameliorated in this area by the presence of seasonal ponds (Emery-Barbier 1995: 377–379; Rosen 1995: 401–402). Although warmer than the earlier Middle Palaeolithic, the local landscape remained dominated by open steppe grasslands, and punctuated by trees along drainages.

Research Themes

As during earlier portions of the Palaeolithic, research themes of the Middle Palaeolithic in Jordan are focused on lithic typology and technology, and on settlement and subsistence systems, as well as some aspects of the debate over the origin of modern humans and the implications this holds for interpretation of various of the archaeological assemblages that have been recovered. With two exceptions, the Levantine Mousterian lithic assemblages of the southern and inland Levant, including Jordan, are classified as Tabun D- or B-type (e.g., Clark *et al.* 1997; Henry 1997: 74; Lindly and Clark 1987; Bisson *et al.* in press), and represent a long-lived complex that is slow to change typologically. As discussed previously, numerous unretouched Levallois points characterize Tabun D-type and B-type; in the arid regions, Tabun D-type points tend to be elongate in form. Recently obtained TL and ESR dates from the site of Ayn Difla in Jordan suggest that Tabun D-type assemblages are much earlier here than previously believed, perhaps in excess of 135,000 years bp (Clark *et al.* 1997); the Tabun B-type appears at later sites in Jordan, such as Tor Faraj and Tor Sabiha, about 69,000 years bp or later.

No hominid remains have yet been recovered from Middle Palaeolithic sites in Jordan to add to the debate in the western Levant regarding the possible existence of two sympatric hominid species (*Homo sapiens neanderthalensis* and *Homo sapiens sapiens*) who apparently made and used similar stone artefacts. This debate, which is polarized into replacement versus continuity viewpoints, has a lengthy history and has not been resolved. The two major viewpoints have been extensively published elsewhere (e.g., Clark and Lindly 1988; Stringer and Andrews 1988) and are only briefly summarized here. Replacement advocates postulate that both hominid species overlapped temporally; archaic humans (*Homo sapiens neanderthalensis*) represent an evolutionary side branch that eventually became extinct. Evidence to support this viewpoint is cited from several sources including molecular genetics (mitochondrial DNA), palaeoanthropology (morpho-metric attributes of hominid fossils) and the archaeological record (chronometric dates, food acquisition techniques). Adherents of this paradigm point out that Neanderthals could not have evolved into modern humans because they survive as a species well after the appearance of moderns, based on both "early" and "late" dates of assemblages associated with Neanderthal fossils (around 122,000 years bp at Tabun and 60,000 years bp at Kebara in the western Levant) and "early" dates for modern human fossils (about 92,000 years bp or earlier at Qafzeh in the western Levant). On the basis of chronometrics alone, this evidence would seem to suggest that the two species co-existed for some tens of thousands of

years. Some researchers have further argued that although both species made and used Levantine Mousterian stone artefacts, there are differences in their subsistence patterns indicating that they occupied somewhat different environmental niches (Shea 2003).

Continuity advocates, on the other hand, argue that the fossils of archaic (Neanderthal) and modern humans from the Levant represent a single evolving population. They point to several lines of evidence including biological factors, aspects of chronological resolution, and behavioral patterning. They attribute variability in skeletal morphology to changes over time, as well as to variation present within the species at any given moment in time (analogous to morphological variation visible in human populations today). Thus, they see the fossil specimens as variable, isolated individuals that must be studied within a population context rather than as individuals. Additionally, they argue that the TL, ESR and other dates associated with various sites are not comparable and can vary greatly depending on which technique is used and what type of sample is dated (e.g., Clark *et al.* 1997). In other words, while the dates obtained from these techniques indicate a relatively long span of time overall, it is difficult to assess the comparison of specific TL dates from one site to specific ESR dates from a different site. The standard deviations associated with dates from different layers at the same site also often overlap considerably; layers that have older or younger mean ages potentially can be virtually "contemporary" when the standard deviations are taken into account. The end result is that neither "species" can be said to predate the other. Finally, based on the competitive exclusion principle of evolutionary ecology, continuity advocates emphasize that it would have been impossible for two sympatric hominid species in the same small region to have co-existed for such a lengthy period of time without inhabiting completely different environmental niches. The association of the same lithic industry with both hominid "species," as well as the same prey animals (similar faunal assemblages), and the use of neighboring site locales in some areas, are all suggestive of a similar adaptation and, therefore, a single hominid line rather than sympatric species.

Another research theme is settlement patterning. Henry's (1995: 107–127) settlement model for the Middle Palaeolithic of southern Jordan is based on the idea of seasonal transhumance. Human groups here during the fall/winter months appear to have utilized a strategy of radial settlement (or logistical mobility)—longer-term, seasonal basecamps with associated ephemeral task camps in nearby localities. During the spring/summer months, they engaged in a circulating settlement pattern (or residential mobility)—a series of successively occupied short-term basecamps. In the Ras al-Naqab area, Tor Faraj represents a low elevation, long-term basecamp during the fall/winter months, and Tor Sabiha one of the series of

Figure 3.4   The Middle Paleolithic site of Ayn Difla, Wadi Hasa.

short-term camps during the spring/summer months. This approach represents a significant departure from settlement models developed for the Middle Palaeolithic of the Negev and Sinai, where researchers have argued that this period was characterized by a year-round radial settlement system that persisted for millennia (e.g., Marks and Friedel 1977). It is clear that the archaeological record of areas of the eastern Levant, such as southern Jordan, has a great deal to contribute towards the understanding of the adaptive flexibility of these early groups of highly mobile hunter-gatherers.

Sites

The earliest chronometrically dated Middle Palaeolithic site in Jordan is the *in situ* deposits from the rockshelter of Ayn Difla in the Wadi Ali tributary drainage to the Wadi Hasa (Figure 3.4). A series of TL, ESR and Th/U dates from samples from several levels indicates that the Tabun D-type artefacts were deposited sometime between about 180,000 to 90,000 years bp (Clark *et al.* 1997). Several seasons of excavation have yielded a relatively large lithic assemblage containing numerous elongated Levallois points, as well as many small flakes and shatter elements. Retouched tools are few, but include examples of burins, notches, and denticulates (Lindly and Clark 1987:

285; Clark *et al.* 1997). The small size of many of the cores suggests that they were discarded when close to the end of their usefulness, and the presence of a wide variety of debitage items, such as the small flakes, shatter, and primary elements (pieces with cortex), indicates that lithic reduction was one activity at this site. Associated faunal remains are quite fragmentary and sparse, but include equids (*Equus*), goat or ibex (*Capra*), and gazelle (*Gazella*) (Clark *et al.* 1988: 235; Lindly and Clark 1987: 289–290). It is likely that the groups who used Ayn Difla intermittently over thousands of years were highly mobile and provisioned themselves by carrying lithic artefacts with them as they traveled from locale to locale (Clark *et al.* 1997).

A microwear analysis of Levallois points from Ayn Difla (Roller and Clark 1997) found no evidence for the use of these artefacts as projectile points. Instead, Levallois points from this site appear to have been utilized for a wide range of functions. These include longitudinal motion, such as slicing or sawing, transverse motion, such as scraping, as well as graving, whittling, and multipurpose motions. Evidence for hafting is present for some of the points.

Assemblages analogous to Tabun D-type are found at Rasfa, a stratified open-air site in the Wadi Zagh in northwestern Jordan (Shea 1998). This site is interesting because it is one of the lowest elevation Middle Palaeolithic sites known, at -37 m below sea level, and is associated with Pleistocene Lake Lisan (the modern remnant of Lake Lisan is the Dead Sea). Several resources, including ready availability of plant foods and animals, seasonal freshwater streams, and high quality flint for stone tools, likely made this site an attractive locale.

Numerous surface Middle Palaeolithic sites are present in the Jafr Basin, where they were associated with a Pleistocene lake and extensive sources of high-quality nodular flint (Quintero and Wilke 1998). The widespread abundance of this exceptional quality flint appears to have resulted in mainly quarry/workshop sites during the Middle Palaeolithic. These are characterized by Levallois technique, testing of nodules as potential cores, and large, side-struck flakes which appear to represent an early removal flake from cores.

Two other *in situ* sites are the rockshelters at Tor Faraj and Tor Sabiha in the Ras al-Naqab region. These sites are archaeologically contemporary and contain Tabun B-type assemblages; both are chronometrically dated to the latter part of the Middle Palaeolithic, about 69,000 years bp (Henry 1995: 37). They are believed to represent different aspects of a Middle Palaeolithic settlement system, with a larger, winter occupied base camp at Tor Faraj, and a smaller, summer short-term camp at Tor Sabiha (Henry 1995: 107–132). Evidence for this settlement model is derived from a variety of sources including the topographic location of the two sites and characteristics of the lithic assemblages. The high elevation location of Tor Sabiha, its limited extent of sheltered area and its eastern exposure are suggestive of locational attributes chosen during summer months; Tor Faraj, in contrast, has a much larger sheltered area, faces south and is at lower elevation (Henry 1995: 123). Artefacts from Tor Faraj tend to be larger and heavier, and elements from the entire process of core reduction are found, including the production of tools, their use and resharpening (Henry 1995: 112–114). These are characteristics of longer-term base camp occupations. Tor Sabiha, on the other hand, yielded lighter weight and smaller artefacts, with lithic reduction evidence pointing to final stage manufacture, use and resharpening of artefacts.

Faunal assemblages from Tor Faraj are limited and poorly preserved; they include gazelle (*Gazella*), equid (*Equus*), and ostrich (*Struthio camelus*) eggshell fragments (Henry 1995: 54). A similar assemblage, with the addition of aurochs (*Bos primigenius*), was recovered from Tor Sabiha. Most of these animals are representative of open steppe-like conditions, while aurochs indicates the presence of locally available water sources (Henry 1995: 58). The faunal species are consistent with the pollen and phytolith data from these sites that also indicate open steppe grasslands interspersed with locally mesic situations.

Microwear studies of lithic artefacts from Tor Faraj and Tor Sabiha also were conducted. At Tor Faraj, the most frequently used artefacts were Levallois points, Levallois debitage and retouched tools (Shea 1995: 97). Comparison of the microwear from these artefacts with traces on experimentally used artefacts indicates that the Tor Faraj assemblage documents evidence of impact, butchering activities, and contact with bone and hafts. A small percentage of the artefacts appear to have been used on soft plant materials and on wood. It is possible that the more xeric, steppe setting of the Ras al-Naqab region contained fewer plant species of use to Middle Palaeolithic humans occupying the Tor Faraj rockshelter than plants near sites in the western Levant that were situated in a Mediterranean forest setting. This may mean that the Tor Faraj groups concentrated more exclusively on hunting and butchering activities than their contemporaries elsewhere (Shea 1995: 97). Microwear on artefacts from Tor Sabiha revealed that similar activities occurred at this high elevation site, with perhaps a greater emphasis on working of animal materials (Lee cited in Henry 1995: 119–120).

The Upper Palaeolithic: c. 45,000– 20,000 years bp

The archaeological record of the Upper Palaeolithic in Jordan, which includes many surface scatters, is relatively well known partly because there are many examples of *in situ* sites compared to earlier periods of the Palaeolithic. Both open-air and rockshelter contexts have been tested in areas such as the Wadi Hasa and the Ras al-Naqab, as well as in the Azraq Basin. Lithic assemblages are identified as belonging to one of three major groupings—an early Upper Palaeolithic that may be transitional from the Middle Palaeolithic, the Ahmarian Complex; and a non-Ahmarian grouping that bears some similarity to both the Ahmarian and to the Levantine Aurignacian (Figure 3.5).

The early Upper Palaeolithic Complex contains Upper Palaeolithic tool types and a technology that features some attributes of Middle Palaeolithic core reduction techniques. The Ahmarian is an elongated blade- and bladelet-based complex, with endscrapers, burins and retouched bladelets. In the early phase, retouched bladelets, such as al-Wad points, are common; in the late phase, Ouchtata retouched bladelets are characteristic. Non-Ahmarian assemblages are typified by a less-refined blade technology that yields rather large, thick debitage, few retouched bladelets and few true Aurignacian tool types. It is dissimilar to the Levantine Aurignacian as defined from rockshelter and cave contexts in the northern and western Levant, which has use of Aurignacian scalar retouch, and production of thick blades and flakes, Aurignacian endscrapers, and carinated and nosed endscrapers. The non-Ahmarian grouping potentially represents variability within the Ahmarian Complex of industries; this is a research question that is in its initial stages of development (Coinman 1998; Coinman and Henry 1995: 194–195; Kerry and Henry 2003; Schyle and Gebel 1997).

Environment

The environment during the Upper Palaeolithic underwent several significant fluctuations. The earlier part of this period (Early Upper Palaeolithic and Early Ahmarian) appears to have been slightly more moist than during the later Middle Palaeolithic (Emery-Barbier 1995: 382), for example, there is evidence of significant Early Ahmarian occupation associated with marsh settings in areas such as the southern Sinai (Phillips 1988). Sites of this period are also found in west-central and southern Jordan. Conditions likely became drier throughout the duration of the Upper Palaeolithic, especially in the period following about 25,000 years bp as world-wide temperatures began to decline with the onset of the last glacial maximum of the Pleistocene. In the Wadi Hasa region, for instance, pollen analyzed from Late Ahmarian sites documents low arboreal pollen, which decreases in frequency through time, while steppic vegetation becomes increasingly dominant (Coinman 1993: 19–20; Olszewski *et al.* 1990: 46). However, a higher water table, which led to increased spring flow and more numerous springs throughout highland areas, helped create many locally ameliorated settings in Jordan where lakes, marshes and seasonal ponds continued in existence from earlier times. These appear to have remained favored locales for Upper Palaeolithic groups.

Figure 3.5   Sites of the Upper Palaeolithic mentioned in the text.

Research Themes

Settlement and subsistence systems are again a key research theme. Two Early Upper Palaeolithic "transitional" sites are known, as well as a small number of Early Ahmarian sites. The majority of the Upper Palaeolithic sites in Jordan, however, appear to be late assemblages, that is, Late Ahmarian or related industries. These Late

Upper Palaeolithic sites have been most frequently found in association with marsh, lake and seasonal pond ecological settings. Henry (1995: 426–427) applies his model of seasonal transhumance between low elevation, fall/winter basecamps, and higher elevation, spring/summer transitory camps—initially documented in the Middle Palaeolithic—to the Upper Palaeolithic in the Ras al-

Naqab region as well. Because his model is dependent on great topographic relief in an area typified by seasonal ponds, however, it is probable that this type of settlement system is not applicable to all areas of Jordan during the Late Upper Palaeolithic. For example, Olszewski (2003: 239–240) suggests that the Late Upper Palaeolithic of the Wadi Hasa area may be a winter to early spring occupation, despite its upland plateau location, with settlement tethered to the lake and marshes present in the eastern part of the drainage. Such areas would have contained a number of attractive resources: freshwater springs, materials for manufacturing baskets, fish, shellfish, waterfowl, and game animals, such as gazelle, equids and aurochs. Radial settlement patterning may also have been present in areas such as the Azraq Basin where analogous lake/marsh conditions existed.

One of the more difficult aspects has been discriminating between the end of the Upper and the beginning of the Epipalaeolithic. In part this is because radiocarbon determinations have suggested that some of the industries of the Late Upper Palaeolithic overlap chronologically with early industries of the Epipalaeolithic (Olszewski 2003: 232). To what extent this simply represents overlap created by the standard deviation age range around the

mean age obtained at various sites is unknown. It is possible, of course, that groups characterized by Upper Palaeolithic lithic assemblages coexisted for some time alongside groups that had developed Epipalaeolithic lithic assemblages. It is important to remember in this context that morphologically different tools could have been used in similar manners or for similar purposes. Thus, two groups manufacturing and using archaeologically distinct tools may have been engaged in very similar overall lifeways. Interpreting the meaning underlying the coexistence of different lithic industries is more problematic, and is a research theme studied more intensively for the Epipalaeolithic period (see section below).

Sites

The Wadi Hasa palaeo-landscape included springs, a lake and marshes (Schuldenrein and Clark 2001, 2003). The Pleistocene lake here probably attained its peak levels about 40,000 years bp, during the Early Upper Palaeolithic, and began to recede beginning about 20,000 years bp. The eastern part of the Wadi Hasa forms a plain, greater than 50 km² in extent, representing the former bed of the lake. Archaeological surveys of the south (Wadi Hasa Survey) and north (Wadi Hasa North Bank Survey and Eastern

Figure 3.6 Excavations at the Upper Paleolithic Site of Thalab Buhayra, Wadi Hasa.

Hasa Late Pleistocene Project) banks of the Hasa system in 1979–1981, 1991–1992 and 1997 yielded 50 Upper Palaeolithic and 19 Upper to Epipalaeolithic sites (Clark *et al.* 1992, 1994; MacDonald *et al.* 1980, 1982, 1983; Olszewski *et al.* 1998: 71). A number of these are *in situ* and include both rockshelters and open-air sites. The distribution of these sites is highly patterned, with most situated within about 4 km of the lake. The density of Upper Palaeolithic sites in the immediate vicinity of Lake Hasa is indicative of the importance of this ecological context. Four Upper Palaeolithic sites have been tested, the Tor Sadaf rockshelter, the open-air sites of Thalab Buhayra (Figure 3.6) and Ayn Buhayra, and the southeast-facing rockshelter at Yutil Hasa (Figure 3.7).

Tor Sadaf, an east-facing rockshelter, contains a sequence of deposits representing two Early Upper Palaeolithic transitional assemblages overlain by the Early Ahmarian Upper Palaeolithic (Coinman *et al.* 1999: 10–12; Fox 2003). The site is in a tributary to the Wadi Hasa, and is one of the few sites of this period to be situated away from Pleistocene Lake Hasa. The lithic assemblage from the lowest levels is called Tor Sadaf A and the assemblage immediately above it is Tor Sadaf B. These document a gradual change in lithic technology from the manufacture of Levallois-like points from single platform cores to the production of true blades characteristic of the Upper Palaeolithic. This gradual change leads to the blade and bladelet industry of the Early Ahmarian, which is characterized by numerous al-Wad points. In addition to lithic artefacts, fragmentary animal bones were also recovered from Tor Sadaf. These are currently under study.

A later phase of the Early Ahmarian Upper Palaeolithic is found at the open-air site of Thalab Buhayra, which is buried in the lacustrine marls along the shore of ancient Lake Hasa (Coinman 2003; Coinman *et al.* 1999: 12–16; Olszewski *et al.* 2001: 41–47). The occupations are remarkable for the quantity of animal bones recovered. These are mainly equids (*Equus*), but also include aurochs (*Bos primigenius*), gazelle (*Gazella* sp.), and wild pig (*Sus scrofa*). Radiocarbon dates of 25,680±100 years bp (Beta-129818) and 24,900±130 years bp (Beta-129817) place activities at this site at the end of the period characterized by the production of al-Wad points (Coinman 2003: 155). The lithic assemblage is unusual in containing Ksar Akil scrapers, which have a serrated edge and are found at only a small number of sites, many other scrapers, and numerous truncations. The occupations at Thalab Buhayra appear to have been quickly buried when

Figure 3.7   The collapsed rockshelter at Upper Paleolithic and Epipaleolithic Yutil Hasa, Wadi Hasa.

lake levels rose and inundated the animal bone marrow extraction and processing locales.

At Ayn Buhayra, a spatially large site on the ancient lakeshore about 1 km northwest of Thalab Buhayra, there is an extensive surface scatter of lithics as well as deeply stratified deposits (greater than 2 m) that span the interval from about 26,000 to 20,000 years bp. At least two stratigraphically and spatially differentiated occupations have been identified. The earlier occupation (Unit C) is characterized by a blade and bladelet technology that yielded retouched pieces, truncations, endscrapers, and microliths, and, more rarely, other tools. Most cores are quite small, suggesting that they were intensively reduced. This assemblage is not a typical Late Ahmarian industry because it contains few Ouchtata bladelets. Marshy sediments were recorded in two of the excavation units; the organics in Unit F were radiocarbon dated to 25,950±440 years bp (Beta-55928) and are presumably correlated with the marsh deposit in Unit C, which yielded the lithic assemblage (Coinman 1993: 19). The later occupation (Units H-I), which is associated with a spring deposit (tufa), yielded radiocarbon dates of 20,300±600 years bp (UA-4395), 20,670±600 years bp (Beta-118757), 23,500±270 years bp (Beta-56424), and 23,560±250 years bp (Beta-55931) (Coinman 2003: 155). The assemblage is a blade and bladelet industry, with microliths, retouched pieces and endscrapers, as well as other tools. It is a typical Late Ahmarian assemblage with numerous Ouchtata bladelets (Coinman 1998, 2003). The fauna consist primarily of equids (*Equus*) and aurochs (*Bos primigenius*), with limited numbers of gazelle (*Gazella* sp.), wild pigs (*Sus scrofa*), ovicaprines, and tortoise (*Testudo graeca*). Among the faunal assemblage are two examples of worked bone and antler/horn (Coinman 1998). One of these tools may have been a device used as a punch to remove blades and flakes from cores; the other has notches along its edge and a groove at its base. The characteristics of the site's assemblages—a full range of tool manufacturing activities and the diversity of tool types—suggest that it functioned as a longer-term base camp.

Yutil Hasa is a small, collapsed rockshelter situated in the narrower reaches of the drainage where the wadi begins to constrict; it is approximately 4 km north of Ayn Buhayra. There is a spring tufa in deposits across the wadi from the rockshelter, and evidence at the site of seeps. Two test units (A and B) yielded Late Ahmarian lithic assemblages and radiocarbon dates of 19,000±1300 years bp (UA-4396) and 22,790±80 years bp (Beta-129813) (Olszewski 2003: 232; Olszewski *et al.* 1990: 38). Pollen evidence indicates a change during the Ahmarian from drier conditions dominated by amaranth and chenopod types to a more mesic setting with trees like oaks (*Quercus*). The lithic assemblage appears to be somewhat similar to the industry from the earlier occupation (Unit C) at Ayn Buhayra, however, the Yutil Hasa assemblage contains Ouchtata bladelets similar to the later occupation at Ayn Buhayra. Cores are limited in frequency and there is minimal diversity in tool types (mainly microliths, retouched pieces and notch/denticulates), suggesting relatively specialized activities such as game hunting and processing. Freshwater springs and the site's location in a narrow section of the Wadi Hasa drainage would have served to attract and constrict the movement of game. The generally well-preserved faunal assemblages document the procurement of gazelle (*Gazella*), equid (*Equus*), aurochs (*Bos primigenius*), and tortoise (*Testudo graeca*).

In addition to these tested sites, there are numerous examples of open-air lithic scatters and additional rockshelters. The lithic scatters range in size from about 25 to 15,000 m². Some of the smaller sites, such as Wadi Hasa Survey 623X, are knapping stations where a limited number of cores were systematically reduced and blanks removed for use elsewhere (Lindly *et al.* 2000). Upper Palaeolithic sites on the plateaus away from the Wadi Hasa and its major tributary drainages are rare; this suggests that use of the plateau areas was incidental compared to the areas in the immediate vicinity of the lake and marshes.

The ecological stability of locally ameliorated situations in the eastern Hasa allowed Upper Palaeolithic groups to exercise alternative settlement options compared to areas such as the Negev or the Ras al-Naqab region (Olszewski and Coinman 1998). Overall, the productivity of lake/marsh resources is high year-round for foraging and collecting activities. Upper Palaeolithic groups in the eastern Hasa likely utilized the immediate vicinity of Lake Hasa as a base for winter, spring and early summer occupation (Olszewski 2003: 239–240). Supplementary hunting and gathering trips into the eastern deserts, where gazelle and other large animals could be procured, were undertaken during the winter. In the late summer and fall, hunter-gatherers followed major tributary drainages south into highland areas characterized by Mediterranean forest where different sets of resources could be exploited. The association of sites with the major tributary drainages suggests that these drainages, due in part to the presence of springs and game, served as travel routes.

In the Ras al-Naqab, somewhat different ecological conditions pertained than in the Wadi Hasa region. As during earlier periods of the Palaeolithic, the Ras al-Naqab area during the Pleistocene was characterized by the presence of seasonal ponds and pools at lower elevations rather than a lake or marshes. The type of settlement patterning here was influenced by this situation, as well as the great topographic relief in the area. Surveys in the Jabal Qalkha section located one Early Upper Palaeolithic and five Early Ahmarian and non-Ahmarian sites (Coinman and Henry 1995). All of these are *in situ* rockshelter sites located at lower elevations, analogous to the site settings of Middle Palaeolithic sites in the area.

The earliest known site of the Upper Palaeolithic in the Ras al-Naqab is the Wadi Aghar, a south-facing rockshelter at the base of a cliff. The sparsity of cultural materials from the excavations suggest that this site was a short-term camp where a limited range of activities occurred. The cultural deposits are relatively shallow and include a rock-lined hearth. The industry from this site has been classified as Early Upper Palaeolithic. Many of the assemblage characteristics are reminiscent of earlier Middle Palaeolithic technology, suggesting that Wadi Aghar is an example of an industry that is transitional between the Middle and Upper Palaeolithic periods (Coinman and Henry 1995: 182–191; Henry 1997: 73), or perhaps similar to the Early Upper Palaeolithic transitional industries from Tor Sadaf in the Wadi Hasa. Lithic manufacture at the site involved the production of relatively large-sized debitage that is typified by elongated blades, many of which are pointed in morphology. Very few bladelets are present, and none are retouched. Cores are relatively numerous and generally are not intensively reduced. Tools are limited in their diversity compared to later Upper Palaeolithic assemblages, but include endscrapers and burins, as well as retouched pieces and notches. The morphology of the elongated pointed blades and technology used to manufacture them strongly suggests that the assemblage from Wadi Aghar represents a local transition from the assemblages of the Ras al-Naqab Middle Palaeolithic sites of Tor Faraj and especially Tor Sabiha.

Early Ahmarian sites are represented by the rockshelters at Tor Hamar (Layers F-G), Tor Aeid, and Jabal Humayma. No radiocarbon dates are available for these sites; all have been relatively dated on the basis of the characteristics of their respective lithic assemblages. At Tor Hamar, the southwest-facing rockshelter is near the confluence of the main wadi channel and several smaller tributaries. Possible attractions include the presence of pools in the wadi that hold water during the winter months, and the fact that the wadi is a route west to the lower elevation locales in the Rift Valley (Coinman and Henry 1995: 138). The lithic assemblage is oriented to the production of elongated debitage, particularly blades and bladelets (Coinman 1998; Coinman and Henry 1995: 162–169). Cores and tools are few in number. The tools consist primarily of burins, retouched flakes, endscrapers, al-Wad points, and other retouched bladelets. A small faunal assemblage includes examples of gazelle (*Gazella*), caprines (*Capra*), equids (*Equus*), and jackal (*Canis aureus*) (Klein 1995: 411). Other items of note are a few shells—*Dentalium*, *Pecten*, *Ancilla*, and a gastropod; shells are rarely found at Upper Palaeolithic sites in the Levant (Reese 1995: 385).

Tor Aeid faces south and is situated above the Wadi Aghar drainage, with a view over the Wadi Qalkha drainage. There are nearby seasonal pools and access to the top

of the cliff. The site contains a lithic assemblage similar to that from Tor Hamar (Layers F-G) and Jabal Humayma (below) (Williams 1997). Retouched pieces are the most common tool type, followed by enscrapers, burins and al-Wad points. Distinctive traits include the use of flakes as blanks for many endscrapers and numerous burins on core-like blanks. The low frequency of tools at both Tor Hamar and Tor Aeid suggest that manufacture of tools, their resharpening and use were not significant activities at either site (Coinman and Henry 1995: 169–178). Tor Aeid is thought to have been a winter camp for small groups (Williams 1997: 146).

The southwest-facing rockshelter of Jabal Humayma was initially described as a "Levantine Aurignacian," or non-Ahmarian site (Coinman and Henry 1995: 152–160). The assemblage described from the early excavations at the site is characterized by large blades and flakes, and a tool component comprised of notches and retouched blades and flakes. A second season of excavation yielded a significant number of al-Wad points, indicating that this site is actually Early Ahmarian, along with numerous retouched pieces, endscrapers, and burins (Kerry 1997). Some differences with "typical Early Ahmarian" assemblages led Coinman (1998) to point out that the earlier Upper Palaeolithic assemblages of the Ahmarian from sites in southern Jordan are quite variable in the details of their technology and typology. This suggests that the definitions used by archaeologists for these industries will need to be refined as more studies are completed. The meaning of this variability is undoubtedly attributable to a complex combination of activity, spatial, and chronological differences between the sites of the Early Ahmarian. Like Tor Aeid, Jabal Humayma may have been a site occupied during the winter (Kerry 1997: 134).

Two sites in the Ras al-Naqab have non-Ahmarian assemblages, Tor Fawaz and Site 440. Tor Fawaz is a south-facing rockshelter overlooking the plain to the east of the Wadi Qalkha (Kerry and Henry 2003). The debitage is much larger than debitage from Early Ahmarian sites in the area, with an emphasis on flakes and blades, and only a minor bladelet component. The technology used to prepare cores, however, is similar to that described for the Early Ahmarian. The most common tools are retouched pieces, followed by notches, endscrapers, and burins. Al-Wad points are extremely rare (Kerry and Henry 2003: 177). Site 440 is across the wadi from Tor Hamar, and thus also situated near the seasonal winter pools and along the access route to the Rift Valley (Coinman and Henry 1995: 143). The lithic assemblage was collected from the surface; no excavation units were dug. The surface sample appears to be unrepresentative. It contains a range of core types, blades, flakes, and largish bladelets. Burins are the most common tool type, and usually are on core-like blanks, much like those from Tor Aeid (Coinman and Henry 1995: 179–181). Archaeological assemblages, such as these from Tor Fawaz and Site 440, highlight the need for a better understanding of lithic technological variability within the Upper Palaeolithic framework (Kerry and Henry 2003: 184).

The settlement strategies of these early Upper Palaeolithic groups in the Ras al-Naqab are thought to continue the seasonal transhumance pattern documented for the Middle Palaeolithic of this region. All six of the Upper Palaeolithic sites, however, are situated at low elevation locales, thus representing only the fall/winter portion of the settlement round (Henry 1995: 426–427). Additionally, all six sites are small rockshelters, with few indications of long-term base camp occupation. Instead, each of these sites appears to be a shorter-term camp, perhaps analogous to a task camp associated with yet undiscovered larger base camps. Alternatively, it is tempting to think that perhaps these sites represent spring/summer higher elevation sites associated with a seasonal round that incorporated movement into the lower elevations of Rift Valley during the summer. This is a pattern that is proposed for some later Epipalaeolithic groups in the region, for example, the Madamaghan (Henry and Shen 1995: 311).

Another mesic area occupied during the Upper Palaeolithic was the Azraq Basin, where both *in situ* and deflated sites dating between about 25,000 and 20,000 years bp have been recorded (Byrd 1988). The assemblages are quite diverse: the Trench 2 materials from Azraq 17 contain many thin bladelets with fine retouch (Byrd 1988: 259), analogous to Ouchtata bladelets of the Late Ahmarian (Coinman 1998); lithics from Wadi Jilat 9 are non-microlithic and include numerous endscrapers and retouched pieces (Garrard *et al.* 1988a: 319), perhaps comparable to the non-Ahmarian assemblages of southern Jordan (Coinman 1998). All of these Upper Palaeolithic assemblages are blade- or bladelet-based, therefore, it is inaccurate to classify them as Levantine Aurignacian. Associated fauna are primarily open steppic types, such as gazelle (*Gazella*) and equids (*Equus*); there are also hares (*Lepus capensis*) and scutes of land tortoise (*Testudo graeca*), which may have served as containers (Garrard *et al.* 1988b: 47). Aurochs (*Bos primigenius*), which favors a more mesic setting, is also present, indicating the availability of wetter settings. Geological studies in the Wadi Jilat indicate that soil erosion suggestive of a drier interval at about 21,000 years bp may have typified the period during which Wadi Jilat 9 was occupied (Garrard *et al.* 1994: 181). This corresponds to general environmental evidence cited above that indicates that drier intervals toward the end of the Upper Palaeolithic period.

There are a number of other documented Upper Palaeolithic sites in Jordan. For a variety of reasons, including modern disturbance, lack of excavation, and lack of study, however, the information from these sites is less complete. Sites include Marazzah North, Marazzah North-East and Abu Aluba in the North Jordan Valley, north of the Dead Sea (Muheisen 1988c: 515). These are open-air sites that have been disturbed by agricultural use of the terraces, as well as natural processes. In the Tabaqat Fahl, open-air Upper Palaeolithic sites are exemplified by Wadi Hammeh 32 and Wadi Hammeh 34 (Edwards *et al.* 1988: 532–535; Macumber and Head 1991: table 1). Only Wadi Hammeh 32 has been briefly reported; it is a severely deflated site with a small collection of lithics. Abu Sharer and Sabra 4 are in the Petra area (Schyle and Uerpmann 1988). In addition to lithics, a small hearth was found at Sabra 4. Finally, in the Azraq Basin, the site of Enoqiyyah is associated with sediments typical of marshes in the area north of the Pleistocene Azraq lake/marsh (Copeland and Hours 1988: 300). Virtually all of these assemblages have been characterized as bearing a resemblance to the Levantine Aurignacian, primarily because there is a large-sized debitage with burins and endscrapers and few bladelets or retouched bladelets. This characterization, however, must be tempered by the knowledge that most of these are surface collections or small samples. When viewed in the context of the variability known to exist within Early Ahmarian assemblages, as well as the non-Ahmarian grouping, it is just as probable that the sites of Marazzah North, North-East, Abu Aluba, Wadi Hammeh 32 and 34, Abu Sharer, Sabra 4, and Enoqiyyah may represent additional examples of the Early Ahmarian/non-Ahmarian industries.

The Epipalaeolithic: c. 22,500–10,300 years bp

Of all the periods of the Palaeolithic, it is this latest period, the Epipalaeolithic, that has yielded the best-known archaeological record in terms of quantity of sites and diversity of site contents (Figure 3.8). This is due in part to the relative recency of the Epipalaeolithic; more sites are preserved because there has been less time for them to have been subjected to erosional processes. Another factor may be increased population size; a greater number of people inhabiting the landscape will both create more sites and perhaps deposit a greater quantity of cultural materials at certain sites. *In situ* sites in rockshelters and in open-air contexts have been located, as well as numerous surface scatters. Perhaps the most striking aspects of the sites of this period, however, are the spatial and chronological variability in their lithic assemblages, the higher frequency of structures such as "dwellings" at sites, and the increased presence of art and ornamentation. In the 12,000 years that comprise the Epipalaeolithic, there are minimally nine recognizable lithic industries and phases in Jordan alone. This total rises to at least 18 industries and phases if sites from both the eastern and western Levant are combined. Some of this variability can be explained as temporal changes in lithic production techniques, and some as related to task specificity at particular sites. Additional arguments have also been made that some typological and technological diversity is due to cultural differences between groups of people or alternatively to the process of lithic reduction itself. These topics are taken up in more detail below.

In Jordan, some Epipalaeolithic lithic assemblages have been classified as Qalkhan, Hamran, Madamaghan and Natufian, although the systematics of the classification framework are still being developed as new sites and areas within Jordan are investigated in greater detail. With the exception of the Natufian industry, there is incomplete agreement between various researchers on the use of this terminology. This has resulted in several, temporary, compromises. For example, Byrd (1994) recognizes specifically named tool types such as the Qalkhan point and La Mouillah point, but chooses to classify assemblages with these and other nongeometric forms of microliths from the Azraq region as "Non-Natufian Microlithic." Neeley *et al.* (2000) follow a similar approach by using "nongeometric Epipalaeolithic" for assemblages in the Wadi Hasa area. Another example is the Madamaghan, which is proposed by Henry (1995: 40) for the Ras al-Naqab area and linked by him to industries of the Mushabian Complex of the Negev and Sinai. Although he defined this industry from the site of Tor Hamar, he chose the site of Wadi Madamagh in the Petra area as the type site assemblage. Because the assemblage from the site of Wadi Madamagh is more similar to assemblages from the Wadi Hasa and the Azraq Basin, Olszewski (2006) has suggested that Madamaghan no longer be used and the term Nebekian (for historical reasons) is more appropriate to describe these Early Epipaleolithic assemblages. Others, such as Edwards *et al.* (1988: 535–537) in the Tabaqat Fahl area, use western Levantine terminology such as Kebaran and Geometric Kebaran. To help clarify these varying viewpoints, the various terminologies that have been applied to particular sites described below will be noted in each site discussion (Table 3.1).

The earliest lithic assemblages of the Epipalaeolithic (Qalkhan, Early Hamran, Nebekian, the Tabaqat Fahl and some Azraq Basin Non-Natufian Microlithic) contain nongeometric forms of microliths. These vary in morphology, for example, arched backed and pointed bladelets, La Mouillah points, Qalkhan points and some microburins typify the Qalkhan (Henry 1995: 219); straight backed bladelets with truncations opposite snaps are typical for the Early Hamran (Henry 1995: 251); arched backed bladelets, La Mouillah points, attenuated "lunates," and abundant microburins are common to the

Qalkhan (Henry 1995)	Madamaghan (Henry 1995)	Nebekian (Olszewski 2006)	Hamran (Henry 1995)	Non-Natufian Microlithic (Byrd 1994)	Non-Microlithic (Byrd 1994)	Natufian (all researchers)
Tor Hamar (E) Wadi Humayma (J406b lower, J405, J407)	Tor Hamar (A–D) Jabal Fatma	Yutil Hasa (C, E) Tor Tareeq (lower) Tor Sageer Tor Hamar (E), Wadi Humayma (J406b lower, J405, J407)	Jabal Hamra (A–C) Jabal Mishraq Jabal Muhayma Wadi Humayma (J406b upper) Quwayra (A–C) Qa Salab (A–C) J21, J22, J26, J31	Uwaynid 14 Uwaynid 18 Wadi Jilat 6 Wadi Jilat 8 Wadi Jilat 22 (Phase B) Azraq 17 Kharaneh IV (A–C)	Wadi Jilat 10 Wadi Jilat 22 (Phase C)	Wadi Judayid Wadi Humayma (J406a)
Uwaynid 14 Uwaynid 18 Wadi Jilat 6	Wadi Madamagh	Uwaynid 14 Uwaynid 18 Wadi Jilat 6 (Phase C)		Wadi Hammeh 26, 31, 33 Wadi Hisban 2 Wadi Hisban 5		Bayda Wadi Mataha
	Wadi Jilat 8	Wadi Madamagh		Yutil Hasa (C, E) Tor Tareeq (lower)		Tabaqa Yutil Hasa (D) WHS 1021
		Wadi Hammeh 26, 31, 33		Tor Hamar		Wadi Hammeh 27 Wadi Hisban 6
				Tabaqat Buma WZ 148		Ayn Saratan Bawwab al-Ghazal
						Qalat Anaza, Jabal Subhi
						Ayn Rahub

Table 3.1 Epipalaeolithic lithic assemblages by researcher.

Nebekian (Olszewski 2006); and arched backed bladelets, La Mouillah points, and numerous microburins characterize some of the Non-Natufian Microlithic in the Azraq area (Byrd 1994: 210–211). All of these assemblages are blade and bladelet technology, and all but the Early Hamran yield very narrow bladelets. Virtually all of these assemblages also contain other tools such as endscrapers on blades, burins, perforators, notches and denticulates, and retouched pieces. Most of these assemblages are either radiometrically dated between 22,500 to 15,000 years bp or are similar typologically and technologically to the dated assemblages.

Beginning c. 15,000 years bp, most Epipalaeolithic assemblages begin to yield geometric forms of microliths, as well as nongeometric types. The industries include the Middle, Late and Final Hamran, as well as the Madamaghan *sensu* Henry (1995: 39–40) and some of the Non-Natufian Microlithic of the Azraq area (Byrd 1994: 210–211). Typical microlithic forms consist of trapeze/rectangles and La Mouillah points, and more rarely triangles. A small number of lunates are also occasionally found. Microburin technique appears to be used in most of these assemblages except for the Middle Hamran (Henry 1995: 39). Blade and bladelet technology continues to predominate, although most bladelets are somewhat wider on average than in earlier assemblages. Scrapers, retouched pieces and notches are included among the other types of tools in these assemblages. An unusual industry includes two sites in the Azraq Basin region with Non-Microlithic assemblages (Byrd 1994: 211–212), in other words, microliths are not the characteristic tool type for these occupations.

The period between about 12,800 to 10,300 years bp is characterized by the Natufian Complex. The lunate is the primary microlithic tool, with Early Natufian assemblages (12,800–11,000 years bp) containing mainly Helwan (bifacially backed) lunates, and Late/Final Natufian assemblages (11,000 to 10,300 years bp) typified by abruptly retouched lunates. Microburin technique is common to most sites of this period of the Epipalaeolithic. Other tools include scrapers, burins, notches and denticulates, and retouched pieces (Henry 1995: 323–327). Although blade and bladelet technology is used, the blanks produced are quite short and wide. There also appears to be a higher incidence of tools on flakes compared to earlier phases of the Epipalaeolithic period.

Environment

Several significant environmental changes occurred during the span of the Epipalaeolithic period. The first of these was the global cooling associated with the approach of the last glacial maximum and its peak c. 18,000 to 17,000 years bp. Available pollen evidence from lake cores (e.g., the Hula core) indicates that this was a cold and relatively dry interval in the Levant, characterized in

many areas by an expansion of steppic vegetation communities (Baruch and Bottema 1991: 16). Certain areas of the eastern Levant, such as the Azraq Basin and the Wadi Hasa, probably witnessed a shrinkage in the lakes and marshes, although freshwater springs continued to flow. Sometime around 15,000 years bp, climatic conditions began to ameliorate as glaciers in the northern latitudes began a relatively rapid retreat. Vegetation communities like the Mediterranean forest became much broader in distribution, as temperatures became somewhat warmer and humidity increased (Baruch and Bottema 1991: 16). A marsh ecology characterized parts of the Azraq Basin, and likely was also characteristic of confluences within the Wadi Hasa drainage system. This climatic optimum, characterized by increasing humidity throughout the period, continued until about 11,500 years bp. From about 11,500 to 10,500 years bp, a period corresponding to the Younger Dryas in the European sequence, climatic conditions worsened considerably as both temperature and humidity decreased. This resulted in an expansion of steppic vegetation communities (Baruch and Bottema 1991: 17). The climatic sequence described here is also supported by pollen analyses derived from archaeological sites (Emery-Barbier 1995: 380–383; Leroi-Gourhan and Darmon 1991).

Research Themes

Four major research themes characterize the study of the Epipalaeolithic: a continuing interest in reconstructing settlement and subsistence patterns; debates concerning the meaning of variability in lithic assemblages that focus primarily on whether distinct cultural groups can be identified; examination of the processes that led to early cultivation and agriculture as a subsistence strategy; and issues related to complex foraging and increased levels of social complexity. The first research theme, settlement and subsistence patterns, involves many of the models explicated for earlier periods of the Palaeolithic. The diversity of settlement strategies documented during the Epipalaeolithic, however, is a potential indication of the greater complexity of group adaptive dynamics. The steppic and desert areas of the western Levant, such as the Negev and Sinai, appear to be characterized by an abandonment of many locales during the earlier part of the Epipalaeolithic; sites of the later Epipalaeolithic (post-16,500 years bp) are well-represented (Goring-Morris 1987: 401–415; Marks and Freidel 1977: 146–149). Most sites in this region of the Levant are small, ephemeral camps, suggesting a highly mobile population. There are examples of Late Natufian sites, however, which contain structures, such as circular, stone-walled dwellings, that may indicate longer-term base camps. In Jordan, the closest apparent parallel to the situation in the Negev and Sinai appears to be in the Black Desert. Extensive surveys by Betts (1998) have located few traces of Epipalaeolithic sites earlier than the Late Natufian phase. One of the Late Natufian sites, Qalat Anaza, has structural elements, such as enclosure walls and possibly hut circles (Betts 1998: 12–15).

In the Ras al-Naqab area, Henry's (1995: 337–343) seasonal transhumance model remains typical for settlement patterning in that region. There are, however, interesting variations compared to earlier periods of the Palaeolithic. For example, both Qalkhan and Madamaghan sites in the lower elevations appear to be winter base camps, but there is an absence of these sites in higher elevations. This suggests that the Qalkhan and Madamaghan transhumance pattern may have involved spring/summer travel to lower, rather than higher, elevations, for instance, to Wadi Arabah. The Hamran sites, on the other hand, follow a strategy of lower elevation winter base camps associated with seasonal lakes, and a higher elevation summer transitory camps. During the succeeding Early Natufian phase, multi-season base camps (e.g., Wadi Judayid J2) are established at somewhat higher elevation settings. The pattern of the Late Natufian appears to involve the use of these upper elevations, but with a return to more mobile strategies involving seasonal camps at lower elevations as well.

The Wadi Hasa region also documents flexibility in settlement strategies throughout much of the Epipalaeolithic period (Olszewski 2000,[1] 2003; Olszewski and Coinman 1998). During the earlier part of the Epipalaeolithic, coinciding with the apparent abandonment of many portions of the Negev and Sinai regions, the lake/marsh microhabitats of the eastern Hasa were subjected to a period of increased environmental fluctuation, associated with the onset, climax and retreat of the last glacial maximum. Resources became more unpredictable, and during some intervals, Lake Hasa was much reduced in size and highly saline. Despite these circumstances, the area continued to be exploited by early Epipalaeolithic (Nebekian) groups. The focus of settlement, as during the Upper Palaeolithic, was within 4 km of remnant Lake Hasa. The settlement strategy appears to be one based on spring to fall occupation of the Hasa region.

A return to more substantial occupation of the eastern Hasa is found beginning about 16,500 years bp, broadly analogous to the re-occupation of the Negev and Sinai during this period. Local ecological conditions rebounded so that the lake and marshes achieved a resource potential comparable to the late Upper Palaeolithic period. Epipalaeolithic groups were characterized by reduced mobility (logistical mobility). As in earlier times, the immediate vicinity of Lake Hasa is the main focus of settlement. The Early Natufian phase which follows represents a distinctive shift in settlement strategy, with occupation focused in areas away from the former Lake Hasa. This is because while local conditions in the Wadi Hasa remained attractive, the lake and marsh regime characteristic of earlier periods appears to be confined to the vicinity of the tributary confluences. Settlement shifted to areas near active springs and probably to sections of the drainage where stands of cereal grasses could be exploited. If so, then harvesting of cereal grasses is likely to have occurred during the spring/summer.

The second research theme of the Epipalaeolithic concerns the interpretation of variability in lithic assemblages. There are two dimensions to this issue: contemporary but distinct assemblages found in geographically different areas (e.g., Hamran in the Ras al-Naqab and "geometric" Early Epipalaeolithic in the Wadi Ziqlab, Wadi Hisban, and Azraq areas), and contemporary but distinct assemblages found within the same region (e.g., Hamran and Madamaghan (*sensu* Henry) in the Ras al-Naqab area). Many of the distinctions that have been noted to date relate to the presence/absence of the microburin technique and to variations within the microlithic class of tools—these include variability in their morphology (i.e., different types), differences in their average length, and patterning in retouch type and placement. Two research positions have crystallized—one favors an explanation based on the presence of different cultural (or "ethnic") groups (e.g., Fellner 1995; Goring-Morris *et al.* 1996; Kaufman 1995), the other posits an explanation based on aspects of lithic reduction (e.g., Neeley and Barton 1994). Although these views appear to be polar opposites to some extent, all of these researchers emphasize the importance that variables such as raw material selection and activity focus played in the production of lithic assemblages. Perhaps the most salient point is the recognition of the fact that how raw material is exploited, including the reduction process, can be a choice that is culturally determined (e.g., Goring-Morris *et al.* 1996). This debate over cultural groups and lithic reduction processes deserves further research, in part because it is likely that elements of both explanations are responsible for the archaeological patterning that is present in Epipalaeolithic industries. Additional information from archaeological data other than the lithic assemblages will be key to clarifying the more subtle aspects of these interpretations.

The third research theme focuses on the shift from simple to complex foraging subsistence systems during the latter part of the Epipalaeolithic. This shift appears to have involved the increased use of stone ground plant foods—acorns and cereal grasses in the Mediterranean forest areas, and cereal grasses in the open parkland and steppic regions. Because later Neolithic groups practiced an agricultural way of life, many researchers have suggested that the origins of agriculture are to be found in the archaeological record of the Late Epipalaeolithic. Concomitant with the increased emphases on certain plant foods in the Late Epipalaeolithic is the emergence of large, multi-season base camps that contain abundant examples of groundstone implements for stone grinding of acorns and cereals, such structures as circular, stone-walled dwellings, bone tools, ornaments and other art, and burials. The most varied and extensive archaeological record of this socioeconomic shift is from sites in the western Levant (e.g., al-Wad and Ayn Mallaha), although a few examples (e.g., Wadi Hammeh 27 and Wadi Mataha) have also been found in Jordan. Perhaps the most

intriguing aspect of this research topic lies in the knowledge that the most complex of these sites are Early Natufian in age and are located primarily in the Mediterranean forest zone. By the Late Natufian, sites appear more often to be transitory camps, except for a few sites in the Negev and Black Desert areas. The distribution of late Natufian

Figure 3.8   Sites of the Epipalaeolithic mentioned in the text.

sites suggests that increased reliance on cereal grasses, which eventually led to their domestication during the Neolithic period, was a development of the steppic areas rather than the more optimal Mediterranean forest zone and that it occurred in a subsistence strategy characterized by simple foraging (Olszewski 2004). Areas such as the Jordan Valley have been suggested as one origin locale for early cultivation (Bar-Yosef and Belfer-Cohen 1989), but others may have been the vast open steppes that dominated much of the ancient landscape of Jordan.

The later Epipalaeolithic is also the focus for the research theme of increased social complexity, particularly during the Early Natufian phase. The large base camps, art, ornamentation, and burial data have suggested to some researchers that Early Natufian societies were characterized by increased population size and density, more ceremonialism, and perhaps social ranking (e.g., Henry 1989: 197–211). For example, certain individuals appear to have been buried with more elaborate grave goods than others; there are also differences between individuals in group burials where one individual of the group is a primary burial and the others are secondary. This might indicate that people with a lower social ranking who predeceased a more important individual were removed from their original graves and re-interred when the higher ranked person died. The majority of the archaeological record utilized by researchers to investigate this topic again is from sites in the western Levant (e.g., al-Wad). The best examples of these types of sites in Jordan are Wadi Hammeh 27, Ayn Saratan, and Wadi Mataha. Few would argue that the Early Natufian phase is not distinct in its archaeological signature. However, not all agree that the level of social complexity necessarily entailed social ranking (e.g., Olszewski 1991). Much of the evidence cited in support of social ranking is derived from excavations conducted in the 1930's when

Figure 3.9   Examples of Early Epipaleolithic microliths from the Wadi Uwaynid, Azraq Region.

excavation techniques and recording methods were not as meticulous. This leaves open to debate the contextual association of various burials and their contents (Belfer-Cohen 1995; Byrd and Monahan 1995).

Sites of the Early Epipalaeolithic

The Early Epipalaeolithic is generally used by Levantine researchers to refer to all Epipalaeolithic complexes prior to the Natufian. In Jordan, these include the Qalkhan, Hamran, Madamaghan (*sensu* Henry), Nebekian, Non-Natufian Microlithic, and Non-Microlithic, as well as assemblages variously attributed to the western Levantine Kebaran and Geometric Kebaran. These sites are widely distributed across many areas of Jordan, for example, the Azraq area, the Wadi Hasa, the Ras al-Naqab, the Tabaqat Fahl, the Wadi Hibsan, the Wadi Ziqlab, and the Petra region (see Figure 3.8).

In the Azraq area, there are a number of open-air sites, including Wadi Uwaynid 14 (middle and upper phases) and 18 (upper phase), Kharaneh IV, and Wadi Jilat 6 and 22. Others are Azraq 17 (Trench 1), and Wadi Jilat 8 and 10. The industries are described as Non-Natufian Microlithic (Byrd 1994: 210–211), although some of the assemblages, especially those from Wadi Uwaynid 14 and 18, and probably Wadi Jilat 6 (Phase C), could be considered Nebekian (Olszewski 2006).

Early chronometrically dated sites are Wadi Uwaynid 14 and 18, which yielded radiocarbon dates associated with diagnostic lithic industries that range from 18,400±250 years bp (OxA-866) at Uwaynid 14 to 19,800±350 years bp (OxA-864) at Uwaynid 18 (Garrard *et al.* 1988a: 325–326). The lithic assemblages are characterized by numerous arched-backed and pointed bladelets, variable quantities of La Mouillah points and truncated backed bladelets, extensive use of the microburin technique, and various larger tools such as scrapers, burins and truncations. At Uwaynid 14 there is a temporal trend toward larger microliths (Figure 3.9) and increased numbers of La Mouillah points. Faunal remains from these two sites include gazelle (*Gazella*), equids (*Equus*), aurochs (*Bos primigenius*), hare (*Lepus capensis)*, and tortoise (*Testudo graeca*). A number of hearths were recorded at Uwaynid 18, and shell beads (*Dentalium*), ochre and a grinding stone were also recovered. These two sites are only 120 m apart, and may represent portions of a single large site that has been divided by erosional channels. They are both situated in palaeosols, indicating somewhat more humid conditions during the periods they were occupied (Garrard *et al.* 1987: 9–15).

At Wadi Jilat 6, the earliest occupation (Phase C) contains a lithic assemblage analogous to those from Uwaynid 14 (middle phase) and Uwaynid 18. Like the Uwaynid sites, the Phase C occupation is associated with a palaeosol indicating more humid climatic conditions (Garrard *et al.* 1988a: 320). The succeeding occupation at Wadi Jilat 6 (Phase B) is also contained within a palaeosol. This phase, like Uwaynid 14 (upper phase), yielded a lithic assemblage characterized by larger microliths, with numerous examples of La Mouillah points. Interestingly, the Phase B assemblage has a low frequency of Qalkhan points (Garrard and Byrd 1992: 50–52), which are used as a marker for the Qalkhan industry in the Ras al-Naqab area (Henry 1995: 38). The Phase B occupation predates c. 16,700–15,500 years bp, based on radiocarbon dates obtained from charcoal samples in the Phase A deposit (Garrard and Byrd 1992: 50). Both the Phase B and C occupations are believed to represent short-term camps. The latest occupation at Wadi Jilat 6 (Phase A) is contained in aeolian silt/loess, indicating dry climatic conditions (Garrard *et al.* 1988a: 320). Somewhat contrary to expectation, it is this occupation that yields the best evidence for a longer-term base camp and/or more frequent site visits. Phase A contains three living floors, two of which are ochre stained; their edges are lipped up, suggesting that they were the floor surfaces for structures such as huts (Garrard and Byrd 1992: 49–50). The lithic assemblage continues to contain numerous microburins, but the microliths are overwhelmingly geometric in form (primarily small triangles). This phase of occupation is radiocarbon dated by several dates between 16,700±140 years bp (AA-5494) and 15,470±130 years bp (AA-5492) (Garrard and Byrd 1992: 50). The three phases at this site yielded faunal assemblages containing gazelle (*Gazella*), equids (*Equus*), hare (*Lepus capnesis*), and tortoise (*Testudo graeca*), as well as rarer fox (*Vulpes*), wolf (*Canis lupus*), aurochs (*Bos primigenius*), wild pig (*Sus scrofa*), and birds, such as ostrich (*Struthio camelus*) and various migratory bird species (Garrard *et al.* 1988a: 320). Other finds include shell beads (*Dentalium, Ancilla, Arcularia,* and *Cerastoderma*), bone points and beads, and groundstone implements (Garrard and Byrd 1992: 52). Seeds of steppic plants such as members of the Chenopodiaceae and Compositae, as well as various grasses, were recovered from Phase A (Garrard *et al.* 1988b: 44). All of these seeds are edible, although use of these for food in Phase A is not documented (Garrard and Byrd 1992: 52).

The site of Kharaneh IV contains several Epipalaeolithic occupations which mirror some, but not all, of the temporal changes seen at sites such as Uwaynid 14 and Wadi Jilat 6. Kharaneh IV is situated roughly between the Uwaynid and the Jilat areas, but slightly farther to the west. Use of the microburin technique is not reported for Phases A–C at this site, which sets it apart from the other Non-Natufian Microlithic assemblages of the Azraq region. There are three phases of Epipalaeolithic occupation;[2] the earliest is Phase A. The Phase A lithics are reminiscent of the western Levantine Early Kebaran, with microgravettes and partially retouched bladelets. The assemblage also contains numerous endscrapers on blades along with burins and additional large tools (Muheisen

1988a: 353–354). Other significant finds include a living floor and hearth, and a faunal assemblage containing equids (*Equus*), gazelle (*Gazella*), tortoise (*Testudo graeca*), and hare (*Lepus capensis*). Phase B also yielded a living floor with a hearth, as well as two burials below the floor. The lithic assemblage contains numerous microliths that are either narrow-pointed forms or truncated and backed; it is considered to be a later Kebaran type industry (Muheisen 1988a: 358). The Phase C occupation contains another living surface and a hearth. The microliths continue to be mainly truncated or backed and truncated types, although there are also a few geometrics such as trapezes. Muheisen (1988a: 365) considers this assemblage to be similar to the western Levantine Geometric Kebaran. The density of cultural materials from each of the phases in conjunction with the presence of living floors, and the burials in Phase B, suggest that Kharaneh IV was a longer-term base camp that was repeatedly visited over the millennia.

Another somewhat atypical site in the Azraq area is Wadi Jilat 22. The earliest two occupations (Phases E and C) are radiocarbon dated to c. 13,500 to 12,800 years bp, and are contained in marsh deposits (Garrard and Byrd 1992: 53–54). These Non-Microlithic assemblages are similar, with a low frequency of microliths, and high frequencies of large tools such as endscrapers, retouched pieces, notches and denticulates, and burins. Use of the microburin technique occurred. The most unusual tool type is the Jilat knife, a pointed blade with a retouched tang. Microwear analyses have determined that these tools functioned as knives rather than projectiles (Garrard and Byrd 1992: 54–56). Jilat knives comprise more than 50% of the Phase C lithic assemblage, indicating that during this phase Wadi Jilat 22 may have been a specialized activity area. The Phase B assemblage is derived from an aeolian silt deposit suggestive of somewhat drier conditions and is microlithic in character, containing La Mouillah points, trapeze-rectangles, triangles, and lunates. Use of the microburin technique is very common. A radiocarbon date of 11,920±180 years bp (OxA-1770) was obtained for this phase (Garrard and Byrd 1992: 53). The faunal assemblage from the phases contains a high frequency of tortoise (*Testudo graeca*) carapace fragments; there are also gazelle (*Gazella*), equid (*Equus*), hare (*Lepus capensis*), wolf/jackal (*Canis*), and fox (*Vulpes*), as well as one caprine bone (Garrard and Byrd 1992: 56). The most striking aspect of the faunal assemblage, however, is the high incidence of bird bones, which include sandgrouse, eagles and mallards (*Anas platyrhyncos*).

Early Epipalaeolithic open-air sites in the Tabaqat Fahl region include Wadi Hammeh 26, 31, and 33 (Edwards *et al.* 1988: 535–541). The largest assemblage is from Wadi Hammeh 26; it contains numerous narrow microliths of the truncated and backed type, and a small number of microburins. Faunal remains include gazelle (*Gazel-*

Figure 3.10 The Early Epipaleolithic Rockshelter of Tor Sageer, Wadi Hasa.

la), pig (*Sus scrofa*), hare (*Lepus capensis*), fox (*Vulpus*), birds, and tortoise (*Testudo graeca*). A radiocarbon date of 19,500±600 years bp (SUA-2101) was obtained from hearth charcoal (Edwards *et al.* 1988: 537). The lithic assemblages from these three sites have been attributed to the western Levantine Kebaran, although the presence of microburins suggests that these assemblages are more appropriated classified using eastern Levantine terminology (e.g., Non-Natufian Microlithic, or Nebekian).

Three sites yielding Early Epipalaeolithic assemblages are known from the Wadi Hasa region; these are the rockshelters at Yutil Hasa (Areas C and E) and Tor Sageer, and the open-air site of Tor Tareeq. The predominant lake environment of the latter part of the Upper Palaeolithic was displaced by ponds and stream-fed marshes during the Early Epipalaeolithic. Yutil Hasa continued to be used as a task camp associated with hunting activities. The Nebekian occupation yielded a lithic assemblage of extremely limited diversity. Tools consist almost exclusively of microliths, which are very narrow and include La Mouillah points, curved (arched-backed), backed and truncated, and "attenuated lunate-types" (Olszewski *et al.* 1994: 131–134). A few scrapers, burins, notches and denticulates, and other large tools also were present. Faunal remains include gazelle (*Gazella*), equids (*Equus*), aurochs (*Bos primigenius*), and tortoise (*Testudo graeca*), as well as a few marine shells. A fragment of a bone awl and a polished bone also were recovered. Current evidence suggests that uses of the rockshelter were of briefer individual duration than during Late Upper Palaeolithic times.

At Tor Sageer (Figure 3.10), a lithic assemblage similar to that from Yutil Hasa Areas C and E was recovered. It includes nongeometric forms of microliths such as backed and truncated, curved backed, "attenuated lunate-types," Ouchtata bladelets, and Dufour bladelets (Olszewski 2003: 234). Larger tools consist of retouched pieces, endscrapers, notch/denticulates, and other forms. Microburin technique is present. Fauna includes equids (*Equus*), gazelle (*Gazella*), ibex (*Capra*), dog/wolf (*Canis*), hare (*Lepus*), tortoise (*Testudo graeca*), and birds. Three radiocarbon dates from a hearth area indicate occupation at Tor Sageer in the interval between about 22,590±80 (Beta-129810) to 20,330±60 (Beta-129809) years bp. In conjunction with the presence of microburins, these radiocarbon dates, as well as those from the Azraq region, clearly indicate that microburin technique does not originate in the Levant with the much later Mushabian Industry, as proposed by Henry and Shen (1995: 295). In fact, it could be argued that microburin technique originates in the eastern Levant, perhaps in Jordan.

The site of Tor Tareeq, a south-facing, open-air site near the former Lake Hasa, is 4 km upstream from Yutil Hasa and has dense, superimposed deposits on the steep terrace in front of the bedrock outcrop. The cultural deposits rest on a sediment complex underlain by lacustrine marl facies typical of a lake edge and pond environment (Schulden-rein and Clark 1994: 37). Faunal remains include gazelle (*Gazella*), equid (*Equus*), aurochs (*Bos primigenius*), hare (*Lepus capensis*), wolf (*Canis lupus*), fox (*Vulpes vulpes*), badger (*Meles meles*), tortoise (*Testudo graeca*), and rock dove (*Columba livia*) (Clark *et al.* 1988: 268), while the pollen profiles include cattail (*Typha*), riparian willow (*Salix*), alder (*Alnus*), and oak (*Quercus*), as well as a substantial Chenopodiaceae component, all of which are indicative of a mosaic of open steppe and lake/marsh environments. Tor Tareeq is described by Neeley *et al.* (2000) as a short-term base camp. The Epipalaeolithic phase of occupation yielded a nongeometric microlithic assemblage with frequent microburins. It is similar in composition to the assemblage from Yutil Hasa, and contains numerous examples of narrow arched-backed bladelets (including curved types), as well as backed and truncated varieties. This early phase occupation features low intensity of core reduction and low ratios of tools to cores, which are thought to represent relatively brief residential occupancy with curation of tools for use off-site. This assemblage has been classified as nongeometric Epipalaeolithic by Neeley *et al.* (2000) and as Nebekian by Olszewski. Radiocarbon dates place this occupation in the interval between about 16,900±500 (UA-4391) to 15,580±250 (UA-4392) years bp.

In the Petra region, the rockshelter site of Wadi Madamagh yielded a lithic assemblage containing narrow microliths in the forms of arched-backed, pointed, and "attenuated lunate type" (Kirkbride 1958). Microburin technique is common. Faunal materials including marine shell were also recovered, and several hearths were documented. This is a large rockshelter (ca. 100 m²); in conjunction with the density of cultural materials it may have been either a base camp or a frequently revisited task locale. New excavations in the rockshelter by Schyle and Uerpmann (1988: 47–52) and a re-examination of the lithics by Byrd (1994: 210) have confirmed its Early Epipalaeolithic character. This site was used by Henry and Garrard (1988: 17–18) as the type site for the Madamaghan industry when they reported the materials from the site of Tor Hamar in the Ras al-Naqab region to the south. The typology used by Kirkbride (1958: 57), which included the term "microlithic lunate-type bladelets," does not refer to true lunates typical of geometric microlith assemblages. Despite the presence of very rare asymmetrical lunates and triangles, the assemblage from Wadi Madamagh is more similar to those from the

Wadi Hasa and the Azraq region than to the Tor Hamar assemblage, forming the basis for Olszewski's (1997) use of the term Nebekian contra Henry's (1995: 40) use of Madamaghan.

Lithic assemblages featuring non-lunate geometric forms of microliths (sometimes referred to as Middle Epipalaeolithic) are documented at two sites, associated with a paleosoil indicative of wetter contexts, in the Wadi Ziqlab. Tabaqat Buma is described as a small camp, c. 150 m², with radiocarbon dates between 14,850±160 (TO-991) to 11,170±100 (TO-987) years bp (Maher *et al.* 2001: 7–13). The small lithic assemblage contains mainly nongeometric forms, but includes a few proto-trapezes, proto-rectangles, and proto-triangles, as well as rare scalene triangles and trapeze/rectangles. The second site, WZ 148, yielded a lithic assemblage that is much clearer in its inclusion of definite geometric microliths, which consist of numerous trapeze/rectangles (Maher *et al.* 2001: 13–16). Other tools include endscrapers, burins, and retouched pieces. Interestingly, microburin technique appears to be incidental, with only one microburin recorded, as well as two microliths with possible remnant microburin scars. Faunal elements comprise red deer (*Cervus elaphus*), fallow deer (*Dama dama*), gazelle (*Gazella* sp.), equids (*Equus* sp.), aurochs (*Bos primigenius*), wild sheep or goat (ovicaprids), Nubian ibex (*Capra nubiana*), wild boar (*Sus scrofa*), fox (*Vulpes*), and tortoise carapaces (*Testudo graeca*). No radiocarbon dates are yet available for this 800 m² site.

The Wadi Hisban is the location of two additional sites with microlith assemblages that typify the latter part of the Early EpiPalaeolithic. Wadi Hisban 2, which is stratigraphically earlier than Wadi Hisban 5, produced very small triangles manufactured using the microburin technique (Edwards *et al.* 1999: 30–36). Wadi Hisban 5, on the other hand, yielded very little evidence for microburin technique, and a microlith assemblage dominated by nongeometric backed and truncated bladelets, with rare geometric trapezes (Edwards *et al.* 1999: 36–41). Although both sites contain stone hearths, radiocarbon results on collagen from burnt bone yielded anomalous dates that are considerably too young. Faunal remains are extremely fragmented and difficult to identify.

A number of Early Epipalaeolithic industries are found in the Ras al-Naqab area—Qalkhan, Madamaghan, and Hamran. Many of the sites are multi-component, containing either a sequence of temporally distinct industries or phases of a particular industry. Sites with Qalkhan assemblages include Wadi Humayma J405, J407, Wadi Humayma J406b (lower), and Tor Hamar (Layer E). The Madamaghan was found at Tor Hamar (Layers A-D) and Jabal Fatma. Hamran sites are Jabal Hamra, Jabal Mishraq, Jabal Muhaymi, Wadi Humayma J406b (upper), J21, J22, J26, and J31.

The two most intensively investigated Qalkhan sites

include one open-air locality (Wadi Humayma) and one rockshelter (Tor Hamar). Lithic assemblages are dominated by nongeometric forms of microliths (e.g., narrow arched-backed and pointed bladelets, La Mouillah points, truncations opposite snaps). Microburin technique is common, and Qalkhan points are the diagnostic element (Henry 1995: 219). There are also a small number of geometric microliths (trapeze/rectangles). Other tools include retouched pieces, notches, scrapers, and chamfered blades. No hearths or faunal remains were recovered from these sites. Because many of the Qalkhan sites are small in size and, with the exception of Tor Hamar, have shallow deposits, they are likely to represent short-term, transitory camps that were revisited on an infrequent basis (Henry 1995: 230).

Both sites yielding Madamaghan assemblages are rockshelters (Tor Hamar and Jabal Fatma). Nongeometric microliths are the dominant tool form and include arched-backed and straight-backed bladelets and La Mouillah points, as well as scalene bladelets. A small proportion of the microliths are geometrics, mainly Helwan lunates (Henry and Garrard 1988: 8; Henry and Shen 1995: 301). Microburin technique is used. Other tools occurring in moderate frequencies are scrapers and retouched pieces. At Tor Hamar (Layers A-D), a diverse assemblage also includes groundstone implements (a pestle, a handstone, a bowl fragment, and mortars), shell (*Dentalium*, *Ancilla*, *Cerithium*, *Conus*, *Cypraea*, *Columbella*, *Gibbula*, *Glycymeris*, *Ostrea*, *Pecten*, and *Arcularia*) and bone points (Henry and Shen 1995: 308–309; Henry and Garrard 1988: 13; Reese 1995: 386). The faunal assemblage from Tor Hamar includes gazelle (*Gazella*), caprines (*Capra*), equids (*Equus*), aurochs (*Bos primigenius*), hare (*Lepus capensis)*, fox (*Vulpes*), jackal (*Canis aureus*), tortoise (*Testudo*), and chukar partridge (*Alectoris chukar*) (Henry and Garrard 1988: 13–14; Klein 1995). Fish scales, as yet unstudied, and ostrich (*Struthio camelus*) eggshell fragments are also reported from Tor Hamar (Klein 1995: 410). The depth of deposits at Tor Hamar suggest that it was consistently revisited over some length of time.

During the Early Hamran, there are both lowland rockshelters (Jabal Hamra Layer C, Jabal Mishraq, and Jabal Muhayma) and highland open-air sites (Wadi Humayma J406b upper, J21 and J22). In these assemblages, the key lithic is nongeometric microliths of the straight-backed and truncated opposite snaps type. Bladelets, including those retouched into tool types, are somewhat wider than in other industries. Retouched pieces, scraper and burins also occur (Henry 1995: 251–255). A small number of groundstone implements including shallow bedrock mortars and a portable mortar (both at Jabal Mishraq) were recorded. Ornamental shells include *Dentalium* and *Mitra*. Perhaps the most intriguing discovery, however, are the panels of petroglyphs at the Jabal Hamra, Jabal Mishraq, and Jabal Muhayma rockshelters. These include

many examples of wild goats; on the basis of desert varnish that has resulted from weathering, and on superimposed ancient Thalmudic script, the petroglyphs are thought to be of great antiquity (Henry 1995: 259–260). The lowland rockshelters have thick cultural deposits and likely represent long-term base camps that were repeatedly visited; on the other hand, the high elevation sites are small in size and have shallow deposits indicative of short-term camps.

The Middle Hamran was found at Jabal Hamra (Layers A and B), Quwayra (Layers B and C), J26 and J31. As during the Early Hamran, lowland sites are rockshelters (Jabal Hamra and Quwayra) and upland sites are open-air (J26 and J31). The nongeometric microlith component occurs in high frequency and continues to contain straight-backed bladelets with truncations opposite snaps. Geometric microliths become more common during this phase and are trapeze/rectangle in form (Henry 1995: 262–264). The tendency toward wider bladelets and bladelet tools also continues during this phase. Microburins are extremely rare, indicating that this technique was not extensively utilized. Retouched pieces and scrapers occur among the larger tools. Groundstone implements have rarely been recovered. Ornamental shell is also rare (*Dentalium* and *Arcularia*) (Reese 1995: 386). The pattern of longer-term base camps at rockshelters at lower elevations and short-term, ephemeral camps at higher altitudes continues.

Quwayra (Layer A) and Qa Salab (Layers A–C) yielded Late to Final Hamran assemblages. Both are lowland rockshelters, representing longer-term base camps. During this phase of the Hamran, trapeze/rectangles are replaced by lunates as the dominant geometric form of microlith. Nongeometric microliths, however, still dominate the tool kit and include straight-backed bladelets with truncations opposite snaps. Relatively wide bladelets continue to be manufactured. Microburin technique becomes more important during these phases, and appears to be related to the emphasis on the production of lunates (Henry 1995: 270–275). Numerous ornamental shells (*Dentalium*, *Glycymeris*, *Pecten*, *Arcularia*, *Mitra*, *Cypraea*, and *Conus*) were also recovered (Reese 1995: 386).

Sites of the Late Epipalaeolithic

Levantine researchers generally refer to all phases of the Natufian as Late Epipalaeolithic. Most of the sites that have been examined in detail in Jordan are Early Natufian in age (Ayn Saratan, Bawwab al-Ghazal, Wadi Hammeh 27, Tabaqa, Yutil Hasa, Bayda, Wadi Mataha, Wadi Judayid), with a few Late Natufian sites found primarily in the Wadi Hisban (Wadi Hisban 6), Petra (Wadi Mataha), the Ras al-Naqab (Wadi Humayma J406a), and Black Desert (Qalat Anaza and Jabal Subhi), as well as one site (Ayn Rahub) in the northern Jordanian highlands north of Irbid (see Figure 3.8).

In the Azraq area, two Late Epipalaeolithic sites were recorded during intensive surveys of the Wadi Jilat, Wadi Uwaynid and central Azraq Basin areas. One is the Early Natufian occupation at Ayn Saratan at a minor spring in the vicinity of the perennial springs at Azraq Shishan (Garrard 1991: 235–236). The hallmark Helwan lunates are an important type in the geometric microlithic component, which also includes bipolar and abruptly backed lunates. Other tools are endscrapers, drills and notches. A few groundstone implements (handstones), shell beads (*Dentalium*), a probable bone sickle haft fragment, and a perforated horn core (aurochs) were recovered (Garrard 1991: 238). The faunal assemblage included aurochs (*Bos primigenius*), equids (*Equus*), gazelle (*Gazella*), hare (*Lepus capensis*), wolf (*Canis lupus*), fox (*Vulpes*), and birds such as pintail (*Anas acuta*) and garganey (*Anas querquedula*). Although no recognizable pit(s) could be discerned, several fragmented human skeletons were recorded. Both male and female adults were present, as well as juveniles and a subadult (Garrard 1991: 240). These appear to be secondary burials. It is probable that Ayn Saratan represents a longer-term base camp.

Bawwab al-Ghazal is also in the vicinity of the springs at Azraq Shishan (Rollefson *et al.* 1999: 2). Several occupations characterize the site, beginning with the Early Natufian (followed by Neolithic and Chalcolithic). A small test trench yielded several hearths, charcoal, and lithics, including Helwan lunates. Further excavations are planned.

In the Tabaqat Fahl region, the Early Natufian site of Wadi Hammeh 27 has also yielded a diverse assemblage, as well as structures and burials indicative of a longer-term base camp occupation. The cultural materials are contained within a humic silty clay indicative of the availability of springs in the vicinity (Edwards 1991: 124). The geometric microlith component is overwhelmingly dominated by Helwan lunates, other microlithic forms include Helwan retouched bladelets and inversely retouched bladelets. Larger tools consist of scrapers, burins, and notches and denticulates. The majority of the studied materials are from Phase I, the uppermost occupation at the site; this occupation is radiocarbon dated to between ca. 12,200±160 (OxA-394) to 11,920±150 (OxA-393) years bp (Edwards 1991: 128). A very diverse array of other stone artefacts, including groundstone, also was recovered. These consist of both basalt and limestone pestles, mortars, mullers, vessel rim fragments, small bowls, and shaft straighteners (Edwards 1991: 129–135). Many of these stone artefacts are decorated with crenellated motifs, grooves, incisions, and zoomorphic designs. There are also three engraved slabs that were used in the construction of one of the structure walls. Two stone-walled structures are known from Phase I—one is curvilinear, the other is U-shaped. Bone artefacts include points, beads, pendants, and six almost complete sickle

hafts, one of which has Helwan lunates in place (Edwards 1991: 136). *Dentalium* shell beads were found in the structures as well as with one of the burials. The skeleton fragments from Phase I represent at least five individuals; there is also one adult primary burial in the underlying Phase III occupation, various human bone fragments, and a pit containing infant teeth in a context above Phase I (Webb and Edwards 2002). The faunal assemblage includes gazelle (*Gazella*), caprines (*Capra*), wild pig (*Sus scrofa*), hare (*Lepus capensis*), birds (at least seven species), equids (*Equus*), aurochs (*Bos primigenius*), red deer (*Dama dama*), roe deer (*Capreolus*), wolf (*Canis lupus*), fox (*Vulpes*), wild cat (*Felis*), tortoise (*Testudo*), freshwater crab (*Potamon potamon*), and various reptiles (Edwards 1991: 146). Identified seeds include grasses, wild barley (*Hordeum spontaneum*), and legumes.

Three sites in the Wadi Hasa have been identified as Early Natufian. One is a rockshelter (Yutil Hasa Unit D), and two are open-air localities (Tabaqa and WHS 1021). As in earlier Palaeolithic times, Yutil Hasa appears to have functioned during the Early Natufian as a task camp associated with hunting activities. Tool diversity and core reduction processes, however, are indicative of somewhat more diverse activities during this phase of occupation than during the Nebekian use of the site (Olszewski 1997; Olszewski *et al.* 1994). The small lithic assemblage contains Helwan lunates, Helwan bladelets, nongeometric microliths, microburins, notches and denticulates, retouched pieces, and a few burins (Coinman *et al.* 1999: 21–22). Faunal remains consist of gazelle (*Gazella*) and aurochs (*Bos primigenius*), and a few marine shell fragments. A series of mortars is present in the bedrock that caps the ridge along which Yutil Hasa is located. Some of these are desert varnished, and it is tempting, on the basis of the emphasis on groundstone implements at other Early Natufian sites, to suggest that these mortars may date to the Natufian utilization of Yutil Hasa.

Approximately 6 km downstream from Yutil Hasa is the site of Tabaqa, tested by Byrd and Colledge (1991) and later by Olszewski *et al.* (1998). The site is situated on a terrace overlooking the confluence of the Wadis Ahmar and Hasa. Investigation of erosional channels in the terrace suggests that the site covers some 5,000 m² or more in area, most of which is buried beneath 1 to 2 m of sterile paludal sediments. The lithic assemblage is characterized by the microburin technique, which was used to produce Helwan lunates. Other tools include a small number of nongeometric microliths, notches and denticulates, retouched pieces, scrapers, and burins (Olszewski *et al.* 1998: 62–64). Charred plant remains yielded grasses, and the faunal assemblage contained gazelle (*Gazella*) and marine shell. A number of groundstone implements such as handstones, bowls, pestles, mortars and querns, as well as stone beads, were also recovered (Byrd and Colledge 1991: 272). Tabaqa appears to be a base camp occupied on a seasonal basis, likely in order to exploit cereal grasses. A possible associated task locale is the nearby site of WHS 1021.

Bayda, a site in the Petra area best known for its Neolithic village and assemblages (see Chapter 3) yielded an Early Natufian occupation some 1.5 m below the Neolithic deposits (Byrd 1989; 1991). Radiocarbon dates indicate that this phase occurred between about 12,910±250 (AA-1463) and 10,910±520 (AA-1462) years bp (Byrd 1991: 248). Lunates are the most frequent microlith type and are dominated by the Helwan type (Byrd 1989: 66–69). Notches and denticulates were very common; tools such as scrapers, retouched pieces truncations, and burins were also present. The faunal assemblage included caprines (*Capra*), gazelle (*Gazella*), aurochs (*Bos primigenius*), and equids (*Equus*) (Hecker 1989:97–99). Marine shell was also recovered; several genera were present—*Dentalium*, *Nerita*, *Strombus*, *Pyrene*, *Clypeomorus*, *Pecten*, *Cypraea*, *Vermetus*, and *Columbella* (Reese 1989: 102–103). Although no structures were recorded, there were several hearths and roasting areas (Byrd 1989: 78–81). Like Tabaqa, Bayda is interpreted as a seasonal base camp that was revisited on numerous occasions. Byrd (1991: 260) suggests the winter season as the most likely option.

Another site in the Petra region is Wadi Mataha, where several phases of Epipalaeolithic occupation from the Geometric Kebaran through the Early and Late Natufian have been recorded (Johnson *et al.* 1999: 254–259). The Early Natufian occupation has a curved stone alignment, likely from a dwelling. Lithics include Helwan lunates and endscrapers. Animal bone consists of caprines (either *Capra aegragrus* or *Capra ibex*) and mountain gazelle (*Gazella gazelle*), as well as birds (mainly *Alcetoris* sp.) and tortoise (*Testudo*), dog (*Canis*), fallow deer (*Dama dama*), hare (*Lepus*), and equid (*Equus*). Marine shell was also recovered, and includes *Dentalium*, worm shell (*Vermitedae*), *Nerita*, and *Olivella*, and appear to mainly derive from the Red Sea. Bedrock mortars are also present, although they cannot be definitively attributed to a specific phase of occupation at the site.

In the Ras al-Naqab region, an Early Natufian site (Wadi Judayid) and a Late Natufian occupation (Wadi Humayma J406a) were documented. Both are open-air sites at relatively high elevation. Wadi Judayid is radiocarbon dated to c. 12,784±650 (SMU-803) to 12,090±800 (SMU-805) years bp (Henry 1995: 321). As expected, geometric microliths are a dominant tool class, containing predominantly Helwan lunates in the Wadi Judayid assemblage and bipolar and abruptly retouched lunates in the Wadi Humayma industry. Microburin technique is common at both sites. Groundstone implements include handstones and mortars (Wadi Judayid) and a grinding slab (Wadi Humayma). Ornamental shell consists of a relatively large assemblage at Wadi Judayid (*Dentalium*, *Nerita*, and gastropods) and a few specimens of *Dental-

ium* and *Arcularia* at Wadi Humayma (Reese 1995: 387). Faunal remains at Wadi Judayid include wild goat (*Capra*) and wild sheep (*Ovis orientalis*), gazelle (*Gazella*), wild ass (*Equus*), aurochs (*Bos primigenius*), hare (*Lepus capensis*), leopard (*Panthera pardus*), fish, and birds (Henry 1995: 327). Wadi Judayid is interpreted as a multi-season base camp and Wadi Humayma as a mid-summer to early fall seasonal camp (Henry 1995: 330–331), perhaps broadly analogous to the seasonal camps at Tabaqa and Bayda.

Late Natufian phase sites were located in the Black Desert region (Betts 1998: 11–35). These include Qalat Anaza and Jabal Subhi, both open-air locales. The chipped stone industries from both sites contain bipolar or abruptly retouched lunates, although nongeometric microlith forms are almost as common. Other tools include retouched pieces, notches, and borers. At Qalat Anaza, two enclosure walls and a circular stone-walled dwelling have been documented. Other items of note are mortars, and shell and stone beads. The faunal assemblage contains gazelle (*Gazella*), ovicaprids, equids (*Equus*), hare (*Lepus capensis*), and canid (*Canis*). Betts (1998: 24, 32) suggests that Qalat Anaza was a seasonal base camp and Jabal al-Subhi, a shorter term occupation. Both sites may have been focused on hunting activities, particularly during the late winter and early spring.

A Final Natufian settlement was recorded at Ayn Rahub in the Jordanian highlands (Muheisen 1988b). The site is an open-air locale on a terrace with several curvilinear and linear walls that probably represent dwellings. There is a high frequency of geometric microliths which consist mainly of bipolar and abruptly retouched lunates. Various nongeometric microliths are also present, as are retouched pieces, and notches and denticulates. Other tools, such as scrapers, burins, and borers, are less frequent. Microburin technique was used. Two groundstone fragments and faunal remains also were recovered (Muheisen 1988b: 482). Fauna includes aurochs (*Bos primegenius*), wild goat (*Capra aegagrus*), mountain gazelle (*Gazella gazella*), European half-ass (*Equus hydruntinus*), onager (*Equus hemionus*), and wolf (*Canis lupus*) (al-Shiyab 1997: 594). The presence of structures probably indicates that Ayn Rahub was a longer-term base camp.

Concluding Remarks

Palaeolithic research in Jordan has both broadened and sharpened our understanding of ancient human groups during the Pleistocene in the Levant. Hundreds of open-air sites and dozens of rockshelter locales are currently documented. Many of these sites are *in situ* and have yielded lithic and faunal assemblages, and occasionally groundstone implements, structures, art, ornaments, and burials. Analyses of the archaeological data from the surveys and excavations have led to new or refined theoretical contributions and have raised a number of additional research questions and directions for future research.

Theoretical Contributions

Investigations into several research themes in Jordan have resulted in theoretical contributions to the study of settlement systems, to the interpretation of variability in lithic assemblages, and to insights into the development of agriculture. All of these contributions have begun with models and ideas developed on the basis of research in the western Levant. In the area of settlement patterning, Henry's (1995: 417–437) seasonal transhumance model adds considerable flexibility to the Negev/Sinai model of long-term, stable radial or circulating settlement systems; each system is hypothesized to last several millennia at a time (Marks and Freidel 1977). The seasonal transhumance model, on the other hand, posits a shift between radiating (fall/winter) and circulating (spring/summer) strategies within an annual cycle that is tied to movement between lower and higher elevational zones. For regions not characterized by great elevational contrast, and particularly for those areas with Pleistocene marsh and lake ecologies in Jordan, Olszewski and Coinman (1998) have proposed another set of settlement strategies. During more mesic periods when the lakes and marshes were highly productive resource locales, settlement systems were likely logistical (radial) and tethered to these "oases" for much of each year. Xeric climatic intervals, when marshes and lakes were much reduced in extent or absent, witnessed residential mobility (circulating) likely tied to the availability and locations of springs in these areas. These strategies were highly flexible and could vary either within a yearly cycle or between years or decades. In particular, settlement strategies characteristic of the late Upper Palaeolithic and Early Epipalaeolithic in the Wadi Hasa region appear to represent a shift from a predominantly fall through early spring occupation during the late Upper Palaeolithic to a spring through fall occupation during the Early Epipalaeolithic (Olszewski 2003).

The documentation and analysis of numerous lithic assemblages in Jordan, particularly those of the Upper and Epipalaeolithic periods, has led to the recognition of great variability in technology and typology. During the Upper Palaeolithic, there are indications that considerable variability exists within the Ahmarian Complex; this currently is treated within the contrast between Ahmarian and non-Ahmarian industries (Coinman 1998). During the Epipalaeolithic, the advent of the microburin technique is now known to have occurred at least as early as 22,500 years bp (Olszewski 2003: 234–236). More importantly, it would appear that this technique is not of North African origin, as previously believed, but is more probably a development of the eastern Levant (perhaps with an origin in Jordan). The variability between Epipalaeolithic lithic assemblages has led to the recognition of several new industries and complexes, such as the Qalkhan, Hamran, and Madamaghan (Henry 1995: 37–40), and the Nebekian (Olszewski 2006). Agreement between researchers on the use of these terms is sometimes less than perfect; this is a reflection of the on-going development of the systematics of classification in Jordan. Interpretation of this lithic variability has been seen as the result of either lithic reduction processes (Neeley and Barton 1994) or a combination of lithic reduction processes and stylistic (ethnic or cultural) traditions (Fellner 1995; Goring-Morris *et al*. 1996; Kaufman 1995).

The Late Epipalaeolithic (Natufian Complex) is widely regarded as a period of intensified cereal grass use and cultivation. This subsistence emphasis is believed to have led to the development of agriculture. The Early Natufian phase has yielded the most dramatic evidence of a complex foraging lifeway, including abundant groundstone implements, dwellings, art, ornamentation, and burials with grave goods. Sites of this phase previously were thought to be present only within the Mediterranean forest vegetation zone, however, several Early Natufian sites in steppic areas of Jordan show that this correlation is no longer valid (Olszewski 2004). The cultivation of cereal grasses during this period may be associated with xeric ecological settings, such as the Jordan Valley, as well as postdating the Early Natufian (Bar-Yosef and Belfer-Cohen 1989; Olszewski 2004). In addition to possible locales in the eastern Jordan Valley, Late Natufian sites in areas such as the Black Desert (Betts 1998) have the potential to address aspects relating to the shift to cultivation and eventually agriculture.

Future Research Directions

In many respects, Palaeolithic research programmes in Jordan are relatively recent. Work that has concentrated on research themes, such as those highlighted above, has suggested many further avenues of investigation. For example, Henry's (1995) Ras al-Naqab projects have revealed the importance of a long-term seasonal transhumance strategy in this region. The most extensively documented segments, however, are the Middle Palaeolithic and the Hamran Complex within the Epipalaeolithic period. Further work at Upper Palaeolithic sites and with sites of the Qalkhan, Madamaghan and Natufian Complexes within the Epipalaeolithic will augment the strength of this model, and perhaps document additional behavioral flexibility as well. The potential of Pleistocene lake/marsh settings, on the other hand, has only barely been realized. Recent fieldwork and on-going analyses in the eastern Wadi Hasa (Coinman 2003; Coinman *et al*. 1999; Olszewski 2003; Olszewski and Coinman 1998; Olszewski *et al*. 1998, 2001) will lead to a better understanding of Upper and Epipalaeolithic hunter-gatherer use of this ecological setting here. Sites of the Azraq Basin also hold great potential to augment our knowledge of marsh/lake resource utilization, particularly during the Epipalaeolithic period (Garrard and Byrd 1992; Garrard *et al.* 1988a; Muheisen 1988a) and the Lower Palaeolithic (Rollefson *et al.* 1997), as do sites from the Tabaqat Fahl region (Edwards *et al.* 1988; Macumber and Edwards 1997). Relatively unexplored Pleistocene lake/marsh settings include the Jafr Basin (Quintero and Wilke 1998). Additional work on Late Natufian Epipalaeolithic sites in areas such as the Black Desert (Betts 1998) will provide data critical to the interpretation of inland adaptations during the period leading to the origin of agriculture.

Specialized studies are also increasingly important to the interpretation of past lifeways. Continued analysis of lithic assemblage variability is likely to result in refinement of both the systematics of classification and interpretive models of reduction processes and stylistic traditions. Documentation of subsistence choices will benefit from more emphasis on the recovery of macrobotanical remains and phytoliths, as well as microwear and residue studies of the edges of stone artefacts. Ultimately, these types of analyzes, in conjunction with theoretical modeling of Palaeolithic behaviorial strategies, will further our anthropological reconstruction of the archaeological record. The Jordanian Palaeolithic record has proven to be of immense value in this regard.

Notes

1. The Middle Epipalaeolithic phase described for the Hasa is now known, on the basis of radiocarbon dates, to be Neolithic in age. Thus, currently, there is no Middle Epipaleolithic in the Hasa region.

2. Phase D was originally attributed to the Middle Epipaleolithic, but research in the Wadi Hasa on a similar lithic assemblage, including radiocarbon dates, indicates that Phase D at Kharaneh IV is Neolithic in age.

Bibliography

Bartl, K., F. al-Khraysheh, and R. Eichmann

2001 Palaeoenvironmental and Archaeological Studies in the Khanasiri Region/Northern Jordan. Preliminary Results of the Archaeological Survey 1999. *Annual of the Department of Antiquities of Jordan* 45: 119–134.

Baruch, U. and S. Bottema

1991 Palynological Evidence for Climatic Changes in the Levant ca. 17,000–9,000 B.P. In O. Bar-Yosef and F.R. Valla (eds.), *The Natufian Culture in the Levant*, 11–20. Ann Arbor: International Monographs in Prehistory.

Bar-Yosef, O. and A. Belfer-Cohen

1989 The Origins of Sedentism and Farming Communities. *Journal of World Prehistory* 3: 447–498.

Belfer-Cohen, A.

1995 Rethinking Social Stratification in the Natufian Culture: The Evidence from Burials. In S. Campbell and A, Green (eds.), *The Archaeology of Death in the Ancient Near East*, 9–16. Oxbow Monograph 51. Oxford: Oxbow Books.

Betts, A.

1998 *The Harra and the Hamad. Excavations and Surveys in Eastern Jordan, Volume 1.* Sheffield: Sheffield Academic Press.

Bisson, M., A. Nowell, C. Cordova, and R. Kalchgruber

in press Human Evolution at the Crossroads: An Archaeological Survey in NW Jordan. *Near Eastern Archaeology* 69(2/3).

Byrd, B.F.

1988 Late Pleistocene Settlement Diversity in the Azraq Basin. *Paléorient* 14: 257–264.

1989 *The Natufian Encampment at Beidha.* Aarhus: Jutland Archaeological Society Publications 23:1.

1991 Beidha: An Early Natufian Encampment in Southern Jordan. In O. Bar-Yosef and F.R. Valla (eds.), *The Natufian Culture in the Levant*, 245–264. Ann Arbor: International Monographs in Prehistory.

1994 Late Quaternary Hunter-Gatherer Complexes in the Levant between 20,000 and 10,000 B.P. In O. Bar-Yosef and R. Kra (eds.), *Late Quaternary Chronology and Paleoclimates of the Eastern Mediterranean*, 206–226. Radiocarbon. Tucson: Department of Anthropology, University of Arizona.

Byrd, B.F. and S.M. Colledge

1991 Early Natufian Occupation along the Edge of the Southern Jordanian Steppe. In O. Bar-Yosef and F.R. Valla (eds.), *The Natufian Culture in the Levant*, 265–276. Ann Arbor: International Monographs in Prehistory.

Byrd, B.F. and C.M. Monahan

1995 Death, Mortuary Ritual, and Natufian Social Structure. *Journal of Anthropological Archaeology* 14: 251–287.

Clark, G.A. and J. Lindly

1988 The Biocultural Transition and the Origin of Modern Humans in the Levant and Western Asia. *Paléorient* 14: 159–167.

Clark, G.A., J. Lindly, M. Donaldson, A. Garrard, N. Coinman, J. Schuldenrein, S. Fish and D. Olszewski

1988 Excavations at Middle, Upper and Epipalaeolithic Sites in the Wadi Hasa, West-Central Jordan. In A.N. Garrard and H.G. Gebel (eds.), *The Prehistory of Jordan*, 209–285. British Archaeological Reports International Series 396. Oxford: British Archaeological Reports.

Clark, G.A., M. Neeley, B. MacDonald, J. Schuldenrein, and K. Amr

1992 Wadi al-Hasa Paleolithic Project-1992: Preliminary Report. *Annual of the Department of Antiquities of Jordan* 36: 13–23.

Clark, G.A., D.I. Olszewski, J. Schuldenrein, N. Rida, and J. Eighmey

1994 Survey and Excavation in the Wadi al-Hasa: A Preliminary Report of the 1993 Season. *Annual of the Department of Antiquities of Jordan* 38: 41–55.

Clark, G.A., J. Schuldenrein, M.L. Donaldson, H.P. Schwarcz, W.J. Rink, and S.K. Fish

1997 Chronostratigraphic Contexts of Middle Paleolithic Horizons at the Ain Difla Rockshelter (WHS 634), West-Central Jordan. In H.G. Gebel, Z. Kafafi and G. Rollefson (eds.), *The Prehistory of Jordan II. Perspectives from 1996*, 77–100. Studies in Near Eastern Production, Subsistence, and Environment. Berlin: *ex oriente*.

Clutton-Brock, J.

1970 The Fossil Fauna from an Upper Pleistocene Site in Jordan. *Journal of Zoology* 161: 19–29.

Coinman, N.R.

1993 WHS 618 – Ain el-Buhira: An Upper Paleolithic Site in the Wadi Hasa, West-Central Jordan. *Paléorient* 19: 17–37.

1998 The Upper Paleolithic of Jordan. In D.O. Henry (ed.), *Prehistoric Archaeology of Jordan*, 39–63. British Archaeological Reports International Series 705. Oxford: British Archaeological Reports.

2003 The Upper Palaeolithic of Jordan: New Data from the Wadi al-Hasa. In A.N. Goring-Morris and A. Belfer-Cohen (eds.), *More Than Meets the Eye. Studies on Upper Palaeolithic Diversity in the Near East*, 151–170. Oxford: Oxbow Books.

Coinman, N.R. and D.O. Henry

1995 The Upper Paleolithic Sites. In D.O. Henry (ed.), *Prehistoric Cultural Ecology and Evolution*, 133–214. New York: Plenum Press.

Coinman, N.R., D.I. Olszewski, K. Abdo, T. Clausen, J. Cooper, J. Fox, M. al-Nahar, E. Richey and L. Saele

1999 The Eastern Hasa Late Pleistocene Project: Preliminary Report on the 1998 Season. *Annual of the Department of Antiquities of Jordan* 43: 9–25.

Copeland, L.

1988 Environment, Chronology and Lower-Middle Paleolithic Occupations of the Azraq Basin, Jordan. *Paléorient* 14: 66–75.

1989a The Artifacts from the Sounding of D. Kirkbride at Lion Spring, Azraq in 1956. In L. Copeland and F. Hours (eds.), *The Hammer on the Rock: Studies on the Early Palaeolithic of Azraq, Jordan*, 171–211. British Archaeological Reports International Series 540. Oxford: British Archaeological Reports.

1989b The Harding Collection of Acheulean Artifacts from Lion Spring, Azraq: A Quantitative and Descriptive Analysis. In L. Copeland and F. Hours (eds.), *The Hammer on the Rock: Studies on the Early Palaeolithic of Azraq, Jordan*, 213–258. British Archaeological Reports International Series 540. Oxford: British Archaeological Reports.

1991 The Late Acheulean Knapping-Floor at C-Spring, Azraq Oasis, Jordan. *Levant* 23: 1–6.

Copeland, L. and F. Hours

1988 The Palaeolithic in North-Central Jordan, An Overview of Survey Results from the Upper Zarqa and Azraq

1982–86. In A.N. Garrard and H.G. Gebel (eds.), *The Prehistory of Jordan*, 287–309. British Archaeological Reports International Series 396. Oxford: British Archaeological Reports.

Edwards, P.C.

1991 Wadi Hammeh 27: An Early Natufian Site at Pella, Jordan. In O. Bar-Yosef and F.R. Valla (eds.), *The Natufian Culture in the Levant*, 123–148. Ann Arbor: International Monographs in Prehistory.

Edwards, P.C., S.J. Bourke, S.M. Colledge, J. Head, and P.G. Macumber

1988 Late Pleistocene Prehistory in the Wadi al-Hammeh, Jordan Valley. In A.N. Garrard and H.G. Gebel (eds.), *The Prehistory of Jordan*, 525–565. British Archaeological Reports International Series 396. Oxford: British Archaeological Reports.

Edwards, P.C., M.J. Head, and P.G. Macumber

1999 An Epipalaeolithic Sequence from Wadi Hisban in the East Jordan Valley. *Annual of the Department of Antiquities of Jordan* 43: 27–48.

Emery-Barbier, A.

1995 Pollen Analysis: Environmental and Climatic Implications. In D.O. Henry (ed.), *Prehistoric Cultural Ecology and Evolution*, 375–384. New York: Plenum Press.

Fellner, R.

1995 Technology or Typology?: A Response to Neeley and Barton. *Antiquity* 69: 381–383.

Field, H.

1960 North Arabian Desert Archaeological Survey, 1925–1950. *Papers of the Peabody Museum* 45(2).

Fox, J.R.

2003 The Tor Sadaf Lithic Assemblages: A Technological Study of the early Upper Palaeolithic in the Wadi al-Hasa. In A.N. Goring-Morris and A. Belfer-Cohen (eds.), *More Than Meets the Eye. Studies on Upper Palaeolithic Diversity in the Near East*, 80–94. Oxford: Oxbow Books.

Garrard, A.N.

1991 Natufian Settlement in the Azraq Basin, Eastern Jordan. In O. Bar-Yosef and F.R. Valla (eds.), *The Natufian Culture in the Levant*, 235–244. Ann Arbor: International Monographs in Prehistory.

Garrard, A.N., D. Baird and B.F. Byrd

1994 Late Paleolithic and Neolithic Chronology in the Azraq Basin. In O. Bar-Yosef and R. Kra (eds.), *Late Quaternary Chronology and Paleoclimates of the Eastern Mediterranean*, 177–199. Tucson: Radiocarbon, Department of Anthropology, University of Arizona.

Garrard, A.N., A. Betts, B. Byrd, and C. Hunt

1987 Prehistoric Environment and Settlement in the Azraq Basin. An Interim Report on the 1985 Excavation Season. *Levant* 19: 5–25.

Garrard, A.N., A. Betts, B. Byrd, and C. Hunt

1988a Summary of Palaeoenvironmental and Prehistoric Investigations in the Azraq Basin. In A.N. Garrard and

H.G. Gebel (eds.), *The Prehistory of Jordan*, 311–337. British Archaeological Reports International Series 396. Oxford: British Archaeological Reports.

Garrard, A.N., and B. Byrd

1992 New Dimensions to the Epipalaeolithic of the Wadi el-Jilat in central Jordan. *Paléorient* 18: 47–62.

Garrard, A.N., B. Byrd and A. Betts

1986 Prehistoric Environment and Settlement in the Azraq Basin. An Interim Report on the 1984 Excavation Season. *Levant* 18: 5–24.

Garrard, A.N., B. Byrd, P. Harvey, and F. Hivernel

1985 Prehistoric Environment and Settlement in the Azraq Basin. Report on the 1982 Survey Season. *Levant* 17: 1–28.

Garrard, A.N. S Colledge, C. Hunt and R. Montague

1988b Environment and Subsistence during the Late Pleistocene and Early Holocene in the Azraq Basin. *Paléorient* 14: 40–49.

Garrard, A.N., N. Stanley Price and L. Copeland

1977 A Survey of Prehistoric Sites in the Azraq Basin, eastern Jordan. *Paléorient* 3: 109–126.

Gilead, I.

1970 Handaxe Industries in Israel and the Near East. *World Archaeology* 2: 1–11.

Goring-Morris, N.

1987 *At the Edge: Terminal Pleistocene Hunter-Gatherers in the Negev and Sinai*. British Archaeological Reports International Series 361. Oxford: British Archaeological Reports.

Goring-Morris, N., D.O. Henry, J.L. Phillips, G.A. Clark, C.M. Barton, and M.P. Neeley

1996 Pattern in the Epipalaeolithic of the Levant: Debate after Neeley & Barton. *Antiquity* 70: 130–147.

Hecker, H.M.

1989 Appendix C. Beidha Natufian: Faunal Report. In B.F. Byrd, *The Natufian Encampment at Beidha*, 97–101. Jutland Archaeological Society Publications 23: 1. Åarhus: Jutland Archaeological Society.

Henry, D.O.

1989 *From Foraging to Agriculture*. Philadelphia: University of Pennsylvania Press.

1995 *Prehistoric Cultural Ecology and Evolution*, 417–437. New York: Plenum Press.

1997 Cultural and Geologic Successions of Middle and Upper Paleolithic Deposits in the Jebel Qalkha Area of Southern Jordan. In H.G. Gebel, Z. Kafafi and G. Rollefson (eds.), *The Prehistory of Jordan II. Perspectives from 1996*, 69–76. Studies in Near Eastern Production, Subsistence, and Environment. Berlin: *ex oriente*.

Henry, D.O. (ed.)

2003 *Neanderthals in the Levant: Behavioral Organization and the Beginnings of Modern Humanity*. London: Continuum.

Henry, D.O. and A.N. Garrard

1988 Tor Hamar: An Epipalaeolithic Rockshelter in Southern Jordan. *Palestine Exploration Quarterly* 120: 1–25.

Henry, D.O. and C. Shen

1995 The Madamaghan Sites. In D.O. Henry (ed.), *Prehistoric Cultural Ecology and Evolution*, 295–317. New York: Plenum Press.

Johnson, D.J., J. Janetski, M. Chazan, S. Witcher, and R. Meadow

1999 Preliminary Report on Brigham Young University's First Season of Excavation and Survey at Wadi al-Mataha, Petra, Jordan. *Annual of the Department of Antiquities of Jordan* 43: 249–260.

Kaufman, D.

1995 Microburins and Microliths of the Levantine Epipalaeolithic: A Comment on the Paper by Neeley and Barton. *Antiquity* 69: 375–381.

Kerry, K.W.

1997 Jebel Humeima: A Preliminary Lithic Analysis of an Ahmarian and Levantine Mousterian Site in Southwest Jordan. In H.G. Gebel, Z. Kafafi and G. Rollefson (eds.), *The Prehistory of Jordan II. Perspectives from 1996*, 125–136. Studies in Near Eastern Production, Subsistence, and Environment. Berlin: *ex oriente*.

Kerry, K.W. and D.O. Henry

2003 Tor Fawaz (J403): An Upper Palaeolithic Occupation in the Jebel Qalkha Area, Southwest Jordan. In A.N. Goring-Morris and A. Belfer-Cohen (eds.), *More Than Meets the Eye. Studies on Upper Palaeolithic Diversity in the Near East*, 171–184. Oxford: Oxbow Books.

Kirkbride, D.

1958 A Kebaran Rockshelter in Wadi Madamagh, near Petra, Jordan. *Man* 63: 55–58.

1966 Five Seasons at the Pre-Pottery Neolithic Village of Beidha in Jordan. *Palestine Exploration Quarterly* 98: 8–72.

Klein, R.G.

1995 The Tor Hamar Fauna. In D.O. Henry (ed.), *Prehistoric Cultural Ecology and Evolution*, 405–416. New York: Plenum Press.

Leroi-Gourhan, A. and F. Darmon

1991 Analyzes polliniques de stations natoufieenes au Proche-Oriente. In O. Bar-Yosef and F.R. Valla (eds.), *The Natufian Culture in the Levant*, 21–26. Ann Arbor: International Monographs in Prehistory.

Lindly, J. and G.A. Clark

1987 A Preliminary Lithic Analysis of the Mousterian Site of Ain Difla (WHS Site 634) in the Wadi Ali, West-Central Jordan. *Proceedings of the Prehistoric Society* 53: 279–292.

Lindly, J., R. Beck and G.A. Clark

2000 Core Reconstructions and Lithic Reduction Sequences at WHS 623X: An Upper Paleolithic Site in the Wadi al-Hasa, West-Central Jordan. In N.R. Coinman (ed.),

The Archaeology of the Wadi al-Hasa, West-Central Jordan, Vol. 2: Archaeological Excavations in the Wadi al-Hasa, 211–226. Tempe: Anthropological Research Papers, Arizona State University.

MacDonald, B., E. Banning and L. Pavlish

1980 The Wadi el Hasa Survey 1979: A Preliminary Report. *Annual of the Department of Antiquities of Jordan* 24: 169–184.

MacDonald, B., A. Bradshaw, L. Herr, M.P. Neeley, and S. Quaintance

2000 The Tafila-Busayra Archaeological Survey: Phase 1 (1999). *Annual of the Department of Antiquities of Jordan* 44: 507–522.

MacDonald, B., L. Herr, M.P. Neeley, S. Quaintance, and A. Bradshaw

2001 The Tafila-Busayra Archaeological Survey: Phase 2 (2000). *Annual of the Department of Antiquities of Jordan* 45: 395–411.

MacDonald, B., G. Rollefson, E. Banning, B. Byrd, and C. d'Annibale

1983 The Wadi el-Hasa Survey, 1982: A Preliminary Report. *Annual of the Department of Antiquities of Jordan* 27: 311–324.

MacDonald, B., G. Rollefson and D. Roller

1982 The Wadi el-Hasa Survey 1981: A Preliminary Report. *Annual of the Department of Antiquities of Jordan* 26: 117–131.

Macumber, P.G.

1992 The Geological Setting of Palaeolithic Sites at Tabaqat Fahl, Jordan. *Paléorient* 18: 31–44.

Macumber, P.G. and P.C. Edwards

1997 Preliminary Results from the Acheulian Site of Mashari'a 1, and a New Stratigraphic Framework for the Lower Palaeolithic of the East Jordan Valley. In H.G. Gebel, Z. Kafafi and G. Rollefson (eds.), 23–43 *The Prehistory of Jordan II. Perspectives from 1996*. Studies in Near Eastern Production, Subsistence, and Environment. Berlin: *ex oriente*.

Macumber, P.G. and M.J. Head

1991 Implications of the Wadi al-Hammeh Sequences for the Terminal Drying of Lake Lisan, Jordan. *Palaeogeography, Palaeoclimatology, Palaeoecology* 84: 163–173.

Maher, L., M. Lohr, M. Betts, C. Parslow, and E.B. Banning

2001 Middle Epipalaeoltihic Sites in Wadi Ziqlab, Northern Jordan. *Paléorient* 27: 5–19.

Marks, A.E. and D. Friedel

1977 Prehistoric Settlement Patterns in the Avdat/Aqev Area. In A.E. Marks (ed.), *Prehistory and Paleoenvironments in the Central Negev, Israel*. Vol. II, 131–158. Dallas: Southern Methodist University Press.

Muheisen, M.

1988a The Epipalaeolithic Phases of Kharaneh IV. In A.N. Garrard and H.G. Gebel (eds.), *The Prehistory of Jordan*, 353–367. British Archaeological Reports International Series 396. Oxford: British Archaeological Reports.

1988b Excavations at 'Ain Rahub, A Final Natufian and Yarmoukian Site near Irbid. In A.N. Garrard and H.G. Gebel (eds.), *The Prehistory of Jordan*, 473–502. British Archaeological Reports International Series 396. Oxford: British Archaeological Reports.

1988c Survey of Prehistoric Cave Sites in the Northern Jordan Valley. In A.N. Garrard and H.G. Gebel (eds.), *The Prehistory of Jordan*, 503–523. British Archaeological Reports International Series 396. Oxford: British Archaeological Reports.

Neeley, M.P. and C.M. Barton

1994 A New Approach to Interpreting Late Pleistocene Microlith Industries in Southwest Asia. *Antiquity* 68: 275–288.

Neeley, M.P., J.D. Peterson, G.A. Clark, and S.K. Fish

2000 WHS 1065 (Tor al-Tareeq), an Epipalaeolithic Site in the Wadi al-Hasa, west-central Jordan. In N.R. Coinman (ed.), *The Archaeology of the Wadi al-Hasa, West-Central Jordan, Vol. 2: Archaeological Excavations in the Wadi al-Hasa*, 245–279. Tempe: Anthropological Research Papers, Arizona State University.

Olson, A.P.

1997 An Initial Technotypological Analysis of J447, an Open-Air Levantine Mousterian Site in Southern Jordan. In H.G. Gebel, Z. Kafafi and G. Rollefson (eds.), *The Prehistory of Jordan II. Perspectives from 1997*, 59–67. Studies in Near Eastern Production, Subsistence, and Environment. Berlin: *ex oriente*.

Olszewski, D.I.

1991 Social Complexity in the Natufian?: Assessing the Relationship of Ideas and Data. In G.A. Clark (ed.), *Perspectives on the Past. Theoretical Biases in Mediterranean Hunter-Gatherer Research*, 322–340. Philadelphia: University of Pennsylvania Press.

1997 From the Late Ahmarian to the Early Natufian: A Summary of Hunter-Gatherer Activities at Yutil al-Hasa, West-Central Jordan. In H.G. Gebel, Z. Kafafi and G. Rollefson (eds.), *The Prehistory of Jordan II. Perspectives from 1996*. Studies in Near Eastern Production, Subsistence, and Environment. Berlin: *ex oriente*.

2000 The Epipalaeolithic in the Wadi al-Hasa: An Overview. In N.R. Coinman (ed.), *The Archaeology of the Wadi al-Hasa, West-Central Jordan, Vol. 2: Excavations at Middle, Upper, and Epipalaeolithic Sites*, 227–243. Tempe: Anthropological Research Papers, Arizona State University.

2003 The Conundrum of the Levantine Late Upper Palaeolithic and Early Epipalaeolithic: Perspectives from the Wadi al-Hasa, Jordan. In A.N. Goring-Morris and A. Belfer-Cohen (eds.), *More Than Meets the Eye. Studies on Upper Palaeolithic Diversity in the Near East*, 230–241. Oxford: Oxbow Books.

2004 Plant Food Subsistence Issues and Scientific Inquiry in the Early Natufian. In C. Delage (ed.), *Views on the Last Hunter-Gatherer Societies in the Near East: The Natufian*

Culture and its Contemporaries. Oxford: British Archaeological Reports International Series.

2006 Issues in the Levantine Epipaleolithic: The Madamaghan, Nebekian and Qalkhan (Levant Epipaleolithic). *Paléorient* 32(1): 19–26.

Olszewski, D.I., G.A. Clark and S. Fish.

1990 WHS 784X (Yutil al-Hasa): A Late Ahmarian Activity Site in the Wadi Hasa, West-Central Jordan. *Proceedings of the Prehistoric Society* 56: 33–49.

Olszewski, D.I. and N.R. Coinman

1998 Late Pleistocene Settlement Patterns in the Wadi al-Hasa, West-Central Jordan. In N.R. Coinman (ed.), *The Archaeology of the Wadi al-Hasa, West-Central Jordan, Vol. 1: Surveys, Settlement Patterns, and the Paleoenvironments of the Wadi al-Hasa*, 177–203. Tempe: Anthropological Research Papers, Arizona State University.

Olszewski, D.I., N.R. Coinman, J. Schuldenrein, T. Clausen, J. Cooper, J. Fox, J.B. Hill, M. al-Nahar, and J. Williams

1998 The Eastern Hasa Late Pleistocene Project: Preliminary Report on the 1997 Season. *Annual of the Department of Antiquities of Jordan* 42: 53–74.

Olszewski, D.I., N.R. Coinman, T.G. Clausen, J.B. Cooper, H. Jansson, M. al-Nahar, U. Schurmans, L.S. Saele, A.J. Sampson, and J.R. Thompson

2001 The Eastern Hasa Late Pleistocene Project. Preliminary Report on the 2000 Fieldseason. *Annual of the Department of Antiquities of Jordan* 45: 39–60.

Olszewski, D.O., M.N. Stevens, R.F. Beck, J. Cooper, and G.A. Clark

1994 The 1993 Excavations at Yutil al-Hasa (WHS 784), An Upper/Epipalaeolithic Site in West-Central Jordan. *Paléorient* 20: 129–141.

Parenti, F., A.H. al-Shiyab, E. Santucci, Z. Kafafi, and G. Palumbo

1997 Early Acheulean Stone Tools and Fossil Faunas from the Dauqara Formation, Upper Zarqa Valley, Jordanian Plateau. In H.G. Gebel, Z. Kafafi and G. Rollefson (eds.), *The Prehistory of Jordan II. Perspectives from 1996*, 7–22. Studies in Near Eastern Production, Subsistence, and Environment. Berlin: *ex oriente*.

Phillips, J.L.

1988 The Upper Paleolithic of the Wadi Feiran, Southern Sinai. *Paléorient* 14: 183–200.

1994 The Upper Paleolithic Chronology of the Levant and the Nile Valley. In O. Bar-Yosef and R. Kra (eds.), *Late Quaternary Chronology and Paleoclimates of the Eastern Mediterranean*, 169–176. Tucson: Radiocarbon, Department of Anthropology, University of Arizona.

Quintero, L.A. and P.J. Wilke

1998 Archaeological Reconnaissance in the al-Jafr Basin, 1997. *Annual of the Department of Antiquities of Jordan* 42: 113–122.

Rees, L.W.B.

1929 The Transjordan Desert. *Antiquity* 3: 389–407.

Reese, D.S.

1989 Appendix D: The Natufian Shells from Beidha. In B.F. Byrd, *The Natufian Encampment at Beidha*, 102–104. Jutland Archaeological Society Publications 23:1. Aarhus: Jutland Archaeological Society.

1995 Shells from the Wadi Hisma Sites. In D.O. Henry (ed.), *Prehistoric Cultural Ecology and Evolution*, 385–390. New York: Plenum Press.

Rhotert, H.

1938 *Vorgeschichtliche Forschungen in Klein Asien und Nordafrika, Band I: Transjordanien*. Stuttgart: Verlag Strecker und Schröder.

Richter, D., H.B. Schroeder, W.J. Rink, P.J. Julig, and H.P. Schwarcz

2001 The Middle to Upper Palaeolithic Transition in the Levant and New Thermoluminescence Dates for a Late Mousterian Assemblage from Jerf al-Ajla Cave (Syria). *Paléorient* 27: 29–46.

Rollefson, G.O.

1981 The Late Acheulean Site at Fjaje, Wadi el-Bustan, Southern Jordan. *Paléorient* 7: 5–21.

1982 Late Acheulean Artifacts from Ain el-Assad ("Lion's Spring") near Azraq, Eastern Jordan. *Bulletin of the American School of Oriental Research* 240: 1–20.

1983 Two Seasons of Excavations at Ain el-Assad near Azraq. *Bulletin of the American School of Oriental Research* 252: 25–34.

1984 A Middle Acheulian Surface Site from Wadi Uweinid, Eastern Jordan. *Paléorient* 10: 127–133.

1985 Late Pleistocene Environments and Seasonal Hunting Strategies: A Case Study from Fjaje, near Shobak, Southern Jordan. In A. Hadidi (ed.), *Studies in the History and Archaeology of Jordan II*, 103–107. Boston: Routledge and Kegan Paul.

Rollefson, G.O., D. Schnurrenberger, L.A. Quintero, R. Watson, and R. Low

1997 'Ain Soda and 'Ain Qasiya: New Late Pleistocene and Early Holocene Sites in the Azraq Shishan Area, Eastern Jordan . In H.G. Gebel, Z. Kafafi and G. Rollefson (eds.), *The Prehistory of Jordan II. Perspectives from 1996*, 45–58. Studies in Near Eastern Production, Subsistence, and Environment. Berlin: *ex oriente*.

Rollefson, G.O., L. Quintero, and P.J. Wilke

1999 Bawwab al-Ghazal: Preliminary Report on the 1998 Testing Season. *Neo-Lithics* 1/99: 2–4.

2001 Azraq Wetlands Survey 2000, Preliminary Report. *Annual of the Department of Antiquities of Jordan* 45: 71–81.

Roller, K.L. and G.A. Clark

1997 Use-Wear Analysis of Levallois Points from the 'Ain Difla Rockshelter, West-Central Jordan. In H.G. Gebel, Z. Kafafi and G. Rollefson (eds.), *The Prehistory of Jordan II. Perspectives from 1996*, 101–109. Studies in Near Eastern Production, Subsistence, and Environment. Berlin: *ex oriente*.

Rosen, A.M.

1995 Preliminary Analysis of Phytoliths from Prehistoric Sites in Southern Jordan. In D.O. Henry (ed.), *Prehistoric Cultural Ecology and Evolution*, 399–403. New York: Plenum Press.

Schuldenrein, J. and G.A. Clark

1994 Landscape and Prehistoric Chronology of West-Central Jordan. *Geoarchaeology* 9: 31–55.

2001 Prehistoric Landscapes and Settlement Geography along the Wadi Hasa, West-Central Jordan. Part I: Geoarchaeology, Human Palaeoecology and Ethnographic Modelling. *Environmental Archaeology* 6: 23–38.

2003 Prehistoric Landscapes and Settlement Geography along the Wadi Hasa, West-Central Jordan. Part II: Towards a Model of Palaeoecological Settlement for the wadi Hasa. *Environmental Archaeology* 8: 1–16.

Schyle, D. and H.G. Gebel

1997 Upper Palaeolithic Siq Umm al-Alda 1, near Wadi Musa, Southern Jordan. In H.G. Gebel, Z. Kafafi and G. Rollefson (eds.), *The Prehistory of Jordan II. Perspectives from 1996*, 149–170. Studies in Near Eastern Production, Subsistence, and Environment. Berlin: *ex oriente*.

Schyle, D. and H.-P. Uerpmann

1988 Paleolithic Sites in the Petra Area. In A.N. Garrard and H.-G. Gebel (eds.), *The Prehistory of Jordan in 1986*, 39–65. British Archaeological Reports International Series 396. Oxford: British Archaeological Reports.

Shea, J.J.

1995 Lithic Microwear Analysis of Tor Faraj Rockshelter. In D.O. Henry (ed.), *Prehistoric Cultural Ecology and Evolution*, 85–105. New York: Plenum Press.

1998 Ar Rasfa, A Levantine Mousterian Site from Northwest Jordan: A Preliminary Report. *Paléorient* 24: 71–78.

2003 Close Encounters: Neanderthals and Modern Humans in the Middle Palaeolithic Levant. *The Review of Archaeology* 24: 42–56.

al-Shiyab, A.H.

1997 Animal Remains from 'Ain Rahub. In H.G. Gebel, Z. Kafafi and G. Rollefson (eds.), *The Prehistory of Jordan II. Perspectives from 1996*, 593–599. Studies in Near Eastern Production, Subsistence, and Environment. Berlin: *ex oriente*.

Stringer, C. and P. Andrews

1988 Genetic and Fossil Evidence for the Origins of Modern Humans. *Science* 239: 1263–1268.

Waechter, J., V. Seton-Williams, D.M. Bate, and L. Picard

date The Excavations at Wadi Dhobai 1937–1938 and the Dhobaian Industry. *Journal of the Palestine Oriental Society* 18: 172–186, 292–298.

Webb, S.G. and P.G. Edwards

2002 The Natufian Human Skeletal Remains from Wadi Hammeh 27 (Jordan). *Paléorient* 28: 103–124.

Whalen, N.M. and C.M Kolly

2001 Survey of Acheulean Sites in the Wadi as-Sirhan Basin, Jordan, 1999. *Annual of the Department of Antiquities of Jordan* 45: 11–18.

Williams, J.K.

1997 Tor Aeid, An Upper Paleolithic Site in Southern Jordan. In H.G. Gebel, Z. Kafafi and G. Rollefson (eds.), *The Prehistory of Jordan II. Perspectives from 1996*, 137–148. Studies in Near Eastern Production, Subsistence, and Environment. Berlin: *ex oriente*.

Zeuner, F., D. Kirkbride and B. Park

1957 Stone Age Exploration in Jordan, 1. *Palestine Exploration Quarterly*: 17–24.

4. The Neolithic Period

Gary Rollefson

Introduction

Beginning in the 1980s the pace of Neolithic research in Jordan surged, and in the past five years since the first version of this synthesis appeared (Rollefson 2001), the rate has not slackened, prompting the necessity for a substantial revision. The results of new surveys (e.g. MacDonald and Sawtell 2002; Henry *et al.* 2001; Amr *et al.* 1998) and subsequent accelerated excavations continue to produce results in considerable quantity, providing rich details and fleshing out previous skeletal frameworks of social and economic relationships within and between farming and herding populations in a variety of environmental settings across the landscape. One of the fundamental outcomes of this work is the documentation of unsuspected but substantial cultural variability across Jordan that spanned the entire Neolithic period.

The beginning and end of the Neolithic are far from clearly defined. The onset is associated with the rise of agriculture, an event that would have profound effects on human population and social organization. This development was a gradual process that had begun much earlier in the Late Epipalaeolithic period, and the resolution between non-selective cultivation and true agriculture is not easily detectable in the archaeological record. But the Neolithic period was also allied with the appearance of changes in the material culture, including the first instance of true arrowheads in the form of al-Khiam and similar projectile points (Bar-Yosef 1981; Nadel *et al.* 1991), and such tangible evidence is of great assistance in deciding if an archaeological site dates to the earliest phases of the Neolithic.

Similarly, the transition from the Neolithic to the Chalcolithic remains obscure. In this instance, material correlates for the change are disputed, partly because of the scarcity of data and partly due to the varied interpre-

Period	Range cal BP[1]
PPNA	12,000 – 11,000
Early PPNB	11,000 – 10,500
Middle PPNB	10,500 – 9,500
Late PPNB	9,500 – 8,900
PPNC	8,900 – 8,300
Pottery Neolithic	8,300 – 6,800?

Table 4.1. Chronological phases of the Neolithic in Jordan.

tations individual scholars draw from particular aspects of the archaeological record (e.g. Goren 1990; Gopher and Gophna 1993: 337; cf. Kafafi 1998; Levy 1995: 226).

In the description and discussion which follows, the chronological phases defined in earlier publications (cf. Bar-Yosef 1981; Rollefson 1989: 169; Weninger *et al.* 2004) and outlined in Table 4.1 will be used.

These periods will be discussed in terms of lithic technology, architecture, subsistence economy and ritual; settlement pattern will also be addressed in so far as it is possible.

The Pre-Pottery Neolithic A

Reflecting the rare number of sites for this period throughout the Levant, only five investigated Jordanian sites (Sabra 1, Iraq al-Dubb, Wadi Faynan 16, Dhra and Zahrat adh-Dhra 2) are assignable with confidence to the PPNA. In the case of Jordan, this mirrors more the insufficiency of surveyed landscape than of the real PPNA presence. All but Iraq al Dubb occur in southern Jordan, so little meaningful interpretation of settlement pattern during this period is possible. Another site (Jabal Qaysa J-24) may in part be PPNA in age, but in view of the limited sounding here, an EPPNB age is also possible.

Lithic Technology and Typology

Confirmed by radiocarbon dates at all sites but Jabal Qaysa J-24, type fossils including Khiamian points, Hagdud truncations and unidirectional blades and blade cores all point to a PPNA time frame for the sites (Gebel 1988: 78 and fig. 6; Henry 1995: 348–49 and fig. 14.3; Kuijt *et al.* 1991: 102–104 and fig. 5; Kuijt 2001a: Table 1, figs. 2–3; Edwards and Higham 2001: Table 1; Sayej 2004a: Table 2; Finlayson *et al.* 2000: Table 3). Small lunates were also found at Iraq al-Dubb, but since the PPNA layers occur above Late Natufian deposits, Kuijt considers that they are probably intrusive into the PPNA layers, and that lunates are not a characteristic component of the PPNA industry (Kuijt 1994b: 2–3, 1996; Kuijt and Mahasneh 1998). The temporary nature of the occupations at Sabra 1 and at Jabal Qaysa J-24 is attested by the restricted nature of the tool kits, and the relatively high percentage of points and other piercing tools indicates their status as camps associated with hunting. The inventory at Iraq al-Dubb still has not been published, but the presence of sickle blades in some quantity (Kuijt *et al.* 1991: 102) suggests a relatively longer stay for the inhabitants of the rockshelter. Substantial architecture at Zahrat adh-Dhra 2, Wadi Faynan 16 and Dhra might point to long-term permanent residence at these sites. Nevertheless, it is claimed that neither Dhra nor Zahrat al-Dhra 2 were continuously occupied for several hundred years, but repeatedly abandoned and resettled (Edwards and Higham (2001: 146).

Projectile points range markedly among the Jordanian sites, ranging from less than 1% at Zahrat al-Dhra 2 (Sayej 2004: 381–383) to nearly a quarter of all retouched tools at Wadi Faynan 16 (Finlayson *et al.* 2000: 16, 21). The Khiamian and Salibiya types are the most diagnostic of the PPNA period projectile point types reported from the Jordanian sites, and they constitute virtually the only

Figure 4.1 Neolithic sites mentioned in the text.

versions of arrowheads at Iraq al-Dubb, Wadi Faynan 16, Dhra,[2] and Sabra 1 (Gebel 1988: figs. 6–9, 10). Notably, use-wear analysis on a large sample of Khiam points from Dhra indicate that a sizeable proportion may have functioned as borers rather than projectile armatures (Goodale and Smith 2001: 3–4). Jabal Qaysa also contains Helwan points (Henry 1995: 348 and fig. 14.3), and this type is also associated with the Early PPNB period (cf. Gopher 1994: 190–199); in the absence of radiocarbon dates at Jabal Qaysa, it is possible that this hunting camp may be from a time near the end of the PPNA or the beginning of the PPNB, or somewhere around 11,150–10,700 BP, and possibly even later in Kuijt's judgment (Kuijt and Chesson 1994: 36–38). That Jabal Qaysa was visited in the early PPNB is supported by the presence of bi-directional naviform blade cores (Henry 1995: fig. 14.6).[3]

Just as there is considerable variation in the presence of point types among the Jordanian sites, this is matched by consequent variation in other tool types. Microliths are conspicuously rare in Dhra, Wadi Faynan 16, and Zahrat al-Dhra 2 in contrast to the northern Jordan Valley. This could indicate mixing of deposits in sites where the Final Natufian underlies PPNA assemblages. Another aspect of typological variability might be that excavations at the sites have encountered differing activity foci. This is one conclusion reached by Pirie based on the analysis of material from Wadi Faynan 16, and she goes on to point out that this has important bearing on the Khiamian-Sultanian controversy. Some argue that the PPNA undergoes a succession of distinct, temporally-restricted cultural entities (e.g., Ronen and Lechevallier 1999: 6), while others contend that the difference in the Khiamian and Sultanian assemblages is more probably related to differences in site function (e.g., Garfinkel 1996). At Wadi Faynan 16, the Khiamian-Sultanian succession appears to be reversed stratigraphically, bringing a new dimension to the debate (Pirie 2001: 4), one that finds support from Dhra, as well (Kuijt 2001a: 123).

Subsistence Economy

Few substantial indications of the subsistence economy practiced by the inhabitants of the PPNA sites are available. Bones are mentioned for both Sabra 1 and Jabal Qaysa, but no species identifications have been provided. At Iraq al-Dubb, preliminary analysis has shown that all animal remains were wild, including in decreasing frequency gazelle, boar, sheep/goat and aurochs for the larger mammals; smaller animals were mostly red fox, wildcat, and lagomorphs. Birds were also preserved, including doves, grouse and pheasant, hawks and waterfowl (Mullen and Gruspier, in Palumbo *et al.* 1990: 114). The recently resumed excavations at Dhra also produced animal bones and plant remains, but analysis is still incomplete. Wadi Faynan 16 produced abundant charred plant remains, mollusks, and faunal remains, but a report on them is forth-

coming. The first season at Zahrat al-Dhra 2 produced only 34 identifiable animal bones, among which *Capra* sp., *Bos primigenius*, badger (*Meles meles*), and crab (*Potamon*) were present (Edwards *et al.* 2002: 12–13).

Plant remains from most of the PPNA sites still have not published. Kuijt *et al.* (1991: 104) mention that botanical analysis for the Iraq al-Dubb is still in progress, but no publication of results has yet appeared; the same may be said for the rest except Zahrat al-Dhra 2, where Meadows has tabulated the results of his research (Edwards *et al.* 2002: 12); wild cereals are occasional to frequent (including some domesticated barley), and pulses, pistachio, and fig nutlets are ubiquitous, all of which indicates that they constituted a significant part of the local diet (Edwards *et al.* 2002: 11).

Architecture

In the south Jabal Qaysa J-24 (Henry 1982, 1995), in the Judayid basin just south of Ras an-Naqab, and Sabra 1 (Gebel 1988), in the Petra region, are small ephemeral campsites with no evidence of architecture. Another temporary PPNA settlement occurred at Iraq al-Dubb, a rockshelter in the Wadi Yabis in northern Jordan (Kuijt *et al.* 1991; Kuijt 1994a). But here, although the rockshelter is small and the terrace in front of it not very extensive, excavations revealed three oval to circular PPNA structures inside the shelter, and the labour invested in the construction indicates that the occupation was at least semi-permanent. The earliest building is known only from a partially exposed mud floor and adjacent mudbricks, a burned post (radiocarbon dated to 11,429±159 BP), and some pit features cut into bedrock. A second building was oval, also with a mud floor, and may have been as large as 1.5 by 3.0 m; the walls of this structure consisted of a single width of cobbles preserved to a height of 70 cm. Details of the third building are barely known since it was not extensively excavated.

PPNA farming villages with at least some degree of permanence are found only in southern Jordan at Zahrat al-Dhra 2, Dhra, and Wadi Faynan 16. Wadi Faynan 16 shows sub-circular semi-subterranean dwellings about 3.5 m in diameter. All the structures in the two soundings indicate two phases of construction, and one house was repeatedly renovated.

Located above the east shore of the Dead Sea at an elevation of c. 40m below sea level (cf. Bennett 1980; Raikes 1980), Dhra covers an area of less than 0.65 ha (Kuijt and Finlayson 2001: 13) and has "extensive evidence for oval or circular structures made of stone and mud" (Kuijt and Mahasneh 1998). A suite of nine radiocarbon dates range from 10,912±222 to 11,549±180 BP (Kuijt and Finlayson 2001: 14). Three well-defined curvilinear structures have been uncovered (including one partially exposed in a tank trench), all ca. 3–3.5 m in diameter. One of the three semisubterranean structures had stone walls standing to a height of 85cm; a low stone feature, possibly a bench, was inside the building (Kuijt and Mahasneh 1998). Another had mud walls standing up to 60 cm; inside were regularly spaced upright stones 35–50 cm high with "notches" created on the uppermost end, evidently to support floor beams raised above the ground (Figure 4.2) (Kuijt and Finlayson 2001: 14).

Zahrat adh-Dhra 2 revealed 17 curvilinear walls of stone emerging through the surface, although these walls did not close to form a surrounded space typical of PPNA houses in Dhra, Wadi Faynan 16, and the northern Jordan Valley sites; they appear to be semi-circular structures instead (Edwards *et al.* 2002: 4, figs. 2, 5–7). Plaster floors and fireplaces occurred inside the arc of the walls, some of which reached 9 m in length.

Ritual

Burned and unburned bones, including some from humans, were reported for Sabra 1 (Gebel 1988: 78; Roehrer-Ertl *et al.* 1988), but there is no clear evidence for an intentional burial.

Iraq al-Dubb produced two burials, both of which were flexed and appear to be complete, although one of them was not completely exposed. One skeleton was of an adult male, the other of an adolescent, and neither had any associated grave goods (Kuijt *et al.* 1991: 106). The two burials inside the shelter could reflect an emotional bond of the social group with the location, even if the occupation of the rockshelter was not a permanent one. Dhra has produced at least one burial (Kuijt, pers. comm.), and Wadi Faynan 16 yielded a subfloor, tightly flexed primary subfloor burial whose skull and mandible were removed and placed alongside the rest of the body; a plan of the burial includes a projectile point in association with the skeleton, but there is no comment on this element in the text (Finlayson *et al.* 2000: 19, fig. 9).

Figurines are rare: the only reported example is a seated human figurine (sex unspecified) of clay from Dhra (Kuijt and Finlayson 2001: 14, fig. 2). A small limestone "plaque" incised with a band of four straight lines, from which more than 14 parallel lines emanate came from Zahrat adh-Dhra 2 (Edwards *et al.* 2002: 6, fig. 8).

The Early Pre-Pottery Neolithic B (EPPNB)

Like the PPNA, evidence for the presence of Early PPNB (EPPNB) settlements in Jordan is relatively rare, known only from the lowest layer at the site of Wadi Jilat 7 (Garrard *et al.* 1994) in the eastern steppe not far from Azraq and from Abu Hudhud (Rollefson 1996) in Wadi Hasa in south-central Jordan.[4]

Lithic Technology and Typology

The most fundamental distinction between the PPNA and PPNB lies in the shift to naviform blade production in the latter period (Cauvin 1987), and the presence of bi-direction-

al blades from such cores characterizes the collections from both Jilat 7, Layer 1 (hereafter 7-1) and Abu Hudhud. No naviform cores were found on the surface of Abu Hudhud, but they account for over 10% of the cores in Jilat 7-1 (Baird 1994: table 2; 1995: 508–509). Reflecting its early date, about a quarter of the 45 Jilat 7-1 projectile points are Khiam and related types, while almost three-quarters are Helwan points; 24 Hagdud truncations were also recovered from this phase. This mix, including the core mixture, is generally similar to the small artefact collection from Jabal Qaysa (Henry 1995: 348), All eight points collected from the surface of Abu Hudhud were Helwan types, but it is possible that the generally smaller Khiamian points and Hagdud truncations may have been overlooked since the collection strategy was not systematic.

The toot kit at Jilat 7-1 was greatly varied (Baird 1994) and indicates that a broad range of activities was undertaken at the site; grinding stones (including mortars, pestles and stone vessels, cf. Wright in Garrard *et al.* 1994: table 2) demonstrate at least a minor degree of permanence for the occupation. Simple and transverse types dominated burins. A single sickle element seems odd for this arid area (Garrard *et al.* 1994: 89), although there is no reason that the tool was necessarily associated with agriculture. The collection of tools from Abu Hudhud, although small, is also diverse (34 pieces among 11 tool classes, in addition to the projectile points and 1 basalt pestle fragment; cf. Rollefson 1996: table 1) and supports the likelihood that Abu Hudhud was at least a semi-permanent settlement.

Architecture

One structure excavated at Jilat 7-1 was rectangular (but with rounded corners) and measured approximately 3 by 3.5 m. Walls were "built from a combination of coursed stones and uprights with rubble packing" (Garrard *et al.* 1994: 75), and other walls of possible contemporaneous structures were located at the edges of the excavated area.

Four small oval or subrectangular structures (c. 3 by 2.5 m) were visible at the surface of Abu Hudhud, and an erosional cut through the site revealed a corner of a building of undetermined size with walls that formed a right angle. It is not clear if the rounded alignments are remnants of house walls or if they were the foundation stones of temporary huts or tents.

Subsistence Economy

Information relating to the exploitation of plant and animal resources is available only from Jilat 7-1. Despite its location in the steppe, the site yielded remains of domesticated einkorn wheat and barley; the rest of the material from flotation samples appears to represent wild seeds, fruits and nuts (Colledge in Garrard *et al.* 1994: 102–105). The animal bones come entirely from wild species (in decreasing frequency hare, gazelle, tortoise and fox; cf. Martin in Garrard *et al.* 1994: table 7). Of particular

Figure 4.2 Reconstruction of Structure 4, Area I, Dhra, Jordan (drawing by Ian Kuijt. By permission).

importance, perhaps, is the absence of any goat and sheep, which indicates that these animals were not available to these hunters (Martin in Garrard *et al.* 1994: 97).

Ritual

No burials were found at Jilat 7-1, but one engraved stone object has been described as having potential calendrical or mathematical functions (Wright in Garrard *et al.* 1994: 92, fig. 10a).

The Middle Pre-Pottery Neolithic B (MPPNB)

The thousand years that constituted the Middle PPNB witnessed what may be taken to reflect a virtual population explosion, for in contrast to the meagre evidence for PPNA and EPPNB settlements in Jordan, later aceramic Neolithic sites are to be found throughout the countryside.

Lithic Technology and Typology

The definition of the PPNB in contradistinction to the PPNA relies most heavily on the widespread adoption of the naviform core-and-blade technique sometime after 11,000 bp. Here again, the EPPNB evidence is critical for evaluating the expanding rate of popularity for naviform blade technology.

Technology

It appears that at MPPNB settlements there is a "dual character" of the lithics industry: one that involves an *ad hoc* execution of the immediate satisfaction of relatively undemanding needs, and another that centres on a sophisticated blade production technique for certain applications (cf. Goring-Morris 1994: 438). Replication experiments have shown the elaborate core preparation and maintenance required of the naviform blade technique (Wilke and Quintero 1994). The narrow range of flint/chert quality used in the process, as well as the restricted distribution of naviform chipping floors, suggests the likelihood that naviform blade production was a specialization practised by relatively few members of the MPPNB Ayn Ghazal community (Quintero and Wilke 1995). Overall, whether dealing with *ad hoc* or specialized naviform blade production, the blade to flake ratio is almost 1:1, a situation that changes dramatically in later periods (cf. Rollefson 1990a, 1997b).

One topic that has received a perceptible degree of debate in the past is the presence, and even dominance, of a high-quality purple-pink flint in many assemblages throughout Jordan and Israel, At the centre of the controversy was whether this glossy material was available as a natural resource or if it represented the results of human modification of poorer quality flint through the means of painstaking heat treatment (e.g. Bar-Yosef 1981, 1991; Nadel 1989: 65–66; Edwards and Thorpe 1986; 85). This issue has been resolved for the northern and central Jordanian highlands, at least, for both outcrops of purple-pink flint and mines to extract the material have been found in the limestone hills of Wadi Huwayjir, about 2 km north of Ayn Ghazal (Quintero 1996), It is likely that outcrops of Huwayjir-type flint occur throughout the southern Levant, and that heat treatment was not resorted to in its processing.

Typology

Projectile Points

As for typology, there may be some territorial differences in the popularity of some MPPNB projectile point types. Although the generalized Byblos and Amuq points are found in both northern and southern Jordan, Jericho points (Gopher's Type A4; cf. Gopher 1994: 36) with pronounced backswept barbs are absent at Bayda, for example, hut they are relatively common at Ayn Ghazal (Eighmey 1992; 99) and Wadi Shuayb (unpublished data). The Abu Gosh point is a variant of the Byblos type, distinguished by a prominent and obliquely pressure-flaked tang (Lechevallier's Type 10; Lechevallier 1978: 53, fig. 17–7; also cf. Eighmey 1992: 97, fig. 8–e); they were nearly four times as popular as Jericho points at Ayn Ghazal (Eighmey 1992; 99, table 2). This type does not exist as a distinct pattern in Mortensen's study of the Bayda inventory, although there are illustrated examples (Mortensen 1970: fig. 16-b, c) that are grouped together in his Type A 11 with points similar to the Munhata point (Eighmey 1992: 95, fig, 8-a; Gopher 1994: fig. 5–18). In any event, Type All points range between 1 and 3% for levels II-VI at Bayda (Mortensen 1970: fig. 19), and a comparable grouping of Abu Gosh and Munhata points at Ayn Ghazal ranges from 19% (PPNC) to 30% (MPPNB) (cf. Eighmey 1992: table 2).

It is also possible that there is a tendency towards the production of more slender and delicate points in southern Jordan in contrast to the longer, bulkier pieces recovered from Wadi Shuayb and Ayn Ghazal. No comparable dimensional data are available to substantiate this subjective observation which is based on published illustrations.

Burins

Data from Ayn Ghazal and Wadi Shuayb show a heavy reliance on burin manufacture, and this tool class, whose function(s) remain(s) enigmatic (Finlayson and Betts 1990), shows a chronologically sensitive pattern in terms of specific type popularity; in the MPPNB period at Ayn Ghazal three-quarters of the burins are of the transverse type, mostly made on naviform blades (Rollefson 1995). The seriational potential of burins appears to hold for both the permanent settlements of northern Jordan and the Jordan Valley, as well as the steppe and desert sites in the eastern part of the country (Rollefson 1988).

Sickles

MPPNB sickles appear to consist principally of long and intact naviform blades that may or may not bear a variety of retouch ranging from fine to moderate serration (Olszewski 1994; Mortensen 1970), and sickle gloss often appears on both lateral edges. The recently completed experimental work on harvesting "green" and "dry" cereal stands with replicated flint blades shows that it is very likely that a significant proportion of blades used as reaping tools on mature, dried-out stalks develop almost no detectable sickle gloss, and it is possible, therefore, that the reliance on the appearance of sickle gloss alone may have resulted in overlooked sickle elements in excavated assemblages (Quintero *et al.* 1997).

Other Tools

Scrapers, borers and knives all may hold important potential for temporal seriation based on the results of sample analyses from Ayn Ghazal (Rollefson *et al.* 1994), but so far these results are not compatible with Mortensen's research (1970), so that it is not clear if differences are due to real regional variation or if the research efforts reflect personal views of typological definition, inclusion and exclusion, or a combination of both aspects. In view of the work by Quintero *et al.* (1997), there is now some reason to suspect that some of the blades ascribed to knives on the basis of edge damage might actually belong to the sickle category, despite the absence of visible gloss; the same observation may apply to Mortensen's results. Axes/celts/adzes, picks, and chisels are extremely rare elements in MPPNB tool kits in both northern and southern Jordan (cf. Rollefson *et al.* 1992: table 4; Mortensen 1970: fig. 53). To date, no tranchet axes have been noted among the MPPNB tools at Ayn Ghazal, and none were noted at Wadi Shuayb. However, Mortensen shows one from Level V, which is MPPNB in date (Mortensen 1970: frig. 49-c); one from Level VI at Bayda and another from Level II (Mortensen 1970: fig. 50 a, b) have been ascribed to the MPPNB, but there are some potential problems with this chronological ascription (see below); the tranchet bit is taken to reflect a tradition of axe manufacture (or at least resharpening) that reaches back to the PPNA and "Early PPNB"[6] periods. The popularity of tranchet axes at MPPNB Jericho, Nahal Oren I–II, and Nahal Lavan 109 (Bar-Yosef 1981: 564, fig. 3) might the indicate that the northern and central highlands of Jordan constitute a regional sector where this tradition of manufacture and resharpening had not been adopted.

Specialization in the production of certain tools was present at Shkarat Msaied, particularly drills that would have been used to manufacture beads (Jensen 2004).

Architecture

Until the beginning of the this century, little was known about MPPNB architecture except for the structures at Ayn Ghazal in northern Jordan (Banning and Byrd 1984, 1987; Byrd and Banning 1988), although some generalizations can be derived from unpublished plans from Wadi Shuayb (cf. Simmons *et al.* 2001, and Bayda in the south (especially Kirkbride 1966, 1967, 1968a). The situation in southern Jordan has since changed dramatically, with important information coming from Ghuwayr I, Ayn Abu Nukhayla, and Shkarat Msaied.

Bayda Levels V–VI

The earliest Neolithic layers at Bayda, whose radiocarbon dates fall comfortably into the MPPNB (cf. Mortensen 1970; 13), already show considerable architectural uniqueness in comparison with architecture from permanent MPPNB settlements anywhere else in the Levant.[7] Circular and semi-subterranean, these one-room structures (c. 4 m in diameter) were clustered into "honeycomb" arrangements of several units each (Kirkbride 1967: 6–8, fig. 1, pls. IB, IIA). Constructed with stone walls interspersed with wooden roof supports, these "post-houses" resemble the circular structures of PPNA Jericho, as Kirkbride noted (1967: 6),[8] differing principally in the construction materials. The major distinctions in the houses in Levels V and VI are that the clustered arrangements that shared common walls in Level VI gave way to free-standing single-room buildings in later Level V, which Kirkbride saw as an indication of a reorganization of social structure; Kirkbride remarked that Level V buildings were also much better constructed, and the size of one of them reached 6.5 m in diameter (1967: 8). Byrd has noted that building size distribution and internal variability suggest that one of the Level V–VI/Phase A buildings may have served a public function (Byrd 1994: 649 and fig. 3).

Bayda Level IV

Continuing an architectural evolution, structures in Level IV maintained the independence and single-room nature of Level V, but they were built on the contemporaneous land surface and had changed to rectilinear shapes (sometimes with rounded corners) that would have been familiar to MPPNB architects in central and northern Jordan. Byrd describes two building sizes (small/medium and large), the latter category associated with "non-domestic" use (Byrd 1994: 650–651, table 3 and fig. 5). The use of relatively thin rectangular stone slabs, leveled and steadied with thin chinking stones, foreshadows dressed-stone construction of LPPNB sites in Jordan,[9]

Shkarat Msaied

Approximately 10 km north of Bayda is Shkarat Msaied (Kaliszan *et al.* 2002), a comparably sized MPPNB compact site (cf. Kinzel 2004: fig. 8) that also has produced circular semi-subterranean houses up to 7 m in diameter (Figure 4.3). As was the case at Bayda, houses occur in clusters, each cluster with shared walls. Some of the houses have plastered floors, others do not; in the northern part of the site, plastered, circular floor hearths are rare. Only one structure is clearly a storage facility, but some smaller room sections may have served this purpose. Entrances into the houses were flanked by thin upright slabs of sandstone, and some structures included stone-pavement platforms. Wall construction is variable, with many walls made of relatively thin rectangular sandstone blocks or less regular geometric boulders, but others had an interior facing of tall, broad slabs of limestone. The use of vertical wooden posts in the walls, which was characteristic of Bayda, is also a common feature at Shkarat Msaied.

Ayn Abu Nukhayla

Located beneath the modern tourist attraction of "Lawrence's Spring" in Wadi Rum, Ayn Abu Nukhayla is a compact, small site (ca. 1200 m²) whose excavations have identified minimally two clusters of curvilinear semi-subterranean structures of more than 3m diameter (Henry *et al.* 2003). The clusters, as at Bayda and Shkarat Msaied, are "honey comb" arrangements of shared walls, although entrances are not clearly defined as in the other two sites. Floors are commonly of beaten earth, although cobble or flagstone pavement floors also occur. Interior storage bins of various geometries exist. The incorporation of posts in the walls of the structures is absent, in contrast to Bayda, which Henry suggests is a consequence of the local environment: trees were less available in Wadi Rum and, essentially, unnecessary; the scarcity of trees as fuel

Figure 4.3 Plan of the MPPNB site of Shkarat Msaied. (By permission of The Shkarat Msaied Neolithic Excavation and Survey Project).

to produce quicklime probably explains the absence of plastered floors at the site (cf. Henry *et al.* 2003: 11–12). The circular, semi-subterranean nature of the architecture at Ayn Abu Nukhayla leads Henry to conclude that the site was only utilized seasonally, and that the same mobile lifeway was, by extension, also characteristic of Bayda V–VI, Shkarat Msaied, the MPPNB sites in Wadi Jilat (Garrard *et al.* 1994; Baird *et al.* 1992), and Nahal Issaron in the Negev (Goring-Morris and Gopher 1983).

Ghuwayr I

This small site, located near the Wadi Faynan/Fidan complex near the northern section of Wadi Araba, does not appear to follow the architectural styles noted at the other MPPNB settlements in southern Jordan. There is a high degree of architectural complexity, including internal staircases and one large exterior stairway. What sets the architecture apart from the other small settlements is that the rooms are all rectangular, some with renovations and rearrangements (e.g., Simmons and Najjar 2000).

Ayn Ghazal MPPNB

Rectangular shapes are the only forms that houses assumed in permanent MPPNB settlements in north and central Jordan, although it must be admitted that the sample of excavated settlements is very small. In any event, no curvilinear structures have been found at MPPNB Ayn Ghazal or Wadi Shuayb, although the situation in the steppe/desert of eastern Jordan reveals both structural forms (and transitional expressions) erected by hunting groups at Wadi Jilat 7 and 26.

The architectural sequence at Ayn Ghazal covers the entire range of the MPPNB (see radiocarbon dates in Rollefson *et al.* 1992; Rollefson 1998a), and there is a clear evolution of architectural standards over the c. 1000-year period. The earliest MPPNB houses (Figure 4.4), were built on the surface and single-roomed (as at Level IV Bayda) and were as large as c. 5 by 8 m (cf. Byrd and Banning 1988: Rollefson and Simmons 1986), with some reaching perhaps 50 m in floor area. Floors were made of a sophisticated lime plaster and massive posts up to 60 cm in diameter supported roofs, and the room had a circular hearth built as an integral part of the floor exactly at its geometric centre (Rollefson 1990b).

Through time, the single-room structures were replaced with two- and even three-roomed houses. The overall area of the buildings was essentially unchanged, although roofs were increasingly supported by stone pillars or "piers" (Byrd and Banning 1988) in place of the thick, tree-trunk-sized roof posts, which were becoming scarcer in the immediate vicinity of the settlement (Rollefson and Köhler-Rollefson 1989). Notably, by the end of the MPPNB period, postholes rarely exceeded 15cm in diameter, and often they were found along wall lines, not in the centre of rooms;

occasionally a number of very small "post holes" (10 cm or less in diameter) were found in some corner areas of rooms, which suggested that such installations as loom areas or storage facilities may have been allotted to some parts of the house. As was the case at Bayda Level IV, the floors were decorated with the application of pigment, sometimes in finger-painted designs of unknown meaning (Rollefson and Simmons 1987).

Throughout the MPPNB area excavated at Ayn Ghazal, the free-standing houses are often built very close together, sometimes to the point that adults would have had trouble passing between them. The slope of the hillside at Ayn Ghazal required that labour-intensive terracing was necessary to provide level ground for house construction, and remnants of terrace walls have been found during the excavation. The isolation of the houses suggests that the (single) families that lived in them were probably independent economic units of production and consumption, although there was probably considerable leeway for kin and friendly support in the event of particular hardship. The independence of the family units is supported by the absence of any courtyard or compound walls that could signal "property rights" or "social boundaries."

MPPNB subsistence

Plant Resources

Although the agricultural species inventory for the MPPNB populations in Jordan was probably not very different from PPNA times, recent evidence suggests that the situation in Jordan and elsewhere in the Levant may not have conformed to the widely held concept of a cereal-based farming economy. From the enormous stocks of charred lentils and peas in a house from MPPNB Ayn Ghazal, they certainly played a more important role in MPPNB diets than they are given credit for; clearly the kinds of processing of harvested crops has effected a powerful under-representation of pulses in MPPNB economies (cf. Rollefson and Simmons 1986: 152; Kislev 1992).

The circumstances of the MPPNB subsistence economy in southern Jordan have been enhanced by the work at Ayn Abu Nukhayla. Although direct macro- or microbotanical evidence of domesticated species has appeared, the abundant presence of grinding stones and "sickle gloss" on blades and bladelets indicate cereal harvesting, which could have happened as a consequence of planting (barley) kernels along the shores of *qa*s just to the east of the site (Henry *et al.* 2003: 25).

In an elegant experimental project, the "domesticated" status of cereal plants in the Levant up to the end if the MPPNB has been called into question (Quintero *et al.* 1997), Sickle gloss was shown to form intensively and rapidly when flint blades were used to cut through "green," partially ripened wheat stalks; blades used to

Figure 4.4 Western room of a two-room MPPNB house at Ayn Ghazal; the doorway connecting the two rooms is top centre. Note the size of the post holes of this c. 10,300 BP lime plaster floor. Scale 1 m; north at left (photo C. Blair).

reap dried wheat were less affected by the development of "sickle sheen." Among the implications of the experimental work, MPPNB and earlier cereal fields may have been populated by substantial proportions of mature plants whose spikes still shattered at maturity, a genetic characteristic that was not successfully controlled until the following LPPNB period (Quintero *et al.* 1997).

Animal Resources

There was a major contrast in terms of the acquisition of meat by the beginning of the MPPNB period. In most PPNA sites in Israel and Jordan, the dominant prey for hunters was gazelle, sometimes overwhelmingly so (cf. Horwitz 1989: fig. 8); this maintained the pattern already established during the Natufian period. But, for people living in the Jordan Valley and in the Jordanian highlands, by 10,300 bp there was a dramatic shift to a focus on goats, if not even earlier (Wasse 2000). It is unfortunate that so little research has been carried out in the EPPNB, for this is when the changeover must have begun.

The prevalence of goats at MPPNB Bayda in southern Jordan may be a direct reflection of the local habitats, for gazelle accounted for only about a quarter of the bones

in one Natufian sample (compared to nearly 70% for goat or ibex) and 0% in another Natufian sample from the site (cf. Hecker 1975; tables 11–12). At Ayn Ghazal goats accounted for half of the animal bones while gazelle reached only about 13% (Köhler-Rollefson *et al.* 1988; table 2); the situation was similar for MPPNB Wadi Shuayb (Simmons *et al.* 2001: tables 7–8). In these last two cases, it is unlikely that the predominance of goat is explained by the immediate environmental circumstances, for the local countryside was probably more densely populated by gazelles than caprines.

The popularity of goats suggests that a different strategy for meat acquisition was in effect by the MPPNB, and that hunting had been supplemented by herding the animals, effectively isolating them from the wild caprine environment and securing them as a living, breathing meat locker. Hecker has referred to this as "cultural control" (Hecker 1975: 306), and Köhler-Rollefson has argued that this manipulation of the species fulfils all the definitional requirements of domestication with the specific absence of genetic change (Köhler-Rollefson 1997; contra Ducos 1994; Horwitz 1989), an outcome of herding that may have been unintentional and unimportant to the earliest populations of goat herders (Köhler-Rollefson and Rollefson 2002). Additional support for an early domestication of goats comes from the presence of goat spherulites in some of the structures at Ayn Abu Nukhayla, which are indications that goats were kept inside the settlement (Henry *et al.* 2003: 24). Regardless of the terminological debate on the status of domestication for MPPNB goats, it is clear that a special relationship between human society and *Capra* sp. had developed early in the MPPNB period, a human predation on a behavioural subservience that was to have a profound effect on settled human populations long before morphologically recognizable *C. hircus* individuals are recognizable in the archaeological record (Köhler-Rollefson and Rollefson 1990).

Beyond the new concentration on keeping and protecting goats, information from Ayn Ghazal (Köhler-Rollefson *et al.* 1988) and Wadi Shuayb reveals that the localities around these settlements consisted of lucrative ecozones that supported a rich variety of animal species; in the case of Ayn Ghazal, more than 50 different species reflected woodland or open woodland, *maquis,* steppe, desert and riverine gallery ecozones until the end of the MPPNB period. Although goatherding accounted for about half of the meat in the diet at Ayn Ghazal, hunting still provided a major part of the daily (perhaps seasonal) meat intake and afforded a probably welcome variety of food; different animals also may have contributed to a wide array of non-nutritional needs as well, such as furs, skins, bone elements for tools and other body parts for other uses.

Ritual

It is tempting to refer to the MPPNB in the Levant as the "classical" period in view of the elaborate expressions of ritual practice. While no monumental structures can be ascribed to the MPPNB,[10] the intricate relationships of birth and renewal, death and burial, post-mortem treatment, and various paraphernalia to realize these themes are unparalleled in the Levantine Neolithic period. Space is too limited for a comprehensive treatment of the ritual aspects of the MPPNB in Jordan, but more detailed accounts are available elsewhere (Rollefson 1983, 1986, 1998b, 2000; Kuijt 2000, 2001b, 2002; Kuijt and Chesson 2004; Gebel *et al.* 2002).

Burials

Kirkbride correctly concluded that the number of MPP-NB burials simply did not conform to population estimates of the settlements, and that an off-site cemetery or other form of post-mortem disposal must have been the norm (Kirkbride 1968b: 272). At Ayn Ghazal, a total of 81 burials of all types (see below) were recovered from the MPPNB layers that spanned about 700 years, which corresponds to just over one burial per decade. Buried beneath the floors of one house that was used over a period of about 400 years (cf. Byrd and Banning 1988) were the remains of 12 individuals, or about one every 33 years (or "long generation").

Subfloor and courtyard burials are well known from MP-PNB sites in the Levant, and normally burials consisted of single interments. Wadi Shuayb's burials contradicted this aspect of post-mortem disposal, for multiple burials of two to four individuals were common (Simmons *et al.* 2001). At Ghuwayr I, an infant with a mother-of-pearl pendant at the neck was buried beneath the floor of a room that had a "cache" of goat and cattle skulls on it (Simmons and Najjar 2000: 7). Other burials in cobble-lined graves, including one that contained three adults and a child, add variability to the situation, although the excavators note that these graves may be intrusive (Simmons and Najjar 2000: 7).

Ayn Ghazal has provided detailed evidence for a variety of burial types. Briefly, they include (a) subfloor or courtyard, decapitated; (b) courtyard, skull intact with the rest of the body; and (c) infant burial (cf. Rollefson 1983; 29–30). The first has been termed the "typical" type (e.g. Rollefson *et al.* 1992: 461), but in view of the remarks in the previous paragraph, this is clearly not the case; in fact, the recovered decapitated burials are probably the exceptional kind of treatment. The second type is even rarer, and the "trash" circumstances these burials involve support the view that in the MPPNB some people died in the community who were not afforded any ritual at all in their disposal (Rollefson 1986: 50).[11] All infants younger than c. 12–15 months were found with skulls intact with the rest of the body, a situation also noted at Bayda (Kirkbride 1967: 9). The "casual" treatment of some infants, also consigned to rubbish pile deposition, was also probably in effect for babies of the people associated with burial type (b), although the circumstances of other infant burials indicate special ritual meaning (Rollefson *et al.* 1992: 463; Rollefson and Simmons 1986: 183). Since all infants below the age of 12–15 months were disposed of with the skull still attached to the body, there may have been a required period of physical and social maturation before public recognition of the child's entry into society, perhaps through some naming ceremony after 12–15 months of age (Rollefson 2000).

Most MPPNB burials included no "grave goods" except the occasional personal ornament, such as a necklace of 40 small bone beads with one woman at Ayn Ghazal (Rollefson 1986: 51) or the cowrie-shell bracelet with a child at Bayda (Kirkbride 1967: 9). A striking exception to this paucity of grave goods was found in 1989 at Wadi Shuayb: in a burial pit with four individuals, a 22 cm-high human female statuette made of marl was placed on the chest of an older adult of undetermined sex; nearby were 20 plaster beads and fragments of smaller figurines (Simmons *et al.* 2001).

Skull Treatment

Headless burials were found at Bayda and Wadi Shuayb, but so far in Jordan MPPNB skulls (e.g. Bienert 1991) have only been recovered at Ayn Ghazal, 13 in all.[12] Three untreated skulls were found in a pit beneath a house floor. (After a close examination, Bonogofsky suggests that these three crania may have once been plastered before they were eventually buried [Bonogofsky 2001a: 167]). A courtyard pit contained four skulls, two of which were evidently untreated, but the other two bore evidence of having the face area covered with lime plaster and bitumen "cosmetics" (eyeliner and pupils). A third plastered skull, found in a bulldozer section with little secure information concerning its context (but probably in a courtyard pit), was skillfully, delicately modeled and incised but reflected no use of bitumen (Simmons *et al.* 1990). Three more modeled skulls, older than 10,200 BP, were placed in a hole dug into sterile basal clay; actually, the skulls themselves were missing, and what had been buried were only the plaster "masks" that once covered the faces (Griffin *et al.* 1998). Three temporal and parietal fragments of a human skull were found on the floor of a house that appears to have been destroyed by fire; the pieces had been scraped clean of flesh and then painted red. Finally, the floor of one room had undergone several renewals, and in one of these the front portions of a decorated skull were shaved off, leaving only the rear portions that were coated with a dark substance, possibly bitumen (Rollefson *et al.* 1999; cf. Rollefson 1983, 1986; Butler 1989; Rollefson and Simmons 1986).[13] Bonogofsky considers that this particular skull was also plastered at one time in view of a "sanding" of the cranium to prepare the surface for plastering (Bonogofsky 2001b: 144).

There was considerable variability in treatment of skulls once they were removed from a burial: (a) possibly no treatment except for reburial elsewhere; (b) painting and perhaps coating of portions with bitumen; (c) re-creation of faces in plaster, with no cosmetics; and (d) re-creation of faces in plaster plus the use of bitumen cosmetics. What this diversity might mean in terms of the potential status differences is conjectural; certainly there is the possibility that a part of the variability could be stylistic evolution over the 1,000-year span of the MPPNB.

Human and Animal Figurines

Bayda and Wadi Shuayb[14] did not produce many small clay human and animal figurines, but they might be relatively numerous at Ghuwayr I (cf. Najjar 2002: figs. 3, 7–8). By contrast, nearly 200 were recovered from MPPNB contexts at Ayn Ghazal. Of the animal figurines, some appear to be whimsical effigies made for or even by children for their amusement (cf. Rollefson 1983; pl. III-7). Other animal figurines almost certainly were involved in rites of magic, such as the "killed" cattle recovered from a subfloor pit (Rollefson 1986: 50, pl. II-4). Schmandt-Besserat (1997) has noted the association

of fire with nearly all the figurines, and the differential firing on many of them, particularly those representing cattle, indicate that they were votive pieces used in ritual activity. It is interesting to note that around the throats of several of the cattle figurines there were depressions formed by spun thread, as if the figurines were "haltered," despite the absence of any bone evidence that cattle at the time were domesticated.

MPPNB human figurines were probably mostly used as talismans for protection (perhaps at special times) from natural or spiritual forces (Rollefson 1998b), but the human form could also be used to display profane human tragedy (cf. Rollefson 1986: 47, pl. 11.3). One class of human figurines includes "fertility figurines", representing obviously pregnant women; the rocker-stamped impressions on these figurines (but not on other types) appear to be unique to Ayn Ghazal (cf. Rollefson 1983: 32, pl. II-3). Whether these figurines were used to promote fertility is a moot point; certainly it must be acknowledged that they may also have been talismans for the protection of mothers during pregnancy and especially at birth.

Lime Plaster Human Statuary

Two caches of lime plaster human statuary were excavated at Ayn Ghazal in 1983 and 1985 (Rollefson 1983, 1986). The 1983 group is stratigraphically the older and consists of 25 or 26 figures (Figure 4.5); two separate radiocarbon samples from between the tightly packed statues produced radiocarbon dates of 9,703±119 BP and 9,724±128 BP. The group recovered in 1985 had been badly disturbed by bulldozer work, and only 10–11 separate pieces (seven restorable) remained in the pit; charcoal stratigraphically older than the statue pit provided a *terminus ante quem* of 9,523±110 BP (Rollefson *et al.* 1992: table 1). It is conceivable that this group actually comes from the first century or two of the LPPNB period.

Tubb and Grissom (1995) have provided technical descriptions of both caches, and no additional comments are needed here. There are close stylistic similarities with two of the plastered skulls from Ayn Ghazal, and it is plausible that the statues and busts represent a step higher in a hierarchy of religious expression, with the skulls representing known ancestors and the statuary symbolizing mythical ancestors that founded clans or even humanity itself (Rollefson 2000).

The two caches differ most noticeably through the presence of three busts from the 1985 group that had two heads rising from a single body (cf. Tubb and Grissom 1995: fig. 10). Interpreting such singular symbolic forms is difficult, but two developments in the southern Levant contemporaneous with the construction of the double-headed pieces include the devastating abandonment of all known permanent farming villages in the Jordan Valley and Israel by the middle of the ninth millennium bp (Rollefson 1987) and the beginning of what might have

Figure 4.5 A female statue (with seven fingers on the left hand) and two busts from the 1983 cache from Ayn Ghazal (photo H. Debaja).

been an intensification of the exploitation of the steppe and desert areas to the east of Ayn Ghazal (cf. Garrard *et al.* 1994; Rollefson and Köhler-Rollefson 1993). In both these situations the people of the Ayn Ghazal community were coming into more intimate contact with once geographically distant groups, and social bonds among them may have been depicted by a union of their respective mythical ancestors.

Other Ritual

The excavators at Shkarat Msaied suggest that the use of slabs of stone standing on end in the walls and at the doorways of the houses at the site may have had some ritual importance, particularly a free-standing piece in front of a raised pavement and another in a rare brown

color erected inside a small (ca. 1m diameter) enclosure (Hermansen and Jensen 2002: 100). Hermansen and Jensen also draw attention to the vertical slab in one of the enclosures at Bayda, which Kirkbride had interpreted as one of three "temples" (Kirkbride 1968: pl. 28A), although the "T" buildings at Bayda have never been securely dated to the MPPNB. Henry also notes similarities of the vertical slabs in buildings at Ayn Abu Nukhayla and the T1 building at Bayda, although he remarks that the presence of domestic equipment on the floors of the structures at Ayn Abu Nukhayla does not suggest ritual use of these spaces (Henry *et al.* 2003: 12).

Settlement Pattern

Numerous aceramic Neolithic sites have been located by recent surveys all across Jordan (e.g. Coinman *et al.* 1988: 56; table 3; Clark *et al.* 1994; Palumbo 1992; Bisheh *et al.* 1993; Wright *et al.* 1989; MacDonald *et al.* 1987; Betts 1992; Garrard *et al.* 1985; Banning *et al.* 1987; Betts 1998), but most of the information has not been subdivided into the Middle and Late PPNB and PPNC phases. In one regard, this is because some surveys were conducted before the M/LPPNB and PPNC distinctions were made; in others, surveys included lithics analysts who were not familiar with the distinctions; finally, in many cases, it is probable that these subtle distinctions cannot be made solely on the basis of surface collections of chipped stone artefacts (cf. Rollefson 1990a: 122–124).

Despite the limited understanding of MPPNB settlement patterns in the broader sense, MPPNB settlements still show a major change of human-land relationships compared to earlier periods. The situation before 10,500 BP is uncertain in terms of permanent settlements, but certainly the free-standing structures at Ayn Ghazal (Rollefson *et al.* 1992), and Wadi Shuayb (Simmons *et al.* 1989) are indicative of permanent residence by a relatively large population, and this is likely the case for Ghuwayr I. While detailed information is scarce, it appears that MPPNB settlements were mostly small or medium-sized, generally smaller than 4–5 ha. In the case of Ayn Ghazal, population estimates range from c. 500 people at the beginning to possibly more than a thousand at the end of the 1000-year range of the MPPNB (cf. Köhler-Rollefson and Rollefson 1990: Table 3). Ayn Ghazal is currently the only source for detailed evidence of population growth in Jordan for the MPPNB period.

The situation in the southern part of Jordan reflects a different settlement pattern. The circular, semi-subterranean nature of the architecture at Ayn Abu Nukhayla leads Henry to conclude that the site was only utilized seasonally, and that the same mobile lifeway was, by extension, also characteristic of Bayda V–VI, Shkarat Msaied, the MPPNB sites in Wadi Jilat (Garrard *et al.* 1994; Baird *et al.* 1992), and Nahal Issaron in the Negev (Goring-Morris and Gopher 1983).

The Late PPNB

Very little was known about the LPPNB period anywhere in the southern Levant, let alone in Jordan, until excavations began at Basta in 1986 (Gebel *et al.* 1988). Since then excavations have probed LPPNB settlements all along the N–S axis of highland Jordan, and they have also been sampled in the eastern steppe/desert region of Jordan. Some of the excavations are so new that little information is available at this time.

Lithic Technology and Typology

There is no major difference in the technological aspects of lithic manufacture in the LPPNB: the specialized naviform and *ad hoc* technologies continued to serve the needs, as they had in the MPPNB period, although Quintero has noted a tendency for naviform cores to lose some of their standardization in the later parts of the LPPNB (Quintero 1998). Typologically there were developments that contributed to a different "look" of the tool kits used by the residents of the region.

Jericho and Abu Gosh points may have been relatively popular in northern Jordan in the earliest part of the LPPNB, but they drop out of the tool kit for most of the period. "Normal" Byblos and Amuq points dominate completely, sometimes with elaborate pressure-flaked retouch. There appears to be a trend to increasingly delicate point manufacture (smaller dimensions altogether), although this has not been statistically tested, and in the south, at least, tangs are often elaborate (cf. Nissen *et al.* 1987: fig. 10; 1991; figs, 3–4). Projectile points from several of the temporary camps in the steppe and desert appear to retain many MPPNB characteristics (especially size) (cf. Betts 1988: fig. 11; Garrard *et al.* 1987: fig. 12; Baird *et al.* 1992: fig. 16).

The burin classes at Ayn Ghazal change from the highly skewed frequencies of the MPPNB to a more even distribution; nevertheless, transverse burin types still outnumber simple, dihedral and truncation burins (Rollefson 1995: table 2).

There also appears to have been a major change in sickle typology. Highly glossed sickle blades accounted for 9% of the formal tools in the MPPNB at Ayn Ghazal (Rollefson *et al.* 1992: table 4), but they made up only 2.9% of the formal inventory in the large 1993–95 LPPNB samples. Similarly, sickles at Basta were also suspiciously low at far less than 1% (Gebel, pers. comm.). In contrast, the number of knives at MPPNB Ayn Ghazal was relatively low at 1.2%, although in the LPPNB this class rose to 29.6%, mostly due to an increase in naviform blades that showed rounded-edge damage and a slight indication of "near gloss" developing within the first millimetre from the edge. This corresponds to the "unglossed" sickles identified by Quintero *et al.* (1997) in their experimental work, and it is likely that these "knives," then, were used for the reaping of dry,

mature cereal crops; as Quintero *et al.* (1997) point out, this is an indication that cereal crops may have become fully domesticated until the LPPNB period.

Specialization is reflected in concentrations of certain stone tools and products. There was a focus on the manufacture of drills at Basit (Rollefson 2002; Rollefson and Parker 2002), most likely associated with bead manufacture. Gebel has identified the complete *chaîne opératoire* of stone ring ("bracelet") production at Baja (Gebel and Bienert 1997: 252–257).

Architecture

The LPPNB period in Jordan saw radical changes in architecture that had held sway for several hundred years, then apparently disappeared for a millennium or more before returning as a common feature of village life in the region after the end of the Neolithic period. Houses in the MPPNB period were single family dwellings with relatively large and open rooms, although houses during this period at Ayn Ghazal showed a continuous increase in room number and corresponding decrease in room size (Rollefson and Köhler-Rollefson 1992). By the last three centuries of the LPPNB period, such houses may have been rare, and in their place larger, multi-family compounds appear to have been constructed to consolidate formerly independent nuclear families into larger and more efficient production and consumption units.

Basta Area B illustrates this phenomenon best (Nissen *et al.* 1991: fig. 1). In one compound, referred to as the "Basta House" arrangement (Nissen *et al.* 2004a: 27), there were 19 rooms that shared common walls around either a large central courtyard or a partially roofed (?) "space" (Figure 4.6). The rooms varied considerably in size, some with interior dimensions of c. 1.5 by 1.5 m, others 2 by 2 m, and yet others 3 by 2 m in inside measurements. Overall, this structure covered more than 150m². At least four, and perhaps five, other multi-roomed compounds shared walls with this immense building, which has been described as "some kind of central building" (Nissen *et al.* 1991: 15). The compact organization reminds one to some degree of prehistoric pueblos in the American Southwest (cf. Gebel and Hermansen 2001: 18), and there is no question that the loose socioeconomic organization of earlier MPPNB settlements had undergone profound alteration.

The situation at Baja is particularly complex in terms of expansion and renovation. Buildings literally "grew up" as floors and ceilings/roofs were raised periodically, reflected in the blocking or partial blocking of windows and entries (Gebel and Hermansen 2004: 17; Kinzel 2004: fig. 2). There also appears to have been an imposing public gate leading into Area B of the settlement, although this entrance was blocked at a later time (Gebel and Hermansen 2004: 17).

Several excavations reflect the change to the Basta-type architecture, including Sifiya in the Wadi Mujib (Mahasneh 1997), Ayn Jammam, southwest of Maan (Waheeb and Fino 1997; cf. Bisheh *et al.* 1993; 121–122), at Baja north of Bayda (cf. Gebel and Bienert 1997), Hemmeh (Makarewicz and Goodale 2004), and possibly in the latest phases at Ghuwayr I (cf. Najjar 1994; Simmons and Najjar 1996). The circumstances in northern Jordan are not so dramatically preserved, although a glimpse of something similar was noted at Wadi Shuayb in 1989, and buildings partially destroyed by bulldozers at Ayn Ghazal also show features of the architectural design seen at Basta (cf. Rollefson 1997a; Rollefson and Kafafi 1996: figs. 2–3).

LPPNB architectural changes also included the first indications of two-storied buildings in Jordan.[15] At Basta one wall is more than 4m high and includes sockets near the centre-line for floor beams; while this suggests

Figure 4.6   Plan of the "Basta house" and adjacent structures. (By permission of the Basta Joint Archaeological Project).

two stories, each roughly 2 m high, it is also possible that this may be a terraced house with the rooms proceeding down the hill slope in 2 m "steps" (Gebel, pers. comm.). Walls preserved to c. 3 m were also found at Ghuwayr I (Najjar, pers. comm.) and Ayn Jammam (Waheeb and Fino 1997).

Two-storey structures are also in evidence at Ayn Ghazal. In one relatively large building in the North Field (partially destroyed by bulldozers), archaeological fill in three rooms recorded the LPPNB destruction of the structure due to fire at the end of the ninth millennium bp. In this fill were hundreds of thousands of charred lentils and peas, burned clay with ceiling beam impressions, and dense amounts of thick, red-painted flour plaster that could only have come from a floor above the ceiling (Rollefson and Kafafi 1996). Another building with room fill that includes second-storey floor plaster can be seen in the bulldozer section of the parking lot in Ayn Ghazal's South Field. Overall, the architectural evidence indicates that the once-independent single-family units that produced and consumed their own food in the MPPNB were forced to adapt to the deteriorating environmental conditions of the latter half of the tenth millennium BP. As population had grown enormously by the end of the MPPNB period, increased demands for fields in the immediate vicinity of settlements could be met only by the establishment of corporate groups, composed minimally of two families (and most likely more)—probably siblings and their spouses—that pooled their resources for equitable distribution among themselves (Rollefson 1997a).

There were other stresses on the social fabric of the Jordanian townspeople of the LPPNB, and this is demonstrated in the emergence and proliferation of buildings that were directed towards religious observations. These shrines and temples are described in a following section.

One final remark on LPPNB architecture involves the presence of subfloor "channels" in buildings in Basta, Sifiya and Khirbat Hammam, either to isolate the floors from damp ground (Nissen *et al.* 1991: 14) or to provide a means of providing a level surface for house construction without the necessity of terracing a hill slope. Such channels were not noted in LPPNB subflooring excavations at Wadi Shuayb. Subfloor channels were noted beneath the floors of an ostensibly LPPNB building (heavily remodeled in the PPNC period) in the South Field of Ayn Ghazal (Rollefson *et al.* 1990: 105 and fig. 7), but it is unlikely that channels could have been present under the large, two-storied house in the North Field, since the floors were very close to bedrock. Altogether, subfloor channels appear to be principally a characteristic of southern Jordan.

Subsistence Economy

Crops planted by LPPNB farmers did not evidently change in any major way; certainly pulses remained a

vital element of the diet, as more than a quarter of a million charred lentils and peas recovered from one house indicate (Neef, pers. comm.; cf. Kafafi and Rollefson 1995: 24). Nevertheless, there appear to be different strategies in the acquisition of plant foods from site to site in Jordan. Neef (2004: 215) remarked that the botanical remains at Basta reflect a low emphasis on the exploitation of either wild or cultivated cereals, with a corresponding reliance on nuts (especially pistachio and almonds) and figs instead (2004: table 4), although he cautioned that this non-conformance with dietary patterns elsewhere in the Levant may be due to specific preservation factors (2004: 215).

Hunting, which had played so prominent a role in the MPPNB subsistence economy, appears to have declined considerably in importance for some communities, perhaps because earlier habitation and exploitation had incurred severe habitat destruction in the immediate vicinity of the settlements (e.g. Köhler-Rollefson and Rollefson 1990). Currently analysed samples from LPPNB Ayn Ghazal show a major reduction in animal species from the rich variety in the MPPNB (cf. Köhler-Rollefson *et al.* 1993: table 1), although admittedly this sample is from the 1988–89 seasons and therefore a comparatively restricted area of the site (c. 60 m²). Nevertheless, preliminary findings of the 1993–95 LPPNB faunal remains indicate a drop in species variability from more than 50 in the MPPNB (Köhler-Rollefson *et al.* 1988) to just over 20 in the LPPNB (cf. von den Driesch and Wodtke 1997). It is important to note that 71% of the LPPNB animal bones are from domesticated ovicaprids (Köhler-Rollefson *et al.* 1993: table 1), so that wild species contributions had fallen by almost 50% in comparison to MPPNB times.[16]

Basta is the only other Jordanian LPPNB settlement with published results of faunal analysis, and the faunal inventory appears to be similar to that at Ayn Ghazal. Although Becker noted that both cattle and pigs appear as domesticated forms at Basta,[17] a more recent publication on the faunal sample from Area A at the site mentions only *B. primigenius*, and *Sus* is not identified as the domestic form (Becker 2004). It is interesting that there are morphologically wild and domesticated forms for both sheep and goats in the faunal collection at Basta (Nissen *et al.* 1991: table 3; 2004: 267–268). She has also remarked that domestic animals accounted for 78–82% of the animal bones at Basta, which is very close to the situation at Ayn Ghazal if the *Bos* and *Sus* remains are accepted as domesticates (see notes 16 and 17 and Köhler-Rollefson *et al.* 1993: table 1). Dogs also held a place in the daily life of LPPNB people (Becker 1991; Quintero and Köhler-Rollefson 1997).

There was a dramatic shift within the domestic animal group at Ayn Ghazal: a revolution in the proportions of goats and sheep. Wasse noted that in the MPPNB the ratio of goats to sheep was roughly 95:5%, but after 500 years by the beginning of the PPNC, this relationship had reversed to a 15:85% ratio, which suggests a major alteration of herd composition during the LPPNB period (Wasse 1997). Although the sample Wasse investigated had potential sampling problems *vis-à-vis* the LPPNB numbers, the larger LPPNB collection from 1993–95 (von den Driesch, pers. comm.) seems to support Wasse's prediction that the late tenth millennium bp witnessed a considerable overhaul of ovicaprid husbandry. Becker has written that the goat to sheep ratio at Basta in the LPPNB stood at 60:40%, which fits neatly between the MPPNB and PPNC extremes at Ayn Ghazal (1991: 64).

This changeover from goat to sheep dominance may have had a major effect on the development of pastoral nomadism (cf. Rollefson and Köhler-Rollefson 1993; Köhler-Rollefson 1992). Faunal remains from the Wadi Jilat and Azraq—sites in areas that are not natural habitats for either sheep or goats—include ovicaprids that appear for the first time, albeit in small numbers, during the LPPNB at c. 9200 BP (Garrard *et al*. 1987; Martin in Garrard *et al*.1994; Baird *et al*. 1992: 27). At issue now is how incipient pastoralism developed, whether as an entirely new aspect of the subsistence economy of local steppe/desert natives (Byrd 1992: 55–56; cf. Perrot 1993; Ducos 1993) or if the herds of sheep and goats, and their herders, were seasonal visitors to the area from permanent farming settlements in the Mediterranean zones of Jordan (e.g. Köhler-Rollefson 1988, 1992; Rollefson and Köhler-Rollefson 1993; Köhler-Rollefson and Rollefson 2002). Bawwab al-Ghazal, a newly discovered LPPNB temporary camp at south Azraq promises to offer good insight into the process of pastoral development (Wilke *et al*. 1997; Rollefson *et al*.1999a).

Ritual

Human Burials

Basta has produced the largest LPPNB mortuary population, comprising 42 individuals (Nissen *et al*. 1987: 96–97; 1991: 18; Berner and Schultz 1997). Burial practices often made use of abandoned rooms and subfloor channels beneath house floors. Skulls were often intact with the rest of the skeleton, although often the cranium was missing from a burial and skulls were found isolated from any body. It was not possible in many cases to determine if the decapitation was intentional or if it was the result of later disturbance. In many other examples, including subfloor burials, it is clear that the skull was intended to remain intact, which is a major departure from the MPPNB instances at Ayn Ghazal. The body was so tightly flexed in some cases that it appears the bodies may have been tied before interment (Nissen *et al*. 1991: 18). There is also evidence to show that red ochre was spread over at least some (parts of) burials at Basta.

Only one burial has been uncovered to date at Ayn

Jammam (Bonogofsky pers. comm.), but its circumstances suggest it may have been a special person. One large room in an LPPNB building included a massive, freestanding stone pillar situated towards the northeast corner that supported the roof. The dead person was placed in the northeast corner, after which walls were built to the ceiling to enclose the burial, effectively decreasing the floor area of the room by nearly 25%.

In view of the broad areas that have been excavated, the number of Ayn Ghazal LPPNB burials is relatively low, but this is mostly because few floors have been taken up. Several of the burials, placed inside rooms, were badly disturbed by later (PPNC?) digging activity that indicates that, as at Basta, abandoned rooms were used for interment. Courtyard burials were relatively common and often resemble MPPNB "trash burials," in the sense that the burial pits are filled with rubbish in addition to the body, and the skull is present. One burial from the East Field showed severe treatment before interment (before death?): every long bone of the skeleton had been broken at least once. Furthermore, a fragment of a flint blade had penetrated the left temporal area, blowing a 2–3 cm section of the interior surface of the cranium into the brain (Rollefson and Kafafi 1996: 22).

Gazelles

Although gazelles had dropped in terms of their former nutritional value, they appear to have taken on some symbolic meaning in both the northern and southern parts of the country in the LPPNB period. At Ayn Jammam, in the same room as the free-standing pillar and the walled-in human burial, a small niche at about eye level in the eastern wall contained the skull of a gazelle arranged so that it stared into the room; on the floor beneath the niche lay a single gazelle horn core (Waheeb, pers. comm.).

There are good indications of a gazelle cult at Ayn Ghazal, too. In one room in the two-storey building in the North Field were five pairs of charred gazelle horns that had fallen from the room above during the conflagration; an isolated gazelle horn was found in the fill of an adjacent room. In the courtyard, behind (uphill and to the west) the building, a small burial pit contained the articulated remains of a juvenile gazelle lying with its head turned back onto its shoulder; the strange thing about this burial is that the feet of the gazelle had been charred before interment (cf. Kafafi and Rollefson 1995: 23; von den Driesch pers. comm.).

Human and Animal Figurines

While figurines have been found at LPPNB sites in Jordan, they are less remarkable than their MPPNB counterparts simply because of their relative rarity. Of note from Basta is a lively collection of at least three human heads (one with phallic implications) (Hermansen 1997; Gebel and Hermansen 1999) and a fragment of a stone mask

(Nissen *et al.* 1987: fig. 16.1) similar to the two better-preserved pieces from Nahal Hemar (Bar-Yosef and Alon 1988: 23–27). There are also animals from Basta, including a small bucranium figurine, a crouched gazelle, a possible boar, and a ram's head figurine that, when inverted, is clearly phallic (Hermansen 1997: pls. 2–3).

Cultic Shrines and Temples

Spectacular architectural remains that undoubtedly are related to ritual activity have been exposed at Ayn Ghazal. Two architectural styles seem to coexist, and they probably had different functions.

Cultic Shrines

Near the two-storey building in the North Field of Ayn Ghazal, an LPPNB building with a four-phase history certainly did nor serve a domestic function, at least not in its final phase of use (Rollefson and Kafafi 1994: 20–24 and figs. 8–10). The first two phases entailed the construction of buildings with an apsidal wall at the western (uphill) end; the adjacent western courtyard consisted of a former MPPNB lime plaster house floor surrounded by the original MPPNB walls (Rollefson and Kafafi 1997). The third phase saw the construction of a straight wall across the width of the apse to counter the collapse of the curved section. The interior design of the building in the first three phases is not known due to the radical changes inflicted by the fourth phase, but it is possible that the structure was essentially "open" and uncluttered with interior "furniture," if the apsidal building that was excavated and re-used by Yarmoukian Pottery Neolithic inhabitants in the Central Field can he used as a model (cf. Rollefson *et al.* 1990: 110–112 and fig. 12). In this regard, there would be similarities with the T-2 and T-3 shrine or sanctuary or temple buildings described by Kirkbride outside the domestic area at Bayda (Kirkbride 1968a: 93–96 and fig. 2).

The concept of the building was completely reorganized in Phase 4 (Figure 4.7). A circular wall enclosed a space 2.5 m in diameter with a doorway leading to the east that led into an antechamber of unknown dimensions. The floors of the earlier structure were cut through in the newest renovation, and a sequence of eight red-painted lime plaster surfaces accumulated in the circular room. The centre of the room was dominated by a hole 60 cm in diameter and c. 40 cm deep. At the edges of the hole the floor plaster began to rise, just as it did along the wall, revealing that at one time there was an installation rising out of the floor at the hole. Beneath the floor were two paired channels about 20 cm wide and 15 cm high formed by limestone slabs resting across the channel sides made of flat limestone slabs set on edge (Rollefson and Kafafi 1994: fig. 10); the channels formed radiating axes in north-south and northeast-southwest directions. Presumably these channels were air ducts to bring air into

the hole from outside to feed a fire in an upraised hearth, although this speculative reconstruction has not been tested by further (damaging) investigation in the field. The unique shape of the building and its uncommon interior arrangements are strong arguments that the building served a ritual function, and the small size and limited access indicate that the structure was probably limited to family (or lineage/clan) observances much in the nature of a cult building or shrine.

In 1996 excavations just 5 m to the south exposed a virtual twin to the cultic building. The walls of the southern room consisted of small, rounded field stones set in thin mortar, in contrast to the sturdy construction techniques in the northern structure. The thin floor, although made of red-painted lime plaster, showed that one reflooring episode had occurred, but the badly damaged surfaces of both of them revealed a very fragile substructure, and with the poor-quality wall construction, the impression one gets is that the shrine had been hastily erected, perhaps with little intention of the need for durability. It is only conjectural at the moment, but it would seem that the southern circular shrine was a successor to the northern one after the latter fell out of use for some reason (Rollefson and Kafafi 1997).

The Upper Temple

A rectangular building erected high on the slope of the central East Field at Ayn Ghazal is clearly distinctive from any domestic LPPNB building at the site. Measuring 4 m (N–S) by at least 5 m (E–W) (the western end was destroyed by erosion), the building is a single-room structure with a dirt floor (one of only two PPNB buildings without a lime plaster floor at Ayn Ghazal; see below). The carefully constructed walls, using rectangular slabs and thin leveling stones similar to the building techniques used in southern Jordan, are preserved to less than a metre high. The following "furniture," or features, identify the structure as a temple (Figure 4.8).

Near the centre of the southern wall two 1.0 by 0.2 by 0.2 m limestone blocks border a 0.5 m-wide patch of brick-red burnt clay about 3.0 cm thick; the eastern end of this altar-like platform is bounded with two large shapeless stones and the western (downslope) side is eroded away.

Directly to the north of this altar is a line of three "standing stones" equidistant from each other and from the southern and northern walls of the temple. The stones stand about 70 cm high, and the central stone tumbled towards the west in antiquity. Midway between the line of the three orthostats and the eastern wall is a red-painted lime plaster hearth, c. 50 cm in maximum dimension, set off from the surrounding floor by seven small limestone slabs.

In the centre of the eastern wall, and an integral part of it, is another orthostat of brilliant white limestone c. 80 cm high and 40 cm wide. The rounded form of this

Figure 4.7 "Twin" LPPNB shrines from Ayn Ghazal. The one on the right is the older, and the circular room is the fourth phase of construction. The one on the left (to the south) was built rapidly and poorly, and it lasted a short time (photo B. Degedeh and Y. Zobi).

"column," plus a knob-like projection at the top, lend an anthropomorphic character to the stone.

The building's interior underwent at least one phase of renovation: a low platform of limestone slabs was built in the space between the north wall and the northernmost standing stone, and this platform was set off from the western side of the room by a thin, single-leaf wall of small limestone blocks. Although the western side of the temple is featureless (bearing in mind erosional damage), easy access to the eastern side would have been only between the central and southern standing stones.

The Lower Temple

Approximately 100 m downhill and southwest of the Upper Temple is another LPPNB structure that clearly served a ritual purpose. The lower example is larger, although erosion has removed much of the western part of both buildings (Figure 4.9). Nevertheless, it is clear that the temple once consisted of several rooms: the eastern room measured 6.5 (N–S) by 3.5 (E–W) m, the partially destroyed western room at least 6.5 (N–S) by 2.5 (E–W) metres. To the east, beyond and adjacent to the eastern room was a small storage (?) chamber excavated into sterile basal clay, measuring 3.0 (N–S) by 1.5m (E–W) and

with walls preserved to at least 1.2 m high.

The internal furniture of the eastern room demonstrates the significance of the space. The "back wall" (east) is preserved to a height of 1.8 m and it is clear that a westward collapse of this wall was the reason for the abandonment of the temple. The floor of the room was clay, apparently obtained from the excavation of the storage chamber east of the temple. Inside the room and against the middle of the eastern wall was an altar nearly 2 m long, consisting of two large limestone slabs c. 60 by 80 by 20 cm that had been set atop three pairs of shaped rectangular "standing stones," each c. 40 cm on a side and roughly 45–70 cm high. In front (west) of the altar was a floor hearth of white (lime?) plaster surrounded by seven limestone slabs, which altogether had a diameter of c. 1 metre. Adjacent to the centre of the northern wall was a small (c. 45 cm on a side) square cubicle made of limestone slabs set on to the clay floor. There were no artefacts in or around this feature, so its function is unknown.

A 1 m-wide doorway in the wall separating the eastern and damaged western rooms (the latter had, evidently, a floor of common dirt) was set off by the thin screen of a single row of stones on the south that quickly (within 60 cm) made a right-angle turn to the north, effectively blocking off all possibility of viewing activity in the east room. The situation implies an example of a "Holy of Holies" much more ancient than ever before conceived (Figure 4.9).

The interior furniture from both these temples set them apart from the shrines in the North Field. It is interesting to note the parallel with Kenyon's PPNB "shrine" at Jericho that incorporated the socketed orthostat in one wall niche (Kenyon 1981: 306–307 and pls. 172–173). The furniture aspect brings to mind the standing slabs in Bayda's T-l building complex, which also had at least two phases of use (Kirkbride 1968a: 95–96 and fig. 2).

The singular nature of these structures is most likely associated with ritual. The persistent, intense burning on the surface of the floor-level altar at Ayn Ghazal is unlike any other feature at the settlement, and burning (and associated smoke and fire) must have been essential elements of the rites practised in the walled surround. The absence of any associated skeletal remains excavated at the three sites, particularly plastered skulls, indicates that the ancestral cult may not have been associated with these buildings.

Settlement Pattern

The lack of distinctions among the general PPNB sites found during surveys conducted in Jordan applies to the LPPNB as well as the MPPNB. Nevertheless, recent excavations have confirmed an earlier prediction that the LPPNB period was a time of population consolidation and site growth that reached "megasite" proportions that would not be seen again until the Chalcolithic period at the earliest (Rollefson 1987, 2005). Although small settlements are present in the LPPNB (such as Tall Rakan [Banning and Najjar 1999], Khirbat Hammam [Peterson 2000], and Hemmeh [Makarewicz and Goodale 2004], and Baja [e.g. Gebel and Hermansen 2004]), it is now apparent that large towns like Ayn Ghazal became established in most of the major wadi systems, including Ayn Jammam at the edge of Wadi Hisma, Basta, Basit (Wadi Musa; Fino 1997), Sifiya (Wadi Mujib; Mahasneh 1997), Ayn Ghazal (southern Wadi Zarqa), Wadi Shuayb (Simmons *et al.* 2001), and perhaps Kharaysin[18] in the northern Wadi Zarqa (Edwards and Thorpe 1986). The emerging pattern of these large centres is intriguing, and it suggests that other towns may be found in other major

Figure 4.8   View to the west (top) of the East Room of the upper LPPNB temple at Ayn Ghazal. The "floor altar" is at upper left, the three "standing stones" at top centre. At right centre is a red-painted lime plaster hearth surrounded by seven stones on a dirt floor (photo B. Degedeh and Y. Zobi).

Figure 4.9 The lower LPPNB temple at Ayn Ghazal. Across the top (east) is a 20 m-plus retaining wall. The East Room of the temple has an altar raised on three pairs of orthostats at the center of the rear (east) wall, in front of which is a white plaster hearth on the dirt floor surrounded by seven stones. A doorway in the wall in the center of the photo is partially blocked by a right-angle screen of stones (photo B. Degedeh and Y. Zobi).

wadi drainages, such as Wadi Dana, Wadi Tafila, Wadi Hasa, Wadi Karak, etc., all along the escarpment from the north to the south of the highland spine of the country. Smaller sites, unfortunately assignable (mostly) to a specific PPNB phase only after excavation, might show dependent relationships with the larger sites in Theissen Polygon studies (cf. Levy 1986).

The reasons for the development of the megasite phenomenon probably lie in great part among the kinds of cultural degradation that slowly but steadily throttled smaller and ecologically sensitive MPPNB settlements, forcing a relocation of the affected populations, in part at least, to farming villages in more tractable environmental circumstances (Rollefson 1987; Köhler-Rollefson and Rollefson 1990). Smaller contemporaneous "subsidiary" villages and hamlets may have existed throughout the arable countryside (and Khirbat Hammam is a possible example; cf. Rollefson and Kafafi 1985; Peterson 2000), but since small sites rarely receive intensive investigation (if any at all), the human geography of Jordan will remain obscure. A few sites in the eastern steppe and desert of

Jordan have been radiocarbon dated to the LPPNB (e.g. Betts 1992; Garrard *et al.*1994), and there was undoubtedly an eastern "push" for part-time exploitation of the area, possibly as the initial stage of pastoral nomadism (Köhler-Rollefson 1992).

What was taking place in Jordan stands in stark contrast to contemporaneous events in the Jordan Valley and Israel. Most long-established farming villages in this western region of the southern Levant were being abandoned wholesale, so that Jericho, Abu Gosh, Munhata, Yiftahel, etc. were mostly deserted by the beginning or middle of the LPPNB period, a part of the environmental circumscription mentioned above. Some of the populations leaving these western villages must have joined relatives on the Jordanian highland, inflating the number of inhabitants in what used to be MPPNB villages like Ayn Ghazal and Wadi Shuayb (Rollefson 1989: 137) or establishing new LPPNB villages and megasites as they moved towards the southern parts of Jordan (Nissen *et al.* 2004b: 23–25, fig. 5). The abandonment tragedy also affected long-lived settlements in the Transjordanian highlands, including Bayda, which has yielded no clear indications of an LPPNB occupation;[20] perhaps many of its residents resettled in nearby Baja or Basta.

Modifications in settlement pattern and adjustments in local resource exploitation were only transient remedies for the problems that had already begun a substantial seismic disturbance to Neolithic lifeways in the MPPNB. After about 500 years of coping with social realignments, the PPNB socio-cultural and socioeconomic patterns had eventually traversed a reweaving process that resulted in a new cultural fabric as distinct from the MPPNB as the MPPNB was different from the PPNA. By the end of the ninth millennium bp, new adjustments set the multidimensional PPNC rearrangement of social, cultural and economic threads that had frayed for some time,

The Pre-Pottery Neolithic C (PPNC)

In her interpretation of the stratigraphy of Jericho and its implications for the region, Kenyon viewed the ninth millennium bp abandonment of the long-lived settlement and the ensuing erosion of the site as evidence for a withdrawal from the southern Levant for up to a thousand years (Kenyon 1979: 46), a suggestion that caught a tenacious hold as the *hiatus palestinien* and that even recently has been recalled as a historical event (Nissen 1993). Investigation of the uninterrupted occupational sequence at Ayn Ghazal first brought the early eighth-millennium bp transitional period between the LPPNB and the Yarmoukian Pottery Neolithic to light, and, in view of its distinctive character in terms of lithic technology and typology, subsistence economy, architecture and ritual, the period was termed the "PPNC" (Rollefson and Simmons 1986: 161). Although the validity of the PPNC as an archaeological "entity" took time for general acceptance in the southern Levant, it has now been recognized at Khirbat Shaykh Ali (Garfinkel 1994) and Atlit Yam (Gopher and Gophna 1993: 307) in Israel, and it is also becoming better known in Jordan such as Hemmeh (Makarewicz and Goodale 2004) in the Wadi Hasa as surveys and excavations have increased the data base there. Unfortunately, most of the information that is available for the PPNC period in Jordan comes only from Ayn Ghazal, although there are indications that some earlier excavations may have unknowingly investigated PPNC deposits.

Lithic Technology and Typology

Comparison of lithic manufacturing techniques for the LPPNB and PPNC phases show changes as striking as between the PPNA and PPNB periods (Cauvin 1987). Every major technological feature (blade:flake ratio, platform type, presence of cortex, etc.) is significantly different (Rollefson 1990a, 1997b), and these contrasts can be directly linked to the relinquishment of the naviform core-and-blade technique (Rollefson *et al.* 1994: 454). The abandonment of this technique is also reflected in the diminution of the use of the pink-purple Wadi Huwayjir flint at Ayn Ghazal, and altogether the evidence demonstrates that specialists in flint tool production (Quintero and Wilke 1995) had lost their calling.[21] Possibly this was due, in part at least, to the decline in the importance of hunting and to the evolution of cereal grains that remained intact with the stalk at maturity.

Typologically, projectile points were much smaller than their MPPNB complements at Ayn Ghazal, although the statistical relationship with the LPPNB in terms of dimensions is not significant, despite a continued trend in these regards. Invasive and even covering unifacial retouch was more characteristic of the PPNC period in contrast to earlier times. Hunted game was dominated by gazelles (Köhler-Rollefson *et al.* 1993: table 1), and this may be partially responsible for the virtually exclusive use of bow-and-arrow delivery systems instead of spear-thrower reliance in the MPPNB (Eighmey 1992).

Burin production was transformed to a nearly equivalent distribution among the four burin classes (Rollefson 1995: table 2), but it should be mentioned that the pre-eminence of truncation burins in the Yarmoukian is foreshadowed by a strong representation in the PPNC. Bifacially retouched knives and tabular knives became typical elements of the tool kit in the PPNC, and scrapers changed dramatically from sidescrapers to transverse scrapers (Rollefson *et al.* 1994: 454–455). There was a trend for retouched tools of all kinds to become shorter, wider and thicker in the PPNC, undoubtedly a consequence of the switch to the increased production of flakes.

Subsistence Economy

Recent research by Wasse (1997) and Von den Driesch and Wodtke (1997) reveals that by the onset of the PPNC at Ayn Ghazal, sheep were in overwhelming supremacy in the ovicaprid herds, and it is possible that cattle and pigs had joined the domestic inventory as well. Hunting had dropped to a minor contribution to the diet (c. 13%; cf. Köhler-Rollefson *et al* 1993: table 1), and most of the mammals came from steppe or desert territory, including gazelle species as well as onager, which had risen to 3% of the bone sample. If the domesticates are removed from consideration, the PPNC faunal inventory at Ayn Ghazal mirrors a very eastern orientation, with few representatives of the Mediterranean forest/woodland or *maquis* zones. This all coincides neatly with the rise in the emphasis on sheep and the model for the intensification of incipient pastoral nomadism (Köhler-Rollefson 1992; Rollefson and Köhler-Rollefson 1993). Further validation for the emergence of pastoral nomadism is provided in the architectural and ritual sections below.

Architecture

PPNC inhabitants clearly reused and renovated standing LPPNB buildings in several areas of Ayn Ghazal (Rollefson *et al.* 1990), which strengthens the idea that there was a transitional period from one phase to the other instead of a replacement of one population by another. It is also quite obvious that the LPPNB standard of two-storeyed, multi-family dwellings was abandoned soon in the PPNC period, and that a novel dual house plan replaced it. One house plan was used by farming families who inhabited Ayn Ghazal year-round; the other was the "corridor building," a platform/storage bunker for relatives who left Ayn Ghazal for months at a time, returning to the town only after the harvest was in.

Smaller and simpler one-room buildings for full-time residents of Ayn Ghazal replaced the composite duplex/triplex houses of the LPPNB. They agreed with the reduced economic circumstances brought on with the cultural degradation of the environment for more than a thousand years at Ayn Ghazal, and they represented one part of a new adaptation to cope with diminished resources in the vicinity of the town. Measuring about 4 by 3 m, the houses were made with thin walls (c. 40 cm thick) and, in complete incongruity with the LPPNB period, with floors made of either dirt or an ersatz plaster made of crushed chalk and mud (*huwwar* in the local Jordanian dialect) (cf. Rollefson and Köhler-Rollefson 1993: fig. 3, upper left). Some storage facilities may have served these farmer families (cf. Rollefson 1993: pl. I-1).

Ayn Ghazal has produced remains of four or five "corridor buildings"—platform/storage bunkers—ranging from mere traces to one building that is substantially intact. The last is a c. 3.5 by 3.5 m semi-subterranean structure with small narrow rooms and proportionally thick walls that clearly supported an upper "storey," although nothing in the room fills below nor in the construction

Figure 4.10 A PPNC corridor building (right, south) and paved ramp (left, north) at Ayn Ghazal. The entrance to the semi-subterranean corridor is at the top of the photo. Notice the small size of the rooms (scale = 1 m) (photo L. Rolston).

of the walls themselves indicates that there was a super-structure in the sense of an upper level of rooms (Figure 4.10). Instead, the broad walls appear to have supported a wood-and-mud roof-cum-platform that could have served as a temporary tent area (Rollefson and Köhler-Rollefson 1993: 36–37 and fig. 2). A floor assemblage of artefacts, found in the cell at the southwest corner of the structure, included axes, loom weights and other heavy duty tools; nothing was found on the floors of the other cells.

Köhler-Rollefson's "Incipient Migratory Pastoralism model" (Köhler-Rollefson 1992) is well supported by the two types of PPNC structures. The platform/storage bunker structures (found only in the South Field) were used by that part of the community that left the settle-ment with their flocks of sheep and goats for extended periods of the annual round, returning only after the har-vest in early summer when the steppe and desert areas dried out and when the animals could forage on the field. During their absence, the herders could store the material not needed on the trip, and relatives could lay up a por-tion of the harvest in anticipation of their return, which would be compensated for by an exchange of sheep and goat products (including fertilizer on the fields) (Köhler-

Rollefson 1992; Rollefson and Köhler-Rollefson 1993).

The PPNC corridor buildings at Ayn Ghazal and those from Levels II and III at Bayda (Kirkbride 1966: figs. 1–2; 1967: fig. 1; Phase C of Byrd 1994) are so similar that they are likely contemporaneous. There is one structural difference: several of the Bayda examples reflect a level of one or more rooms built above the semi-subterranean basement cells (Byrd 1994: fig. 8; Kirkbride 1966: 15), while this was not evident at Ayn Ghazal; nevertheless, this suggests local functional variability and is a weak argument against the overall congruence of the design and probable functions of the structures in both parts of Jordan. What is a problem at the moment is the MPPNB age Kirkbride assigned to Levels II and III on the basis of radiocarbon dates (Kirkbride 1966: 72).

Two radiocarbon dates of 8711±280 BP (Sam-ple AA-1165) and 8765±158 BP (Sample AA-5205) uphold the PPNC ascription to the Ayn Ghazal corri-dor buildings; three other charcoal samples from the fill in and around the PPNC structure are LPPNB in age and probably reflect the disturbance caused by the PPNC builders as they excavated down to an LPPNB red-painted plaster floor for their own use: four other radiocarbon dates support the general PPNC time frame at Ayn Ghazal (cf. Rollefson *et al.* 1992: table 1). The three dates from Levels II–III at Bayda, which ranged in assay results of 10,194±28 BP (GrN-5062), 9956±179 BP (P-1382), and 9592±212 bp (K-1085), all came from the *same* piece of charcoal, and chronologically the charcoal is contradictingly older than samples from stratigraphically earlier contexts. As Kirkbride mentioned, "the large pits excavated to contain the semisubterranean corridor buildings of Levels II and III had largely obliterated the underlying level" (1966: 19), which undoubtedly created an enormous amount of material from mixed contexts, including an earlier charred log that ended up in Level II "fill." In sum, there is a strong possibility that a major PPNC occupation occurred at Bayda that was not recognized in field work or laboratory analysis, possibly due to the mixed nature of the earlier artefacts combined with contemporary discards of the early ninth millennium BP.

The large open buildings from Phase C at Bayda, to which Byrd assigns a public, non-domestic function (Byrd 1994: 656–657, fig. 9), have not been found at Ayn Ghazal or Wadi Shuayb. On the other hand, public "architecture" of a sort has been uncovered at Ayn Ghazal that indicates not only non-domestic utilization, but a high degree of public cooperation in community planning and construction. One of these public works is the "Great Wall," a relatively massive bulwark 1.4m wide and preserved to a height of four to five courses that ran roughly east—west for more than 11 m in the Central Field;[22] this wall separated two *huwwar*-plastered courtyards, which in themselves were not characteristically domestic arrangements. The entire system remains enigmatic and only future excavation can resolve the meaning of this situation (cf. Figure 4.12).

The "walled street," a public thoroughfare that roughly paralleled the Great Wall about 22 m to the north, is the second element of public construction (Figure 4.11). Approximately 2.5 m wide, the street progressed from the roadside bulldozer cut uphill for a distance of c. 9 m before it was destroyed by later Yarmoukian activity. In this stretch there were two gateways, set off from the street by a curb of a single line of stones, that led into courtyards to the north (Rollefson and Kafafi 1994: 13–14, figs. 4 and 7).

Settlement Pattern

As mentioned earlier, early eighth-millennium presence in the southern Levant was unknown prior to 1984, and it is evident that the material culture characteristics of PPNC period are still unfamiliar for some recent excavators. PPNC occupations are not easily detectable on the basis of surface collections of lithic artefacts; the PPNC phenomenon is more than simply a change in lithic pro-

Figure 4.11 The stepped, walled street at Ayn Ghazal is in the centre of the photo. At the top is the modern highway, and to the left (north) is a Yarmoukian "tent" structure (photo Y. Zobi).

duction (while fundamental, this change may not be easily recognizable to many surveying teams). But as the extent of PPNC identifiers becomes better known, the distribution of PPNC sites will probably increase accordingly.

PPNC occupations are already documented at Ayn Ghazal , Wadi Shuayb, Hemmeh (Rollefson 1999; Makarewicz and Goodale 2004), and the recently discovered site of Sayyeh in the Wadi Zarqa drainage has revealed a PPNC horizon beneath a Yarmoukian deposit (Kafafi *et al.* 1999). PPNC layers are also possible at Basta, although Gebel considers the post-LPPNB aceramic layers to fall outside the parameters of the PPNC (Gebel 2002b). The architecture at Bayda now suggests a major PPNC occupation there in the early ninth millennium BP. Architectural characteristics at Sifiya (personal observation), Ghuwayr I (personal observation) and Ayn Jammam (Waheeb and Fino 1997) also suggest possible PPNC presence near the end of each local occupation. Smaller farming sites in the western highlands of Jordan or pastoral sites in the steppe and desert are problematic, since they would have produced decreased numbers of distinctive artefacts; their smaller sizes would be easier to miss on surveys or, if detected, they would have been more difficult to assign to a post-PPNB ascription because of transitional characteristics in many cases.

Human Burials

At Ayn Ghazal later cultural activity had disturbed many of the 37 burials excavated from PPNC layers; in addition, numerous scattered human bones have also turned up in PPNC contexts, and these might represent many LPPNB and even MPPNB interments dislodged by PPNC pit-digging activity.

PPNC burials are distinctive from earlier norms in several ways: (a) multiple interments in the same pit occur commonly; (b) secondary burials, previously very rare at Ayn Ghazal at least, became as popular as primary burials; (c) decapitation of skeletons was no longer practised, which argues that the ancestor cult had changed considerably, if it had not been abandoned altogether; and (d) grave offerings, in the form of pig bones, were common elements in burial pits.

The situation involving multiple interments in the same burial pit may have its origin in the LPPNB, for some of the subfloor channels at Basta contained several individuals; on the other hand, it is also possible that these circumstances represented repeated reopening of the channels in successive burial rites (Nissen *et al.* 1991: 18). The situation for multiple burial pits in pre-PPNC times will remain ambiguous until more complete field reports are forthcoming. At Ayn Ghazal, the earliest (?) PPNC burials were placed beneath house floors, a carryover from LPPNB times, but in these instances the differences clearly pointed to PPNC alterations of earlier practices. First, two pits contained two and three individuals, respectively, and, as they were primary burials, it is likely that they had died at about the same time. One implication might be that diseases had taken hold of the large settlements.[23]

The burial of people who had died elsewhere and were transported back for interment became a routine rite at Ayn Ghazal in the PPNC period, and roughly half of the interments are of this type.

Characteristically, many of the smaller bones (wrist, ankle, ribs, etc.) are missing in such interments; on the other hand, in one case the secondary burial was represented simply by a skull with no other skeletal elements present. A common interpretation of secondary burials holds that people who died outside the permanent village were brought back to the settlement, perhaps after a considerable period of time, and in the process some bones were lost along the way. When viewed from the perspective of Köhler-Rollefson's "Incipient Migratory Pastoralism" model (Köhler-Rollefson 1992), the secondary burials could represent the part-time herder segment of the community, an interpretation supported by an especially high incidence of secondary burials in the corridor-building complex in the South Field.[24]

The presence of the isolated skull as one secondary burial in the South Field is unique at Ayn Ghazal; there is no evidence from the other burials that skull decapitation was still practised by the first half of the eighth millennium bp. In view of the number of subfloor burials at LPPNB Basta, where skulls were routinely included with the rest of the skeleton, the decline in the importance of

the skull cult may have already begun by the last quarter of the ninth millennium bp.

A novel PPNC change in the post-mortem treatment of the dead was the inclusion of pig bones with some people. So far this appears to be known only at Ayn Ghazal. A detailed correlation has not yet been undertaken, but there is some indication that the pig bone offerings are principally associated with the corridor-building complex in the South Field, although there are some instances in the "permanent village" area in the Central Field as well. If the distribution of pig bone grave offerings is restricted in both the "herder" (South Field) and "permanent farmer" (Central Field) sectors at Ayn Ghazal, we may have the earliest solid evidence of clan-based totemism in the Levant.

Human and Animal Figurines

PPNC deposits in Jordan have not been rich in human and animal figurines. Mention should be made of an elegant carved limestone figurine, painted red, of a stylized pregnant woman 14 cm long from Ayn Ghazal (Kafafi and Rollefson 1995: fig. 7). It is unique in its form, size, and material, and there is some reason to believe it was placed on a special platform in a courtyard (Schmandt-Besserat 1998). Besides this, other examples (in clay) are rare and not otherwise exceptional.

The Aceramic-Ceramic Neolithic Transition

Kenyon proposed that the return of farmers to the southern Levant was a recolonization by people who, after perhaps a thousand years, had invented a fired-pottery technology (Kenyon 1979: 45–46). This entire scenario has now been shown to be of interest in the history of archaeological investigation, but it is also wrong. The stratigraphic evidence at Ayn Ghazal alone (and also at Wadi Shuayb) is strong testimony to a consistent transition from the LPPNB through the PPNC to the Yarmoukian period in terms of architectural use (Rollefson and Köhler-Rollefson 1993; Rollefson 1993).

The development of lime plaster technology satisfied all the prerequisites for the emergence of a pottery technology, and this pre-adaptation had been in place in the southern Levant since at least the beginning of the MPPNB (Rollefson 1990b). Indeed, as early as the mid-ninth millennium well-fired potsherds were found at Tall Assouad in northern Syria (Cauvin 1974) and at Ayn Ghazal (Rollefson and Simmons 1986). But these examples were exceptional; the tradition of pottery manufacture is certainly a characteristic that began near the latter half of the ninth millennium bp. Several instances of the transition from the Pre-Pottery to the Pottery Neolithic phases are shown in architectural use at Ayn Ghazal (Rollefson 1993). The stratigraphic and architectural evidence is strong testimony that there was a consistent occupation and evolution from the PPNC into the Yarmoukian period.

The Pottery Neolithic

The situation concerning the character of the Pottery Neolithic has become very complex over the past decade, and the simple scheme devised on the basis of the Jericho sequence in the 1950s is no longer tenable, not only for Jordan but for the entire southern Levant. As described above, the emergence of a ceramic technology was a local development in the area, and in view of the size and geographic diversity of the southern Levant, it should not be surprising that the trajectories of ceramic traditions did not follow a unilineal succession.

As was the case for so much of the aceramic Neolithic of Jordan, the ceramic Neolithic period remains poorly documented in the sense that the information at hand comes from only a few excavations, and these have been very different in terms of how intensively the Pottery Neolithic layers were investigated and reported. Among the most basic issues that remain to be resolved are how many distinct ceramic traditions there were, how they are distinguished, how long they lasted and how many may have been contemporaneous traditions.

The Yarmoukian

The most widely and firmly attested Pottery Neolithic entity in Jordan is the Yarmoukian tradition, a direct outgrowth of the earlier PPNC (Rollefson 1993). This ceramic tradition is defined by its distinctive ceramics, including the typical banded herringbone impression (Kafafi 1993). At present it appears that the Yarmoukian is restricted to the northern part of Jordan, having been reported from Ayn Rahub, near Irbid (Gebel and Muheisen 1985; Muheisen *et al.* 1988), Jabal Abu Thawwab between Amman and Jarash (Kafafi 1988); Wadi Shuayb (Simmons *et al.* 1989), Ayn Ghazal (e.g. Kafafi 1990), Seyyeh near Zarqa (Kafafi *et al.* 1999), Tall Rakan in the Wadi Ziqlab (Banning and Najjar 1999), and Umm Meshrat I and II southeast of Madaba (Cropper *et al.* 2003a; 2003b). The only radiocarbon date from the Pottery Neolithic in Jordan comes from Ayn Rahub, which at 8278±80 BP (Muheisen *et al.* 1988: 498) falls near the beginning of the Yarmoukian period; there is absolutely no indication of when the Yarmoukian ended.

Lithic Technology and Typology

There was little change in lithic technology from the PPNC to the Yarmoukian: flakes dominated the assemblage, and what blades were produced (usually short and relatively broad) came from relatively irregular-unidirectional blade cores. The use of high-quality Wadi Huwayjir-type flint with pink-to-purple hues disappeared altogether, although some of the projectile points and sickle blades appear to have been made on pink-purple flint naviform blades scavenged from earlier cultural deposits at Ayn Ghazal.

Projectile points became very small in general, and complete bifacial retouch was commonly used to shape them. Sickle blades have a deeply denticulated cutting edge formed by wide adjacent notches, and usually the tools are blade fragments that were backed and truncated at one or both ends. The high gloss on these sickle elements indicates they were not used on mature (dry) cereals, and although more research is necessary to determine their use, the cutting of reeds for mats and basketry should be considered.

Burins are heavily dominated by truncation types, particularly burins on concave truncations (Rollefson 1995). The similarities with burin sites from the steppe and desert in eastern Jordan suggest a general similarity in function throughout the region, although the use of burins of any kind remains enigmatic (cf. Finlayson and Betts 1990).

Architecture

The variability in Yarmoukian architecture is difficult to assess in view of the limited exposures of structures in Jordan. No coherent architecture was encountered in the restricted trenches at Wadi Shuayb and Ayn Rahub, and no preliminary reports have yet appeared for Sayyeh. Reliance must be placed, then, on the limited information from Abu Thawwab and the more extensive finds at Ayn Ghazal. The fragmentary nature of the architecture at Jabal Abu Thawwab is such that little more can be said except that the Yarmoukian layers had both rectilinear and curvilinear structures; of the latter, one building had a diameter projected to be c. 4 m (Kafafi 1985: 125, 2001: 23–28; cf. Kafafi 1986).

Permanent structures at Ayn Ghazal are mostly rectilinear, and the largest building discovered so far has three or four rooms and measures at least 4.3 by 8.8 m (Figure 4.11; Kafafi and Rollefson 1995: 14–15). The sturdy walls were built of undressed stone set in mud mortar, and one of the dirt floors was coated with a large square area of *huwwar*. Hearths and firepits were located outside in the spacious courtyards, sometimes associated with *arishas* (shaded areas). A small (2 by 1 m) oval "kitchen" outhouse (Figure 4.12) was uncovered in one courtyard (Kafafi and Rollefson 1995: 16).

A circular building was only partially exposed in the 1996 season of excavation at Ayn Ghazal, and consequently there are doubts as to any interior features (Rollefson and Kafafi 1997). The wall of the exposed arc was extraordinarily thick (c. 80 cm), and the diameter would have been c. 5.5 to 6.0 m with a floor area of c. 12.5 m²: one is not dealing with a flimsy outhouse. A doorway 80 cm wide opened to the south, complete with a threshold of flat limestone slabs and, just inside, a stone with a door socket almost 20 cm in diameter. The function of the structure remains uncertain, but since there were circular domestic structures at Jabal Abu Thawwab, it is possible this is

Figure 4.12 The large Yarmoukian dwelling at Ayn Ghazal is at lower right, much later than the Great Wall and other structures in the upper half of the photo. The Great Wall was PPNC but used and modified by later Yarmoukian residents. Note the "empty" courtyard to the left (north) of the house.

simply a robust house with a floor plan that developed later in the Yarmoukian occupation of the settlement. It appears that the round "house" is stratigraphically later than the rectangular house described above.

Other architectural elements used by the Yarmoukian inhabitants reflect the continuous use of the settlement across the transitional period from the PPNC. One of these is the reuse and slight modifications of the "Great Wall" and the Walled Street originally constructed in the first half of the eighth millennium bp. Stretching back to much earlier horizons in their persistent zeal for digging pits, the Yarmoukians also encountered the lime plaster floor of an LPPNB apsidal building, which they cleared and used for their own purposes, ostensibly associated with some public function in view of the restricted presence of Yarmoukian fine ware inside and immediately outside the former late ninth-millennium building (Rollefson *et al.* 1990: 110–112).

The final kind of architecture associated with the Yarmoukian occupation at Ayn Ghazal is also the latest in the sequence. Foreshadowed, perhaps, by the solid round house of the later Yarmoukian levels at the site, at least two examples of circular temporary buildings have been exposed in the latest Yarmoukian layers (Rollefson and Kafafi 1994: 16–17; Rollefson and Simmons 1987: 105). The structures were outlined with a single row of stones that appear to have acted as anchors for walls made of animal skins or woven mats/cloth; the interior space had a diameter of between 4–5

and 5.0m. It is possible that these structures are forerunners of the Bedouin tent, erected by the last Yarmoukian visitors to Ayn Ghazal, who brought their herds of sheep and goats to the sweet water of the spring after the settlement had become a ghost town (cf. Figure 4.11).

Yarmoukian Subsistence Economy

Faunal resources are well represented and reflect a heavy dominance by sheep and goat herding. Pig and cattle were likely additions to domesticated species, although hunting was still practised (albeit at a much lower intensity compared to the MPPNB). Wild animals were primarily from steppe and desert species, including gazelle and *Equus* sp. (Köhler-Rollefson *et al.* 1988, 1993; ash-Shiyab 1997; Wasse 1997), although notably the hunting of wild goat appears to have increased (Von den Driesch and Wodtke 1997), possibly since the domestic animals were away from the settlement for long periods.

Despite intensive sampling for flotation analysis at Ayn Ghazal, the only palaeobotanical results reflect that animal dung appears to have been the major fuel of the time. Fortuitously, remains from Ayn Rahub analyzed by Neef were more productive and show that emmer (and less frequently einkorn) wheat and hulled barley were the principal cereal crops, in addition to flax as a fibre or oil source. Wood charcoal was exclusively from the deciduous oak species *Quercus ithahurensis*. Other "weedy" species included medick, mallow, clover, milk vetch and the thistles *Centaurea* and *Cartliamus* (Neef, in Muheisen *et al.* 1988: 497).

Yarmoukian Settlement Pattern

Trying to determine a settlement pattern based on the limited amount of available information is inappropriate, but some aspects should be brought up that may reflect reality. First, the areal extent of Wadi Shuayb was at its greatest (c. 14 ha?), based on surface indications and on pottery in roadcuts, during the Yarmoukian period, and at Ayn Ghazal Yarmoukian structures were distributed over at least 12 ha. This is in contrast to the small size of such sites as Jabal Abu Thawwab, which likely did not exceed a couple of hectares at the most.

Secondly, although Wadi Shuayb and Ayn Ghazal were larger (in both area and probably population) than other known Yarmoukian settlements, it is clear that population densities in the permanent towns had dropped considerably over the period since the MPPNB and LPPNB heydays. At Ayn Ghazal, for instance, spaces between houses were more than 15m (how much more remains unknown), and perhaps the total size of the 12 ha Yarmoukian population may have been even less than the original number of inhabitants in the 2 ha MPPNB settlement.

Finally, there is no reason to assume that the regional population of northern Jordan declined during the Yarmoukian period. In his survey around Jabal Abu Thawwab,

Kafafi (pers. comm.) located numerous Yarmoukian hamlets within a short distance of each other, reflecting a dispersal of former human concentrations into a more diffuse scatter across the countryside. Banning's "both sides of the surface" survey in the Wadi Ziqlab, where he has looked not only for archaeological evidence on the ground but beneath it as well, has shown that many sites, especially small ones alongside drainages, are obscured by natural processes (e.g. Banning 1996); they normally do not show up on traditional survey projects.

The Pottery Neolithic A tradition in Jordan

There is a clear distinction between the Yarmoukian tradition and the pottery recovered from Jericho Layer IX (variously termed Pottery Neolithic A [PNA], "Jericho IX" and "Lodian"), and one of the easiest features to recognize is the use of slips and a red pigment applied in geometric motifs (e.g. Kenyon 1979: 62 and fig. 4). The Jericho style is clearly an entity characteristic of the area west of the Jordan River and north of the Negev (Gopher and Gophna 1993: fig. 10). This early Jericho pottery has also appeared in minor quantities among the pottery repertoires of Ayn Ghazal and Wadi Shuayb (Kafafi 1998), but at Khirbat Dharih (cf. Site 524 in MacDonald *et al.* 1982: 121) and Dhra (Bennett 1980; cf. Kuijt and Finlayson 2002) in southern Jordan it appears to have constituted the major ceramic tradition.

The recent excavations at Dhra have revealed poorly preserved rectangular buildings (Kuijt and Finlayson 2002: fig. 1) in contrast to Bennett, who saw close similarities to PNA pit dwellings at Jericho (Bennett 1980: 33; cf. Kenyon 1979: 60–63); no hints of the size of this permanent (?) farming village have been suggested, although it may have been relatively large (cf. Raikes 1980: 56–60). Indications of pit dwellings also occurred in the road cut at Site 524 in Wadi Laban just north of Tafila (MacDonald *et al.* 1982), but unfortunately highway construction in 1982 destroyed the remainder of the settlement before any excavations could be undertaken.

The Wadi Rabah Tradition in Jordan

Although defined as a ceramic tradition in 1958 in Israel (Kaplan 1958; cf. Gopher and Gophna 1993), recognition of this tradition east of the Jordan Valley has been a recent event. Banning (1996: 35) appears to have uncovered three farmsteads in Wadi Ziqlab whose pottery and sickle blades are similar to Wadi Rabah sites elsewhere (Banning *et al.* 2002; Banning *et al.* 1996: figs. 6 and 7; Banning 1995: 5, 7). Kafafi (1998) assigned the "Middle Levels" of Abu Hamid[25] to the Wadi Rabah, although the "Lower Levels" were described as belonging to the Ghrubba tradition. In view of the broadly similar definitions of the Ghrubba and Wadi Rabah pottery wares and types (with bow-rim jars, hole-mouth jars and painted designs (compare Kafafi 1998 and Gopher and Gophna 1993: 329–333), it might be the case that the excavations at Abu Hamid have defined two successive phases of the Wadi Rabah entity (cf. Dollfus and Kafafi 1993: 246–249, 254).

It is not yet clear how widely the Wadi Rabah levels at Abu Hamid may have extended, but in view of the large size (c. 6.6 ha; Dollfus and Kafafi 1988: 23) of the seventh-millennium BP. Chalcolithic settlement in the highest levels, Abu Hamid could have been at one end of the settlement scale as opposed to the farmstead settlements in the Wadi Ziqlab (Banning 1996).

Dollfus and Kafafi note that the hunting of animals played a "minimal" role in the subsistence economy, with bones of wild animals reaching only 10% of the faunal remains (Dollfus and Kafafi 1993: 245). This pattern was already established as early as the beginning of the PPNC (Köhler-Rollefson *et al.* 1993). No quantification is available yet, but the hunting of red and fallow deer, aurochs and wild boar is also reported for the Wadi Ziqlab sites (Banning *et al.* 1996: 43).

Other Ceramic Neolithic Sites in Jordan

Among the latest Pottery Neolithic entities is the Qatifian, originally defined on the basis of pottery in the Nahal Besor in Israel (Gilead and Alon 1988). A final phase of this development appears to be at the base of the stratigraphy of Tulaylat Ghassul (Lovell 2001: 49). At Ayn Waida, near the PPNA/Jericho IX site of Dhra at the edge of the Dead Sea plain, a small (0.6 ha) settlement also produced Qatifian-like pottery in association with rectangular structures of massive construction (Kuijt and Chesson 2002). A radiocarbon date indicates that the village was established around 7200 BP, about 600 years after the Jericho IX village was occupied (Kuijt and Chesson 2002: 120).

There are other sites with Pottery Neolithic layers (and some with layers containing pottery of an unknown period) from Jordan that cannot be assigned to one of the generally accepted ceramic Neolithic phases. In some cases the samples were too small or suspicious to make a judgment. Such was the case at Basta, for example, where the quantity and nature of the potsherds could not be assessed (Gebel pers. comm.). At Ayn Jammam, pottery fragments have been found on the surface, and, while they appear to be Neolithic, the small sample does not neatly conform to any of the major definitions.

A Pottery Neolithic site in Wadi Faynan is reported in some detail in terms of its circumstances, lithics and pottery (Najjar *et al.* 1990; Simmons and Najjar 2002), but the authors have intentionally not attempted to ascribe the ceramic assemblage to a general entity, noting that there was little decorated material. Reports of a Qatfian (a late Pottery Neolithic/early Chalcolithic group) presence at "Faynan" (Goren 1990: 102–105) actually refer to a small surface collection from Wadi Fidan 4, an Early Bronze I site, and do not relate to the site described by Najjar *et al.* (Adams 1997: 653–655, pers. comm. 2005). Based on the illustrated pottery and lithics (especially sickles), Najjar *et al.* may be dealing with a variant of the Wadi Rabah tradition (1990: figs. 10, 12–13).

There are other issues concerning the Pottery Neolithic, not the least of which is deciding when the Neolithic ends and the Chalcolithic begins. The "Ghassulian culture," for example, remains enigmatic in terms of its identity (e.g. Lovell 2001; Bourke 1997; Kafafi 1998). The same problem has concerned the reality of the Pottery Neolithic B (PNB) designation, particularly in view of the similarities in ceramic repertoires with the Wadi Rabah and Ghassulian assemblages. Certainly, a prominent element of uncertainty lies in the restricted (geographically, stratigraphically and statistically) nature of the various assemblages found so far, but another concern must deal with treating the transitional nature of culture change. The onset of the Neolithic itself will never be defined in the field, since the Neolithic period was a process, one that was a series of transitions of other processes set in motion long before the "beginning" of the PPNA. In the same way, the "end" of the Neolithic and the "beginning" of the Chalcolithic will remain as much a matter of opinion as of any specifically identifiable feature to distinguish the two periods.

The "Aceramic Pottery Neolithic of the Desert"

It is not uncommon that interest in human society—political, economic, even archaeological—has focused on areas where human population has been greatest: those areas are usually where dramatic events took place and are most recognizable for the historic and prehistoric records. But focusing a spotlight on one part of the stage automatically dims action that takes place elsewhere, even when this activity is an essential part of the entire drama.

The unfarmable steppe and desert of Jordan were occupied from the beginning of Jordan's prehistoric record, and they remained important areas of exploitation in the PPN and PN periods as well. Most of our information comes from the concerted efforts of Garrard and his team (e.g. Garrard *et al.* 1996, with references) and the independent investigations of Betts (e.g. Betts 1986, 1992, 1998 with references). Although the steppe and desert regions could not sustain human groups in permanent settlements, there appears to have been a "permanent occupation" of the area by either transient herders with their sheep and goats or, in Byrd's view, of resident hunters and gatherers who adopted pastoralism in response to pressures from farming and hunting groups to the west (1992).

Most of the sites from the desert and steppe areas are temporary camps with the shallowest of accumulated deposits. One site near Jabal Tharwa consisted of a single circular arrangement of stones approximately 7m in diameter (Wasse and Rollefson 2005); the similarity with the final Yarmoukian "tent" structures at Ayn Ghazal is striking. Jabal Naja was occupied around 8226±106 BP (Finlayson and Betts 1990: 13) (thus generally Yarmoukian in age), and the focus on burin production is one that is shared not only in terms of a tool class (burins), but also by a burin class (concave truncation burins), with other sites throughout the arid eastern region (Betts 1988; Rollefson 1988). The association of these camps with ephemeral structures that may have been corrals suggests they were inhabited by pastoralists, but the focus on burin production remains puzzling. Betts has suggested that the burins were not intentional tools but "cores" for the production of small splinters ("burin spalls") to be used as drill bits for manufacturing stone and bone beads (Finlayson and Betts 1990: 19–20). There are other possible uses of burin spalls (Rollefson, Quintero and Wilke 1999) that might be associated with pastoral camps, but field research has not been undertaken so far to test these hypotheses.

While undoubtedly seasonal camps, Jabal Tharwa 2 and Wisad are substantial compounds that, based on arrowhead shapes, are probably Late Neolithic, but little more precision can be provided except that the points do not correspond to Yarmoukian canons, so these sites are probably datable to the middle to late eighth millennium. The size of the structures (up to 7 m diameter) indicates multifamily groups of people, and several larger pens for animals (up to 15 m diameter) reflect sizeable herds, presumably ovicaprids (Wasse and Rollefson 2005).

Concluding Remarks

The results that have been generated by the research projects over the past two decades are impressive in their scale and detail. The composition of the general evolution of Neolithic socioeconomic and sociocultural systems has taken on a fully formed outline, stretching from the earliest part of the PPNA through more than 7000 years up to the onset of metal-producing cultures. Some areas require emphatic efforts, such as the poorly known EPPNB and the later phases of the ceramic Neolithic, but at least some starting points have been identified for that research.

It is clear that, despite their obvious contacts with the Jordan Valley and Israel, the inhabitants of the highland zones and steppe/desert areas in Jordan directed their developments independently, taking advantage of local resources and opportunities to adjust continually to their own impacts on the environment. This is most clearly shown in the case of the smooth passage through the tenth millennium BP in Jordan, while tumultuous disruptions rocked the settlements in the Rift and areas to the west; in fact, the conditions in Jordan were comfortable enough that a sizeable proportion of the populations forced to abandon their villages in the west were able to emigrate eastwards, expanding established villages like Wadi Shuayb and Ayn Ghazal and founding new towns themselves.

At least three "provinces" appear to have characterized Jordan during the tenth millennium (and perhaps throughout the entire Neolithic period), including the northern section (from Ayn Rahub to Ayn Ghazal), the southern part (from Wadi Rum up to Sifiya in the Wadi Mujib) and the eastern steppe and desert areas that covered two-thirds of the country. These "territories" are identifiable by architectural traits and, to some degree, by lithic typology (especially in projectile points) and ceramic technology/typology. There may also have been real differences in the ritual arena in these three territories as well, although in terms of the elaborate statuary from Ayn Ghazal, this would be an argument based on "silence" from the south, an argument that could quickly be refuted in the next season of excavations.

The emergence of enormous settlements near the middle of the tenth millennium BP—at the change from the MPPNB to the LPPNB—is a phenomenon that is principally characteristic of Jordan,[26] and the population concentrations must have set in operation a chain of social stresses and organizational adaptations to cope with both external and internal pressures. Part of the response could have been the scenario described by Köhler-Rollefson in her pastoralism model, wherein a new system arose that immediately reduced stress on local ecosystems by removing both humans and animals from the area for large parts of the year, beginning a process that would come to characterize the entire Levantine region for the rest of its history.

Another element of change during the existence of the town phenomenon undoubtedly had to do with social relationships between neighbours and not-so-close neighbours. As permanent populations grew, a new surprise was in store: for the first time a resident of a town could encounter another resident who may have been more or less a stranger. As competition for farm land became keener, older methods from MPPNB times may not have been effective in settling conflicting claims for fields and resources; and these conflicts may have arisen within and not just between kin groups. The growth of multi-family houses is one reflection of this kind of stress, as is the apparent disappearance of the ancestor cult by the end of the LPPNB. The late tenth-millennium temples at Ayn Ghazal (and perhaps the Tl complex at Bayda) show no connections with plastered skulls, burials or statues. Instead, there may have been a turning outward from kin groups, and from the community, towards an external, spiritual means of resolving problems that grew among strangers and kinfolk alike.

The concentration on later Neolithic developments is only about 15–20 years old, and the revelations of work in Wadi Ziqlab and Jabal Abu Thawwab have shown the directions that continued research should take. The tantalizing scatters of as yet under-researched ceramic Neolithic sites in the southern part of Jordan have some indications that the social patterns of the country—and the Levant in general—were much more complex than was imagined in the early 1980s.

The accelerated field research and theoretical ruminations in the past generation have provided prehistorians with the means to approach questions that were not even considered in the early 1970s.[27] This is true for Jordan's entire prehistoric record, of course, but the richness of the data from the Neolithic period has generated enormous anthropological excitement, and remarkable, solid progress in the understanding of our food-producing predecessors is promised in the near future.

Notes

1. Except where specifically mentioned, all dates are expressed as cal BP dates calculated according to Weninger *et al.* 2004.

2. At Dhra, among the more than 300 points recovered by 2001, Khiam points outnumber Salibiya points by two to one (and there are two Jordan Valley points as well) (Goodale and Smith 2001: 1).

3. Notable among the projectile points at Bayda, 13 are Khiam points, mostly from the lower layers (Levels VI-IV), where they reflect 2–3% of the points (Mortensen 1970: 21–22, fig. 19).

4. Kuijt (1997) and Sayej (2004b) hold a different view concerning the presence of the EPPNB in Jordan, indicating that this period of development did not occur south of the Euphrates Valley, where it was first defined by Cauvin (cf. Cauvin 1987). It is possible that the EPPNB was indeed not present in southern Jordan, but the case seems different for Jordan north of the Wadi Hasa.

5. Bayda produced seven Helwan points; in the lowest layers (V and VI) they accounted for 1.0–1.5% (Mortensen 1970: 23, fig. 19).

6. Note that this use of the term "Early PPNB" antedates Cauvin's (1987) tripartite division of the PPNB period; Bar-Yosef's use of the term (1981: 564) does not necessarily reflect a reference restricted to the mid- to late tenth millennium bp.

7. Byrd summarized the architectural developments at Bayda in which he uses "phases;" essentially Byrd's Phase A is equivalent to Kirkbride's Levels V–VI, Phase B to Level IV, and Phase C to Levels 1-III (Byrd 1994).

8. The potential for a PPNA or EPPNB presence at Bayda is strong in view of the occurrence of Khiam and Helwan points (see notes 3 and 5), despite the

"young" radiocarbon dates in Level VI (cf. Weinstein 1984: 328–329).

9. The structures from Bayda Levels II and III/Phase C are discussed later in the PPNC section.

10. Incomplete information from Ghuwayr 1, which has a series of MPPNB and M/LPPNB dates, suggests one relatively large building where there may have been one room, at least, associated with ritual activities in view of three niches and what may have been an altar (Simmons and Najjar 1996).

11. Another "type" of burial may be represented by a single example. It is a courtyard burial, but unlike "typical" decapitated burials or "trash" burials, the 15-year-old woman appears to be in a secondary location: the long bones were neatly stacked, next to which lay the mandible; ribs and vertebrae were scattered among the long bones and jaw.

12. This total does not include the skulls that were still attached to "trash burials" or infants.

13. The identity of the substance has not been confirmed; there are superficial similarities with three coated skulls at Nahal Hemar (Yakar and Hershkovitz 1988; Arensburg and Hershkovitz 1989), but what had been first described as bitumen has since been identified as collagen (Bar-Yosef pers. comm.; Nissenbaum pers. comm.).

14. The rarity of figurines at Wadi Shuayb is explainable, in part at least, by the restricted area of MPPNB excavations (cf. Simmons *et al.* 1989, 2001).

15. Two-storied buildings are claimed for the MPPNB levels at Cafer Höyük in southeast Turkey (Molist and Cauvin 1991: 107–109, fig. 15), although the bottom storey could be a basement storage area. Other two-storied buildings may occur in eastern Anatolia during the LPPNB period.

16. The decline in wild species in the diet may, in fact, have been much more dramatic if cattle and pigs had become domesticated during this period, possibilities that remain unverified (von den Driesch and Wodtke 1997).

17. Von den Driesch has noted that the cattle and pigs from LPPNB (and PPNC) Ayn Ghazal are still morphologically wild, in her opinion, although the residents at Ayn Ghazal may have been keeping them in corrals/stalls (von den Driesch and Wodtke 1997), which could constitute the beginning phases of domestication.

18. Edwards and Thorpe (1986) caution that the 36 ha distribution of artefacts on the steep slopes of Wadi Zarqa at Kharaysin may reflect erosion and deflation. How large the actual settlement was requires extensive excavation probes.

19. Kenyon once implied that the southern Levant had been abandoned by farming people for up to a millennium after the misty end of the PPNB occupation at Jericho (Kenyon 1979: 45–46), a contention that has been popular among prehistorians for a long time since. It is unlikely that the Jordan Valley and the western areas of Israel were devoid of farming communities during the LPPNB and even the PPNC periods; see below.

20. The earlier discussion of possible LPPNB temples or shrines at Bayda does not conflict with a desertion of the site as a permanent farming settlement. The temples and shrines may have served as focal points of returning pilgrims among the emigrant populations for generations.

21. This situation is also shown by the disappearance of dense chipping floors that had characterized restricted loci in MPPNB and LPPNB courtyards.

22. The eastern end was truncated by bulldozer work connected with highway construction; the western end lies somewhere under unexcavated sediments (see Rollefson *et al.* 1990: 108–109; Rollefson *et al.* 1992: fig. 6). It is probable that although the Great Wall was used by PPNC (and Yarmoukian) residents, the initial construction was in the LPPNB period.

23. Preliminary analysis of one PPNC skeleton has revealed bone disease associated with chronic tuberculosis, and another late LPPNB skeleton also suggests a similar pathology (Najjar *et al.* 1996). Epidemic tubercular death would probably have been too rapid for bone pathologies to develop in most cases, and it is not surprising that tuberculosis appears in the Neolithic since goats, sheep and cattle are vectors for the disease.

24. Contributing to the absence of some of the bones in secondary burials under these circumstances, if someone died in the steppe/desert in the earlier part of the pastoral visit, the body may have been left for excarnation (including under stone cairns) for several months, and this may have attracted the attention of scavengers that could have been responsible for the disappearance of bones that were not necessarily small.

25. A radiocarbon sample from the "very top of these levels" gave a date of 6867±79 BP, while the overlying Chalcolithic levels yielded three dates between 6551±57 and 6421±50 BP (Dollfus and Kafafi 1993: 244–245).

26. Large (greater than 10 ha) settlements are also known from Syria (e.g. Tall Abu Hurayra) and the Jordan Valley (Beisamoun and Khirbat Sheikh Ali), but in these areas the towns are exceptions to the "normal" settlement sizes (cf. Rollefson 1987, 1999; Gebel and Rollefson 1997).

27. Or, if they were considered, they certainly had precious little information from which to develop answers.

Bibliography

Amr, K., A. al-Momani, S. Farajat and H. Falahat
1998 Archaeological Survey of the Wadi Musa Water Supply and Wastewater Project Area. *Annual of the Department of Antiquities of Jordan* 42: 503–548.

Arensburg, B. and I. Hershkovitz
1989 Artificial Skull "Treatment" in the PPNB Period: Nahal Hemar. In I. Hershkovitz (ed.), *People and Culture in Change,* 115–133; British Archaeological Reports International Series 508. Oxford: British Archaeological Reports.

Baird, D.
1993 Neolithic Chipped Stone Assemblages from the Azraq Basin, Jordan, and the Significance of the Neolithic of the Arid Zones of the Levant. Unpublished PhD dissertation, University of Edinburgh.
1994 Chipped Stone Production Technology from the Azraq Project Neolithic Sites. In H. Gebel and S. Kozlowski (eds.), *Neolithic Chipped Stone Industries of the Fertile Crescent,* 525–542. Berlin: *ex oriente.*
1995 Chipped Stone Raw Material Procurement and Selection in the Azraq Basin: Implications for Levantine Neolithic Cultural Developments. In K. Amr, F. Zayadine and M. Zaghloul (eds.), *Studies in the History and Archaeology of Jordan V,* 505–514. Amman: Department of Antiquities.

Baird, D., A. Garrard, L. Martin and K. Wright
1992 Prehistoric Environment and Settlement in the Azraq Basin: An Interim Report on the 1988 Season. *Levant* 24: 1–31.

Banning, E.
1995 Herders or Homesteaders ? A Neolithic Farm in the Wadi Ziqlab, Jordan. *Biblical Archaeologist* 58.1: 2- 13.
1996 Highlands and Lowlands: Problems and Survey Frameworks for Rural Archaeology in the Near East. *Bulletin of the American Schools of Oriental Research* 301: 25–46.

Banning, E. and B. Byrd
1984 The Architecture of PPNB 'Ain Ghazal, Jordan. *Bulletin of the American Schools of Oriental Research* 255: 15–20.
1987 Houses and the Changing Residential Unit: Domestic Architecture at PPNB 'Ain Ghazal. *Proceedings of the Prehistoric Society* 53: 309–325.

Banning, E. and M. Najjar
1999 Excavations at Tell Rakan I, a Neolithic Site in Wadi Ziqlab, Jordan. *Neo-Lithics* 2/99: 1–3.

Banning, E., R. Dods, J. McCorriston, S. Monckton, and P. Sheppard
1987 Report on the Wadi Ziqlab Project 1986 Season of Excavations. *Annual of the Department of Antiquities of Jordan* 31: 321–342.
1996 The 1992 Excavations in Wadi Ziqlab, Jordan. *Annual of the Department of Antiquities of Jordan* 40: 29–50.
2002 Excavations at al-Basatin, Wadi Ziqlab, Jordan. *Neo-Lithics* 2/02: 13–14.

Bar-Yosef, O.
1981 The 'Pre-Pottery Neolithic' in the Southern Levant. In J. Cauvin and P. Sanlaville (eds.), *Préhistoire du Levant,* 551–569. Paris: Centre National de la Recherche Scientifique.
1991 Raw Material Exploitation in the Levantine Epi-Paleolithic. In A. Montet-White and S. Holen (eds.), *Raw Material Exploitation among Prehistoric Hunters and Gatherers,* 235–250. Publications in Anthropology 19. Lawrence: University of Kansas.

Bar-Yosef, O. and D. Alon
1988 Nahal Hemar Cave: The Excavations. *'Atiqot* 18: 1–30.

Becker, C.
1991 The Analysis of Mammalian Bones from Basta, a Pre-Pottery Neolithic Site in Jordan: Problems and Potential. *Paléorient* 17: 59–75.
2004 On the Identification of Sheep and Goats: The Evidence from Basta. In H.J. Nissen, M. Muheisen and H.G.K. Gebel (eds.), *Basta I. The Human Ecology,* 219–310. *biblioteca neolithica Asiae meridionalis et occidentalis.* Berlin: *ex oriente.*

Bennett, C.M.
1980 Soundings at Dhra', Jordan. *Levant* 12: 30–39.

Berner, M. and M. Schultz
1997 The Physical Anthropology of the Late PPNB Population of Basta. *Neo-Lithics* 2/97: 7.

Betts, A.
1986 The Prehistory of the Basalt Desert, Transjordan: An Analysis. Unpublished PhD dissertation, University College, London, Institute of Archaeology.
1988 1986 Excavations at Dhuweila, Eastern Jordan: A Preliminary Report. *Levant* 20: 7–21.
1992 Eastern Jordan: Economic Choices and Site Location in the Neolithic Periods. In M. Zaghloul, K. Amr, F. Zayadine, R. Nabeel and N. Rida Tawfiq (eds.), *Studies in the History and Archaeology of Jordan IV,* 111–114. Amman: Department of Antiquities.
1998 *The Harra and the Hamad. Excavations and Surveys in Eastern Jordan,* Vol. I. Sheffield Archaeological Monographs 9. Sheffield: Sheffield Academic Press.

Bienert, H.-D.
1991 Skull Cult in the Prehistoric Near East. *Journal of Prehistoric Religion* 5: 9–23.

Bisheh, G., S. Farajat, G. Palumbo and M. Waheeb

1993 Archaeological Rescue Survey of the Ras an-Naqab–Aqaba Highway Alignment, 1992. *Annual of the Department of Antiquities of Jordan* 37: 119–131.

Bonogofsky, M.A.

2001a *An Osteo-Archaeological Examination of the Ancestor Cult During the Pre-Pottery Neolithic B Period in the Levant.* Unpublished doctoral dissertation, Department of Near East Studies. Berkeley: University of California.

2001b Cranial Modeling and Neolithic Bone Modification at 'Ain Ghazal: New Interpretations. *Paléorient* 27: 141–146.

Bourke, S.

1997 The 'Pre-Ghassulian' Sequence at Teleilat Ghassul: Sydney University Excavations 1975–1995. In H.G.K. Gebel, Z. Kafafi and G. Rollefson (eds.), *The Prehistory of Jordan II: Perspectives from 1997*, 395–418. Berlin: ex oriente.

Butler, C.

1989 The Plastered Skulls of 'Ain Ghazal: Preliminary Findings. In I. Hershkovitz (ed.), *People and Culture in Change,* 141–146. British Archaeological Reports International Series 508. Oxford: British Archaeological Reports.

Byrd, B.

1992 The Dispersal of Food Production across the Levant. In A. Gebauer and T. Price (eds.), *Transitions to Agriculture in Prehistory,* 49–61. Madison: Prehistory Press.

1994 Public and Private, Domestic and Corporate: The Emergence of the Southwest Asian Village. *American Antiquity* 59: 639–66.

Byrd, B. and E. Banning

1988 Southern Levantine Pier Houses: Intersite Architectural Patterning during the Pre-Pottery Neolithic B. *Paléorient* 14: 65–72.

Cauvin, J.

1974 Les débuts de la céramique sur le Moyen-Euphrate: nouveaux documents. *Paléorient* 2: 199–205.

1987 Chronologies relative et absolue dans le Néolithique du Levant Nord et d'Anatolie entre 10.000 et 8.000 bp. In O. Aurenche, J. Evin and F. Hours (eds.), *Chronologies du Proche Orient*, 325–342. British Archaeological Reports International Series 379. Oxford: British Archaeological Reports.

Clark, G.A., D. Olszewski, J. Shuldenrein, N. Rida and J.D. Eighmey

1994 Survey and Excavation in Wadi el-Hasa: A Preliminary Report on the 1993 Season. *Annual of the Department of Antiquities of Jordan* 38: 41–55.

Coinman, N., G. Clark and J. Lindly

1988 A Diachronic Study of Paleolithic and Early Neolithic Site Placement Patterns in the Southern Tributaries of the Wadi el-Hasa. In B. MacDonald (ed.), *The Wadi el Hasa Archaeological Survey 1979–1983, West-Central Jordan,* 48–86. Waterloo: Wilfrid Laurier University.

Cropper, D., C. Foley and U. Linnamae

2003a Results from the Preliminary Investigations at Umm Meshrat I and II. *Neo-Lithics* 1/03: 15–21.

Cropper, D., C. Foley and G. Rollefson

2003b Umm Meshrat I and II: Two New Late Neolithic Sites along the Wadi ath-Thamad, Jordan. In F. Ninow (ed.), *Wort und Stein. Studien zur Theologie und Archäologie,* 15–32. Frankfurt: Peter Lang.

Dollfus, G. and Z. Kafafi

1988 *Abu Hamid. Village du 4e millenaire de la vallée du Jourdain.* Amman: Economic.

1993 Recent Researches at Abu Hamid. *Annual of the Department of Antiquities of Jordan* 37: 241–262.

Ducos, R.

1993 Proto-élevage et élevage au Levant sud au VIIe millénaire B.C.: Les données de la Damascene. *Paléorient* 19: 153–173.

1994 À propos du modèle du pastoralisme PPNC proposé par G. Rollefson et I. Köhler-Rollefson. *Paléorient* 20: 165–166.

Edwards, P., J. Meadows, G. Sayej and M. Metzger

2002 Zahrat Adh-Dhra': A New Pre-Pottery Neolithic A Site on the Dead Sea Plain in Jordan. *Bulletin of the American Schools of Oriental Research* 327: 1–15.

Edwards, P. and T. Higham

2001 Zahrat adh-Dhra' and the Dead Sea Plain at the Dawn of the Holocene. In A. Walmsley (ed.), *Australians Uncovering Ancient Jordan. Fifty Years of Middle East Archaeology,* 139–152. Sydney: University of Sydney.

Edwards, R. and S. Thorpe

1986 Surface Lithic Finds from Kharaysin, Jordan. *Paléorient* 12: 85–87.

Eighmey, J.

1992 A Functional Analysis of Projectile Points from the Neolithic Site of 'Ain Ghazal, Unpublished MA thesis, San Diego State University.

Finlayson, B. and A. Betts

1990 Functional Analysis of Chipped Stone Artefacts from the Late Neolithic Site of Gabal Na'ja, Eastern Jordan. *Paléorient* 16: 13–20.

Finlayson, B., S. Mithen, D. Carruthers, A. Kennedy, A. Pirie, and R. Tipping

2000 Dana-Faynan-Ghuwayr Prehistory Project. *Levant* 32: 1–26.

Fino, N.

1997 Al-Baseet, a New LPPNB Site Found in Wadi Musa, Southern Jordan. *Neo-Lithics* 3/97: 13–14.

Garfinkel, Y.

1994 The PPNC Flint Assemblage from Tel 'Ali. In H. G. Gebel and S. K. Kozlowski (eds.), *Neolithic Chipped Stone Industries of the Fertile Crescent,* 543–562. Berlin: ex oriente.

1996 Critical Obervations on the So-Called Khiamian Flint Industry. In S.K. Kozlowski and H.G. Gebel (eds.), *Neolithic*

Chipped Stone Industries of the Fertile Crescent, and Their Contemporaries in Adjacent Regions, 15–21. Berlin: ex oriente.

Garrard, A., S. Colledge and L. Martin

1996 The Emergence of Crop Cultivation and Caprine Herding in the 'Marginal Zone' of the Southern Levant. In D. Harris (ed.), *The Origins and Spread of Agriculture and Pastoralism in Eurasia,* 204–226. London: University College.

Garrard, A., B. Byrd, P. Harvey and F. Hivernel

1985 Prehistoric Environment and Settlement in the Azraq Basin: A Report on the 1982 Survey Season. *Levant* 17: 1–28.

1987 Prehistoric Environment and Settlement in the Azraq Basin: An Interim Report on the 1985 Excavation Season. *Levant* 19: 5–26.

1994 Prehistoric Environment and Settlement in the Azraq Basin: An Interim Report on the 1987 and 1988 Excavation Seasons. *Levant* 26: 73–109.

Gebel, H.G.

1988 Late Epipaleolithic-Aceramic Neolithic Sites in the Petra Area. In A. Garrard and H. Gebel (eds.), *The Prehistory of Jordan,* 67–100. British Archaeological Reports International Series 396. Oxford: British Archaeological Reports.

2002a Walls. Loci of Forces. In H.G. Gebel, B.D. Jensen and C.H. Jensen (eds.), *Magic Practices and Ritual in the Near Eastern Neolithic,* 119–132. Berlin: ex oriente.

2002b The Neolithic of the Near East. An Essay on a Polycentric Process and Other Research Problems. In A. Hausleiter, S. Kerner and B. Muller-Neuhof (eds.), *Material Culture and Mental Spheres: Internationales Symposium für Hans J. Nissen.* Alter Orient und Altes Testament 293: 313–324. Münster: Ugarit Verlag.

Gebel, H.G. and H.-D. Bienert

1997 Ba'ja Hidden in the Petra Mountains. Preliminary Report on the 1997 Excavations. In H.G. Gebel, Z. Kafafi and G.O. Rollefson (eds.), *The Prehistory of Jordan II. Perspectives from 1997,* 221–262. Berlin: ex oriente.

Gebel, H.G. and Hermansen, B.

1999 A Third Little Head from LPPNB Basta, Southern Jordan. *Neo-Lithics* 2/99: 11–12.

2001 LPPNB Ba'ja 2001. A Short Note. *Neo-Lithics* 2/01: 15–20.

2004 Ba'ja 2003: Summary on the 5th Season of Excavation. *Neo-Lithics* 2/04: 15–18.

Gebel, H.G., B.D. Hermansen and C.H. Jensen (eds.)

2002 *Magic Practices and Ritual in the Near Eastern Neolithic.* Studies in Near Eastern Production, Subsistence and Environment 8. Berlin: *ex oriente*.

Gebel, H.G. and M. Muheisen

1985 Note on 'Ain Rahub, a New Late Natufian Site Near Irbid, Jordan. *Paléorient* 11: 107–110.

Gebel, H.G. and G. Rollefson (eds.)

1997 Central Settlements in Neolithic Jordan, *Neo-Lithics* 2/97.

Gebel, H.G., M. Muheisen, H. Nissen, N. Qadi and M. Starck

1988 Preliminary Report on the First Season of Excavations at the Late Aceramic Neolithic Site of Basta. In A. Garrard and H.G. Gebel (eds.), *The Prehistory of Jordan,* 101–134. British Archaeological Reports International Series 396. Oxford: British Archaeological Reports.

Gilead, I. and D. Alon

1988 Excavations of Protohistoric Sites in the Nahal Besor and the Late Neolithic of the Northern Negev. *Mitekufat Haeven* 21: 109–130.

Goodale, N. and S. Smith

2001 Pre-Pottery Neolithic A Projectile Points at Dhra', Jordan: Preliminary Thoughts on Form, Function, and Site Interpretation. *Neo-Lithics* 2/01: 1–5.

Gopher, A.

1994 *Arrowheads of the Neolithic Levant.* Winona Lake, WI: Eisenbrauns.

Gopher, A. and R. Gophna

1993 Cultures of the Eighth and Seventh Millennia bp in the Southern Levant: A Review for the 1990s. *Journal of World Prehistory* 7: 297–353.

Goren, Y.

1990 The 'Qatifian Culture' in Southern Israel and Transjordan: Additional Aspects for its Definition. *Mitekufat Haeven* 23: 100–112.

Goring-Morris, N,

1994 Aspects of the PPNB Lithics Industry of Kfar Hahoresh, near Nazareth, Israel. In H.G. Gebel and S.K. Kozlowski (eds.), *Neolithic Chipped Stone Industries of the Fertile Crescent,* 427–444. Berlin: ex oriente.

Goring-Morris, N. and A. Gopher

1983 Nahal Issaron: A Neolithic Settlement in the Southern Negev: Preliminary Report of the Excavations in 1980. *Israel Exploration Journal* 33: 149–162.

Griffin, R., C. Grissom and G. Rollefson

1998 Three Late 8th Millennium Plastered Faces from Ain Ghazal, Jordan. *Paléorient* 24: 59–70.

Hecker, H.

1975 *The Faunal Analysis of the Primary Food Animals from Pre-Pottery Neolithic Beidha (Jordan).* Unpublished PhD dissertation, Columbia University. Ann Arbor: University Microfilms.

Henry, D.

1982 The Prehistory of Southern Jordan and Relationships with the Levant. *Journal of Field Archaeology* 9: 417–444.

1995 *Prehistoric Cultural Ecology and Evolution: Insights from Southern Jordan.* New York: Plenum.

Henry, D., C. Cordova, J. White, R. Dean, J. Beaver, H. Ekstrom, S. Kadowaki, J. McCorriston, A. Nowell and L. Scott-Cummings

2003 The Early Neolithic Site of Ayn Abu Nukhayla, Southern Jordan. *Bulletin of the American Schools of Oriental Research* 330: 1–30.

Henry, D., K. Kerry, J. Beaver and J. White

2001 Survey of Prehistoric Sites, Wadi Araba, Southern Jordan. *Bulletin of the American Schools of Oriental Research* 323: 1–19.

Hermansen, B.D.

1997 Art and Ritual Behaviour in Neolithic Basta. In H.G.K. Gebel, Z. Kafafi and G.O. Rollefson (eds.), *The Prehistory of Jordan II. Perspectives from 1997*, 333–343. Berlin: ex oriente.

Hermansen, B.D. and C.H. Jensen

2002 Notes on Some Features of Possible Ritual Significance at MPPNB Shaqarat Mazyad, Southern Jordan. In H.G. Gebel, B.D. Jensen and C.H. Jensen (eds.), *Magic Practices and Ritual in the Near Eastern Neolithic*, 91–101. Berlin: ex oriente.

Horwitz, L.

1989 A Reassessment of Caprovine Domestication in the Levantine Neolithic: Old Questions, New Answers. In I. Hershkovitz (ed.), *People and Culture in Change*, 153–181. British Archaeological Reports International Series 508. Oxford: British Archaeological Reports.

Jensen, C.H.

2004 Production areas at MPPNB Shkarat Msaied, Southern Jordan. *Neo-Lithics* 2/04: 22–226.

Kafafi, Z.

1985 Late Neolithic Architecture from Jabal Abu Thawwab, Jordan. *Paléorient* 11: 125–127.

1986 Second Season of Excavations at Jabal Abu Thawwab (er-Rumman), 1985, Preliminary Report. *Annual of the Department of Antiquities of Jordan* 30: 57–68.

1988 Jabal Abu Thawwab, a Pottery Neolithic Village in North Jordan. In A. Garrard and H.G. Gebel (eds.), *The Prehistory of Jordan*, 451–471. British Archaeological Reports International Series 396. Oxford: British Archaeological Reports.

1990 Early Pottery Contexts from 'Ain Ghazal, Jordan. *Bulletin of the American Schools of Oriental Research* 280: 15–30.

1993 The Yarmoukians in Jordan. *Paléorient* 19: 101–114.

1998 The Late Neolithic in Jordan. In D. Henry (ed.), *The Prehistoric Archaeology of Jordan*, 127–138. British Archaeological Reports International Series 705. Oxford: Archaeopress.

2001 *Jebel Abu Thawwab (er-Rumman), Central Jordan. The Late Neolithic and Early Bronze Age I Occupations.* Biblioteca neolithica Asiae meridionalis et occidentalis. Berlin: ex oriente.

Kafafi, Z., I. Caneva and G. Palumbo

1999 The Neolithic Site of es-Sayyeh: Preliminary Report on the 1999 Season. *Neo-Lithics* 3/99: 10–12.

Kafafi, Z. and G. Rollefson

1995 The 1994 excavations at Ayn Ghazal: Preliminary Report. *Annual of the Department of Antiquities of Jordan* 39: 13–29.

Kaliszan, L., B.D. Hermansen, C. Jensen, T. Skudbøl, M. Bille, P. Bangsgaard, A. Ihr, M. Sørensen and Bente Markussen

2002 Shaqarat Mazyad—The Village on the Edge. *Neo-Lithics* 1/02: 16–19.

Kaplan, J.

1958 Excavations at Wadi Raba. *Israel Exploration Journal* 8: 149–160.

Kenyon, K.

1979 *Archaeology in the Holy Land*. 4th edn. London: Benn.

1981 *Excavations at Jericho, III*. London: British School of Archaeology in Jerusalem.

Kinzel, M.

2004 Some Notes on the Reconstruction of PPNB Architecture. *Neo-Lithics* 2/04: 18–22.

Kirkbride, D.

1966 Five Seasons at the Pre -Pottery Neolithic Village of Beidha in Jordan. *Palestine Exploration Quarterly* 98: 8–72.

1967 Beidha 1965: An Interim Report. *Palestine Exploration Quarterly* 99: 5–14.

1968a Beidha 1967: An Interim Report. *Palestine Exploration Quarterly* 100: 90–96.

1968b Beidha: Early Neolithic Village Life South of the Dead Sea. *Antiquity* 42: 263–274.

Kislev, M.

1992 Agriculture in the Near East in the Vllth Millennium bc. In P. Anderson (ed.), *Préhistoire de l'agriculture: Nouvelles approches expérimentales et ethnographiques*, 87–93. Monographie de CRA 6. Paris: Centre National de la Recherche Scientifique.

Köhler-Rollefson, I.

1988 The Aftermath of the Levantine Neolithic Revolution in Light of Ecologic and Ethnographic Evidence. *Paléorient* 14: 87–93.

1992 A Model for the Development of Nomadic Pastoralism on the Transjordanian Plateau. In O. Bar-Yosef and A. Khazanov (eds.), *Pastoralism in the Levant*, 11–18. Madison: Prehistory Press.

1997 Proto-Élevage, Pathologies and Pastoralism: A Post-Mortem on Goat Domestication. In H.G. Gebel, Z. Kafafi and G. Rollefson (eds.), *The Prehistory of Jordan II: Perspectives from 1997*, 557–566. Berlin: ex oriente.

Köhler-Rollefson, I. and G. Rollefson

1990 The Impact of Neolithic Man on the Environment: The Case of 'Ain Ghazal, Jordan. In S. Bottema, G. Entjes-Nieborg and W. van Zeist (eds.), *Man's Role in the Shaping of the Eastern Mediterranean Landscape*, 3–14. Rotterdam: Balkema.

2002 Brooding about Breeding: Social Implications for the Process of Animal Domestication. In R. Cappers and S. Bottema (eds.), *The Dawn of Farming in the Near East*, 177–181. Berlin: ex oriente.

Köhler-Rollefson, I., W. Gillespie and M. Metzger

1988 The Fauna from Neolithic Ain Ghazal. In A. Garrard and H. Gebel (eds.), *The Prehistory of Jordan,* 423–430. British Archaeological Reports International Series 396. Oxford: British Archaeological Reports.

Köhler-Rollefson, I., L. Quintero and G. Rollefson

1993 A Brief Note on the Fauna from Neolithic Ain Ghazal. *Paléorient* 19: 95–97.

Kuijt, I.

1994a Pre-Pottery Neolithic A Settlement Variability: Evidence for Sociopolitical Developments in the Southern Levant. *Journal of Mediterranean Archaeology* 7: 165–192.

1994b A Brief Note on the Chipped Stone Assemblage from 'Iraq ad-Dubb, Jordan. *Neo-Lithics* 2/94: 2–3.

1996 Where Are the Microlithics? Lithic Technology and Neolithic Chronology as Seen from the PPNA Occupation at Dhra, Jordan. *Neo-Lithics* 2/96: 7–8.

1997 Trying to Fit Round Houses into Square Holes: Re-examining the Timing of the South-Central Levantine Pre-Pottery Neolithic A and Pre-Pottery Neolithic B Transition. In H.G. Gebel, Z. Kafafi and G. Rollefson (eds.), *The Prehistory of Jordan II: Perspectives from 1997,* 193–202. Berlin: ex oriente.

2000 Keeping the Peace: Ritual, Skull Caching and Community Integration in the Levantine Neolithic. In I. Kuijt (ed.), *Life in Neolithic Farming Communities: Social Organization, Identity, and Differentiation,* 137–163. New York: Kluwer Academic/Plenum Press.

2001a Lithic Inter-assemblage Variability and Cultural-Historical Sequences: A Consideration of the Pre-Pottery Neolithic A Occupation of Dhra', Jordan. *Paléorient* 27: 107–125.

2001b Meaningful Masks: Place, Death and the Transmission of Social Memory in Early Agricultural Communities of the Near Eastern Pre-Pottery Neolithic. In M. Chesson (ed.), *Social Memory, Identity and Death: Interdisciplinary Perspectives on Mortuary Rituals,* 80–99. Washington: American Anthropological Association.

2002 Reflections on Ritual and the Transmission of Authority in the Pre-Pottery Neolithic of the Levant. In H.G. Gebel, B.D. Hermansen and C.H. Jensen (eds.), *Magic Practices and Ritual in the Near Eastern Neolithic,* 81–90. Studies in Early Near Eastern Production, Subsistence, and Environment 8. Berlin: ex oriente.

Kuijt, I. and M. Chesson

1994 Investigations at Jabal Queisa, Jordan (1993): A Reconsideration of Chronology and Occupational History. *Annual of the Department of Antiquities of Jordan* 38: 33–39.

2002 Excavations at 'Ain Waida', Jordan: New Insights into Pottery Neolithic Lifeways in the Southern Levant. *Paléorient* 28: 109–122.

2004 Lumps of Clay and Pieces of Stone: Ambiguity, Bodies, and Identity as Portrayed in Neolithic Figurines. In S. Pollack and R. Bernbeck (eds.), *Archaeologies of the Middle East: Critical Perspectives,* 152–183. London: Blackwell.

Kuijt, I. and B. Finlayson

2001 The 2001 Excavation Season at the Pre-Pottery Neolithic A Site of Dhra', Jordan: Preliminary Results. *Neo-Lithics* 2/01: 12–15.

2002 The 2002 Excavation Season at Dhra', Jordan: Preliminary Results from the Jericho IX and Pre-Pottery Neolithic A Components. *Neo-Lithics* 2/02: 17–21.

Kuijt, I., J. Mabry and G. Palumbo

1991 Early Neolithic Use of Upland Areas of Wadi el-Yabis: Preliminary Evidence from the Excavations of 'Iraq ad-Dubb, Jordan. *Paléorient* 17: 99–108.

Kuijt, I. and H. Mahasneh

1998 Dhra': An Early Neolithic Village in the Southern Jordan Valley. *Journal of Field Archaeology* 25: 153–161.

Lechevallier, M.

1978 *Abou Gosh et Beisamoun.* Mémoires et Travaux du Centre de Recherches Préhistoriques Française de Jérusalem No. 2. Paris: Association Paléorient.

Levy, T.

1986 The Chalcolithic Period. *Biblical Archaeologist* 49: 83–106.

1995 Cult, Metallurgy and Rank Societies–Chalcolithic Period (ca. 4500–3500 BCE). In T. Levy (ed.), *The Archaeology of Society in the Holy Land,* 226–243. London: Leicester University Press.

Lovell, J.

2001 *The Late Neolithic and Chalcolithic Periods in the Southern Levant. New Data from the Site of Teleilat Ghassul, Jordan.* British Archaeological Reports International Series 974. Oxford: Archaeopress.

MacDonald, B., G.A. Clark, M. Neeley, R. Adams and M. Gregory

1987 Southern Ghor and Northeast 'Arabah Archaeological Survey 1986, Jordan: A Preliminary Report. *Annual of the Department of Antiquities of Jordan* 31: 391–418.

MacDonald, B., G. Rollefson and D. Roller

1982 The Wadi el-Hasa Survey 1981. Preliminary Report. *Annual of the Department of Antiquities of Jordan* 26: 117–131.

MacDonald, B. and W. Sawtell

2002 The Tafila-Busayra Archaeological Survey: Phase 3 (2001). *Annual of the Department of Antiquities of Jordan* 46: 477–484.

Mahasneh, H.

1997 Es-Sifiya: A Pre-Pottery Neolithic B Site in the Wadi el-Mujib, Jordan. In H.G. Gebel, Z. Kafafi and G. Rollefson (eds.), *The Prehistory of Jordan II. Perspectives from 1997,* 203–214. Berlin: ex oriente.

Makarewicz, C. and N. Goodale

2004 Results from the First Excavation Season at el-Hemmeh: A Pre-Pottery Neolithic Site in the Wadi el-Hasa, Jordan. *Neo-Lithics* 2/04: 5–11.

Molist, M. and J. Cauvin

1991 Les niveaux inférieures de Cafer Höyük (Malatya, Turquie): Stratigraphie et architectures (fouilles 1984–1986). *Cahiers de l'Euphrates* 5–6: 85–114.

Mortensen, P.

1970 A Preliminary Study of the Chipped Stone Industry from Beidha. *Acta Archaeologica* 41: 1–54.

Muheisen, M., H.G. Gebel, C. Hannss and R. Neef

1988 Ain Rahub, a New Final Natufian and Yarmoukian Site near Irbid. In A. Garrard and H.G. Gebel (eds.), *The Prehistory of Jordan*, 472–502. British Archaeological Reports International Series 396. Oxford: British Archaeological Reports.

Nadel, D.

1989 Flint Heat Treatment at the Beginning of the Neolithic Period in the Levant. *Journal of the Israel Prehistoric Society* 22: 61–67.

Nadel, D., O. Bar-Yosef and A. Gopher

1991 Early Neolithic Arrowhead Types in the Southern Levant: A Typological Suggestion. *Paléorient* 17: 109–120.

Najjar, M.

1994 Ghwair I, a Neolithic Site in Wadi Feinan. *The Near East in Antiquity* 4: 75–85.

2002 Symbolism in the Iconography of the Neolithic of Wadi Faynan, Jordan. In H.G. Gebel, B.D. Hermansen and C.H. Jensen (eds.), *Magic Practices and Ritual in the Near Eastern Neolithic*, 103–109. Studies in Early Neolithic Production, Subsistence, and Environment 8. Berlin: ex oriente.

Najjar, M., A. al-Shiyab and I. al-Sarie

1996 Cases of Tuberculosis at 'Ain Ghazal, Jordan. *Paléorient* 22: 123–128.

Najjar, M., A. Abu Dayya, E. Suleiman, G. Weisgerber and A. Hauptmann

1990 Tell Wadi Feinan: The First Pottery Neolithic Tell in the South of Jordan. *Annual of the Department of Antiquities of Jordan* 34: 27–56.

Neef, R.

2004 Vegetation and Plant Husbandry. In H. Nissen, M. Muheisen and H.G. Gebel (eds.), *Basta I. The Human Ecology*, 187–218. Biblioteca neolithica Asiae meridionalis et occidentalis. Berlin: ex oriente.

Nissen, H.

1993 The PPNC, the Sheep and the 'Hiatus Palestinian'. *Paléorient* 19: 177–183.

Nissen, H., M. Muheisen and H.G. Gebel

1987 Report on the First Two Seasons of Excavation at Basta (1986–1987). *Annual of the Department of Antiquities of Jordan* 31: 79–119.

1991 Report on the Excavations at Basta 1988. *Annual of the Department of Antiquities of Jordan* 35: 13–40.

Nissen, H., M. Muheisen, and H.G. Gebel (eds.)

2004a *Basta I. The Human Ecology. biblioteca neolithica Asiae meridionalis et occidentalis.* Berlin: ex oriente.

2004b Editor's Introduction. In H. Nissen, M. Muheisen, and H.G. Gebel (eds.), *Basta I. The Human Ecology*, 7–34. Biblioteca neolithica Asiae meridionalis et occidentalis. Berlin: ex oriente.

Olszewski, D.

1994 The PPN Glossed Blades from Ain Ghazal, Jordan (1982–85 and 1988–89 Seasons). In H.G. Gebel and S.K. Kozlowski (eds.), *Neolithic Chipped Stone Industries of the Fertile Crescent*, 467–478. Berlin: ex oriente.

Palumbo, G.

1992 The 1990 Wadi al-Yabis Survey Project and Soundings at Khirbat Umm el-Hedamus. *Annual of the Department of Antiquities of Jordan* 36: 25–41.

Palumbo, G., J. Mabry and I. Kuijt

1990 The Wadi at-Yabis Survey: Report on the 1989 Field Season. *Annual of the Department of Antiquities of Jordan* 34: 95–118.

Perrot, J.

1993 Remarques Introductives. *Paléorient* 19: 9–21.

Peterson, J.

2000 Test Excavations at PPNB/PPNC Khirbet Hammam, Wadi el-Hasa, Jordan. *Neo-Lithics* 1/00: 4–6.

Pirie, A.

2001 Wadi Faynan 16 Chipped Stone: PPNA Variability at One Site. *Neo-Lithics* 2/01: 5–9.

Quintero, L.

1996 Flint Mining in the Pre-Pottery Neolithic: Preliminary Report on the Exploitation of Flint at Neolithic 'Ayn Ghazal in Highland Jordan. In S. Kozlowski and H.G. Gebel (eds.), *Neolithic Chipped Stone Industries of the Fertile Crescent and their Contemporaries in Adjacent Regions*, 233–242. Berlin: ex oriente.

1998 *Evolution of Lithic Economies in the Levantine Neolithic: Development and Demise of Naviform Core Technology.* Unpublished PhD dissertation, Department of Anthropology, University of California-Riverside.

Quintero, L. and I. Köhler-Rollefson

1997 The 'Ain Ghazal Dog: A Case for the Neolithic Origin of *Canis familiaris* in the Near East. In H.G. Gebel, Z. Kafafi and G. Rollefson (eds.), *The Prehistory of Jordan II: Perspectives from 1996*, 567–574. Berlin: ex oriente.

Quintero, L. and P. Wilke

1995 Evolution and Economic Significance of Naviform Core-and-Blade Technology in the Southern Levant. *Paléorient* 21: 17–34.

Quintero, L., P. Wilke and J. Waines

1997 Pragmatic Studies of Near Eastern Neolithic Sickle Blades. In H.G. Gebel, Z. Kafafi and G.O. Rollefson (eds.), *The Prehistory of Jordan II : Perspectives from 1997*, 263–286. Berlin: ex oriente.

Raikes, T.

1980 Notes on Some Neolithic and Later Sites in Wadi Araba and the Dead Sea Valley. *Levant* 12: 40–60.

Roehrer-Ertl, O., K.-W. Frey and H. Newseley

1988 Preliminary Note on Early Neolithic Human Remains from Basta and Sabra. In A. Garrard and H.G. Gebel (eds.), *The Prehistory of Jordan,* 135–136. British Archaeological Reports International Series 396, Oxford: British Archaeological Reports.

Rollefson, G.

1983 Ritual and Ceremony at Neolithic Ain Ghazal (Jordan). *Paléorient* 9: 29–38.

1986 Neolithic Ain Ghazal (Jordan): Ritual and Ceremony II. *Paléorient* 12: 45–52.

1987 Local and Regional Relations in the Levantine PPN Period: Ain Ghazal, Jordan, as a Regional Centre. In A. Hadidi (ed.), *Studies in the History and Archaeology of Jordan III,* 29–32. Amman: Department of Antiquities.

1988 Stratified Burin Classes at 'Ain Ghazal: Implications for the Desert Neolithic of Jordan, In A. Garrard and H.G. Gebel (eds.), *The Prehistory of Jordan,* 437–449. British Archaeological Reports International Series 396. Oxford: British Archaeological Reports.

1989 The Late Aceramic Neolithic of the Levant: A Synthesis. *Paléorient* 15: 168–173.

1990a Neolithic Chipped Stone Technology at 'Ain Ghazal, Jordan: The Status of the PPNC Phase. *Paléorient* 16: 119–124.

1990b The Uses of Plaster at Neolithic 'Ain Ghazal, Jordan. *Archeomaterials* 4: 33–54.

1993 The Origins of the Yarmoukian at 'Ain Ghazal, *Paléorient* 19: 91–100.

1995 Burin Variability at Neolithic 'Ayn Ghazal, Jordan. In K. Amr, F. Zayadine and M. Zaghloul (eds.), *Studies in the History and Archaeology of Jordan V,* 515–518. Amman: Department of Antiquities.

1996 Abu Hudhud (WHS 1008): An EPPNB Settlement in the Wadi el-Hasa, Southern Jordan. In S. Kozlowski and H.G. Gebel (eds.), *Neolithic Chipped Stone Industries of the Fertile Crescent and their Contemporaries in Adjacent Regions,* 159–160. Berlin: ex oriente.

1997a Changes in Architecture and Social Organization at 'Ain Ghazal. In H.G. Gebel, Z. Kafafi and G. Rollefson (eds.), *The Prehistory of Jordan II: Perspectives from 1997,* 287–308. Berlin: ex oriente.

1997b A Further Note on the Blade: Blade Ratio as a Neolithic Phase Discriminator. *Neo-Lithics* 1/97: 20.

1998a Expanded Radiocarbon Chronology from 'Ain Ghazal. *Neo-Lithics* 2/98: 8–10.

1998b Neolithic 'Ain Ghazal: Ritual and Ceremony III. *Paléorient* 24: 43–58.

2000 Ritual and Social Organization at Neolithic 'Ain Ghazal. In I. Kuijt (ed.), *Life in Neolithic Farming Villages,* 165–190. New York: Kluwer Academic/Plenum.

2001 The Neolithic Period. In B. MacDonald, R. Adams, and P. Bienkowski (eds.), *Archaeology of Jordan,* 67–105. Sheffield: Sheffield Academic Press.

2002 Bead-Making Tools from LPPNB al-Basît, Jordan. *Neo-Lithics* 2/02: 5–7.

2005 Emerging Complexity in LPPNB Social Organization. In Bienert, H.-D., H.G. Gebel and R. Neef (eds.), *Central Settlements in Neolithic Jordan.* Berlin: ex oriente.

Rollefson, G., M. Forstadt and R. Beck

1994 A Preliminary Typology of Scrapers, Knives and Borers from 'Ain Ghazal. In H.G. Gebel and S. Kozlowski (eds.), *Neolithic Chipped Stone Industries of the Fertile Crescent,* 445–466, Berlin: ex oriente.

Rollefson, G. and Z. Kafafi

1985 Khirbat Hammam: A PPNB Village in die Wadi el-Hasa, Southern Jordan. *Bulletin of the American Schools of Oriental Research* 258: 63–69.

1994 The 1993 Season at 'Ain Ghazal: Preliminary Report. *Annual of the Department of Antiquities of Jordan* 38: 11–32.

1996 The 1995 Season at 'Ayn Ghazal: Preliminary Report. *Annual of the Department of Antiquities of Jordan* 40: 11–28.

1997 The 1996 Season at 'Ayn Ghazal: Preliminary Report. *Annual of the Department of Antiquities of Jordan* 41: 27–48.

Rollefson, G. and I. Köhler-Rollefson

1989 The Collapse of Early Neolithic Settlements in the Southern Levant. In I. Hershkovitz: (ed.), *People and Cultures in Change,* 73–89. British Archaeological Reports International Series 508. Oxford: British Archaeological Reports.

1992 Early Neolithic Exploitation Patterns in the Levant: Cultural Impact on the Environment. *Population and Environment* 13: 243–254.

1993 PPNC Adaptations in the First Half of the 6th Millennium bc. *Paléorient* 19: 33–42.

Rollefson, G. and M. Parker

2002 Craft Specialization at al-Basît, Wadi Musa, Southern Jordan. *Neo-Lithics* 1/02: 21–23.

Rollefson, G. and A. Simmons

1986 The Neolithic Village of 'Ain Ghazal, Jordan: Preliminary Report on the 1984 Season. *Bulletin of the American Schools of Oriental Research Supplement* 24: 145–164.

1987 The Life and Death of Ain Ghazal. *Archaeology* 40: 38–45.

Rollefson, G., Z. Kafafi and A. Simmons

1990 The Neolithic Village of 'Ain Ghazal: Preliminary Report on the 1988 Season. *Bulletin of the American Schools of Oriental Research Supplement* 27: 95–116.

Rollefson, G., L. Quintero and P. Wilke

1999 Bawwab al-Ghazal: Preliminary Report on the Testing Season 1998. *Neo-Lithics* 1/99: 2–4.

Rollefson, G., D. Schmandt-Besserat and J. Rose

1999 A Decorated Skull from MPPNB Ain Ghazal. *Paléorient* 24: 99–104.

Rollefson, G., A. Simmons and Z. Kafafi

1992 Neolithic Cultures at Ain Ghazal, Jordan. *Journal of Field Archaeology* 19: 443–470.

Ronen A. and M. Lechevallier

1999 Save the Khiamian! *Neo-Lithics* 1/99: 2–3.

Sayej, G.

2004a Lithic Production at the Pre-Pottery Neolithic A Site of Zahrat adh-Dhra' and Its Context. *Studies in the History and Archaeology of Jordan VIII*, 379–387. Amman: Department of Antiquities.

2004b The Lithic Industries of Zahrat adh-Dhra' 2and the Pre-Pottery Neolithic Period of Southern Jordan. Unpublished PhD thesis, Department of Archaeology, La Trobe University, La Trobe, Australia.

Schmandt-Besserat, D.

1997 Animal Symbols at Ain Ghazal. *Expedition* 39: 48–58.

1998 A Stone Metaphor for Creation. *Near Eastern Archaeology* 61: 109–117.

al-Shiyab, A.H.

1997 Animal Remains from 'Ain Rahub. In H.G. Gebel, Z. Kafafi and G. Rollefson (eds.), *Prehistory of Jordan II: Perspectives from 1997*, 593–600. Berlin: ex oriente.

Simmons, A. and M. Najjar

1996 Current Investigations at Ghwair I, a Neolithic Settlement in Southern Jordan. *Neo-Lithics* 2/96: 6–7.

2000 Preliminary Report on the 1999–2000 Excavation Season at the Pre-Pottery Neolithic Settlement of Ghwair I, Southern Jordan. *Neo-Lithics* 1/00: 6–8.

2002 Preliminary Report of the Tell Wadi Feinan Neolithic Testing Project. *Neo-Lithics* 1/02: 19–21.

Simmons, A., Z. Kafafi, G. Rollefson and K. Moyer

1989 Test Excavations at Wadi Shu'ayb, a Major Neolithic Settlement in Central Jordan. *Annual of the Department of Antiquities of Jordan* 33: 27–42.

Simmons, A., A. Boulton, C. Butler, Z. Kafafi and G. Rollefson

1990 A Plastered Human Skull from Neolithic 'Ain Ghazal, Jordan. *Journal of Field Archaeology* 17–1: 107–10.

Simmons, A., G. Rollefson, Z. Kafafi, R. Mandel, M. an-Nahar, J. Cooper, I. Köhler-Rollefson and K. Durand

2001 Wadi Shu'eib, A Large Neolithic Community in Central Jordan: Final Report of Test Investigations. *Bulletin of the American Schools of Oriental Research* 321: 1–39.

Tubb, K. and C. Grissom

1995 'Ayn Ghazal: A Comparative Study of the 1983 and 1985 Statuary Caches. In K. Amr, F. Zayadine and M. Zaghloul (eds.), *Studies in the History and Archaeology of Jordan V*, 515–518. Amman: Department of Antiquities.

Von den Driesch, A. and U. Wodtke

1997 The Fauna of 'Ain Ghazal, a Major PPN and Early PN Settlement in Central Jordan. In H.G. Gebel, Z. Kafafi and G. Rollefson (eds.), *Prehistory of Jordan II: Perspectives from 1997*, 511–556. Berlin: ex oriente.

Waheeb, M. and N. Fino

1997 'Ayn el-Jammam: A Neolithic Site near Ras en-Naqb, Southern Jordan. In H.G. Gebel, Z. Kafafi and G. Rollefson (eds.), *The Prehistory of Jordan II: Perspectives from 1997*, 215–220. Berlin: ex oriente.

Wasse, A.

1997 Preliminary Results of an Analysis of Sheep and Goat Bones from 'Ain Ghazal, Jordan. In H.G. Gebel, Z. Kafafi and G.O. Rollefson (eds.), *The Prehistory of Jordan II: Perspectives from 1997*, 575–592. Berlin: ex oriente.

2000 *The Development of Goat and Sheep Herding During the Levantine Neolithic.* Unpublished PhD thesis, Institute of Archeology. London: University College London.

Wasse, A., and G. Rollefson

2005 The Wadi Sirhan Project: Report on the 2002 Archaeological Reconnaissance of Wadi Hudruj and Jabal Tharwa. *Levant* 37: 1–20.

Weinstein, J.

1984 Radiocarbon Dating in the Southern Levant. *Radiocarbon* 26: 297–366.

Weninger, B., O. Jöris, and U. Danzeglocke.

2004 *The Cologne Radiocarbon Calibration & Paleoclimate Research Package.* http://www.calpal-online.de/

Wilke, P. and L. Quintero

1994 Naviform Core-and-Blade Technology: Assemblage Character as Determined by Replicative Experiments. In H.G. Gebel and S.K. Kozlowski (eds.), *Neolithic Chipped Stone Industries of the Fertile Crescent*, 33–60. Berlin: ex oriente.

Wilke, P., L. Quintero and G. Rollefson

1997 Bawwab el-Ghazal: A Temporary Station of Hunting Pastoralists in the Eastern Jordanian Desert. *Neo-Lithics* 3/97: 12–14.

Wright, K., R. Schick and R. Brown

1989 Report on a Preliminary Survey of the Wadi Shu'eib. *Annual of the Department of Antiquities of Jordan* 33: 345–350.

Yakar, R. and I. Hershkovitz

1988 Nahal Hemar. The Modeled Skulls. *'Atiqot* 18: 59–63.

5. The Chalcolithic Period

Stephen J. Bourke

Introduction

Attempting an overview of Chalcolithic material culture from a specifically Jordanian perspective is bedevilled by the uneven coverage of much of the country. Relatively intensive investigation of the Jordan Valley in general, and the site of Tulaylat Ghassul in particular, contrasts with a still superficial knowledge of settlement and landuse in the verdant north/central uplands and the marginal zones to the east and south. An equal consideration of all regions of Jordan is not yet possible, as intensive exploration of upland and marginal zones is still in its infancy.

Nevertheless, there is value in an assessment of the Chalcolithic from a Jordanian perspective, as much of the current debate (Gilead 1988; Levy 1995) on Chalcolithic socio-economic development is sourced almost exclusively to material from sites located in the northern Negev. This skews debate, often to the detriment of much newly discovered data from the central/southeastern Levant (Gopher and Tsuk 1996; Gal *et al.* 1997). A Jordanian perspective will only highlight the need for a more even distribution of research effort, and the limited value of generalizations sourced to a single region of what is both geomorphologically and culturally a sharply dissected landscape.

This being said, any assessment of the Jordanian Chalcolithic will still be dominated by Jordan Valley data, although new work in the uplands to the east (Kamleh 2000; Kafafi and Vieweger 2000; Lovell 2002, 2007), in the copper-rich Faynan region (Levy and Adams *et al.* 2001), and the marginal lands to the south (Khalil *et al.* 2003) will eventually change this picture. Even so, the database is at present unavoidably skewed towards Jordan Valley discoveries, and it should be noted at the outset that this has the potential to downvalue the importance of southern and eastern transhumant groups in the cultural processes identified during this period.

After introductory remarks on history of research and chronology, our procedure will be to outline settlement patterns, economic and subsistence developments, and material cultural remains (including burial customs and trade patterns), initially with reference to the evidence from Tulaylat Ghassul, and then from a Jordan Valley perspective, before integrating observations so derived with the more limited data from upland/marginal areas.

History of Research

Concerted study of the Chalcolithic period in Jordan began with the first excavations at Tulaylat Ghassul. The eight seasons of excavation by the Pontifical Biblical Institute (1929–1938) uncovered spectacular remains of a hitherto little-known Chalcolithic civilization (Mallon *et al.* 1934; Koeppel *et al.* 1940). Mallon and Koeppel distinguished four main phases of occupation (Ghassul I–IV), with the latest (Ghassul IV) spread over some 20 hectares. The failure to investigate the earlier three phases (Ghassul I–III) in any detail and the significance of this omission went largely undetected in the enthusiastic description of the newly discovered Ghassul IV culture, which rapidly became the exemplar for the entire south Levantine Chalcolithic, thereafter known as the Ghassulian culture.

The next major development in Jordanian Chalcolithic studies was the publication of Nelson Glueck's extensive wartime surveys east of the Jordan, which documented the spread of prehistoric settlement throughout the uplands and out into the eastern marginal zones (Glueck 1951), although an uncritical acceptance of Glueck's rapid field identifications led to much subsequent confusion, and the probable over-estimation of upland Chalcolithic settlement intensity. Shortly after Glueck's publication, Henri de Contenson and James Mellaart carried out a much more intensive survey in the Jordan Valley as part of the Point IV Irrigation Project, and sampled seven of the more prominent prehistoric mounds (Leonard 1992). Soundings at Tall Shuna North, Abu Habil, Saidiyya Tahta, Tall Umm Hammad and Ghrubba uncovered a string of well-established Chalcolithic settlements along the eastern edge of the valley, and revealed the presence of both "Ghassulian" and "non-Ghassulian" Chalcolithic assemblages in the northern part of the valley (de Contensen 1960a; Mellaart 1962). The publication of these important discoveries was much delayed and presented piecemeal when finally published, which led to many important observations made at the time being ignored.

As the 1950s unfolded, Mellaart's publication of the Early Chalcolithic Ghrubba material (1956), with its apparent Halafian links and implied population movements down the Wadi Zarqa, and de Contensen's (1961) suggestion that the Early Chalcolithic of Tall Shuna North was no more than "Ghassulian influenced" underlined the need to better understand the early occupational sequence (Ghassul I–III) at the type-site of Tulaylat Ghassul. Responding to this need, North's single season of renewed excavations at Tulaylat Ghassul in 1959/1960 focussed on exploring the early horizons at the site (North 1961). His conclusions appeared unequivocal. North reaffirmed the fourfold division of occupation at the site, and notwithstanding the great depth of occupation documented across the site, claimed no significant difference in culture between the first three phases and the last, flatly denying any evidence for a developmental sequence at the site.

Hennessy's return to Ghassul in 1967 marks a turning point in the study of the Chalcolithic period in Jordan. Planned as a long-term project, excavations were interrupted after a single season by the Arab-Israeli War of that

Figure 5.1   Chalcolithic sites mentioned in the text. See Figure 5.2 for details of the Jordan Valley and surrounding region and Figure 5.3 for southern Israel and the Dead Sea Region of Jordan.

year. Even so, Hennessy's findings were revolutionary, and totally unexpected in the light of North's then quite recent pronouncements. Hennessy (1969) described a nine-stage sequence, and outlined a clear cultural progression from basal deposits which he characterized as a local manifestation of the Jericho ceramic Neolithic (Lovell 2001b). Hennessy concluded that the Ghassulian culture developed smoothly out of this local Late Neolithic precursor, passing through readily distinguished developmental stages, before culminating in the well known Classic Ghassulian culture so brilliantly revealed by Pontifical Biblical excavators.

In the years immediately after the Six-Day War, Hennessy's conclusions were rapidly assimilated into the doctoral literature of a "younger brigade" of scholars (Moore, Lee and Elliot), although established researchers (Perrot, Kenyon, Lapp and Mellaart) continued to view the Ghassulian as a short-lived foreign inspired culture. A growing knowledge of Late Neolithic culture at Jericho allowed Moore (1973) to establish convincing links between the stone tool traditions of Jericho and Ghassul, which outweighed vague ceramic links with the Syro-Mesopotamian northeast. At the same time, a "Northern Chalcolithic" culture was codified in both assemblage and distribution by de Vaux (1966). Soon after, Kaplan (1969) reinforced de Vaux's advocacy of an indigenous origin for this "Northern Chalcolithic" by nominating the newly codified Wadi Rabah Neolithic as the likely parent, an impression Kirkbride (1969) and Copeland's (1969) survey work in the Lebanese Baqaa, and Dunand's research at Byblos (1973), was held to support. As Kaplan viewed Late Neolithic Jericho as a degenerate variety of the Wadi Rabah Neolithic, once Moore (1973) had linked the basal Ghassul assemblage to the Jericho Late Neolithic, an indigenous origin for the Ghassulian seemed inescapable.

The great changes in the political landscape after the Six-Day War prompted renewed interest in regional survey. Although opportunistic small-scale surveys had begun to exploit Glueck's database in the late 1950s and early 1960s, it was Mittmann's North Jordan Survey that began the systematic checking of Glueck's database in the uplands of the North Jordan Plateau (Mittmann 1970; Boling 1988; Kamleh 2000). This revealed a strictly limited Chalcolithic presence in the western uplands, along the wadi systems. The documentation of settled agricultural communities in some numbers on the plateau threw into sharp focus the need to determine the relationship (if any) between the Jordan Valley and Upland Plateau settlements.

As conditions normalized in the Jordan Valley in 1975, the intensive Joint Survey Project (Ibrahim *et al.* 1976; Ibrahim *et al.* 1988) did for the Jordan Valley floor what Mittmann had done for the plateau, doubling the number of sites known from earlier Point IV days. The JSP began

to illustrate the close relationship of Chalcolithic site clusters and the lateral wadi systems linking the valley and the plateau, whilst at the same time contrasting Chalcolithic settlement patterns with those of the succeeding Early Bronze Age. Hereafter, intensive survey of the Jordan Valley lateral wadi systems began to "knit together" the often large valley-base settlements, smaller foothill settlements and the little-known upland sites into what are arguably regional associations (Betts 1992).

At the same time, survey work in the West/Central (Hesban 1973–76: Ibach 1987) and Southern Plateau (Central/Southern Moab 1978–82: Miller [ed.] 1991) regions and in the Wadi Arabah (East Arabah/Faynan 1978–79: Raikes 1980) intensified, revealing scattered Chalcolithic settlements throughout the uplands and along the lateral wadis running into the northern Wadi Arabah and south Jordan Valleys. Of particular importance was intensified work in the Fidan/Faynan wadi systems, focusing on the large copper deposits in this region, and intensified work in the South East Dead Sea plain (Expedition to the Dead Sea Plain 1973–74: Rast and Schaub 1974; Arab Potash Company Townships: McCreery 1978/79). Surveys across the southern plateau (Wadi Hasa Survey 1979–83: MacDonald *et al.* 1988), in the Arabah (Southern Ghor and Northeast Arabah Survey 1985–86: MacDonald *et al.* 1992) and in the southern lowlands (Aqaba-Maan Survey 1980–92: Munro *et al.* 1997) intensified during the early 1980s, and continues to the present day.

Whilst expanded survey work gradually began to reveal the distribution of Chalcolithic settlements throughout the verdant west uplands, along with some form of presence out into the marginal zones, renewed excavations began to collect the physical evidence needed to address the strengthening economic/environmental concerns of the 1970s and early 1980s. The single most important development for Chalcolithic studies was Hennessy's return to Tulaylat Ghassul.

After relocating from Jerusalem to Sydney, Hennessy led three seasons of renewed excavations at Tulaylat Ghassul between 1975 and 1977 (Hennessy 1982). It was during these seasons that he greatly expanded the size of trenches into the earliest phases of occupation at Ghassul, which strengthened his first impressions of a Neolithic ancestry for the Ghassulian, and allowed him to outline a meticulously stratified "pre-Classic" Ghassulian sequence (Bourke 1997b). However, the Sydney expedition is probably best known for the discovery of the Late Chalcolithic Sanctuary complex on the southwestern fringe of the site (Seaton 2000, 2006), and the famous polychrome figured "Processional" wall painting (Hennessy 1978; Cameron 1981). Hennessy's suggested indigenous Late Neolithic origin for the Ghassulian culture is now widely accepted (Mazar 1990; Gilead 1990; Stager 1992; Levy 1993; Lovell 2001b).

The decade of the 1980s saw a flowering of new projects

researching Chalcolithic settlements in the Jordan Valley. The more prominent were Hanbury-Tenison's on Jabal Sartaba (1980–83) as part of the Pella Excavation Project, Leonard's at Katarit al-Samra (1982), Helms' at Tall Umm Hammad (1982–84), Gustaveson-Gaube's problematic excavations at Tall Shuna North (1984–85), and most importantly Dollfus and Kafafi's excavations at Abu Hamid (1986–92). The first two projects (Jabal Sartaba, Tall Umm Hammad) concentrated on latest Chalcolithic deposits (Hanbury-Tenison 1986; Betts [ed.] 1992). Most published material from Abu Hamid is of a similar date, although there is undoubtedly a very long sequence at the site (Dollfus and Kafafi 1993; Lovell *et al.* 1997, 2004). Gustaveson-Gaube's assemblages from Tall Shuna North should be seen as part of the pre-Ghassulian "Early Chalcolithic" culture discussed by de Contenson (Baird 1987; de Contenson 1960b, 1964; Leonard 1992; Baird and Philip 1994). Together, these projects greatly expanded the Chalcolithic database and promoted a more nuanced assessment of Jordan Valley material culture.

At the same time intensified survey work in the lateral wadis of the east Jordan Valley enriched understanding of Chalcolithic settlement patterns, underscoring the relationship of site location and winter (and perhaps spring) floodwater utilization, employed in tandem with the exploitation of permanent springs. Surveys in the Wadi Arab (1978: Kerestes *et al.* 1977/78; 1983: Hanbury-Tenison *et al.* 1984), Wadi Ziqlab (1981–95: Banning *et al.* 1989, 1996, 1998), Wadi Yabis (1987–92: Mabry and Palumbo 1988, 1992; Palumbo *et al.* 1990), Wadi Sarar (1987–88: Mabry 1989), Wadi Kufranjah (1985: Green 1986), Wadi Zarqa (1978: Kerestes *et al.* 1977/78; 1980–82: Gordon and Villiers 1986), Wadi Nimrin (Simmons *et al.* 1989), the Wadi Hisban (Iktanu Survey 1966–67: Prag 1974; Hesban Survey 1973–74: Ibach 1987), and the Naur-Dead Sea/Wadi Kufrayn (Coughenour 1976) wadi systems developed an increasingly comprehensive view of the relationship of geography and Chalcolithic site location.

The first intensive work in the northern uplands occurred at this time, with surveys of the Irbid-Ramtha (1983–84: Lenzen and McQuitty 1983; Lenzen 1986), Ajlun-Kufranjah (1986: Green 1986), Jarash-Husn (1984: Leonard 1987), Jarash Region (1982–88: Sapin 1992; 1984: Hanbury-Tenison 1987), Baqah Valley (1977–87: McGovern 1989), Ayn Ghazal (1987: Simmons and Kafafi 1992), Greater Amman (1987–88: Abu Dayyah *et al.* 1991) and Sahab (1983–86: Gustaveson-Gaube and Ibrahim 1986) regions the most notable for early period remains. On the eastern periphery, Helms' (1972–76: Betts [ed.] 1991) pioneering Wadi Rajil-Jawa area survey, Betts's more extensive Black Desert Survey (1979–86: Betts 1986), and Garrard's Wadi Jilat Survey (1981–88: Garrard 1998) carried knowledge far into the marginal zones.

The ten years after Hennessy's excavations at Ghassul were marked by several major syntheses important for Chalcolithic studies, among them the final publication of the Jericho Neolithic (Kenyon and Holland 1982, 1983) and Kafafi's (1982) study of the Jordanian Ceramic Neolithic, the collection (and eventual publication) of much of Mellaart's material from Point IV soundings by Leonard (complete 1985, published 1992), Hanbury-Tenison's wide-ranging synthesis of the Jordanian Late Chalcolithic (1986) and Levy's (Levy ed. 1987) first synthetic study of the excavations at Shiqmim. Together, these represented a sea-change in knowledge, for Kafafi and Hanbury-Tenison's syntheses of Jordanian Neolithic and Chalcolithic material created the first thoroughgoing consensus on the extent and nature of these two periods, with which the ever-increasing body of survey and excavation data could be integrated, and against which Palestinian Neolithic and Chalcolithic discoveries could be viewed.

Excavations in the Jordan Valley over the last fifteen years has tended to be relatively small scale problem-oriented studies at previously investigated sites. Among these, renewed work at Tall Shuna North (1991–1994: Baird and Philip 1994), deep soundings on the main Tall of Pella (1992–97: Bourke *et al.* 1998, 2003) and renewed work at Tulaylat Ghassul (1994–99: Bourke *et al.* 1995, 2000, in press) may be highlighted. Work on the plateau has been more restricted but grows steadily. Ibrahim's pioneering soundings at Sahab, southeast of Amman (1972–77) began detailed work on the Chalcolithic in that region (Ibrahim 1984). This was strengthened by Amr and Najjar's work northeast of Amman at Wadi Qattar (1989; Amr *et al.* 1993), Kerner's work further to the east at Abu Snesleh (1990–92: Kerner *et al.* 1992), and Ji's work in the northwest at Iraq al-Amir (1997; Ji and Lee 1999, 2000, 2002). Najjar's excavations at Tall Wadi Faynan (1988; Najjar *et al.* 1990) began exploration of the Neolithic/Chalcolithic strata at what is probably the central settlement in the crucial Faynan copper ore region, although Hauptmann's important metallurgical analyses had been going on for some time (1984–88; Hauptmann 2000). Exploration of the Faynan region intensified throughout the 1990s, with several large projects exploring the region (Barker *et al.* 1997, 1998; Wright *et al.* 1998; Simmons and Najjar 1997; Adams 1999; Levy and Adams *et al.* 2001). Henry's soundings at the Judayid Basin sites of Quaysa and Jill (1979–83: Henry 1995), Hart's at Khirbat Qurayn North (1985: Hart 1987) and Khalil's more substantial investigations at Magass (1985–95: Khalil 1987, 1995; 1998–2003: Khalil and Eichmann 1999, 2001; Khalil *et al.* 2003) began concentrated work on the great variety of Chalcolithic cultures in the south, whilst Betts" soundings at Hibr (1989: Betts 1992) and survey work in the Black Desert (Betts [ed.] 1998), did the same for the eastern marginal zones. Rollefson's intensive prehistoric surveys in the Azraq Wetlands (2000: Rollefson *et al.* 2001) completes this picture of marginal zone occupation.

Recent survey work has become more tightly focussed, and increasingly constitutes urgent rescue work ahead of roadworks and industrial/housing developments. Surveys along the Wadi Ajib in the far northeast (Betts *et al.* 1995, 1996), the Pella Hinterland (Watson 2004, 2006; Watson and O'Hea 1996), the Zarqa headwaters (Palumbo *et al.* 1996; Kafafi *et al.* 1997; Caneva *et al.* 2001), the Hesban uplands (Prag 1991; Ji and Lee 1999, 2000, 2002), the eastern Dead Sea shore (Amr *et al.* 1996), the central/east Kerak plateau (Mattingly 1996), the south lowlands (Bisheh *et al.* 1993; Waheeb 1996) and the southern plateau (MacDonald 2004; MacDonald *et al.* 2000, 2001, 2002) cover a wide range of environments, many under imminent threat. This inevitably results in an ever-more uneven coverage. Surveys typically sample the urban fringe and the pristine far horizons, while ignoring the perhaps compromised but less threatened middle distance. The institution of a long-term Cultural Resource Management program in 1987, along with the development of the Jordan Antiquities Database and Information System site list (JADIS: Palumbo 1994; Savage 2007), will be crucial in counterbalancing the flood of emergency rescue work with a long-term program of intensified regional survey.

A major trend in recent times has been the increased employment of technical/analytical studies. Ceramic and metallographic studies have been revolutionized by petrographic, chemical and technological studies (Roux and Courty 1997; Rehren *et al.* 1997). Petrographic, chemical and use-wear studies on ground and flake stone assemblages seek data on quarry sources, manufacturing technique and function (Philip and Williams-Thorpe 2000, 2001; Quintero *et al.* 2002). After much preliminary survey, detailed investigation of the Faynan copper sources will soon provide a reliable archaeological background to the Bochum Museum's metallurgical studies (Hauptmann 2000; Adams 1999; Levy and Adams *et al.* 2001). A heightened awareness of the need to document the economic underpinnings of Chalcolithic society has given a new prominence to geochemical, climatalogical, zoological and botanical studies (Neef 1990; Hourani 2002; Fall *et al.* 1998; Falconer *et al.* 2003; Meadows 2004). Cross-cultural analysis is now more commonly sourced to a suite of radiometric dates than a ceramic typological analysis (Braun 2001; Bourke *et al.* 2001, 2004; Burton and Levy 2001). Sharp sub-regional assemblage variability and differential rates of culture change are generally acknowledged factors in the increasingly dissected cultural landscapes of Chalcolithic Jordan (Kerner 2001; Lovell 2001a; Blackham 2002).

Even though research efforts remain dominated by Jordan Valley data, excavation of upland and marginal zone settlements steadily grows, and will inevitably allow for a more balanced summary of Chalcolithic settlement data than currently possible. Adequate coverage of the Jordan Valley is certainly possible today, but even allowing for the increasing activity outside the Valley, no more than an impression of regional settlement patterns is currently available. The summary offered below is neither definitive nor synthetic, rather an impression of work very much in progress.

Relative and Absolute Chronology

There is no demonstrable link between the historical chronologies of Egypt or Mesopotamia and the Chalcolithic of Jordan. There are a variety of local south Canaanite objects that some feel reflect knowledge of the predynastic cultures of Egypt (Commenge and Alon 2002), and even more tenuous parallels with Syro-Mesopotamian prehistoric assemblages have been drawn from time to time (Kaplan 1960). Vague cultural parallels provide insufficient evidence on which to base even a rudimentary relative chronology. Regional relative chronologies must be sourced to radiometric data, but until very recently the number of dates available for the south Levantine Chalcolithic were too concentrated on the Negev for widespread application outside that area (Levy 1992; Gilead 1994). However, the situation has changed significantly over the last ten years, as the steady rise in the number of analytical studies sourced to radiocarbon dates illustrates (Joffe and Dessel 1995; Burton and Levy 2001).

A select list of Jordanian radiocarbon determinations, along with a restricted number from adjacent regions for comparative purposes can be found in Table 5.1. It is now generally accepted that the Jordanian Chalcolithic develops relatively smoothly out of the local Late Neolithic cultures. Broadly speaking, the vast majority of Jordanian Chalcolithic assemblages fall within the late seventh/sixth millennium BP or the fifth/early fourth millennium cal BC, the cultural phasing being roughly delimited by the large suite of Late Neolithic dates from Wadi Ziqlab 200 (Banning *et al.* 1996) and a comparable suite of early Early Bronze I dates from Tall Shuna North (Bronk Ramsey *et al.* 2002).

From the radiometric determinations in Table 5.1, it can be seen that any attempt to divide the Jordanian Chalcolithic into multiple sub-phases is premature. There is currently little radiometric support for discerning a "post-Ghassulian" phase within the Jordanian sequence (contra Hanbury-Tenison 1986: 117–118), although there is some (albeit controversial) support for a "post-Ghassulian" afterglow in the northern Negev and West Dead Sea area (Gilead 1994; Joffe and Dessel 1995; Burton and Levy 2001). There is strong radiometric support for defining a "pre-Ghassulian" cultural phase at Tulaylat Ghassul (Bourke *et al.* 2001, 2004b) and Abu Hamid (Lovell *et al.* 1997, 2004) in the south, and at Pella (Bourke *et al.* 2003, 2004a) and Tall Shuna North (Bronk

Site	Site Phase	Lab	Date b.p.	Date B.C.	Period
Ziqlab 200	E33	TO-3409	6900 ± 70	5740	Late Neo
Nizzanim	Early Neo	Hv-8509	6740 ± 90	5620	Late Neo
Tsaf	I	RT-508A	6720 ± 460	5590	Late Neo
Ziqlab 200	F34	TO-3411	6670 ± 60	5560	Late Neo
Chagar Bazar	Level 11/12	P-1487	6665 ± 75	5550	Late Halaf
Tall Laylan	Period VIa	UM-1817	6580 ± 100	5480	Early Ubaid
Wadi Faynan	Prof. B	HD-10567	6410 ± 115	5350	Late Neo
Ziqlab 200	G34	TO-3412	6380 ± 70	5320	Late Neo
Wadi Faynan	Prof. B	HD-12335	6360 ± 45	5300	Late Neo
Ziqlab 200	E33	TO-3410	6350 ± 70	5275	Late Neo
Abu Hamid	Lower	Ly-6174	6200 ± 80	5165	Late Neo
Ziqlab 200	E33	TO-3408	6190 ± 70	5135	Late Neo
Abu Hamid	Lower	Ly-6254	6190 ± 55	5135	Late Neo
Abu Hamid	Lower	Ly-6255	6160 ± 70	5100	Late Neo
Abu Hamid	Lower	Ly-6259	6135 ± 80	5075	Late Neo
H Turkman	Period IVB	GrN-13038	6110 ± 80	5060	Late Ubaid
Wadi Faynan	Baulk	HD-12338	6110 ± 75	5050	Neo/Early Chalc
Ras Shamra	Period IIIC	P-389	6100 ± 175	5020	Post-Halaf
Qatif Y3	Late Neo	PTA-2968	6040 ± 80	4930	Late Neo
Abu Hamid	Middle ?	GrN-16357	6030 ± 60	4920	Neo/Early Chalc
Sukas	G11: layer 58	K-936	5910 ± 100	4860	Neo/Early Chalc
Ghassul	AXI 10.15	OZD 025	5900 ± 70	4850	Late Neo
Ghassul	AXI 9.37	OZD 026	5850 ± 115	4740	Late Neo
Ghassul	AXI 13.7	OZD 024	5790 ± 85	4685	Late Neo
Turkman	Period IVB	GrN-13041	5760 ± 80	4670	Late Ubaid
Shiqmim	Upper Vill.	RT-649B	5750 ± 180	4660	Early/Late Chalc
Merimda	Early	W-4355	5750 ± 100	4660	Early Chalc
Pella	32D 42.37	OZD 020	5750 ± 65	4660	Early Chalc
Abu Hamid	Upper ?	GrN-16358	5745 ± 35	4650	Early/Late Chalc
Ziqlab 200	Area A	TO-1086	5740 ± 110	4625	Early/Late Chalc
Wadi Faynan	Sq. A loc.23	HD-12337	5740 ± 35	4625	Early/Late Chalc
Pella	32F 17.18	OZD 022	5730 ± 85	4615	Early Chalc
Pella	32D 80.3	OZD 018	5725 ± 85	4610	Early Chalc
Jabal Quaysa	J24	SMU-804	5720 ± 150	4605	Early/Late Chalc
Shiqmim	Phase IV	OxA-2523	5710 ± 140	4600	Early/Late Chalc
Abu Hamid	Upper ?	GrN-14623	5670 ± 40	4570	Early/Late Chalc
Abu Hamid	Middle	Ly-6249	5655 ± 210	4580	Early Chalc
Pella	28A 44.7	OZD 021	5655 ± 90	4580	Early Chalc
Golan	Site 21	RT-1864	5655 ± 60	4555	Early/Late Chalc
Abu Hamid	Upper ?	GrN-17496	5650 ± 40	4550	Early/Late Chalc
Abu Hamid	Middle	Ly-6248	5650 ± 75	4550	Early Chalc
Ghassul	GII 66.55	OZD 031	5605 ± 80	4510	Early Chalc
Abu Hamid	Middle	Ly-6251	5580 ± 95	4485	Early Chalc
Ghassul	AXI 11.14	OZD 028	5580 ± 65	4485	Early Chalc
Pella	32F 16.2	OZG 609	5580 ± 50	4485	Early Chalc
Ghassul	GII 64.4	OZD 032	5575 ± 70	4480	Early Chalc
Ghassul	QI 13.1	OZD 030	5550 ± 165	4455	Late Chalc
Shiqmim	Phase IV	OxA-2526	5540 ± 150	4445	Late Chalc
Thawwab	"Post-Neo"	GrN-15192	5540 ± 110	4445	Late Chalc
Golan	Faras Silo	RT-718	5540 ± 110	4445	Late Chalc
Shiqmim	Phase III	OxA-2521	5530 ± 130	4435	Late Chalc
Ghassul	N I 11.7	OZD 029	5525 ± 90	4430	Late Chalc
Ghassul	GII 55.11	OZD 033	5455 ± 60	4350	Late Chalc
Abu Snesleh	Chalc	Hv-20791	5445 ± 195	4340	Late Chalc
Gilat	Phase III	RT-860A	5440 ± 180	4335	Late Chalc
Nahal Qanah	Gold Dep.	RT-861E	5440 ± 100	4335	Late Chalc
Pella	Area XIV	SUA-2391	5430 ± 60	4325	Late Chalc
Bir Safadi	Lower	M-864A	5420 ± 350	4315	Late Chalc
Shiqmim	Phase III	OxA-2525	5385 ± 130	4280	Late Chalc
Qalat Mudiq	Layer IV	IRPA-168	5380 ± 210	4275	Late Ubaid
Wadi Faynan	Sq.A loc.8	HD-12336	5375 ± 30	4270	Late Chalc
Shiqmim	Phase II	RT-859D	5370 ± 180	4265	Late Chalc
Ghassul	GIII 10.10	OZD 034	5340 ± 70	4235	Late Chalc
Ghassul	A II	GrN-15194	5330 ± 25	4220	Late Chalc
Abu Hamid	Middle ?	Ly-6257	5325 ± 140	4215	Late Chalc
Hemamieh	Badarian	WSU-1728	5290 ± 130	4180	Badarian
Horvat Beter	Early	W-254	5280 ± 150	4170	Late Chalc
Bir Safadi	Middle	M-864B	5270 ± 300	4160	Late Chalc
Harbush	Golani	RT-525	5270 ± 140	4160	Late Chalc
Ghassul	E XXIII	GrN-15195	5270 ± 100	4160	Late Chalc
Merimda	Late	WSU-1846	5260 ± 90	4150	Early Delta
Shiqmim	Phase I	RT-554A	5250 ± 140	4140	Late Chalc
Abu Hamid	Upper ?	Ly-6258	5205 ± 95	4100	Late Chalc
Tall Shuna N.	E II 43	GrN-15200	5125 ± 25	4020	Late Chalc
Bir Safadi	Upper	M-864C	5120 ± 350	4015	Late Chalc
Tall Shuna N.	E I 12/3	GrN-15199	5115 ± 25	4010	Late Chalc
Ghassul	A II (Baulk)	GrN-15196	5110 ± 90	4005	Late Chalc
Horvat Beter	Late	PTA-4312b	5100 ± 130	3995	Late Chalc
Hab.Kabira	Uruk	GrN-00000	5085 ± 65	3980	Early Uruk
Shiqmim	Phase I	OxA-2520	5060 ± 140	3950	Late Chalc
Naqada KH1	Early Naq.	SMU-360	5030 ± 100	3920	Naqada I
Naqada NT	Early Naq.	WSU-2257	4990 ± 80	3880	Naqada I
Naqada KH3	Early Naq.	TX-2340	4970 ± 70	3860	Naqada I
Harbush	Golan	RT-1862	4945 ± 65	3830	Late Chalc
Shiqmim	Phase I	RT-1339	4940 ± 70	3825	Late Chalc
Maadi	Early	KN-3574	4940 ± 60	3825	Late Delta
Nahal Mishmar	Hoard Mat	W-1341	4880 ± 250	3760	Late Chalc
Maadi	Early	R-1425	4860 ± 70	3740	Late Delta
Harbush	Golan	RT-1866	4810 ± 90	3690	Late Chalc
Gilat	Phase II	RT-860B	4800 ± 135	3680	Late Chalc
Hierakonpolis	Site 29	WIS-1183	4800 ± 75	3680	Naqada II
Mishmar	Hoard Mat	I-285	4780 ± 100	3660	Late Chalc
Hierakonpolis	Site 29	WIS-1169	4760 ± 80	3640	Naqada II

Table 5.1   Radiocarbon dates for the Jordanian Chalcolithic.

Ramsey *et al.* 2002) in the north. From a south Levantine perspective, the Jordanian Chalcolithic should be seen as later than the Qatifian (Kuijt and Chesson 2003), and the early phases of the Munhata/Rabah complex, and contemporaneous with the later Rabah ("Tsafian") and the northern Negev Besoran complexes (Gilead 1988, 1990), although the Negev Beersheban Chalcolithic may extend slightly beyond the timeframe of the Jordanian Ghassulian (Burton and Levy 2001). In the wider world, at least partly contemporary are the Merimda/Omari (Delta) cultures and the Badarian/Naqada I (Valley) cultures in Egypt (Hassan 1985; Hendrickx 2006), the poorly differentiated Syrian Chalcolithic (Hole 2001), and the northern Mesopotamian varieties of the later Ubaid (Joffe 2000).

Settlement Patterns

In spite of the great increase in survey work over the last generation, the record is still largely deficient in detail, published in a most preliminary form, largely uncorrected for geomorphological processes, and biased towards large sites and more visible remains. Even so, a general pattern to settlement distribution can be discerned. Highest settlement densities occur in the Jordan Valley, with a more restricted but still considerable spread into the foothills and the western margins of the upland plateau. Plateau settlements are concentrated either close by the heads of the many lateral wadis leading into the lowlands, or along the margins of the better watered upland valleys. Coverage becomes ever more sparce as one moves farther east and south along the seasonal wadis into more marginal environmental zones.

The Jordan Valley

Major Chalcolithic settlements are positioned on the alluvial fans of the main side wadis that enter the Valley from the uplands to the east. Settlement size seems broadly correlated with the size of associated alluvial fans, and is perhaps more tightly correlated with the subset of this area suitable for floodwater irrigation. Smaller sites are found along the upper courses of each wadi system, larger and more closely packed in the western half, smaller and less numerous the farther east into the uplands one goes. There are no significant settlements between the

Figure 5.2   Detail of Chalcolithic site locations in the Jordan
Valley and surrounding regions.

Wadis Zarqa and Nimrin (Bourke 2002b). The absence
of major lateral wadis between these two main wadi sys-
tems strengthens the argument correlating settlement size
and alluvial floodplain area. There are major Chalcolithic
settlements at Tall Shuna North (Wadi Arab), Tall Fendi
(Wadi Ziqlab), Pella (Wadi Jirm), Tall Abu Habil (Wadi
Yabis), Abu Hamid (Wadi Ajlun), Tall Handaquq North
(Wadi Sarar), Saidiyya Tahta (Wadi Kufranjah), Katarit al-
Samra/Tall Umm Hammad (Wadi Zarqa), Ghrubba/Tall
Ghanam (Wadi Nimrin), Tall Malih (Wadi Kufrayn),
Tulaylat Ghassul (Wadi Ramah/Djaffara) and Tall
Azaymeh (Wadi Azaymeh). This pattern continues south
along the eastern shore of the Dead Sea with Zara 25
(Wadi Ayn Umm Hudayb), Bab adh-Dhra APC (Wadi
Kerak) and Tall Wadi Faynan (Wadi Faynan) the more
prominent settlements.

Overall, there are more than a hundred Chalcolithic
period sites known for the East Jordan Valley alone, with
less than ten percent larger than two hectares. Whilst several sites are quite large (over 10 hectares) and some mid-
sized (around five hectares), there is no clear evidence for
the existence of a settlement system reflecting rank-size
distribution patterns (Bourke 2002b). Given the correlation between site magnitude and associated floodplain
size, and the absence of any clear evidence for pronounced
economic specialization, growth is likely to be correlated
with irrigated agricultural potential. However, where at
least some form of stratification can be inferred, it is associated exclusively with the largest sites (Ghassul, Abu Hamid), which suggests that the largest sites may have served
as cultural (if not necessarily economic) central places.

Of the major settlements, Chalcolithic deposits have
been intensively investigated at Tall Shuna North, Pella,

Abu Hamid and Tulaylat Ghassul, and more limited
soundings have been made at Tall Fendi, Abu Habil, Saidiyya Tahta, Tall Umm Hammad and Ghrubba. Materials
drawn from surface survey, restricted soundings and large
scale area excavations all suggest that the Zarqa/Nimrin
"settlement gap" marks an effective border between relatively distinct Early Chalcolithic cultural assemblages
in the north and south valley, a distinctiveness much
reduced (if not entirely removed) in the Late Chalcolithic
period. It seems likely that the Early Chalcolithic sites of
the north Valley are more closely associated with the later
Rabah/Tsafian complex (Gophna and Sadeh 1988/89;
Garfinkel *et al.* 2006a) than sites in the south. Early Chalcolithic sites of the southern valley have their precursors
in the Early Chalcolithic assemblages at Tulaylat Ghassul (Bourke 1997b), and seem likely to derive from the
cultural mosaic represented by the Jericho Late Neolithic
(Moore 1973), although some maintain that the poorly
defined northern Negev Qatifian culture is a more appropriate parent culture (Goren 1990; Garfinkel 1999; Kuijt
and Chesson 2003).

The Jordanian Uplands and the Marginal Zones

Once the recalibration of Glueck's pottery reading is
noted (for Middle Chalcolithic read Ghassulian, for Late
Chalcolithic read Early Bronze I), the non-intensive format of most early (and some modern) survey projects fac-
tored in, and the tendency to characterise most fourth
millennium upland sites as "Chalcolithic/Early Bronze
Age" (with most turning out to be Early Bronze I when
scrutinized closely), a very superficial survey of the up-
land/inland Chalcolithic would suggest a rough count of
around 140 sites reported in one form or another. Most
are quite small (under a hectare in size), with the vast
majority linked to wadi systems in the western half of the
upland plateau.

There is a cluster of around 25 sites in the northern
uplands, with concentrations on the Irbid/Ramtha Plain
(Lenzen and McQuity 1983) around the largest site of Sal
(Kamleh 2000; Kafafi and Vieweger 2000), some located
along the western escarpment, others along the inland
wadi systems, and a few far into the eastern Harra (Betts
1992; Betts [ed.] 1998) or in the Azraq Oasis (Rollefson *et
al.* 2001). A variety of surveys (Leonard 1987; Hanbury-
Tenison 1987; Sapin 1992) have identified another 10
small sites between Husn and Jarash, 10 more between
Jarash and Amman, and a cluster of around 20 in the
environs of Amman, with Sahab the largest (Ibrahim
1984), and Wadi Qattar (Amr *et al.* 1993)/Abu Snesleh
(Lamprichs 1998; Kerner 2001) smaller sites to the northeast and southwest respectively. All sites of any size are
positioned adjacent to wadis, or at the confluence of two
wadi systems. The Hesban/Madaba Plains survey area has
produced perhaps another 25 sites, most small and clustered along the western escarpment wadis (Ibach 1987;

Mortensen and Thuesen 1998), or located in and around the later Early Bronze tell sites (Harrison 1997). The various Karak Plateau surveys (Miller [ed.] 1991; Mattingly 1996) account for another 10, mostly small and more definitely associated with the western escarpment and the lateral wadis. The East Dead Sea Plains (Rast and Schaub 1974; McCreery 1978/79), the Wadi Hasa and northeast Arabah (MacDonald *et al.* 1988, 1992) and the Wadi Faynan regions (Barker *et al.* 1997, 1998; Simmons and Najjar 1997; Adams 1999; Levy and Adams *et al.* 2001) are linked to another 10–15 sites. Most are small, concentrated in the Faynan/Fidan region, dominated by Tall Wadi Faynan, and even more closely wedded to the eastern wadi systems. The foothills and the lowlands of the Hisma (Henry 1995) reveal a similar number of noticably smaller sites (such as Wadi Quaysa), probably correlated with specialist pastoral activities. Further to the southeast, a cluster of small sites in the Jafr Basin would suggest low-level pastoral activity alongside flint mining on an industrial scale (Quintero *et al.* 2002). Another ten sites can be documented along the Edomite plateau (Hart and Faulkner 1985), with the spring-fed site of Khirbat Qurayn North the largest in the region (Hart 1987). A further 10 sites can be identified in the Aqaba/Maan survey region (Jobling 1989), although all are small and similar in type to those of the Hisma/Jafr regions. Close by the south coast, the surprisingly large site of Tall Magass (Khalil 1995; Khalil and Eichmann 1999, 2001), dominates the Red Sea coastal region. Although some of the material from this site may be Chalcolithic, the majority seems better associated with the Early Bronze IA sites in the Arabah or around Timna (Görsdorf 2002; Kerner 2003; Brückner *et al.* 2002; Khalil *et al.* 2003).

Few upland sites have been investigated in any detail, making material cultural characterization perilous and diachronic analysis impossible. The recent work at Khawarij (Lovell 2007; Lovell *et al.* 2006, in press) provides the first thoroughgoing exploration of northern upland culture. Further south, work at Sahab in particular, Wadi Qattar and Abu Snesleh provide reasonable coverage of the Amman region. Farther to the south, the more isolated activity at Tall Wadi Faynan, Hart's sounding at Khirbat Qurayn North, Henry's detailed characterization of the Hisma Basin sites and Quintero *et al.*'s pioneering work in the Jafr Basin represent small islands of knowledge in an ocean of survey results. Comments below represent the barest of preliminary impressions of an extremely varigated data set.

North Plateau Sites

In the past (Mittmann 1970, Hanbury-Tenison 1986; Boling 1988), the north plateau sites were reported to be a mixture of small settled villages (if close by water sources) or pastoral encampments (if removed from water sources). It is unlikely that site function can be so eas-

ily correlated with permanent water source, although a shifting mosaic of sedentary, nomadic and transhumant lifeways is not unreasonable. Optimal locations are all occupied, and even minor wadi systems are utilized. Some marginal zones are exploited to a limited extent. The impression is one of an even if sparsely occupied landscape, but with no obviously neglected econiches. Material cultural associations are very poorly understood. Ceramics are reported to be predominantly coarse red slipped wares, with painted decoration quite rare (Kamleh 2000; Kafafi and Vieweger 2000). Associations with the Golan Chalcolithic (Epstein 1998) is hinted at by architectural similarities (Lovell *et al.* inpress) and ground stone inventories (Ibrahim and Mittmann 1998), but a comprehensive description of the North Jordanian Upland cultures is yet to be developed.

Epstein (1998) viewed the Golan Chalcolithic culture as a distinct sub-regional grouping, with few links to the better-known Ghassulian of the Jordan Valley. The Golan subsistence regime is dominated by olive cultivation and transhumant pastoralism. Olive cultivation became increasingly important as the Chalcolithic economy developed (Epstein 1993), and settlement studies relate a Late Chalcolithic expansion into the Palestinian uplands with spreading olive cultivation (Finkelstein and Gophna 1993; Fall *et al.* 1998). A similar scenario may well be at least partly applicable to the north Jordanian uplands (Kamleh 2000; Lovell 2002, 2007; Falconer *et al.* 2003). It is possible that the Golan and adjacent Irbid/Ramtha plain settlements are to be associated in one sub-regional unit, with one segment of the society practicing transhumant pastoralism, journeying from the central Golan (Arabic, Jawlan) in summer to the eastern Harra in win-

Figure 5.3   Detail of Chalcolithic site locations in southern Israel and the Dead Sea region of Jordan.

ter, and the balance (particularly in larger sites northeast of Irbid) practicing a sedentary mixed farming regime, enriched by a developing emphasis on horticulture (Bienert and Vieweger 1999, 2000).

Radiocarbon dating for the Golan Chalcolithic (Carmi *et al.* 1995, 1998) would see it confined to the last quarter of the fifth and first half of the fourth millennium cal BC. As latest dates for Rasm Harbush are as late as any south Levantine Chalcolithic settlement site (Burton and Levy 2001), it seems unlikely that the Golan Chalcolithic complex came to an end significantly before the Beersheban of the northern Negev. If the Irbid/Ramtha complex can be related to the Golan Chalcolithic, then a similar relatively Late Chalcolithic chronology may be proposed for the majority of the sites in that region.

Central Plateau Sites

The site of Sahab, southeast of Amman, would appear to be a mature settled agricultural community. The material culture is said to have particular links with the Classic Ghassulian sites, with painted pottery a more common occurrence than in northern plateau assemblages. The presence of large storage silos (Ibrahim 1987) suggests communal storage of grain surpluses, and the discovery of a seal fragment may hint at regulated inter-regional trade (Ibrahim 1983; Bourke 2002a, 2002b). Although the excavator favours immigration into the uplands from the Jordan Valley as the preferrred explanation for the origin of the Sahab area settlements (Ibrahim 1987), Late Neolithic settlement is known in the region (Kafafi 1992; Kerner 2001), and the Wadi Qattar Chalcolithic site may contain an early Chalcolithic component (Amr *et al.* 1993). Kerner's work at Late Chalcolithic Abu Snesleh (Kerner *et al.* 1992) contrasts somewhat with Sahab, perhaps illustrating the more restricted assemblage of a small community in the more marginal (northeastern) niche. Given the relatively low frequency of sickle blades and the high frequency of tabular scrapers (Lehmann *et al.* 1991), it is possible that the pastoral component played a more central role at Snesleh. Material culture and radiometric data favour association with the larger Sahab community (Kerner 2001).

The South

The Chalcolithic settlements in the Wadi Faynan have only recently begun to be explored intensively (Adams 1999; Levy and Adams *et al.* 2001). Najjar's work at Tall Wadi Faynan has identified the likely main focus of Neolithic/Chalcolithic occupation in the region (Najjar *et al.* 1990). Radiometric data would suggest an extensive Chalcolithic period occupation at the site (particularly in Area A). Neolithic/Chalcolithic material culture is still poorly known, but published Neolithic ceramic material (Najjar *et al.* 1990) has reasonably close form parallels in the early assemblages at Tulaylat Ghassul (Hen-

nessy 1982), and the lithic assemblage suggests a mixed farming regime, probably based on floodwater irrigation (Barker *et al.* 1997). A surface figurine fragment may suggest tenuous links with Yarmukian culture (Najjar *et al.* 1990: 32–33), although radiometric data would suggest a later association, not inconsistent with Ghassulian parallels (Hennessy 1969). Kafafi (1993) suggested an association with the PNA-related sequences at Dhra and Dharih, which seems more likely than Goren's (1990) suggested links with the Negevite Qatifian (Bourke 1997b), although such an affiliation has found support in recent typological study (Garfinkel 1999) and excavations (Kuijt and Chesson 2003).

Khalil's work at the well established mixed farming village of Tall Magass, slightly inland from the southern coast, stands in high contrast to the seasonal "Timnian" pastoral encampments, if Henry's detailed analysis of the Hisma Basin occupation (Henry 1995) is typical of the region as a whole. Magass is a relatively large village site with apparent architectural and ceramic links to the more established settlements of the north (Khalil 1992). The most common explanation for the apparently anomalous developments at Tall Magass is (presumably Timnan) copper exploitation (Khalil and Riederer 1998), although the local microenvironment seems capable of supporting mixed farming, perhaps with a high pastoral component (Khalil 1995). However, more recent excavations at Magass (Khalil and Eichmann 1999, 2001; Khalil *et al.* 2003) and associated sites such as Hujayrat Ghuzlan (Kerner, in Khalil *et al.* 2003, 175–182; Kerner 2003) suggest most significant occupation dates to the earliest phases of the Early Bronze Age (Görsdorf 2002). While a small Chalcolithic component may well be present at Magass (as at Arad V), it seems probable that the majority of the "Magass-related" south coastal settlements are post-Chalcolithic in date.

Summary

Chalcolithic settlement is widespread throughout Jordan. A major concentration in the Jordan Valley, directly associated with floodwater management strategies, is suggested by surveys old and new. Recent research suggests lowland floodwater harvesting commenced in Late Neolithic times (Kuijt *et al.* 2007), although groundwater exploitation has a considerable prehistory (Garfinkel *et al.* 2006b). Upland Chalcolithic occupation is widespread, although still tending to concentrate along wadi systems, the western escarpment and optimal farmlands, suggesting floodwater management was an important factor in upland settlement location as well. Both settlement number and site size increase (on average) from Late Neolithic levels and a greater variety of upland habitats are exploited, suggesting a more flexible combination of pastoral/agricultural/horticultural components in the latter period. Even so, settlement numbers are small in comparison to the subsequent Early Bronze Age, where a considerable increase in settlement number occurs. In the south, Chalcolithic settlements are few and far between, small in scale, and more firmly tied to the west escarpment wadi systems, with seasonal encampments more numerous in the marginal areas further east. Due to well recognized uncertainties within the survey database, we cannot yet speak of changing settlement patterns over the course of the Chalcolithic. However, Wadi Qattar hints at an early Chalcolithic occupation of the central plateau, and isolated ceramic elements from Karak Plateau sites would seem to support this.

Economic Activity

Introduction

The developmental status of the Chalcolithic economy is controversial. Until recently it was common to contrast an economically vibrant interactive Early Bronze Age with an insular subsistence-level Chalcolithic. However, the key economic differences (niche exploitation of fruits, intensified production via irrigation, deep-plough promoted agricultural expansion, long-distance trade in cash crops facilitated by equid domestication) once held to differentiate the two economies can no longer be sustained in the light of new work at Ghassul and elsewhere (Bourke *et al.* 2000, 2003, in press; Lovell 2007).

There is considerable evidence for olive harvesting, both in the valley floor (Meadows in Bourke *et al.* 2000: 83–84; Meadows 2001, 2005) and in the hill regions (Willcox 1992) from Late Neolithic times (Meadows in Bourke *et al.* 2003). This develops into full-blown cultivation by the Late Chalcolithic period (Meadows 2001: 14–16), probably throughout the eastern foothills (Mabry and Palumbo 1992; Lovell 2002). Floodwater irrigation systems are well documented in the Negev (Levy [ed.] 1987; Levy 1995), and are likely to have existed in the south Jordan Valley as well (Glueck 1951; Zohary and Speigal-Roy 1975; Prag 2007). Settlement pattern and (particularly in the south) rainfall data provide compelling circumstantial evidence favouring widespread employment of simple floodwater management schemes. It is more difficult to determine the timing for the introduction of deep plough agriculture, although zoopathological evidence would suggest this dates from the Late Chalcolithic period in the western Negev (Grigson 1995). At Tulaylat Ghassul, cattle numbers approach the 20 percent deep-plough "threshold" (Wapnish and Hesse 1991: 26–27) from mid-Chalcolithic times (Mairs in Bourke *et al.* 2000, 2003), and it seems that limited use of the deep plough occurred in the Jordanian uplands at least by the Late Chalcolithic (Amr *et al.* 1993: 274). The domestication of the donkey is now well documented in Late Chalcolithic times (Grigson 1995; Mairs in Bourke *et al.* 2000: 79), as has been

implied for some time by Late Chalcolithic clay models (Epstein 1985). Fig and date were most probably domesticated by the Late Chalcolithic (Grigson 1995; Meadows in Bourke *et al.* 2000: 83; Meadows 2001, 2005).

It is difficult to argue that the Jordanian Late Chalcolithic economy differs noticeably from that of the succeeding Early Bronze Age in key features and economic potential. However, it is undeniable that the intensity of certain aspects of economic activity (deep plough agriculture, tree crops, copper metallurgy, trade) altered over the course of the Early Bronze Age. This may be due in part to novel social regulatory mechanisms and heightened levels of inter-regional interaction in the EBA. However, the key elements of the EBA economy are present in the preceeding Chalcolithic, so if one wishes to argue that EBA economic activity represents a departure from previous norms, current evidence suggests that any such change must be recognized as one of degree or intensity, and not a change in fundamental economic forms.

Case Study: Husbandry and Agricultural Practices at Tulaylat Ghassul

The six metre deep thousand year long occupational sequence at Tulaylat Ghassul is grouped into six major archaeological horizons of unequal length (Bourke 1997a, 1997b). The entire sequence is to be characterized by relatively slow material cultural progression from one mosaic of attributes to another, with two main instances of more pronounced cultural change. The first occurs between the Late Neolithic and Early Chalcolithic phases, Hennessy Phases H/I and G (Hennessy 1969, 1982; Bourke 1997a, 1997b, 2002b, in press), witnessing major changes to architectural forms and ceramic and lithic toolkits, towards something more definitely ancestral to the later "Classic Ghassulian" assemblage (Bourke 1997b). The second major change is that between the Middle "pre-Ghassulian" (Hennessy E/D) and Late "classic Ghassulian" (Hennessy Phases C/A) respectively (Hennessy 1969, 1982; Bourke 1997a, 1997b). This may be characterized by the development of specialized lithic toolkits, enriched ceramic repertoires, distinct architectural forms, large storage facilities, formalized cult activity and bureaucratic regulatory devices (Bourke 2002b).

These two main alterations to the material cultural assemblage (discussed in more detail in appropriate sections below) probably reflect episodes of heightened economic and social change. The first (between Ghassul H/I and G) may well be characterized as the time when intensified agricultural practices were adopted. The second (between Ghassul D and C) is probably the time at which significant social change towards a more stratified economically diverse society becomes visible in the material record. More speculatively, socio-economic change may be the by-product of diversified and intensified irrigation-assisted agricultural practices. These essentially economic processes may have promoted the development of more specialized production and managerial elites and more elaborate social regulatory devices on the one hand, whilst producing the significantly enhanced agricultural surpluses needed to sustain and buttress the developing managerial elites.

Zoological and Botanical Evidence

Over the course of the thousand year sequence major changes in husbandry practices occur (Mairs in Bourke *et al.* 2000, 2003; Figure 5.5). The marked increase in aged cattle and absence of neonates from Early Chalcolithic times onwards suggests a shift towards some form of milk production regime. The sudden change in pig harvesting patterns in the Early Chalcolithic signals their adoption as a (if not the) main domestic meat protein source. The gradual reduction in neonate and aged ovicaprines from the Middle Chalcolithic period onwards may well suggest the development of increasingly sophisticated herd management strategies, accompanied by a gradual shift of emphasis in fibre production regimes (McCorriston 1997). A move towards a more intensified wool production regime by later Chalcolithic times is implied by the sharply increased sheep numbers relative to goat. One

possible interpretation of Late Chalcolithic husbandry patterns would see flock pasturing offsite for a significant part of the year (thus removing neonatal remains from the bone assemblage), as more and more fieldspace on the nearby floodplain was given over to intensified agriculture (which in turn came to place pressure on flax production regimes). Flocks returned during the shearing season to feed upon the field stubble.

There is a clear impression of increasing agricultural intensification and the exploitation of more productive strains of wheat and barley over time (Meadows in Bourke *et al.* 2000: 83–84). There is a tendency towards crop diversification over time, with legumes and fruits steadily increasing in importance (Meadows in Bourke *et al.* 2000: 84). As well, there is the suggestion of a major alteration in field management strategies in the Late Chalcolithic, with the development of green field fallowing (Meadows in Bourke *et al.* 2000, 2003; Meadows 2005). Distinct spatially segregated crop processing regimes develop by the Late Chalcolithic. The exploitation of tree crops from an early stage, and evidence for domestication of olive (and possibly fig) from mid-Chalcolithic times underlines the growing importance of fruit yield over time (Meadows 2001, 2005).

Given the probable annual rainfall for the Chalcolithic

Figure 5.4   Plan of Univesity of Sydney excavation areas at Tulaylat Ghassul.

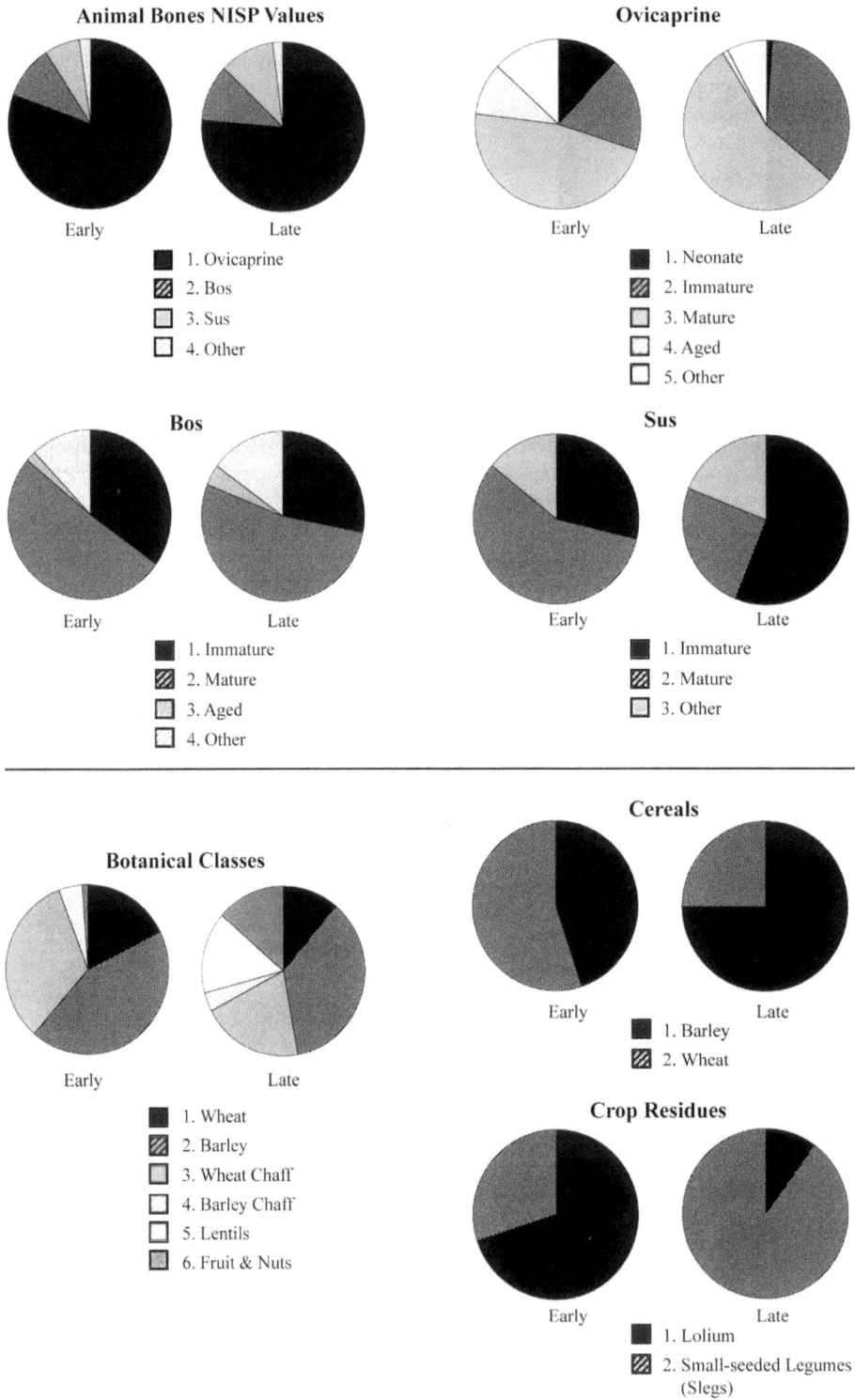

Figure 5.5 Faunal and botanical data from Sydney University Ghassul excavations.

south Jordan Valley, even allowing for a (still-controversial) modest increase from altered summer monsoon patterns, it is difficult to see how the increasingly sophisticated production regime at Ghassul was achieved in the absence of some form of floodwater management/irrigation (Prag 2007). Evidence is only suggestive and admittedly largely circumstantial at present, although specific irrigation weed types and seed morphology vectors are currently under investigation. Irrigation is likely to have begun as simple management of the winter wadi floodwaters as they spread across the alluvial fan (Kuijt *et al.* 2007). More elaborate irrigation regimes may have drawn on springwater sources in spring/summer, although increased summer rainfall early in the Chalcolithic is a distinct possibility if the monsoonal rain systems did shift north in this period (Hole 1997; Weiss 2001). However, the sophisticated mixed farming regimes of Late Chalcolithic Ghassul would seem to require a more structured management of competing demands for what probably became an increasingly scarce resource, particularly if the monsoonal systems shifted south towards the end of the Chalcolithic (Goodfriend 1991).

Ghassul in Context

The picture of agriculture and husbandry at Tulaylat Ghassul is significantly more complete than for most other Chalcolithic sites in Jordan, although many share features with Ghassul. All major Jordan Valley sites display a mixed farming regime by the Late Chalcolithic. The contemporaneous botanical and zoological assemblages at Pella, Abu Hamid and Ghassul can be viewed as essentially similar. Olive cultivation is fundamental to all, as is a mixed wheat/barley cereal crop. The more productive (if more environmentally fragile) varieties of wheat (emmer) and barley (six-row) dominate cereal assemblages. Legumes are an important source of protein, which may allow one to speculate on the introduction of green field fallowing in all Jordan Valley sites by this time. Flax is grown as an important specialized crop, and fruit crops are now a significant part of the assemblage.

At Abu Hamid (Dollfus and Kafafi [eds.] 1988), the increase in pig numbers in comparison with those at Ghassul is more a consequence of the wetter conditions in the mid-Valley than any significant variation in husbandry practice. This point is reinforced by the even greater importance of pig in the swampy conditions at Tall Shuna North (Baird and Philip 1994). Not surprisingly, the slightly drier conditions in the foothill regions around Pella result in reduced pig numbers in comparison with Tall Shuna North (Mairs in Bourke *et al.* 1998, 2003). Environmental variability rather than differential husbandry practice is the likely explanation for slight assemblage variability up and down the valley (Grigson 1995). Equids are a consistent presence, as are small numbers of deer and gazelle, but the main food animals are

cattle, ovicaprines and pig. The age-class harvest patterns at Ghassul, Abu Hamid and Pella are very similar, with an implied emphasis on cattle and ovicaprine milk production, and pig as an important domestic meat protein source. The absence of ovicaprine neonatal classes at Abu Hamid implies winter pasturing at some remove from the main site (Dollfus and Kafafi [eds.] 1988: 28), and provides further evidence for the existence of a well-established pastoral component by Late Chalcolithic times.

Although evidence from the Late Chalcolithic uplands is very slight, the Golan assemblages include cereals, legumes and olives and a mixed husbandry regime (Epstein 1998), which is likely to be similar to most north Jordan plateau sites (Lovell 2007, Lovell *et al.* in press). The Sahab assemblage includes cereals, olives and legumes, and a mixed husbandry regime (Ibrahim 1987). The material from Wadi Qattar includes cereals and fruits, and a husbandry regime in which ovicaprines predominate. Of particular interest are observations on cattle age classes which suggest the employment of aged animals for secondary milk production and possible deep-plough agriculture (Amr *et al.* 1993: 274). A similar state of affairs exists at Abu Snesleh, with the zoological assemblage suggesting a greater reliance on ovicaprines and hunted species (Kerner 2001, pers. comm.), a state of affairs more in keeping with the transhumant assemblages of the Hisma (Henry 1995) and the Eastern Desert margins (Betts 1992).

It is more difficult to determine if the Early Chalcolithic assemblages at Ghassul are in any way representative of the country as a whole, due mainly to the absence of adequate comparative data. There is a limited amount of evidence from Tall Shuna North (Baird and Philip 1994) and Pella (Bourke *et al.* 2003) which hints at more variation in earlier Chalcolithic assemblages. Whilst olive seems to have been a constant presence within the plant assemblage from Neolithic times (Meadows 2005), the evidence for domestication only manifests itself from Late Chalcolithic times onwards (Meadows 2001). The relatively late appearance of domesticated olive (and other tree crops?) into the north Jordan Valley (Bourke 2002b) may well suggest that horticulture in general came later to the north Jordan Valley than to the south. However, the presence of tree crops in the Golan (Epstein 1993), the eastern foothills (Willcox 1992) and north/central upland zones (Amr *et al.* 1993) by Late Chalcolithic times suggests that once introduced into the northern Jordan Valley, domesticated tree crops spread into the foothill zones and eastern uplands quite rapidly (Lovell 2002, 2007).

Interpretation

The move from simple economic description to socioeconomic reconstruction is likely to remain hazardous for some time to come. However, all but extreme minimalists should acknowledge that significant socio-economic change does occur over the course of the Chalcolithic period (Levy 1995, 1996; Bourke 2002b). Practitioners will continue to differ over the economic significance of observed changes (Levy [ed.] 1987; Gilead 1988), the potential and actual social change that need be inferred from such economic changes (Levy 1995; Yoffee 1993), and the degree of continuity between Late Chalcolithic and Early Bronze Age socio-economic regimes (Hanbury-Tenison 1986; Joffe 1993).

The relatively undifferentiated Late Neolithic and Early Chalcolithic economic systems of the Jordan Valley settlements would suggest little economic and minimal social differentiation, a tribal society in which autonomous nuclear household production units were the norm (Kafafi 1993; Gopher and Gophna 1993; Banning 1998; Garfinkel and Matskevich 2002; Horwitz 2002). Over time, intensified and specialized agricultural practices, buttressed by an increasing reliance on labour intensive and elite-regulated floodwater irrigation systems, may have led to the development of distinct (and perhaps competing) social classes, primarily sourced to the production of

increased agricultural surpluses. It may be that the exploitation of high-yield cereals alongside more traditionally exploited cultivars, and the development of specialized husbandry and horticultural activities alongside simple mixed farming regimes, marks the crucial diversification of economic activity during the Late Chalcolithic period (Bourke 2002b).

The evidence from Ghassul would suggest a gradual and piecemeal transformation of a relatively undifferentiated Early Chalcolithic society into one in which specialized economic activity existed alongside a more undifferentiated economic mode in the Late Chalcolithic. The very large grain storage systems at Ghassul, Abu Hamid, Pella and Sahab illustrate the significance of large scale stored agricultural produce to at least one segment of society by Late Chalcolithic times. It may well be that the much-discussed "restructuring" of Early Bronze Age society (Philip, this volume) represents no more than the triumph of one pre-existing mode of labour mobilization, that of extended family households over nuclear family units (Flannery 2002). The greater economic power of

Figure 5.6   Plan of Pontifical Biblical Institute excavations.

these extended family units may in turn have promoted the spread of individualizing chiefdoms, as these emphasized service over lineage. Traditional lineage-oriented chiefdoms would have been at a considerable disadvantage in the diversifying economic landscape of the later Chalcolithic (Earle 2002; Stein 1998).

Architecture

Settlement Layout and Domestic Architecture

Few settlements have been extensively excavated. Very large surface areas were excavated by the first Pontifical Biblical Institute mission at Tulaylat Ghassul (over 12,000 m²), but not carefully, so that the association of architectural units across large and apparently featureless courtyards and their combination into general phase plans is rarely as secure as published settlement plans imply. However, without the evidence from Ghassul there is virtually no information on any but the latest settlements at most sites (Tall Shuna North, Pella, Abu Hamid and Sahab), and with the exception of Abu Hamid, even these exposures rarely extend beyond one or two dwelling units. As with many other aspects of the Jordanian Chalcolithic, a close consideration of the evidence from Tulaylat Ghassul is central to any attempt at synthesis.

Late Chalcolithic Domestic Architecture and Settlement Layout at Tulaylat Ghassul

Most reviews of Ghassulian architecture (Lee 1973; Mazar 1990; Gonen 1992; Porath 1992) seem agreed on a number of points. Houses are rectilinear in form (Figure 5.6), and simply constructed of handformed sundried bricks, sometimes set upon a single course of undressed fieldstone foundations, or otherwise built directly onto prepared rammed clay surfaces. Dwellings were flat roofed and constructed from wood beams, reed battens and mudplaster, with no second storey apparent. Walls were carefully plastered (often many times over), and not uncommonly painted, mostly in a monochrome buff but occasionally in brilliant polychrome. As generally envizaged, the basic architectural unit consisted of a roofed broadroom dwelling (5 x 5 m) with an attached (10 x 5 m) open or partly roofed courtyard, together forming one unit on average 15 by 5 m in extent. The roofed dwelling was thought to have been used primarily for sleeping, with the majority of food preparation, cooking and craft activities taking place in the courtyards, in which the majority of hearths and storage pits were generally located. These simple housing units (assumed to be the dwellings of nuclear families) were arranged in irregular clumps around larger open more public spaces ("plazas"), which were linked together by narrow winding alleyways. The implication of this traditional account of architectural form and settlement plan is that there was little or no architectural differentiation, reflecting the

conditions existing in a large but undifferentiated farming village.

A glance at Mallon's Tulayl 1 settlement plan (Mallon *et al.* 1934) would seem to reinforce this impression of an undifferentiated village, but a close examination of plans and photographs of individual dwellings suggests variation not apparent from a consideration of the "sanitized" settlement top-plans alone. There is considerable variation in the size, shape and construction of individual dwellings, and in the size and layout of attached courtyards. Some of the housing units appear quite substantial, particularly those with stone wall footings. These are often equipped with stone and plaster-lined storage pits, brick benches, free standing mudbrick bins, and centrally positioned flat stone anvils. Other structures appear relatively small and undistinguished in their fittings. Further support for this suggested architectural differentiation is drawn from a consideration of Koeppel's little studied top-plans from the better-documented excavations on Tulayl 3 (Koeppel *et al.* 1940).

Even the most cursory view of the Tulayl 3 Phase IVA/B top plans illustrates the substantial variation in unit type, with several large multi-room complexes associated with numerous one and two room storage units (Koeppel *et al.* 1940; Lee 1973). The multi-room complexes often have brick-built free-standing bins, stone-lined storage pits and large ceramic pithoi placed along the interior walls and in the corners of generally trapesoidal courtyards, or within the simple "row house" storage and work rooms, these latter arranged in lines, all opening into the courtyards. A number of the larger "plazas" have small structures at their centre, perhaps for the feeding (or watering) of livestock. Nowhere can one discern the idealized simple housing units. Several large multi-room complexes dominate the Tulayl 3 settlement plan, with considerable variability in the size and elaboration of individual dwelling units, courtyard size and storage capacity. Overall, the impression is one of considerable variability, certainly not consistent with the traditional view of standardized Chalcolithic architectural form and undifferentiated settlement plan.

The generally accepted view that elaborate figured polychrome wall paintings do not correlate with higher quality artefactual assemblages (Koeppel *et al.* 1940) should be reconsidered. Whenever it is possible to determine context with some confidence, both building form and artefact types do suggest a functional and qualitative difference associated with the presence of wall paintings (Koeppel *et al.* 1940: 82; Lee 1973: 339; Elliot 1977; Cameron 1981), whether this be measured by elaboration of construction, quantity and quality of artefacts, storage capacity, or number of activity areas (Lee 1973; Elliot 1977; Bourke 2002b). All else being equal, the presence of wall paintings probably does imply a special-function for the structure in question, with cultic-ritual use probable

(Joffe 1998; Garfinkel 1998). It should be remembered that Hennessy did find large quantities of polychrome wall painting fragments in association with his Sanctuary buildings, although these were not recoverable.

Current Excavations at Ghassul (1994–99): The Area H Complex

Current investigations on the westernmost hillock of Tulayl 6 (Area H, Figure 5.4) have explored an area approximately 30 x 15 m in extent (H II–IV), and fully excavated two phases of a Late Chalcolithic broadroom dwelling (5 x 7 m) and walled courtyard (13 x 7 m) complex (Bourke 1997a: 255; Bourke *et al.* 2000: 55–58). The walls of the two-room complex were carefully constructed of handmade bun-shaped bricks, built on a single course of fieldstone foundations. Interior wall surfaces were thickly mud-plastered. Small plaster-lined pits were situated in two corners, and a collection of stone tools (tabular scrapers and flint chisels) were recovered from a third corner. Rammed clay pathways ran around the north and west exteriors of the dwelling, and a doorway opened directly onto the western "street," whilst a second opened into the northwestern corner of the attached courtyard. The courtyard was probably roofed along its northern end, and featured a large centrally placed hearth, a number of stone and brick bins built against the western courtyard wall, a number of shattered storage vessels placed in small depressions against the eastern wall, a paved (and perhaps roofed) work area in the southeast corner, and a doorway in the southwestern corner. Outside the southwestern courtyard entrance, less well preserved features probably indicate the presence of a series of stone and brick fodder bins and a shallow, rectangular plaster-lined water trough, set around the north and western perimeters of a small pebble-paved "plaza." The cobbled surface of the "plaza" led up to the courtyard entrance, and ran south to an adjoining east/west alleyway, which ran along the southern exterior wall of the complex, separating this housing unit from others to the south and west.

The courtyard area seems to have been the main work and storage area. A collection of tabular scrapers were found together, along with several chisels, small hammerstones, and what may be resharpening debitage, all in a discrete area beside the northern wall. Open areas immediately beside the central stone-lined hearth preserved a rich collection of animal bones, including all major domesticates, but with sheep outnumbering goats by seven to one. Botanical samples hint at the storage of cereals and flax in the northeastern courtyard area, and fodder crops in the south and in the exterior "plaza" bins. Overall, the impression is one of a well designed, solidly built and well maintained multi-purpose dwelling, with discrete sheltered interior work and storage areas and external stock feeding facilities, all linked together by well maintained cobbled or rammed earth pathways. Current excavations in the northern (Area G), central (Area N), southern (Area A) and eastern (Area Q) areas of the site further reinforce this impression of well ordered multi-purpose dwellings, displaying non-standardized ground-plans, a variety of construction techniques and numerous special-purpose work and storage areas (Bourke *et al.* in press).

Late Chalcolithic Domestic Architecture at Ghassul: A Summary

This review of Late Chalcolithic architectural evidence from Tulaylat Ghassul reveals a rather different picture to that generally portrayed. Whilst much architecture was rectilinear, curved walls, "corrals" and windbreaks were common. Rectangular, trapesoidal and triangular courtyards were all found together. Single, double and multi-room complexes were all known, alongside various combinations of small, medium and large rooms. Some floor surfaces and passageways were cobbled, but most employed prepared rammed clay surfaces for interiors, and less prepared compacted soil layers for alleyways. The majority of dwelling floors occurred at approximately the same level as exterior surfaces, but a few were semi-subterranean, and these were generally cobbled. Distinct activity and storage areas were revealed by material cultural and environmental datasets. Thick mudplaster was widely employed to seal walls and roofs, and line pits and bins. Mostly this plaster was unpainted, but occasionally walls were decorated in brilliant mineral polychomes, often displaying an elaborate complex symbolism, the interpretation of which is much complicated by multiple overpaintings and differential wear.

Early Chalcolithic Domestic Architecture at Tulaylat Ghassul

Far less is known about the architecture of the early phases at Tulaylat Ghassul. Although a large area of Tulayl 3 was excavated into Stratum III layers, little coherent architecture or settlement layout can be recovered from the fragmentary plans produced by Koeppel and Lee (Koeppel 1938; Lee 1973). Hennessy excavated about half of two 5 x 7 m trenches (A II and A III) into sterile sands during renewed work in the 1970s (Hennessy 1982, 1989; Bourke 1997b, 2002b; Lovell 2001a). In these two trenches, Hennessy uncovered four coherent phases of rectilinear mudbrick on stone architecture. These architectural phases were associated with plastered pits and bins, a number of distinct activity areas (including a complete flint-knapping/bone tool preparation area), one associated with an elaborate polychrome wall painting (Cameron 1981). Only with the earliest two phases (Hennessy's "Late Neolithic" Phases H and I) does the architecture change to semi-subterranean round dwellings.

Figure 5.7   Chalcolithic Domestic architecture. 1. North Shuna; 2. Abu Hamid; 3. Jabal Sartaba, Pella; 4. Abu Snesleh; 5. Tall Fendi; 6. Sahab.

The current excavations have explored two small areas of Early Chalcolithic architecture (Bourke 1997b; Bourke *et al.* 2000, in press). In 5 x 5 m trench G II, a neatly constructed complex of storage bins (two rows of 2 x 1 m brick bins) was uncovered. They were built against the north eastern corner of a large room, or perhaps a roofed courtyard. One row of three bins contained quantities of flax, legume and cereal residues respectively. Two in the second row produced immature pig teeth (perhaps suggesting use as farrowing pens), and the last held a quantity of beads and a collection of bone and stone awls (Bourke *et al.* 2000: 52–53). Excavations in 5 x 5 m trench A XI (the eastern half of Hennessy's original trench A I), uncovered three phases of rectilinear architecture equivalent to Hennessy Phases D–F. Along with portions of two well constructed mudbrick rooms (one in the northwest, the other in the southeast corner), numerous thickly plastered fire pits in the southwest corner were found to contain a rich assortment of cereal and fruit remains (Bourke *et al.* 2000: 40–42).

Current excavations have explored meaningful areas of three main phases of rectilinear architecture below the "classic" Late Chalcolithic Ghassulian horizon (Bourke 1997b; Bourke *et al.* 2000, in press). Observations match those from Hennessy's deep probes (Hennessy 1977, 1982, 1989). Carefully constructed rectilinear units seem to be a feature of the architecture of Ghassul from the beginning of the Chalcolithic period.

Chalcolithic Domestic Architecture at Other Sites

Abu Hamid

Over 2000 m² of Late Chalcolithic architecture has been uncovered in two main excavation fields at Abu Hamid (Dollfus and Kafafi [eds.] 1988; Dollfus and Kafafi 1989, 1993; Lovell *et al.* 2004). The main architectural themes reflect those at Ghassul. Multi-room rectilinear architecture, built of handmade mudbricks set on a single course of field stone foundations are featured (Figure 5.7.2 left). The settlement seems well laid out, with considerable distances (large "plazas", Figure 5.7.2 right) existing between dwelling units (Dollfus and Kafafi eds. 1988 figs. 16 and 18–20; Lovell *et al.* 2004: fig.3). Most units display the "dwelling and courtyard" design, although rows of contiguous smaller rooms become more common over time, and are associated with the larger open "plazas." Most work and bulk storage areas are located in enclosed courtyards or small "row houses" associated with them. There does seem to be differentiation between complexes, with more substantial "broadroom" units associated with lines of much smaller "row houses," as at Ghassul. The famous very large storage jar/grain silo (Dollfus and Kafafi [eds.] 1988: 46) was found in a small semi-subterranean "row house" associated with one of the more substantial complexes. Other small "row house" rooms are associ-

ated with storage jars, food preparation and specialized flint working (Dollfus and Kafafi 1993: 244–245). Thick plaster-lined bins and pits are common, and distinct work areas have been detected within structures. Overall, this seems a very similar settlement landscape to that reflected in Koeppel's Level IV plans from the Tulayl 3 excavations at Ghassul. Details of internal layout and function can be matched by the findings of the more recent Sydney University work at Ghassul.

The appropriate stratigraphic relationship of the Abu Hamid Early Chalcolithic "Middle Phase" architecture to the Tulaylat Ghassul sequence remains unclear, although association with Ghassul Phase D/G assemblages is likely (Bourke *et al.* 2001; Lovell 2001a; Lovell *et al.* 2004). The information gained from the relatively large scale "Middle Phase" excavations is uniquely important, as it provides something of a backdrop against which the Late Chalcolithic norms at both sites may be viewed. The main "Middle Phase" variations would seem to be less evidence for plaza "row houses" and more for "stand-alone" multi-cellular complexes, organized in a more dispersed built environment. The walls of the "Middle Phase" complexes are built of well formed plano-convex bricks set on field-stone foundations. Plans consist of large open rectangular living rooms with defined work areas, linked by narrow passageways to smaller rectangular rooms associated with storage or special activities. Mudbrick benches, partition walls, plastered stone-lined subterranean pits and above-ground built storage bins, plastered polychrome painted walls and plastered pillar bases, pebble paved zones and semi-circular boundary walls all feature in architectural units which were constantly remodelled, built over and subdivided as needs altered. As well, there is the suggestion that special-purpose industrial areas existed in the north and east of the southern sector in "Middle Phase" times.

The existence of stand-alone multi-room multi-purpose complexes in "Middle Phase" times (ca. 4500 BC) would seem to imply at least some tendency towards diversified economic activity, centralized redistribution of agricultural products and craft specialization. Comparison of Middle and Upper Phase settlements would suggest a strengthening of this tendency over time, with more provision for large scale grain storage, more easily identified (and more numerous) activity areas and more distinctive craft specialization (Roux and Courty 1997), featuring in Upper Phase (ca. 4000 BC) plans.

Pella

Late Chalcolithic architecture has been exposed in two main locations at Pella, the first an isolated farmstead (Area XIV) on the western slopes of the Jabal Sartaba hillside (Figure 5.7.3) about a kilometre southeast of the main settlement (Hanbury-Tenison 1986: 178–181), and between the Jabal Sartaba groundplans and the upland "row-house" layouts of the Golan Chalcolithic (Hanbury-Tenison in McNicoll *et al.* 1992: 24), and those discovered in his survey work east of Jarash (Hanbury-Tenison 1986: 114).

On the main mound of Khirbat Fahl, several small probes and one large trench has resulted in the exposure of approximately 250 m² of a multi-use area, that is dominated by a massive grain storage complex (Figure 5.8, Bourke 1997c; Bourke *et al.* 2003). The central southern area of the exposure (trench XXXIID, 25 x 8 m in extent) contains a network of six (two rows of three) storage silos. Each is 1 m wide and 1–2 m deep. Several are thickly plastered and three are ceramic-lined. Immediately to the northeast is a rectangular stone and mudbrick platform (Figure 5.8) some 2.5 m thick, raised approximately half a metre above the surrounding surfaces, and exposed over 5 m of its length (Bourke *et al.* 2003). The structure was originally thought to be a major wall, but is now viewed as the stone foundations and mudbrick flooring of the east end of a grain storage facility. Excavations in the area of the platform recovered a massive burnt deposit of pre-sorted (99% clean) wheat grain product (Meadows in Bourke *et al.* 2003). The platform storage complex also featured areas of neat stone-slab paving along the interior north face of the platform, stone stairs built into the eastern end, and stretches of pebble paving around the plaster-lined silos. Associated with the platform were a series of neatly constructed small rectilinear rooms to the west, a gently curving courtyard border wall to the east, and numbers of small thickly plastered bins and pits to the south. All of this material dates to the early Late Chalcolithic period, and is to be compared with the classic Ghassulian phases at Tulaylat Ghassul, the Upper Phase assemblages at Abu Hamid, and the "Ghassulian-related" assemblage from Neve Ur. Overall, the Late Chalcolithic evidence from Pella indicates intensive cultivation of the olive and centralized storage of grain in a prosperous well regulated Late Chalcolithic settlement.

The Early Chalcolithic presence at Pella is less well known. A limited sounding (5 x 7 m) in the western edge of the Area XXXII exposure was taken down to bedrock during the 1997 field season (Bourke *et al.* 2003: figs. 17–18). The majority of the Early Chalcolithic exposure is dominated by a walled courtyard area, much disturbed by multi-phase plaster-lined storage pits. The courtyard features several stone and mudbrick bins built against the northern boundary wall, which has an entrance in its centre. Two stone-lined silos fill the centre of the courtyard, surrounded by several smaller relatively shallow plaster-lined bins, areas of hard orangey-yellow plastered floor and at least two plaster-lined flat circular pillar-supports, perhaps suggesting that at least the northern half of the courtyard was roofed. Associated fragmentary architecture in the north and west consists of small rectilinear mud-

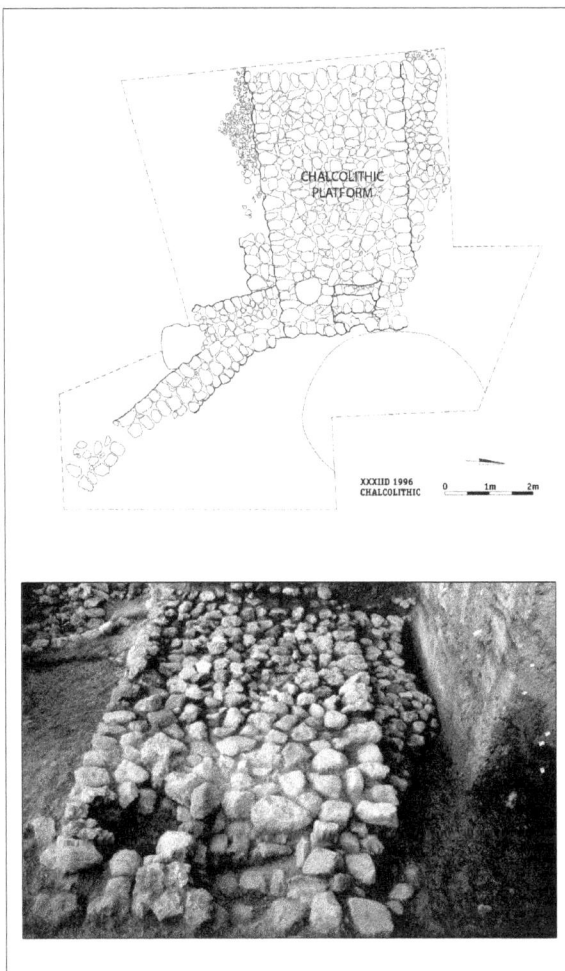

Figure 5.8 Platform at Pella.

the second a series of wall lines and silos set around a large stone and mudbrick platform (Area XXXII, Figure 5.8) located on the central south side of the main mound of Khirbat Fahl (Bourke *et al.* 2003: figs. 5–7). The first settlement (Area XIV) seems likely to have been the site of a dispersed agricultural complex, with at least three distinct units, one (at least) of which was strongly geared towards the production and storage of olives as fruit and oil (Bourke 1997c). Very shallow occupation deposits and uneven sharply sloping bedrock resulted in the recovery of fragmentary plans and virtually no superstructures, but enough was preserved to reveal the familiar rectilinear multi-room enclosed courtyard groundplan, featuring small "row houses" given over to special activity areas (olive processing and storage), with many stone-lined pits, plaster-lined bins and silos, and stone and mudbrick benches located in the courtyards (Hanbury-Tenison in McNicoll *et al.* 1992: 21–22). Material culture and radiometric dating suggests a Late Chalcolithic date (Hanbury-Tenison 1986:112–113). Hanbury-Tenison drew parallels brick bin-like structures, perhaps used for food storage (in the west) and preparation (in the north). The associated material assemblage seems to have more affinities with the "Northern Chalcolithic" assemblages at Tall Farah North and Tall Shuna North, than with the Early Chalcolithic assemblages at Abu Hamid and Tulaylat Ghassul (Bourke *et al.* 2003).

Tall Shuna North

Three expeditions (de Contensen/Mellaart, Gustaveson-Gaube, Baird and Philip) have excavated Chalcolithic period remains at Tall Shuna North, and together they have exposed approximately 100 m² of pre-Bronze Age deposits. The recent detailed investigations by Gustaveson-Gaube (Area E 1984–85) and Baird (Area D 1991–94), working on the western edge of the central tell close by one another, uncovered approximately 85 m² of a tightly packed rectilinear multi-cellular complex of large and small rooms built around a roughly square courtyard (Figure 5.7.1) (Baird and Philip 1994). Structures were built from hand-formed mudbricks laid on fieldstone foundations, and provided with beaten earth floors. Plaster-lined pits, semi-circular brick silos and patches of cobbled surface, several associated with discrete storage or activity areas, were positioned within the courtyard. The complex was rebuilt several times, with walls and installations added as required, and seems to have been in use for some considerable period of time.

The chronological positioning of the Shuna Chalcolithic assemblages has been much debated, but the presence of "Tsafian" Lattice Painted pottery (Leonard 1992; Baird and Philip 1994: 123–124) within the assemblage suggests an Early Chalcolithic date, as do a recent suite of radiometric data (Bronk-Ramsey *et al.* 2002). Architectural layout and assemblages from Gustaveson-Gaube and Baird's "Shuna Chalcolithic" are quite similar to the recently excavated Early Chalcolithic materials from Pella (Bourke *et al.* 2003: 344; Bourke *et al.* 2004a: 122–123). Most importantly, the Shuna Early Chalcolithic seems likely to be the first reliably excavated exemplar of de Vaux's "Northern Chalcolithic" assemblage east of the Jordan River. Many isolated, generally poorly stratified assemblage "scraps," have been assigned to this "Northern Chalcolithic" culture over the years (de Vaux 1966), but hitherto the combination of poor description and uncertain context robbed these observations of much significance, even though their likely status as indigenous successor to local Ceramic Neolithic cultures had long been recognized (de Vaux 1966; Perrot 1968; Kaplan 1969). Baird and Philip's meticulous investigations give promise of the first thorough description and evaluation of this potentially widespread pre-Ghassulian Early Chalcolithic culture (Baird 1987; Baird and Philip 1994).

The Central Uplands: Sahab and Snesleh

Ibrahim's pioneering investigations at Sahab in the early 1970s provided the first reliable excavated sequence of the upland Late Chalcolithic culture, which was suggested as deriving from earlier Chalcolithic Jordan Valley exemplars, with some Damascene elements (Ibrahim 1984: 257–258; 1987: 73–75). Approximately 150 m² of Late Chalcolithic architecture was exposed in Ibrahim's Area E excavations (Figure 5.7.6). Architectural form and constructional technique is close to Ghassulian exemplars (Ibrahim 1987: 73). Wall constructions are primarily of hand-formed mudbricks set on fieldstone foundations. Layouts display the familiar central courtyard with associated rectilinear small "row-house" flanking rooms, not unlike the Golan and Jabal Sartaba layouts (Hanbury-Tenison 1986). Several of the small rooms are closely packed with storage pits, and a number of very large stone-lined storage silos are located within the courtyard. This provides reasonable evidence for large scale storage of what seems to have been a considerable agricultural surplus. The Area E complex was modified a number of times, suggesting some time depth to the occupation. Ibrahim believes that the layout of the complex implied occupation by an extended family unit (1987: 73). The material assemblage has links to the classic Ghassulian (Hennessy Phase A-C) and the Abu Hamid "Upper Phase" assemblages.

Closely associated with survey work in the region around Sahab southeast of Amman, the more recent Abu Snesleh excavations of the early 1990s (Lehmann *et al.* 1991; Kerner *et al.* 1992) have uncovered approximately 100 m² of a similarly dated Late Chalcolithic settlement. Fragmentary remains of a rectangular broadroom structure were recovered (Figure 5.7.4, Lamprichs 1998: fig. 22). Construction utilizes quite large roughly squared stone blocks, but otherwise suggests a very similar technique to that employed at Sahab. The rectilinear broadroom, associated courtyard and centrally positioned storage installation suggest a similar layout (and function) as well. Overall, the architectural layout and material cultural homogeneity of the central upland region in the Late Chalcolithic period favours the existence of a thinly spread (Gustaveson-Gaube 1986; Bernbeck *et al.*1995) system of extended-family run farmsteads in the countryside surrounding the larger central settlement of Sahab (Kerner 2001).

The Contrasting South: Jabal Jill and Tall Magass

Henry's investigations in the Hisma Basin have documented a number of the semi-permanent campsites of transhumant pastoralists (Henry 1995: 356) who occupied the region during the Fourth Millennium BC. The architectural form and layout differs sharply from that of the permanent farming communities on the plateau. Henry divides the transhumant pastoral sites of the Judayid Basin into two main categories, ephemeral camps and "long-term" camps. Architectural remains of the latter at Jabal Jill (J14), and less coherent traces at Jabal Quaysa (J 24) consist of loosely associated groups of circular structures stretching over an excavated area of approximately 200 m². Constructions feature semi-subterranean stone-lined single room roundhouses, which contain stone-lined hearths, storage pits and discrete work and food-preparation areas (Henry 1995: 358–361). They are associated with large circular "corrals," smaller circular storage facilities and patches of pebble pavement. Individual architectural form and settlement layout contrast sharply with the architecture of the permanent farming villages of the north plateau and the south coast. This may be attributed in some degree to variant subsistence regime, and cultural associations with either the southwestern Timnian complex (Henry 1995; Rothenberg 1999), or cultures of the northwestern Hijaz.

Khalil's recently renewed excavations at the south coastal site of Tall Magass (Khalil and Eichmann 1999, 2001; Khalil *et al.* 2003), now four kilometres north of Aqaba but perhaps closer to the shore in antiquity, have uncovered approximately 150 m² of a four phase (I–IV) agricultural/industrial settlement in two distinct fields (A/C and B) of excavation (Khalil 1987, 1992, 1995). The architectural technique and layout are typical of the permanent settlements of the north/central uplands, and sharply in contrast with the transhumant camps immediately to the north and east. Layout duplicates the familiar plan of central courtyard with multiple tightly packed clusters of associated small rooms, storage bins and work areas. Fieldstone foundations, hand-formed mudbricks, stone and plaster-lined storage pits, large mudbrick and stone storage silos, and what may well be ceramic firing pits and small-scale copper smelting facilities, all feature in a picture of densely packed industrial (?) activity areas, storage facilities and domestic food preparation areas (Khalil 1995). Some structures include numbers of small storage bins, very similar in form to those uncovered at Tulaylat Ghassul in Area G II (Bourke *et al.* 2000: fig.10).

The south Jordanian material assemblage is still little known (Genz 1997), and the relative chronology of the Magass "culture" assemblage is controversial (Kerner 2003; Kerner in Khalil *et al.* 2003). However, it remains possible that at least the earliest phases of the diverse range of domestic, storage and industrial/manufacturing facilities at Tall Magass date to the latest phases of the Chalcolithic period, although what proportion of the sequence this may entail remains unclear, as the radiometric data currently available span both Chalcolithic and Early Bronze I periods (Görsdorf 2002). Even so, the overall pattern revealed by Khalil's excavations is one of a permanent mixed farming/small industrial settlement, set in a hinterland dominated by semi-permanent pastoral camps (Jobling 1989: 16–24). Khalil's soundings at Hujayrat

Ghuzlan, slightly over a kilometre further east up the Wadi Yutm, suggest that by the Early Bronze Age more of the hinterland settlements had become agricultural villages exploiting the winter wadi floodwaters (Khalil *et al.* 2003).

Cultic Architecture. Case Study: The Tulaylat Ghassul Sanctuary Area

Introduction

Only one building complex in Jordan has ever been identified as purpose-built for Chalcolithic cultic activities, and that is the Tulayl 5 (Hennessy Area E) Sanctuary Complex at Tulaylat Ghassul (Figure 5.9, Hennessy 1982: 56; Seaton 2006). Over the course of three field seasons (1975–77) Hennessy opened 16 trenches in and around the Sanctuary Complex, fully excavating the two nominated sanctuary buildings (Sanctuaries A and B), stretches of the northern and western Temenos Enclosure walls, and a 10 x 5 m area 15 metres to the north of the Temenos wall (Hennessy 1982, 1989). The current Sydney University expedition has carried out four further seasons (1994–99) of renewed investigations, opening four additional trenches in and around the Sanctuary Complex, for the most part in areas unexplored by Hennessy. A major semi-circular structure linked to Sanctuary A (Figure 5.9) (Installation C), a shallow gateway (Installation D) in the northwest corner of the later Stone Temenos wall, and an earlier phase Mudbrick Temenos wall were added to Hennessy's discoveries, and a number of internal phasing issues clarified (Bourke *et al.* 2000: 43–50, in press).

Architectural Form and Cult Practice: Some Contextual Remarks

Recent debate over the form and variety of Chalcolithic cult practice (Joffe *et al.* 2001; Gilead 2002; Seaton 2006; Levy [ed.] 2006) has been dominated by both architecture and assemblages drawn from the northern Negev (Gilat/Shiqmim) and the West Dead Sea regions (En Gedi and Nahal Mishmar). Initial suggestions that the Ghassul wall paintings were indicators of cultic activity were hamstrung by Koeppel's (1940: 46) insistence that associated architectural contexts were unexceptional and associated assemblages undistinguished. North suggested that Koeppel's apparently authoritative denial of any unusual architectural contexts for the famous wall paintings had more to do with poor attention to detail than any clear determination of standardized architectural forms (North 1961: 35–36). North argued that the Tiger Fresco came from a cultic context, suggesting that it be associated with a semi-subterranean stone-lined "throne" feature (North 1961: 36). However, a close consideration of the published photographs make it more likely that North's apparently linked features (wall painting and stone-lined silo) are associated with unrelated superimposed struc-

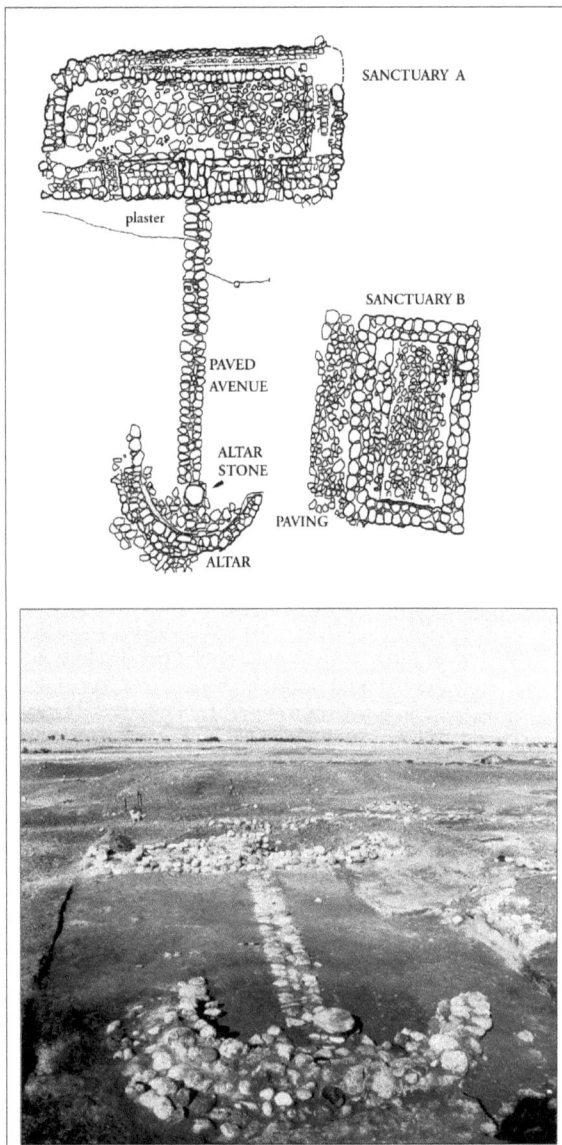

Figure 5.9   Plan and photo of sanctuary area at Ghassul.

tures (Blackham 1999).

Nonetheless, there are distinct clusters of what may reasonably be interpreted as cultic or ritual paintings in separate building complexes on Tulayl 3 (Koeppel *et al.* 1940; Elliot 1977: 19–20), and on Tulayl 1 (Hennessy 1978; Cameron 1981; Hennessy 1989). The most spectacular of these is the multi-roomed broadroom complex (Building 78) uncovered by Mallon in Square B 7 in the centre of Tulayl 3 (Mallon *et al.* 1934). It contained the famous "Bird" and "Notables" paintings in a context including a built altar, offering pits and a small storage room (Room 81) off to the east. Most importantly Room 81 contained over thirty broken cornet cups (Koeppel *et al.* 1940; Cam-

eron 1995). The recent suggested association of alcohol consumption, cult practice and developing social stratification may have relevance here (Joffe 1998). Further support for a cultic function is drawn from the subject matter of the Notables painting, which illustrates an explicitly ritual and hierarchical event (Stager 1992). An associated semi-circular horseshoe-shaped structure (installation 75a) is positioned in the centre of an enclosed courtyard (Area 77) to the west of Building 78. This layout of enclosed courtyard and associated multi-room complex remained largely unaltered from earlier Stratum III times. Given the central role of a large star in the Notables painting, it seems probable that the building in which the famous "star" painting was discovered (Building 10) had a cultic function as well, although much of this latter complex lay north of the Pontifical Biblical Institute excavation area and was never fully investigated.

Hennessy's Processional painting (Figure 5.10, Cameron 1981) was discovered in 1977, during the excavation of a broadroom and courtyard complex not unlike Mallon's Building 78, although Hennessy's Area A broadroom structure is less well preserved and was only partly excavated. However, the discovery of a cornet cup deposit within the structure strengthens the link between ritual drinking and/or libation offerings and cult practice (Hennessy 1977; Bourke 2002b). The architectural features loosely associated with the Pontifical Biblical Institute wall paintings—a central internally sub-divided broadroom with ancilliary storage chambers, exterior paved areas, enclosed courtyards and semi-circular offering installations—were too rarely found to be codified as a cultic architectural template. This changed with Hennessy's discoveries in Area E (Hennessy 1982) and the full publication of the previously excavated En Gedi sanctuary (Ussishkin 1980). They made it possible to define just such a template—central broadrooms, enclosed courtyard with semi-circular offering installations (Ottosson 1980; Hennessy 1982, 1989; Seaton 2000, 2006).

Cultic Architecture: Conclusions

Notwithstanding this late tendency towards a standardised cultic architectural complex, a variety of cultic installations co-existed across the site during the Late Chalcolithic period at Ghassul. These variant architectural forms may point to a variety of contemporary cults (Amiran 1989; Fox 1997), although similar offering assemblages (anthropomorphic and zoomorphic figurines/vessels, fenestrated stands, mortars, pestles and numerous cornet cups) from En Gedi, Gilat and Ghassul would imply broadly similar cult practice at each site. Minor variations may have a chronological explanation, and may be due to later codification of earlier less formalized practices (Bourke 2002b). Equally, changing economic (Joffe 1998) or environmental (Prag 1995; Hole 1997) conditions may have elicited different responses from heterar-

Figure 5.10 Processional wall painting from Ghassul.

chical religious communities as circumstances changed.

Material Remains

Ceramics

It is not yet possible to provide an adequate description of ceramic assemblages spanning the entire Chalcolithic period. Much is known about the latest Chalcolithic assemblages, generally (but not always) to be related in varying degrees of association with the classic Ghassulian assemblage (Figure 5.11, Mallon *et al.* 1934; Koeppel *et al.* 1940; Lee 1973; Elliot 1978), recently summarized by form (Garfinkel 1999) and chronological positioning (Stager 1992). Early Chalcolithic assemblages are far less well known at present, although recent work at Ghassul (Lovell 2001a), Abu Hamid (Lovell *et al.* 2004) and Pella (Bourke *et al.* 2003) begins to redress the balance. The present summary will confine itself to highlighting major trends visible in what are very much ongoing analyzes.

The classic Ghassulian Late Chalcolithic assemblage is dominated numerically by medium sized holemouth or short-necked storage jars and holemouth cooking pots. Distinctive forms, such as cornet cups, fenestrated stands, necked churns, ceramic spoons and very large storage containers are not unknown in earlier assemblages (Garfinkel 1999; Lovell 2001a; Blackham 1999, 2002), but become more common as time progresses. Most ceramic classes can be divided into forms associated with the two basic activities of food preparation/consumption and processing/storage. Large-scale feasting and other forms of conspicuous consumption (Joffe 1998), and the bulk storage and redistribution of agricultural produce (Earle [ed.] 1991), are recognized as important indicators of emerging stratified societies. Defining ceramic assemblages that

may be associated with such activities provides an important line of evidence in ongoing analyses of Chalcolithic societal development. Identifying specialized types (large storage vessels) and mass produced cooking (holemouth cooking pots) and feasting vessels (cornets) is one way to advance analysis. In the Early Chalcolithic assemblages there are few specialized ceramic forms (Garfinkel 1999), but with the onset of the Late Chalcolithic horizons at Tulaylat Ghassul, Abu Hamid and Pella in the lowlands and at Sahab in the highlands, such specialized forms become more common.

Another indicator of developing specialized production regimes within the ceramics industry may be novel manufacturing processes and inter-regional distribution networks, both of which become more visible over time. Early Chalcolithic assemblages display little evidence of standardized form/fabric repertoires, manufacturing techniques or elaborate distribution networks (Lovell 2001a; Garfinkel and Matskevich 2002). However, recent work on the Late Chalcolithic Ghassul (Lovell 2001a), Abu Hamid (Roux and Courty 1997) and Pella (Lovell 2000) assemblages would suggest the development of form-specific manufacturing (Lovell, pers.comm.) and firing (Edwards and Segnit 1984) techniques. Whilst the impact of specialized potting activities within the total ceramic assemblage remains relatively small, when coupled with limited chemical-analytical evidence (Goren 1989, 1995; Bourke 2002a) for an expanding regional distribution network in the Late Chalcolithic, and the incidence of potter's marks on a variety of ceramic forms (Garfinkel 1999; Bourke 2002b), one may posit the existence of a growing professional element working alongside the more common household production regimes, at least by the second half of the Late Chalcolithic period. As with agricultural diversification, it seems probable that an initially small professional component expanded steadily over time, as markets and the capacity to service them grew hand in hand.

The presence of unique ceramic forms may also be an indicator of specialized potting activity. Obvious examples of such material are the well known anthropomorphic and zoomorphic vessels from the Gilat and En Gedi sanctuaries (Joffe *et al.* 2001). Similar vessels have been found within the sanctuary complex at Ghassul (Seaton 2000, 2006), Abu Hamid (Dollfus and Kafafi 1995), and recently at Qulah (Milevski 2002). Whilst such vessels reveal much about particular cult practices (Amiran 1989; Fox 1997), they also draw attention to distinctive potting traditions. The ceramic ossuaries, found in a variety of prosaic container, anthropomorphic/zoomorphic and architectural forms (Perrot and Ladiray 1980; Gal *et al.* 1999), are another prominent example of specialized ceramic production. Another form of specialized production would appear to be the Gilat "torpedo jar" (Alon and Levy 1989; Goren 1995), and the distinctive

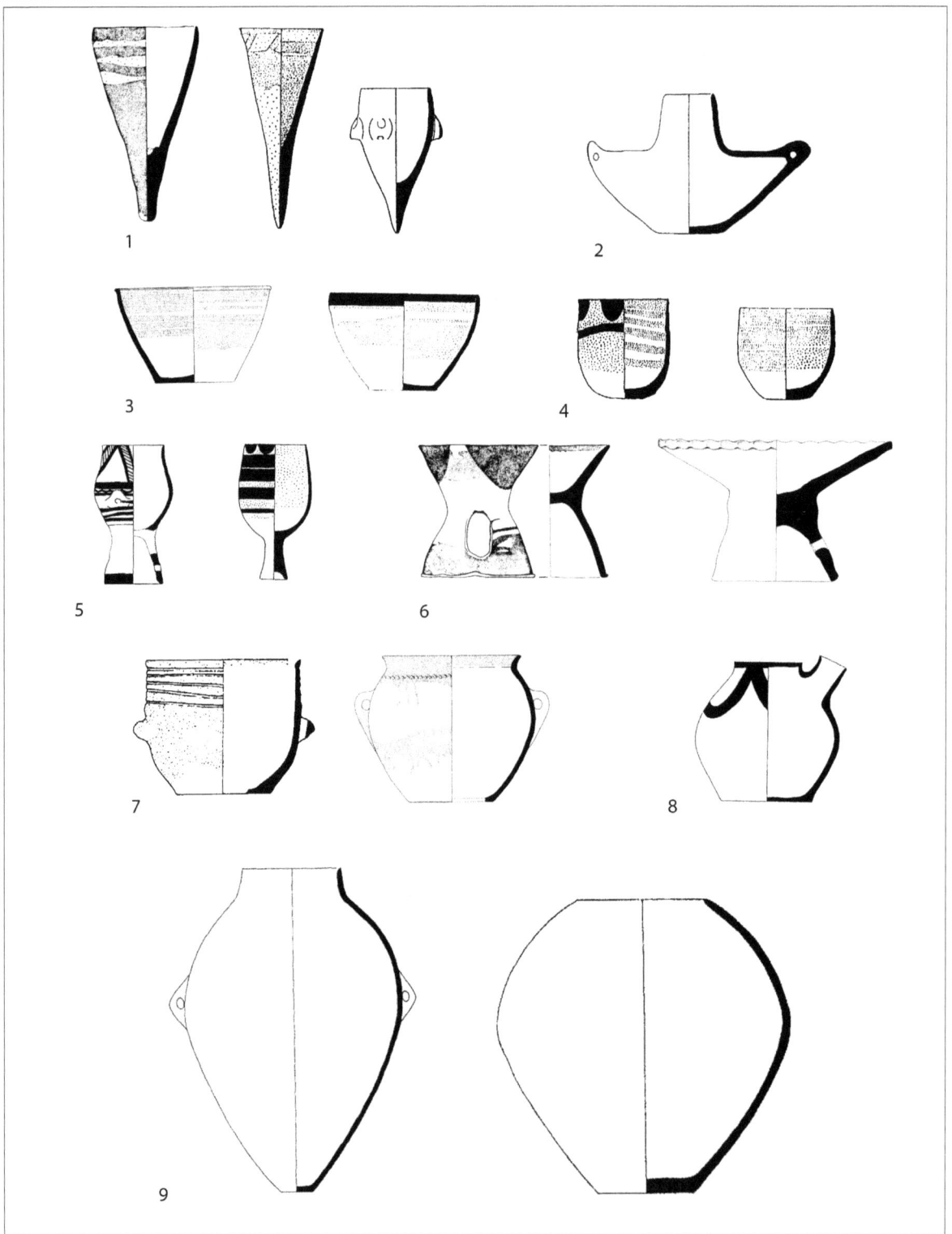

Figure 5.11 Pottery types from Ghassul. 1. Cornets; 2. Churn; 3. Bowls; 4. Cups; 5. Goblets; 6. Fenestrated Stands; 7. Jars; 8. Spouted Jar; 9. Storage jars.

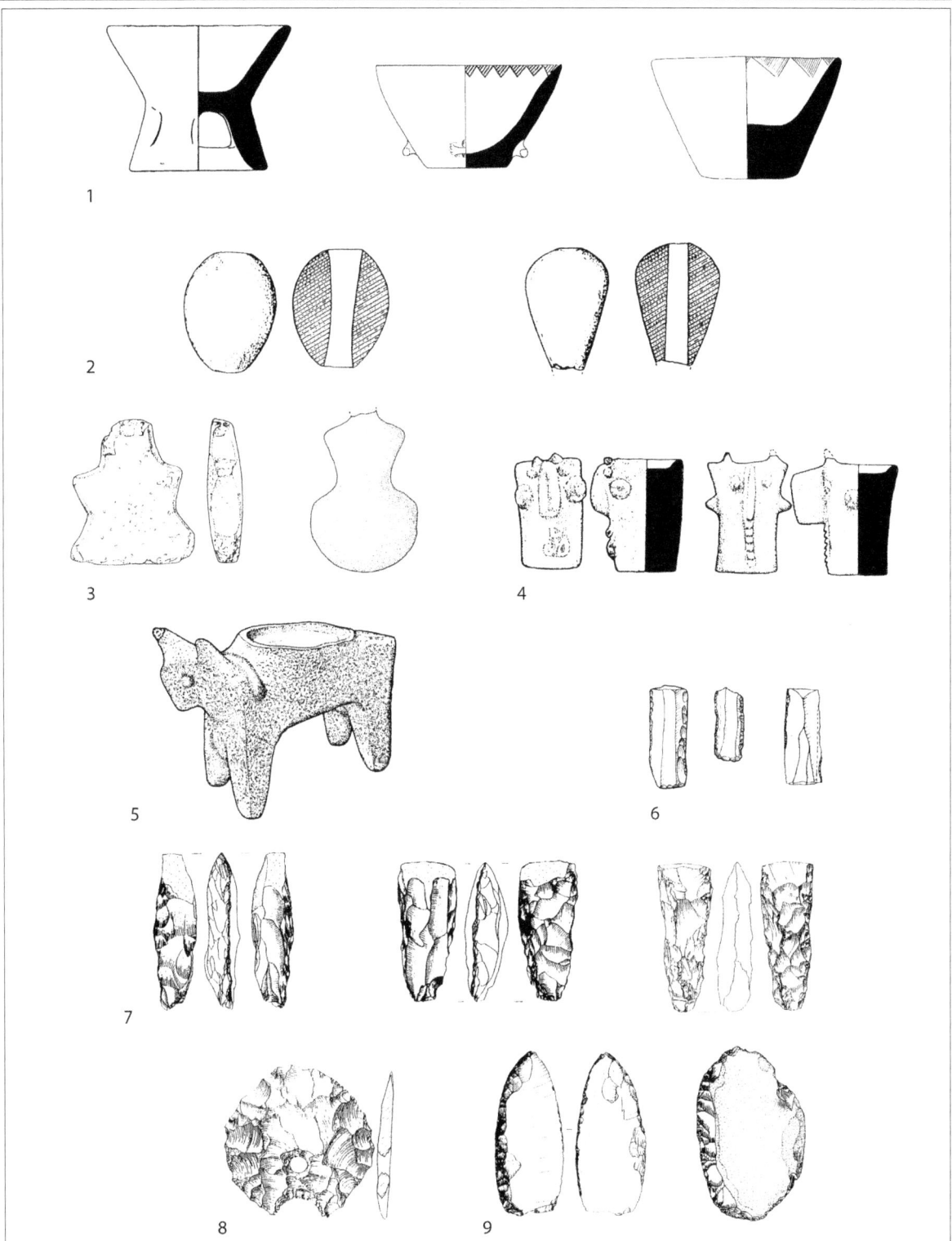

Figure 5.12 Ground and Flaked stone. 1. Basalt bowls; 2. Maceheads 3. Violin-shaped figurines; 4. Basalt anthropoid figurine; 5. Basalt zoomorphic figurine; 6. Sickle blades; 7. Chisels; 8. Holed-disk tool; 9. Fan scrapers.

Negevite "Cream Ware" ceramics (Amiran 1955; Blackham 1999). More evidence for specialized production in the Late Chalcolithic will be revealed when petrographic and chemical analyses move away from generic classification of regional assemblages (a necessary first step), and begin to focus on inter-regional analyses of distinctive form-classes (eg. very fine cornets, wheel-finished flasks, "V-shaped" bowls, "streaky-wash" ware), which are an increasingly numerous component of regional Late Chalcolithic assemblages as the period unfolds.

Most variation between Chalcolithic ceramic assemblages is confined to decorative regimes. Surface decoration varies widely both temporally and spatially (Lovell 2001a; Kerner 2001; Blackham 2002), and is often employed to differentiate assemblages chrono-spatially. Whilst it is probable that culturally significant information is encoded within sharply contrasting decorative regimes, undue emphasis should not be given to minor variations of motif placement or execution within broadly similar ceramic assemblages (Mellaart 1975; Garfinkel 1999), as such "variations on a theme" are more likely to signify within-group differentiation rather than significant cultural contrasts.

Stone Tools

Earlier Chalcolithic lithic assemblages are poorly defined, although current work on the long sequences from Tall Shuna North, Pella, Abu Hamid and Tulaylat Ghassul will eventually produce better defined assemblages, which will fill a large technological gap between the relatively well known Late Neolithic and Late Chalcolithic assemblages. The Late Chalcolithic Ghassulian assemblage (Figure 5.12.6–9) is often characterized by the presence of distinctive tool forms such as the chisel, the fan-scraper and the backed blade (Rosen 1997). Although related and probably ancestral forms of many typical Late Chalcolithic artefacts can be traced back to Late Neolithic precursors, careful techno-typological and frequency analyses of distinctive tool types characterize the Ghassulian lithic assemblage effectively. However, all Late Chalcolithic lithic assemblages are not equally well known, and it would certainly be premature to assume that contemporary lithic assemblages can be viewed as broadly similar without further detailed study. Individual lithic toolkits will (at least to some extent) reflect the requirements and resources of local environments, suggesting that any attempt to define a generic "Late Chalcolithic" lithic assemblage would involve unjustified generalization. Our procedure will be to describe prominent features of the lithic assemblage at Ghassul, recognizing that contemporaneous regional variations in the type and frequency of individual forms (tabular scrapers, holed disks) or manufacturing techniques (Baird 1987) are already well documented in the literature.

At Tulaylat Ghassul, the generic chisel form includes

a number of distinctive sub-classes defined by the presence or absence of hafting, hafting format, edge shape, length and butt condition (Lee 1973: 247–250). Hennessy's first season at Ghassul produced a large Late Chalcolithic lithic assemblage, but a very restricted sample of Early Chalcolithic material. Stockton's report on the 1967 material (Hennessy 1969:17) should be regarded as a detailed statement on the Late Chalcolithic (Phase A–C) assemblage only. His remarks on the earlier phased materials were based on very small samples and should be treated with caution. Habgood's detailed study of Ghassulian lithics (Habgood 1983) made use of Hennessy's 1975–77 Early Chalcolithic lithic assemblages, as well as Stockton's 1967 study. Habgood concluded that chisels were present throughout the Chalcolithic sequence, and that they were both more abundant and more typologically variable in Late Chalcolithic times. As well, a tendency towards greater overall body length, reduced body thickness, and increased blade width was observed during Late Chalcolithic times (Habgood 1983). Typological and technological studies are consistent with a variety of chopping, cutting and manufacturing uses (Lee 1973: 250).

Fan scrapers are another distinctive tool type found within the Late Chalcolithic toolkit (Lee 1973: 253–254). Whilst rare in earlier Chalcolithic assemblages, they are common in later toolkits (Hennessy 1969: 17–18; Habgood 1983), often displaying distinct intra-site distributional patterning (Bourke *et al.* 2000: 58). In south Levantine assemblages, they are made from a distinctive brown cortical flint, very probably sourced to the Jafr Basin (Quintero *et al.* 2002) in the east Jordanian desert. It had earlier been assumed that much of the brown cortical flint employed in Chalcolithic/EBA scraper manufacture was sourced to the western Negev (Rosen 1997: 75). Rosen has suggested that the geometric fall-off in frequency distribution for brown cortical flint (Rosen 1983: 80–81; Baird 1987: 476) was strongly suggestive of a Negevite source for EBA scrapers. However, recent Ghassul data reinforces earlier observations (Helms 1987b) that Jordanian Chalcolithic scraper distributions did not fit Rosen's logarithmic fall-off model nearly so well as subsequent EBA assemblages (Rosen 1997:105–106). It seems probable that the Jafr sources were far more important in Late Chalcolithic flint procurement strategies (Hanbury-Tenison 1986; Henry 1995; Khalil *et al.* 2003:166–168) than hitherto suspected (Quintero *et al.* 2002). The fan scraper has a relatively limited typological variation (Rosen 1997: 74), and function is likely to have been multi-purpose, as butchering knives (McConaughy 1979), hafted cutting tools (Lee 1973), and perhaps sheep shears (Henry 1995: 372–373).

The backed blade is another hallmark of the later Chalcolithic assemblages. Ghassulian blade manufacturing techniques tended to produce small to medium prismatic blades, fashioned from single-platform local wadi cobbles (Rosen 1997: 45–48). Backing is usually a unifacial abrupt hard hammer retouch, whilst infrequent working edge retouch varies from very slight ("nibbling") to a light serration. Retouch is general only on sickle blades, which commonly display silica sheen (Hennessy 1969: 18; Lee 1973: 250–251). Sickle blades tend to be between 5–8 cm long, rectangular in shape, truncated and reworked at each end, and triangular in section (Rosen 1997: 50).

There is some suggestion that the proto-Canaanean blade manufacturing technology begins towards the end of the Chalcolithic period (Hanbury-Tenison 1986: 146–150; Baird 1987: 476–478; Rowan and Levy 1994: 167–168), so that a limited presence of Canaanean technology may be consistent with a Chalcolithic date. However, Canaanean technology is rare in pre-Bronze Age assemblages (Rosen 1997: 50–55; Zbenovich 1998: 198–199), and concentrated in the very latest Chalcolithic/early EBA horizons at Tall Shuna North (Baird 1987: 478–479) and Tall Magass (Hanbury-Tenison 1986: 147; Rowan and Levy 1994: 168).

The perforated disc and/or star-shaped tool is one of the more enigmatic Chalcolithic tool types. It is made from a large flake, similar in initial production regime to the tabular scraper. Shapes range from semi-circular to rounded, with a multi-pronged or star-shaped variant. The primary flake is often retouched bifacially to thin the body, and abruptly retouched to shape the blunt side of asymmetrical tools. Most feature a central hole pecked through the body from one side. Distribution is concentrated in southern Syria, northern Palestine and upland north Jordan, with isolated examples found in north Jordan Valley sites (Hanbury-Tenison 1986: 142–143; Epstein and Noy 1988; Rosen 1997: 85). The few well dated examples are concentrated in the latest phases of the Chalcolithic period. Function remains unclear, but suggestions range from the prosaic use as a cutting tool (Epstein and Noy 1988), a wool carding device (Nasrallah 1948) to the ceremonial/symbolic (Hanbury-Tenison 1986; Rosen 1997). The pronged or star-shaped disc may have functioned as an actual weapon or perhaps as a symbol of authority. Parallels with the famous Nahal Mishmar star-shaped copper standards (Bar-Adon 1980: 47–50), or the more familiar mace/standards with holed disc-shaped tops (Bar-Adon 1980: 84–87), may well be relevant.

The bulk of the Chalcolithic lithic assemblage is made up of "ad hoc" tools (notches and denticulates, awls and borers, side scrapers and retouched flakes), with more than half the assemblage classed as debitage (Hikade in Bourke *et al.* 2003: fig.53). Chronological and typological distinctiveness of such tool categories within Chalcolithic assemblages remains unclear. It is probable that larger flake tools, abruptly retouched steep side scrapers, end scrapers, burins and bladelet tools are better associated with early Chalcolithic assemblages, although this remains speculative (Hennessy 1969: 18; Baird 1987: 476–478; Rosen 1997:

67). The "ad hoc" elements may represent less-specialized tool elements fashioned as needed for a range of "generic" tasks. At Tulaylat Ghassul, "ad hoc" elements show no particular spatial patterning, although high lithic frequencies in one area (F II) may indicate warehousing of primary materials or the presence of a lithic "workshop" area.

Ground Stone

A prominent feature of the Chalcolithic ground stone assemblage (Figure 5.12. 1–5) are the basalt bowl forms (Hanbury-Tenison 1986: 162–163; Gonen 1992: 57–58; Gilead [ed.] 1995: 310–311), although other stone materials (phosphorite and limestone) are occasionally utilized. The most common products are the wide flaring-rim flat-based "V-shaped" bowl form. These are often decorated with shallow diagonally incised triangular motifs, pendent from rim interiors (Bourke *et al.* 2000: fig. 23). A less common variation on this bowl form features the addition of a fenestrated foot or bar-ring stand, which together form a high-footed chalice. These fenestrated vessels occasionally display elaborate horizontal ridged decoration at the body/base join, and cross-hatched light incision on leg exteriors. Many vessels (both simple and elaborate) are highly polished on interior surfaces.

A second distinctive product of the Chalcolithic ground-stone industry are the basalt sculptured figurative vessels. These can be both anthropomorphic and zoomorphic, although the cylindrical anthropomorphic "pillar figures" are the better known. Pillar figures (Epstein 1975, 1988) feature prominent facial features (ears, eyes, nose), and usually include a shallow bowl at the top of the figure. Zoomorphic figures of horned bovines or caprines with a shallow bowl on the back are less well known but equally spectacular (Ibrahim and Mittmann 1998). Pillared figures (anthropomorphic and zoomorphic) are generally considered products of the "Golan" Chalcolithic culture (Epstein 1988; Ibrahim and Mittmann 1998), which spans the lowlands of the eastern Galilee, the Golan and Damascus basin, and south into upland north Jordan (Epstein 1978a; Hanbury-Tenison 1986).

Ghassul has been suggested as a major basalt vessel manufacturing centre in the past (Gilead and Goren 1989; Gilead [ed.] 1995), but recent petrological and chemical studies suggest that whilst utilitarian tools derived from the local Sweimeh outcrops, fine bowls were made from north Jordanian upland basalts (Philip and Williams-Thorpe 2000, 2001). Large (and virtually unexplored) north Jordanian sites such as Sal (Kafafi and Vieweger 2000) are littered with basalt vessels made from outcrops close by the site (Philip and Williams-Thorpe 1993), and at least some of the distinctive figurative vessels are probably to be sourced to this region (Kamleh 2000; Ibrahim and Mittmann 1998). Philip and Williams-Thorpe's most recent chemical analyses (2000, 2001) suggest that a major production centre for fine basalt bowls and figurative pieces is to be located on the north Jordan plateau. Whilst the fine bowl forms seem to have been widely traded, the figured basalt pieces are rarely found outside their Central Levantine core area. However, one non-figurative cylindrical vessel, a solid concave-sided pillar with characteristic shallow bowl on top, was recently discovered in the Ghassul sanctuary area (Seaton 2000; Bourke *et al.* 2000). Although the Ghassul pillar may be unrelated to the Golan sculptures (Hanbury-Tenison 1986: 163), the similarity to rare undecorated (early?) pillar figures (Epstein 1975: 55) suggests that it might be. Given Epstein's suggested cultic context for the Golan pillar figures (Epstein 1978a), the sanctuary context of the Ghassul pillar may be especially significant (Bourke *et al.* 2000: 46–49).

Ground and polished stone maceheads are a characteristic feature of the Chalcolithic stone assemblage (Bar-Adon 1980: 116; Hanbury-Tenison 1986: 164; Gonen 1992: 58). They have been found at Magass (Khalil 1992: 144–145), Ghassul (Mallon *et al.* 1934: 71; Lee 1973: 276–7), Abu Hamid (Dollfus and Kafafi 1989: 107 and fig. 9), Pella (Bourke *et al.* 1994: 91–93) and Tubna (Banning *et al.* 1998: 153). Most maceheads are either spherical or pear-shaped, with drilled central perforations. A variety of stones were employed in their manufacture, although limestone, calcite and haematite are the most common. Whilst the limestone is likely to derive from local sources (Bender 1974), and the haematite may be sourced to the Ajlun region (Hauptmann, pers. comm.), the calcite is probably imported from the Eastern Desert of Egypt (Lucas and Harris 1962).

The majority of Chalcolithic maceheads are made from high prestige (copper), rare (haematite) or imported (calcite) materials, making them far more likely to be markers of status (Blackham 1999: 62) than simple weapons of war. Their presence in assemblages need not imply militarization of society (Levy 1995: 243), but probably serves as further evidence for developing social stratification (Cialowicz 1989). At Ghassul, the recent discovery of a miniature haematite macehead, a siltstone stamp seal, a mother-of-pearl pectoral and several miniature ceramic vessels closely associated within a large multi-purpose complex, may provide a further indication of the link between maceheads (particularly miniatures) and elite activity (Bourke *et al.* 2000: 71–74).

Miscellaneous ground stone objects bulk large within the Chalcolithic assemblage, and range from quite large coarse stone mortars, through various-sized discoid spindle whorls, to a variety of shaped semi-precious polished and bored stone beads (Lee 1973: 263–283). The majority of the roughly fashioned stone mortars, pestles, hoes, picks and hammerstones derive from local limestone, basalt and flint sources. Stone spindle whorls are generally discoid shaped with a bored central hole, and derive from local limestones. Beads are made from a wide variety of materials, ranging from locally available limestones, through semi-precious haematite, carnelian and greenstone, to exotic imported serpentinite and calcite examples (Bourke *et al.* 1995: 49–53; Bourke 2002a: 155–156).

Worked Bone, Ivory and Shell

At Ghassul and at other valley sites, the bone tool assemblage seems to derive from local domesticates (Lee 1973: 284–293; Hanbury-Tenison 1986: 164–165), with ovicaprine metapodials the predominant material used (Bourke *et al.* 1995: 49–50, 2000: 74). Most are fashioned into a variety of more or less keenly sharpened points, needles, burnishers and spatulae. The majority of such points, awls and needles were probably used in hide, fibre and food preparation. A minority of the more finely worked and highly polished bone points were likely to have been used as hair or clothing pins, perhaps in association with numerous small flat disk beads and polished trapesoidal bone pendants, as jewellery items. To be included among jewellery items are several highly polished miniature violin-shaped pendants known from Pontifical Biblical Institute (Scham 1997: 108) and recent Sydney University excavations (Figure 5.15.12; Bourke *et al.* 2000: fig. 22:7). More enigmatic, possibly mnemonic pieces are known (Levy and Golden 1996: 155–157; Scham 1997: 108), although such challenging interpretations remain contentious. Several small highly polished and skillfully worked hippopotamus tusk ivory pendants were recovered from Pontifical Biblical Institute excavations (Lee 1973: 288–289). Tortoise shell was occasionally used for bead and pendant manufacture (Lee 1973: 285), although both ivory and tortoise are rare in the bone assemblage.

At Ghassul, both worked and unworked shell occurs within an assemblage dominated by local Melanopsis and Unio species (Lee 1973: 305–316; Hanbury-Tenison 1986: 165; Reese 1998). The Pontifical Biblical Institute excavators found several pieces of Red Sea mother of pearl (Maleagrina margaritifera) shaped into crescent pectorals with holes at each end, and a further pectoral (Figure 5.15.13) was found in recent Sydney University excavations (Bourke *et al.* 2000: 71). Numbers of the Nilotic Aspatharia (found by both expeditions) may have been employed as tools and ornaments (Reese *et al.* 1986). Examples of the less frequently found Glycymeris, Cardium, Conus and Tridacna were probably also employed as jewellery (Lee 1973). In southern Jordan Tall Magass profits from its proximity to the Red Sea sources of several shell families, with considerable evidence for shell bead manufacture recovered from the site (Khalil 1992: 144).

Metallurgy and Faience

Copper tools are rare and occur in Late Chalcolithic assemblages only. At Ghassul, two complete and several fragmentary chisel-like flattened axes were found during Mallon's excavations on Tulayl 1 (Figure 5.15.5; Mallon *et al.* 1934: 75). They seem quite similar in overall dimensions to polished narrow-pointed flint chisel forms, and probably served a similar function (Rosen 1997). As well, several quite large fishhook-shaped implements were recovered. Their function remains unclear, but seems probably architectural. Mallon's early chemical analysis (Mallon *et al.* 1934: 77) returned the surprising result of a high tin content. Recent re-examination of two of the axes by Hauptmann has found the original analyses to have been in error. The axes were made from a nearly pure copper, suggesting an unsurprising association with Faynan ores (Hauptmann, pers. comm.). Otherwise, with the exception of a number of simple pin fragments, copper tools remain very rare at Ghassul.

Copper of any sort is equally rare at Abu Hamid (Dollfus and Kafafi 1989: 106), Pella (Bourke *et al.* 2003) and Tall Shuna North (Rehren *et al.* 1997), and generally confined to pin fragments. However, the situation at Tall Magass is noticably different. Here copper ore, slag in small quantities and metallic copper finds are considerably more common (Khalil 1992: 144–147; Khalil and Riederer 1998). The site is likely to have benefited from its proximity to Timnan ores, the source of some (but probably not all) of the copper at Magass (Khalil 1992: 147; Khalil and Riederer 1998: 7). Links with Timnan ores might imply an Early Bronze Age date for the levels in which copper appears (Rothenberg 1999), an interpretation recently supported by radiometric (Görsdorf 2002) and ceramic (Kerner 2003) evidence.

If copper distribution is accepted as a useful indicator of inter-regional interaction, then the rarity of copper tools and the absence of any of the more specialized arsenical/antimony copper alloy objects in Jordan would seem to imply that Jordanian sites were not part of Negevite copper distribution networks (Bourke 2002a). However, as the arsenical/antimony objects are regarded by many as special status objects (Tadmor *et al.* 1995; Gopher and Tsuk [eds.] 1996), their absence from Jordan could equally be accounted for by variant cult practices. A chronological element may also be at work. Copper production in general, and especially the production of arsenical/antimony alloy objects, would seem to be confined to the latest phases of the Beersheban Chalcolithic (Joffe and Dessel 1995). If new dates for the end of significant occupation at Ghassul have any more general application, then many Jordanian sites may well have been in sharp decline or already abandoned by late Beersheban times (Bourke *et al.* 2001, 2004).

A number of pale brown faience disk beads have been recovered in recent excavations at Tulaylat Ghassul. Faience remains very rare in all but the latest Chalcolithic contexts, and the small quantities known to exist at Tulaylat Ghassul (Bourke *et al.* 1995: 52–53) may well

derive from Egypt (Peltenburg 1987: 11–12; 1995: 36–37), although local production associated with small-scale copper smelting should not be discounted.

Seals, Tokens and Potmarks

Stamp seals (Figure 5.13) are very rare elements in Late Chalcolithic assemblages (Ben-Tor 1995: 365–366), and their significance in south Levantine contexts remains unclear (Hanbury-Tenison 1986: 100). In Syro-Mesopotamia, similar seals are viewed as unambiguous indicators of centralizing tendencies in the economic sphere, and growing complexity in the social sphere (Schmandt-Besserat 1992). A detailed analysis of the spiral-incised stamp seal from Grar (Ben-Tor 1995) has identified it as phyllite, a non-local grey-green soapstone equivalent of likely Syrian origin (Ben-Tor 1995: 361–362). Further, Ben-Tor has suggested that most other spiral-incised stamp seals found west of the Jordan are made of this material, implying all are imports (Ben-Tor 1995: 366). Whilst this provocative suggestion needs to be confirmed by petrographic analysis, it holds the implication that as occasional imports into the Late (perhaps very late) southern Levantine Chalcolithic, such seals need not hold any significance for local socio-economic development.

At Ghassul, recent excavations discovered a carefully crafted square cross-hatch incised siltstone stamp seal, found in a reliable Late Chalcolithic context, in association with a haematite macehead and mother-of-pearl jewellery (Bourke *et al.* 2000: 71). This is quite unlike the small conical circle-incised stamp seals found in Mallon's excavations (Mallon *et al.* 1934; Lee 1973; Elliot 1978), but is very close to the seal fragment found at Sahab (Ibrahim 1983: 44). Helms' (1991: 113–117, 333) synthesis of the early Jordanian glyptic evidence would suggest that cross-hatch incised seal findspots are concentrated in the south Jordan Valley, and are products of that region. The cross-hatch motif on the Sahab seal might suggest an economic link between the eastern upland regions and the south Jordan Valley, consistent with Sahab's general cultural affiliations (Ibrahim 1987: 73–75). The distribution of the round spiral-incised seals may imply the existence of a second, coastal maritime network (Mellaart 1975: 158; Keel 1989: 3–4; Ben-Tor 1995).

However one interprets the significance of the spiral and cross-hatch incised seals, they remain rare in the south Levantine Chalcolithic, and if they are to be seen as the first indicators of a nascent bureaucratic system, further evidence of record keeping might be expected (Bourke 2002b: 12–14). In Syro-Mesopotamia, a variety of small geometric counters (Schmandt-Besserat 1992) and an increased frequency of incised and stamped potmarks (Helms 1991), are two of the more prominent indicators of such a tendency, and both are present in the Late Chalcolithic assemblages of the Jordan Valley (Lee 1973; Helms 1987a).

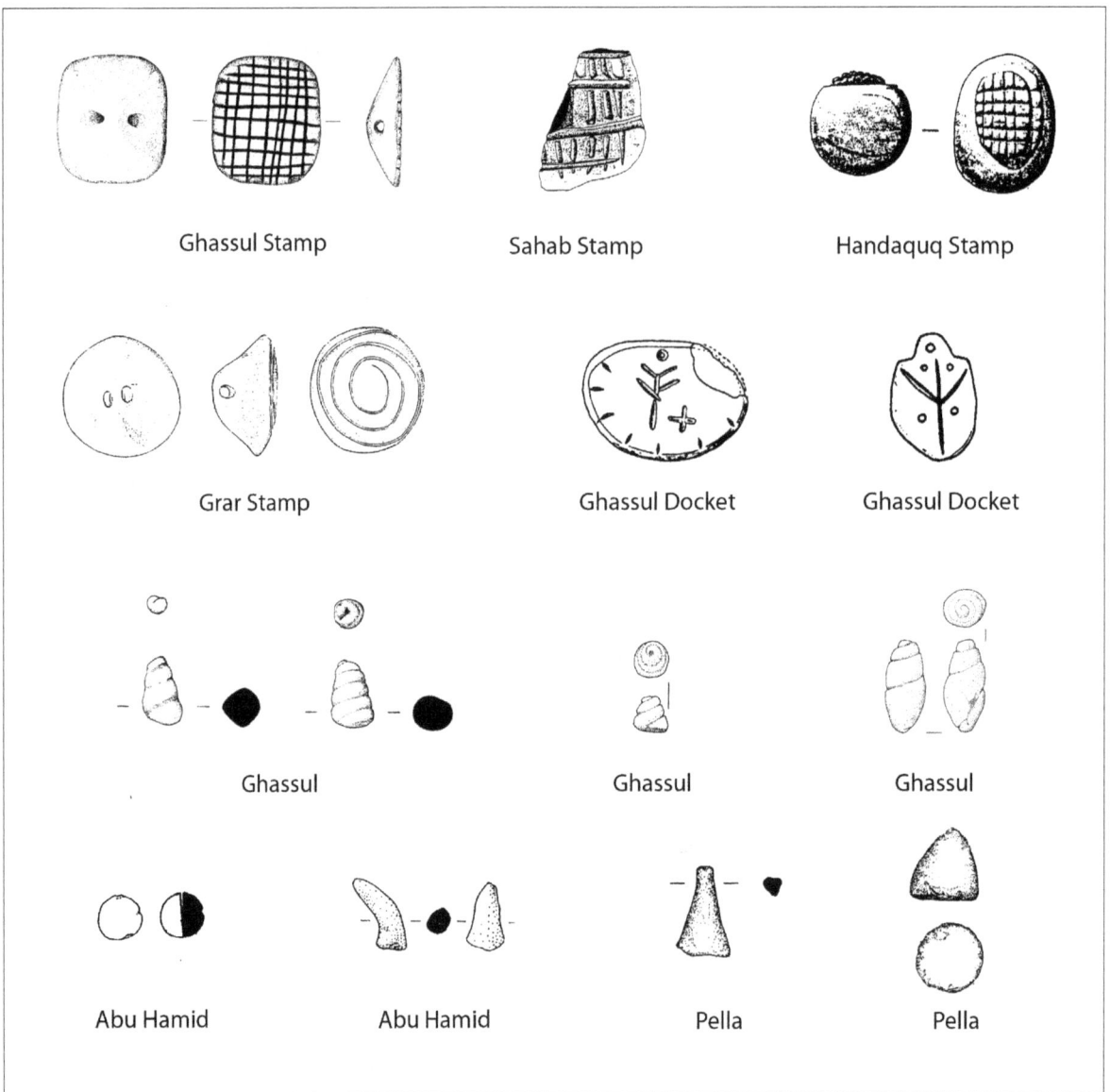

Figure 5.13 Stamps, Dockets and Tokens at Tulaylat Ghassul, Sahab, Tall Handaquq North, Grar, Abu Hamid and Pella.

Numerous small ceramic or stone tokens have been documented as precursors to writing in Syro-Mesopotamia (Schmandt-Besserat 1992), and a few isolated examples have been discovered in Jordanian Chalcolithic contexts. Two stone spiral grooved conoid tokens (Schmandt-Besserat 1992: 204, Cone Type 1:38) were recovered off a floor in recent work at Ghassul (Bourke *et al.* 2000: 71). These may be associated with several stone conoids with incised circles around their bases (Lee 1973: 278–279, LB 61), quite close to Schmandt-Besserat's Punctated Base Conoids (1992: 204, Cone Type 1:25). These very small pieces have often been identified as stamp seals (Elliot 1978), but are perhaps better seen as tokens. As well,

a number of small limestone flattened spheroids with incised points set around their rim (Lee 1973: 276–77, LB 513 h–i) identified as small loom weights, may possibly be seen as Spheroid Punctated tokens (Schmandt-Besserat 1992: 206, Cone Type 2:6A). At Abu Hamid, a number of animal "horns" published with ceramic figurine fragments (Dollfus and Kafafi 1989, 106; 1995: 451, Cone Type 1:2), may be ceramic conoid tokens (Schmandt-Besserat 1992: 203, Cone Types 1:3 and 1:14), and a small partly perforated ceramic ball (Dollfus and Kafafi 1989: Cone Type 9:3), may be a Notched Sphere token (Schmandt-Besserat 1992: 206, Cone Type 2:7). From Pella comes a Ceramic Truncated Cone token (Schmandt-Besserat

1992: 203, Cone Type 1:13) and a Ceramic Flattened Cone token (Schmandt-Besserat 1992: 203, Cone Type 1:2), both from storage contexts (Bourke 2002b: 12–14).

Detecting further examples of south Levantine tokens will not be a straightforward procedure, as an element of subjectivity in identification will remain until an agreed-upon corpus is constructed. This is unlikely to be identical to Schmandt-Besserat's Syro-Mesopotamian corpus, although it probably will emulate essential features. It remains to be seen if an increased sensitivity to the potential significance of small clay objects in the wake of Schmandt-Besserat's synthetic study produces many more examples than the few offered above. However, the rich harvest of tokens and sealings produced in Syro-Mesopotamian destruction deposits (Akkermans and Duistermaat 1997; Campbell 2000) suggests that taphonomic factors play a very significant role in the preservation of unfired tokens and sealings. Whilst the isolated finds documented above do not allow us to claim a greatly increased concern for record-keeping in the Jordanian Late Chalcolithic, they do suggest a first movement in this direction, perhaps under the influence of northern developments.

Incised potmarks are a relatively common occurrence on Late Chalcolithic pottery vessels at Ghassul. These marks are generally very simple devices, such as crosses of various forms, circles in isolation or with a variety of associated linear ornament, diagonal and upright cross-hatched patches or simple tree motifs (Mallon *et al.* 1934: 121–122; Lee 1973; Helms 1987c). On rare occasions these incised marks can include zoomorphic figures (North 1964). Perhaps to be associated with the increased incidence of potmarks are a number of docket-like geometric stone plaques, generally with a suspension hole at their centre-top, known from Pontifical Biblical Institute excavations (Lee 1973: 278–279, LB 62; Schmandt-Besserat 1992: 219, 7: 20–23).

All potmarks, plaques and zoomorphic incised figures are confined to the latest phases at Ghassul. With caution, one may associate such tendencies with the first predynastic Egyptian steps towards hieroglyphic recording practice (Baines 1988; Schmandt-Besserat 1992: 167–183; Schulman 1992: 412–415). Again, one must be careful not to overstate the case for developing bureaucratic practice in Late Chalcolithic Ghassul, as the examples offered above remain isolated cases. Even so, the weight of evidence (seal, token and potmark) is consistent with a heightened concern for recording practices in Late Chalcolithic Jordan. The indicators are fitful at present, but the corpus of bureaucratic recording devices steadily grows.

Wall Paintings

Wall painting was one of the most distinctive, and artistically brilliant features of the Chalcolithic period in Jordan (Cameron 1981). At Tulaylat Ghassul, when first discovered by Mallon in 1931, the polychrome figured wall paintings (Figure 5.10) seemed a uniquely early manifestation of artistic brilliance (Mallon *et al.* 1934: 129–141). Mellaart's subsequent magnificent discoveries at Neolithic Çatal Hüyük (Mellaart 1967, 1975), and the full publication of the Hierakonpolis T.100 material (Payne 1973; Kemp 1973, 1989), demonstrated that such endeavour had a very long history. Rather than being a spectacular anomaly, the Chalcolithic paintings from Ghassul represent a brilliant episode in a long developmental process. However, one must guard against the tendency to relate the earlier (Çatal Hüyük) and later (Hierakonpolis) manifestations via the medium of Ghassul (Cameron 1981: 32–35), as there is no demonstrable direct link between the three artistic traditions. New discoveries, such as those at Arslantepe (Frangipane 1997), make a nonsense of such sweeping associations.

Numerous wall painting fragments and assorted pieces of painted plaster have been found over the course of the four phases of field excavation at Ghassul. In her detailed consideration of the Ghassul paintings, Cameron (1981: 3) isolates seven main paintings for detailed consideration, although it must be emphasized that many more fragments of painted wall decoration are known from across the site. Of the seven highlighted paintings, three (the Notables, Star and Bird friezes) were found during the first Pontifical Biblical Institute excavations (Mallon *et al.* 1934: 129–140), and another two (the Geometric and Tiger friezes) in subsequent Pontifical Biblical Institute work (North 1961: 32–36; Blackham 1999). Hennessy found the geometric Zig-Zag fragment in 1967 (Hennessy 1969: 7), and the polychrome Procession frieze in 1977 (Hennessy 1978; see Figure 5.10, p.131).

The Ghassul wall paintings are generally painted onto a brilliant white through yellow-buff fine lime wash, laid over a more substantial mudplaster backing. Paints are generally mineral based, and probably applied to a still-damp surface. Colours include deep scarlet, dark blue, black, green, yellow and a range of browns, all typically well preserved. As each wall shows evidence of multiple overpaintings, and each individual mural began with a new fine lime wash, the adhesion of each overpainting to previous murals is generally poor, and flakes of various depths easily detach. It is quite common to lift a fragment of painting which displays elements of up to five overpaintings on the preserved surface. This complicates interpretation, and much confusion has resulted from a failure to differentiate between the various overpainting phases, often with hilarous results—the "walrus fangs" reconstructed on many of the "spook" masks are the result of earlier cornet cup motifs combined with later "spook" masks (Cameron 1981: 10). Much laboured interpretation of apparently related motifs on such paintings as the Star fresco is misguided, as preserved motifs often represent a palimpsest of between five and twenty unrelated overpaintings.

The first of Cameron's paintings, the "Notables frieze" (Cameron 1981: 4), is drawn from the bottom half metre strip of an approximately five metre long painting. The painting illustrates the feet of a series of large seated figures, facing a much smaller figure, standing in front of a large painted star. The second, the famous "star" frieze (Cameron 1981: 5), consists of an approximately two metre wide eight-pointed polychrome decorated star, apparently associated with a selection of architectural, zoomorphic, geometric and masked anthropomorphic motif fragments, many of which are overlapped by the central Star motif. The third painting, the "Bird" frieze (Cameron 1981: 6), was immediately recognized as being executed in a noticeably different style to the previous finds. The rendering of the plumage on a partridge-like fowl is naturalistic (almost impressionistic) in style, and sharply different to the crisp linear technique of the preceding murals. Unfortunately little associated contextual motifs were recovered from this five metre long stretch of painting.

North's second-phase Pontifical Biblical Institute work first discovered the large "Geometric" frieze (Cameron 1981: 7–8). Important points here are North's observations on the unique combination of raised hollow plastic ornament (craters) with geometric lined decoration (North 1961: 35), and Cameron's controversial suggested parallel with the famous Vulture Frieze at Çatal Hüyük (Cameron 1981: 20–21), with all that this seems to imply for shared funerary excarnation rituals (Cameron 1995: 118). North's second discovery, the famous polychrome "Tiger" frieze (North 1961: 6; Cameron 1981: 9), consists of a confusing array of overlapping segments of unrelated motifs, apparently dominated by a large striped animal. Here Cameron's suggested reconstruction (Cameron 1981: 28–31) of an elaborately dressed male figure in place of North's "tiger" is more plausible.

Hennessy's monochrome "Zig-Zag" fragment came from a large Phase B broadroom discovered in 1967 (Hennessy 1969: 7; Cameron 1981: 12). It was part of a larger painting, but only a small metre-square piece was recoverable. The preserved fragment seems to be of a house-like structure (Cameron 1981: 31). The house form illustrated appears to have an opening in its short side, and as the typical Late Chalcolithic dwelling units at Tulaylat Ghassul were broadrooms, it seemed at least possible that the structure illustrated was an ossuary. Hennessy discovered the famous "Processional" frieze in early 1977, lifted it during the second 1977 field season, and had it conserved in Amman in 1978. This scene, also much complicated by multiple overpaintings, appears to show a procession of elaborately attired masked figures, the largest carrying a sickle-shaped object, promenading towards a walled complex, shown in plan to the left of the procession (Cameron 1981: 13). It only remains to be noted that Hennessy found large amounts of shattered

wall painting fragments associated with the Area E sanctuary buildings, along with what can plausibly be reconstructed as a painter's workshop in trench F V, outside the complex to the northeast (Hennessy 1978). However, no substantial wall painting fragments were recoverable during excavations in the sanctuary precinct.

Recently renewed excavations at Ghassul have recovered small pieces of painted plaster in a number of locations, and one half metre square fragment, found in 1995 in trench N II, northeast of Hennessy's Area A (Seaton in Bourke *et al.* 2000: 65–66). The "Garlanded Sickle" fragment shows a red sickle-shaped object, with white garlands threaded through circular holes in the object. It is vaguely similar to the perforated sickle-like objects discovered at Nahal Mishmar (Bar-Adon 1980:16–21), one of which retained traces of red colour and fragments of fibre. It is possible that the Garlanded Sickle painting and the Mishmar Perforated sickles relate in some way to the sickle-like object held by the lead figure in Hennessy's "Processional" frieze (Cameron 1981: 27; Figure 5.10).

For fifty years, the Ghassul wall paintings were unique in the Chalcolithic of Jordan (Cameron 1981: 3), but a find from Abu Hamid has demonstrated that polychrome wall painting was not confined to one site in the south Jordan Valley (Dollfus and Kafafi 1993: 251–253). The Abu Hamid fragment consists of a series of linear and filled geometric motifs painted onto an off-white background. It is similar in design, technique and execution to several of the smaller geometric fragments from Ghassul.

The wall paintings from Ghassul are a uniquely important record of ancient socio-cultic behaviour, as well as representing an important landmark in the history of art. Art speaks with an immediacy matched by few other media, and the quality of the painting and the apparent naturalism of the Ghassulian subject matter serves only to emphasize a feeling of accessibility. However, interpretation of subject matter and evaluations of cultural significance are far more troubled territory than earlier analysts acknowledged (Cameron 1981: 32–35; Mellaart 1998: 37–39; Hodder and Matthews 1998: 50–51). Even so, it is probable that at least some of the more famous Ghassulian wall paintings (the Star, Notables and Processional paintings) do illustrate aspects of cult practice.

Figurines

Stylized human and animal figurines (Figure 15. 11–12) are a feature of the Jordanian Chalcolithic, and both have a long history in the region (Mellaart 1975; Garfinkel 1995; Gopher and Orelle 1996; McAdam 1997). The most distinctive is the "violin-shaped" figurine. The small to medium sized figurines are made predominantly of ground and polished limestone, although a variety of stone types, including calcite, marble, greenstone and sandstone have been recorded (Levy and Golden 1996: 153–156). Miniature violin pendants in ivory and bone are known from Ghassul (Lee 1973: 279. e–f; Bourke *et al.* 2000: fig. 22: 7) and in greenstone from Abu Hamid (Dollfus and Kafafi [eds.] 1988: 49, fig. 80). The extreme stylization of most violin figurines is in sharp contrast with more naturalistic, but much rarer basalt (Shiqmim) and ivory (Abu Matar/Bir Safadi) figurines from the northern Negev (Levy and Golden 1996: 154–155).

The majority of violin-figurine find contexts west of the Jordan have been interpreted as cultic (Perrot 1959; Alon and Levy 1989; Levy and Golden 1996; Levy [ed.] 2006: 753–804). The sheer concentration (59) of such figurines at Gilat would seem to be support for such a contention (Levy and Golden 1996: 155). Violin figurines are known from Ghassul (Lee 1973: 278, LB 72), Abu Hamid (Dollfus and Kafafi 1995: 454–455) and Pella (Bourke *et al.* 2003: fig. 39: 1). Whilst none are from an explicitly cultic context, at Ghassul Lee's (1973) Tulayl 3 findspot co-ordinates are consistent with a relationship to the Building 78 cult complex (Elliot 1977; Bourke 2002a: 160). The Pella findspot lies near later (MBA) cult installations, and associated with a Chalcolithic complex which may have been a cultic focus (Bourke *et al.* 1998: 180–181). The context of the Abu Hamid figurines remains to be clarified, although association with the zoomorphic bull rhyton and the macehead cache should not be ruled out (Dollfus and Kafafi [eds.] 1988; Dollfus and Kafafi 1995: 455). However, no violin figurines were found associated with Hennessy's Sanctuary complex (Seaton 2000), none are reported from upland Chalcolithic sites, and no Jordan Valley site has recorded anything like the concentration of figurines reported at Gilat. The presence of violin figurines in Jordan Valley assemblages may represent items of exchange rather than indigenous products (Alon and Levy 1989: 209; Dollfus and Kafafi 1995: 455), perhaps indicating some form of cult association between a Gilat central place and Jordan Valley peripheries (Levy [ed.] 2006).

Animal figurines are very common within early and later Chalcolithic assemblages, and both technique and subject matter hark back to Neolithic examplars (Garfinkel 1995; McAdam 1997). The majority are small and fashioned by hand, although bone tools are occasionally used to pick out finer details. Many Neolithic figurines are unfired (McAdam 1997: 135), but most Chalcolithic examples are generally well fired. Although identifying types is a manifestly subjective endeavour, it would appear that the majority of Ghassul's figurines represent domestic ovicaprines and cattle, and a variety of deer, dog and bird species. Animal and bird figurines are also known from Abu Hamid (Dollfus and Kafafi 1995: 451–455) and animal figurines from Pella.

Function is not obvious beyond simple representation, but the fact that many of the figurines found at Ghassul are broken at the neck or mid-body may be significant, given the apparent "ritual killing" of many of the Ayn Ghazal figurines (McAdam 1997: 131–135). Whilst damage to the largely unfired Neolithic figurines from Ayn Ghazal may be due to their original fragility, the well-fired Chalcolithic examples (Mallon *et al.* 1934: 83–87) suggest something more than simple wear and tear may be occurring. However, at Ghassul contextual details do not support any specialized function, with most figurine fragments derived from rubbish deposits. Many show traces of burning, but this may relate to often ashy depositional contexts. Function as ornaments (Levy 1993), talleys (Schmandt-Besserat 1992; McAdam 1997) or protective talismans are all possible. Whatever function the animal figurines may have served, they document a concern for a relatively limited number of species, in a lively plastic art tradition.

Burial Customs

Subfloor shallow pit burials are the norm for neonatal and young child burials in the Chalcolithic southern Levant (Hanbury-Tenison 1986: 205–231; Gonen 1992: 74–78). Around forty neonatal and child burials are known from Tulaylat Ghassul (Lee 1973: 332–338; Elliot 1977: 22; Hennessy 1969: 7; Blackham 1999: 37–38), some buried in jars and others roughly contained by large storage jar sherds. They are generally to be located beneath floors in room corners. However, early suggestions that this practice documents child sacrifice (Mallon *et al.* 1934: 49–50; Lee 1973: 334–336) are likely to be incorrect. Similar child burials are known from Pella (Hanbury-Tenison 1986) and Tall Shuna North (Baird and Philip 1994). Burial analysis is commonly employed to explore socioeconomic developmental status. Child burials with disproportionate amounts of grave goods at Shiqmim (Levy and Alon 1982: 52–53) and Nahal Qanah (Gopher and Tsuk 1996: 226) are claimed as evidence for an ascribed status regime in Late Chalcolithic times, but such evidence is not particularly compelling (Hanbury-Tenison 1986: 220–224).

Intramural adult burials are very rare in Jordanian Chalcolithic sites (Elliot 1977: 21–22; Hanbury-Tenison 1986: 224), and extramural cemeteries are both rare and difficult to define (Joffe 2003). It is commonly observed that select elements of the ruinfields at Adaymeh (Figure 5.14), located two kilometres southeast of Ghassul, constitute the most likely cemetery for Ghassul (Mallon *et al.* 1934; Stekelis 1935; Hanbury-Tenison 1986). Adaymeh was excavated by Stekelis in 1933 (Stekelis 1935) concurrently with Pontifical Biblical Institute work at Ghassul. Confusion has arisen from the intermixture of a number of distinct and perhaps unrelated elements within the one three hectare ruinfield. The first component is a large cist grave cemetery, consisting of several hundred metre-long stone-lined rectangular pits, containing either tightly flexed primary inhumations or secondary burials consisting of long-bone and skull clusters. The cist cemetery may

Adaymah

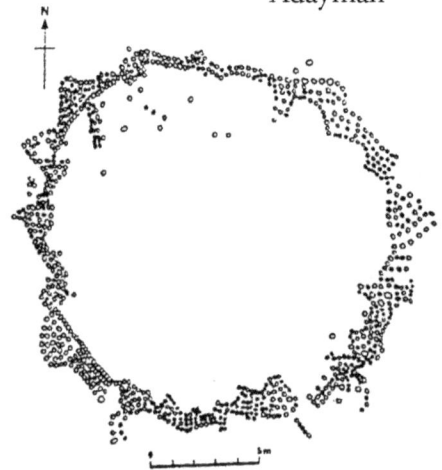

Bab adh-Dhra enclosure

Adaymah enclosure

Bab adh-Dhra cairns

Adaymah tumulus

Figure 5.14 Burial architecture at Adaymeh and Bab adh-Dhra.

be associated with a series of five metre wide stone and rubble tumuli, as some overlay cist graves, while others do not. A relationship is generally assumed, but the evidence is defective. To the south of the cist/tumuli complex lies a 30 m wide sub-round stone enclosure, apparently unrelated to a nearby series of dolmen clusters (Hanbury-Tenison 1986: 218–219).

Attempting to assess functional relationships across the ruinfield is made difficult by the limitations of sixty year old evidence, and present inability to re-examine the primary data, which lies within a military zone. Prag (1995: 76–77) differentiates Late Chalcolithic cist burials from Early Bronze I dolmen fields, and follows Stekelis (1935: 67–69), Elliot (1977: 19) and Hanbury-Tenison (1986: 218) in dating the large enclosure to the Chalcolithic. However, the ceramic evidence for association between Adaymeh and Ghassul remains slight, and the possibility remains that the cist, tumuli and enclosure complex could equally well have served a semi-nomadic (perhaps even post-Ghassulian) component of Chalcolithic society, in just such a way as the dolmen complexes are thought to have served a later transhumant people (Prag 1995: 83–84).

The few other Chalcolithic cemeteries known in Jordan appear to share features with Shiqmim (Levy and Alon 1985; Hanbury-Tenison 1986), and Adaymeh (McCreery 1978/79; Clarke 1979). Around thirty roughly rounded cairn tombs were discovered about a kilometre south of Bab adh-Dhra in 1977 (Figure 5.14; McCreery 1978/79), and investigated shortly thereafter as a rescue excavation (Clarke 1979). The cairn tombs appear to be larger versions of the Adaymeh cists, except that each appears to be covered with a stone and rubble tumulus, somewhat similar to the Adaymeh tumuli (Clarke 1979: 60–69). As well, Clarke investigated two large 25 m wide enclosures, broadly similar to the one discovered at Adaymeh by Stekelis (Clarke 1979, 69–73). The Bab adh-Dhra structures appear to be directly related to the cairn tombs, and associated with funerary activities, strongly implying that the Adaymeh enclosure was used for a similar activity (Clarke 1979: 75–76). Date and cultural affiliation of the Bab adh-Dhra structures was difficult to determine due to the paucity of finds and their generally poor condition. However, Clarke felt that the best parallels lay with the Ghassulian Chalcolithic (Clarke 1979: 73–74). It has been recently suggested that many of these Bab adh-Dhra tumuli date to the early Middle Bronze Age (Edwards *et al.* 2004: 194–195). However, the heavily eroded cooking pot fabrics deployed as evidence are difficult to date in isolation. Detailed survey and excavation are required to settle the matter.

Very little is known about Chalcolithic funerary activity. However, if the few fragmentary examples have been interpreted correctly, then funerary culture may have included open-air enclosures (perhaps for primary excar-nation) in association with cist and tumulus graves (for ultimate secondary burial). This culture seems broadly consistent around the Dead Sea periphery, as an enclosure similar to those at Adaymeh and Bab adh-Dhra is known from the Nahal Mishmar region (Bar-Adon 1980: 12–13). Moorey (1989: 179) has raised the possibility that the copper "crowns" from Nahal Mishmar (Bar-Adon 1980: 24–39) are better interpreted as model funerary enclosures. He further suggested that the prominent large birds associated with the more elaborate "crowns" allude to a function as excarnation areas. It may be that the often assumed link between the Nahal Mishmar hoard and the En Gedi sanctuary is unnecessary (Bar-Adon 1980: 202), and that the hoard is to be associated with funerary activities in the Nahal Mishmar region itself. The existence of a Dead Sea enclosure and cist/tumulus funerary culture is suggested by the distributional evidence, and may be contrasted with a coastal/central upland cave and ossuary funerary culture (Hanbury-Tenison 1986: 205–212; Perrot and Ladiray 1980; Gopher and Tsuk 1996; Gal *et al.* 1997; van den Brink 1998; Joffe 2003).

Trade and Foreign Relations

Much has been written on traded materials and their apparent illustration of far-flung foreign relations during the Chalcolithic period (Hanbury-Tenison 1986: 95–103; Bourke 2002a; Commenge and Alon 2002). Little is known about the earlier phases of the Chalcolithic in Jordan, and comments are generally confined to vague observations on ceramic parallels with the Halafian north (Kaplan 1960; Mellaart 1975; Gophna and Sadeh 1988/89) or the Badarian south (Kaplan 1959; Kantor 1992; Friedman 1999). Such statements rarely document actual imports, far less method or motivation. If inter-regional trade did exist in the early Chalcolithic period, it was a very minor component of material variability and not developmentally significant. In the later Chalcolithic period, evidence does exist for relatively widespread materials exchange (Figure 5.15). Care should be taken to distinguish between relatively high volume within-region trade in bulk commodities (hard stone, copper, ceramics) and small scale inter-regional exchange of exotics. Regional trade in basalt, alabaster and haematite is well documented, and likely to be of some significance. However, the economic importance of inter-regional trade in exotic items of adornment (shell, faience, ivory and semi-precious stones) should not be over-emphasised. The vast majority of the Jordanian Late Chalcolithic material assemblage derived from the immediate hinterland of each site, and is locally manufactured.

Whilst the bulk of all ceramic assemblages seem to be locally made, distinctive manufacturing techniques at Abu Hamid (Roux and Courty 1997), and physico-chemical analysis at Ghassul (Edwards 1997; Bourke 2002a) suggests that a small percentage of Late Chalcolithic ceram-

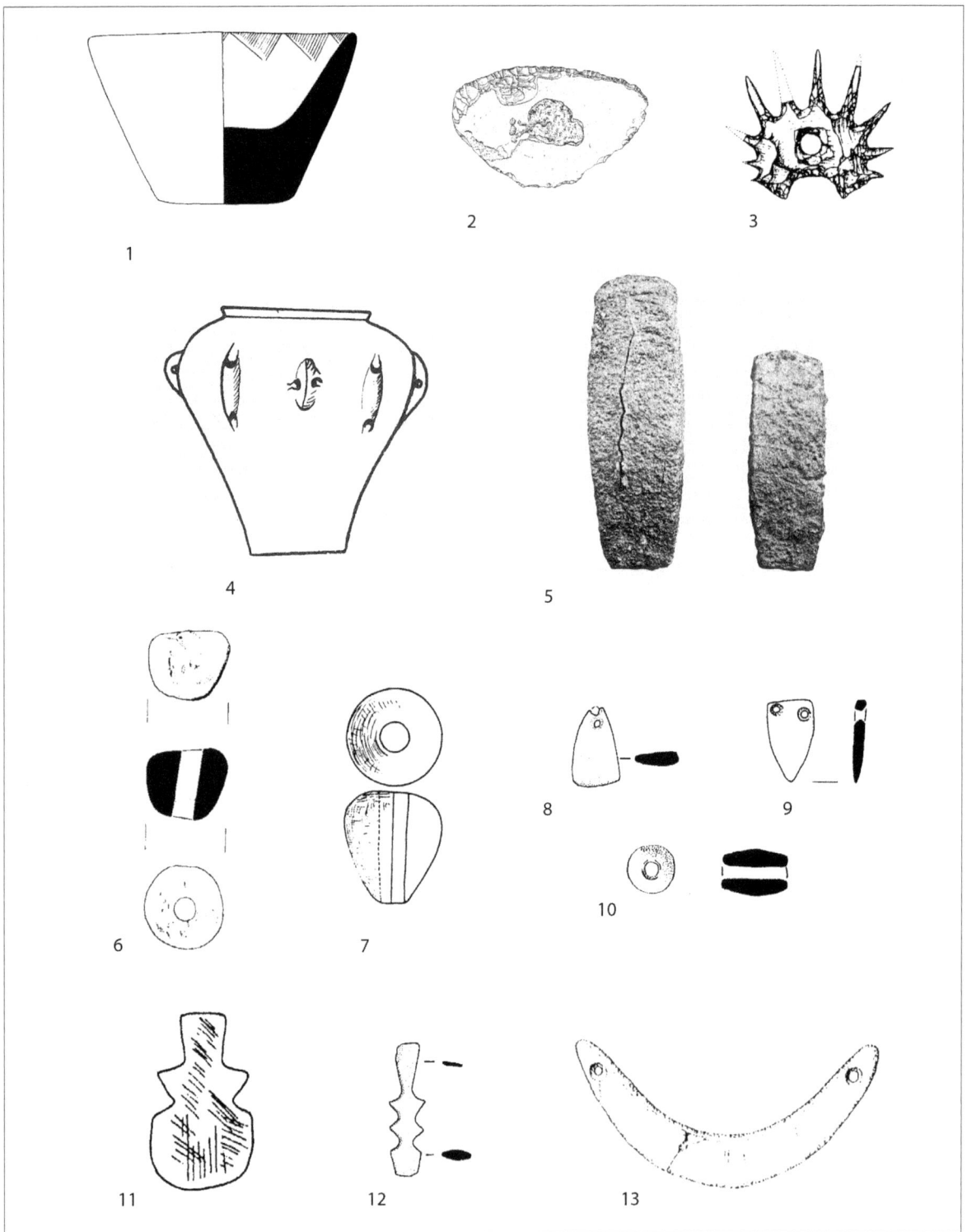

Figure 5.15 Traded items. 1. Basalt bowl; 2. Fan scraper; 3. Star-shaped tool; 4. Creamware jar; 5. Copper tools; 6. Haematite macehead; 7. Alabaster macehead; 8. Greenstone pendant; 9. Alabaster pendant; 10. Serpentine bead; 11. Alabaster violin-shaped figurine; 12. Ivory pendant; 13. Mother of Pearl Pendant.

ics derive from the north Jordan valley and the upland regions to the north and east of the Jordan Valley. The presence of the distinctive Cream Ware at Ghassul (Bourke *et al.* in press, Blackham 1999) suggests a small but distinctive inter-regional element in this exchange. Whilst basalt suitable for utilitarian tools was exploited from a number of locations throughout Jordan (Philip and Williams-Thorpe 1993), basalt suitable for elaborate vessel manufacture is sourced to the northern Jordan uplands (Philip and Williams-Thorpe 2000, 2001). Although lithic assemblages were largely crafted from locally available resources (Baird 1987; Rollefson 1992), the raw material for a not insignificant percentage of fine flint tools probably derives from the Jafr Basin (Quintero *et al.* 2002). Haematite is sourced to the upland regions of central Jordan, and alabaster, marble and serpentinite all probably derive from the Eastern Desert of Egypt (Bourke 2002a). Virtually all Jordan Valley copper comes from the Faynan region (Hauptmann pers. comm.), although south Jordanian sites may draw some copper from Timna (Rothenberg 1999). Much exotic shell derives from the Red Sea, and a smaller percentage from Mediterranean and Nilotic sources (Lee 1973; Reese *et al.* 1986; Reese 1998).

There is considerable evidence for regional movement of relatively bulky materials (basalt, haematite, copper and flint) and inter-regional movment of fine items of adornment (semi-precious stone, faience, ivory and shell), but there is little reason to posit systematic long-distance reciprocal trade between Jordanian Chalcolithic sites and centres in lower Egypt, northern Syria or southern Mesopotamia (Bourke 2002a). A low intensity "down the line" exchange is more likely, but such cannot be held to have played an important role in the local economies. However, the bulk of the evidence for inter-regional exchange is concentrated in the latest Chalcolithic phases at most sites (Khalil *et al.* 2003), so it would seem reasonable to suggest that intensity of contact (both regional and inter-regional) increases over time, to reach its greatest heights at the very end of the Chalcolithic period.

Chalcolithic Society

The developmental status of south Levantine Chalcolithic society remains controversial (Levy 1995; Yoffee 1993). Arguments over the archaeological correlates of social transformation have intensified as the sophisticated field projects of the 1980s move from preliminary description to final publication (Gilead 1995; Levy [ed.] 2006). At one level, discussion is strictly anthropological, and concerns itself with re-visiting undoubtedly over-rigid developmental typologies (Yoffee 1993; Rothman 1994). At another level, prehistorians continue to explore archaeological cultures with reference to evolving anthropological theory (Yoffee 1995; Levy 1996) because the desire to identify significant socio-economic developmental vectors in pre-state formations remains a priority of all research

into complex society (Stein 1998; Levy [ed.] 2006).

Current research agendas in the fifth millennium BC Middle East acknowledge the need to abandon over-rigid typological "checklists," whilst preserving the broad concept of middle-range societies with distinctive developmental features (Stein 1998: 4–7). Refinements to monolithic organizational classes (simple/complex or individualizing/group-oriented chiefdoms) have been generally accepted (Stein 1998: 8–10), and much attention is now focused on the mechanisms through which sub-chiefly lineage groups compete with each other for power (Savage 1997). Researchers recognize the need to evaluate the varying significance of enhanced agricultural surpluses (Stein 1994a), rural/urban interaction (Falconer and Savage 1995), inter-regional exchange (Algaze 1993), craft specialization (McCorriston 1997), writing and literacy (Baines 1988) and cult practice (Alon and Levy 1989) in this competition for influence and power. This is never straightforward, and in the relatively impoverished cultural landscapes of the southern Levant, particularly challenging.

It would be premature to do more than sketch the barest outline of Jordanian Chalcolithic social organization at present, as many important field projects are currently in publication phase (Tall Shuna North, Pella, Abu Hamid, Tulaylat Ghassul). We can do no more than describe changes from Neolithic norms (Gopher 1995; Gopher and Gophna 1993), and (with less confidence) begin to identify potential agencies in such change. Our ignorance of Early Chalcolithic norms is profound (Garfinkel 1999; Garfinkel and Matskevich 2002), and this hamstrings thoroughgoing processual analysis. Our treatment will concentrate on the better known later Chalcolithic cultures in general and the site of Ghassul in particular, because this is where the majority of our evidence is located. Contrasting individual features of the Late Neolithic and the Late Chalcolithic assemblages is feasible, but accurately assessing the degree of inter-relatedness of a suite of individual changes (contingency) is an ongoing difficulty. This is an important caveat, because it renders difficult (if not impossible) the evaluation of the degree of inter-relatedness of individual changed states. The Late Chalcolithic cultures are the endpoint of a millennium-long process during which individual strands of the socio-economic mix may have altered at differing times and at differing rates. Without the long perspective of well-dated Early Chalcolithic developmental sequences, we risk viewing changed individual elements as related when they are not, or fail to identify genuinely contingent features due to an inadequately refined time perspective (Bourke 2002b).

Economy and Society

Increasing differentation, specialization and intensification of economic activity from early in Late Chalcolithic times (ca. 4200 BC) is consistent with the ecofactual evidence recently documented at Tulaylat Ghassul (Bourke 1997b, 2002b). One interpretation of the Ghassul evidence would see the Late Chalcolithic economy as one in which a number of distinctive subsistence strategies exist in parallel, some generalist and focused on subsistence, and others more specialized in high yield (but environmentally fragile) monocultures (Meadows 2001, 2005; Mairs in Bourke *et al.* 2000, 2003). Given that high-yield cereals, pulses and fruits have a relatively short storage life, the motivation to move away from traditional subsistence regimes towards the production of specialized agricultural surpluses would suggest heightened internal demand for these products. The motivation to produce larger surpluses remains a matter of debate, although it is consistent with increasing levels of elite competition (D'Altroy and Earle 1985; Earle 1987). The architectural evidence at Ghassul for increasing numbers of specialized storage facilities in association with multi-room complexes, is no longer in doubt (Bourke 2002b; Bourke *et al.* 2000, in press). This tendency towards large storage facilities is also seen at Abu Hamid (Dollfus and Kafafi eds. 1988), Pella (Bourke *et al.* 1998, 2003), Tell Tsaf (Garfinkel et al. 2006a), and Sahab (Ibrahim 1984).

While an increased ability to store agricultural surpluses is widespread, the absence of many of the additional trappings of a "typical" chiefdom must be acknowledged. There are few signs of overt architectural differentiation (Blackham 1999), although creation of distinctive cultic establishments does occur (Seaton 2000, 2006; Bourke 2002b; Bourke *et al.* 2000, in press). Differential mortuary practices are not well documented east of the Jordan (Joffe 2003). There is little evidence for marked concentrations of elite wealth or symbols of authority (Levy 1995). Inter-regional traded goods remain only a minor factor in the local economy, with long-distance imports confined to jewellery items consistent with modest levels of wealth display (Bourke 2002a). In short, if one seeks to view Late Chalcolithic society as some form of chiefdom (Levy 1995), then it must be acknowledged to be a chiefdom with few of the traditional trappings. This circumstance need not be the impediment it is often said to be (Gilead 1988), as contemporaneous Ubaid-period southern Mesopotamia provides an instructive parallel in form and circumstance (Stein 1994a). Stein views Ubaid society as consisting of a series of small group-oriented "egalitarianising" chiefdoms (Stein 1994a: 42–43), which derived much of their wealth and power through the ability to mobilize labour from extended kinship groups to generate a reliable agricultural surplus (Flannery 2002). Such a developmental scenario has a number of striking material cultural parallels with the Late Chalcolithic of Jordan (Bourke 2002b). In the Jordan Valley, the early domestication and subsequent intensive exploitation of olive fruit and oil (Meadows 2001), and the early devel-

opment of a significant pastoral component (Mairs in Bourke *et al.* 2000, 2003) were key factors in the development of a reliable agricultural surplus.

Within this landscape, several additional factors may have played a part in Ghassul's rise to prominence. Landform and climate combine to circumscribe settlement distribution in the south Jordan Valley, suggesting a variant on Carneiro's Circumscription Hypothesis (Carneiro 1970; Falconer and Savage 1995). A review of settlement patterns in the south Jordan Valley (Bourke 2002b) reveals a series of wadi-related segmentary distributions (Stein 1994b), with the largest settlement typically on the alluvial floodplain adjacent to winter floodwater-producing wadis (Falconer 1994). If the close-knit network of wadi systems between Nimrim and the Dead Sea are viewed as a region, then Ghassul enjoys an acknowledged primacy over all other settlements within this region. Such primacy is typically accounted for through the concentration of unique services (economic, cultic and trade) on the primate centre (Falconer and Savage 1995: 40). Tulaylat Ghassul may well have enjoyed an enhanced regional cultic function (Cameron 1981; Seaton 2000, 2006). Intensified regional and more limited inter-regional exchange is well documented at Late Chalcolithic Ghassul (Philip and Williams-Thorpe 2000, 2001; Reese 1998; Bourke 2002a). The present state of the evidence is in keeping with Stein's (1994b: 11–12) segmentary-state model for the Jeziran countryside, with the largest settlement exercising a limited and selective control over an effectively autonomous hinterland. There is sufficient evidence to suggest that the Jordan Valley wadi-mouth settlements in general, and Tulaylat Ghassul in particular, enjoyed heightened levels of internal organization in comparison with smaller hinterland settlements.

Conclusion: The Demise of the Ghassulian Chalcolithic

The view of the Jordanian Chalcolithic offered above relies heavily on evidence drawn from Jordan Valley sites in general and Tulaylat Ghassul in particular. Emphasis on the relatively developed material cultural circumstance at Ghassul recurs throughout this overview. This emphasis is due in part to Ghassul being the most intensively investigated Chalcolithic site in Jordan, but it also reflects the absence of comparative data from other sites that have been well explored. Looking ahead to the imminent publication of several major field projects, future overviews should be able to achieve a considerably more balanced (and nuanced) assessment of the countryside as a whole. As it is, this overview largely reflects the concerns and biases of the last fifty years, perspectives that are changing rapidly with the onset of an ever-more comprehensive coverage of the landscape, and a greatly enhanced analytical toolkit.

The demise of the Jordanian Chalcolithic, and the relat-

ed question of the degree of continuity with the successor cultures of the Early Bronze Age will continue to bedevil scholars for some time to come. At present the fashion in Early Bronze Age studies is to question the traditional view of a relatively sophisticated Early Bronze Age "walled town culture," once viewed as representing a sharp departure from the preceding Chalcolithic "village-based society." Arguments advanced herein for a modest complexity in later Chalcolithic society (if accepted) result in a further narrowing of the distance between Chalcolithic and Early Bronze Age socio-economic norms. Modest stratification based on elite control of agricultural surpluses was not unique to the Early Bronze Age, as this was an important element in the Late Chalcolithic agricultural transformation. Even so, significant change between the periods does occur. The rich symbolic landscape of the Late Chalcolithic vanishes forever.

It may be that Jordanian Late Chalcolithic society can be viewed as one in which "traditional" ruling elites, which sourced their power to the control of specialized religious knowledge, gradually came into competition with an emerging elite whose power was more directly sourced to the control of agricultural surpluses. Whilst there is no evidence for heightened levels of conflict or destruction, it is possible that in the increasingly harsh environmental regime of the latest Chalcolithic, leadership in society shifted from those who manifestly could not control the environment, to those who had at least developed a viable means of coping with changed circumstances. If this is so, the gradual socio-political marginalizing of the old "ritual" elite may have resulted in an actual physical displacement of these religious elites and their symbolic paraphernalia to the marginal environments of the west Dead Sea region.

All evidence currently available suggests that the Ghassulian Chalcolithic had its origins in the village societies of the Late Neolithic Jordan Valley, some time in the Sixth Millennium cal BC. It seems likely that a sharp climatic alteration intervened to halt the gradual economic progression evidenced in the long sequence at Ghassul. While hardier economic elements survived to build a new society in the succeeding Early Bronze Age, a great many of the most brilliant artistic elements were lost forever. If radiometric data are an accurate guide, the Chalcolithic Ghassulian culture that grew up by the shores of the Dead Sea around 4500 cal BC came to an end around 3800 cal BC in much the same environment as it began. Today the landscape is harsh and barren, but strangely attractive to all who work in it.

Bibliography

Abu Dayyah, A., J. Greene, I. Haj Hassan and E. Suleiman

1991 Archaeological Survey of Greater Amman, Phase I: Final Report. *Annual of the Department of Antiquities of Jordan* 35: 361–395.

Adams, R.B.

1999 The Development of Copper Metallurgy During the Early Bronze Age: Evidence from the Faynan Region, Southern Jordan. Unpublished PhD Thesis Sheffield University.

Akkermans, P. and K. Duistermaat

1997 Of Storage and Nomads: The Sealings of Late Neolithic Sabi Abyad, Syria. *Paléorient* 22: 17–44.

Alon, D. and T. Levy

1989 The Archaeology of Cult and the Chalcolithic Structures at Gilat. *Journal of Mediterranean Archaeology* 2: 163–221.

Algaze, G.

1993 Expansionary Dynamics of some early Pristine States. *American Anthropologist* 95: 304–333.

2001 Initial Social Complexity in Southwestern Asia: The Mesopotamian Advantage. *Current Anthropology* 42: 199–233.

Amiran, R.

1955 The 'Cream Ware' of Gezer and the Beersheba Late Chalcolithic. *Israel Exploration Journal* 4: 240–245.

1989 The Gilat Goddess and the Temples of Gilat, En-Gedi and Ai. In P. de Miroschedji (ed.), *L'Urbanisation de la Palestine a l'age du Bronze ancien*. British Archaeological Reports International Series 527, 53–61. Oxford: British Archaeological Reports.

Amr, K., M. Najjar, S. Kerner, K. Rielly and D. McCreery

1993 Wadi al-Qattar Salvage Excavation 1989. *Annual of the Department of Antiquities of Jordan* 38: 263–278.

Amr, K., K. Hamdan, S. Helms and L. Mohamadieh

1996 Archaeological Survey of the East Coast of the Dead Sea Phase I: Suwayma, az-Zara and Umm Sidra. *Annual of the Department of Antiquities of Jordan* 40: 429–450.

Avner, U., I. Carmi and D. Segal

1994 Neolithic to Bronze Age Settlement of the Negev and Sinai in light of Radiocarbon dating: A View from the southern Negev. In O. Bar-Yosef and R. Kra (eds.), *Late Quaternary Chronology and Paleoclimates of the Eastern Mediterranean*, 265–300. Tucson, AZ: Radiocarbon.

Baines, J.

1988 Literacy, social organization and the archaeological record: The case of Early Egypt. In J. Gledhill, B. Bender and M. Larsen (eds.), *State and Society: The Emergence and Development of Social Hierarchy and Political Centralisation*, 192–214. London: Unwin-Hyman.

Baird, D.

1987 A Preliminary analysis of the Chipped Stone from the 1985 excavations at Tell esh-Shuna North. *Annual of the Department of Antiquities of Jordan* 31: 461–480.

Baird, D. and G. Philip

1994 Preliminary Report on the Third (1993) Season of Excavations at Tell esh-Shuna North. *Levant* 26: 111–133.

Banning, E.

1998 The Neolithic Period: Triumphs of Architecture,

Agriculture, and Art. *Near Eastern Archaeology* 61: 188–237.

2002   Consensus and Debate on the Late Neolithic and Chalcolithic of the Southern Levant. *Paléorient* 28: 148–155.

2007   Late Prehistory in Wadi Ziqlab, al-Kura, Jordan: From Sedentism to Olive Oil Factories. In T. Levy, P-M. Michele Daviau, R. Younker and M. Shaer (eds.), *Crossing Jordan: North American Contributions to the Archaeology of Jordan*, 37–46. London: Equinox.

Banning, E., R. Dods, J. Field, S. Maltby, J. McCorriston, S. Monckton, R. Rubenstein and P. Sheppard

1989   Wadi Ziqlab Project 1987: A Preliminary Report. *Annual of the Department of Antiquities of Jordan* 33: 43–58.

Banning, E., D. Rahimi, J. Siggers and H. Ta'ani

1996   The 1992 Season of Excavations in Wadi Ziqlab, Jordan. *Annual of the Department of Antiquities of Jordan* 40: 29–50.

Banning, E., M. Blackham and D. Lasby

1998   Excavations at WZ 121, a Chalcolithic site at Tubna in the Wadi Ziqlab. *Annual of the Department of Antiquities of Jordan* 42: 141–159.

Bar-Adon, P.

1980   *The Cave of the Treasure.* Jerusalem: Israel Exploration Society.

Barker, G., O. Creighton, D. Gilbertson, C. Hunt, D. Mattingly, S. McLaren, and D. Thomas

1997   The Wadi Faynan Project, Southern Jordan: A Preliminary Report on the Geomorphology and Landscape Archaeology. *Levant* 29: 19–40.

Barker, G., R. Adams, O. Creighton, D. Gilbertson, J. Grattan, C. Hunt, D. Mattingly, S. McLaren, H. Mohamed, P. Newson, T. Reynolds and D. Thomas

1998   Environment and Landuse in the Wadi Faynan, Southern Jordan: The Second Season of Geoarchaeology and Landscape Archaeology. *Levant* 30: 5–25.

Bender, F.

1974   *Geology of Jordan.* Berlin: Contributions to the Regional Geology of the Earth.

Ben-Tor, A.

1995   A Stamp Seal and a Seal Impression of the Chalcolithic Period from Grar. In I. Gilead (ed.), *Grar: A Chalcolithic Site in the Northern Negev*, 361–375. Beersheva: Ben Gurion University.

Bernbeck, R., R. Lamprichs, G. Lehmann and S. Kerner

1995   Wasserspeicherung in der jordanischen Steppe. *Das Altertum* 40: 163–174.

Betts, A.

1986   The Prehistory of the Black Desert, Transjordan. Unpublished PhD. thesis, University of London.

1992   Tell el-Hibr: A Rock Shelter Occupation of the Fourth Millennium BCE in the Jordanian Badiya. *Bulletin of the American Schools of Oriental Research* 287: 5–23.

Betts, A. (ed.)

1991   *Excavations at Jawa 1972–1986.* Edinburgh: Edinburgh University.

1998   *The Harra and the Hamad: Excavations and Surveys in Eastern Jordan*, Vol. 1. Sheffield: Sheffield Academic Press.

Betts, A., S. Eames, M. Schroder and A. Husan

1995   Archaeological Survey of the Wadi al-Ajib, Mafraq District. *Annual of the Department of Antiquities of Jordan* 39: 149–168.

Bienert, H-D. and D. Vieweger

1999   Archaeological Excavations at the Late Neolithic site of ash-Shalaf: A Preliminary Report on the 1998 Season. *Annual of the Department of Antiquities of Jordan* 43: 49–68.

2000   Archaeological Excavations at the Late Neolithic site of ash-Shalaf: A Preliminary Report on the 1999 Season. *Annual of the Department of Antiquities of Jordan* 44: 109–118.

Bisheh, G., S. Farajat, G. Palumbo and M. Waheeb

1993   Archaeological Rescue Survey of the Ras an-Naqb–Aqaba Highway Alignment, 1992. *Annual of the Department of Antiquities of Jordan* 37: 119–134.

Blackham, M.

1999   Teleilat Ghassul: An Appraisal of Robert North's Excavations (1959–1960). *Levant* 31: 19–64.

2002   *Modeling Time and Transition in Prehistory: The Jordan Valley Chalcolithic (5,500–3,500 BC).* Oxford: Archaeopress.

Boling, R.

1988   *The Early Biblical Community in Transjordan.* Sheffield: Sheffield Academic Press.

Bourke, S.

1997a   The Urbanisation Process in the South Jordan Valley: Renewed Excavations at Teleilat Ghassul 1994/1995. In A. Hadidi (ed.), *Studies in the History and Archaeology of Jordan I*, 249–259. Amman: Department of Antiquities of Jordan.

1997b   The 'pre-Ghassulian' sequence at Teleilat Ghassul. In H.G. Gebel, Z. Kafafi and G.O. Rollefson (eds.), *The Prehistory of Jordan II: Perspectives from 1997*, 395–417. Berlin: ex oriente.

1997c   Pre-Classical Pella in Jordan: A Conspectus of Ten Year's Work (1985–1995). *Palestine Exploration Quarterly* 129: 94–115.

2002a   Teleilat Ghassul: Foreign Relations in the Late Chalcolithic Period. In E. van den Brink and T. Levy (eds.), *Egypt and the Levant: Interrelations from the 4th through the Early 3rd Millennium B.C.E.*, 154–164. London: Leicester University Press.

2002b   The Origins of Social Complexity in the South Jordan Valley: New Evidence from Teleilat Ghassul, Jordan. *Palestine Exploration Quarterly* 134: 2–27.

in press   The Late Neolithic/Early Chalcolithic Transition at Teleilat Ghassul: Context, Chronology and Culture. *Paleorient* 33/1.

Bourke, S., R. Sparks, K. Sowada and L. Mairs

1994 Preliminary Report on the Fourteenth Season of Excavation by the University of Sydney at Pella in Jordan. *Annual of the Department of Antiquities of Jordan* 38: 81–126.

Bourke, S., P. Seaton, R. Sparks, J. Lovell and L. Mairs

1995 Preliminary Report on a First Season of Renewed Excavations at Teleilat Ghassul by the University of Sydney, 1994. *Annual of The Department of Antiquities of Jordan* 39: 31–64.

Bourke, S., R. Sparks, K. Sowada, P. McLaren and L. Mairs

1998 Preliminary Report on the University of Sydney's Sixteenth and Seventeenth Seasons of Excavations at Pella (Tabaqat Fahl) in 1994/95. *Annual of the Department of Antiquities of Jordan* 42: 179–211.

Bourke, S., P. Seaton, R. Sparks, J. Lovell, L. Mairs and J. Meadows

2000 Preliminary Report on a Second and Third Season of Renewed Excavations at Teleilat Ghassul by the University of Sydney, 1995/1997. *Annual of the Department of Antiquities of Jordan* 44: 37–89.

Bourke, S., E. Lawson, J. Lovell, U. Zoppi, Q. Hua and M. Barbetti

2001 The Chronology of the Ghassulian Chalcolithic Period in the Southern Levant: New 14C Determinations from Teleilat Ghassul, Jordan. *Radiocarbon* 43: 1217–1222.

Bourke, S., R. Sparks, P. McLaren, K. Sowada, L. Mairs, J. Meadows, T. Hikade and W. Reade

2003 Preliminary Report on the University's Eighteenth and Nineteenth Seasons of Excavations at Pella (Tabaqat Fahl) in 1996/97. *Annual of the Department of Antiquities of Jordan* 47: 335–388.

Bourke, S.J., E. Lawson, Q. Hua and U. Zoppi

2004a The Chronology of the Late Neolithic and Early Chalcolithic periods in the North Jordan Valley: New 14C Determinations from Pella in Jordan. In T. Higham, C. Bronk-Ramsey and C. Owen (eds.), *Radiocarbon and Archaeology. Proceedings of the 4th Symposium, Oxford 2002*, 119–125. Oxford: Oxbow Books.

Bourke, S., U. Zoppi, Q. Hua, J. Meadows and S. Gibbins

2004b The End of the Chalcolithic Period in the South Jordan Valley: New 14C Dates from Teleilat Ghassul, Jordan. *Radiocarbon* 46: 315–323.

Bourke, S. and J. Lovell

2004 Ghassul, Chronology and Cultural Sequencing. *Paleorient* 30/1: 179–182.

Bourke, S., J. Lovell, P. Seaton, R. Sparks, L. Mairs and J. Meadows.

in press Preliminary Report on a Fourth Season of Renewed Excavations at Teleilat Ghassul by the University of Sydney, 1999. *Annual of the Department of Antiquities Jordan* 51.

Braun E.

2001. Proto, Early Dynastic Egypt and Early Bronze I–II of the Southern Levant: Some Uneasy 14C Correlations. *Radiocarbon* 43: 1279–1296.

Bronk-Ramsey, C., T. Higham, D. Owen, A. Pike and R. Hedges

2002 Radiocarbon dates from the Oxford AMS system: Datelist 31. *Archaeometry* 44: 1–149.

Burton, M. and T. Levy

2001 The Chalcolithic Radiocarbon Record and Its Use in Southern Levantine Archaeology. *Radiocarbon* 43: 1223–1246.

Cameron, D.

1981 *The Ghassulian Wall Paintings*. London: Kenyon-Deane.

1995 The Ghassulian Wall Paintings. *Bollettino del Centro Camuno di Studi Preistorici* 28: 114–120.

Campbell, S.

2000 The Burnt House at Arpachiyeh: A Reexamination. *Bulletin of the American Schools of Oriental Research* 318: 1–40.

Caneva, I., M. Hatamleh, Z. Kafafi, M. Munzi, G. Palumbo, F. Parenti, A. al-Shiyab, M. Wilson, B. Bianchi, P. Conti and N. Qadi

2001 The Wadi az-Zarqa/Wadi ad-Dulayl Archaeological Project: Report on the 1997 and 1999 Fieldwork Seasons. *Annual of the Department of Antiquities of Jordan* 45: 83–118.

Carmi, I., C. Epstein and D. Segal

1995 Radiocarbon dates from Chalcolithic Sites in the Golan. *Atiqot* 27: 207–209.

Carneiro, R.

1970 A Theory for the Origin of the State. *Science* 69: 733–738.

Cialowicz, K.

1989 *Les tetes de massues des périodes Prédynastique et Archaique dans la Vallée du Nil*. Kracow: University of Kracow.

Clark, V.

1979 Investigations in a Prehistoric Necropolis near Bab edh-Dhra. *Annual of the Department of Antiquities of Jordan* 22-23: 57–77.

Commenge, C. and D. Alon

2002 Competitive Involution and Expanded Horizons: Exploring the Nature of Interaction between the Northern Negev and Lower Egypt (4500–3600 BCE). In E. van den Brink and T. Levy (eds.), *Egypt and the Levant: Interrelations from the 4th through the Early 3rd Millennium B.C.E.*, 139–153. London: Leicester University Press.

Contenson, H. de

1960a Three Soundings in the Jordan Valley. *Annual of the Department of Antiquities of Jordan* 3-4: 12–98.

1960b La Chronologie relative du Niveau le plus Ancien de Tell esh Shuna. *Mélanges de l'Université Saint-Joseph* 37: 57–75.

1961 Remarques sur le Chalcolithique Recent de Tell esh-Shuna. *Revue Biblique* 68: 546–556.

1964 The 1953 Survey in the Yarmouk and Jordan Valleys. *Annual of the Department of Antiquities of Jordan* 8–9: 30–46.

Copeland, L.

1969 Neolithic Village Sites in the South Beqaa, Lebanon. *Mélanges de l'Université Saint-Joseph* 45: 85–114.

Coughenour, R.

1976 Preliminary Report on the Exploration and Excavation of Mugharet el Warda and Abu Thawab. *Annual of the Department of Antiquities of Jordan* 21: 71–76.

D'Altroy, T. and T. Earle

1985 Staple Finance, Wealth Finance and Storage in the Inka Political Economy. *Current Anthropology* 26: 187–206.

Dollfus, G. and Z. Kafafi (eds.)

1988 *Abu Hamid: Village Du 4ème Millénaire de la vallée du Jordain.* Amman: l'Institut français d'archéologie du Proche-Orient.

Dollfus, G. and Z. Kafafi

1989 Abu Hamid. In D.Homes-Fredericq and J.B. Hennessy (eds.), *Archaeology of Jordan 2.* Vol. II. 1 Field Reports. Surveys and Sites A–K, 102–113. Leuven: Peeters.

1993 Recent Researches at Abu Hamid. *Annual of the Department of Antiquities of Jordan* 37: 241–262.

1995 Representations Humains et Animales sur le site d'Abu Hamid. In K. Amr, F. Zayadine and M. Zaghloul (eds.), *Studies in the History and Archaeology of Jordan V,* 449–457. Amman: Department of Antiquities.

Donahue, J., B. Peer and R.T. Schaub

1997 The Southeastern Dead Sea Plain: Changing Shorelines and their Impact on Settlement Patterns through Historical Periods. In Ghazi Bisheh (ed.), *Studies in the History and Archaeology of Jordan VI,* 127–136. Amman: Department of Antiquities.

Dunand, M.

1973 *Fouilles de Byblos* V. Paris: Maisonneuve.

Düring, B.

2001 Social Dimensions in the Architecture of Neolithic Çatalhöyük. *Anatolian Studies* 51: 1–18.

Earle, T.K.

1987 Chiefdoms in Archaeological and Ethnohistorical Perspective. *Annual Review of Anthropology* 16: 279–308.

2002 *Bronze Age Economics.* Boulder:Westview Press.

Earle, T.K. (ed.).

1991 *Chiefdoms: Power, Economy and Ideology.* Cambridge: Cambridge University Press.

Edwards, P., S. Falconer, P. Fall, A. Ariotti and T. Swoveland

2004 Archaeology and Environment of the Dead Sea Plain: Preliminary Results of the Third Season of Investigations by the Joint La Trobe University/Arizona State University Project. *Annual of the Department of Antiquities Jordan* 48:181–202.

Edwards, W.I.

1997 *Report on Teleilat Ghassul Petrography 1995–96.* Sydney: Teleilat Ghassul Project.

Edwards, W.I. and E.R. Segnit

1984 Pottery Technology at the Chalcolithic Site of Teleilat Ghassul. *Archaeometry* 26: 69–77.

Elliot, C.

1977 The Religious Beliefs of the Ghassulians. *Palestine Exploration Quarterly* 109: 3–25.

1978 The Ghassulian Culture in Palestine: Origins, Influences and Abandonment. *Levant* 10: 37–54.

Epstein, C.

1975 Basalt Pillar Figures from the Golan. *Israel Exploration Journal* 25: 193–201.

1978a Aspects of Symbolism in Chalcolithic Palestine. In P. Moorey and P. Parr (eds.), *Archaeology in the Levant: Essays for Kathleen Kenyon,* 23–35. Warminster: Aris and Phillips.

1978b A New Aspect of Chalcolithic Culture. *Bulletin of the American Schools of Oriental Research* 229: 27–45.

1985 Laden Animal Figurines from the Chalcolithic Period in Palestine. *Bulletin of the American Schools of Oriental Research* 258: 53–62.

1988 Basalt Pillar Figures from the Golan and the Huleh Region. *Israel Exploration Journal* 38: 205–223.

1993 Oil Production in the Golan Heights during the Chalcolithic Period. *Tel Aviv* 20: 133–146.

1998 *The Chalcolithic Culture of the Golan.* Jerusalem: Israel Antiquities Authority.

Epstein, C. and T. Noy

1988 Observations concerning Perporated tools from Chalcolithic Palestine. *Paléorient* 14: 133–144.

Falconer, S.

1994 Village Economy and Society in the Jordan Valley: A Study of Bronze Age Rural Complexity. In G.Schwartz and S. Falconer (eds.), *Archaeological Views from the Countryside: Village Communities in Early Complex Societies,* 121–142. Washington: Smithsonian Institution.

Falconer, S. and S. Savage

1995 Heartlands and Hinterlands: Alternative Trajectories of Early Urbanisation in Mesopotamia and the Southern Levant. *American Antiquity* 60: 37–58.

Falconer, S., P. Fall, M. Metzger and L. Lines

2003 Bronze Age Rural Economic Transitions in the Jordan Valley. *Annual of the American Schools of Oriental Research* 58: 1–17.

Fall, P., L. Lines and S. Falconer

1998 Seeds of Civilisation: Bronze Age Rural Economy and Ecology in the Southern Levant. *Annals of the Association of American Geographers* 88: 107–125.

Finkelstein, I.

1990 Early Arad-Urbanism of the Nomads. *Zeitschrift des Deutschen Palästina-Vereins* 106: 34–50.

1995 Two Notes on Early Bronze Age Urbanisation and Urbanism. *Tel Aviv* 22: 47–69.

Finkelstein, I. and R. Gophna

1993 Settlement, Demographic, and Economic Patterns in the Highlands of Palestine in the Chalcolithic and Early Bronze Periods and the Beginning of Urbanism. *Bulletin of the American Schools of Oriental Research* 289: 1–22.

Flannery, K.

2002 The Origins of the Village Revisited: From Nuclear to Extended Households. *American Antiquity* 67: 417–433.

Fox, N.

1997 The Striped Goddess from Gilat: Implications for the Chalcolithic Cult. *Israel Exploration Journal* 47: 212–225.

Frangipane, M.

1997 A 4th-Millennium Temple/Palace Complex at Arslantepe-Malatya. North-South Relations and the formation of Early State Societies in the northern regions of Greater Mesopotamia. *Paléorient* 23: 45–73.

Friedman, R.

1999 'Badari Grave Group 569'. In W. Davies (ed.), *Studies in Egyptian Antiquities. A Tribute to T.G.H. James,* 1–11. British Museum Occasional Paper 123. London: British Museum Press.

Gal, Z., H. Smithline and D. Shalem

1997 A Chalcolithic Burial Cave in Peqi'in, Upper Galilee. *Israel Exploration Journal* 47: 145–154.

1999 New Iconographic Aspects of Chalcolithic Art: Preliminary Observations on Finds from the Peqi'in Cave. *'Atiqot* 37: 1–16.

Galili, E. and J. Sharvit

1994/5 Evidence of Olive Oil Production from the Submerged Site at Kfar Samir, Israel. *Mitkufat Haevan* 26: 122–133.

Garfinkel, Y.

1992a The Material Culture in the Central Jordan Valley in the Pottery Neolithic and Early Chalcolithic Periods. Unpublished PhD thesis, Hebrew University Jerusalem.

1992b *The Pottery Assemblages of the Sha'ar Hagolan and Rabah Stages of Munhatta (Israel).* Les Cahiers du Centre de Recherche Français de Jerusalem 8. Paris: Association Paléorient.

1993 Tel 'Eli. *Excavations and Surveys in Israel, Vol. 12,* 19. Jerusalem: Israel Exploration Society.

1995 *Human and Animal Figurines from Munhatta (Israel).* Les Cahiers du Centre de Recherche Français de Jerusalem 6. Paris: Association Paléorient.

1998 Dancing and the Beginning of Art Scenes in the Early Village Communities of the Near East and Southeast Europe. *Cambridge Archaeological Journal* 8: 207–237.

1999 *Neolithic and Chalcolithic Pottery of the Southern Levant.*

Qedem 39. Jerusalem: The Hebrew University.

Garfinkel, Y. and Z. Matskevich

2002 Abu Zureiq. A Wadi Rabah Site in the Jezreel Valley: Final Report of the 1962 Excavations. *Israel Exploration Journal* 52: 129–166.

Garfinkel, Y. and M. Miller

2002 *Sha'ar Hagolan Volume 1: Neolithic Art in Context.* Oxford: Oxbow Books.

Garfinkel, Y., D. Ben-Shlomo, M. Freikman and A. Vered

2006a The Renewed Excavations at Tel Tzaf: A Site in the Jordan Valley from the Intermediate Chalcolithic Period. *Qadmoniot* 39/132: 78–86.

Garfinkel, Y., A. Vered and O. Bar-Yosef

2006b The domestication of water: the Neolithic well at Sha'ar Hagolan, Jordan Valley, Israel. *Antiquity* 80: 686–696.

Garrard, A.

1998 Environment and Cultural Adaptations in the Azraq Basin: 24000–7000 BC. In D. Henry (ed.), *The Prehistoric Archaeology of Jordan,* 139–148. British Archaeological Reports International Series 705. Oxford: Archaeopress.

Garrard, A., A. Betts, B. Byrd and C. Hunt

1987 Prehistoric environment and settlement in the Azraq Basin: An interim report on the 1985 excavation season. *Levant* 19: 5–25.

Genz, H.

1997 Problems in defining a Chalcolithic for Southern Jordan. In H.G. Gebel, Z. Kafafi and G.O. Rollefson (eds.), *The Prehistory of Jordan II: Perspectives from 1997,* 441–448. Berlin: ex oriente.

Gilead, I.

1988 The Chalcolithic Period in the Levant. *Journal of World Prehistory* 2: 397–443.

1990 The Neolithic-Chalcolithic transition and the Qatifian of the northern Negev and Sinai. *Levant* 22: 47–63.

1994 The History of the Chalcolithic Settlement in the Nahal Beer Sheva Area: The Radiocarbon Aspect. *Bulletin of the American Schools of Oriental Research* 296: 1–13.

2002 Religio-Magic Behaviour in the Chalcolithic Period of Palestine. In E. Oren and S. Ahituv (eds.), *Aharon Kempinski Memorial Volume: Studies in Archaeology and Related Disciplines,* 39–54. Beer-Sheva: Studies by the Department of Bible and Ancient Near East 15. Beersheva: Ben Gurion University.

Gilead, I. (ed.)

1995 *Grar: A Chalcolithic Site in the Northern Negev.* Beersheva: Ben Gurion University.

Gilead, I. and Y. Goren

1986 Stations of the Chalcolithic Period in Nahal Sekher, Northern Negev. *Paléorient* 12: 83–90.

1989 Petrographic analyses of fourth Millennium BC pottery and stone vesels from the northern Negev, Israel. *Bulletin of the American Schools of Oriental Research* 275: 5–14.

Glueck, N.

1951 *Explorations in Eastern Palestine IV (1945–49).* Annual of the American Schools of Oriental Research. New Haven: American Schools of Oriental Research.

Goodfriend, G.

1991 Holocene Trends in ^{18}O in Landsnails from the Negev Desert. *Quaternary Research* 35: 417–426.

Gonen, R.

1992 The Chalcolithic Period. In A. Ben-Tor (ed.), *The Archaeology of Ancient Israel,* 40–80. New Haven: Yale University Press.

Gopher, A.

1995 Early Pottery Bearing Groups in Israel—The Pottery Neolithic Period. In T. Levy (ed.), *The Archaeology of Society in the Holy Land,* 205–225. Leicester: Leicester University Press.

Gopher, A. and R. Gophna

1993 Cultures of the Eighth and Seventh Millennia B.P. in the southern Levant: A Review for the 90s. *Journal of World Prehistory* 7: 297–353.

Gopher, A. and E. Orelle

1996 An Alternative Interpretation for the Material Imagery of the Yamukian, a Neolithic Culture of the Sixth Millennium BC in the Southern Levant. *Cambridge Archaeological Journal* 6: 255–279.

Gopher, A. and T. Tsuk,(eds.)

1996 *The Nahal Qanah Cave.* Tel Aviv: Tel Aviv University.

Gophna, R and S. Sadeh

1988/9 Excavations at Tel Tsaf: An Early Chalcolithic site in the Jordan Valley. *Tel Aviv* 15/16: 3–36.

Gordon, R. and L. Villiers

1986 Telul edh Dhahab and its Environs. Surveys of 1980 and 1982. A Preliminary Report. *Annual of the Department of Antiquities of Jordan* 30: 275–289.

Goren, Y.

1989 Contacts between Transjordan and Israel during the Chalcolithic Period-Evidence from the Petrography of Pottery, Stone and Metal Artefacts. *Mitkufat Haevan* 22: 148–150.

1990 The Qatifian Culture in southern Israel and Transjordan. *Mitkufat Haevan* 23: 100–112.

1995 Shrines and Ceramics in Chalcolithic Israel: The View through the Petrographic Microscope. *Archaeometry* 37: 287–305.

Görsdorf J.

2002 New ^{14}C Datings of Prehistoric Settlements in the South of Jordan. In R. Eichmann (ed.), *Neuere Forschungen im Vorderen Orient,* 333–339. Berlin: Deutsches Archäologisches Institut.

Greenberg, R.

2002 *Early Urbanisations in the Levant: A Regional Narrative.* London: Leicester University Press.

Greene, J.

1986 *Ajlun-Kufrinji Archaeological Survey.* Amman: Department of Antiquities of Jordan.

Grigson, C.

1995 Plough and Pasture in the Early Economy of the Southern Levant. In T. Levy (ed.), *The Archaeology of Society in the Holy Land,* 245–268. London: Leicester University Press.

Gustavson-Gaube, C.

1986 Tall as Shuna North 1984–85. *Archiv für Orientforschung* 31: 218–222.

Gustavson-Gaube, C. and M. Ibrahim

1986 Sahab Survey 1983. *Archiv für Orientforschung* 31: 283–286.

Habgood, P.

1983 Report on the Lithic Assemblage from the 1975–77 Excavations at Teleilat Ghassul. Sydney: Teleilat Ghassul Project.

Hanbury-Tenison, J.

1986 *The Late Chalcolithic to Early Bronze I Transition in Palestine and Transjordan.* British Archaeological Reports International Series 311. Oxford: British Archaeological Reports.

1987 Jerash Region Survey 1984. *Annual of the Department of Antiquities of Jordan* 31: 129–157.

Hanbury-Tenison, J., S. Hart, P. Watson and R. Faulkner

1984 Wadi Arab Survey 1983. *Annual of the Department of Antiquities of Jordan* 28: 385–424.

Harrison, T.

1997 Shifting Patterns of Settlement in the Highlands of Central Jordan during the Early Bronze Age. *Bulletin of the American Schools of Oriental Research* 306: 1–37.

Hart, S.

1987 Five Soundings in Southern Jordan. *Levant* 19: 33–47.

Hart, S. and R. Faulkner

1985 Preliminary Report on a Survey in Edom. *Annual of the Department of Antiquities of Jordan* 29: 255–277.

Hassan, F.

1985 Radiocarbon Chronology of Neolithic and Predynastic sites in Upper Egypt and the Delta. *The African Archaeological Review* 3: 95–116.

Hauptmann, A.

1989 The Earliest Periods of Copper Metallurgy in Feinan/Jordan. In A. Hauptmann, E. Pernicka and G. Wagner (eds.), *Old World Archaeometallurgy,* 119–135. Bochum: Deutschen Bergbau-Museum.

Helms, S.

1987a A Question of Economic Control during the Proto-Historical Era of Palestine/Transjordan. In A. Hadidi (ed.), *Studies in the History and Archaeology of Jordan III,* 41–51. Amman: Department of Antiquities of Jordan.

1987b Jawa, Tell Um Hammad and the EB I/Late Chalcolithic Landscape. *Levant* 19: 49–82.

1987c A Note on Some 4th Millennium Stamp Seal Impressions from Jordan. *Akkadica* 52: 29–31.

1991 Stamped, Incised and Painted Designs. In A. Betts (ed.), *Excavations at Jawa 1972–1986*, 113–124. Edinburgh: Edinburgh University.

Hennessy, J.B.

1969 Preliminary Report on a First Season of Excavations at Teleilat Ghassul. *Levant* 1: 1–24.

1977 *Teleilat Ghassul: An Interim Report*. Sydney: Sydney University.

1978 City Below the Sea. *Hemisphere* 22:30–35.

1982 Teleilat Ghassul and its Place in the Archaeology of Jordan. In A. Hadidi (ed.), *Studies in the History and Archaeology of Jordan I*, 55–58. Amman: Department of Antiquities of Jordan.

1989 Ghassul, Teleilat. In D.Homes-Fredericq and J.B. Hennessy (eds.), *Archaeology of Jordan 2*. Vol. II. 1 Field Reports. Surveys and Sites A–K, 230–241. Leuven: Peeters.

Henry, D.

1995 *Prehistoric Cultural Ecology and Evolution: Insights from Southern Jordan*. New York: Plenum.

Hodder, I. and R. Matthews

1998 Çatalhöyük: the 1990s Seasons. In R. Matthews (ed.), *Ancient Anatolia*, 43–51. London: British Institute at Ankara.

Hodder, I. and Cessford, C.

2004 Daily Practice and Social Memory at Çatalhöyük. *American Antiquity* 69: 1/–40.

Hole, F.

1997 Evidence for Mid-Holocene Environmental Change in the Western Khabur Drainage, Northeastern Syria. In H. Nüzhet Dalfes, George Kukla, and Harvey Weiss (eds.), *Third Millennium BC Climate Change and Old World Collapse*, 39–66. Berlin: Springer.

2001 A Radiocarbon Chronology for the Middle Khabur, Syria. *Iraq* 63: 67–79.

Horwitz, L.

2002 Fauna from the Wadi Rabah site of Abu Zureiq. *Israel Exploration Journal* 52: 167–178.

Hourani, F.

2002 Le cadre paléogéographique des premieres sociétés agricoles dans la vallée du Jourdain. Etude de l'impact des événements climatiques de l'Holocene aancien sur la dyanmique du peuplement humain. Unpublished PhD. thesis, Institut national agronomique Paris-Grignon.

Hourani, F. and M-A. Courty

1997 L'Évolution morpho-climatique de 10 500 à 5 500 BP dans la vallée du Jourdain. *Paléorient* 23: 95–105.

Ibach, R.

1987 *Hesban 5. Archaeological Survey of the Hesban Region: Catalogue of Sites and Characterisation of Periods*. Berrien Springs, MI: Andrews University.

Ibrahim, M.

1983 Siegel und Siegelabdrucke aus Sahab. *Zeitschrift des Deutschen Palästina-Vereins* 99: 43–53.

1984 Sahab. *Archiv für Orientforschung* 29: 256–260.

1987 Sahab and its foreign relations. In A. Hadidi (ed.), *Studies in the History and Archaeology of Jordan III*, 73–81. Amman: Department of Antiquities of Jordan.

Ibrahim, M. and S. Mittmann

1998 Eine chalkolithische Stiersculptur aus Nordjordanien. *Zeitschrift des Deutschen Palästina-Vereins* 114: 101–105.

Ibrahim, M., J. Sauer and K. Yassine

1976 The East Jordan valley Survey. *Bulletin of the American Schools of Oriental Research* 222: 41–66.

1988 The East Jordan Valley Survey, 1976: Part 2. In K.Yassine (ed.), *Archaeology of Jordan: Essays and Reports*, 189–207. Amman: University of Jordan.

Ji, C.

1997 The Chalcolithic and Early Bronze Cemeteries near Iraq al-Amir and the Preliminary Report on Salvage Excavations. *Annual of the Department of Antiquities of Jordan* 41: 49–68.

Ji, C. and J. Lee

1999 The 1998 Season of Archaeological Survey in the Regions of Iraq al-Amir and Wadi al-Kafrayn: A Preliminary Report. *Annual of the Department of Antiquities of Jordan* 43: 521–542.

2000 A Preliminary Report on the Dhiban Plateau Survey Project 1999: The Versacare Expedition. *Annual of the Department of Antiquities of Jordan* 44: 493–506.

2002 The Survey in the Regions of Iraq al-Amir and Wadi al-Kafrayn, 2000. *Annual of the Department of Antiquities of Jordan* 46: 179–196.

Jobling, W.

1989 Aqaba-Ma'an Archaeological and Epigraphic Survey. In D. Homes-Fredericq and J.B. Hennessy (eds.), *Archaeology of Jordan 2*. Vol. II.1 Field Reports. Surveys and Sites A–K, 16–24. Leuven: Peeters.

Joffe, A.

1993 *Settlement and Society in Early Bronze Age I and II Southern Levant*. Sheffield: Sheffield Academic Press.

1998 Alcohol and Social Complexity in Ancient Western Asia. *Current Anthropology* 39: 297–322.

2000 Egypt and Syro-Mesopotamia in the 4th Millennium: Implications of the New Chronology. *Current Anthropology* 41:113–123.

2003 Slouching towards Beersheva: Chalcolithic Mortuary practices in Local and Regional Context. In B.A. Nakhai (ed.), *The Near East in the Southwest: Essays in Honor of William G. Dever*, 45–67. Annual of the American Schools of Oriental Research 58. Boston: American Schools of Oriental Research.

Joffe, A and J.-P. Dessel

1995 Redefining Chronology and Terminology for the Chalcolithic of the Southern Levant. *Current Anthropology* 36: 507–518.

Joffe, A., J.P. Dessel and R. Hallote

2001 The 'Gilat Woman': Female Iconography, Chalcolithic Cult, and the End of Southern Levantine Prehistory. *Near Eastern Archaeology* 64: 9–23.

Kafafi, Z.

1982 The Neolithic of Jordan. Unpublished PhD. thesis, Free University, Berlin.

1992 Pottery Neolithic Settlement Patterns in Jordan. In M. Zaghloul, K. Amr, F. Zayadine, R. Nabeel and N. Rida Tawfiq (eds.), *Studies in the History and Archaeology of Jordan IV*, 115–123. Amman: Department of Antiquities.

1993 The Yarmoukians in Jordan. *Paléorient* 19: 101–114.

Kafafi, Z., G. Palumbo, A. Al-Shiyab, F. Parenti, E. Santucci and M. Hatamleh

1997 The Wadi az-Zarqaʻ/Wadi ad-Dulayl Archaeological Project. Report on the 1996 Fieldwork Season. *Annual of the Department of Antiquities of Jordan* 41: 9–26.

Kafafi, Z. and D. Vieweger

2000 Geoelectric and Archaeological Work at Sal, Jordan: A Preliminary report on the 1999 Season at the Chalcolithic and Early Bronze Age Site. *Annual of the Department of Antiquities of Jordan* 44: 173–192.

Kamleh, J.

2000 *Der Zeiraqon-Survey (1989–1994). Mit Beiträgen zur Methodik und zur geschichtlichen Auswertung archäologischer Oberflächenuntersuchungen in Palästina.* Wiesbaden: German Palestinian Society.

Kantor, H.

1992 The Relative Chronology of Egypt and Its Foreign Correlations before the First Intermediate Period. In R. Ehrich (ed.), *Chronologies in Old World Archaeology*, 3–21. Chicago: University of Chicago.

Kaplan, J.

1959 The Connections of the Palestinian Chalcolithic culture with Prehistoric Egypt. *Israel Exploration Journal* 9: 134–136.

1960 The Relation of the Chalcolithic Pottery of Palestine to Halafian Ware. *Bulletin of the American Schools of Oriental Research* 159: 32–36.

1969 'Ein el- Jarba: Chalcolithic Remains in the Plain of Esdraelon. *Bulletin of the American Schools of Oriental Research* 194: 2–39.

Keel, O.

1989 *Studien zu der StampSiegeln aus Palastina.* Vol. II. Gottingen: Orbis Biblicus et Orientalis.

Kerestes, T., J. Lundquist, B. Wood, and K. Yassine

1977/78 An archaeological survey of the Three Reservoir Areas in Northern Jordan, 1978. *Annual of the Department of Antiquities of Jordan* 22: 108–135.

Kemp, B.

1973 Photographs of the Decorated Tomb at Hierakonpolis.

Journal of Egyptian Archaeology 59: 36–43.

1989 *Ancient Egypt: Anatomy of a Civilisation.* Routledge, London.

Kempinski, A.

1992 Chalcolithic and Early Bronze Age Temples. In A. Kempinski and R. Reich (eds.), *The Architecture of Ancient Israel*, 53–59. Jerusalem: Israel Exploration Society.

Kenyon, K. and T. Holland

1982 *Excavations at Jericho* IV. London: British School of Archaeology in Jerusalem.

1983 *Excavations at Jericho* V. London: British School of Archaeology in Jerusalem.

Kerner, S.

2000 The Chalcolithic Period. In H.-D. Bienert and B. Müller-Neuhof (eds.), *At the Crossroads: Essays on the Archaeology, History and Current Affairs of the Middle East*, 35–46. Amman: German Protestant Institute.

2001 *Das Chalkolithikum in der südlichen Levante: Die Entwicklung Handwerklicher Spezialisierung und ihre Beziehung zu Gesellschaftlicher Komplexität.* Berlin: Deutsches Archäologisches Institut.

2003 The Pottery of Hujeirat al-Ghuzlan 1998 to 2003: A First Impression. *Orient & Occident.* Newsletter of the German Protestant Institute of Archaeology in Amman 8: 18–20.

Kerner, S., R. Bernbeck, R. Lamprichs and G. Lehmann

1992 Excavations in Abu Snesleh: Middle Bronze Age and Chalcolithic Architecture in Central Jordan. In S. Kerner (ed.). *The Near East in Antiquity* 3, 43–54. Amman: German Protestant Institute.

Khalil, L.

1987 Preliminary Report on the 1985 excavation at el-Maqass-Aqaba. *Annual of the Department of Antiquities of Jordan* 31: 481–485.

1992 Some technological features from a Chalcolithic site at Magass-Aqaba. In M. Zaghloul, K. Amr, F. Zayadine, R. Nabeel and N. Rida Tawfiq (eds.), *Studies in the History and Archaeology of Jordan IV*, 143–148. Amman: Department of Antiquities.

1995 A Second Season of Excavations at al-Magass-Aqaba. *Annual of the Department of Antiquities of Jordan* 39: 65–80.

Khalil, L. and R. Eichmann

1999 Archaeological Survey and Excavation at Wadi al-Yutum and Tall al-Magass Area, Aqaba: A Preliminary Report on the First Season 1998. *Annual of the Department of Antiquities of Jordan* 43: 501–520.

2001 Archaeological Survey and Excavation at the Wadi al-Yutum and Magass Area, al-Aqaba: A Preliminary Report on the Second Season in 2000. *Annual of the Department of Antiquities of Jordan* 45: 195–204.

Khalil, L., R. Eichmann and K. Schmidt

2003 Archaeological Survey and Excavations at the Wadi al-Yutum and al-Magass Area—al-'Aqaba (ASEYM): A

Preliminary Report on the Third and Fourth Seasons Excavations at Tall Hujayrat al-Ghuzlan in 2002 and 2003 Wadi al-Yutum. *Annual of the Department of Antiquities of Jordan* 47:159–182.

Khalil, L. and Riederer

1998 Examination of Copper Metallurgical Remains from a Chalcolithic Site at el-Magass, Jordan. *Damaszener Mitteilungen* 10: 1–9.

Kirkbride, D.

1969 Early Byblos and the Beqa'a. *Mélanges de l'Université Saint-Joseph* 45: 45–60.

Koeppel, R.

1938 Die achte Grabung in Ghassul. *Biblica* 19: 260–266.

Koeppel, R., R. Mallon and R. Neuville

1940 *Teleilat Ghassul II*. Rome: Pontifical Biblical Institute.

Kuijt, I. and M. Chesson

2002 Excavations at Ain Waida, Jordan: New Insights in Pottery Neolithic Lifeways in the Southern Levant. *Paléorient* 28:109–122.

Kuijt, I., B. Finlayson and J. MacKay

2007 Pottery Neolithic landscape modification at Dhra'. *Antiquity* 81: 1–13.

Lamprichs, R.

1998 *Abu Snesleh. Ergebnisse der Ausgrabungen 1990 und 1992*. Berlin.

Lee, J.

1973 Chalcolithic Ghassul: New Aspects and Master Typology. Unpublished PhD. thesis, The Hebrew University, Jerusalem.

Lehmann, G., R. Lamprichs, S. Kerner and R. Bernbeck

1991 The 1990 Excavations at Abu Snesleh: Preliminary Report. *Annual of the Department of Antiquities of Jordan* 35: 41–63.

Lenzen, C.

1986 Tall Irbid and Beit Ras. *Archiv für Orientforschung* 31: 164–166

Lenzen, C. and A. McQuitty

1983 A Preliminary Survey of the Irbid-Beit Ras Region, northwestern Jordan. *Annual of the Department of Antiquities of Jordan* 27: 656.

Leonard, A.

1987 The Jarash-Tell el-Husn Highway Survey. *Annual of the Department of Antiquities of Jordan* 31: 343–390.

1989 A Chalcolithic Fine Ware from Kataret es-Samra in the Jordan Valley. *Bulletin of the American Schools of Oriental Research* 276: 3–14.

Leonard, A. (ed).

1992 *The Jordan Valley Survey, 1953: Some Unpublished Soundings Conducted by James Mellaart*. Annual of the American Schools of Oriental Research 50. Winona Lake: Eisenbrauns.

Levy, T.

1992 Radiocarbon dating of the Beersheba culture and Predynastic Egypt. In E.C.M. van den Brink (ed.), *The Nile Delta in Transition: 4th–3rd Millennium BC*, 345–356. Jerusalem: Privately Published.

1993 Ghassul, Tuleilat el. In E. Stern (ed.), *New Encyclopaedia of Archaeological Excavations in the Holy Land*, 506–511. Jerusalem: Carta.

1995 Cult, Metallurgy and Rank Societies—Chalcolithic Period (ca. 4500–3500 BCE). In T. Levy (ed.), *The Archaeology of Society in the Holy Land*, 226–244. London: Leicester University Press.

1996 Anthropological Approaches to Protohistoric Palestine: A Case Study from the Negev Desert. In J. Seger (ed.), *Retrieving the Past: Essays on Archaeology and Research in Honor of Gus van Beek*, 163–178. Winona Lake: Eisenbrauns.

Levy, T. (ed.)

1987 *Shiqmim I: Studies Concerning Chalcolithic Societies in the Northern Negev Desert, Israel*. British Archaeological Reports International Series 356. Oxford: British Archaeological Reports.

2006 *Archaeology, Anthropology and Cult: The Sanctuary at Gilat, Israel*. London: Equinox.

Levy, T. and D. Alon

1982 The Chalcolithic Mortuary site near Mezad Aluf, northern Negev desert: A Preliminary study. *Bulletin of the American Schools of Oriental Research* 248: 37–59.

Levy, T. and J. Golden

1996 Syncretistic and Mnemonic Dimensions of Chalcolithic Art: A New Human Figurine from Shiqmim. *Biblical Archaeologist* 59: 150–159.

Levy, T., R. Adams, A. Witten, J. Anderson, Y. Arbel, S. Kuah, J. Moreno, A. Lo and M. Wagonner

2001 Early Metallurgy, Interaction, and Social Change: The Jabal Hamrat Fidan (Jordan) Research Design and 1998 Archaeological Survey: Preliminary Report. *Annual of the Department of Antiquities of Jordan* 45: 159–188.

Levy, T., M. Burton and Y. Rowan

2006 Chalcolithic Hamlet Excavations near Shiqmim, Negev Desert, Israel. *Jouurnal of Field Archaeology* 31: 41–60.

Lovell, J.

2000 Pella in Jordan in the Chalcolithic Period. In D. Baird and G. Philip (eds.), *Ceramics and Change in the Early Bronze Age of the Southern Levant*, 59–71. Sheffield: Sheffield Academic Press.

2001a *The Late Neolithic and Chalcolithic Periods in the Southern Levant: New data from Teleilat Ghassul, Jordan*. British Archaeological Reports International Series 974. Oxford: Archaeopress.

2001b An Indigenous Development: Basil Hennessy and the Late Neolithic at Teleilat Ghassul. In A. Walmsley (ed.), *Australians in Jordan. 50 Years of Excavation and Survey*, 31–42. Sydney: University of Sydney.

2002 Shifting Subsistence Patterns: Some Ideas about the end of the Chalcolithic in the Southern Levant. *Paléorient* 28: 89–102.

2007 The Wadi ar-Rayyan Archaeological Project (WRAP): Investigating the Chalcolithic-Early Bronze Age Transition. In F. Khraysheh (ed.), *Studies in the History and Archaeology of Jordan IX*, 457–466. Amman: Department of Antiquities.

Lovell, J., Z. Kafafi and G. Dollfus

1997 A Preliminary Note on the Ceramics from the Basal Levels at Abu Hamid. In H.G. Gebel, Z. Kafafi and G.O. Rollefson (eds.), *The Prehistory of Jordan II: Perspectives from 1997*, 361–370. Berlin: ex oriente.

Lovell, J., G. Dollfus and Z. Kafafi

2004 The Middle Phases at Abu Hamid and the Wadi Rabah Horizon. In *Studies in the History and Archaeology of Jordan VIII*, 263–274. Amman: Department of Antiquities of Jordan.

Lovell, J., J. Meadows, T. Adams, D. Thomas, T. Richter, H. Miller, C. Elias, I. McRae and M. Balawaneh

2006 The Second Preliminary Report of the Wadi Rayyan Archaeological Project: The First Season of Excavations at el-Khawarij. *Annual of the Department of Antiquities Jordan* 50: 33–59.

Lovell, J., D. Thomas, H. Miller, K. Wesselingh, A. Kurzawska, I. McRae, C. Elias, E. Obeidat and A. Abu Shmeis

in press The Third Preliminary Report of the Wadi Rayyan Archaeological Project: The Second Season of Excavations at el-Khawarij. *Annual of the Department of Antiquities Jordan* 51.

Lucas, A and J.R. Harris

1962 *Ancient Egyptian Materials and Industries*. 4th edn. London: Edward Arnold.

McAdam, E.

1997 The Figurines from the 1982–5 Seasons of Excavations at Ain Ghazal. *Levant* 29: 115–152.

McConaughy, M.

1979 Formal and Functional Analysis of Chipped Stone Tools from Bab edh-Dhra. Unpublished PhD thesis, University of Pittsburgh.

McCorriston, J.

1997 The Fibre Revolution: Textile Extensification, Alienation and Social Stratification in Ancient Mesopotamia. *Current Anthropology* 38: 517–549.

McCreery, D.

1978/9 Preliminary Report of the Arab Potash Company Township Archaeological Survey. *Annual of the Department of Antiquities of Jordan* 22–23: 150–162.

McNicoll, A., P. Edwards, J. Hanbury-Tenison, J.B. Hennessy, T. Potts, R. Smith, A. Walmsley and P. Watson.

1992 *Pella in Jordan 2*. Mediterranean Archaeology Supplement 2. Sydney

Mabry, J.

1989 Investigations at Tell el-Handaquq, Jordan (1987–88).

Annual of the Department of Antiquities of Jordan 33: 59–95.

Mabry, J. and G. Palumbo

1988 The 1987 Wadi el-Yabis Survey. *Annual of the Department of Antiquities of Jordan* 32: 275–305.

1992 Environmental, Economic, and Political Constraints on Ancient Settlement Patterns in the Wadi al-Yabis Region. In M. Zaghloul, K. Amr, F. Zayadine, R. Nabeel and N. Rida Tawfiq (eds.), *Studies in the History and Archaeology of Jordan IV*, 67–72. Amman: Department of Antiquities.

MacDonald, B.

2004 The Tafila-Busayra Archaeological Survey, West-Central Jordan: Phases 1, 2 and 3 (1999, 2000 and 2001 Seasons). *Studies in the History and Archaeology of Jordan VIII*, 275–284. Amman: Department of Antiquities.

MacDonald, B. (ed.)

1988 The Wadi el-Hasa Archaeological Survey 1979–1983, West-Central Jordan. Waterloo: Wilfrid Laurier University Press.

1992 The Southern Ghors and Northeast 'Arabah Archaeological Survey. Sheffield: J.R. Collis Publications.

MacDonald, B., A. Bradshaw, L. Herr, M. Neeley and S. Quaintance

2000 The Tafila-Busayra Archaeological Survey: Phase 1 (1999). *Annual of the Department of Antiquities of Jordan* 44: 507–522.

MacDonald, B., L. Herr, M. Neeley, S. Quaintance and A. Bradshaw

2001 The Tafila-Busayra Archaeological Survey: Phase 2 (2000). *Annual of the Department of Antiquities of Jordan* 45: 395–412.

MacDonald, B. and W. Sawtell

2002 The Tafila-Busayra Archaeological Survey: Phase 3 (2001). *Annual of the Department of Antiquities of Jordan* 46: 477–484.

Mallon, A., R. Koeppel and R. Neuville

1934 *Teleilat Ghassul I*. Rome: Pontifical Biblical Institue.

Mattingly, G.

1996 Al-Karak Resources Project 1995: A Preliminary Report on the Pilot Season. *Annual of the Department of Antiquities of Jordan* 40: 349–368.

Mazar, A.

1990 *Archaeology of the Land of the Bible*. New York: Doubleday.

McGovern, P.

1989 Baq'ah Valley Project-Survey and Excavation. In D.Homes-Fredericq and J.B. Hennessy (eds.), *Archaeology of Jordan 2*. Vol. II.1 Field Reports. Surveys and Sites A–K, 25–44. Leuven: Peeters.

Meadows, J.

1998 *Ghassul Archaeobotany Report, 1997 Season*. Sydney: Teleilat Ghassul Project.

2001 Olive Domestication at Teleilat Ghassul. In L. Hopkins and A. Parker (eds.) *Archaeology of the Near East: An Australian Perspective*, 13–18. Sydney: ACL.

2005 Early Farmers and their Environment: Archaeobotanical studies of Neolithic and Chalcolithic sites in Jordan. Unpublished PhD thesis, La Trobe University, Melbourne.

Mellaart, J.

1956 The Neolithic Site of Ghrubba. *Annual of the Department of Antiquities of Jordan* 3: 24–40.

1962 Preliminary Report of the Archaeological Survey in the Yarmouk and Jordan Valley. *Annual of the Department of Antiquities of Jordan* 6–7: 126–158.

1967 *Çatalhöyük: A Neolithic Town in Anatolia.* Thames and Hudson, London.

1975 *The Neolithic of the Near East.* Thames and Hudson, London.

1998 Çatalhöyük: the 1960s Seasons. In R. Matthews (ed.), *Ancient Anatolia. Fifty Years' Work by the British Institute of Archaeology at Ankara*, 35–41. London: British Institute of Archaeology at Ankara.

Milevski, I.

2002 A New Fertility Figurine and New Animal Motifs from the Chalcolithic in the Southern Levant: Finds from Cave K-1 at Quleh, Israel. *Paléorient* 28: 133–141.

Miller, J. (ed.)

1991 *Archaeological Survey of the Kerak Plateau.* Atlanta: Scholars Press.

Mittmann, S.

1970 *Beiträge zur Siedlungs und Territorialgeschichte des Nördlichen Ostjordanlandes.* Wiesbaden: German Palestinian Society.

Moore, A.

1973 The Late Neolithic in Palestine. *Levant* 5: 36–68.

Moorey, P.R.S.

1989 The Chalcolithic Hoard from Nahal Mishmar, Israel, in context. *World Archaeology* 20: 171–189.

Mortensen, P. and I. Thuesen

1998 The Prehistoric Periods. In M. Piccirillo and E. Alliath (eds.), *Mount Nebo: New Archaeological Excavations 1967–1997*, 84–99. Jerusalem: Franciscan Printing Press.

Munro, R., R. Morgan,and W. Jobling

1997 Optical dating and landscape chronology at ad-Disa, southern Jordan, and its potential. In G. Bisheh (ed.), *Studies in the History and Archaeology of Jordan VI*, 97–104. Amman: Department of Antiquities.

Najjar, M., A. Abu Dayya, E. Suleiman, G. Weisgerber and A. Hauptmann

1990 Tell Wadi Feinan: The First Pottery Neolithic Tell in the South of Jordan. *Annual of the Department of Antiquities of Jordan* 34: 27–51.

Nasrallah, J.

1948 Une station ghassoulienne du Hauran. *Revue Biblique* 55: 81–103.

Neef, R.

1990 Introduction, development and environmental implications of olive culture. In S. Bottema, G. Entjes-Nieborg and W. van Zeist (eds.), *Man's Role in the Shaping of the Eastern Mediterranean Landscape*, 295–306. Rotterdam: Balkema.

Nigro, L. and B. Panciroli

2001 Materiali archeologici dai primi scavi del Pontificio Istituto Biblico a Tuleilat el-Ghassul (1929–1938) nei Musei Vaticani. *Bollettino dei Monumenti, Musei e Gallerie Pontificie* 21: 11–73.

North, R.

1961 *Ghassul 1960 Excavation Report.* Rome: Pontifical Biblical Institute.

1964 Ghassul's New-Found Jar-Incision. *Annual of the Department of Antiquities of Jordan* 8–9: 68–74.

Ottosson, M.

1980 *Temples and Cult Places in Palestine.* Uppsala: Uppsala University.

Palumbo, G.

1994 JADIS. The Jordan Antiquities Database and Information System. A Summary of the Data. Amman: Department of Antiquities of Jordan.

Palumbo, G., J. Mabry and I. Kuijt

1990 The Wadi el-Yabis Survey: Report on the 1989 Field Season. *Annual of the Department of Antiquities of Jordan* 34: 95–118.

Palumbo, G., M. Munzi, S. Collins, F. Hourani, A. Peruzzetto and M. Wilson

1996 The Wadi az-Zarqa/Wadi ad-Dulayl Excavation and Survey Projects. *Annual of the Department of Antiquities of Jordan* 40: 375–427.

Payne, J.

1973 Tomb 100: The Decorated Tomb at Hierakonpolis confirmed. *Journal of Egyptian Archaeology* 59: 31–35.

Peltenburg, E.

1987 Early Faience: Recent Studies, Origins and Relations with Glass. In M. Bimson and I. Freestone (eds.), *Early Vitreous Materials,* 5–29. London: British Museum.

1995 Kissonerga in Cyprus and the Appearance of Faience in the East Mediterranean. In S. Bourke and J-P. Descoeudres (eds.), *Trade, Contact and the Movement of Peoples in the Eastern Mediterranean: Studies in Honour of J. Basil Hennessy. Mediterranean Archaeology*, 31–41. Sydney: Meditarch.

Perrot, J.

1959 Statuettes en ivoire et autres objets en ivoire et os provenent des gisements prehistoriques de la région de Beershéba. *Syria* 36: 8–19.

1968 La prehistoire Palestinienne. *Supplément au Dictionnaire Archéologique de la Bible* 8: 286–446.

Perrot, J. and D. Ladiray

1980 Tombes a ossuaires de la region cotiere Palestinienne au IVe millenaire l'ere chretienne. Paris: Association Paléorient.

Philip, G. and O. Williams-Thorpe

1993 A Provenance Study of Jordanian Basalt Vessels of the Chalcolithic and Early Bronze Age I Periods. *Paléorient* 19: 51–63.

2000 The Production and Distribution of Ground Stone Artefacts in the Southern Levant during the 5th–4th Millennia BC: Some Implications of Geochemical and Petrographic Analysis. In P. Matthiae, A. Enea, L. Peyronel and F. Pinnock (eds.), *Proceedings of the First International Congress on the Archaeology of the Ancient Near East*, 1379–1396. Rome: University of Rome La Sapienza.

2001 The production and consumption of basalt artefacts in the southern Levant during the 5th–4th millennia BC: a geochemical and petrographic investigation. In A. Millard (ed.), *Archaeological Sciences '97: Proceedings of the conference held at the University of Durham 2–4 September 1997*, 11–30. British Archaeological Reports International Series 939. Oxford: Archaeopress.

Porath, Y.

1992 Domestic Architecture of the Chalcolithic Period. In A. Kempinski and R. Reich (eds.), *The Architecture of Ancient Israel*, 40–50. Jerusalem: Israel Exploration Society.

Prag, K.

1974 The Intermediate Early Bronze–Middle Bronze Age: An Interpretation of the Evidence from Transjordan, Syria and Lebanon. *Levant* 6: 69–116.

1991 A Walk in the Wadi Hesban. *Palestine Exploration Quarterly* 123: 48–61.

1995 The Dead Sea Dolmens: Death and the Landscape. In S. Campbell and A. Green (eds.), *The Archaeology of Death in the Ancient Near East*, 75–85. Oxford: Oxbow Books.

2007 Water Strategies in the Iktanu Region of Jordan. In F. Khraysheh (ed.), *Studies in the History and Archaeology of Jordan IX*, 405–412. Amman: Department of Antiquities.

Quintero, L., P. Wilke, and G. Rollefson

2002 From Flint Mine to Fan Scraper: The Late Prehistoric Jafr Industrial Complex. *Bulletin of the American Schools of Oriental Research* 327: 17–48.

Raikes, T.

1980 Notes on some Neolithic and later sites in Wadi Araba and the Dead Sea Valley. *Levant* 12: 40–60.

Rast, W. and R.T. Schaub

1974 Survey of the Southeastern Plain of the Dead Sea, 1973. *Annual of the Department of Antiquities of Jordan* 19: 5–53.

Reese, D.

1998 A First Study of Teleilat Ghassul Shell Remains 1994–97. Sydney: Teleilat Ghassul Project.

Reese, D., H.K. Mienis and F.R. Woodward

1986 On the Trade of Shells and Fish from the Nile River. *Bulletin of the American Schools of Oriental Research* 264: 79–84.

Rehren, T., K. Hess, and G. Philip

1997 Fourth millennium BC Copper Metallurgy in Northern Jordon: The Evidence from Tell esh-Shuna. In H.G. Gebel, Z. Kafafi and G.O. Rollefson (eds.), *The Prehistory of Jordan II: Perspectives from 1997*, 625–640. Berlin: ex oriente.

Rollefson, G.

1992 Chipped Stone Tools from Pella. In A. McNicoll, P. Edwards, J. Hanbury-Tenison, J.B. Hennessy, T. Potts, R. Smith, A. Walmsley and P. Watson (eds.), *Pella in Jordan 2*, 231–241. Mediterranean Archaeology Supplement 2. Sydney: Meditarch.

Rollefson, G., L. Quintero, and P. Wilke

2001 Azraq Wetlands Survey 2000: Preliminary Report. *Annual of the Department of Antiquities of Jordan* 45: 71–82.

Rosen, S.A.

1983 Tabular Scraper Trade: A Model for material culture dispersion. *Bulletin of the American Schools of Oriental Research* 249: 79–86.

1989 The Origins of Craft Specialisation: Lithic Perspectives. In I. Hershkovitz (ed.), *People and Culture in Change*, 107–114. British Archaeological Reports International Series 508. Oxford: Archaeopress.

1997 *Lithics after the Stone Age*. Walnut Creek: Altamira.

Rothenberg, B.

1999 Archaeometallurgical Researches in the southern Arabah 1959–1990. Part 1: Late Pottery Neolithic to Early Bronze IV. *Palestine Exploration Quarterly* 131: 68–89.

Rothman, M.

1994 Evolutionary Typologies and Cultural Complexity. In G.Stein and M. Rothman (eds.), *Chiefdoms and Early States in the Near East: The Organisational Dynamics of Complexity*, 1–22. Monographs in World Archaeology 18. Madison: Prehistory Press.

Roux, V. and M-A. Courty

1997 Les bols elabores au tour d'Abu Hamid: Rupture technique au 4e millenaire avant J.-C. dans le Levant-Sud. *Paléorient* 23: 25–43.

Rowan, Y. and T. Levy

1994 Proto-Canaanean Blades of the Chalcolithic Period. *Levant* 26: 167–174.

Sapin, J.

1992 De l'occupation à l'utilisation de l'espace à l'aube de l'age du bronze dans la région de Jérash et sa périphérie orientale. In M. Zaghloul, K. Amr, F. Zayadine, R. Nabeel and N. Rida Tawfiq (eds.), *Studies in the History and Archaeology of Jordan IV*, 169–174. Amman: Department of Antiquities.

Savage, S.

1997 Descent Group Competition and Economic Strategies in Predynastic Egypt. *Journal of Anthropological Archaeology* 16: 226–268.

2007 Controlling Space at the Regional Level: Geographic Information Systems (GIS) and JADIS in Jordan. In T. Levy, P-M. Michele Daviau, R. Younker and M. Shaer (eds.), *Crossing Jordan: North American Contributions to the Archaeology of Jordan*, 37–46. London: Equinox Publishing.

Scham, S.

1997 Shiqmim's Violin-Shaped Figurines and Ghassulian Bone Artifacts. *Biblical Archaeologist* 60: 108.

Scham, S. and Y. Garfinkel

2000 Perforated Rods-A New Chalcolithic Ivory Type. *Bulletin of the American Schools of Oriental Research* 319: 1–5.

Schick, T.

1998 *The Cave of the Warrior. A Fourth Millennium Burial in the Judaean Desert.* Jerusalem: Israel Antiquities Authority.

Schmandt-Besserat, D.

1992 *Before Writing, Vol. 1. From Counting to Cuneiform.* Austin: University of Texas.

Schulman, A.

1992 Still More Egyptian Seal Impressions from 'En Besor. In E.C.M. van den Brink (ed.), *The Nile Delta in Transition: 4th–3rd Millennium BC*, 395–417. Jerusalem: Privately Published.

Seaton, P.

2000 Aspects of New Research at the Chalcolithic Sanctuary Precinct at Teleilat Ghassul. In P. Matthiae, A. Enea, L. Peyronel and F. Pinnock (eds.), *Proceedings of the First International Congress on the Archaeology of the Ancient Near East*, 1503–1514. Rome: University of Rome La Sapienza.

2006 Chalcolithic Cult and Risk Management at Teleilat Ghassul: The Area E Sanctuary. Unpublished PhD thesis, University of Sydney, Sydney.

Segal, D., I. Carmi, Z. Gal, and H. Smithline

1998 Dating a Chalcolithic Burial Cave in Peqi'in, Upper Galilee, Israel. *Radiocarbon* 40: 707–712.

Simmons, A. and Z. Kafafi

1992 The Ain Ghazal Survey: Patterns of Settlement in the Greater Wadi az-Zarqa Area, Central Jordan. In M. Zaghloul, K. Amr, F. Zayadine, R. Nabeel and N. Rida Tawfiq (eds.), *Studies in the History and Archaeology of Jordan IV*, 77–82. Amman: Department of Antiquities.

Simmons, A. and M. Najjar

1998 Al-Ghuwayr I, A Pre-Pottery Neolithic Village in Wadi Faynan, Southern Jordan: A Preliminary Report on the 1996 and 1997/98 Seasons. *Annual of the Department of Antiquities of Jordan* 42: 91–101.

Simmons, A., Z. Kafafi, G. Rollefson and K. Moyer

1989 Test Excavations at Wadi Shu'eib, a Major Neolithic Settlement in Central Jordan. *Annual of the Department of Antiquities of Jordan* 33: 27–42.

Stager, L.

1985 The first fruits of civilisation. In J. Tubb (ed.), *Palestine in the Bronze and Iron Age*, 172–188. London: Institute of Archaeology.

1992 The Periodisation of Palestine from the Neolithic through Early Bronze times. In R. Ehrich (ed.), *Chronologies in Old World Archaeology*, 22–60. Chicago: University of Chicago.

Stein, G.

1994a Economy, Ritual and Power in 'Ubaid Mesopotamia. In G.Stein and M. Rothman (eds.), *Chiefdoms and Early States in the Near East: The Organisational Dynamics of Complexity*, 35–46. Monographs in World Archaeology 18. Madison: Prehistory Press.

1994b Segmentary states and Organisational Variation in early complex societies. In G.Schwartz and S. Falconer (eds.), *Archaeological Views from the Countryside: Village Communities in Early Complex Societies*, 10–18. Washington: Smithsonian Institution.

1998 Heterogeneity, Power and Political Economy: Some Current Research Issues in the Archaeology of Old World Complex Societies. *Journal of Archaeological Research* 6: 1–44.

Stein, G. and Rothman, M. (eds.)

1994 *Chiefdoms and Early States in the Near East: The Organisational Dynamics of Complexity.* Monographs in World Archaeology 18. Madison: Prehistory Press.

Stekelis, M.

1935 *Les Monuments Mégalithiques de Palestine.* Paris: Archives de L'Institut de Paleontologie Humaine.

Tadmor, M., D. Kedem, F. Begemann, A. Hauptmann, E. Pernicka and S. Schmitt-Strecker

1995 The Nahal Mishmar Hoard from the Judean Desert: Technology, Composition and Provenance. *'Atiqot* 27: 95–148.

Tzori, N.

1958 Neolithic and Chalcolithic Sites in the Valley of Beth Shan. *Palestine Exploration Quarterly* 90: 44–51.

1967 On two pithoi from the Beth Shan region of the Jordan Valley. *Palestine Exploration Quarterly* 99: 101–103.

Ussishkin, D.

1980 The Ghassulian Shrine at En-Gedi. *Tel Aviv* 7: 1–44.

Van den Brink, E.

1998 An Index to Chalcolithic Mortuary Caves in Israel. *Israel Exploration Journal* 48: 165–173.

Vaux, R. de

1966 Palestine during the Neolithic and Chalcolithic Periods. In I.E.S. Edwards, C.J. Gadd, N.G.L. Hammond (eds.), *The Cambridge Ancient History*, vol. I, 498–538. Cambridge: Cambridge University Press.

Waheeb, M.

1996 Archaeological Excavation at Ras en-Naqb-Aqaba Road Alignment: Preliminary Report (1995). *Annual of the Department of Antiquities of Jordan* 40: 339–348.

Wapnish, P. and B. Hesse

1991 Faunal Remains from Tel Dan: Perspectives on animal production at a village, urban and ritual center. *Archaeozoologia* 4: 9–86.

Watson, P.

2004 Cultural Identity and Wine Production in Northern Jordan: A Case Study in Context. In *Studies in the History and Archaeology of Jordan VIII*, 485–502. Amman: Department of Antiquities of Jordan.

2006 Changing Patterns of Settlement and Land Use in the Hinterland of Pella (Jordan) in Late Antiquity. In A. Lewin and P. Pellegrini (eds.), *Settlements and Demography in the Near East in Late Antiquity*, 171–191. Pisa: Instituti Editoriali e Poligrafici Internationali.

Watson, P. and M. O'Hea

1996 Pella Hinterland Survey 1994: Preliminary Report. *Levant* 28: 63–76.

Weiss, H.

2001 Beyond the Younger Dryas: Collapse as Adaptation to Abrupt Climate Change in Ancient Western Asia and the Eastern Mediterranean. In G. Bawden and R. Reycraft (eds.), *Environmental Disaster and the Archaeology of Human Response*, 75–98. Albuquerque: Maxwell Museum of Anthropology.

Wilcox, G.

1992 Preliminary Report on the Plant Remains from Pella. In A. McNicoll, P. Edwards, J. Hanbury-Tenison, J.B. Hennessy, T. Potts, R. Smith, A. Walmsley and P. Watson (eds.), *Pella in Jordan 2*, 253–256. Mediterranean Archaeology Supplement 2. Sydney: Meditarch.

Wright, K., M. Najjar, J. Last and N. Moloney

1998 The Wadi Faynan 4th and 3rd Millennia Project, 1997: Report on the First Season of Test Excavations at Wadi Faynan 100. *Levant* 30: 33–60.

Yoffee, N.

1993 Too Many Chiefs? (or, Safe Texts for the 90s). In N. Yoffee and A. Sherratt (eds.), *Archaeological Theory: Who Sets the Agenda?*, 60–78. Cambridge: Cambridge University Press.

1995 Conclusion: A Mass in celebration of the conference. In T. Levy (ed.), *The Archaeology of Society in the Holy Land*, 542–548. London: Leicester University Press.

Zbenovich, V.

1998 Review of S. Rosen, Lithics after the Stone Age. *Mitkufat Haevan* 28: 197–204.

Zohary, D. and P. Spiegel-Roy

1975 The beginnings of fruit growing in the Old World. *Science* 187: 319–327.

6. The Early Bronze Age I–III

Graham Philip

Introduction

In the previous version of this contribution (Philip 2001), I used the opportunity provided by the request to produce an overview of the evidence for the Early Bronze Age in Jordan to put forward an interpretation of the data which differed from the "city-states" model which has dominated the literature in recent decades (e.g. Ben-Tor 1992; Esse 1991; Mazar 1990; Richard 1987). It is encouraging to note that since that account was written other scholars have raised similar concerns regarding the appropriateness of the traditional approach (e.g. Greenberg 2002, 2003; Harrison and Savage 2003; Nicolle 1999). As a result, in the current version of this chapter, I have sought to take account both of the substantial amount of new evidence which has appeared since the late 1990s and shifts in scholarly approaches to the interpretation of small scale complex societies in the region. Once more, however, it is important to stress that this review should not be regarded as anything other than a framework that others may wish to critique, revise, develop, or even contradict.

Early Bronze Age Studies in the Southern Levant

Origins of the City-State Model

Until recently scholars have viewed the Early Bronze Age within a broadly neo-evolutionary, and region-wide, framework (Ben-Tor 1992; Esse 1989a, 1991; Finkelstein 1995a; Mazar 1990; Richard 1987). Thus the sequence was understood as a period of increasing complexity during EB I, leading to the appearance of a stratified society during EB II–III, and decline during EB IV (see Esse 1989a: table 1; Palumbo, this volume). In regional terms, EB II–III society was seen as comprising a series of broadly homologous city-states, each based around a walled urban centre. These are sometimes viewed as "peer-polities" (Finkelstein 1995a). In recent years, scholars have challenged various aspects of this model, but before examining the critique, we must first consider the way in which the previous interpretation took form.

The key point is that the idea of Early Bronze Age city-states in the southern Levant became entrenched in the literature (e.g. Albright 1949: 74) many years before scholars began to debate the material correlates of urbanism and stratified societies and apply these to data from the Ancient Near East (Adams 1966; Flannery 1972; Service 1962, 1975; Wright 1977). As a result, the presence at these sites of the classic characteristics of state societies—regional polities, social stratification, elite control of the economic base, administrative systems—was never actually demonstrated, it was simply assumed.

In fact, the idea of Early Bronze Age city-states appears to have derived from two sources. Firstly, Wright's (1961: 81) remark that the Early Bronze Age represented "the beginning of the city-state system" makes it clear that Early Bronze Age urbanism was really a projection back in time of the situation in the Late Bronze Age as revealed by documentary sources that indicate the existence of small city-states, based around the main urban centres (Bunimovitz 1995: 326; Moran 1992). This model also appears to fit the Middle Bronze Age data (Ilan 1995: 301), and scholars have assumed a broad equivalence between the Early Bronze Age walled settlements and the urban communities of the second millennium BC (Finkelstein 1995a: 55; de Miroschedji 1999: 12). The EB III is, however, separated from the Middle Bronze Age by a gap of several centuries, characterized by a very different form of socio-economic organization (Palumbo, this volume). There is, therefore, no reason to *assume* continuity of social or political organization between the two periods. The second source was the widely held belief that developments in the southern Levant should comprise a parallel, if smaller scale, version of processes of urbanization and state development taking place in contemporary Mesopotamia and Egypt (Kenyon 1979: 84–86; Wright 1961: 81). In this regard, Ben-Tor's (1992: 86) analogy that places the southern Levant at the edge of a pond, receiving the outer ripples of a stone (urbanism) thrown into the south Mesopotamian centre, is particularly revealing. There was, therefore, an expectation that urban settlements existed, one that was readily satisfied by the presence of walled sites.

Leaving detailed points for later, attention should be drawn to three broader critiques which have been developed in recent years. Greenberg (2003) has argued on the basis of detailed analysis of the occupational sequences of key EBA sites in Palestine, that the grand regional narrative of linear evolution which has underpinned most work to date is simply inconsistent with the evidence, and that the real picture is one of diverse and fragmentary regional sequences, with ample evidence for false starts and sporadic realignments. On a rather different tack, others have argued that the traditional references to the Mesopotamian world are inappropriate, and that more relevant analogies can be drawn with the smaller-scale contemporary societies of the Aegean (Chesson and

Philip 2003; Joffe 2004). Finally, many of our assumptions regarding the formation, development and nature of state-level societies in Mesopotamia itself have come under increasing scrutiny in recent years (Stein 1998, 2001; Rothman 2004).

Evidence for the Existence of City-States

While scholars working within the framework of traditional Palestinian "historical" or "biblical" archaeology (e.g. Kenyon 1979; Mazar 1990) appear to have taken for granted the "fact" of Early Bronze Age city-states, others have sought to situate Palestinian city-states within a

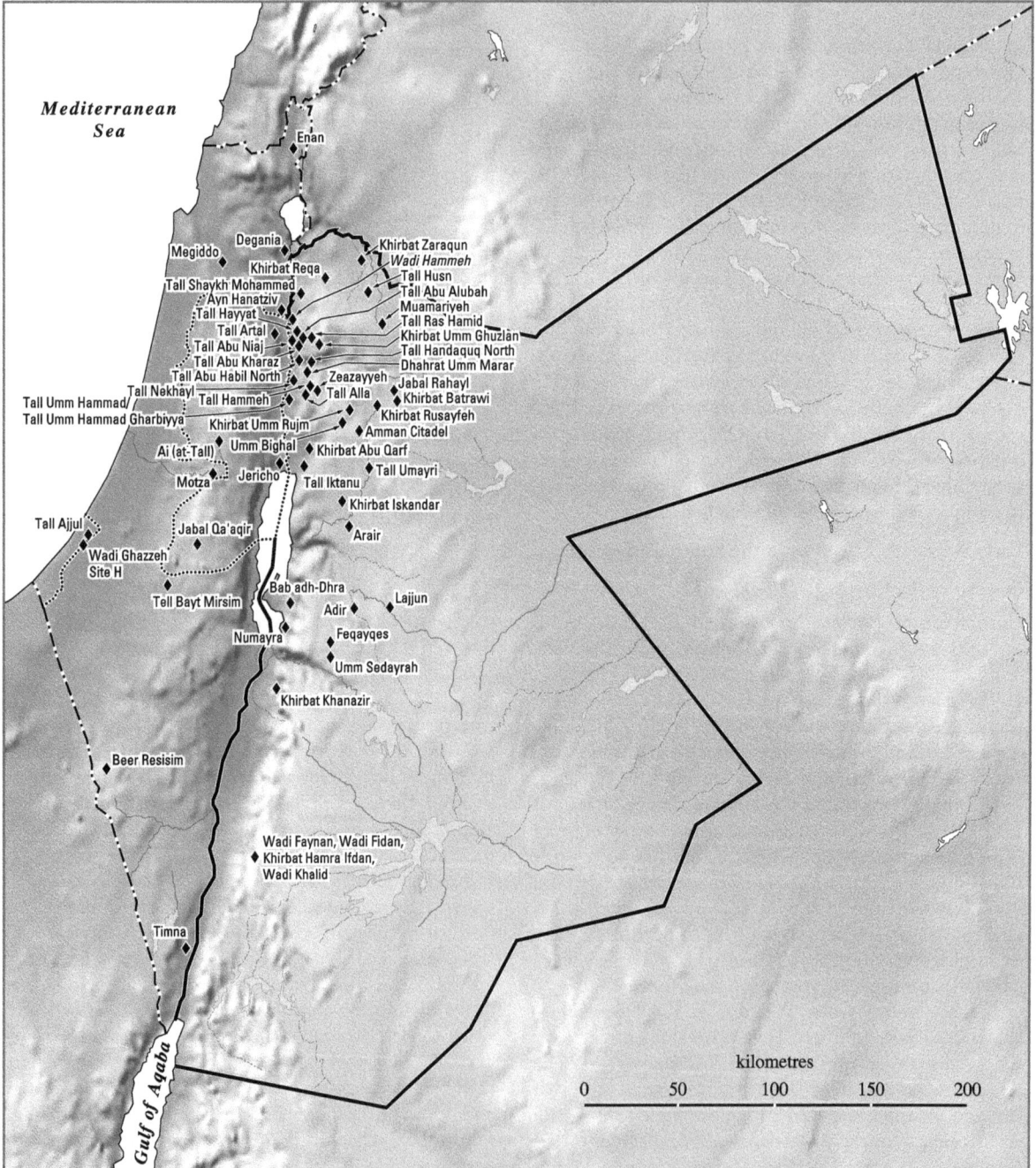

Figure 6.1   Early Bronze Age I–III sites mentioned in the text.

broader theoretical debate, and to identify specific correlates of complexity and urbanism within the regional data (Esse 1989a: fig. 1; de Miroschedji 1989: fig. 1; Joffe 1993). These include the presence of public architecture, including defensive and administrative structures, evidence for the growth of social, political and settlement hierarchies, and various forms of economic specialization including both crafts and subsistence practices.

Esse (1989a), for example, argued that Early Bronze Age Palestine represented an instance of Secondary State Formation (Price 1978). Thus, the development of small-scale polities controlled by local elites took place in response to connections with the more developed state of Egypt, which presented opportunities for incipient local elites to enhance their power by exploiting strategic economic niches. The "urban" centres thus constituted regional foci of specialization and control. Such a coincidence of political and economic power is widely assumed in neo-evolutionary literature (e.g. Flannery 1972). The image of the Early Bronze Age city-states as peer polities put forward by Finkelstein (1995a, after Renfrew and Cherry 1986) paints a picture of hierarchical, territorial, political and economic units each organized around a walled central place. Once the reality of such polities was accepted, their existence provided a ready-made explanation for a host of socio-economic developments, such as agricultural intensification, the construction of major public architecture and decreasing regionalism in material culture, topics which have therefore rarely been examined individually.

The reality is less clear-cut, however. De Miroschedji (1989: 73–74) stressed the diversity of developmental trajectories in the different regions of Palestine, a point amplified in an overview of settlement data by Finkelstein and Gophna (1993), and recent regional studies (e.g. Adams 2002; Greenberg 2002; Kamlah 2000). Secondly, de Miroschedji (1989: 70–71) observes that the patterning of aspects of material culture, the production and distribution of pottery and chipped stone for example, suggests that some areas of the economy operated at a spatial level far more extensive than the likely extent of any single political unit. Both points raise doubts about the reality of the existence throughout the southern Levant of a series of homologous city-states each acting as a regional focus for political, economic and ritual power. This review of the evidence from Jordan presents an ideal opportunity to devise an alternative analytical framework for the study of the Early Bronze Age in the southern Levant.

Critique of the City-State Model

There are clear discrepancies between the empirical data from the Early Bronze Age southern Levant and the criteria taken as indicative of complex urban-based polities elsewhere in western Asia. Major problem areas include the following.

Urbanism

The small size of many walled settlements indicates concentrations of population well below those generally understood as indicative of urban communities. Territorial populations too appear significantly below the absolute levels generally associated with the existence of states (Falconer 1987, 1994; Joffe 1993). In addition, the episodic and/or short-lived nature of the occupation at many walled sites (Dessel and Joffe 2000: 41; Fischer 2000: 222–228; Greenberg 2003) points to developmental trajectories which were highly contingent and argues against these forming core elements within long-term regional economic and political structures.

Settlement Structure

The presence of regional settlement hierarchies is generally seen as a necessary condition for the existence of states (Flannery 1972: 412; Wright 1977: 383). These cannot be demonstrated convincingly using the settlement data from the Early Bronze Age southern Levant (Falconer and Savage 1995; Harrison 1997). While intensive surveys indicate that settlement was organized around a number of local clusters, analysis of the evidence from the Amman and Madaba areas does not support the idea that local clusters comprised highly integrated political or economic units (Harrison and Savage 2003).

Administrative and Control Systems

Many models of state formation have stressed the importance of administration to complex organizations (Flannery 1972; Wright and Johnson 1975). In the southern Levant, however, although there is evidence for the application of cylinder seals to ceramic containers, this falls far short of the kind of evidence that would be required to argue for a genuine administrative system, such as writing or sealing practices designed to track commodity flows in a systematic manner (Joffe 2001: 359–360).

Elites

Socio-political hierarchies are viewed as an essential component of states (Service 1975; Wright 1977). The forms of evidence considered indicative of such hierarchies elsewhere in southwest Asia, however, are absent in the southern Levant, such as large public buildings with reception facilities and service areas, a highly differentiated burial record and the presence and uneven distribution of "wealth" items. Palace B at Tell Yarmouth in southern Palestine, a large public building, has been compared to palaces from other regions of western Asia (de Miroschedji 1999: 10–11), although it differs from these in several key respects. These suggest that it represents a locally developed form (Nicolle 1999: 63), and as demonstrated by the manner in which cylinder seals were used (see p. 207), the existence of a degree of formal similarity between material from the southern Levant and that from

Mesopotamia is not in itself evidence of functional equivalence. Moreover, it dates to a late stage of EB III, and so cannot be used to argue for the existence of palace-based elites throughout the EB II–III period.

One approach (e.g. Joffe 1993) has been to contextualize the model by developing concepts of complexity and urbanism suited to small-scale societies, arguing that, seen in terms of local environmental and subsistence conditions, Early Bronze Age walled settlements represent significant concentrations of both population and human energy. In this usage, the local "urban" units are seen as agglomerated, nucleated and differentiated settlements, representing not a distinct "tier" in a hierarchy, but rather lying at one end of a continuum of forms of settlement and organization (Joffe 1993: 64–65). "Palaces" are re-interpreted as elite residences, although features such as defensive walls and cultic structures are still accorded a high priority in terms of understanding the political and economic roles of these sites. This may well prove a benefitial approach, but it requires us to posit a quantitatively different form of "urbanism" for which material correlates and conceptual frameworks have yet to be established. It may be more fruitful to examine economic, political and social complexity without linking these to urbanism, and thus avoiding all the unspoken assumptions inherent in the latter term (Chesson and Philip 2003).

Alternative Interpretations

The Chiefdom Model

One obvious alternative is the chiefdom model, which has proved a useful heuristic device for the analysis of ancient societies, and which has been applied to the data from Chalcolithic Palestine and a range of fifth- through third-millennium BC societies from other parts of the Near East (T.E. Levy 1986, 1995a; Stein and Rothman (eds.) 1994). This form of political organization is characterized by a modest degree of social and economic stratification and involves regional populations in the thousands or tens of thousands (Johnson and Earle 1987; Earle 1987, 1991), figures that appear appropriate for Early Bronze Age Jordan. However, the concept originated as one stage in a neo-evolutionary sequence of societal "types" (Service 1962). As a distinct set of organizational characteristics was attributed to each stage, this can result in a lack of sensitivity to the subtleties of individual historical trajectories (Crumley 1987; Paynter 1989; Yoffee 1993), suggesting that a less rigid analytical tool may be required.

Middle-Range Societies

The notion of middle-range societies, developed by Feinman and Neitzel (1984) on the basis of ethnographic data, was designed to conceptualize a spectrum of organizational forms intermediate between mobile gatherer-hunter groups and bureaucratic states, and thus subsumes the chiefdom. Many of the characteristics of middle-range societies appear germane to the Early Bronze Age data from Jordan; political organization is highly variable and there is a clear correlation between the total population of a society and the number of levels of political decision-making. Ethnographic data indicated that no groups including less than 4000 members (a level unlikely to have been attained by any of the walled sites in Jordan, see below) revealed more than two levels of decision-making (Feinman and Neitzel 1984: 69). Methods of transferring leadership positions vary considerably, although neither purely achieved power nor inflexible hereditary forms are common. There is, however, a tendency for positions to remain within certain family lines, a point perhaps connected with inherited economic advantage. The evidence revealed a high degree of administrative flexibility, however, and economic inequalities observed did not always equate to political rank (Feinman and Neitzel 1984; Hastorf 1990: 148). Recent work in western Asia and elsewhere indicates that significant areas of economic activity could exist outside the operational arena of political power (Stein and Blackman 1993; Wattenmaker 1994; Potter and King 1995; J.E. Levy 1995), and there is now a trend towards approaches that seek to "unpack" the various components of complexity, political and economic structures in particular (Netting 1990). Given the variety of organizational forms characteristic of middle-range societies, Feinman and Neitzel (1984) suggest that the model can be best employed as a means to explore the interrelationships between different aspects of the given society, by using the archaeological data to investigate key dimensions of social organization.

Staple Finance

D'Altroy and Earle (1985) have defined two organizational modes that describe the economic basis of political power in chiefdoms, wealth finance and staple finance. In the former, political power is based upon the control and manipulation of access to valued substances or products, something for which Early Bronze Age Jordan has produced little evidence. More relevant perhaps is staple finance in which power derives from the control and manipulation of the products of subsistence production, an organizational feature generally associated with societies characterized as agricultural, collective and territorial, and which may prove of value in terms of the southern Levant. Archaeological criteria by which staple finance might be recognized include evidence for intensified agricultural production, and the availability of storage and transport facilities (Schwartz 1994; Stein 1994). This concept appears particularly appropriate given the emphasis placed in recent work on the key role played by the production, storage and movement of agricultural products within Early Bronze Age societies (Stager 2001; Genz 2002).

Heterarchy

As Stein (1998: 6–7) has observed, discussion of the nature of power in ancient complex societies has shifted away from an interest in hierarchical structures, which are focused upon elite strategies for winning and maintaining political and economic power, and towards approaches which utilize Crumley's concept of "heterarchy." Crumley (1979: 144) defines a heterarchical system as one in which "each element is either unranked (relative to other elements) or possesses the *potential* for being ranked in a number of different ways, depending on systemic requirements." The result is to emphasize the idea of power relations which, while certainly complex, are flexible, contingent and constantly fluctuating.

The idea of hierarchy as order has underpinned the city-state model, and has structured most discussions of the nature of Early Bronze Age societies in the southern Levant. This has been despite the fact that the existence of hierarchy cannot be readily demonstrated through the data (see below). The problem may lie not with the evidence, but in the appropriateness of the assumptions integral to a hierarchical model, which may ignore the degree to which significant elements of social and economic complexity can arise from non-hierarchical relationships. Examples include those between groups differentiated on the basis of kinship, household, age or gender. Using the heterarchy concept, instead of seeking to explain the evidence in terms of a single organizational principle, we are free to think in terms of overlapping, and at times contradictory, organizational forms (Crumley 1987, 1995).

We should view inter-group relations, including structures of power and domination, not as fixed within an overarching framework, but as transient and contingent. Thus, we must therefore reject the simple unifocal perspective implied by elite-dominated regional centres in favour of altogether more complex forms of organization in which different types of relationships (e.g. cultic, exchange, kinship), constituted at different scales (e.g. household, intra-community, inter-community) may cross-cut each other and/or be organized along quite different lines. Such an approach appears well suited to situations in which there is clear evidence for the exercise of power on a considerable scale, but where the data do not provide the traditional indicators of elite-driven state societies, and has therefore played a key role in recent discussions of the south Levantine Early Bronze Age (Chesson 2003; Harrison 1997; Harrison and Savage 2003; Philip 2001).

Complexity and the Corporate Village

Archaeologists working in the Levant have traditionally contrasted "urban" sites, characterized as large diverse centres for the provision of specialist services, with villages, seen as small homogenous units supplying primary products, but dependent upon urban centres for specialist goods and services. As Schwartz and Falconer (1994: 2) observe, however, villages are both more complex, and socially and economically diverse, than has generally been assumed. Nevertheless, the notion of village complexity appears to offer a useful way of comprehending Early Bronze Age Jordan.

One potentially valuable insight into the nature of Early Bronze Age communities is offered by the corporate village, an organizational form identifiable in Late Bronze Age documentary sources from the Levant dealing with agricultural communities (Magness-Gardiner 1994, with references; Schwartz and Falconer 1994). In such communities land was held in a variety of communal forms—within a single family, between several families, as village lands—and external demands for tax and labour obligations were met jointly. The apparent inconsistency between the clear evidence for coordinated large-scale projects (e.g. defensive walls) and limited indications for the existence of institutionalized elites in the Early Bronze Age can be explained by the proposition that investment activities requiring cooperation beyond the level of individual households were undertaken on a corporate basis by a variety of organizational units, including kinship groups and the entire community. It is worth making the point that, in the absence of elites indulging in conspicuous consumption, village communities may have been able to retain sufficient surplus production to finance investments in valuable communal infrastructure, such as agricultural and defensive works and collective burial monuments. This model, which shares certain features with Renfrew's (1974) idea of "group-oriented chiefdoms," appears to offer the basis of a new approach to the evidence from Early Bronze Age Jordan.

A recent study by Chesson (2003), drawing upon the ideas of Lévi-Strauss, has suggested that communities were organized internally in terms of "houses." These are understood as corporate groups, generally constituted on the basis of kinship ties, often making reference to real or fictitious ancestors and comprised of one or more households (the latter being the basic building blocks of EBA societies). Each house would hold "an estate made up of both material and immaterial wealth,which perpetuates itself through transmission of its name, its goods and its titles down a real or imaginery line" (Lévi-Strauss 1982: 174, after Chesson 2003: 82). These units would undertake collaborative activities to support the success and reproduction of the house and its estate. Clearly, such a system would contain the potential to result in significant inequality between houses, through differential access to productive resources such as land and labour, and perhaps varying degrees of influence and authority within the wider community.

The key to maintaining such a system over time, and avoiding a fatal transition towards institutionalized inequality, may have lain within what has been termed a "corporate power strategy" (Blanton *et al.* 1996), through which power is distributed across different groups and sectors within society in a heterarchical fashion. An appropriate "group-centred" ideology combined with effective networks of resistance to potential attempts by particular individuals or interests to monopolize power would contribute to the long-term stability of the system. This is not to argue that such systems were egalitarian (Sweet 1960, cited in Schwartz and Falconer 1994: 6). Disparities might take the form of differential access to land and livestock as well as status and reputation (all hard to detect in the archaeological record) rather than conspicuous consumption, and are more strongly related to staple than wealth finance. Following Renfrew (1974) and Blanton *et al.* (1996: 6–7), archaeological correlates of a corporate village organization might include defences, irrigation works, certain categories of public building (but not palaces), group-centred burial monuments, a lack of "prestige" goods in spite of technological innovation in the production of utilitarian artefacts, and minimal evidence for the systematic differentiation of individuals. These criteria, which centre on the deployment of wealth in projects of value to the community rather than its consumption as a facet of elite lifestyles, appear highly relevant to the Early Bronze Age data from the southern Levant.

Nor is the corporate village model a "static" phenomenon, unable to account for diachronic change. Evidence from later periods (Joffe 1993: 48, with references) suggests that a village would have included elements from several different "houses," with these having differing degrees of wealth, prestige and extra-community connections. The shifting pattern of cooperative and competitive interaction between these groups would have provided an important internal dynamic for change. In addition, Magness-Gardiner (1994: 44–45) has noted that successful units will tend to expand at the expense of the less successful ones, leading to the development of villages of greater and lesser importance, and a diversity of village forms, a point also made by Nicolle (1999: 46–54).

Clearly, damage to the agricultural base, or other localized problems, would directly affect a community's ability to "reinvest," and could result in potentially rapid changes in fortune. Thus, in a system in which the individual corporate village constituted the highest-order organizational unit, we might expect a relatively stable region-wide structure, but a high degree of instability in the case of its separate components. In this light, the evidence for significant discontinuities in the occupational record of individual sites and regions (Gophna 1995; Greenberg 2003; Portugali and Gophna 1993) conforms to the expectations of a dynamic corporate village model.

Review of the Evidence

Chronology

The Establishment of Absolute Chronologies

An Egyptian historical chronology based upon the sequence of royal dynasties exists from the end of the fourth millennium BC. In theory, this permits the accurate dating of artefacts from certain Egyptian contexts, often the graves of named individuals. Thus, material of Egyptian origin, when recovered at sites outside Egypt, or Levantine artefacts from reliable Egyptian contexts, can provide synchronisms that allow the correlation of Levantine archaeological deposits with Egyptian historical chronology. Limitations of this method include the rarity of finds of Egyptian origin in Jordan, and the possibility that these may have entered the archaeological record long after the date of their production.

Historical dating provides good evidence only for the end of EB I. A growing corpus of Egyptian material, including pottery and *serekhs,* several of which can be read as Narmer, first king of Dynasty 1, have been recovered from late EB I contexts in southern Palestine (Brandl 1992; Levy 1995a: 31; van den Brink 1996). These provide a firm correlation between the beginning of Egyptian Dynasty 1 and the end of EB I. The beginning of EB II can be equated with a relatively early point within the Egyptian First Dynasty, as vessels of forms diagnostic of EB II first appear in the tomb of the Pharaoh Djer. Egyptologists' dates for the beginning of the First Dynasty, however, have ranged between c. 3100 and 2900 BC (see Kantor 1992; Wilkinson 1996: 9–15 for details). Current Egyptological opinion appears to favour a date between 3100 and 3000 BC for the beginning of Dynasty 1 (Hendrickx 1996: table 9; Wilkinson 1999: 27), which would place the beginning of EB II at the very end of the fourth millennium BC, in good agreement with the radiocarbon evidence (see below).

It is generally believed that the beginning of EB III equates with the Egyptian Third Dynasty, so the EB II/III transition has been traditionally placed c. 2700–2650 BC (Stager 1992: 41; Joffe 1993: 68), although this should be regarded as no more than an estimate (see below). The linkage with Egyptian chronology is looser than that of EB II because many of the Levantine ceramic forms found in contexts of Egyptian Third Dynasty and later have a relatively long duration in the Levant (see Esse 1991: 103–116; Stager 1992: 37–39 for discussion). Stager (1992: fig. 16) gives correlations between EB II–III Palestine and the Egyptian dynastic sequence.

Radiocarbon Dating

Despite concerns from some quarters (e.g. Braun 2001), radiocarbon dating is assuming an ever greater importance in the construction of chronologies in the region (Avner and Carmi 2001; Bourke *et al.* 2001; Burton and

Levy 2001). It has two key advantages over a chronology built upon historical synchronisms:

1. The method allows the extension of absolute dating to a period well before the upper limit of the Egyptian historical chronology; absolute dates for the EB I period are dependent upon radiocarbon.

2. Radiocarbon dates are taken on decayed organic material, which, unlike Egyptian imports, can be recovered from most sites. In combination, the two methods now provide a reasonably secure absolute chronology for the main phases of the Early Bronze Age.

A growing body of radiocarbon dates indicates that the Chalcolithic period as traditionally defined terminates in the first few centuries of the fourth millennium BC (Burton and Levy 2001). Most recent studies have placed the beginning of the Early Bronze Age around 3500 BC (Braun 2001; Joffe 1993; Stager 1992: 40), although radiocarbon dates from excavations at Tall Shuna suggest that in the north Jordan Valley at least the EB I period may have begun by 3600 BC. (Bronk Ramsey *et al.* 2002: 83–84).

Radiocarbon Dates from Jordan

Although the corpus of Early Bronze Age I–III radiocarbon dates from Jordan is growing rapidly, many dates suffer from poor documentation of the samples and the archaeological contexts from which they were obtained, which can render them hard to interpret. The selected groups here, therefore, have well-documented dates from clear chronological horizons.

A series of dates from early EB I deposits from Tall Shuna falls between 3650 and 3350 BC; those from the later EB I deposits fall between 3400 and 3000 BC (Bronk Ramsay *et al.* 2002: 83–84), while a group of late EB I/EB II dates from Tall Abu Kharaz (Fischer 1998: 219–220) cluster between 3350 and 2900 BC. Five dates, including four from charcoal and one from grape seeds, collected from the exclusively EB III site of Numayra (Rast and Schaub 1980: table 3) fall between 2900 and 2500 BC (Table 6.1).

The Establishment of Relative Ceramic Chronologies

Many sites lack both reliable radiocarbon dates and Egyptian material. In these cases, pottery is the prime dating indicator. On the whole, Early Bronze Age pottery from Jordan is comparable to that from Palestine, the ceramic chronology of which has been the subject of regular discussion, founded upon the studies of Wright (1937) and Amiran (1969); a more recent overview has been provided by Stager (1992). Developments in EB I and II Palestine are described by Joffe (1993), and the traditional EB I–III ceramic chronology summarized by Stager (1992). A more recent collection of papers (Philip

Period	Absolute dates BC
Early EB I	3600–3400/3300
Late EB I	3400/3300–3100/3000
EB II	3100/3000–2850/2750
EB III	2850/2750–2400/2300

Table 6.1 Estimate of absolute dates for EB I–III, based upon calibrated radiocarbon measurements.

and Baird 2000a) includes a number of studies which document the pottery sequences at individual sites, or the space-time distribution of particular ceramic styles.

EB I

While the definition and nomenclature of the EB II and III periods have been reasonably uncontentious, the terminology and definition of EB I has been a source of scholarly disagreement. The underlying reason for this is that EB I pottery differs markedly from region to region. The traditional two-phase terminology of EB IA and IB for this period (Stager 1992) is avoided here for two reasons:

1. Material tends to be assigned to one or other of these categories on the basis of its place within a localized ceramic sequence. In the absence of radiocarbon dates, however, it is not clear that material termed EB IA or IB in one area is necessarily contemporary with that described by the same term elsewhere.

2. Increasingly refined chronological control has meant that in southern Palestine some scholars now recognize three (Stager 1992: 31–32) and others four phases of EB I (e.g. Yekutieli 2000). Until reliable correlations have been established between different regional pottery sequences, it seems better simply to allocate material to an earlier or later position within its own regional sequence.

Two main phases of EB I have been recognized in north Jordan. In general terms, Early EB I is defined on the basis of "Grey Burnished Ware" and what have been termed "Impressed-Slash Wares" by Stager (1992: 29–30). The best published example of a northern early EB I assemblage to date is that from Yiftahel in Palestine (Braun 1997). Late EB I is characterized by vessels bearing what has been termed "Band Slip" or "Grain Wash" decoration, well documented at En Shadud in Palestine (Braun 1985).

A refined picture of regional ceramic chronology is dependent upon long stratified sequences, such as those from Tall Umm Hammad (Betts 1992), Tall Shuna (Baird and Philip 1994) and Bab adh-Dhra (Rast and Schaub 2003), the first two in the Jordan Valley, the latter located in the Southern Ghor, southeast of the Dead Sea. All three sites have provided evidence for a long EB I period, and each has revealed the existence of two chronologically distinct EB I ceramic phases, a view which has gained further support from the renewed excavation at the key Palestinian site of Megiddo (Joffe 2000: 183). The contrasts between the different sequences, however, highlight the degree of ceramic regionalism present in the later fourth millennium BC.

EB II

This period witnessed a decline in ceramic regionalism, with pottery becoming increasingly homogenous throughout the southern Levant. This process is well demonstrated in the Faynan area of southern Jordan, where a distinctive local EB I assemblage is replaced by EB II material "typical of the developed mainstream" (Adams 2003: 16). While this makes it relatively easy to recognize EB II material, it is not yet possible to correlate EB II sequences at different sites to provide an internal ceramic chronology for the period. Thus, there exists no clear basis for recognizing internal subdivisions within EB II, other than the relative stratigraphic positions of groups of material at individual sites. In Palestine, two main EB II ceramic regions, north and south, have been defined (Stager 1992; Joffe 1993). In general, the northern region is characterized by the presence of vessels in a wide variety of shapes made in highly-fired "Metallic" Ware, and the southern by red-slipped and burnished vessels made from softer fabrics (Greenberg and Porat 1996; Greenberg 2000). Provisional evidence suggests that these divisions are broadly applicable to Jordan, where Metallic Ware occurs in radiometrically-dated contexts at Tall Abu Kharaz in the Jordan Valley (Fischer 2000). That said, lacking the independent verification of radiocarbon dates at a number of sites, we currently have no way of determining whether Metallic Ware appeared at all sites at the same time, and so the assignation of deposits to EB II on the basis of the presence of Metallic Ware has a certain circularity. In particular, we have little idea as to how long Metallic Ware remained in production, or how it was distributed, and it is not impossible that the key indicator of EB II was a short-lived, or unevenly distributed, style of pottery.

Recently, the validity of traditional ceramic distinctions between EB I and II has been called into question. Work at Tall Abu Kharaz has revealed that jars bearing Band Slip decoration and vessels in Metallic Ware, hitherto believed diagnostic of late EB I and EB II respectively, occurred together on the same floors (Fischer and Toivonen-Skage 1995: 587, figs. 3–4; Fischer 2000), indicating their contemporaneous usage. Moreover, the observation of storage vessels bearing painted decoration in the Band Slip style in EB II–III contexts at Khirbat Zaraqun (Genz 2000, 2002: 33–34), confirms that such material should not be taken as an unequivocal indicator of late EB I occupation. This point may require some reconsidera-

tion of settlement pattern data, as the presence of sherds bearing the very distinctive Band Slip decoration is likely to have been a key factor in the assignation of surface-collected material to late EB I.

EB III

The beginning of EB III in the north Jordan Valley is generally seen as marked by the appearance of the distinctive Khirbat Kerak ware (Stager 1992: 39; Mazar *et al.* 2000: 259–260), although other ceramic changes have also been observed (Greenberg 2000: 184–191), and until a secure radiocarbon chronology is established, there will remain an element of circular reasoning in the Khirbat Kerak ware = EB III linkage (Philip 1999: 34). Whatever the case, the restricted spatial distribution of this pottery form (Esse 1991: 138–140, fig. 25; de Miroschedji 2000a) renders Khirbat Kerak ware unsuitable as a universal indicator of EB III. While abundant at Tall Shuna (Leonard 1992), it is not common on the north Jordanian plateau (Genz 2002: 30–31, tables 6–7), and even in the Jordan Valley appears only sporadically south of Beth Shan (Esse 1991: 138–139). Sites as far south as Madaba and the Southern Ghor, however, show occasional imports or particular bowl forms that appear to have been influenced by features of Khirbat Kerak ware, and which should be broadly contemporary with the northern material (Harrison 2000a: 114–114, figs. 5.14.32, 5.15.12; Schaub and Rast 1989: 439).

Khirbat Kerak ware apart, substantial groups of (typologically) EB III pottery have now been published from three sites, namely, Bab adh-Dhra, Tall Umayri and Khirbat Zaraqun (Genz 2002; Harrison 2000a, 2000b; Rast and Schaub 2003; Schaub and Rast 1989), with a smaller quantity published from Tall Handaquq (S) (Chesson 2000). While it is now possible to distinguish between EB II and EB III assemblages in many cases, there are still problems in making reliable chronological correlations between assemblages from different sites and regions on ceramic grounds alone. The EB III/IV transition is usually placed around 2350 BC, although in the absence of good radiocarbon evidence this is really no more than a convention.

It should be clear from the above that the dating of sites through ceramic criteria is less precise than is often assumed. While material can generally be assigned to a phase such as EB II, these are generally of several centuries' duration, and it is very difficult to place ceramic assemblages to a specific point within such a phase (Dessel and Joffe 2000: 38–39). In practice, the presence at a site of material dating to any one period (EB II, say) does *not* imply continuous occupation during the whole of that period, although this appears to be the assumption in much of the literature. This fiction has underplayed the point that occupations measured in terms of a few generations, or one or two centuries, perhaps followed by periods of desertion and subsequent re-occupation, were probably common, even at the major fortified sites (Greenberg 2003). It is worth bearing in mind that in the absence of clear stratigraphic indicators for abandonment, punctuated occupations may go unnoticed, in particular if desertion and re-occupation took place *within* a single ceramic phase. If correct, this points to a more fluid settlement and political universe than has generally been envisaged for the Early Bronze Age, and it is therefore hard to see individual sites as playing a critical role in structuring long-term, regional social and economic relationships. A situation such as this can be better related to a flexible, heterarchical world of corporate villages and middle-range societies than to the institutionalized power structures generally associated with city states.

The Material Remains: Architecture

Archaeological field-work has been focused mainly upon walled sites; far less is known about the material culture and spatial organization of smaller settlements. The inherent bias within the available data has, therefore, conditioned the following discussion of architectural remains, the aim of which is to summarize the available information, before returning to consider its significance for our overall interpretation of the nature of the local Early Bronze Age.

Walls and Defensive Structures

With the exception of Jawa, the earliest well-dated fortification walls presently known in Jordan are the EB II defences at Bab adh-Dhra, although more information is available on examples dating to EB III. As in Early Bronze Age Palestine (Kempinski 1992a: 72), fortifications grew by accretion, with walls subject to successive phases of thickening or other forms of elaboration. For example, at Bab adh-Dhra an EB III stone wall, appears to have replaced an earlier mud-brick structure (Rast and Schaub 2003: 168), while the thickening of walls over time by the addition of extra layers of stone is well illustrated at Khirbat Zaraqun (Figure 6.2). Building materials generally reflect what was locally available, for example, sandstone at Numayra, limestone at Khirbat Zaraqun, and at Bab adh-Dhra a combination of wadi cobble and angular limestone boulders, depending upon which was most immediately to hand on that particular part of the site (Rast and Schaub 2003: 283).

The main wall at Bab adh-Dhra, which dates to EB III, was at least 7 m wide at the base, and bore traces of a decayed mud-brick superstructure. It was built in sections some 15–20 m long separated by transverse walls, a technique widely paralleled in Palestine (e.g. Amiran *et al.* 1978: 11–12, pl. 178), with the number of stone foundation courses varying according to local topography (Rast 1995: 126). Variation in the type of stone used for the cores of different sections (Rast and Schaub 2003: 283)

may indicate that construction was divided between different groups of workers, or that the wall was constructed in stages, a possible contrast to the more unified building operations hypothesized for key Palestinian sites (de Miroschedji 1989: 68). At Numayra (Coogan 1984), two parallel walls constituted the inner and outer wall-faces, while the space in between was filled with rubble. Here, too, there is evidence for transverse sections, but placed at some 7 m intervals.

Semi-circular towers of the kind known from several EB II sites in Palestine (Braun 1996; Kempinski 1992a: 72) are as yet unknown in Jordan. A number of walled sites do, however, exhibit rectangular towers or bastions. Bab adh-Dhra has produced evidence for two EB III towers in Field XI, a prominent location in the northeastern part of the site (Rast and Schaub 2003: 253). These were built using a combination of stone, mud-brick and timber beams set between small stones (Rast and Schaub 2003: 254, fig. 10.2). It is not clear, however, whether this structure was connected to the circuit wall. Regularly spaced rectangular towers formed part of the enclosure system at Tall Handaquq (N) in the Jordan Valley (Mabry *et al.* 1996: 123), while a rectangular bastion some 30m in length protected the main entrance at Khirbat Zaraqun (Genz 2002: 10; Figure 6.2). This was constructed by the addition of extra layers of stone, resulting in a final width of more than twice that of other parts of the circuit wall. The presence of a rectangular tower at the 1 ha site of Numayra indicates that these were not just a feature of the larger settlements. At Pella, a 20 metre long stretch of walling located at the eastern edge of the tell, just inside the Middle Bronze Age town wall, has been interpreted as part of an Early Bronze Age perimeter wall (Bourke 1997: 99). This construction, which shows two distinct phases, is dated between late EB I and the end of EB II. The presence of what appear to be two rectangular towers or revetments would appear to negate the idea of generalized shift from EB II semi-circular to EB III rectangular towers that has been claimed on the basis of the Palestinian evidence (Kempinski 1992a: 72). What may be a continuation of this wall has been uncovered in Area XXXII along the southern edge of the Tall (Bourke 1997: 99–100, figs. 4–5).

The complexity of the Early Bronze Age occupation at Pella is exemplified by the presence of a large stone platform in a prominent location on the summit of Tall Husn, a natural hill located across Wadi Jirm from the main tell (Bourke *et al.* 1994: 98, figs. 8–9; Bourke 1997: 100–103, fig. 8), and that appears to represent some sort of defended complex. The extensive Early Bronze Age remains include two rubble platforms with roughly-dressed stone faces, each measuring 15 by 15 m and with traces of a possible mud-brick superstructure. The two platforms were separated by an east-west corridor and there appears to have been a possible gateway at the southern end flanked by two square towers (Gibbins 2001: 89–92). Evidence for processing and storage functions occurs in the form of plaster-lined pits and grinding equipment. A hoard of copper objects was found within the destruction debris of the final use of the structure. The whole complex is dated to EB II, and its floruit would appear broadly in line with that of the rest of the site which spans late EB I and EB II (Bourke 1997: 104, 2000: 252).

In concept at least, this unit is reminiscent of EB III stone platforms known at such sites as Tell Yarmouth (de Miroschedji 1988: 52–53), and the massive stone structures documented at Khirbat Zaraqun (see p. 171). The contrast between the walls around the main tell, which defend the settlement, and the Tall Husn structure is intriguing. The latter is located close to a perennial spring, and in addition to offering wide vistas in several directions would have formed a particularly impressive monument for travellers coming from the east (Gibbins 2001: 94). This was of course the location of numerous upland settlements and extensive tomb fields and so Tall Husn would have been a conspicuous feature on a key route used by traders and pastoralist groups moving from the plateau westwards to the Jordan Valley and Palestine.

We should be wary of assuming, however, that all walls were intended for defence. A case in point is Jabal Mutawwaq (Hanbury-Tenison 1989a: 137) where analysis revealed that the enclosure wall consisted of a single course of long, undressed stone blocks, set end-to-end. Both its construction and the presence of domestic units outside the circuit (Hanbury-Tenison 1989b: 57) argue against a defensive function. I will return to this point when I review the wider social and symbolic significance of fortified settlements (see p. 179).

Gates

The EB III gate at Bab adh-Dhra was of direct-entry design, without towers or other defensive elaboration, prior to the construction of a blocking wall in its final phase (Rast and Schaub 2003: 276–278, fig. 10.27). At Jawa in the steppe, however, the EB I Upper Fortifications included gate G 1, which featured a pair of small piers projecting slightly beyond the exterior face of the wall to create a small chamber (Helms 1981: 103–105, fig. 38; Betts 1991: 34–35, fig. 37), while a paved gateway opening between two rubble buttresses has recently been encountered within the EB II platform structure at Tall Husn near Pella (Bourke 1997: 102, figs. 8–9). The sole instance of a large Early Bronze Age gate complex that has been investigated in detail, however, is the main gate at Khirbat Zaraqun (Figure 6.2). This consists of a corridor 15 m long by 2 m broad, which passes between two towers and two rectangular rooms, before opening into a triangular open area within the upper settlement. This gate revealed three constructional phases, while another gate in the southwestern wall of the site revealed

two separate phases of use prior to its being built over (Mittmann 1994; Ibrahim and Mittmann 1994). Such frequent modification of defensive structures is characteristic of EB III building in Palestine (Kempinksi 1992a: 73). It is not clear whether the successive stages represented real technical improvements, necessary repairs and refurbishment, or were more connected with embellishment for the purposes of display and prestige.

In addition to the main gates, the circuit wall of Khirbat Zaraqun is periodically interrupted by small gaps, some 1 m in width, which are interpreted as posterns, a feature familiar from Palestinian sites (Helms 1975). While these might have a military function, Herzog (1986: 30) sees posterns as allowing easy access to the exterior, avoiding what would otherwise have been frequent, lengthy detours via the major entrances. The most obvious explanation is that posterns were included to facilitate access to cultivated areas and the movement of livestock. Thus, defensive concerns appear to have been tempered with regard to the demands of daily agricultural life.

Water Systems

Water storage structures are a well-documented feature of Early Bronze Age walled sites in Palestine (Ben-Tor 1992: 104). The capture of seasonal precipitation would have been even more vital in parts of the Jordanian plateau where some settlements were located close to the limits of dry farming.

A series of tunnels cut into the limestone bedrock deep below the site of Khirbat Zaraqun allowed access to an underground water source. While there is no conclusive evidence for an Early Bronze Age date for this system, the physical relationship of the system to the walled Early Bronze Age settlement, and the importance of water storage facilities at other Early Bronze Age sites in the region, are highly suggestive. A more elaborate water management system has been documented at Jawa, located in the arid basalt *harra* some 160 km east of the Jordan Valley (Helms 1981; Betts 1991), where there is evidence for the use of stone-built dams designed to channel water into storage pools via canals. The main catchment at Jawa is Wadi Rajil, which carries winter run-off from the Jabal Arab lying to the north. Despite the lack of direct stratigraphic connections between it and the settlement, the excavator is surely correct in dating the water system to the Early Bronze Age (Betts 1991: 54). However, the exact nature and duration of the occupation remains a matter of debate (Betts 1991; Braemer 1993; McClelland and Porter 1995). The water management system at Jawa is not unique however. Structures designed to capture seasonal run-off have also been documented at the walled site of Khirbat Umbashi and the nucleated village of Khirbat Dabab, both located east of the Jabal Arab in south Syria (Braemer 1999), a development which hints at the growing importance of livestock-herding groups in the region

Figure 6.2   Plan of excavated area of Khirbat Zaraqun, showing walls, main gate, streets and cultic complex. Note the contrast between the latter and the more densely built-up area to the east (redrawn by Y. Beadnell).

during the later fourth and early third millennia BC.

Helms (1982: 109) draws attention to common construction techniques linking the Jawa water system to the fortification walls found at various Early Bronze Age settlements, and would view the site as an example of "transmigrant urbanism," that is, a short-term occupation by incomers from more developed areas. Rather than interpreting Jawa as an isolated engineering marvel in the steppe, however, what is remarkable about the site is the excellent preservation of the structural remains. This is attributable to its location in the steppe where it has been relatively little affected by subsequent colluviation processes, later settlement or stone robbing. Thus, Jawa is a uniquely well-preserved instance of water management techniques that may have been quite widely practised during the later fourth millennium BC.

While parallels are rare, Mabry *et al.* (1996: 124) have argued that two stone-built dams spanning Wadi Sarar near the large Early Bronze Age site of Tall Handaquq (N) date no later than the fourth millennium BC, and are connected with efforts to retain water and silt brought down by seasonal floods. It is probably no coincidence that Early Bronze Age settlements in the Jordan Valley are concentrated along the major side wadis (Ibrahim *et*

al. 1988: 171), the places most suitable for water capture techniques. While physical evidence for water management systems in the valley remains limited, this may reflect the impact of post-Early Bronze Age geomorphological processes—in particular the complex combination of aggradation and erosion which wadis appear to have undergone (Donahue 2003: 49–50; Mabry 1989: 59), and the build-up of colluvium along the valley floor (Banning 1996)—in addition to later building and agricultural activities. Other topographical features that may indicate water storage activities include a large depression within the site of Tall Handaquq (N), and a substantial basin detected at Tall Jalul near Madaba (Mabry *et al.* 1996: 124, fig. 2; Harrison 1997). There appears to be a limited but suggestive body of evidence for both on-site water storage and for major structures designed to exploit seasonal water surpluses. The evidence for EBA flax cultivation at Bab adh-Dhra in the Southern Ghor, however, is regarded as indicative of irrigation (McCreery 2003: 457).

Internal Organization of Walled Settlements

A number of Palestinian Early Bronze Age sites appear to show a division into an acropolis area, containing key public buildings, and a lower town, comprising domestic structures (Kempinski 1992a: 79). The implied difference has been seen as indicative of social differentiation. A similar arrangement of upper and lower town appears to have characterized a number of walled sites in Jordan, such as Tall Hammam and Tall Handaquq (S) in the Jordan Valley, and Lajjun on the Karak Plateau (Prag 1991: 60; Chesson 1998; Miller 1991: 102). This was not universal, however, since at Numayra the entire central area was occupied by domestic structures (Coogan 1984). Clearly, all walled settlements did not have the same function.

Khirbat Zaraqun is the only site where a sufficiently large contiguous area (5000 m², see Figure 6.2) has been excavated to permit discussion of internal organization (Mittmann 1994). The site shows good evidence for systematic planning and appears to have been divided into an upper town, located east of the main gate, containing cult structures and other public buildings, and a lower town to the south. The latter revealed a regular network of streets, with dwelling units separated by narrow passageways.

There is little to suggest that Early Bronze Age walled settlements in Jordan were intended to function as centres of specialist manufacturing activity. No walled site has yet produced a clearly defined industrial installation, or even a marked concentration of manufacturing debris, suggesting that much craft activity was undertaken outside the walled areas. This suggestion receives confirmation from the survival until the early 1970s of significant concentrations of flint-working debris in the fields below the walled site of Bab adh-Dhra (Rast and Schaub 2003: 6–7). In addition, work at that site has revealed evidence for significant extramural occupation, including activity of EB III date, that is, contemporary with the floruit of the walled settlement (Rast and Schaub 2003: 251). Thus it is possible that the traditional tendency of excavators to concentrate their efforts upon intramural occupation has skewed the data, and that extramural activity may have formed a significant part of the picture.

Public buildings

Cult Structures from Settlements

While Chalcolithic cult structures appear both within settlements and as isolated units (T.E. Levy 1995a: 235–236), their concentration within settlements in EB I and within the central areas of walled sites (that is, differentiated from domestic occupation) by EB II–III has been taken as indicative of increasing centralized control over religious activity (de Miroschedji 1989: 69). Khirbat Zaraqun has revealed an excellent example of such a cult area (Figure 6.2), located just southeast of the main entrance (Mittmann 1994; Ibrahim and Mittmann 1994). This consisted of an enclosure containing four "broadroom" structures, both elements (enclosure and broadroom layout) characteristic of Early Bronze Age cultic buildings in Palestine (Ben-Tor 1992: 101; Kempinski 1992b: 57–58, fig. 1).

These buildings were of different sizes, and formed a rough circle around a courtyard. The southern structure had a shallow anteroom placed before the "cella" and is interpreted as a temple by excavators. On the floor were two flat stone slabs, which would have functioned as the bases for timber roof supports, partly embedded in the limestone-marl floor. Benches of plastered stone lined the walls. Three other "broadroom" structures surrounded the courtyard; that in the northeast corner revealed indications of a possible staircase giving access to the roof or an upper storey in an annex against the rear wall. At the eastern side of this area, a circular stone-built platform was located. Some 6.5 m in diameter and bearing traces of lime plaster rendering, the platform was preserved to between 0.5 m and 1.0 m in height, with access gained via several steps on its eastern side. The cultic nature of this area is confirmed by the existence of a very similar structure, Altar 4017, in the EB III cultic area at Megiddo in northern Palestine (Finkelstein and Ussishkin 2000: 73). The presence of two such similar structures might suggest not only shared architectural styles, but even a degree of common cult practices between the two sites. What have been interpreted as "cult" structures, however, are not restricted to upper towns. Building 1.3 located in the lower town at Khirbat Zaraqun, in architectural terms a domestic structure, has also been viewed as "cultic" because it produced a number of figurines. The excavators have suggested that this structure represented the focus of some sort of domestic cult, in contrast to the "official" practices represented by the main "cultic" area in the upper city.

Sanctuary A at Bab adh-Dhra (Rast and Schaub 2003: 321–335, fig. 10.57) stood on an elevated position in the southwest part of the site and, as with the cult area at Khirbat Zaraqun, was located close to the main wall. It consisted of a rectilinear building, oriented north-south with a door in the (long) west side. Internally, the structure was divided by a low mud-brick stairway into a lower area at the south, to which the entrance gave access, and a raised area at the northern end, this paved with flagstones which produced a charred timber beam marked with a number of plaster-filled notches. The building stood within a courtyard which was paved in mud-brick. The base of a stone altar was located around 7 m west of the building, while two small, sunken, circular, clay-lined bowls located symmetrically on the east and west sides of the building contained quantities of ash. The area produced one seal impression and an unusual number of flint tabular scrapers. Further support for the non-domestic nature of this structure comes from the presence on the same spot of an earlier structure, the excavators' Sanctuary B. This structure (Rast and Schaub 2003: 157–165, fig. 8.2) appears to have been of similar size and orientation to the later building although it preserved evidence for a line of five stone bases, bearing the remains of timber roof supports. The ceramic assemblage from this building was different in composition from that of more obviously domestic areas (Rast and Schaub 2003: 165), while the clear continuity between the two structures further emphasizes their unusual nature. In that light, the excavators' interpretation of these as cult structures seems credible.

There is little in Sanctuaries A or B to suggest that these structures reflect aspects of cultic practice that were under the direct physical control of elites. Moreover, the presence of a second possible cult area located in Field XVI (Rast and Schaub 2003: 291–295, fig. 10.33), raises interesting issues. The association of this structure with cult is less clear as it consisted simply of a plastered room which produced a carefully cut column-base, the base of a unique ceramic chalice, and an imported siltstone palette, an unusual but not definitively cultic assemblage. The presence directly above these remains of an installation consisting of two large flat slabs surrounded by a circular wall (Rast and Schaub 2003: 398–399, fig. 12.1) in the vicinity of which a number of horn cores were recovered, may indicate however continuity of special purpose activity in this particular area. If anything, the evidence from Bab adh-Dhra points to cult and ritual activity as being protean in nature, rather than having any simple or direct association with the exercise of political power

Standing Stones

Groups of free-standing stone monoliths, often viewed as of cultic significance, are known from the Chalcolithic site of Gilat (Alon and Levy 1989: 182–184; Levy *et al.* 2006: 110, pl. 5.28–29) and in arid areas of southern Palestine (Avner 1984, 1990). Several examples from south-central Jordan, however, are located within, or close to, Early Bronze Age walled settlements.

A short way from the walled site of Lajjun east of Karak, Glueck (1934: 45, fig. 19) reported a group of 16 uncut limestone blocks, each around 1.5 m high and erected on end to form a gentle curve. At Adir, some 10 km to the southwest, Glueck (1934: 45–47, figs. 19–21) recorded three much larger monoliths. One, 4.5 m high, remained erect, while two others, each 3.8 m in length, were lying on the ground. Albright (1924: 10) recorded the presence of monoliths at Bab adh-Dhra, although these have since been destroyed, while others exist at Khirbat Iskandar (Richard and Boraas 1984: fig. 5). Several groups of standing stones from southern Jordan appear to reveal a spatial association with Early Bronze Age settlements. A monolithic pillar standing upon an artificial stone terrace in Ghor adh-Dhra, east of the Dead Sea, has been dated to the Early Bronze Age (Korber 1993), although the associated material remains unpublished. It

is not clear, however, whether the apparent concentration of monolithic sites in south-central Jordan reflects their original distribution or a lower rate of destruction there compared with areas to the north and west that have seen more intensive subsequent land-use.

Standing stones in Jordan have traditionally been dated to EB IV, a view apparently based upon Glueck's early surveys in "Moab" (see Mattingly 1983: 482–483), and it has often been assumed that these "open-air" monuments were associated with nomadic groups (see Graesser 1972 for general discussion). However, the location of examples both within and close to EBA II–III and EB III–IV sites on the Karak Plateau such as Lajjun (Chesson *et al.* 2005: 24, fig. 13), clarifies both their dating and association with sedentary communities. Note also that extra-mural settlement around Bab adh-Dhra was by no means restricted to the EB IV period (Rast and Schaub 2003: 6–7). Moreover, the alleged association of stone monoliths with mobile groups would appear qualified by their presence in cult structures located at the heart of major towns of the second-millennium BC (Ottosson 1980; Kempinski 1992b: 174–175). The incorporation of a pre-existing row of free-standing worked stone slabs within the wall of a substantial EB I building at Hartuv in Palestine (Mazar and de Miroschedji 1996: 6–10, figs. 5–6) underscores the connection between superficially very different architectural forms, namely roofed rectangular structures, and open-air monoliths. Given the ability of humans to transform and reinterpret structures, attempts to associate either type of monument with a particular social group would appear overly simplistic.

Cult Structures: Discussion

Individual units appear relatively small, and there is no indication of storage or administrative facilities directly associated with cultic installations. Many structures take the form of broadrooms, with roofs supported on wooden pillars resting upon stone bases. The discovery of a large cult installation at EB III Khirbat Zaraqun appears to support Joffe's (1993: 83) argument that there was, at least by EB III, a tendency to locate certain aspects of cult activity within central areas of larger sites, as at Khirbat Zaraqun and Megiddo. This could be interpreted as indicative of growing control over these agricultural communities by emergent elites, who sought to utilize cult connections as part of a strategy of legitimation.

This may only be one part of the story, however, and alternative interpretations are possible. The variety of potential Early Bronze Age "cultic" structures, ranging from single rooms to large complexes, as well as a range of open-air sites of a very different physical nature, suggests the simultaneous existence of multiple spheres of cult activity, not all of which would have been equally well integrated with systems of political control. Moreover, while one building from Khirbat Zaraqun has offered some evidence for cult furnishings, it remains the case that the majority of so-called cult structures have produced far less in the way of distinctive paraphernalia than have their second-millennium BC equivalents. The absence from Early Bronze Age cult areas of the offering pits, and large quantities of portable artefacts so characteristic of second-millennium BC cult sites (Philip 1988; Ilan 1992), is interesting, and suggests that the practices conducted within and around cultic buildings differed between the two periods. Given the close relationship between Middle Bronze Age grave goods and contemporary cultic offerings (Philip 1988: 193), the rarity of small non-ceramic objects in both Early Bronze Age graves and cult sites may not be fortuitous (see further discussion under burial evidence, p. 193).

Administrative Structures

In comparison to their defences, the preserved public architecture from Early Bronze Age sites in the southern Levant is relatively unimpressive (Kempinski 1992a: 78; Joffe 1993: 84). Recently a large EB IIIB architectural complex has been identified at Tell Yarmouth (de Miroschedji 1999: 10–12). The structure includes numerous rooms, significant storage facilities and a hypostyle hall (de Miroschedji 2002a: 89–90, fig. 2). Despite its size, however, there is nothing to indicate that either this building, or Building 3177 at Megiddo which is also sometimes identified as a palace, was functionally equivalent to the administrative complexes seen in third millennium BC Syria, as at Tall Mardikh (Nicolle 1999: 62–63). The latter has revealed evidence for reception suites, bureaucratic archives, specialized craft workshops, and stockpiles of valuable imports (Archi 1991; Mazzoni 1991; Pinnock 1991) none of which are yet documented in Palestine or Jordan. While the building at Tell Yarmouth has revealed two successive architectural phases, both fall within EB IIIB in ceramic terms, and it is likely that this structure represents a relatively late development within the regional EBA sequence, and so does not constitute evidence for the presence of elites in the region throughout EB II–III. In fact, the absence of Syrian-style palaces from sites in the southern Levant, despite the evidence for "public works" in the form of defensive and water management systems, points to a form of socio-political organization in the south that was qualitatively different from that of Syria.

In the southern Levant, large, non-domestic structures regularly take the form of rectangular halls with a central row of pillars, a design that persists right through EB I–III (Marquet-Krause 1949: fig. C; de Miroschedji 1988: 38, fig. 2; Mazar and de Miroschedji 1996; Mazar 1997: 148). Only one excavated Early Bronze Age structure from Jordan falls into this category, a building complex located to the east of the cultic area at Khirbat Zaraqun (Figure 6.2). This consists of a large "broadroom" with thick walls, perhaps indicative of the presence of an upper storey.

Adjoining it is a complex of small rooms, which produced many small finds and medium-sized storage vessels. While provisionally termed a "palace" (Mittmann 1994), the finds included a large assemblage of ceramic containers, suggesting that the structure functioned more in connection with work and storage than with official reception and government. Another large building was located in the lower town, connected with the gate. Measuring 11.5 m long by 5.0 m broad, and with a row of four stone pillar bases on the floor, this building appears not unlike the so-called "Palace" at Ai, now generally interpreted as a temple of some kind (Callaway 1993: 41).

Pillared halls have been variously interpreted as temples, palaces and storage complexes, and it may be that this was no more than an architectural form employed for structures fulfilling a range of functions. Perhaps the notion of a clear distinction between buildings having cultic, administrative or elite residential functions is inappropriate in an Early Bronze Age context. These structures might be better termed "non-domestic" or "special purpose" complexes (Mazar and de Miroschedji 1996: 13). As such, they may have taken the form of individual buildings able to serve a variety of the community's needs, an interpretation that appears in accord with the cross-cutting power structures envisaged under a heterarchical model.

A connection between large structures and storage is seen in a late EB I pillared hall recently excavated at Beth Shan (Mazar 1997), which contained large amounts of carbonized grain and lentils and many broken jars. The pattern is reinforced by recent evidence from Tall Saidiyya. Here, an EB II multi-roomed installation included a sunken room which contained the remains of 12 or 13 large storage jars, suggesting the need to keep a commodity cool, most likely olive oil (Tubb and Dorrell 1993, 1994). The presence of almost 200 pierced bivalve shells within one room has led the excavator to suggest their employment within some sort of recording system connected to storage activities (Tubb and Dorrell 1994: 63). While evidence for specialized craft production is scant, the data strongly suggest that certain non-domestic structures within Early Bronze Age walled settlements played an important role vis-à-vis the storage of agricultural products, such as grain, lentils and liquids. In this light, the fortifications would have offered the critical elements of both external security and internal control, points perhaps significant on both physical and ideological levels.

The evidence from the EB III period points to a growing emphasis upon centralized storage at a supra-household scale, and increasing evidence of an element of political control. The example of Khirbat Zaraqun, where a significant concentration of storage jars (among other ceramic forms) was identified in Building 0.8 in the so-called "upper city" (Genz 2002: 96, table 60, pl. 24–52), is confirmed by parallels from Palestine, such as a concentration of pithoi in Palace B at Tell Yarmouth (de Miroschedji 1999: 11), and the major EB III building at Khirbat Karak which is best understood as a structure for the centralized, large-scale storage of grain (Mazar 2001). Such evidence for the mobilization and concentration of significant quantities of agricultural products is consistent with the expectations of the staple-finance model outlined earlier.

To summarize, large architectural complexes of possible "cultic" or administrative function are not well documented before EB III. If these are indicative of growing inequality, or even of an emergent elite (Joffe 1993: 85–87), then the creation of supra-household storage facilities and defensive walls predates this political development, and should be seen as related to the actions of corporate village communities.

Domestic Structures

EB I

In contrast to the wide distribution of "rectangular halls," Early Bronze Age domestic structures assumed a variety of forms. A tradition of free-standing curvilinear structures is documented in the early EB I of northern Palestine (Ben-Tor 1992: 62–64). A distinctive feature of those from Yiftahel in Galilee was the presence of an internal area of stone paving (Braun 1989b: 4, fig. 4). An arrangement of slabs observed in the partly exposed early EB I Building 5 at Tall Shuna (Baird and Philip 1994: 116, fig. 5) may indicate the presence of similar units at sites in northern Jordan.

While small rural sites such as Yiftahel may well have been composed largely of low-density, free-standing, curvilinear structures (Braun 1989a: fig. 4), larger settlements have revealed greater architectural diversity. In addition to Building 5 described above, the early EB I phase at Tall Shuna has revealed a circular structure some 5.5 m in diameter, built of mud-brick on stone foundations (Figure 6.3), with a stone slab in the centre forming the base for a timber roof support. Building 9 appears to have been one of several circular structures, grouped closely in the central area of the site, revealing a greater density of structures than that seen in many "rural" sites. There is an interesting correspondence between the form of this structure and circular built tombs occurring at Bab adh-Dhra ascribed to EB IB (e.g. Schaub 1982: 73). Small circular structures (diameter c. 2–3 m) were also identified at the small settlement of Jabal Abu Thawwab, where they occurred alongside rectilinear architecture (Kafafi 2001: 65–89, figs. 24–32). The rectilinear buildings had plastered floors with storage jars occasionally set into these. There was, however, no evidence of installations within the circular buildings, which were probably used for household-level storage.

The early EB I period at Tall Shuna also produced Building 13, a rectilinear multi-roomed structure, more akin to the later EB I buildings from the site (Figure 6.4) and EB I structures from nearby sites like Tell Kitan in Palestine (Eisenberg 1993: 879–880). Among the noteworthy features of Building 13 are plastered hearths positioned in the corners of rooms and the presence in the floor of irregular stone pillar bases, indicative of substantial roofed areas—illustrating a connection between local domestic and public architectural forms. The evidence from Tall Shuna, therefore, argues against a "normative" view of EB I domestic structures as dominated by a single architectural style. Furthermore, the variety noted at Tall Shuna is in sharp contrast to the more homogenous architecture seen at smaller sites, such as Yiftahel and Abu Thawwab, suggesting that there was a real difference in both architectural diversity and the density of occupation between the larger, long-lived EB I sites, such as Tall Shuna, and the shorter occupations evidenced at small rural sites. This fact emphasizes the pivotal role played by the larger northern EB I settlements in the restructuring of post-Chalcolithic society (Joffe 1993: 46). The location of Tall Shuna and other large early EB I sites, such as Tall Umm Hammad (Betts 1992), on major wadi systems offering considerable irrigation potential is also likely to form part of this picture.

Occupation at a far lower density is seen at the fourth-millennium BC site of Jabal Mutawwaq east of Jarash, where surface remains suggest the presence of several hundred ovoid structures dispersed over some 28 ha. Some lie within and others outside the so-called enclosure wall. Individual units are 6–10 m in length with foundations of long stone slabs and a doorway in one of the long sides flanked by upright pillars, a feature also seen in the entrance to one of the rectangular halls at Hartuv in Palestine (Mazar and de Miroschedji 1996: 9, fig. 5). The contrast between such low-density arrangements of relatively homogenous units and the more heterogeneous make-up of higher density occupations may well indicate the greater functional diversity and socio-economic complexity of the latter, which would appear to anticipate the role of the later EB II–III walled settlements.

The walled site of Jawa in the steppe presents yet another contrast. Here, small subcircular structures with walls coated in yellow clay plaster have been interpreted as dwellings. A structure in square UT1 consisted of a subcircular main room, with two smaller compartments. Flat stones in the centre of the floor may have provided a base for roof supports (Betts 1991: 35–36, figs. 39–40). There is little in the evidence from Jawa, however, to suggest that this architecture represented an indigenous steppe tradition, and it is better seen as an adaptation of familiar western techniques to suit locally available building materials and environmental conditions. The walled EB II settlement of Arad in the arid northern Negev has been interpreted by Finkelstein (1990; 1995b: 80–82) as a community of sedentarized pastoralists, facilitating inter-

Figure 6.3   Tall Shuna, circular EB I structure, Building 9; note stone base for central roof support (G. Philip).

action between the populations of the south Palestinian steppe and the Mediterranean zone. This view gains support from distinctions observed between the architecture and material of Arad and that of Ai located in the Mediterranean zone north of Jerusalem (Ilan 2001). Despite this contrast, Nicolle's (1999: 47) division of walled sites into villages and pastoralist enclosures may be seeking to impose binary categories on a continuum. In this context it is interesting to observe that the architecture of Arad, with its compounds, rectilinear structures and evidence of planning (Ben-Tor 1992: 62–63), is substantially different from that so far revealed at Jawa, suggesting that there may be significant differences between the ways in which southern and eastern parts of the steppe were incorporated into the wider regional system.

EB II–III

The domestic architecture of EB II–III is characterized by rectilinear, multi-roomed structures generally built of mud-brick on stone foundations, sometimes with internal benches. The influence of locally available materials on building practices is neatly illustrated by the fact that

buildings at Numayra are made in local sandstone, while those at nearby Bab adh-Dhra are built almost entirely of mud-brick, reflecting its position on marl deposits (Rast 1995: 127). This procedure extended to the latter site's local funerary architecture as well, with stone foundations restricted to major architectural units.

Typical domestic installations include a variety of ovens and hearths and large jars sunk into floors (Herr *et al.* 1991: 11). At Tall Abu Kharaz (Fischer 1993, 1994), structures are terraced to deal with the sloping topography, and are separated by narrow pebbled streets. Overall, the evidence appears to suggest that multi-roomed, rectilinear structures, separated by narrow alleyways were the norm for EB II–III sites, although the picture would be more satisfactory were more undefended "rural" sites to be excavated to complement the evidence from the fortified settlements. While general accounts focus attention upon the predominance of "broadroom" architecture during EB II–III (Ben-Tor 1992: 62–64), many domestic structures do not appear to conform to this category. The main common feature of domestic architecture throughout the Mediterranean zone appears to be the rectilinear plan, within which there exists a considerable degree of variety.

Tall Umayri has revealed multi-roomed EB III domestic complexes that might be described as consisting of groups of "long" rooms. Artefacts reflect subsistence-related activities—grinding stones, storage jars and debris from chipped-stone working—while a range of spindle whorls indicates textile production (Herr *et al.* 1991: 10–11) within domestic structures. Multi-roomed rectilinear complexes also characterized the central area at Numayra where several such units were separated by open areas. This site also revealed evidence for roofing techniques using wooden beams covered in reeds and grasses tied together with ropes to produce a kind of thatch (Coogan 1984). Installations such as hearths, stone mortars and storage jars were set into the ground, while the large assemblage of storage vessels, and a number of pits and unfired clay silos, indicate that a significant amount of agricultural produce was stored within individual dwelling complexes. Viewed as a whole, the evidence suggests that many aspects of production and storage were undertaken at the level of individual households.

Numayra, at 1 ha, is small for a walled site, and, despite the emphasis on storage seen within domestic units, has not produced any structure equivalent to the pillared halls seen at some other sites. There is clearly no direct functional equivalence between a small, walled site such as Numayra in the Southern Ghor and much larger settlements such as Khirbat Zaraqun, located in areas with far greater agricultural potential.

Early Bronze Age Walled Settlements: Organization, Significance and Diversity

While some walled sites were clearly more than simple agglomerations of domestic units, there is no evidence at present from Jordan for the palace complexes or specialist workshops seen in Syria. Rather, the major architectural units appear to have been multi-purpose pillared halls, a form derived from domestic architectural traditions, and which may have been connected with the storage of agricultural products. The architectural evidence suggests a society that, while sufficiently corporate to make substantial investments in common facilities, remained heterogeneous and fragmented in many aspects of subsistence, residence and cultic activity.

The traditional focus upon the presence of defensive walls as a criterion for indicating "significance" has distracted attention from the fact that even the largest Early Bronze Age walled sites in Jordan encompass no more than 10–20 ha which is small by the standards of "urbanism"

Figure 6.4   Tall Shuna, later EB I rectilinear structure, Building 3; note stone bases for uprights supporting roofed areas (G. Philip).

present in Syria and Mesopotamia (Falconer 1987; Joffe 1993). A consideration of the population levels of Jordanian walled settlements should provide some indication of their likely socio-political organization. Falconer (1994: 312) argues that a settlement should only be defined as "urban" when its population lies beyond that which can be supported from its immediate agricultural sustaining area. A common method of reckoning the populations of ancient sites is the use of estimates based upon site areas. Calculation is complicated, however, by the contrasting figures employe ed by scholars to estimate population per unit area, which range between 100 and 250 persons per ha (Esse 1991: 162; Harrison 1997). Using Falconer's figure of 1.5 ha of land per person, and an agricultural sustaining area of 3–4 km radius from the site, both derived from ethnographic sources (see Falconer 1994: 312 for details), it is possible to estimate where the urban/rural boundary would lie using population densities of 100 and 250 persons per ha (Table 6.2).

Given the difficulty of relating site area to population (Esse 1991; Harrison 1997) and the very different agricultural potentials of the hinterlands of individual sites, these figures are of heuristic value only. It is immediately apparent, however, that only by using the maximum estimate for population density and the minimum agricultural sustaining area (3 km radius) does the limit for "urban" fall below 8 ha In reality, the limit probably lies some way above this, with the result that few if any of the Early Bronze Age walled sites in Jordan would be classed as "urban" on this basis (for site areas, see Table 6.3). In fact, they should be seen as non-urban agricultural communities, a situation aptly summed up in Falconer's (1987) phrase "Heartland of Villages," a conclusion in accord with the architectural evidence treated above.

Using the figures quoted above, population estimates for a 10 ha settlement would lie in the range of 1000–2500 persons. A number of cross-cultural studies suggest that communities with populations exceeding 2500 seem to be associated with a significant degree of organizational complexity (Feinman 1995: 260). At the other end of the spectrum, figures quoted by Upham (1990: 12) suggest 400 individuals as providing the upper limit for the population of most non-hierarchical sedentary societies. Under most of the estimates cited above, the population of nearly all Jordanian Early Bronze Age walled sites would fall between these thresholds, and would be classed

as "middle range" societies according to the criteria of Feinman and Neitzel (1984). Of critical importance for our understanding of the Early Bronze Age data is the point that, with groups of this size, there is no automatic connection between *political* leadership and control over strategic *economic* resources, a position in keeping with the ideas of kinship-based groups and heterarchy.

Continuity of Settlement Between EB II and EB III

These two are frequently treated together in settlement studies (Gophna and Portugali 1988; Finkelstein and Gophna 1993), and perceived as the floruit of the Early Bronze Age city-state system (Esse 1989a: table 1). The tendency to treat EB II and III as a unit, however, may have concealed very real changes taking place within this lengthy period, a point that has already been made by Joffe (1993). In practice, sites showing settlement continuity through EB II–III (e.g. Bab adh-Dhra) are the exception. Many sites show only partial Early Bronze Age sequences, often relatively short periods of florescence punctuated by significant phases of decline or abandonment (see Table 6.3). Some of the largest EB I settlements, such as Tall Shuna and Tall Umm Hammad, did not develop into major EB II centres, while many walled EB II sites—Pella, Tall Abu Kharaz, Tall Saidiyya, for example—show little sign of significant EB III occupation. On the other hand, some sites with substantial EB II–III remains, for example Khirbat Zaraqun, reveal little evidence for significant occupation during EB I (Kamlah 2000: 187). In Palestine the picture is comparable. Major settlements, such as Megiddo and Beth Shan (Greenberg 2003) lack significant EB II occupations, despite the presence of substantial EB I and EB III remains, while other important sites, such as Arad and Tall Farah North (Amiran and Ilan 1996: 1; de Miroschedji 1993a: 437), were abandoned before the end of EB II. A case in point is Greenberg's (2002: 74–78) recent analysis of settlement data from the Huleh basin which has revealed just such a pattern of settlement discontinuity and change through the EB I–III.

There has been a tendency in the literature to assume that the presence of EB II or EB III occupation means that the site was occupied throughout the entire EB II or EB III periods. Implicit in this view is the notion that walled sites were fundamental structural components of the political and economic organization of their local

Sustaining area (radius in km)	Sustaining area (ha)	Sustainable population	Threshold 100 persons/ha	Threshold 250 persons/ha
3	2850	1900	19.0	7.6
4	5000	3350	33.5	13.4

Table 6.2   Threshold area for defining an urban site, using sustaining areas of both 3 and 4 km radius and population estimates of 100 and 250 persons/ha.

regions. To my knowledge, however, no walled site in Jordan has yet produced the large number of successive stratigraphic phases of domestic occupation that would be expected to result from the continuous intensive use of mud-brick architecture over several centuries. Long continuous occupations require to be demonstrated on stratigraphic grounds, rather than simply being assumed on the basis of our still inadequate knowledge of local ceramic sequences.

The large number of sites which do not show smooth transitions between periods should make us cautious about assuming continuity of occupation within periods (Dessel and Joffe 2000: 38). This provides further evidence for viewing individual walled settlements as something less than permanent structural features of the Early Bronze Age landscape. It would perhaps be better to view their expansion, continuance and contraction as contingent upon particular, and perhaps short-lived, combinations of circumstances within individual localities.

Unstable hierarchies and highly fluid systems of political control are common features of middle-range societies (Paynter 1989: 381–383; Earle 1991: 4). Thus, regional polities, where they existed, may have been short-lived political phenomena, deriving material support from the local subsistence base, but not constituting deeply rooted features of local socio-economic organization, and certainly not indicative of institutionalized, elite-dominated resource extraction. A constantly mutating system of this kind might explain some of the apparent oddities of site location noted by Finkelstein (1995a) in his discussion of theoretical site territories in EB II–III Palestine. It might also account for the significant number of large EBA II–III sites that did not reappear as important settlements in the Middle and Late Bronze Ages.

Having considered the characteristics of these sites, we are left to conclude that walls cannot be taken to indicate political control. Rather, defences are more likely to have resulted from corporate activity. The evidence from the interiors of these sites suggests that they were focused around residence, protection of the community and secure storage for its agricultural products. While security was clearly an issue, walls also inscribed the presence of these communities into the landscape in an imposing and highly visible manner. Thus the sites also functioned as the material expression of the permanent, secure place in the landscape to which communities may have aspired but which the settlement record suggests was not always achieved (Philip 2003: 115–116). Nicolle (1999: 44) has made a similar point concerning the function of fortifications in the case of enclosure sites which he sees having served the twin functions of defence for the community and its livestock, and of making symbolic statements regarding rights to territory.

Settlement and Subsistence

Subsistence Economy

The fourth millennium BC saw a number of important developments in the subsistence economy of the southern Levant. This was not a case of the introduction of new crops or animals, as many of the innovations characteristic of the EBA are first documented in the Chalcolithic (Bourke, this volume). What was new was the way in which practices were intensified and integrated to permit a significant increase in agricultural production, and thus feed into the reshaping of both the basic economy and the ways through which power could be expressed. The major areas of change were:

a. Irrigation agriculture. Although likely to have been practised during the Chalcolithic (Bourke 2002), irrigation agriculture appears to have been more widely adopted during the Early Bronze Age (A.M. Rosen 1995: 33–35; McCreery 2003).

b. Extensive cultivation, using the ox-drawn plough (Kolska-Horwitz and Tchernov 1989; Grigson 1995).

c. A substantially increased emphasis on tree crops, the olive and vine in particular (Stager 1985; Lipschitz *et al.* 1991; Finkelstein and Gophna 1993: Genz 2003a).

d. The large-scale employment of the donkey as a pack animal (Ovadia 1992; Grigson 1995).

e. The greater availability of metal tools for agricultural maintenance and general construction purposes. Evidence in this case comes as much from a decline in the frequency of heavy chipped-stone tools such as axes, adzes and chisels at the beginning of the Early Bronze Age, as from the corpus of surviving metalwork (S.A. Rosen 1997a: 161–162).

The effective exploitation of most of the above innovations would have required a degree of long-term investment.

The ability to commit resources in this manner has been linked to the stimulus provided by Egyptian demand for the products of the Levant (Esse 1989a; Joffe 1993; Finkelstein and Gophna 1993; T.E. Levy 1995a). The argument is that the appropriation of produce and, thus, control over investment decisions was increasingly concentrated in the hands of emergent local political elites, who functioned as coordinating mechanisms for production, and as channels through which products were collected and transported to the Egyptian market. According to this view, changes in subsistence practices were linked to local political change. Increasing agricultural production to a level beyond that required for immediate subsistence needs would have provided an opportunity for surpluses to be deployed in a variety of projects. The manner in which such surpluses were

Site name	Site area (ha)	Periods of occupation
Jawa	c. 5 (upper town)	EB I (Betts 1991: fig. 5)
Khirbat Zaraqun	8	EB III (Genz 2002: 7)
Pella/Husn	8	EB I–II (Bourke 1997)
Tall Abu Kharaz	4	EB I–II (Fischer 1994)
Tall Handaquq (N)	7 (fortified) 25–30 (scatter)	EB I–II (Mabry *et al.* 1996)
Tall Saidiyya	8	EB I–II (Tubb and Dorrell 1994)
Tall Handaquq (S)	15	EB IB–III (Chesson 1998: 20)
Tall Hammam	15	EB III (Prag 1991: 65)
Tall Umayri	4.25	EB III (Harrison 1997)
Bab adh-Dhra	4.5+	EB I–III (Rast and Schaub 2003: 6)
Numayra	1	EB III (Coogan 1984)

Table 6.3   Excavated walled Early Bronze Age sites in Jordan (site areas and periods of occupation) listed from north to south.

deployed, however, would have been a factor of socio-political organization, the social relations of production in Marxian terms.

The unique archaeological record of the Early Bronze Age constitutes the material results of these choices, and so the lack of evidence for conspicuous consumption and the emergence of elites contrasts with the strength of evidence for investment in a variety of community-centred projects (defences, irrigation works, storage facilities, etc). The manner in which surpluses were deployed appears consistent with the anticipated outcome of decision-making on a corporate basis (Schwartz and Falconer 1994; Blanton *et al.* 1996), in which investment in community-level projects was favoured over individual consumption. If elites are indeed lacking for much of the EBA, some alternative coordinating mechanism is required to account for the scale of change observed. In fact, an explanation which does not require the presence of elites has recently been advanced by Chesson (2003: 86). In her view, the large-scale organizational structures required to drive these changes were situated either at the level of kinship-based "houses," each encompassing a number of residential households, or that of cooperative action between a number of houses, in particular when it was necessary to undertake major tasks such as the construction of defences or significant agricultural infrastructure.

Of course, the environmental diversity of Jordan was such that irrigation, tree crops and extensive plough agriculture were not equally suited to all areas. Regional differentials are also seen in Early Bronze Age Palestine where there existed a contrast between the coastal plain, suited for cereal growing, and the upland areas of the West Bank, seen as more suited to tree crops and seasonal grazing (A.M. Rosen 1995: 38; Falconer and Savage 1995: 51). It can be argued, therefore, that the supra-regional changes in settlement and economy that are documented (see below) could only have resulted from the effective integration of the productive capacities of different regions.

Irrigation

In a region in which rainfall was highly seasonal, and in which raising livestock was likely to be an important component of subsistence strategies, structural evidence for the collection of water cannot automatically be taken as indicative of irrigation agriculture. The structural indications from Tall Handaquq (N) at present constitute the only physical evidence for the existence of major water catchment systems outside the basalt *harra*. Support is provided by the recovery of grains of naked bread wheat of a sufficiently large size to suggest irrigation agriculture (Mabry *et al.* 1996: 142). In addition, the botanical record from Bab adh-Dhra, located on Wadi Karak in the arid Southern Ghor, indicates the cultivation of cereals and pulses, suggesting some sort of irrigation. Additional evidence in the form of linseeds, of a size too great to have been cultivated without irrigation (McCreery 2003: 457), provides further support for this view. Although no structural remains of Early Bronze Age water systems were found, the existence of a system perhaps involving the channelling of spring flows or captured run-off water would have increased considerably the agricultural potential of the area, and would go a long way towards explaining the growth of a walled settlement in that particular location.

Simple floodwater irrigation systems are documented from earlier Chalcolithic settlements located along watercourses, such as Wadi Beersheva (T.E. Levy 1995b: 230; A.M. Rosen 1989, 1991, 1995) and in the Jordan valley (Bourke 2002: 5), indicating that the necessary technology was already available at the beginning of the Early Bronze Age. The site of Jawa in the steppe has revealed both structural and botanical evidence (e.g. the presence of six-row barley that could not have been grown locally without irrigation) for the practice of small-scale irrigation (Helms 1982: 105; Wilcox 1981). Regardless of whether the water captured at Jawa was used for cultivation or for raising livestock alone, the presence of dams and pools at a fourth-millennium BC site far out in the steppe is strong evidence for the employment of similar techniques elsewhere in Jordan.

Another argument in favour of irrigation agriculture in the Jordan Valley is the sheer number and size of Early Bronze Age settlements and their concentration along the major tributary wadis. Many of these sites are located in areas where annual precipitation is below 300 mm, which, when interannual variability is taken into account (Esse 1991: 11), would render reliable cultivation of most cereals and pulses problematic (Lipschitz 1989: 274). Within these regions, it is hard to see how the population concentrations implied by sites covering 10 ha or more could have been sustained without the increased agricultural production that irrigation would have provided (A.M. Rosen 1995: 33). In fact, the investment and long-term commitment to a location implied by irrigation may have played a part in the development of walled communities in these key locations.

A dependence upon irrigation agriculture might also provide a clue to the lack of significant post-EB III occupation at many of the larger Early Bronze Age sites in the Jordan Valley. Although too little geomorphological work has yet been undertaken to establish a general pattern, significant episodes of post-Early Bronze Age erosion, observed at Bab adh-Dhra and Numayra in the Southern Ghor (Donahue 2003: 48–50) and at Tall Handaquq (N) farther north (Mabry 1989: 59), may have reduced irrigation potential through the downcutting of the nearby water courses. A.M. Rosen (1995: 36) has observed that erosional processes towards the end of the Early Bronze Age appear to have rendered floodwater irrigation difficult at certain Palestinian Early Bronze Age sites, perhaps significantly reducing the carrying capacity of the local agricultural base in these locations. Were it established that the two sets of processes were related, this would constitute important evidence for our understanding of both the origins, and eventual decline, of Early Bronze Age subsistence and settlement patterns in the region.

Tree Crops

Not all large Palestinian Early Bronze Age sites were in locations offering the possibility of irrigation agriculture (A.M. Rosen 1995: 36). Perhaps as much as half of the "built-up" area in EB II–III Palestine was concentrated in the upland areas of Galilee and the West Bank (Broshi and Gophna 1984; Palumbo 1990: 44), a pattern strikingly different from that of the Middle and Late Bronze Ages. This shift appears to be connected with the expansion of upland olive and grape cultivation (Stager 1985; Finkelstein and Gophna 1993). Recent data from Khirbat Zaraqun (Riehl 2004: 110–112) indicates the cultivation of wheat and barley, alongside lentil, olive, flax, grape, and fig. Her observation that olive wood dominated

the charcoal record is particularly interesting in light of Genz's (2003a: 61) comment that in many areas the native tree cover would have consisted of oak species, as this points to significant olive cultivation in the vicinity of the site. In Jordan, the upland areas along the northwestern margins of the plateau, where precipitation was highest, would have had good potential for the cultivation of tree crops, and recent work (Lovell in press) has identified the presence of olive among other crops at a Late Chalcolithic settlement in the Wadi Rayyan, suggesting a similar presence in the EBA.

Olive cultivation did not begin in the Early Bronze Age as there is archaeobotanical evidence for both cultivation and oil extraction from Chalcolithic Tulaylat Ghassul (Bourke 2002: 9), and artefactual data—basalt basins and ceramic spouted vats—from Late Chalcolithic settlements in the Jaulan (Hebrew, Golan) (see Epstein 1993: table 1). The EBA evidence, recently reviewed by Genz (2003a: 60–64, table 1), however, is even more convincing and may point to a significant change in the scale and importance of production. Botanical evidence includes the presence of olive pits at many sites and the predominance of olive among the wood charcoal samples at EB II Tall Saidiyya (Cartwright and Clapham 1993) and EB III Khirbat Zaraqun (Riehl 2004). The latter argues for local cultivation, on the grounds that the wood is likely to have originated from the pruning and felling of trees located at no great distance from these sites. In addition, new ceramic forms characteristic of the Early Bronze Age include jugs, juglets, narrow-necked storage jars and "vats" interpreted as oil separators, all of which indicate an increased emphasis upon the handling of liquid commodities (Stager 1985: 176–177; Esse 1991: 119–124; Genz 2003a: 64–65).

The evidence for wine production is less clear. The presence of grape-vine charcoal at Tall Saidiyya (Cartwright 2002: 104) points to local cultivation as the wood is insufficiently desirable as timber to make it worth bringing from a distance. Also, charred grape seeds appear in EB I contexts at both Bab adh-Dhra (McCreery 2003) and Tall Shuna (Holden pers. comm.), in keeping with the evidence from Palestine (Lipschitz 1989: 274). As the native habitat of the grape lies far to the north (Zohary and Hopf 1993), this should indicate its deliberate introduction at these sites. The presence of carbonized grape seeds cannot be taken, however, as direct evidence for wine production. They may simply represent fresh grapes (Genz 2003a: 67) or even raisins, as Cartwright (2002: 104) believes to have been the case with charred grape remains from EB II Tall Saidiyya. Moreover, the absence of distinctive drinking vessels from the Jordanian ceramic repertory prior to the EB IV period, when cups inspired by Syrian styles appear (Bunimovitz and Greenberg 2004), might also indicate that wine was not introduced until the late third millennium BC.

How do tree crops fit into the development of the economy as a whole? The first point is that the history and social and economic impacts of the olive and the vine were different, and the two should not be conflated. Olive oil is a high-value product suitable for storage, for further processing (e.g. as scented oils), for use as an (expensive) fuel or culinary product, and as an exchange commodity. Furthermore, fruit trees are propagated by cuttings and grafting (Lipschitz *et al.* 1991: 441), techniques different from those required by cereals and pulses. Also unlike cereals, olive trees require six to seven years between planting and fruiting (Zohary and Hopf 1993). Thus productive olive cultivation requires a major investment some years in advance of any anticipated return, although that return will be repeated annually for many decades if appropriately maintained. To be successful, stability and security are the prerequisites of olive cultivation (Zohary and Hopf 1993: 134–137). In ideological terms these conditions are consistent with a situation in which it was accepted that the value of a particular tract of land could be changed (i.e. increased) through the application of labour, and that particular individuals or groups could develop long-term rights to specific tracts of land.

The presence of "oil extraction equipment" in many houses in the Golan (Epstein 1993: 143) implies a domestic level of production. In the Early Bronze Age, however, there is evidence for a marked intensification of production, underlined by storage facilities for liquid products at EB II Tall Saidiyya (Tubb and Dorrell 1993, 1994) and EB III Khirbat Zaraqun (Genz 2003a: 68), suggesting that some walled sites may have acted as focal points for the collection and storage of a variety of agricultural products. In the absence of clear evidence for an elite-directed economy, at least during EB I and II, kinship or community-based corporate groups appear to offer an alternative organizational mechanism.

Oils and fats are also likely to have provided the basis for a variety of scents. Recent analytical work has revealed the presence of vegetable oils in jars of Levantine forms found in First Dynasty cemeteries in the Nile Valley (Serpico and White 1996) and would appear to indicate some sort of trade in fine oils. Possible evidence for the presence of wood resins, such as cedar or pine, in at least one imported one-handled jug (Serpico and White 1996: 136) argues for the production and export of scents, thus combining two local specialities (oil and scented wood species) to create an added-value product.

Large-scale production of olives in upland areas, however, presupposes that a proportion of the product was destined for consumption elsewhere. In this case, there would have been profit in having collection points either in or en route to likely areas of consumption. The presence of an oil storage structure at Tall Saidiyya in the Jordan Valley, alongside olive-wood charcoal, stone crushing basins and a quality of crushed olive pits (Tubb and Dorrell 1993, 1994; Cartwright 2002: 104–109) points to a degree of lowland cultivation and oil production, although it is also possible that a proportion of the produce of upland areas was taken for storage at, and distribution from, the larger walled sites in the lowlands, perhaps being ultimately destined for key harbour sites along the coast, as envisaged by Stager's (2001) "Port Power" model. This sees the mechanism responsible for mobilizing commodities as essentially commercial, and does not require an overarching regional system of political or military control. It is possible that production was stimulated by external demand from Egypt, at least during EB I (Finkelstein and Gophna 1993). Firm evidence for large-scale Egyptian demand for such products during EB II–III, however, remains limited. The absence of evidence for olive cultivation at Wadi Fidan 4 in the Faynan region of southern Jordan (Meadows 2001: 157–159), despite the practice of floodwater farming to counter the aridity of the area (olives have been grown locally under irrigation in recent years), suggests that efforts were concentrated upon the production of those crops best suited to the local regime (e.g. wheat and barley), and that whatever the importance of olives in moister locations, this was not sufficient to push local farmers towards their cultivation.

Rather than envisaging massive external demand as the key driver for crop cultivation, it may be better to develop Manning's (1993: 47) point that emergent elites may seek to produce their own high-value resources for exchange or for display and consumption. It requires little imagination to view the individual "houses" within village communities as being to some extent in competition, a point reinforced by Chesson's (1999, 2001) work on the burial evidence from Bab adh-Dhra. Given the lack of evidence for "wealth" in the form of imports and fine craft goods, it is possible that such competition was centred around the production, stockpiling and consumption of valuable products such as olive oil. The inclusion of a large number of jugs and juglets in Early Bronze Age burials (see Burials, p. 196) might be regarded as just such an act of conspicuous consumption, simultaneously providing for the deceased and maintaining the value of these products by removing substantial quantities from circulation (Meillassoux 1968; Gregory 1982). It is worth noting that Early Bronze Age jugs and juglets are ubiquitous, occurring in tombs at sites both within and outside those areas best suited for the cultivation of tree crops, suggesting that their significance was recognized on a regional rather than local scale. Even were these vessels to be placed empty in tombs, the symbolism may still have been as described above.

Plough Agriculture

The faunal assemblages from both EB I Tall Shuna and EB III Khirbat Zaraqun revealed a significant cattle component (Tables 6.4 and 6.5), suggesting that developments in Jordan were in line with those in Palestine, where introduction of the ox-drawn plough during the Early Bronze Age is now widely accepted (Grigson 1995: 267–268). As part of a general trend towards increased output, the productivity of areas of the plateau suitable for dry farming, but offering little potential for irrigation agriculture or the intensive cultivation of tree crops, could have been transformed by plough cultivation. The adoption of the ox-drawn plough has been suggested as one reason for Early Bronze Age settlement expansion in the Madaba Plains (Harrison 1997), and would have been equally valuable in other upland regions, such as the Hauran and the Karak Plateau, which also show significant settlement expansion at this time (see Settlement, p. 189).

Conditions in these regions would have suited the planting of relatively large areas of low-density cereal crops. Such extensive agriculture, perhaps employing a fallowing strategy rather than the more labour-intensive rotation with pulses (Halstead 1995: 13), would have provided sufficient output to support the local population, without requiring such high levels of labour input as to render the whole system difficult to maintain. Periodic demand for additional labour for harvesting, for example, might have been met through drawing on the labour of part-time specialists, such as potters or metalsmiths, or those engaged mainly in animal herding, to whom stubble grazing may have been highly attractive.

The adoption of the ox-drawn plough permits both increased output and the growth of wealth disparities within a community (Sherratt 1981; Gilman 1991). Furthermore, the training and maintenance requirements of oxen impose a significant "entry cost," which effectively places ownership out of the reach of small land-holders (Halstead 1995: 17). Thus, plough agriculture appears to benefit larger landowners disproportionately through increased outputs combined with the ability to control others' access to the critical resource of cattle. It appears, then, that the very strategy that seems to have permitted settlement expansion over significant areas of the Jordanian plateau was structured so as to result in growing inequality. This assumes, however, that access to plough animals was mediated through patron–client relationships. Once more, the notion of corporate communities composed of a variety of kinship-based units, would provide an alternative way of gaining access to, and meeting the costs of, draught animals. As with irrigation agriculture, however, this strategy holds considerable potential for exacerbating initial differences between groups in terms of size and resources, and thus wealth and prestige, and may hold the seeds of important social changes.

Animal Raising

The key to interpreting livestock-raising strategies lies in understanding the overall herd structure, that is, the proportions of different species. In Jordan, however, animal-raising strategies would have been partly determined by local environmental conditions (Kolska-Horwitz and Tchernov 1989: 287–288; Grigson 1995: 251–255, figs. 6a–c), with sites in the more arid areas generally showing low frequencies of cattle and pig. Detailed information is currently available from only two sites: EB I Tall Shuna and EB III Khirbat Zaraqun (Croft 1994; Dechert 1995).

Remarks

The marked presence of pig at Tall Shuna is probably related to the distinctive environment of the Jordan Valley, a point reinforced by the presence of significant quantities of pig bone at Chalcolithic Tulaylat Ghassul and Pella (Bourke 2002: 9, this volume). The pattern of decline from Chalcolithic into later EB I documented at Tall Shuna, however, is in line with the general regional pattern (Grigson 1995: 254). The other striking characteristic is the increase in the percentage of cattle bone from early to late EB I, which would render bovids the major contributor to meat production. Particularly important is the fact that the late EB I period sees cattle exceed 20%, which has been suggested as a threshold figure indicative of the use of the ox-drawn plough (Hesse and Wapnish 1991: 26–27). This shift appears to coincide with a significant increase in settlement size.

EB III Khirbat Zaraqun, located close to the steppe edge, provides a very different faunal sample. The low percentage of pig reflects the site's location on the plateau where the water and shade which they prefer were not readily available. Here, too, cattle are present at a level consistent with plough agriculture, although preliminary evidence from sites in the Madaba region (Table 6.5) and the Karak Plateau (Chesson *et al.* 2005: 40–42, table 3) reveals cattle bone at far lower levels. Given that the 20% cattle-bone threshold is attained in Middle Chalcolithic deposits at Tulaylat Ghassul (Bourke, this volume), a date at which the use of the ox-drawn plough is hard to accept, there are grounds for suggesting that this figure needs to be adjusted to take account of the variety of environmental conditions existing within Jordan, and the possible range of animal procurement strategies in use.

The predominance of sheep and goat at many sites reinforces their vital role in the Early Bronze Age subsistence economy, in particular in the more arid areas. The presence of roughly-equal proportions of male and female sheep at Khirbat Zaraqun might suggest a herd kept mainly to provide wool (Dechert 1995) rather than dairy products. A contrasting pattern is seen in the goat bones, with adult females outnumbering males by 15 to 1. The shortage of evidence for the slaughter of young males, normally indicative of a dairy herd (Grigson 1995: 256–257), is striking. While this might in part result from the difficulty of differentiating between the sex of immature animals (Dechert 1995: 85), it is also possible that caprid bone from Khirbat Zaraqun represents but one part of a more complex, and perhaps geographically dispersed, stock-raising system. At Khirbat Zaraqun, the sheep to goat ratio is 55 to 45, in marked contrast to the ratio of 75 to 25 documented at Tell Yarmouth in Palestine (Davis 1988: 145). The presence of a broadly similar ratio on Early Bronze Age sites on the Karak Plateau, close to the limits of dry-farming suggests that the higher proportion of goat bone at Khirbat Zaraqun is an artefact of its proximity to the steppe. Wapnish and Hesse (1988; Hesse and Wapnish 1991) have stressed that faunal remains are directly indicative of animal consumption patterns rather than local herd structures. Caprines are both valuable and mobile, and may be produced and consumed within different economies, and the complex patterning of faunal remains seen at Khirbat Zaraqun may indicate the consumption on-site of mature female animals deriving from herds kept by groups exploiting the steppe, which had arrived at the site through exchange. A link of some sort with the steppe is confirmed by the presence of the remains of both ostrich and wild equid (Dechert 1995).

The evidence from Jawa (Betts 1991) demonstrates clearly the existence of connections between the steppe and areas to the west. Furthermore, recent research in the Syrian Hauran (Braemer *et al.* 1993; Braemer and Échallier 1995) suggests a role for Early Bronze Age sites in that area in connection with animal-herding strategies. Although caprine herding in the Jordanian steppe has a long history (Garrard *et al.* 1996), the degree of integration between steppe and farming groups remains unclear. One effect of agricultural intensification in the moister areas of Jordan may have been to encourage the development of increasingly close economic links between the west and a steppe economy focused on livestock raising, thus adding an additional block to an increasingly integrated regional economy, and one more element to a heterarchical organization.

The notion of a regionally-specialized economy integrated through upland–lowland relationships has been advanced for Palestine (Esse 1991: 156–158; Finkelstein and Gophna 1993), and interactions between the larger sites in the Jordan Valley and the uplands, and perhaps steppic areas to the east, may reflect a similar structure of regional economic specialization, albeit in some cases more a difference of degree than of kind. Physical evidence includes the presence of upland species such as plum and almond at Bab adh-Dhra (McCreery 2003: 460), but more significant may be the generalized east-west distribution of Early Bronze Age ceramic style zones (see Pottery, p. 200–201).

Equids and Transport

The evidence discussed above suggests an intensified, multi-component Early Bronze Age subsistence econo-my, involving new products and technology, the growth of centralized storage and regional specialization within an increasingly integrated economy. The effective operation of such a system would have required a reliable and economical means of transport, the lack of which would have acted as a significant constraint upon interregional connections. Pack animals, the donkey in particular, would have offered just such a mechanism. While animal transport may well have begun during the Chalcolithic (Epstein 1985; Grigson 1987, 1995: 258; Bourke 2002: 12), the evidence (and requirement) for pack donkeys becomes more plentiful during EB I (Ovadiah 1992: 20–22). In addition to transporting produce, donkeys would also have offered a means of transporting water, tools and building materials to both settlements and to agricultural land, and their employment on a substantial scale would surely have constituted a significant enabling factor in wider economic developments. Actual faunal evidence is limited, although domestic equids were present at Khirbat Zaraqun (Dechert 1995). This, however, is the case in many periods (Ovadiah 1992: table 1), and probably results from the limited role of equids as sources of meat (Grigson 1995: 258), with the result that their remains were rarely incorporated within on-site domestic refuse deposits.

Discussion

Although the existence of major structures with a significant storage function is documented (see Administrative Structures, p. 174), there is also ample evidence for storage of cereals and pulses at household level. Examples include a plaster-lined bin at EB II Tall Saidiyya (Tubb and Dorrell 1993), both jars and wooden containers at Tall Abu Kharaz (Fischer 1993: 285), and several thousand chickpeas in an EB III domestic structure at Tall Umayri (Herr *et al.* 1991: 10). The small circular buildings documented at sites such as Tall Shuna and Jabal Abu Thawwab (see p. 175) are also likely to be connected with storage at a domestic level. Many aspects of Early Bronze Age agriculture offered scope for increasing production through the investment of human labour—irrigation and water storage, terracing, extensive weeding. In the absence of clear evidence for elite control over agricultural production or storage, we should perhaps view kinship-based corporate groups as the means of coordinating economic activity on a supra-household level.

The Changing Economy and Power Potentialities

In a recent account (Philip 2003: 107–108) I have sought to explain how the changes in the agricultural economy would have modified peoples' understanding of, and attitudes to, the landscape. In brief, the opportunities offered by new crops would have differentially altered the potential value of various tracts of land. Equally, the degree of long-term investment required to increase the potential output (such as planting trees, construction and irrigation works, training plough oxen) may have led to increasing acceptance of the notion of land ownership. Moreover, access to good quality, well managed land, by generating quantities of valued products would have offered a new route to power. I have also suggested that changes to the agricultural regime would have changed the ideological dimension of landscape with new forms of activity undertaken at different times of the year, and in new locations, thus contributing to the "revaluation" of the landscape. Further, the revised patterns of activity and movement within and across the terrain would have reshaped the ways in which the landscape was viewed and understood.

As important as land for the intensification of agricultural production in the manner outlined above was the ability to deploy human labour (Knapp 1990, 1993: 88). In the absence of convincing evidence for the existence of institutionalized elites of the kind that are documented in other parts of the Near East during the fourth and third millennia BC (Joffe 1993: 84–86; Chesson and Philip 2003: 9), kinship or community-based groups are the most likely means of obtaining the resources necessary to undertake projects, requiring a significant outlay (Chesson and Philip 2003: 11). Under such circumstances groups would surely have developed strong ties to particular tracts of land, and a sense of long-term solidarity that would have been closely tied to, even physically inscribed in, the local landscape.

As the likelihood of obtaining the desired outputs was dependent upon appropriate inputs (the ability to invest, access to suitable land, organizational skills, the strategic deployment of labour), land would have become what marxists have termed an "instrument of labour" (Meillassoux 1972: 99). Under such circumstances there is a clear ideological connection between the present-day group, which functions by building upon resources arising from the labour of the ancestors and who "created" the familiar landscape, and future generations who will glean the fruits of today's efforts (Meillassoux 1972: 99–100). Thus the pursuit of productive activity requiring long-term investment and a continuing supply of labour, creates a direct connection between past, present and future gen-

Site	Cattle %	Pig %	Caprines %
Khirbat Zaraqun	20	0.7	70
Tall Madaba	3	—	97
Qarn Qubish	c. 5	—	c. 95

Table 6.5 Percentages of identified bone fragments for main species represented at Khirbat Zaraqun and sites in the Madba region (after Dechert 1995; Harrison and Savage 2003: 45–46).

erations. This situation would surely have promoted the reproduction of multi-generational economic or labour units, structured around a combination of real and fictitious kinship ties of the kind outlined by Chesson (2003), which would have assumed the functions of planning and coordination all too often attributed to elites. The existence of multiple houses may have served to hinder the development of monopoly control with economic production remaining rooted in such groups, ensuring a degree of overall stability within the system, while political power shifted between groups and between settlements according to a host of local factors.

Many of the apparently sharp contrasts between the archaeology of the Chalcolithic and Early Bronze Age periods can be accounted for through their different subsistence possibilities, and the associated settlement structures and artefacts. Other differences may be explained by the contrasting modes through which power was expressed. For example, a whole range of characteristic Chalcolithic prestige artefacts (T. E. Levy 1993, 1995b), termed "ritual paraphernalia" by Joffe (1993: 37), disappears from the archaeological record at the end of the period. This may simply reflect their diminished significance in an EBA world in which land, labour and stored commodities offered new routes to power, which emphasized the economic activity of individual communities rather than the acquisition of prestige items through long-range networks. Under such circumstances, walled settlements might be understood not only as a means of protection for a community and its stored agricultural produce, but also as a key element in political strategies concerned with the inter-community competitive expression of power through the deployment of resources to create and embellish highly visible monuments.

Settlement Evidence

The subsistence data reviewed above provides a basis for reaching an understanding of Early Bronze Age settlement evidence. The new subsistence possibilities are likely to have had a significant and highly varied impact upon the economic potential of different regions of Jordan, with the result that regional settlement organization should be expected to differ quite substantially from that of previous periods.

Period	Cattle %	Pig %	Caprines %	Total bones
Chalcolithic	15.0	46.3	38.7	313
Early EB I	13.0	37.2	49.7	223
Late EB I	28.1	19.1	52.8	335

Table 6.4 Percentages of identified bone fragments for main species represented at Tall Shuna (after Croft 1994).

Limitations of the Data

Before examining regional settlement data in detail, it is appropriate to discuss the limitations of the available evidence.

a. Good survey data are only available for a small percentage of Jordan: in many areas basic evidence for settlement distribution is lacking. As a result, certain areas for which information is available must be asked to "stand for" larger, unsurveyed regions.

b. In many cases, evidence is published in preliminary form only. Furthermore, this comes from surveys undertaken with varied aims, resources and field methodologies. The result is that data from different areas are not always directly comparable. Thus, the inter-regional comparisons attempted below are no more than broad interpretative statements, based on the sketchy information available. Our knowledge of the distribution of small sites in particular is skewed towards those few areas that have been subject to systematic, intensive survey coverage (Harrison 1997: figs. 2–3). Elsewhere, only the largest sites are generally documented.

c. Many of the larger settlements represent multi period occupations, which present familiar problems (Joffe 1993: 13–14), such as the over-representation of material from the latest or most extensive phase of occupation, and a tendency to quote a single figure for site area regardless of fluctuations through time.

d. The dating of survey evidence is dependent upon the interpretation of surface pottery. Chronological precision is thus limited both by our knowledge of the local ceramics and the size and composition of the available sample. Many sites can be characterized only as EB II–III, which presents problems for the analysis of settlement organization, all the more so given the possibility that individual sites may have been occupied for quite short spells within these long periods (Dessel and Joffe 2000: 38–39). Re-evaluation of dates is rarely possible as few researchers have published ceramic evidence on a site-by-site basis.

e. In Jordan's highly dissected terrain, geomorphological processes are likely to have had a significant and uneven impact upon the nature of the visible settlement record (Joffe 1993: 12; Banning 1996). For example, heavy post-EBA sedimentation occurring in the vicinity of Tall Umayri, southwest of modern Amman, (Schnurrenberger 1991: 372–374) is likely to have considerably reduced the visibility of Early Bronze Age settlement in this area. Few published surveys, however, appear to have attempted to counter this by the use of appropriate sampling techniques, and their results may not reflect closely original settlement distributions.

Regional Settlement Data

North Jordan Plateau

Kamlah (2000: 144, diag. 2) notes that various surveys have indicated that in northern Jordan the EBA represents a significant peak of settlement, one which is not surpassed until the Iron Age. It is clear from fairly coarse surveys that northwestern Jordan supported a number of relatively large Early Bronze Age settlements, reflecting its favourable environment (Mittmann 1970: 256–264). More detailed information has come from a recent survey in the vicinity of Khirbat Zaraqun which reveals EBA settlement to have been focused upon the valleys and grouped in two main clusters. These were centred upon the walled settlements of Khirbat Zaraqun (8 ha) and Khirbat Rahub (10 ha), located only a few kilometers apart and into which there was a degree of population agglomeration in the later stages of the period (Kamlah 2000: 186–189, fig. 14). As Kamlah notes, however, this may only be part of the picture, as the whole system may simply represent the hinterland of possible larger centres at Tall Irbid and Tall Husn. Additional support for this view comes from the presence of EB sites of similar size to Khirbat Zaraqun on the plateau northwest of Irbid.

The situation documented in the Wadi Ajib located only 60 km to the east is rather different. Here Early Bronze Age settlement is quite limited (Betts *et al.* 1995, 1996), while there is a major expansion during the Middle Bronze Age (Eames 2003: 94, fig. 6). The contrast between this pattern and the clear EBA settlement peak seen in the Zaraqun survey is striking and highlights the very different settlement histories which could pertain in regions only a few tens of kilometres apart.

The Jordan Valley

Low rainfall and the infrequency of reliable springs ensured that major Early Bronze Age sites were primarily located at the edge of the valley floor, at the points where the major side wadis enter the valley from the eastern escarpment (Ibrahim *et al.* 1988: 171). Most of the wadi systems reveal one major settlement, frequently walled (Table 6.6). A.M. Rosen's (1995) suggestion that Early Bronze Age sites on the coastal plain of Palestine were positioned to exploit seasonal wadi floodwaters appears highly suggestive, and the positioning of major settlements within the Jordan Valley might imply the use of similar irrigation techniques.

The lack of intensive surveys renders it hard to reconstruct local settlement organization in detail. Most field projects have concentrated upon the excavation of individual sites, paying little attention to the regional settlement context. Exceptions include survey work in the "Zarqa triangle," and in the area immediately north of the Dead Sea (Helms 1992; Prag 1992). In the former, EB

I occupation is dominated by the extensive, apparently unwalled site of Tall Umm Hammad alongside which existed a number of smaller dispersed communities. EB II–III saw, however, a marked concentration of population upon the walled site of Tall Handaquq (S). This was followed in EB IV by a return to smaller dispersed settlements. A similar trend was reported from a survey of the lower Zarqa Basin to the east (Gordon and Villiers 1983). Work in the southern part of the Jordan Valley (Prag 1992: 155) reveals a similar picture, with EB II–III witnessing the appearance of walled sites and a corresponding decline in the actual number of settlements compared to EB I. These areas appear to demonstrate the pattern of population agglomeration familiar from the Palestinian data (Esse 1991; Joffe 1993), although a contrasting pattern is seen in some areas of the valley. In the north, for example, at Tall Shuna, an early EB I settlement estimated at c. 7 ha, was succeeded by a larger late EB I settlement, which, covering c. 16–20 ha, was larger than many EB II–III walled sites. There is little evidence for a substantial EB II occupation in this area, however. Here, then, the agglomeration process (if such there was—no reliable survey data are available) took place rather earlier, and there appears to have been local settlement disruption during EB II. The site also revealed an EB III occupation, characterized by the presence of Khirbat Kerak ware, no less extensive than the c. 7.5 ha estimated for the early EB I (Baird and Philip forthcoming). This is all the more surprising in the light of the paucity of EB II evidence, and may raise questions concerning the reliability of the ceramic criteria used to define occupational periods (see Philip and Baird 2000b).

With the exception of Tall Shuna, however, there is an apparent absence of major EB III settlements on the east side of the northern part of the valley. Tall Shuna apart, the most northerly fortified EB III settlement is Tall Handaquq (S), a marked change in settlement distribution compared to EB II, which saw the presence of several fortified sites in this part of the valley (Table 6.6). A similar contraction in settlement numbers between EB II and EB III is also documented in the Coastal Plain and Jezreel regions (Palumbo 1990: 47, fig. 19), where it has been interpreted as indicating the concentration of population into a small number of ever-larger centres. The southern part of the valley, however, sees an increase in the number of walled settlements during EB III, a situation more in line with that seen in southern Palestine (Finkelstein 1995a: 63). The different patterns of settlement development within the Jordan Valley may reflect not just subsistence factors, but may be related to those processes governing the appearance of Khirbat Kerak ware (Philip 1999) (see Pottery, p. 202).

Upland Areas

Ajlun

The highly localized variations in geomorphology and ground cover conditions characteristic of dissected upland territories can have a striking effect upon site recovery rates (Banning 1996: 29–31). While this renders many details of settlement development in the Ajlun highlands uncertain, the broad outlines of the region's settlement history are now becoming clear. Although both Neolithic and Chalcolithic occupation is known in this region (Kuijt *et al.* 1991; Banning *et al.* 1994) and there is evidence for Chalcolithic olive cultivation in the moister more westerly parts of the uplands (Lovell in press), survey work suggests a major expansion of settlement during EB I–II. Among other things, this period sees the appearance of walled enclosures. An example of the quadrangular enclosures characteristic of the more westerly parts of the Ajlun highlands is Ras Umm Zrayk which consists of a stone wall forming three sides of a rectangle measuring 85 x 50 m (Braemer and Sapin 2001: 80–81, fig. 6). The fourth side is open and is defined by the edge of a steep slope to the south. There is a concentration of EB I/II ceramics located, not inside the enclosure, but on a small natural terrace just outside the northwest corner of the walls. This might represent camping occupation or a concentration of activities undertaken outside the walled enclosure; it might also indicate the pattern of rubbish disposal. These sites appear to have parallels among the enclosures which Zertal (1993) has reported from the uplands of the West Bank.

Chronology is something of an issue. Sapin (1992: 171) has argued for an abatement of settlement with EB III, while Mabry and Palumbo (1988: 289) observe that the ceramic criteria for distinguishing EB II and III material in this area remain uncertain. Increasing activity appears to reflect the expansion of arboriculture on the one hand, and a greater emphasis on pastoral strategies on the other. The relative importance of, and nature of the relationship between, these two activities remains uncertain. The broad contemporaneity of this development with the growth of large Early Bronze Age settlements in the lowlands supports the view that these processes were related to the development of an increasingly integrated, if politically unstructured, regional economy.

An example is the polygonal enclosure of Majnuna (Braemer and Sapin 2001: 78–79, fig. 4). This hexagonal enclosure, some 40 m across, is located just above the steep northern slopes of the Wadi Jarash. It is composed of lengths of rectilinear wall, including large orthostatic blocks, and is located among other stone structures such as long stretches of linear walling and a range of stone tumuli and dolmens. Such structures are often associated with the development of pastoral herding strategies (see p. 194)

The Steppe Edge and the Wadi Zarqa

In contrast to the Mediterranean environment of the western uplands, the steppe edge offers rather different subsistence possibilities (Sapin 1985), and here the evidence for Early Bronze Age activity appears very different from the tell sites characteristic of the lowland areas. A good example is Jabal Abu Rudniyya (Braemer and Sapin 2001: 74–76, fig. 3). The site consists of a complex of structures including two circular enclosures, each positioned in a natural bowl in the hills, overlooking a wadi bed. The circles are separated by a projecting spur of land on top of which was positioned a large megalithic tomb. The largest circle was of diameter c. 100 m and formed from wall segments constructed using large, roughly-shaped stones. It revealed evidence of additional structures both within and external to the walls, and a quantity of EB I pottery. The smaller circle was of similar construction and had rather better evidence for internal structures. Rectilinear buildings noted in the vicinity of the circles are interpreted as domestic units, while circular features appear designed to capture water for livestock. Although not all structures in the area are necessarily contemporary (pottery from several periods is present), there is good evidence to indicate that a significant proportion of the whole, including the circles and water capture structures, is of Early Bronze Age origin, and should be interpreted as enclosures and dwellings used on a seasonal basis by pastoralist groups.

Braemer and Sapin (2001: 78) observe that comparable structures have been recorded in many areas along the steppe edge including Wadi Zarqa, the Jordan Valley escarpment around Madaba, and the Southern Ghor, which might point to large scale pastoralist activity during the EBA. There also appears to be a connection between the distribution of such stone structures and that of visible stone burial monuments. While uncertainty as to the dating and function of the various sites prevents us from viewing them all as aspects of a single phenomenon, there is no doubt that the later fourth millennium witnessed a significant increase in the visibility of mobile groups along the margins of the steppe.

While their presence probably reflects some particular aspect of the manner in which the stock-rearing and agricultural components of the population were integrated during the EB I period, the emphasis upon visibility suggests that semi-mobile groups were seeking to inscribe themselves in the landscape in a manner similar to that which has been posited for contemporary agricultural groups (Philip 2003: 120–121, see p. 197). This may indicate that mobile groups were developing a growing sense of rights to particular territories, marking their association with regular routes and seeking to reproduce those rights through the creation of culturally-defined "places" in an anthropogenic landscape. If correct, this points to a considerable degree of ideological overlap between agricultural and pastoral populations, and might suggest that, in contrast to the situation in later periods, the two groups were relatively little distinguished.

The presence of numerous EB I sites in the Wadi Zarqa, Rumman and Jarash areas, some of which appear to show ceramic links with both the central Jordan Valley and the steppe site of Jawa (Gordon and Villiers 1983: 288; Hanbury-Tenison 1987; Helms 1987: 55–60; Betts 1991: 74–75, 1992: 47–48), may provide evidence of patterns of movement and territory. In contrast, EB II–III sedentary occupation, at least in the lower Zarqa Basin, appears less extensive, and agglomeration of population within the single enclosed site of at-Tall (area 2.4 ha) cannot account for the general decline in overall settled area in the valley. That said, ceramic parallels between the Zarqa and Jordan Valleys noted in EB I continue into EB II (Chesson *et al.* 1995: 120, fig. 3), where the walled EB II settlement of Tall Sukhne (area 3.5 ha) was occupied, although intermittently (Chesson *et al.* 1995: 116). The contrast between the strength of EB I occupation in the lower Zarqa Valley, and apparent EB II peak documented by Chesson *et al.* (1995: 122) in the middle Zarqa Basin, indicates (assuming this is not an artefact of differing survey methodologies, or a ceramic recognition issue) the differentiated nature of human activity even within adjacent sections of the same valley system. A further contrast is provided by recent survey work at Jabal Khanasiri, west of Mafraq and 25 km north of the Zarqa, which produced no evidence at all of EBA settlement (Bartl *et al.* 2002).

Central Jordan Plateau

Recent survey west of Amman (Chang-Ho and Lee 2002: 194) has revealed in addition to burials in the form of dolmens and rock-cut tombs, fairly intensive evidence of Chalcolithic-EBA settlement in the area between Wadi Shuayb and the Wadi Kufrayn. This includes fortified sites in prominent locations; the form these take is not yet clear, but they highlight the significance of the plateau-edge and escarpment landscapes. The variety of site types is further expanded by the ceremonial site of Murayghat located southwest of Madaba, which consists of a series of stone circles and rectangles (Savage and Rollefson 2001: 223–224), a scatter of pottery and lithics over 25 ha, and a group of over one hundred dolmens. The site is dated by ceramics to EB I with the concentration of small jars and bowls suggesting offerings of some kind (Savage and Rollefson 2001: 227, fig. 6).

As in the Zaraqon area, surveys in the Madaba Plain (Harrison 1997) also identified the presence of settlement clusters with a trend towards agglomeration of population into larger settlements during EB II–III, as noted elsewhere in the southern Levant (Gophna and Portugali 1988; Esse 1991; Finkelstein and Gophna 1993; Joffe 1993; Falconer 1994). Tall Madaba, with an *estimated*

Early Bronze Age area of 13–16 ha, would have constituted a regional centre as large as all but the biggest of those known from Palestine (Finkelstein 1995a). In this case, the present day absence of Early Bronze Age settlement beyond the 250 mm isohyet (Harrison 1997: 16) confirms the association of sedentary activity with the limits of dry farming, although it appears likely that settlements in these areas would have practised, through necessity, a more resilient subsistence strategy than those in the side wadis of the Jordan Valley.

Both quantitative studies of settlement data (Harrison 1997: fig. 9) and the broad homogeneity of material culture point to limited inter-site economic differentiation, and betoken a low level of settlement integration. While site locations and material evidence point to a limited degree of local specialization (Harrison and Savage 2003: 47–48), there is little to support notions of centralized production so the situation is best understood as having comprised a distributed economy. Thus, while large sites exist, they do not form the upper tier of a clearly structured hierarchy, but may be better viewed as possibly short-lived epiphenomena.

Several of the larger EB II–III sites on the plateau developed from smaller Late Chalcolithic/EB I occupations (Harrison 1997: table 3), suggesting settlement expansion from the wadi systems on to the plateau during the later fourth millennium, and which given the nature of the plain, would almost certainly have been connected with extensive plough-based cereal cultivation. Moving beyond the Madaba cluster, Harrison and Savage (2003: 40) have characterized settlement in the highlands of Jordan generally as consisting of a heterarchical settlement network composed of small, regional communities each represented by a distinct settlement cluster, which was only loosely integrated with neighbouring clusters.

The Karak Region

Chesson *et al.* (2005) have confirmed an EB I presence on the Karak Plateau, followed by a significant expansion during EB II which sees the appearance of walled settlements. Sites generally range between 4 and 11 ha in area. The fact that most sites were occupied only for part of the period makes it hard to sustain notions of an EB II–III settlement hierarchy (*contra* Steele 1990: 16) and it is better to view the Karak Plateau as one more example of a poorly-integrated heterarchical structure. The paucity of material dating between the EB IV period and the Iron Age II, a gap of some twelve hundred years, highlights the fact that Early Bronze Age settlement in this area extends significantly farther east than is the case in many other periods. Also, somewhat counter-intuitive is the continuity of occupation from EB III into EB IV witnessed in the region. This transition is usually seen as marking a significant change in settlement patterns and organization (Palumbo 1990: 98–102). The reason may lie in Palumbo's (1990: 58–59) suggestion that locations near the limits of dry farming were not well suited to highly-intensive agricultural strategies, so communities in such locations practiced low-intensity crop production combined with steppic grazing to provide the basis for a resilient food system (La Bianca 1990: 20). Such a low-intensity structure may have been less likely to collapse under pressure than the highly specialized EB III economies which appear to have existed to the north and west.

The Wadi Hasa and Settlement in the Southern Arid Zone

Surveys in recent years have provided a considerable body of evidence for Early Bronze Age occupation in areas of southern Jordan where local annual precipitation is insufficient to support widespread intensive agricultural activity. The few large Early Bronze Age settlements in this area are restricted to alluvial terraces situated adjacent to major wadis draining the plateau to the east (Donahue 1981: 140) and which offer some potential for irrigation. In that sense, they resemble the larger settlements of the Jordan Valley to the north.

Survey in Wadi Hasa and the Southern Ghor indicates, however, the presence of a significant number of Early Bronze Age "campsites" and "corrals" in areas less obviously suited for agriculture, and which are thereby taken to indicate pastoralist activity. In this case there appears to be a marked predominance of EB I over EB II–III settlement (MacDonald *et al.* 1988: 155–166, tables 24–26, 1992: 61–71), the reverse of the situation documented in the Karak Plateau and Madaba Plains. The discrepancy may be partly methodological. For example, the reporting of lithic scatters in the Southern Ghor (Neeley 1992) contrasts with their absence from the catalogues of Chalcolithic–Early Bronze Age sites recorded in the Karak Plateau (Miller 1991). The presence of EB II–III sites in areas with good agricultural potential, however, renders the absence of indications of contemporary evidence from smaller sites rather odd. In fact, this raises the question of the relationship between site function and the range of diagnostic material present. Of the 38 sites in Wadi Hasa listed as EB I (MacDonald *et al.* 1988: table 4), no less than 30 produced 10 or fewer diagnostic sherds. Given the small samples, and an environment favouring small or seasonally occupied settlements, the Early Bronze Age ceramic inventory is likely to have been impoverished and to lack the classic EB II–III diagnostic forms, a point borne out by the presence of 29 sites in the Southern Ghor classed as "Early Bronze Age" without further qualification (MacDonald *et al.* 1992: 71).

MacDonald *et al.* (1988: 166) also note that some of the EB I "camp sites" resemble those known from Sinai and the Negev, which are traditionally dated to EB II on the basis of their alleged association with Arad (Beit-Arieh 1981). The obvious solution to this confused situation lies in the work of Avner and Carmi (2001) in the

Negev which has used radiocarbon evidence to demonstrate that the fairly basic assemblages characteristic of arid zone sites cannot be used to date occupation any more precisely than within a broad Chalcolithic–Early Bronze Age range. Thus, the data from southern Jordan should be reinterpreted as evidence for a continuous exploitation of the region throughout these periods, a scenario more in keeping with settlement evidence from areas to the north and west.

That said, fourth–third-millennium BC evidence from southern Jordan is far more striking than that of the second millennium (see MacDonald *et al.* 1988: tables 168–170), with evidence, such as pens and corrals, presumably connected with animal management activities especially prevalent. This would appear in keeping with the idea expressed above of the growth of a specialized animal-raising economy in the arid zone during the Early Bronze Age. The faunal evidence from Jabal Jill (Henry 1995: 368–369), which produced 74% caprine and 25% gazelle bones, implies an unusual combination of herding and hunting strategies, and might indicate the extent to which caprine raising for "export" had become integrated within the subsistence strategies of diverse steppe-based communities.

Southern Jordan

A number of EBA sites are now documented in the Petra area, where they are generally located in defensive locations 800–1200 m above sea level. Excavations at one of these, Umm Saysban (Lindner *et al.* 2001, 304–308, fig. 44), revealed rectangular structures of probable EB II/III date made from sandstone slabs. The concentration of storage jars and grinding installations, and absence of cooking and serving vessels in these buildings suggest a storage function, perhaps used on a seasonal basis.

Jordan contains major copper deposits in the Faynan area, east of Wadi Araba, ores that were employed at Chalcolithic settlements in Wadi Beersheva (Shalev 1994). Work by the German Mining Museum since 1985 has produced evidence for ancient mining and smelting from a number of periods, including the continuous exploitation of the Faynan ores throughout the Early Bronze Age (Hauptmann *et al.* 1992; Hauptmann 2000). The evidence for copper extraction, including the geological characteristics and distribution of the ores, the technology of mining operations, smelting methods and various technical aspects of copper production has now been presented in detail by Hauptmann (2000).

Initial activity appears to have been undertaken on a fairly small scale and focused upon readily accessible ores, with stone hammers used to cut open gallery mines into the relatively accessible Massive Brown Sandstone deposits. Copper was smelted in relatively small quantities with copper prills extracted from the lumps of slag by crushing,

Site	Wadi system	Periods of occupation	Nature of occupation	Subsequent occupation
Tall Shuna	Wadi Arab	EB I, EB III	Large unwalled EB I, smaller EB III	Hell
Tall Sakhineh	Small wadi S. of Wadi Arab	EBA	?	MB, LB, Iron
Tall Arab *	Wadi Ziqlab	EBA	?	MB, LB, Iron
Pella/ Tall Husn	Wadi Jirm	EB I–II	Walled EB I–II	Major MBA and LBA
Tall Husn	Wadi Jirm	EB II ?	Major structure, EBII	Small MB/LB
Tall Abu Kharaz	Wadi Yabis	EB I–II	Walled 4 ha	Smaller LBA
Ad-Debab*	Wadi Zarqa	Chalco-EB	?	EB IV, Classical
Tall Handaquq (N)	Wadi Sarar	EB I–II	Walled 7 ha, with larger sherd scatter	None
Tall Saidiyya	Wadi Kufranjah	EB II	Walled? 8 ha	Small, end of LBA
Tall Handaquq (S)	Wadi Zarqa	EB IB–III ?	Walled, 15 ha	None
Tall Umm Hammad	Wadi Zarqa	EB I	Unwalled, 20 ha scatter	EB IV
Tall Qos*	Wadi Rajib	EB I–II ?	?	Iron Age
Tall Hammam	Wadi Kufrayn	EB III	Walled, 15 ha ?	MB/LB
Tall Mustah*	Wadi Kufrayn	?	?	LBA, Byz
Bab adh-Dhra'	Wadi Karak	EB I–III	Walled, 4–8 ha	None
Numayra	Wadi Numayra	EB III	Walled, 1 ha	None

*The information is derived from Ibrahim *et al.* (1988), with no subsequent confirmation.

Table 6.6   Early Bronze Age sites on the east side of the Jordan Valley (listed from north to south).

perhaps followed by further re-heating. The EB II period, however, witnessed important changes in copper production. The less accessible but richer ores of the Dolomite-Limestone Shale deposits were now accessed by digging vertical shafts several metres down from the surface. The shafts were expanded at the bottom to form galleries allowing access to ores located deeper within the rock formation, while the practice of leaving pillars to support the roof allowed galleries to become quite extensive. Fifty-six such mines were documented in the Wadi Khalad alone (Hauptmann 2000).

There was also a move towards smelting close to the mines. Larger smelting furnaces were used, often set into the windward side of natural rises. The example of Wadi Faynan 9 revealed a series of furnaces built one over the other indicating repeated use of the same location over an extended period (Hauptmann 2000: 74–77, fig. 49). Analysis of charcoal from smelting operations indicates that this derived mostly from species native to a Mediterranean forest environment, suggesting that timber continued to be available locally. Metal was probably extracted from slag after smelting by crushing the lumps with stone hammers. Evidence takes the form of rock-cut mortars and the large spreads of slag at locations such as Ras an-Naqb (Hauptmann 2000: 85–86, figs. 59–60).

It is only recently, however, that study of settlements in the area has provided the evidence required to view copper production in its wider social and economic context. Adams (2002) has recently offered an integrated review of the development of both settlement and metallurgy in the area during the Early Bronze Age.

The later fourth millennium BC (EB I) village site of Wadi Fidan 4 represents a small agricultural settlement, whose inhabitants practiced floodwater irrigation alongside the small-scale production of copper (Adams 2002: 25; Meadows 2001). The pottery reflects mainly local stylistic features, and the raw material was obtained from nearby wadi beds (Adams 2003: 15). There is evidence (ore, crushed slag, crucible fragments, remains of small clay-built hearths, copper droplets) for the processing on-site of small quantities of copper probably using a crucible technology (Adams 1999; 2002: 26). At this stage it is possible that both ore and processed copper were traded, and there is evidence to suggest that Faynan ores may have reached Maadi in the Nile Valley as well as Chalcolithic sites in the Beersheva Basin (Hauptmann and Pernicka 1989: 137–141).

Evidence for the EB II period comes from the site of Barqa al-Hatiya, in particular through Adams' (1999, 2003) re-evaluation of the original excavator's report (Fritz 1994) and subsequent re-excavation of the site in 1993 by M. Flender as part of the German Mining Museum team (unpublished). This isolated rectilinear building stands on a hill, the summit of which is covered with remains of slag and other metallurgical debris, reaching

a depth of 50 cm in places. Both ceramics and radiocarbon evidence point to a date in the earlier third millennium BC. In contrast to the highly-regionalized pottery from Wadi Fidan 4, the ceramic assemblage from this site includes many forms characteristic of the EB II, or transitional EB II/III elsewhere in the southern Levant. In addition, vessels of local production are now joined by pottery imported from sites to the west. The increasing sophistication of the material culture, and the evidence for closer integration with wider regional developments appears consistent with the increase in both scale and sophistication of the extractive metallurgy at this time, as was documented by Hauptmann (2000). It appears, then, that Faynan copper was assuming a much greater role in the regional economy.

Developments during EB III and later are represented by the specialist manufacturing site of Khirbat Hamra Ifdan in the Wadi Fidan. Dated by both pottery and radiocarbon to late EB III–EB IV (Adams 2000), the site is best seen as a specialist manufacturing location. It has yielded extensive evidence for the production of copper artefacts, including crucible fragments and a large number of broken clay moulds intended for the production of tools such as axes, pins, chisels, but also bar-shaped metal ingots (Adams 1999, chapter 7, 2002; Levy and Adams *et al.* 2002: 429, table 3). These items look as if they were intended for onward distribution, and are very similar to examples found on sites and metal hoards from the Negev, dated to the later third millennium BC. The distribution of these ingots may indicate that Faynan copper was being exported on a large scale to sites to the north and west, perhaps even as far as Egypt (Adams 2002: 33; 2006). Again there appears to have been an increase in the scale and sophistication of metallurgical operations in the region. It is not yet clear, however, whether these developments can be correlated with changes in political control (Adams 1999, 2002; Genz 2001).

There is now good evidence for early EB I occupation in the Aqaba region at the south end of the Wadi Arabah, with the site of Tall Magass, some 4 km north of Aqaba, having produced evidence for copper working. Egyptian contacts are indicated by a fragment of a siltstone palette (Brückner *et al.* 2002: 323, fig. 70). Similar material and additional evidence for metalworking in the form of copper ore, slag and crucible fragments comes from Hujayrat Ghuzlan, located some 3 km north of Aqaba (Khalil and Eichmann 2001: 200). The presence of flax at this site seems to point to irrigation agriculture in the local wadis.

The Steppe as an Economic Centre

One of the surprises of recent years has been the identification of evidence for the large-scale, specialist production of blanks for the manufacture of tabular flint scrapers around the Pleistocene lake basin at Jafr, in southeast

Jordan. Here, fieldwork (Quintero *et al.* 2002) has identified a number of quarrying sites (tabular flint nodules are bedded in the local Eocene limestone) and numerous areas around these where the ground surface is strewn with flint nodules, many showing the removal of several cortical flakes. The evidence (Fujii 2000, 2001; Quintero *et al.* 2002) confirms this as a genuine specialist operation, with one quarry site (among several dozen) which covered 12 ha having an estimated production of seven hundred and fifty thousand blanks. Given the scale of production, and the frequency of the scrapers at sites in the west, the industry must have been of considerable economic significance.

The low annual precipitation (c. 50 mm) suggests that flint extraction was a winter activity, undertaken by seasonal inhabitants. The structures associated with these operations survive as round or oval stone walled buildings, or in some cases arrangements of upright limestone slabs. There are also various cairns nearby. An example, the site of Qa Abu Tulahya West, is currently under investigation and has been described by the excavator (Fujii 2001: 35) as a "pseudo-settlement," that is a site composed of imitation domestic structures which were not truly functional. If this interpretation is proved correct, it may constitute yet another instance of groups exploiting the arid zone, adopting modes of expression or behaviour characteristic of agricultural groups in order to establish a claim to areas of landscape and their associated resources. Transport on the scale required may only have become possible with the domestication of the donkey, this being a further example of the synergies which we see as the result of developments in several aspects of technology.

Major Patterns in Settlement Data

The distribution of Early Bronze Age settlement is in striking contrast to patterns seen during the second millennium BC, which demonstrate much reduced settlement in many parts of the plateau. In the area south of Amman for example, it is only with the Iron Age II period that we see the re-emergence of a sedentary component resembling that documented for EB II–III (Chesson *et al.* 2005; MacDonald *et al.* 1988; Miller 1991). Equally, the few Middle Bronze Age sites located in the Jordan Valley south of Wadi Zarqa (Najjar 1992) offer a sharp contrast to the more southerly extent of walled EB II–III settlements (Ibrahim *et al.* 1988; Prag 1992: 155).

While this may reflect environmental changes towards the end of the third millennium BC, the data for the Holocene is patchy (Goldberg 1994: 99), and the various strands of palaeoenvironmental evidence are by no means in agreement (see papers in Bar-Yosef and Kra 1994, and discussion in A.M. Rosen 1995). Moreover, any particular climatic shift would have had a differential impact upon the various regions of Jordan. Increased rainfall may cause erosion of agricultural soils in one area and better crop growth in another. On the whole, environmental models operate at a scale well beyond the level at which such developments were perceived, and responded to, in human terms.

In fact, it may be useful to consider the reason for the development of the distinct Early Bronze Age settlement pattern in the first place. It can be argued that this is indicative of a form of socio-economic organization in the Early Bronze Age that was not simply resurrected during the Middle and Late Bronze Ages. In Palestine too, a significant number of large Early Bronze Age centres were not reoccupied in the second millennium BC (Broshi and Gophna 1986; Falconer 1987; Finkelstein and Gophna 1993), suggesting that there existed a qualitative difference between the settlement landscapes of the third and second millennia BC.

Studies of settlement data (Falconer 1994: 315–317; Falconer and Savage 1995; Harrison 1997; Harrison and Savage 2003) suggest that the Early Bronze Age is characterized by poorly integrated settlement systems, free to integrate in a variety of ways, rather than supporting a rigid hierarchical structure. There was also significant regional differentiation, pointing to a flexible system in which local settlement clusters had divergent trajectories, perhaps reflecting social or environmental developments taking place at a limited spatial scale.

As the existence of regional settlement hierarchies focused around the largest sites has not generally been demonstrated, analyses framed in terms of "central places" (e.g. Finkelstein 1995a) may be inappropriate for Early Bronze Age Jordan. Rather, the settlement landscape may be better described as a patchwork in which much activity was structured around individual communities or local settlements clusters, but which were linked to wider economic activities, perhaps in a relatively unsystematic way. Examples of the latter might include the acquisition of copper or specialist flint products, or the movement outwards of agricultural commodities such as olive oil.

Under such a system, the demonstrable evidence for interregional contact would have resulted from contacts at a day-to-day or perhaps seasonal level, facilitated by routine or regular patterns of social and economic interaction between members of individual communities. Such a system could have functioned without the involvement of large economic institutions, or elites based at a few key sites. This is not to deny the possible existence of larger political and economic units, but to suggest that these appeared sporadically, were possibly short-lived, and were superimposed upon a much broader resilient network of local communities following their own courses of development (Falconer and Savage 1995: 55).

Such a construct would appear consistent with the notion of walled sites as representing an ideological resource, the visible inscription of communities in a symbolically-charged landscape rather than economic central places

(Philip 2003: 115). In such a reconstruction they would have symbolized a community's rights of access to a particular territory, with their prominence and monumentality implying a degree of permanence for such claims that was often contradicted by the occupational histories of individual sites. Such an explanation might have been meaningful to groups practising a range of subsistence strategies, and might explain the apparent crossover in symbolic expressions between predominantly agricultural and mainly pastoralist communities.

Mobile Groups

A form of mobile animal herding, closely integrated with a sedentary agricultural economy, described as village-based transhumance, has been documented during the fifth millennium BC in southwestern Palestine (T.E. Levy 1992: 73; 1995: 232). Settlement evidence in both the southern and eastern arid zones suggests, however, the emergence during the Early Bronze Age of significant, if regionally differentiated, systems of specialized livestock management providing secondary animal products for sedentary communities.

Given that settlements in the Jordan Valley and much of the plateau had reasonable access to grazing resources, we might suspect that some of these communities were also quite extensively involved with mobile animal herding. This would have constituted a rather different system from the more specialized animal management posited for groups exploiting the arid zone. These more localized processes of nomadization and sedentarization, perhaps fluctuating year-to-year, region-to-region, would have provided a relatively fine-tuned response to local environmental, economic and socio-political factors. The on-site storage of agricultural staples, combined with the possibility of seasonal variations in the size of the resident population, may have given added emphasis to wall construction as a means of protecting valuable community resources.

Highland–Lowland–Steppe Connections and the Growth of a Regional Economy

There is both ceramic (east–west style zones) and economic evidence to argue for connections between settlement development in upland and lowland areas. I have suggested that different regions followed agricultural strategies best described as "subsistence plus" with each developing a specialist component suited to the local environment. Each would, therefore, have contributed specific resources to an increasingly integrated regional economy. Intensive horticulture in the valley would have exploited the potential of floodwater irrigation while requiring a significant labour force. Extensive plough agriculture would have rendered possible the production of agricultural surpluses in suitable areas of the plateau. The cultivation of fruit trees in well-watered upland zones would have supplied

a product suitable for exchange, perhaps with the larger valley bottom sites, while the development of a mobile pastoralist component would have catered for sedentary communities' need for animal products, as well as providing a pool of additional labour that could be drawn upon as required. Critically, these changes appear to have taken place in the absence of convincing evidence for the existence of institutionalized elite power.

The Material Remains: Burial Data
A Case Study: Graves from Bab adh-Dhra

The sole Jordanian cemetery producing material from all periods of the Early Bronze Age is located just outside the walled settlement of Bab adh-Dhra. Despite some local characteristics, examples selected from this site will be used as the basis for discussion. EB IA burials occur in shaft and chamber graves (Figure 6.5). Tomb A 78 (Schaub and Rast 1981) consisted of a vertical circular shaft opening into four chambers, the entrance to each of which was closed by a blocking stone. The disarticulated skeletal remains of several individuals formed a pile in the centre of each chamber. Skulls were usually placed to the left of the pile, while grave goods, mainly ceramic vessels, were placed around the edge of the chamber or to the right of the entrance. The graves contained both adult and child burials, and are assumed to represent family groups. Finds were dominated by pottery, mostly bowls (50–60%), jars and juglets with wide necks (Figure 6.8.1–2). Other artefacts, such as limestone maceheads, shell bracelets, basalt bowls and clay figurines (Figure 6.12), occur less frequently. EB IB tombs (Schaub and Rast 1989) are characterized by shafts opening into a single chamber, with entrances that include a threshold stone flanked by stone orthostats. A similar practice has been observed at the EB I pillared hall at Hartuv (Mazar and de Miroschedji 1996), suggesting an overlap between structures used by the living and the dead. EB IB graves contain more articulated burials, and disarticulated remains when found, are not placed in the deliberate piles characteristic of EB IA. Some EB IB graves are circular, mud-brick structures with a semi-circular forecourt; the apparent resemblance to the entrance shaft of contemporary rock-cut tombs may be intentional.

EB II–III funerary architecture consists of rectangular mud-brick structures 7–11 m long and 4–7 m broad, termed "charnel houses" (Figure 6.6). The entrance was in the long side and had a stone threshold, giving the tombs a close resemblance to the layout of the so-called "broad-room" house. In many cases, two monoliths flanked the entrance, a feature with parallels in both stone-built tombs and other architectural units. Some EB II charnel houses were circular, with walls corbelled inwards and a central slab, presumably the base for a roof support. While these carry over certain design features from shaft and chamber graves, parallels with circular architecture at northern sites, such as Tall Shuna (Figure 6.3) are also close. Char-

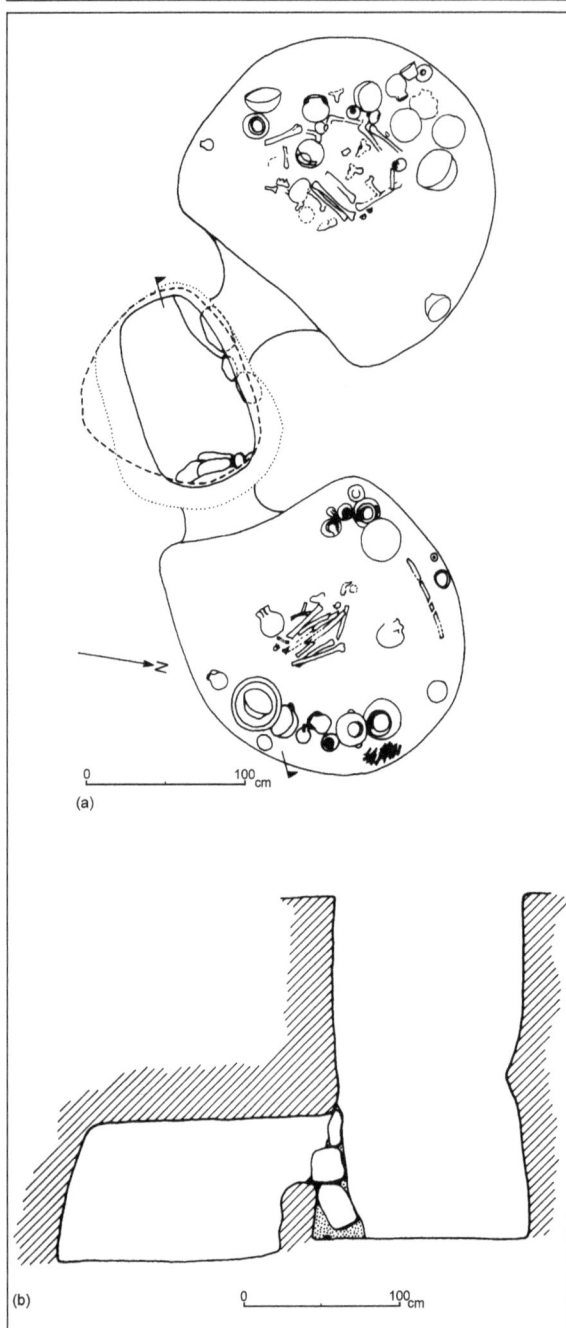

Figure 6.5   Bab adh-Dhra Tomb A76, an EB IA shaft grave:
a. plan; b. section (drawn by Y. Beadnell).

possibly connected with the transport or laying out of the deceased. All other burials, including 161 skulls, were disarticulated and clustered in piles along the external and internal walls.

Discussion

EB IA disarticulated burials have been interpreted as indicating periodic visits to the site by non-sedentary groups (Schaub 1981: 81; Khazanov 1984; Dever 1987), with the dead transported in a decomposed state. Palumbo (1990: 122), however, makes the point that many sedentary communities also practise disarticulated burial. In fact, discrepancies between numbers of skulls and long bones recovered from individual tombs at Bab adh-Dhra, and the stylized arrangement of both skeletal material and artefacts—see also Jericho Tomb A 94 (Kenyon 1960: 20) and an EB I tomb at Ayn Assawir in Palestine (Mazar 1990: 98)—appear suggestive not of mobility, but of specific practices involving human remains. The handling, movement, even veneration of ancestral remains are phenomena well documented in both the ethnographic and archaeological literature from other parts of the world (Barrett 1988). Anthropological research (Van Gennep 1960; Turner 1969; Bloch 1971) suggests that structures designed for long term reuse, allowing regular access to the community of the deceased, would permit the symbolic presence of the ancestors to be drawn into the world of the living. Thus, tombs would provide foci for links with the ancestral group, with the interment of an individual understood as part of a process, a link in a chain. The maintenance of an ancestral unit would help explain the sheer number of individuals interred within single funerary structures, and it seems reasonable to suggest that multiple successive burial was connected to the developing importance of kin-based groups as corporate units (Chesson 1999; Harrison 2001).

Built-Stone Tombs

The type most commonly associated with the Early Bronze Age are the so-called dolmens (Figure 6.7), which consist of a chamber built from roughly-worked stone uprights, supporting a capstone: chambers can be up to 2–3 m in length. Although dating stone burial monuments is difficult because of later disturbance and reuse, there is a general consensus that many date to the fourth and third millennia BC (Prag 1995; Zohar 1992). Their main concentrations are along the escarpment and eastern slopes of the Jordan Valley, from the region northeast of the Dead Sea to the hills east of Pella (Watson 1996), and on the plateau where numerous examples are documented in the area east of Jarash (Sapin 1992; Hanbury-Tenison 1989a). Traditionally, scholars have connected "megalithic" monuments in the Levant with pastoralist groups (Zohar 1992: 52–55), although there is an association between the distribution of built stone monuments

nel houses could contain more than 100 disarticulated burials, in some cases forming distinct layers, suggesting an extended period of use. One large, long-lived tomb, A 22 (Rast and Schaub 1980), included six articulated burials, three of those associated with the remains of what may have been a pallet or bed made of poles and matting,

Figure 6.6   Bab adh-Dhra Tomb A55, an EB II–III charnel house used for multiple successive interment over an extended period; doorway to left of picture, blackened area beyond scale produced burnt linen cloth covering pottery and bones (photo by R.T. Schaub).

and of EB I settlements in the area northeast of the Dead Sea (Prag 1995: 79), a point reinforced by the locations of surveyed dolmen fields in Wadi Yabis (see Palumbo *et al*. 1990: 480).

As the corpus of examples has developed, the variety of burial monuments has cast doubt on the applicability of the traditional dichotomy between underground shaft and chamber graves, and above-ground built stone tombs (Philip 2003: 118–119). Both dolmens and shaft tombs occur together at Jabal Mutawwaq (Hanbury-Tenison 1989a: 137–139), and we are probably dealing with structures "whose form may not be fixed but rather embody ideas which themselves may be variable and changing" (Bradley 1993: 71–72). Moreover, connections between stone-working techniques employed on superficially different structures, such as the monolithic door jambs in Hall 134 at Hartuv in Palestine (Mazar and de Miroschedji 1996) and the entrances to charnel houses at Bab adh-Dhra and stone-lined cists at Safi-Nage (Waheeb 1995: figs. 1–2), raise questions concerning their ascription to distinct sections of the population.

Further doubt has been cast upon the simple association of shaft tombs with sedentary groups and dolmens with pastoralists through the excavation of a largely undisturbed late EB I dolmen near Tall Umayri, (Dubis and Dabrowski 2002). This structure contained the remains of more than 20 individuals, and a range of burial goods that would have been perfectly at home in a contemporary shaft and chamber grave. The shared features of these two burial forms appear at least as strong as the contrasts. In practice, as Prag (1995: 83) has observed, "megalithic monuments are so widely distributed and so numerous as to suggest that they represented the "normal" mode of burial for the dead of a large part of the population over an extended period."

In addition to commonality in terms of assemblages, and association with ancestors, it is worth bearing in mind that both classes of monument are likely to have constituted visible elements in the landscape. This is obvious in the case of built-stone tombs, and the EB II–III charnel houses at Bab adh-Dhra which would have looked rather like houses from a distance, quite literally the dwellings

Figure 6.7 Dolmen, Jabal Mutawwaq (G. Philip).

of the ancestors (Chesson 1999, 2001). Even at Jericho, where shaft and chamber graves remained the norm right through the Early Bronze Age, the rarity of tombs cutting into earlier examples suggests that they were marked above-ground.

Burial Equipment

This suggestion finds support in the stereotypical nature of the grave goods, which are dominated by ceramics, the forms and fabrics of which overlap to a great extent with those of domestic pottery. The rarity of metal goods is particularly striking in the light of evidence for Early Bronze Age copper exploitation at Faynan (Adams and Genz 1995; Adams 1999, 2002; Hauptmann 2000), and for copper-working at individual sites (Rehren *et al.* 1997). The grave repertoire appears to have excluded many forms of artefact. Of particular note is the rarity of those things most closely associated with the marking of individuals in EB IV and Middle Bronze Age graves—pins, jewellery, weapons, meat offerings—items placed close to the body and presumably associated with specific individuals (Hallotte 1996; Baxevani 1995; Ilan 1995; Philip 1995b). This might suggest that EBA burial sought deliberately to subsume individuals within the group.

Cooking and large storage vessels are also rare in graves. These do, however, contain a significant number of small

bowls and narrow-necked jugs and juglets (Schaub 1996: 234, table 1), best characterized as vessels for food consumption, and containers for such valuables as oil, wine or scents. Given the apparent significance of oil production to the wider economy, it may be that these vessels and their contents expressed in burial contexts messages concerning access to the critical agricultural resources of land, labour and investment. The attribution of symbolic value to locally-produced substances is consistent with arguments presented earlier concerning a new emphasis upon the mobilization of agricultural products.

The presence of numerous walled settlements alongside "collective" burial practices lacking obvious wealth differences supports the view that kinship-based groups were the core component of Early Bronze Age social and economic organization. In the absence of convincing evidence for institutionalized elites, it would appear that these groups provided the basis for undertaking major delayed return investments, and working in cooperation could have created material remains superficially akin to those produced by stratified state societies.

The stereotypical form and long-term continuity of collective tombs argue that they were closely involved in the reproduction of the social structure (Chesson 1999, 2001), and by providing an ideological context for living corporate groups they may have served to maintain a system of rights and obligations and to provide a legitimating "past" for current social realities. Mortuary practices may, therefore, have served the interests of an incipient elite by reproducing structures of authority through the promotion of an "egalitarian" or "group-centred" ideology, akin to Renfrew's (1974) concept of group-orientated chiefdoms. Such an ideology may have served to play down the reality of growing inequality of access to power and resources, a point perhaps reflected in Chesson's (1999) distinction between "Greater" and "Lesser" houses. Differentiated in terms of size, number of burials and range of grave offerings, these appear to provide evidence for growing disparities between the power of different corporate groups during EB III. This situation appears entirely compatible with the internal dynamics of heterarchically organized corporate village communities.

Morris' (1991) notion that ancestors could have a continuing engagement with the affairs of their descendants, as participants in social, political and economic relationships, and in particular with the transmission of descent and property, fits well with the organization of EBA communities as described above. That being so we might expect that burial monuments, as both the repositories of the ancestors and prominent landscape features, would have constituted an important element of symbolic capital which could have been mobilized to suit differing local requirements. An obvious function would have been to bring the ancestors into physical and symbolic relationships with the landscape and thus symbolize the continuity and legitimacy of a group's rights. If some megalithic tombs belonged to sedentary rather than mobile populations, then their very presence in the uplands might relate to the development of these landscapes for agriculture, with all the movement and activity which this would have entailed.

Although occupation at many settlements may have been short-lived or punctuated, that does not mean that local communities ceased to exist, although the scale and visibility of their daily activities may have been reduced. While stone walls would have rendered even abandoned settlements significant landscape features, the conspicuous presence of ancestral tombs may have allowed the past to be mobilized in such a way as to permit communities to sustain claims to resources, even during periods of decline, when they may have been incapable of maintaining a fortified settlement.

Early Bronze Age Social and Cultural Landscapes

The Early Bronze Age saw the incorporation of various novel features within the topography of Jordan: walled human settlements, dams and irrigated fields, orchards, extensive new areas of ploughed arable land, numerous built-stone tombs, and presumably a variety of paths and routes whereby people, animals and commodities could move across the landscape. It is important, therefore, to consider the sheer physical impact of Early Bronze Age activity, and the degree to which the pre-existing landscape would have been modified. Theoretical discussions (Thomas 1991; Bradley 1993; Tilley 1994) have stressed that humans not only create and modify landscapes but that these, in turn, constitute social and ideological symbols that play a role in influencing people's comprehension and experience of the world.

Thus, while the growth of large Neolithic settlements and the domestication of caprines may have impacted significantly upon the environment (Rollefson 1993, this volume; Garrard *et al.* 1996), this would have been the cumulative, perhaps imperceptible, result of short-term subsistence choices. The highly visible Early Bronze Age modifications were deliberate constructions, and created a landscape that had been formed by human choices and action, and the development of which was open to day-to-day perception and judgment. From the later fourth millennium BC onwards, the inhabitants of Jordan would have moved within a landscape much of which originated in the Early Bronze Age. Recognizing the way in which the built environment alters, even forms, people's perceptions (Thomas 1991), it can be suggested that the Early Bronze Age sees the inscription into the landscape of both living groups and their past, through the creation of a world in which space was structured by highly visible human creations.

Material Remains: Portable Artefacts

Implicit in much writing on Levantine archaeology is the assumption that craft specialization evolved concomitant with increasingly complex and centralized political development (e.g. Adams 2002: 30; Greenberg 2002: 90–91), although "most models for the organization of production are based on the analysis of complex—especially state—societies, and therefore do not adequately address the economic and political conditions found in smaller scale societies" (Costin 2001: 309). In light of the above statement, and the widely-held assumptions regarding the state-level organization of Early Bronze Age societies in the southern Levant, this should come as no surprise.

Early doubts as to whether such a reconstruction was really consistent with the evidence (S.A. Rosen 1993, 1997b), have been amplified more recently (Chesson and Philip 2003; Harrison and Savage 2003). Various criteria have been suggested to distinguish between specialization and basic household-level production (e.g. Feinman *et al.* 1984; Costin 1991). On the basis of such criteria, for example, standardization of form and technique and restricted availability of raw materials, a number of products, such as Canaanean blades and Metallic Ware pottery appear likely to have been produced by specialists for wide distribution, a point reinforced by their suitability for transportation.

Specialization in what are essentially utilitarian products often indicates production for domestic consumption, with certain households or communities producing for other units (Costin 1991: 13). Such a system does not require the existence of urban communities or elites to function, and need not be indicative of stratification or inequality. For example, it is hard to imagine how the distribution of tabular flint blanks produced in the Jafr Basin (Quintero *et al*. 2002) could be tied to any kind of formal political control. While these, and products such as Canaanean flint blades or Metallic Ware storage vessels were specialist items of economic significance, and produced in restricted locations, their space-time distributions far exceed those likely to have been associated with individual political units.

While craft specialization has often been seen as an important component of hierarchical organizations, with the growth of attached specialists working for elites and producing high-status goods seen as a typical facet of complex societies (e.g. Blumfiel and Earle 1987), there is little evidence for high-status manufactured goods from Early Bronze Age Jordan. Nor is there much to indicate large concentrations of manufacturing activities within major settlements. Thus, the data indicate that various segments of the economy were organized quite differently, with significant areas of production and procurement having little or no relationship to matters of political power. Yet again, we appear to be witnessing potentially heterarchical relationships rather than a single organizational principle, the city-state.

Pottery

Although knowledge has increased considerably in recent years (see Philip and Baird 2000a), ceramic development in Early Bronze Age Jordan remains broadly compatible with the scheme for the southern Levant outlined by Stager (1992). The key theoretical difficulty, however, is that until recently much discussion was conducted using the ceramic categories defined in Wright's (1937) classic study of Early Bronze Age Palestinian ceramics, which was largely concerned with the space-time organization of the material. For those researchers who remained focused upon the reconstruction of the region's culture history, this problem went largely unnoticed (Dessel and Joffe 2000: 37). However, those who sought to ask "anthropological" questions were constrained by a dataset that had been designed to address a very different set of concerns.

The core difficulty is that while our basic ceramic categories are abstractions created by twentieth century archaeologists primarily as organizational devices, these are often assumed, implicitly, to map directly onto real past entities (on this problem see Barrett's [1994] comments on the status of the "beaker" phenomenon in European prehistory). Chronology apart, much of the traditional literature has concentrated upon pottery as a "cultural" indicator (e.g. Kenyon 1979), or as evidence for inter-

regional (i.e. cultural) contacts (Hennessy 1967; Ben-Tor 1986; Stager 1992: 40–41). Researchers have appeared reluctant to move beyond traditional questions and methodologies (Philip and Baird 2000b: 3–4) and continue to work with traditional typologies based upon shape and decoration. With the exception of the pioneering work of Franken (1974), studies of fabric and manufacturing techniques are a recent innovation, and have remained essentially descriptive (e.g. Beynon *et al*. 1986), or have resorted to traditional "pots to people" explanations for patterns demonstrated on the basis of petrographic data (Greenberg and Porat 1996).

Fortunately, the various dimensions of pottery as an investigative tool are becoming apparent and researchers are beginning to consider the socio-economic implications of patterns of ceramic production and distribution (Goren and Zuckermann 2000; Greenberg 2000). In particular, recent work in Jordan has highlighted the accretive, multi-component nature of the ceramic assemblages recovered from many sites (Betts 1991: 103–107; Genz 2002; London 1991; Rast and Schaub 2003), which cannot, therefore, be directly equated with individual "cultures."

EB I

The internal development of the EB I period is particularly well documented in Jordan, with three recently excavated sites—Tall Shuna, Tall Umm Hammad and Bab adh-Dhra—having produced clear evidence for two distinct ceramic subphases.

The bulk of the early EB I assemblage from Tall Shuna consists of handmade vessels in a coarse, poorly levigated fabric bearing a light orange wash. Shapes are simple, including conical bowls with straight sides and simple jar forms; decoration is restricted to heavy thumb impressions. Rounded ledge handles, thumb impressed around the edge, are characteristic. Hole-mouth cooking pots show a distinctive calcite temper, beneficial in the control of thermal shock, and may bear impressed ovoids or slashes on the rim.

The most distinctive component of the pottery assemblage of the earlier EB I phase in the north is Grey Burnished Ware (GBW), although it comprises a small percentage of the total repertoire. Vessels have a grey-black, highly burnished surface and are restricted to large bowl forms, sometimes bearing plastic decoration (see Goren and Zuckermann 2000: fig. 10.2). Petrographic evidence suggests that GBW was a specialized product, but manufactured at more than one centre (Goren and Zukermann 2000: 169–170). GBW is characteristic of northern Palestine and Transjordan. Its distribution extends onto the plateau (Kamlah 2000: 97), but does not reach Jawa in the east. In the Jordan Valley, GBW occurs as far south as Tall Umm Hammad (Betts 1992: 76–77), but was not reported from the extensive EB I occupations recorded in the Jarash and Rumman regions (Hanbury-

Tenison 1987; Gordon and Knauf 1987), from Jabal Abu Thawwab (Douglas and Kafafi 2000: 110; Kafafi 2001) or the Dead Sea region (Rast and Schaub 2003).

The later EB I pottery from Tall Shuna consisted of large vessels, such as hole-mouth jars and pithoi, bearing bands of streaky red wash known as Band Slip decoration, and small vessels, mainly bowls and closed containers, with red-slipped and burnished surfaces. Hemispherical bowls replaced straight-sided forms, and impressed decoration is less common. New developments include Crackled Ware, which appears to represent a late descendant of GBW (Esse 1989b; Rowan 1994). The early and late EB I ceramic repertoires from Tall Shuna have good parallels respectively at Yiftahel (Braun 1997) and En Shadud (Braun 1985) in northern Palestine.

Band Slip pottery is often described as a "ware" (e.g. Stager 1992: 30), although it is better understood as a decorative technique, which can occur on a range of forms and fabrics (Genz 2000; Joffe 2000: 184). It is distributed across a broad east–west band extending from the north Jordan plateau and the Syrian Hauran (Genz 2002; Braemer and Échallier 2000: 406) through the Esdraelon Valley to the Mediterranean coast (Scheftelowitz 2002: 97). On the east side of the Jordan Valley it is well represented at Tall Abu Kharaz (Fischer 2000), and while its southern limit appears to lie in the area of the Wadi Zarqa (Kamlah 2000: fig. 6), there are sporadic occurrences at more southerly sites, such as Tall Iktanu (Prag 1993: 269). While there is a marked association between this decorative technique and storage vessels, the technique is not exclusive to any single form, and there is a degree of change through time (Genz 2002: 33–34, table 10).

A long EB I sequence from Tall Umm Hammad in the central part of the Jordan Valley (Betts 1992: 17–21) also reveals two distinct ceramic phases. The earlier part (Stage 2) includes a large number of hole-mouth jars bearing impressed or slashed decoration along or just below the rim, as seen at Tall Shuna. One particular variant, apparently produced in a single fabric, bears four pushed-up ledge handles on the shoulder (Figure 8.3) (Betts 1992: 47). This distinctive form has been recognized elsewhere in the central Jordan Valley (Mabry 1989: 61), in the uplands to the east where it has been used as a chronological marker for early EB I (Hanbury-Tenison 1987; Betts 1992: 48; Braemer and Sapin 2001) and as an import at Jawa in the basalt *harra* (Betts 1991: 72), where it provides clear evidence for a connection between the central Jordan Valley and the *badia* during EB I. The physical transport of pottery from the central Jordan Valley to the steppe may well be indicative of patterns of seasonal mobility between these areas (Helms 1987). The absence of such vessels from Tall Shuna at the northern end of the Jordan Valley points again to interaction framed in east–west rather than north–south terms.

Red-slipped and burnished surface treatment appears restricted to loop-handled juglets and small hemispherical bowls, and appears to increase in frequency with time (Betts 1992: 99). Also characteristic of this phase are large GBW bowls (Betts 1992: 76–77, genre 45). Noteworthy is the presence of what may be a related form, deep bowls with everted rim (Betts 1992: 78–79, genre 48). These share certain characteristics of size and shape with GBW, but lack the distinctive surface treatment, and have general parallels at Jabal Abu Thawwab (Douglas and Kafafi 2000: 107–108, figs. 6.6–7). This raises the possibility that by focusing upon the distinctive colour of GBW vessels scholars may have missed their real significance, namely their size and shape. There might be a functional equivalence of large open bowls generally, including the large bowl forms from early EB I Bab adh-Dhra (Rast and Schaub 2003: 85, figs. 5.2 and 5.6) where GBW is lacking. As a result, we may have underestimated the significance of the widespread adoption of a group of large vessels, the appearance of which may be indicative of changing attitudes to food consumption. GBW and other large bowls may be connected with an early stage in the social practices which were to develop around the platter-bowls which are so characteristic of EB II–III assemblages (Bunimovitz and Greenberg 2004: 21).

Tall Umm Hammad Stage 3 produced a later EB I assemblage, although the exact relationship between stages 2 and 3 remains unclear, owing to the limited excavation area and the possibility of a local stratigraphic break (Philip 1995b: 166). Traits distinctive of stage 3 include a decline in the proportion of hole-mouth jars bearing impressed decoration, with many now undecorated, and the appearance on others of Band Slip decoration. Red-slipped and burnished surface treatments become increasingly common and a number of new shapes appear, including high-necked jars, platters with inverted rims and spouted bowls.

This stage also sees the appearance of the distinctive Tall Umm Hammad Sharqiyya (TUH) ware (Leonard 1992: 83; Betts 1992: 107, repertoire 6), which appears in a heavy red fabric as large bowls and jars bearing multiple applied bands with thick thumb-impressed and moulded decoration. The distribution of this material during the EB I period is restricted to the central Jordan Valley (see Betts 1992: 56 *inter alia*) with an extension westwards to Tall Farah North where it was termed Pré-Urbaine-D (de Miroschedji 1971: 38–40, fig. 14). It was not detected by surveys in districts east of the valley (Hanbury-Tenison 1987; Gordon and Knauf 1987) despite earlier ceramic connections between these areas, however, and is not present at either Pella or Tall Abu Kharaz (Bourke 2000; Fischer 2000). Both the appearance and limited distribution of TUH ware suggest that it represents a localized product, while the range of shapes in which it occurs indicates a connection with storage. The contrast between the limited distribution of TUH ware and the far more widely occuring Band Slip decoration highlights the complexity of EB I ceramic patterning and the need to accommodate the simultaneous operation of a variety of processes at contrasting scales.

At Bab adh-Dhra the later EB I witnesses the appearance of vessels bearing Line Group painted decoration, a style which consists of parallel lines of red or brown paint applied directly to the surface of small vessels. Pottery bearing this type of decoration extends across south-central Palestine from Ai (at-Tall) to Arad (Schaub 1982; Stager 1985; 1992: 29), through the south Jordan Valley (Prag 1989: 38–40), and onto the plateau where it extends from Amman to the Karak region (Brown 1991: 173; Dubis and Dabrowski 2002). Further south, the ceramics of the Faynan and Aqaba regions remain poorly understood, although recent evidence points to these as representing descendants of local Chalcolithic styles (Adams 1999, 2002, 2003).

At all three sites the key changes from earlier to later EB I ceramics can be summarized as follows: increasing evidence of openness to styles and practices reflecting contacts in the wider region, greater technical skill including a higher standard of vessel finish and firing, and the employment of a wider range of fabrics in a more selective fashion for the production of specific vessel forms. These are classic indicators of increasing craft specialization. Despite the adoption at late EB I Bab adh-Dhra of styles and techniques documented elsewhere—the use of crushed limestone temper in cooking vessels (Philip and Baird 2000b:11; Rast and Schaub 2003: 132), and "duck bill" ledge handles—local traditions remained strong, however, and some of the more elaborate variations documented at more northerly sites remained absent (Rast and Schaub 2003: 146).

While ceramic regionalism is generally taken as characteristic of EBI, the term as traditionally employed amounts to the recognition of a few distinctive features within a complex of cross-cutting ceramic assemblages; some are styles of painting, while others appear to be associated with specific combinations of vessel form and fabric. In reality, it appears that ceramic "regions" are constituted at different spatial scales. While the distinctive material from Bab adh-Dhra, or that from contemporary southern Jordan both appear to be confined to spatially restricted areas, elements of the ceramics from Tall Shuna and Tall Umm Hammad appear to be distributed across large areas of the north. Equally, in comparison to Tall Shuna, late EB I Bab adh-Dhra reveals a much more restricted range of fabrics, suggesting that the two assemblages result from rather different patterns of production and procurement.

Certain broad patterns are already clear, however. The main elements of traditional "regionalism"—GBW, Band Slip and Line Group decoration—are manifest spatially as extensive east–west distributions, but their north–

south limits are more restricted. Even pottery of more localized distribution appears to follow this pattern with the four lugged jars known from Jawa and the central Jordan Valley absent at sites both to the north and south, while Tall Umm Hammad Sharqiyya ware appears concentrated along the axis of Wadis Zarqa and Fara. These ceramic distributions might appear counter-intuitive, in that they cut across natural topographic boundaries, while evidence for north–south communications along the valley floor or plateau is less apparent. This argues for some wider role for an east–west axis, one that might be connected to growing economic integration between the lowland, upland and steppe regions with their different subsistence potentials. It is also worth observing that, despite the differences in specific styles, many of the key *functional* ceramic categories are present at agriculture-based settlements throughout Jordan, suggesting that a rich and complex network of shared values and practices underpinned day-to-day activities among Early Bronze Age communities.

EB II

Pottery of this period from Palestine appears to fall into two broad groups, namely, Metallic Wares in the north and "local" softer, red-slipped and burnished pottery in central and southern areas (Greenberg and Porat 1996: 137), a characterization that is broadly applicable to Jordan.

Metallic Ware

The characteristics of Metallic Ware are now well known (Greenberg and Porat 1996; Greenberg 2002: 43–48). It is a red or grey fabric, fired to a temperature between 850 and 950 degrees C, and used to produce thin-walled vessels with a matt surface and a distinctive metallic ring when struck. The ware is believed on petrographic grounds to originate from a single clay body located in the Lower Cretaceous formation, which outcrops at the foot of Jabal Shaykh (Mount Hermon). The ware is used to produce a wide range of vessel forms. Metallic Ware vessels dominate EB II assemblages in northern Palestine and comprise 50–70% of the ceramic assemblage at EB II sites as far south as the Jezreel Valley (Greenberg 2002: 48). That a major component of the pottery occurring at northern EB II sites was imported from this source indicates both large-scale production and a significant degree of economic integration. Cooking pots, however, do not appear in Metallic Ware, and were presumably manufactured locally.

Greenberg and Porat (1996: 20) argued that the extensive distribution of Metallic Ware during EB II is connected with changing political structures in northern Palestine. There are good arguments against this view, however. Metallic Ware was utilized on a spatial scale far greater than that of any posited individual polity, while there is

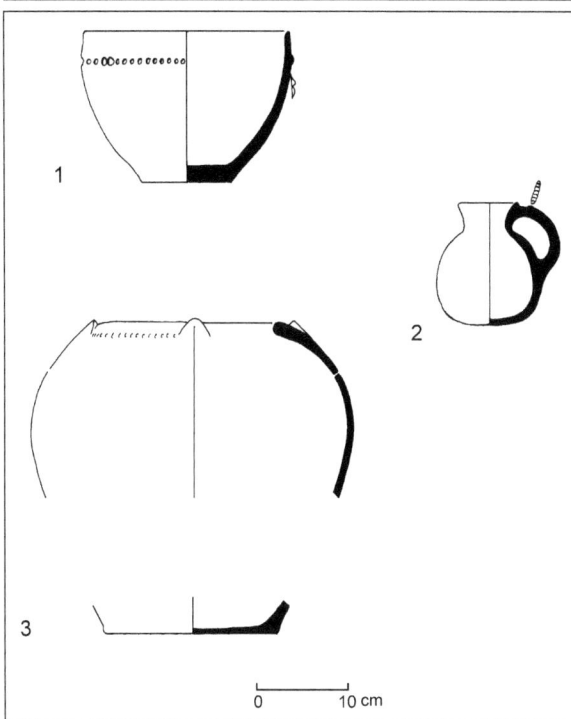

Figure 6.8 EB I pottery (drawn by Y. Beadnell).
1: Bab adh-Dhra, EB IA bowl with conical projec-
tions; below rim. 2: Bab adh-Dhra, EB IA jug. 3:
Tall Umm Hammad, EB IA hole-mouth jar with
pushed-up lug handles of a type occurring at sites
in Wadi Zarqa and Jawa in the steppe.

now growing evidence from western Asia indicating that
significant areas of specialized economic activity were
organized independently of the existence of political
hierarchies (Stein and Blackman 1993; Wattenmaker
1994; S.A. Rosen 1997b). Costin (1991: 13) has suggested that items manufactured by independent specialists tend to be utilitarian, used by most households and
available without restriction, while specialists attached to
elites tend to produce luxury items and wealth-generating
goods. Metallic Ware belongs to the first rather than the
second of these categories, while the distinctive concentration of production is simply explained by the restricted physical distribution of the required raw materials, a
factor that Costin (1991: 13–15) has acknowledged as
playing a key role in determining the basis of production. Thus the distribution of Metallic Ware is probably
better explained as the summative outcome of numerous small-scale transactions undertaken at community or
household level, rather than as an indication of any overarching political organization. In this sense, it represents
an incremental advance along the trajectory of increasing
regional economic interaction that was already well under
way during EB I.

More recently Greenberg (2002: 92–93) has posited a

connection with what he terms the EB II agricultural-
commercial complex, which he sees as connected to settlement growth in the Huleh Basin during EB II, and
ultimately resulting from a movement of people into the
area from the north Jordan Valley. A significant quantity
of Metallic Ware, however, has been reported from Tall
Abu Kharaz in the north Jordan Valley (Fischer 2000;
Fischer and Toivonen-Skage 1995), where it appears
as platters, jugs and juglets, and large storage jars with
pattern-combed decoration, Tall Handaquq (N) (Mabry
1989: 79, fig. 10.17), and Tall Sukhne in Wadi Zarqa
(Chesson *et al.* 1995), revealing the eastward extent of
this ceramic form. In the case of Abu Kharaz, for which
most information is available, the presence of platters
suggests that the pottery itself was a commodity rather
than simply a container, a point reinforced by the relatively low weights of individual vessels (Greenberg and
Porat 1996: 19). Local ceramic production remained
important at these sites, however, and included a range of
bowls, jugs and amphoriskoi, as well as large storage vessels, bearing red-painted decoration executed in a variety
of styles. Whatever the reason in the Huleh Basin, the
evidence from Jordan points towards a simple commercial
explanation with this high quality, light (i.e. portable),
mass produced (so presumably cheap) pottery coming to
supplement, or even displace, elements of local production. Given that the Early Bronze Age appears to have
been marked by the movement of people, livestock and
commodities on a significant scale, there is no reason why
this should not apply equally to ceramics.

Non-metallic Wares

In southern Palestine, Metallic Ware vessels are rare
(Greenberg 1996: 137) and they have not yet been reported from sites in south-central Jordan, where red-slipped
and burnished vessels made in softer fabrics predominate.
Here, despite similarities with Metallic Ware in terms
of vessel shape, production appears to have been almost
entirely localized as exemplified by the pottery from Bab
adh-Dhra. The site's EB II assemblage revealed an increase
in narrow-necked jugs and juglets, presumably an indication of the importance of specialized liquid products, and
the appearance of wide shallow platters. The latter were often made in a basalt-tempered fabric, while the fine-wares
contained Nubian Sand (Rast and Schaub 2003: 224).
While neither of these are likely to have been immediately
local to the site, they are certainly consistent with geology
of the general area. Thus, the decline in ceramic regionalism characteristic of EB II presumably reflects an increasing commonality of economic and perhaps social practices
resulting from growing inter-regional communication.

The presence at Barqa al-Hatiya in Wadi Faynan of EB
II/III pottery in "standard" shapes (Adams 1999, chapter
6, 2003) reveals the extent to which a particular set of
ceramic forms had become established in domestic con-

texts throughout the southern Levant by the earlier third millennium BC. The suggestion that the distinctive arkosic fabrics which occur in cooking pots from Arad are likely to have originated in the Faynan area (Adams 1999, chapter 6, 2003: 17), when taken alongside the absence of such vessels from Bab adh-Dhra (Rast and Schaub 2003), indicates that the east-west orientation of communication networks continued to apply to both southern and northern parts of the region.

I would not read too much into the apparent domination of Metallic Ware in the north. Rather than posit a division into a Metallic Ware sphere and the rest, I would see the former as indicating that the products of one particular production centre (which happened to have access to a high-quality clay body that was well suited to the manufacture of a very wide range of forms, and good fuel supplies) were able to gain a competitive advantage over alternative products, within a specific area and for a period of time. The fall-off pattern simply indicates the way in which that advantage was gradually negated by the impact of distance upon the cost of transport and the support which could be expected from social or cultural networks.

EB III

In general terms, the EB III period sees a continuation of the trend towards greater convergence of regional ceramic assemblages, with one exception.

Khirbat Kerak Ware

This highly-distinctive form of pottery has a soft fabric, resulting from firing at a relatively low temperature. Vessels have a highly-burnished red or black surface, with relief decoration in some cases, and occur in shapes foreign to the ceramic traditions of the southern Levant (Philip 1999: 38–40, figs. 4–5). While generally seen as the hallmark of the EB III period in northern Palestine, the distribution of Khirbat Kerak ware is concentrated in the northern part of the Jordan Valley (Esse 1991; Philip 1999). The only substantial excavated assemblage from Jordan is that from Tall Shuna, where the wide range of vessel forms, including pot-stands, vessel lids and portable hearths, as well as shapes more typical of the local industry, such as bowls and platters (Figure 6.9), suggest the presence of a production centre (Philip 1999: 43).

Esse (1991: table 4, fig. 25) notes that occurrences of Khirbat Kerak ware outside the "core" area of the north Jordan Valley tend to be restricted to the smaller bowl forms. While this appears to hold in the case of southern sites, the presence of a one-handled vessel at Khirbat Zaraqun (Mittmann 1994: 10) and part of a stand and a piece of an incised vessel from a tomb at Arqub adh-Dhahr (Parr 1956, nos. 208, 214), suggests that we have much to learn concerning the distribution of Khirbat Kerak ware on the north Jordan plateau. Scholars have generally interpreted Khirbat Kerak ware in terms of

the arrival of new population groups, ultimately of east Anatolian origin (Hennessy 1967: 79; Esse 1991: 139–140). There are difficulties with this view however (Philip 1999: 35–36). It is noteworthy that Khirbat Kerak ware lacks many of the ceramic forms most closely associated with the "classic" Early Bronze Age agricultural economy—jugs and juglets, storage vessels, large platter bowls—and Philip (1999) has argued that scholars seeking to explain the appearance of this pottery should focus upon the socio-economic status of the user communities.

Other Aspects of EB III Ceramics

EB III pottery in the local tradition is now well represented throughout Jordan (Figure 6.11.1–5): on the plateau at Khirbat Zaraqun near Irbid (Genz 2002) and at Tall Umayri south of Amman (Harrison 2000a, 2000b); in the Jordan Valley at Tall Handaquq (S) (Chesson 2000); and at Bab adh-Dhra and Numayra in the Southern Ghor (Schaub and Rast 1989; Rast and Schaub 2003). Specific forms that appear to be diagnostic of EB III include deep bowls with flattened inverted rims (hammer-rimmed), red-brown slipped and burnished platters with inverted or vertical rims, bearing a small external groove below the rim, and juglets with piriform (pear-shaped) bodies and narrow stump bases, all clearly developments from familiar EB I–II forms.

EB III material from north Jordan is typified by that from the final occupation phase at Khirbat Zaraqun. This

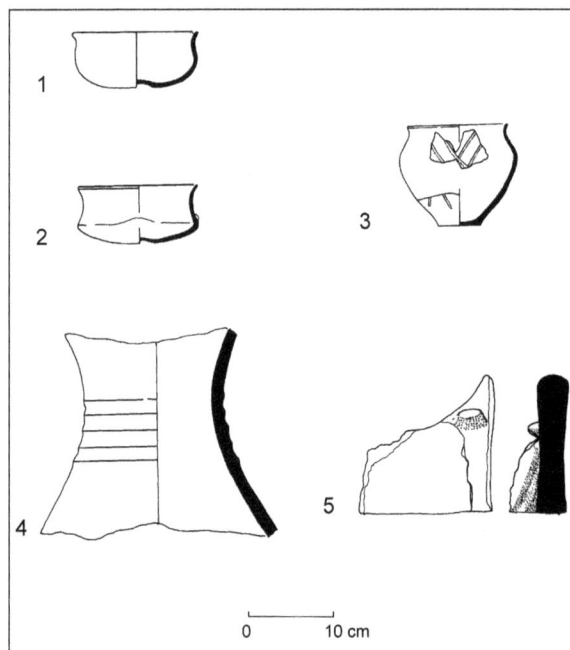

Figure 6.9 Khirbat Kerak ware vessels from Tall Shuna (drawn by Y. Beadnell). 1–2: Bowls. 3: Jar. 4: Pot-stand. 5: Part of portable horseshoe-shaped hearth.

site provides not only a characteristic assemblage, but also real insight into the role of ceramics within the economy and daily life. Storage vessels were common. Necked jars with loop handles could hold contents up to a volume of 20–30 litres, while large pithoi, some as much as 1 m in height, could hold well over 100 litres, up to 140 litres in some cases (Genz 2002: 90, table 58, abb. 6–7). Some were in a fabric resembling what appears to be Metallic Ware, and bore vertical combing and horizontal applied rope decoration at the neck. These may represent the continuation in a narrower range of forms of the Metallic Ware industry of the EB II period. The continued appearance in clear EB III contexts of Band Slip decoration on large storage vessels (Genz 2000: 280) has important implications for its use as a dating criterion. Deep-combed inverted rim bowls with spout and loop handles (Genz 2002: abb. 5d) may be connected with olive oil production (Stager 1985: 176–177; Esse 1991: 119–124), although some have expressed doubts as to this interpretation (de Miroschedji 2000b: 326).

A considerable quantity of ceramics relating to the latest occupational phase at Khirbat Zaraqun were restorable, providing an insight into the distribution of different vessel types (Genz 2002: 96–100, tables 60–69). The assemblage from the administrative complex in the Upper City included a high proportion of storage jars (Figure 6.10), while that from the lower settlement, assumed to reflect domestic activity, revealed a markedly higher proportion of cooking and serving vessels. The association between administrative buildings and the bulk storage of agricultural products is very clear in this case (Genz 2003a: 68). That said, the upper city lacked large quantities of obviously special purpose vessels, perhaps suggesting that pottery played relatively little part in the marking of status in daily life. It is therefore worth noting that juglets, which are such a characteristic feature of EB II–III grave assemblages (Rast and Schaub 1989), constituted no more than 1% of the settlement ceramics (Genz 2002: 28, table 4). We must conclude that these vessels played a particular role in mortuary contexts, perhaps because of the "value" which arose from their association with precious commodities such as fine or scented oils. Presumably these were deemed appropriate offerings for the dead, either at the time of interment, or perhaps in ceremonies connected with the commemoration of the ancestors.

In general, EB III material from south-central Jordan (Figure 6.11.1–5) compares well typologically with that from central and southern Palestine (Harrison 2000b: 360). The EB III repertoire of the central-southern plateau is typified by that from Tall Umayri, and consists of a variety of jars, including examples of both flaring and hole-mouth forms, a range of platter bowls, some with inturned rims, and small bowls decorated with vertical bands of red paint (Harrison 2000a, 2000b). Small–medium-sized bowls and hole-mouth jars are dominant

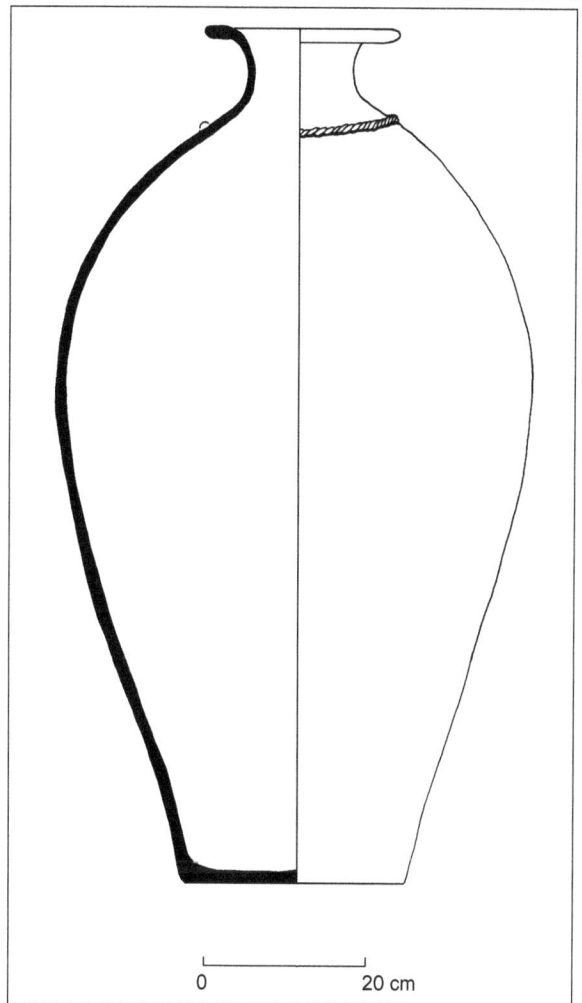

Figure 6.10 Khirbat Zaraqun, large EB III storage jar; note that the applied rope-like clay band at the neck lies in the place where a seal impression would be placed (drawn by Y. Beadnell).

numerically, while the use of ledge handles on storage jars and the presence of jars with a "combed" exterior bearing a white chalky slip are characteristic of southern sites (Harrison 2000b: 353–355). Overall, both northern and southern assemblages appear to represent direct continuations of local EB II traditions, rendering Khirbat Kerak ware all the more distinctive in comparison.

A technical study by London *et al.* (1991) has revealed that at Tall Umayri a range of pot-forming techniques and fabrics were employed for different vessel types, leading London (1991: 394) to suggest that different parts of the ceramic repertoire were produced by different potters, possibly working on different bases. Petrographic studies of EB II–III pottery from sites in the Southern Ghor (Rast and Schaub 2003) indicate a mainly local production, with some movement of specific products between

Bab adh-Dhra and Numayra, but with little evidence for a significant input of material from outside the Southern Ghor area. It is striking that assemblages, which in the case of individual sites develop from the coalescence of a number of different strands of ceramic production, appear quite similar when viewed on a site-to-site comparative basis. This reinforces the idea that the underlying pattern of demand reflected a fairly uniform set of requirements, itself indicative of quite similar social and economic practices.

Stone

Chipped Stone

Studies of Early Bronze Age chipped stone have focused upon the most distinctive artefact types, the so-called Canaanean blades and tabular scrapers.

Sickles

The sickle elements known as Canaanean blades were long parallel-sided blades of distinctive trapezoidal cross-section, struck from a prepared, single platform core (S.A. Rosen 1997a: 46–49). The resulting long blades could be snapped to produce shorter segments 4–6 cm in length, which were mounted in groups of five to six, set into notches on a wooden handle; a partly preserved example was recovered from destruction debris at Tall Abu Kharaz (Fischer 1994: fig. 11.4). EB I examples from Tall Iktanu revealed polish on one edge, believed to be indicative of the reaping of grasses, while the opposite edge frequently bore traces of bitumen intended to fix the blade to a haft (McCartney 1996: 145).

This blade form does not derive from earlier local flint-working traditions, but is related to a technological complex spanning the Levant, north Syria and Anatolia. In the southern Levant, blades are usually made from brown, fine-grained, Eocene flint nodules, and caches of unretouched examples found at several sites in Palestine and at Tall Iktanu in Jordan provide evidence for their distribution as unfinished blades (McCartney 1996: 145; S.A. Rosen 1997a: 141). This fact, plus the lack of manufacturing debris recovered from most excavations, suggests specialized production. The absence of evidence for production at major tell sites, with the exception of EB III Tell Halif (Futato 1996), argues, however, that manufacture was not organized by political elites, and that these blades constitute a good example of a utilitarian specialist product produced and distributed independently of political power structures (Hayden 1994: 200). The predominant use of Eocene flint for blade production appears to confirm Costin's (1991: 13–15) suggestion that (as with Metallic Ware) crafts organized on such a basis may be based upon raw materials of uneven distribution. Rosen's point that production was largely based within rural set-

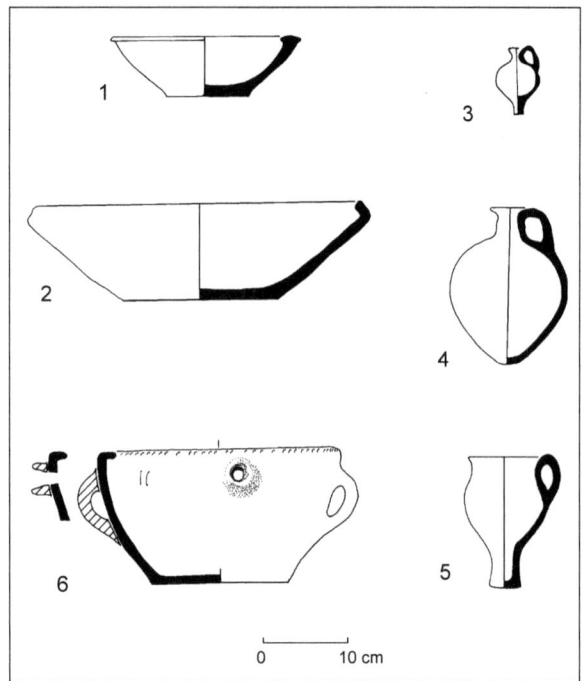

Figure 6.11 EB III pottery from Bab adh-Dhra (1–5). 1–2: Platter-bowls with inverted rim. 3–5. Jug forms with characteristic pointed and stump bases. 6: Khirbat Zaraqun, vat, possibly used in the processing of olive oil (drawn by Y. Beadnell).

tlements is consistent with such an interpretation, and is supported by their continued occurrence during EB IV (S.A. Rosen 1997a: 108 and 143), at which point major centres had effectively disappeared.

At Bab adh-Dhra, Canaanean blades occur in small quantites from EB IB onwards, and they are present at EB III Numayra (McConaughty 1980, 2003). Production debris is absent, however, and the raw material appears to be largely non-local in origin (McConaughty 2003: 479). In contrast, those blades made using local raw materials are of triangular cross-section and appear to have developed from local Chalcolithic traditions (McConaughty 2003: 504). Similar blades are found in the arid areas of southern Palestine (S.A. Rosen 1997a: 141), suggesting, as does the paucity of Canaanean blades reported from sites on the Karak Plateau (Chesson *et al.* 2005: 44), that despite the superficial cultural homogeneity which characterized the southern Levant during EB II–III, innovations could be taken up differentially. Parts of southern Jordan, then, appear to have retained particular flint-working local traditions.

Tabular Scrapers

Tabular scrapers (S.A. Rosen 1997a: 71–79) are a feature of Chalcolithic assemblages and consist of large retouched flakes, showing the deliberate retention of cortex over most of the dorsal surface. They vary in shape and measure on average 15–20 cm long by 1 cm thick (Futato 1996: 61). The previously known quarry sites are concentrated in the southern Negev and Sinai, and have recently been joined by evidence for large-scale production in the Jafr region of southeast Jordan, where a connection between the long-range distribution of such tools and the activities of pastoral groups has been confirmed (Quintero *et al.* 2002).

As regards function, they are best seen as hand-held knives, suitable for resharpening, and used for a range of activities (Quintero *et al.* 2002: 46). The idea that some were used as butchering tools may find support in their occurrence in what are interpreted as cult contexts at Bab adh-Dhra and several Palestinian sites (S.A. Rosen 1997a: 74). Another possible use is for the shearing of wool-bearing sheep (Henry 1995: 372). It may not be fortuitous that the massive expansion in their production is broadly contemporary with a significant increase in the scale and visibility of human activity in the steppe, a landscape well suited to exploitation by animal-herding groups. Whatever the case, it is clear that tabular scrapers and Canaanean blades were produced and distributed on rather different bases, and that neither of these economically-significant products provides convincing evidence for centralized economic direction.

Ad Hoc Production

In the case of both Tall Umm Hammad and Bab adh-Dhra (Betts 1992: 122–123; McConaughty 2003: 487) on-site flint working was limited to the fashioning of "irregular" tools from flakes struck from local cherts obtained as wadi cobble. Flake cores were numerous at the latter site, but blade cores have not been recovered (McConaughty 2003: 480), which indicates that specialist blade production was undertaken off site. One possible location was provided by the extensive scatters of chipped stone debris in the fields below the site noted by Rast and Schaub (1974: 4). Sadly, the area was bulldozed before it could be recorded. Thus, there existed a separation between "imported" specialized and *ad hoc* tools, produced locally as required, presumably at a household level. The apparent lack of an equivalent element in late fourth-millennium BC, chipped stone assemblages from Mesopotamia (Pope and Pollock 1995) highlights the organizational differences between the economies of the two areas.

Groundstone

The groundstone industry of the Early Bronze Age has not been subject to a comprehensive study and is often inadequately reported in archaeological publications. By analogy with earlier periods (Hanbury-Tenison 1986; Wright 1993), one would expect this to include a sub-stantial body of heavy food-processing tools, mortars, rubbers, pounders and so on. The stone chosen appears to vary according to local availability. There also existed a range of finely-manufactured basalt vessels, generally with flat bases and flaring walls that tapered towards the rim (Beebe 1989; Braun 1990). These appear in both grave and settlement contexts (Figure 6.12.2).

Our understanding of the procurement and use of groundstone for artefact production has changed significantly in recent years. It is clear from sites such as Tall Shuna (where basalt completely dominates the repertory of groundstone tools) that when this rock type was readily available it was by far the favoured material for the production of tools such as grinders, rubbers etc. As the case of Bab adh-Dhra demonstrates very well, when basalt was less immediately available, other rock-types available in the vicinity such as sandstone, or even limestone, would be employed (Lee 2003: 632). In essence this part of the economy can be seen as very much a local enterprise.

In contrast, the basalt vessels which are a very characteristic feature of the EB I period in particular (Beebe 1989; Braun 1990), appear to have been obtained on a quite different basis. Recent geochemical studies (Philip and Williams-Thorpe 2001; Rutter *et al.* 2003; Rutter and Philip in press) have indicated that despite the extensive range of basalt outcrops available in the southern Levant, the material used for bowl production derived from a very limited range of sources, with a particular concentration upon material from the north Jordan Valley and the area around Jabal Shaykh (Mount Hermon). Vessels made in basalt from these sources are now documented from sites in north Jordan, Palestine, and Maadi in Egypt. Clearly there existed an extensive network for the distribution of these artefacts. The EB I vessels examined from sites and cemeteries in the Southern Ghor and Faynan areas (Figure 6.12.2) are, however, chemically distinct from the remaining material. These appear to have originated, not in the north, but from basalt outcrops located on the Karak Plateau. This smaller-scale, regional distribution system may represent an attempt by communities in south-central Jordan to create a local equivalent, in emulation of a network to which they may have had limited access, and points to a real sense of local identity in this area.

Metals

Copper

The most frequently used metal was copper; the repertoire of artefacts is similar to that from Palestine. Weapons occur in a few EB III tombs, and include narrow-bladed daggers with a wooden handle attached by rivets (Philip 1989: 103–104, type 2) and crescent-shaped axes from Bab adh-Dhra (Figure 6.12.1) (Philip 1989: 45–46, type 1). With the exception of a single tin–bronze weapon

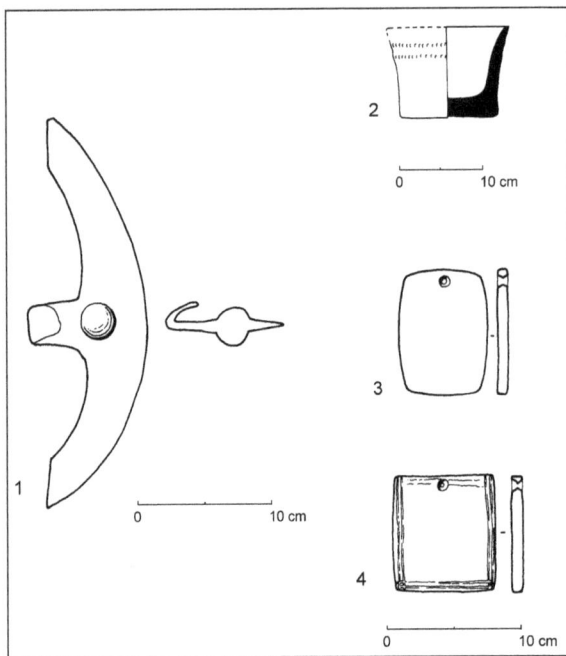

Figure 6.12 Metal and groundstone artefacts from Bab adh-Dhra (drawn by Y. Beadnell). 1: Crescentic Axe from Bab adh-Dhra, Tomb A 44, EB III. 2: Basalt vessel from Bab adh-Dhra, Tomb A 70, EB IA. 3–4: Siltstone palettes from EB II–III graves at Bab adh-Dhra.

from Bab adh-Dhra, this being of a type with its best parallels in the north (Maddin *et al.* 2003: 514, 520, table 17.1), they are all made from unalloyed copper. Characteristic metal tools include flat axes and chisels, along with a variety of awls and other smaller items. Recent finds include an EB II "hoard" of metal objects from Pella (Bourke 1997), recently also confimed as copper rather than bronze (Philip *et al.* 2003: 86–87), an axe and chisel from domestic contexts at Tall Abu Kharaz (Fischer 1993: 285), and a group of EB III copper adzes from Numayra (Rast and Schaub 1980: 44).

The most important recent development with regard to copper metallurgy in Early Bronze Age Jordan has been the revelation of the scale of mining and metal production at Faynan (Hauptmann 2000; Adams 1999, 2002). Copper-working, as opposed to extraction, was, however, widely dispersed throughout the southern Levant (Golden 2002: 235). In southern Jordan, evidence for metalworking occurs at Tall Magass and Hujayrat Ghuzlan near Aqaba (Khalil 1992: 144; Khalil and Eichmann 2001: 200). At the opposite end of Jordan, a late EB I midden deposit at Tall Shuna has produced metalworking debris including round-based crucibles, small rectangular moulds and metal prills (Rehren *et al.* 1997). The moulds from this site appear designed not to cast tools, but small rectangular copper blocks or thin ingots, perhaps designed

for hammering to form copper sheet, or to produce small billets of standard size for subsequent redistribution. Later copper-working evidence comes from Room 15 in the EB III settlement of Numayra (Coogan 1984: 77) and, taken together, the dispersed nature of artefact production and the consistent artefact repertoire argues for widely-held culturally-determined notions of appropriate forms, that is, the communication and sharing of concepts at a spatial level well beyond that of potential political units.

Recent archaeometallurgical research (Hauptmann *et al.* 1999) suggests that contrary to previous assumptions, the main source of the copper used at the EB II site of Arad in the northern Negev was not Sinai, but Faynan. When considered alongside Adams' (2003: 17) suggestion that the distinctive arkosic-tempered ceramics from Arad also originated in Faynan, the evidence for links between the two areas becomes very clear. The continued importance of the area as a copper source into EB III–IV has been clarified by the discovery at Khirbat Hamra Ifdan of a major production centre for not only copper tools, but also metal ingots (see Palumbo this volume, Figure 12, p. 253). In fact, ingots from EB IV sites in southern Palestine can be shown on geochemical grounds to have derived from Faynan ores (T.E. Levy and Adams *et al.* 2002: 435, fig. 7).

It would be misleading, however, to assume the existence of a single monolithic copper industry deriving all raw material from Faynan. The copper recovered from Tall Shuna contained both arsenic and nickel at around 2%, a composition incompatible with any ore yet identified at Faynan (Rehren *et al.* 1997). Further confirmation comes from lead-isotope analysis of five EB II copper objects from Pella which revealed isotopic compositions compatible with copper sources on Cyprus and in the Taurus Mountains, as well as Faynan (Philip *et al.* 2003: 86–87, table 4). Thus while Faynan copper may well have been of great importance to consumers in southern Palestine and Jordan, sites in the north may have had access to metal from a wider range of sources.

Most of the models employed by archaeologists for the reconstruction of past communities tend to associate large scale, specialist production with the existence of some form of economic and political control (e.g. Adams 2002: 30). However, there is as yet no material evidence from Faynan for the existence of a central place, or even a local elite who might have controlled copper production. Admittedly, it is possible that major Early Bronze Age structures are buried below later deposits, for example at the large and virtually untouched site of Khirbat Faynan, or that given the limitations imposed by the aridity of the area, control over copper resources was exercised in a manner that left little direct archaeological evidence.

There are, however, other arguments against elite control. The hoards from Kfar Monash in Palestine and Pella in Jordan (Hestrin and Tadmor 1963; Bourke 1997) indicate that metal artefacts were in circulation in some quantity by the EB I–II periods. Genz (2001), however, has noted the contrast between the scale of evidence for copper production at EB II–III Faynan, the relatively low number of metal artefacts appearing in contemporary graves, and the lack of evidence for a clear association between metalworking and any of the non-domestic architectural units thus far excavated in Jordan. Moreover, the concentration of metal weapons from burials at Bab adh-Dhra in tombs of clear EB III date (Maddin *et al.* 2003: 518), might suggest that these artefacts were only beginning to assume their "conventional" role as markers of high status in the latter stages of the Early Bronze Age.

Taken together, these arguments could be used to argue against political control over the copper industry and that the production and circulation of metal aretfacts, like that of chipped stone and ceramics, was undertaken by independent specialists, perhaps organized at the level of kinship group or community. Although the evidence suggests that this might have begun to change during EB III, it seems that for much of the Early Bronze Age metal may have circulated through everyday social and economic networks, that is, within the fabric of everyday life, not as a special commodity, access to which was strictly controlled by elites. The contrast between the paucity of metalwork in grave contexts and the marked emphasis upon containers for storing agricultural products provides a clear pointer as to the principles underlying notions of "appropriateness" as constructed by Early Bronze Age communities.

Gold and Silver

Both gold and silver artefacts are rare in the southern Levant. Neither metal occurs locally; the nearest gold sources are in Egypt, silver in Anatolia (Moorey 1994). Several pieces of gold leaf jewellery come from EB II–III charnel house A 22 at Bab adh-Dhra, while a group of gold beads and tiny gold spacers appears to belong to a necklace (Rast and Schaub 1980: fig. 14). Silver artefacts are known from late EB I contexts at Tall Shuna (a pin and a fragment of silver sheet) and Bab adh-Dhra (Philip and Rehren 1996). Analysis (Rehren *et al.* 1996) has revealed both silver artefacts from Tall Shuna to be artificial alloys, containing a few per cent each of gold and copper, the latter presumably added to harden the metal (Moorey 1994: 238). The use of gold–silver alloys by ancient craftsmen, suggests that smiths had little idea of the exact nature of their material, and perhaps indicates the presence within the region of a supply of partly recycled precious metal "stock." The presence of silver or gold artefacts does not, therefore, constitute evidence for direct contacts with either Egypt or Anatolia.

Seals and Sealings

Seal impressions from the southern Levant appear exclus-

ively on sherds from ceramic storage containers. They were formed by rolling a cylinder seal repeatedly to impress a continuous band of design on the vessel's shoulder (Figure 6.13.2). The technique has good parallels in Early Bronze Age Syria (Collon 1987: 113; Mazzoni 2003, with further references). At first glance, the sealing of containers would appear to provide a means of administrative control over commodity storage, and so be consistent with a system of staple finance. In Mesopotamia, however, seals were employed in such a manner as to link sealing events with individual transactions and thus constitute a complete administrative system—door sealings, bale and basket tags, bullae, etc. (Collon 1987: 113). The evidence from Jordan is different (Joffe 2001: 359–360).

The corpus of Early Bronze Age sealings from Jordan has grown to more than 160, recovered from at least 15 sites (Vieweger 1997: 151; Flender 2000). Geographically, sealings are not distributed evenly across the region, but show a marked concentration in north Palestine and Jordan (Flender 2000: 297, fig. 17.2). The largest single group from Jordan comes from Khirbat Zaraqun which has produced more than 140 seal impressions, made using around 120 different seals (Flender 2000: 295). The sheer variety and lack of repeated designs make it hard to see this as evidence of an administrative system. Moreover, when seals are compared at a regional level, the absence of motifs specific to individual sites implies that whatever information was encoded it must have been highly generalized (Greenberg 2001: 193).

Moreover, vessels were only impressed once, and this prior to firing. As a result, whatever information was encoded in seal impressions must have been decided within the potter's workshop (Joffe 2001: 361). In fact, by far the majority of the seal impressions from Khirbat Zaraqun occurred on jars of one type, so-called Metallic Ware pithoi (Figure 6.10). These are large coil-built storage vessels with a capacity of around 100 litres (Flender 2000: 296). A strong association between seal impressions and Metallic Ware jars is also seen in Palestine (Greenberg 2001: 189), and petrographic data suggest that this very distinctive class of vessel was produced and distributed from a single location in the region of Jabal Shaikh/Mount Hermon (Greenberg and Porat 1996; Greenberg 2001: 191–192). As it is hard to see how the marking of vessels in the potters' workshop could be adapted to the specific requirements of administrative practices at individual sites, we must look for other, rather more mundane explanations.

Many Metallic Ware pithoi were not seal-impressed. Instead they bore applied clay rope-decoration in the same position around the base of the neck (Figure 6.10), that is, at the potentially weak neck-body junction. In fact, it is possible that sealing had no communicative function at all, but simply served a technical purpose connected to vessel manufacture. In this case, the use of seals by Metal-

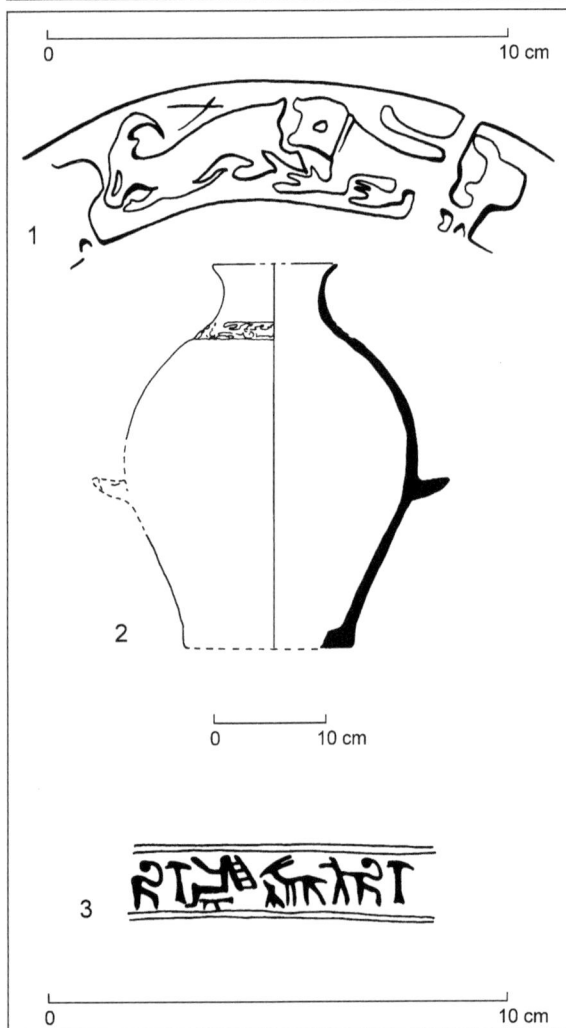

Figure 6.13 Sealing practices from EBA Jordan (drawn by Y. Beadnell). 1: Sealing employing zoomorphic motif, Bab adh-Dhra, No. 1301. 2: Position of seal impression on storage vessel; note how the seal has been rolled around the neck of the vessel.
3: Impression of cylinder seal bearing design which includes a seated female figure, Bab adh-Dhra, No. 2823.

from Tall Umayri (Harrison 2000a: 152, fig. 52.9; Daviau 1991: 6.24:17) and the Karak Plateau (Brown 1991: 179, no. 64), plus a small but significant group from Bab adh-Dhra (Lapp 2003) (Figure 6.13.1, 3). In this area impressions are fewer and the association between sealing and Metallic Ware no longer holds. The seals and sealings from Bab adh-Dhra demonstrate that practices in this area differed in many ways from those in the north. Impressions appear on vessels made in a range of local ceramic wares, and while these mostly appeared on large closed vessels there is not the clear association with a particular vessel type that is documented at Khirbat Zaraqun (Lapp 2003: 525, 545).

Such inconsistency of practice clearly argues against a single systematic function for sealing in the south, and Lapp (2003: 548–549) thinks that the overall lack of pattern points to sealing as a decorative device. There is also some evidence which suggests that elements of the seal designs occurring at Bab adh-Dhra are drawn from Egyptian imagery rather than from that of the north, with at least one seal (Bab adh-Dhra No. 2823, Figure 6.13.3) having good Egyptian First Dynasty parallels (Lapp 2003: 526, 551).

Sealing in Early Bronze Age Jordan cannot be deployed as convincing evidence for complex administrative systems but represents no more than an idea adopted from what Joffe (1993: 56) has termed "a distant and undifferentiated Syro-Mesopotamian world," stripped of its original meaning and subsequently reinterpreted in a local context. If practices in north Jordan represented an attenuated version of those of Syro-Mesopotamia, then those documented in the south were yet one more stage removed.

Other Artefacts

Although a number of additional artefact forms are reported from Early Bronze Age sites in Jordan, the range and variety is quite limited. There do exist inter-site distinctions in the material, however, presumably related to the kind of diversity of local practices that might underlie distinctive regional ceramic and architectural styles.

Bone, Clay, Shell and Stone

Two particular classes of artefact stand out, both of which are frequently treated as *objets d'art* (Ben-Tor 1992: 121). The function and significance of decorated bone tubes, distributed widely throughout Syria and the Levant remains uncertain, although Genz favours an interpretation as cosmetic containers (see Zarzecki-Peleg 1993; Genz 2003b). Examples from Jordan, include one from Tall Shuna, probably of EBA date, and several EB III instances from Khirbat Zaraqun, that is, a largely northern distribution. An EB III bull's head from Charnel House A 21 at Bab adh-Dhra (Wilkinson 1989: 458, fig. 262.2) belongs to a group of small carved bovine heads known

lic Ware potters might simply indicate their appropriation of a practice which they knew to be associated with ceramic jars in Syria, but of which they had a limited understanding. An example of one very basic way in which sealing might have conveyed information is provided by Flender (2000: 303), who has suggested that the difference between sealed vessels and those with rope decoration could have been determined by touch, and that this might have provided the basis of a very simple way of differentiating between vessels storing two different classes or qualities of product in poorly-lit storage complexes.

In south-central Jordan, seal impressions are known

from EB II–III contexts in Palestine (de Miroschedji 1993b). One might speculate that, lacking other types of animal figurine in the Early Bronze Age, the choice of bovids indicates an association with draft animals and, thus, with agricultural productivity.

Unbaked clay figurines with upraised arms are so far unique to graves at Bab adh-Dhra (Wilkinson 1989) and may represent a phenomenon of particular significance at that site. Contacts with the Red Sea area are revealed through shell bracelets that occur in EB I tombs at Bab adh-Dhra, at Tall Magass near Aqaba (Khalil 1992: 1.3, 1.6–8), and in great numbers at Safi-Nage (Adams pers. com.). The beads from the former site reveal the wide geogrpahical range of material acquired, including copper ore from Faynan, shells from both the Mediterranean and Red Seas, and several in hippopotamous and one made from elephant ivory (Broeder and Skinner 2003: 591–592).

Similar artefacts are found in Palestine, Sinai and Egypt (Wilkinson 1989) and highlight contacts with the arid zone to the south. Seven "schist" or "grey stone" palettes, mostly perforated and of rectangular shape, were recovered from EB II–III graves at Bab adh-Dhra (Figure 6.12.3–4; Wilkinson 1989: 453–455, fig. 261). These resemble the Egyptian stone cosmetic palettes discussed by Petrie (1921), made from grey siltstone (Klemm and Klemm 1993: 369). Similar palettes are known from Chalcolithic and Early Bronze Age sites in Palestine and are believed to be Egyptian imports (Ben-Tor 1992: 94), although "local" examples occur in such materials as limestone and granite (Hennessy 1967: 32; Brandl 1992: 447). At Bab adh-Dhra, the apparent lack of palettes in local stone suggests that it may have been important to produce palettes in stones with particular characteristics of colour and texture. Additional examples are reported from the Early Bronze Age occupation at Tall Umayri (Geraty *et al.* 1986: 135).

Jacobs (1996: 130) notes that a number of such palettes found in the southern Levant come from EB III contexts, which would place them several centuries later than their closest stylistic parallels from Egypt, a pattern that extends to those from Bab adh-Dhra. This apparent chronological discrepancy receives support from recent work at Minshat Abu Omar (Kroeper 1996: 72), where palettes do not occur after MAO IV, that is, First to mid-Second Dynasty (Kroeper 1996: 81–82, fig. 8). Although reducing the gap somewhat, these are still considerably earlier than the EB III dates of some examples from the Levant. Palettes found in the southern Levant are frequently perforated (Wilkinson 1989: fig. 269; Jacobs 1996: figs. 1, 3, 6), which is rarely the case with Egyptian examples, suggesting that this type of artefact may have been reinterpreted in a Levantine context, and may not simply represent the direct adoption of an Egyptian custom.

Evidence for Connections with Egypt

One of the major changes in our understanding of Palestinian archaeology in recent years has been the growing evidence for a significant Egyptian involvement in the region during the later fourth millennium BC. However, in contrast to the sheer quantity of Egyptian and Egyptianising material from sites in southwestern Palestine (de Miroschedji 2002b, with further references), the evidence from EB I Bab adh-Dhra and the apparent insularity of Wadi Fidan 4 do not point towards large-scale Egyptian connections with south Jordan. In fact, prior to the expansion of copper production in Faynan it is hard to see what was available in Jordan that the Egyptians could not have readily obtained elsewhere in the Levant. The situation may have changed in the third millennium BC, and Adams (2002) has argued that the key factor driving the increase in copper production at Faynan in EB II was increased demand from Egypt. While this is certainly a possibility, and there is some evidence to support a possible trade route from Faynan across the Negev to Egypt in the later third millennium BC (Adams 1999, 2000; Levy and Adams *et al.* 2002), the evidence which would confirm such a trade in the earlier periods is not yet available.

Items such as the siltstone palettes discussed above, or the occasional pots, stone vessels or maceheads from sites in the Jordan Valley or Southern Ghor (e.g. Papadopoulos *et al.* 2001: 198, fig.4; Fischer 2002) provide no firm basis for a significant Egyptian role in Early Bronze Age Jordan. That said, we must be careful to consider evidence for Egyptian contact of a kind rather more subtle than that documented in southwestern Palestine. There is just such evidence from northern Palestine and the Jordan Valley. An unusual group of Egyptian-style ceramic vessels made using local clays at Early Bronze Age Megiddo, only 30 km west of the Jordan River (Joffe 2000: 170) is intriguing for what it implies about patterns of demand. An EB II style jug from Khirbat Karak on Lake Tiberias, which bears an incised hieroglyphic graffito (Greenberg and Eisenberg 2002: 214) might indicate the presence of an Egyptian agent of some kind in the north Jordan Valley in the early third millennium BC. It is possible, therefore, that there may have been some mechanism for Egyptian demand reaching into Jordan, despite the absence of any echoes of the more obvious settlement activity documented in the south.

Jordan During Early Bronze Age I–III: An Image

This chapter has put forward an alternative to the traditional city-state model for the Early Bronze Age. In the absence of clear evidence for the presence of institutionalized elites, it is argued that the distinctive archaeological record of Early Bronze Age Jordan indicates, in the main, prosperous village communities, in which a well developed agricultural base provided the resources necessary for undertaking major projects on a corporate basis. Within these communities, wealth was understood in terms of land and productive facilities, a significant change in the symbolism of power compared to the preceding Chalcolithic.

Individual households, and larger supra-household kinship-based groups, are seen as constituting the basic units of action at many levels. While a staple finance model appears to offer the most appropriate way to conceive the political economy, there remains a lack of clarity as to who controlled the commodities collected. Many aspects of the economy, including much craft production, is, however, seen as focused upon independent specialists. Evidence for attached specialists is hard to identify. There is little to indicate that economic and political power were systematically linked in such a way as to offer a basis for sustained monopolistic control. Greater regional interaction over time is attributed to demand resulting from increasing economic specialization, intended to produce additional resources for investment rather than for elite consumption.

There is evidence from Palestine for growing centralization and inequality during EB III (Joffe 1993: 86–87; de Miroschedji 1999), and this may reflect the growing consolidation of disparities in wealth and power between different kin groups, a point perhaps reflected in burial practices at Bab adh-Dhra which hint at growing disparities between the better and less well provisioned charnel houses (Chesson 1999, 2001). While the evidence from Tell Yarmouth, Megiddo and Khirbat Zaraqun suggests that during EB III more effort was being devoted to the construction of public architecture, and also points to a growing system of control over agricultural products, many areas of Jordan, such as the Madaba region and the Karak Plateau, appear to have remained outside this process. While this is not the place to discuss the demise of EB III society in the southern Levant (see Palumbo, this volume), it is worth emphasizing that it is in the latter areas where we see the best evidence for continuity of settlement into EB IV.

In fact, the outstanding characteristic of this period is the relatively slow rates of change apparent in many aspects of material culture. This may be attributable to the absence of the elite-driven, competitive dynamic that appears so influential in the transformation of society, economy and material culture in later periods (see Sherratt and Sherratt 1991). One might suggest that the evidence from the southern Levant, Jordan in particular, provides a rare glimpse of the form taken by complex societies in the area when exploitative, conspicuously consuming elites, the presence of whom is so clear in contemporary Mesopotamia, did not exist. Because of this, Chesson and Philip (2003) have recently suggested that the most useful archaeological comparisons for the southern Levant

in the Early Bronze Age may lie not to the north and east but in Cyprus and the Aegean.

Interludes of occupation at many walled sites appear to have been relatively short, or punctuated, suggesting that these did not represent the core structuring elements of the local economic system. By viewing walled settlements as part of a wider landscape including cemeteries, cult sites and agricultural plots we can begin to take a more holistic and richly textured view of the period. The existence of major east-west ceramic style zones has been noted more than once. While these clearly hint at systems of communication running from the Jordanian plateau towards the Mediterranean coast, in line with Stager's (2001) suggestion that economic networks existed to draw resources from inland areas to the Mediterranean, we must remember that these would have run in both directions. Just as recent research has emphasized the importance of access to the Mediterranean for developments in Palestine (Marcus 2002; de Miroschedji 2002b; Philip 2002), the scale of developments in the arid zone during the EBA, a region to which agricultural settlements in western Jordan had prime access, suggests that it would be a mistake to view Jordan simply as a hinterland.

The extent of both defended sites and burial monuments in marginal areas along the Rift Valley escarpment and along the eastern fringes of the arid zone indicates that walled settlements were not simply associated with communities practising intensive agriculture, but had become a symbolic statement, a resource capable of being reworked in a variety of contexts. Moreover, as the evidence grows for the economic importance of groups exploiting the steppe and their connections with societies to the west, we can begin to see a context within which these ideas might have been developed.

In trying to understand Early Bronze Age Jordan we should probably think less in terms of fixed locations, and more of patterns of movement. We need to imagine a landscape that was experienced by individuals and groups as they moved around it, rather than one which was envisaged from a single focal point. The main ceramic style zones were constituted at a spatial scale well beyond that encompassed by individual settlement clusters. If these form a guide to regular patterns of communication, however, then the numerous groups of burial monuments located along the Jordan Valley escarpment would have formed an integral component of the landscape through which significant numbers of people would have moved. The location of fortified sites in prominent positions, high above key east-west wadi courses might also be seen in the same light.

Acknowledgements

I am grateful to Dr Russell Adams for inviting me to produce an updated version of my 2001 chapter from *The Archaeology of Jordan*. Having begun, I immediately realized how much new information had appeared since the previous version was finalized, and I now wish that I had not agreed quite so rapidly. I have attempted, however, to reflect the main advances in knowledge since the late 1990s, as far as time and resources have allowed, and must simply ask the reader's forbearance for any significant omissions.

I also owe a real debt to various Directors and staff of the Department of Antiquities of Jordan, who have encouraged and facilitated my research in many ways over the years, and to the British Institute at Amman for Archaeology and History (now the Council for British Research in the Levant), which provided both the opportunity and means to investigate many of the issues raised here through archaeological field work at the EB I site of Tall Shuna. I am grateful also to Mrs Yvonne Beadnell, who prepared the original line-drawings, many of which are reprinted here. Finally, I should acknowledge the supportive role of my family, who have shown immense forbearance in the face of sustained archaeological provocation.

Bibliography

Adams, R.

1999 The Development of Copper Metallurgy During the Early Bronze Age of the Southern Levant: Evidence from the Faynan Region, Southern Jordan. Unpublished PhD Thesis, Department of Archaeology and Prehistory, Sheffield University.

2000 The Early Bronze Age III–IV Transition in Southern Jordan: Evidence from *Khirbet Hamra Ifdan*. In G. Philip and D. Baird (eds.), *Ceramics and Change in the Early Bronze Age of the Southern Levant*, 379–401. Sheffield: Sheffield Academic Press.

2002 From Farms to Factories: The Development of Copper Production at Faynan during the Early Bronze Age. In B. S. Ottaway and E. C. Wagner, *Metals in Society*, 24–35. British Archaeological Reports International Series 1061. Oxford: Archaeopress.

2003 External Influences at Faynan during the Early Bronze Age: A Re-analysis of Building 1 at Barqa el-Hetiye, Jordan. *Palestine Exploration Quarterly* 127: 8–20.

2006 Copper Trading Networks Across the Wadi Arabah During the Later Early Bronze Age. In P. Bienkowski and K Galor (eds.) *Crossing the Rift: Resources, Routes, Settlement Patterns and Interaction in the Wadi Arabah*, 137–144. Council for British Research in the Levant Monograph. London: Council for British Research in the Levant.

Adams, R. and H. Genz

1995 Excavations at Wadi Fidan 4, a Chalcolithic Village Complex in the Copper Ore District of Feinan, Southern Jordan. *Palestine Exploration Quarterly* 127: 8–20.

Adams, R. McC.

1966 *The Evolution of Urban Society*. Chicago: Aldine.

Albright, W.F.

1924 The Archaeological Results of an Expedition to Moab and the Dead Sea. *Bulletin of the American Schools of Oriental Research* 14: 2–12.

Albright, W.F.

1949 *The Archaeology of Palestine*. Harmondsworth: Penguin.

Alon, D. and T.E. Levy

1989 The Archaeology of Cult and the Chalcolithic Sanctuary at Gilat. *Journal of Mediterranean Archaeology* 2: 163–221.

Amiran, R.

1969 *Ancient Pottery of the Holy Land*. Jerusalem: Masada.

Amiran, R. and O. Ilan

1996 *Early Arad II: The Chalcolithic and Early Bronze IB Settlements and Early Bronze II City: Architecture and Planning. Sixth to Eighteenth Seasons of Excavations, 1971–1978, 1980–1984*. Jerusalem: Israel Exploration Society.

Amiran, R. U. Paran, Y. Shiloh, R. Brown, Y. Tsafrir and A. Ben-Tor

1978 *Early Arad: The Chalcolithic Settlement and Early Bronze Age City I: First–Fifth Seasons of Excavations 1962–1966*. Jerusalem: Israel Exploration Society.

Archi, A.

1991 Ebla: la formazione di uno stato del III millennio a.C. *La Parola del Passato* 46: 195–219.

Avner, U.

1984 Ancient Cult Sites in the Negev and Sinai Deserts. *Tel Aviv* 11: 115–131.

1990 Ancient Agricultural Settlement and Religion in the Uvda Valley in Southern Israel. *Biblical Archaeologist* 53: 125–141.

Avner, U. and I. Carmi

2001 Settlement Patterns in the Southern Levant Deserts during the 6th–3rd millennia BC: a revision based on 14C dating. *Radiocarbon* 43: 1203–1216.

Baird, D. and G. Philip

1994 Preliminary Report on the Third (1993) Season of Excavations at Tell esh-Shuna North. *Levant* 26: 111–133.

Banning, E.B.

1996 Highlands and Lowlands: Problems and Survey Frameworks for Rural Archaeology in the Near East. *Bulletin of the American Schools of Oriental Research* 301: 25–46.

Banning, E.B., D. Rahimi and J. Siggers

1994 The Late Neolithic of the Southern Levant: Hiatus, Settlement Shift and Observer Bias. *Paléorient* 20: 151–164.

Bartl, K., R. Eichmann, and F. Khraysheh

2002 Archäologische Oberflächenuntersuchungen im Gebiet des Jabal al Khanasiri/Nordjordanien. Vorläufiger Bericht der Kampagne 1999. In I.R. Eichmann (ed.), *Ausgrabungen und Surveys im Vorderen Orient 5*, 79–146.

Rahden: Deutsches Archäologisches Institut Orient Abteilung/Verlag Marie Leidorf.

Bar-Yosef, O. and R. Kra (eds.)

1994 *Late Quaternary Chronology and Paleoclimates of the Eastern Mediterranean.* Radiocarbon. Tucson: The University of Arizona Press.

Barrett, J.

1988 The Living, the Dead and the Ancestors: Neolithic and Early Bronze Age Mortuary Practices. In J. Barret and I. Kinnes (eds.), *The Archaeology of Context in the Neolithic and Bronze Age: Recent Trends,* 30–41. Sheffield: J.R. Collis Publications.

1994 *Fragments from Antiquity: An Archaeology of Social Life in Britain, 2900–1200 BC.* Oxford: Blackwell.

Baxevani, E.

1995 The Complex Nomads: Death and Social Stratification in EB IV Southern Levant. In A.C. Green and S. Campbell (eds.), *The Archaeology of Death in the Ancient Near East,* 85–95. Oxbow Monograph 51. Oxford: Oxbow.

Beebe, H.K.

1989 Basalt Bowls. In R.T. Schaub and W.E. Rast (eds.), *Bab edh-Dhra: Excavations in the Cemetery Directed by Paul W. Lapp (1965–67).* Reports of the Expedition to the Dead Sea Plain, Jordan, vol. I. Winona Lake, IN: Eisenbrauns.

Beit-Arieh, I.

1981 A Pattern of Settlement in Southern Sinai and Southern Canaan in the Third Millennium BC. *Bulletin of the American Schools of Oriental Research* 243: 31–55.

Ben-Tor, A.

1986 The Trade Relations of Palestine in the Early Bronze Age. *Journal of the Economic and Social History of the Orient* 29: 1–27.

1992 The Early Bronze Age. In A. Ben-Tor (ed.), *The Archaeology of Ancient Israel.* New Haven: Yale University Press.

Betts, A.V.G. (ed.).

1991 *Excavations at Jawa 1972–1986.* Edinburgh: Edinburgh University Press.

1992 *Excavations at Tell Um Hammad: The Early Assemblages (EB I–II).* Edinburgh: Edinburgh University Press.

Betts, A.G., S. Eames, M. Schroeder, A. al-Q. al-Husan

1995 Archaeological Survey of the Wadi al-'Ajib, al-Mafraq. *Annual of the Department of Antiquities of Jordan* 39: 149–168.

Betts, A.G., S. Eames, S. Hulka, M. Schroeder, J. Rust and J.B. McLaren

1996 Studies of Bronze Age Occupation in the Wadi al-'Ajib, Southern Hauran. *Levant* 28: 27–39.

Beynon, D.E., J. Donahue, R.T. Schaub, and R.H. Johnston

1986 Tempering Types and Sources for Early Bronze Age Ceramics from Bab edh-Dhra'. *Journal of Field Archaeology* 13: 297–305.

Blanton, R.E., G. Feinman, S.A. Kowalewski and P.N. Peregrine

1996 A Dual-Processual Theory for the Evolution of Mesoamerican Civilization. *Current Anthropology* 37: 1–31.

Bloch, M.

1971 *Placing the Dead.* London: Seminar.

Blumfiel, E. and T.E. Earle

1987 Specialization, Exchange and Complex Societies: An Introduction. In E. Blumfiel and T.E. Earle (eds.), *Specialization, Exchange and Complex Societies,* 1–10. Cambridge: Cambridge University Press.

Bourke, S.J.

1997 Pre-Classical Pella in Jordan: A Conspectus of Ten Years' Work (1985–1995). *Palestine Exploration Quarterly* 129: 93–115.

2000 Pella in the Early Bronze Age. In G. Philip and D. Baird (eds.), *Ceramics and Change in the Early Bronze Age of the Southern Levant,* 233–253. Sheffield, Sheffield Academic Press.

2002 The Origins of Social Complexity in the Southern Levant; New Evidence from Teleilet Ghassul, Jordan. *Palestine Exploration Quarterly* 134: 2–27.

Bourke, S.J., R.T. Sparks, K.N. Sowada and L.D. Mairs.

1994 Preliminary Report on the University of Sydney's Fourteenth Season of Excavations at Pella (Tabaqat Fahl) in 1992. *Annual of the Department of Antiquities of Jordan* 38: 81–126.

Bourke, S.J., E. Lawson, J. Lovell, U. Zoppi, M. Barbetti and Q. Hua

2001 The Chronology of the Ghassulian Chalcolithic Period in the Southern Levant: New 14C Determinations from Teleilat Ghassul, Jordan. *Radiocarbon* 43: 1217–1222.

Bradley, R.

1993 *Altering the Earth: The Origins of Monuments in Britain and Continental Europe.* Society of Antiquaries of Scotland Monograph Series No. 8. Edinburgh: Society of Antiquaries of Scotland.

Braemer, F.

1993 Review of A.V.G. Betts. *Excavations at Jawa 1972–1986. Syria* 70: 283–286.

1999 Le changement dans les habitats de la steppe du Proche-Orient au IIIe millénaire. In F. Braemer, S. Cleziou and A. Coudart, *Habitat et Société,* 181–199. Actes des XIX Recontres Internationales d'Archéologie et d'Histoire d'Antibes. Antibes: Éditions APDCA.

Braemer, F. and J.-C. Échallier

1995 La marge désertique en Syrie du Sud au IIIe Millénaire: éléments d'appréciation de l'évolution du milieu. In *L'Homme et la Dégradation de l'Environnement,* 345–356. XVe Recontres Internationales d'Archéologie et d'Histoire d'Antibes. Juan-les-Pins: Éditions APDCA.

2000 A Summary Statement on the Early Bronze Age Ceramics from Southern Syria, and the Relationship of this Material with that of Neighbouring Regions. In G.

Philip and D. Baird (eds.), *Ceramics and Change in the Early Bronze Age of the Southern Levant*, 403–410. Sheffield: Sheffield Academic Press.

Braemer, F., J.-C. Échallier and A. Taraqji

1993 Khirbet el Umbashi (Syrie): rapport préliminaire sur les campagnes 1991 et 1992. *Syria* 70: 415–30.

Braemer, F. and J. Sapin

2001 Modes d'occupation de la steppe dans le Levant sud-est au Bronze Ancien. Les strucutres liées au pastoralism. In B. Geyer, *Conquête de la steppe et appropriation des terres sur les marges arides du Croissant fertile*. Travaux de la Maison de l'Orient Méditerranéen 36: 69–88. Lyon.

Brandl, B.

1992 Evidence for Egyptian Colonization in the Southern Coastal Plain and Lowlands of Canaan during the EB I Period. In E.C.M. van den Brink (ed.), *The Nile Delta in Transition: 4th–3rd Millennium BC*, 441–476. Jerusalem: Israel Exploration Society.

Braun, E.

1985 *En Shadud: Salvage Excavations at a Farming Community in the Jezreel Valley, Israel*. British Archaeological Reports International Series 249. Oxford: British Archaeological Reports.

1989a The Transition from the Chalcolithic to the Early Bronze Age. In P. de Miroschedji (ed.), *L'Urbanisation de la Palestine à l'âge du Bronze Ancien*, 7–29. British Archaeological Reports International Series 527. Oxford: British Archaeological Reports.

1989b The Problem of the Apsidal House. *Palestine Exploration Quarterly* 2: 1–43.

1990 Basalt Bowls of the EB I Horizon in the Southern Levant. *Paléorient* 16: 87–96.

1996 Salvage Excavations at the Early Bronze Age Site of Me'ona: Final Report. *'Atiqot* 28: 1–39.

1997 *Yiftah'el: Salvage and Rescue Excavations at a Prehistoric Village in Lower Galilee, Israel*. Israel Antiquities Authority Reports No. 2. Jerusalem: Israel Antiquities Authority.

2001 Proto, Early, Dynastic Egypt and the EB I–II of the southern Levant: Some Uneasy 14C Correlations. *Radiocarbon* 43: 1279–1295.

Broeder, N. H. and H. C. Skinner

2003 Jewelry and Ornaments. In W. E. Rast and R. T. Schaub (eds.), *Bâb edh-Dhrâʿ: Excavations at the Town Site (1975–81)*, 566–598. Reports of the Expedition to the Dead Sea Plain, Jordan 2. Winona Lake, IN: Eisenbrauns.

Bronk Ramsey, C., T. F. G. Higham, D.C.Owen, A.W.G.Pike, R.E.M. Hedges

2002 Radiocarbon Dates fron the Oxford AMS system: Archaeometry Datelist 31. *Archaeometry* 44(3): 1–149.

Broshi, M. and R. Gophna

1984 The Settlements and Population of Palestine during the Early Bronze Age II–III. *Bulletin of the American Schools of Oriental Research* 253: 41–53.

Broshi, M. and R. Gophna

1986 Middle Bronze Age II Palestine: Its Settlements and Population. *Bulletin of the American Schools of Oriental Research*. 261: 73–90.

Brown, R.

1991 Ceramics from the Kerak Plateau. In J.M. Miller (ed.), *Archaeological Survey of the Kerak Plateau*, 169–280. American Schools of Oriental Research Archaeological Monographs 1. Atlanta: Scholars Press.

Brückner, H., R. Eichmann, L. Herling, K. Heiko, S. Kerner, L. Khalil and R. Miqdadi

2002 Chalcolithic and Early Bronze Sites Near 'Aqaba, Jordan. Archaeological Survey and Excavation in the Wadi al-Yutum and Tell al-Magass Area (ASYEM). A Preliminary Report on the First Season 1998. In. I.R. Eichmann (ed.), *Ausgrabungen und Surveys im Vorderen Orient* 5, 215–331. Rahden: Deutsches Archäologisches Institut Orient Abteilung/Verlag Marie Leidorf.

Bunimovitz, S.

1995 On the Edge of Empires: The Late Bronze Age 1500–1200 BC. In T.E. Levy (ed.), *The Archaeology of Society in the Holy Land*, 320–331. London: Leicester University Press.

Bunimovitz, S. and R. Greenberg

2004 Revealed in Their Cups: Syrian Drinking Customs in Intermediate Bronze Age Canaan. *Bulletin of the American Schools of Oriental Research* 334: 19–31.

Burton, M. and T.E. Levy

2001 The Chalcolithic Radiocarbon Record and Its Use in Southern Levantine Archaeology. *Radiocarbon* 43: 1223–1246.

Callaway, J.A.

1993 Ai. In E. Stern (ed.), *The New Encyclopedia of Archaeological Excavations in the Holy Land*, I: 39–45. Jerusalem: Israel Exploration Society.

Cartwright, C.

2002 Grape and Grain; Dietary Evidence from an Early Bronze Age Store at Tell es-Sa'idiyyeh, Jordan. *Palestine Exploration Quarterly* 134: 98–117.

Cartwright, C. and A. Clapham

1993 Appendix C. The Archaeobotanical Remains from Tell es-Sa'idiyeh, Jordan. In J.N. Tubb and P.G. Dorrell, Interim Report on the Sixth Season of Excavations. *Palestine Exploration Quarterly* 125: 73–74.

Chang-Ho, C., J. and J.K. Lee

2002 The Survey in the Regions of 'Iraq al-Amir and Wadi al-Kafrayn, 2000. *Annual of the Department of Antiquities of Jordan* 46: 179–195.

Chesson, M.S.

1998 Preliminary Result of Excavations at Tell el-Handaquq South (1993–1996). *Palestine Exploration Quarterly* 130: 20–34.

1999 Libraries of the Dead: Early Bronze Age Charnel Houses and Social Identity at Urban Bab edh-Dhra', Jordan.

Journal of Anthropological Archaeology 18: 137–164.

2000 Ceramics and Daily Life in the EBA Household: Form, Function and Action in Residential Compounds at Tell el-Handaquq, South Jordan. In D. Baird and G. Philip (eds.) *Ceramics and Change in the Early Bronze Age of the Southern Levant*, 365–378. Sheffield: Sheffield Academic Press.

2001 Embodied Memories of Place and People: Death in an Early Urban Society. In M.S. Chesson (ed.), *Social Memory, Identity and Death: Ethnographic and Archaeological Perspectives on Mortuary Rituals*, 100–113. Archaeological Papers of the American Anthropological Association 10. Arlington, VA: American Anthropological Association.

2003 Households, Houses, Neighborhoods and Corporate Villages: Modeling the Early Bronze Age as a House Society. *Journal of Mediterranean Archaeology* 16: 79–102.

Chesson, M. and G. Philip

2003 Tales of the City? 'Urbanism' in the Early Bronze Age Levant from Mediterranean and Levantine Perspectives. *Journal of Mediterranean Archaeology* 16: 3–16.

Chesson, M., M. Flender, H. Genz, F. Hourani and G. Palumbo

1995 Tell es-Sukhne North: An Early Bronze Age II Site in Jordan. *Paléorient* 21: 113–123.

Chesson, M. S., C. Makarewicz, I. Kuijt, I. and C. Whiting

2005 Results of the 2001 Kerak Plateau Early Bronze Age Survey. *Annual of the American Schools of Oriental Research* 59: 1–62. Boston, MA: American Schools of Oriental Research.

Collon, D.

1987 *First Impressions: Cylinder Seals in the Ancient Near East.* London: British Museum.

Coogan, M.D.

1984 Numeira 1981. *Bulletin of the American Schools of Oriental Research* 255: 75–82.

Costin, C.L.

1991 Craft Specialization: Issues in Defining, Documenting and Explaining the Organization of Production. *Archaeological Method and Theory* 3: 1–56.

2001 Craft Production Systems. In G. Feinman and D. Price (eds.), *Archaeology at the Millennium: A Sourcebook*, 273–333. New York: Kluwer Academic.

Croft, P.

1994 Some Preliminary Comments on the Animal Remains from the First Three Seasons at Shuna. In D. Baird and G. Philip, Preliminary Report on the Third (1993) Season of Excavations at Tell esh-Shuna North. *Levant* 26: 130–131.

Crumley, C.L.

1979 Three Locational Models: An Epistemological Assessment for Anthropology and Archaeology. In M.B. Schiffer (ed.), *Advances in Archaeological Method and Theory* 2: 141–173. New York: Academic Press.

1987 A Dialectical Critique of Hierarchy. In T.C. Patterson and C.W. Gailey (eds.), *Power Relations and State Formation*, 155–169. Washington: American Anthropological Assocation.

1995 Heterarchy and the Analysis of Complex Societies. In R.M. Ehrenreich, C.L. Crumley and J.E. Levy (eds.), *Heterarchy and the Analysis of Complex Societies*, 1–5. Archaeological Papers of the American Anthropological Association. Arlington: American Anthropological Association.

D'Altroy, T. and T.E. Earle

1985 State Finance, Wealth Finance and Storage in the Inka Political Economy. *Current Anthropology* 26: 187–206.

Daviau, P.M.M.

1991 Field D: The Lower Southern Terrace. In L.G. Herr, L.T. Geraty, Ø.S. LaBianca and R.W. Younker (eds.), *Madaba Plains Project: The 1987 Season at Tell el-'Umeiri and Vicinity and Subsidiary Studies*, 87–155. Berrien Springs, MI: Andrews University.

Davis, S.J.M.

1988 The Mammal Bones: Tel Yarmouth 1980–1983. In P. de Miroschedji (ed.), *Yarmouth I: Rapport sur les trois premiéres campagnes de fouilles à Tel Yarmouth (Israël)*, 143–49. Paris: Éditions Recherche sur les Civilisations.

Dechert, B.

1995 The Bone Remains from Hirbet ez-Zeraqon. In H. Buitenhuis and H.-P. Uerpmann (eds.), *Archaeozoology of the Near East 2*, 79–87. Leiden: Bachhuys.

Dessel, J. P. and A.H. Joffe

2000 Alternative Approaches to Early Bronze Age Pottery. In G. Philip and D. Baird (eds.), *Ceramics and Change in the Early Bronze Age of the Southern Levant*, 31–58. Sheffield: Sheffield Academic Press.

Dever, W.G.

1987 Funerary Practices in EB IV (MBI) Palestine: A Study in Cultural Continuity. In J.H. Marks and R.M. Good (eds.), *Love and Death in the Ancient Near East: Essays in Honor of Marvin H. Pope*, 9–19. Guildford: Four Quarters.

Donahue, J.

1981 Geologic Investigations at Early Bronze Sites. In W.E. Rast and R.T. Schaub (eds.), *The Southeastern Dead Sea Plain Expedition: An Interim Report of the 1977 Season*, 137–154. Annual of the American Schools of Oriental Research 46. Cambridge: American Schools of Oriental Research.

2003 Geology and Geomorphology. In W. E. Rast and R. T. Schaub (eds.), *Bab edh-Dhra: Excavations at the Town Site (1975–81)*, 18–55. Reports of the Expedition to the Dead Sea Plain, Jordan 2. Winona Lake, IN: Eisenbrauns.

Douglas, K. and Z. Kafafi

2000 The main aspects of the EB I pottery from Jebel Abu Thawwab, north Jordan. In G. Philip and D. Baird (eds.) *Ceramics and Change in the Early Bronze Age of the Southern Levant*, 101–111. Sheffield: Sheffield Academic Press.

Dubis, E. and B. Dabrowski

2002 Field K: The Dolmen and Other Features on the South Slopes of Tall al-'Umayri. In L. G. Herr (ed.), *Madaba Plains Project 5. The 1994 Season at Tall al- 'Umayri and Subsequent Studies*, 171–177. Berrien Springs, MI: Andrews University Press in cooperation with the Institute of Archaeology.

Earle, T.E.

1987 Chiefdoms in Archaeological and Historical Perspective. *Annual Review of Anthropology* 16: 279–308.

Earle, T. E. (ed.)

1991 *Chiefdoms, Power, Economy and Ideology*. Cambridge: Cambridge University Press.

Eames, S.

2003 Between 'The Desert and the Sown': The Hauran as a Frontier Zone in the Middle Bronze Age. *Palestine Exploration Quarterly* 135: 88–107.

Eisenberg, E.

1993 Tell Kitan. In E. Stern (ed.), *The New Encyclopedia of Archaeological Excavations in the Holy Land*, II: 878–881. Jerusalem: Israel Exploration Society.

Epstein, C.

1985 Laden Animal Figurines from the Chalcolithic Period in Palestine. *Bulletin of the American Schools of Oriental Research* 258: 53–62.

1993 Oil Production in the Golan Heights during the Chalcolithic Period. *Tel Aviv* 20: 133–146.

Esse, D.L.

1989a Secondary State Formation and Collapse in Early Bronze Age Palestine. In P. de Miroschedji (ed.), *L'urbanisation de la Palestine à l'âge du Bronze Ancien*, 81–96. British Archaeological Reports International Series 527. Oxford: British Archaeological Reports.

1989b Village Potters in Early Bronze Age Palestine: A Case Study. In A. Leonard Jr. and B.B.Williams (eds.), *Essays in Ancient Civilization Presented to Helene Kantor*, 77–92. Studies in Ancient Oriental Civilization 47. Chicago: University of Chicago Press.

1991 *Subsistence, Trade and Social Change in Early Bronze Age Palestine*. Studies in Ancient Oriental Civilization 50. Chicago: University of Chicago Press.

Falconer, S.E.

1987 Heartland of Villages: Reconsidering Early Urbanism in the Southern Levant. Unpublished PhD dissertation, The University of Arizona, Tucson.

1994 The Development and Decline of Bronze Age Civilization in the Levant: A Reassessment of Urbanism and Ruralism. In C. Mathers and S. Stoddart (eds.), *Development and Decline in the Mediterranean Bronze Age*, 305–333. Sheffield Archaeological Monographs 8. Sheffield: J.R. Collis.

Falconer, S.E. and S. Savage

1995 Heartlands and Hinterlands: Alternative Trajectories of Early Urbanization in Mesopotamia and the Southern Levant. *American Antiquity* 60: 37–58.

Feinman, G.M.

1995 The Emergence of Inequality: A Focus on Strategies and Processes. In T.D. Price and G.M. Feinman (eds.), *Foundations of Social Inequality*, 255–280. New York: Plenum.

Feinman, G.M. and J. Neitzel

1984 Too Many Types: An Overview of Sedentary Prestate Societes in the Americans. In M. Schiffer (ed.), *Advances in Archaeological Method and Theory* 7, 39–102. New York: Academic Press.

Feinman, G.M., S.A. Kowalewski and R.E. Blanton.

1984 Modelling Ceramic Production and Organizational Change in the Pre-Hispanic Valley of Oaxaca. In S.E. van der Leuw and A.C. Pritchard (eds.), *The Many Dimensions of Pottery*, 297–333. Amsterdam: Universiteit van Amsterdam.

Finkelstein, I.

1990 Early Arad: Urbanization of the Nomads. *Zeitschrift des Deutschen Palästina-Vereins* 106: 34–50.

1995a Two Notes on Early Bronze Age Urbanization and Urbanism. *Tel Aviv* 22: 47–69.

1995b *Living on the Fringe: The Archaeology and History of the Negev, Sinai and Neighbouring Regions in the Bronze and Iron Ages*. Monographs in Mediterranean Archaeology. Sheffield: Sheffield Academic Press.

Finkelstein, I. and R. Gophna

1993 Settlement, Demographic and Economic Patterns in the Highlands of Palestine in the Chalcolithic and Early Bronze Periods and the Beginning of Urbanism. *Bulletin of the American Schools of Oriental Research* 289: 1–22.

Finkelstein, I., D. Ussishkin and B. Halpern. (eds.)

2000 *Megiddo III: the 1992–1996 seasons*. Tel Aviv: Institute of Archaeology Tel Aviv University.

Fischer, P.M.

1993 Tell Abu al-Kharaz: The Swedish Jordan Expedition 1991, Second Season Preliminary Excavation Report. *Annual of the Department of Antiquities of Jordan* 37: 279–306.

Fischer, P.M.

1994 Tell Abu al-Kharaz: The Swedish Jordan Expedition 1992, Third Season Preliminary Excavation Report. *Annual of the Department of Antiquities of Jordan* 38: 127–146.

1998 Tall abu al-Kharaz. The Swedish Jordan Expedition 1997, Eighth Season Preliminary Excavation Report. *Annual of the Department of Antiquities of Jordan* 42: 213–223.

2000 The Early Bronze Age at Tell Abu al-Kharaz, Jordan Valley: A Study of Pottery Typology and Provenance, Radiocarbon Dates and Synchronization of Palestine and Egypt. In G. Philip and D. Baird (eds.), *Ceramics and Change in the Early Bronze Age of the Southern Levant*, 201–232. Sheffield: Sheffield Academic Press.

2002 Egyptian-Transjordanian Interaction during Predynastic and Protodynastic Times: the Evidence from Tell

Abu al-Kharaz, Jordan Valley. In E.C.M. van den Brink and T.E. Levy (eds.), *Egypt and the Levant: Interrelations from the 4th through the Early 3rd Millennium BCE*, 323–333. London, Leicester University Press.

Fischer, P.M. and E. Toivonen-Skage

1995 Metallic Burnished Early Bronze Age Ware from Tall Abu al-Kharaz. In K. 'Amr, F. Zayadine and M. Zaghloul (eds.), *Studies in the History and Archaeology of Jordan V,* 587–98. Amman: Department of Antiquities.

Flannery, K.V.

1972 The Cultural Evolution of Civilizations. *Annual Review of Ecology and Systematics* 3: 399–426.

Flender, M.

2000 Cylinder Seal Impressed Vessels of the Early Bronze Age III in Northern Palestine. In G. Philip and D. Baird (eds.), *Ceramics and Change in the Early Bronze Age of the Southern Levant*, 295–314. Sheffield: Sheffield Academic Press.

Franken, H.J.

1974 *In Search of the Jericho Potters: Ceramics from the Iron Age and from the Neolithicum*. Amsterdam: North-Holland.

Fritz, V.

1994 Vorbericht über die Grabungen in Barqa el-Hetiye im Gebeit von Fenan, Wadi el-'Arabah, Jordanien. *Zeitschrift des Deutschen Palästina-Vereins* 110: 125–150.

Fujii, S.

2000 Qa' Abu Tulayha West, an Interim Report of the 1999 Season. *Annual of the Department of Antiquities of Jordan* 44: 149–171.

2001 Qa' Abu Tulayha West 2000, an Interim Report on the Fourth Season. *Annual of the Department of Antiquities of Jordan* 45: 19–37.

Futato, E.M.

1996 Early Bronze III Canaanean Blade/Scraper Cores from Tell Halif, Israel. In J.D. Seger (ed.), *Retrieving the Past: Essays on Archaeological Research and Methodology in Honor of Gus W. Van Beek*, 61–74. Winona Lake, IN: Eisenbrauns.

Garrard, A.N., S. Colledge and L. Martin

1996 The Emergence of Crop Cultivation and Caprine Herding in the 'Marginal Zone' of the Southern Levant. In D. Harris (ed.), *The Origins and Spread of Agriculture and Pastoralism in Eurasia*, 204–226. London: University College London Press.

Genz, H.

2000 Grain-wash Decoration in Early Bronze Age III? The Evidence from Khirbet ez-Zeraqon. In G. Philip and D. Baird (eds.), *Ceramics and Change in the Early Bronze Age of the Southern Levant*, 279–286. Sheffield: Sheffield Academic Press.

2001 The Organization of Early Bronze Age Metalworking in the Southern Levant. *Paléorient* 26: 55–65.

2002 *Die frühbronzezeitliche Keramik von Hirbet ez-Zeraqon: mit Studien zur Chronologie und funktionalen Deutung frühbronzezeitlicher Keramik in der südlichen Levante.* Abhandlungen des Deutschen Palästinavereins; Bd. 27,2 Deutsch-jordanische Ausgrabungen in Hirbet ez-Zeraqon, 1984–1994. Endberichte Bd. 5. Wiesbaden: Harrossowitz.

2003a Cash Crop Production and Storage in the EBA Southern Levant. *Journal of Mediterranean Archaeology* 16: 59–78.

2003b *Ritzverzierte Knochenhülsen des dritten Jahrtausends im Ostmittelmeeraum. Eine studie zu den frühen Kulturverbindungen zwischen Levante und Ägäis*. Abhandlungen des Deutschen Palästina Veriens Band 31. Wiesbaden: Harrosswitz.

Geraty, L.T., L.G. Herr and Ø.S. LaBianca

1986 Madaba Plains Project. A Preliminary Report of the 1984 Season at Tell el-'Umeiri and Vicinity. *Bulletin of the American Schools of Oriental Research, Supplementary Series* 24: 117–119.

Gibbins, S.

2001 Early Bronze Age fortifications on Tell Husn (Pella). In A. Walmsley (ed.), *Australians Uncovering Ancient Jordan. Fifty Years of Middle Eastern Archaeology*, 89–94. Sydney, Research Institute for Humanities and Social Sciences, The University of Sydney and the Department of Antiquities of Jordan.

Gilman, A.

1991 Trajectories towards Social Complexity in the Later Prehistory of the Mediterranean. In T.E. Earle (ed.), *Chiefdoms, Power, Economy and Ideology*, 146–168. Cambridge: Cambridge University Press.

Glueck, N.

1934 *Explorations in Eastern Palestine I*. Annual of the American Schools of Oriental Research 14: 1–113. New Haven: American Schools of Oriental Research.

Goldberg, P.

1994 Interpreting Late Quaternary Continental Sequences in Israel. In O. Bar-Yosef and R.S. Kra (eds.), *Late Quaternary Chronology and Paleoclimates of the East Mediterranean*, 89–103. Radiocarbon. Tucson: The University of Arizona.

Golden, J.

2002 The Origins of the Metals Trade in the Eastern Mediterranean: Social Organization of Production in the Early Copper Industries. In E.C.M. van den Brink and T.E. Levy (eds.), *Egypt and the Levant: Interrelations from the 4th through the Early 3rd Millennium BCE*, 225–238. London: Leicester University Press.

Gophna, R.

1995 Early Bronze Age Canaan: Some Spatial and Demographic Observations. In T.E. Levy (ed.), *Archaeology of Society in the Holy Land*, 269–280. London: Leicester University Press.

Gophna, R. and Y. Portugali

1988 Settlement and Demographic Processes in Israel's Coastal Plain from the Chalcolithic to the Middle

Bronze Age. *Bulletin of the American Schools of Oriental Research* 269: 11–28.

Gordon, R. and L. Villiers

1983 Telul edh-Dhahab and its Environs: Survey of 1980 and 1982: Preliminary Report. *Annual of the Department of Antiquities of Jordan* 27: 275–289.

Gordon, R.L. Jr and E.A. Knauf

1987 Er-Rumman Survey 1985. *Annual of the Department of Antiquities of Jordan* 31: 289–298.

Goren, Y. and S. Zukermann

2000 An Overview of the Typology, Provenance and Technology of the Early Bronze Age I 'Grey Burnished Ware'. In G. Philip and D. Baird (eds.), *Ceramics and Change in the Early Bronze Age of the Southern Levant*, 165–182. Sheffield: Sheffield Academic Press.

Graesser, C.F.

1972 Standing Stones in Ancient Palestine. *Biblical Archaeologist* 35: 34–64.

Greenberg, R.

1996 The Early Bronze Age Levels. In A. Biran (ed.), *Dan I: A Chronicle of the Excavations, the Pottery Neolithic, the Early Bronze Age and the Middle Bronze Age Tombs*, 83–160. Jerusalem: Nelson Glueck School of Biblical Archaeology.

2000 Changes in Ceramic Production between Early Bronze Age II and III in Northern Israel, based on the Pottery of Tel Hazor and Tel Dan. In G. Philip and D. Baird (eds.), *Ceramics and Change in the Early Bronze Age of the Southern Levant*, 183–200. Sheffield: Sheffield Academic Press.

2001 Early Bronze Age II–III Palestinian Cylinder Seal Impressions and the North Canaanite Metallic Ware jar. In S.R. Wolff (ed.), *Studies in the Archaeology of Israel and Neighbouring Lands in Memory of Douglas L. Esse*, 189–198. Chicago: The Oriental Institute of the University of Chicago.

2002 *Early Urbanizations in the Levant: a Regional Narrative*. New York: Leicester University Press.

2003 Early Bronze Age Megiddo and Bet Shean: Discontinuous Settlement in Sociopolitical Context. *Journal of Mediterranean Archaeology* 16: 17–32.

Greenberg, R. and E. Eisenberg

2002 Egypt, Bet Yerah and Early Canaanite Urbanization. In E.C.M. van den Brink and T.E. Levy (eds.) *Egypt and the Levant: Interrelations from the 4th through the Early 3rd Millennium BCE*, 213–224. London: Leicester University Press.

Greenberg, R. and N. Porat

1996 A Third Millennium Levantine Pottery Production Center: Typology, Petrography and Provenance of the Metallic Ware of Northern Israel and Adjacent Regions. *Bulletin of the American Schools of Oriental Research* 301: 5–24.

Gregory, C.

1982 *Gifts and Commodities*. London: Academic Press.

Grigson, C.

1987 Shiqmim: Pastoralism and Other Aspects of Animal Management in the Chalcolithic of the Northern Negev. In T.E. Levy (ed.), *Shiqmim I: Studies Concerning Chalcolithic Societies in the Northern Negev Desert, Israel (1982–1984)*, 219–241. British Archaeological Reports International Series 356. Oxford: British Archaeological Reports.

1995 Plough and Pasture in the Early Economy of the Southern Levant. In T.E. Levy (ed.), *Archaeology of Society in the Holy Land*, 245–68. London: Leicester University Press.

Hallotte, R.S.

1996 Mortuary Archaeology and the Middle Bronze Age Southern Levant. *Journal of Mediterranean Archaeology* 8: 93–122.

Halstead, P.

1995 Plough and Power: The Economic and Social Significance of Cultivation with the Ox-drawn Ard in the Mediterranean. *Bulletin on Sumerian Agriculture* 8: 11–22.

Hanbury-Tenison, J.W.

1986 *The Late Chalcolithic–Early Bronze I Transition in Palestine and Transjordan*. British Archaeological Reports International Series 311. Oxford: British Archaeological Reports.

1987 Jarash Region Survey 1984. *Annual of the Department of Antiquities of Jordan* 31: 129–157.

1989a Jebel Mutawwaq 1986. *Annual of the Department of Antiquities of Jordan* 33: 137–144.

1989b Desert Urbanism in the Fourth Millennium. *Palestine Exploration Quarterly* 121: 55–63.

Harrison, T.

1997 Shifting Patterns of Settlement in the Highlands of Central Jordan during the Early Bronze Age. *Bulletin of the American Schools of Oriental Research* 306: 1–38.

2000a Field D: The Lower Southern Terrace. In L.G. Herr (ed.), *Madaba Plains Project 4. The 1992 Season at Tall al-'Umayri and Subsequent Studies*, 95–154. Berrien Springs, MI: Andrews University Press in cooperation with the Institute of Archaeology.

2000b The Early Bronze III Ceramic Horizon for Highland Central Jordan. In G. Philip and D. Baird (eds.), *Ceramics and Change in the Early Bronze Age of the Southern Levant*, 347–364. Sheffield: Sheffield Academic Press.

2001 Early Bronze Age Social Organization as Reflected in Burial Patterns from the Southern Levant. In S. R. Wolff (ed.), *Studies in the Archaeology of Israel and Neighbouring Lands in Memory of Douglas L. Esse*, 215–236. Chicago: The Oriental Institute of the University of Chicago.

Harrison, T. P. and S. H. Savage

2003 Settlement Heterogeneity and Multivariate Craft Production in the Early Bronze Age Southern Levant. *Jour-

nal of Mediterranean Archaeology 16: 33–57.

Hastorf, C.

1990 One Path to the Heights: Negotiating Political Inequality in the Sausa of Peru. In S. Upham (ed.), *The Evolution of Political Systems: Sociopolitics in Small-Scale Sedentary Societies*, 146–175. Cambridge: Cambridge University Press.

Hauptmann, A.

2000 *Zur frühen Metallurgie des Kupfers in Fenan/Jordanien* Bochum: Deutsches Bergbau-Museum.

Hauptmann, A., F. Begemann and S. Schmidt-Strecker

1999 Copper Objects from Arad: Their Composition and Provenance. *Bulletin of the American Schools of Oriental Research* 314: 1–17.

Hauptmann, A., G. Weisgerber and E.A. Knauf

1983 Archäometallurgische und bergbauarchäologische Untersuchungen im Gebiet von Fenan, Wadi Arabah (Jordanien). *Der Anschnitt* 37: 163–195.

Hauptmann, A. and E. Pernicka

1989 Chemische und mineralogische Analyse einiger Erz und Kupferfunde von Maadi. In I. Rizkana and J. Seeher *Maadi 3: The Non-lithic Small Finds and the Structural Remains of the Predynastic Settlement*, 137–140. Mainz an Rhein: Philipp von Zabern.

Hauptmann, A., F. Begemann, E. Heitkemper, E. Pernicka and S. Schmitt-Strecker

1992 Early Copper Produced at Feinan, Wadi Araba, Jordan: The Composition of Ores and Copper. *Archaeomaterials* 6: 1–33.

Hayden, B.

1994 Village Approaches to Complex Societies. In G.M. Schwartz and S.E. Falconer (eds.), *Archaeological Views from the Countryside: Village Communities in Early Complex Societies*, 198–206. Washington: Smithsonian Institution.

Helms, S.W.

1975 Posterns in Early Bronze Age Fortifications of Palestine. *Palestine Exploration Quarterly* 107: 133–150.

1981 *Jawa: Lost City of the Black Desert*. London: Methuen.

1982 Paleo-Beduin and Transmigrant Urbanism. In A. Hadidi (ed.), *Studies in the History and Archaeology of Jordan I*, 97–113. Amman: Department of Antiquities.

1987 Jawa, Tell um Hamad and the E.B.I/Late Chalcolithic Landscape. *Levant* 19: 49–81.

1992 The 'Zarqa Triangle': A Preliminary Appraisal of Protohistoric Settlement Patterns and Demographic Episodes. In M. Zaghloul, K. 'Amr, F. Zayadine, R. Nabeel and N. Rida Tawfiq (eds.), *Studies in the History and Archaeology of Jordan IV*, 129–135. Amman: Department of Antiquities.

Hendrickx, S.

1996 The Relative Chronology of the Naqada Culture: Problems and Possibilities. In J. Spencer (ed.), *Aspects of Early Egypt*, 36–69. London: British Museum.

Hennessy, J.B.

1967 *The Foreign Relations of Palestine during the Early Bronze Age*. London: Colt Archaeological Institute.

Henry, D.O.

1995 *Prehistoric Cultural Ecology and Evolution: Insights from Southern Jordan*. New York: Plenum.

Herr, L.G., L.T. Geraty, Ø.S. LaBianca and R.W. Younker

1991 *Madaba Plains Project 2: The 1987 Season at Tell el-'Umeiri and Vicinity and Subsidiary Studies*, 87–155. Berrien Springs, MI: Andrews University.

Herzog, Z.

1986 *Das Stadttor in Israel und in den Nachbarländern*. Mainz am Rhein: Von Zabern.

Hesse, B. and P. Wapnish

1991 Faunal remains from Tel Dan: Perspectives on Animal Production at a Village, Urban and Rural Centre. *ArchaeoZoologia* 4(2): 9–86.

Hestrin, R. and M. Tadmor

1963 A Hoard of Tools and Weapons from Kfar Monash. *Israel Exploration Journal* 13: 265–288.

Ibrahim, M. and S. Mittmann

1994 Excavations at Khirbet ez-Zeraqon 1993. *Newsletter of the Institute of Archaeology and Anthropology, Yarmouk University* 16: 11–15.

Ibrahim, M., K. Yassine and J.A. Sauer

1988 The East Jordan Valley Survey 1975 (Parts 1 and 2). In K. Yassine (ed.), *The Archaeology of Jordan: Essays and Reports*, 159–207. Amman: Department of Archaeology, University of Jordan.

Ilan, D.

1992 A MBA Offering Deposit from Tel Dan. *Tel Aviv* 19: 247–266.

1995 The Dawn of Internationalism: The Middle Bronze Age. In T.E. Levy (ed.), *Archaeology of Society in the Holy Land*, 297–319. London: Leicester University Press.

Ilan, O.

2001 Household archaeology at Arad and Ai in the Early Bronze Age. In S. R. Wolff (ed.), *Studies in the Archaeology of Israel and Neighbouring Lands in Memory of Douglas L. Esse*, 317–354. Chicago: The Oriental Institute of the University of Chicago.

Jacobs, P.F.

1996 A Cosmetic Palette from Early Bronze III at Tell Halif. In J.D. Seger (ed.), *Retrieving the Past: Essays on Archaeological Research and Methodology in Honor of Gus W. Van Beek*, 123–134. Winona Lake, IN: Eisenbrauns.

Joffe, A.H.

1993 *Settlement and Society in the Early Bronze I and II Southern Levant: Complementarity and Contradiction in Small-Scale Complex Society*. Sheffield: Sheffield Academic Press.

2000 The Early Bronze Age Pottery from Area J. In I. Finkelstein, D. Ussishkin and B. Halpern (eds.), *Megiddo III:*

the 1992–1996 Seasons, 161–185. Tel Aviv: Institute of Archaeology Tel Aviv University.

2001 Early Bronze Age Seal Impressions from the Jezreel Valley and the Problem of Sealing in the Southern Levant. S.R. Wolff (ed.), *Studies in the Archaeology of Israel and Neighbouring Lands in Memory of Douglas L. Esse*, 355–375. Chicago: The Oriental Institute of the University of Chicago.

2004 Athens and Jerusalem in the Third Millennium: Culture, Comparison and the Evolution of Social Complexity. *Journal of Mediterranean Archaeology* 17: 247–267.

Johnson, G. and T. Earle

1987 *The Evolution of Human Society: From Forager Group to Agrarian State*. Stanford: Stanford University Press.

Kafafi, Z. (ed.)

2001 *Jebel Abu Thawwab (Er-Rumman), Central Jordan: the Late Neolithic and Early Bronze Age I occupations*. Bibliotheca neolithica Asiae meridionalis et occidentalis. Monograph of the Institute of Archaeology and Anthropology (Yarmouk University) 3. Berlin: *ex oriente*.

Kamlah, J.

2000 *Der Zeraqon-Survey 1989–1994. Mit Beiträgen zur Methodik und geschichtlichen Auswertung archäologischer Oberflächenuntersuchungen in Palästina*. Abhandlungen des Deutschen Palästinavereins; Bd. 27,1. Deutsch-jordänische Ausgrabungen in Hirbet ez-Zeraqon, 1984–1994. Endberichte Bd. 2 Wiesbaden: Harrassowitz.

Kantor, H.

1992 The Relative Chronology of Egypt and its Foreign Correlations before the First Intermediate Period. In R.W. Ehrich (ed.), *Chronologies in Old World Archaeology*, 3–21. Chicago: University of Chicago Press.

Kempinski, A.

1992a Fortifications, Public Buildings and Town Planning in the Early Bronze Age. In A. Kempinski and R. Reich (eds.), *The Architecture of Ancient Israel from the Prehistoric to the Persian Periods*, 68–80. Jerusalem: Israel Exploration Society.

1992b The Middle Bronze Age. In A. Ben-Tor (ed.), *The Archaeology of Ancient Israel*, 159–210. New Haven: Yale University Press.

Kenyon, K.M.

1960 *Excavations at Jericho* I. London: British School of Archaeology in Jerusalem.

1979 *Archaeology in the Holy Land*. 4th edn. London: Benn.

Khalil, L.

1992 Some Technological Features from a Chalcolithic Site at Magass-Aqaba. In M. Zaghloul, K. 'Amr, F. Zayadine, R. Nabeel and N. Rida Tawfiq (eds.), *Studies in the History and Archaeology of Jordan IV*, 143–148. Amman: Department of Antiquities.

Khalil, L. and R. Eichmann

2001 Archaeological Survey and Excavation at the Wadi al-Yutum and Magass area — al-Aqaba (ASEYM): a Pre-

liminary Report on the Second Season in 2000. *Annual of the Department of Antiquities of Jordan* 45: 195–204.

Khazanov, A.M.

1984 *Nomads and the Outside World*. Cambridge: Cambridge University Press.

Klemm, R. and D. Klemm

1993 *Steine und Steinbrüche im Alten Ägypten*. Berlin: Springer.

Knapp, A.B.

1990 Production, Location and Integration on Bronze Age Cyprus. *Current Anthropology* 31: 147–176.

1993 Social Complexity: Incipience, Emergence, and Development in Bronze Age Cyprus. *Bulletin of the American Schools of Oriental Research* 292: 85–108.

Kolska-Horwitz, L. and E. Tchernov

1989 Animal Exploitation in the Early Bronze Age of the Southern Levant: An Overview. In P. de Miroschedji (ed.), *L'urbanisation de la Palestine à l'âge du Bronze Ancien*, 279–296. British Archaeological Reports International Series 527. Oxford: British Archaeological Reports.

Korber, C.

1993 Edh-Dhra' Survey 1992. *Annual of the Department of Antiquities of Jordan* 37: 550–553.

Kroeper, K.

1996 Minshat Abu Omar: Burials with Palettes. In J. Spencer (ed.), *Aspects of Early Egypt*, 70–92. London: British Museum.

Kuijt, I., J. Mabry and G. Palumbo

1991 Early Neolithic Use of Upland Areas of Wadi el-Yabis: Preliminary Evidence from the Excavations of 'Iraq ed-Dubb, Jordan. *Paléorient* 17: 99–108.

LaBianca, Ø.S.

1990 *Sedentarization and Nomadization: Food System Cycles at Hesban and Vicinity in Transjordan*. Berrien Springs, MI: Andrews University.

Lapp, N.

2003 Cylinder Seals, Impressions and Incised Sherds. In W. E. Rast and R. T. Schaub (eds.), *Bâb edh-Dhrâ': Excavations at the Town Site (1975–81)*, 522–565. Reports of the Expedition to the Dead Sea Plain, Jordan 2. Winona Lake, IN: Eisenbrauns.

Lee, J.R.

2003 Worked Stones. In W. E. Rast and R. T. Schaub (eds.), *Bâb edh-Dhrâ': Excavations at the Town Site (1975–81)*, 622–637. Reports of the Expedition to the Dead Sea Plain, Jordan 2. Winona Lake, IN: Eisenbrauns.

Leonard, A.

1992 *The Jordan Valley Survey, 1953: Some Unpublished Soundings Conducted by James Mellaart*. Annual of the American Schools of Oriental Research 50. Winona Lake, IN: Eisenbrauns.

Lévi-Strauss, C.

1982 *The Way of the Masks*, (translated S. Modelski). Seattle: University of Washington Press.

Levy, J.E.

1995 Heterarchy in Bronze Age Denmark: Settlement Pattern, Gender and Ritual. In R.M. Ehrenreich, C.L. Crumley and J.E. Levy (eds.), *Heterarchy and the Analysis of Complex Societies*, 41–53. Archaeological Papers of the American Anthropological Association 6. Arlington: American Anthropological Association.

Levy, T.E.

1986 Archaeological Sources for the History of Palestine: The Chalcolithic Period. *Biblical Archaeologist* 49: 82–108.

1992 Transhumance, Subsistence and Social Evolution in the Northern Negev Desert. In O. Bar-Yosef and A. Khazanov (eds.), *Pastoralism in the Levant: Archaeological Material in Anthropological Perspectives*, 65–82. Madison, WI: Prehistory.

1993 Production, Space and Social Change in Protohistoric Palestine. In A. Holl and T.E. Levy, *Spatial Boundaries and Social Dynamics: Case Studies from Food-Producing Societies*, 63–82. Ann Arbor: International Monographs in Prehistory.

1995a Cult, Metallurgy and Rank Societies: Chalcolithic. In T.E. Levy (ed.), *Archaeology of Society in the Holy Land*, 226–243. London: Leicester University Press.

1995b New Light on King Narmer and the Protodynastic Egyptian Presence in Canaan. *Biblical Archaeologist* 58: 26–36.

Levy, T.E., R.B. Adams, A. Hauptmann, M. Prange, S. Schmitt-Strecker and M. Najjar

2002 Early Bronze Age Metallurgy: A Newly Discovered Copper Manufactory in Southern Jordan. *Antiquity* 76: 425–437.

Levy, T.E., D. Alon, Y. Rowan and M. Kersal

2006 The Sanctuary Sequence: Excavations at Gilat 1975–77, 1989, 1990–92. In T.E. Levy (ed.), *Archaeology, Anthropology and Cult. The Sanctuary at Gilat, Israel*, 95–212. London: Equinox.

Lindner, M., U. Hubner and H. Genz

2001 The Early Bronze Age Settlement on Umm Saysaban North of Petra (Jordan) and its Topographical Context. Report on the 1998/1999 Survey. *Annual of the Department of Antiquities of Jordan* 45: 287–310.

Lipschitz, N.

1989 Plant Economy and Diet in the Early Bronze Age in Israel: A Summary of Present Research. In P. de Miroschedji (ed.), *L'urbanisation de la Palestine à l'âge du Bronze Ancien*, 269–278. British Archaeological Reports International Series 527. Oxford: British Archaeological Reports.

Lipschitz, N. R., Gophna, M. Hartman and G. Biger

1991 The Beginning of Olive (*Olea europaea*) Cultivation in the Old World: A Reassessment. *Journal of Archaeological Science* 18: 441–453.

London, G.A.

1991 Aspects of Early Bronze and Late Iron Age Ceramic Production at Tell el-'Umeiri. In L.G. Herr, L.T. Geraty, Ø.S. LaBianca and R.W. Younker (eds.), *Madaba Plains Project 2: The 1987 Season at Tell el-'Umeiri and Vicinity and Subsidiary Studies*, 383–419. Berrien Springs, MI: Andrews University.

London, G.A., H. Plint and J. Smith

1991 Preliminary Petrographic Ananlysis of Pottery from Tell el-'Umeiri and Hinterland Sites 1987. In L.G. Herr, L. T. Geraty, Ø. S. LaBianca and R. W. Younker (eds.), *Madaba Plains Project 2: The 1987 Season at Tell el-'Umeiri and Vicinity and Subsidiary Studies*, 423–439. Berrien Springs, MI: Andrews University.

Lovell, J.

in press The Wadi Rayyan Archaeological Project (WRAP): Investigating the Chalcolithic–Early Bronze Age Transition. Studies in the History and Archaeology of Jordan *IX*. Amman: Department of Antiquities of Jordan.

Mabry, J.

1989 Investigations at Tell el-Handaquq, Jordan (1987–88). *Annual of the Department of Antiquities of Jordan* 33: 59–95.

Mabry, J. and G. Palumbo

1988 The 1987 Wadi el-Yabis Survey. *Annual of the Department of Antiquities of Jordan* 32: 275–306.

Mabry, J.M.L. Donaldson, K. Gruspier, G. Mullen, G. Palumbo, M. N. Rawlings and M.A. Woodburn

1996 Early Town Development and Water Management in the Jordan Valley: Investigations at Tell el-Handaquq North. *Annual of the American Schools of Oriental Research* 53: 115–154. Cambridge: American Schools of Oriental Research.

MacDonald, B. (ed.)

1988 *The Wadi el Hasa Archaeological Survey, 1979–1983, West-Central Jordan*. Waterloo: Wilfrid Laurier University.

1992 *The Southern Ghors and Northeast 'Arabah Archaeological Survey*. Sheffield Archaeological Monographs 5. Sheffield: J.R. Collis.

Maddin, R., J. D. Muhly and T. Stech

2003 Metallurgical Studies on Copper Artefacts from Bâb adh-Dhrâ'. In W. E. Rast and R. T. Schaub (eds.), *Bâb adh-Dhrâ': Excavations at the Town Site (1975–81)*, 513–521. Reports of the Expedition to the Dead Sea Plain, Jordan 2. Winona Lake, IN: Eisenbrauns.

Magness-Gardiner, B.

1994 Urban–Rural Relations in Bronze Age Syria: Evidence from Alalakh Level VII Palace Archives. In G.M. Schwartz and S.E. Falconer (eds.), *Archaeological Views from the Countryside: Village Communities in Early Complex Societies*, 37–47. Washington: Smithsonian Institution.

Manning, S.W.

1993 Prestige, Distinction and Competition: The Anatomy of Socioeconomic Complexity in Fourth to Second Millennium B.C.E. Cyprus. *Bulletin of the American Schools of Oriental Research* 292: 35–58.

Marcus, J.

2002 Early Seafaring and Maritime Activity in the Southern Levant from Prehistory through the Third Millennium BCE In E.C.M. van den Brink and T.E. Levy (eds.), *Egypt and the Levant: Interrelations from the 4th through the Early 3rd Millennium BCE*, 403–417. London: Leicester University Press.

Marquet-Krause, J.

1949 *Les fouilles de Ai (et-Tell) 1933–1935*. Paris: Geuthner.

Mattingly, G.L.

1983 Nelson Glueck and Early Bronze Age Moab. *Annual of the Department of Antiquities of Jordan* 27: 481–489.

Mazar, A.

1990 *Archaeology of the Land of the Bible 10,000–586 B.C.E.* New York: Doubleday.

1997 The Excavations at Tel Beth Shean during the Years 1989–94. In N.A. Silberman and D.B. Small (eds.), *The Archaeology of Israel: Constructing the Past, Interpreting the Present*, 144–165. Sheffield: Sheffield Academic Press.

2001 On the Significance of the Early Bronze III Granary Building at Beit Yerah. In S.R. Wolff (ed.), *Studies in the Archaeology of Israel and Neighbouring Lands in Memory of Douglas L. Esse*, 447–464. Chicago: The Oriental Institute of the University of Chicago.

Mazar, A. and P. de Miroschedji

1996 Hartuv, an Aspect of the Early Bronze I Culture of Southern Israel. *Bulletin of the American Schools of Oriental Research* 302: 1–40.

Mazar, A., A. Ziv-Esudri and A. Cohen-Weinberger

2000 The Early Bronze Age II–III at Tel Beth Shean: Preliminary Observations. In G. Philip and D. Baird (eds.) *Ceramics and Change in the Early Bronze Age of the Southern Levant*, 255–278. Sheffield: Sheffield Academic Press.

Mazzoni, S.

1991 Ebla e la formazione della cultura urbana in Siria. *La Parola del Passato* 46: 163–194.

2003 Ebla: Crafts and Power in an Emergent State of Third Millennium BC Syria. *Journal of Mediterranean Archaeology* 16: 173–191.

McCartney, C.

1996 A Report on the Chipped Stone Assemblage from Tell Iktanu, Jordan Valley. *Levant* 1996: 131–156.

McClelland, T.L. and A. Porter

1995 Jawa and North Syria. In K. 'Amr, F. Zayadine and M. Zaghloul (eds.), *Studies in the History and Archaeology of of Jordan V*, 49–65. Amman: Department of Antiquities.

McConaughty, M.A.

1980 Chipped Stone Tools from Bab edh-Dhra'. *Bulletin of the American Schools of Oriental Research* 240: 53–58.

2003 Chipped Stone Tools at Bâb edh-Dhrâ'. In W.E. Rast and R.T. Schaub (eds.), *Bâb edh-Dhrâ': Excavations at the Town Site (1975–81)*, 437–512. Reports of the Expedition to the Dead Sea Plain, Jordan 2. Winona Lake, IN: Eisenbrauns.

McCreery, D.W.

2003 The Paleoethnobotany of Bâb edh-Dhrâ'. In W. E. Rast and R. T. Schaub (eds.), *Bâb edh-Dhrâ': Excavations at the Town Site (1975–81)*, 449–463. Reports of the Expedition to the Dead Sea Plain, Jordan 2. Winona Lake, IN: Eisenbrauns.

Meadows, J.

2001 Arid-zone Farming in the Fourth Millennium BC: the Plant Remains from Wadi Fidan 4. In A. Walmsley (ed.), *Australians Uncovering Ancient Jordan. Fifty Years of Middle Eastern Archaeology*, 153–164. Sydney: Research Institute for Humanities and Social Sciences, The University of Sydney and the Department of Antiquities of Jordan.

Meillassoux, C.

1968 Ostentation, Destruction, Reproduction. *Economie et Societé* 2: 760–772.

1972 From Reproduction to Production: A Marxist Approach to Economic Anthropology. *Economy and Society* 1: 93–105.

Miller, J.M. (ed.)

1991 *Archaeological Survey of the Kerak Plateau*. American Schools of Oriental Research Archaeological Monographs 1. Atlanta: Scholars Press.

Miroschedji, P. de

1971 *L'époque préurbaine en Palestine*. Cahiers de la Revue Biblique 13. Paris: Gabalda.

1988 *Yarmouth I: rapport sur les trois premiéres campagnes de fouilles à Tel Yarmouth (Israël) (1980–1982)*. Paris: Éditions Recherche sur les Civilisations.

1989 Le processus d'urbanisation en Palestine au Bronze Ancien: chronologie et rythmes. In P. de Miroschedji (ed.), *L'urbanisation de la Palestine à l'âge du Bronze Ancien*, 63–80. British Archaeological Reports International Series 527. Oxford: British Archaeological Reports.

1993a Tell el-Far'ah North: Neolithic to Middle Bronze Age. In E. Stern (ed.), *The New Encyclopedia of Archaeological Excavations in the Holy Land* 1, 433–438. Jerusalem: Israel Exploration Society.

1993b Notes sur les têtes de taureau en os, en ivoire et en pierre du Bronze Ancien de Palestine. In M. Heltzer, A. Segal and D. Kaufman (eds.), *Studies in the Archaeology and History of Ancient Israel in Honour of Moshe Dothan*, 29–39. Haifa: Haifa University.

1999 Yarmouth: The Dawn of City-States in Southern Canaan. *Near Eastern Archaeology* 62: 2–19.

2000a La céramique de Khirbet Kerak en Syro-Palestine: état de la question. In C. Marro (ed.), *Chronologies des pays du Caucase et de l'Euphrate aux IVème-IIIème millénaires*, 255–278. Paris: Boccard.

2000b An Early Bronze Age III Pottery Sequence for Southern Israel. In G. Philip and D. Baird (eds.), *Ceramics and Change in the Early Bronze Age of the Southern Levant*, 315–346. Sheffield: Sheffield Academic Press.

2002a Tell Yarmuth 1999. *Israel Exploration Journal* 52: 87–95.

2002b The socio-political dynamics of Egyptian-Canaanite interaction in the Early Bronze Age. In E.C.M. van den Brink and T.E. Levy (eds.), *Egypt and the Levant. Interrelations from the 4th through the Early 3rd Millennia B.C.E.*, 39–57. London: Leicester University Press.

Mittmann, S.

1970 *Beitrage zur siedlungs-und territorialgeschichte des nordlichen Ostjordanlandes*. Wiesbaden: Harrassowitz.

1994 Hirbet ez-Zeraqon: Eine Stadt der frühen Bronzezeit in Nordjordanien. *Archaeologie in Deutschland*, 10–15.

Moorey, P.R.S.

1994 *Ancient Mesopotamian Materials and Industries*. Oxford: Clarendon Press.

Moran, W.

1992 *The Amarna Letters*. Baltimore: Johns Hopkins University.

Morris, I.

1991 The Archaeology of Ancestors: the Saxe/Goldstein hypothesis Revisited. *Cambridge Archaeological Journal* 1: 147–69.

Najjar, M.

1992 The Jordan Valley (East Bank) during the Middle Bronze Age in the Light of New Excavations. In M. Zaghloul, K. 'Amr, F. Zayadine, R. Nabeel and N. Rida Tawfiq (eds.), *Studies in the History and Archaeology of Jordan IV*, 149–154. Amman: Department of Antiquities of Jordan.

Neeley, M.P.

1992 Lithic Period Sites. In B. MacDonald (ed.), *The Southern Ghors and Northeast 'Arabah Archaeological Survey*, 25–52. Sheffield Archaeological Monographs 5. Sheffield: J.R. Collis.

Netting R. McC.

1990 Population, Permanent Agriculture, and Polities: Unpacking the Evolutionary Portmanteau. In S. Upham (ed.), *The Evolution of Political Systems: Sociopolitics in Small-Scale Sedentary Societies*, 21–61. Cambridge: Cambridge University Press.

Nicolle, C.

1999 *L'époque des premiers bourgs fortifiés pertinence de l'existence d'un processus d'urbanisation dans le Levant sud au troisième millénaire*. Bibliotheque archeologique et historique (Institut francais d'archeologie du Proche-Orient) v. 156. Beirut: Institut francais d'archeologie du Proche-Orient.

Ottosson, M.

1980 *Temples and Cult Places in Palestine*. Uppsala: Almquist and Wiksell International.

Ovadia, E.

1992 The Domestication of the Ass and Pack Transport by Animals: A Case of Technological Change. In O. Bar-Yosef and A.M. Khazanov (eds.), *Pastoralism in the Levant: Archaeological Materials in Anthropological Perspectives*, 19–28. Madison, WI Prehistory Press.

Palumbo, G.

1990 *The Early Bronze IV in the Southern Levant: Settlement Patterns, Economy and Material Culture of a 'Dark Age'*. Contriibuti e materiali di archeologica orientale III. Rome: Universita di Roma 'La Sapienza'.

Palumbo, G., J. Mabry and I. Kuijt

1990 Survey in the Wadi el-Yabis. *Syria* 67: 479–481.

Papadopoulos, T. J., L. Kontorli-Papadopoulos, and D. Politis

2001 Rescue excavaitons at an-Naq' and Tulaylat Qasr Musa al-Hamid 2000. *Annual of the Department of Antiquities of Jordan* 45: 189–193.

Parr, P.

1956 A Cave at Arqub El Dhahr. *Annual of the Department of Antiquities of Jordan* 3: 61–73.

Paynter, R.

1989 The Archaeology of Equality and Inequality. *Annual Review of Anthropology* 18: 369–399.

Petrie, W.F.

1921 *Corpus of Prehistoric Pottery and Palettes*. London: British School of Archaeology in Egypt.

Philip, G.

1988 Hoards of the Early and Middle Bronze Ages in the Levant. *World Archaeology* 20: 190–208.

1989 *Metal Weapons of the Early and Middle Bronze Ages in Syria-Palestine*. British Archaeological Reports International Series 526, 2 vols. Oxford: British Archaeological Reports.

1995a Warrior Burials in the Ancient Near Eastern Bronze Age: The Evidence from Mesopotamia, Western Iran and Syria-Palestine. In A.C. Green and S. Campbell (eds.), *The Archaeology of Death in the Ancient Near East*, 140–154. Oxbow Monograph 51. Oxford: Oxbow.

1995b Jawa and Tell Um-Hammad: Two EBA Sites in Jordan. *Palestine Exploration Quarterly* 127: 161–170.

1999 Complexity and Diversity in the Southern Levant during the Third Millennium bc: The Evidence of Khirbet Kerak Ware. *Journal of Mediterranean Archaeology* 12: 26–57.

2001 The Early Bronze I–III Age. In B. MacDonald, R. Adams and P. Bienkoswki (eds.), *The Archaeology of Jordan*, 163–232. Sheffield: Sheffield Academic Press.

2002 Contacts between the 'Uruk' World and the Levant during the Fourth Millennium BC: Evidence and Interpretation. In J. N. Postgate (ed.), *Artefacts of Com-*

plexity. Tracking the Uruk in the Near East, 207–235. Warminster, Aris and Phillips.

2003 The Early Bronze Age of the Southern Levant: A Landscape Approach. *Journal of Mediterranean Archaeology* 16: 103–131.

Philip, G. and D. Baird (eds.)

2000a *Ceramics and Change in the Early Bronze Age of the Southern Levant*. Sheffield: Sheffield Academic Press.

2000b Early Bronze Age Ceramics in the Southern Levant: An Overview. In G. Philip and D. Baird (eds.), *Ceramics and Change in the Early Bronze Age of the Southern Levant*, 3–30. Sheffield: Sheffield Academic Press.

Philip, G. and T. Rehren

1996 Fourth Millennium bc Silver from Tell esh-Shuna, Jordan: Archaeometallurgical Investigation and Some Thoughts on Ceramic Skeuomorphs. *Oxford Journal of Archaeology* 15: 129–150.

Philip, G. and O. Williams-Thorpe

2001 The Production and Consumption of Basalt Artefacts in the Southern Levant during the 5th–4th Millennia BC: A Geochemical and Petrographic Investigation. In A. R. Millard (ed.), *Proceedings of Archaeological Sciences 1997*, 11–30. Oxford: Archaeopress.

Philip, G., P.W. Clogg, D. Dungworth, S. Stos

2003 Copper Metallurgy in the Jordan Valley from the 3rd to the 1st Millennia BC: Chemical, Metallographic and Lead Isotope Analyses of Artefacts from Pella. *Levant* 35: 71–100.

Pinnock, F.

1991 Considerazioni sul sistema commerciale di Ebla protosiriana. *La Parola del Passato* 46: 270–284.

Pope, M. and S. Pollock

1995 Trade, Tools and Tasks: A Study of Uruk Chipped Stone Industries. *Research in Economic Anthropology* 16: 227–265.

Portugali, J. and R. Gophna

1993 Crisis, Progress and Urbanization: The Transition from Early Bronze I to Early Bronze II in Palestine. *Tel Aviv* 20: 164–186.

Potter, D.R. and E.M. King

1995 A Heterarchical Approach to Lowland Maya Socioeconomics. In R.M. Ehrenreich, C.L. Crumley and J.E. Levy (eds.), *Heterarchy and the Analysis of Complex Societies*, 17–32. Archaeological Papers of the American Anthropological Association 6. Arlington: American Anthropological Association.

Prag, K.

1989 Preliminary Peport on Excavations at Tell Iktanu, Jordan. *Levant* 21: 33–45.

1991 Preliminary Peport on Excavations at Tell Iktanu, and Tell el-Hammam, Jordan 1990. *Levant* 23: 55–66.

1992 Bronze Age Settlement Patterns in the South Jordan Valley: Archaeology, Environment and Ethnology. In M. Zaghloul, K. 'Amr, F. Zayadine, R. Nabeel and N.

Rida Tawfiq (eds.), *Studies in the History and Archaeology of Jordan IV*, 155–160. Amman: Department of Antiquities.

1993 The Excavations at Tell Iktanu 1989 and 1990: The Excavations at Tell al-Hammam 1990. *Syria* 70: 269–273.

1995 The Dead Sea Dolmens: Death and the Landscape. In S. Campbell and A. Green (eds.), *The Archaeology of Death in the Ancient Near East*, 75–84. Oxbow Monographs 51. Oxford: Oxbow.

Price, B.J.

1978 Secondary State Formation: An Explanatory Model. In R. Cohen and E.R. Service (eds.), *The Origins of the State*, 161–186. Philadelphia: Institute for the Study of Human Issues.

Quintero, L. A., P. J. Wilke and G.O. Rollefson

2002 From Flint Mine to Fan Scraper: The Late Prehistoric Jafr Industrial Complex. *Bulletin of the American Schools of Oriental Research* 327: 17–48.

Rast, W.E.

1995 Building on Marl: The Case of Bab adh-Dhra'. In K. 'Amr, F. Zayadine and M. Zaghloul (eds.), *Studies in the History and Archaeology of Jordan V*, 123–128. Amman: Department of Antiquities.

Rast, W.E. and R.T. Schaub

1974 Survey of the Southeastern Plain of the Dead Sea, 1973. *Annual of the Department of Antiquities of Jordan* 19: 5–53.

1978 A Preliminary Report of the Excavations at Bab edh-Dhra 1975. In D.N. Freedman (ed.), *Preliminary Excavation Reports: Bab edh-Dhra', Sardis, Meiron, Tell el-Hesi, Carthage (Punic)*, 1–32. Annual of the American Schools of Oriental Research 43. Cambridge: American Schools of Oriental Research.

1980 Preliminary Report of the 1979 Expedition to the Dead Sea Plain, Jordan. *Bulletin of the American Schools of Oriental Research* 240: 21–63.

1981 *The South Eastern Dead Sea Plain Expedition: An Interim Report of the 1977 Season*. Annual of the American Schools of Oriental Research 46. Cambridge: American Schools of Oriental Research.

2003 *Bab edh-Dhra: Excavations at the Town Site (1975–81)*. Reports of the Expedition to the Dead Sea Plain, Jordan 2. Winona Lake, IN: Eisenbrauns.

Rehren, T., K. Hess and G. Philip

1996 Auriferous Silver in Western Asia: Ore or Alloy? *Journal of the Historical Metallurgy Society* 30: 1–10.

1997 Fourth Millennium BC Copper Metallurgy in Northern Jordan: The Evidence from Tell esh-Shuna. In H.-G. Gebel, Z. Kafafi and G.O. Rollefson (eds.), *Prehistory of Jordan. II. Perspectives from 1997*, 625–640. Studies in Early Near Eastern Production, Subsistence and Environment 4. Berlin: *ex oriente*.

Renfrew, A.C.

1974 Beyond a Subsistence Economy: The Evolution of Social

Organizations in Prehistoric Europe. In C.M. Moore (ed.), *Reconstructing Complex Societies: An Archaeological Colloquium*, 69–95. Bulletin of the American Schools of Oriental Research Supplements 20. Cambridge: American Schools of Oriental Research.

Renfrew, A.C. and J.F. Cherry

1986 *Peer Polity Interaction and Socio-Political Change.* Cambridge: Cambridge University Press.

Richard, S.L.

1987 The Early Bronze Age: The Rise and Collapse of Urbanism. *Biblical Archaeologist* 50: 22–43.

Richard, S.L. and R.S. Boraas

1984 Report of the 1981–82 Season of the Expedition to Khirbet Iskander and its Vicinity. *Bulletin of the American Schools of Oriental Research* 254: 63–87.

Riehl, S.

2004 Archaeobotany at the Early Bronze Age settlement of Hirbet ez-Zeraqon. *Zeitschrift des Deutschen Palästina Vereins* 120: 101–120.

Rollefson, G.O.

1993 PPNC Adaptations in the First Half of the Sixth Millennium B.C. *Paléorient* 19: 33–42.

Rosen, A.M.

1989 Environmental Change at the End of the Early Bronze Age. In P. de Miroschedji (ed.), *L'urbanisation de la Palestine à l'age du Bronze Ancien*, 247–255. British Archaeological Reports International Series 527. Oxford: British Archaeological Reports.

1991 Early Bronze Age Tel Erani: An Environmental Perspective. *Tel Aviv* 18: 192–204.

1995 The Social Response to Environmental Change in Early Bronze Age Canaan. *Journal of Anthropological Archaeology* 14: 26–44.

Rosen, S.A.

1993 Metals, Rocks, Specialization and the Beginning of Urbanism in the Northern Negev. In A. Biran and J. Aviram (eds.), *Biblical Archaeology Today 1990: Pre-Congress Symposium Supplement: Population, Production and Power*, 41–56. Jerusalem: Israel Exploration Society.

1997a *Lithics after the Stone Age: A Handbook of Stone Tools from the Levant.* London: Altamira.

1997b Craft Specialization and the Rise of Secondary Urbanism: A View from the Southern Levant. In W.E. Aufrecht, N.A Mirau and S.W. Gauley (eds.), *Urbanism in Antiquity: From Mesopotamia to Crete*, 82–91. Journal for the Study of the Old Testament Supplement Series 244. Sheffield: Sheffield Academic Press.

Rothman, M.S.

2004 Studying the Development of Complex Society: Mesopotamia in the Late Fifth and Fourth Millennia BC *Journal of Archaeological Research* 12: 75–119.

Rowan, D.

1994 The Early Bronze Age Ceramics from Area A. In D. Baird and G. Philip, Preliminary Report on the Third

(1993) Season of Excavations at Tell esh-Shuna North. *Levant* 26: 124–129.

Rutter, G.P. and G. Philip

In press Beyond Provenance Analysis: the Movement of Basaltic Artefacts through a Social Landscape. In J. Ebeling and Y. Rowan (eds), *New Approaches to Old Stones: Recent Studies of Ground Stone Artefacts.* Approaches to Anthropological Archaeology. Winona Lake, IN: Eisenbrauns.

Rutter, G.P., D.G. Pearson, G. Philip, J.M.D. Day, and C.J. Ottley

2003 The Use of ICP-MS in Provenancing Igneous Stone Artefacts: Examples from the Southern Levant. In G. Holland and S.D. Tanner (eds), *8th International Conference on Plasma Source Mass Spectrometry* (Durham Sept. 2002), 209–220. Cambridge: Royal Society of Chemistry.

Sapin, J.

1985 Prospection géo-archéologique de l'Ajlûn 1981–82: example de recherche intégrante. In A. Hadidi (ed.), *Studies in the History and Archaeology of Jordan II*, 217–227. Amman: Department of Antiquities.

Sapin, J.

1992 De l'occupation à l'utilisation de l'espace à l'aube de l'âge du Bronze dans le région de Jerash et sa péripherie orientale. In M. Zaghloul, K. 'Amr, F. Zayadine, R. Nabeel and N. Rida Tawfiq (eds.), *Studies in the History and Archaeology of Jordan IV*, 169–174. Amman: Department of Antiquities.

Schaub, R.T.

1981 Ceramic Sequences in the Tomb Groups at Bab edh-Dhra. In W.E. Rast and R.T. Schaub (eds.), *The Southeastern Dead Sea Plain Expedition: An Interim Report of the 1977 Season*, 69–118. Annual of the American Schools of Oriental Research 46. Cambridge: American Schools of Oriental Research.

1982 The Origins of the Early Bronze Age Walled Town Culture of Jordan. In A. Hadidi (ed.), *Studies in the History and Archaeology of Jordan II*, 67–75. Amman: Department of Antiquities.

1996 Pots as Containers. In J.D. Seger (ed.), *Retrieving the Past: Essays on Archaeological Research and Methodology in Honor of Gus W. Van Beek*, 231–243. Winona Lake, IN: Eisenbrauns.

Schaub, R.T. and W.E. Rast

1981 Patterns of Burial at Bab edh-Dhra. In W.E. Rast and R.T. Schaub (eds.), *The Southeastern Dead Sea Plain Expedition: An Interim Report of the 1977 Season*, 45–68. Annual of the American Schools of Oriental Research 46. Cambridge: American Schools of Oriental Research.

1984 Preliminary Report of the 1981 Expedition to the Dead Sea Plain, Jordan. *Bulletin of the American Schools of Oriental Research* 254: 35–60.

1987 Ceramic Vessels as Evidence for Trade and Communication during the Early Bronze Age in Jordan. In A.

Hadidi (ed.), *Studies in the History and Archaeology of Jordan III*, 247–250. Amman: Department of Antiquities.

1989 *Bab edh-Dhra: Excavations in the Cemetery Directed by Paul W. Lapp (1965–67)*. Reports of the Expedition to the Dead Sea Plain, Jordan, I. Winona Lake, IN: Eisenbrauns.

1992 A Reassessment of Nelson Glueck on Settlement on the Jordan Plateau in Early Bronze III and IV. In M. Zaghloul, K. 'Amr, F. Zayadine, R. Nabeel and N. Rida Tawfiq (eds.), *Studies in the History and Archaeology of Jordan IV*, 161–168. Amman: Department of Antiquities.

Savage, S.H. and G.O. Rollefson

2001 The Moab Archaeological Resource Survey: Some Results from the 2000 Field Season. *Annual of the Department of Antiquities of Jordan* 45: 217–236.

Scheftelowitz, N.

2002 Pottery: Early Bronze Age. In A. Kempinski, N. Scheftelowitz and R. Oren, *Tell Kabri The 1986–1993 Excavation Seasons*, 96–108. Tel Aviv: Tel Aviv University Sonia and Marco Nadler Institute of Archaeology. Emery and Clare Yass Publications in Archaeology.

Schnurrenberger, D.W.

1991 Preliminary Comments on the Geology of the Tell el-'Umeiri Region. In L.G. Herr, L. T. Geraty, O. S. LaBianca and R. W. Younker (eds.), *Madaba Plains Project 2: The 1987 Season at Tell el-'Umeiri and Vicinity and Subsequent Studies*. Berrien Springs, MI: Andrews University

Schwartz, G.M.

1994 Rural Economic Specialization and Early Urbanization in the Khabur Valley, Syria. In G.M. Schwartz and S.E. Falconer (eds.), *Archaeological Views from the Countryside: Village Communities in Early Complex Societies*, 19–36. Washington: Smithsonian Institution.

Schwartz, G.M. and S.E. Falconer

1994 Rural Approaches to Social Complexity. In G.M. Schwartz and S.E. Falconer (eds.), *Archaeological Views from the Countryside: Village Communities in Early Complex Societies*, 1–9. Washington: Smithsonian Institution.

Serpico, M. and R. White

1996 A Report on the Analysis of the Contents of a Cache of Jars from the Tomb of Djer. In J. Spencer (ed.), *Aspects of Early Egypt*, 128–139. London: British Museum.

Service, E.

1962 *Primitive Social Organization*. New York: Random House.

1975 *Origins of the State and Civilizations*. New York: Norton.

Shalev, S.

1994 The Change in Metal Production from the Chalcolithic Period to the Early Bronze Age in Israel and Jordan. *Antiquity* 68: 630–637.

Sherratt, A.

1981 Plough and Pastoralism: Aspects of the Secondary Products Revolution. In I. Hodder, G. Isaac and N. Hammond (eds.), *Pattern of the Past*, 261–305. Cambridge: Cambridge University Press.

Sherratt, A. and E. Sherratt

1991 From Luxuries to Commodities: The Nature of Mediterranean Bronze Age Trading Systems. In N.H. Gale (ed.), *Bronze Age Trade in the Mediterranean*, 351–386. Studies in Mediterranean Archaeology 90. Jonsered: Åströms Förlag.

Stager, L.

1985 The First Fruits of Civilization. In J.N. Tubb (ed.), *Palestine in the Bronze and Iron Ages: Papers in Honour of Olga Tufnell*, 172–188. London: Institute of Archaeology.

1992 The Periodization of Palestine from Neolithic through Early Bronze Times. In R.W. Ehrich (ed.), *Chronologies in Old World Archaeology*, 22–41. Chicago: University of Chicago Press.

2001 Port Power in the Early and the Middle Bronze Age: The Organziation of Maritime Trade and Hinterland Production. In S.R. Wolff (ed.), *Studies in the Archaeology of Israel and Neighbouring Lands in Memory of Douglas L. Esse,* 625–638. Chicago: The Oriental Institute of the University of Chicago.

Steele, C.S.

1990 Early Bronze Age Socio-Political Organization in Southwestern Asia. *Zeitschrift des Deutschen Palästina-Vereins* 106: 1–33.

Stein, G.

1994 Segmentary States and Organizational Variations in Early Complex Societies: A Rural Perspective. In G. Schwartz and S.E. Falconer (eds.), *Archaeological Views from the Countryside: Village Communities in Early Complex Societies*, 10–18. Washington: Smithsonian Institution.

1998 Heterogeneity, power, and political economy: some current research issues in the archaeology of Old World complex societies. *Journal of Archaeological Research* 6: 1–44.

2001 Understanding Ancient State Societies in the Old World In G. Feinman and D. Price (eds.), *Archaeology at the Millennium: A Sourcebook*, 353–79. New York: Kluwer.

Stein, G. and M.J. Blackman

1993 The Organizational Context of Specialised Craft Production in Early Mesopotamian States. *Research in Economic Anthropology* 14: 29–59.

Stein, G. and M.S. Rothman, (eds.)

1994 *Chiefdoms and Early States in the Near East. The Organizational Dynamics of Complexity*. Madison, WI: Prehistory Press.

Sweet, L.

1960 *Tell Touqan: A Syrian Village*. Anthropological Papers of the Museum of Anthropology, University of Michigan

No. 14. Ann Arbor, MI: University of Michigan.

Thomas, J.

1991 *Rethinking the Neolithic*. Cambridge: Cambridge University Press.

Tilley, C.

1994 *A Phenomenology of Landscape: Places, Paths and Monuments*. Oxford: Berg.

Tubb, J.N. and P.G. Dorrell

1993 Tell es-Sa'idiyeh: Interim Report on the Sixth Season of Excavations. *Palestine Exploration Quarterly* 125: 50–74.

1994 Tell es-Sa'idiyeh 1993: Interim Report on the Seventh Season of Excavations. *Palestine Exploration Quarterly* 126: 52–67.

Turner, V.

1969 *The Ritual Process*. New York: Cornell University Press.

Upham, S. (ed.)

1990 *The Evolution of Political Systems: Sociopolitics in Small-scale Sedentary Societies*. Cambridge: Cambridge University Press.

Van den Brink, E.

1996 The Incised Serekh-Signs of Dynasties 0–1, Part 1: Complete Vessels. In J. Spencer (ed.), *Aspects of Early Egypt*, 140–58. London: British Museum.

Van Gennep, A.

1960 *The Rites of Passage*. Chicago: University of Chicago Press.

Vieweger, D.

1997 An Early Bronze Age Handle with Cylinder Seal Impression from Dayr Qiqub, Jordan. *Levant* 29: 147–52.

Waheeb, M.

1995 The First Season of the An-Naq' Project, Ghawr As-Safi. *Annual of the Department of Antiquities of Jordan* 39: 553–55.

Wapnish, P. and B. Hesse

1988 Urbanization and the Organization of Animal Production at Tell Jemmeh in the Middle Bronze Age Levant. *Journal of Near Eastern Studies* 47.2: 81–94.

Watson, P.

1996 Pella Hinterland Survey 1994: Preliminary Report. *Levant* 28: 63–76.

Wattenmaker, P.

1994 State Formation and the Organization of Domestic Craft Production at Third Millennium bc Kurban Höyük, Southeast Turkey. In G. Schwartz and S. Falconer (eds.), *Archaeological Views from the Countryside: Village Communities in Early Complex Societies*, 109–20. Washington: Smithsonian Institution.

Wilcox, G.H.

1981 Plant Remains. In S.W. Helms, *Jawa: Lost City of the Black Desert*, 247–48. London: Methuen.

Wilkinson, A.

1989 Objects from the EB II and III Tombs. In R.T. Schaub and W.E. Rast, *Bab edh-Dhra: Excavations in the Cemetery Directed by Paul W. Lapp (1965–67)*, 444–72. Reports of the Expedition to the Dead Sea Plain, Jordan, vol. I. Winona Lake, IN: Eisenbrauns.

Wilkinson, T.A.H.

1996 *State Formation in Egypt: Chronology and Society*. British Archaeological Reports International Series 651. Oxford: Tempus Reparatum.

1999 *Early Dynastic Egypt*. London: Routledge.

Wright, G.E.

1937 *The Pottery of Palestine from the Earliest Times to the End of the Early Bronze Age*. New Haven: American Schools of Oriental Research.

1961 The Archaeology of Palestine. In G.E. Wright (ed.), *The Bible and the Ancient Near East: Essays in Honor of William Foxwell Albright*, 73–112. London: Routledge and Kegan Paul.

Wright, H.T. 1977. Recent Research on the Origin of the State. *Annual Review of Anthropology* 6: 379–97.

Wright, H.T. and G.A. Johnson

1975 Population, Exchange and Early State Formation in South Western Iran. *American Anthropologist* 77: 267–91.

Wright, K.I.

1993 Early Holocene Ground Stone Assemblages in the Levant. *Levant* 25: 93–111.

Yekutieli, Y.

2000 Early Bronze Age I pottery in southwestern Canaan. In G. Philip and D. Baird (eds.), *Ceramics and Change in the Early Bronze Age of the Southern Levant*, 129–152. Sheffield: Sheffield Academic Press.

Yoffee, N.

1993 Too Many Chiefs? (or, Safe Texts for the 90's). In N. Yoffee and A. Sherratt (eds.), *Archaeological Theory: Who Sets the Agenda*, 60–78. Cambridge: Cambridge University Press.

Zarzecki-Peleg, A.

1991 Decorated Bones of the Third Millennium B.C.E. from Palestine and Syria: Stylistic Analysis. *Israel Exploration Journal* 43: 1–22.

Zertal, A.

1993 Fortified Enclosures of the Early Bronze Age in the Samaria Region and the Beginning of Urbanization. *Levant* 25: 18–31.

Zohar, M.

1992 Megalithic Cemeteries in the Levant. In O. Bar-Yosef and A.M. Khazanov (eds.), *Pastoralism in the Levant: Archaeological Materials in Anthropological Perspectives*, 43–63. Madison, WI Prehistory Press.

Zohary, D. and M. Hopf

1993 *Domestication of Plants in the Old World: The Origins and Spread of Cultivated Plants in Western Asia, Europe and the Nile Valley*. 2nd edn. Oxford: Clarendon Press.

7. The Early Bronze Age IV

Gaetano Palumbo

Introduction

The Early Bronze Age IV (c. 2350–2000 bc) is characterized in Jordan by an extensive occupation of both fertile and arid environments, in what seems to be an essentially rural occupation of the landscape, and with a typical absence of urban centres. This characteristic makes the entire period a "rural interlude" between the Early Bronze II–III and the Middle Bronze Ages, periods when the urban element of those societies appeared to be much stronger. The same situation is reflected in Israel and Palestine, as well as southern Lebanon and Syria, while in northern Syria large urban centres (such as Ebla [Tall Mardikh]) flourished precisely during the last quarter of the third millennium bc.

The cause of this apparent sudden demise of the Early Bronze Age urban environment was sought in the past in the arrival of nomadic groups from the desert fringes and the Syrian steppes (identified with the Amorites). A combination of new archaeological data from surveys and excavations and a different interpretative perspective, centred on socioeconomic factors rather than political episodes, has modified the nomadic invasion theory in favour of an approach oriented to a model of "ruralization" of the cultural landscape of the Levant (Falconer 1994, 1995). This "ruralization" can be interpreted as an answer to the internal crisis of the urban structure that dominated the cultural landscape of the Levant during the first seven centuries of the third millennium bc (Dever 1995; Palumbo 1990).

Terminology and Theoretical Models

Early Bronze Age IV (EB IV) is only one of several "labels" used to identify the chronological and cultural phase covering approximately the last three centuries of the third millennium bc. The adoption of the EB IV terminology stresses the idea that, especially in Jordan, this period seems to have more important links with the previous, rather than the following periods. The phase was recognized as early as 1932 by Albright (1932), who called it Middle Bronze (MB) I and placed it in absolute dates between 2100 and 1900 bc. Glueck, in his *Survey of Eastern Palestine* (1934, 1935, 1939, 1951), followed the same terminology, while Wright introduced the EB IV terminology for the first time, identifying a phase immediately preceding Albright's MB I, which he recognized at several locations, including Tomb 351 at Jericho, and the assemblage at Wadi Ghazzeh Site H (Wright 1937:

78–81). None of the complexes Wright mentions are earlier than Albright's "MB I," with the exception of Tomb 351 at Jericho, and stratum J at Tell Beth Mirsim, both rather late EB III in date, and Wadi Ghazzeh Site H, which dates to Late Chalcolithic/Early Bronze I (Dever 1973: 39). With the excavations at Jericho by Kenyon came also the formulation of the nomadic invasion theory and the creation of another term to describe the period: "Intermediate Early Bronze–Middle Bronze" (EB–MB) (Kenyon 1951: 106; 1956: 41–42). Kenyon's "Amorite hypothesis," which sees in the arrival of populations from the Syrian steppes the cause for the collapse of urbanization at the end of EB III in Palestine, met the favour of many scholars. The theory, however, was not completely original, since already in 1938 Wright had expressed an opinion linking the Amorites with the changes observed between the EB III and the following periods. This opinion was also repeated by Albright (1940) and De Vaux (1946), but it was Kenyon who linked the archaeological evidence found at several late third-millennium cemeteries in Palestine and formulated the "Amorite hypothesis" that was at the base of the nomadic model until recently. The core of the theory claims that the Amorites, a Semitic, non-indigenous population, entered Palestine and occupied the hill country, while the native Canaaneans, who were responsible for the urban Early Bronze Age civilization, were confined to the coastal plain (Kenyon 1956: 41). Very little is said about the regions east of the Jordan by Kenyon, but the absence of excavations, with the exception of Bab adh-Dhra, could not help her in establishing the facts for her theory. At Jericho she compiled a strict typology of tomb types that she attributed to separate ethnic groups (Kenyon 1960: 180–259; 1965: 33–161).

While some scholars adhered to Kenyon's "pure" invasion theory (Lapp 1966: 111–16;[1] Kochavi 1963a: 141–42), many others adopted a more moderate view, where infiltrations of nomadic groups, rather than invasions, are at the base of the changes observed in the archaeological record (Amiran 1960: 224-225; Dever 1970: 145; 1971: 211–225; Prag 1974: 106–107; Tufnell 1958: 41–42).

While not clearly supporting or denying the"Amorite hypothesis," Amiran added an interesting contribution to the debate, identifying a series of pottery groups, or "families," which she named in a variety of ways and dated to different phases within the period. She finally defined her position in a 1974 paper where she presented three basic families: the Southern Group, the Northern Group and the Bethel Group. In contrast with previous positions, she saw these families as largely contemporary (1974: 2).

The acceptance of this basic division by many scholars is connected with its strong emphasis on regionalism, which is still today understood as one of the most distinct characteristics of this period's material culture.

Between 1971 and 1973 Dever expanded the "families" subdivision pioneered by Amiran, improving it by taking into consideration the entire material culture of the regions investigated, and not only the pottery typology. Dever recognized seven families: Northern (N); North-Central (NC); Jericho/Jordan Valley (J); Southern (S); Central Hills (CH); Coastal (C); and Jordan (TR). He did

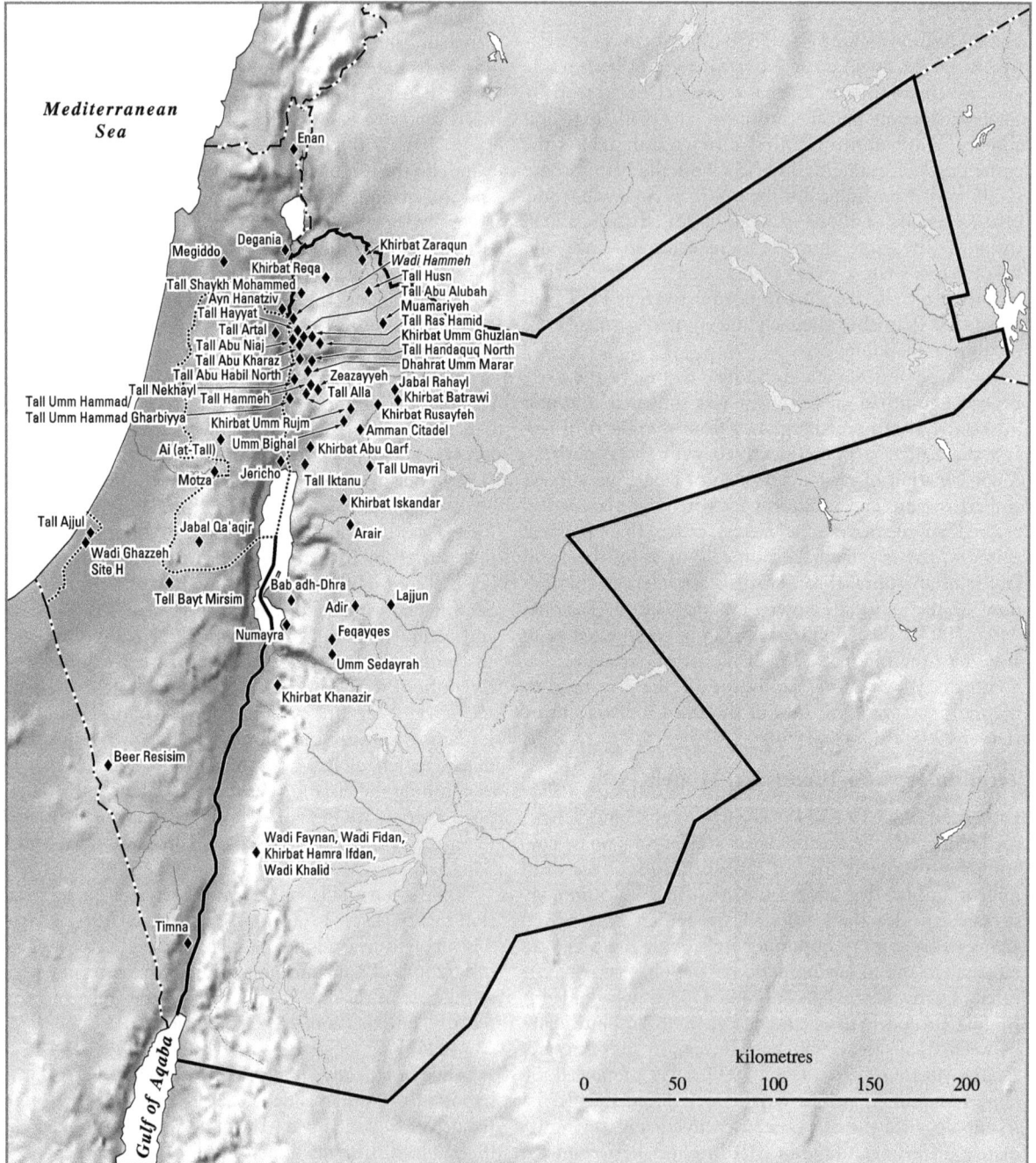

Figure 7.1   Early Bronze Age IV sites mentioned in the text.

not believe in rigid boundaries between the groups, and thought that the families largely overlapped chronologically, even if he dated the TR to an earlier phase than the N, NC, J and CH, and put the S to the terminal phase of the period. He rejected his original MB I terminology to adopt the EB IV terminology, which he also subdivided into three phases (A, B, C) (Figure 7.2).

In 1980 Dever basically confirmed this division and chronology, formulating his theory on pastoral nomadism. In developing this theory, he adopted the fundamental studies by Liverani (1970, 1973) and Rowton (1967), where the historicity of the Amorites was put in doubt by stringent arguments denying the existence of nomadic groups originating in northern Syria, where instead a sophisticated urban culture and a high degree of sedentarization existed at the end of the third millennium bc.

Liverani showed, in fact, that our knowledge of the presence of "savage nomads" in Syria derived from the propaganda of the Mesopotamian cities that described the MAR-TU as people "not knowing houses, not knowing cities," "eating raw meat, they do not have houses, and when they die, they are not buried," "tent dwellers."[2] However, these nomads were only the pastoral groups living at the fringe of the desert, sometimes pushing their way into the fertile grounds of Mesopotamia: the population in Syria during the last quarter of the third millennium bc mainly included urban dwellers and agricultural communities. Another argument pushed forward by Liverani was that the kind of nomadism represented in Kenyon's Amorite hypothesis is of the historical Central Asian "type" (Patai 1951; Bacon 1954; Khazanov 1978; 1984: 44–53), not applicable to Syria-Palestine, where nomadism is of a pastoral type characterized by short movements and transhumance (Fabietti 1982; Khazanov 1984: 53–59).[3]

The concept of "dimorphic society," introduced by Liverani to describe the social structure of Syria during this period, derives from Rowton's reconstruction of Old Babylonian society at Mari. Rowton used this term to describe the characteristics of a social web where the nomadic/pastoral and the agricultural/sedentary elements are in symbiosis. In the case of Mari's society during the eighteenth century bc, and northern Syrian society at the end of the third millennium bc as analysed by Liverani, the sedentary component was urbanized, adding another variable to the complex system of social relations (Rowton 1967).[4]

The concept of dimorphic society and a more careful look at the phenomenon of pastoral nomadism in ancient Middle Eastern societies are at the basis of a revival of theoretical studies, which can be placed in the decade between the mid-1970s and the mid-1980s, concerning the Early Bronze Age IV. Dever, for example, moved from the MB I to the EB IV terminology, changing also his theoretical perspective. From a moderate version of the

"Amorite hypothesis," that looked to the Jabal Bishri area in central Syria for the source of the nomadic invasions, he came to support the pastoral nomadism model and the concept of a "dimorphic society," describing its effects as "the brief triumph of the desert over the sown" (1980: 58).

This model of pastoral nomadism sees wider mobility by part of the nomads and access to "forbidden" areas formerly controlled by the central power as a consequence of the disintegration of the Early Bronze Age urban structure.[5] The new type of settlement, based on seasonal transhumance, prevailed throughout the EB IV according to Dever, especially in the more marginal zones of Palestine and Jordan. He conceded, however, that greater settlement stability could have existed in such areas as the Jordan Valley. Dever's archaeological surveys and excavations at Jabal Qa'aqir applied this model to an area he designated the "Hebron and Khirbat Kirmil Hills–Negev Complex" (Dever 1972, 1981; Gitin 1975), where he conducted a series of excavations (Dever 1975a) in the Hebron Hills, and at Beer Resisim in the Central Negev (Cohen and Dever 1978, 1979, 1981; Dever 1983, 1985). Dever interpreted the sites of the Hebron area as summer camps and cemeteries of semi-nomadic populations who spent their winter months in the Central Negev (1980: 57).

Thompson (1975, 1979) believes not only that the continuity of cultural traditions and settlement between the Early Bronze Age I–III and the EB IV are substantial, but also that most of the settlement during EB IV was sedentary and based on agriculture. His extreme position, however, was based on an acritical reading of the site lists and showed little familiarity with both the archaeological evidence and the various types of nomadism found in the region.

In the same years, Prag developed her view of the EB IV as a period of change derived not from invasions, but from infiltrations of nomadic groups or true "pastoral migrations" from Syria toward the main valleys (Huleh, Jordan and Jezreel). For Prag, these nomadic movements were also a consequence of the decline of the Early Bronze Age urban civilization (Prag 1984: 67; 1985).

In the 1980s and 1990s, several excavations and survey data have helped to advance the understanding of the period.

Falconer and Magness-Gardiner (1984, 1989) based their observations on the data coming from two excavations they conducted in the Jordan Valley, at Tall Hayyat and Tall Abu Niaj. The variety of subsistence strategies identified in their excavations suggested that the model of pastoral nomadism cannot serve, alone, as an explanation for the type of mixed economic solutions adopted by the EB IV people. In his dissertation, Falconer (1987a) expanded this intuition in a model that sees pastoralism as part of a rural economic system, formed by various components, sometimes in balance, other times in conflict, but basically representing an element of stability in a region where cities could not develop into the well-organized structure visible in Mesopotamia or Syria. Dever called this the "rural-nomadic" model (1992: 88). With different nuances, it is still the model most accepted today.

For Richard and Long (who based their work on the results of their excavations at Khirbat Iskandar, the only true "urban" EB IV settlement excavated so far in the southern Levant)[6] the importance of pastoral nomadism was limited to local or regional boundaries. Richard sees, in the change occurring at the end of Early Bronze Age III in the society's organization and production subsystems, a reaction to an irreversible crisis in the larger urban system. The direction of change is not from a sedentary to a nomadic way of life, but from an urban to a non-urban and pastoral production system, the latter being more typical of villages and small centres (Richard and Boraas 1988; Richard 1987). Richard's model is based on the theory of chiefdoms as described by Service (1962), but this adaptation has been unconvincing so far.

In another contribution, Long (1986) and Richard and Long (1989) adapted a model formulated by Bates and Lees (1977: 837–839), which suggests that decline in the specialization of an economic system is followed by decline in the agricultural and pastoral modes of production. Instead of fluctuation between different types of subsistence strategies, such as agriculture and pastoralism, fluctuation should be seen in terms of different degrees of specialization. In this case, rather than shifts from one subsistence strategy to another, as implied by the pastoral nomadism model, the whole system would have been more amalgamated and less specialized.

More sophisticated than Long and Richard's contribution is the model formulated by Finkelstein (1989). He goes beyond the "dimorphic society" approach, introducing a "multimorphic" approach, which would better explain the causes of urban civilization's collapse. While he believes that the EB IV period in the southern Levant is characterized by the collapse of the specialization system (following, even if not explicitly, Bates and Lees), he stresses, quite rightly, the importance of the marginal nomadic or semi-nomadic pastoral groups for the understanding of this period, and identifies in the "visibility" of these groups, from an archaeological point of view, the consequence of a partial sedentarization dictated not by a political power, but by more autonomous productive strategies, since no agricultural surplus was available any more from the sedentary communities (Finkelstein 1989: 135–136). Between 1992 and 1995 Finkelstein further refined his theory, adopting Lemche's (1985) definition of a "polymorphous society." By doing so he also denied the chronological variations seen by Dever in his pottery "families" and added trade as one of the factors that encouraged the sedentarization of pastoral nomads, citing the evidence provided by recent work in the copper-

mining area of Faynan. He also stressed the difficulty in tracing the "archaeological line" between agriculturalists practising herding and herders practising agriculture, especially in areas of traditional settlement (Finkelstein 1992: 134; 1995: 99).

My general work on the EB IV of the southern Levant (Palumbo 1990) introduced the concept of "diversified levels of specialization," following Marfoe's approach (1979). This is an improvement over both the dimorphic/multimorphic and the specialization/despecialization models, in that it is not a "linear" model, but explains variation in terms of "shifts along a spectrum of available economic strategies and sociocultural roles" (Marfoe 1979: 8). In this perspective, the entire Early Bronze–Middle Bronze transition can be explained in terms of adaptations to changing physical and political conditions. Both the Early Bronze urban "collapse" and the Middle Bronze urban rise can be explained in this context, but the model has a special significance in explaining the variety of adaptive strategies that are observed throughout the southern Levant during the last quarter of the third millennium bc. It is the rural, rather than the pastoral aspect of production that really differentiates this period from the more "urban" EB II–III and Middle Bronze periods, and it is this "rural response" to urban collapse that underlines the capability of "ruralism" to survive stress and continue virtually unchanged through periods of urban control (Palumbo 1990: 130–131, see also Falconer 1994).

Similar conclusions were reached by Esse (1991: 175), who, in his analysis of the evolution of the cultural, economic and social landscape of northern Palestine during the Early Bronze Age, maintained that throughout this period the entire spectrum of adaptive strategies existed: what changed from one period to another was their balance, and in EB IV he sees the dominance of the pastoral component.

LaBianca (1990) observed in the data gathered during the Hisban/Madaba Plains project a recurrence of phases in which settlement is more stable against phases in which it is more dispersed, following responses to changing political or environmental circumstances. He called these "cycles of intensification and abatement," and they can be easily adapted to explain what happened in the region between the Early and the Middle Bronze Ages.

This stress on the "rurality" of the Early and Middle Bronze Age cultures of the southern Levant has been partially accepted by Dever in his latest contributions to this argument (1992, 1995). There, Dever admits that the data from Jordan support a more diversified economic environment, but he stresses that regionalism and pastoral nomadism are better explanations for the situation in Cisjordan. In a revision of the models concerning the EB IV, he concludes that the archaeological evidence is not sufficient to test the applicability of chiefdom models (Service 1962; Carneiro 1981) to the situation in the southern

Levant during the EB IV. He rejects the model of "multimorphic society" as formulated by Finkelstein, finding it excessively particularizing. Dever prefers to resort to a tribal model that can explain the pastoral nomadic social structure of such regions as the Hebron Hills, the regionalism evidenced in various aspects of the material culture, and the presence of separate groups in cemeteries, such as Jericho and Jabal Qa'aqir. As for the rural agricultural villages, Dever speaks about a "rural" model that incorporates pastoral nomadism. He sees the villages as an outgrowth of tribal societies, clan-like conglomerates with a largely egalitarian social structure. According to Dever, the EB IV is a period in which the strong regional component is the reflection of a social division based on semi-nomadic tribal groups that partly sedentarize, creating new economic and social units. Dever agrees with Joffe's (1991) view of "alternating phases of low-level and higher-level organization, a pattern of socio-political complexity spiralling upwards and downwards around the domestic mode of production" as being the essential characteristic of social evolution in this region (Dever 1992, 1995). While not directly related to the EB IV of the southern Levant, a series of articles written by Buccellati on the problem of the identification and role of the Amorites in third-millennium societies of Syria has some methodological relevance here. His reconstruction of the rural landscape of Terqa, Mari, and Ebla (1990a, 1990b, 1992, 1993) sees the Amorites as an anomalous rural class, independent from the urban centres, but substantially Mesopotamian in character. Defining the role of the Amorites, Buccellati identifies in them a class of peasants/herders, a consequence of "nomadization of the peasants" that occupies a precise niche in the ecological landscape of the upper Euphrates. This approach is in contrast to Rowton's symbiotic model, and introduces a new point of view in the definition of "ruralism" in the emerging urban societies of the third millennium bc. Even more radical is the contribution to the debate presented by Marx (1992), who disputes the existence of pastoral nomads in the Levant as a separate entity, since they are an integral part of the economy and structure of urban societies.

The latest theoretical contributions to the topic, by Long (2003) and Richard (2003), do not add new elements to the debate. Long and Richard insist on the specialization/despecialization model, although in a more contextual, postprocessual approach. I also repeated, in 2001, the position that characterized my earlier research, on a variety of adaptation strategies to changing environmental, political, and cultural roles (Palumbo 2001).

Chronology

While the absolute date of the entire period is commonly accepted (2350/2300–2000 bc), roughly corresponding to the First Intermediate Period in Egypt, and the end of the Akkad dynasty and the Ur III period in Mesopotamia,

the internal division of the period is still open to debate.

The tripartite division proposed by Dever (1980) was until recently the most accepted one. According to this division, EB IVA, dated between 2350 and 2200 bc, is only represented by Family TR, or Transjordan. EB IVB, dated between 2200 and 2100 bc, is represented by Families N (North), NC (North-Central), J (Jordan Valley), and CH (Central Hills), the latter going into EB IVC (2100–2000 bc), mostly represented by Family S (Southern) (Figure 7.2). The challenge to this view comes from several excavations conducted in Jordan: these excavations include Falconer and Magness-Gardiner's at Tall Hayyat and Tall Abu Niaj; Richard, Boraas and Long's at Khirbat Iskandar; Prag's at Tall Iktanu; Rast and Schaub's at Bab adh-Dhra; and Adams and Adams and Levy at Khirbat Hamra Ifdan in the Faynan district of southern Jordan.

Falconer and Magness-Gardiner's tentative solution to the problem of apparent overlap of Families traditions was to consider Tall Hayyat as on the border zone between two different but contemporary pottery traditions (Families J and NC) (Falconer and Magness-Gardiner 1984: 57–58). Helms (1986: 46) not only sees the Southern Family as contemporary to most of the other regional groups,[7] but also recommends not a tripartite but a bipartite division (Helms 1989: 32).[8] At Khirbat Iskandar red-slipped wares (typical of the Transjordan Family) were found in stratigraphic association with pottery types and decorations of the Southern Family (Richard and Boraas 1988: 124),[9] and handleless storage jars were found together with folded "envelope" ledge-handle jars, two "signatures" that do not appear together in Dever's classification. For Richard and Boraas, this is due not to chronological differences, but to regional variations in contemporaneous pottery traditions.

At Tall Iktanu there are some substantial differences between the two archaeological phases (1 and 2, 1 being the most ancient) recognized by Prag. Totally absent in Phase 2 are the red-slipped ware and the large bowls with grooves under the inverted rim, the most common type in southern Transjordanian repertoires, which is missing in the repertoires of sites north of the Zarqa River. In Phase 1 band-combed and painted wares are lacking (they are not common in Phase 2, either).[10]

Besides these characteristics, there are also some pottery types or decorations prevailing in one phase or in the other, explained by Prag in chronological terms. This includes the presence of incised decoration on Phase 1 jars, and the differences in the folded "envelope" ledge-handle types, which in Phase 1 tend to have smaller and spaced flaps, while in Phase 2 they are usually larger and overlapping. Prag tried to establish some correlations with other sites in Transjordan and with the Jericho Tall and tombs using this sequence (1974: 77–81; 1986). These correlations seem to be valid mainly for the southern sites, such as Arair and Adir, and much less for the sites north

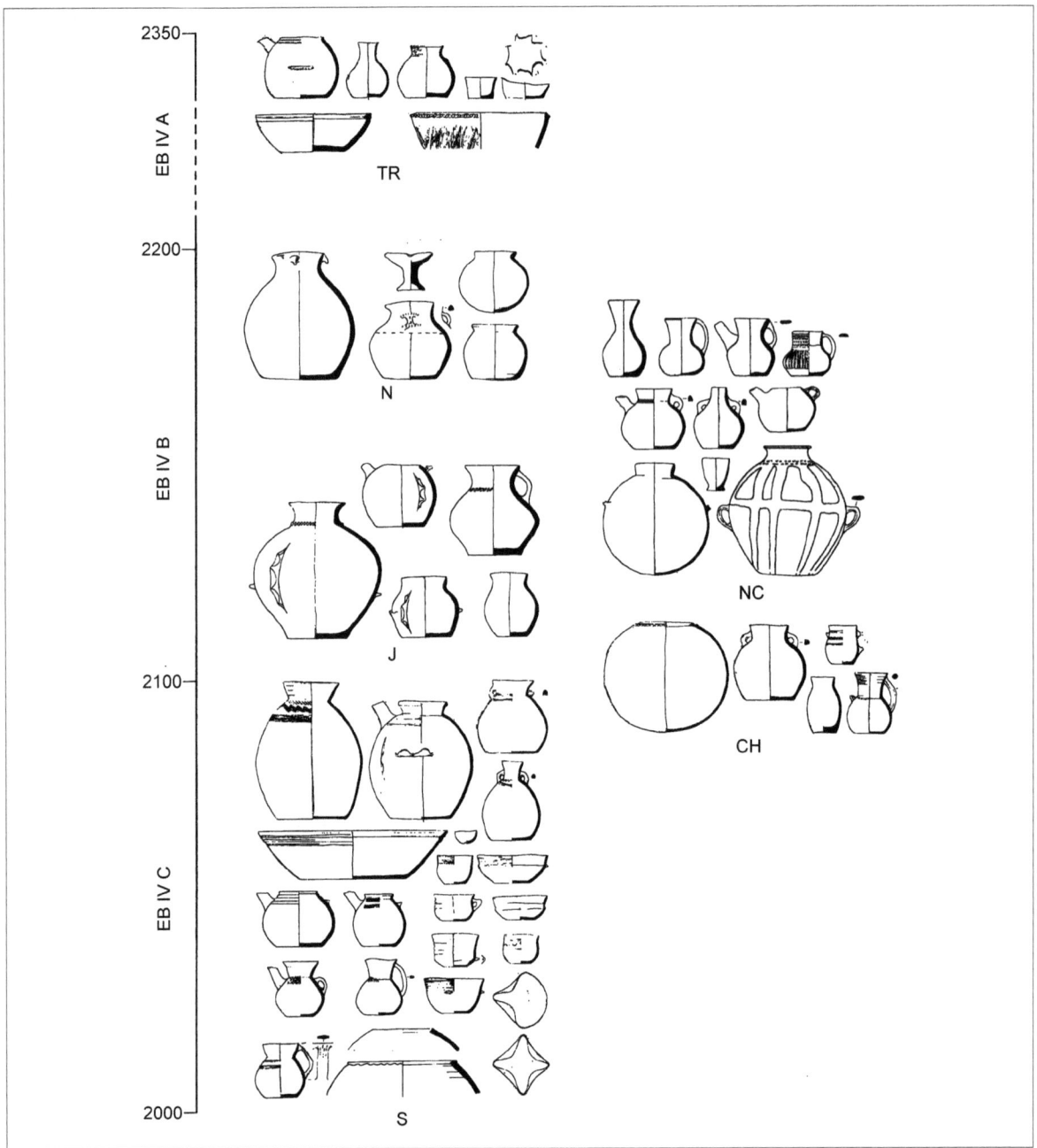

Figure 7.2   Pottery chronology according to Dever (source Palumbo 1990).

of the Zarqa River, whose repertoires frequently diverge from those at Tall Iktanu.

The four stages (5–8) identified by Helms at Tall Umm Hammad can also be divided into two main periods. Stage 5 is characterized by pottery types defined by Helms as the "regional equivalent of the red burnished, rilled, and other wares described as EB IVA," some of which are paralleled at Tall Iktanu, Phase 1 (Helms 1989: 29). In stages

6–8, the pottery is mainly of EB IVB types, but includes also EB IVC (i.e. Southern Family) types. The earlier examples of the pottery from these stages are paralleled by types known at Tall Iktanu, Phase 2 (Helms 1989: 29).

At Bab adh-Dhra, Rast and Schaub (2003) identified three layers in stratum I, attributed to the EBIV. An early and a late phase are described by Rast and Schaub (2003: 443–444) on the basis of changes in the pottery assemblage. One of the most evident changes is the diminishing number of holemouth jars and the increase of necked jars from the earliest to the latest phases of stratum I, especially in field X of the town site. Similarly the earlier phase is characterized by bowls with rolled rims, while the later phase sees an increase of turned-down rilled bowls. The correlation with other sites are between stratum IC (the earliest of the three identified at Bab adh-Dhra) and Arair VIb and Khirbat Iskandar Phase 1, while stratum IA has parallels with Arair VIa and Khirbat Iskandar Phase 3. Parallels with Phase 6 of Khirbat Hamra Ifdan and with Tall Umm Hammad Stage V, are not numerous and cannot be more precise than a generic parallel to stratum I of Bab adh-Dhra.

More recently Adams has suggested a chronological revision of the dating of many of the Central Negev Highland sites based upon his analysis of the radiocarbon dated ceramic phases at Khirbat Hamra Ifdan, in the Faynan district of southern Jordan. At Khirbat Hamra Ifdan, a large multi-phased copper manufacturing site, the dominance of Red-slipped (Family TR) forms virtually identical to those from sites such as En Ziq in contexts radiocarbon dated to a clear EBA III date suggests that the dating of phases at many sites in the Central Negev Highlands should be revised to EBIII, rather than EBIV in date (Adams 2006). At Khirbat Hamra Ifdan, the presence of mixed Family TR and Family S pottery styles only occurs in the final "abandonment phase" of the site (Adams 1999, 2000), and supports the data from Khirbat Iskandar and also that of Goren's petrographic analysis (1996), which also clearly indicates some revision is needed to the ceramic chronology and regionalism suggested by Dever and others.

It is not clear whether the long occupational sequence (five phases) at Khirbat Iskandar is also reflected by several pottery phases, or whether the stylistic evolution at that site is more continuous than at Tall Iktanu. Mixed pottery styles were found in the B8–B7 storerooms at this site (Richard and Boraas 1988: 124–127), including red-slipped and burnished vessels, considered among the earlier EB IV types, together with unslipped greyware types with incised or combed decoration, similar to Dever's Family S types.

Two phases were also identified by Olávarri at Arair (levels VIb and VIa), so distinct in their characteristics that they were assigned to the "Intermediate Bronze I and II," respectively (Olávarri 1969).[11] Levels VIb and VIa roughly correspond to Phases 1 and 2 at Tall Iktanu as shown by parallels in the pottery repertoire.

Table 7.1 shows a suggested association of basic pottery characteristics and their prevalence in certain stratified contexts. This simplified sequence (which by no means excludes the presence of "earlier" or "later" types from the contexts mentioned, but it rather shows a prevalence of certain characteristics in those same contexts) shows that

a division of the EBIV in Transjordan in at least two phases is justified. Whether this evolution of pottery types has only chronological implications, or it is associated also to changes in material culture, it is matter of speculation and would need more excavated material and good stratified sequences. Another conclusion is that Dever's Families are largely contemporary, or with important overlappings. The geographic "areas of influence" of Families are also being reconsidered in the light of the contemporary presence of different Families at several sites.

Settlement Patterns

One of the reasons for the reconstruction of the EB IV as a period of pastoral nomadic way of life has been the lack of clear "settlements" to be dated to this period, and, on the other hand, a very large number of cemeteries without an apparent association with occupation layers at nearby sites, which often seem to be abandoned during EB II–III or occupied only during the beginning of the Middle Bronze Age.

This very general picture does not correspond to the facts, especially in Jordan. Over the past 15 years, a number of survey and excavation projects have tackled the problem of EB IV settlement, succeeding in the identification of a myriad of little rural sites, a few villages, and at least one "town": Khirbat Iskandar. My general analysis of the EB IV in the southern Levant (Palumbo 1990) collected information on 258 sites in Jordan. Of these, only 29 were cemeteries, a pattern opposite to the tenet of the pastoral nomadic model, according to which the cemeteries are the only "visible" archaeological sites of a semi-nomadic culture. Another small number of sites (nine) had both surface or stratified remains and a cemetery or tombs. Finally, only 20 of the total number of sites could be defined as a "settlement," on the basis of either excavated remains or the importance of the material culture record found. At that time, only nine sites with consistent EB IV remains had been excavated, producing also a stratigraphic sequence.

These sites were Tall Abu Niaj, Adir, Arair, Bab adh-Dhra (fields X and XVI), Tall Hayyat, Tall Iktanu, Khirbat Iskandar, Tall Umm Hammad, and Zaraqun.[12] Since then, work has continued at some of those sites (Tall Abu Niaj, Tall Iktanu, Khirbat Iskandar, and Zaraqun), and started at others (Jabal Rahayl, Khirbat Hamra Ifdan).

The JADIS (Jordan Antiquities Database and Information System) database, developed from 1990 to 1994 at the Department of Antiquities of Jordan, has allowed a more thorough investigation of published and unpublished records, and the addition of information from recent archaeological projects. While only a handful of these sites have been confirmed as having occupational remains of the period, a look at the distribution of EB IV find-spots in Jordan is useful to observe possible variations from the previous and following periods. As a matter

Pottery types	Early types							Late types							
	Tall Umm Hammad 5-6	Khirbat Hamra Ifdan 5b	Bab adh-Dhra IC	Khirbat Iskander Early phase	Arair VIb	Adir C/B	Tall Iktanu I	Bab adh-Dhra I B-A	Arair VIa	Adir A	Khirbat Hamra Ifdan 6	Khirbat Iskandar Late phase	Tall Umm Hammad 7-8	Tall Iktanu 2	Tall Abu Niaj
Rounded rim holemouth jars	■	■	■	■	■	■	■								
Short necked jars	■	■	■	■	■	■	■								
Small, spaced flaps in folded ledge-handles	■	■	■	■	■	■	■								
Red slipped wares		■	■	■	■	■	■								
Rolled rim bowls		■	■	■	■	■	■	■							
Rounded rim grooved holemouth jars			■	■	■	■	■	■	■						
Rilled teapots/bowls				■	■	■	■	■	■	■					
Inverted rilled-rim platter bowls				■	■	■	■	■	■	■	■				
Grooved bowls					■	■	■	■	■	■	■	■			
Recessed rim grooved holemouth jars							■	■	■	■	■	■	■		
Deep bowls with flattened rims								■	■	■	■	■	■	■	
Everted rim jars									■	■	■	■	■	■	
Band-combing										■	■	■	■	■	■
Large overlapping flaps in ledge-handles											■	■	■	■	■
Painted wares												■	■	■	■

Table 7.1   Early and Late EBIV pottery types and their presence in stratified contexts.

of fact, this variation is quite evident in comparing both absolute numbers and the distributional charts. A general pattern of site dispersion is evident at the end of the EB II–III period: the absolute number of sites increases from EB III to EB IV, and decreases again from EB IV to MB IIA. From the more general perspective of EB II–III and the Middle Bronze Age, however, the number of sites is actually less in EB IV than in the other periods. This has led many scholars to conclude that the EB IV marked a period of site abandonment and nomadization. In reality, it is only the site size that drops drastically from EB II–III to EB IV: in the Madaba region median site size drops from 4.4 to 2.3 ha (Harrison 1997: 17), and in northern Palestine the drop is even more dramatic: from 3.2 to 0.84 ha (Esse 1991: 151–152).

On the contrary, the occupation of EB III and MB IIA sites shows a marked association with EB IV presence: both in the Jordan Valley and northern Jordan (north of the Zarqa River), for example, about 45% of the EB III sites are abandoned, and 50% or more continue into the EB IV. The same proportion is also valid for the MB IIA, with 45% of the sites not showing EB IV presence, against over 50% with both EB IV and MB IIA remains. It is interesting to note that this "smooth" transition is especially valid in Jordan, while in Cisjordan there are drastic variations from region to region.[13]

This phenomenon could be explained in two ways: "ground visibility" or "archaeological visibility" of pastoral sites. "Ground visibility" of ephemeral sites, such as pastoral camps, is much higher in desert areas than in cultivated or vegetated zones. The "archaeological visibility" of pastoral sites instead derives from a shift in economic and productive strategies, which in periods of crisis become more varied and less mobile. This means that sites that were previously occupied for brief periods, thus leaving scant or no traces, are now settled for longer periods of time, leaving a more evident record (Finkelstein 1989: 135; 1995: 98–100).

The pattern of settlement observed in Jordan shows some differences between the valleys and the plateaus, and between northern and southern regions. These differences are also reflected in the material culture, especially in the pottery types found on the surface or deposits of settlements and cemeteries.

Jordan Valley

Settlements on the east bank of the Jordan Valley are of various types, including open sites such as Tall Abu Niaj (Figure 7.3), Tall Hayyat, Tall Umm Hammad, Zeazayyeh (Ibrahim *et al.* 1988: 191, site 144), all situated on low ground, or Tall Iktanu (Prag 1974, 1986, 1988, 1989), located on higher ground, but probably not for defensive purposes. A site located on a hilltop, probably in a more defensive location, is Dhahrat Umm Marar (Ibrahim *et al.* 1976: 50), where possible traces of fortifications are visible on the surface. Their common characteristic is proximity to a spring or a watercourse, and the presence of good agricultural soils in their vicinity. Traces of less permanent occupation are found at sites with more consistent remains from both earlier and more recent periods, such as Tall Abu Alubah (Mabry and Palumbo 1988: site 23), Tall Abu Habil North, Tall Abu Kharaz, Khirbat Abu Qarf, Tall Alla (near Tall Dayr Alla), Tall Handaquq North (Mabry 1989), and others.[14]

It is not rare to find cemeteries (characterized by shaft and cist tombs) associated with "permanent" sites: the best examples illustrating this situation are given by the sites of Tall Abu Niaj and Tall Umm Hammad (Helms 1983, 1986; Tubb 1985).

Northern Jordan

One hundred and twenty-three sites are known from this region, but unfortunately it is not easy to evaluate the real intensity of the settlement, since almost all evidence comes from surface surveys or accidental discoveries.[15] Few sites in this region have been excavated: at Khirbat Zaraqun the EB II and III settlement was fortified, but during the EB IV a sedentary village with well-built houses existed on this site. At Jabal Rahayl, soundings revealed both EB II and EB IV phases (Palumbo *et al.* 1996). Several other sites, many of which are situated on hilltops, have substantial remains visible on the surface. Hilltop location predominates in this region: 44% of the habitation sites are located in this position and another 26% on slopes or ridges.

Some of these sites were probably even fortified, as in the cases of Jabal Rahayl (Palumbo e*t al.* 1996) (Figure 7.4), Khirbat Rusayfeh (Glueck 1939), and Khirbat Batrawi (Palumbo e*t al.* 1996) or at least surrounded by enclosure walls. Resayfeh was unfortunately destroyed by the cemetery of the nearby village. Both Albright

and Glueck describe the site as clearly fortified (Albright 1934: 15; Glueck 1939: 205–206), with many traces of walls visible on the surface. Their reading of the pottery as EB IV has been confirmed by the discovery of a tomb, and by the collection of surface material (Palumbo and Peterman 1993).

The presence of these sites in this area of Jordan is very interesting. They are all close to the Zarqa River, a permanent watercourse. They are also very close to the 200 mm isohyet, which marks the minimum amount of rainfall for the practice of dry farming. These sites could be examples of defended settlements in an area where the relationships between sedentary and nomadic components of the society were probably less peaceful than in other regions of the country. In this same region, there are also clear examples of sedentary rural settlements in open areas (valleys, plateaus), showing that in some cases there was no need either to occupy defended positions or to compete for the land.[16]

There are 12 cemeteries or tomb locations known in northern Jordan, most in the Amman area. Unfortunately, the urban growth of the capital does not allow us to understand whether these cemeteries were associated with

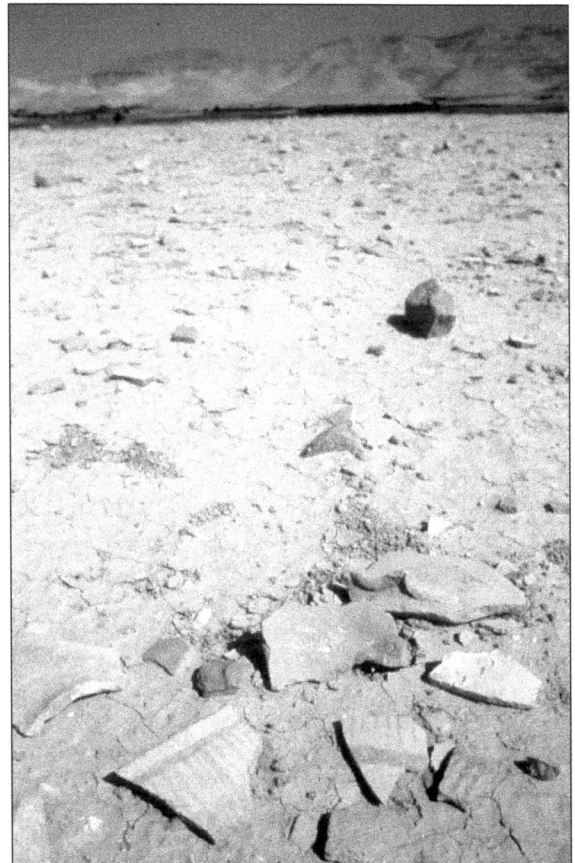

Figure 7.3 Tall Abu Niaj: surface pottery scatter.

Figure 7.4   General view of Jabal Rahayl, looking east from Jabal Asi.

settlements. Occupational remains have been identified so far only on the Amman Citadel.

In conclusion, it is clear that occupation in northern Jordan had an agricultural basis. Sedentary villages played an important role in this economy, even if the pastoral component of the society was probably very strong, especially along the eastern fringes of the plateau, where the limited amount of rainfall and the absence of permanent water courses means that the exploitation of natural resources is limited to pasture.

Central and Southern Jordan

In central Jordan the continuity of settlement between the EB II/III and IV is very clear. The continuity in types of settlement is especially attested by the ongoing urban tradition in the EB IV culture. Khirbat Iskandar is the only excavated EB IV site with fortifications built or at least reused during this period (Figure 7.5). Richard believes that the fortifications at Iskandar went out of use during a later phase of the EB IV settlement.[17] It confirms that in this region certain conditions existed allowing the survival of EB II/III cultural traditions, which flourished only in the first phases of the EB IV period and died out gradually towards the end of the millennium. It is not surprising that the first and most unequivocal evidence of EB IV sedentary occupation comes from this region. Glueck

had already ascertained the importance of sites like Khirbat Iskandar, Arair, Adir, Bab adh-Dhra, Feqayqes and Lajjun (Figure 7.6) for the occupational history of the region during the EB IV. The topographic location of the sites seems to favor a defensive attitude with 38% of the sites on hilltops or ridges, and another 25% on slopes. Only 24% are in a more open position on the plateau or on terraces. Only a few cemeteries (four) have been found in this region. This is probably due to the small number of accurate surveys made in the region.

Human settlement in central Jordan during the EB IV had an important agricultural and sedentary base. At Bab adh-Dhra the occupation of field X shows houses and courtyards, part of a village showing a reduced occupation, although with substantial continuity from the previous period (Rast and Schaub 2003: 448).

Khirbat Iskandar cannot be considered an exception to the rule of undefended villages in Jordan during the EB IV. New research is needed to understand both the pattern of fortified settlements and their significance in a political and economic structure based almost exclusively on local rural organization. But in this case, too, we cannot rule out the idea that Khirbat Iskandar, and probably Adir and Lajjun, could have been centres of sedentary rural activity "on the border line" with a more turbulent and unstable desert region. The presence of pastoral settlements in this region can probably be identified at several sites with traces of EB IV occupation but no architectural remains, found especially in south-central Jordan by Mattingly and his survey team (1984).

In southern Jordan the situation is rather different. MB II presence has been tentatively identified by MacDonald *et al.* at only two of the 20 EB IV sites known in this region (Rababeh: 1982: 44; SGNAS Site 198: 1992).

The few sites found do not permit statistics on their topographic location, but the trend in southern Jordan seems to contrast with the situation observed in central Jordan, where defense was highly valued in the choice of settlement location. In southern Jordan only two out of 13 sites are on high locations, all the others on lower slopes, terraces, plateaus or even valley bottoms. Very few surveys have been made in the southernmost areas of this region. The writer's 1990 summary work on EB IV had expressed the hope that more surveys in the southernmost regions of Jordan could clarify the apparently complete absence of EB IV occupation only a few kilometres south of Wadi Hasa.[18] The work of Adams in the Faynan area has started to modify this picture, confirming an active exploitation of the copper mines during the EB II–IV (Adams 1999, 2000, 2002). Haiman (1996) and Goren (1996) go as far as relating the EB IV settlement of the Negev and northern Sinai to the copper trade from the

Faynan area to Egypt, while Adams suggests that this began much earlier in the EB II, and continued throughout the remainder of the EB until copper sources from Cyprus begin to fill the wider market for copper across the entire Near East. The petrographic analysis of pottery found at sites in the Negev conducted by Goren shows two main sources: the Judaean Hills south of Jerusalem and central/southern Jordan (including the Faynan area). This second group makes up 38% of the entire EB IV ceramic repertoire found in the Negev so far. With the percentage of "foreign" imports reaching 80% in the Negev, half of which originated in Jordan, it is clear that the transhumance model proposed by Dever must be reassessed (in his key site, Beer Resisim, the majority of the pottery has a Jordanian origin). Adams petrographic analysis of the EB pottery from Khirbat Hamra Ifdan (Figure 7.7) supports Goren's analysis, but also indicates that there are significant problems with the dating of the Central Negev Highland sites based upon correlations with the pottery of the well-dated sequences at Khirbat Hamra Ifdan (Adams 2006).

Besides the sites in the Faynan area, the only other important EB IV site in southern Jordan is Khirbat Khanazir (Abu Ishribsheh), a large cemetery spread out along the base of hills above the Wadi Arabah for about 2 km (MacDonald *et al.* 1987: 406; MacDonald 1995;

Figure 7.5   General view of Khirbat Iskandar, looking north.

Khouri 1988: 113). Surface remains consist of exclusively EB IV pottery and of rectangular tombs with very well-preserved walls up to 1 m high. Surveys have so far failed to reveal the presence of settlements in the vicinity, as no trace of EB IV occupation was identified by Rast and Schaub on the tell proper (1974: 12–13). This site should perhaps be interpreted as a seasonal settlement, no different from most of the Negev sites.

Material Culture

Public and Domestic Architecture

With few exceptions, there is no real evidence of urban planning at EB IV settlements, even if layouts can be recognized at sites with more important architectural remains. Even the domestic architecture cannot be easily characterized, given the range, but also the scarcity, of architectural remains. Substantial remains, however, do exist, especially in Jordan. It is on the basis of these remains that it has been possible to recognize a rural component in EB IV societies that cannot be characterized as exclusively pastoral.

Town Planning

Very few sites can provide information on the composition and structure of settlement. Excavations at Khirbat Iskandar, Tall Umm Hammad, Tall Abu Niaj, and at Bab

adh-Dhra's extramural areas, however, have revealed elements that can perhaps be defined as an attempt at spatial organization.

At Tall Iktanu excavation and the survey of buildings visible on the surface made a reconstruction of the village plan possible. Prag observes that there is a clear order in this plan. Streets are narrow (c. 2 or 3 m wide), and they divide areas formed by several habitation units. The streets converge towards the centre of the settlement, where no excavation or survey has been made to date. When Prag was writing in the early 1970s, Tall Umm Hammad was known only for its surface pottery scatter, identified by Glueck (1951: 318–329). Prag cited this site as a typical example of an EB IV nomadic camp, on the basis of the large area covered by the sherd scatter. She also did not believe Glueck's hypothesis that the site was more sedentary than a nomadic encampment (1974: 96–97).

Recent excavations at Tall Umm Hammad, directed by Helms, have proved Glueck's interpretation correct. Tall Umm Hammad was a village formed by habitation areas separated by narrow streets (c. 2 m wide), with a pattern very similar to that observed by Prag at Tall Iktanu (Helms 1986: 30). As at Iktanu, there is also evidence for several building phases (at least two at Tall Iktanu, and three at Tall Umm Hammad). At Tall Umm Hammad the foundation walls were made of mudbricks, and it is for this

Figure 7.6 Menhir alignment at Lajjun.

Figure 7.7   Aerial view of the copper production site at Khirbat Hamra Ifdan in the Faynan region. Photo courtesy of R. Adams and T. Levy, Jabal Hamrat Fidan Project.

reason that no traces of architecture had been observed on the surface by previous investigators. The same situation was observed during the test excavation at Tall Abu Nlaj. This site is situated on a *qattara* hill near the Ghor, in the Jordan Valley. Its surface is strewn with thousands of pottery sherds, but none of the mudbrick architectural remains were visible before excavation.

Another site with possible evidence of town planning is Khirbat Iskandar, the only excavated EB IV site with fortifications belonging to this period. Domestic structures found at the site seem to be organized around courtyards, but the arrangement of these structures and their relations to the streets is still not clear since the area exposed by excavation is still limited (Richard and Boraas 1988: 115). In general, there are several analogies with what has already been observed at Tall Iktanu and at Tall Umm Hammad, while the presence of fortifications adds an important element to the structure of settlements in the central and northern areas of the southern Levant.

Public Buildings

This type of building, including defensive works and fortifications, is extremely rare during this period. Khirbat Iskandar's fortifications are the only ones excavated to date, while the soundings conducted at Jabal Rahayl

(Palumbo *et al.* 1996) are of too limited extent to confirm the presence of true fortifications there.

Fortifications or enclosures may be present at a handful of other sites: Dhahrat Umm Marar, Khirbat Batrawi, Khirbat Rusayfeh, Adir, and Arair. The date of the fortification at Lajjun is certainly EB II–III, but it is still possible that there was an EB IV reuse.

At Khirbat Iskandar, clear evidence of fortifications belonging to the EB IV comes from area B (Richard and Boraas 1988). The building technique observed here recalls a characteristic recorded at Bab adh-Dhra and Numayra. There, the fortification wall is built by filling the space between two lines of large stone blocks with smaller stones and rubble. Every 8 m (7 m at Bab adh-Dhra and Numayra; Rast and Schaub 1978: 10; 1980: 40–42) a perpendicular wall was inserted in order to strengthen the structure. In area C a structure formed by a series of parallel long rooms is interpreted as a gate, or at least as a building of a certain importance. One of the rooms is paved and provided with benches along its inner perimeter. This entire structure is very different from those domestic units found in area B.

The other "public" structure known before the most recent excavations is the Bab adh-Dhra "cultic" structure, excavated by Rast and Schaub in Field XVI. Remains of this structure belong to four different phases of use, which could possibly be related to the four occupation phases found in the Field X domestic area. The structure is characterized by terracing and retaining walls, and by a series of small rooms with well-built walls and plastered surfaces. A pedestal stone was found reused in a wall of phase 3. This stone is very similar to those found at Ai (at-Tall) in Sanctuary A (Callaway 1972: 247). According to the excavators, however, the best evidence for the cultic use of the area comes from phase IV, to which belongs an "altar" composed of a large flat stone set on a platform of smaller stones inside a room, and an "offering table" outside this building built with a flat stone slab set on a mudbrick wall five courses high and three rows wide. On this slab were more than a dozen horns of animals, some of which were identified as sheep/goat (Schaub and Rast 1984: 57–58, 2003:398–400).

The Adir temple, excavated by Albright in 1933 (Albright 1934: 13–18; Cleveland 1960: 77–97), is an isolated structure, almost completely destroyed by the foundations of a modern house. EB IV pottery was found in the area, but the stratigraphic evidence is not conclusive. In fact, an EB IV date for this structure was suggested by Albright only because of its position near some monoliths, one of which is still standing.

Domestic Structures

As noted above, domestic units seem to be built in "blocks" formed by four or more houses. These blocks are separated by narrow alleys, as at Tall Iktanu, Tall Umm Hammad, Bab adh-Dhra (Rast and Schaub 1978: 21), and, possibly, Khirbat Iskandar. At all of the above-mentioned sites, the typical domestic structure is characterized by a series of small square or rectangular, sometimes interconnecting, rooms built around a central courtyard. The latter was probably not roofed, because the available wood beams could not span that space. At Bab adh-Dhra the style is different. The houses are single rooms of *Breitraum* type, which finds its roots in the EB II/III construction styles.[19] The houses found at other sites are more or less rectangular, and their length often surpasses 10 m. According to Helms this architectural style finds its origins in the building traditions of the Early Bronze Age II/III, or is directly derived from Syrian influences. Prag made the same hypotheses, with reference to the temple and private houses at Megiddo (Helms 1986: 32; Prag 1971: 304). There are several building techniques reflecting the different local availability of materials. At Jericho, Tall Iktanu, Khirbat Iskandar and Bab adh-Dhra foundation walls were built with unhewn stones, and walls were erected using mudbricks or *terre pisée*. At Tall Umm Hammad and at Tall Abu Niaj even the foundations were made of mudbrick.

Cemeteries and Tombs

Only 25% of identified EB IV cemeteries are found close to habitation sites with occupations dated to the same period. This figure is drastically different from the percentage calculated for the EB II/III period, as 64% of cemeteries or single tombs have been found in proximity to a settlement. The reason for this must be found in the uneven archaeological record, and in the fact that many isolated discoveries of EB IV tombs have been made during construction works, often not followed by surveys to identify possible settlement remains.

The main EB II/III cemeteries were also in use during the EB IV, such as at Bab adh-Dhra (Schaub and Rast 1989) and Jericho (Kenyon 1960, 1965). As for the general structure of cemeteries, the EB IV period is characterized by the first constant use of areas expressly designated for the burial of the deceased. During EB II/III the expansion of cemetery areas was very rare, due to the practice of collective burial or family tombs.[20] During EB IV the widespread reintroduction of the single burial in a shaft tomb, already known but used sporadically during the EB II/III period, and the abandonment of the practice of burials in natural caves were two factors that contributed to the modification of the basic concept of a cemetery, from burial ground to "city of the dead."

Typical EB IV mortuary structures are shaft tombs dug in a chalky, soft and compact rock (Figure 7.8). There are several types of shaft tombs. The most common type has a circular or ovoid shaft, about 2 m deep, with a small entrance leading to the chamber. The entrance is sometimes blocked by a stone slab. The chamber has a circular shape, 2 or 3 m in diameter, and a low ceiling. Sometimes a lamp niche is present. There are a number of variants to this type: (a) the shaft or chamber shape (oblong, rectangular, irregular); (b) the presence of one or more steps, or a short corridor leading into the chamber; (c) the dimensions can vary for the shaft's depth from 1 to 5 m; and (d) the chamber's diameter, from less than a metre to over 6 m. Multiple chamber tombs are common. In these, chambers may be separate (having just the shaft in common, such as the Amman Sport City tomb: Zayadine 1978: fig. 2). Construction of a shaft tomb must have been a labour-intensive enterprise, and various considerations point to the existence of professional groups of grave diggers, a sort of economic specialization that, together with other characteristics, such as village pottery production, characterizes EB IV as a period of diversified economic specializations.

Shaft tombs are the most common mortuary structure during the EB IV, but they are not the only ones. In the regions where the soft limestone is absent the tombs are above ground, built with stone slabs or piled rocks. These structures are known as dolmens and cairns. A tumulus sometimes covers the built structure. In Jordan they belong mainly to the Late Chalcolithic/EB I period, but their reuse during EB IV has been confirmed at various sites. In the Golan, the earliest date of use of dolmens seems to be EB IV (Epstein 1985). These monuments are not exclusive to the desert or to the basalt areas in Palestine-Jordan, but are also found where shaft tombs are common. For this reason, it has been suggested that tumuli and cists might have contained primary burials,

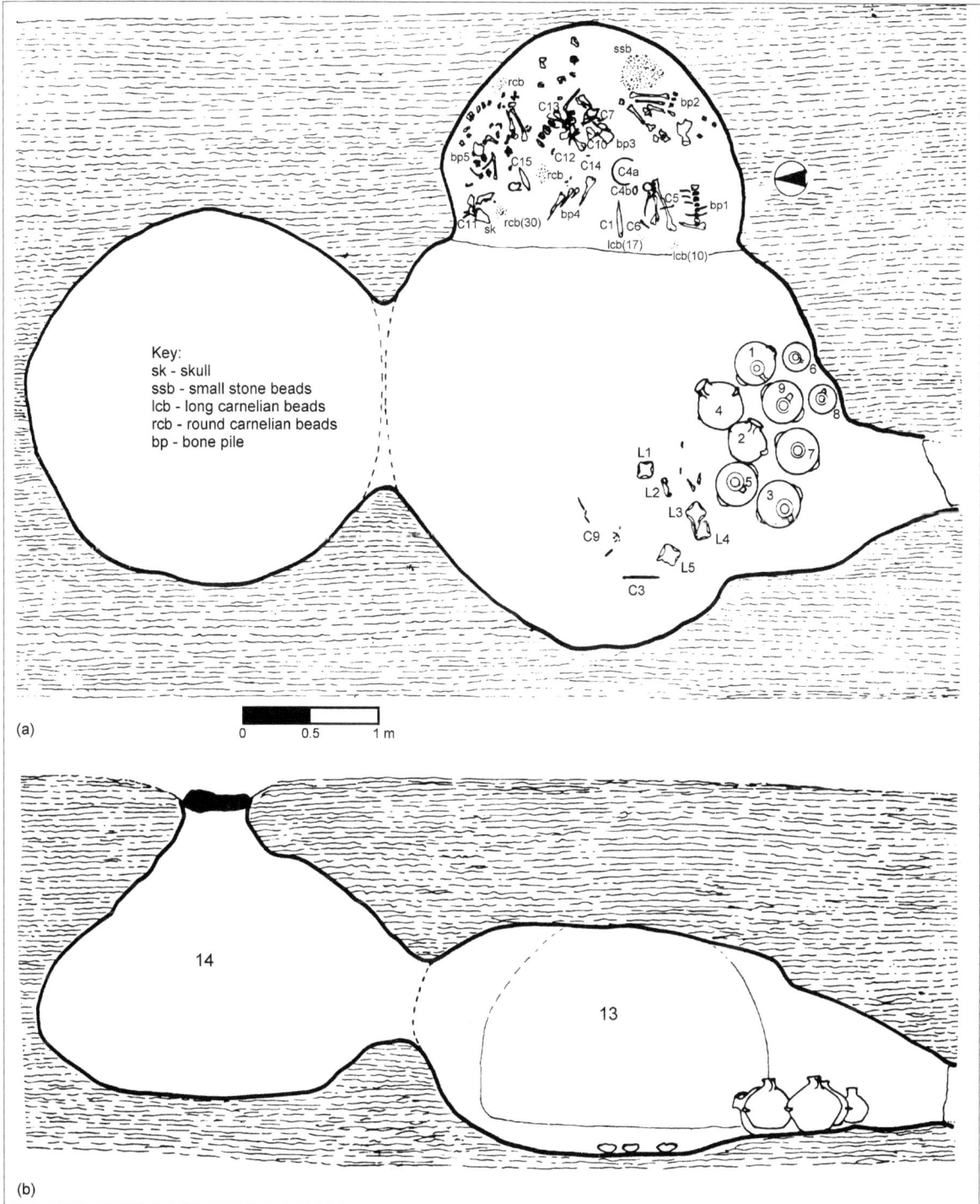

Figure 7.8   Shaft tomb at Tall Umayri (from ADAJ 37, 1993).

which were then collected and reburied in shaft tombs (London 1987: 73). Cairns are also peculiar to the southern regions, while dolmens are more common in the north. Being very visible, these monuments have been constantly reused or robbed through time, so that today it is difficult to date them.[21]

On the Jordanian plateau, dolmens are often found close to EB IV settlements, as at Khirbat Umm Ghuzlan, in Wadi Yabis (Figure 7.9). Indirect proof of an EB IV date for the construction or reuse of at least some dolmens can also be seen in the "built" shaft tomb (i.e. a tomb with slab lining) found at Degania, just south of the Sea of Galilee (Kochavi 1973: 51), and at Tall Ajjul, near Gaza (Petrie 1932: pl. LIII: 1516, 1517).

The entire set of data concerning the megalithic monuments points to a use, if not construction, of many of these structures during the EB IV period. Unfortunately, not a single undisturbed burial has been found. For this reason, the dolmens are an interesting typological addition to the assemblage of mortuary structures in the southern Levant dating to this period, but they still do not provide useful information on the mortuary practices performed in them. The same can be said for the cairns found in the southern Jordan Valley (Tall Iktanu) and the Southern Ghors (Bab adh-Dhra). Their EB IV date is indicated by the presence of habitation sites of the same

period in their vicinities, and by the accurate dating of some objects found within the tombs.[22] Finally, the peculiarity of the tombs found at Khanazir should be mentioned as parallels are found outside of Jordan, in the Negev, for the built above ground "shaft tombs" and in the Gulf area for the rectangular built tombs.

Mortuary Practices

The variety and complexity of mortuary practices in EB IV might be interpreted as signs of a complex social structure. For many scholars, this variability has a chronological basis (Dever 1987), while for others it has to do with the presence of different familiar or tribal groups with different mortuary traditions in the same area (Kenyon 1960). More recent work maintains that these variations cannot be explained by chronology or differences in material culture alone, and that they reflect the deceased's social status (Palumbo 1990).

Body Treatment

Three types of body treatment are found throughout Palestine and Jordan during EB IV: secondary disarticulated; primary flexed; and primary extended or semi-flexed. Primary flexed burials were rare during the EB I–III, when extended and disarticulated burials prevailed. During the EB IV disarticulated burials prevail, followed by

Figure 7.9   Dolmen at Khirbat Umm Ghuzlan.

the flexed burial, while the extended or semi-flexed burial is quite rare.

Disarticulated burials are often the only type of body treatment found in EB IV cemeteries. Disarticulation was probably caused by decay of bodies in the open air, or temporary burial and reinterment. Bones in disarticulated burials are usually found in one or more piles in the centre of the burial chamber or at the bottom of the chamber itself. Sometimes they are found with no order in the chamber. It is very rare to find a complete disarticulated skeleton. The bones most commonly found are the long bones and the skulls. This could be considered an indirect proof of temporary burial, followed by gathering of some bones to represent the whole body in the final interment. Secondary burial has been considered by some scholars as distinctive of nomadic societies. The opposite, however, is true, since it is more common among sedentary societies in various regions of the world and throughout history.

Primary flexed burial is less frequent, but it has been recorded all over the country, in its two variants (on the left and on the right side). At Jericho more than a quarter of the EB IV burials belong to this type.[23] The body is generally turned towards the chamber entrance, with arms bent and placed against the chest, in foetal position. Based on a study conducted on tombs of this type in the Jericho cemetery, it has been suggested that burials on the right side are those of males, and those on the left side are those of females (Palumbo 1986, 1987). In the absence of anthropological studies, this interpretation is based on the association with grave goods (weapons are found in association with burials flexed on the right, no offerings or few objects, such as pins and spindle whorls, in association with burials flexed on the left), an association that has no exceptions so far in the numerous tombs and ten sites in the southern Levant where this burial type is present.

Only one tomb in Jordan (Wadi Hammeh Tomb 80E) has been found with an extended burial. Ten more tombs found in Israel and Palestine have this type of burial (Palumbo 1990). Notwithstanding its rarity, this burial is maintained as a "type" because its constant association with "rich" graves gives additional significance to this particular body treatment, representing, perhaps, a symbolic expression of social status.

Another very distinctive characteristic of EB IV mortuary practices, and rarely found during the EB II/III and Middle Bronze periods, are the large numbers of single interments, as well as the limited number of people buried in the same chamber (no more than four or five) in the case of multiple burials. During both the EB II/III and the Middle Bronze Age, the common practice was collective burial, containing in some cases hundreds of bodies. Not only were burials usually collective during these periods, but grave goods as well were left without association with separate burials. In the EB IV collective burials, in contrast, the single interments do not lose their individuality, since there was a clear attempt to assign grave goods to each one of the burials present in the tomb. The relation between the type of burial and the type of grave goods associated with it was certainly more important during EB IV than in the previous and following periods. As we will see, there was also a relation between grave goods and type of tomb. These three categories of analysis (burials, grave goods and tomb architecture) are, thus, important for reconstructing EB IV mortuary practices in their wider context, rather than in an isolated, typological perspective.

Grave Goods

Pottery is the object most commonly found in tombs. Pottery types include lamps, small jars, amphoriskoi and large jars. Bowls, cups (more frequent in the southern regions) and spouted vessels are types found less frequently. In general it is rare to find a large number of vessels within a tomb. Sometimes weapons, pins or beads are found in the tomb. Weapons include daggers, knives, spearheads and axes (the latter have been found in very few tombs). When a dagger is present, a single specimen is usually placed close to the body of the deceased.

Animal bones are also found in tombs, and they are certainly the remains of food offerings given to the deceased. The bones are almost always of sheep and goat. Data is still scant on the association between animal offerings and "prestige" burials, an association that has been observed by London at the cemetery of Jabal Qa'aqir, on the West Bank (London 1987).

Tombs containing human remains but totally deprived of grave goods are not uncommon. In other tombs, the only objects found are a few beads and, sometimes, a copper pin. Copper belts and "crowns" have also been found on the bodies of primary burials in the Jericho cemetery. These were certainly "prestige" items representing the deceased's higher social status (Shay 1983: 34).

There are no standards in the method of placing the grave goods in the tomb chamber. Pottery is usually found near or close to the chamber walls, while weapons and personal equipment (pins, combs, beads) are closer to the body of the deceased. Daggers and knives were probably tied to a leather belt worn by the deceased. This hypothesis is suggested by the position of the dagger in primary burials, commonly found at the deceased's waist or shoulder.

The clearest example of a relation between grave goods and architectural elements of the tomb is provided by the presence of a lamp niche in many tomb chambers. At Jericho, the lamp niche was often used, but sometimes no lamps were found in the tomb, even if a niche was. In other cases, lamps were among the grave goods, but they were not placed in the niche or there was no niche, so that this relation is not as secure as might be expected.

There are basic differences between EB I–III and EB IV mortuary practices. Differences are found already in the tomb types: dolmens, cairns and shaft tombs represent three different burial traditions, the first two surviving in Jordan and the Negev desert from the Late Chalcolithic and Early Bronze Age I periods, the third finding its full development in EB IV all across the southern Levant, but also originating in the Early Bronze Age cultures of this same region. In EB IV, the predominance of single depositions, of "true" disarticulated burials (as opposed to the "derived secondary" burials of EB I–III, above), and of a particular care in the allotment of grave goods to each burial in case of multiple burials, are all elements that are not found on this scale in EB I–III mortuary practices. The differences *within* the EB IV mortuary practices are also important, because they could be interpreted as symbolic expressions of social status. The evidence in favour of this interpretation is found in the almost constant association of primary burials with "richer" grave goods (above), and in an even finer distinction between primary extended and primary flexed burials, with the former exhibiting the "richest" grave goods in the Jericho cemetery (Palumbo 1987). Present evidence is not adequate to draw conclusions about the structure of EB IV society. That social status was ascribed at birth is demonstrated, in my opinion, by the presence at Jericho of differential body treatment in child burials, which are always disarticulated and without grave goods, except for two tombs,[24] where they are flexed on their right side and provided with a simple grave assemblage. The "visibility" of children and infant burials, and, even more, their differential body treatment is commonly considered a characteristic emerging with the increase of hierarchical aspects (Brown 1982: 29), but data is still inconclusive for demonstrating that the formation of social hierarchies was a common phenomenon throughout the southern Levant.

Aspects of Material Culture: Pottery Production, Styles and "Families"

Pottery typology has been for many scholars one of the keys to the understanding of the chronological problems of this period. Unfortunately, the stratigraphic sequence still missing between EB III and EB IV leaves much of this research in an abstract layer.

The division of pottery types into "families" by Amiran and, later, by Dever, has been for the past 30 years a fixed point in the understanding of the period. This reconstruction has been used for chronological considerations, as well as for the understanding of the period as a nomadic interlude with localized craft productions. Recent research, however, is changing this view. The evidence of strong "regionalism" in the EB IV pottery styles is unquestionable. The decline of urban-based workshops and urban-controlled regional and interregional trade is certainly one of the causes of the development of isolated pottery traditions.

A chronological revision, however, is in order to accommodate recent archaeological evidence and eliminate the gaps left by the original reconstruction. Dever was probably conscious of these limitations to his theory, since he never explicitly mentioned the existence of "gaps" in entire regions. In 1995, however, he admitted that chronological revisions were necessary, even if he seemed to maintain his general sequence, allowing for larger overlaps between families (Dever 1995).

Three of Dever's original "Families" are present in Jordan: Families J, NC, and TR.

Family J or Jericho/Jordan Valley is present both in Jordan and the West Bank, and is mainly found in Jordan Valley sites between the area a few kilometres south of Beth Shan and the northern shores of the Dead Sea. To the east, Dever included also the Jordanian plateau between the area south of Tall Husn (which he considers of NC influence) and the Amman area (but see below for the suggested addition of another group for the Amman/Zarqa area). To the west, Dever recognized J Family types in the eastern flank of the Central Hills. This family is characterized by the Jericho tomb assemblages, the materials from Tall Iktanu, and the pottery found at sites in the central and southern Jordan Valley. The most common forms are the large ovoid jar with two folded-envelope ledge-handles (Kenyon 1965: fig. 16.9), ovoid jugs with a vertical handle (Kenyon 1965: fig. 15.8), the spouted hole-mouth jar, the amphoriskos (Kenyon 1965: fig. 15.6), and the small jar without handles (Kenyon 1965: fig. 15.2).

Decoration is limited to a coil applied to jar necks and decorated with nail or finger impressions.

Family NC, or North-Central, is mostly based, according to Dever, in northern Israel, covering the Jezreel Valley, the Beth Shan area and lower Galilee. In Jordan, pottery of this type has been found at Tall Husn, near Irbid, and in the northern Jordan Valley. The hallmark of this pottery group is its painted decoration, consisting of red lines, sometimes grouped in series, decorating the interior and exterior of several forms. Some of the forms also exhibit a "Syrian" flare, without doubt derived from contacts with the north. The most characteristic forms are the ovoid jar with vertical handles, basins with ledge-handles below the rim (Palumbo 1990: fig. 37, 39), small "trickle-painted" cups and plates (Wightman 1988: fig. 12), amphoriskoi, and jugs with squat body and very high flared neck and long vertical handle (Wightman 1988: fig. 8)

Family TR, or Transjordan, was initially designated by Dever to cover the pottery found in southern Jordan as a result of the examination of Glueck's survey material and of Bab adh-Dhra tomb A54. In 1980, however, Dever also assigned to family TR the material coming from northeastern Jordan and the eastern flank of the

Jordanian plateau (Dever 1980: 48). Pottery found at Bab adh-Dhra (Schaub and Rast 1989; Rast and Schaub 2003), Khirbat Iskandar (Richard 1983, 1990; Richard and Boraas 1984, 1988), Khirbat Khanazir (MacDonald *et al.* 1987: 407), Adir, Feqayqes, Lajjun and Umm Sedayrah (Palumbo 1990: figs. 54–58) has widened the small repertoire of forms, initially characterized in Dever's classification by platter bowls, amphoriskoi, spouted hole-mouth jars and handleless flasks. New forms include the burnished red-slipped amphoriskos, the jar with incised decoration and large platter bowls, frequently red-slipped and burnished. Family TR types are the ones that are typologically closer to EB II–III forms.

In 1993 Palumbo and Peterman added a new family to this repertoire. The new classification derived from the analysis of pottery groups in the Amman and Zarqa areas that exhibit homogeneous repertoire of forms and decorations, while at the same time lack the hallmarks of the other "families" that are present in Jordan. This group was named Family AZ (or Amman/Zarqa). It is characterized by strap handle jugs, storage jars with a strap handle and folded-envelope ledge-handles (both of them are the hallmark of this group) and a limited repertoire of amphoriskoi and ovoid storage jars, often with incised decoration on the neck and shoulder (Palumbo and Peterman 1993: figs. 1, 5). The boundaries of this "family" have been so far recognized in the upper Zarqa drainage and the Amman region, but may extend north to the vicinity of Irbid and south to the Madaba area, as the discovery of an EB IV cemetery with this kind of pottery in the vicinity of Tall Umayri may demonstrate (Waheeb and Palumbo 1993) (Figure 7.10).

Recent scientific analyses of different pottery groups in Jordan and Israel have produced interesting results that provide important insights into pottery production and trade in EB IV societies.

Falconer's neutron activation analysis of a limited sample of sherds collected on the surface and from controlled excavation at a few EB IV Jordan Valley sites (from north to south: Tall Hammeh, Tall Hayyat, Tall Abu Niaj, Dhahrat Umm Marar and Tall Umm Hammad Gharbiyya) showed quite unexpected results. One of the sites, Tall Abu Niaj, emerges as a manufacturing and distributing centre of fine ware, such as "trickle-painted" cups. The predicted pattern for these sites was that of autonomous pottery production, as a result of the very limited nature of the economic relationship between villages during the period (Falconer 1987a, 1987b). Falconer's analysis clearly showed that pottery production was primarily local. In the case of the pottery produced at Tall Abu Niaj, however, the data show that not only was this a centre for the manufacture of fine "trickle-painted" ware, but also that this type of pottery was distributed among villages in the area. The only site among those examined by Falconer where a "trickle-painted" bowl sherd has not been found

is Tall Umm Hammad Gharbiyya, which is also the farthest site from Tall Abu Niaj.

A similar experiment of neutron activation analysis has been conducted by Yellin and Perlman on a pottery tomb group from Tall Artal (a site only 5 km from Tall Abu Niaj, on the west bank of the Jordan), which was compared with other vessels from Ayn Hanatziv and Megiddo.[25] The analyses showed that most of the Artal vessels, a jug from tomb 89 at Ayn Hanatziv, and one amphoriskos from Megiddo tomb 1098A came from the same production centre. One may suggest that this pottery also originated in Abu Niaj, but in the absence of analyses of the clay found near Artal this remains a hypothesis. Falconer (1987a) believes that both sites may have specialized in the production of fine wares. This interpretation is stimulating, being in character with the main thesis formulated by Falconer, according to which there was a differentiated rural economy prior to the advent of Middle Bronze Age urbanism, and that small villages were dependent on larger ones for exchange and trade of goods (1987b: 257–258). The presence of two fine-ware manufacturing places so close to each other cannot be considered a contradiction, but confirms instead the fundamentally disarticulated and autonomous character of EB IV intersite organization.

The petrographic analyses conducted by Goren (1996) on northern Negev and southern Jordanian pottery also show a much wider presence of "foreign" imports in local pottery assemblages, to the extent that these imports are sometimes the majority.

At this point, the idea of strong regional boundaries should probably be modified in favour of a less abstract concept of cultural exchange between neighbouring communities. Exchange of actual goods was probably an ordinary phenomenon. Pottery vessels and their contents were perhaps among the most important items traded. From this perspective, the presence of the same form of vessel or pottery decoration at several sites could be attributed to trade from a single or a few manufacturing centres, and not to a regional style influencing the potters' production. The modified view of regionalism proposed here would include, on the one hand, a more integrated pattern of relations among communities, and, on the other, the existence of some sorts of "regional centres," at least in pottery production. The concept of "Central Place" as applied by Johnson to Mesopotamian and Persian situations (1972, 1973) does not find its application here, since the economic integration of EB IV communities in the southern Levant never reached a level where a Central Place distribution occurred or an administrative power emerged. The re-emergence of local production (and exchange?) centres after the EB III crisis, however, might be postulated on the basis of the latest research. When (and if) these centres were able to create around them a net of depending villages cannot yet be demonstrated, and it is still a matter of pure speculation.

Metal, Flint, and Stone Tools

Metal Sources and Mining

Until recent research in the Faynan area was conducted, there was very scarce evidence confirming mining activities during the EB IV (Rothenberg 1978: 14). In the Timna area mining activities were only assumed on the basis of indirect evidence, such as the discovery of copper ingots in several Negev and northern sites, but the evidence attesting mining activities in the Faynan area during the EB IV is now clear.[26] Archaeological research in this region is revealing more intense and larger scale exploitation of the copper ores than in the Timna area (Hauptmann and Weisgerber 1987: 422). In both regions the earliest evidence for mining and copper smelting is attributed to the EB I period.

The discovery of several copper hoards and copper artefacts across Palestine confirms an extensive trade in this metal. In 1985, Stech, Muhly and Maddin concluded that copper and tin were imported into Palestine via

Figure 7.10 "Family AZ" pottery from a tomb at Tall Umayri (from ADAJ 37, 1993).

Syria, possibly from Anatolia, where both these metals are found. The presence of tin in high percentages in some of the artefacts analysed is not considered natural by these scholars, who believe that these artefacts are of true tin bronze. Tin, however, is present in relatively high percentages in the Faynan copper ores.

It is difficult to understand whether small percentages of elements other than copper are part of the copper ore or were introduced during the smelting process; arsenic and lead, for example, are often present in varying quantities in the copper objects, but this might be due to the characteristics of these elements, since arsenic tends to become volatile under reducing conditions during smelting, so that the variations in arsenic content "could be produced by different atmospheres at several points during production" (Stech *et al.* 1985: 78). Lead, on the other hand, tends to concentrate in different points of the copper artefact, so that there might be strong variations in lead content in the same artefact (79). For this reason, the deliberate use of arsenic as an alloy to produce bronze is not yet certain. According to Khalil, however, addition of arsenic to copper was deliberate, in order to produce a better material (1984: 168); his analyses of daggers from Tall Ajjul and Jericho generally show consistent percentages of arsenic that he attributes to an alloying procedure. Moorey and Schweizer (1972) also believe in the existence of arsenical bronze during the third millennium bc in the southern Levant. The presence of tin as an alloy, on the other hand, is now certain for at least one class of EB IV artefact, the dagger.

Until a few years ago, it was commonly believed that no bronze technology was achieved in Palestine until the Middle Bronze Age (Moorey and Schweizer 1972: 193; Gerstenblith 1983: 96–98), even if the presence of a bronze artefact, the dagger from Jericho Tomb G83a, was already recognized, but treated as an isolated and possibly imported artefact (Moorey and Schweizer 1972: 195). The discovery of an EB IV tomb near Enan, in the Huleh Valley, and the analysis of the metal objects found in it, showed that while the artefacts other than the daggers were made of arsenical copper, the daggers were made of tin bronze (Eisenberg 1985: 65; Stech *et al.* 1985: 79), thus providing the Jericho dagger with a more secure context. Stech *et al.* (1985: 76) believe that tin bronze technology was introduced to Syria-Palestine via Anatolia, where it was known already during the EB II (also Muhly 1985: 284–285 and references there). The sporadic presence of bronze objects found in Syria, however, must be corrected by the epigraphical evidence. At Ebla, in fact, bronze was well known during the period of the state archives (Tall Mardikh (Ebla) IIB1—c. 2400–2300 bc), and in several texts mentioning the import of copper and tin these two metals appear frequently in the constant proportion of nine to one (Matthiae 1989: 272). Matthiae points out that this proportion corresponds to that used in the alloy-ing procedure in more advanced technological development of bronze production.

The introduction of bronze technology represents an advance in EB IV over the preceding periods and confirms this as a period of increasing specialization and technological advancement, even if in village rather than urban contexts.

No smelting furnaces dated to the EB IV have been found in the southern Levant to date. It might be assumed that the technology of copper smelting did not change dramatically during the third, and possibly early second millennium bc, so that Early Bronze and MB II furnaces can be taken as an example for the EB IV period as well. There is no evidence for the use of skin or pot bellows and tuyères to allow the ventilation of the slag during smelting. Hauptmann reconstructs, for the Faynan furnaces, a technique for natural ventilation known in Mesoamerica, where stone slabs form a grating in the front of the furnace, allowing the air to reach the slag. At the same time, clay sticks (which have been found near these furnaces) were used to strengthen the wall and chimney of the smelting furnace.

Pot bellows, however, are known in Palestine from MB II contexts at Tell Beth Mirsim (Davey 1979: 106, fig. 3.3),[27] and from mid-third-millennium bc contexts in northern Syria (Beit-Arieh 1985: 116). Skin bellows were apparently in use in Egypt as early as the nineteenth century bc.[28] This evidence is important not only for its early date, but also because of the context in which the possible bellows are represented, probably representing a group of itinerant metalsmiths. That metalsmithing could be a specialized activity belonging to nomadic groups is a current opinion not only for this early period, but also for late second millennium bc situations (Beit-Arieh 1985: 115). Stech *et al.* (1985) explain the typological uniformity of metal artefacts during the EB IV by the presence of nomadic metalsmiths, while Gerstenblith, (1983: 97) referring to the Middle Bronze Age situation, would rather attribute this uniformity, which is also evident in metal types of that period, to the spread of ideas along trade routes, rather than to actual itinerant metalworkers.

Metal Artefacts

There are only a few basic categories of metal artefacts, stylistically similar to the EB II–III metal types: weapons, tools and ornamental/functional artefacts. The first category is the most common, and includes daggers, spearheads and axes. Tools are much rarer to find, being almost exclusively simple adzes and chisels. Pins are the most common artefact that can be included in the ornamental/functional category, besides bracelets and rings. Copper belts and "crowns," more rare, may be added to this category.

Weapons

These are usually found in funerary contexts. The dagger is the most common type of weapon associated with a burial. The relationship between grave goods and position of the body in the tomb has been treated in another section.

Several types of daggers have been identified so far, but the basic one is clearly related to the EB II/III type, consisting of a flat, elongated blade, not ribbed, with four to six rivets at the hilt attachment. Dagger shapes show a greater variation than in the previous periods. Besides the daggers with rounded tip, no mid-rib, and almost parallel sides (Kenyon 1965: 52, fig. 24.7), there are also pointed daggers with tapering sides and narrow hilt attachment (Kenyon 1956: 51, fig. 10.5–9; Oren 1973: 174, fig. 20.17), daggers with a pronounced rib (Waheeb and Palumbo 1993: 160, fig. 7.1) (Figure 7.11) and even short, triangular-blade daggers, which announce MB IIA types (Negbi 1966: 23, fig. 2.2; Eisenberg 1985: 67, fig. 7.39).

Spearheads are less frequently found than daggers, but they do appear in many tomb offerings across the southern Levant, sometimes as the only weapon in the grave assemblage, but more frequently found in association with a dagger, as at Amman (Zayadine 1978), Tall Umayri (Waheeb and Palumbo 1993) and at a number of sites in Palestine (Palumbo 1990). They have different shapes: elongated with a leaf-shaped point and round section (Kenyon 1965: 84, fig. 41.11, 13), very narrow, with quadrangular section (Figure 7.11) (Waheeb and Palumbo 1993: 160, fig. 7.3, Kenyon 1965: 84, fig. 41.15), all with curled tangs, or similar to daggers, with tapering sides, more or less pronounced mid-rib, and both curled (Tzaferis 1968: pl. 1A, incorrectly identified as daggers) and riveted tang (Eisenberg 1985: 68, fig. 8). Spears were probably deposited in the tombs complete with their shafts; traces of olive wood have been identified attached to a spearhead found in a tomb at Motza (Bahat 1975).

Arrowheads have been found in very limited number in a few tombs, especially in northern Palestine (see list and parallels in Palumbo 1990: 110). They have a leaf-shaped point and a short tang, circular or square in section.

Fenestrated battle-axes are a rare find in EB IV tombs, especially at northern sites, but they are a particularly interesting artefact, being a typological development of the EB III lunated, or "epsilon" axe, and preceding the classic MB II "duckbill" axe.[29] They have not been found in Jordan so far (see Palumbo 1990: 110–111 for a list of axes found in Israel). While they are mostly found in funerary contexts, an axe found at Megiddo is particularly important, since it was found in a wall of temple 4040, stratum XIV (Loud 1948: pl. 128: 3), allowing the dating of the stratum and the temple to the EB IV. It is interesting to note that while this type of axe disappears in Palestine in the fol-

lowing MB IIA period, substituted by the "duckbill" axe, in Syria both the "fenestrated" and the "duckbill" axe are found even side-by-side in MB II contexts.[30]

Tools

Metal objects belonging to this category are extremely rare. Flint tools were more widely used for different purposes. The only metal tools I am aware of are simple chisels, flat adzes (none of which, however, has been found in Jordan, Palumbo 1990: 111), and small awls (found at Tall Umayri, Waheeb and Palumbo 1993: 160, fig. 7.4).

Ornaments

Metal objects with an ornamental/functional purpose are not very common, if we exclude the pins, which are fairly common in grave assemblages, especially in the northern regions of the country.

Pins occur in four varieties: (1) short, pointed at both ends, round or square in section; (2) with simple curled heads and round section; (3) with broad shaft heads, a circular perforation and round section; and (4) with hemispherical head, elongated perforation and round section. All these four types were contemporary, since they have been found together in a tomb near Enan (Eisenberg 1985: 70, fig. 10.53, 59, 61, 62). They have various sizes, between 5 and 10 and 25 and 30 cm. Less common are longer pins, such as a 49.5 cm pin from Enan (Eisenberg 1985: 70, fig. 10.64). Only pins of type 1 are found all across Palestine, but pins of type 2 have also been found at Tall Umayri, south of Amman (Waheeb and Palumbo 1993: 160, fig. 7.5–6). The distribution of the more complex types is limited almost exclusively to the north, and their close parallels with pins found in Syria, especially in the Hama Region (Prag 1974: 95), witness a strong northern influence on the production of these objects, if not an actual origin in Syrian workshops.[31]

Rings and bracelets have been found exclusively in grave assemblages in northern regions (Palumbo 1990:112). They usually have open ends, sometimes overlapping. More elaborate patterns are less common. According to Epstein (1985) and Eisenberg (1985), the origin of these objects must be sought in Syria, where the best comparisons are found. At Umayri (Waheeb and Palumbo 1993: 156–157, figs. 4.5, 5.7) a bronze band or ring was "wrapped" around a jar and a jug handle, a unique find so far.

Until a salvage excavation of an EB IV tomb near Tall Umayri in 1992, in which a belt and possibly a buckle were found, belts and "crowns" made of copper were known only from Jericho. The belt (Waheeb and Palumbo 1993: 161, fig. 8) is decorated in repoussé with parallel lines of dots.

Flint Tools and Implements

Flint tools production in the EB IV period can be considered as a survival of Chalcolithic and Early Bronze Age traditions. The most common tool found in EB IV contexts is the so-called "Canaanean" sickle blade, which finds its origin in the EB I period. The term "Canaanean" identifies a technique common throughout the Early Bronze Age, which has been described in detail by Rosen (1983, 1997). Already Neuville (1930) and, in greater detail, Crowfoot Payne (1948) had identified the common characteristics of Canaanean blades, and specifically their trapezoidal cross-section, the two parallel lines on the dorsal side running near the centre of the blade itself, the prepared and narrow striking platform, a deep negative bulb of percussion and two spurs on either side. Besides technological considerations, Canaanean blades are char-

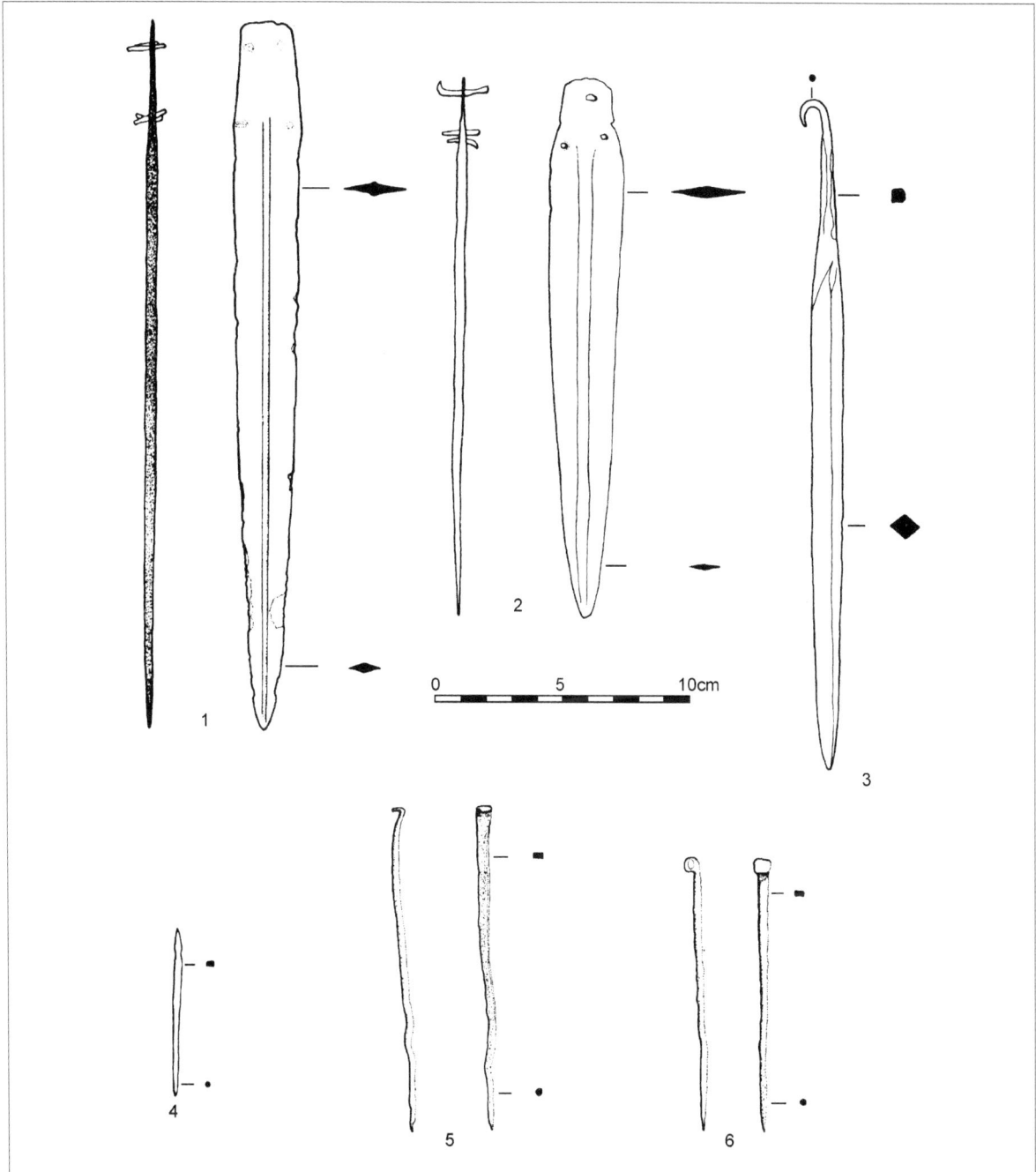

Figure 7.11 Weapons from a tomb at Tall Umayri (from ADAJ 37, 1993).

acterized by the extremely good quality of the flint used to produce them. This, and the fact that tools made out of Canaanean blades were used and resharpened several times, mean that this type of flint product was not made at every site, and must have been an important trade item throughout the Early Bronze Age.

Early Bronze Age Canaanean blade workshops have been identified at several sites (Rosen 1997: 108), almost all of them small villages. The production and trade of this item seems to be a village-based activity throughout the Early Bronze Age, and an activity that certainly continues in the EB IV, as the presence of this tool type at several sites demonstrates. Data is still insufficient, however, to confirm the existence of a few centres of blade production during the period. The rare presence of tabular flint scrapers in EB IV contexts (Palumbo 1990: 115), an Early Bronze II/III type, confirms the substantial continuity of lithic technologies and patterns of flint tool production from the "urban" EB II/III into the "rural" EB IV. In other words, this type of specialization, and possibly the local trade network connected with it, was not affected by the collapse of the urban civilization at the end of the EB III, since these production and trade activities were probably independent of urban control.

Canaanean sickle blades were produced by snapping segments from longer blades. They were not retouched during first use, but sickle sheen, which often appears on one or both edges (Prag 1971; Rosen 1982; Betts 1984), and some edge sharpening and resharpening, show that the segments were reversed in the sickle haft after some use. Five to seven segments were probably used in each sickle, which was about 30 cm long on current estimates. Bitumen might have been used to secure hafting on the sickle. Bitumen traces were found in the EB IV strata of Tall Iktanu (Prag 1971: 261).

Blade width seems to increase through time, reaching maximum broadness at the end of the Early Bronze Age (Waechter 1958; Crowfoot Payne 1983; Betts 1984). According to Rosen, however, variations in blade width have a local rather than a chronological significance, in the sense that they might be due to the activity of different regional production centres (1983: 26). At Tall Umm Hammad Gharbiyya, EB IV types also have more pronounced trapezoidal cross-sections (Betts 1984).

Reaping knives were made out of complete, or at least longer sections, of Canaanean blades. They are usually longer than 10 cm, and their use as tools is witnessed by the sheen appearing along one or both edges. They have been found at several EB IV sites, such Tall Abu Niaj and Tall Nekhayl (Palumbo 1990: 114), Jericho (Crowfoot Payne 1983), Tall Iktanu (Prag 1971) and sites in Israel. These blades show lustre and abrasion along both edges up to the distal end, but stopping 2–3 cm above the butt. According to Crowfoot Payne, then, this means that the blade was end hafted, or, as an alternative, held in the hand, possibly with wrappings, such as leather or other materials, around the butt (1983: 723; also Prag 1971; Rosen 1983).

There are no clear examples of complete EB IV lithic assemblages published yet, so it is not known what the proportion is at different sites between Canaanean and simple sickle blades. The presence and proportion of other tool types, such as scrapers and chisels, is also generally unknown. Besides some dissertation material (Hammond 1977), there is very little published on the technological aspect of local flint production. Such a study would provide interesting insights, since Canaanean technology is less common at some sites than expected. McConaughy (1979) and Rosen (1983) have already observed that at Bab adh-Dhra only about 15% of the sickle blades are technologically Canaanean, and that this technology becomes very rare in the Negev. Prag seems to think that Canaanean industry is absent or very degenerate at such northern and central Jordan sites as Khirbat Umm Rujm, Muamariyeh, Adir and Arair (Prag 1971).[32] Evidence from Jabal Rahayl (Palumbo 1990) also indicates that Canaanean technology is rare in northeastern Jordan.

In the Jordan Valley the Canaanean blade is very common, but here too with some interesting variants. At Tall Iktanu Phase 1 only a few flints have been recorded, none of which are Canaanean, while in Phase 2 the only flint tools found are sickle blades, mainly of the Canaanean type (Prag 1971). They are also common at Tall Umm Hammad (Prag 1971; Betts 1984), as they are at other central Jordan Valley sites, such as Tall Nekhayl (Glueck 1951: pl. 112.1) and Zeazayyeh (Palumbo 1990: 114). The differences between Tall Abu Niaj and Dhahrat Umm Marar are not limited to the pottery repertoires, but are found in the lithic assemblages as well. Tall Abu Niaj is characterized by a typical blade industry on a very fine flint. At least two-thirds of this industry is Canaanean. Particularly interesting in this surface collection is the presence of two backed blades, very uncommon elsewhere. At Dhahrat Umm Marar surface flints are much rarer, and the assemblage is predominantly, but not exclusively, characterized by sickle blades. The flint used for the sickle blades is not as fine as at Tall Abu Niaj, and, most importantly, the technology is probably not Canaanean (Palumbo 1990: 115). This raises the question, unresolved for the pottery assemblage, whether the differences between these two neighbouring sites are of a regional or chronological character. Prag tried to reach some conclusions by comparing Iktanu's and other Palestinian and southern Jordanian assemblages, but the available evidence was not sufficient for postulating more than just preliminary thoughts. She concludes that the earlier stage of the EB IV (her EB–MB) period, characterized by a degeneration of the Early Bronze Age lithic traditions, was followed by a revival of those same traditions at a later stage of the period. Her impressions were based on the presence–absence patterns of the lithics at a few excavated sites rather than on the study of intra-site variations in the technology and in the assemblages.

Fragments of basalt or limestone querns are a common surface find at many EB IV sites, witnessing, together with the sickle blades, an important agricultural component at these settlements. Unfortunately, no precise information is given on the quantities and size of quern fragments found on the surface. At Jabal Rahayl, north of Zarqa, they are very common, but also shattered in small fragments; at Muamariyeh, as well, they are present in quantity, together with rubbing implements (also Prag 1971: 266). Prag found fragments of querns at several of her survey sites (1971). They are a common feature at Jordan Valley sites, such as Tall Abu Niaj, Dhahrat Umm Marar, Tall Nekhayl, Zeazayyeh, Tall Umm Hammad Gharbiyya and Tall Iktanu. They have been found at many sites in central Jordan, such as Khirbat Iskandar, Adir and Feqayqes, together with other pounding and grinding implements (Richard 1983). Querns and rubbing stones coming from archaeological deposits are much rarer: one quern and one rubbing stone were found together in a Phase 2 room at Tall Iktanu (Prag 1971: fig. 59.1), while querns have been found at Bab adh-Dhra Fields IX and X (Rast and Schaub 1978: 19, 21).

Mortars were found at Bab adh-Dhra Fields IX and X (Rast and Schaub 1978: 19, 21), Tall Iktanu (Prag 1971: fig. 59. 3–4) and Khirbat Iskandar (Richard 1983). Pestles are also reported from the latter site.

Limestone or basalt rings are large (10 cm in diameter or larger), doughnut shaped and their possible function has been discussed at some length by Prag (1971: 267–268). Their most probable function was as digging stick weights, and quite interestingly they have been found only in Jordan and at Jericho.[33]

Smaller perforated stones were probably spindle-whorls. Their shape is totally different from the digging stick weights, having a more flattened aspect. The hole is also much smaller in proportion to the surface. This tool also has only been found in EB IV contexts in Jordan and at Jericho (see Palumbo 1990: 117).

Stone and Shell Ornaments

Stone beads have been found at several sites in grave assemblages (Palumbo 1990: 117 n. 80). They are of different shapes and materials: disc, barrel-shaped, biconical and cylinder-shaped. The stone used for their production includes agate, carnelian, chalcedony, quartz, calcite and alabaster.

Frit beads are not uncommon in EB IV grave assemblages, and they are always found in association with stone beads. Bone beads are rare, but they are also very fragile, and they might not have survived intact among the grave goods. Shell beads have also been found at a few sites, including Jericho.

Shell or bone plaques of oblong shape and two perforations at their extremities have been found at several sites, mainly, but not exclusively, in grave assemblages (Palumbo 1990: 118).

Economy

Agriculture

Far from being a period of exclusive animal husbandry, EB IV sites are revealing evidence of plant cultivation. Cereals, pulses and fruits were all cultivated, especially where water was easily available. At Tall Hayyat and Tall Abu Niaj, Falconer and Magness-Gardiner found wheat, barley and a variety of legumes and fruits, including grape and fig. Not common, but also present, was the olive. At Jericho a similar variety was found by Kenyon: wheat and barley, lentils, peas and chick-peas, together with grapes, figs, dates and pistachios. In Bab adh-Dhra's stratum I the most common remains were from figs and barley, with high presence of olive, wheat and fig (Rast and Schaub 2003: 455)

As a general observation, there is a smaller number of cultivated plant species found at EB IV sites than in the previous and following periods, perhaps an indication of a more limited production, concentrated on garden-like crops. The presence of grapes and fruits is significant, because these only reproduce by cloning, and only give fruit after several years. All this implies a settled human element (Grigson 1995: 259).

Pastoralism and Husbandry

One of the elements used to substantiate the presence of a strong pastoral nomadic component in EB IV was the large number of sheep and goat bones found, especially in mortuary contexts. This picture may be misleading and the result of the use of these animals as food offerings in funerary rites. In reality, high percentages of cattle and pig bones have been found at several villages, including Tall Abu Niaj. Sheep/goat only prevail at sites in the desert, an environment that is more favourable to these animals. In the case of the presence of cattle and pig, clearly we cannot speak of pastoral nomads. This is also another element that has allowed scholars to look beyond the pastoral nomadic model to describe the economic basis of EB IV societies. Pastoral nomadism may have been an option at sites in the desert or marginal areas. In other cases sheep/goat husbandry may have taken the form of transhumance between winter and summer pastures conducted by specialized shepherds belonging to settled communities. In some cases, sheep/goat pastoralism may have been a purely local, village-based activity that excluded nomadic movements or even transhumance. There is an evident change from EB II–III to IV in the percentage of sheep/goat versus cattle and pig, and this is probably due to the fact that small, semi-isolated communities may tend to limit the herding of animals more dependent on humans for their care, especially if there are limited opportunities to sell or exchange these animals for other products.

Trade

Evidence of trade during the EB IV is found in almost every material culture component, from pottery to metal and flint tools. The presence at several sites in northern Israel and as far south as Khirbat Iskandar (Richard 1990: 36) of Syrian "caliciform" grey-painted teapots, goblets and cups (Dever 1980; Mazzoni 1985) indicates that these items were treasured and often deposited in grave assemblages.

The contacts between Syria, especially the Hama Region (Prag 1974; Mazzoni 1985), and Palestine are clear, even if they are limited to sites in the northern regions of Palestine. The reasons why this diffusion did not reach sites farther south than Megiddo (with very few exceptions) has probably to do with the fact that these villages were at the margins of an active trade network among the urban communities of northern Syria, and that these communities did not have interest in expanding their area of influence south of the Damascene. It certainly cannot be said that the southern Levant was involved in long-distance international trade during the EB IV. The sites in Palestine touched by the exchange of goods with northern regions were not able to start a process of *internal* diffusion of these foreign goods, probably because a true "central market place" with redistributive functions was missing.

Much more important for the economy of the southern Levantine EB IV and for its future development into the Middle Bronze Age was the function of local trade (Falconer 1987a, 1987b; Rosen 1983, 1997). As we have seen, Falconer (1987b: 252) showed through neutron activation analysis of clays and pottery from various sites in the Jordan Valley that, while utilitarian pottery is locally produced, finer wares tend to be produced at one or a few sites and distributed to the neighbouring communities. This pattern coincides with the conclusions reached by Rosen (1983, 1997), who believes that the so-called "Canaanean" blades were produced at a few specialized centres and then traded. It is quite interesting to note that a village in the Jordan Valley, Tall Abu Niaj, could be one of these specialized centres of *both* pottery and flint production. Copper production at Faynan also played an important role in the continuation of a trade pattern across the Negev, and perhaps into Sinai and the Nile Delta. This is demonstrated by the discovery at a number of Negev sites of pottery produced in Jordan, as well as from evidence for a highly developed industry for the production of copper ingots (Figure 7.12) at Khirbat Hamra Ifdan, suggesting a commoditization of the copper trade during the later Early Bronze Age (Adams 1999, 2002)

While the disappearance of international trade at the end of EB III was a logical consequence of the crisis of the "urban" system, the persistence of a village exchange system from the EB II/III (Rosen 1997) into the EB IV shows that the rural economy at its basic level did not change throughout the Early Bronze Age.

EB IV in its Historical Context

The emphasis on the urban characteristics of EB II and III is one of the reasons why the importance of the small rural settlement and of its relationships with the larger sites and the nomad or pastoral groups has been underestimated in the literature. The crisis that affects all urban centres during the EB III does not change the traditional village production and craft systems, which seem to survive in the EB IV, especially in Jordan. Settlement patterns, however, are disrupted, and this is probably due to a process of nucleation of the population during the EB II–III periods, which led to the abandonment of villages.

The abandonment of rural villages might also be due to a "flight" of some segments of the population towards less controllable subsistence strategies, such as pastoral activities. The beginning and the subsequent development of the economic crisis was perhaps caused by several factors, such as drought, intersite competition, interruption of trade routes, as well as by the inadequate system of rural villages supplying the main centres. When this crisis reached its peak, the segment of population more closely linked to rural production began to move in the opposite direction, into the countryside again, reoccupying the abandoned villages or founding new ones. For the next three centuries the population reverted to a simpler subsistence economy (with the exceptions noted above of some specialized pastoral, pottery and metal production systems) that had apparently disappeared during the predominance of an urban-based economy, and instead re-emerged in all its pervasive force during the eclipse of the urban system.

From this perspective, the "rural" EB IV cannot be considered foreign to the Early Bronze Age cultures of the southern Levant. Joffe (1993) maintains that the "domestic unit of production" was the *basic* economic system of the entire Early Bronze Age. The beginnings of the urban exploitation did not affect a specialized production system, except, perhaps, during the EB III, when some sort of demographic and possibly political centralization occurred. But as soon as the crisis process started, it was probably natural for most of the population to revert to the basic and traditional subsistence strategies. Exaggerating the terms of the question, we may say that the Early Bronze Age urbanization was achieved only *at the expense* of the rural basis. The collapse of the system started when the needs of the "cities" surpassed the carrying capacity of the rural villages. What may be considered as the first "experiment" in the southern Levant in the exploitation of a population segment ended as a result of being pushed too far, too early.

According to this interpretation of collapse, the social and cultural change observed during the EB IV period is a consequence of the crisis of the urban structure and of the reaction started by the rural basis of those same structures. The main characteristics of the EB IV culture in the southern Levant are few and well defined: (a) the prevailing economy is the rural/household specialized production; (b) there is no large-scale international trade; (c) regional trade is limited to a few craft/goods production specialized centres; (d) settlement is dispersed and characterized by mobility in some marginal areas and sedentism in other regions; and (e) there is a strong tendency towards regionalization of cultural traits. To some scholars, these characteristics are typical of a nomad–pastoral culture. The transhumant model (Dever's Negev-Hebron Hills Complex), limited to the region between the Negev and the South-Central Hills, can be used to describe a situation where a rural pastoral component prevailed.

In other regions there is a more balanced relationship between sedentary and pastoral elements of the society, such as in the Jordan Valley and on the plateaus of northern and central Jordan. The economic choice of the people living in more favourable areas of the country was to diversify production, in order to be able to withstand periods of crisis. The combination of agriculture and pastoralism, and the selection of one or the other system as the main production activity during certain periods are not due to the prevailing of one segment of the population over another, but rather to a well thought-out deci-

sion of the same rural population, which remains open to shifting from one system to another, as deemed necessary by the circumstances, and to maintain diversified levels of specialization within its own economic structure (Marfoe 1979).

These interpretations can be applied to the situation of the entire southern Levant, and can be used to restructure the concept of "dimorphic society," which has been used by many to presume the success of the nomadic "element" during periods of unbalanced relationships between the two components of the society. The dichotomy congenital in the concept of "dimorphic society" is too rigid, as Kamp and Yoffee (1980: 93) already observed. There is no justification, then, for using a "dimorphic" approach, when it is clear that relationships and exchanges between groups were much more complex.[34] This interaction must have been even more evident during periods of crisis; from this perspective, the "ruralization" of some elements of the urban component, the dispersion of village dwellers into smaller productive units (farms or hamlets at a domestic level of production) and the adoption of a mode of production more oriented towards pastoralism could have been accompanied by a corresponding sedentarization of nomadic groups that could have taken advantage of a weakened and disappearing urban power, or forced by a decrease in agricultural surplus to practise their own farming.

On the basis of the available evidence, the characteristics of the EB IV period can be reconstructed with an economy based on the integrating both pastoralism and agriculture, and trade on a local basis, perhaps on a larger scale in the north. This region was probably in the sphere of influence of urban centres in central and northern Syria, which were flourishing during this period. Local trade may have been favoured by the presence of large villages more active in specialized craft production.

Some trends towards labour division can be seen in the specialized production and trade of pottery, "Canaanean" blades, metal weapons, in the mining and metalsmithing activities in the Timna and Faynan areas, and in the presence of "professional" groups charged with the construction of the large shaft tombs at several sites.

Traces of a complex social structure can be identified in the mortuary practices. The presence of similar differentiated mortuary practices at several sites in the southern Levant might be due to the existence of a common "ideology" and of a common social structure, besides ethnic and/or tribal differences.

As regards settlement patterns, the available evidence shows a dispersed pattern of settlements, not only in marginal areas, such as the Negev Highlands, but also where water and good agricultural soil is present. The rural landscape of EB IV in the southern Levant is one of small villages filling available ecological niches. Depending on the environmental constraints and the economy practised

Figure 7.12 Ingot hoard from Khirbat Hamra Ifdan. Photo courtesy of R. Adams and T. Levy., Jabal Hamrat Fidan Project.

at these sites, some of them were certainly less stable and more ephemeral than others. Thus, villages in central Jordan or the Jordan Valley were probably occupied permanently, with a mixed economy based on agriculture and herding, perhaps integrated by local trade and specialized pottery, flint, or metal production, as might have been the case with Tall Abu Niaj in the Jordan Valley. The sites involved in this production may have acted as "regional centres" for trade or exchange between neighbouring communities. Traces or perhaps remnants of long-distance trade may be seen in the Syrian commodities reaching Palestinian sites in the north. The presence of fortifications or enclosures at a few sites implies the existence of small towns or regional centres and may be interpreted, according to Richard and Boraas, as a survival of Early Bronze Age traditions and as a "readaptation to a level of political autonomy probably best explained by the chiefdom model" (1988: 128). Without pushing the evidence too far, it should be noted, however, that the distribution of EB IV "forted" sites is marginal to the main agricultural regions, such as the Huleh Valley, the Jezreel and the Jordan Valley, and generally located between the 200 and 300 mm isohyet. It is possible that in these marginal regions there was higher competition for land between sedentary and mobile pastoral groups, which resulted in more defensive behaviour by the sedentary communities. At this point, the growth of both regional craft production and trading centres, and "military," or at least defended agricultural outposts, created a hierarchical settlement system, which eventually was also reflected in the social structure (above). This may have been the basis for the development of a new urban culture.

The "continuity" between EB II/III and EB IV does not mean that there was a sharp interruption in settlement patterns and cultural traits between the latter period and the Middle Bronze Age. We have seen that in some regions there is even more continuity in settlement location between EB IV and MB IIA than between EB III and IV. The importance of trade for the development of the Middle Bronze Age urban culture, in Gerstenblith's opinion (1983), is perhaps overemphasized. There is no doubt that trade may have played an important role in the development of the new urban civilization, but certainly not as a single, or even the main factor. Social and cultural change at the beginning of the second millennium bc can be seen as the result of the influence of political, climatic, economic and technological factors on a economic (the rural/domestic specialized production) and social base (where the beginnings of social stratification can be seen) that were ready to receive and develop the new trends. From this perspective, the renewed success of the urban structure in the southern Levant can be considered a local development of trends derived from the economic and social traditions of both the "urban" EB II/III and the "rural" EB IV societies. We have recognized

these trends mainly in the adaptive ability of rural settlement and production strategies, as well as in the existence, during the EB IV, of a type of social structure that was able to develop into a more stratified component, where the administrative and, later, urban elites played a pivotal role in the formation of a new structured society. Finkelstein interprets this process as a shift back to the "multimorphic society," and the emergence of a stronger rural system (1989: 137). The fact that Falconer (1987b) also sees in the MBA the superimposition of towns on a rural landscape shows a convergence of interpretations on the role that the rural component of society played in the economic and political development between the Early and Middle Bronze Ages in this area.

In conclusion, far from being a Dark Age, the EB IV emerges in these interpretations as a period in which its system of specialized local production and mixed agricultural strategy, as well as technological innovations (such as the widespread introduction of tin bronze technology), served to reinforce the role of the rural component of the society, and laid the basis for the development of a renewed and stronger urban culture.

Notes

1. See Palumbo (1990: 10–11) for a detailed presentation of Lapp's argument on the origin of nomadic invasion from the movements of Transcaucasian Kurgans.

2. On the relationships between Ur III urban elites and pastoral nomadic people as seen from the "centre," see Buccellati (1966); Liverani (1970, 1973; 1988: 298–307); De Geus (1971); Haldar (1971); Kamp and Yoffee (1980).

3. On the emergence of specialized pastoral production in the southern Levant, see Lees and Bates (1974); Sherratt (1981); Levy (1983); Rosen (1988).

4. The concept of "dimorphic society" became a central theme in a long series of articles by the same author. Through the years, he fossilized his theory into a overly rigid dichotomy between nomads and sedentary peoples (Rowton 1973, 1976, 1977). See Kamp and Yoffee (1980: 93–94) for a criticism of Rowton's position.

5. The causes of this collapse are generically listed by Dever. He mentions "political misfortunes, economic reverses, a series of natural calamities such as drought or pestilence, over-population of urban centres and exhaustion of natural resources, or some combination of these and other factors" (Dever 1980: 58). The aim of Dever's analysis was not to look for causes, but rather to show that the priority of a pastoral economy and the dispersion of human settlement were consequences of much more important events than just an "invasion."

6. Excavations at Khirbat Iskandar are directed by S. Richard. Preliminary reports in Richard (1990); Richard and Boraas (1988); Richard and Long (1995).

7. In his analysis of Tall Umm Hammad pottery repertoire, Helms reached the conclusion that many different styles influenced pottery production at this site.

8. Helms criticizes only the chronology proposed by Dever, judging as "convincing and comprehensive" the typological analysis (1989: 32). See also Helms and McCreery 1988: 341.

9. Found in the B8–B7 storerooms.

10. Only little more than a dozen band-combed fragments and a few painted hole-mouth jar rims.

11. Because of the typological and stylistic characteristics of the pottery repertoire, Olàvarri himself would have preferred to use the terms EB IVA and EB IVB, but he refrained from doing so to avoid confusion (1969: 259).

12. Tall Abu Niaj: Falconer and Magness-Gardiner 1984; 1989; Adir: Cleveland 1960; Arair: Olàvarri 1969; Bab adh-Dhra: Rast and Schaub 1981; Schaub and Rast 1989; Tall Hayyat: Falconer and Magness-Gardiner 1984, 1989; Tall Iktanu: Prag 1986, 1988, 1989; Khirbat Iskandar: Richard 1990; Richard and Boraas 1988; Richard and Long 1995; Tall Umm Hammad: Helms 1986; Khirbat Zaraqun: Ibrahim and Mittmann 1987.

13. On the Coastal Plain, for example, only 8% of the EB III sites are also occupied in EB IV, and only 20% of the MB IIA sites also have EB IV occupation, a situation in contrast with the Hebron region, where 70% of EB III sites are reoccupied in EB IV, and 75% of the MB IIA sites have an EB IV presence (Palumbo 1990: 48–62).

14. For all of these sites: Ibrahim *et al.* 1976: 48–49; 1988: 191–192.

15. Glueck 1939, 1951; Mittmann 1970; Prag 1971 (Shueib-Hisban Survey); Ibach 1978 (Hisban Survey); Gordon and Villiers 1983; Kerestes *et al.* 1978; Banning 1985 (Wadi Ziqlab Survey); Mabry and Palumbo 1988; Palumbo *et al.* 1990 (Wadi Yabis Survey); Palumbo *et al.* 1996 (Wadi Zarqa Survey).

16. See for example the sites of Muamariyeh and Khirbat Reqa. Both are quite large (about 4 ha); the first is spread on both sides of a wadi and on the hill slopes close to it, and the second is on a plateau on the edge of a valley (Glueck 1951: 82–84, 180–181).

17. The Iskandar fortifications are dated to phases C and D of occupation. In phase B they were probably abandoned, and by phase A they were certainly out

of use (Richard and Boraas 1988: 112–113).

18. Surveys in the Wadi Hasa and Southern Ghors region were carried out by MacDonald *et al.* (1980, 1982, 1987, 1988, 1992).

19. Rast and Schaub's (1978: 22) work in Bab adh-Dhra's Areas IX and X outside of the EB II/III city wall showed that at this site there was also a consistent sedentary occupation during EB IV.

20. The only exception is the large cemetery at Bab adh-Dhra, where during EB I and part of EB II, shaft tombs containing single or a few burials were the norm. But at this site, too, the typical EB II/III mortuary practice was collective burial, represented here by charnel houses, some of which contained hundreds of bodies.

21. Some of them still have a "mysterious" character. See, for example, the large tumulus at Rujm Hiri, in the Golan, surrounded by a triple wall circle, which has been interpreted as a cultic site (Zohar 1989). A large tumulus surrounded by stone cairns was identified near Kufr Abil during the 1989 Wadi Yabis survey season (Palumbo *et al.* 1990).

22. The Bab adh-Dhra cairns were empty (Rast and Schaub 1978: 29), like those dug in several Negev sites.

23. Flexed burials on the right side have been found in Jordan at Amman and Bab adh-Dhra. Flexed burials on the left side have been observed at Umm Bighal (near Amman) and Bab adh-Dhra.

24. Tombs L8 and M12 (Kenyon 1965).

25. With the exception of a lamp from Tall Artal, all the specimens tested are "trickle-painted" ware. Appendix in Hess 1984: 55–60.

26. See the jar sherd used as a lamp found 22 m below the surface in copper mine no. 43 at Wadi Khalad (Hauptmann and Weisgerber 1987: 424, 426, fig. 5.1), and the sites identified by R. Adams, with evidence of smelting and production activities at Khirbat Hamra Ifdan.

27. See also the reconstruction made by Beit-Arieh of pot or stone bellows operation on the basis of the Rekhmi-Re wall painting at Thebes (1985: 94, fig. 4), dated to the Eighteenth Dynasty.

28. They are represented with a group of Asiatics in the Tomb of Khnum-hotpe III at Beni Hasan (Davey 1979: 111 and references there).

29. For the typological development of this weapon, with parallels from Palestine and Syria, see Dever (1975b: 30).

30. As at Ebla, Hypogeum Q.78.B1 and Q.78.C, Tomb of the Lord of the Goats (Mardikh IIIB, c. 1750–1700

bc) (Matthiae 1980: fig. 10, 11, 12; 1984: pl. 83). A complete mould for a fenestrated axe has been found at Ebla in Tomb D3712, of the Old Syrian period (c. 1850–1750 bc) (Weiss 1985: 183, 243). The axes from Hypogeum Q.78.C belong, however, to a rather different type from the "classic" fenestrated axes, since their blade is already quite elongated. Matthiae classifies the axes on the basis of their width–length ratio as "large" (fenestrated), "medium" and "long" (duckbill) types (1980). To the "medium" type he attributes the axes found at Ebla, which could have a possible Iranian origin (1980: 59).

31. An extensive discussion on the parallels with Syria is in Prag (1974: 93–95).

32. Richard reports the presence of "the typical Early Bronze Age sickle blades of the characteristic trapezoidal shape" at Khirbat Iskandar (1983: 51), but whether these blades are Canaanean or not is not explicitly stated.

33. Tall Iktanu, Muamariyeh, Tall Umm Hammad Gharbiyya, Tall Shaykh Mohammed (Prag 1971); Zeazayyeh, Tall Ras Hamid (Palumbo 1990: fig. 59: 1, 6); Jericho Tombs N4 and M5 (Kenyon 1965: 60, fig. 29: 1–2).

34. On the same lines is Finkelstein's (1989) definition of "multimorphic society," which is applied, however, only to the "urban" Early Bronze and Middle Bronze societies, since he sees EB IV as a period of collapsing specializations.

Bibliography

Adams, R.B.

1999 The Development of Copper Metallurgy During the Early Bronze Age of the Southern Levant: Evidence from the Faynan Region, Southern Jordan. Unpublished PhD Thesis, Sheffield University.

2000 The EBA III–IV Transition in southern Jordan: Evidence from Khirbat Hamra Ifdan. In G. Philip and D. Baird (eds.), *Ceramics and Change in the Early Bronze Age of the Southern Levant*, 379–401. Levantine Archaeology 2. Sheffield Academic Press.

2002 From Farms to Factories: The development of copper production at Faynan, southern Jordan, during the Early Bronze Age. In B.S. Ottaway and E.C. Wagner (eds.), *Metals and Society*, 21–32. British Archaeological Reports, International Series. Oxford: Archaeopress.

2003 External influences at Faynan during the Early Bronze Age: A re-analysis of Building 1 at *Barqa el-Hetiye*, Jordan. *Palestine Exploration Quarterly* 135: 6–21.

2006 Copper Trading Networks Across the Arabah During the Later Early Bronze Age. In P. Bienkowski and K. Galor (eds.) *Crossing the Rift: Resources, Routes, Settlement Patterns and Interaction in the Wadi Arabah*, 137–144. Council for British Research in the Levant Monograph. London: Council for British Research in the Levant.

Albright, W.F.

1932 *The Excavation of Tell Beit Mirsim I*. Annual of the American Schools of Oriental Research 12. New Haven, CT: American Schools of Oriental Research.

1934 Soundings at Ader: A Bronze Age City of Moab. *Bulletin of the American Schools of Oriental Research* 53: 13–18.

1940 *From the Stone Age to Christianity*. Baltimore, MD: The Johns Hopkins University Press.

Amiran, R.

1960 Pottery of the Middle Bronze Age I in Palestine. *Israel Exploration Journal* 10: 204–225.

1974 A Tomb-Group from Geva'—Carmel. *'Atiqot* 7: 1–12 (Hebrew Series).

Bacon, E.E.

1954 Types of Pastoral Nomadism in Central and Southwest Asia. *Southwestern Journal of Anthropology* 10: 44–68.

Bahat, D.

1975 A Middle Bronze Age Tomb Cave at Motza. *Eretz Israel* 12: 18–23 (Hebrew).

Banning, E.B.

1985 Pastoral and Agricultural Land Use in the Wadi Ziqlab, Jordan: An Archaeological and Ecological Survey. Unpublished PhD Thesis, University of Toronto.

Bates, D.G. and S.H. Lees

1977 The Role of Exchange in Productive Specialization. *American Anthropologist* 79: 824–841.

Beit-Arieh, I.

1985 Serabit al-Khadim: New Metallurgical and Chronological Aspects. *Levant* 17: 89–116.

Betts, A.

1984 Chipped Stone Tools. *Levant* 16: 52.

Brown, J.A.

1982 The Search for Rank in Prehistoric Burials. In R. Chapman and K. Randsborg (eds.), *The Archaeology of Death*, 25–37. Cambridge: Cambridge University Press.

Buccellati, G.

1966 *The Amorites of the Ur III Period*. Naples: Oriental Institute.

1990a 'River Bank,' 'High Country' and 'Pasture Land:' The Growth of Nomadism on the Middle Euphrates and the Khabur. In S. Eicher, M. Wäfler and D. Warburton (eds.), *Tell al-Hamidiyah*, II: 87–117. Göttingen: Vandenhoek and Ruprecht.

1990b The Rural Landscape of the Ancient Zor: The Terqa Evidence. In B. Geyer (ed.), *Techniques et pratiques hydro-agricoles traditionnelles en domaine irrigué*, 159–169. Paris: Geuthner.

1992 Ebla and the Amorites. *Eblaitica* 3: 83–104.

1993 Gli Amorrei e l' 'addomesticamento' della steppa. In O. Rouault and M.G. Masetti-Rouault (eds.), *L'Eufrate e il tempo: Le civiltà del Medio Eufrate e della Gezira siriana*, 67–69. Milan: Electa.

Callaway, J.A.

1972 *The Early Bronze Age Sanctuary at 'Ai (et-Tell)*. London: Quarritch.

Carneiro, R.L.

1981 The Chiefdom: Precursor of the State. In G.D. Jones and R.R. Kurtz (eds.), *The Transition to Statehood in the New World*, 37–79. Cambridge: Cambridge University Press.

Cleveland, R.L.

1960 The Excavation of the Conway High Place (Petra) and Soundings at Khirbet Ader. *Annual of the American Schools of Oriental Research* 35: 59–97. New Haven, CT: American Schools of Oriental Research.

Cohen, R. and W. G. Dever

1978 Preliminary Report of the Pilot Season of the 'Central Negev Highlands' Project. *Bulletin of the American Schools of Oriental Research* 232: 29–45.

1979 Preliminary Report of the Second Season of the 'Central Negev Highlands' Project. *Bulletin of the American Schools of Oriental Research* 236: 41–60.

1981 Preliminary Report of the Third and Final Season of the 'Central Negev Highlands' Project. *Bulletin of the American Schools of Oriental Research* 243: 57–77.

Crowfoot Payne, J.

1948 Some Flint Implements from 'Affula. *Journal of the Palestine Oriental Society* 21: 72–78.

1983 The Flint Industries of Jericho. In K.M. Kenyon and T.A. Holland (eds.), *Excavations at Jericho. V. The Pottery Phases of the Tell and Other Finds*, 682–758. London: British School in Jerusalem.

Davey, C.J.

1979 Some Ancient Near Eastern Pot Bellows. *Levant* 11: 101–111.

De Geus, G.H.J.

1971 The Amorites in the Archaeology of Palestine. *Ugarit Forschungen* 3: 41–60.

De Vaux, R.

1946 Les Patriarches Hébreux et les découvertes modernes, I. *Revue Biblique* 53: 321–348.

Dever, W.G.

1970 The 'Middle Bronze I Period' in Syria-Palestine. In J.A. Sanders (ed.), *Near Eastern Archaeology in the Twentieth Century: Essays in Honor of Nelson Glueck*, 132–163. Garden City, NY: Doubleday.

1971 The Peoples of Palestine in the Middle Bronze I Period. *Harvard Theological Review* 64: 197–226.

1972 A Middle Bronze I Site in the West Bank of the Jordan. *Archaeology* 25: 231–233.

1973 The EB IV–MB I Horizon in Transjordan and Southern Palestine. *Bulletin of the American Schools of Oriental Research* 210: 37–63.

1975a A Middle Bronze I Cemetery at Khirbat al-Kirmil. *Eretz Israel* 12: 18–33 (Hebrew).

1975b MB IIA Cemeteries at 'Ain es-Samiyeh and Sinjil. *Bulletin of the American Schools of Oriental Research* 217: 23–36.

1980 New Vistas on the EB IV (MB I) Horizon in Syria-Palestine. *Bulletin of the American Schools of Oriental Research* 237: 35–64.

1981 Cave G26 at Jabal Qa'aqir: A Domestic Assemblage of Middle Bronze I. *Eretz Israel* 15: 22–32 (Hebrew).

1983 Be'er Resisim: A Late Third Millennium B.C.E. Settlement. *Qadmoniot* 16: 52–57 (Hebrew).

1985 Village Planning at Be'er Resisim and Socio-Economic Structure in Early Bronze Age IV Palestine. *Eretz Israel* 18: 18–28 (Hebrew).

1987 Funerary Practices in EB IV (MB I) Palestine: A Study in Cultural Discontinuity. In J.H. Marks and R.M. Goods (eds.), *Love and Death in the Ancient Near East: Essays in Honor of Marvin H. Pope*, 9–19. London: Guilford.

1992 Pastoralism and the End of the Urban Early Bronze Age in Palestine. In O. Bar-Yosef and A. Khazanov (eds.), *Pastoralism in the Levant: Archaeological Materials in Anthropological Perspective*, 83–92. Madison, WI: Prehistory Press.

1995 Social Structure in the Early Bronze IV Period in Palestine. In T.E. Levy (ed.), *The Archaeology of Society in the Holy Land*, 282–296. London: Leicester University Press.

Eisenberg, E.

1985 A Burial Cave of the Early Bronze Age IV (MB I) near 'Enan. *'Atiqot* 17: 59–74 (English Series).

Epstein, C.

1985 Dolmen Excavated in the Golan. *'Atiqot* 17: 20–58 (English Series).

Esse, D.L.

1991 *Subsistence, Trade, and Social Change in Early Bronze Age Palestine*. Chicago, IL: Oriental Institute.

Fabietti, U.

1982 *Nomadi del Medio Oriente*. Torino: Loescher.

Falconer, S.E.

1987a Heartland of Villages: Reconsidering Early Urbanism in the Southern Levant. Unpublished PhD Thesis, University of Arizona, Tucson.

1987b Village Pottery Production and Exchange: a Jordan Valley Perspective. In A. Hadidi (ed.), *Studies in the History and Archaeology of Jordan* III, 251–259. Amman: Department of Antiquities.

1994 The Development and Decline of Bronze Age Civilisation in the Southern Levant: A Reassessment of Urbanism and Ruralism. In C. Mathers and S. Stoddart (eds.), *Development and Decline in the Mediterranean Bronze Age*, 305–333. Sheffield: Sheffield Academic Press.

1995 Rural Responses to Early Urbanism: Bronze Age Household and Village Economy at Tell el-Hayyat, Jordan. *Journal of Field Archaeology* 22(4): 399–419.

Falconer, S.E. and B. Magness-Gardiner

1984 Preliminary Report of the First Season of the Tell al-Hayyat Project. *Bulletin of the American Schools of Oriental Research* 255: 49–74.

1989 Hayyat (Tell al-). In D. Homès-Fredericq and J.B. Hennessy (eds.), *Archaeology of Jordan*. II.1. *Field Reports: Surveys and Sites A–K*, 254–261. Akkadica Supplementum 7. Leuven: Peeters.

Finkelstein, I.

1989 Further Observations on the Socio-Demographic Structure of the Intermediate Bronze Age. *Levant* 21: 129–140.

1992 Pastoralism in the Highlands of Canaan in the Third and Second Millennia B.C.E. In O. Bar-Yosef and A. Khazanov (eds.), *Pastoralism in the Levant,* 133–142. Madison, WI: Prehistory.

1995 *Living on the Fringe*. Sheffield: Sheffield Academic.

Gerstenblith, P.

1983 *The Levant at the Beginning of the Middle Bronze Age*. American Schools of Oriental Research Dissertation Series, 5. Winona Lake, IN: Eisenbrauns.

Gitin, S.

1975 Middle Bronze I 'Domestic Pottery' at Jabal Qa'aqir: A Ceramic Inventory of Cave G23. *Eretz Israel* 12: 46–62.

Glueck, N.

1934 *Explorations in Eastern Palestine* I. Annual of the American Schools of Oriental Research 14. New Haven, CT: American Schools of Oriental Research.

1935 *Explorations in Eastern Palestine* II. Annual of the American Schools of Oriental Research 15. New Haven, CT: American Schools of Oriental Research.

1939 *Explorations in Eastern Palestine* III. Annual of the American Schools of Oriental Research, 18–19. New Haven, CT: American Schools of Oriental Research.

1951 *Explorations in Eastern Palestine* IV. Annual of the American Schools of Oriental Research, 25–28. New Haven, CT: American Schools of Oriental Research.

Gordon, R.L. and L.E. Villiers

1983 Telul edh-Dhahab and its Environs: Surveys of 1980 and 1982: A Preliminary Report. *Annual of the Department of Antiquities of Jordan* 27: 275–289.

Goren, Y.

1996 The Southern Levant in the Early Bronze Age IV: The Petrographic Perspective. *Bulletin of the American Schools of Oriental Research* 303: 33–72.

Grigson, C.

1995 Plough and Pasture in the Early Economy of the Southern Levant. In T. Levy (ed.), *The Archaeology of Society in the Holy Land,* 245–263. London: Leicester University Press.

Haiman, M.

1996 Early Bronze Age IV Settlement Pattern of the Negev and Sinai Deserts: View from Small Marginal Temporary Sites. *Bulletin of the American Schools of Oriental Research* 303: 1–32.

Haldar, A.

1971 *Who Were the Amorites?* Leiden: E.J. Brill.

Hammond, W.M.

1977 The Raw and the Chipped: An Analysis of Correlations between Raw Materials and Tools of a Lithic Industry from Tell el-Hesi, Israel. Unpublished PhD Thesis, Columbia University.

Harrison, T.P.

1997 Shifting Patterns of Settlement in the Highlands of Central Jordan during the Early Bronze Age. *Bulletin of the American Schools of Oriental Research* 306: 1–38.

Hauptmann, A.

1986 Archaeometallurgical and Mining-Archaeological Studies in the Eastern 'Arabah, Feinan Area, 2nd Season. *Annual of the Department of Antiquities of Jordan* 30: 415–419.

2000 *Zur frühen Metallurgie des Kupfers in Fenan/Jordanien.* Der Anschnitt Beiheft 11. Bochum: Deutsches Bergbau Museum.

2007 *The Archaeometallurgy of copper: evidence from Faynan, Jordan*. Natural Science in Archaeology 1. Berlin: Springer.

Hauptmann, A. and G. Weisgerber

1987 Archaeometallurgical and Mining-Archaeological Investigations in the Area of Feinan, Wadi 'Arabah (Jordan). *Annual of the Department of Antiquities of Jordan* 31: 419–437.

Helms, S.W.

1983 The EB IV (EB–MB) Cemetery at Tiwal esh-Sharqi, in the Jordan Valley, 1983. *Annual of the Department of Antiquities of Jordan* 27: 55–85.

1986 Excavations at Tell Um Hammad, 1984. *Levant* 18: 25–49.

1989 An EB IV Pottery Repertoire at Amman, Jordan. *Bulletin of the American Schools of Oriental Research* 273: 17–36.

Helms, S.W. and D.W. McCreery

1988 Rescue Excavations at Umm el-Bighal: The Pottery. *Annual of the Department of Antiquities of Jordan* 32: 319–347.

Hess, O.

1984 MBI Tombs at Tel 'Artal. *Bulletin of the American Schools of Oriental Research* 253: 55–60.

Ibach, R.

1978 Expanded Archaeological Survey of the Hesban Region. *Andrews University Seminar Studies* 16: 201–213.

Ibrahim, M. and S. Mittmann

1987 Tell el-Mughayyir and Khirbat Zeraqoun. *Newsletter of the Institute of Archaeology and Anthropology of Yarmouk University* 4: 3–6.

Ibrahim, M., J.A. Sauer and K. Yassine

1976 The East Jordan Valley Survey, 1975. *Bulletin of the American Schools of Oriental Research* 222: 41–66.

1988 The East Jordan Valley Survey, 1976 (Part Two). In K. Yassine (ed.), *Archaeology of Jordan: Essays and Reports*, 189–207. Amman: Department of Archaeology, University of Jordan.

Joffe, A.H.

1991 Early Bronze I and the Evolution of Social Complexity in the Southern Levant. *Journal of Mediterranean Archaeology* 4: 3–58

1993 *Settlement and Society in the Early Bronze Age I and II, Southern Levant*. Sheffield: Sheffield University.

Johnson, G.A.

1972 A Test of the Utility of Central Place Theory to Archaeology. In P. Ucko, R. Tringham and G.W. Dimbleby (eds.), *Man, Settlement, and Urbanism*, 769–785. London: Duckworth.

1973 *Local Exchange and Early State Development in Southwestern Iran*. Anthropological Papers 51. Ann Arbor: Museum of Anthropology, University of Michigan.

Kamp, K.A. and N. Yoffee

1980 Ethnicity in Ancient Western Asia during the Early Second Millennium B.C.: Archaeological Assessments and Ethnoarchaeological Prospectives. *Bulletin of the American Schools of Oriental Research* 237: 85–104.

Kenyon, K.M.

1951 Some Notes on the History of Jericho in the Second Millennium B.C. *Palestine Exploration Quarterly* 83: 101–138.

1956 Tombs of the Intermediate Early Bronze–Middle Bronze at Tell el-Ajjul. *Annual of the Department of Antiquities of Jordan* 3: 41–55.

1960 *Excavations at Jericho*. I. *The Tombs Excavated in 1952–1954*. London: British School of Archaeology in Jerusalem.

1965 *Excavations at Jericho*. II. *The Tombs Excavated in 1955–1958*. London: British School of Archaeology in Jerusalem.

1966 *Amorites and Canaanites*. London: Oxford University.

Kerestes, T.M., J.M. Lundquist, B.G. Wood, and K. Yassine

1978 An Archaeological Survey of Three Reservoir Areas in Northern Jordan, 1978. *Annual of the Department of Antiquities of Jordan* 22: 108–135.

Khalil, L.

1984 Metallurgical Analyses of Some Weapons from Tell el-'Ajjul. *Levant* 16: 167–170.

Khazanov, A.M.

1978 Characteristic Features of Nomadic Communities in the Eurasian Steppes. In W. Weissleder (ed.), *The Nomadic Alternative*, 119–126. The Hague: Mouton.

1984 *Nomads and the Outside World*. Cambridge: Cambridge University Press.

Khouri, R.G.

1988 *The Antiquities of the Jordan Rift Valley*. Amman: Al-Kutba.

Kochavi, M.

1963a Har Yeruham. *Israel Exploration Journal* 13: 141–142.

1963b The Excavations at Tel Yeruham. *Yediot* 27: 284–292 (Hebrew).

1973 A Built Shaft Tomb of the MB I at Degania 'A'. *Qadmoniot* 6: 50–53 (Hebrew).

LaBianca, O.S.

1990 *Sedentarization and Nomadization: Food System Cycles at Hesban and Vicinity in Transjordan*. Hesban 1. Berrien Springs, MI: Andrews University.

Lapp, P.W.

1966 *The Dhahr Mirzbaneh Tombs*. New Haven, CT: American Schools of Oriental Research.

Lees, S.H. and D.G. Bates

1974 The Origins of Specialized Pastoral Nomadism: A Systemic Model. *American Antiquity* 39: 187–193.

Lemche, N.P.

1985 *Early Israel*. Leiden: E.J. Brill.

Levy, T.E.

1983 The Emergence of Specialized Pastoralism in the Southern Levant. *World Archaeology* 15: 15–36.

Levy, T.E., R.B. Adams, A. Hauptmann, M. Prange, S. Schmitt-Strecker and M. Najjar

2002 Early Bronze Age Metallurgy: A Newly Discovered Copper Manufactory in Southern Jordan. *Antiquity* 76: 425–437.

Liverani, M.

1970 Per una considerazione storica del problema amorreo. *Oriens Antiquus* 9: 5–27.

1973 The Amorites. In D.J. Wiseman (ed.), *Peoples of Old Testament Times*, 100–133. Oxford: Clarendon.

1988 *Antico Oriente: Storia Società Economia*. Bari: Laterza.

London, G.A.

1987 Homage to the Elders. *Biblical Archaeologist* 50: 70–74.

Long, J.C.

1986 Sedentism in Early Bronze IV Palestine-Transjordan: An Analysis of Sociocultural Variability in the Late Third Millennium bc. Paper presented at the Annual Meetings of the American Schools of Oriental Research, Atlanta, GA.

2003 Theory in Archaeology: Culture Change at the End of the Early Bronze Age. In S. Richard (ed.) Near Eastern Archaeology. A Reader, 308–318. Winona Lake, IN: Eisenbrauns.

Loud, G.

1948 *Megiddo II, Seasons of 1935–1939*. Oriental Institue Puplication 162. Chicago, IL: Oriental Institute.

Mabry, J.

1989 Investigations at Tell el-Handaquq, Jordan (1987–88). *Annual of the Department of Antiquities of Jordan* 33: 59–95.

Mabry, J. and G. Palumbo

1988 The 1987 Wadi el-Yabis Survey. *Annual of the Department of Antiquities of Jordan* 32: 275–305.

MacDonald, B.

1995 EB IV Tombs at Khirbat Khanazir: Types, Construction, and Relation to Other EB IV Tombs in Syria-Palestine. In K. 'Amr, F. Zayadine and M. Zaghloul (eds.), *Studies in the History and Archaeology of Jordan V*, 129–134. Amman: Department of Antiquities.

1982 The Wadi el-Hasa Survey 1979 and Previous Archaeological Work in Southern Jordan. *Bulletin of the American Schools of Oriental Research* 245: 35–52.

MacDonald, B. (ed.)

1988 *The Wadi el-Hasa Archaeological Survey 1979–1983, West-Central Jordan*. Waterloo, ON: Wilfrid Laurier University.

1992 *The Southern Ghors and Northeast 'Arabah Archaeological Survey*. Sheffield Archaeological Monographs 5. Sheffield: J.R. Collis.

MacDonald, B., E.B. Banning and L.A. Pavlish

1980 The Wadi el-Hasa Survey 1979: A Preliminary Report. *Annual of the Department of Antiquities of Jordan* 24: 169–183.

MacDonald, B., R.B. Adams, G. Clarke, M. Neeley, and M. Gregory

1987 Southern Ghors and Northeast 'Arabah Archaeological Survey 1986, Jordan: A Preliminary Report. *Annual of the Department of Antiquities of Jordan* 31: 391–413.

Marfoe, L.

1979 The Integrative Transformation: Patterns of Sociopolitical Organization in Southern Syria. *Bulletin of the American Schools of Oriental Research* 234: 1–42.

Marx, E.

1992 Are There Pastoral Nomads in the Middle East? In O. Bar-Yosef and A. Khazanov (eds.), *Pastoralism in the Levant*, 255–260. Madison, WI: Prehistory Press.

Matthiae, P.

1980 Sulle asce fenestrate del 'Signore dei Capridi'. *Studi Eblaiti* 3(3–4): 53–62.

1984 *I Tesori di Ebla*. Bari: Laterza.

1989 *Ebla, un Impero Ritrovato*. Torino: Einaudi.

Mattingly, G. L.

1984 The Early Bronze Age Sites of Central and Southern Moab. *Near East Archaeological Society Bulletin, New Series* 23: 69–88.

Mazzoni, S.

1985 Elements of the Ceramic Culture of Early Syrian Ebla in Comparison with Syro-Palestinian EB IV. *Bulletin of the American Schools of Oriental Research* 257: 1–18.

McConaughy, M.

1979 Formal and Functional Analyses of Chipped Stone Tools from Bab edh-Dhra. Unpublished PhD Thesis, University of Michigan, Ann Arbor, Michigan.

Mittmann, S.

1970 *Beiträge zur Siedlungs-und Territorial-Geschichte des Nördlichen Ostjordanlandes*. Wiesbaden: Abhandlungen des Deutschen Palästina vereins.

Moorey, P.R.S. and F. Schweizer

1972 Copper and Copper Alloys in Ancient Iraq, Syria and Palestine: Some New Analyses. *Archaeometry* 14: 177–197.

Muhly, J.D.

1985 Sources of Tin and the Beginnings of Bronze Metallurgy. *American Journal of Archaeology* 89: 275–291.

Negbi, O.

1966 *Canaanite Burial Caves at Hanita*. Hanita: Kibbutz Hanita (Hebrew).

Neuville, R.

1930 Notes de préhistoire Palestinienne. *Journal of the Palestine Oriental Society* 10: 64–75.

Olávarri, E.

1969 Fouilles à Aro' er sur l' Arnon. *Revue Biblique* 76: 230–259.

Oren, E.D.

1973 *The Northern Cemetery of Beth Shan*. Leiden: E.J. Brill.

Palumbo, G.

1986 Per un'analisi delle sepolture contratte del Bronzo Antico IV di Gerico. *Contributi e Materiali di Archeologia Orientale* 1: 287–306.

1987 'Egalitarian' or 'Stratified' Society? Some Notes on Mortuary Practices and Social Structure at Jericho in EB IV. *Bulletin of the American Schools of Oriental Research* 267: 43–59.

1990 *The Early Bronze Age IV in the Southern Levant: Settlement Patterns, Economy, and Material Culture of a 'Dark Age'*. Contributi e Materiali di Archeologia Orientale III. Roma: Università di Roma 'La Sapienza'.

2001 The Early Bronze Age IV. In B. MacDonald, R. Adams, and P. Bienkowski (eds.), *The Archaeology of Jordan*, 163–232. Sheffield: Sheffield Academic Press

Palumbo, G. and G. Peterman

1993 Early Bronze Age IV Ceramic Regionalism in Central Jordan. *Bulletin of the American Schools of Oriental Research* 289: 23–32

Palumbo, G., J. Mabry and I. Kuijt

1990 The Wadi el-Yabis Survey: Report on the 1989 Field Season. *Annual of the Department of Antiquities of Jordan* 34: 95–118.

Palumbo, G., M. Munzi, S. Collins, F. Hourani, A. Peruzzetto and M.D. Willson

1996 The Wadi az-Zarqa/Wadi ad-Dulayil Excavations and Survey Project: Report on the October–November

1993 Fieldwork Season. *Annual of the Department of Antiquities of Jordan* 40: 375–427.

Patai, R.

1951 Nomadism: Middle Eastern and Central Asian. *Southwestern Journal of Anthropology* 7: 401–414.

Petrie, W.F.

1932 *Ancient Gaza,* II. London: British School of Archaeology in Egypt.

Prag, K.

1971 A Study of the Intermediate Early Bronze–Middle Bronze Age in Transjordan, Syria and Lebanon. Unpublished PhD dissertation, St Hugh's College, University of Oxford.

1974 The Intermediate Early Bronze–Middle Bronze Age: An Interpretation of the Evidence from Transjordan, Syria and Lebanon. *Levant* 6: 69–116.

1984 Review Article: Continuity and Migration in the South Levant in the Late Third Millennium: A Review of T.L. Thompson's and Some Other Views. *Palestine Exploration Quarterly* 116: 58–68.

1985 Ancient and Modern Pastoral Migration in the Levant. *Levant* 17: 81–88.

1986 The Intermediate Early Bronze–Middle Bronze Age Sequences at Tell Iktanu Reviewed. *Bulletin of the American Schools of Oriental Research* 264: 61–72.

1988 Kilns of the Intermediate Early Bronze–Middle Bronze Age at Tell Iktanu: Preliminary Report, 1987 Season. *Annual of the Department of Antiquities of Jordan* 32: 59–72.

1989 Preliminary Report on the Excavations at Tell Iktanu, Jordan, 1987. *Levant* 21: 33–45.

Rast, W.E. and R.T. Schaub

1974 Survey of the South Eastern Plain of the Dead Sea, 1973. *Annual of the Department of Antiquities of Jordan* 19: 5–53.

1978 A Preliminary Report of Excavations at Bab edh-Dhra', 1975. In D.N. Freedman (ed.), *Preliminary Excavation Reports: Bab edh-Dhra', Sardis, Meiron, Tell el-Hesi, Carthage (Punic),* 1–39. Cambridge, MA: American Schools of Oriental Research.

1980 Preliminary Report of the 1979 Expedition to the Dead Sea Plain, Jordan. *Bulletin of the American Schools of Oriental Research* 240: 21–61.

1981 *The Southeastern Dead Sea Plain Expedition: An Interim Report of the 1977 Season.* Annual of the American Schools of Oriental Research 46. Cambridge, MA: American Schools of Oriental Research.

2003 *Bab edh-Dhra. Excavations at the Town site (1975–1981).* Winona Lake, IN: Eisenbrauns

Richard, S.

1983 Report on the 1982 Season of Excavations at Khirbet Iskander. *Annual of the Department of Antiquities of Jordan* 27: 45–53.

1987 The Early Bronze Age in Palestine: The Rise and Collapse of Urbanism. *Biblical Archaeologist* 50: 22–43.

1990 The 1987 Expedition to Khirbet Iskander and its Vicinity: Fourth Preliminary Report. In W.E. Rast (ed.), *Preliminary Reports of ASOR-Sponsored Excavations 1983–1987.* Bulletin of the American Schools of Oriental Research Supplement 26, 33–58. Baltimore, MD: American Schools of Oriental Research.

2003 The Early Bronze Age in the Southern Levant. In S. Richard (ed.) *Near Eastern Archaeology: A Reader,* 286–302. Winona Lake, IN: Eisenbrauns.

Richard, S. and R.S. Boraas

1984 Preliminary Report of the 1981–82 Seasons of the Expedition to Khirbet Iskander and its Vicinity. *Bulletin of the American Schools of Oriental Research* 254: 63–87.

1988 The Early Bronze IV Fortified Site of Khirbet Iskander, Jordan: Third Preliminary Report, 1984 Season. In W.E. Rast (ed.), *Preliminary Reports of ASOR-Sponsored Excavations 1982–1985.* Bulletin of the American Schools of Oriental Research Supplement, 25, 107–130. Baltimore, MD: American Schools of Oriental Research.

Richard, S. and J.C. Long

1989 Specialization/Despecialization: A Model to Explain Culture Change at the End of the Early Bronze Age, ca. 2350–2000 B.C. Paper read at the Annual Meetings of the American Schools of Oriental Research, Anaheim, CA.

1995 Archaeological Expedition to Khirbet Iskander and its Vicinity, 1994. *Annual of the Department of Antiquities of Jordan* 39: 81–92.

Rosen, S.A.

1982 Flint Sickle-Blades of the Late Prehistoric and Early Historic Periods in Israel. *Tel Aviv* 9: 139–145.

1983 The Canaanean Blade and the Early Bronze Age. *Israel Exploration Journal* 33: 15–29.

1988 Notes on the Origins of Pastoral Nomadism: A Case Study from the Negev and Sinai. *Current Anthropology* 29: 498–506.

1997 *Lithics after the Stone Age.* Walnut Creek, CA: Altamira.

Rothenberg, B.

1978 Chalcolithic Copper Smelting. *Archaeo-Metallurgy* 1: 1–23.

Rowton, M.B.

1967 Physical Environment and the Problem of the Nomads. In J.R. Kupper (ed.), *La civilisation de Mari,* 109–121. Paris: Les Belles Lettres.

1973 Autonomy and Nomadism in Western Asia. *Orientalia* 42: 242–258.

1976 Dimorphic Structure and the Tribal Elite. *Studia Instituti Anthropos* 30.

1977 Dimorphic Structure and the Parasocial Element. *Journal of Near Eastern Studies* 36: 181–198.

Schaub, R.T. and W.E. Rast

1984 Preliminary Report of the 1981 Expedition to the Dead Sea Plain, Jordan. *Bulletin of the American Schools of*

Oriental Research* 254: 35–60.

1989 *Bab edh-Dhra: Excavations in the Cemetery Directed by Paul W. Lapp (1965–1967).* Winona Lake, WI: Eisenbrauns.

Service, E.R.

1962 *Primitive Social Organization.* New York: Random House.

Shay, T.

1983 Burial Customs at Jericho in the Intermediate Bronze Age: A Componential Analysis. *Tel Aviv* 10: 26–37.

Sherratt, A.

1981 Plough and Pastoralism: Aspects of the Secondary Products Revolution. In I. Hodder, G. Isaac and N. Hammond (eds.), *Patterns of the Past: Studies in Honor of David Clarke*, 261–305. Cambridge: Cambridge University.

Stech, T., J.D. Muhly and R. Maddin

1985 Metallurgical Studies on Artefacts from the Tomb Near 'Enan. *'Atiqot* 17: 75–82 (English Series).

Thompson, T.L.

1975 *The Settlement of Sinai and the Negev in the Bronze Age.* Wiesbaden: Harrassowitz.

1978 The Background of the Patriarchs: A Reply to Dever and Clark. *Journal for the Study of the Old Testament* 9: 2–43.

1979 *The Settlement of Palestine in the Bronze Age.* Wiesbaden: Harrassowitz.

Tubb, J.N.

1985 Excavations in the Early Bronze Age Cemetery of Tiwal esh-Sharqi: A Preliminary Report. *Annual of the Department of Antiquities of Jordan* 29: 115–130.

Tufnell, O. *et al.*

1958 *Lachish IV: The Bronze Age.* London: Oxford University.

Tzaferis, V.

1968 A Middle Bronze I Cemetery in Tiberias. *Israel Exploration Journal* 18: 15–19.

Waechter, J.

1958 Flint Implements. In O. Tufnell (ed.), *Lachish IV: The Bronze Age*, 325–27. London: Oxford University.

Waheeb, M. and G. Palumbo

1993 Salvage Excavations at a Bronze Age Cemetery near Tell el-Umeiri. *Annual of the Department of Antiquities of Jordan* 37: 147–163.

Weiss, H. (ed.)

1985 *Ebla to Damascus: Art and Archaeology of Ancient Syria.* Washington, DC: Smithsonian Institution.

Wightman, G.J.

1988 An EBIV Cemetery in the North Jordan Valley. *Levant* 20: 139–159.

Wright, G.E.

1937 *The Pottery of Palestine from the Earliest Times to the End of the Early Bronze Age.* New Haven, CT: American Schools of Oriental Research.

1938 The Chronology of Palestinian Pottery in Middle Bronze I. *Bulletin of the American Schools of Oriental Research* 71: 27–34.

Zayadine, F.

1978 An EB–MB Bilobate Tomb at Amman. In P.R.S. Moorey and P.J. Parr (eds.), *Archaeology in the Levant: Essays in Honor of Kathleen M. Kenyon*, 59–66. Warminster: Aris and Phillips.

Zohar, M.

1989 Rogem Hiri: A Megalithic Monument in the Golan. *Israel Exploration Journal* 39: 18–31.

8. The Middle Bronze Age

Steven Falconer

Introduction

The beginning of the Middle Bronze Age (c. 2000 bc) was signalled by the rapid rejuvenation of towns and cities atop the stratified tells of the southern Levant. While some communities were founded anew, many sites that had lain abandoned during the collapse of urbanism in the last centuries of the Early Bronze Age were now reoccupied, expanded and refortified. Although the cultural heritage of the entire Bronze Age is commonly ascribed to the Canaanites of the Old Testament (Dever 1987; Joffe 1993) and other ancient texts (e.g. Matthiae 1981: 187), the archaeological record for the Middle Bronze Age represents "a major break in terms of technology, trade, and social and political institutions from the preceding period" (Gerstenblith 1983: 123). In contrast, the technological and stylistic continuity of material culture through the Middle Bronze Age and into the Late Bronze Age is striking. Recent archaeological syntheses focused west of the Jordan River (e.g. Dever 1987; Mazar 1990; Ilan 1995) emphasize pronounced increases in regional population density, and in the number and size of Levantine cities, all of which reached levels by the end of the Middle Bronze Age (c. 1500 bc) that remained unsurpassed until the Roman and Byzantine periods more than a millennium later (Broshi 1979).

In the lands of modern Jordan, the Middle Bronze Age represents a fundamental archaeological paradox. While this period represents the high point of urbanized Canaanite society in the southern Levant generally, material evidence of Middle Bronze Age society remains relatively elusive east of the Jordan River. On the basis of his pioneering explorations, Glueck (1970: 21) surmised that between major proliferation of settlement in the Early Bronze and the Iron Ages, Jordan witnessed "a gap in the history of permanent sedentary occupation, lasting from the end of the twentieth to the beginning of the thirteenth century bc." In light of a growing abundance of archaeological research conducted since the 1970s, we may now view Glueck's assessment as an exercise in hyperbole. In many areas of Jordan, Middle Bronze Age settlements *are* less numerous and substantial than those that preceded or followed them. However, a variety of excavations and surveys provide tantalizing glimpses of Middle Bronze Age town and village life that augment our appreciation of Canaanite society, and may help explain the apparently modest Middle Bronze Age settlement and population densities east of the Jordan.

Chronology and Nomenclature

The beginning and end dates traditionally assigned to the Middle Bronze Age derive, in large part, from the dynastic history of ancient Egypt. Between roughly 2300 and 2000 bc centralized pharaonic authority apparently collapsed during the "First Intermediate Period" of Egypt, with serious political and economic ramifications for neighbouring societies. The contemporaneous time span in the southern Levant included periods labeled "EB IV" and "MB I" by Albright (1962, 1966). Alternative nomenclatures now prevail in which the entire interval is labelled "EB IV" or "Intermediate Early Bronze–Middle Bronze," for example (see Chapter 7).

The beginning of the Middle Bronze Age is correlated axiomatically with the end of the First Intermediate Period and the ascension of Egypt's Twelfth Dynasty c. 1991 bc, which reestablished centralized government and widespread commercial exchange in the eastern Mediterranean (see, e.g., Weinstein 1975, 1981). Albright's pioneering chronology divided MB II into sub-periods A, B and C, which spanned roughly the same time range as Egypt's Middle Kingdom and "Second Intermediate Period" (see Table 8.1). During five centuries of considerable population increase (see Broshi and Gophna 1986), the rebirth of Levantine towns in MB IIA was followed by their expansion into fortified cities in MB IIB and C, culminating with the apex of Canaanite urban development c. 1500 bc. Middle Bronze IIC coincided with another era of political turmoil in Egypt during which the Fifteenth Dynasty of "Asiatic" or "Hyksos" kings ruled much of Lower Egypt. Military disruptions associated with the collapse of Hyksos power, and possibly their expulsion into the southern Levant, provide an end point for the Middle Bronze Age that is marked archaeologically by the destruction of many Canaanite cities (Weinstein 1991).

In addition to presumed political linkages, the tripartite Middle Bronze Age chronology has hinged on selected innovations in city fortifications as implicit material reflections of the process of urbanization. For example, following their appearance at a few sites in MB IIA, the virtual ubiquity of rampart fortifications (i.e. featuring an earthen core and banked slopes constructed against town walls or tell slopes) among the cities of the southern Levant is cited as a hallmark of MB IIB (Dever 1976: 16; Mazar 1990: 198). A variant form of rampart fortification, known as a glacis, first materialized in MB IIB (a single MB IIA example is reported from Tell Poleg, Israel)

(Mazar 1990: 202). These hard-packed ramparts lay at the foot of masonry fortification walls and usually had a coating of lime, creating a smooth steep impediment to ladders or siege equipment. Similarly, the construction of Cyclopean walls (i.e. characterized by huge unhewn stonework), following town destructions in the late seventeenth century bc, was used as a defining feature of MB

IIC a generation ago (e.g. Mazar 1968: 91), but tends to be disregarded as a chronological marker today.

The most striking regional innovations in town architecture emerged at the beginning of MB IIB. Hence, there has been a general tendency to emphasize the more readily visible distinctions between MB IIA and B, while downplaying contrasts between MB IIB and C. For

Figure 8.1 Sites mentioned in the text.

Egypt	Years bc	Southern Levant			
		Albright	Israeli	Kenyon	Dever
Second Intermediate (14th–17th Dynasties)	c. 1650–1500	MB IIC	MB IIB	MB II	MB III
Middle Kingdom (12th and 13th Dynasties)	c. 1800–1650	MB IIB	MB IIB	MB II	MB II
	c. 2000–1800	MB IIA	MB IIA	MB I	MB I

Table 8.1   Middle Bronze Age chronology and nomenclature (Source: Dever 1987: 149).

example, most Israeli archaeologists subsume Albright's MB IIB and C within "MB IIB," citing greater continuity than disjunction in material culture and architecture. Following this reasoning, Kenyon (1973) also suggested two Middle Bronze Age sub-periods, to be relabelled "MB I" and "MB II." Subsequently, Gerstenblith (1983: 2–3) and Dever (1987) have returned to a tripartite Middle Bronze chronology that includes sub-periods I, II and III. Since most literature retains Albright's nomenclature, this chapter will follow suit. In fact, the terminological controversy summarized above obscures a more important consensus that the Middle Bronze Age, however it is subdivided and labelled, witnessed the dramatic reappearance and more gradual florescence of Canaanite cities and urbanized society.

More fundamentally, Ilan (1995: 299) has called for an independent, radiocarbon-based Middle Bronze Age chronology based on the scarcity of chronologically sensitive Egyptian material culture in the Levant, the present abundance of alternative chronological schemes (as noted above) and the poorly understood geographical variability that marks some Middle Bronze Age evidence. As a chronological caveat, we should note the potential tautology of using Egyptian political transitions to define Middle Bronze Age chronology for the Levant, and subsequently explaining the major junctures within the Middle Bronze Age on the basis of Egyptian political dynamics. Unfortunately, an independent Middle Bronze Age chronology will not emerge until a sufficiently robust collection of radiocarbon dates (with the inherent uncertainties of standard deviations and recalibration) can counteract the allure of apparently firm, historically based dates from Egypt and elsewhere. Presently, data for historically independent chronologies (radiocarbon or otherwise) are embryonic at best.

Material Culture

The beginning of the Middle Bronze Age featured dramatic discontinuities in material culture and settlement patterns. For example, the hand-built pottery of the Early Bronze Age was replaced by a new repertoire of wheel-thrown vessel forms, and bronze tools augmented a metal industry limited previously to copper. As Dever noted two decades ago, "the break between [the Early and Middle Bronze ages] in terms of their material culture is one of the most abrupt and complete in the entire cultural

sequence of Palestine" (1976: 5). Previous attributions of this disjunction to the arrival of new populations, especially the Amorites (Mazar 1968; Kenyon 1973; Dever 1976), in the southern Levant do not figure prominently in Middle Bronze Age research at present (but cf. Mazar 1990: 189; Ilan 1995: 300–301).

The innovation of the fast potter's wheel permitted a broadened range of technically more sophisticated vessel forms, many with Syrian parallels, but very few of which derive from EB IV ceramics. Basic vessel forms, which provide the basis for regional ceramic chronologies developed over the last century, display striking continuity through the Middle Bronze Age and into the Late Bronze Age, as an important aspect of Canaanite material culture. Middle Bronze Age fineware pottery is particularly indicative of the increasing importance of regional ceramic exchange. This aspect of ceramic technology became particularly accentuated in the ceramic trade relations between the Levant and Cyprus in the Late Bronze Age.

A notable characteristic of MB IIA pottery is burnished red slip decoration, particularly common on small vessels. Painted motifs, again often on smaller forms and modestly sized jars, often feature horizontal black or red bands. While some studies suggest derivation of Levantine painted styles from similar examples of "Khabur Ware" from northern Syria (e.g. Dever 1976; Gerstenblith 1983: 59–64), others argue that this Levantine decorative tradition is independent (Tubb 1983).

During MB IIB, red slip decoration gradually gave way to white or cream slips, again primarily on smaller vessel forms. Tall Yehudiyeh Ware, a distinctive dark greyish-black ceramic with punctate decoration, was used primarily to manufacture juglets. Chemical analysis of Tall Yehudiyeh vessels from a variety of locales suggests its manufacture at two centres, one in the eastern Nile Delta and the second at or near Afula, in modern northern Israel (Kaplan 1980). Its widespread occurrence along the Mediterranean seaboard and on Cyprus attests to a growing regional trade in pottery and other commodities.

The pottery of MB IIC features two distinct fineware traditions: Chocolate-on-White Ware and Bichrome Ware. Chocolate-on-White vessels are found most commonly in the northern Jordan Valley, where many apparently were manufactured (Knapp 1993). Bichrome Ware, characterized by its red and black painted decoration, is found more widely distributed throughout the southern Levant. Chemical analyses suggest that most Bichrome vessels were made on Cyprus (Mazar 1990: 259–261). Both of these decorative traditions continue into the Late Bronze Age as parts of a larger Canaanite cultural continuity through the second millennium bc (Mazar 1990: 261).

Human Impact on the Bronze Age Environment

Before considering the social implications of regional settlement patterns, it is imperative that we consider evidence for the increasingly humanized environmental setting to which Middle Bronze Age urbanism contributed and in which it flourished. The natural environmental setting for Levantine agrarian prehistory was far from pristine. A variety of evidence from Ayn Ghazal attests to severe *localized* deforestation as early as the Pre-Pottery Neolithic (e.g. Rollefson and Kohler-Rollefson 1992; Rollefson *et al.* 1992). A second wave of agricultural innovation, featuring intensive orchard cultivation, did not become pronounced until the third and second millennia bc, roughly 5000 years after the domestication of cereals and legumes (N.F. Miller 1991). Palynological analysis of lake cores taken along the Jordan Rift (see Baruch 1990) suggests that the major impetus for the anthropogenic vegetation so characteristic of Jordan and the eastern Mediterranean stems from agricultural intensification to serve emerging urban markets. This trend was most pronounced during several centuries of Roman rule, but had deeper roots lying at least as early as the Middle Bronze Age (Falconer and Fall 1995).

The domestication of several strategic orchard taxa, including olive (*Olea europea*), grape (*Vitis vinifera*) and fig (*Ficus carica*) began in the Levant during the fourth millennium bc (Zohary and Spiegel-Roy 1975; Neef 1990). Olive, arguably the most important fruit tree of the eastern Mediterranean, was valued primarily as a producer of oil for eating and cooking, ointments and fuel for lamps (Zohary 1982). Olive oil could be stored for long periods, and consequently was a valued trade commodity and a symbol of wealth throughout the Mediterranean basin beginning in the Early Bronze Age (Zohary and Hopf 1988). Olive fruits were not pickled and eaten whole until the Hellenistic and Roman periods (Stager 1985).

The grape vine, a similarly versatile orchard taxon, produced fruits that could be eaten fresh, dried to make raisins, or pressed to render juice and wine (Zohary 1982). Figs, which could be dried, stored and eaten year round, supplied fresh foodstuffs rich in sugar. Olive oil, wine and dried figs could be sealed in pottery jars, stored and transported, making them particularly suitable for regional exchange (Stager 1985). By the beginning of the Middle Bronze Age, olive, grape and fig had long been established as the three main horticultural taxa in areas of rain-fed

agriculture throughout the eastern Mediterranean (Zohary and Hopf 1988).

Analysis of pollen from a 5 m sediment core recovered from the southeastern portion of the Sea of Galilee permits the reconstruction of surrounding vegetation before, during and after the Middle Bronze Age (see Baruch 1990). The pollen assemblages from this core are divided into six zones that illustrate the general course of human environmental impact along the Jordan Rift.

The most striking feature of the Sea of Galilee pollen diagram (Figure 8.2) is a massive peak in olive pollen deposition in Zone Y slightly before 2000 years ago. This peak, coupled with sharply reduced amounts of oak pollen (both deciduous *Quercus boissieri* and evergreen *Q. calliprinos*), graphically reflects an era of widespread forest clearance and particularly large-scale olive oil production to serve the markets of the Roman empire. The deposition of grape pollen provides an impressive reflection of the importance of vineyards on surrounding hill slopes, since grape vines are very modest pollen producers.

Interestingly, the pronounced impact of Roman arboriculture appears to be part of a longer process of culturally induced environmental flux beginning at least 5000 years ago. The two lowest pollen zones from the Sea of Galilee show an aggregate trend of decreased arboreal pollen (primarily oak, but also pistachio [*Pistacia atlantica*] and pine [*Pinus halepensis*]), suggesting long-term forest clearance. In Zone X1, at the core's base, pollen from dense oak forest declines, and olive pollen increases to a modest peak roughly contemporaneous with the Early and Middle Bronze Ages. Following a subsequent short-term regeneration of oak forest, dwindling oak pollen frequencies, a slight olive peak and the first appearance of grape pollen in Zone X2 (c. 3000 bp) implicate renewed forest clearance and the cultivation of orchards and vineyards during the Iron Age.

Given its low production levels, the absence of grape pollen from Zone X1 does not rule out significant Bronze Age vineyard horticulture. Indeed, the earliest evidence of grape cultivation in the southern Levant appears as carbonized seeds excavated from Early Bronze sites, including Numayra (McCreery 1980) and Jericho (Hopf 1983). Fig, the region's third major economic taxon, is a wasp-pollinated tree and therefore does not appear in Levantine pollen records. However, the earliest fig pips date to the Chalcolithic (Hopf 1983) and the Early Bronze Age (McCreery 1980), and evidence of fig cultivation is widespread by the Middle Bronze Age (Lines 1995).

These palynological data for economic and wild taxa alike suggest the beginnings of regional disturbance of natural taxa, including significant deforestation. Extrapolating from the Sea of Galilee pollen record, we may envision a Middle Bronze Age landscape still characterized by large tracts of oak/pistachio woodland (see also Gophna *et al.* 1986; Liphschitz *et al.* 1989). However, with the rise of urban markets and the regional commerce that they must have facilitated, the settlements of the southern Levant now actively remoulded their surrounding countrysides. Lowlands and river valleys became increasingly checkered with annual subsistence crops, while perennial fruit-bearing trees and vines encroached on neighbouring uplands (Stager 1985). The distinctly anthropogenic character of modern Middle Eastern landscapes has been achieved only after several subsequent millennia of human impacts. The regional transformation of that landscape, however, is one of the abiding legacies of Levantine urbanism, which enjoyed its first heyday during the Middle Bronze Age (Fall *et al.* 1998, 2002, 2004).

Levantine Towns and Cities

With some sense of the environmental setting in which it developed, we may consider the dynamics of Middle Bronze Age settlement in the southern Levant generally, and in the surveyed locales of Jordan more specifically. While much of the regional populace continued to live in small rural sites, practising seasonal pastoralism and sedentary farming, vanishingly few EB IV sites remained occupied into the Middle Bronze Age. In addition, and in stark contrast to EB IV settlements, relatively large towns and cities, often fortified, appeared atop the region's stratified tells. Many of these larger communities were built on the remains of EB II or III settlements that had remained unoccupied during EB IV.

Interpretive scenarios focused west of the Jordan River argue that Middle Bronze Age towns developed first along the Mediterranean coastal plain and lowland valleys

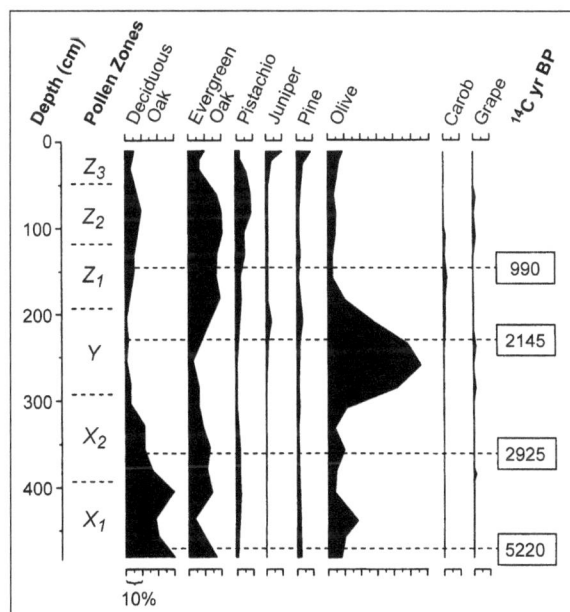

Figure 8.2   Arboreal pollen frequencies from the Sea of Galilee sediment core (after Baruch 1990).

communicating with the coast (Gerstenblith 1983: 118; Mazar 1990: 176–178; Ilan 1995: 301). Indeed, MB IIA walled towns dotted the Levantine coast between Ashkelon to the south and Ras Shamra (ancient Ugarit) in Syria (Kenyon 1973: 84; Ilan 1995: 301). Traditional interpretations hold further that substantial inland towns did not emerge until later in MB IIA (e.g. Shechem) or in MB IIB (e.g. Jericho) (Gerstenblith 1983: 118–119; Mazar 1990: 197–198).

The coastal distribution of towns has been attributed to mercantile influences, especially from Egypt, delivered via maritime or overland trade (Gerstenblith 1983: 109–126; Gophna 1984). Foreign missions have been interpreted from Egyptian statuary found at Levantine coastal sites and from Egyptian documentary evidence (Mazar 1968: 73; Posener 1971: 549). More recently, Bunimovitz (1989: 47–74; see Ilan 1995: 302) has suggested a united Middle Bronze Age coastal polity. However, critical reviews point out the limited archaeological data on which these arguments are built (e.g. Weinstein 1975), and infer a series of localized polities lying along the east–west river drainages that linked the hills of Palestine with the coastal plain (Ilan 1995: 302).

Excavated Settlements in Jordan

While the general coastal orientation of the largest Middle Bronze Age towns is apparent (Falconer 1994), and although evidence from MB IIA is poorly represented in Jordan (Dornemann 1983: 15), excavations at a variety of sites east of the Jordan River provide new insights on Middle Bronze Age settlements ranging from small hamlets to sizable towns, some of which date to the very beginning of the period. The overview below begins with excavated evidence from the Jordan Valley and the Dead Sea Plain, then considers the archaeologically known towns of the northern and central Transjordanian plateau, as well as the two examples of Middle Bronze Age settlement in the eastern desert of Jordan. Subsequently, a review of several major regional surveys provides a broadly painted portrait of how localized settlement trends in Jordan relate to the more comprehensive settlement patterns reported west of the Jordan River.

Jordan Valley

Only four Middle Bronze Age settlements in the Jordan Valley have been excavated to a significant extent, and many other sites show an apparent hiatus in occupation during the period (e.g. Tall Abu Kharaz, Tall Saidiyya). Three of the four excavated sites, Tall Dayr Alla, Tall Nimrin and Tall Hayyat, lie in the *ghor*, the rich agricultural area covering the broad Pleistocene terrace above the active floodplain of the Jordan River, which is known in Arabic as the *zor*. Pella, at present the best-known Middle Bronze Age town in Jordan, lies in the first line of foothills lying immediately overlooking the *ghor* from the east.

Pella

The site of ancient Pella lies adjacent to the modern village of Tabaqat Fahl and commands a permanent spring in the adjacent Wadi Jirm. Its settlement history extends back to the Neolithic and features extensive ruins dating to the Roman period, during which Pella was a member of the league of cities known as the Decapolis.

Given the particularly lengthy occupation of the site, Middle Bronze Age data derive from deep soundings with limited lateral exposure (see Figure 8.3). For example, before being discontinued and backfilled, the West Cut at Pella (Area VIII) produced MB IIB–C sherds at a depth of 14 m below the modern tell surface (Smith 1993: 1177). Elsewhere, Middle Bronze Age ceramics come from stratified sedimentary fill in Areas XXV and XXVIII along Pella's south slope (e.g. Smith and McNicoll 1986: 113, fig. 20). Pella's role as a major town early in the Middle Bronze Age is attested further by two apparently cornering sections of a massive mudbrick town wall in the East Cut (Area III, plots D and F) (Smith and Potts 1992: 35, 40–44, fig. 7). The excavators are wary of assigning a specific construction date for this architecture, the earliest known pre-classical fortification at Pella, since contemporaneous deposits have produced no reconstructible pottery thus far (Potts *et al.* 1988: 131). Currently available sherd assemblages suggest a construction date in MB IIA (Smith 1993: 1176). Excavations in 1997 revealed an additional stretch of Middle Bronze fortification wall in Area XXVIII, approximately 300 m west of Area III (Bourke, pers. comm.). Jointly, these walls hint at a Middle Bronze Age defensive system that encompassed the entire main mound at Pella, an area of perhaps 8 ha. By applying an estimated population density of 200–300 people per hectare, which is derived from a plethora of ethnographic accounts of traditional Middle Eastern communities (see especially Kramer 1982: 155–181), Pella might have housed about 2000 people. The likelihood that Pella was a substantial fortified town early in the Middle Bronze Age is strengthened by its inclusion (as Pihilum) among the presumably bothersome and ritually cursed cities of the Egyptian Execration Texts (Smith 1973: 23; see discussion below).

While Areas VIII, XXV and XXVIII have produced MB IIB and C ceramics, the best stratified evidence for these periods comes from the East Cut (Area III). Here the entire Middle Bronze Age sequence is represented in strata X–VI, and plots III C and F reveal MB IIB mudbrick domestic architecture just inside the town wall (Smith and Potts 1992: 44–47, fig. 8).

In addition to its tell deposits, Pella has produced abundant mortuary evidence from off-site tombs. While MB IIA burials are lacking, the contents of later tombs suggest significant international connections, especially at the end of the Middle Bronze Age and into the Late Bronze Age.

A single infant jar burial dating to MB IIB was excavated in Area VIII on the tell (Smith 1973: 367), and a variety of tombs, most previously looted or eroded, have been surveyed west and southwest of Pella, but remain unexcavated (Smith 1993: 1177). More fruitful excavations have investigated Middle and Late Bronze Age cemeteries east of the tell (Area II) and on the north slope of neighbouring Tall Husn (Area XI), which lies on the south side of Wadi Jirm. These cemeteries include chamber and cist tombs, many spanning the MB IIC/LB I transition. For example, Tombs 1 (in Area II) and 62 (in Area XI) feature abundant Chocolate-on-White chalices, jugs and bowls (Smith 1973: 170, l. 46; Potts *et al.* 1988: 206), like those traded between Pella and distant markets to the west and north (Knapp 1993). The three burial chambers in Tomb 62 produced over 2000 vessels, abundant personal ornaments and the skeletal remains of more than 100 individual burials, suggesting significant material affluence and long-term use by the people of Pella (Potts *et al.* 1988: 205, figs. 9, 10).

Tall Dayr Alla

Tall Dayr Alla, which lies near the confluence of the Zarqa and Jordan Rivers, may be equated with ancient Succoth of the Old Testament and Talmud (van der Kooij and Ibrahim 1989: 75–76). An excavated exposure of less than 100m² at the southeast foot of the tell reveals the earliest known Middle Bronze Age remains at the site: a substantial mudbrick town wall preserved to a height of 2.5 m (van der Kooij and Ibrahim 1989: 75–76). This wall in Tall Dayr Alla's Phase IV dates, based on associated Tall Yehudiyeh Ware, no earlier than MB IIB. Domestic architecture, including mudbrick walls and courtyards, is also found in Phase IV and the subsequent Phase V. If the entire tell was inhabited during MB II, Tall Dayr Alla would represent a small fortified town a few hectares in size, with a population on the order of 1000 inhabitants.

Tall Nimrin

Lying near the mouth of Wadi Shuayb in the modern town of South Shuna, Tall Nimrin contains nearly 6 m of stratified remains from the Middle Bronze Age. Unlike Tall Dayr Alla, Nimrin provides stratified domestic architecture and material culture dating to MB IIA, apparently reflecting an unfortified village. Massive stone-founded mudbrick fortification walls date later in the Middle Bronze Age, and remain preserved up to 4 m in height, with a glacis along their exterior. This monumental architecture was constructed in two phases, the first in late MB IIB and the second in MB IIC (Flanagan *et al.* 1994: 217–218). Interestingly, this massive wall system may have protected a village perhaps only 1 ha in size (200–300 inhabitants), which was abandoned abruptly in the sixteenth or early fifteenth century bc (Flanagan *et al.* 1994: 217–219).

Tall Hayyat

The low mound of Tall Hayyat lies amid the *ghor* approximately 2 km east of the Jordan River and 7 km southwest of Pella. Tall Hayyat embodies a Middle Bronze Age hamlet that measured about one-half hectare and would have housed no more than 150 inhabitants. Excavations have exposed 400m² of Hayyat's surface area and proceeded through 4.5 m of cultural deposition at the mound's centre (Falconer and Magness-Gardiner 1989; Falconer and Fall 2006).

Habitation at Tall Hayyat began very late in EB IV and continued through six major strati-graphic/architectural phases to late MB IIC. An ephemeral EB IV stratum (Phase 6) lies at the tell's base. Tall Hayyat's earliest architecture consists of a small, centrally located mudbrick shrine dating to early MB IIA (Phase 5), which is the first in a stratified series of mudbrick temples that are enlarged and elaborated in Phases 4–2 (MB IIA, B and C, respectively). These sanctuaries become much larger than Hayyat's dwellings, show remarkable continuity between phases and provide examples of the "Migdal" temples known primarily from cities in the Levant, Syria and Lower Egypt (see Figure 8.4 and discussions in Magness-Gardiner and Falconer 1994, and Falconer and Fall 2006).

In each stratum, a surrounding wall clearly segregates each temple compound from mudbrick household structures. Domestic architecture was not found in Phase 5, but in Phases 4, 3 and 2 the areas outside each temple compound feature houses, walled courtyards and alleyways. In addition, Tall Hayyat revealed an intact MB IIA (Phase 4) pottery kiln on its southern slope (see Falconer 1987). Phase 1, dating to late MB IIC, produced only fragments of domestic architecture and no evidence of a temple.

Figure 8.3 Excavation areas on the main mound of Pella and adjoining hillsides (after Smith 1993: 1174).

Patterns of faunal, floral and ceramic deposition reveal several salient aspects of village economy at Tall Hayyat. In turn, these data provide a glimpse of urban–rural relations in the Jordan Valley. Hayyat's economic evidence hints at a few increased connections with external markets, which we might expect for such a community (see Falconer 1995; Fall *et al.* 1998). For example, between Phases 5 and 3 sheep became more commonly husbanded than goats, presumably because sheep generate secondary products, especially wool, with greater market value. Increased remains of marketable fruit (e.g. olive, grape and figs) and ceramic serving vessels made by craft specialists also hint at greater exchange of agricultural and manufactured products.

However, these trends are overshadowed by data suggesting accentuated economic autonomy at Tall Hayyat. For instance, despite the market potential of their wool, sheep remained important sources of meat for domestic consumption. Tall Hayyat also featured a surprisingly robust element of household pig herding that increased markedly through time. Finally, the ceramic repertoire shows that the manufacture of cooking pots became increasingly localized, storejars became more commonly suitable as short-term containers, rather than transport of marketable goods, and the storage functions of Tall Hayyat's temples increasingly resembled those of households (Falconer 1995; Fall *et al.* 1998; Falconer and Fall 2006).

In sum, most of the evidence from Tall Hayyat implies increasing economic self-reliance throughout the Middle Bronze Age. Growing local investment is reflected in the increased size and elaboration of Tall Hayyat's temple and domestic architecture (see discussion in Magness-Gardiner and Falconer 1994; Falconer 1995). Likewise, this village performed activities otherwise concentrated in cities, including the manufacture of copper alloy tools, weapons and figurines (Falconer and Magness-Gardiner 1989). The farmers of Tall Hayyat apparently exploited some opportunities presented by town and city markets, but simultaneously ensured community autonomy in the face of the inevitable liabilities of urbanism.

Dead Sea Plain

The only Middle Bronze Age sites known in the Jordan Rift south of Tall Nimrin are found at Zahrat adh-Dhra and Dayr Ayn Abata southeast of the Dead Sea. The settlement at Zahrat adh-Dhra 1 is marked by visible stone architecture along a northwest–southeast-trending ridge in the Plain of Dhra, east of Bab adh-Dhra (Edwards *et al.* 1998). The remains of numerous rectangular structures and curved enclosures are spread widely over approximately 6 ha. Excavations directed by the author in the winter of 1999/2000 suggest intermittent occupation in MB II A and B (see Edwards *et al.* 2001; Fall *et al.* 2007). Severe downcutting followed this occupation (or may have ended it), as shown by the erosion of Middle Bronze

Age structures into the steep-sided wadis to the northeast and southwest (Edwards *et al.* 2002, 2004). This evidence suggests the site originally extended over a much larger area (see Berelov 2006).

At least 19 Middle Bronze Age single-and double-chamber cairn tombs lie north of the Byzantine monastery at Dayr Ayn Abata, on the steep slopes overlooking the modern town of Safi in the Southern Ghor (Politis 1990, 1993, 1995, 1997). Although these tombs have been looted heavily, their assemblages suggest a date late in MB II.

Northern Plateau: Tall Irbid, Abila, Jarash, Dahr Mudayna

Excavations along the west and northeast sides of Tall Irbid have exposed a three-tier mudbrick city wall system, the earliest of which dates to c. 2000 bc (Lenzen and McQuitty 1989: 299–300). Tall Irbid extends over approximately 20 ha and, if fully encircled by walls, embodies a Middle Bronze Age fortified town formerly inhabited by perhaps 5000 people.

Abila and Jarash, two members of the classical Decapolis in the general vicinity of Irbid, have also produced substantial amounts of Middle Bronze Age pottery (Braemer 1987; Mare 1991: 206). At Jarash, living surfaces just above bedrock include abundant Chocolate-on-White Ware, indicating a use date in MB IIC. At both sites, which extend over very large areas in later periods, the extent of Middle Bronze Age settlement is unknown.

At Dahr Mudayna, a modest ridgetop site northwest of Jarash, limited soundings again reveal Chocolate-on-White Ware, as well as substantial amounts of MB IIA and B pottery (Kafafi and Knauf 1989).

Central Plateau: Amman, Tall Safut, Abu Snesleh, Sahab, Tall Jalul, Tall Umayri

A deep sounding on the lower terrace of the citadel of Amman reveals a stone-founded city wall dating to Middle Bronze II B and C (Greene and Amr 1992: 116–117). A glacis on the upper terrace apparently also dates to the latter part of the Middle Bronze Age (Dornemann 1983: 18; Zayadine *et al.* 1987: 308), although little associated material culture has been published. Although its size during the second millennium bc is difficult to estimate, the citadel may have measured 10 ha, with a population of 2000–3000 people.

More impressive remains are reported from Middle Bronze Age chamber tombs in the vicinity of Amman. These tombs, which feature pottery dating between late MB IIB and the beginning of the Late Bronze Age, include ornate bronze and beaded jewellery, scarabs and alabaster vessels (Piccirillo 1978; Najjar 1991). A single MB IIB–C tomb has also been reported near Mount Nebo in Wadi Abu Naml (Dornemann 1983: 17).

Middle Bronze IIB–C fortifications with an associated

glacis are also attested at Sahab, lying southeast of Amman, approximately halfway between the modern capital and the edge of the eastern desert (Ibrahim 1987: 76; 1989). The extent of these walls is uncertain and, if comparable to Sahab's Late Bronze Age fortifications, would have enclosed a few hectares at most (see Ibrahim 1989: 519).

Two nearby caves, used as tombs, produced human remains and ceramic assemblages dating to MB IIB or C. Sahab's modest size, fortifications and location suggest that it may have served as an outpost on the desert fringe, possibly comparable to those of the *limes* system during the Roman and Byzantine periods (Ibrahim 1987: 76).

Figure 8.4   Temple and domestic architecture excavated in phases 5–2 at Tall Hayyat (after Magness-Gardiner and Falconer 1994: fig. 5).

Tall Safut, perched at the southern edge of the Baqah Valley northwest of Amman, has also revealed deposition identified as a glacis (Maayah 1960: 115). Following subsequent tentative acceptance of this interpretation (Dornemann 1983: 19), these deposits most recently have been reassessed as part of the site's natural geology (Wimmer 1989: 513).

Middle Bronze Age domestic architecture is reported from Abu Snesleh, a settlement of uncertain size lying east of Amman at the desert margin. Limited soundings have exposed a stone-founded mudbrick house with an assemblage of domestic pottery similar to the more abundant MB IIB and C collections from sites west of the Jordan River (Lehmann *et al.* 1991).

In the vicinity of Madaba, surveys of two major *tulul* have revealed abundant Middle Bronze Age pottery. While excavations have begun only recently at Tall Jalul, several field seasons at Tall Umayri have exposed a beaten earth rampart along its western slope. Pottery related to the construction of the rampart (including Chocolate-on-White Ware), as well as that recovered from the eastern portion of the site, suggests that Tall Umayri was a fortified settlement in MB IIB and C (Herr *et al.* 1991: 159, 166). The tell's full extent of approximately 6.5 ha suggests that it may represent a moderately sized town with about 1600 inhabitants.

Eastern Desert: Jawa, Tall Rukeis

The only excavated Middle Bronze Age sites in Jordan's eastern desert are fortified settlements at Jawa and Tall Rukeis. The latest architecture at Jawa includes a stone "citadel" measuring somewhat less than 1 ha, and dating to the Middle Bronze Age (Helms 1975: 22–26; 1976: 2–7; 1977: 23–27). This unusual stone structure features two stories of cell-like rooms arrayed around a central walled courtyard and flanked by three covered corridors with stone roof supports. The citadel's floor plan was readily apparent from the surface (see Helms 1976: fig. 3), necessitating only limited excavation. Following its construction, apparently in MB IIA, the citadel may have served as a caravanserai for overland trade between Syria or Mesopotamia and the Levant (Helms 1975: 26).

Tall Rukeis, near the Syrian border, is associated with several small Middle Bronze Age farmsteads along the Wadi Ajib, which drains south from the Jabal Druze (Betts *et al.* 1996; Betts 1998). Excavations reveal two phases of Middle Bronze architecture, including basalt fortifications with a chambered gate and small-scale domestic structures, possibly for storage. Agricultural features on the landscapes around both Tall Rukeis and Jawa suggest intensive Bronze Age water conservation in this agriculturally marginal environment.

Regional Settlement Patterns in the Southern Levant

The most widely published and analyzed Bronze Age set-

tlement data presently derive from a variety of archaeological surveys that have covered approximately 14,000 km² between the Mediterranean and the Jordan Valley (see Ibrahim *et al.* 1976, 1988; Broshi and Gophna 1984, 1986; Gophna and Portugali 1988; Joffe 1991; Finkelstein and Gophna 1993; Falconer 1994; Falconer and Savage 1995). These studies show that the number of archaeologically detectable settlements increased substantially between MB IIA and MB IIB–C. However, this trend incorporated only modest growth in sedentary populations, and a noticeable *decrease* in average site size to c. 2 ha in MB IIB–C (Falconer 1994). These characteristics indicate a form of growth primarily involving smaller settlements. This inference is corroborated by two additional trends: a substantial drop in the percentage of the regional populations living in towns (i.e. sites larger than 10 ha), and a rise in the number of rural villages (i.e. sites smaller than 5 ha) (Falconer 1994). In concert, these trends describe a process of growth manifested primarily in a proliferation of villages and hamlets, especially in the hills of Palestine and in the Jordan Valley.

Rank-size Analysis

Rank-size analysis provides a particularly economical method for comprehending Middle Bronze Age settlement patterns and comparing them with the Levant's first expression of urbanism in the Early Bronze Age. This method assesses regional political and economic integration by correlating the size and rank of communities in a settlement system. The "rank-size rule" holds that for regions "with a long tradition of urbanism, which are politically and economically complex," the size of any *n*-ranked place may be predicted by dividing the size of the largest place by *n* (Berry 1961: 582; Zipf 1949). In other words, in politically mature regions with well-integrated economic systems the largest city is expected to have twice the population of the second-ranked city, three times the population of the third-ranked city, and so on. When plotted logarithmically, the settlement sizes within such a system will describe a straight line, log-normal distribution in accordance with the rank-size rule.

Interestingly, archaeological settlement patterns seldom conform to the expectations of the rank-size rule, and their interpretation usually stems from the manner in which they depart from log-normal (e.g. Johnson 1977, 1980; Paynter 1983). For example, "primate" rank-size distributions are characterized by a first-ranked place (a "primate" city) that is much larger than predicted by the rank-size rule (Jefferson 1939). Primate rank-size curves, which tend to dip below a log-normal line, reflect extreme interdependence between communities. In contrast, "convex" rank-size curves, which rise above a log-normal line, commonly derive from the pooling of multiple settlement systems or from systems characterized by poor integration, in which community sizes are less hierarchical than predicted by the rank-size rule (Johnson 1977: 497, 1980).

In light of the pre-eminence normally ascribed to fortified Bronze Age cities in the southern Levant (e.g. Dever 1987), we might anticipate accordingly primate rank-size settlement distributions. However, Early and Middle Bronze Age survey data collected from the Jordan Valley west to the Mediterranean produce a series of *convex* departures from log-normal for both the Early and Middle Bronze Ages (Falconer and Savage 1995; Fall *et al.* 1998; see Figure 8.5). Although the MB IIB–C data describe a closer approximation of log-normal than seen for MB IIA, both curves suggest consistently poor political and economic integration in the southern Levant generally, the pooling of multiple localized settlement enclaves, or both.

The Egyptian Execration Texts provide an indirect, but intriguing, reflection of Levantine regional politics that may help us interpret these patterns. These texts consist of sherds (the "Berlin Texts") and statuette fragments (the "Brussels Texts") inscribed with lists of Asiatic localities (cities or regions) and their rulers who were cursed as adversaries of Pharaoh. The Berlin Texts, dated to the reign of Sesostris III (Posener 1971: 541), have been correlated with MB IIA in Palestine (Mazar 1968: 75). These texts enumerate 20 territories associated with 30 "rulers." The larger collection of Brussels Texts dates approximately one generation later, and enumerates 62 territories and a similar number of rulers (Posener 1971: 541, 555). Among the Brussels Texts, perhaps dating to early MB IIB, more numerous territories suggest the spread of towns and cities, while more frequent single rulers imply slightly more centralized "city-states" (Posener 1971: 541; Mazar 1968: 75, 81). When viewed in tandem, these documentary and survey accounts hint at the gradual coalescence of small local polities, but more fundamentally portray a highly fragmented Levantine political landscape.

Localized Settlement Patterns in the Jordan Valley

At present, regional survey coverage in Jordan tends to be intensive, but geographically discontinuous (see discussion below). Fortunately, Bronze Age settlement patterns in the Jordan Valley, a clearly circumscribed region of approximately 1700 km², are illuminated by archaeological surveys covering both sides of the Jordan River (see Ibrahim *et al.* 1976, 1988; Broshi and Gophna 1984, 1986; Joffe 1991; Falconer and Savage 1995).

Early and Middle Bronze Age rank-size curves for the Jordan Valley are effectively log-normal, showing statistically insignificant convex departures (Figure 8.6). In contrast to the southern Levant generally, this log-normality suggests more effective economic and political integration, the existence of very few localized settlement systems, or both. During the Early Bronze Age, the Jordan Valley enjoyed settlement densities comparable to, or greater than, those found anywhere in the southern Levant, including

the heavily populated Mediterranean coastal plan (Joffe 1991; Falconer and Savage 1995). Following the EB IV collapse, Middle Bronze Age settlements redeveloped, but on a much-reduced scale. Middle Bronze Age sites are strikingly smaller in number and size than their Early Bronze Age predecessors. During the Middle Bronze Age, the Jordan Valley's population grew slightly, while the number of settlements roughly doubled between MB IIA and B–C (Broshi and Gophna 1986; Falconer 1994).

Archaeological survey investigations to the east and south of the Jordan Valley have tended to be discontinuous, with the coverage defined within individual wadi drainages or in the hinterlands surrounding focal sites. Although these surveys are not amenable to a rank-size analysis for a contiguous region, their results do show a number of common patterns, most notably a drop in settlement density between the Early and Middle Bronze Ages.

The following discussion summarizes the results from a number of surveys conducted along drainages into the Jordan Valley and Wadi Arabah, then considers surveys conducted on the Transjordanian plateau. This overview emphasizes settlement distinctions in the regional urbanism of the Early and Middle Bronze Ages. In light of this, and because its evidence is reported inconsistently, EB IV settlement is, regrettably, excluded. Likewise, since our focus lies on domestic sites, evidence from very ephemeral or special activity sites (e.g. sherd scatters) is omitted.

Figure 8.5 Rank-size distributions for Early Bronze III and Middle Bronze IIB–C settlements of known size in the southern Levant. For EB III: K-=.406, p<.01; For MB IIB–C: K-= .479, p<.01. Data from Ibrahim *et al.* (1976, 1988), Broshi and Gophna (1984, 1986), Gophna and Portugali (1988), Joffe (1991) and Finkelstein and Gophna (1993) (after Falconer and Savage 1995: fig. 8).

Figure 8.6 Rank-size distributions for Early Bronze II, Middle Bronze IIA and Middle Bronze IIB–C settlements of known size in the Jordan Valley. For EB II: K-= .219,p = .69; For MB IIA: K-= .231, p = .29; For MB IIB–C: K-= .308, p = .24. Data from Ibrahim *et al.* (1976, 1988), Broshi and Gophna (1984, 1986), Joffe (1991).

Several surveys have been conducted in the major wadis that drain the Transjordanian plateau into the Jordan River. Systematic coverage of wadi bottoms and adjacent hills is reported for Wadi Arab (Hanbury-Tenison 1984) Wadi Ziqlab (Banning and Fawcett 1983), Wadi Hammeh (Petocz and Villiers 1984) and Wadi Yabis (Mabry and Palumbo 1988). Although field methods varied between surveys, each project utilized some form of systematic sampling in designating areas for pedestrian reconnaissance.

Likewise, these surveys use different chronological categories to report their results. For example, the Wadi Arab and Wadi Ziqlab surveys combine data for EB II and III settlements, as well as for the Middle and Late Bronze Ages.

Given their comparably systematic sampling methods, it is interesting to note significant variability in site frequencies between drainages. For example, Wadis Arab and Yabis reveal modest, but roughly comparable, Early and Middle Bronze Age settlement frequencies. However, Wadi Ziqlab produced no Early Bronze Age sites and only low-density Middle–Late Bronze Age sherd scatters (Banning and Fawcett 1983), while in Wadi Hammeh, Early and Middle Bronze Age evidence is limited to Pella, aside from a single small Early Bronze tell (Petocz and Villiers 1984).

Survey Coverage of the Transjordanian Plateau

On the Transjordanian Plateau between the upper courses of the Yarmouk and Zarqa Rivers, a non-systematic survey of Roman roads reports the widespread occurrence of Middle Bronze Age sites, and isolated soundings confirm the presence of stratified Middle Bronze Age remains at several of them (Mittmann 1970).

Two surveys on the central Transjordanian Plateau reveal a substantial drop in settlement between the EB I–III periods and the Middle Bronze Age. Non-random survey coverage of the lands within a 10 km radius of Hisban revealed Early Bronze Age sherds on the surface of 46 sites, while Middle Bronze Age remains were limited to 10 sites, most of which are quite small (Ibach 1987: 3, tables 3.5, 6). Sizeable Middle Bronze Age occupations were limited to Tall Umayri and Tall Jalul, both of which also feature substantial evidence from the Early Bronze Age.

The Madaba Plains Survey investigated 55 visible sites within a 10 × 10 km quadrat around Tall Umayri, of which 10 were occupied during EB I–III, while only two provided evidence from the Middle Bronze Age (Boling 1989). Additional reconnaissance of a 1.5% random sample within this area revealed 11 further Early Bronze Age settlements, but only two other Middle Bronze Age sites.

A survey of 875 km² on the Karak plateau documented 28 sites that may have been EB II–III habitations (i.e. with five or more surface sherds) and 15 such sites dating to the Middle Bronze Age (J.M. Miller 1991: 308; Brown 1991: 185). Again, these sites, especially those dating to the Middle Bronze Age, are commonly quite small.

Farther south, the Wadi Hasa Survey has sampled varying portions of the 600 km² drainage with a combination of pedestrian and vehicular coverage, documenting dozens of EB I sites, but very few from any other periods within the Bronze Age (MacDonald (ed.) 1988: 166–168; Clark *et al.* 1994).

Overview of Settlement Pattern Data

Table 8.2 summarizes site counts and densities for six major surveys conducted during the last 20 years in Jordan, in which systematic sampling detected a significant number of Middle Bronze Age sites. When viewing these data, several caveats merit recognition. First, the essential criteria for identifying sites, especially domestic sites, vary between surveys. Miller's criterion of domestic sites having five or more diagnostic sherds is a rare exercise in explicit definition (J.M. Miller 1991). Second, Table 8.2 hints at variability in survey intensity, especially in light of the general inverse correlation of total survey coverage and site density. It appears, not surprisingly, that more localized surveys may detect smaller, more ephemeral sites that are overlooked by more ambitious, but less intensive reconnaissance. Likewise, more localized surveys may be more lenient in the criteria used to define a "site." Further, the temporal conflation that inevitably accompanies survey chronologies takes different forms from survey to survey.

Survey	Area Surveyed (km²)	EB Sites (no./100 km²)	MB Sites (no./100 km²)
East Jordan Valley	700	40a (5.7)	27 (3.9)
Wadi Arab	25	4a (16)	3c (12)
Wadi Yabis	186	13b (7.0)	14 (7.5)
Hisban	314	46b (14.6)	10 (3.2)
Madaba Plains	100	11b (11.0)	2 (2.0)
Karak Plateau	875	28a (3.2)	15 (1.7)

Table 8.2 Early and Middle Bronze Age site counts and densities in Jordan. Source: Data from Ibrahim *et al.* 1976, 1988; Hanbury-Tenison 1984; Mabry and Palumbo 1988; Ibach 1987; Boling 1989; J.M. Miller 1991. Notes: a = EB II–III; b=EB I–II; c = MB–LB.

Most significantly here, an "Early Bronze Age" site designation subsumes EB I, II and III for some surveys, but only EB II and III for others.

Even with these cautions in mind, two major settlement trends, one chronological and the other geographical, emerge fairly clearly. First, with the exception of the near-equality of sites from the Early and Middle Bronze Ages reported by the Wadi Yabis Survey, there is a consistent drop in settlement density between these two periods in the other major surveyed regions of Jordan. This characteristic is particularly pronounced for the surveys of the central and southern regions of the Transjordanian plateau. Secondly, Middle Bronze Age site densities, which are highest in Wadis Arab and Yabis along the northern Jordan Valley, again dwindle to extremely low values on the central and southern plateau, with no sites reported to date south of Wadi Hasa.

Conclusions

The review above clarifies the relative paucity of evidence for Middle Bronze Age society in Jordan. However, rather than accept Glueck's premature impression of a regional settlement hiatus during this period, a number of tantalizing trends in our available data cry out for more substantial field investigations. First, although most of the excavated remains and virtually all of the mortuary evidence date to MB IIB and C, a number of sites reveal substantial occupations during MB IIA. These communities stretch from Pella in the Jordan Valley to the eastern desert at Jawa. Secondly, Middle Bronze Age communties in Jordan ranged from small cities of 10–20 ha (e.g. Pella, Tall Irbid, possibly the Amman Citadel), to towns with 1000–2000 inhabitants (e.g. Tall Dayr Alla, Tall Umayri, Sahab), to villages with a few hundred occupants at most (e.g. Tall Hayyat, Tall Nimrin). Thirdly, following the fortification of some communities in MB IIA (Pella, Tall Irbid, Amman Citadel), virtually all known settlements apparently were ringed by protective walls during MB IIB–C (with the exceptions of smaller sites like Tall Hayyat, Abu Snesleh and Dahr Mudayna). Thus, the commonly cited coastal orientation for the development of Middle Bronze Age settlement and society (e.g. in Gerstenblith 1983; Mazar 1990; Falconer 1994; Ilan 1995) must be modified to accommodate the widespread, and often fortified, spectrum of communities east of the Jordan River.

Regional survey data, as discontinuous as they may be, highlight major distinctions between the Bronze Age settlement trajectories of Palestine and Israel to the west versus those of Jordan to the east. West of the Jordan River, the Middle Bronze Age may be characterized as an apex of pre-classical urbanism and population density with some justification (e.g. Dever 1987; Mazar 1990). However, to the east, its regional patterns reflect a recession of sedentary settlement that follows the advent of urbanism in the Early Bronze Age. Additionally, there is a fairly clear north–south fall-off pattern in Middle Bronze settlement densities, suggesting the possible importance of northerly economic and political ties stemming from the Beth Shan and Jezreel Valleys and the connections to the Mediterranean that they represent. In this regard, it is not altogether surprising that the northern towns of Pella and Tall Irbid potentially represent two of the most substantial centres of Middle Bronze Age society in Jordan.

In sum, while Jordan does not present evidence of settlement or population densities comparable to those in modern Palestine and Israel (with the possible exception of the northern Jordan Valley), it can no longer be characterized as a largely blank map during the Middle Bronze Age. Rather, it should be reconsidered as a thinly veiled mosaic of communities, whose larger integration within Canaanite society may not simply follow the relatively well-documented patterns of urbanization west of the Jordan River, but now must be explored on a broader stage stretching from the Mediterranean to the eastern desert.

Bibliography

Albright, W.F.

1962 The Chronology of MB I (Early Bronze–Middle Bronze). *Bulletin of the American Schools of Oriental*

Research 168: 36–42.

1966 Remarks on the Chronology of Early Bronze IV–Middle Bronze II A in Phoenicia and Syria-Palestine. *Bulletin of the American Schools of Oriental Research* 184: 26–35.

Banning, E.B. and C. Fawcett

1983 Man–land Relationships in the Ancient Wadi Ziqlab. *Annual of the Department of Antiquities of Jordan* 27: 291–309.

Baruch, U.

1990 Palynological Evidence of Human Impact on the Vegetation as Recorded in Late Holocene Lake Sediments in Israel. In S. Bottema, G. Entjes-Nieborg and W. van Zeist (eds.), *Man's Role in the Shaping of the Eastern Mediterranean Landscape*, 283–293. Rotterdam: Balkema.

Berelov, I.

2006 *Occupation and Abandonment of Middle Bronze Age Zahrat adh-Dhra' 1, Jordan.* British Archaeological Reports International Series 1493 Oxford: British Archaeological Reports.

Berry, B.J.L.

1961 City Size Distributions and Economic Development. *Economic Development and Culture Change* 9: 573–588.

Betts, A.

1998 *The Harra and the Hamad: Excavations and Surveys in Eastern Jordan, vol. I.* Sheffield Archaeological Monographs. Sheffield: J.R. Collis.

Betts, A., S. Eames, S. Hulka, M. Schroder, J. Rust and B. Mclaren

1996 Studies of Bronze Age Occupation in the Wadi al-'Ajib, Southern Hauran. *Levant* 27: 27–39.

Boling, R.G.

1989 Site Survey in the el-'Umeiri Region. In L.T. Geraty, Larry G. Herr, Øystein S. Labianca and Randall W. Younker (eds.), *Madaba Plains Project I: The 1984 Season at Tell el-'Umeiri and Vicinity and Subsequent Studies*, 98–188. Berrien Springs, MI: Andrews University.

Braemer, F.

1987 Two Campaigns of Excavations on the Ancient Tell of Jerash. *Annual of the Department of Antiquities of Jordan* 31: 525–529.

Broshi, M.

1979 The Population of Western Palestine in the Roman–Byzantine Period. *Bulletin of the American Schools of Oriental Research* 236: 1–10.

Broshi, M. and R. Gophna

1984 The Settlements and Population of Palestine During the Early Bronze Age II–III. *Bulletin of the American Schools of Oriental Research* 253: 41–53.

1986 Middle Bronze Age II Palestine: Its Settlements and Population. *Bulletin of the American Schools of Oriental Research* 261: 73–90.

Brown, R.

1991 Ceramics from the Kerak Plateau. In J. M. Miller (ed.), *Archaeological Survey of the Kerak Plateau,* 169–279. Atlanta, GA: Scholars.

Bunimovitz, S.

1989 The Land of Israel in the Late Bronze Age: A Case Study of Socio-Cultural Change in a Complex Society. Unpublished Ph.D. dissertation, Tel Aviv University (Hebrew with English Summary).

Clark, G.A., D.I. Olszewski, J. Schuldenrein, N. Rida and J.D. Eighmey

1994 Survey and Excavation in Wadi el-Hasa: A Preliminary Report of the 1993 Field Season. *Annual of the Department of Antiquities of Jordan* 38: 41–55.

Dever, W.G.

1976 The Beginning of the Middle Bronze Age in Syria-Palestine. In F.M. Cross, W.E. Lemke and P.D. Miller (eds.), *In Magnalia Dei: The Mighty Acts of God, Essays on the Bible and Archaeology in Memory of G. Ernest Wright*, 3–38. Garden City, NY: Doubleday.

1987 Palestine in the Middle Bronze Age: The Zenith of the Urban Canaanite Era. *Biblical Archaeologist* 50(3): 149–177.

Dornemann, R.

1983 *The Archaeology of the Transjordan in the Bronze and Iron Ages.* Milwaukee, WI: Milwaukee Public Museum.

Edwards, P.C., P. Macumber and M.K. Green

1998 Investigations into the Early Prehistory of the East Jordan Valley: Results of the 1993/4 La Trobe University Survey and Excavation Season. *Annual of the Department of Antiquities of Jordan* 42: 15–39.

Edwards, P.C., S.E. Falconer, P.L. Fall, I. Berelov, C. Davies, J. Meadows, C. Meegan, M.C. Metzger and G.J. Sayej

2001 Archaeology and environment of the Dead Sea Plain: preliminary results of the first season of investigations by the joint La Trobe University/Arizona State University Project. *Annual of the Department of Antiquities, Jordan* 45: 135–157.

Edwards, P.C., S.E. Falconer, P.L. Fall, I. Berelov, J. Czarzasty, C. Day, J. Meadows, C. Meegan, G.J. Sayej, T. Swoveland and M. Westaway

2002 Archaeology and environment of the Dead Sea Plain: preliminary results of the second season of investigations by the joint La Trobe University/Arizona State University Project. *Annual of the Department of Antiquities, Jordan* 46: 51–92.

Edwards, P.C., S.E. Falconer, P.L. Fall, A. Ariotti and T. Swoveland

2004 Archaeology and environment of the Dead Sea Plain: preliminary results of the third season of investigations by the joint La Trobe University/Arizona State University Project. *Annual of the Department of Antiquities, Jordan* 48: 1–21.

Falconer, S.E.

1987 Village Pottery Production and Exchange: A Jordan Valley Perspective. In A. Hadidi (ed.), *Studies in the History and Archaeology of Jordan III,* 251–259. Amman: Department of Antiquities.

1994 The Development and Decline of Bronze Age Civilisation in the Southern Levant: A Reassessment of Urbanism and Ruralism. In C. Mathers and S. Stoddart (eds.), *Development and Decline in the Mediterranean Bronze Age,* 305–333. Sheffield: Sheffield Academic Press.

1995 Rural Responses to Early Urbanism: Bronze Age Household and Village Economy at Tell el-Hayyat, Jordan. *Journal of Field Archaeology* 22(4): 399–419.

Falconer, S.E. and P.L. Fall

1995 Human Impacts on the Environment during the Rise and Collapse of Civilization in the Eastern Mediterranean. In D.W. Steadman and J.I. Mead (eds.) *Late Quaternary Environments and Deep History: A Tribute to Paul S. Martin,* 84–101. Hot Springs, SD: The Mammoth Site.

2006 *Bronze Age Rural Economy and Village Life at Tell el-Hayyat, Jordan.* Oxford: British Archaeological Reports, International Series 1586.

Falconer, S.E. and B. Magness-Gardiner

1989 Bronze Age Village Life in the Jordan Valley: Archaeological Investigations at Tell el-Hayyat and Tell Abu en-Ni'aj. *National Geographic Research* 5(3): 335–347.

Falconer, S.E. and S.H. Savage

1995 Heartlands and Hinterlands: Alternative Trajectories of Early Urbanization in Mesopotamia and the Southern Levant. *American Antiquity* 60(1): 37–58.

Fall, P.L., L. Lines and S.E. Falconer

1998 Seeds of Civilization: Bronze Age Rural Economy and Ecology in the Southern Levant. *Annals of the Association of American Geographers* 88(1): 107–125.

Fall, P.L., S.E. Falconer and P.C. Edwards

2007 Living on the edge: settlement and abandonment on the Dead Sea Plain. In T.E. Levy, P.M.M. Daviau, R.W. Younker and M. Shaer (eds.), *Crossing Jordan: North American Contributions to the Archaeology of Jordan,* 225–232. London: Equinox Publishing.

Fall, P.L., S.E. Falconer, L. Lines, and M. Metzger

2004 Environmental impacts of the rise of civilization in the southern Levant. In C.L. Redman, P.R. Fish, S.R. James, and J.D. Rogers (eds.), *Prehistoric Human Impact: Global Perspectives on Environmental Degradation,* 261–291. Washington, D.C.: Smithsonian Institution Press.

Finkelstein, I. and R. Gophna

1993 Settlement, Demographic and Economic Patterns in the Highlands of Palestine in the Chalcolithic and Early Bronze Periods and the Beginning of Urbanism. *Bulletin of the American Schools of Oriental Research* 289: 1–22.

Flanagan, J.W., D.W. McCreery and K.N. Yassine

1994 Tell Nimrin: Preliminary Report on the 1993 Season. *Annual of the Department of Antiquities of Jordan* 38: 205–244.

1996 Tall Nimrin: Preliminary Report on the 1995 Excavation and Geological Survey. *Annual of the Department of Antiquities of Jordan* 40: 271–292.

Gerstenblith, P.

1983 *The Levant at the Beginning of the Middle Bronze Age.* American Schools of Oriental Research Dissertation Series, no. 5. Winona Lake, IN: American Schools of Oriental Research.

Glueck, N.

1970 *The Other Side of the Jordan.* 2nd edn. Cambridge, MA: American Schools of Oriental Research.

Gophna, R.

1984 The Settlement Landscape of Palestine in the Early Bronze Age II–III and Middle Bronze Age. *Israel Exploration Journal* 34: 20–31.

Gophna, R. and J. Portugali

1988 Settlement and Demographic Processes in Israel's Coastal Plain from the Chalcolithic to the Middle Bronze Age. *Bulletin of the American Schools of Oriental Research* 269: 11–28.

Gophna, R., N. Liphschitz and S. Lev-Yadun

1986 Man's Impact on the Natural Vegetation of the Central Coastal Plain of Israel during the Chalcolithic Period and the Bronze Age. *Tel Aviv* 13(14): 71–84.

Greene, J.A. and K. 'Amr

1992 Deep Sounding on the Lower Terrace of the Amman Citadel: Final Report. *Annual of the Department of Antiquities of Jordan* 36: 113–144.

Hanbury-Tenison, J.W.

1984 Wadi Arab Survey 1983. *Annual of the Department of Antiquities of Jordan* 28: 385–424.

Helms, S.W.

1975 Jawa 1973: A Preliminary Report. *Levant* 7: 20–38.

1976 Jawa Excavations 1974: A Preliminary Report. *Levant* 8: 1–35.

1977 Jawa Excavations 1975: Third Preliminary Report. *Levant* 9: 21–35.

Kaplan, M.

1980 *The Origin and Distribution of Tell el-Yehudiyeh Ware.* Studies in Mediterranean Archaeology 42. Göteborg: Paul Åström.

Herr, L.G., L.T. Geraty, O.S. LaBianca and R.W. Younker

1991 Madaba Plains Project: The 1989 Excavations at Tell el-'Umeiri and Vicinity. *Annual of the Department of Antiquities of Jordan* 35: 155–180.

Hopf, M.

1983 Jericho Plant Remains. In K.M. Kenyon and T.A. Holland (eds.), *Excavations at Jericho V,* 576–621. London: British School of Archaeology in Jerusalem.

Ibach, R.D.

1987 *Archaeological Survey of the Hesban Region.* Berrien Springs, MI: Andrews University.

Ibrahim, M.M.

1987 Sahab and its Foreign Relations. In A. Hadidi (ed.), *Studies in the History and Archaeology of Jordan III,* 73–81. Amman: Department of Antiquities.

1989 Sahab. In D. Homès-Fredericq and J. B. Hennessy (eds.), *Archaeology of Jordan.* II.2. Field Reports: Sites L–Z, 516–520. Akkadica Supplementum 8. Leuven: Peeters.

Ibrahim, M.M., J. Sauer and K. Yassine

1976 The East Jordan Valley Survey, 1975. *Bulletin of the American Schools of Oriental Research* 222: 41–66.

1988 The East Jordan Valley Survey, 1976 (Part Two). In K. Yassine (ed.), *Archaeology of Jordan: Essays and Reports,* 189–207. Amman: Department of Archaeology, University of Jordan.

Ilan, D.

1995 The Dawn of Internationalism—The Middle Bronze Age. In T. E. Levy (ed.), *The Archaeology of Society in the Holy Land,* 297–319. London: Leicester University.

Jefferson, M.

1939 The Law of the Primate City. *Geography Review* 29: 226–232.

Joffe, A.H.

1991 Settlement and Society in Early Bronze I and II Canaan. Unpublished Ph.D. dissertation, University of Arizona, Tucson.

1993 *Settlement and Society in the Early Bronze I and II Southern Levant.* Sheffield: Sheffield Academic Press.

Johnson, G.A.

1977 Aspects of Regional Analysis in Archaeology. *Annual Review of Anthropology* 6: 479–508.

1980 Rank-size Convexity and System Integration: A View from Archaeology. *Economic Geography* 56(3): 234–247.

Kafafi, Z.A. and E.A. Knauf

1989 Dahr el-Medineh. In D. Homès-Fredericq and J.B. Hennessy (eds.), *Archaeology of Jordan.* II.1. Field Reports: Surveys and Sites A–K, 198–200. Akkadica Supplementum 7. Leuven: Peeters. Astrom.

Kenyon, K.

1973 Palestine in the Middle Bronze Age. In *Cambridge Ancient History,* 2, Part 1, 77–116. 3rd edn. Cambridge: Cambridge University.

Knapp, A.B.

1993 *Society and Polity in Bronze Age Pella: An Annales Perspective.* Sheffield: Sheffield Academic Press.

Kramer, C.

1982 *Village Ethnoarchaeology: Rural Iran in Archaeological Perspective.* New York: Academic Press.

Lehmann, G., R. Lamprich, S. Kerner and R. Bernbeck

1991 The 1990 Excavations at Abu Snesleh. *Annual of the Department of Antiquities of Jordan* 35: 41–65.

Lenzen, C. and A.M. McQuitty

1989 Irbid (Tell). In D. Homès-Fredericq and J. B. Hennessy (eds.), *Archaeology of Jordan.* II.1. Field Reports: Surveys and Sites A–K, 298–300. Akkadica Supplementum 7. Leuven: Peeters.

Lines, L.

1995 Bronze Age Orchard Cultivation and Urbanization in the Jordan River Valley. Unpublished PhD Dissertation, Arizona State University, Tempe.

Liphschitz, N.R. Gophna and S. Lev-Yadun

1989 Man's Impact on the Vegetational Landscape of Israel in the Early Bronze Age II–III. In P. de Miroschedji (ed.), *L'urbanisation de la Palestine á l'âge du Bronze Ancien,* 263–268. British Archaeological Reports International Series 527. Oxford: British Archaeological Reports.

Ma'ayah, F.

1960 Recent Archaeological Discoveries in Jordan. *Annual of the Department of Antiquities of Jordan* 4/5: 114–116.

Mabry, J. and G. Palumbo

1988 The 1987 Wadi el-Yabis Survey. *Annual of the Department of Antiquities of Jordan* 32: 275–305.

MacDonald, B. (ed.)

1988 *The Wadi el-Hasa Archaeological Survey 1979–1983, West Central Jordan.* Waterloo, Ontario: Wilfrid Laurier University.

Magness-Gardiner, B. and S.E. Falconer

1994 Community, Polity, and Temple in a Middle Bronze Age Levantine Village. *Journal of Mediterranean Archaeology* 7(2): 127–164.

Mare, H.

1991 The 1988 Season of Excavation at Abila of the Decapolis. *Annual of the Department of Antiquities of Jordan* 35: 203–221.

Matthiae, P.

1981 *Ebla: An Empire Rediscovered.* New York: Doubleday.

Mazar, A.

1990 *Archaeology of the Land of the Bible.* New York: Doubleday.

Mazar, B.

1968 The Middle Bronze Age in Palestine. *Israel Exploration Journal* 18: 65–97.

McCreery, D.W.

1980 The Nature and Cultural Implications of Early Bronze Age Agriculture in the Southern Ghor of Jordan: An Archaeological Reconstruction. Unpublished PhD dissertation, University of Pittsburgh.

Miller, J.M. (ed.)

1991 *Archaeological Survey of the Kerak Plateau.* Atlanta, GA: Scholars Press.

Miller, N.F.

1991 The Near East. In W. van Zeist, K. Wasylikowa and K.-E. Behre (eds.), *Progress in Old World Paleoethno-botany: A Retrospective View on the Occasion of 20 Years of the International Work Group for Palaeoethnobotany,* 133–160. Rotterdam: Balkema.

Mittmann, S.

1970 Beiträge zur Siedlungs-und Territorial Geschichte des Nördlichen Ostjordanlandes. Wiesbaden: Harrassowitz.

Najjar, M.

1991 A New Middle Bronze Age Tomb at the Citadel of Amman. *Annual of the Department of Antiquities of Jordan* 35: 105–34.

Neef, R.

1990 Introduction, Development and Environmental Implications of Olive Culture: The Evidence from Jordan. In S. Bottema, G. Entjes-Nieborg and W. van Zeist (eds.), *Man's Role in the Shaping of the Eastern Mediterranean Landscape,* 295–306. Rotterdam: Balkema.

Paynter, R.W.

1983 Expanding the Scope of Settlement Analysis. In J. Moore and A. Keene (eds.), *Archaeological Hammers and Theories,* 233–275. New York: Academic Press.

Petocz, D. and L. Villiers

1984 Wadi Hammeh Survey. *Annual of the Department of Antiquities of Jordan* 28: 77–81.

Piccirillo, M.

1978 Una tomba del Bronzo Medeo ad Amman. *Liber Annuus* 28: 73–86.

Politis, K.

1990 Excavations at Deir 'Ain 'Abata, 1990. *Annual of the Department of Antiquities of Jordan* 34: 377–387.

1993 The 1992 Season of Excavations and the 1993 Season of Restorations at Deir 'Ain 'Abata. *Annual of the Department of Antiquities of Jordan* 37: 503–520.

1995 Excavations and Restorations at Dayr 'Ain 'Abata, 1994. *Annual of the Department of Antiquities of Jordan* 39: 447–491.

1997 Excavations and Restorations at Dayr 'Ain 'Abata, 1995. *Annual of the Department of Antiquities of Jordan* 41: 341–350.

Posener, G.

1971 Syria and Palestine ca. 2160–1780 B.C.: Relations with Egypt. In *Cambridge Ancient History,* 1, part 2, 532–558. 3rd edn. Cambridge: Cambridge University.

Potts, T.F., S.J. Bourke, P.C. Edwards, F. Richards and G.J. Wightman

1988 Preliminary Report on the Eighth and Ninth Seasons of Excavation by the University of Sydney at Pella (Tabaqat Fahl), 1986 and 1987. *Annual of the Department of Antiquities of Jordan* 32: 115–49.

Rollefson, G. and I. Kohler-Rollefson

1992 Early Neolithic Exploitation Patterns in the Levant: Cultural Impact on the Environment. *Population and Environment* 13: 243–254.

Rollefson, G., A. Simmons and Z. Kafafi

1992 Neolithic Cultures at 'Ain Ghazal, Jordan. *Journal of Field Archaeology* 19: 443–470.

Smith, R.H.

1973 *Pella of the Decapolis,* I. Wooster, OH: Wooster College.

1993 Pella. In E. Stern (ed.), *The New Encyclopedia of Archaeological Excavations in the Holy Land,* 1174–1180. Jerusalem: Israel Exploration Society.

Smith, R.H. and A.W. McNicoll

1986 The 1982 and 1983 Seasons at Pella of the Decapolis. In *Bulletin of the American Schools of Oriental Research Supplement* 24: 89–116. Philadelphia: American Schools of Oriental Research.

Smith, R.H. and T.F. Potts

1992 The Middle and Late Bronze Ages. In A.W. McNicoll P.C. Edwards, J. Hanbury-Tenison, J.B. Hennessy, T.F. Potts, R.H. Smith, A. Walmsley and P. Watson (eds.), *Pella in Jordan 2,* 35–81. Sydney: University of Sydney.

Stager, L.E.

1985 The Firstfruits of Civilization. In J.N. Tubb (ed.), *Palestine in the Bronze and Iron Ages: Papers in Honor of Olga Tufnell,* 172–188. London: Institute of Archaeology.

Tubb, J.N.

1983 The MB II A Period in Palestine: Its Relationship with Syria and its Origin. *Levant* 15: 49–62.

Van der Kooij, G. and M.M. Ibrahim

1989 *Picking Up the Threads … A Continuing Review of Excavations at Deir Alla, Jordan.* Leiden: University of Leiden.

Weinstein, J.M.

1975 Egyptian Relations with Palestine in the Middle Kingdom. *Bulletin of the American Schools of Oriental Research* 217: 116.

1981 The Egyptian Empire in Palestine: A Reassessment. *Bulletin of the American Schools of Oriental Research* 241: 128.

1991 Egypt and the Middle Bronze II C/Late Bronze IA Transition in Palestine. *Levant* 23: 105–115.

Wimmer, D.

1989 Safut (Tell). In D. Homès-Fredericq and J. B. Hennessy (eds.), *Archaeology of Jordan.* II.2. Field Reports: Surveys and Sites L–Z, 512–515. Akkadica Supplementum 8. Leuven: Peeters.

Zayadine, F., M. Najjar and J.A. Greene

1987 Recent Excavations on the Citadel of Amman (Lower Terrace). *Annual of the Department of Antiquities of Jordan* 31: 299–311.

Zipf, G.K.

1949 *Human Behavior and the Principle of Least Effort: An Introduction to Human Ecology*. Reading, MA: Addison-Wesley.

Zohary, D. and M. Hopf

1988 *Domestication of Plants in the Old World*. Oxford: Clarendon.

Zohary, M.

1982 *Plants of the Bible*. Cambridge: Cambridge University.

Zohary, M. and P. Spiegel-Roy

1975 Beginnings of Fruit Growing in the Old World. *Science* 187: 319–27.

9. The Late Bronze Age

John Strange

Introduction

The Late Bronze Age in Jordan is divided into LB I, IIA and IIB. These divisions are dictated partly by the archaeological finds, to a certain extent also by political realities and, ultimately, by the terminology of the archaeology of the Levant, especially that of Palestine west of the river Jordan. Jordan itself may be divided into northern Jordan, that is, the northern plains from the Yarmuk River to the mountains south of Jarash, or to Wadi Zarqa; central Jordan, the area south of this to Wadi Hasa; southern Jordan, the area south of Wadi Hasa; the Jordan Valley from Tall Shuna (N) to the Dead Sea; and, finally, the desert to the east.

The Nature of the Evidence

The Late Bronze Age is the first period in the history and archaeology of Jordan from which we find a small body of written evidence. This is due to the fact that the Egyptians took an interest in the area. The Egyptian texts, although sporadic and accidental, give some possibility of reconstructing certain aspects of the history and archaeology of Jordan that would otherwise be impossible. The most important texts are the toponym lists from Egyptian temples, which, however, regrettably largely omit Jordanian toponyms, royal stelae that are important especially for the later part of the period, and, finally, biographical texts and accidental references in administrative documents and the like (for the character of the sources cf. Redford 1982).

The published evidence of the material culture of the period is disappointingly meagre compared to other periods in the history of Jordan. Only a few of the excavated sites are published in final form, for example, the excavation of the Late Bronze Age temple at Tall Dayr Alla, the Baqah Valley, parts of the Pella excavations, and the Amman Airport temple. Otherwise, only preliminary publications exist, if at all.

Origins

On the basis of material culture, the Late Bronze Age is a continuation of the Middle Bronze Age and there is no discernable cultural break. This is best seen, for example, from the pottery forms and technology. Examples of the former are carinated and pedestalled bowls, dipper juglets, amphorae, and, not least, Chocolate-on-White Ware (Fischer 1999) that overlap the transition between the periods. Regarding this transition, pottery is still produced at the beginning of the Late Bronze Age using the true potter's wheel. At the Amman Airport temple, imported pottery ranged from the late Middle Bronze Age through the Late Bronze Age (c. 1700–1200 bc), with many of the pieces being heirlooms, while the local pottery seems to date exclusively to the thirteenth century bc (Herr 1997).

This evidence also seems to indicate continuity in population groups as does continuity in architecture and the arts. Pella is a further example of this, showing a smooth transition from the Middle Bronze Age to the Late Bronze Age (McNicoll *et al.* 1992: 35, pls. 47–50, 53–59). At Pella, heirlooms, such as the ivory inlaid box from the Middle Bronze Age (McNicoll *et al.* 1992: 35, 59–63), point to continuation of both people and culture, as does Tomb 62, which was probably used by a family or clan during both the late Middle and early Late Bronze Ages (McNicoll *et al.* 1992: 69–81). At Irbid, moreover, the Middle Bronze Age city wall survived and was continued to be used into the Late Bronze Age (Lenzen *et al.* 1985). Finally, surveys have shown that a large proportion of settlements of the Middle Bronze Age survived into the Late Bronze Age (see, for example, Najjar 1992).

Chronology and Dating Evidence

Here the low Egyptian chronology (Kitchen 1987: 52) will be used wherever possible for all historical dates.

The Late Bronze Age is usually said to begin c. 1550 bc, a conventional date derived from Egyptian chronology and history. It is, however, difficult to pinpoint the beginning of the period archaeologically, as the transition from the Middle Bronze Age is not marked by a uniform destruction horizon or the like (see, however, Weinstein 1991; cf. Thompson 1994: 205–208). The urban system of the Middle Bronze Age II crumbled in western Palestine over a period of 100–120 years (Naaman 1994: 184), and, by analogy, the same would probably also be the case east of the Jordan. The Middle Bronze/Late Bronze Age transition period lasts from c. 1600 bc to c. 1500 bc: Chocolate-on-White pottery overlaps the transition, which spans a very long period, perhaps as much as a century. It therefore seems reasonable to date the beginning of the true Late Bronze Age from the Egyptian conquest. This brought Jordan into the international system of the Late Bronze Age (see below), and prepared for the real innovation of the period, namely, the abundant trade with other areas of the Levant and the Eastern Mediterranean world as reflected in the import of Cypriot and Mycenaean pottery and, conversely, the probable export of such commodities as wine or olive oil from Jordan to the west. This, of course, again makes the date of the beginning of the period dependent on the Egyptian evidence and mixes archaeological and historical reasoning. It must be remembered, however, that the divisions of the Bronze Age are to a large extent conventional and artificial, created after a tripartite system in European prehistory. The Egyptian conquest of Palestine, including Jordan, took place just after the co-regency of Hatshepsut and Tuthmosis III (1479–1457 bc) in Tuthmosis III's twenty-second year (the year of Hatshepsut's death), or 1457 bc. Since the transition period more or less coincides with

Figure 9.1   Late Bronze Age sites mentioned in the text.

parts of the Late Bronze I period, the beginning of the Late Bronze Age can be dated between 1550 and 1450 bc. LB I would be partially the Middle Bronze Age/Late Bronze Age transition period.

The date of the end of the Late Bronze Age is also uncertain because of another transition period that is evident, for example, in archaeological evidence at Tall Dayr Alla (Franken 1964b: 418–420), Tall Fukhar (Strange 1993, 1997) and at Tall Saidiyya (Tubb 1988b: 65; for a summary of the period see van der Steen 1997, 2004). There is solid archaeological evidence that the temple at Tall Dayr Alla was destroyed at the end of the period, and since nothing later than LB IIB material (for example, no Mycenaean pottery later than Mycenaean IIIb and its local imitations) was found in the destruction level (Franken 1992), this is a convenient benchmark. An important artefact from the destruction level is a faience vase with the cartouche of Queen Tewosret, or Tausert (1188–1186 bc) (Franken 1992: 30–31), giving the date 1188 bc as *terminus a quo* (Kitchen 1987: 52). With some reservations Franken dates the destruction to just after the first decade of the twelfth century bc (1992: 176–177). At Tall Saidiyya Stratum XII, the Late Bronze Age/Iron Age transition period is characterized by a possible Egyptian residence, a palace built in Egyptian style, and a cemetery with signs of very strong Egyptian influence (Tubb 1990: 26–37), including finds that may connect this cemetery with the presence of Sea Peoples (e.g. Tubb 1990: 33). After this any Egyptian presence in Jordan seems to end, and as will be argued below, the Late Bronze Age of Jordan coincides more or less with the Egyptian domination of the country. It is possible to take the transition period together with the Late Bronze Age and claim that the Egyptian presence at Tall Saidiyya marks the end of the Late Bronze Age. It is also possible, however, to take the presence of Sea Peoples as a sign of the beginning of the Iron Age. In this chapter the former alternative is preferred.

There is evidence at Tall Fukhar for the end of the Late Bronze Age, as the palace there was apparently abandoned and then occupied by squatters, before it was destroyed in a violent conflagration and replaced by a village of the Late Bronze Age/Early Iron Age transition period or Early Iron IA period with no Mycenaean pottery. The only Philistine sherd ever found in the highlands of Jordan was in fill in the subsequent stratum, that is, the early Iron I period. This seems to give a *terminus ante quem* of c. 1050 bc for the beginning of this period (Strange 1997: 402–403), and the dates c. 1550–1450 bc to c. 1200–1150 bc for the beginning and end of the Late Bronze Age respectively, with a transition period included both at the beginning and at the end of the period.

The LB I period is contemporary with part of the transition period and the LB I proper, roughly from 1550–1450 to c. 1400 bc, just before the Amarna period. The next century, the fourteenth century bc, the LB IIA period,

is the period of the waning of Egyptian dominance in the area, as may be seen from the Amarna letters, which, however, refer mostly to western Palestine. The LB IIB comprises the rest of the Late Bronze Age, from c. 1300 bc to the end in the first decades of the twelfth century bc. It should be noted that the periods are defined also by the corresponding periods in western Palestine. For a summary of these dates see Table 1 below.

Radiocarbon Dates

Very few radiocarbon dates from Late Bronze Age Jordan have been published, and those that have are not particularly useful due to the fact that they are in general too high for the period (for a selction see Table 2). This may be due to the character of the specimens investigated, since they come mostly from carbonized wood used for roof constructions. Since the timber used in construction is invariably older, and sometimes considerably older, than the building, to say nothing of its destruction, the radiocarbon date of the specimen would necessarily be expected to be older than the pottery and other artefacts in the destruction layer.

Radiocarbon dates falling within the Late Bronze Age are known from the Faynan Region, the largest copper production centre of the southern Levant (Bartlett 1997: 190; Hauptmann 2000: 66; Levy and Adams *et al.* 2004: 870; Levy *et al.* 2005b: 135). However, the context of these dates is still controversial, since a number of them come from either extensive and long-lived slag piles from copper smelting, or from archaeological levels of structures at Khirbat en-Nahas, the dating of which is still hotly contested (Van der Steen and Bienkowski 2005, 2006; Levy et al 2005a, 2006; Finkelstein 2005). In general it is probably correct to assume that although some of these dates from metal processing residues and structures fit the terminal phase of the Late Bronze Age, that in fact their is still no conclusive evidence of a Late Bronze Age occupation of the region or of smelting in Wadi Faynan prior to the Iron Age (Hauptmann and Weisgerber 1992: 63).

At Irbid excavations have shown a destruction from c. 1200 bc supported by radiocarbon dates, these, however, not yet published (Lenzen and McQuitty 1998: 268).

At Tall Zera a destruction level from the fortifications gave a radiocarbon date between 1450–1300 BC (Viewger and Häser 2005: 4).

Period	Dates
Middle/Late Bronze Age transition	1600 to c. 1500 bc
Late Bronze Age I	1550–1450/1400 bc
Late Bronze Age II	1450/1400–c. 1050 bc
Iron Age I	begins c. 1050 bc

Table 9.1   Division of periods during the Late Bronze Age.

Environment

Beginning about the sixteenth century bc, the climate in Palestine seems to have been much drier than that of the preceding centuries of the Middle Bronze Age. Evidence for this relative drought comes both from a substantial drop in olive production, as well as a lowering of the water table indicated by a shift of settlement in Western Palestine, dependent on wells (Lipschitz 1986: 37–58; 1996: 139–145; Thompson 1994: 204–205). In contrast to the period after 1000 bc, this relative drought probably culminated around 1200 bc, when the period was dominated by a sub-Atlantic period of aridity with both a decrease in rainfall of approximately 20% and rising temperatures of 2–3°C. Evidence for this is drawn from coastal Syria, the Great Syrian steppe, the Dead Sea Basin and Jordan (Shehadeh 1985: 26–27; Nützel 1976: 11–24; Neuman and Parpola 1987: 161–182; van Zeist 1985: 199–204; Thompson 1994: 215–221). This relative drought would have affected the marginal areas to the east and the south most severely, and would, to a large extent, account for the change in settlement pattern that can be observed in Jordan, as well as contributing to the economic decline during the Late Bronze Age.

At Pella, oak is less frequent compared to the periods before the Bronze Age; instead willow and/or poplar, *Ziziphus* sp., almond, hackberry and olive are found, perhaps indicating that degradation of forests on the lower slopes had started. This could also be due, however, to climatic influences or selection (McNicoll *et al.* 1992: 255).

Historical Background

The Late Bronze Age was the first truly international age in the Eastern Mediterranean and the Levant. During this period the world was divided into spheres of interest, each dominated by a great king, and the interaction between these kings and their spheres of interest was regulated by means of a complicated system of trade relations, cultural exchanges, dynastic marriages and treaties (Liverani 1987; Merrillees 1986; Strange 1986: 2–7). The Levant and its hinterland as far north as Ugarit lay in the Egyptian sphere of interest in the early part of the Late Bronze Age. To the north, the Hittite Empire sought to expand. This resulted in a series of exhausting wars between the two states, ending in a treaty between Egypt and Hatti in 1254 bc and defining the border between the two in Lebanon. This left Egypt in control of Palestine, Transjordan and the areas in south Lebanon and around Damascus. In the Mediterranean, the Mycenaean Empire was the major power. Cyprus, which was probably independent in the early part of the Late Bronze Age but later became a colony of the Mycenaeans, played the role of trade emporium. To the east, Mitanni was a great power in the earlier part of the Late Bronze Age and, throughout the whole period.

Tall Dayr Alla, carbonized roof beam
(Franken 1992: 177)

	95.4%		68.3%
	(2 sigma)		(1 sigma)
	1292–1266 bc		1510–1478 bc
	1522–1296 cal. bc		1460–1382 bc
			1344–1320 cal. bc

Baqah Valley Project
(McGovern *et al.* 1986: 333-34)

	calibrated dates
Upper burial layer of a LB II age cave	1590–1520±60 bc
	1710–1690±70 bc
LB II pit (with LBA I pottery)	1910–1780±60 bc
+	2290–2190±70 bc
top of pit	2090±70 bc

These radiocarbon dates are too high to say anything meaningful about the chronology of the Late Bronze Age (McGovern *et al.* 1986: 333-34).

Tall Fukhar, destruction level, probable roof material
(Carbon-14 Dating Laboratory, National Museum, Copenhagen)

Sample	*14C b*	*1950 BC cal.*	*±stand. dev BC cal*	*13C promille PBD*
1. Charred banches (*Olea europea*)	3380±90	1680	1750–1520	–21.0
2. Part of an oakbeam	3210±90	1490–1450	1530–1400	–22.8
3. Charred heartwood (*Quercus* sp.)	3610±90	1940	2120–1790	–24.2
4. Charcoal (*Olea europea* L.)	3260±65	1520	1610–1440	–21.5
Average of 1, 2 and 4	3280±45	1520	1610–1510	

No. 3 is heartwood and could be considerably older than the outer layers reflecting the felling of the tree and the subsequent use of the beam. Here again, the dates seem much too high, placing the construction of the palace in the LB I period, but they reflect the age of the timber used in the construction of the building.

Carbonized grain from the destruction layer dated by pottery to 1300–1150 BC at Irbid
(Ambers *et al.* 1989: 28)

cal. 14C date bpcal	*14C date BC*	*13C*
3040±HO	1395–1260	–20.0

According to McQuitty (Lenzen, Gordon and McQuitty 1985; Lenzen and McQuitty 1988: 268) the sample was taken from the grain cache that probably dates to within one year of the destruction of the building and places it firmly within the traditional Late Bronze Age rather than the Late Bronze Age/Iron Age transition.

Table 9.2   Radiocarbon dates from the Late Bronze Age.

Assyria and Babylonia were important trade partners but did not act directly politically in the Levant.

At the outset of the Late Bronze Age, Egypt conquered Jordan, as may be seen from the great list at Karnak where at least toponyms nos. 89–101 should be situated in Jordan, although the precise identification of names is in most cases impossible (Helck 1971: 127–128; Smith 1973: 23–32; Aharoni 1979: 173, 159; Redford 1982: 115–119; Knauf and Lenzen 1987: 49–53; Lenzen and Knauf 1987: 54–59, but see Timm 1989: 53–56). At Soleb, some names are given in a list from Amenophis III (1390–1352): *smt* in Shasu, *yhw* in Shasu, *trbr* in Shasu, *bt'* (?). They also, however, cannot be identified with any certainty (Giveon 1971: 27). The degree of Egyptian domination is difficult to assess. No doubt the main interest of the Egyptian kings was to control the area militarily to avoid unpleasant surprises and protect the Jordan Valley and western Palestine, and to protect the trade routes. Another interest lay in tapping the wealth of the country by trade or tribute (cf. Redford 1993: 209–213; Knapp 1993: 40–49). For the character of the Egyptian empire and their way of exploiting it see Panagiotopoulos (2000).

The southern part of the country, south of Wadi Hasa, was probably neglected, and at present there is no evidence of settled occupation in the Late Bronze Age. It is noteworthy, especially in view of the Egyptian activity at Timna on the other side of Wadi Arabah, that there was no exploitation of the copper ore deposits in Wadi Faynan during the Late Bronze Age (Hauptmann and Weisgerber 1992: 63). Southern Jordan, which was later to become the kingdoms of Moab and Edom, was inhabited by the Shasu, nomadic elements known from the Egyptian texts and reliefs (Giveon 1971; Bienkowski 1991: 14).

In the Amarna period Egyptian domination continued, as is evidenced by the Amarna Letters which mention several toponyms east of the Jordan (for example, Pella, controlled by King Mutbalu, the main city in a city-state bordering on the city-state of Ashtaroth [Tall Ashtara] controlled by King Ayyub [Amarna Letter no. 256; see Albright 1943: 9–15; Helck 1971: 184; Aharoni 1979: 159–160; Knapp 1993: 42–48]). Here again the identification of the names is not certain. It seems, at least to judge from the evidence from western Palestine, that Egyptian influence was weakened considerably in the course of the fourteenth century bc, although the evidence of the Amarna Letters can be interpreted in different ways.

During the Nineteenth Dynasty however, Egypt reasserted and strengthened its hegemony beginning with the campaigns of Sethos I (1294–1279), who, after provocation from the Shasu, campaigned in northern Palestine, southern Lebanon and Syria and apparently northern Jordan (Kitchen 1982: 20–24). This was followed by campaigns of Ramesses II (1279–1213) (Redford 1993: 179–191; Knapp 1993: 48; cf. the Egyptian policy in western Palestine where Weinstein assesses the evidence to be a military occupation [1982: 17–22]). A list of Asiatic names on a statue of Ramesses II from the temple at Luxor includes Moab (no. 14), together with Hatti, Naaharina and Assur. The list mixes great states with smaller ones, and while the mention of Mitanni is suspicious, it does mention Moab as a political entity outside the realm of Egypt, confirming evidence of a state in Jordan (cf. Timm 1989: 5–9). A relief in the court of the Luxor temple of Ramesses II shows two prisoners from Moab taken after the plunder of Butartu (Bienkowski 1991: 14).

The stelae erected by Sethos I and Ramesses II at Beth Shan also testifies to military expeditions across the Jordan River, again with a number of toponyms (Aharoni 1979: 166–170). The upper part of a stele erected by Sethos I was found at Tall Shihab on the Yarmuk, c. 28 km northeast of Irbid (Erman 1893: 100–101). Moreover, a stele with the cartouche of Ramesses II was set up at Shaykh Sa'ade, c. 30 km northwest of Dar'a (Weinstein 1982: 20). Both stelae, which are on the route to Damascus, indicate Egyptian presence. This coincides with the beginning of the LB IIB period, found for example at Tall Fukhar (Strange 1994: 537; 1997) and at Irbid (Lenzen *et al.* 1985: 152). Also the possible Egyptian governor's palace at Tall Saidiyya testifies to the importance of Jordan to the Egyptians in this period (e.g. Tubb 1988c).

At the end of the LB II period, the Egyptians withdrew from Jordan and concentrated their efforts on Cisjordan. The cities in the country east of the river were left to their own fate. Evidence for this may perhaps be seen for example at Tall Fukhar (Strange 1997). In the following period, the early Iron Age, there is no historical evidence concerning Jordan. Only later, in the Iron Age II, do we again find any historical evidence.

The purported biblical material on the history of Jordan in the Late Bronze Age, although it is in itself abundant and important in some respects, is also in many respects manifestly contradictory to the archaeological finds (MacDonald 1994). Thus, in the present state of biblical research, this material is, from a historical and chronological point of view, so unsatisfactory that it is probably safer to disregard it completely as historical evidence pertaining to the Late Bronze Age.

Settlement Patterns

Since Glueck's explorations more than fifty years ago a great deal of archaeological survey work has been conducted in Jordan (Figure 9.1). As a result of these efforts, a fairly reliable description of the pattern of settlement can be drawn. Such a description must, however, be taken with caution, as every survey in itself is often incomplete, and because the various surveys have not been conducted by the same standards and methods. Furthermore pottery, which is the main dating tool of a survey, is not always sufficiently diagnostic to allow accurate conclusions, and there is, as in all research, a tendency to find what is sought for. Also, very little material from excavations has been published from the Late Bronze Age except for preliminary publications. Only the excavations at Tall Abu Kharaz and parts of the excavations at Pella, the temple of Tall Dayr Alla, and part of the Baqah Valley Project have been published in final form. Thus, there is very little stratigraphically dated material to check the dates of the pottery found by the surveys.

A convenient departure point may be the data collected in JADIS (Palumbo 1994), although the data are to some extent useless in the opinion of the editor, who observes (Palumbo 1994: 1.15) that the information is biased towards the Iron Age and Classical periods. It can be seen from Palumbo's table (Palumbo 1994: 1.14) that from the Early Bronze Age 1102 sites are listed, from the Middle Bronze Age 290 sites, from the Late Bronze Age 295, from the Iron Age I–II 1614 sites, from the Roman period 2306 sites, and from the Byzantine period 2299 sites (Palumbo 1994: 1.14). This suggests that rather than observing an explosion of human occupation, we are seeing a biased data collection strategy. More than a third of the sites listed provide inadequate information on the period(s) of occupation. Finally, the information in JADIS is biased towards the cultivated areas (Palumbo 1994: 1.15). Palumbo concludes that the data cannot be used for settlement pattern studies. It is more useful for a sociological and historical profile of archaeological research. The voids in the research still need to be filled by intensive archaeological surveys.

JADIS divides Jordan into 15 sectors. This makes its use somewhat awkward, because the sections do not stem from the natural geographical regions of the country, but are derived from the mechanical use of the UTM coordinates and consequently cut across these regions. Thus, the Jordan Valley is treated together with the Western Hills in sections 1, 2 and 4. As a result, the sites in the valley cannot be separated easily from those in the mountains. Roughly speaking, sectors 1, 2 and 3 are situated in northern Jordan; sectors 4, 5, 6, 7, 9 and 10 in central Jordan; sectors 11, 12, and 14 in southern Jordan; and, finally, sectors 7, 8, 13 and 15 are situated in the desert to the east.

It should be kept in mind that the lists in JADIS do not give the relative size of the settlements in the individual periods. Moreover, we simply do not know the population density of Jordan, for instance, in the Late Bronze Age as compared to the Middle Bronze or Iron Ages.

Still, despite all these caveats, it may be possible to deduce some trends in the settlement from the JADIS data and then compare and control them with more precise surveys and knowledge gained from excavations.

First of all, as would be expected, the settlements are concentrated in the western and northern parts of the country in the Late Bronze Age: northern Jordan, 117 sites with 102 sites surviving from earlier, and 15 newly founded; central Jordan, 176 sites with 89 surviving and 87 new; southern Jordan, 18 sites with 7 surviving and 11 new; the desert, 4 sites with 1 surviving and 3 new; and the Jordan Valley, part of sectors 1, 2 and 4, part of 124 sites with 101 surviving and 23 new. The data on southern Jordan should be seriously questioned (see below).

Secondly, a decrease in the number of settlements from the Middle Bronze to the Late Bronze Age can be observed in most parts of the country. Only in sectors numbers 6, 9, 10 in central Jordan, together with sector number 11 in southern Jordan, is an increase listed, and these data should be treated with suspicion, as will be seen below.

Finally, an enormous increase in the number of settlements may be seen from the Late Bronze to the Iron Age (both I and II) all over the country. This increase does not necessarily reflect an increase in the number of inhabitants. It may simply be a spreading of the population from the larger centres of the Late Bronze Age. By and large, the above observations are corroborated by the various surveys and soundings that have been published over the last 25 years. Mittmann found a decrease in settlement in northern Jordan from the Middle Bronze to the LB I period and a further decrease in the LB II period (Mittmann 1970: 256–264). The main cities in the north were occupied during the Late Bronze Age. Irbid (possibly Gintot Lenzen and Knauf 1987) for example, was a large town in the LB IIC period (1300–1150 bc). This is attested by a temple, a basalt city wall incorporated from the Middle Bronze Age, and major public structures and tombs. The major occupational phase in the history of the city was c. 1200 bc when the city covered the entire tell and which ended in a destruction that was not manmade (Dajani 1964; Lenzen 1986, 1992; Lenzen *et al.* 1985: 153–154; Lenzen and Knauf 1986; 1987: 60).

Although sparse information has been published, it appears that Quwayliba (Abila) was occupied in the Late Bronze period (Mare 1989: 474–477). Tomb material from the site has been published (Kafafi 1984).

At Tall Fukhar massive fortifications and a large public building with imported luxury wares show that the city was important in the Late Bronze Age. The settlement spread over the entire tell with a densely settled lower town which was later abandoned at the end of the Late Bronze Age when settlement shrank to a village at the top of the tell (see below).

Moreover, a scarab from the Nineteenth Dynasty was found (Ottosson 1992; Strange 1997: 402; Eggler and Keel 2006: 288–289). There are reports of Late Bronze Age pottery, today unfortunately lost, from Tall Husn (Lenzen and Knauf 1987: 61; Sauer 1986: 6; cf. Leonard 1987b: 359–360, 363).

The Zeraqon survey showed a centralization of settlements during the Late Bronze Age in the area around Wadi Shellale (Kamleh 2000: 195).

The eastern most settlement in northern Jordan seems to be reflected in a tomb at Mafraq, but this is from the end of the Late Bronze Age or from the Late Bronze Age/Iron Age transition period (Piccirillo: 1976: 27–30) and may be seen as a harbinger of the more dense settlement in the Iron Age. A survey failed to find Bronze Age in a 100 km square large area west of Mafraq (Archäologisher Anzeiger 2000: 620). In the Jarash region Braemer found an increase in settlements—though not accompanied by an increase in population—from the Middle Bronze to the Late Bronze Age, indicating a spreading of settlements to the mountains (Braemer 1992). There seems, moreover, to be a major settlement phase on new sites in the middle of the second millennium bc (Braemer 1987: 529). It must be kept in mind that the Jarash region is adjacent to, or could even be considered part of, central Jordan, where the JADIS data shows an increase in settlement. In Jarash itself, the Late Bronze Age levels were found on bedrock and included well-preserved floors of which four belong to the end of the period. Pottery included Chocolate-on-White and White Slip Ware (Braemer 1987: 525–528), perhaps indicating that the settlement lasted the whole period.

In central Jordan, the Ajlun highlands and the Jordan plateau attest to only a few sites occupied (Gordon and Knauf 1987: 294–297; Mabry and Palumbo 1992). In Wadi Yabis, there is a decline from the Middle Bronze to the Late Bronze Age. Farther south, the plateau shows occupation in the Late Bronze Age in an abated state and town settlements are relatively rare. At Tall Nimrin—where three seasons of excavation have failed to produce clear evidence from the Late Bronze and early Iron Ages—the presence of late Iron Age walls built immediately over MB II structures suggest an occupational gap during the second half of the second millennium bc (Flanagan et al. 1992: 535–536). Sahab and Umm Dananir were small in size (Herr 1992). Moreover, sites like Umm Qanafah, Madaba and Amman were occupied (Prag 1992).

Late Bronze Age tombs are attested at Amman (Dajani 1966). Moreover, on the *Qalah* (citadel), the Late Bronze Age has been found on the first and second plateau, indicating that the town was possibly as large and important as during the later Iron Age, and may have been walled. Associated pottery included Chocolate-on-White and white burnished wares from the beginning of the period (Dornemann 1983: 105–121; 1997: 99; Zayadine et al. 1987: 308).

A remarkable temple was found at the former Amman civil airport (Hennessy 1966), and at Mabrak, 4 km southeast of the airport, an analogous square, but probably domestic, building was found, dating from the same period (Yassine 1988; see also below).

Northwest of Amman, in the Baqah Valley, numerous settlements from the Late Bronze Age were found. Tall Umm Dananir in particular must be mentioned, with a *quadratbau*-type structure, possibly cultic, and an overlapping sequence of Late Bronze Age tombs with imports (McGovern 1992; see also below). Tall Safut, overlooking a major entrance to the Baqah Valley, has a perimeter wall, possibly a Middle Bronze Age defence in continued use into the LB II period (Wimmer 1987a: 280), and a probable sanctuary (Wimmer 1989: 514). In the destruction layer, a chalice with barley and a bronze figurine of a god were found (Wimmer 1987a: 280–281).

West of Amman the region of Iraq al-Amir and Wadi Kufrayn have yielded LB-pottery from 4 out of 174 sites (Ji and Lee 1999: 438).

Only 6 of the 155 sites surveyed within 16 km of Tall Hisban have possible Late Bronze Age pottery. Only two major sites, Tall Jalul and Tall Umayri, show evidence from the period. Tall Jalul has both LB I and II sherds in fills (Herr et al. 1994: 161), and the pottery from the period at Tall Umayri shows close parallels to that at Tall Jalul (Ibach 1987: 157). At Balua there are Late Bronze Age remains in the area immediately east and west of the *khirbat*. The main site, the find spot of the Balua stele (see below), is though to date primarily to the Iron Age (Worschech et al. 1986: 292; Worschech 1997: 270).

There is evidence of occupation at Khirbat Arair at the end of the Late Bronze Age (Olávarri 1997: 178). A settlement from the Late Bronze Age lies below the Iron Age fortress at Lahun, where houses with clay ovens, silos, grinding stones, cooking pots and storage jars were excavated and a scarab from the Twentieth Dynasty was also found (Homés-Fredericq 1989: 354; 1997: 155). On the Dhiban Plateau after a gap during the Middle Bronze Age and the LB I period, there seems to have been a resurgence of settlement in the Late Bronze Age II with sherds at 10 out of 421 sites, with the settlement probably continuing into the Iron Age (Ji and Lee 2000: 504–505)

Sedentary occupation in the area between Wadi Mujib and Wadi Hasa is perhaps corroborated by the Egyptian epigraphic evidence where we find Moab mentioned on temple walls at Luxor (cf. above). Sahab, 12 km southeast of Amman, has evidence of Late Bronze Age occupation in the form of a Late Bronze/Iron Age tomb (Dajani 1970), a thirteenth century building, and a town wall, 75 m of which has been uncovered (Ibrahim 1974: 60–61; 1975: 78–80). The town seems to have had unbroken occupation from the Middle Bronze to the Iron Age I period (Ibrahim 1989: 516), with the pottery from the Late Bronze Age covering the period up to the late thirteenth century (Ibrahim 1987: 76–77).

Late Bronze Age sites are lacking north and northeast of Amman in the Ayn Ghazal and Wadi Zarqa area, but these regions are close to the desert (Simmons and Kafafi 1992: 81).

Betts' (1989) survey in the northeast desert region of Jordan shows that it was not occupied during the Late Bronze Age.

The northern half of the Jordan Valley, from the Yarmuk River to Wadi Rajib, shows 6 out of 106 surveyed sites occupied in the Late Bronze Age: Tall Meqbereh and Tall Abu Kharaz (associated or twin sites); Tall Sakhineh; Tall Saidiyya and Tall Keraymeh (two more associated sites); and Tall Mazar (Yassine *et al.* 1988: 167–174). Pella should also be mentioned, although it is not in the survey.

Three of the above-listed sites have been excavated. Pella, the most important and most northerly located of the three, produced evidence of rich Late Bronze Age remains (Bourke *et al.* 1994: 104–109).

Tall Abu Kharaz has yielded buildings from LB I, transition layers from LB I and II, a temple from LB IIA and walls built during the period and reused in the Iron Age (Fischer 1991, 1993, 1994, 1997a, 2006a).

At Tall Mazar domestic installations from the Late Bronze Age were found, but no architectural remains (Yassine 1989).

Tall Saidiyya had rich Late Bronze Age deposits, including most notably a possible Egyptian governor's residence from the thirteenth century (Stratum XII), an elaborate water system and a Late Bronze Age cemetery (Tubb 1986; Tubb *et al.* 1996: 24–27).

The southern half of the Jordan Valley, from Wadi Rajib to the Dead Sea, had 14 out of 118 surveyed sites occupied in the Late Bronze Age: Tall Nekhayl South; Tall Ghazaleh; Tall Kharabeh; Tall Qadan; Tall Qadan South; Tall Dayr Alla; Tall Rabi; Tall Abu Nijrah; Tall Argadat; Katarit al-Samra, Ayn Bassah; Tall Tahune; Jazayir; and Tall Mustah (Yassine *et al.* 1988: 190–197).

Of these sites two, Katarit al-Samra and Tall Dayr Alla, have been examined more closely. A cemetery was found at the former and the tell has material from the Middle Bronze/Late Bronze Age transition, and much from the LB I and II, including Cypriot imports. A Late Bronze tomb yielded material, including imports, from throughout the period, especially from the thirteenth century (Leonard 1979, 1986).

At Tall Dayr Alla a temple, renovated several times, existed throughout the Late Bronze Age. The site seems to have been a trading station, probably controlled by the Egyptians (Franken 1992).

It appears that the Jordan Valley south of Ayn Bassah (which is near Katarit al-Samra) was virtually uninhabited during the Late Bronze Age. Only three sites, at Wadi Nimrin and Wadi Kufrayn, were found to be settled farther south (Yassine *et al.* 1988). South of the Dead Sea, in the Southern Ghors and Northeast Arabah, no Late Bronze Age sites are found (MacDonald 1992a: 71).

There is very little evidence of occupation on the plateau between Wadi Mujib and Wadi Hasa. The Late Bronze Age was attested at five sites by Miller (1979), revisiting sites earlier surveyed by Glueck, but soundings at one of these have not confirmed that survey's identification of Late Bronze Age pottery (Bienkowski *et al.* 1997; Bienkowski and Adams 1999). Of these five sites the most important is Balua. The same is true in the northwest Ard Karak, where Worschech survey (1992) found Late Bronze Age pottery at only four sites, after a sudden decline from the Middle Bronze Age.

In southern Jordan, south of Wadi Hasa, no site has yielded definite Late Bronze Age pottery in stratified sequences (Bienkowski 1996; Bienkowski *et al.* 1997; Bienkowski and Adams 1999). MacDonald (MacDonald ed. 1988: 166–170 and pl. 6) report Late Bronze Age pottery at three sites and Late Bronze/Iron Age pottery at five sites. There is no definitive proof of smelting during the second millennium bc in Wadi Faynan (Hauptmann and Weisgerber 1992: 63), although "Midianite" pottery has been found recently in the Faynan Landscape Survey and from excavations at Khirbat en-Nahas (Adams, pers. com.), as well as at at the Iron Age House at Barqa al-Hatiya (Fritz 1994). There are also reports of "Midianite pottery" from the far south (Jobling 1981: 31). This pottery, however, should, according to some writers, perhaps be dated to the Iron Age, or even spanning the Late Bronze Age/Iron Age (cf. Fritz 1994: 144–145; Rothenberg and Glass 1983; but see below). It should not be assumed, however, that southern Jordan was empty. The area was probably inhabited by nomads who were caravaneers and lived by herding, and who left no trace (cf. above on the Egyptian evidence of the Shasu).

Summing up, it seems that the number of settlements in Jordan was small in the Late Bronze Age. It was certainly less than in the previous period. Only in confined areas, for example, around Jarash, did the number of settlements increase. This is probably due to a dissemination of the population and resettlement from other towns. The southern parts of central Jordan were apparently thinly populated, with the southern part of the Jordan Valley and Jordan south of Wadi Hasa completely empty of permanent settlements, but probably inhabited by nomadic pastoralists, if not necessarily Shasu. At the end of the period there seems to have been a resurgence of settlement in the western parts of Central Jordan.

Material Culture

Woodwork, Bone and Ivory

A large number of objects of ivory and bone have been found (e.g. McGovern *et al.* 1986: 243–246; Tubb 1988b: 67; Franken 1992: 33–34, 42–43, 45–46, 58, 60, 64–65; McNicoll *et al.* 1982: 43, 46–48, 102–103; 1992: pl. 72). The production is best represented by the Lion Box from Pella (Potts 1987; Bienkowski 1991: 104–105; McNicoll *et al.* 1992: 59–62). The wooden frame has perished completely, but the shape can be reconstructed from the position of the carved ivory panels when it was found. On the lid, there is a unique representation of two rampant lions roaring at each other with their front paws resting on two *uraei* whose bodies intertwine between the lions' legs forming a kind of ornament. Also on the lid is a winged sundisc with two *uraei*, and on the sides there are panels with *Djed* pillars. The box is Egyptian in inspiration, but also shows influence from other places, for example, Syria and Mesopotamia, and was probably made either as a Hyksos work from the Nile Delta or in the Levant between the eighteenth and sixteenth centuries bc, which, strictly speaking, makes it an heirloom from the Middle Bronze Age (Potts 1987: 69–70). Also from Pella comes a box decorated with a continuous frieze of *Djed* pillars with possibly wooden panels with other motifs; it was probably manufactured at the same workshop as the Lion Box, perhaps even by the same craftsman (McNicoll *et al.* 1992: 62–64 and pl. 38). Finally, an ivory cosmetic box in the shape of a fish found inside a bronze bowl in the cemetery at Tall Saidiyya must be singled out (Tubb 1988b: 64, 66; Bienkowski 1991: 104–105).

Spindle Whorls and Handle

These categories of domestic items have been largely neglected, but those from the Baqah Valley Project are discussed briefly by McGovern *et al.* (1986: 243–44).

Figure 9.2 Glass pendant in form of a fertility figurine, Tall Fukhar.

Glass

Pendant of glass in form of a fertility type figurine (Strange 1997: 402 and fig. 7) (Figure 9.2); raw glass ingot (Bourke *et al.* 2003: 361).

Bronzework

McGovern *et al.* (1986: 245–257, 268; see also 278–283 for the metallurgy) gives a typology of copper-base artefacts found in the Baqah Valley from the Late Bronze Age. This can be supplemented by published material from the temple at Tall Dayr Alla, Pella and several artefacts from other sites: *anklets and bracelets* (McGovern *et al.* 1986: 246, 250–255; McNicoll *et al.* 1992: 77); *earrings* (McGovern *et al.* 1986: 247, 250–253); *rings* (McGovern *et al.* 1986: 248, 250–255, 286–287; McNicoll *et al.* 1992: 77, pl. 61); *pendants* (Franken 1992: 33–34); *daggers* (McGovern *et al.* 1986: 248, 256–257); *knives* (Franken 1992: 33–34; McNicoll *et al.* 1992: 77, pl. 61); *spearpoints* (Franken 1992: 33–34; McNicoll *et al.* 1982: 43); *arrowheads* (McGovern *et al.* 1986: 249, 256–257; Franken 1992: 33–34; McNicoll *et al.* 1992: 77); *bolts* (Bourke *et al.* 1999:53 with fig. 6); *scales for armour* (Franken 1992: 31–33); *pins* (McNicoll *et al.* 1992: 77); *toggle pins* (McGovern *et al.* 1986: 249, 250–251, 254–257; McNicoll *et al.* 1982: 46–48; 1992: 77, pl. 61); *hooks* (Franken 1992: 33–34); *tweezers* (McNicoll *et al.* 1982: 43, 47; 1992: 77); *spatulae* (Franken 1992: 66–67); *rods* (McGovern *et al.* 1986: 249, 254–255); *needles* (Franken 1992: 31, 33–34, 91, 94); *figurines* (Wimmer 1987a: 280; Franken 1992: 42, 44); *lamps* (Strange 1997: 402) (Figure 9.3); *bowls* (McGovern *et al.* 1986: 268); *tableware*: from the cemetery at Tall Saidiyya came a bronze wine set, a platter, a jug and a strainer (Tubb 1988b: 69–70; Bienkowski 1991: 94–95); *cymbals* (Bourke *et al.* 2003: 359 with fig. 40, 1–2).

Stone Objects

Alabaster jars (e.g. McNicoll *et al.* 1982: pl. 109; McGovern *et al.* 1986: 270; Franken 1992: 59, 64, 91, 94); *tazza of serpentinite of Egyptian type* (Bourke *et al.* 1994: 92, 109–110); *Egyptian stone vessels* (Hankey 1974: 168–175); *objects made of Cretan limestone* (Hankey 1974: 175–176); *beads* (McGovern *et al.* 1986: 202–242); *basalt bowls, mortars, rubbing stones and querns* (Hankey 1974: 177; McGovern 1986: 269–270; Franken 1992: 30–31, 34–35, 76, 78, 88–89; McNicoll *et al.* 1992: 77); also *ostrich eggs* (McGovern *et al.* 1986: 271), *shells etc.* (Reese in McGovern *et al.* 1986: 320–332).

Sculpture

Two monuments from the end of the Late Bronze Age stand out. From Rujm Abd comes a basalt stela, showing a warrior god with a spear and a kilt, made in the thirteenth–twelfth centuries bc. The kilt is similar to those worn by tributaries in Egyptian private tombs from the

Figure 9.3   Bronze lamp, Tall Fukhar.

Eighteenth and Nineteenth Dynasties (Zayadine 1991: 36–37). The relief is similar to those showing fertility and/or warrior gods from northwest Syria.

The stela from Balua (Figure 9.4) (Ward andMartin 1964: 14; Zayadine 1991: 35, 37) is in sharp relief with three standing figures. On the left is a standing figure with a loincloth. He is wearing the double crown of Upper and Lower Egypt. He holds a *was*-sceptre in his left hand and an obscure object, which he is giving to the figure in the middle, in his right hand. The middle figure is turned with lifted hands to receive the object. He is in gala dress worn by kings from the Amarna period onwards (Ward and Martin 1964: 14). His headdress is known from Egyptian scenes where it is used by Shasu Bedouin (Giveon 1971: pl. V, D-F); he is evidently the local king of Moab. A goddess is standing to the right. She wears a common dress, known from the Eighteenth Dynasty onwards, worn both by members of the royal family and by goddesses, and an *'atef* -crown, normally worn by a male god in Jordan (Daviau and Dion 1994: 162–165). In her right hand, she holds an *ankh*-sign. The scene is strongly reminiscent of Egyptian reliefs showing the living king, with a goddess in attendance, adoring the head of the pantheon (Ward and Martin 1964: 17). Two symbols are shown above the shoulders of the king in the middle. The one before the face of the king could be an orb and a crescent and should be associated with Baal-Saphon, while the one behind the king is a crescent and should be associated with the goddess who would thus be a moon goddess (Ward and Martin 1964: 16). In my opinion, the relief depicts an Egyptian scene— namely, the investiture of the local king by the two main deities of the local pantheon, probably El, Baal-Saphon or Kemosh and Astarte or Anat— transferred to Moab. It is executed by an artist who knew Egyptian art, but was not an Egyptian himself (Ward and Martin 1964: 14). The relief is thus evidence of an artistic tradition in Jordan at least at the end of the Late Bronze Age (for the inscription above the relief see below. The early dating is feasible in view of the mention of Moab as a political entity in the list in the temple of Luxor (cf. above). It should, however, be mentioned that the stela is dated to the tenth century bc by Worschech (1997: 270;

see also Timm 1989: 92–93 for the latest discussion).

Apart from these large pieces of art and some bronze figurines (see below), most of the sculptures known from the Late Bronze Age are miniature art, that is, a large number of scarabs and cylinder seals, or imprints, found in excavations of tells or in tombs (e.g. Ward 1964, 1966; McGovern *et al.* 1986: 284–294; Tubb 1988b: 71; Franken 1992: 28–33, 41–42, 58–59, 64–67, 76–78; McNicoll *et al.* 1992: 77–78, pl. 39; Eggler and Keel 2006: 288–289). A seal from Tall Abu Kharaz, showing the tree of life with antithetic ibexes, must be mentioned because of its religious significance, representing the Tree of Life (Fischer 1994: 133, 137).

Pottery

The most obvious characteristic of the pottery of the Late Bronze Age is the continuity of forms from the Middle Bronze Age, together with new developments. Chocolate-on-White Ware continues into the LB I period in the northern part of the country (Fischer 1999). It is found, for example, at Pella (Hennessy 1985; Fischer 2003), Tall Abu Kharaz (Fischer 1991: 86–87; 1993: 292–294; 1995: 112–113; 1997b: 135–136; 1999: 1–29; 2003: 51–66), Katarit al-Samra (Leonard 1979, 1986), the Baqah Valley (McGovern *et al.* 1986: 76, 89 nos. 4–5, 173–174), Quwayliba (McGovern *et al.* 1986: 76), Amman (McGovern *et al.* 1986: 76), Tall Fukhar (McGovern 1997: 424; Strange 1997: 402) and was possibly produced in Katarit al-Samra (McGovern 1997: 424). The lamp, in the form of a flat bowl pinched on one side, is another example of a type of pottery that continued from the Middle Bronze Age.

New forms are also found, for example, the cooking pot with sharp carination and triangular rims, and the pilgrim flask, as well as forms that were copied from imports such as pyxides and stirrup jars. Technically, during the LB I period, more and more pottery, not only the large pieces, but also jugs and bowls, were made by coiling instead of on a true potter's wheel. This method becomes predominant in the LB II period (McGovern *et al.* 1986: 168–169, 174–177). In the Baqah Valley in the LB I period, the fine wares were tempered with 5–10% quartz and/or calcite, and are very well fired (at c. 900 degrees C); in the LB II period, the absolute amount of temper increases to as high as 20%, and the vessels are fired at a lower temperature; the slow wheel is still in use (McGovern *et al.* 1986: 145). Burnishing becomes rare and more and more vessels are decorated with painting, making the Late Bronze Age pottery the most colourful pottery in the Bronze and Iron Ages. The decoration is often bichrome, painted in horizontal or vertical straight and wavy bands, bowls often with concentric circles, but also with metopes or motifs; a well-known one seems to be the Tree of Life (Franken 1992: 92, 138, 184; Fischer 1991: 87; Strange

2004:23) with attendant animals or worshippers (Potts *et al.* 1988: 138; Franken 1992: 82, 124, 130; Bourke *et al.* 2003: 353 with fig. 31).

The repertoire includes the following forms (the list is not exhaustive concerning forms, and includes only the more important and published find assemblages, the Baqah Valley, Pella; Tall Saidiyya, Tall Dayr Alla, Tall Abu Kharaz, and for the Mycenaean imports especially the Amman Airport Temple):

Bowls, open and rounded, many of them carinated, and/ or pedestalled (Figure 9.5.1–5) (McGovern *et al.* 1986: 86–89, 94–95, 98, 117, 168–70; McNicoll *et al.* 1982: pls. 105, 107, 109, 111, 117, 119; 1992: pls. 28, 43, 44, 47, 48; Pritchard 1980: 81; Tubb 1988b: 42; Fischer 1991: 88–89; 1993: 291–292; Franken 1992: 29, 39, 44, 48–49, 54, 62, 68, 77, 80–81, 85–86, 90, 99–100); *kraters* (Figure 9.5.9) (McGovern *et al.* 1986: 120–125, 148–149; McNicoll *et al.* 1992: pl. 49; Fischer 1991: 88–89; Franken 1992: 77); *chalices* (Figure 9.5.6) (McGovern *et al.* 1986: 88–89, 118–119; Franken 1992: 29); *cups* (Pritchard 1980: 81); *Goblets* (Figure 9.5.8) (Fischer 1991: 88–89; Franken 1992: 40, 54–55, 62, 68); *jars* (Figure 9.5.7, 10) (McGovern *et al.* 1986: 88–89, 148–149; McNicoll *et al.* 1982: pls. 105, 117, 119; 1992: pls. 28, 44, 48; Pritchard 1980: 83; Tubb 1988b: 42; Franken 1992: 39–40, 77–78, 86–87, 93, 99); *storage jars* (Figure 9.5.12–13) (McGovern *et al.* 1986: 88–89, 132–135, 167–169; Pritchard 1980: 83; Tubb 1988b: 58, 67; Fischer 1991: 94–95; Franken 1992: 94; for the *collared rim jar* and its use see Wengrow 1996); *amphoriskoi* (Figure 9.5.11) (McGovern *et al.* 1986: 89–90; Pritchard 1980: 81); *jugs and juglets* (Figure 9.5.14–16, 19) (McGovern *et al.* 1986: 90–91, 124–133, 167–169; McNicoll *et al.* 1982: pls. 105, 107, 113, 117, 119; 1992: pls. 28, 48; Pritchard 1980: 81, 83; Tubb 1988b: 42; Tubb 1990: 30; Fischer 1991: 90–91; Franken 1992: 39–40, 44, 50, 55, 62, 68, 77, 81–83, 86, 91, 99–100); *strainer jugs* (Figure 9.5.17) (McGovern *et al.* 1986: 136–37; Franken 1992: 82); *pilgrim flasks* (Figure 9.6.1) (McGovern 1986: 136–137; Pritchard 1980: 83; Tubb 1988b: 67; Franken 1992: 29, 55, 68, 99–100); *pilgrim flasks with figural painting* (Franken 1992: 55, 57: man with dog leading a goat; *pyxides* (Pritchard 1980: 81; Tubb 1988a: 42); *lamps* (Figure 9.5.18) (McGovern *et al.* 1986: 92–93, 138–145, 148–149, 168–170; McNicoll *et al.* 1982: pls. 109, 113; Pritchard 1980: 83; Tubb 1988b: 67; Fischer 1991: 92–93; Franken 1992: 29, 39, 49, 54, 62, 77, 80, 90, 99); *cooking pots* (Figure 9.6.2–3) (McGovern *et al.* 1986: 136–137, 169–170; McNicoll *et al.* 1982: pl. 119; 1992: pls. 28, 34, 45, 48; Tubb 1988b: 42–43; Tubb 1990: 30; Fischer 1991: 94–95; 1993: 291–292; Franken 1992: 81, 85, 99); *cult vessels* (Figure 9.6.6–7) (Fischer 1991: 92–93; Franken 1992: 30, 41, 56–57, 68, 83; Bourke 2003:352); *Chocolate-on-White* (Figure 9.6.4–5) (Leonard 1981; Hennessy 1985; McGovern *et al.* 1986: 173–174; McNicoll *et al.* 1992: 74, pls.

56–57; Fischer 1993: 292–294); *miscellaneous (cup-and-saucer, anthropomorphic vessel, zoomorphic vessel, storage vessel, clay tablets* [Figure 9.6.10], *funnel)* (McGovern *et al.* 1986: 268–269; Franken 1992: 29, 38, 41, 44, 51, 55, 59, 62–64, 66, 77, 83; Fischer 1994: 133, 137; Bourke 2003: 345); *figures* (Bourke *et al.* 1992: 11; Franken 1992: 34–35; Kamlah 1993).

Mycenaean storage jars (Hankey 1974: 145–147); *Mycenaean kraters* (Hankey 1974: 147–149; Herr 1983b: 229); *Mycenaean jugs* (Pritchard 1980: 81, 62); *Mycenaean squat jars or alabasters* (Hankey 1974: 149–150), *Mycenaean stirrup jars* (Hankey 1974: 150–155; McGovern *et al.* 1986: 194–198; Pritchard 1980: 83; Tubb 1988b: 67; Franken 1992: 40); *Mycenaean flasks* (Hankey 1974: 155–156); *Mycenaean pyxides* (Pritchard 1980: 81); *Mycenaean open vessels* (Hankey 1974: 156–157). Also a few sherds of *Minoan vessels* were found (Hankey 1974: 157–158). *Cypriot White slip ware* (McGovern *et al.* 1986: 196–200; Fischer 1991: 90–91); *Cypriot Base Ring Wares* (McGovern *et al.* 1986: 196–200; Pritchard 1980: 81; Fischer 1991: 90–91). *Faience* (Franken 1992: 45–46, 58–61, 64–67; Bourke *et al.* 2003: 359); *knob,* possibly a wall decoration (Strange 1997: 404) (Figure 9.7). For sherd typology see Dornemann (1983: 20–22); McGovern *et al.* (1986: 64–201); Franken (1992: 115–

Figure 9.4 The panel from the Balua stela (Ward and Martin 1964: pl. 3).

Figure 9.5 Late Bronze Age pottery 1. Bowl, Late Bronze Age IA (McGovern *et al.* 1986: 87, 1). 2. Bowl, Late Bronze Age IA (McGovern *et al.* 1986: 87, 2). 3. Bowl, Late Bronze Age IB (McGovern *et al.* 1986: 87, 2). 4. Bowl, Late Bronze Age II (McGovern *et al.* 1986: 101, 8). 5. Bowl, Late Bronze Age II (McGovern *et al.* 1986: 105, 2). 6. Chalice, Late Bronze Age II (McGovern *et al.* 1986: 119, 9). 7. Jar, Late Bronze Age IA (McGovern *et al.* 1986: 88, 5). 8. Goblet, Late Bronze Age II (Franken 1992: 125, 3). 9. Krater, Late Bronze Age II (McGovern *et al.* 1986: 125, 3). 10. Jar, Late Bronze Age II (McGovern *et al.* 1986: 127, 3). 11. Amphoriskos, Late Bronze Age II (McGovern *et al.* 1986: 91, 1). 12. Storage jar, Late Bronze Age II (Tall Fukhar). 13. Storage jar, Late Bronze Age IA (McGovern *et al.* 1986: 89, 7). 14. Juglet, Late Bronze Age IA (McGovern *et al.* 1986: 91, 8). 15. Juglet, Late Bronze Age IB/IIA (McGovern *et al.* 1986: 131, 4). 16. Juglet, Late Bronze Age II (McGovern *et al.* 1986: 131, 5). 17. Strainer jug, Late Bronze Age II (Franken 1992: 82). 18. Lamp, Late Bronze Age II (McGovern *et al.* 1986: 138, 3). 19. Jug, Late Bronze Age II (McGovern *et al.* 1986: 127, 13).

Figure 9.6 Late Bronze Age pottery 2. 1. Pilgrim flask, Late Bronze Age II (Franken 1992: 68). 2. Cooking pot, Late Bronze Age I (Bourke *et al.* 1992: pl. 45). 3. Cooking pots, Late Bronze Age II (Tall Fukhar). 4. Chocolate-on-White Ware, Late Bronze Age I (Hennessy 1985: 101). 5. Chocolate-on-White Ware, Late Bronze Age I (Hennessy 1985: 101). 6. Fenestrated cult vessel, Late Bronze Age II (Franken 1992: 30). 7. Cult vessel (kernos), Late Bronze Age II (Franken 1992: 68). 8. Mycenaean stirrup jar, Mycenaean IIIB (McGovern *et al.* 1986: 197, 2). 9. Cypriot White Slip II milk bowl (McGovern *et al.* 1986: 197, 11). 10. Inscribed clay tablet, Late Bronze Age II (Franken 1964a: 377). 11. Fertility figurine, Late Bronze Age (Bourke *et al.* 1994: 111). 12. Faience vase with cartouche of Taousert (Tewosret) (Franken 1992: 31).

148); for technology see also Vilders (1993, 1995). For forms see also Hendrix *et al.* (1996: 146–158); for the published pottery up to 1995, see Herr and Trenchard 1996.

Social and Political Organization

Very little is known about the social and political organization in the Late Bronze Age. It seems, however, from the distribution of the larger settlements, in so far as it is possible to deduce this from the published material, that the city-state organization of the Middle Bronze Age survived the Egyptian conquest and was maintained during the whole period, probably under Egyptian hegemony. This can also be inferred from the Amarna Letters, for example, EA 256, concerning Pella (Albright 1943: 10–15), and the Balua stela. The former, however, pertains only to a single incident and only to the northernmost part of Jordan. The latter may perhaps point to the beginning of the territorial states known later from the Iron Age (see below). The Egyptians had a person who was either a local king, at least seen from his own point of view, or something like a modern *mukhtar*, seen from the Egyptian point of view, in charge of each of these city-states. Some were possibly Egyptian envoys. However, the names of the petty kings in the Amarna Letters are all either Semitic or Hurrian. The kings were, therefore, probably indigenous.

The two temples at the Amman Airport and at Tall Dayr Alla in central Jordan suggest some tribal meeting points where non-sedentary people gathered, either to bury their dead or to trade with the Egyptians. This does not, however, necessarily point to any tribal confederation or amphictyonic organization, as was formerly pos-tulated for the early Israelites, but rather to some (vague) arrangement, perhaps in the latter case under Egyptian supervision. (For the temple at Tall Dayr Alla see further below). Alternatively, the temple at the Amman Airport, together with one found at Tall Umm Dananir, could simply be located at some distance from the community using them.

In the later part of the period, LB IIB, the finds at Tall Saidiyya may point to a real Egyptian colonization with a garrison of mercenaries to protect an Egyptian governor (Tubb 1988c). Events in the northern part of the country, however, where for example, the palace at Tall Fukhar was destroyed and not rebuilt, show that at this stage the Egyptian presence was probably confined to the Jordan Valley, abandoning the rest of the country. It is interesting to note that the sedentary population in cities, such as Sahab, Jarash, Amman, lived there simultaneously with the non-sedentary population frequenting the temple at the Amman Airport.

This points to a situation where society was changing, with city-states and their satellites in the mountains, living together with the nomads, the Shasu, who were probably the only people living in the south. Only later in the Iron Age was this situation replaced by the kingdoms of Ammon, Moab and Edom, although the Balua stela and the occurrence of Moab in Egyptian lists point to the beginnings of this development already in the LB IIB period.

Subsistence

Flora

Grain, *Hordeum vulgare f. distichon* (two row-hulled barley) and *Triticum dicoccun* (emmer), from the Late Bronze IIB has been found at Irbid (Lenzen *et al.* 1985). Although the period is poorly represented at Pella, two row-hulled barley and emmer, horse bean, grape, grass, bitter vetch, broad bean, chick-pea, lentils, oak, almond, willow/poplar, Christ's-thorn, olive and hackberry are attested. Proportionally, fewer weeds and grass are found than before, suggesting perhaps more sophisticated crop-processing techniques (McNicoll *et al.* 1992: 255, endplate 10–11).

Fauna

The bones of sheep/goat, dog, equid, and cattle are reported from Baqah Valley Cave A2 (from the LB I period). Sheep/goat, dog, cattle and donkey (also rodents, bird, snake, frog and turtle) accounted for 57.97% of the bone material and reflect grave offerings of food for the dead. From Cave B3 (from the LB II period), the bones of sheep/goat, equid and cattle are reported. Here again, the majority of bones are of sheep/goat (and rodent, bird, frog, turtle, fish). Finally, a pit from the LB II period at Tall Umm Dananir contained the bones of cattle, equid, sheep/goat and carnivore remains (McGovern *et al.* 1986: 315–316).

Figure 9.7 Glazed "knob," possibly wall decoration, Tall Fukhar.

Taken as a whole, the published material is too sparse to conclude anything about subsistence in the Late Bronze Age. However, the evidence from the imported pottery, as well as the evidence for exports of wine or oil (see below), makes it certain that there was a surplus of agricultural production for trade or tribute.

Technology

Pritchard discovered and partially examined a water system at Tall Saidiyya (1985: 57–59). The lowest part, a semicircular chamber fed by an underground spring, was later cleared (Miller in Tubb 1988b: 84–88). Finally, a type of gallery, paved with flat cobbles, and surrounding the top of the pool to the north with access from the northern circuit roadway on the tell, was found. The excavated pottery proved the water system belonged to Stratum XII, the Egyptian phase, to which the Egyptian residency also belongs (Tubb *et al.* 1996: 35–36).

Architecture

Houses

Very few complete plans of buildings from the Late Bronze Age have been published. Parts of buildings, however, are known.

A large building, probably a local ruler's palace, was found at Pella (Figure 9.8.1). It was built in the LB I period and was, according to the excavators, in use until early in the LB IIB period, that is from the late fifteenth and during the first half of the fourteenth centuries bc (c. 1420–1350). It had trench-built walls, having foundations of massive fieldstones with a superstructure of mudbricks, with thick plaster floors in the courtyard and in the adjacent rooms. The building measured c. 15 by 15 m and had a courtyard with two rows of rooms in its first phase to the north and to the south. In a later phase, characterized by a series of ashy floors, two or three more rooms with stone and mudbrick walls were built against the eastern and western walls of the courtyard making it smaller. One of the rooms was a lavatory with drainage. Two decorated Egyptian ivory boxes, two fragments of cuneiform tablets, scarabs and a seal impression were found in the building. The plan is best compared to the form called "Governor's Residency" (Bourke *et al.* 1994: 104–107).

Another possible governor's residency, from a later period (area AA, Stratum XII), was found at Tall Saidiyya. The Egyptian-style plan and the construction method, with deep foundations of mudbrick, led the excavator to classify it as an Egyptian Governor's Residency (Tubb and Dorrell 1991: 69).

A palace complex (in the same Stratum XII) was found next to the outer wall at Tall Saidiyya (Figure 9.8.2). The building consisted of a series of rooms, courtyards and rooms on both sides of a passageway leading through to the city wall. A pair of interconnecting vaulted cisterns and a pool with a system of channels were found in the building, while in the pool a large number of Egyptian-type store-jars were found (Tubb and Dorrell 1993: 57, 59–61; Tubb 1997: 453–454).

A large monumental building from the LB IIA and IIB periods was partially uncovered at Tall Fukhar (Figure 9.8.3; Strange 1997: 402). It is either a temple or a palace, probably the latter. Its length is at least 40 m, while the breadth cannot as yet be determined. The outer walls are very thick, c. 1.5 m, with a 1.5m foundation of large stones and a mudbrick superstructure. Together both stand up to a height of 2.1 m. There was a thick white plaster floor in the rooms, with later floors above it. The destruction layer inside the building is 2 m thick, and the nature of the debris suggests that the building had an upper floor. The two rooms that have been partially excavated have entrances to other rooms to the south and to the north where the main entrance is presumably located. A staircase, only half of which has been excavated, has five steps leading down from an outer court. It is flanked by a doorpost or 'pillar' built of large boulders measuring 1x 1 m square. The front of the building with its entrance suggests a "Bit Hilani"-type building.

A kitchen, dated by the finds to the LB I period, was found at Tall Abu Kharaz. In it were found a bowl and jug, with metopic pattern, a spouted krater with "double base ring," a large krater and a storage jar with two handles (Fischer 1993: 283).

At Tall Fukhar part of a lower city showed a street with at least two houses and part of other houses (Figure 9.9). They were probably built in the LB I period, although no foundation trenches were found to date from that age, but a significant amount of LB I pottery was found in later fills in the houses. The latest phase coincided with the palace found on top of the tell (see Figure 9.8.3 and below). House A had five rooms around a courtyard and perhaps one or two more, however unexcavated or destroyed, as the house was situated along the scarp. In rooms 1 and 2 two tabuns and a storage jar were found, and in room 5 a bench and a mortar *in situ* suggesting a floor. In the courtyard (room 6) a large tabun was found in a corner. House B had five rooms around a courtyard, again probably with more rooms unexcavated. Room 2 was a kitchen with a saddle quern lying on a bed of stones in the floor, a mortar *in situ* and a tabun made of a collared rim jar upside down, of a kind found later both here as well as at other sites. Other walls indicate houses situated up towards the crest of the tell.

At Tall Umayri a LB II house was found to have been built in phase 13 after a LB I hiatus; it contained two rooms with a beaten earth surface, next to this remains of another building were excavated with a beaten earth surface running up to a wall of large boulders. From the next phase (phase 12) a large pit, a garbage depository was dug with mostly LB sherds but a few from the Iron I period (Herr *et al.* 1999: 105–106).

Figure 9.8   Late Bronze Age building plans. 1. Pella, palace from Late Bronze Age I (Bourke et al. 1992: 10). 2. Tall Saidiyya, western palace complex with aqueduct from Late Bronze Age II (Tubb and Dorrell 1994: 57). 3. Tall Fukhar, palace from Late Bronze Age IIB. 4. Tall Dayr Alla, cella with other rooms in temple from Late Bronze Age II (Franken 1992: 24). 5. Amman Airport, square temple from Late Bronze Age II (Hennessy 1966: 58).

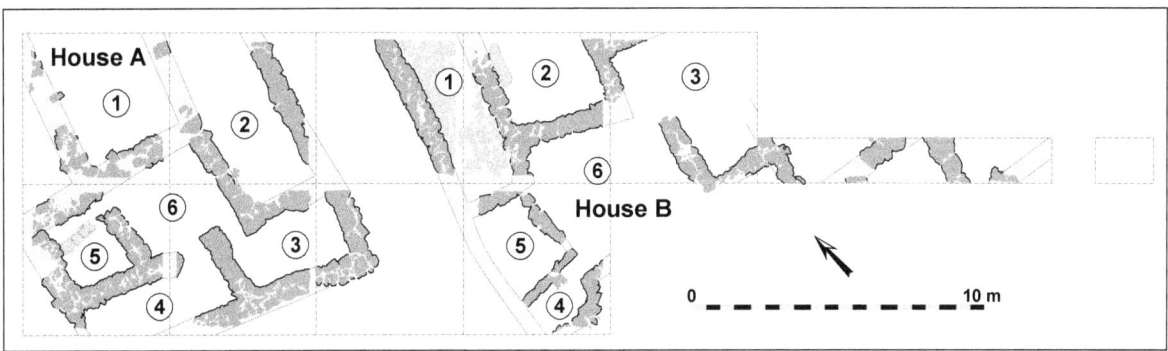

Figure 9.9   Houses at Tall Fukhar.

Temples

An interesting class of buildings is the square buildings (*Quadratbau*) found at three places, all in the vicinity of Amman: at the Amman Airport from the LB IIA–B period, a little before 1300 and in use to before 1200 bc (Figure 9.8.5; Hennessy 1966; 1989: 169–177; Herr 1983a, 1983b); at Mabrak of an uncertain date (not strictly a square but a rectangular building; Yassine 1988: 61–64); and at Tall Umm Dananir from the LB IB–II period (from c. 1500–1200 bc; McGovern 1989: 35). The first two have been completely cleared, while only a quarter has been excavated of the Tall Umm Dananir building. The excavator, however, is certain it is a square building. The three buildings have a central room with a number of corridor-like rooms around it along the outer walls. The Amman Airport building and the Tall Umm Dananir one are temples. The use of the Mabrak structure is not determined. The pottery, nondescript body sherds, are probably from the Late Bronze Age and the proximity and likeness to the other buildings make it likely that it was also intended to be a temple, although apparently never finished and used. The excavator, however, believes it to be a domestic structure for everyday use (Yassine 1988).

A temple (Figure 9.8.4) was found at Tall Dayr Alla. It is not earlier than the sixteenth century and existed into the twelfth century bc when it was destroyed by an earthquake (Franken 1992: 176). It was built on an eight m-high platform. The cella was another metre above the other rooms of the temple. The building belongs, in its latest phase, to the *Langbau* type with a non-axial or indirect entry (Franken 1992: 166). In its excavated segment, it had walls four to five bricks wide and two pillar bases on the 15 m-long axis. West of the cella, and separated from it by a brick wall, there was a complex of storerooms stacked with a workaday repertoire of large deep bowls, jugs and jars; east of the cella, there was a small courtyard, and beyond that several rooms were dug. In one of the rooms there were 12 clay tablets, indicating a temple archive, while in other rooms finer pottery, cylinder

seals, scarabs, faience flasks, alabaster dishes, beads and Mycenaean imports were found. The building had been renewed regularly by adding a thick layer of fresh clay and stone to the pillar base. Because of the lack of space on the tell for ordinary houses, the temple has been interpreted as a shrine for traders who frequented the spot (van der Kooij 1993: 339–340; Franken 1961: 361–368 and pls. 2–12; Franken 1992: 23–103).

A rectangular temple from the LB IIA period (trench III, Stratum 3) measuring c. 6.8 x 5.2 m, was excavated at Tall Abu Kharaz. Its outer walls were c. 0.75 m wide. The building was oriented northwest–southeast, and was open to the northwest where stone slabs were found which supported a roof. A wall (wall 7) runs to the outer northwest wall. Together they create an enclosure of c. 6 m². The inner space of the larger room is 20m², and the excavator found it surprising that no roof supports were found in the centre of the room (could it be that the room was an open space, and that the little room at the northwestern corner was the only covered part of the temple, a kind of propylaion?). A square altar was built in the eastern part of the enclosure and a bench in its northeastern part. A rich repertoire of pottery was found in the temple: fine quality vessels, pedestalled bowls, bowls and carinated bowls, decorated jugs and juglets, a goblet, a stand, as well as Cypriot imports, among them a Cypriot early White Slip bowl with a possible Kalavassos provenance from c. 1375 bc (Fischer 1991: 79–80; 1993: 282–283).

At Pella a very large fortress temple was found, only partially excavated although; it was built in the MB/LB transition period (c. 1600 bc) with close parallels with fortress temples at Megiddo and Shechem; especially with the latter, perhaps due to the documented links between the royal houses of Pella and Shechem. It was severely damaged in an earthquake probably early in the LB II period and was destroyed at the end of the Bronze Age (c. 1150 bc); it was later rebuilt and survived well into the Iron Age (Bourke *et al* 2003: 346–353 with fig. 23).

Foreign Relations and Trade

Jordan was in intensive contact with the outside world

during the Late Bronze Age, and a few examples of artefacts from various excavations will suffice to demonstrate
this. Mesopotamian material has been found, including a
cylinder seal (probably made in Babylon) at the Amman
Airport temple (Hennessy 1989: 176); fragments of two
tablets with cuneiform writing at Pella (McNicoll *et al.*
1992: 199–201); a glass pendant in the form of a fertility-
type figurine (Figure 9.2) and a unique knob (Figure 9.7),
possibly a wall decoration at Tall Fukhar (Strange 1994;
1997: 402 and fig. 6). Moreover, Egyptian *unguentaria*
have been found at Pella (Homés-Fredericq and Franken
1986: 135), an Egyptian calcite cylindrical jar found in
a cultic context at Pella (Bourke *et al.* 2003: 357 with
fig. 39.4) and Egyptian pottery at Tall Saidiyya (Pritchard 1980: 7–8). Mycenaean and Cypriot pottery has
been found in the Baqah Valley (McGovern *et al.* 1986:
194–201). The trade followed a network that can be
reconstructed with some confidence, with the main "gateway" being Pella. Commodities probably came from Beth
Shan, Megiddo and ultimately from Tell Nami (attested
as an export emporium for Jordan), Tell Abu Hawam
or Akko on the Mediterranean coast (Artzy 1994: 132;
Leonard 1987a: 265; Knapp 1993: 24–28, 87). From Pella, the goods went down the Jordan Valley to Tall Saidiyya
and farther to Tall Dayr Alla and Amman. Alternatively,
there was a route to Irbid and from there south to Tall
Umm Dananir and Amman, from where the route forked
to Sahab and to Madaba (Leonard 1987a: 265). But there
must have been other gateways. The "Midianite" ware
found at the Amman Airport temple (Hennessy 1989:
171), although this piece must be seen as an isolated find
(Parr 1982: 129), and in the south of Jordan (Jobling
1981: 110, pl. 31), demonstrates that there must have
been a caravan route from the south. This may also possibly be reflected in the find of a large scarab bought in Wadi
Musa (Ward 1973: 45–46) from the reign of Amenhotep
III. This route was probably operated or "protected" by
the Shasu from Arabia to Amman where the goods could
then be taken via the network described above north to
Irbid and down to the Jordan Valley. A similar route may
have existed from the north, through Damascus (another
possible gateway). This is the best explanation for the
finds from the palace at Tall Fukhar where several items,
some of them unique in Jordan, were imports from Syria
or Mesopotamia (Strange 1997). Since Tall Fukhar lies
northwest of Ramtha, just north of the later Roman road
from the coast to Bostra, there must have been easy access
to Irbid, with a link to Pella. Alternatively, the road could
have gone directly from Ramtha to Jarash, the Baqah Valley and Amman on what was later called the King's Highway and *Via Nova Traiana* (cf. Knapp 1993: 26–27).

Other trade routes of less importance must have existed. For example, pottery of special types was imported to
Tall Fukhar from southern Palestine in the MB II period
(cooking pot and a jar/goblet), the LB II period (cooking

pot), and the Iron IB period (collared rim jar and Philistine bowl) (McGovern 1997: 423–424), suggesting a
route probably across the highlands of Palestine to either
Tall Saidiyya or to Pella and from there to Irbid and farther
east; later the Roman road from Irbid to Dera'a crossed
the Wadi Shellale just south of Tall Fukhar. Moreover, the
spread of the Chocolate-on-White Ware, probably from
a single production centre in the northern Jordan Valley
(McGovern 1997: 424), shows a local network of trade
routes in Jordan itself.

The nature of the imports can only be guessed at, as
we do not know for certain what was transported in the
Mycenaean and Cypriot vessels. It has been suggested,
partly because of the closed forms, that the Mycenaean
vessels contained specialty oils and unguents (Leonard
1987a: 262–264). As for the Cypriot pottery, we can only
guess at what was transported in the milk bowls, an open
and rather shallow form. Perhaps they were imported as
tableware for their beauty. Merrillees has suggested that
Cypriot Base Ring *bil bils* may have been formed in imitation of the opium poppy, and used for wide-spread trade
in opium to Egypt and the Near East (1962: 287–292).
At least one class of imported vessels, that is, the chariot
vases, were probably imported for their intrinsic value
(Hankey 1974: 147), but they are from the latest phase of
the Late Bronze Age, and so far found in Jordan only at
the Amman Airport temple.

We have some idea of what was exported since wine and
oil are mentioned in Egyptian texts as commodities from
Asia (Helck 1971: 396–397, 398–402; Redford 1993:
212). This idea may be supported by the finds of the collared rim jar in Jordan and Palestine. The jars were probably used for the transport of these liquids, possibly on
camels, from production centres in Jordan to the harbours
of Tell Nami and Tell Naharija on the Mediterranean coast
(Wengrow 1996: 12–23; Artzy 1994: 132, 136–138).

Pella is mentioned in Papyrus Anastasi IV: 16, 6–17, 4
as a supplier of chariot parts in the LB II period (Smith
1973: 32). Other possible export products could have
been grain and cattle (Helck 1971: 370–372).

Defence

Tall Fukhar had massive walls built of medium-large
stones in the LB II period. Any traces of a gate were
unfortunately robbed in the Late Bronze Age/early Iron
Age transition period or in the early Iron Age (Ottosson
1992: 517, see however, Ottosson 2000 for a different
interpretation).

Irbid was initially defended in the LB IA period by a
basalt wall that was a survival from the Middle Bronze
Age. This wall was incorporated into the city in the LB
II period and another wall, of which 48 m was excavated,
was built outside the former wall. A tower also seemed to
belong to the city's defences (Lenzen 1992; Lenzen *et al.*
1985: 153–155).

A town wall from the Middle Bronze Age was found at Pella. It seems, however, that it was out of use in the Late Bronze Age and the town was no longer fortified, as it was then repeatedly mentioned in Egyptian texts as conquered (Smith 1973: 24–32; McNicoll *et al.* 1992: 40–41, 47). Perhaps it points to a status of peace under Egyptian hegemony.

Tall Safut had a perimeter wall founded on bedrock with a very narrow foundation trench (Wimmer 1987a: 280; 1987b: 165) during the Late Bronze period. Sahab was defended by a town wall of which 75 m has been uncovered. The complete wall appears to have been symmetrical, with rounded angles and resembling a kind of super-ellipse. It existed from the fifteenth into the late thirteenth centuries bc. However, only its foundations, sunk into earlier deposits in the form of a deep trench lined on both sides with large and medium-sized stones, were found (Ibrahim 1975: 78–80; 1987: 76; 1989: 519).

In Stratum XII at Tall Saidiyya, a casemate city wall, with a very large building behind it, was found. A near-vertical trench had been cut into the slope of the mound, and in the bottom large, flat stones were placed, above which a thick layer of pisé had been poured. Into this bedding were set the lowest courses of brickwork. The casemate wall's external and internal leaves are 1.10 m and 1.20 m thick respectively and the entire structure has a width of 3.5 m. The compartments were filled with rubble and the entire complex was buttressed (Tubb 1988a: 41–45; Tubb and Dorrell 1993: 57–60). In Stratum XII the site had as its main entry an indirect access approach, namely, a pebble-paved road ascended the tell from the northeast. The road entered the city through a four metre-wide vaulted mudbrick gate through the casemate wall. Beyond the rear of the wall, the street turned 90 degrees by means of a gate chamber that is not yet fully explored (Tubb *et al.* 1996: 31–33).

A city wall, originally built in the Early Bronze Age, but re-used in the Late Bronze Age, was found at Tall Abu Kharaz (Fischer 1996: 520; 2006a: 18, 163–213).

The existence of fortifications around all the major cities excavated may indicate unrest or warlike conditions in the Late Bronze Age. This is corroborated by Amarna Letter 256 in which the king of Pella describes serious disturbances (Albright 1943: 10–15). If such fortifications did indeed exist, then the situation in Jordan was the opposite of that in Palestine, where sites were unfortified during the Late Bronze Age (Gonen 1984).

Burial Customs

Various burial customs were in use in the Late Bronze Age in Jordan, they are here classified accoding to Gonen's system (Gonen 1992).

Cave Burials

The usual custom was to place the bodies in a cave (Gonen 1992: 9–15) with their grave goods. A cave could be used over a long period of time and was often reused from an earlier period, perhaps indicating continuity.

Tomb 62 at Pella dates from the Middle Bronze II–Late Bronze I period. It consists of three rock-cut chambers (3.15 x 3.78; 2.79 x 3.30; and 1.80 x 2.04 m) with a short dromos; a step led up from chamber one to chamber two. The cave, before serving as a tomb, had been used for processing food in the Middle Bronze Age. The roofs of the chambers had fallen in and had crushed much of the pottery in the tomb, but still hundreds of vessels survived intact. The individuals buried in the tomb numbered 100–150, which probably was an extended family or clan; nothing in the tomb suggests great wealth or status. The grave goods comprised more than 2000 artefacts including bowls, jars and jugs, juglets, lamps and imported Cypriot wares. The many Chocolate-on-White vessels must be singled out. Along with the pottery, gold, silver and bronze utensils, such as toggle pins, earrings, pendants, bracelets, tweezers, arrowheads, a knife, beads of various materials, scarabs, cylinder seals, stone vessels, clay artefacts, bone implements, a shell ring and a shark's tooth were found. The tomb testifies to a continuity from the Middle to the Late Bronze Age at Pella (Potts *et al.* 1985: 193, 205–208; Smith and Hennessy in McNicoll *et al.* 1992: 69–81; Knapp 1993).

Tomb 1 from the east cemetery at Pella is another tomb from the Middle Bronze/Late Bronze transition period. It is dated, according to the excavators, to c. 1600–1550/25 (Smith 1973: 170–171).

Tombs 20 and 21 at Pella come from the very beginning of the Late Bronze Age, that is, the LB IA period, or close to 1550. The original chambers seem to have been kidney shaped with a small side chamber. The main chamber was used for seven burials that were very badly preserved because of flooding and collapse. As a result, four pots floated in from an earlier Middle Bronze Age tomb. Grave goods included bowls, jars, pithoi, jugs and juglets, lamps, alabaster cosmetic jars, one with lid, a basalt axe head or hammer head, beads, a gold ring, incised bone inlays and fragments, bronze toggle pins, a javelin with tweezers and scarabs. Much of the pottery is Chocolate-on-White Ware. The side chamber of Tomb 21 contained two bowls, a jar and a bronze toggle pin (McNicoll *et al.* 1982: 40, 43–49).

Cave A2 in the Baqah Valley dates to the LB I period. Only a quarter of the cave was excavated. It had two chambers, an elliptical one measuring c. 5.2 x 3.4 m and, adjoined to it by a short passage, another chamber measuring c. 5.2 x 5.5 m. The entrance to the cave was through a triangular opening measuring c. 1.1 x 0.6 m. The cave had two distinct layers of burials: layer 2b, 0.5 m thick, representing a thick layer of disarticulated burials from the LB IA period; and layer 2a, representing a disturbed layer with much LB IB material. The grave goods included pottery, beads, shellbeads, cylinder seals, scarabs, spindle-whorls, anklets or bracelets, earrings, toggle pins, and ostrich egg fragments. More than two-thirds of the datable artefacts belong to the LB IA period (Brown and McGovern in McGovern *et al.* 1986: 32–44).

Tombs 13 and 14 from Quwayliba are dated to LB I–II. Only the pottery has been published and it is locally made except for one piece, a dark-grey jug that is an import (Kafafi 1984: fig. 5.6).

A tomb from LB I–II was found at Katarit al-Samra (Leonard 1981: 179–195). Other tombs from the Middle Bronze/Late Bronze period are Tombs 91, 94 and 95 from Pella (Edwards *et al.* 1990: 86).

Cave B3 in the Baqah Valley dates to the LB II period. It measures c. 9 x 4 m. The entrance was horizontal, elliptical, at a steep angle to the hillside and had probably been closed by a large boulder. The grave contained two burial layers, which together contained a minimum number of 64 individuals. The upper layer contained the remains of at least eight individuals of which three had been intentionally placed around an inverted bichrome bowl, and a blackened cooking pot, suggesting that a funerary meal or offering had been prepared in the tomb. A 1 cm thick sterile layer separated this upper layer from the lower one. In the latter, one of the burials had a necklace of glass and copper beads with a pair of carnelian beads. The grave goods comprised about 300 vessels (Brown and McGovern in McGovern *et al.* 1986: 44–53).

Tomb D from Irbid is from the Late Bronze/Iron Age transition period (between 1350 and 1100 bc, in the excavator's opinion). Here again, the grave goods are abundant (Dajani 1964: 99–101).

A Late Bronze/Early Iron Age period tomb was found at Sahem. The tomb contained 78 ceramic vessels as well as beads, pendants, buttons, a female stone figurine and three clay figurines (Fischer 1997).

Pit Burials

A very large cemetery with pit burials (Gonen 1992: 15–20) and jar burials was found on the lower segment of Tall Saidiyya. The burials date to the LB IIB period, that is, the twelfth century bc, contemporary with the Egyptian residency of Stratum XII. The graves are simple pit burials, sometimes marked or lined with stones or mudbricks and contained in excess of 500 individuals. Graves are cut into a 30–40 cm thick silt deposit overlying an occupation from the Early Bronze Age. One tomb could even be described as a shaft tomb. It was not possible to determine the exact level from which the graves had been cut, and the continued use of the same area created considerable disturbance and intercutting of graves (Pritchard 1980: 10–30; Tubb 1988b: 73–80; 1990: 29–37, 38–42;

1991: 190; 1997: 453; Tubb and Dorrell 1991b: 84–86; 1993: 67–72; 1994: 65–66; Tubb *et al.* 1996: 36–39). The publication of Pritchard (1980: 32–34) gives a catalogue, with illustrations, of the grave deposits that include bowls, jars, storage jars, jugs and juglets, flasks, goblets, lamps, pyxides, imported stirrup jars, base ring jugs, together with bronze-work, bracelets, anklets, beads, scarabs, seals, alabaster and ivory (Pritchard 1980: 31–103). Tubb notes further grave goods, including a very fine bronze wine set, and a surprising number of Egyptian burial customs (Tubb 1988a: 63–71; 1990: 36).

Bench Burials

Bench burial caves have rock-cut benches or stone and earth benches constructed around the walls of the cave (Gonen 1992: 23–24). The benches were used for multiple burials over a long period of time. The bones of earlier burials were removed to make room for new burials. At least one bench burial cave is known, Cave C from Sahab. It dates to the Late Bronze Age–Iron Age periods (from the fourteenth to the ninth centuries bc, according to the excavator). The cave measures c. 8.2 x 4.5 m and is c. 1.8 m high. Near its southeast corner there is a chimney-like construction reaching the surface and perhaps indicating that the cave was used earlier as a dwelling (an alternative explanation could be an installation for libations in connection with ancestor worship like at Pella, see below). A rock-cut bench, c. 50 cm high, is located along its south side and on its northern side there is another bench, c. 1.5 m wide and 20 cm high. A pavement runs from the entrance eastwards to a recess in which the chimney is situated and another pavement runs from the centre of the cave to the benches. The entrance to the cave was reached by several steps. There is no information on the number of burials in the cave, but apparently it was in use throughout the entire period. Grave goods included bowls, jugs and juglets, dippers, cooking pots, flasks, pyxides, lamps, zoomorphic figurines and imported stirrup vases; other objects included ostrich eggs, daggers and knives, toggle pins, arrowheads, bracelets, anklets, earrings and finger rings, kohl sticks, pendants, stone objects and seals and stamps. These latter objects are, however, not dated (Dajani 1970: 29–32, 34, 53–64).

Structural Tombs

A number of structural tombs (Gonen 1992: 27–28) were found in the cemetery at Tall Saidiyya. They were built-up chambers made of horizontally laid and bonded mudbricks and were lined up in two parallel rows in an east–west direction. The tombs were obviously planned in advance and were intended to be visible above the ground (Tubb 1988b: 60). The roof construction has gone, but it is tempting to suggest a corbelled roof like the five corbelled tombs found in western Palestine (Gonen 1992: 27).

Jar or Pithos Burial

A number of jar burials (Gonen 1992: 30) have been found at the Late Bronze Age cemetery at Tall Saidiyya. Single jar burials have been found with infants or foetuses, sometimes with grave goods, such as beads, amulets, bracelets and anklets; very often textiles showed that the bodies were wrapped, as also indicated by fibulae. The jars were sealed with a bowl or the base of another jar. Twenty-seven examples of double pithos burials of adults were also found: two extremely large jars were joined shoulder-to-shoulder after the necks had been removed and the junction was sealed using additional store jar sherds or stones. A variation was to cover the body with sherds from store jars and set the head inside a jar. As this type of burial, double pithos, is very rare in Palestine both east and west of the Jordan River, the excavator has connected these burials with a population of alien elements, perhaps Sea Peoples while the city was under Egyptian control (Pritchard 1980: 10–30; Tubb 1988b: 73–80; 1990: 31–42; 1991: 190; 1997: 453; Tubb and Dorrell 1991: 84–86; 1993: 67–72; 1994: 65–66; 1997: 453; Tubb *et al.* 1996: 36–39). Some peculiar burial customs were also attested in this cemetery. In one instance, additional skulls were re-buried with the original interment (Tubb 1988b: 63). Often, an inverted bowl, commonly of bronze, was placed on the pelvis in a position showing that it had covered the genitals of the deceased. In one case, the body had been placed face down. Bones of fish were found on the back of the skull. The hands met at the pelvis, and over them a bronze bowl with a ivory cosmetic box in the shape of a fish had been placed. In another grave, a javelin was found on the chest of the deceased with the point in the direction of the throat (Tubb 1988b: 63–66). Whatever these practices mean, they all bear witness to an extraordinary care for the deceased and probably a belief in an afterlife.

No examples have yet been found from Jordan in the Late Bronze Age for the other burial types in Gonen's typology (intramural burial, loculi burial, bilobate cave burial, open-pit burial, larnax burial, coffin burial).

Cremation

A rock pile, originally a stone-built incinerator, was found close to the square building at the Amman Airport temple. A number of bones, 95% of which were human, were scattered around it. All the human bones showed definite signs of burning, but not one of the animal bones had been burned. The excavator interpreted the finds as a temple for human sacrifice or a mortuary temple (Hennessy 1989: 171–177). Later excavators, however, have interpreted the place as a sanctuary for the cremation of the dead due to the finds of imported ceramics, fine ceramic vessels, bronze weapons and gold jewellery. This might be typical tomb furniture of a ritual centre connected with the dead and their cremation and burial, mainly for nomadic groups, as there was no sign of occupation in the vicinity (Herr 1983a: 9–11). Cremation did not, however, seem to be connected with the square temple at Tall Umm Dananir.

Religion and Ritual

A number of representations of gods are attested in the material from the Late Bronze Age.

At Tall Safut, a male figurine made of bronze (92.8% copper, 5.45% tin and 1.75% other elements) was found. The figurine is a seated, smiling deity with a crown and with forearms extended and wrapped in gold. Two bronze pegs suggest it had been attached to some wooden structure. The eyes are hollow and may have been inlaid (Wimmer 1987a: 280; 1987b: 165 and pl. 12). Probably it is an El-type, like the seated gods from Ugarit.

A male god with a spear in his hand and wearing a kilt is carved on a basalt stela found at Rujm Abd. This god is probably a Baal type warrior god (Zayadine 1991: 36–37; see also above).

There is the depiction of a male god wearing the Egyptian double crown along with a goddess and the local king on the Balua stele (Ward and Martin 1964: pls. 1 and 3). The male god is possibly El, Baal-Saphon or Kemosh, while the goddess could be either Ashtarte or Anat (see above).

A fertility-type goddess, with Hathor hairstyle, swollen abdomen and holding her breasts, was excavated from the destruction level of the palace at Tall Fukhar. The hair has been restored, from fragments found together with the figurine (Strange 1997: 402; Figure 9.2). The goddess, probably an heirloom, conforms to a type well attested in the LB I period in the Near East and probably manufactured in Mesopotamia (McGovern 1985: 30). The goddess is probably an Egyptianized Astarte (cf. Keel and Uehlinger 1993: 74–80, 110–122).

A clay figurine, showing a woman covering her pubic hair with the right hand and holding her breast with the left, and a mould for clay figurines with pronounced pubic hair and holding two plants were found at Tall Fukhar (Kamlah 1993: 107–114). Both are representations of Astarte (cf. Kamlah 1993: 109; Keel and Uehlinger 1992: 74–80, 110–122). The mould perhaps indicates the popularity of the goddess, since the plaquettes seem to have been locally produced. Another example of a clay plaquette with an Astarte figurine comes from Pella (Figure 9.6.11; Bourke *et al.* 1994: 110–112).

These figurines, which have countless parallels in other countries of the Ancient Near East (cf. Keel and Uehlinger 1993; 1993: 55–110), show that religion in Jordan conformed to the well-known type of fertility religion that was spread all over Syria-Palestine in the Late Bronze Age. It is, however, not possible at the present stage of research to describe the religion in detail. For example, we do not know whether the attempts above of attributing names of specific gods or goddesses to the figurines are more than guesswork since we do not know if there was continuity in the names of gods from the Late Bronze Age to the Iron Age, when we do know some of the names. Nor do we know if the names of the gods and goddesses in Jordan were the same as those of similar gods and goddesses in other parts of Syria-Palestine (e.g. the Ugaritic texts). We might expect a good deal of variation from place to place.

A glimpse of the cult can be obtained from the Amman Airport temple. When the temple was built, the operations commenced with digging a foundation trench, providing the site with a level surface. The outside walls were then placed on this surface in the form of a square. After the first course had been laid, the whole interior was packed with a fill (15–20 cm) of yellow clay and terra rossa. In this fill, there were frequent pockets of burnt clay, ashes and bone, evidence of a series of dedication offerings, consisting of a burnt offering together with small pieces of gold jewellery, beads, scarabs, cylinder seals, bone and ivory pieces and pottery fragments. Next, the inner walls were positioned, together with a cylindrical altar, in the centre of the building. The foundation trench was finally filled in and a number of arrow or small javelin heads were offered at the end (Hennessy 1966: 157).

A similar kind of ritual is attested at the square building at Tall Umm Dananir (McGovern 1989: 35).

A painted fenestrated stand from a pit in the fortress temple at Pella (Figure 9.8.1 p. 296) was richly decorated with adorants holding a ceremonial staff, with Tree of Life and caprides and ostriches perhaps, according to the excavator, pointing to the ceremonies in the temple (Figure 9.10; Bourke *et al.* 2003: 352–353 with fig. 31).

At Pella a remarkable example of ancestor worship with links to MB/LB burials and to Megiddo was found in a building with two building phases (MB IIC/ LB IA and LB IB/ LB IIA) in the shape of plaster lined bins with a number of ceramic vessels and ceramic funnels, possibly decommissioned funerary libation vessels (Bourke *et al.* 1998: 194–196; 2003: 342 and 345).

Writing

A number of hieroglyphic inscriptions, on monuments, on seals, and imprints from seals, have been found in Jordan from the Late Bronze Age.

Most important is the Balua stela from the thirteenth or early twelfth century bc. It was probably executed by a local craftsman in Moab. The inscription at the top of the stela, above the relief, is so badly worn that it is not possible to read it in full and only parts and single hieroglyphs can be read. The best publication is by Ward and Martin (1964), who conclude that the inscription was probably executed by the same artist, who was not an Egyptian but

Figure 9.10 Fenestrated stand from Pella (Bourke *et al.* 2003: 352).

knew enough of the Egyptian culture to make a relief and inscription in Egyptian style. Timm (1989: 93) maintains that the writing is not Egyptian, but perhaps Minoan or Cypro-Minoan. But he seems to date the stela to the Iron Age, and would then presumably have to connect it with the Sea Peoples. On balance and in view of the occurrence of Moab as a political entity on an inscription in the Luxor temple, it appears to me that the text is at least an attempt to produce an Egyptian inscription.

Two fragments of cuneiform tablets have been found at Pella, and on the basis of the stratigraphic context, they should be dated to the earlier part of the Late Bronze Age between 1550 and 1450 bc. They are too fragmentary to give any meaning, and it is not possible to determine where they were written (McNicoll *et al.* 1992: 299–301). They do, however, testify to knowledge of cuneiform writing at Pella, as does the later letter from Pella found at Tall Amarna (no. 256) (Albright 1943: 10–15).

The only examples of indigenous writing come from Tall Dayr Alla (Figure 9.6.10). In the debris of the temple, 11 tablets were found with a script that has until now defied all attempts at decipherment (Franken 1964a; 1964b: 421 and pl. V; 1965: 150–152; 1992: 57–59, 62–63; van den Branden 1965: 129–150; van der Kooij 1993: 339). The tablets are undoubtedly in a local script and probably served economic purposes. Perhaps the very existence of a local script shows a certain independence from the Egyptian overlords at the site at this specific time as the end of Egyptian hegemony drew to its close.

Summary of the Period

The Late Bronze Age shows a waning of settlement in most areas of Jordan compared to the Middle Bronze Age. This abatement is probably due to the deterioration of the climate, which became drier over the period, but could also partly be due to Egyptian exploitation. Jordan was most heavily settled in the north and the west in the mountains along the Jordan Valley and in the valley itself. The southern part of the valley and the southern part of Jordan south of Wadi Hasa were virtually empty, inhabited only by nomadic people.

Jordan was more or less under Egyptian rule during the entire period. The country was in close contact with other areas, and evidence of trade in the form of imported pottery and other artefacts is found all over the country. This contact is probably due to Egyptian overlordship bringing the international trade network into contact with populations, first and foremost at Pella. As a result, the material culture seems heavily influenced from abroad, but it has, for example, in the pottery decoration, a colourfulness that, together with the pottery of Palestine, seems to be indigenous. At the same time, the Egyptians exploited the country heavily, and material culture suffered from it.

The country seems to have been divided into city-states, each with a kind of king or Egyptian *mukhtar*. In spite of the Egyptian hegemony, however, there seems to have been a state of warfare or at least a state of manoeuvring between the small city-states. Evidence for this situation may be the numerous defences around the cities, and in one instance at least in an historical source, a letter found at Amarna (EA256). The Egyptian kings from time to time also needed to reassert their power in the area. At the very end of the period, when Egyptian influence was waning, there seem to be indications of the emergence of new kingdoms such as Moab. Whether this is also found farther to the north cannot be said with certainty. However, in view of the string of fortified settlements in what was later Ammon—Tall Umm ad-Dananir, Tall Safut, Amman, Tall Umayri, and Tall Sahab—it is possible that the Ammonite kingdom developed earlier than Moab and existed already early in the Late Bronze Age since settlement in Jordan has usually been from north to south (LaBianca and Younker 1995: 406–407). It seems that the central part of Jordan around Amman was an exception to the overall abatement of settlement in the period.

Bibliography

Aharoni, Y.

1979 *The Land of the Bible.* Tr. and ed. A.F. Rainey. London: Burns and Oates.

Albright, W.F.

1943 Two Little Understood Amarna Letters from the Middle Jordan Valley. *Bulletin of the American Schools of Oriental Research* 89: 7–17.

Ambers, J., K. Matthews and S. Bowman

1989 British Museum Natural Radiocarbon Measurements I. *Radiocarbon* 31: 15–32.

Archäologishe Anzeiger

2000 Jahresbericht 1999.

Artzy, M.

1994 Incense, Camels and Collared Rim Jars: Desert Trade Routes and Maritime Outlets in the Second Millennium. *Oxford Journal of Archaeology* 13: 121–47.

Bartlett, J.R.

1997 Edom. In E.M. Meyers (ed.), *The Oxford Encyclopedia of Archaeology in the Near East* 2: 189–90. New York: Oxford University Press.

Betts, A.V.G.

1989 Black Desert Survey. In D. Homés-Fredericq and J.B. Hennessy (eds.), *Archaeology of Jordan.* II.1. *Field Reports: Surveys and Sites A–K,* 45–48. Akkadica Supplementum 7. Leuven: Peeters.

Bienkowski, P.

1996 Soundings in the Wadi Hasa, 1995. *Palestine Exploration Quarterly* 128: 87.

Bienkowski, P. (ed.)

1991 *Treasures from an Ancient Land: The Art of Jordan.* Stroud: Alan Sutton.

Bienkowski, P. and R. Adams

1999   Soundings at Ash-Shorabat and Khirbat Dubab in the Wadi Hasa, Jordan: The Pottery. *Levant* 31: 149–172.

Bienkowski, P., R.B. Adams, R. Philpott and L. Sedman

1997   Soundings at Ash-Shorabat and Khirbat Dubab in the Wadi Hasa, Jordan: The Stratigraphy. *Levant* 29: 41–70.

Bourke, S.J., R.T. Sparks, K.N. Sowada and L.D. Mairs

1994   Preliminary Report on the University of Sydney's Fourteenth Season of Excavation at Pella (Tabaqat Fahl) in 1992. *Annual of the Department of Antiquities of Jordan* 38: 81–126.

Bourke, S.J., R.T. Sparks, K.N. Sowada, P.B. Mclaren and L.D. Mairs

1998   Preliminary Report on the University of Sydney's Sixteenth and Seventeenth Seasons of Excavations at Pella (Tabaqat Fahl) in 1994/95. *Annual of the Department of Antiquities of Jordan* 42: 179–211.

Bourke, S.J., R.T. Sparks and L.D. Mairs

1999   Bronze Age Occupation on Tell Husn (Pella). Report on the University of Sydney's 1994/95 Seasons. *Mediterranean Archaeology* 12: 51–66.

2003   Preliminary Report on the University of Sydney's Eighteenth and Nineteenth Seasons of Excavations at Pella (Tabaqat Fahl) in 1996/7. *Annual of the Department of Antiquities of Jordan* 47: 335–388.

Braemer, F.

1987   Two Campaigns of Excavations on the Ancient Tell of Jerash. *Annual of the Department of Antiquities of Jordan* 31: 525–530.

1992   Occupation du sol dans la région de Jérash aux périodes du Bronze Récent et du Fer. In M. Zaghloul, K. 'Amr and F. Zayadine (eds.), *Studies in the History and Archaeology of Jordan IV,* 191–98. Amman: Department of Antiquities.

Dajani, R.W.

1964   Iron Age Tombs from Irbid. *Annual of the Department of Antiquities of Jordan* 8–9: 99–101.

1966   Jabal Nuzha Tomb at Amman. *Annual of the Department of Antiquities of Jordan* 11: 48–52.

1970   A Late Bronze–Iron Age Tomb Excavated at Sahab, 1968. *Annual of the Department of Antiquities of Jordan* 15: 29–34, 53–64.

Daviau, P.M.M. and P.E. Dion

1994   El, the God of the Ammonites? The Atef-Crowned Head from Tell Jawa, Jordan. *Zeitschrift des Deutschen Palästina-Vereins* 110: 158–167.

Dornemann, R.H.

1983   *The Archaeology of Transjordan in the Bronze and Iron Ages.* Milwaukee, WI: The Milwaukee Public Museum.

1997   Amman. In E.M. Meyers (ed.), *The Oxford Encyclopedia of Archaeology in the Near East,* I: 99–102. New York: Oxford University Press.

Edwards, P.C., S.J. Bourke, K.A. Da Costa, J.C. Tidmarsh, A.G. Walmsley and P.M. Watson

1990   Preliminary Report on the University of Sydney's Tenth Season of Excavations at Pella (Tabaqat Fahl) in 1988. *Annual of the Department of Antiquities of Jordan* 34: 57–93.

Eggler, J. und Keel, O.

2006   *Corpus der Siegel-Amulette aus Jordanien.* Orbis Biblicue et Orientalis. Series Archaeologica XVIII. Fribouirg: Akademie Press.

Erman, A.

1893   Die Denkmal Ramses' II im Ostjordanland. *Zeitschrift für Ägyptische Sprache und Altertumswissenschaft* 31: 100–101.

Finkelstein, I

2005   Khirbet en-Nahas, Edom and Biblical History. *Tel Aviv* 32: 119–125

Fischer, P.M.

1991   Tell Abu Kharaz. The Swedish Jordan Expedition 1989: First Preliminary Report from Trial Soundings. *Annual of the Department of Antiquities of Jordan* 34: 67–103.

1993   Tell Abu Kharaz. The Swedish Jordan Expedition 1991: Second Season Preliminary Report. *Annual of the Department of Antiquities of Jordan* 37: 279–305.

1994   Tell Abu Kharaz. The Swedish Jordan Expedition 1992: Third Season Preliminary Report. *Annual of the Department of Antiquities of Jordan* 38: 127–145.

1995   Tall Abu Al-Kharaz. The Swedish Jordan Expedition 1993. Fourth Season Preliminary Excavation Report. *Annual of the Department of Antiquities of Jordan* XXXIX: 93–119.

1996   Tell Abu al-Kharaz. In P.M. Bikai and V. Egan (eds.), Archaeology in Jordan. *American Journal of Archaeology* 106: 507–535.

1997a   Tall Abu Kharaz. The Swedish Jordan Expedition 1995–1996. Sixth and Seventh Season Preliminary Excavation Report. *Annual of the Department of Antiquities of Jordan* XLI: 129–144.

1997b   A Late Bronze to Early Iron Age Tomb at Sahem, Jordan. *Abhandlungen des Deutschen Palästina-Vereins* 21. Wiesbaden: Harrassowitz.

1999   Chocolate-on-White Ware: Typology, Chronology, and Provenance: The Evidence from Tell Abu al-Kharaz, Jordan Valley. *Bulletin of the American Schools of Oriental Research* 313: 1–29.

2003   Chocolate-on-White Ware: Further Observations and Radiocarbon Dates. *Ägypten und Levante* XIII: 51–68.

2006a   *Tell Abu al-Kharaz in the Jordan Valley. Volume II: The Middle and Late Bronze Ages.* Österreichische Akademie der Wissenshaften. Denkschriften der Gesamtakademie, Band XXXIX. Wien.

2006b   The Rise and Fall of the Middle and Late Bronze Age Societies of Tell Abu al-Kharaz. In *The Chronology of the Jordan Valley.* Österreichische Akademie der Wissenshaften. Denkschriften der Gesamtakademie, Band XL. Wien.

Flanagan, J.W., D.W. McCreery and K.N. Yassine

1992 Preliminary Report of the 1990 Excavation at Tell Nimrin. *Annual of the Department of Antiquities of Jordan* 36: 89–111.

Franken, H.J.

1961 The Excavations at Deir 'Alla in Jordan. *Vetus Testamentum* 11: 361–372.

1964a Clay Tablets from Deir 'Alla, Jordan. *Vetus Testamentum* 14: 377–379.

1964b Excavations at Deir 'Alla, Season 1964. *Vetus Testamentum* 14: 417–422.

1965 A Note on How the Deir 'Alla Tablets Were Written. *Vetus Testamentum* 15: 150–152.

1992 *Excavations at Tell Deir 'Alla: The Late Bronze Age Sanctuary.* Leuven: Peeters.

Fritz, V.

1994 Vorbericht über die Grabungen in Barqa el-Hetiye im Gebiet von Fenan, Wadi el-'Araba (Jordanien) 1990. *Zeitschrift des Deutschen Palästina-Vereins* 110: 125–50.

Giveon, R.

1971 *Les Bédouins Shosou des Documents égyptiens.* Documenta et Monumenta Oriens Antiqui 12. Leiden: E.J. Brill.

Gonen, R.

1984 Urban Canaan in the Late Bronze Period. *Bulletin of the American Schools of Oriental Research* 253: 61–73.

1992 *Burial Patterns and Cultural Diversity in Late Bronze Age Canaan.* American Schools of Oriental Research Dissertation Series 7. Winona Lake, WI: Eisenbrauns.

Gordon, R.L. Jr. and E.A. Knauf

1987 Er-Rumman Survey 1985. *Annual of the Department of Antiquities of Jordan* 31: 289–298.

Hankey, V.

1974 A Late Bronze Age Temple at Amman. I: The Aegean Pottery. II: Vases and Objects made of Stone. *Levant* 6: 131–134.

Hauptmann, A.

2000 *Zur Frühen Metallurgie des Kupfers in Fenan/Jordanien.* Der Anschnitt supplement 11. Bochum: Deutsches Bergbau-Museum.

Hauptmann, A. and G. Weisgerber

1992 Periods of Ore Exploitation and Metal Production in the Area of Feinan, Wadi Arabah, Jordan. In M. Zaghloul, K. 'Amr and F. Zayadine (eds.), *Studies in the History and Archaeology of Jordan IV,* 61–66. Amman: Department of Antiquities.

Helck, W.

1971 *Die Beziehungen ägyptens zu Vorderasien im 3. und 2. Jahrtausend v.Chr.* Ägyptologische Abhandlungen 5. Wiesbaden: Harrassowitz.

Hendrix, R.E., P.R. Drey and J.B. Storfjell

1996 *Ancient Pottery of Transjordan.* Berrien Springs, MI: Institute of Archaeology/Horn Archaeological Museum and Andrews University.

Hennessy, J.B.

1966 Excavation of a Late Bronze Age Temple at Amman. *Palestine Exploration Quarterly* 98: 155–162.

1985 Chocolate on White Ware in Pella. In J.N. Tubb (ed.), *Palestine in the Bronze and Iron Ages: Papers in Honour of Olga Tufnell,* 100–113. London: Institute of Archaeology.

1986 Pella. In D. Homés-Fredericq and H. J. Franken, *Pottery and PottersóPast and Present,* 134–138. Tübingen: Attempto.

1989 Amman Airport. In D. Homés-Fredericq and J.B. Hennessy (eds.), *Archaeology of Jordan.* II.1. *Field Reports: Surveys and Sites A–K,* 167–178 Akkadica Supplementum 7. Leuven: Peeters.

Herr, L.G.

1983a *The Amman Airport Excavations, 1976.* The Annual of the American Schools of Oriental Research 48. Winona Lake, WI: Eisenbrauns.

1983b The Amman Airport Structure and the Geopolitics of Ancient Transjordan. *Biblical Archaeologist* 46: 223–229.

1992 Shifts in Settlement Patterns of Late Bronze and Iron Age Amman. In M. Zaghloul, K. 'Amr and F. Zayadine (eds.), *Studies in the History and Archaeology of Jordan IV,* 175–176. Amman: Department of Antiquities.

1997 Amman Airport Temple. In E.M. Meyers (ed.), *The Oxford Encyclopedia of Archaeology in the Near East,* I: 102–103. New York: Oxford University Press.

Herr, L.G. and W.C. Trenchard

1996 *Published Pottery of Palestine.* Atlanta, GA: Scholars Press.

Herr, L.G., L.T. Geraty, O.S. LaBianca and R.W. Younker

1994 Madaba Plains Project: The 1992 Excavations at Tell el-'Umeiri, Tell Jalul, and Vicinity. *Annual of the Department of Antiquities of Jordan* 38: 147–172.

Herr, L.G., D.R. Clark, L.T. Geraty and O.S. LaBianca

1999 Madaba Plains Project: Excavations at Tall al-'Umayri, 1998. *Annual of the Department of Antiquitiesof Jordan* 43: 99–125.

Homés-Fredericq, D.

1989 Lehun. In D. Homés-Fredericq and J.B. Hennessy (eds.), *Archaeology of Jordan.* II.2. *Field Reports: Surveys and Sites L–Z,* 349–359. Akkadica Supplementum 8. Leuven: Peeters.

1997 *Lehun.* Bruxelles: Imprimerie Cultura Wetteren.

Homés-Fredericq, D. and H.J. Franken

1986 *Pottery and Potters, Past and Present.* Tübingen: Attempto.

Homés-Fredericq, D. and J.B. Hennessy (eds.)

1989 *Archaeology of Jordan.* II. *Field Reports, Surveys and Sites.* Akkadica Supplementum 7–8. Leuven: Peeters.

Ibach, R.D.

1987 *Archaeological Survey of the Hesban Region. Hesban* 5. Berrien Springs, MI: Institute of Archaeology and Andrews University.

Ibrahim, M.M.

1974 Second Season of Excavation at Sahab, 1973. *Annual of the Department of Antiquities of Jordan* 19: 55–61.

1975 Third Season of Excavations at Sahab, 1975 (Preliminary Report). *Annual of the Department of Antiquities of Jordan* 20: 69–82.

1987 Sahab and its Foreign Relations. In A. Hadidi (ed.), *Studies in the History and Archaeology of Jordan III*, 73–81. Amman: Department of Antiquities.

1989 Sahab. In D. Homès-Fredericq and J.B. Hennessy (eds.), *Archaeology of Jordan*. II.2. *Field Reports: Surveys and Sites L–Z*. Akkadica Supplementum 8. Leuven: Peeters.

Ji, Chang-ho C., and Jong K. Lee

1999 The 1998 Season of Archaeological Survey in the Regions of 'Iraq al-'Amir and Wadi al-Kafaryn. A Preliminary Report. *Annual of the Department of Antiquities of Jordan* 43: 521–539.

2000 Preliminary Report on the Dhiban Plateau Survey Project, 1999: The Versacare Expedition. *Annual of the Department of Antiquities of Jordan* 44: 493–506.

Jobling, W.J.

1981 Preliminary Report on the Archaeological Survey between Ma'an and 'Aqaba. *Annual of the Department of Antiquities of Jordan* 26: 105–111.

Kafafi, Z.

1984 Late Bronze Pottery from Qwelbe (Jordan). *Zeitschrift des Deutschen Palästina-Vereins* 100: 12–29.

Kamlah, J.

1993 Tell el Fuhhar (Zarqu?) und die pflanzenhaltende Göottin in Palästina Ergebnisse des Zeraqon-Surveys 1989. *Zeitschrift des Deutschen Palästina-Vereins* 109: 101–127.

2000 *Zeraqôn-Survey 1988–1994*. Abhandlungen des Deutschen Palästina-Vereins Band 27,1. Wiesbaden: Harrassowitz Verlag.

Keel, O. and Ch. Uehlinger

1993 *Göttinnen, Götter und Gottessymbole*. Quaestiones Disputatae 134. Freiburg: Herder.

Kitchen, K.A.

1982 *Pharaoh Triumphant: The Life and Times of Ramesses II*. Warminster: Aris and Phillips.

1987 The Basics of Egyptian Chronology in Relation to the Bronze Age. In P. Åström (ed.), *High, Middle or Low?: Acts of an International Colloquium on Absolute Chronology Held at the University of Gothenburg 20th–22nd August 1987*, 37–55. Gothenburg: P. Åström.

Knapp, A.B.

1993 *Society and Polity at Bronze Age Pella: An Annales Perspective*. JSOT/ASOR Monograph Series 6. Sheffield: Sheffield Academic Press.

Knauf, E.A. and C.J. Lenzen

1987 Notes on Syrian Toponyms in Egyptian Sources II. *Göttinger Miszellen* 98: 49–53.

LaBianca, Ø.S. and R.W. Younker

1995 The Archaeology of Society in Late Bronze/Iron Age Transjordan (ca. 1400–500 BCE). In T.E. Levy (ed.), *The Archaeology of Society in the Holy Land*, 399–415. London: Leicester University Press.

Lenzen C.J.

1986 Tell Irbid and Tell Ras. *Archiv für Orientforschung* 33: 164–166.

1992 Tell Irbid. In D.N. Freedman (ed.), *Anchor Bible Dictionary*, III, 456–57. New York: Doubleday.

Lenzen, C.J. and E.A. Knauf

1986 Tell Irbid and Beit Ras, 1983–86. *Liber Annuus* 36: 361–363.

1987 Notes on Syrian Toponyms in Egyptian Sources I. *Göttinger Miszellen* 96: 59–64.

Lenzen, C.J., R.L. Gordon and A.M. McQuitty

1985 Excavations at Tell Irbid and Beit Ras. *Annual of the Department of Antiquities of Jordan* 29: 151–159.

Lenzen, C.J. and A.M. McQuitty

1988 The 1984 Survey of the Irbid/Bet Ras Region. *Annual of the Department of Antiquities of Jordan* 32: 265–274.

Leonard, A. Jr.

1979 Kataret es-Samra: A Late Bronze Age Cemetery in Transjordan? *Bulletin of the American Schools of Oriental Research* 234: 53–65.

1981 Kataret es-Samra: A Late Bronze Age Cemetery in Transjordan? *Annual of the Department of Antiquities of Jordan* 25: 179–95.

1986 Kattaret as-Samra. *Archiv für Orientforschung* 33: 166–167.

1987a The Significance of the Mycenaean Pottery Found East of the Jordan River. In A. Hadidi (ed.), *Studies in the History and Archaeology of Jordan III*, 261–266. Amman: Department of Antiquities.

1987b The Jarash–Tell el-Husn Highway Survey. *Annual of the Department of Antiquities of Jordan* 31: 343–390.

Levy, T., R. Adams, M. Najjar, A. Hauptmann, J.D. Anderson, B. Brandl, M.A. Robinson and T. Higham

2004 Reassessing the chronology of Biblical Edom: new excavations and 14C dates from Khirbat en-Nahas (Jordan). *Antiquity* 302: 865–879.

Levy, T., M. Najjar and T. Higham

2005a How many fortresses do you need to write a preliminary report? http://www.wadiarabahproject.man.ac.uk/titlepage/news/Antiquity/WAP%20review.htm#review.

Levy, T., M. Najjar, J. van der Plicht, N. Smith, H.J. Bruins and T. Higham

2005b Lowland Edom and the High and Low Chronologies. In T. Levy and T. Higham (eds.), *The Bible and Radiocarbon Dating: Archaeology, Text and Science*, 129–163. London: Equinox.

Levy, T., T. Higham and M. Najjar

2006 Response to van der Steen and Bienkowski. *Antiquity*

80 (http://antiquity.ac.uk/ProjGall/levy/index.html)

Lipschitz, N.

1986 Overview of the Dendrochronological and Dendroarchaeological Research in Israel. *Dendrochronologia* 4: 37–58.

1996 Olives in Ancient Israel in View of Dendroarchaeological Investigations. In M. Heltzer and D. Eitam (eds.), *Olive Oil in Antiquity*, 139–145. Padova: Sargon (originally issued at Haifa University 1988).

Liverani, M.

1987 The Collapse of the Near Eastern Regional System at the End of the Bronze Age: The Case of Syria. In M. Rowlands, M. Larsen and K. Kristiansen (eds.), *Centre and Periphery in the Ancient World*, 66–73. Cambridge: Cambridge University Press.

Mabry, J. and G. Palumbo

1992 Environmental, Economic and Political Constraints on Ancient Settlement Patterns in the Wadi al-Yabis Region. In M. Zaghloul, K. 'Amr and F. Zayadine (eds.), *Studies in the History and Archaeology of Jordan IV*, 67–72. Amman: Department of Antiquities.

MacDonald, B.

1992a Settlement Patterns Along the Southern Flank of Wadi al-Hasa: Evidence from 'The Wadi Hasa Archaeological Survey'. In M. Zaghloul, K. 'Amr and F. Zayadine (eds.), *Studies in the History and Archaeology of Jordan IV*, 73–76. Amman: Department of Antiquities.

1992b The Southern Ghors and the Northeast Arabah Archaeological Survey. Sheffield Archaeological Monographs 5. Sheffield: J.R. Collis.

1994 Early Edom: The Relation between the Literary and Archaeological Evidence. In M.D. Coogan, J.C. Exum and L.E. Stager (eds.), *Scripture and Other Artefacts: Essays on Archaeology and the Bible in Honor of Philip J. King*, 230–46. Louisville, KY: Westminster/John Knox Press.

MacDonald, B. (ed.)

1988 *The Wadi el Hasa Archaeological Survey 1979–1983, West Central Jordan.* Waterloo, ON: Wilfrid Laurier University.

Mare, H.

1989 Quweilbeh. In D. Homés-Fredericq and J.B. Hennessy (eds.), *Archaeology of Jordan*. II.2. *Field Reports: Surveys and Sites L–Z*, 472–486. Akkadica Supplementum 8. Leuven: Peeters.

McGovern, P.E.

1985 *Late Bronze Age Palestinian Pendants.* JSOT/ASOR Monograph Series 1. Sheffield: Sheffield Academic.

1989 Baqah Valley Survey. In D. Homés-Fredericq and J.B. Hennessy (eds), *Archaeology of Jordan*. II.1. *Field Reports: Surveys and Sites A–K*, 25–44. Akkadica Supplementum 7. Leuven: Peeters.

1992 Settlement Patterns of the Late Bronze and in the Greater Amman Area. In M. Zaghloul, K. 'Amr and F. Zayadine (eds.), *Studies in the History and Archaeology of Jordan IV*, 179–183. Amman: Department of Antiquities.

1997 A Ceramic Sequence for Northern Jordan: An Archaeological and Chemical Perspective. In G. Bisheh, M. Zaghloul and I. Kehrberg (eds.), *Studies in the History and Archaeology of Jordan VI*, 421–425. Amman: Department of Antiquities.

McGovern, P.E. (ed.)

1986 *The Late Bronze and Early Iron Ages of Central Transjordan: The Baqah Valley Project.* University Museum Monograph 65. Philadelphia: The University Museum.

McNicoll, A., R.H. Smith and J.B. Hennessy

1982 *Pella in Jordan 1: An Interim Report on the Joint University of Sydney and The College of Wooster Excavations at Pella 1979–81.* Canberra: Australian National Gallery.

McNicoll, A.W., R.H. Smith, P.M. Watson, and S. Gordon

1992 *Pella in Jordan 2.* Mediterranean Archaeology Supplement 2. Sydney: University of Sydney.

Merrillees, R.S.

1986 Political Conditions in the Eastern Mediterranean during the Late Bronze Age. *Biblical Archaeologist* 49: 42–50.

Miller, J.M.

1979 Archaeological Survey South of Wadi Mujib: Glueck's Sites Revisited. *Annual of the Department of Antiquities of Jordan* 23: 79–92.

Mittmann, S.

1970 *Beiträge zur Siedlungs und Territorialgeschichte des nördlichen Ostjordanlandes.* Abhandlungen des Deutschen Palästinavereins. Wiesbaden: Harrassowitz.

Na'aman, N.

1994 The Hurrians and the End of the Middle Bronze Age in Palestine. *Levant* 26: 175–187.

Najjar, M.

1992 The Jordan Valley (East Bank) during the Middle Bronze Age in the Light of New Excavations. In M. Zaghloul, K. 'Amr and F. Zayadine (eds.), *Studies in the History and Archaeology of Jordan IV*, 149–153. Amman: Department of Antiquities.

Neuman, J. and S. Parpola

1987 Climatic Change and Eleventh–Tenth Century Eclipse of Assyria and Babylonia. *Journal of Near Eastern Studies* 46: 161–182.

Nützel, W.

1976 The Climatic Changes of Mesopotamia and Border Areas. *Sumer* 32: 11–24.

Olávarri, E.

1997 'Ara'ir. In E.M. Meyers (ed.), *The Oxford Encyclopedia of the Archaeology in the Near East*, I: 177–178. New York: Oxford University Press.

Ottosson, M.

1992 Tell el-Fukhar. *American Journal of Archaeology* 96: 516–518.

2000 Tall Fukhar: The Gate. *Svensk Exegetisk Årsbok* 65: 182–190.

Palumbo, G. (ed.)

1994 *JADIS: The Jordan Antiquities Database and Information System: A Summary of the Data.* Amman: Department of Antiquities of Jordan and the American Center of Oriental Research.

Panagiotopoulos, D.

2000 Tributabgaben und Huldigungsgeschenke aus der Levante. Die Ägyptische Nordexpansion in der 18. Dynastie aus Strukturgeschichtlichen Sicht. *Ägypten und Levante* X: 139–158.

Parr, P.

1982 Contacts between North West Arabia and Jordan in the Late Bronze and Iron Ages. In A. Hadidi (ed.), *Studies in the History and Archaeology of Jordan I,* 127–133. Amman: Department of Antiquities.

Piccirillo, M.

1976 Una Tomba del Ferro I a Mafraq. *Liber Annuus* 26: 27–30.

Potts, T.F.

1987 A Bronze Age Ivory-Decorated Box from Pella (Pahel) and its Foreign Relations. In A. Hadidi (ed.), *Studies in the History and Archaeology of Jordan III,* 59–71. Amman: Department of Antiquities.

Potts, T.F., P.C. Colledge and P.C. Edwards

1985 Preliminary Report on a Sixth Season of Excavation by the University of Sydney at Pella in Jordan (1983/84). *Annual of the Department of Antiquities of Jordan* 29: 181–210.

Potts, T.F., S.J. Bourke, P.C. Edwards, F. Richards and G.J. Wightman

1988 Preliminary Report on the Eighth and Ninth Seasons of Excavation by the University of Sydney at Pella (Tabaqat Fahl), 1986 and 1987. *Annual of the Department of Antiquities of Jordan* 32: 115–149.

Prag, K.

1992 Bronze Age Settlement Patterns in the South Jordan Valley: Archaeology, Environment and Ethnology. In M. Zaghloul,K. 'Amrand F. Zayadine (eds.), *Studies in the History and Archaeology of Jordan IV,* 155–160. Amman: Department of Antiquities.

Pritchard, J.B.

1980 *The Cemetery at Tell es-Sa'aidiyeh, Jordan.* University Museum Monograph 41. Philadelphia: The University Museum.

1985 *Tell es-Sa'idiyeh: Excavations on the Tell, 1964–1966.* University Museum Monograph 60. Philadelphia: The University Museum.

Redford, D.B.

1982 Contact between Egypt and Jordan in the New Kingdom: Some Comments on Sources. In A. Hadidi (ed.), *Studies in the History and Archaeology of Jordan I,* 115–119. Amman: Department of Antiquities.

1993 *Egypt, Canaan, and Israel in Ancient Times.* Princeton: Princeton University.

Rothenberg, B. and J. Glass

1983 The Midianite Pottery. In J.F.A. Sawyer and J.A. Clines (eds.), *Midian, Moab and Edom,* 65–124. Journal for the Study of the Old Testament. Supplement Series 24. Sheffield: University of Sheffield.

Sauer, J.A.

1986 Transjordan in the Bronze and Iron Ages: A Critique of Gluek's Synthesis. *Bulletin of the American Schools of Oriental Research* 263: 1–26.

Shehadeh, N.

1985 The Climate of Jordan in the Past and Present. In A. Hadidi (ed.), *Studies in the History and Archaeology of Jordan II,* 24–37. Amman: Department of Antiquities.

Simmons, A.H. and Z. Kafafi

1992 The 'Ain Ghazal Survey: Patterns of Settlement in the Greater Wadi az-Zarqa Area, Central Jordan. In M. Zaghloul, K. 'Amr and F. Zayadine (eds.), *Studies in the History and Archaeology of Jordan IV,* 77–82. Amman: Department of Antiquities.

Smith, R.H.

1973 *Pella of the Decapolis I.* Wooster, OH: The College of Wooster.

Strange, J.

1986 The Transition from the Bronze Age to the Iron Age in the Eastern Mediterranean and the Emergence of the Israelite State. *Scandinavian Journal of the Old Testament* 1: 1–19.

1993 Tell el-Fukhar. *American Journal of Archaeology* 97: 484–487.

1994 Tell el-Fukhar. *American Journal of Archaeology* 98: 521–559.

1997 Tall Fukhar 1990–1993. In G. Bisheh, M. Zaghloul and I. Kehrberg (eds.), *Studies in the History and Archaeology of Jordan VI,* 399–406. Amman: Department of Antiquities.

2003 Tell el Fukhar. *American Journal of Archaeology* 107: 461–63.

2004a Jordan between Mesopotamia and Egypt in the Bronze and Iron Ages. *Studies in the History and Archaeology of Jordan VII,* 427–432.

2004b Tell el-Fukhar—et nordisk project i Jordan. *Bibliana* 5 no. 2: 17–25.

Thompson, T.L.

1994 (1992) *Early History of the Israelite People from the Written and Archaeological Sources.* Leiden: E.J. Brill.

Timm, S.

1989 *Moab Zwischen den Mächten: Studien zu historischen Denkmälern und Texten.* " Agypten und Altes Testament 17. Wiesbaden: Harrassowitz.

Tubb, J.N.

1986 Tell es-Sa'idiyeh: Interim Report of the Second Season

of Excavations. *Annual of the Department of Antiquities of Jordan* 30: 119–129.

1988a Tell es-Sa'idiyeh: Third Season Interim Report. *Annual of the Department of Antiquities of Jordan* 32: 41–58.

1988b Preliminary Report on the First Three Seasons of Renewed Excavations on Tell el-Sa'idiyeh. *Levant* 20: 23–88.

1988c The Role of the Sea Peoples in the Bronze Industry of Palestine/Transjordan in the Late Bronze/Early Iron Age Transition. In J. Curtis (ed.), *Bronze-Working Centres of Western Asia c. 1000–539 b.c.* London and New York: Kegan Paul in association with the British Museum.

1990 Preliminary Report on the Fourth Season of Excavations at Tell es-Sa'idiyeh in the Jordan Valley. *Levant* 22: 21–42.

1991 Preliminary Report on the Fifth Season of Excavations on Tell es-Sa'idiyeh. *Annual of the Department of Antiquities of Jordan* 35: 181–194.

1997 Tell es-Sa'idiyeh. In E.M. Meyers (ed.), *The Oxford Encyclopedia of Archaeology in the Near East*, IV: 452–455. New York: Oxford University Press.

Tubb, J.N. and P.G. Dorrell

1991 Tell es-Sa'idiyeh: Preliminary Report on the Fifth Season of Excavations. *Levant* 23: 67–86.

1993 Tell es-Sa'idiyeh: Interim Report on the Sixth Season of Excavation. *Palestine Exploration Quarterly* 125: 50–74.

1994 Tell es-Sa'idiyeh 1993: Interim Report on the Seventh Season of Excavation. *Palestine Exploration Quarterly* 129: 52–67.

Tubb, J.N., P.G. Dorrell and F.J. Cobbing

1996 Interim Report on the Eighth (1995) Season of Excavations at Tell es-Sa'idiyeh. *Palestine Exploration Quarterly* 128: 16–40.

Van den Branden, A.

1965 Essai de déchiffrement des inscriptions de Deir 'Alla. *Vetus Testamentum* 15: 129–150.

Van der Kooij, G.

1993 Tell Deir Allah. In E. Stern (ed.), *The New Encyclopedia of Archaeological Excavations in the Holy Land* I, 338–342. Jerusalem: The Israel Exploration Society/Carta.

Van der Steen, E

1996 The Central East Jordan Valley in the Late Bronze and Early Iron Ages. *Bulletin of the American Schools of Oriental Research* 302: 51–74.

1997 Pots and Potters. *Annual of the Department of Antiquities of Jordan* 41: 81–93.

2004 *Tribes and Territories in Transition*. Orientalia Lovaniensia Analecta 130. Leuven: Peeters.

Van der Steen, E and P. Bienkowski

2005 Review of "Reassessing the chronology of Biblical Edom." http://www.wadiarabahproject.man.ac.uk/title page/news/Antiquity/WAP%20review.htm#review.

2006 Radiocarbon dates from Khirbat en-Nahas: a methodological critique. *Antiquity* 80 (http://antiquity.ac.uk/ProjGall/levy/index.html)

Viewieger, D. und Häser, J.

2005 Der Tell Zerā'a im Wadi el-'Arab. *Zeitschrift des Deutschen Palästina-Vereins* 123: 1–27.

Vilders, M.

1993 Some Remarks on the Production of Cooking Pots in the Jordan Valley. *Palestine Exploration Quarterly* 125: 149–156.

1995 Some Technological Features of Tall Saidiyya Cooking Pots. In K. 'Amr, F. Zayadine and M. Zaghloul (eds.), *Studies in the History and Archaeology of Jordan V*, 597–601. Amman: Department of Antiquities.

Ward, W.A.

1964 Cylinders and Scarabs from a Late Bronze Age Temple at Amman. *Annual of the Department of Antiquities of Jordan* 8–9: 47–55.

1966 Scarabs, Seals and Cylinders from Two Tombs at Amman. *Annual of the Department of Antiquities of Jordan* 11: 5–18.

1973 A Possible New Link between Egypt and Jordan during the Reign of Amenhotep III. *Annual of the Department of Antiquities of Jordan* 18: 45–46.

Ward, W.A. and M.F. Martin

1964 The Balua Stele: A New Transcription with Palaeographical and Historical Notes. *Annual of the Department of Antiquities of Jordan* 8: 5–29.

Weinstein, J.M.

1982 The Egyptian Empire in Palestine: A Reassessment. *Bulletin of the American Schools of Oriental Research* 241: 1–28.

1991 Egypt and the Middle Bronze IIC/Late Bronze IA Transition in Palestine. *Levant* 23: 105–115.

Wengrow, D.

1996 Egyptian Taskmasters and Heavy Burdens: Highland Exploitation and the Collared-Rim Pithos of the Bronze/Iron Age Levant. *Oxford Journal of Archaeology* 15: 307–326.

Wimmer, D.H.

1987a The Excavations at Tell Safut. In A. Hadidi (ed.), *Studies in the History and Archaeology of Jordan III*, 279–282. Amman: Department of Antiquities.

1987b The Safut Excavations 1982–85 Preliminary Report. *Annual of the Department of Antiquities of Jordan* 31: 159–171.

1989 Safut (Tell). In D. Homés-Fredericq and J.B. Hennessy (eds.), *Archaeology of Jordan*. II.2. *Field Reports: Sites L–Z*, 512–515. Akkadica Supplementum 8. Leuven: Peeters.

Worschech, U.

1992 Ancient Settlement Patterns in the Northwest Ard al-Karak. In M. Zaghloul, K. 'Amr and F. Zayadine (eds.), *Studies in the History and Archaeology of Jordan IV*, 83–

88. Amman: Department of Antiquities.

1997 Balua. In E.M. Meyers (ed.), *The Oxford Encyclopedia of Archaeology in the Near East*, I: 269–270. New York: Oxford University.

Worschech, U.F.C., U. Rosenthal and F. Zayadine

1986 The Fourth Season in the Northwest Ard el-Kerak and Soundings at Balua 1986. *Annual of the Department of Antiquities of Jordan* 30: 285–301.

Yassine, K.

1988 El-Mabrak: An Architectural Analogue of the Amman Airport Building. In K. Yassine (ed.), *Archaeology of Jordan: Essays and Reports*, 61–64. Amman: University of Jordan.

1989 Tell el Mazar. In D. Homés-Fredericq and H.J. Hennessy (eds.), *Archaeology of Jordan*. II.2. *Field Reports: Sites L–Z*, 381–384. Akkadica Supplementum 8. Leuven: Peeters.

Yassine, K.H., J. Sauer and M. Ibrahim

1988 The East Jordan Valley Survey, 1975. In K.H. Yassine (ed.), *Archaeology of Jordan: Essays and Reports*, 159–207. Amman: University of Jordan.

Zayadine, F.

1991 Sculpture in Ancient Jordan. In P. Bienkowski (ed.), *Treasures from an Ancient Land: The Art of Jordan*, 31–61. Stroud: Alan Sutton.

Zayadine, F., M. Najjar and J.A. Greene

1987 Recent Excavations on the Citadel of Amman (Lower Terrace): A Preliminary Report. *Annual of the Department of Antiquities of Jordan* 31: 299–310.

Zeist, W. van

1985 Past and Present Environment of the Jordan Valley. In A. Hadidi (ed.), *Studies in the History and Archaeology of Jordan II*, 199–204. Amman: Department of Antiquities.

10. The Iron Age

Larry Herr and Mohammed Najjar

Introduction

The Iron Age in Jordan saw the settlement of a variety of population groups or "tribes" in the arable parts of the Jordanian plateau and their gradual coalescence into formal "national" states with their own monarchies and governmental bureaucracies. Although the Jordan Valley and the northern plateau (north of Wadi Zarqa) had been constantly and relatively heavily settled throughout the Bronze Age, the plateau south of the Wadi Zarqa had been comparatively empty during the Middle and Late Bronze Ages. Settlement began again in the Amman region toward the end of the Late Bronze Age; in the Karak region during Iron Age I; and in the Tafila and Aqabah regions during the second half of Iron II. Settlement thus spread gradually in a southward direction throughout the Iron Age.

Stratigraphic excavations at Iron Age sites that exposed significant remains did not occur until the 1980s, except for those of Glueck at Tall Khalayfi (Pratico 1993) and Bennett at Umm Biyara (Bienkowski 1990), Tawilan (Bennett and Bienkowski 1995), and Busayra (Bienkowski 1990). Even the extensive excavations at Dhiban in the 1950s and 1960s (Tushingham 1993 and cited sources) and Tall Hisban in the 1960s and 1970s (Merling and Geraty 1994) produced only fragmentary Iron Age remains, albeit with copious pottery in secondary contexts. Moreover, most of these excavations produced only a few finds from Iron I. Indeed, that period has only begun to be exposed significantly in the last decade (Ji 1995).

In assigning sites to specific sub-periods of the Iron Age below, we have suggested somewhat nuanced datings for several sites based on the ceramic assemblages. Much progress has occurred recently on the pottery of Jordan, allowing us to redate older excavated materials. For instance, we now have very consistent groupings of different types of collared pithoi into assemblages with equally different cooking pots, jugs, bowls and jars. Simply to find a collared pithos is no longer enough to ascribe a settlement to the early Iron I period (as did, for instance, Sauer [1986: 10]; for the typological history of the collared pithos in Jordan see Herr [2001]).

No attempt has been made to isolate all survey sites that have produced Iron Age pottery. Moreover, surveyed sites do not always tell an accurate story. Whereas one survey suggested Late Bronze to Iron Age settlement for one particular site in the south, excavation found nothing except a few examples of Iron II pottery in secondary deposits

(Bienkowski *et al.* 1997, Bienkowski and Adams 1999).

Although not mentioned specifically as a bibliographic source, the results of many of the Iron Age sites appear in Homès-Fredericq and Hennessy (1989).

Late Bronze Age/Iron I Transition (Late Thirteenth–Early Twelfth Centuries bc)

Egyptian sources for the early Iron Age include Papyrus Anastasi VI during the reign of Merneptah (c. 1206 bc), which mentions the Shasu, apparently nomads from a region that included southern Jordan. On the basis of this and earlier inscriptions from the reign of Ramesses II, Kitchen has come to the conclusion that "Moab, and especially Edom, should be considered mainly as 'tented kingdoms'" (1992: 27).

The only other textual sources relevant to this period are later reports and/or remembrances of the biblical documents. These include stories of the origins of the Ammonites and Moabites (Gen 19.38), the defeat of King Og in a battle that mentions his astounding iron bed (Deut 3.1–11), and a series of wars with Israel and the Transjordanian states about who was to control the land east of Jordan (e.g. the Jephthah story in Judges 11) and even that to the west (e.g. the stories of Ehud against the Moabites in Judges 4 and Gideon against the Midianites in Judges 6).

This sub-period is defined ceramically by a mixture of early Iron I and Late Bronze Age pottery. A few sites on the plateau continued from the Late Bronze Age (Abila (?), Amman, the Baqah Valley, Umm Dananir, Tall Fukhar, Irbid, Jarash, Tall Safut (?), Sahab (if the tomb reflects a contemporary settlement), and Tall Umayri. This suggests a peaceful continuity from the Late Bronze Age into the Iron Age, at least in the north where most of these sites occur. A similar picture obtains for the Jordan Valley at Pella and Tall Saidiyya only (Tall Dayr Alla seems to have been uninhabited at this point).

Most of the finds on the plateau come from tombs (Sahem, Amman, Sahab, the Baqah Valley and Madaba); fragmentary architectural remains are reported for Abila(?), Tall Hisban (Sauer 1986), Irbid, and Jarash (the published collared pithos is similar to those from Tall Umayri [compare Braemer 1987: fig. 2.8 with Clark 1997: figs. 4.14–20]); isolated and/or secondary pottery finds seem to come from Arair, Umm Dananir(?), Rujm Henu(?), Tall Safut(?), Tall Jalul (Younker, pers. comm.), and Tall Jawa South (Daviau, pers. comm.). The finds at

Tall Hisban include a small cistern and a long trench cut into bedrock, possibly a deep, narrow moat at the edge of the hilltop (LaBianca and Ray, pers. comm.). Preliminary reports from Tall Irbid indicate a very thick destruction level (up to 4 m) that covered the city wall, a tower, and a two-storied public building that contained cultic vessels.

Lahun has produced a casemate wall and four houses, some of which are pillared. The remains seem to date to a broader time than just the transitional period, but not enough pottery has been published to make independent decisions (Homès-Fredericq 1997b). Whereas the remains are very shallow, several episodes of rebuilding in the houses suggest a long period of time for the settlement (Homès-Fredericq 1992: 190). Farther south the remains

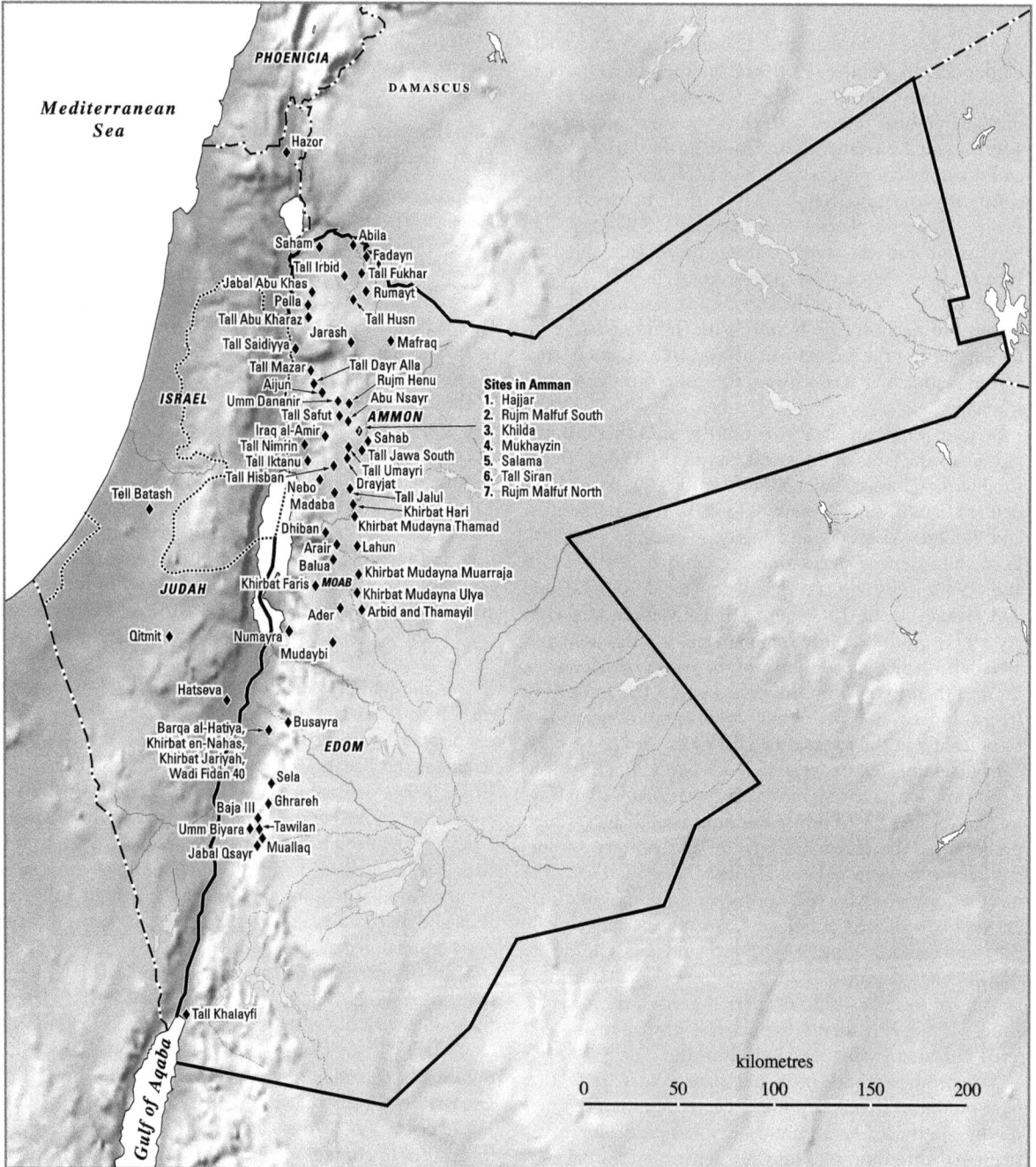

Figure 10.1 Iron Age sites mentioned in the text.

Abila (?)	Walls (Mare 1992 and other references there)
Amman	Tomb (Dajani 1966a); pottery (most is Iron IIC, Hadidi 1970: pl. 1.11)
Arair V	Houses (Olávarri 1965: fig. 1.1–4)
Baqah Valley	Tombs (McGovern 1986)
Khirbat Umm Dananir (?)	Unpublished pottery (McGovern 1986: 61)
Jarash (?)	Floor fragments; no published pottery (Braemer 1987)
Lahun	Fortified village; casemate wall; four houses (Homès-Fredericq 1997b)
Madaba	Tomb (Harding and Isserlin 1953)
Pella	Town with destruction (end of LB); village (McNicoll *et al.* 1982; Bourke 1997: 103–13)
Rujm Henu (?)	Unpublished pottery (McGovern 1983: 126)
Sahab	Tomb (Dajani 1970)
Sahem	Tomb (Fischer 1997)
Tall Fukhar	Re-used palace?; house walls (Strange 1997)
Tall Hisban 21	Rock-cut trench; cistern (Fisher 1994)
Tall Irbid Phase 2	City wall; tower; cultic building (Lenzen 1988); Tomb B (Dajani 1966b)
Tall Safut (?)	Unpublished pottery (Wimmer 1987: 281)
Tall Saidiyya XIV–XV	Tombs (Pritchard 1980); wall and cobbled surface (Tubb *et al.* 1996)
Tawilan	Pottery (Hart 1995: 60, fig. 6.19.11)
Tall Umayri	Fortification system; four-room house; other houses(Clark 1997)

Table 10.1 Excavated sites with at least preliminary reports on the Late Bronze Age/Iron I transition .

are very sparse. At Tawilan a cooking pot from this period and a Midianite potsherd were found in mixed contexts.

The best-preserved remains so far come from Tall Umayri (Clark 1994; Herr *et al.* 1997b). The defensive system (Figure 10.2) included a dry moat cut out of the original ridge upon which the site was founded (14); a retaining wall (12) supporting a massive rampart that repaired a crack in bedrock probably caused by an earthquake (9); and a defensive wall surrounding the site at the top of the rampart (8), which has been traced for approximately 70 m with two interruptions.

Inside the town walls were the remains of two houses (Figure 10.3). Building B, preserved over 2 m high in places by a massive brick destruction layer from the upper storey of the building, was a four-room house with post bases separating the long rooms (Room B2). The broadroom (Room B3) contained almost 40 collared pithoi lining the walls of the room and from the collapsed upper storey (Figure 10.5, top, shows the rim of one of these vessels). Six bronze weapons in the destruction debris of the room suggest that the site was destroyed by military attack. A paved annex to the east (Room B1), surrounded by a narrow wall interspersed with post bases, may have been an animal pen. Another building to the south (Building A) contained more collared pithoi in the broadroom (Room A3). In the paved area of Room A2 was a standing stone with a votive altar or table in front, but in the nearby courtyard were domestic remains, sug-

gesting a house with a small shrine.

Parallels to the objects from these structures are found mostly in the highland regions north of Jerusalem and range from pottery to potters' marks to seals. Similarities are notably less extensive in the Jordan Valley. Tall Umayri, however, was larger and somewhat more prosperous than the sites west of the Jordan Valley. The finds probably reflect socioeconomic or lifestyle connections with the highlands of western Palestine. The limited assemblage of the finds suggests a simple economic system brought about by tribal groups beginning a lengthy sedentarization process in the highland areas of Jordan that was more-or-less free of prior occupation. A major catalyst of this initial settlement may have been the north–south trade routes.

In the Jordan Valley, the most important site is Pella, although generally the Iron Age is not very clear there. The remains published as coming from the end of the Late Bronze Age are considered to be transitional, if the pottery published in 1982 also comes from that horizon (McNicoll *et al.* 1982: 121–127); it should, however, be noted that much of the pottery seems to be from later Iron I, as well. Tall Dayr Alla seems to have been uninhabited until slightly later. The large and rich cemetery at Tall Saidiyya with LB IIB and Iron I pottery and other objects suggests a significant town or city there. Indeed, recent excavations have uncovered tantalizing hints of its existence, but the exposure is very small. The Jordan Valley

Figure 10.2 Schematic section of the western defences at Tall Umayri. Iron IIC: No. 13, addition to retaining wall. Late Bronze/
Iron I transitional period: Nos. 1–7. features of Building A (compare with Figure 10.3); No. 8, defensive wall; No. 9,
beaten earth rampart; No. 12, retaining wall; No. 14, bottom of moat; MBIIC: No. 10, beaten earth rampart;
No. 15, bottom of moat.

sites generally produced finds of a much more varied and
luxurious repertoire than the plateau sites.

Iron I (Twelfth–Eleventh Centuries bc)

New sites include, most significantly, those toward the
southern edges of settlement in the regions of Madaba
and Karak, continuing the gradual southward movement
of settlements throughout Iron I. This period includes
several subphases of activity that overlap throughout the
period. Not all the sites listed above were contemporary.

On the northern plateau, Tall Fukhar seems to continue re-using the Late Bronze palace (see Strange, this
volume), while Abila may have extended into this time
period as well. Phase 1 at Tall Irbid, which lasted into
Iron IIB, included a rebuilt city wall and domestic buildings associated with an industrial installation, which the
excavators suggest was for wine. However, the published
evidence for all three sites in this region is sparse.

In central areas, the sites of Tall Umayri and Tall Hisban
continue into the middle of the Iron I period. At the
former site, a storeroom was built on top of the bricky
destruction of the transitional town and at least 18 collared pithoi were embedded in the fallen bricks (Herr
et al. 1997b: fig. 3 bottom, shows an example of one of
these vessels). At Tall Hisban, the bedrock trench (moat?)
was filled with a layer of Iron I pottery representing forms
from the late twelfth and eleventh centuries bc. This
would suggest the trench was no longer in use. The Iron I
pottery from Sahab is virtually identical to that from Tall
Umayri at this time (for one example among many, com-

pare the collared pithos from Tall Umayri at the bottom
of Figure 10.5 (Herr *et al.* 1997b) with an example from
Sahab published by Ibrahim 1978: 116, 119). Of special
interest are the seal impressions on the rims of many of
the Sahab collared pithoi. One rim with a seal impression was found at Tall Umayri. None of the house plans
at Sahab were complete, but enough was uncovered to
characterize the rooms as rectangular and mostly paved
with flagstones (Ibrahim 1974: pls. 15, 18 for the house
plans).

Other central plateau sites which may have continued from the previous period were Amman (incoherent
walls), Madaba (if the late tomb can infer a settlement),
Tall Safut (also without published pottery), and probably
Lahun, though here also published pottery is lacking.
New sites may include Hajjar (a farm or tower, but no
published pottery), Iraq al-Amir town (fills and a possible
fortification wall; note that P. Lapp apparently identified
Iron IIC pottery as Iron I) and Rujm Malfuf South (the
pottery is unpublished). A few potsherds from the period
have been published from Dhiban.

Towards the end of this period settlements were appearing in the Karak region at two very similar sites,
Khirbat Mudayna Ulya and Khirbat Mudayna Muarraja.
Because the ruins are visible on the surface, it is easy to
describe the city walls, towers, town gates, dry moats sev-
ering the sites from neighbouring hills, and the roadways
approaching the sites. Four-room houses are visible and
are sometimes preserved as high as the lintels spanning
the doors. In some cases large slabs of stone are still visible

Abila (?)	Walls (Mare 1992 and other references there)
Amman (?)	Unpublished pottery (Zayadine *et al.* 1987: 308; Najjar 1997); pottery (Dornemann 1983: 97)
Arair (?)	Houses? (Olávarri-Goicoechea1993: 93)
Dhiban	Pottery in secondary deposits (Winnett and Reed 1964: pl. 76.11–13)
Hajjar (?)	Walls (Thompson 1972)
Iraq al-Amir (?)	Fills and possible fortification wall (N. Lapp 1983: 10; 1989: fig. 9b.1–2, 20–23; the rest belong to Iron IIC and later—no. 8 is Roman)
Jarash	Pottery in secondary deposits (Braemer 1986: fig. 15.9–10 [no. 8 is probably LB])
Khirbat Mudayna Ulya	Houses, city walls and gate; eleventh century only (C. Routledge 1995)
Khirbat Mudayna Muarraja	City walls, gate, towers, houses (Olávarri 1978; 1983)
Lahun (?)	Fortified village; casemate wall; four houses (Homès-Fredericq 1997b)
Madaba	Tomb (Piccirillo 1975; Thompson 1986)
Pella VII	Village wall fragments (Bourke 1997)
Rujm Malfuf South (?)	Unpublished pottery (Thompson 1973)
Sahab	Domestic house fragments; collared pithoi burials; burial cave (Ibrahim 1987: 77–78)
Tall Abu Kharaz	Citadel? (Fischer 1994: 130)
Tall Dayr Alla	Phases A to G or H; bronzesmith workshop; pits (Franken 1969)
Tall Fukhar	Reused palace?; house walls; Philistine potsherd (Strange 1997)
Tall Hisban 20–19	Pottery in rock-cut trench (Sauer 1994)
Tall Irbid Phase 1	City wall; houses; wine installation (Lenzen 1988)
Tall Mazar (?)	Courtyard building with cultic objects (Yassine 1988: 115–135)
Tall Nimrin	Wall fragments (Flanagan *et al.* 1994: 212–216)
Tall Safut (?)	Mudbrick installation; unpublished pottery (Wimmer 1989)
Tall Saidiyya XII	Parts of the cemetery (Pritchard 1980, e.g. figs. 16.2, 3; 30.2; 31.1, etc.—brown and black juglets); administrative complex; steps to water source (Tubb *et al.* 1996: 24–27)
Tall Umayri	Storerooms and destruction layer (Clark 1989: 249–250 [Phases 5 and 4; Phase 4 was misdated to early Iron II])

Table 10.2 Excavated sites with at least preliminary reports on the Iron I period.

spanning the rooms of the houses with a corbelling technique. The pottery from the excavations seems to date to the eleventh century bc.

The Jordan Valley site of Pella continued from the earlier period, but the wall fragments are not as yet easily interpreted. Tubb *et al.* (1996) seem to suggest that stone terraces at Tall Saidiyya may lead to entrances to the stepped structure, excavated by Pritchard, which descended to the water source at the foot of the site. The closest parallels to this latter feature are found in Mycenaean Greece (Mycenae and Tiryns). A large residency or administrative complex, possibly with Egyptian connections, was also found there. Three major sites began at this time: Tall Abu Kharaz, Tall Dayr Alla, and Tall Mazar. There may have been a citadel at Tall Abu Kharaz, but the initial report has not been pursued in later seasons of excavation. At Tall Dayr Alla Phases A–G or H all belong to the Iron I period. The first four phases (A–D) include a possibly itinerant bronze-smith's workshop on top of the

Late Bronze sanctuary and probably date to the twelfth century bc. Nearby deposits of clay were used for moulds and the metal was fired in a large oven. Pear-shaped pits were also found around the smithy, as were small wall fragments. Some of the painted pottery has been connected with Philistine ware (Sauer 1986: 12 and fig. 12). The excavators suggest Phase C ended in an earthquake. Phases E–G/H were characterized by a much heavier settlement, but with walls often only one brick wide and founded on a layer of reeds. Phase H produced a major building of uncertain use. Towards the end of the period, an open-court sanctuary was constructed on the lower mound at Tall Mazar with three rooms at the end of a large courtyard. The pottery, much of which was found together outside the door to one of the rooms, dates to the end of Iron I and the beginning of Iron II (Yassine 1988: 122–124). A few wall fragments and pottery appeared at Tall Nimrin.

Figure 10.3 Plan of the Late Bronze/Iron I Transitional period architecture at Tall Umayri. Building A has the shrine in Room A2; Building B is the four-room house (Drawn by D. Clark, L. Herr, J. Lawlor, R. McBain and W. Pillar.

Iron II (Tenth–Sixth Centuries bc)

The most extensive textual sources for Iron II comprise passages from the Deuteronomistic history of the Hebrew Bible, which were written considerably later and, therefore, reflect later historical and theological concerns, especially through the eyes of the kingdom of Judah (Hübner 1992). They chronicle a series of wars between Israel and the Transjordanian states (e.g. 2 Sam 10.7–8; 11.1; 12.26–31; 17.27). Other references mention ambassadors of the kings of Edom, Moab, Ammon, Tyre and Sidon in Jerusalem (Jer. 27.1), probably to arrange a rebellion against Babylon. Many of the prophets castigate the Transjordanian kingdoms for social, political, economic and military offences against Judah. The only Egyptian reference comes from the triumphal reliefs of Shoshenq 1 (945–924 bc) commemorating his successful campaign into Palestine and Transjordan. Names in rows H and V of the topographical list have been identified with Transjordanian sites (Kitchen 1992: 29). From the ninth century bc onwards Egyptian influence in the area was confined to certain artistic elements in the material culture (Kitchen 1992: 30).

Among Assyrian sources the Black Obelisk of Shalmaneser III (858–824 bc) records that "Basa, son of Ruhubi from Ammon" was part of a rebellion (Pritchard 1969: 279; but cf. Millard 1992).

The fact that extant Assyrian texts do not refer to Ammon during the next 110 years suggests that there was little or no contact between them. The Building Inscription of Tiglath-Pileser III (744–727 bc) lists 18 kings who sent tribute to Assyria, including Sanipu of Bit Ammon, Salmanu of Moab, and Qaushmalaku of Edom (Pritchard 1969: 282). These three nations were again listed among

Figure 10.4 Isometric drawing of the Late Bronze/Iron I transitional four-room house at Tall Umayri as reconstructed from the finds in 1996 (drawing by Phonda Root).

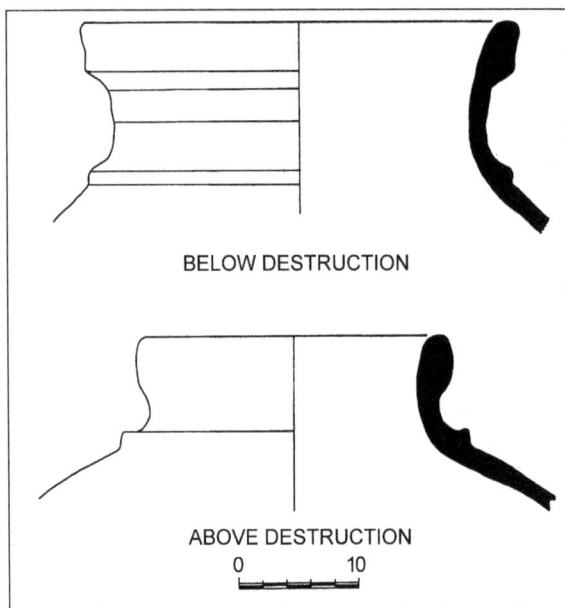

Figure 10.5 Comparison of collared pithos rims from below the destruction of the Late Bronze/Iron I transitional period top) and those above the destruction (bottom).

the tributaries of Sennacherib (704–681 bc): "Buduili from Bet Ammon, Kammusnadbi from Moab, and Aia'rammu from Edom" (Pritchard 1969: 287). Among the 22 kings listed on Cylinder C of Ashurbanipal (668–633 bc) were "Amminadbi king of Bet Ammon, Qaushgabri, king of Edom, Musuri, king of Moab" (Pritchard 1969: 298). Several other texts speak of tribute from the Transjordanian countries in the seventh century bc (see Pritchard 1969: 287–300). Most of the tribute was precious metals such as silver and gold, so we must assume a relatively stable economy in order to meet the demand of such tribute. On the other hand, Assyrian rule stimulated political and socioeconomic stability. It allowed development of national cultures within the broad context of the Assyrian empire and fostered close contact with a wide network of vassal states and provinces (Bienkowski 1992b: 5). The political independence of the vassal states seems to have been assured as long as the tribute was paid. The Assyrian sources apparently suggest that actual Assyrian presence in Moab and Edom did not begin until the reign of Ashurbanipal; nor did they deport anyone from (at least) Moab and Edom (Millard 1992).

After the collapse of the Neo-Assyrian empire in 612 bc and a short rule by Egypt, the Babylonians controlled the region under Nebuchadrezzar II (605–562 bc). In the 580s bc Baalis, the king of Ammon, was a member of an anti-Babylonian rebellion. Josephus states that Ammon and Moab were reconquered in 582/1 bc (*Ant.* 10.9.7). After the collapse of the Neo-Babylonian empire the Transjordanian nations probably became provinces

within the Persian empire. Finds from Tall Umayri suggest this was the case for Ammon, at least (Herr 1997b: 325–327).

Iron IIA (Tenth Century bc)

The early centuries of Iron II are presently very difficult to document in Jordan. Specifically, the tenth century assemblage of pottery is not easy to isolate, making many of the attributions here uncertain. Some could be placed slightly earlier in Iron I. Roughly half of the material attributed to this period comes from tombs, many of which contain mixed ceramic assemblages. Because of these uncertainties and the lack of any significant, large excavations, we cannot make generalizations regarding settlement patterns or zones of material culture. In spite of this dearth of materials, it is possible that, already by this time, we can suggest incipient national groups that controlled parts of the plateau. The following suggestions of population (sociopolitical) groups are based on material culture, inscriptions, the Deuteronomist's accounts in the Bible and later geopolitical developments that reflect continuity of settlement: Israelites (possibly alternating with Aramaeans) seem to have controlled the northern plateau of Irbid and Ajlun; Ammonites began grouping in the region around Amman; other Israelite groups were in the Madaba Plain; Moabites occupied the Dhiban and Karak regions; and Edomites and possibly related groups (e.g. possible groups called Temanites and Midianites etc.) seem to have continued primarily a non-sedentary way of life south of Wadi Hasa. The Israelites probably controlled most of the Jordan Valley.

Northern Plateau

Already by the early ninth century bc the Bible remembers strong antagonisms between Israel and the Aramaeans of Damascus in this region. This geopolitical situation may remember earlier (tenth century bc) claims to the region by both groups. However, during the tenth century bc, the material culture is not well enough established to differentiate between the two societies. Moreover, the population (demography) of the area probably did not change when the geopolitics altered. The sites of the region are either very recently excavated or incompletely published. It is, therefore, very difficult to be sure of their dates and the precise nature of their finds.

The mudbrick "fortress" at Rumayth VIII contained finds largely of a domestic nature. The outer wall of an apparent casemate construction was only 1.25–1.50 m thick and does not inspire certainty that the structure was a fortress. More likely it was simply a small walled settlement, primarily domestic in nature. A small recessed gate pierced the north wall. Because the two subphases were each destroyed by fires it is possible to speculate, among other scenarios, that the border conflicts between Israel and Damascus may have caused them. Sauer confirms

Amman	Tomb G? (Dornemann 1983: 49–50); pottery from soundings mixed with earlier and later forms (Dornemann 1983: 90, 170)
Arair V (?)	Fortress (Olávarri 1965: 85, 87; Olávarri-Goicoechea 1993: 93)
Balua (?)	Storage area; pottery (Worschech and Ninow 1994)
Fadayn (Fedein) (?)	Fortress? (Humbert 1989)
Khirbat Mudayna Ulya (?)	Houses, city walls and gate (C. Routledge 1995)
Khirbat Mudayna Muarraja (?)	City walls, gate, towers, houses (Olávarri 1978, 1983)
Lahun (?)	Fortress for agricultural storage (Homès-Fredericq 1997b)
Madaba	Tomb (Piccirillo 1975; Thompson 1986)
Mafraq	Tomb (Piccirillo 1976)
Nebo?	Tomb (Saller 1966)
Pella VI (?)	Houses with plaster walls, benches, floors, and bins; destruction; tomb (Bourke 1997: 111–113)
Rumayth VIII	Fortress (P. Lapp 1975:114–115)
Sahab	Tomb (Dajani 1970: 33–34)
Tall Dayr Alla H–K	Tower and city wall; houses; jar with insects (Franken 1969)
Tall Hisban	Pottery (Sauer 1994: 239–244)
Tall Husn (?)	Casemate wall? and destruction (Leonard 1987: 359–369)
Tall Irbid	Tomb C (Dajani 1966b); city wall; houses; wine installation (Lenzen 1988)
Tall Mazar	Courtyard building (Yassine 1988: 115–135)
Tall Nimrin	Wall fragments, pottery (Flanagan *et al.* 1994: 212–216)
Tall Saidiyya X–IX	Open courtyard; re-used walls of Stratum XI tower (Tubb 1988: 34–37)

Table 10.3 Excavated sites with at least preliminary reports on the Iron IIA period.

that some of the unpublished pottery was red-slipped and burnished (1986: 14). Another possible fortress was found at Fadayn, but the results are very sketchy.

Irbid Tomb C contained earlier pottery, but some seems to date to this period. The excavations at Tall Irbid have apparently produced a continuous settlement from Iron I to Iron IIB with the same remains described above in the Iron I section. Another tomb was found at Mafraq that has parallels to the tenth century bc ceramic corpus at Hazor (Sauer 1986: 14). The preliminary publication of the sounding at Tall Husn tentatively suggests an early Iron II casemate wall possibly destroyed slightly later (Leonard 1987: 369); some of the pottery seems to belong to this phase (Leonard 1987: figs. 16g; 18a, c, m).

North Central Plateau

The Bible talks about Ammonite kings as contemporaries of David and Solomon, but tenth century bc remains are tantalizing at best on the Amman Citadel where a tomb and small soundings seem to have uncovered ill-defined remains. There also appears to be another tomb at Sahab, re-used from Late Bronze/Iron I times. It is very likely that excavations at Tall Umayri will uncover Iron IIA remains. Large amounts of pottery at Tall Hisban indicate the presence of occupation but all architectural and living

remains were destroyed by later inhabitants, unless the large reservoir dates to this period (Sauer 1994: 241–242; see Iron IIB for more details on its construction).

Madaba Plateau

The tombs at Madaba and Nebo seem to belong to this period and imply settlements at those sites. Nearby Tall Jalul will probably produce tenth century bc remains. The border fortresses at Lahun and Arair were most likely connected geopolitically with the Israelite groups to the north because both sites seem situated ideally to protect access from the south. Dhiban may not have been settled, but we await a better understanding of Moabite pottery.

South Central Plateau

At Balua, eleventh–tenth century bc collared pithoi were discovered in a storage area (Worschech and Ninow 1994: 202; the date is Herr's).

Southern Plateau

We are still not convinced that there was sedentary occupation in the region south of Wadi Hasa. Some have argued for it (Sauer 1986; Finkelstein 1992; but compare Bienkowski 1992a and Herr 1997) partially by misunderstanding the ceramics of Transjordan (Finkelstein) and by the simple assumption that there must be something there (Sauer, pers. comm.). So far there is no clear published evidence that would alter the views of Bienkowski (1992b: 7–8) and others that no Iron Age settlements have been excavated in the region dating before the eighth century bc (but see below regarding recent fieldwork in the Wadi Arabah). Glueck's early publications on Tall Khalayfi at the northern tip of the Gulf of Aqaba misdated a type of hand-made pottery called "Negev Ware" by restricting it to the tenth century bc. A recent reappraisal has placed the earliest remains there in the eighth century bc (Pratico 1993).

Jordan Valley

All four Jordan Valley sites in our list are in the northern part. Pella included houses with a remarkably extensive use of plaster on walls, benches, floors and bins. For the two destructions involved, the excavators suggest a military attack for the first one (Shoshenq? [Shishak]) and an earthquake for the second. A courtyard at Tall Saidiyya was paved with cobbles with depressions that contained large amounts of animal bones and a substance analysed as dung; there were significant amounts of pig bones suggesting an animal pen. The presence of the pig bones could indicate a population of non-Semites or that the Semitic prescription against pigs simply was not practised consistently, or, indeed, was not well known or enforced at that time.

Yassine dates the pottery on the floor of Room 101 in the courtyard building at Tall Mazar to the tenth century bc (1988: 122–124). This would represent the final stage of the building that was probably built towards the end of Iron I. The pottery seems to have fallen from shelves, while the chalices suggest a cultic function for the room. At Tall Dayr Alla, the phases are somewhat difficult to ascribe to centuries because of their relatively large number. It would seem, however, that the round mud-brick tower and associated thick city wall belong here. The excavators suggest this may have been part of a gate complex (van der Kooij 1993). Tall Nimrin has also apparently produced finds from this period.

Wadi Arabah

As early as 1990, the excavations of Fritz (1994) at Barqa al-Hatiya in the Faynan region, uncovered a well-preserved Iron Age house (Fritz 1994). Fritz dated the structure on the basis of the "collared-rim jars" to Iron Age I, while a single radiometric date placed it in Iron Age IIB. Because it now seems evident that collared pithoi continued into Iron Age II in Jordan (Herr 2001), the later date is preferable.

In 1990, Fritz also conducted limited excavations at Khirbat en-Nahas, discovering a structure that corresponds closely with the Iron Age house at Barqa. Hauptmann's team also attained radiometric dates for several of the very extensive copper smelting slag heaps at Khirbat en-Nahas, which were dated from the mid-twelfth to late ninth centuries and at Khirbat Jariyah, which were dated from the twelfth to late tenth centuries (Hauptmann 2000, 66 and summarized in Levy and Adams *et al.* 2004, table 1). These dates have limited usefulness, however, since the carbon samples come from wood used as fuel which may be significantly earlier than the smelting activity with which they are associated.

In 1997, excavations were conducted in the Wadi Fidan 40 cemetery by Levy and Adams (Levy *et al.* 1999). It was found to be a large Iron Age cemetery of what appears to be a nomadic/pastoralist population. The graves produced limited artefactual assemblages outside of stone and glass beads, iron and bronze-alloy jewelry (bracelets, anklets and toe rings), animal hide shrouds and wooden bowls. The cemetery was dated by a single high precision radiocarbon date, to the late Iron Age IIA (Levy and Adams *et al.* 1999, 303). This population—there are literally thousands of graves—may not have been directly related to the copper mining of the Faynan region: of the many hundreds of stone beads, not one was a copper mineral (Adams pers. comm.).

Achaeological surveys of the Faynan Basin (Barker *et al.* 1999; Barker *et al.* [eds.] 2007) and the Wadi Fidan (Levy *et al.* 2001) have revealed extensive Iron Age occupation throughout the wadi system, supporting the evidence from excavations.

Recently, surveys of the Wadi Guwayab and Wadi Jariyah, and excavations at Khirbat en-Nahas by Levy and Adams have provided further significant evidence of extensive Iron Age occupation related to the exploitation of copper mines in the Faynan region. The radiometric dates at Khirbat en-Nahas range between the mid-eleventh–early eighth centuries BC (Levy *et al.* 2004, 870; Levy *et al.* 2005, table 10.1) but cannot be confirmed as yet from published ceramic assemblages.

The density, diversity and extent of the Iron Age occupation throughout the Faynan Basin suggest a re-settlement of the region as early as the Iron Age II with multi-faceted activity patterns, including industrial activity, agriculture, domestic occupation and cemeteries.

Iron IIB (Ninth–Eighth Centuries bc)

With Iron IIB we are able to construct a much more precise synthesis of the people and their culture than we could for Iron IIA. Several major sites have been excavated in several parts of the country and we have more precise historical sources as well (above).

Northern Plateau

After initially being held by Israel, this region probably went to the Aramaeans of Damascus during the ninth century bc wars between the two nations recorded by the Deuteronomist in 2 Kings. The fortified enclosure at Rumayth was bolstered with an outer wall in Stratum VII and a small gate was constructed in the east wall. The heavy destruction, dated by P. Lapp to the mid-ninth century bc, left some of the walls standing 2.5 m high. Both Strata VI and V expanded beyond the fortified enclosure of Stratum V by adding houses in the southeast but their walls were only 50 cm wide. A copper-refining kiln with copious amounts of slag was discovered here. The houses of Stratum V may have been destroyed by Tiglath-Pileser III. At Tall Irbid the earlier houses and thick wall, which probably was part of a fortification system, apparently continued into this period. Some of the Iron II pottery excavated at Tall Husn by Leonard seems early in the period (e.g. Leonard 1987: fig. 16 g, j, p). Only one of the potsherds published by Braemer could be Iron IIB (1987: fig. 2.9—the krater does not seem to have reached the full hole-mouth form of Iron IIC).

Central Plateau

The pottery of Moab (best seen at Dhiban) may be similar to that from Tall Hisban at this time (Sauer 1994: 245), suggesting that Moab may have reached as far north as the southern hills around Amman. Certainly the Mesha Inscription indicates such a scenario. North of Tall Hisban the Ammonites seem to have been the primary group at Tall Umayri and Tall Jawa South.

This period is very weakly witnessed in the Amman region, although pottery and wall fragments have been found at several sites (Amman, Hajjar, Tall Safut, and Tall Umayri). The Amman Citadel Inscription records a major building project at Amman in the second half of the ninth century bc. The statue head of a deity, probably Milkom or Il, seems to come from this time. At Sahab, Ibrahim found a "pillared house" that he equates with the four-room houses west of the Jordan. He notes parallels to the pottery from both Iron IIB and IIC. The most extensively exposed site so far is Tall Jawa South. A casemate wall fortified the settlement and a possible four-or six-chambered gate seems to have pierced the fortifications in the south-

Amman	Possible pottery (Dornemann 1983: 170–71); Citadel Inscription (Thompson and Zayadine 1973)
Arair V–IV	Fortress; reservoir (Olávarri 1965)
Balua	Public building (Worschech 1989)
Busayra	Pottery (Finkelstein 1992—most of these are Iron IIB forms)
Dhiban	Podium for palace?; tower; Mesha Inscription (Tushingham 1972, 1990)
Hajjar	Pottery (Thompson 1972)
Jarash (?)	Pottery? (Braemer 1987: fig. 2.9)
Khirbat Faris	Pottery (Johns *et al.* 1989)
Lahun (?)	Fortress (Homès-Fredericq 1997b)
Madaba	Tomb portions (Thompson 1986)
Mudayna Thamad	City wall; six-chamber gate (Daviau, pers. comm.)
Mazar	Pottery (Yassine 1989)
Nebo	Pottery (Saller and Bagatti 1949)
Pella VI (?)	Houses with plaster walls, benches, floors and bins; destruction; tomb (Bourke 1997; Sauer 1994: 245 and Rumeith VII–V references there) Fortress; casemate wall; houses;
Tall Abu Kharaz 3–4	City wall; towers; pit (Fischer 1995: 102–103; 1996: 103–104)
Tall Dayr Alla IX–VI	Houses; Balaam Inscription (Franken and Ibrahim 1989; van der Kooij 1993)
Tall Hisban	Water reservoir (Sauer 1994: 244–246)
Tall Husn	Pottery (Leonard 1987)
Tall Irbid	City wall; houses; wine installation (Lenzen 1988)
Tall Jalul	Paved road; gate (Herr *et al.* 1996: 71–74)
Tall Jawa South	Houses; casemate wall; gate (Daviau 1996a: 84–90)
Tall Khalayfi IC	Casemate fortress (Pratico 1993: 71)
Tall Nimrin	Pits; pottery (Dornemann 1990: fig. 5.8–22; Flanagan and McCreery 1990: 148)
Tall Safut Sahab (?)	copper-refining kiln (P. Lapp 1975: 115–119) Destruction layer; pottery (Wimmer 1987: 281) Pillared house? (Ibrahim 1987: 78–79)
Tall Saidiyya	VIII–IV Block of houses (Pritchard 1985; Tubb and Dorrell 1991)
Tall Umayri	Wall fragments (Herr *et al.* 1994: 149–150)

Table 10.4 Excavated sites with at least preliminary reports on the Iron IIB period.

east. A large building was composed of four parallel long rooms, but the finds on the floor were not specific enough to suggest a clear function for any of the rooms. In another area, a large warren of at least eleven rooms contained mostly domestic finds. Some of the walls were constructed in the *a telaio* technique whereby segmented or pillared orthostats alternated with uncoursed stone fill.

In the southern part of the region there are many sites that seem to date to this time. The most important site of the area was Dhiban where the Mesha Inscription was discovered at the end of the nineteenth century; it is the longest inscription from the southern Levant and records the Moabite rebellion against Israel (also told from an Israelite perspective in the Bible, 2 Kings 3). At the site of Dhiban itself, later construction has made the early Iron II period virtually impossible to detect outside the pottery in secondary deposits. But there may have been a podium for a palace or temple and a tower. Much of the Iron II pottery from Dhiban seems to date to this period, but Moabite pottery is not well known. The six-chamber gate recently found at Mudayna Thamad had a length of 13.7 m (Daviau 1996b). Beams from the roof were carbon dated to about 800 bc (Daviau, pers. comm.). The finds reflect storage and worship, as well as game playing. For a site this small, the gate represents considerable investment of labour. Besides the casemate wall connected with the six-chamber gate, there was a lower wall encircling the site part way down the slope, perhaps built on a natural promontory. At Arair, Olávarri suggests that the fortress of Stratum V was destroyed by Mesha in the late ninth century bc, and then rebuilt immediately after (Stratum IV). The new fortress had a thick wall surrounding it made up of three parallel walls filled with debris. On the northern side, most vulnerable to attack, a double wall was added. Typical of the constructions Mesha records on his stela, a reservoir found at the northwestern foot of the fortress may have belonged to his works.

The northernmost extremity of Moab was apparently Tall Hisban, which, according to Sauer (above), had pottery more akin to Dhiban than Amman. Certainly the biblical remembrance of Heshbon belonging to Moab (Isa. 16.8–9) may stem from this geopolitical situation. In any case, like Dhiban, the Iron IIB remains at Tall Hisban have been destroyed by later occupants, leaving only pottery in secondary deposits. Tall Jalul may contain some of the best remains, but they seem to be limited to the two stone-paved approach roads and outer (?) gate, preliminarily dated to the ninth and eighth centuries bc. A small fortress at Lahun, overlooking Wadi Mujib, had a main gate in the north and a smaller postern in the south; four towers stood at each of the corners. It is difficult to date the fortress, but some of the pottery appears to be early Iron II (Homès-Fredericq 1992: 196), but some goes into Iron IIC (Homès-Fredericq 1992: 197). Portions of the tombs from Madaba and Nebo seem to extend from Iron IIA into very early Iron IIB.

South Central Plateau

Parts of a large public building were excavated at Balua that produced pottery apparently from Iron IIB and C. This city is the largest site on the Karak Plateau from the Iron II period. The excavators suggest that King Mesha began the major buildings in the ninth century bc, but much more of the site needs to be exposed and published before a clear stratigraphy can be suggested. At Khirbat Faris a few of the published Iron II sherds could be Iron IIB (Johns *et al.* 1989: fig. 23.4, 5, 8).

South Plateau

Very few settlements from this period existed on the southern Edomite Plateau. Indeed, all we have for certain are the Iron II collared pithoi published by Bennett from Busayra in various articles and then grouped by Finkelstein as "Iron I" (1992). We now know, however, that in Transjordan this ceramic form continued throughout Iron II (Herr 2001). Many of the major buildings at the site may have begun toward the end of the eighth century and continued into Iron IIC (see that period for a more detailed description).

Although it does not belong to this region, we will consider Tall Khalayfi here because of its Edomite connections. The earliest building, Glueck's Casemate Fortress IC, seems to have dated to the eighth century, but the attribution of the pottery to strata was impossible to reconstruct (for renewed excavations, see Mussell 1999). It consisted of a four-room building surrounded by a casemate wall (Pratico 1993: 172), and may have functioned as a storage depot for trade on the Red Sea.

Jordan Valley

In the Jordan Valley were several prosperous excavated sites. Because the valley is so long, it may have been associated with several geopolitical entities. Many of the vessels from Tomb 89 at Pella belong to the early centuries of Iron II (Bourke 1997: 112), but the evidence for a contemporary settlement is vague at best. Several metres of later material usually cover Iron Age deposits. Bourke suggests a modest settlement on the northwest slopes of Jabal Abu Khas. At Tall Abu Kharaz early Iron II pottery was found in Strata 4 and 3, which included two towers, a city wall encircling the upper part of the mound and a pit with a metal figurine of a deity. All phases of the large block of 10 houses and the streets flanking it uncovered by Pritchard at Tall Saidiyya belong to this period. The houses contained brick pillars separating some of the rooms, which often contained loom weights arranged in rows, suggesting they were attached to looms when the houses were destroyed. At Tall Mazar and Tall Nimrin early Iron II pottery has been found, but *in situ* remains elude excavators.

The most remarkable find from Tall Dayr Alla IX, dated

to around 800 bc, is the Balaam Inscription found on plaster fragments that had fallen from the wall of a house. It recounts a vision seen by the same prophet Balaam mentioned in the Bible (Num. 22–24). The language and script of the inscription are problematic; scholars are divided as to whether they are Ammonite or Aramaic (Hoftijzer and van der Kooij 1991). An earthquake apparently destroyed the several houses found in this stratum. After two ephemeral phases, Tall Dayr Alla VI produced the remains of several more houses and a storeroom containing many ceramic vessels from the eighth century.

Iron IIC (Seventh–Sixth Centuries bc)

It is from the Iron IIC finds that we have the best evidence for the separation of nationalities based on material culture. As national awareness of the political, social and ideological/religious levels rose, so did its expression in the archaeological record, especially in terms of writing, language, religious art and pottery. In Jordan, the material culture of Iron IIC seems to continue into the early Persian period, perhaps as late as the late fifth century bc (Sauer 1986: 18; Herr 1995). Because there are so many sites from this period, we have decided to present a true synthesis and not mention the finds site-by-site (Herr 1997a for more details).

Northern Plateau

This part of the country seems to have been largely bereft of settlement. The Assyrian destruction seems to have destroyed the local will to establish significant settlements in the area.

Central Plateau and Jordan Valley

This was the era of greatest prosperity for Ammon, whose geographical boundaries seem to have stretched southward through most of the Madaba Plain to the Wadi Wala drainage system. Ammonite material culture is found at Tall Umayri, Tall Jawa South, Hisban 16, Tall Jalul, and on the surface at Khirbat Hari on the bank of a tributary of Wadi Thamad. We probably may include sites in the Jordan Valley east of the river as Ammonite, though their material culture is not as homogeneous as sites on the plateau: Tall Dayr Alla VI, Tall Mazar, Tall Nimrin and Tall Saidiyya IV. The northern border of Ammon may also have extended beyond Wadi Zarqa (biblical Jabbok River) to include possible sites in the Ajlun area. The desert was a natural boundary on the east (Herr 1992).

The settlement pattern of Ammon was centered on Amman where, unfortunately, no major multi-season excavation has yet taken place on the Iron Age remains. Small fragments of city fortifications, building walls of houses and a possible palace, and collections of material culture including fine pottery and a volute (Proto-Ionic) capital, all speak of a thriving royal city. Surrounding it were smaller towns, such as Tall Safut on the north, Iraq al-Amir on the west, Tall Jawa South, Sahab, and, later, Tall Umayri on the south, and the Jordan Valley sites on the west. Smaller villages or agricultural sites were in the hinterland, such as the scores of farmsteads in the highlands around Amman (Younker 1991b), including Mukhayzin and Salama. Some of these smaller sites were fortresses (e.g. Rujm Henu and Drayjat; see Kletter 1991); that is, they were situated in strategic locations, were somewhat larger than the agricultural sites, and had no associated agricultural installations, for example, winepresses. Ammon was thus a large city-state with its major capital city surrounded by scattered towns/villages, fortresses and rural farmsteads.

Rainfall in the highlands is sufficient for dry farming. Grain was produced in the valleys and plains, while orchards and vegetables grew on the hillsides and flocks grazed in the open spaces between fields and on the eastern steppe bordering the desert. Later, when the Babylonians took over the area and the Ammonite king Baalyasha (a seal impression of one of his officials was found at Tall Umayri [Herr 1985]) conspired against them with a prince of Judah (Jer. 40.14), the Babylonians conquered them and placed them under tribute (Josephus, *Ant.* 10.9.7). The administrative site of Tall Umayri was apparently built at that time to oversee the crown's investment in wine production at scores of farmsteads in the hinterland to pay this tribute (many of the rural sites in Tall Umayri's hinterland were associated with one or more winepresses).

No Ammonite site has been excavated extensively enough to gain a clear picture of an urban plan. The best glimpse is Tall Umayri, but it was not a normal residential site and was founded very late in the period. It included administrative buildings in the southwestern quarter of the site with domestic structures housing the officials to the north and east. There was no city wall, but a monumental entrance structure with a small shrine (standing stone and basin) were found facing the valley where the King's Highway most likely passed. But no streets have been found. Tall Jawa South was a fortified residential site with houses inside a casemate wall, but here also nothing can be said about street plans.

An idea of architectural plans of Ammonite buildings is beginning to emerge. The rectangular plan of the Ammonite fortresses is best seen at Rujm Henu in the Baqah Valley and Drajyat south of Tall Umayri. Most of these fortress sites were inhabited in later centuries, making clear descriptions difficult. The palace of the Ammonite kings or at least a major administrative building may have been found at Amman in the east-central part of the site by a French–Jordanian team (Zayadine *et al.* 1989: 362). Certainly the building was an important one with very large walls surrounding a courtyard paved with a high-quality plaster floor. The rich finds and their international flair (a clay mask, Phoenician ivories, a green glass

Abila	Burial; domestic remains (Mare 1991)
Abu Nusayr	Tomb (Abu Ghanimeh 1984)
Adir (?)	Wall fragments (Cleveland 1960)
Amman	Palace?; wall fragments; tombs (Dornemann 1983; Zayadine *et al.* 1987, 1989); wall fragments; storeroom, storage pits (Najjar 1997)
Arbid	Farmstead (B. Routledge 1995)
Baja III	Acro-site (Lindner and Farajat 1987)
Balua	Houses; pottery (Worschech 1989: 202–203)
Busayra	Palace; city wall (Bienkowski 1990)
Dhiban	Pottery (Tushingham 1972)
Drayjat	Fortress (Younker *et al.* 1990: 11–14)
Ghrareh	Fortress; four-room house (Hart 1989)
Hajjar	Circular tower (Thompson 1972, 1977)
Iraq al-Amir	Fortification wall; pottery (N. Lapp 1989: 285, 288)
Jabal Qsayr	Acro-site (Lindner *et al.* 1996b)
Khilda	Circular tower and house (Najjar 1992)
Khirbat Mudayna Thamad	Casemate city wall; six-chamber gate (Daviau 1996b)
Lahun	Town settlement (Homès-Fredericq 1992)
Madaba	City wall (Harrison, pers. comm.)
Muallaq	Fortress (Lindner *et al.* 1996a)
Mudaybi	Fortress; volute capitals (Mattingly 1997)
Mukhayzin	Watchtower (Thompson 1984)
Nebo	Tomb (Saller and Bagatti 1949; Saller 1966)
Rujm Henu	Fortress (Clark 1983; McGovern 1993: 146)
Rujm Malfuf South	Farmstead? (Thompson 1973)
Sahab	Wall fragments (Ibrahim 1987: 79, here dated to the eighth and seventh centuries bc)
Salama	Farmstead? (Lenzen and McQuitty 1989; Bikai 1993: 521)
Sela	Neo-Babylonian inscription (Dalley and Goguel 1997)
Tall Abu Kharaz 1–2	City wall; towers; pit (Fischer 1995: 102–103; 1996: 103–104)
Tall Dayr Alla VI	Houses; pits (van der Kooij 1993: 341)
Tall Hisban 16	Wall fragments; reservoir (Fisher 1994; Lugenbeal and Sauer 1972)
Tall Iktanu (?)	Fortress; watchtower; silos (Prag 1989; 1990: 122)
Tall Jalul	Tripartite pillared building; pillared house (Younker *et al.* 1997: 232)
Tall Jawa South	Casemate wall; house (Daviau 1996a: 90–93)
Tall Khalayfi	Offset-inset wall; gate fortress (Pratico 1993: 26–28; Mussell 1999)
Tall Mazar	Tombs (Yassine 1984)
Tall Nimrin	Pottery; wall fragments (Dornemann 1990)
Tall Safut	City wall; houses (Wimmer 1987)
Tall Saidiyya IV	Pits (Pritchard 1985)
Tall Siran	Bottle inscription (Thompson and Zayadine 1973)
Tawilan	Houses; unfortified (Bennett and Bienkowski 1995)
Thamayil	Farmstead (B. Routledge 1995)
Tall Umayri	Administrative buildings; houses; monumental entry (Herr 1991, 1997a)
Tall Umayri	Five farmsteads and one fortress (Geraty et al. 1988: 226-28; Younker *et al.* 1990: 11–13; 1993: 209; 1996: 68)
Umm Biyara	Houses (Bienkowski 1990)
Umm Dananir	Cobbled courtyard; ostracon (McGovern 1993: 147)

Table 10.5 Excavated sites with at least preliminary reports on the Iron IIC period.

goblet, lapis lazuli fragments, and perhaps four double-faced Hathor heads) suggest a palatial interpretation. The administrative buildings at Tall Umayri had very thick walls (up to 2 m) and were constructed with basements. One of the buildings was constructed in the four-room plan. A tripartite pillared building at Tall Jalul is the first one found in Transjordan. City walls included casemate structures at Tall Jawa South and the fortress of Rujm Henu. A very thick solid wall was uncovered in 1998 at Madaba and another solid wall seems to have circled Amman; the latter also possibly included a circular tower. A city gate was discovered at Tall Jawa South, but its plan has not yet been published. A house at Tall Umayri, only partially excavated, may have had a four-room plan with a cobbled longroom and a cobbled broadroom. But the form is otherwise rare in Ammon; indeed, there does not seem to be a typical Ammonite house plan. One of the houses at Tall Jawa South contained two stairways and monolithic pillars separating some of the eleven rooms (Daviau 1996a: 90–93). Another flight of steps was found at Khilda; it led to a platform at the level of the second floor. Other house fragments have been found at Tall Dayr Alla VI, Tall Jalul, Tall Safut and Sahab. Several houses have over ten interconnected rooms. It is possible that these are basements supporting a more coherent plan in the upper storey.

Of the 150 buildings that have been identified as "Ammonite monumental structures" (35 circular "towers," 122 rectangular "fortresses"), only about 6% have been excavated. Much debate has centred around them regarding function (were they fortresses or towers connecting a military defence system, or were they agricultural facilities, and/or settlements?) and date (were they Iron Age, Roman, or Byzantine or multi-period?). The best suggestion seems to be that of Younker (1991b) and others who say that the buildings on hilltops with strategic views in many directions functioned militarily, while those on hillsides overlooking valleys and next to orchards were farmsteads. Many of them were initially built in the Iron Age, but were re-used in one or more later periods. Some, on the other hand, were not Iron Age at all, as was apparently the case with Rujm Malfuf North.

Ammonite pottery entered its most distinctive and superior phase in Iron IIC as potting technologies improved, perhaps from Assyrian inspiration. Very few of the typical vessel forms found in Ammon have been discovered outside the region. Several excavations on the Ammonite plateau have produced a great amount of Ammonite pottery in the last two decades, including Tall Hisban (first defined by Lugenbeal and Sauer 1972), Rujm Henu, Tall Umayri, Tall Jawa South and Tall Jalul. The Jordan Valley sites of Tall Dayr Alla and Tall Saidiyya have it too, but not in the same proportions, and it is almost completely lacking from Pella (perhaps because the site was not occupied; Bourke 1997: 113). Several types of fine wares included elegant shallow bowls or plates, sometimes rivalling the much later Nabataean ware for fineness; there were also decoratively burnished bowls, some with a grey burnish made with a manganese tool; but the most distinctive development occurred with a variety of burnished black bowls called, fittingly enough, "black-burnished ware."

The imported items found in the palace at Amman, as well as the Ammonite black-burnished bowl from Tell Batash in Judah (Kelm and Mazar 1985: fig. 16.4), indicate active trade patterns. There was a major north–south road in Transjordan traditionally called the "King's Highway;" and at least two other roads must have crossed the Jordan Valley from Amman to Jerusalem and the Samaria region. Trade on the King's Highway is represented in the lists of goods on the Tall Hisban ostraca (soon to be published in full in a book of collected essays by F.M. Cross). The sites in the Jordan Valley may have seen more traded items than those on the plateau because they were on both north–south and east–west routes. The tombs at Tall Mazar illustrate this with their Assyrian, Judaean and Phoenician vessels (Yassine 1984). There are also indications from sites on the plateau for trade with Phoenicia: artistic motifs suggest Phoenician themes (Bordreuil 1973); pottery from tombs in Amman (Gal 1995: 90–91); and a seal written in Ammonite script mentioning Astarte of Sidon (below). The lenticular body of a New Year Flask from Egypt, made of a greenish-turquoise faience, was found in a storage cave near an agricultural site in the Tall Umayri region (Younker 1991a: fig. 12.122.15). These vessels were traded all over the Mediterranean during the Saite (26th) dynasty (seventh–sixth centuries bc) (Homès-Fredericq 1992: 198).

Ammonite scribes developed their own distinctive writing style after borrowing the Aramaic script at the beginning of Iron IIB (Cross 1975; Herr 1980). The formal script is characterized by vertical stances; the heads of some letters opened very late in the seventh century, following an Aramaic development that began a century earlier. The most important inscription of the period is the Siran Bottle, which contained eight lines of Ammonite semi-cursive writing of around 600 bc. It mentions at least three kings of Ammon (Thompson and Zayadine 1973; Cross 1973). There are also scores of seals with several found *in situ* at Tall Umayri and one of its agricultural farmsteads (Aufrecht 1989). The most famous one is the seal impression of an official of an Ammonite king named Ba'alyasha (Herr 1985). There were also several ostraca found in the fill of the Tall Hisban 16 reservoir; several of them represent receipts of trade items. The Ammonite script gave way to Aramaic in the middle of the sixth century bc (Cross 1975).

The Ammonite language belonged to the "Canaanite" family of Northwest Semitic, but contained what appears to be an element of Arabic, especially in names, perhaps because of Ammon's proximity to the eastern desert.

Ammonite differs from neighbouring Hebrew and Moabite in small but not insignificant ways (Jackson 1983: 108). One difference seems to have been a different pronunciation of sibilants (Hendel 1996).

The religion of Ammon centred around its god Milkom, who may be depicted by several male statues and figurines wearing the *atef* crown (Daviau and Dion 1994). Like Yahweh in Judah he was probably an Il (Hebrew = El) deity; his iconographic symbol of a bull with huge horns is ubiquitous on Ammonite seals (Aufrecht 1989). A seal written in Ammonite script that mentions Astarte of Sidon suggests that Ammonites also worshipped Astarte. No Ammonite temples have been found, but small shrines or cultic corners were found at Tall Umayri (a standing stone with a basin at the entrance to the settlement) and perhaps in the palace at Amman.

There is less evidence of large, monumental art than in Iron IIB, although some of the statues mentioned above may have come from Iron IIC. Tall Umayri produced fragments of a life-sized ceramic statue or anthropomorphic cultic object in 1998 (unpublished as yet). Fertility goddess figurines, some with eyes bugged out and noses made by pinching the clay between thumb and forefinger, are the most frequent human types of figurines, while horses with riders, bovines and lions are the most frequent animals depicted. Seals also present iconographic scenes. One example from Tall Umayri, though it is extremely small, is so nicely carved we can suggest that the species of bird on the seal was an orange-tufted sunbird, a small nectar-feeding bird still seen today (Herr 1997b). The seal impression of the official of Ba'alyasha contained the depiction of a flying scarab beetle, probably a royal symbol as it was in Judah on the *lmlk* jars (Younker 1985).

The several tombs found in the Amman region were chambers cut into bedrock cliffs, much like those from the Jerusalem area. A very large cemetery in the Jordan Valley at Tall Mazar, which was made up mostly of pit graves, produced a cornucopia of finds, including pottery, glass, stone and metal vessels, bronze weapons, jewellery, beads, seals and bone and shell objects (Yassine 1984).

A water system has been known at the Citadel of Amman as early as 1889 (Conder 1889: 34). Further investigations have been conducted since the beginning of the twentieth century (Dornemann 1983: 90; Zayadine *et al.* 1989: 357, fig. 1–2). The underground water system consists of a large plastered cistern (c. 700 m³) that is most likely later in date and a 23 m long passageway carved in the native rock, leading from the top of the cistern. The difference in the altitude between the entrance of the shaft and the floor of the reservoir exceeds 17 m. The occupation in the area went back to MB II and Iron Age periods (Dornemann 1983: 90), making it possible that the water system was in use during these periods. Among other water systems, the most significant was the reservoir at Tall Hisban that continued in use from Iron IIB. It measured 17 x 17

m in size and was 7 m deep and could have held around 2000 m³ of water (about 2 million litres). The interesting feature of the reservoir was that it was so near the top of the mound and, even though every drop of rainfall could have been channelled into it, it would have needed thousands more donkey loads of water to fill it.

South Central Plateau

From the few excavations that have been conducted in Moab it would seem that the most significant remains come from Iron IIB. But the pottery of Moab is not well enough known for us to subdivide Iron II easily. Moreover, very recently excavated sites are beginning to produce results from Iron IIC. The Moabite remains from Khirbat Mudayna Thamad represent the northeastern border. Some feel that Moab was eclipsed at this time by Arab tribes (Olávarri-Goicoechea 1993: 93). However, an Egyptian New Year Flask was found at Lahun confirming trade on the King's Highway during Iron IIC. The houses at Balua have only been partially excavated and we do not have enough to suggest coherent plans.

A monumental gate (at least four chambers) was uncovered at Mudaybi that contained four or more large volute (proto-Ionic) capitals (Drinkard 1997). This large fortress is surrounded by a huge fortification wall and was apparently intended to guard approaches to the Karak region through the Fajj, a natural roadway connecting the King's Highway with the Desert Highway to the east.

A few (under 30) Moabite seals from this time, whose owners carry the theophoric element Kemosh in their names, indicate that at least some organized entity of Moab existed. In fact, one seal refers to its owner as a *mazkir* or official "recorder," probably of the government (Israel 1987). Moabite writing was similar to Hebrew but with larger heads on some letters and a squatter look overall; some letters were also similar to Aramaic or Ammonite. A beautifully preserved papyrus contains a short inscription in Moabite writing that refers to a *marzeah* (Bordreuil and Pardee 1990), usually interpreted as a funerary feast. Some scholars, however, doubt the authenticity of the document because it was purchased on the antiquities market and is in remarkably good shape for an ancient document. Isolated farmsteads have been excavated at Thamayil and Arbid.

The Moabite language was very closely related to Hebrew, except for a few differences, such as - *'in* for the masculine plural ending instead of Hebrew- *'im* (Jackson 1983: 108). The best inscription for Moabite is the Mesha Stela that is dated to Iron IIB; it is virtually identical to what we know of Hebrew of that period.

Southern Plateau

Almost all Iron Age remains in Edom date to this period, when the Edomites also expanded to the west into the southern Negev. The core territory of Edom, however, was southeast of the Dead Sea around the capital city of Busayra situated on a ridge with a stunning view overlooking deep wadis. Here were the only major public architectural remains so far found in Edom, except for the fortresses at Tall Khalayfi and Hazeva 5–4. Tawilan was a small town, while Muallaq seems to have been a fortress. There were also several small settlements in out-of-the-way locations high on rugged mountain tops, such as Umm Biyara in Petra, Sela, Baja III and Jabal Qsayr, as well as others located by surveys but not yet excavated (Lindner 1992). The difficult access to these "acro-sites" reminds one of the rocky fastness of which the biblical texts sometimes speak of Edom (2 Chron. 25.12). Because these sites were made up of residences and not fortresses, they present a problem of interpretation. Why were they inhabited? Were conditions so bad that people simply moved there to live? How could they support themselves 300 m above the floor of (later) Petra at Umm Biyara? Were these sites constructed much like the *ghorfas* of the Berbers in North Africa, as places of retreat during military invasions or raids? In fact, the small rooms, low doors and lack of streets at Umm Biyara remind one of the Lilliputian features of the *ghorfas*.

Edom was located in a narrow strip of cultivable land where dry farming could occur in the highlands east of the Wadi Arabah, which reach over 1500 m in altitude. Outside this strip the climatic conditions are that of a semi-desert at best where there was probably a strong element of nomadic pastoralism. This difficult climate is probably what inhibited Edomite sedentarism in the earlier parts of the Iron Age even though we have them mentioned by name on Egyptian inscriptions of the Late Bronze Age (Kitchen 1992).

Because of the specialized nature of Edomite sites, it is difficult to draw a good picture of a typical Edomite urban plan. A solid city wall surrounded Busayra with a simple opening in the wall 2 m wide for a gate (probably a postern). In the middle of the site were two phases of a monumental building, possibly a temple in the Assyrian style. A portion of another public building was excavated to the south that may have been a palace, again in the Assyrian style. Some even suggest the Assyrians may have constructed the buildings for themselves, but there is little other evidence for a dominant physical Assyrian presence. Residential areas probably surrounded the monumental buildings. The residential town of Tawilan was unwalled but excavations were too limited to gain a good picture. No streets are visible in the plans, leaving one with the impression of a warren of walls and rooms. The acro-site of Umm Biyara also reminds one of a warren. The excavations were fairly widespread, but no streets were found. The plan of the fortress at Tall Khalayfi is clear during two phases following the eighth century bc phase (Pratico 1993). A new thick wall enclosed the Iron IIB structure into a large area probably including a few residences.

The architecture of the possible temple at Busayra has a plan much like Assyrian buildings, with large open courts surrounded by rooms; but much of the building lies below a modern school and cannot be excavated. The thickness of the walls and the size of the rooms suggest the structure was a very important one. After entering the probable temple in the courtyard, one could turn to the right and walk up a series of broad stairs and enter a long room that may have been the cella. Two stone bases flanked the entrance at the top of the stairs and may have been to support columns or statues. Because of the presence of pottery statuary at other Edomite shrines in the west (Qitmit and Hazeva 5— see below), the latter suggestion may be correct, although no statuary has been found at Busayra. Other rooms flanked the central structure in this monumental compound. The central building in the fortress at Tall Khalayfi was a large version of a four-room house. When they existed, city walls tended to be solid, such as Busayra; those of fortresses could be casemate or solid (offset-inset). Too few complete or coherent houses have been excavated at Edomite sites to be certain if there was a typical Edomite house plan or not; however, one four-room example was uncovered at Ghrareh. At times, it is also difficult to separate one house from its neighbour. Several rooms at Tawilan had pillars. One feature of houses in Edom appears to be their close connection to neighbouring buildings. The warren-like nature of their residences at Tawilan and Umm Biyara may reflect a lack of privacy or an intense awareness of kinship. A few door lintels were preserved at Umm Biyara; their low height of about 1.3–1.5 m probably indicates economy or a temporary/emergency type of settlement rather than the short stature of the people.

Edomite architecture lacked ashlar masonry at Busayra. Mudbrick was used at Tall Khalayfi where stone would have had to be brought from several kilometres away; flat slabs of stone were used at Umm Biyara because they were ready at hand.

Edomite painted pottery, found in great quantities at Busayra but also elsewhere, is characterized by multi-coloured bands and geometric patterns; it is distinctive and easily recognizable. Even the unpainted pottery such as jugs and cooking pots can be clearly identified as Edomite.

Another aspect of Iron II pottery in the southern reaches of Jordan is called Negev ware. It was handmade and is found from southern Jordan to Sinai. But rather than identifying it with Edomites, it should more properly be identified with the pastoral–nomadic lifestyle of the desert people; any group living in the area could have made it.

Trade is probably best represented at the Edomite fortress at Tall Khalayfi, situated at the tip of the Gulf of Aqaba. Although it is presently located about half a kilometre from the coast, in antiquity the coastline was farther inland. Its main building was probably a well-fortified storehouse or emporium for receiving and sending shipped goods. Other Edomite trade probably passed through its holdings to the west. Hazeva 5–4 was located at a junction of the north–south road in the Wadi Arabah with an east–west route leading from the King's Highway via Wadi Hasa/Wadi Faynan and northern Edom to Gaza. Holding these sites would have secured the Arabian caravan trade in Edomite hands.

Like Moabite, Edomite script is characterized by a syncretistic use of some letters in a Hebrew style and others in an Aramaic style and two letters that sometimes are written upside down. Many of the names in this script use the theophoric element Qaus (or Qôs), the Edomite deity. Several seals have been found at sites in both Jordan and the Negev, and ostraca were found at Tall Khalayfi and Busayra. The Edomite language, based on these and other ostraca, is closely related to Hebrew and Moabite within the "Canaanite" family of Northwest Semitic. Indeed, one scholar has recently stated that there are no features that would suggest Edomite was an independent dialect from Hebrew (Vanderhooft 1995). One of the most astounding finds from the territory of Edom was the discovery of a Neo-Babylonian cuneiform inscription high on the cliff at Sela. There was probably a major road descending from the highlands to the Wadi Faynan area at this point.

Because of the sensational sculptural finds west of the Wadi Arabah at Qitmit and Hazeva 5–4, we can now say more about the iconography and visual aspects of Edomite religion than any other group among the nations of the southern Levant. The religion of their national deity, Qaus (or Qôs was probably very much like that of Yahweh in Judah, Milkom in Ammon and Kemosh in Moab. If he was the one depicted on the statues found at Qitmit (his name figures prominently in the inscriptions found there; Beit-Arieh 1995) and Hazeva, he had a barrel chest, a beard and moustache, and was dressed in a pointed headdress and possibly a fringed garment. The three rooms of the rectangular structure at Qitmit suggest a triad of deities, including no doubt the goddess Asherah (or Astarte) whose figurines were found at Qitmit. Among the animal figurines from Qitmit was a stunning example of a cherub, or sphinx, leading us to suggest a similarity to the Jerusalem cult of Yahweh whose primary iconography was the cherub (a guardian composite beast).

Water was always a problem in Edom. Its relative scarcity did not allow its inhabitants to reach the same prosperity as their northern neighbours and it limited the rate at which they could sedentarize. Springs could be found in the low valleys, but in the acro-sites the people needed to depend completely on cisterns. Indeed, the name Umm Biyara means "Mother of Cisterns."

Conclusion

The two primary aspects of settlement patterns in Jordan during the Iron Age were the gradual growth of "national" or "group" awareness among territorial segments of society and the gradual spread of occupation from north to south.

Bibliography

Abu Ghanimeh, K.

1984 Abu Nseir Excavations. *Annual of the Department of Antiquities of Jordan* 28: 305–310.

Aufrecht, W.E.

1989 *A Corpus of Ammonite Inscriptions*. Lewiston: Mellon.

Barker, G.W., R.B. Adams, O.H. Creighton, D. Crook, D.D. Gilbertson, J.P. Grattan, C.O. Hunt, D.J. Mattingly, S.J. McLaren, H.A. Mohammed, P. Newson, C. Palmer, B. Pyatt, T.E.G. Reynolds, R. Tomber.

1999 Environment and Land Use in the Wadi Faynan, Southern Jordan: the Third Season of Geoarchaeology and Landscape Archaeology (1998). Levant 31: 255–292.

Barker, G.W. D. Gilbertson, and D. Mattingly (eds)

2007 Archaeology and Desertification: The Wadi Faynan Landscape Survey, Southern Jordan. Levant Supplementary Series. Council for British Research in the Levant in Association with Oxbow Books.

Beit-Arieh, I.

1995 *Horvat Qitmit: An Edomite Shrine in the Biblical Negev*. Tel Aviv: Sonia and Marco Nadler Institute of Archaeology.

Bennett, C.-M. and P. Bienkowski

1995 *Excavations at Tawilan in Southern Jordan*. British Monographs in Archaeology 8. Oxford: Oxford University Press.

Bienkowski, P.

1990 Umm el-Biyara, Tawilan and Buseirah in Retrospect. *Levant* 22: 91–109.

1992a The Beginning of the arkerIron Age in Edom: A Reply to Finkelstein. *Levant* 24: 167–170.

1992b The Beginning of the Iron Age in Southern Jordan: A Framework. In P. Bienkowski (ed.), *Early Edom and Moab: The Beginning of the Iron Age in Southern Jordan*, 1–12. Sheffield Archaeological Monographs 7. Sheffield: J.R. Collis.

Bienkowski, P. and R.B. Adams

1999 Soundings at Ash-Shorabat and Khirbat Dubab in the Wadi Hasa. Jordan: the Pottery. *Levant* 31: 149–72.

Bienkowski, P., R.B. Adams, R.A. Philpott and L. Sedman

1997 Soundings at Ash-Shorabat and Khirbat Dubab in the Wadi Hasa, Jordan: the Stratigraphy. *Levant* 29: 41–70.

Bikai, P.M.

1993 Khirbet Salameh 1992. *Annual of the Department of Antiquities of Jordan* 37: 521–532.

Bordreuil, P.

1973 Inscriptions sigillaires ouest-sémitique. *Syria* 50: 181–185.

Bordreuil, P. and D. Pardee

1990 Le papyrus du marzeah. *Semitica* 38: 49–68.

Bourke, S.J.

1997 Pre-Classical Pella in Jordan: A Conspectus of Ten Years' Work. *Palestine Exploration Quarterly* 129: 94–115.

Braemer, F.

1986 Etudes complémentaires. In F. Zayadine (ed.), *Jerash Archaeological Project 1981–1983*, 61–66. Amman: Department of Antiquities.

1987 Two Campaigns of Excavations on the Ancient Tell of Jarash. *Annual of the Department of Antiquities of Jordan* 31: 525–529.

Clark, D.R.

1989 Field B: The Western Defense System. In L.T. Geraty L.G. Herr, Ø.S. Labianca and R.W. Younker (eds.), *Madaba Plains Project 1: The 1984 Season at Tell el-'Umeiri and Vicinity and Subsequent Studies*, 244–257. Berrien Springs, MI: Andrews University/Institute of Archaeology.

1994 The Iron I Defense System at Tell el-'Umeiri, Jordan. *Biblical Archaeologist* 57: 241–242.

1997 Field B: The Western Defensive System. In L.G. Herr L.T. Geraty, Ø.S. Labianca and R.W. Younker (eds.), *Madaba Plains Project 3: The 1989 Season at Tell el-'Umeiri and Vicinity and Subsequent Studies*, 53–98. Berrien Springs, MI: Andrews University/Institute of Archaeology.

Clark, V.A.

1983 The Iron IIC/Persian Pottery from Rujm al Henu. *Annual of the Department of Antiquities of Jordan* 27: 143–163.

Cleveland, R.L.

1960 The Excavation of the Conway High Place (Petra) and Soundings at Khirbet Ader. *Annual of the American Schools of Oriental Research* 34–35: 79–97.

Conder, C.R.

1889 *The Survey of Eastern Palestine: Memoirs of the Topography, Orography, Hydrography, Archaeology, etc. The 'Adwan Country*. London: Palestine Exploration Fund.

Cross, F.M.

1973 Notes on the Ammonite Inscription from Tell Siran. *Bulletin of the American Schools of Oriental Research* 212: 12–15.

1975 Ammonite Ostraca from Heshbon: Heshbon Ostraca IV–VIII. *Andrews University Seminary Studies* 13: 1–20.

Dajani, R.W.

1966a Jabal Nuzha Tomb at Amman. *Annual of the Department of Antiquities of Jordan* 11: 48–51.

1966b Four Iron Age Tombs from Irbid. *Annual of the Department of Antiquities of Jordan* 11: 88–101.

1970 A Late Bronze–Iron Age Tomb Excavated at Sahab, 1968. *Annual of the Department of Antiquities of Jordan* 15: 29–34.

Dalley, S. and A. Goguel

1997 The Sela' Sculpture: A Neo-Babylonian Rock Relief in Southern Jordan. *Annual of the Department of Antiquities of Jordan* 41: 169–176.

Daviau, P.M.

1996a The Fifth Season of Excavations at Tall Jawa (1994): A Preliminary Report. *Annual of the Department of Antiquities of Jordan* 40: 83–100.

1996b Wadi eth-Themed. *American Center of Oriental Research Newsletter* 8(1): 5–6.

Daviau, P.M. and P.E. Dion

1994 El, the God of the Ammonites? The Atef-Crowned Head from *Tell Jawa*, Jordan. *Zeitschrift des Deutschen Palästina-Vereins* 110: 158–167.

Dornemann, R.H.

1983 *The Archaeology of the Transjordan in the Bronze and Iron Ages*. Milwaukee: Milwaukee Public Museum.

1990 Preliminary Comments on the Pottery Traditions at Tell Nimrin, Illustrated from the 1989 Season of Excavations. *Annual of the Department of Antiquities of Jordan* 34: 153–181.

Drinkard, J.F.

1997 New Volute Capital Discovered. *Biblical Archaeologist* 60: 249–250.

Finkelstein, I.

1992 Edom in the Iron I. *Levant* 24: 159–166.

Fischer, P.M.

1994 Tell Abu al-Kharaz: The Swedish Jordan Expedition 1992: Third Season Preliminary Excavation Report. *Annual of the Department of Antiquities of Jordan* 38: 127–145.

1995 Tall Abu al-Kharaz: The Swedish Jordan Expedition 1993: Fourth Season Preliminary Excavation Report. *Annual of the Department of Antiquities of Jordan* 39: 93–119.

1996 Tall Abu-Kharaz: The Swedish Jordan Expedition 1994: Fifth Season Preliminary Excavation Report. *Annual of the Department of Antiquities of Jordan* 40: 101–110.

1997 *A Late Bronze to Early Iron Age Tomb at Sahem, Jordan*. Wiesbaden: Otto Harrassowitz.

Fisher, J.R.

1994 Hesban and the Ammonites during the Iron Age. In D. Merling and L.T. Geraty (eds.), *Hesban after 25 Years*, 81–96. Berrien Springs, MI: Andrews University/Institute of Archaeology.

Flanagan, J.W. and D.W. McCreery

1990 First Preliminary Report of the 1989 Tell Nimrin Project. *Annual of the Department of Antiquities of Jordan* 34: 131–152.

Flanagan, J.W. and D.W. McCreery

1994 Tell Nimrin Preliminary Report on the 1993 Season. *Annual of the Department of Antiquities of Jordan* 38: 205–244.

Franken, H.J.

1969 *Excavations at Tell Deir 'Alla I.* Leiden: E.J. Brill.

1992 *Excavations at Tell Deir 'Alla: The Late Bronze Age Sanctuary.* Louvain: Peeters.

Franken, H.J. and M.M. Ibrahim

1989 Deir 'Alla (Tell). In D. Homès-Fredericq and J.B. Hennessy (eds.), *Archaeology of Jordan.* II.1. *Field Reports: Surveys and Sites A–K*, 201–205. Akkadica Supplementum 7. Leuven: Peeters.

Fritz, V.

1994 Vorbericht über die Grabungen in Barqa el-Hetiye im Gebiet von Fenan, Wadi el-'Araba (Jordanien) 1990. *Zeitschrift des Deutschen Palästina-Vereins* 110: 125–50

Gal, Z.

1995 The Diffusion of Phoenician Cultural Influence in Light of the Excavations at Hurvat Rosh Zayit. *Tel Aviv* 22: 89–93.

Geraty, L.T, L.G. Herr and Ø.S. LaBianca

1988 The Joint Madaba Plains Project: A Preliminary Report on the Second Season at Tell el-'Umeiri and Vicinity. *Andrews University Seminary Studies* 26: 217–252.

Hadidi, A.

1970 The Pottery from the Roman Forum at Amman. *Annual of the Department of Antiquities of Jordan* 15: 11–15.

Harding, G.L. and B.S.J. Isserlin

1953 An Early Iron Age Tomb at Madeba. *Palestine Exploration Fund Annual* 4: 27–33.

Hart, S.

1989 Ghrareh. In Homès-Fredericq and J.B. Hennessy (eds.), *Archaeology of Jordan.* II.1. *Field Reports: Surveys and Sites*, 241–245. Akkadica Supplementum 7. Leuven: Peeters.

1995 The Pottery. In C.-M. Bennett and P. Bienkowski (eds.), *Excavations at Tawilan in Southern Jordan*, 53–66. British Monographs in Archaeology 8. Oxford: Oxford University Press.

Hauptmann, A.

2000 *Zur frühen Metallurgie des Kupfers in Fenan/Jordanien.* Der Anschnitt Beiheft 11. Bochum: Deutsches Bergbau Museum.

Hendel, R.S.

1996 Sibilants and *sibbolet* (Judges 12:6). *Bulletin of the American Schools of Oriental Research* 301: 69–76.

Herr, L.G.

1980 The Formal Scripts of Iron Age Transjordan. *Bulletin of the American Schools of Oriental Research* 238: 21–34.

1985 The Servant of Baalis. *Biblical Archaeologist* 48: 169–172.
1992 Shifts in Settlement Patterns of Late Bronze and Iron Age Ammon. In S. Tell, G. Bisheh, F. Zayadine, K. 'Amr, and M. Zaghloul (eds.), *Studies in the History and Archaeology of Jordan IV*, 175–178. Amman: Department of Antiquities.

1995 The Late Iron II–Persian Ceramic Horizon at Tall Umayri. In K. 'Amr, F. Zayadine and M. Zaghloul (eds.), *Studies in the History and Archaeology of Jordan V*, 617–619. Amman: Department of Antiquities.

1997a The Iron Age II Period: Emerging Nations. *Biblical Archaeologist* 60: 114–183.

1997b Epigraphic Finds from Tall Umayri during the 1989 Season. In L.G. Herr, L.T. Geraty, Ø.S. Labianca and R.W. Younker (eds.), *Madaba Plains Project 3*: 323–329. Berrien Springs, MI: Andrews University/Institute of Archaeology.

2001 The History of the Collared Pithos at Tell el-'Umeiri, Jordan. In Samuel R. Wolff (ed.), *Studies in the Archaeology of Israel and Neighboring Lands in Memory of Douglas L. Esse*, 237–250. Studies in Ancient Oriental Civilization 59. Chicago: Oriental Institute.

in prep The Iron Age Pottery. In J.A. Sauer and L.G. Herr (eds.), *Hesban: The Ceramic Remains.* Berrien Springs, MI: Andrews University/Institute of Archaeology.

Herr, L.G., L.T. Geraty, O.S. LaBianca and R.W. Younker

1994 Madaba Plains Project: The 1992 Excavations at Tell el-'Umeiri, Tell Jalul, and Vicinity. *Annual of the Department of Antiquities of Jordan* 38: 147–172.

Herr, L.G., L.T. Geraty, O.S. LaBianca, R.W. Younker and D.R. Clark

1996 Madaba Plains Project 1994: Excavations at Tall Umayri, Tall Jalul, and Vicinity. *Annual of the Department of Antiquities of Jordan* 40: 63–81.

1997 Madaba Plains Project 1996: Excavations at Tall Umayri, Tall Jalul and Vicinity. *Annual of the Department of Antiquities of Jordan* 41: 145–167.

Herr, L.G., L.T. Geraty, Ø.S. Labianca and R.W. Younker (eds.)

1991 *Madaba Plains Project 2: The 1987 Season at Tell el-'Umeiri and Vicinity and Subsequent Studies.* Berrien Springs, MI: Andrews University/Institute of Archaeology.

1997 *Madaba Plains Project 3: The 1989 Season at Tall Umayri and Vicinity and Subsequent Studies.* Berrien Springs, MI: Andrews University/Institute of Archaeology.

Hoftijzer, J. and G. van der Kooij (eds.)

1991 *The Balaam Text from Deir 'Alla Re-Evaluated—Proceedings of the International Symposium Held at Leiden, 21–24 August 1989.* Leiden: E.J. Brill.

Homès-Fredericq, D.

1992 Late Bronze and Iron Age Evidence from Lehun in Moab. In P. Bienkowski (ed.), *Early Edom and Moab: The Beginning of the Iron Age in Southern Jordan*, 187–202. Sheffield Archaeological Monographs 7. Sheffield: J.R. Collis.

1997a Lehun. In E.M. Meyers (ed.), *The Oxford Encyclopedia of Archaeology in the Near East*, III, 340–341. New York: Oxford University Press.

1997b *Lehun et la voie royale.* Brussels: Comité Belge de fouilles en Jordanie/Belgisch comité voor Opgravingen in Jordanie.

Homès-Fredericq, D. and J.B. Hennessy (eds.)

1989 *Archaeology of Jordan*. II. *Field Reports: Surveys and Sites*. Akkadica Supplementum 7–8. Leuven: Peeters.

Hübner, U.

1992 *Die Ammoniter: Untersuchungen zur Geschichte, Kultur und Religion einer Transjordanischen Volkes im 1. Jahrtausend V. Chr.* Wiesbaden: Otto Harrassowitz.

Humbert, J.-B.

1989 Fedein (el). In D. Homès-Fredericq and J.B. Hennessy (eds.), *Archaeology of Jordan*. II.1. *Field Reports: Surveys and Sites A–K*, 221–224. Akkadica Supplementum 7. Leuven: Peeters.

Ibrahim, M.M.

1974 Second Season of Excavation at Sahab, 1973. *Annual of the Department of Antiquities of Jordan* 19: 55–61.

1978 The Collared-Rim Jar of the Early Iron Age. In P.R.S. Moorey and P. Parr (eds.), *Archaeology in the Levant: Essays for Kathleen Kenyon*, 117–126. Warminster: Aris & Phillips.

1987 Sahab and its Foreign Relations. In A. Hadidi (ed.), *Studies in the History and Archaeology of Jordan III*, 73–81. Amman: Department of Antiquities.

Israel, F.

1987 Studi Moabiti I: Rassegna di epigrafia Moabita e i sigilli. In G. Bernini and V. Brugnatelli (eds.), *Studi Camito-semitici e Indeuropei*, 101–138. Rome: Unicopli.

Jackson, K.P.

1983 *The Ammonite Language of the Iron Age*. Chico, CA: Scholars Press.

Ji, C.-H.C.

1995 Iron Age I in Central and Northern Transjordan: An Interim Summary of Archaeological Data. *Palestine Exploration Quarterly* 127: 122–140.

Johns, J., A. McQuitty, and R. Falkner

1989 The Faris Project: Preliminary Report upon the 1986 and 1988 Seasons. *Levant* 21: 63–95.

Kelm, G.L. and A. Mazar

1985 Tel Batash (Timnah) Excavations, Second Preliminary Report (1981–1983). *Bulletin of the American Schools of Oriental Research Supplement* 23: 93–120.

Kitchen, K.A.

1992 The Egyptian Evidence on Ancient Jordan. In P. Bienkowski (ed.), *Early Edom and Moab: The Beginning of the Iron Age in Southern Jordan*, 21–34. Sheffield Archaeological Monographs 7. Sheffield: J.R. Collis.

Kletter, R.

1991 The Rujm El-Malfuf Buildings and the Assyrian Vassal State of Ammon. *Bulletin of the American Schools of Oriental Research* 284: 33–50. Lapp, N.L.

1983 Introduction. In N.L. Lapp (ed.), *The Excavations at Araq el-Emir*, 1–11. Annual of the American Schools of Oriental Research 47. Winona Lake, IN: American Schools of Oriental Research/Eisenbrauns.

1989 'Iraq el Amir. In D. Homès-Fredericq and J. B. Hennessy (eds.), *Archaeology of Jordan*. II.1. *Field Reports: Surveys and Sites A–K*, 280–288. Akkadica Supplementum 7. Leuven: Peeters.

Lapp, P.W.

1975 Excavations at Tell er-Rumeith. In N.L. Lapp (ed.), *The Tale of the Tell: Archaeological Studies*, 111–119. Pittsburg, PA: Pickwick.

Lenzen, C.J.

1988 Tell Irbid and its Context: A Problem in Archaeological Interpretation. *Biblische Notizen* 42: 27–35.

Lenzen, C.J. and A.M. McQuitty

1989 Salameh (Khirbet). In D.Homès-Fredericq and J.B. Hennessy (eds.), *Archaeology of Jordan*. II.2. *Field Reports: Sites L–Z*, 543–546. Akkadica Supplementum 8. Leuven: Peeters.

Lenzen, C.J., R.L. Gordon and A.M. McQuitty

1985 Excavations at Tell Irbid and Beit Ras, 1985. *Annual of the Department of Antiquities of Jordan* 29: 151–159.

Leonard, A.

1987 The Jarash-Tell el-Husn Highway Survey. *Annual of the Department of Antiquities of Jordan* 31: 343–390.

Levy, T.E., R.B. Adams and R. Shafiq

1999 The Jabal Hamrat Fidan Archaeological Project: Excavations in the Wadi Fidan 40 Cemetery, Jordan (1997). *Levant* 31: 299–314.

Levy, T.E., R.B. Adams, A.J. Witten, J. Anderson, Y. Arbel, S. Kuah, J. Moreno, A. Lo and M. Wagonner

2001 Early Metallurgy, Interaction, and Social Change: The Jabal Hamrat Fidan Archaeological Project Research Design and 1998 Survey. *Annual of the Department of Antiquities of Jordan* 45: 45–76.

Levy, T.E., R.B. Adams, M. Najjar, A. Hauptmann, J.D. Anderson, B. Brandl, M.A. Robinson and T. Higham

2004 Reassessing the chronology of Biblical Edom: new excavations and 14C dates from Khirbat en-Nahas (Jordan). *Antiquity* 302: 865–879.

Levy, T.E. , M. Najjar, J. van der Plicht, N. Smith, H. Bruins and T. Higham

2005 Lowland Edom and the High and Low Chronology: Edomie State Formation, the Bible and recent archaeologicval research in southern Jordan. In T.E. Levy and T. Higham (eds.), *The Bible and Radiocarbon dating: Archaeology, Text and Science*, 129–163. London: Equinox Publishing.

Lindner, M.

1992 Edom outside the Famous Excavations: Evidence from Surveys in the Greater Petra Area. In P. Bienkowski (ed.), *Early Edom and Moab: The Beginning of the Iron Age in Southern Jordan*, 143–166. Sheffield Archaeological Monographs 7. Sheffield: J.R. Collis.

Lindner, M. and S. Farajat

1987 An Edomite Mountain Stronghold North of Petra (Ba'ja III). *Annual of the Department of Antiquities of Jordan* 31: 175–185.

Lindner, M., E.A. Knauf, J.P. Zeitler and H. Hubl

1996b Jabal al-Qseir: A Fortified Iron II (Edomite) Mountain Stronghold in Southern Jordan, its Pottery and its Historical Context. *Annual of the Department of Antiquities of Jordan* 40: 137–166.

Lugenbeal, E.N. and J.A. Sauer

1972 Seventh–Sixth Century B.C. Pottery from Area B at Heshbon. *Andrews University Seminary Studies* 10(1): 21–69.

Mare, W.H.

1991 The 1988 Season of Excavation at Abila of the Decapolis. *Annual of the Department of Antiquities of Jordan* 35: 203–221.

1992 The Abila Excavation: The Seventh Campaign at Abila of the Decapolis. *Near East Archaeological Society Bulletin* 37: 10–18.

Mattingly, G.L.

1997 A New Agenda for Research on Ancient Moab. *Biblical Archaeologist* 60: 214–221.

McGovern, P.E.

1983 Test Soundings of Archaeological and Resistivity Survey Results at Rujm al-Henu. *Annual of the Department of Antiquities of Jordan* 27: 105–141.

1986 *The Late Bronze and Early Iron Ages of Central Transjordan: The Baqʻah Valley Project, 1977–1981*. Philadelphia: The University Museum.

1993 Baqʻah Valley. In E. Stern, (ed.), *The New Encyclopedia of Archaeological Excavations in the Holy Land*, I: 338–342. Jerusalem: Israel Exploration Society.

McNicoll, A.W., R.H. Smith and J.B. Hennessy (eds.)

1982 *Pella in Jordan I*. Canberra: Australian National Gallery.

Merling, D. and L.T. Geraty (eds.)

1985 *Tell es-Saʻidiyeh: Excavations on the Tell, 1964–1966*. University Museum Monograph 60. Philadelphia, PA: The University Museum/University of Pennsylvania.

1994 *Hesban after 25 Years*. Berrien Springs, MI: Andrews University/Institute of Archaeology.

Millard, A.

1992 Assyrian Involvement in Edom. In P. Bienkowski (ed.), *Early Edom and Moab: The Beginning of the Iron Age in Southern Jordan*, 35–39. Sheffield Archaeological Monographs 7. Sheffield: J.R. Collis.

Mussell, M-L.

1999 Tell el-Kheleifeh. *ACOR Newsletter* 11(1): 5–6.

Najjar, M.

1992 Rescue Excavations at Khilda/Amman. *Annual of the Department of Antiquities of Jordan* 36: 420–409 (Arabic).

1997 The 1990–1992 Excavations. In A. Koutsoukou *et al.* (eds.), *The Great Temple of Amman: The Excavations*, 1–22. Amman: American Center of Oriental Research.

Olávarri, E.

1965 Sondages a ʻAroʻer sur l'Arnon. *Revue Biblique* 72: 77–94.

1978 Sondeo Arqueologico en Khirbet Medeineh junto a Smakieh (Jordania). *Annual of the Department of Antiquities of Jordan* 22: 136–149.

1983 La campagne de fouilles 1982 à Khirbet Medeinet al-Muʻarradjeh pres de Smakieh (Kerak). *Annual of the Department of Antiquities of Jordan* 27: 165–178.

Olávarri-Goicoechea, E.

1993 Aroer (in Moab). In E. Stern (ed.), *The New Encyclopedia of Archaeological Excavations in the Holy Land*, I, 92–93. Jerusalem: Israel Exploration Society.

Piccirillo, M.

1975 Una tomba del ferro I a Madaba. *Liber Annuus* 25: 199–224.

1976 Una Tomba del Ferro I a Mafraq (Giordania). *Liber Annuus* 26: 27–30.

Prag, K.

1989 Iktanu (Tell). In D. Homès-Fredericq and J. B. Hennessy (eds.), *Archaeology of Jordan*. II.1. *Field Reports: Surveys and Sites A–K*, 275–280. Akkadica Supplementum 7. Leuven: Peeters.

1990 Preliminary Report on the Excavations at Tell Iktanu. *Annual of the Department of Antiquities of Jordan* 34: 119–130.

Pratico, G.D.

1993 *Nelson Glueck's 1938–1940 Excavations at Tell el-Kheleifeh: A Reappraisal*. Atlanta, GA: Scholars Press.

Pritchard, J.B.

1980 *The Cemetery at Tell es-Saʻidiyeh, Jordan*. Philadelphia, PA: The University Museum.

Pritchard, J.B. (ed.)

1969 *Ancient Near Eastern Texts*. 3rd edn. Princeton: Princeton University.

Routledge, B.

1995 Archaeological Explorations in the Vicinity of Khirbat ath-Thamayil 1992. *Annual of the Department of Antiquities of Jordan* 39: 127–147.

Routledge, C.

1995 Pillared Buildings in Iron Age Moab. *Biblical Archaeologist* 54: 236.

Saller, S.J.

1966 Iron Age Tombs at Nebo, Jordan. *Liber Annuus* 16: 165–298.

Saller, S.J. and B. Bagatti

1949 *The Town of Nebo (Khirbet el-Mekhayyat)*. Studium Biblicum Franciscanum 7. Jerusalem: Franciscan.

Sauer, J.A.

1986 Transjordan in the Bronze and Iron Ages: A Critique of Glueck's Synthesis. *Bulletin of the American Schools of Oriental Research* 263: 1–26.

1994 The Pottery at Hesban and its Relationships to the History of Jordan: An Interim Hesban Pottery Report, 1993. In D. Merling and T. Geraty (eds.), *Hesban after 25 Years*, 225–282. Berrien Springs, MI: Andrews University/Institute of Archaeology.

Strange, J.

1997 Tall al-Fukhar 1990–1991: A Preliminary Report. In G. Bisheh *et al.* (eds.), *Studies in the History and Archaeology of Jordan VI*, 399–406. Amman: Department of Antiquities.

Thompson, H.O.

1972 The 1972 Excavation of Khirbet al-Hajjar. *Annual of the Department of Antiquities of Jordan* 17: 47–72.

1973 Rujm el-Malfuf South. *Annual of the Department of Antiquities of Jordan* 18: 47–50.

1977 The Ammonite Remains at Khirbet al-Hajjar. *Bulletin of the American Schools of Oriental Research* 227: 27–34.

1984 The Excavation of Rujm el-Mekheizin. *Annual of the Department of Antiquities of Jordan* 28: 31–38.

1986 An Iron Age Tomb at Madaba. In L.T. Geraty and L.G. Herr (eds.), *The Archaeology of Jordan and Other Studies: Presented to Siegfried H. Horn*, 331–363. Berrien Springs, MI: Andrews University.

Thompson, H.O. and Zayadine, F.

1973 The Tell Siran Inscription. *Bulletin of the American Schools of Oriental Research* 212: 5–12.

Tubb, J.N.

1988 Tell es-Sa'idiyeh: Preliminary Report on the First Three Seasons of Renewed Excavations. *Levant* 20: 23–88.

Tubb, J.N. and P.G. Dorrell

1991 Tell es-Sa'idiyeh: Interim Report on the Fifth (1990) Season of Excavations. *Levant* 23: 67–86.

Tubb, J.N. P.G. Dorrell and F.J. Cobbing

1996 Interim Report on the Eighth (1995) Season of Excavations at Tell es-Sa'idiyeh. *Palestine Exploration Quarterly* 128: 16–40.

Tushingham, A.D.

1972 *The Excavations at Dibon (Dhiban) in Moab.* Annual of the American Schools of Oriental Research 40. Cambridge: American Schools of Oriental Research.

1990 Dhiban Reconsidered: King Mesha and his Works. *Annual of the Department of Antiquities of Jordan* 34: 183–192.

1993 Dibon. In E. Stern (ed.), *The New Encyclopedia of Archaeological Excavations in the Holy Land*, I, 350–352. Jerusalem: Israel Exploration Society.

Van der Kooij, G.

1993 Deir 'Alla, Tell. In E. Stern (ed.), *The New Encyclopedia of Archaeological Excavations in the Holy Land*, I, 338–342. Jerusalem: Israel Exploration Society.

Vanderhooft, D.S.

1995 The Edomite Dialect and Script: A Review of Evidence. In D.V. Edelman (ed.), *You Shall not Abhor an Edomite for he is Your Brother: Edom and Seir in History and Tradition*, 137–158. Atlanta, GA: Scholars Press.

Wimmer, D.H.

1987 The Excavations at Tell Safut. In A. Hadidi (ed.), *Studies in the History and Archaeology of Jordan III*, 279–282. Amman: Department of Antiquities.

1989 Safut (Tell). In D. Homès-Fredericq and J.B. Hennessy (eds.), *Archaeology of Jordan*. II.2. *Field Reports: Sites L–Z*, 512–515. Akkadica Supplementum 8. Leuven: Peeters.

Winnett, F.V. and W.L. Reed

1964 *The Excavations at Dibon (Dhiban) in Moab.* Annual of the American Schools of Oriental Research 36–37. New Haven, CT: American Schools of Oriental Research.

Worschech, U.

1989 Preliminary Report on the Second Campaign at the Ancient Site of el-Balu' in 1986. *Annual of the Department of Antiquities of Jordan* 33: 111–121.

Worschech, U. and F. Ninow

1994 Preliminary Report on the Third Campaign at the Ancient Site of el-Balu' in 1991. *Annual of the Department of Antiquities of Jordan* 38: 195–203.

Yassine, K.

1984 *Tell el Mazar I: Cemetery A.* Amman: The University of Jordan.

1988 *Archaeology of Jordan: Essays and Reports.* Amman: University of Jordan/Department of Archaeology.

1989 Mazar (Tell el). In D. Homès-Fredericq and J.B. Hennessy (eds.), *Archaeology of Jordan*. II.2. *Field Reports: Sites L–Z*, 381–384. Akkadica Supplementum 8. Leuven: Peeters.

Younker, R.W.

1985 Israel, Judah, and Ammon and the Motifs on the Baalis Seal from Tell el-'Umeiri. *Biblical Archaeologist* 48: 173–183.

1991a The Judgment Survey. In L.G. Herr, L.T. Geraty, Ø.S. LaBianca, R.W. Younker (eds.), *Madaba Plains Project 2: The 1987 Season at Tell el-'Umeiri and Vicinity and Subsequent Studies*, 269–334. Berrien Springs, MI: Andrews University/Institute of Archaeology.

1991b Architectural Remains from the Hinterland Survey. In L.G. Herr, L.T. Geraty, Ø.S. LaBianca, R.W. Younker (eds.), *Madaba Plains Project 2: The 1987 Season at Tell el-'Umeiri and Vicinity and Subsequent Studies*, 335–341. Berrien Springs, MI: Andrews University/Institute of Archaeology.

Younker, R.W., L.T. Geraty, L.G. Herr and Ø.S. LaBianca

1990 The Joint Madaba Plains Project: A Preliminary Report of the 1989 Season, Including the Regional Survey and Excavations at el-Dreijat, Tell Jawa, and Tell el-'Umeiri. *Andrews University Seminary Studies* 28: 5–52.

1993 The Joint Madaba Plains Project: A Preliminary Report of the 1992 Season, Including the Regional Survey and Excavations at Tell Jalul and Tell el-ʻUmeiri. *Andrews University Seminary Studies* 31: 205–238.

Younker, R.W., L.T. Geraty, L.G. Herr, Ø.S. LaBianca and D. Clark

1996 Preliminary Report of the 1994 Season of the Madaba Plains Project: Regional Survey, Tall Umayri, and Tall Jalul Excavations. *Andrews University Seminary Studies* 34: 65–92.

1997 Preliminary Report of the 1996 Season of the Madaba Plains Project: Regional Survey, Tall Umayri and Tall Jalul Excavations. *Andrews University Seminary Studies* 35: 227–240.

Zeitler, J.P., E.A, Knauf and M. Lindner

1996a An Edomite Fortress and a Late Islamic Village near Petra (Jordan): Khirbat al-Muʻallaq. *Annual of the Department of Antiquities of Jordan* 40: 111–135.

Zayadine, F., J.-B. Humbert and M. Najjar

1987 Recent Excavations on the Citadel of Amman (Lower Terrace): A Preliminary Report. *Annual of the Department of Antiquities of Jordan* 31: 299–311.

1989 The 1988 Excavations on the Citadel of Amman, Lower Terrace, Area A. *Annual of the Department of Antiquities of Jordan* 33: 357–363.

11. The Persian Period

Piotr Bienkowski

Chronology and Historical Background

The absolute chronology of the Persian period in Transjordan can be fixed at 539–332 BC. In 539 BC Cyrus II, king of Persia, entered Babylon, and it is generally accepted that Syria and Palestine submitted to him in the same year, immediately following the fall of Babylon (Dandamaev 1989: 60–61; Lemaire 1994a: 11–13). Alexander the Great arrived in Phoenicia in 332 BC and, despite some local opposition, that date can be used conveniently as marking the end of the Persian period (cf. Eph'al 1988: 147).

However, it is unclear if the Persians had effective control of Transjordan for the whole period. There are no ancient written sources that refer to Transjordan during the period. In the Persian sources, the area from the Euphrates to southern Palestine, including Transjordan, is known by the territorial term "Beyond the River" (though the term had already been used in Neo-Assyrian and Neo-Babylonian times, Eph'al 1988: 141). During the fourth year of the rule of Cyrus in Babylonia, a united province was created consisting of Babylonia and "Beyond the River" (Dandamaev 1989: 60–61; Eph'al 1988: 153). There appears to have been little administrative change in the transition from Neo-Babylonian to Persian rule. Since the entire Neo-Babylonian empire came under the rule of a single governor, this suggests that for the time being Persian rule in the Levant maintained the same administrative patterns as in the Neo-Babylonian period (Hoglund 1992: 5; Stern 1990: 221; Aharoni 1979: 411).

Unfortunately, the administrative position of Transjordan in Neo-Babylonian times, and what happened to the Iron Age kingdoms of Ammon, Moab and Edom, is not at all clear. Ammon and Moab are not mentioned in any contemporary inscriptions. According to Josephus (Ant. 10.9.7), Nebuchadnezzar conquered Ammon and Moab in 582/581 BC, and most scholars interpret this as meaning that Ammon and Moab were annexed at this point and were, henceforth, ruled directly from Babylon (e.g. Ahlström 1993: 801). Josephus does not explicitly state this, however; indeed, although he mentions the exile of Jews to Babylon in the same passage, he makes no mention of the exile of Ammonites or Moabites, which might be expected to have automatically followed a full annexation.

Edom may appear in the Nabonidus Chronicle for his third year, 553 BC, but the signs are broken and the exact reading is not certain (Beaulieu 1989: 166, 169; Grayson 1975: 105, 282). What is normally restored is: "He/they encamped against the land of Edom" or "against the city of Edom." This is usually understood as meaning a siege of Busayra, Edom's capital, and the annexation of Edom (Bartlett 1989: 157–161; Ahlström 1993: 805), but the evidence is scarcely conclusive.

Ammon, Moab and Edom may, therefore, have been annexed by the Neo-Babylonians, but conclusive proof is lacking, although admittedly it is unlikely that they survived as independent kingdoms into the Persian period (Eph'al 1988: 142).

After 486 BC, "Beyond the River" became a satrapy in its own right (Eph'al 1988: 153–155; Lemaire 1994a: 13).[1] A sub-unit of a satrapy was a province, ruled by a governor. The only certain provinces within the satrapy of "Beyond the River" in the sources are Judah and Samaria in Palestine (Eph'al 1988: 158; Lemaire 1994a: 16–24, 41–46).

There is some evidence that Ammon might have been a Persian province. The Book of Nehemiah mentions someone called "Tobiah, the servant, the Ammonite" (Neh. 2.10, 19), and it has been suggested that "servant" refers to a fuller title "servant of the king," and that Tobiah was a Persian official, perhaps even a governor (e.g. Eph'al 1988: 152; Lemaire 1994a: 48–50), but this is uncertain. Three stamped impressions on jars from Tall Umayri, written in Aramaic and dating to the late sixth or early fifth century BC, have been interpreted as the Ammonite equivalent of the Yehud stamps from Judah, which contained the name of the Persian province and probably served as a stamp on goods in the Persian provincial tax system (Herr 1992, 1993: 35; Lemaire 1994b: 264). If this is correct, the Tall Umayri stamps, two of which read "Shuba Ammon" and one "Aya Ammon," may name governors or treasurers of the Persian province of Ammon. Evidence from elsewhere suggests that governors were members of the local ethnic groups (Eph'al 1988: 151–152), so there is no need to envisage a large influx of native Persians or of Persian material culture.

Of course, even if there was a Persian province of Ammon, we do not know what its borders were,[2] nor do we know the status of Edom and Moab. A common view (e.g. Lemaire 1994a: 28) is to deny the existence of a Persian province of Edom/Idumaea on the grounds that southern Transjordan and southern Judah would have been under the control of the Qedarite Arabs mentioned by Herodotus 3.5 (Lemaire 1994a: 24–27), although Idumaea may have been created as a province later, in the fourth century BC (Eph'al 1984: 199; Graf 1990: 139–143; see now Bartlett 1999). Nevertheless, the cuneiform tablet excavated at Tawilan, north of Petra in Edom, but written in Harran, 900 km away in north Syria, dating to the accession year of one of the Achaemenid kings named Darius (see below; Dalley 1995: 67–68), does imply that whatever Edom's status, there were no barriers to communication and commerce with the rest of the Persian empire.

Lemaire tentatively suggests the existence of a province called Moab situated essentially east of the Dead Sea, although he acknowledges that direct evidence is non-existent (1994a: 46–47). The proposal that the legend on

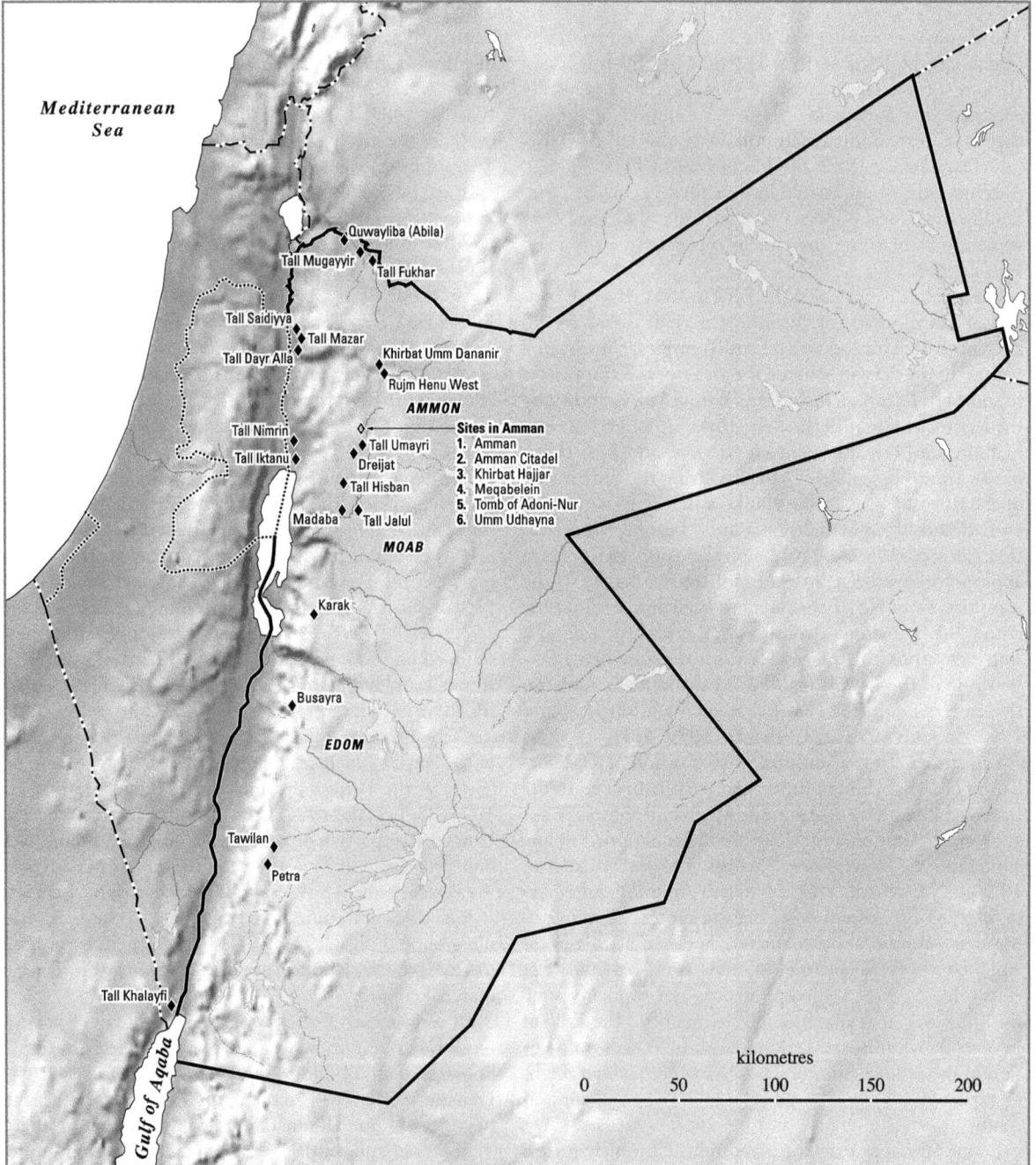

Figure 11.1 Persian period sites mentioned in the text.

a pseudo-Athenian coin, previously attributed to Gaza and read *b'm*, now be read *m'b* and attest to the existence of a Moabite mint, is scarcely conclusive (Lemaire 1994b: 282). The inclusion of Moab (*m'b*), in the "Hierodulen" texts from Main in South Arabia, as a location associated with the commercial activities of the Mineans, does not necessarily imply that this was the name of a province, although Ammon (*'mn*) is also included (Lemaire 1994a: 47; Graf 1990: 143). Lemaire's (1994a: 52–53) tentative hints that there were also Persian provinces of Gilead, Qarnini and Haurina in northern Transjordan are even more speculative; they are based not on direct evidence but on the assumption that these had already existed as Assyrian provinces, which is arguable (Bienkowski 2000).

Graf (1993: 156–160) attempts to reconstruct a Persian royal road system in Syria-Palestine, including Transjordan. From Damascus, his proposed route links Bostra, Amman, Hisban, Karak, Busayra, Tawilan, Fardakh and Tall Khalayfi. These are sites which have all allegedly yielded Persian-period finds and which are along the route of the later Via Nova Traiana, the Roman imperial road constructed between AD 111 and 114. Graf suggests that it may have had a Persian predecessor, but much of the evidence is tenuous: there are no specifically Persian-period finds from Karak or Fardakh (which is included only because the name seems to be of Persian derivation), and there is no evidence for an actual road, although at this period even a royal road would have been a dirt track that is hard to detect archaeologically (cf. Graf 1993: 165–166).

Eph'al has argued that at the beginning of the Persian period southern Transjordan was still viewed as part of the empire, but when it appears again in the sources in the Early Hellenistic period, this region was not included in the empire created by Alexander and his successors (1984: 205, 1988: 163). In the third century BC, during the Ptolemaic rule of Coele Syria, it is clear that the region of Ammon was under Ptolemaic rule, former Edom was under Nabataean control, and the status of Moab is uncertain. Eph'al proposes that Persian rule in Transjordan collapsed after the death of Darius II in 404 BC, when there were anti-Persian activities, fomented by Egypt, in the Levant and Cyprus and rebellions and internal struggles within the central government. However, by 344 BC the Phoenician revolt against Persia had been defeated, and Persia reconquered Egypt in 342 BC (Dandamaev 1989: 270–273). It is, thus, likely that Transjordan was under Persian rule at that time (and it has been suggested that the Persians may have fortified their southern frontier at this point, cf. Lemaire 1994: 28–30). Nevertheless, the situation remains unclear, and it is impossible to be certain if Transjordan was under Persian control for the whole period or not. In any case, by the time of Alexander's conquest it would seem that Persian rule in the Levant was minimal and nominal: the opposition to Alexander in Tyre and Gaza came from local elements, not from Persia itself (Eph'al 1988: 147).

A relative archaeological chronology cannot yet be constructed for the Persian period in Transjordan. Some scholars refer to "Early Persian" or "Late Persian," but these distinctions appear to be based on the proportion of Iron II or Hellenistic ceramic types in levels judged to be Persian, and not on well stratified and dated assemblages of unambiguous Persian material.

Settlement Patterns

On the basis of his surveys in Transjordan in the 1930s, Glueck concluded that there was a full gap in occupation from the end of Iron II to the Hellenistic and Nabataean periods (cf. conveniently Sauer 1986 with full bibliography). Until recently, this idea of a Persian-period occupation gap in most of Transjordan was generally accepted and it was concluded, on very little evidence, that Edom and Moab at least were overrun by nomadic Arab tribes (Ezekiel 25.4's "people of the East," cf. Eph'al 1988: 163; Lemaire 1994a: 51; see for example Sapin 1996, who envisages an extensive semi-nomadic and pastoralist population between the fifth and third centuries BC during a phase of climatic aridity). These tribes tended to be identified with the Qedarite Arabs who were regarded as having jurisdiction over "the sparsely populated areas that were not occupied by a settled people" (Stern 1990: 223).

Archaeological evidence for Persian-period settlement in Transjordan was not widespread enough to counter this view, and Albright (1954) seems to have been alone in recognising the continuity of late Iron Age Ammonite material culture, especially the pottery, into later periods. Although there were isolated tomb deposits and a few other finds in Transjordan dated to the Persian period —mostly foreign imports, a few inscriptions, and tenuous parallels from Palestine—there was no proper excavated sequence of material that could be shown unambiguously to date to the period. It was suggested that the pottery from the Hisban excavations of the 1970s might continue from Iron II into the Persian period, but since no stratigraphic sub-phasing could be established there, this did not constitute convincing evidence (Herr 1995; Sauer 1994: 246–248). There appeared to be four Persian phases at Tall Dayr Alla from the excavations of the mid-1980s (van der Kooij 1987), but little hard evidence has yet been published.

The ongoing excavations at Tall Umayri have now provided good stratigraphic evidence for continuity from Iron II to the Persian period (cf. Herr 1995, 1999). Two continuously occupied strata bridge the sixth century BC: the second stratum reused the walls of the first and has been dated to the late sixth and early fifth centuries BC. This stratigraphic evidence from Tall Umayri for continuity between Iron II and the Persian period now allows us to draw together the ever-increasing evidence for the Persian period in Jordan into a more coherent and defensible framework.

The pattern that is now evident is continuity from Iron II, through the Persian period and perhaps into the Hellenistic period (Homès-Fredericq 1996; Bienkowski 2001, 2002: 350–351). Many surveys and excavations have identified little or no diagnostic Persian material, but in fact it must be acknowledged that in some of these at least there might be an element of continuity from Iron II into the Persian period without much of a definable change in the material culture.

The map of Persian-period sites in Transjordan now covers the whole area from north to south. The excavated sites that have identified material dated to the Persian period (Figure 11.1) are listed below with bibliographic references, although the use of the term "Iron II/Persian" by excavators is confusing: it either masks uncertainty as to the precise chronological span of the material, or reflects genuine continuity between the Iron II and Persian periods.

Excavations (North to South)

Quwayliba/Abila (Mare 1989: 474): Persian-period sherds identified in Area A.

Tall Mugayyir (Ibrahim and Mittmann 1986: 171): Persian-period sherds identified, in association with a "fort," "way station" or "caravanserai" dating from the Iron Age to the Hellenistic period.

Tall Fukhar (Ottosson 1993: 100; Strange 1997): "Iron IIC/Persian" silos or bins and some building remains.

Tall Saidiyya (Pritchard 1985: 60–68, 86–87; Tubb and Dorrell 1994: 52–59; Tubb, Dorrell and Cobbing 1996: 22, 25 fig.12): Stratum III square building of the Persian period, dated primarily by an Aramaic inscription with letters characteristic of the late sixth to fourth centuries BC, plus two ostraca, with recent excavations suggesting earlier phases of the building, and some Persian-period graves.

Tall Mazar (Yassine 1984, 1988b, 1988c; Yassine and Teixidor 1988): cemetery, grain silos, houses; ostracon and seals dated to the Persian period.

Tall Dayr Alla (van der Kooij 1987; van der Kooij and Ibrahim 1989: 89–90): Phase V buildings, Phase IV, Phase III wall foundations and small pits, Phase II pit all probably Persian, dated by fifth century BC Attic lamp (Phase V), fourth century BC Greek "fish-plate" (Phase III), and inscribed ostraca dated between 500 and 400 BC.

Khirbat Umm Dananir (McGovern 1989: 40–42): "Iron IIC/Persian" courtyard with oven, and inscribed storage jar.

Rujm Henu West (Clark 1983): "Iron IIC/Persian tower."

Amman Citadel (Greene and 'Amr 1992: 126 and fig. 7: 6): "Iron III/Persian"–Early Hellenistic pottery lid in deep sounding.

Khilda (Yassine 1988a): two rock-cut tombs dating between the seventh and fifth centuries BC, possibly associated with an Ammonite tower.

Meqabelayn tomb (Harding 1950: pls. 13: 3, 15: 11; Sauer 1986: 18): sand-core glass dated to c. 500 BC, and pottery similar to Tall Mazar.

Umm Udhayna (Hadidi 1987): rock-cut tomb with characteristic Persian metalwork and fifth century BC Attic lekythoi.

Rujm Selim (Geraty et al. 1988): building with perimeter wall, courtyard and four rooms first constructed in Iron II (Phase 6). The overlying Phase 5 is dated to late Iron II/early Persian: the courtyard was levelled with fill dirt and possibly cobbled. Inside the building were found domestic objects such as loom weights, spindle whorls and sherds from a water jug dated to the Persian period. After Phase 5 there was a gap until Phase 4 in the Late Hellenistic period.

Tall Umayri (Herr et al. 1991a: 13, 241–242; Herr 1992, 1993, 1995; Herr et al. 1994: 155; Younker et al. 1996: 77–79): three stamped jar impressions possibly of the Persian province of Ammon, dated to the late sixth century BC, and Attic sherds of the fifth century BC, found in an administrative building with evidence of continuity from late Iron II.

Drayjat (Younker et al. 1990: 13): "fort" perhaps originally dating to Iron II, cleared to bedrock and new walls constructed in the Late Persian/Early Hellenistic period, creating rooms within the building.

Tall Nimrin (Flanagan, McCreery and Yassine 1992: 98–100, 1994; Dempsey 1993): one locus with two phases of occupation and partially preserved structures of the Persian period, together with eight ostraca, sixth–fourth centuries BC.

Tall Iktanu (Prag 1989: 40–44, figs. 8–11): fort.

Hisban (Sauer 1994: 246–248; Cross and Geraty 1994: 172–174; Merling 1994: 215–216; Ray 2001: 168): Stratum 16, covering the Iron IIC/Persian periods (c. 700–500/450 BC according to Ray 2001, but see below), consisted of various walls, and its association with imported Attic pottery and Persian-period ostraca may indicate that it was a small town involved in administrative activities. The destruction date of Stratum 16 is unclear, and Ray (2001: 147) states that it could be anywhere between the early sixth century (i.e. destruction by Nebuchadnezzar II in 582 BC, within Iron II) and the mid-fifth century BC (i.e. Xerxes in 486–484 BC, within the Persian period). Following that there is a gap until the Late Hellenistic Stratum 15 fortress at the beginning of the second century BC, the construction of which involved the denuding of the entire summit of the mound to bedrock. However, Sauer (1994: 247) dated the Stratum 16 pottery to the sixth–fourth centuries BC, which would extend that stratum to the end of the Persian period. There are also hints of an even later date, with Sauer

(1994: 248) leaving open the possibility that the Stratum 16 pottery extended into the Early Hellenistic period, as late as the third century BC. If that was the case, the gap between Strata 16 and 15 begins to disappear, and there is the possibility of continuity between the Iron II, Persian and Hellenistic occupations (for the Hellenistic strata cf. Mitchel 1992; Ray 2001: 159–162).

Madaba (Harrison 1994: 429): "Persian–Hellenistic" sherds noted without further details.

Tall Jalul (Younker *et al.* 1996: 72–73; Younker and Merling 1999): parts of at least three late Iron II/Persian-period buildings were found in Fields C and D, with pottery including imported Attic ware. The Field D building seems to have consisted of rooms surrounding a central courtyard, with pillars supporting the ceiling. One of the Field C buildings sealed a burial cave containing 14 skeletons, with late Iron II/Persian pottery. In Field B the latest phase of an entrance road associated with an outer gatehouse is a repaving dating to the late Iron II/Persian period (sixth–fifth centuries BC). In Field A were found several pits, some sections of walls, and a stretch of pavement (dated to the fifth–fourth centuries BC).

Busayra (Bienkowski 2002: 350–351): three late fourth century BC Attic sherds were excavated, two of them stratified in the last phase of the Area A public building, below the destruction level, indicating that the building—and possibly the Area C public building too—continued in use at least to the end of the Persian period. Five Hellenistic sherds were also found, one of which was stratified with the two Attic sherds: unless it is a stray, this would date the end of the Area A public building to c. 200 BC, at the end of the Early Hellenistic period, thus giving a 500 year time span for the use of the building, from late Iron II, through the Persian period and well into the Hellenistic period.

Tawilan (Bienkowski 1990; Bennett and Bienkowski 1995): cuneiform tablet dated to the accession year of one of the Achaemenid kings named Darius, found in an accumulation deposit overlying the main occupation.

Tall Khalayfi (DiVito 1993: 58–63): ostraca dated to fifth and fourth centuries BC.

A Phoenician coin found inside the tower at Khirbat Hajjar and dated to c. 400 BC was explained as a post-occupational deposit by the excavator (Thompson 1972: pl. 7, 1977: 31). The tomb of Adoni-Nur in Amman (Harding and Tufnell 1953) is essentially seventh century BC, but Attic imports and sand-core glass dating to c. 500 BC may suggest that its use continued into the Persian period (Sauer 1986: 18).

Surveys

Given the problems of identifying characteristic Persian-period material in Transjordan, surveys are unreliable for locating Persian-period settlement. Many surveys have recorded finding no diagnostic Persian-period sherds.

Surveys that claim some Persian-period material are:

Baqah Valley Survey (McGovern 1989: 40–42): three sites dated to 'Iron IIC/Persian' (c. 650–400 BC).

Dhiban Plateau Survey (Ji and Lee 2000a: 494, table 1): pottery of the Persian period was collected at 13 sites, that is, 3.09% of the sites explored (although "Iron II" is also referred to as "Iron II/Persian," with 53 sites, or 12.59%, Ji and Lee 2000a: 504). A decline is suggested for the late Persian period, before a settlement increase in the Hellenistic period to a level slightly higher than in the Iron II/Persian period.

East Jordan Valley Survey (Yassine, Ibrahim and Sauer 1988: 175–177, 198–199): Thirteen sites identified, but with only small quantities of Persian-period sherds. There appears to be some continuity between Iron II, Persian and Hellenistic periods, with sherds of all three periods found at six of the sites.

Heshbon Survey (Ibach 1987: 158–168): pottery of the "Iron II/Persian" period (c. 900–500 BC) was collected at 63 sites, that is, 43 % of the sites explored by the survey. The "Late Persian" period (c. 500–250 BC) was almost completely unrepresented in the survey. Only one site, Tall Jalul, yielded three sherds of the period, and this is now being excavated (see above).

Iraq al-Amir and Wadi Kafrayn Surveys (Ji 1998; Ji and Lee 1999; 2000b: 182, table 3): pottery of the Persian period was collected at 26 sites, that is, 12.04% of the sites explored by the survey (although "Iron II/Persian" was collected at 35 sites, or 16.20%).

Karak Plateau Survey (Miller 1991): pottery of the "Iron IIC/Persian" period (c. 540–332 BC) was collected at 20 sites (Miller 1991: 310). However, diagnostic Persian-period pottery was very rare (Brown 1991: 203–205).

Tafila–Busayra Archaeological Survey (MacDonald *et al.* 2004): the Persian period is described as "poorly represented" in the survey (MacDonald *et al.* 2004: 418). Sherds identified as Persian/Hellenistic were collected from one random square (MacDonald *et al.* 2004: 58, 79), and a reading of "Late Persian/Hellenistic" was assigned to sherds from another random square (MacDonald *et al.* 2004: 58, 128–129; one cooking pot sherd illustrated (MacDonald *et al.* 2004: 129: no. 5).

Tall Umayri Hinterland Survey (Herr *et al.* 1991a: 278): one "Early Persian" sherd from Site 69.

Wadi Yabis Survey (Mabry and Palumbo 1989: 94–96): diagnostic "Persian/Hellenistic" pottery was confirmed at four sites. Three of these showed continuity from the Iron II period.

Pottery

Local pottery, indistinguishable from Iron II pottery, has been excavated in contexts associated with imported Greek pottery of the fifth and fourth centuries BC at Tall Umayri, Tall Jalul, Umm Udhayna, Khilda, Tall Dayr Alla (Homès-Fredericq 1996: 74) and Busayra (for Greek ceramic imports into Palestine, see Stern 1982: 136–141). There is no doubt at all, therefore, that there is continuity from Iron II into the Persian period in Transjordan; much of the Iron II pottery repertoire can thus be regarded as still being in use in the Persian period. Here, only those pottery forms that appear to be new to or characteristic of the Persian period will be highlighted, and particularly those that come from the well-stratified and dated contexts at Tall Umayri and Tall Dayr Alla (cf. Hendrix *et al.* 1997: 202).[3]

At Tall Umayri, local pottery was found in stratified contexts associated with fifth century BC imported Attic sherds, suggesting a date within the Persian period. Many of these local forms were nevertheless typical of the late Iron II corpus, but other forms appear to have Persian parallels, especially to recent, well-stratified assemblages at Tell Hesi and Gezer (Herr 1995): triangular jar rims on a variety of forms, necked kraters, particular bowl types, flat lamps, and chevron decoration (Figure 11.2). Totally absent were characteristic Persian types such as sausage jars, high-necked cooking pots and amphorae. Other typical Persian types were very rare, such as mortaria and shallow rounded bowls. Some of these have been found elsewhere in Transjordan. Sausage jars occur at Tall Saidiyya (Figure 11.3), Umm Udhayna and Meqabelayn, some with pointed bases, some disc-based. Amphorae (straight-shouldered jars) are found at Umm Udhayna and Tall Saidiyya. Mortaria have been found at Tall Saidiyya and at Tall Dayr Alla, where the pottery is also in contexts associated with fifth and fourth century BC imported Greek pottery. Bag-shaped perfume juglets are found at Tall Saidiyya (Figure 11.4). At Tall Dayr Alla, a form characteristic of the Persian levels appears to be a long narrow bottle, narrower than late Iron II types; cf. van der Kooij and Ibrahim 1989: 107 no.149, illustrated on p.104). The most common Persian-period form at Tall Nimrin was a storage jar with a simple, thickened, slightly everted rim (Flanagan, McCreery and Yassine 1994: 236 fig.19: 6–9). Sauer has concluded that typical features of the Hisban "Iron IIC–Persian" assemblage, paralleled elsewhere, include widely spaced interior black wheel-burnishing, short-necked cooking pots, and offset-rimmed, red-burnished bowls (Sauer 1994: 246–248).

As in the Iron II period, there is likely to be regional variation within Transjordan, but this cannot yet be demonstrated.

Architecture

Domestic

The only identifiable domestic architecture comes from Tall Mazar, Tall Dayr Alla, Khirbat Umm Dananir and Tall Umayri. The first three had architecture based on courtyards containing tabuns or silos; at Mazar Stratum II and Tall Dayr Alla Phase V, the courtyards were sur-rounded by mud-brick walls, occasionally on stone foundations. Later Persian-period phases at Tall Mazar and Tall Dayr Alla seem to consist of pits. Tall Mazar Stratum I, the final occupation phase dated to the fourth century BC, consisted of deep, rounded storage pits and silos, many lined with bricks, stones or mud-bricks. The pits were cylindrical, barrel- or cone-shaped, and were found filled with chaff, charred grains, pottery, copper and stone vessels. Tall Dayr Alla Phase III consisted of heavy wall foundations and small pits, while Phase II was virtually one huge pit.

At Tall Fukhar, more than twenty stone-lined silos or bins were scattered over the whole excavated area, and possibly connected with building remains, although this could not be proved (Strange 1997). Some of the silos were paved and covered.

Building C at Tall Umayri had domestic materials such as small ash lenses, basalt grindstones, spindle whorls, jar stoppers, oven fragments and mammal ribs on the floors of seven interconnected rooms (Herr *et al.* 1991a: 17–19, 1991b: 157–158). Stairs led down into one room, and another room had two pillars. The building's position immediately to the north of the administrative Buildings A and B tempts speculation that Building C may have housed the bureaucrats (pers. comm. L. G. Herr). Dating to the very beginning of the Persian period at Tall Umayri is a possible tent or shack platform made of flimsy walls, built on the edge of the moat (Herr *et al.* 1994: 155).

Public

Buildings identified as public or administrative and possibly dating to the Persian period have been excavated at Tall Saidiyya Stratum III (Figure 11.5), Tall Umayri, Tall Jalul, Drayjat (Figure 11.6) and Busayra (Figures 11.7–11.8). There are similarities between the Busayra and Tall Saidiyya buildings: they appear to be in the "open-court" style known from the Neo-Assyrian period in Mesopotamia and the Levant. At Tall Saidiyya, the courtyard was stone-paved, at Busayra the courtyards of the Area A and C buildings were plastered. However, below the Tall Saidiyya stone courtyard were two phases of weathered plaster associated with pits and one phase of a pebbly surface, which appear to be earlier phases of the building, dated by the excavator to the sixth century BC (Tubb and Dorrell 1994: 54–57). The Tall Saidiyya courtyard was surrounded by rooms on all four sides; the Busayra Area C building had a series of rooms parallel to the court, the remainder of the plan being unexcavated, while the Area A building had rooms on three sides of the courtyard. The excavator concluded that the Tall Saidiyya building was for defence, although small finds suggested activities such as spinning, weaving, sewing and milling.

It should be noted that the only evidence presented so far for dating the Tall Saidiyya "fortress" to the Persian

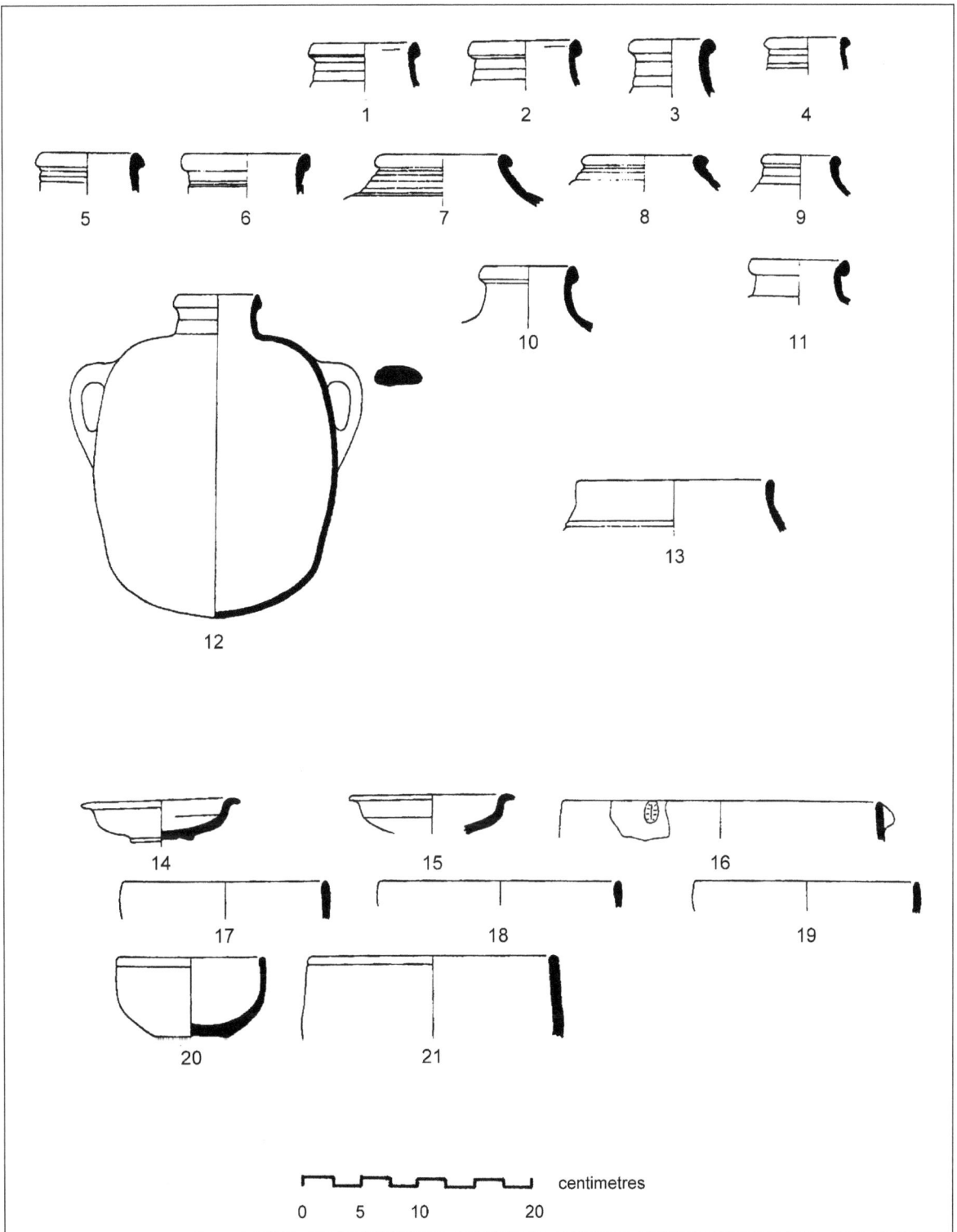

Figure 11.2 Pottery from stratified contexts at Tall Umayri which has Persian-period parallels: 1–12, triangular jar rims (from Geraty *et al.* 1989: 321, nos. 9–17, 22–24). 13, necked krater (from Geraty *et al.* 1989: 325 no. 11). 14–21, bowls (from Herr *et al.* 1991: 42 nos. 24–25, 31 nos. 22–27).

period is an inscription on an incense burner from the floor of one room (see below), dated by the shape of the letters between the late sixth and fourth centuries BC (Pritchard 1985: 67). Evidence for dating the earlier phases of the building has yet to be published (Tubb and Dorrell 1994: 52–59).

The Area A building at Busayra, probably a temple, was originally constructed in Iron II on a stone platform, but two Attic sherds in the final pre-destruction deposit prove that it continued in use to the late fourth century BC. The plan was based on two wings, one the temple proper with a possible sanctuary approached from a courtyard, the other wing perhaps a storage/administrative annexe (Bienkowski 2002: 94–95).

The final phase of the Busayra Area C building, originally probably an Iron II palace or residence, may also have continued in use into the Persian period, although this dating is based on stratigraphic analogy with the Area A building and not on direct evidence (Bienkowski 2002: 475–478). The earlier Iron II building was raised on a stone platform, with a large plastered courtyard or recep-

Figure 11.4 Bag-shaped perfume juglet from Tall Saidiyya.

tion room with rooms on at least one side. These rooms had extensive plaster and stone-paved floors, a bathroom, and storage areas. In the later (Persian?) phase the spaces were subdivided and new doorways were added, and a possible gatehouse with a piered gate was built on the opposite side of the courtyard.

A rectangular structure at Drayjat (Figure 11.5), originally probably Iron II but remodelled in the Late Persian/Hellenistic period, may have been a fort and is of similar size to the Tall Saidiyya building (Younker *et al.* 1990: 13, 33 pl. 6). It was built of massive unhewn and partially hewn stones; the excavators suggested that the interior walls supported a second storey.

Two buildings at Tall Umayri have been described as administrative, and seem in their later phases to have continued from Iron II into the Persian period. Building A was apparently a single room with thick walls; Building B was planned like a four-room house but with monumental walls and a basement. The large building at neighbouring Tall Jalul has two or three rows of stone pillars supporting the roof, which had collapsed into the rooms; the associated artefacts included an incense stand/altar, a stone roof roller, basalt food preparation vessels and iron tools (Younker *et al.* 1996: 72–73, 89 pl. 16), perhaps suggesting a function beyond the strictly administrative.

Hoglund (1992: 165–205) argues that there is a distinctive type of "fortress" dating to the mid-fifth century

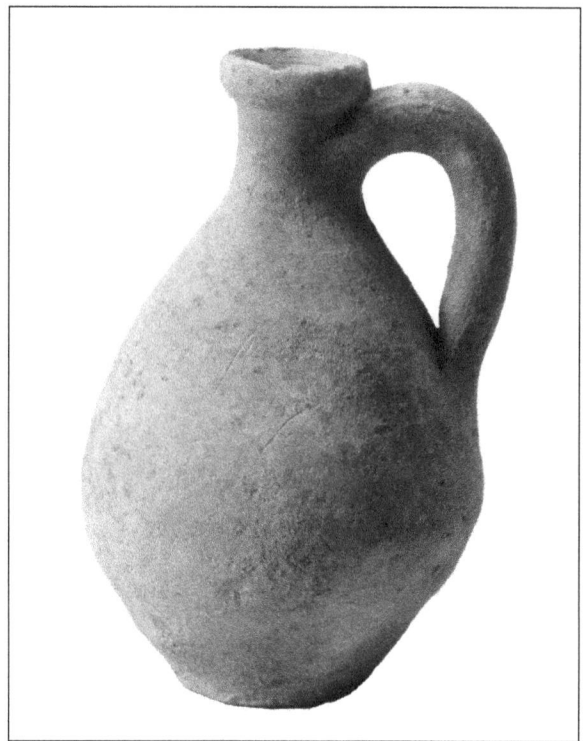

10 cms

Figure 11.3 Sausage-shaped torpedo jar from Tall Saidiyya.

BC that housed Persian garrisons as a result of insecurity in the Levant because of the Egyptian revolt and the Delian league's involvement. He includes Tall Saidiyya, and amends Pritchard's date of 420 BC upwards to the mid-fifth century BC. However, the excavations at Tall Saidiyya (Tubb and Dorrell 1994: 52–59) have shown that Pritchard's Stratum III square building was the culmination of several earlier levels of a courtyard building, perhaps of Persian date but maybe earlier. These earlier levels may not fit into Hoglund's suggested chronology, or his proposed construction specification for a garrison. Furthermore, the Persian-period administrative building at Tall Umayri also continues from the Neo-Babylonian period (Herr 1993), suggesting that such administrative buildings simply re-used existing structures.

Burial Customs

Apart from isolated tombs, the only cemetery dated to the Persian period that has been excavated and fully published is that north of the mound at Tall Mazar (Yassine 1984). In general, there appears to be a continuation of Iron II burial practices (themselves little published from Transjordan) and similarities with Persian-period burials in Palestine (see Yassine 1999).

Eighty-five graves were excavated at Tall Mazar, dated to the sixth–fifth centuries BC (possibly, therefore, beginning still within the Neo-Babylonian period). With some exceptions, the bodies were oriented east–west, heads to the east and faces to the south, with males extended and females flexed (Yassine 1984: 8–9).

Five types of burial were found at Tall Mazar (Yassine 1984: 6–7):

Figure 11.5 Stratum III building at Tall Saidiyya Stratum III (after Pritchard 1985: fig. 185).

Figure 11.6 Building at Drayjat, originally probably Iron II but remodelled in the late Persian/Hellenistic period (after Younker *et al.* 1990: 33 pl. 6).

1. The majority were simple pit burials, with the body wrapped in a cloth or mat and laid in a pit, a type also common in Palestine (Stern 1982: 86).
2. Brick-lined tombs (3).
3. Tombs lined with stone on one side, the body laid on the earth, possibly with a wooden cover (6).
4. Infant storage jar burial (1).
5. Larnax burial, i.e. a clay burial coffin shaped like a bathtub (1).

Associated with the male burials were generally pottery and metal objects (vessels, arrowheads, spearheads, swords and knives); female burials tended to have bracelets, necklaces, bronze and silver earrings, and beads of faience, glass and carnelian. Animal bones accompanying one burial were tentatively identified by the excavator as a pet or joints of meat (Yassine 1984: 36).

The Persian-period cemetery on the lower tell at nearby Tall Saidiyya (Tubb, Dorrell and Cobbing 1996: 22) generally had grave pits dug among the Early Bronze Age buildings. The excavator notes that these Persian-period burials were identical in every respect to the Late Bronze Age burials in the same area, and could be chronologically distinguished only on the basis of any diagnostic material. Unfortunately, the inventories of graves at Tall Saidiyya published in the preliminary reports do not indicate their date, so it is uncertain which graves belong to the Persian period. However, the few graves specifically noted in the preliminary reports as Persian-period are pit burials with the same orientation as those at Tall Mazar and similar grave goods. One of the graves contained four stamp seals (Tubb, Dorrell and Cobbing 1996: 25 fig.12, although only three are noted in the inventory on p.38).

Four isolated rock-cut tombs have also been dated to the Persian period: Meqabelayn (Harding 1950),[4] Umm Udhayna (Hadidi 1987), and two poorly recorded tombs at Khilda (Yassine 1988a). Meqabelayn, Umm Udhayna and Khilda Tomb 2 consisted of burial chambers with benches. Meqabelayn had a shallow central pit, while Umm Udhayna had a main chamber with 15 skeletons, probably multiple successive burials, and other burials

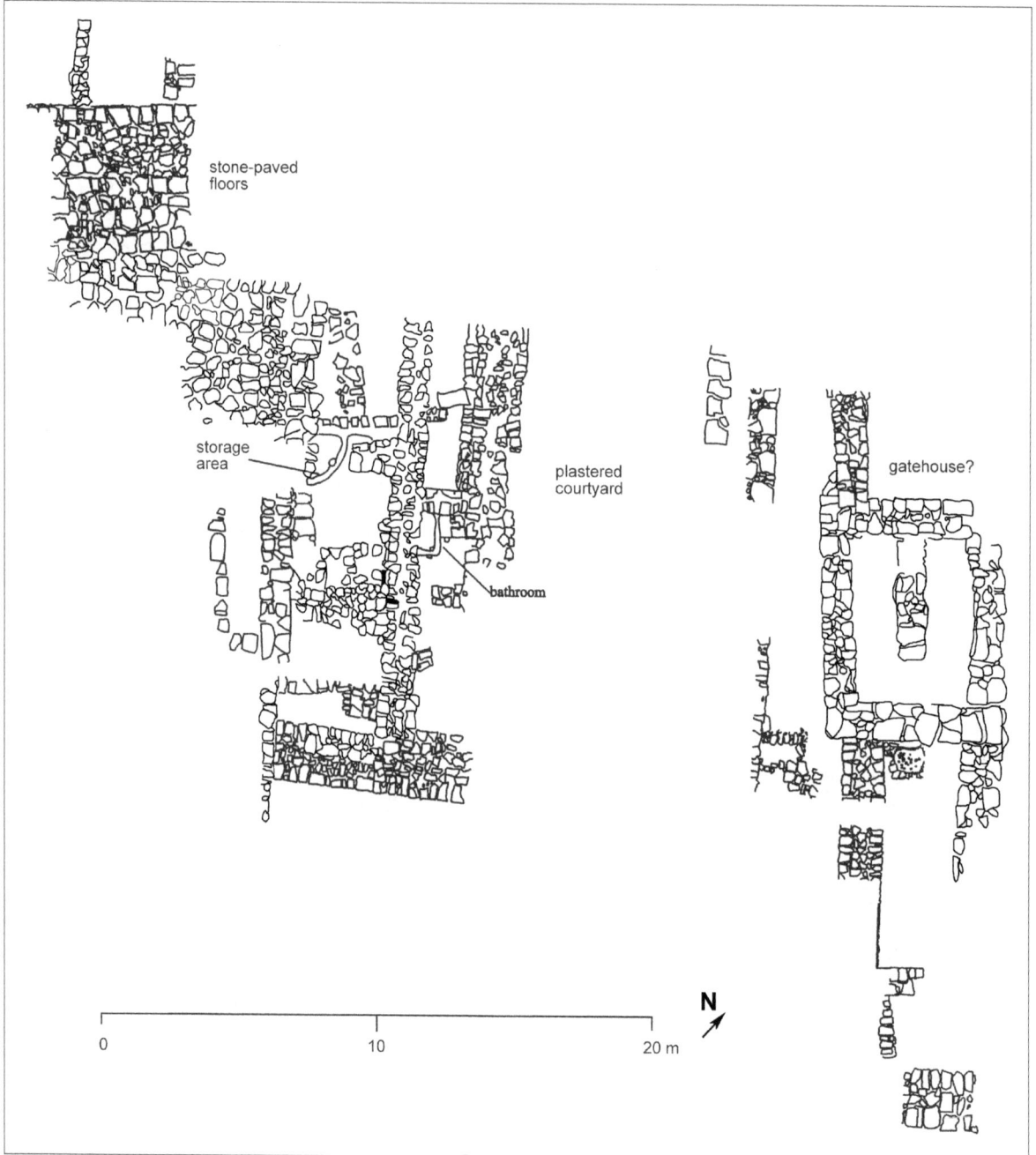

Figure 11.7 Final phase of Area C building at Busayra, probably a palace (drawing by Piotr Bienkowski).

Figure 11.8 Final phase of Area A building at Busayra, originally Iron II, but which may have continued as late as the fourth century BC (drawing by Piotr Bienkowski).

scattered on the benches. The associated finds in each case are similar to those known from Tall Mazar and Tall Saidiyya.

Material Culture

Very few objects found in Transjordan are diagnostically "Persian." There are occasional discoveries of fine pieces such as a pair of painted terracotta riders from the Meqabelayn tomb (Bienkowski 1991: 45 pl. 46 in colour), a silver earring from the Umm Udhayna tomb (Bienkowski 1991: 103 pl. 124 in colour), or an elaborately decorated and inscribed limestone incense burner from Tall Saidiyya (Pritchard 1985: 66–68 and fig.18: 22), which arguably are Persian-period, but the most common small finds on all sites are bronze objects. The vast majority of these can only be dated broadly Iron II–Persian, since they are common or at least occur already in Iron II contexts but probably continue in use into the Persian period.

Bronze bowl types are essentially the same as those in Palestine (Stern 1982: 144–145). The two most common types at Tall Mazar, Khilda, Umm Udhayna, Meqabelayn and Tall Saidiyya are: a) flat, carinated, with an everted rim; and b) round, slightly carinated, with a convex base and omphalos, normally decorated in relief with floral patterns. Both types appear first in late Iron II contexts in Palestine and continue into the Persian period, the latter being the common bowl of the Persian period according to Stern. A third type found at Tall Mazar is a deep rounded bowl without an umbo, also a common Persian-period type (Amiran 1972), with parallels in Palestine and Syria. An unusual bronze dish from Umm Udhayna has a handle comprising two horses' heads (Zayadine 1986: 147).

Two types of bronze strainer are found at Tall Mazar, Umm Udhayna and Khilda: a) a possibly earlier Iron Age type with horizontal handles and deep carinated bowl; and b) a possibly later (?Persian) type with an upright handle and deep but plain round bowl. A third type at Tall Mazar has a duck-head terminal and floral stem, similar to Persian-period types in Palestine (Amiran 1972; Stern 1982: 147).

Triangular and/or bow-shaped bronze fibulae are found at Tawilan, Busayra, the Meqabelayn tomb, the Umm Udhayna tomb, Tall Umayri, Tall Saidiyya, Tall Mazar and Tall Dayr Alla. These occur first in the eighth and seventh centuries BC, but continue in use through the Persian period and even later throughout the Near East.

Standard Iron II–Persian leaf-shaped bronze arrowheads are common, but "Irano-Scythian" trilobe bronze arrowheads, often regarded as diagnostic of the Persian period, are found at Tawilan, Busayra, Tall Umayri, Tall Mazar and Tall Dayr Alla. However, although "Irano-Scythian" arrowheads are found throughout the limits of the Persian empire, the type first appears in Assyrian-period contexts and must be dated broadly seventh–fourth centuries BC (cf. Stern 1982: 154–156).

Circular bronze mirrors with long tapering plain tangs are found at Umm Udhayna, Tall Meqabelayn, Tall Saidiyya and Tall Mazar. In Palestine, these appear at the very end of the Iron Age and are popular in the Persian period (Stern 1982: 147).

Rings and bracelets formed from bent copper or copper alloy/bronze rods or occasionally sheet bronze are found at Tawilan, Busayra, Tall Khalayfi, Tall Dayr Alla, Tall Saidiyya and Tall Mazar. This type can be dated broadly Iron II–Persian, but in fact this simple shape appears in many periods, and is even found in Islamic-period tombs.

A unique piece is a bronze censer with a lid, supported by a stand in the shape of a human female figure on a tripod base, from the Umm Udhayna tomb (Khalil 1986; Zayadine 1986: 144–145; Bienkowski 1991: 96 pl. 115 in colour). The incised decoration appears to be in Achaemenid style. The hairstyle is particularly distinctive because of its "trimmed" style in which the pattern of small curls appears at the end of wavy strands. These strands in turn radiate from the circular ring holding the stem of the incense bowl. The curls are represented with a grid pattern. This hair arrangement is depicted on the terracotta reliefs of bearded males at Susa and Persepolis.

Inscriptions and Seals

The only inscribed document from Transjordan officially dated within the Persian period is the cuneiform tablet from Tawilan (Dalley 1995: 67–68). This is a legal document drawn up in Harran, dated to the accession year of one of the Achaemenid kings named Darius (i.e. 521, 423 or 335 BC), containing testimony to the disputed sale of two rams. The name and patronymic of the man responsible for the testimony are both compounded with the divine name "Qos;" other names cited are Aramaic or Babylonian. Unfortunately, the tablet was not found in an occupation deposit at Tawilan and so cannot be used unambiguously to date settlement at the site into the Persian period (Bennett and Bienkowski 1995: 102–103).

Inscriptions from Transjordan from late Iron II, especially the sixth century BC, are difficult to date precisely, but Lemaire (1994b: 262) concludes that no Ammonite, Moabite or Edomite inscription proper dates to the Persian period. Aramaic inscriptions, on the other hand, are well attested (Lemaire 1994b: 262–266).

A limestone incense burner from Tall Saidiyya, decorated with geometric designs, a horse and a human figure, was inscribed in Aramaic *lzkwr*, "(belonging) to Zakkur," and dated palaeographically between the late sixth and fourth centuries BC (Pritchard 1985: 66–68).

Ostraca from Tall Saidiyya, Tall Mazar, Tall Dayr Alla, Tall Nimrin, Hisban, and Tall Khalayfi, dated palaeographically to the Persian period, have mostly short Aramaic inscriptions, some of which can be identified as records of goods, often with personal names, although generally they are not very informative. They date between the late sixth and fourth–third centuries BC, and demonstrate that Aramaic had largely replaced the national scripts in Transjordan by the end of the sixth century BC (Cross and Geraty 1994: 172).

The personal names compounded with divine names on ostraca form the only evidence for religion from this period. As well as on the Tawilan tablet, Edomite "Qos" occurs in a name on a late sixth century BC ostracon from Hisban (Cross and Geraty 1994: 173 [A6]), and "Qos," Canaanite "Baal" and Phoenician "Eshmun" on fifth–early fourth century BC ostraca from Tall Khalayfi (DiVito 1993, Reg. Nos. 2070-1). "Milkom" and "El" occur on an ostracon from Tall Mazar (Yassine and Teixidor 1988: 141), and "El" on a fifth century BC ostracon from Tall Dayr Alla (van der Kooij and Ibrahim 1989: 69–70). "Yahweh" may occur in a fourth to third century BC ostracon from Tall Mazar (Yassine and Teixidor 1988: 137).

Three stamped jar impressions from Tall Umayri (Herr 1992) were found associated with the public buildings. They are written in Aramaic script and have been dated to the late sixth century BC. Their reading is not certain, but Herr suggests that two with the same inscription read "Shuba Ammon." By analogy with the *yhd/yhwd* stamps from Judah, which probably served as a stamp on goods in the Persian provincial tax system, Herr suggests that Shuba might be the name of the governor or treasurer of the Persian province of Ammon. A third stamped jar impression was found during the 1994 excavations, with a different name, "Aya" (Lemaire 1994b: 264).

Stamp and cylinder seals from Tall Umayri (Porada 1989: 381–384), Tall Mazar (Yassine 1984: 103–107 and fig. 9: 1, 6, 1988c: 150 no. 302), Khilda (Yassine 1988a: 21, 30 fig. 8: 4) and Tall Saidiyya (Tubb, Dorrell and Cobbing 1996: 25 fig. 12),[5] have good parallels to fifth century BC examples elsewhere. Porada (1989: 381) suggests that, while the inspirations may come from genuinely Achaemenid seals, in most cases the designs and workmanship appear to be local. Although insufficient Persian-period seals have yet been found in Transjordan to define a local style, many of those identified so far have human or animal figures in Achaemenid style but with significant differences of detail unparalleled elsewhere. Other seals found in supposedly Persian-period contexts, either at these sites or at Umm Udhayna, have parallels in the late Iron II period (Neo-Babylonian, earlier sixth century BC).

From the Iron Age to the Hellenistic Period

Until recently the evidence for Persian-period settlement in Jordan was sparse and stratigraphically unclear, allowing even the latest commentators to conclude that sedentary life had disappeared from large parts of the country. Recent evidence shows clear proof for continuity of at least some settlements from Iron II through the Persian period and possibly even into the Hellenistic period. Although there is also some evidence that Ammon was a Persian province, there is no evidence for the status of Edom or Moab within the Persian empire, and no basis for the claim that Busayra and Tall Khalayfi were integrated into the Persian administrative system (Elayi and Sapin 1998: 155). Nevertheless, it is now generally accepted that the Iron Age kingdoms of Ammon, Moab and Edom are best interpreted as "tribal kingdoms" rather than centralized states, with a mixture of settled and pastoralist populations, and their "capitals" were essentially centres of supra-tribal authorities (LaBianca and Younker 1985; Bienkowski and van der Steen 2001). Settlement in the major centres continued into the Persian period and maybe later, and it is likely that the supra-tribal authorities continued to represent their areas and tribes under the Persians and possibly even the Ptolemies (Bienkowski 2002: 482; Berlin 1997: 11).

Little research has been undertaken to synthesize evidence for the Hellenistic period in Jordan (cf. Smith 1990; Berlin 1997; Ji 2001; Ji and Lee 2004; Tidmarsh 2001). We must beware of occasional terminological and chronological confusion, since of course the Nabataean period was coterminous with the Hellenistic, but, certainly in its earlier stages, Nabataean culture was confined to southern Jordan—and it should be stressed that Hellenistic pottery can be identified quite separately on Nabataean sites. The clearest chronological definitions are based on historical, not archaeological, criteria: the Hellenistic period begins conventionally in 332 BC with Alexander the Great's arrival in Phoenicia, with Jordan under the rule first of the Ptolemies from Egypt (c. 301–198 BC) and then the Seleucids from Syria (c. 198–63 BC); it ends with Pompey's conquest of Syria in 63 BC (for the Nabataeans, see the chapter by Schmid, this volume).

There is still no conclusive archaeological evidence concerning continuity between Edomite and Nabataean settlements (Bartlett 1990; Bienkowski 1990). Busayra was occupied from Iron II until at least the end of the Persian period, and possibly into the Hellenistic period (the dating depends on a single stratified third century BC Hellenistic sherd, which may conceivably be a stray, although four more unstratified sherds were found; cf. Bienkowski 2002: 350–351), but Nabataean pottery found unstratified at the site dates between the first century BC and the second century AD, and is not associated with the Iron II/Persian settlement (Bienkowski 2002: 348). Neither Tall Khalayfi—apart from a surface find of a Rhodian jar handle dating to c. 200 BC (Pratico 1993: 62)—nor Aila (Roman Aqaba, Parker 1997: 39) have yielded evidence for the Hellenistic period.

Farther north there was some continuity of settlement from Iron II through the Persian period and into the Hellenistic period, at least at Tall Umayri (Herr 1993), Dreijat (Younker *et al.* 1990: 13), Tall Saidiyya (Pritchard 1985), and Fukhar (Strange 1997: 403–405), and possibly at Hisban (see above). Until recently, the relative paucity of Early Hellenistic sites, compared with the comparative density of preceding Iron II and following Late Hellenistic settlement, was attributed to initial stagnation due to Ptolemaic domination and a possible period of drought, followed by Seleucid fostering of new trade routes and a cooler, wetter climate (Smith 1990). This apparent pattern always appeared suspect, since the contemporary records of Polybius (Paton 1922), Zenon (Edgar 1925) and Strabo (Jones 1917) betray no indication of depressed economic, social or demographic conditions in this region. Ji (2001) draws attention to accumulating evidence for the building of villages, villas, small farmsteads and garrisons across the Jordanian plateau and the Jordan Valley in the Early Hellenistic period, a process apparently pre-dating the changes in urban centres in the Late Hellenistic period (Barghouti 1982). Nevertheless, Hellenistic settlement patterns are still not clear, and surveys in central and northern Jordan have suggested differences between regions (Ji 1998; Ji and Lee 1999). On the Jordanian Plateau and in the north Jordan Valley there may have been a gap in the late Persian period, but in the Early and particularly the Late Hellenistic period there was a considerable increase in settlements. In the south and central Jordan Valley, however, there seems to have been continuity from the Persian into the Early Hellenistic period, but thereafter a gap until the Roman period.

It is difficult to assess how much confidence can be placed in these survey results, given the still sketchy knowledge of Hellenistic-period pottery in different regions, and the lack of a published stratified corpus of Early Hellenistic pottery from Jordan (Smith 1990: 125; cf. Ji and Lee 2004). Without doubt, though, there was some continuity from the Persian, through the Hellenistic and into the Roman period. Certainly during the Hellenistic period several "Greek" cities in Jordan were founded—Gadara, Abila, Pella, Gerasa and Philadelphia—which with others formed what at the beginning of the Roman imperial era became the federation known as the Decapolis (see the chapter by Freeman, this volume).

Notes

1. Lemaire 1994a supersedes his earlier fundamental study of the Persian administration of Palestine and Transjordan (1990).

2. Lemaire (1994a: 51) proposes that the borders of the Persian province of Ammon corresponded to the borders of the Ammonite kingdom in the seventh and sixth centuries BC, in his view the area around modern Amman plus the central Jordan Valley. Unfortunately, the precise borders of the Iron Age kingdom of Ammon are uncertain (cf. Hübner 1992: 131–157); indeed, it is likely that they were highly fluid and changeable.

3. Most of the pottery from Transjordan with Persian par-

allels is still unpublished or illustrated only by photographs, so line drawings are difficult to illustrate here. The author thanks Dr. L.G. Herr for his assistance with the material from Tall Umayri and for his permission to reproduce pottery drawings in Figure 11.2 originally published by him in Geraty *et al.* 1989 and Herr *et al.* 1991a; Jonathan Tubb for his permission to use previously unpublished photographs of pottery from Tall Saidiyya (Figures 11.3–11.4).

4. The date of the Meqabelayn tomb has been much discussed (cf. Stern 1982: 79–80). It could date anytime between the late seventh and early fifth centuries BC, with Stern preferring a mid-sixth century BC date.

5. An unpublished conical stamp seal from Tall Saidiyya Grave 27 (cf. Tubb 1988: 74), probably to be dated to the beginning of the Persian period, depicts a horned animal with a long tail, in front a leaf or a stylized (Egyptian?) feather, and above a winged scarab. I am grateful to the excavator, Jonathan Tubb, for permission to refer to this object prior to its publication.

Bibliography

Aharoni, Y.

1979 *The Land of the Bible: A Historical Geography*. Second edition, trans. and ed. A. F. Rainey. London: Burns and Oates.

Ahlström, G.W.

1993 *The History of Ancient Palestine from the Palaeolithic Period to Alexander's Conquest*. D. Edelman (ed.). Journal for the Study of the Old Testament Supplement Series 146. Sheffield: Sheffield Academic Press.

Albright, W.F.

1954 Notes on Ammonite History. In *Miscellanea Biblica B. Ubach*, 131–136. Montserrat.

Amiran, R.

1972 Achaemenian Bronze Objects from a Tomb at Kh. Ibsan in Lower Galilee. *Levant* 4: 135–138.

Barghouti, A.N.

1982 Urbanization of Palestine and Jordan in Hellenistic and Roman Times. In A. Hadidi (ed.), *Studies in the History and Archaeology of Jordan I*, 209–229. Amman: Department of Antiquities.

Bartlett, J.R.

1989 *Edom and the Edomites*. Journal for the Study of the Old Testament Supplement Series 77. Sheffield: Sheffield Academic Press.

1990 From Edomites to Nabataeans: The Problem of Continuity. *Aram* 2: 25–34.

1999 Edomites and Idumaeans. *Palestine Exploration Quarterly* 131: 102–114.

Beaulieu, P-A.

1989 *The Reign of Nabonidus, King of Babylon: 556–539 BC*. New Haven: Yale University.

Bennett, C-M. and P. Bienkowski

1995 *Excavations at Tawilan in Southern Jordan.* Oxford: Oxford University Press.

Berlin, A.M.

1997 Between Large Forces: Palestine in the Hellenistic Period. *Biblical Archaeologist* 60: 2–51.

Bienkowski, P.

1990 The Chronology of Tawilan and the 'Dark Age' of Edom. *Aram* 2: 35–44.

2000 Transjordan and Assyria. In L.E. Stager, J.A. Greene and M.D. Coogan (eds.), *The Archaeology of Jordan and Beyond: Essays in Honor of James A. Sauer*, 44–58. Winona Lake: Eisenbrauns.

2001 The Iron Age and Persian Periods in Jordan. In *Studies in the History and Archaeology of Jordan VII*, 265–274. Amman: Department of Antiquities.

2002 *Busayra: Excavations by Crystal-M. Bennett 1971–1980.* Oxford: Oxford University Press.

Bienkowski, P. (ed.)

1991 *Treasures from an Ancient Land: The Art of Jordan.* Stroud: Alan Sutton.

Bienkowski, P. and E. van der Steen

2001 Tribes, Trade and Towns: A New Framework for the Late Iron Age in Southern Jordan and the Negev. *Bulletin of the American Schools of Oriental Research* 323: 21–47.

Brown, R.M.

1991 Ceramics from the Kerak Plateau. In J.M. Miller (ed.), *Archaeological Survey of the Kerak Plateau*, 169–279. Atlanta: Scholars Press.

Clark, V.A.

1983 The Iron IIC/Persian Pottery from Rujm al-Henu. *Annual of the Department of Antiquities of Jordan* 27: 143–163.

Cross, F.M. and L.T. Geraty

1994 The Ammonite Ostraca from Tell Hesban. In D. Merling and L.T. Geraty (eds.), *Hesban after 25 Years*, 169–74. Berrien Springs: Institute of Archaeology/Siegfried H. Horn Archaeological Museum.

Dalley, S.

1995 The Cuneiform Tablet. In C.-M. Bennett and P. Bienkowski, *Excavations at Tawilan in Southern Jordan*, 67–68. Oxford: Oxford University Press.

Dandamaev, M.A.

1989 *A Political History of the Achaemenid Empire.* Leiden: E.J. Brill.

Dempsey, D.

1993 An Ostracon from Tell Nimrin. *Bulletin of the American Schools of Oriental Research* 289: 55–58.

DiVito, R.A.

1993 The Tell el-Kheleifeh Inscriptions. In G. Pratico, *Nelson Glueck's 1938–1940 Excavations at Tell el-Kheleifeh: A Reappraisal*, 51–63. Atlanta: Scholars Press.

Edgar, C.C.

1925 *The Zenon Papyri.* 4 vols. Cairo.

Elayi, J. and J. Sapin

1998 *Beyond the River: New Perspectives on Transeuphratene.* Sheffield: Sheffield Academic Press.

Eph'al, I.

1984 *The Ancient Arabs: Nomads on the Borders of the Fertile Crescent 9th–5th Centuries B.C.* Jerusalem: Magnes.

1988 Syria-Palestine under Achaemenid Rule. *The Cambridge Ancient History* 4: 139–164. Second ed. Cambridge: Cambridge University Press.

Flanagan, J.W., D.W. McCreery and K.N. Yassine

1992 Preliminary Report of the 1990 Excavation at Tell Nimrin. *Annual of the Department of Antiquities of Jordan* 36: 89–11.

1994 Tell Nimrin: Preliminary Report on the 1993 Season. *Annual of the Department of Antiquities of Jordan* 38: 205–244.

Geraty, L.E., L.G. Herr and Ø.S. LaBianca

1988 The Joint Madaba Plains Project: A Preliminary Report on the Second Season at Tell el-'Umeiri and Vicinity (June 18 to August 6, 1987). *Andrews University Seminary Studies* 26: 217–252.

Geraty, L.E. L.G. Herr, Ø.S. LaBianca and R.W. Younker

1989 *Madaba Plains Project 1: The 1984 Season at Tell el-'Umeiri and Vicinity and Subsequent Studies.* Berrien Springs: Andrews University.

Graf, D.F.

1990 Arabia during Achaemenid Times. In H. Sancisi-Weerdenburg and A. Kuhrt (eds.), *Achaemenid History IV: Centre and Periphery*, 131–148. Leiden: Nederlands Instituut voor het Nabije Oosten.

1993 The Persian Royal Road System in Syria-Palestine. *Transeuphratène* 6: 149 –168.

Grayson, A.K.

1975 *Assyrian and Babylonian Chronicles.* Locust Valley: Augustin.

Greene, J.A. and K. 'Amr

1992 Deep Sounding on the Lower Terrace of the Amman Citadel: Final Report. *Annual of the Department of Antiquities of Jordan* 36: 113–144.

Hadidi, A.

1987 An Ammonite Tomb at Amman. *Levant* 19: 101–120.

Harding, G.L.

1950 An Iron-Age Tomb at Meqabelein. *Quarterly of the Department of Antiquities of Palestine* 14: 44–48.

Harding, G.L. and O. Tufnell

1953 The Tomb of Adoni Nur in Amman. *Palestine Exploration Fund Annual* 6: 48–75.

Harrison, T.P.

1994 A Sixth–Seventh Century Assemblage from Madaba, Jordan. *Annual of the Department of Antiquities of Jordan* 38: 429–46.

Hendrix, R.E., P.R. Drey and J.B. Storfjell

1997 *Ancient Pottery of Transjordan: An Introduction Utilizing Published Whole Forms.* Berrien Springs, MI: Institute of Archaeology/Horn Archaeological Museum, Andrews University.

Herr, L.G.

1992 Two Stamped Jar Impressions of the Persian Province of Ammon from Tell el-'Umeiri. *Annual of the Department of Antiquities of Jordan* 36: 163–166.

1993 What Ever Happened to the Ammonites? *Biblical Archaeology Review* 19/6: 26–35, 68.

1995 The Late Iron II–Persian Ceramic Horizon at Tell el-'Umeiri. In K. 'Amr, F. Zayadine and M. Zaghloul (eds.), *Studies in the History and Archaeology of Jordan V*, 617–619. Amman: Department of Antiquities.

1999 The Ammonites in the Late Iron Age and Persian Period. In B. MacDonald and R.W. Younker (eds.), *Ancient Ammon*, 219–237. Studies in the History and Culture of the Ancient Near East. Leiden: E.J. Brill.

Herr, L.G., L.T. Geraty, Ø.S. LaBianca and R.W. Younker

1991a *Madaba Plains Project 2: The 1987 Season at Tell el-'Umeiri and Vicinity and Subsequent Studies.* Berrien Springs, MI: Andrews University.

Herr, L.G., L.T. Geraty, Ø.S. LaBianca and R.W. Younker

1991b Madaba Plains Project: The 1989 Excavations at Tell el-'Umeiri and Vicinity. *Annual of the Department of Antiquities of Jordan* 35: 155–179.

1994 Madaba Plains Project: The 1992 Excavations at Tell el-'Umeiri, Tell Jalul, and Vicinity. *Annual of the Department of Antiquities of Jordan* 38: 147–172.

Hoglund, K.G.

1992 *Achaemenid Imperial Administration in Syria-Palestine and the Missions of Ezra and Nehemiah.* Atlanta, GA: Scholars.

Homès-Fredericq, D.

1996 Influences diverses en Transjordanie à l'époque achéménide. *Transeuphratène* 11: 63–76.

Hübner, U.

1992 *Die Ammoniter: Untersuchungen zur Geschichte Kultur und Religion einer Transjordanischen Volkes im 1. Jahrtausend v. Chr.* Wiesbaden: Harrassowitz.

Ibach, R.D.

1987 *Archaeological Survey of the Hesban Region.* Berrien Springs, MI: Andrews University.

Ibrahim, M. and S. Mittmann

1986 Al-Mugayyir. *Archiv für Orientforschung* 33: 167–172.

Ji, C-H. C.

1998 Archaeological Survey and Settlement Patterns in the Region of 'Iraq al-'Amir, 1996: A Preliminary Report. *Annual of the Department of Antiquities of Jordan* 42: 587–608.

2001 'Iraq al-'Amir and the Hellenistic Settlements in Central and Northern Jordan. *Studies in the History and Archaeology of Jordan* 7: 379–389.

Ji, C-H. C. and J. K. Lee

1999 The 1998 Season of Archaeological Survey in the Regions of 'Iraq al-'Amir and Wadi al-Kafrayn: A Preliminary Report. *Annual of the Department of Antiquities of Jordan* 43: 521–539.

2000a. A Preliminary Report on the Dhiban Plateau Survey Project 1999: The Versacare Expedition. *Annual of the Department of Antiquities of Jordan* 44: 493–506.

2000b. The Survey in the Regions of 'Iraq al-Amir and Wadi al-Kafrayn, 2000. *Annual of the Department of Antiquities of Jordan* 44: 179–195.

2004 From the Tobiads to the Hasmoneans: The Hellenistic Pottery, Coins, and History in the Regions of 'Iraq al-Amir and the Wadi Hisban. In F. al-Khraysheh (ed.), *Studies in the History and Archaeology of Jordan VIII*, 177–188. Amman: Department of Antiquities.

Jones, H.L.

1917 *The Geography of Strabo.* 8 vols. Cambridge, MA: Harvard University.

Khalil, L. A.

1986 A Bronze Caryatid Censer from Amman. *Levant* 18: 103–110.

Kooij, G. van der

1987 Tell Deir 'Alla (East Jordan Valley) During the Achaemenid Period: Some Aspects of the Culture. In H. Sancisi-Weerdenburg (ed.), *Achaemenid History I: Sources, Structures and Synthesis*, 97–102. Leiden: Nederlands Instituut voor het Nabije Oosten.

Kooij, G. van der, and M.M. Ibrahim (eds.)

1989 *Picking Up the Threads…A Continuing Review of Excavations at Deir Alla, Jordan.* Leiden: University of Leiden Archaeological Centre.

LaBianca, Ø.S. and R.W. Younker

1985 The Kingdoms of Ammon, Moab and Edom: The Archaeology of Society in Late Bronze/Iron Age Transjordan (*ca.* 1400–500 BCE). In T.E. Levy (ed.), *The Archaeology of Society in the Holy Land*, 399–415. London: Leicester University Press.

Lemaire, A.

1990 Populations et territoires de la Palestine à l'époque perse. *Transeuphratène* 3: 31–74.

1994a Histoire et administration de la Palestine à l'époque perse. In E-M. Laperrousaz and A. Lemaire (eds.), *La Palestine à l'Époque Perse*, 11–53. Paris: Les Éditions du Cerf.

1994b Épigraphie et numismatique palestiniennes. In E-M. Laperrousaz and A. Lemaire (eds.), *La Palestine à l'Époque Perse*, 261–287. Paris: Les Éditions du Cerf.

Mabry, J. and G. Palumbo

1989 Wadi Yabis Survey, 1987. In D. Homès-Fredericq and J. B. Hennessy (eds.), *Archaeology of Jordan II/1. Field Reports: Surveys and Sites A–K*, 91–97. Akkadica Supplementum 7. Leiden: Peeters.

MacDonald, B., L.G. Herr, M.P. Neeley, T. Gagos, K. Moumani, and M. Rockman

2004 *The Tafila–Busayra Archaeological Survey 1999–2001, West-Central Jordan*. Archaeological Reports 9. Boston, MA: American Schools of Oriental Research.

Mare, W.H.

1989 Quweilbeh (Abila). In D. Homès-Fredericq and J.B. Hennessy (eds.), *Archaeology of Jordan II/2. Field Reports: Sites L–Z*, 472–487. Akkadica Supplementum 8. Leiden: Peeters.

McGovern, P.E.

1989 Baq'ah Valley Survey. In D. Homès-Fredericq and J. B. Hennessy (eds.), *Archaeology of Jordan II/1. Field Reports: Surveys and Sites A–K*, 25–44. Akkadica Supplementum 7. Leiden: Peeters.

Merling, D.

1994 The 'Pools of Heshban': As Discovered by the Heshban Expedition. In D. Merling and L.T. Geraty (eds.), *Hesban After 25 Years*, 211–223. Berrien Springs: Institute of Archaeology/Siegfried H. Horn Archaeological Museum.

Miller, J.M. (ed.)

1991 *Archaeological Survey of the Kerak Plateau*. Atlanta, GA: Scholars.

Mitchel, L.A.

1992 *Hesban 7: Hellenistic and Roman Strata*. Berrien Springs, MI: Andrews University Press.

Ottosson, M.

1993 The Iron Age of Northern Jordan. In A. Lemaire and B. Otzen (eds.), *History and Traditions of Early Israel: Studies Presented to Eduard Nielsen*, 90–103. Leiden: E.J. Brill.

Parker, S.T.

1997 Preliminary Report on the 1994 Season of the Roman Aqaba Project. *Bulletin of the American Schools of Oriental Research* 305: 19–44.

Paton, W.R.

1922 *Polybius*. 6 vols. London: Heinemann.

Porada, E.

1989 Two Cylinder Seals from'Umeiri, Nos. 49 and 363. In L.T. Geraty, L.G. Herr, Ø.S. LaBianca and R.W. Younker (eds.), *Madaba Plains Project I: The 1984 Season at Tell el-'Umeiri and Vicinity and Subsequent Studies*, 381–384. Berrien Springs, MI: Andrews University.

Prag, K.

1989 Preliminary Report on the Excavations at Tell Iktanu, Jordan, 1987. *Levant* 21: 33–45.

Pratico, G.D.

1993 *Nelson Glueck's 1938–1940 Excavations at Tell el-Kheleifeh: A Reappraisal*. Atlanta, GA: Scholars.

Pritchard, J.B.

1985 *Tell es-Sa'idiyeh: Excavations on the Tell, 1964–1966*. Philadelphia, PA: University of Pennsylvania.

Ray, P.J.

2001 *Tell Hesban and Vicinity in the Iron Age*. Berrien Springs, MI: Andrews University Press.

Sapin, J.

1996 Réflexions sur des stratégies et des techniques d'adaptation dans la Transjordanie du 1er millénaire. *Transeuphratène* 11: 45–61.

Sauer, J.A.

1986 Transjordan in the Bronze and Iron Ages: A Critique of Glueck's Synthesis. *Bulletin of the American Schools of Oriental Research* 263: 1–26.

1994 The Pottery at Hesban and its Relationship to the History of Jordan: An Interim Hesban Pottery Report, 1993. In D. Merling and L.T. Geraty (eds.), *Hesban After 25 Years*, 225–281. Berrien Springs, MI: Institute of Archaeology/Siegfried H. Horn Archaeological Museum.

Smith, R.H.

1990 The Southern Levant in the Hellenistic Period. *Levant* 22: 123–130.

Stern, E.

1982 *Material Culture of the Land of the Bible in the Persian Period 538–332 B.C.* Warminster: Aris and Phillips.

1990 New Evidence on the Administrative Division of Palestine in the Persian Period. In H. Sancisi-Weerdenburg and A. Kuhrt (eds.), *Achaemenid History IV: Centre and Periphery*, 221–226. Leiden: Nederlands Instituut voor het Nabije Oosten.

Strange, J.

1997 Tall al-Fukhar 1990–1991: A Preliminary Report. In G. Bisheh, M. Zaghloul and I. Kehrberg (eds.), *Studies in the History and Archaeology of Jordan VI*, 399–406. Amman: Department of Antiquities.

Thompson, H.O.

1972 The 1972 Excavation of Khirbet el-Hajjar. *Annual of the Department of Antiquities of Jordan* 17: 47–72.

1977 The Ammonite Remains at Khirbet el-Hajjar. *Bulletin of the American Schools of Oriental Reaearch* 227: 27–34.

Tidmarsh, J.

2001 The Problem of Early Hellenistic Jordan. In A. Walmsley (ed.), *Australians Uncovering Ancient Jordan*, 191–206. Sydney: University of Sydney.

Tubb, J.N.

1988 Tell es-Sa'idiyeh: Preliminary Report on the First Three Seasons of Renewed Excavations. *Levant* 20: 23–88.

Tubb, J.N. and P.G. Dorrell

1994 Tell es-Sa'idiyeh 1993: Interim Report on the Seventh Season of Excavations. *Palestine Exploration Quarterly* 126: 52–67.

Tubb, J.N., P.G. Dorrell and F.J. Cobbing

1996 Interim Report on the Eighth (1995) Season of Excavations at Tell es-Sa'idiyeh. *Palestine Exploration Quarterly* 128: 16–40.

Yassine, K.

1984 *Tell el-Mazar Cemetery A*. Amman: University of Jordan.

1988a Ammonite Fortresses, Date and Function. In K. Yassine (ed.), *Archaeology of Jordan: Essays and Reports*, 11–31. Amman: Department of Archaeology, University of Jordan.

1988b Tell El Mazar Field I: Preliminary Report of Areas G, H, L, and M. In K. Yassine (ed.), *Archaeology of Jordan: Essays and Reports*, 73–113. Amman: Department of Archaeology, University of Jordan.

1988c Ammonite Seals from Tell el-Mazar. In K. Yassine (ed.), *Archaeology of Jordan: Essays and Reports*, 143–155. Amman: Department of Archaeology, University of Jordan.

1999 Burial Customs and Practices in Ancient Ammon. In B. MacDonald and R.W. Younker (eds.), *Ancient Ammon*, 137–151. Studies in the History and Culture of the Ancient Near East. Leiden: E.J. Brill.

Yassine, K., M.M. Ibrahim and J. Sauer

1988 The East Jordan Valley Survey, 1975 and 1976. In K. Yassine (ed.), *Archaeology of Jordan: Essays and Reports*, 159–207. Amman: Department of Archaeology, University of Jordan.

Yassine, K. and J. Teixidor

1988 Ammonite and Aramaic Inscriptions from Tell el-Mazar. In K. Yassine (ed.), *Archaeology of Jordan: Essays and Reports*, 137–142. Amman: Department of Archaeology, University of Jordan.

Younker, R.W. and D. Merling

1999 Tall Jalul. *ACOR Newsletter* 11.1: 6–7.

Younker, R.W., L.T. Geraty, L.G. Herr, and Ø.S. LaBianca

1990 The Joint Madaba Plains Project: A Preliminary Report of the 1989 Season, including the Regional Survey and Excavations at El-Dreijat, Tell Jawa, and Tell el-'Umeiri (June 19 to August 8, 1989). *Andrews University Seminary Studies* 28/1: 5–52.

Younker, R.W., L.T. Geraty, L.G. Herr, and Ø.S. LaBianca and D. Clark

1996 Preliminary Report of the 1994 Season of the Madaba Plains Project: Regional Survey, Tall al-'Umayri, and Tall Jalul Excavations. *Andrews University Seminary Studies* 34/1: 65–92.

Zayadine, F.

1986 L'époque perse-achéménide. In *La Voie Royale: 9000 Ans d'Art au Royaume de Jordanie*, 142–151. Paris: Association Française d'Action Artistique.

12. The Hellenistic Period and the Nabataeans

Stephan G. Schmid

The Hellenistic Period

In general terms, the Hellenistic Period, c. 330–30 BC, can be considered one of the best known historical periods of Antiquity. The three hundred years between the death of Alexander the Great (323 BC) and the fall of the last of the great Hellenistic kingdoms, Egypt, to the Romans (30 BC) produced an overwhelming amount of historical documents and material culture.[1] This general observation is true for almost all of the Mediterranean as well as for neighbouring regions, such as Mesopotamia and Iran, parts of the Seleucid kingdom, and for Egypt, home of the Ptolemies.[2] However, when turning to Transjordan, there is much less reason for optimism. As a matter of fact, despite some historical notions, the archaeological record for the Hellenistic period is extremely poor.

For instance, survey projects in central Jordan revealed that the Persian and the Hellenistic periods are by far the less well attested in terms of physical presence and density of occupation (Mattingly 1990; Hart and Falkner 1985; Hart 1985, 1986A, 1987). It is very likely that the same picture is true for the whole of Jordan, although there are definitely some sites with continuity from the Iron Age until the later Hellenistic period, but in general terms settlement patterns seem to indicate a clear decrease in sites (on the Persian period see Bienkowski this volume; for the Hellenistic period see Smith 1990). The Decapolis, a political union of several ancient cities in northern Jordan, southern Syria and Israel, is taken as one element to demonstrate the highly developed status of that area in the Hellenistic period, since it is often believed that this formation is the direct result of Pompey the Great's intervention and re-structuring of the Near East in 64/3 BC (for example Bowersock 1983: 30–31). However, it has recently become clear that the Decapolis as a political body did not exist before the first century AD (Wenning 1994; Millar 1993: 408–14; Graf 1992a; Lichtenberger 2003). Still, most of these cities did indeed provide us with a few remains of the Hellenistic period, but they are difficult to interpret and seem much less important than the remains of the Roman period. In the following, a short overview of the most important remains belonging to the Hellenistic period is given.

In general terms, Transjordan, Palestine, Phoenicia and parts of southern Syria were strongly contested between several of the diadochs, the immediate successors of Alexander.[3] After the battle of Ipsos in 301 BC, the whole area, known as Coele Syria, came under Ptolemaic rule.

During the entire third century BC the Ptolemies and the Seleucids fought several "Syrian wars" in order to control Coele Syria. During the fourth (or the third, according to the system of counting them) Syrian war of 221–217 BC, the Seleucids conquered most of that area but immediately lost it again. The fifth (or fourth) Syrian war of 201–195 BC finally gave them the supremacy over Coele Syria. Since the Seleucid kingdom began to weaken soon after these events, local powers such as the Maccabees, the Hasmoneans and the Nabataeans extended their influence and control upon areas formerly under Ptolemaic and then Seleucid rule.

Gadara

Gadara, modern Umm Qays (Weber 2002), is situated at a very important strategic point on a high plateau, where one overlooks and controls the Yarmuk Valley and several roads (see Figure 12.1 for location). From the late fourth-century BC onwards, several intellectuals are reported to be from Gadara, such as the Cynic Menippos (late fourth-century BC), the poet Meleagros (late second–early first century BC), or the Epicurean Philodemos (first century BC), especially known through the finds of his texts in the so-called Villa dei Papiri in Herculaneum (Weber 2002: 59–67 for further references; Guzzo 1999; Dorandi 1995). However, these learned men absolved most if not all of their careers abroad and, therefore, their lives can not attest a great deal about the size and importance of their hometown. Although the name of the city goes back to the Semitic toponym "Gader", archaeological and historical evidence for a pre-Hellenistic settlement is very small. During the third century BC the city belonged to the Ptolemies. To this period belong a few sherds of imported Greek and Egyptian pottery and, possibly, some remains of a fortification that can be assumed according to a reference in Polybios (5, 71, 3), which refers to the temporary conquest of Gadara by the Seleucid Antiochos III in 211 BC (Weber 2002: 60–2; Lichtenberger 2003: 83–86; Hoffmann and Bührig 2000: 186–187). A few years later, i.e. shortly after 200 BC, Gadara came under Seleucid control. This was probably the starting point for a considerable improvement of size and infrastructure of the settlement that most likely was given the status of a *polis* (city) at the same time (Weber 2002: 62–64; Hoffmann 2001). Due to construction of a parking lot to meet the demands of growing tourism, an important section of the city walls was completely exposed in 1996 and 1997 (Figure 12.2). This, together with geophysical measurements and survey activities, led to a rather concise picture of the complete course of the city walls and even some hints as to the city grid, that seems based on the well known rectangular prototypes of Greek cities. The walls circumscribe an area of about 225 x 300 m and include the peak of the acropolis hill, a topo-graphical feature that can be observed on several other occasions (Weber 2002: 314 fig. 34; Hoffmann 2001: 394 fig. 6; Hoffmann and Bührig 2000: 206 fig. 26). So far, no information regarding details of the space within the walls, such as plans of houses or other buildings has become available.

To the north of the city walls, on a promontory about

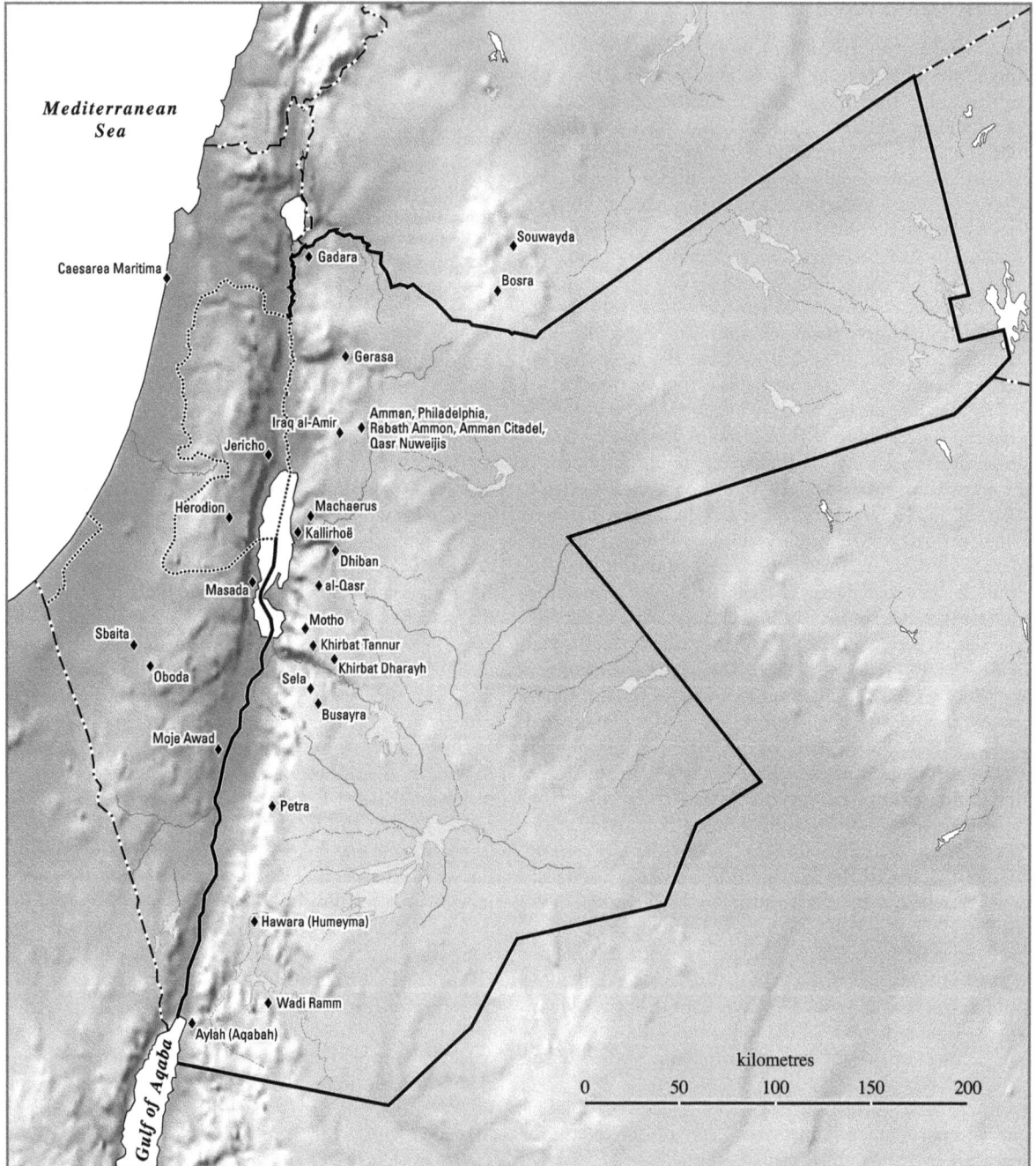

Figure 12.1 Hellenistic period and Nabataean sites mentioned in the text.

Figure 12.2 Gadara/Umm Qays, stretch of the city wall.

125 m *extra muros*, a separate compound for a small temple was errected. The beginning of the construction goes back to the first half of the second century, apparently shortly after the city walls were completed, but work was not accomplished until the early first century BC (Weber 2002: 335–337; Hoffmann 1999).[4] Despite the lack of inscriptions, there is a good chance that the Doric temple was dedicated to Zeus, the god favoured by the Seleucids.

Gerasa

Gerasa, modern Jarash, follows to some extent a similar pattern to Gadara. Here too, the Semitic name and dispersed finds indicate a much older, pre-Hellenistic settlement (Lichtenberger 2003: 191; Seigne 1997a: 995).[5] Like in the case of Gadara, the Seleucid conquest around 200 BC must have contributed to an increasing development, which went together with the attribution of the *polis*-status as Antiocheia on the Chrysorrhoas ("the gold-bearer," which means the nearby river). While the city plan and the sumptuous buildings all belong to the Roman and even Byzantine periods, some information about the Hellenistic nucleus can be obtained. The acropolis of that settlement has to be located on the hill near the river, now the location of the museum, formerly known as "camp hill" (Figure 12.3). Soundings in that area revealed an interesting sequence of pottery and, to a lesser extent, structures that

cover the MB IIC to the Iron II periods and then again from the mid-second century BC onwards with a hiatus from the seventh to the early second century BC (Braemer 1987). These results are likely to confirm the constructive impact of the Seleucid conquest and to disqualify pseudo-historical constructions from (late) Roman times according to which Alexander the Great or his general Perdikkas was the founder of the city (Lichtenberger 2003: 191–192). It is from that same area that some extremely scanty indications for Hellenistic dwellings are reported (Seigne 1997b: 76).

As at Gadara, an important sanctuary was installed on the slopes of a nearby hill *extra muros*. Some 120 m southwest of the acropolis, on the site of a cave that served pre-Hellenistic cultic purposes, a first altar was installed in the second century BC, followed by a second one and soon after a first small temple, both in the first century BC (Seigne 2002: 12–15, 1997a, 1993).[6] According to the decoration of the first temple showing reliefs of thunderbolts, it was dedicated to Zeus. These structures were considerably enlarged from the early first century AD onwards and were to become a huge sanctuary on two artificial terrasses. The configuration is the same as in Gadara, with a nearby extra-mural sanctuary on a separate promontory, facing the acropolis on an opposite hilltop. According to one interesting hypothesis, the sanctuary of Artemis, erected in the first

Figure 12.3 Gerasa/Jarash, view towards the acropolis hill from the temple of Zeus.

half of the second century AD on a hill formerly occupied by a necropolis, is the transformation of a much older cult, maybe going back to the pre-Hellenistic Semitic occupation of the site, that initially was located on the acropolis hill (Seigne 1992).

Recent excavations on the northern stretch of the Roman city walls revealed a tomb of the Hellenistic period that contained a nice selection of pottery comprising a *lagynos* and several zoomorphic vases. The pottery and a coin point to the late second or early first century BC for the burial (Kehrberg and Manley 2002: especially 197–199).[7]

Philadelphia

Philadelphia, modern Amman, presents to some extent similar evidence to Gadara and Gerasa, as far as historical and archaeological information can be obtained.[8] Passages in the Hebrew Bible as well as some dispersed archaeological evidence confirm the importance of Rabbath-Ammon, the capital of the Ammonites during the Iron Age. During the Persian period occupation was apparently far from dense (MacDonald and Younker 1999; Hübner 1992). After Alexander's campaign the city was symbolically refounded by Ptolemy II Philadelphos (see below) and remained under Ptolemaic control

until the late third century BC. The first conquest of the city by the Seleucids in 218/7 BC did not last for long, but from 200 BC onwards the city belonged to the Seleucid kingdom (MacAdam 1992; Zayadine 1990b). Although the Ptolemies lost their supremacy over Transjordan with the fourth Syrian war, the Seleucids did not always exercise direct control, since on several occasions local tyrants and Nabataean kings are quoted as the lords of Philadelphia, until the city gained its independence after 63 BC. Unfortunately, the precise relationships between the Seleucids, the local tyrants (depending on the Seleucids or on the Nabataeans?) and the Nabataeans (depending on the Seleucids?) are not always clear.[9]

Several seasons of excavation on the citadel hill have revealed terracing walls and occupation levels belonging to the Hellenistic period; however, important later structures prevent the obtaining of a concise picture of the occupational pattern (Greene and 'Amr 1992; Zayadine and Humbert 1992: 233–238, 242–247; Zayadine and Humbert and Najjar 1989; Zayadine and Najjar and Greene 1987; Bennett 1979; Zayadine 1977–78; Zayadine 1973). Not only a Hellenistic occupation of the Amman Citadel is therefore attested, but several coins of Ptolemy II Philadelphos (283–246 BC), the founder of Hellenistic Philadelphia, were discovered related to floors of that period (Zayadine and Humbert and Najjar 1989: 362–363),[10] attesting an early Hellenistic occupation that is missing in most other places, even if it is likely to have been rather small. The presence of the Nabataeans, although historically attested, is somewhat enigmatic. Archaeological evidence from the citadel is restricted to a few sherds belonging to the first century AD.[11] However, there is a rather well supplied corpus of typical Hellenistic pottery from the soundings on the citadel. Since the earliest known pottery of the Nabataeans, belonging to the late second and early first century BC, does show exactly the same forms and the same brownish-reddish surface slips, it can not be excluded that some genuine Nabataean pottery will be found within the samples from Philadelphia.[12]

It is true that the overall evidence for the Hellenistic period in the region of the future Decapolis cities within the borders of modern Jordan is rather disappointing. On the one hand, this situation may be partially explained by the difficult access to the structures corresponding to the second and first century BC, in most cases covered by the important building programs of the Roman period. On the other hand, all the results obtained so far point indeed to rather small settlements. If there is something like a general pattern, one could describe it as follows. Early occupations belonging to the third century BC and, therefore, to the period of Ptolemaic supremacy are, if ever, only indirectly attested, for example by Polybios' mention of a city wall in the case of Gadara being attacked by the Seleucids at the end of the third century BC. Other evidence from the Roman period that indicates for instance a foundation under Alexander the Great or Perdikkas in the case of Gerasa, are very likely to be historizing constructs without any evidence. The only exception is offered by Philadelphia, where the historically attested re-foundation by Ptolemy II Philadelphos seems to find archaeological support, bearing in mind the long time of circulation of some coin types. In general terms, most of Coele Syria and especially the region east of the Jordan was apparently in decline during the third century BC. This can be explained, within other arguments, by a certain disinterest of the Ptolemies that, like their Assyrian and Persian forerunners, were focusing on a small coastal corridor in order to link Egypt with Syria (Smith 1990; on the preceeding periods see Hackl and Jenni and Schneider 2003: 9–12). From the early second century BC onwards, with the Seleucid takeover, fortified acropoleis begin to appear, often together with a new extra-mural sanctuary dedicated to Zeus and an elevation to the status of a *polis*. Despite the impact of the Seleucid rule, the hellenization of these cities was somewhat discrete. At least this is the conclusion when looking at the artistic production. At Pella, the main corpus of "classical" sculpture in the round or in relief is imported and/or belongs already to the Roman period, with very few exceptions (Weber

1993). The same is true for Gadara and in general terms for all of the Decapolis cities (Weber 2002). The relief decoration of the first small temple of Zeus at Gerasa is, despite the purely Greek iconography, characterized by its somewhat clumsy execution that has nothing in common with the elegant reliefs and capitals of the Roman period found within the same city, an observation that can also be extended to most of the other places under examination (Dentzer-Feydy 1992). As a result, the "Greek" cities of the area were probably not much different from other, more local settlements. No matter to what degree the area was undergoing a proper hellenization, the economic situation clearly improved from the second century BC onwards, as can be shown by the increasing imports from Syria, Asia Minor and mainland Greece, as reflected by stamped amphora handles and fine ware pottery (for the evidence from Gadara see Kenrick 2000).

As we shall see below, more or less the same general picture, i.e. rather scarce material evidence for the third and second centuries BC and a remarkable increase within all domains of material culture from the late first century BC onwards, can be observed in the case of Nabataean culture and one can ask whether this is pure coincidence.

The best evidence for a massive Hellenistic cultural impact during the Hellenistic period properly is offered by the Qasr Abd at Iraq al-Amir, situated between Amman and the Jordan Valley (Figure 12.4; Will *et al.* 1991; Nielsen 1994: 138–146, 282–284; see also below on the relation with Nabataean rock-cut façades). The monument, probably a kind of summer residence, can be attributed to Hyrcanus of the Tobiads' dynasty and is, therefore, dated to the years 182–175 BC. The familiy of the Tobiads was already in charge of the Ammanitis during the Ptolemaic supremacy, as a passage in the Zenon archive may suggest.[13] The building, identified as Hyrcanus' property called Tyros according to Flavius Josephus (*Ant.* 12.4.11), clearly stands in the tradition of Hellenistic palace architecture showing Near Eastern influence. As general aspects we can point out a lower, massive storey, with only a single entrance, combined with an upper storey with several windows and *intercolumnia*. Further, there is the rich figurative decoration with a family of lions on the edges of the first floor and fragments of eagles probably adorning the edges of the second floor. Of special interest for our further consideration is a particular feature of the Qasr Abd. The entire building was placed in an artificial lake, accessible only by a path from the East (Will *et al.* 1991: 37–38, n. 157, maps 1–4). The lake was filled by water from sources on the slopes surrounding the building and brought underground to two fountains, in the form of panthers, on the east side of the palace, close to its northeastern corner, and on the west side, close to its northwestern corner (Will *et al.* 1991: 211–218). Therefore, the whole monument would have had the aspect of a ship floating in a

Figure 12.4 Iraq al-Amir, Qasr Abd.

lake that was filled by itself. It does not matter whether or not the retaining walls for the lake were ever completed and, therefore, whether or not the lake was ever filled. The idea behind the installation is clear and it is this point that leads to further reflection. This makes it a good comparison for the luxury ship of Ptolemy IV, the *thalamegos*, which will be discussed below. An affiliation to Alexandria is also confirmed by the architectural elements, primarily by the capitals (Will *et al.* 1991: 149–208 especially 167–178; Fischer 1990b: 7–11).[14] Alternatively, there are some characteristics in the general aspect of the façade that put Qasr Abd in a close relationship with known palace architecture from Macedonia and Asia Minor (Will *et al.* 1991: 277–286; on related architecture see Brands 1996; Siganidou 1996; Nielsen 1994: 81–99; Heermann 1986; Pandermalis 1976).

To a similar context of strongly Hellenized luxury architecture belong the many palaces and palace like buildings of Herod the Great, although they are one and a half century younger than the Qasr Abd (Japp 2000; Netzer 1996b, 1999; Lichtenberger 1999; Roller 1998; Nielsen 1994: 181–208; for historical aspects related to Herod and his family see Kokkinos 1998). While the seaside palace at Caesarea Maritima takes over the same general aspect of floating in the water as does the Qasr Abd, combined with a huge central peristyle courtyard, typical of Hellenistic

architecture, two buildings situated in Transjordan shall be mentioned here. The forteress of Machaerus (Misneqa, near Mukawir) was an important outpost of the Herodian defense against the Nabataeans on the eastern shore of the Dead Sea (Figure 12.5). According to the main historical source, Flavius Josephus (*War* 7.6.1–4), the prominent hilltop was already occupied during the Hasmonean period under Alexander Jannaeus (103–76 BC), destroyed by the Romans in 57 BC and then rebuilt by Herod the Great.[15] The archaeological excavations were able to confirm most of Josephus' account, including the massive ramps built by the Roman besiegers during the Jewish revolt in AD 72, when Machaerus was destroyed. While the outline of the Hasmonean structure is somewhat obscure, the plan of the Herodian palace-fortress is easier to understand. We find all the important aspects of the different cultural influences that caracterized the Heriodian reign. The main element in the northwestern half of the hilltop is a huge peristyle courtyard, built over a subterranean cistern. This combination is clearly borrowed from Hellenistic architecture and is reminiscent of, for instance, the rich houses of Delos (Trümper 1998; Hoepfner *et al.* 1999: 515–524). As the central element of luxury architecture, combining practical purposes with aspects of dominating a rather hostile (= arid) sourounding, the cistern and peristyle element will be perfected in the early first century AD within the "Villa Iovis", the palace of the Roman emperor Tiberius on the Italian island of Capri (Krause 2003). This latter structure shows to what extent the Herodian buildings were important trend-setters, probably being themselves just a glimpse of Alexandrian luxury architecture and related buildings.[16] The idea of abundant luxury at Machaerus was pursued further by the construction of a huge pressure-aqueduct that had to cross an important difference of level in order to bring the water to the top of the hill. This water was used, along with other uses, to supply a typical Roman bath installation with a hypocaustum heating system. Although only fragmentarily preserved, wall paintings and mosaics (the earliest found so far in Transjordan) attest to elaborate interior decoration (Fittschen 1996; Foerster 1995a; for comparable Mosaics from other Herodian buildings see Foerster 1995b; Ovadiah 1994). All these features, i.e. peristyle, bath installation with hypocaustum heating, mosaics and wall paintings are integral part of most other palaces of Herod the Great.

The other building ascribed to Herod's presence in Transjordan is a huge villa complex at Kallirrhoë (Ayn Zara) at the eastern shore of the Dead Sea. According to Flavius Josephus (*Ant.*17.6.5; *War* 1.33. 5), Herod was seeking relief from his, eventually deadly, illness in this ancient spa (Strobel and Wimmer 2003; Clamer 1997; Japp

2000; Netzer 1996b, 1999; Lichtenberger 1999; Roller 1998; Nielsen 1994).[17] The villa that is identified with a residence of Herod is a rectangular complex measuring roughly 75 x 35 m and organized around two peristyle courtyards. In the northeastern part the peristyle is surrounded on three sides by porticoes with the central one giving access to a huge room on the northwestern side, either a triclinium or a reception hall. This room has a corridor on its back and lateral sides. The position and the form of that room strongly recall similar rooms at Herod's first palace at Jericho and to some extent also within the seaside palace at Caesarea Maritima. The northeastern part apparently had a Hasmonean forerunner, while the southwestern aisle was added in the Herodian period. The southwestern part shows a similar peristyle with porticoes on three sides. Here too and in a similar position as on the other part, a central room on the northwestern side dominates the structure. Exactly opposite that main room a basin with steps giving access was constructed, maybe once directly related to one of the hot springs of the area. Since the whole structure is poorly preserved, the interior decoration is almost completely lost. Fragments of moulded stucco decoration show that it surely belonged to a high standard, since exactly the same decoration elements were found in other Herodian palaces and in richly decorated Nabataean dwellings from Petra.[18] The Herodian building phase shows again a perfect syn-

Figure 12.5 Machaerus.

thesis between elements of Hellenistic luxury architecture and elements that can be found within the Roman *villegiatura*. The arrangement with two peristyle courtyards corresponds perfectly to Vitruvius' description of the rich Greek houses of the Hellenistic period (Zoppi 1991–92; Raeder 1988; Reber 1988), with one part that was open to visitors and where the owner held his receptions and banquets (the *andronitis*) and an other part where the family lived and where visitors usually had no access (the *gynaikonitis*). This principle is also present within the palaces of the Hellenistic kingdoms such as the palaces of the Macedonian kings at Pella and Vergina in northern Greece or the palaces of the Attalids at Pergamon (Brands 1996; Hoefner 1996; Nielsen 1994) and can be found as well within the palace of the Flavian emperors on the Palatine at Rome (Zanker 2002, with older references). The strong integration of aspects like the beautiful view on the springs of the oasis or on the Dead Sea can be found within other Herodian buildings (Caesarea Maritima, Masada and others more) and are typical features of Roman *villae* (Förtsch 1996).

The Nabataeans

Nabataean studies, both in the field of archaeology and history, have expanded in recent decades. Evidence for this comes from the increasing numbers of exhibitions and publications devoted to the subject.[19] However, there are still many unanswered questions including details of chronology and general interpretation.[20] The aim here, therefore, is to report on the current state of research in most of the categories usually dealt with within Nabataean culture and to propose some general thoughts about the development of Nabataean art and culture between the end of the fourth century BC and the annexiation of the Nabataean kingdom by Rome in AD 106.

A people called Nabataeans are first mentioned in 312/311 BC (Diodorus 19.94.1; 95.1–97.6). Diodorus, writing in the first century BC, describes an attempt by Athenaios, a general of Antigonos Monophthalmos, one of the successors of Alexander the Great, to conquer the Nabataeans.[21] He is most probably referring to Hieronymos of Kardia, who as a historian participated in this campaign and was, therefore, an eyewitness of this first reported contact between the Nabataeans and the Hellenistic world. As the Nabataeans apparently did not have any historiography of their own, we are, other than partial information given by inscriptions, strongly dependent on the picture of them as drawn by Greeks and Romans. The first account of 312/311 BC depicts the Nabataeans as both nomads and skilful traders between South Arabia and the Syro-Phoenician coast. The description contains all the typical characteristics of nomads, including laws forbidding them to build houses, cultivate plants, practise agriculture, and so on. Their behaviour, while engaging with Greek troops and their mercenaries, is characteristically

nomadic: they left behind their goods and families on a rocky stronghold and were on their way to an annual meeting where they conducted trade and other business. This is a typical non-sedentary feature that can be witnessed in more or less the same fashion even today on market days in Arab villages, bringing together the nomads from the surrounding areas to exchange their goods (Altorki and Cole 1989: 60–64). Special attention is given to Diodorus' mention of the rocky stronghold with only one easily defensible access. This description would fit Umm Biyara, one of the characteristic rocks surrounding the city of Petra.

Some scholars claim that Sela near Busayra would fit better the geographical description and distances that Diodorus gives.[22] Some scholars believe that Diodorus' description may not reflect the Nabataeans of 312 BC but rather a collection of *topoi* used by Greeks and Romans in general to describe distant peoples not well known to them (see the remarks by Bosworth 2002: 169–209, especially 184–209 on the Nabataeans). However, this position involves at least two serious problems concerning the history and the archaeology of the Nabataeans. The first problem is determining where the Nabataeans were *before* 312 BC. Present archaeological evidence does not support the presence of the Nabataeans in central or southern Jordan, where the text seems to locate them, at such an early date. Formerly, the theory of a material continuity between Edomites and Nabataeans was occasionally supported but recently has lost most of its attraction, mainly because there is little archaeological evidence from excavations or surveys (in favour of continuity: Bartlett 1979; against or at least sceptical: Bartlett 1990; Bienkowski 1990; Mattingly 1990; Hart and Falkner 1985; Hart 1987). Recent reconsideration of Crystal Bennet's excavation at Busayra led, however, to an interesting new proposal. According to this, imported Attic pottery of the late fourth century BC and Hellenistic sherds of the third and second centuries BC were found together with pottery types that previously were thought to be exclusively of Iron Age date. If this should be confirmed on a wider scale, the gap between Edomite and Nabataean presence would narrow considerably (Bienkowski 2002: 90). For the time being, however, it seems more likely that the Nabataeans were not an indigenous population of these areas but immigrated around the middle of the first millennium BC. Recent studies based on historical and linguistic evidence favour north or northeast Arabia rather than South Arabia as their place of origin (Hackl and Jenni and Schneider 2003: 15–19; Graf 1990; Knauf 1986; Milik 1982).

The second problem involves tracing the Nabataeans *after* 312 BC. Although there are historical sources making clear that they have to be located in central and south Jordan (Diodorus 3.42.5; 3.43.4–5; 2 Macc. 5.8; 1 Macc. 5.25; 9.35; Josephus, *Ant.* 12.8.3), there seems to be almost no material evidence that could be assigned to the Nabataeans during the third and second centuries BC.

It is only c. 100 BC that material culture identified as Nabataean appears (Schmid 2001a and 2001b). There are some older finds, especially from Petra, reported and connected with the Nabataeans, for example, stamped amphorae handles and occasionally black glazed pottery. However, in most cases these finds are apparently intrusive and are, therefore, not of value (Schneider 1996: 130–132, 141–142; Parr 1960: 135).[23] It is true that some of the Historical references could point to a certain organization and social structure already in use before the late second century BC. First, one of the papyri from the Zenon archive mentions Nabataeans in the Hauran already in the third century BC, i.e. still during Ptolemaic supremacy (Zenon papyrus PSI 406: Hackl and Jenny and Schneider 2003: 364–367). This does not mean they were exercing any control of that area, but it testifies to their widespread presence, probably related to commercial activities, at a time for which there is no archaeological evidence so far. The other reference is found in an epigram by Poseidippos of Pella (first half of the third century BC), where a "Nabataean (…) king of the Arabs, fighting on horseback" is mentioned (Hackl and Jenni and Schneider 2003: 586–587).[24] The rather lacunary text offers some problems, i.e. space for interpretation. For instance, the "horse" is not definitely attested but completed; however, there seems to be sufficient evidence for the reading. Whether "Nabataean" and "king of the Arabs" have to be understood as belonging together is not clear either, although rather probable. And finally, as with all Greek and Roman references to the institution of kingship in peripheral areas, we do not really know whether this kind of kingship does correspond to what a Greek would have associated with it or merely to a kind of "chief" of an Arab tribe, i.e. a shaykh. Another text may cause more serious "problems" when compared to the archaeological evidence. In an honorific inscription from Priene dating to c. 130 BC, a delegation from that city to "Petra in Arabia" is mentioned (Hackl and Jenni and Schneider 2003: 126–127 no. A.005.01; Roche 1996: 83 no. 10; Wenning 1987: 23 no. 5).[25] This means that there must have been a minimum of permanent infrastructure that qualified Petra as a kind of city in the eyes of the Greeks from Asia Minor already in 130 BC. However, as exposed above, the absence of serious archaeological evidence does not (yet) support such an idea of development within the late second century BC. On the one hand, maybe recent excavation at the area of Qasr al-Bint could sharpen the picture about a presumed Hellenistic occupation of Petra's later city center.[26] On the other hand, after what we observed in the case of the Hellenistic cities in northern Jordan and what we learned by Diodorus' account, one would rather look for a elevated acropolis-like structure, no matter whether this is located on top of Umm Biyara or on the hill of Khabis that was believed to be the acropolis of Petra by all early visitors until it turned out that most of the visible structures date to the Crusader period (see Figure 12.7 for location).

The Earliest Material Culture and the Process of Settlement

Definitive evidence of a Nabataean material culture does not occur before the end of the second or the beginning of the first century BC. The most readily available evidence may be obtained from coins because there is usually little doubt about their date and ethnic attribution (on the coinage of the Nabataeans, see Schmitt-Korte 1997: 101–104; 1991: 135–148; Weiser and Cotton 1996: 268–285; Schmitt-Korte and Price 1994; Peter 1993; Schmitt-Korte 1990; Schmitt-Korte and Cowell 1989; and Meshorer 1975). The earliest, anonymous mints are attributed to Aretas II (120/110–96 BC) (Peter 1996: 91–93 and n.413 cat. nn. 1 and 2; Bowsher 1990; Meshorer 1975: 9–12, 85–86 pl. 1 cat. nn. 1–4. sup. 1.) or Aretas III (87/84.62 BC) (Schmitt-Korte 1990: 125–126). Recent finds support the earlier dating (Weiser and Cotton 1996: 268, n.240; Kushnir-Stein and Gitler 1992–93). The earliest coins, clearly modelled on Hellenistic prototypes, were minted in Damascus by Aretas III from 84 BC onwards, but probably quite soon afterwards (after 72 BC?) in Petra (Meshorer 1975: 12–16, 86–87 pl. 1 cat. nn. 5–8; Schmitt-Korte and Price 1994: 95–96; Augé 1990: 131–132).[27] Not only is the style of the first Nabataean coins purely Hellenistic but they also contain Greek inscriptions. This sudden initialization of a coin mint requires an explanation that will be attempted later. Here it is sufficient to point out that the minting of coins means that there must have been some kind of infrastructure. This appears to be the case since even an irregular minting requires a political and economic overlord and a superimposed organization, both of which are difficult to imagine in the case of the non-sedentary infrastructure of a people. In this context the title "king" of the Nabataeans must be mentioned. If the hypothesis that Knauf proposes is correct and Aretas III was the first to use the title "king," in the Hellenistic meaning of the term, in the early first century BC, this could indeed prove a structural change in Nabataean society (Knauf 1997: 15–16 and n. 25 for the older references).[28]

A similar picture is obtained by looking at characteristic Nabataean pottery. Again, none of this pottery can be dated before the late second or early first century BC (Schmid 1995: 637–638, 640–641, 1996a: 127–129, 1996b: 161–162, 164, 168, 1997b: 134, 2000b). Decisive chronological evidence is provided by the fact that along with the earliest Nabataean pottery, fragments of the so-called Eastern terra sigillata A (ESA) are found. Such pottery was not produced before the very end of the second-century BC. The first fine-ware Nabataean pottery, with its smoothly rounded shapes and frequently occurring reddish or brownish slip, imitates the late Hellenistic pottery of the Near East (Figure 12.6.1–5; on this phenomenon see also Schmid 1996a: 130, n.17; Hannestad 1983: 83–120; both have additional references). In fact, if this pottery were not known to have been found in Nabataean territory, its shape and surface treatment would not be distinctive from any other pottery of the Hellenized east.[29] The most outstanding feature of this pottery, mostly in the form of bowls, is the painting, which consists of simple lines on the inner body of the vessel (Figure 12.6). Moreover, it occurs at a time and in an environment that was not favourable at all for painted pottery. In Greece and the Near East, painted pottery was produced to a much lesser extent in the Hellenistic Age and began to be habitually replaced by stamped or mould-made decoration, such as the so-called Megarian bowls or Eastern terra sigillata. This development was due to economic conditions. Stamped and mould-made pottery could be produced in much larger quantities, that is, in an almost industrial way in the modern sense of the word. Therefore, these categories of mould-made bowls and terra sigillata became major export articles in the second and first centuries BC and are found all over the Mediterranean. In contrast, Nabataean pottery apparently was not produced for export, even though the potters achieved a very high technical level as we shall see later. While the shapes of the Nabataean fine-ware pottery of the first half of the first century BC are entirely Hellenistic, a determination of the painting as shown in Figure 12.6 is much more difficult as no immediate prototypes can be found. Keeping in mind the presumed immigration of the Nabataeans from the northern or northeastern part of the Arabian Peninsula around the middle of the first millennium BC, there may, however, be a surprising explanation. It is precisely on the southern shores of the Arabian-Persian Gulf and in Iran that very similar painting on pottery is found, dating from the second millennium BC to the fourth century BC (Boucharlat and Lombard 1985, 1991; Boucharlat and Mouton 1993a, 1993b; de Cardi 1984; Stevens 1994; Haerinck 1983: 98–100). Moreover, some Nabataean pottery forms clearly seem to be based on Mesopotamian, north Arabian even Iranian prototypes (Schmid 1996a: 130–134; 2000b: 118–121). This may be the first *archaeological* evidence for the origin of the Nabataeans. It must be mentioned that from this first stage of Nabataean pottery onwards there are already closed vessels like the amphora (Figure 12.6.5), indicating that this pottery was not, as believed earlier, used for cultic purposes, but for everyday life, that is, eating, drinking and storage.

The same general picture as seen in fine-ware pottery occurs in pottery lamps. Again, no lamps dating before the very late second century BC are known from any stratified Nabataean context. The earliest lamps are either imports or more or less accurate

imitations of common late Hellenistic types (Zanoni 1996: 311–313, nn. 1 and 2).

With the sudden introduction of these pottery categories around 100 BC, the material culture of the Nabataeans not only has its beginning but develops amazingly to include, in its later phases, huge architectural complexes, both of profane and sacral use, as well as the eye-catching rock-cut tomb façades of Petra (see below). When we try to understand the fact that the Nabataeans appear to have lived in central and southern Jordan from the time of their presumed immigration, that is, in the middle of the first millennium BC, or from their first mention in 312/311 BC at the latest, until the introduction of their material culture, as described above, without leaving many traces for at least 200 years, one explanation seems best.

As we have seen, Diodorus' description depicts the Nabataeans as nomads or semi-nomads. If so, then the Nabataeans would have had almost no need for a "normal" material culture. Of course, during the entire span of this nomadic period there may have been other categories of material culture such as textiles, for example carpets and the like, or wooden tools and idols that are not preserved.[30] The absence of other categories can easily be explained by their nomadic lifestyle. For instance, nomads do not produce pottery simply because they are never long enough in one place where clay sources, water for the production of pottery, and wood for firing are available in large quantities (Schmid 2001a). In this case, our evidence would suggest that their settlement took place around 100 BC when they were forced to create a more permanent infrastructure in order to remain competitive in trade. The end of the second and beginning of the first-century BC was marked by the decline of the Seleucid dynasty. This led to a power vacuum in the Syro-Phoenician area. This, in turn, led also to the rise of the Hasmoneans and other local powers, on the one hand, (Hackl and Jenni and Schneider 2003: 36–43; Wolski 1999, especially 83–116; Sherwin-White and Kuhrt 1993: 217–229; Fischer 1980, 1990a). and to an increase of Ptolemaic long-distance trade, due mostly to the discovery of the direct sea route from South Arabia to India, on the other (Drexhage 1988: 7–9).[31] Both events may have encouraged the Nabataeans to start settling on a more permanent basis in order to fill partially the gap left by the Seleucids and to challenge the Ptolemies in long-distance trade.[32] It was also during this time that historical sources report the Nabataeans as being increasingly involved in supra-regional conflicts with their neighbours. Around 93 BC the Nabataean king Obodas I defeated the Hasmonean Alexander Jannaeus (Josephus, *Ant.* 13.13.5; *War* 1.4.4; Bowersock 1983: 23–24; Hammond 1973: 17). The battle of Motho (c. 84 BC) between the Nabataeans and the Seleucids deserves special mention: it is not entirely clear who won the battle but the Seleucid king Antiochus XII died

1-5   plain pottery of phase 1 (c. 100-50 B.C.)

6-13   plain and painted pottery of phase 2 (c. 50 B.C. - A.D. 20)

14-26   plain, stamped and rouletted pottery of phase 3 (c. A.D. 20-100)

27   painted pottery of phase 3b (c. A.D. 70/80-100)
28. 29   painted pottery of the 2ᵐ and 3ʳᵈ centuries A.D.

Figure 12.6 Nabataean pottery.

(Josephus, *Ant.* 13.15.1; *War* 1.4.7; Bowersock 1983: 24–25; Wenning 1993b: 30–31). This resulted in the temporary takeover of Damascus by the Nabataeans under king Aretas III (Josephus, *Ant.* 13.15.2; *War* 1.4.8; Bowersock 1983: 25–26; Hammond 1973: 18) and had an important influence on the creation of Nabataean coinage, as indicated above, since some of the first Nabataean coins were struck in Damascus.

The presumed settlement of the Nabataeans then led to the creation of their material culture, but as there was no immediate preceding local material culture, the Nabataeans did the logical thing. They oriented their new culture according to the mainstreams of the contemporary Hellenistic world in its Near Eastern variant as it was on display in major Hellenistic cities, such as Alexandria in Egypt and Seleucia in Syria, as well as at the trading places they frequented, for example Rhodes, Kos, Priene, Milet and Delos. These and other places, according to inscriptions, are known to have been visited by Nabataeans or to have maintained contacts with the Nabataeans, as in the case of Priene (Schmid 2004a; Wenning 1987: 22–24; Roche 1996: 73–99).

No architectural remains of this earliest phase of Nabataean settlement are presently known. It is possible that the former nomads continued living for a while in tents before they started building houses (Stucky 1996: 14–17). Or, for example, as in Petra, they lived in caves (Nehmé 1997a; Nehmé 1997b: 66–70). Since caves cannot be precisely dated, the chronological relation between houses and inhabited caves is not clear. However, some small fragments of painted stucco found in an early first century BC context illustrate that there was already, during this early stage of settlement at Petra, a form of "architecture," whether built or carved in the rock is unknown, that could be decorated with paintings (Schmid 2001a). What a possible intermediate stage between nomadism and settlement would have looked like may be illustrated on the top of the rock of Sela, a candidate for the "national stronghold" (see above). At several places at Sela, there are not only many huge rock-cut cisterns but also carvings in the higher rocks. These appear to be related to two postholes a few metres in front of them. Maybe the carvings and the postholes were used for the installation of temporary structures, using wooden beams, resulting in a mixture of tents and houses (see the proposed reconstruction in Schmid 2001c: 370 fig. 11.2). However, as long as there are no systematic excavations at Sela (there are, however, some illicit ones), this interpretation and primarily the date of these carvings must remain hypothetical. Another, indirect, indication for a kind of "monumental" architecture as early as the first half of the first century BC can be found while looking at the water supply of Petra. Cleaning and excavation of the Siq in the 1990s revealed a first gravity flow channel that belongs to the first half of the first century BC (Bellwald *et al.* 2003: 33–45, 52). A

very similar channel was unearthed immediately north of the "Temenos Gate" leading to the Qasr al-Bint in summer 2004 (Figure 12.8; cf. Figure 12.7 for location).[33] Constructed from irregular small stones and covered with a thick layer of whitish hydraulic mortar on the inner side, the roughly 42cm wide channel runs from the area of the later "baths" towards the Wadi Mousa. At least one rather big cistern was related to that channel as becomes clear from the edge visible on Figure 12.8. The chronology of the gravity flow channel can be established by two means. On the one hand it is cut off by a wall dating to the third quarter of the first century BC (see below). On the other hand, the fill of the channel consisted of homogeneous Nabataean pottery of the later second-and early first century BC. It seems, therefore logical to suppose that the channel was constructed and in use during the first half of the first century BC. Both stretches of early first century BC water supply systems, in the Siq and in the city center, lead to the assumption that there must have been other structures and first tentatives to organize the entire area.

As the Nabataeans did not produce any historiography of their own, we are greatly restricted in our knowledge of their sociocultural organization. It should be sufficient to point out that ethnographic studies show that with the process of settlement a stronger specialization in terms of trade, crafts and administration is observed, leading, of course, to the creation of different social groups within a society (Altorki and Cole 1989). In the earlier stages of settlement there were people within the community that could be called part-time sedentarized because they were involved in long-distance camel trade and, therefore, on the road for about six months of the year, while others were permanent residents (Altorki and Cole 1989: 67–82).[34] With the introduction of new means of transport, most of the former camel raiders had to change their occupation and new social differentiation resulted (Altorki and Cole 1989: 101–102, 208–231).[35] In part, the same can be concluded in the case of the Nabataeans. With their definitive settlement c. 100 BC at least in and around Petra, some specialization had necessarily taken place (Schmid 2001a). In order to maintain their economic wealth, that is, the supply of spices and other goods from South Arabia for sale in the ports of the eastern Mediterranean, some would have travelled throughout the peninsula for most of the year.[36] Others would have specialized in crafts and industry as can be seen in the case of pottery, because Nabataean pottery is certainly the product of professional potters from its first stage onwards (Schmid 2001a).

That the early first century BC was indeed a period of increasing Nabataean presence and permanent installation in southern Jordan is further indicated by the foundation of sites such as Hawara (modern Humayma) and Aila (modern Aqabah). According to historical and archaeo-

Figure 12.7 Map of Petra. 1. Colonnaded Street; 2. Temenos; 3. "Upper Market;" 4. "Middle Market;" 5. "Lower Market;" 6. Great Temple; 7. Byzantine Tower; 8. Byzantine Church; 9. "Royal Palace;" 10. Temple of the Winged Lions; 11. Temenos Gate; 12. Baths; 13. Altar; 14. Qasr al-Bint; 15. Unfinished Tomb; 16. Museum; 17. "Columbarium;" 18. Tomb of the Broken Pediment; 19. Tomb 229; 20. Triclinium; 21. Tomb 258; 22. Roman Soldier Tomb; 23. Medallion and Block Relief; 24. Garden Temple; 25. Lion Fountain; 26. "Obelisks;" 27. High Place.

Figure 12.8 Petra: excavations near the Temenos Gate.

logical evidence, both sites were founded in the 80s or 70s of the first century BC, although—like for the rest of Nabataean culture—a massive development took place but in the later first century BC.[37] The case of Hawara (Humayma) is especially interesting when considering the water supply system of the site and comparing with the early evidence from Petra as discussed above. All cases clearly show that by the early first century BC the Nabataeans were fully familiar with water management systems as developed in the Hellenistic Mediterranean of the third- and second centuries BC (Oleson 1992, 1994).

The Monumentalization of the Material Culture

The Chronological Basis: Pottery and Coins

As mentioned above, no definite remains of architecture from the early period of Nabataean culture survive. The same is true for sculpture. It seems that the Nabataeans, in their first stage of settlement and production of material culture, adopted only "smaller" categories, such as coins, pottery and terracotta. The Nabataean pottery is probably the best indicator of change and continuity since it is found in abundance and reflects easily recognizable fashions.

According to this view, the first period or phase of Nabataean pottery, as represented in Figure 12.6.

1–5, lasts for roughly two generations, from c. 100 BC until the middle of the first century BC. After this sudden initiation, a development started, leading to a distinctive Nabataean style. However, external influences are not uncommon. These can be observed in fine-ware pottery in the late first century BC when some characteristic prototypes from the Roman thin-walled and sigillata pottery are adopted, but only temporarily (Figure 12.6.13; Schmid 1996a: 132–133). The main shapes, primarily open drinking bowls and plates, probably used for eating, of the second half of the first century BC and the beginning of the first century AD, are in most cases developed versions of the initial vessels of the earlier phases, but showing sharper forms and thinner walls (Figure 12.6.6–7). However, there is a decisive change in the decorative patterns around 50 BC. The simple lines of the first phase are replaced by floral motifs, especially rows of leaves and fine limbs, across the inner body of the vessel (Figure 12.6.9–10). One of the characteristics of these bowls is the absence of a foot or any other standing device. As there are almost no stands found in Nabataean pottery, this means that such painted bowls were held in the hand when being filled. This is a clear indication of their function as drinking bowls, as can be seen in Greek pottery types as well, for instance in the case of *rhyta*. In general terms, the spectrum of Nabataean fine ware covers aspects of daily life well. There is a huge quantity of plates and drinking bowls (about 75%) and a smaller, but representative, quantity of flasks, jugs and other shapes that were used for serving and storage (Figure 12.6). Of course, cooking pots and other vessels that were used for the preparation and storage of food must be added to these forms of "table ware."

The occasional adoption of foreign pottery shapes also leads to one of the characteristic changes in the decoration of Nabataean bowls. Around 25 BC a flat bowl with a stepped wall is introduced into the pottery spectrum. It is clearly borrowed from Iranian or Mesopotamian prototypes, where this form was already common for centuries (Schmid 1996a: 131 and n. 31–33; 2000b: 148–149). Since this addition to the vessel wall made it difficult to apply the radial decoration as shown in Figure 12.6, the decorative system changes into concentrically applied floral motives (Figure 12.6.10). Interestingly, even when the stepped wall disappears a few years later, the concentric decoration remains. A further development sees an increasing *horror vacui* of the painters, trying to cover completely the vessel's body with increasingly smaller motifs, such as dots, "eyes," small leaves, and so on (Figure 12.6.10). This characteristic decoration, no longer in the bright red of the earlier painting, but in rather brownish and violet colours, marks the turning of the centuries, that is, about the first 30 years of Aretas IV's reign (9 BC–AD 40).

As observed, Nabataean pottery of the second half of the first century BC is quite sensitive to what could be called "international fashion." It shows at the same time, nevertheless, the first tendencies towards a distinctive Nabataean style.

Similar features can be observed in Nabataean coin minting. On the occasion of the Nabataeans' first reported clash with the western world in 312/311 BC, Diodorus reports that the Nabataeans were using "Syrian" letters. This certainly means that they were writing in Aramaic, the *lingua franca* of the entire Near East at the time. The fact that their first coins bear Greek inscriptions underlines how strong and complete must have been the sudden input of Hellenistic culture at the time of their settlement. Therefore, the most remarkable step towards a typical Nabataean coin minting is certainly the change from Greek to Aramaic legends, already during the first century BC. The international component, however, is shown by the style of the coins, especially the portraits of Nabataean kings. For instance, the coins of Aretas IV (9 BC–AD 40) show the king's head in a style similar to contemporary Roman coins, although he wears the traditional Nabataean haircut with long curls at the neck.[38] A further sign of a certain Romanization in Nabataean coinage may be seen by the fact that from the year 14/13 BC on, coins of Obodas III and Aretas IV show the king crowned with a (laurel?) wreath. Earlier all the

Nabataean kings were shown exclusively diademed according to the customs of Hellenistic kings. Obodas III minted coins with both types of portraits during the last five years of his reign,[39] as did Aretas IV for the first four years of his reign.[40] However, after 5 BC Nabataean kings are shown exclusively with the wreath on their coins.

Although the chronological coincidence is rather striking, it is difficult to decide whether or not the above-described situation may be more than just fashion: the years from 14/13–10/9 BC were marked by an intense struggle between the Nabataeans and Herod the Great (Josephus, *Ant.* 15.10.2; 16.9.1–10.9; Meshorer 1975: 32–33; Millar 1993: 39–40; Bowersock 1983: 49–54; Hammond 1973: 23–26). Augustus consistently supported Herod with one exception, namely, when the Nabataean "prime minister" Syllaios made him believe that Herod had been the aggressor (Josephus, *Ant.* 16.9.2–3; on Syllaios see also Josephus, *Ant.* 16.7.6; Kokkinos 1998: 177–205 especially 182–84). Therefore, the overall situation for the Nabataeans in this conflict was rather uncomfortable during the last years of Obodas III and the early reign of Aretas IV, because Rome was on the side of their Jewish opponents. The situation was so bad that Augustus was apparently thinking about donating the Nabataean kingdom to Herod. It is said that only the continuing problems within Herod's family kept Augustus from doing so (Josephus, *Ant.* 16.10.9 [353–55]). Considering their situation, it must have seemed appropriate for the Nabataean kings to show their devotion to Rome and the *princeps* at least initially. It could very well be that Obodas III and Aretas IV did so by replacing the traditional Hellenistic diadem with the typical Roman wreath. In light of this, it is certainly no coincidence that the ambassadors sent to Rome by Aretas IV brought Augustus an expensive golden wreath, symbol of the ruler's legitimization. It is also significant that Augustus did not accept the gift because he was angry at the Nabataean ruler for ascending to the throne without asking for his approval. This puzzling event shows that, indeed, there must have been a kind of dependence on Rome at the time (Josephus, *Ant.* 16.9.4 [296]).

Architecture: Houses and Temples

Pottery and coin minting, therefore, clearly show the reception of international fashion on the one hand and the development towards a distinct Nabataean style on the other. The most striking feature in Nabataean material culture of the late first century BC and the early first-century AD, however, is the tendency towards monumentalization. As mentioned above, there are hardly ever any traces of architecture and sculpture in the previous periods. Again, as in the case of pottery and coins, we witness an increase of these categories apparently falling in the last quarter of the first century BC, with an additional boost in the early years of Aretas IV. Some hints point to a beginning of this development as early as the third quarter of the first century BC. This is most probably the date of the first built houses observed so far on the hill of Zantur in the western quarter of Petra (Kolb and Keller 2001: 317–319).[41] The massive and carefully constructed wall in the above mentioned trench near the "Temenos Gate", running approximately in north–south direction or more precisely parallel to the Wadi Mousa, belongs to the third quarter of the first century BC according to the pottery from the foundation trench. This wall probably corresponds to a similar structure south of the "Temenos Gate" that was discovered by Parr in the late 1950s (Parr 1960: 132 pl. 22b). In a later phase, that wall was a stylobate for a row of columns of which the first half-column base still is *in situ* (Figure 12.8). As we shall see below, that phase probably belongs to the last quarter of the first century BC. However, the construction of the wall goes back another quarter of a century and attests monumental building activity in the city center, although the precise plan of this building or these buildings can not yet be drawn.

The last quarter of the first century BC saw an important increase in building activities. Several houses excavated so far at Petra date to this period (Stucky 1996: 17–21, 48–49 and n. 195 referring to older excavations, especially at Khatute and Khubtha; Kolb 1997: 62–63.). From examples presently known, it becomes clear that there is a kind of social differentiation, as houses clearly differ in size and ornamentation. If we try to trace back the structure and ground plan of these early houses we witness a phenomenon similar to that of the earliest Nabataean pottery and coins. Here again, there are strong indications that the Nabataeans were inspired by the current type of (late) Hellenistic houses in the Near East. One of the most characteristic features in this context is certainly the peristyle courtyard, as seen in the houses at az-Zantur and Khatute (see Figure 12.7 for their locations). While the house at Khatute gives an almost perfect example of a Hellenistic peristyle house, including the huge cistern under the main courtyard, such as are on display, for instance, on the island of Delos (Hoepfner *et al.* 1999: 515–524; Trümper 1998), the case seems to be somewhat different for the house at az-Zantur. There, the open areas allowing light and fresh air to circulate into the inner rooms behind the columns are not in the centre of the house but rather pushed towards the periphery. This, as well as the not very systematic alignment of the smaller rooms, may well be the original Nabataean contribution to their house types.[42] However, very prominent examples like the famous villa at Boscoreale (Italy) or some houses from Pergamon show that even in such cases the courtyards could be decentrated.[43] In general terms, it seems that living in Petra during the early imperial years was not much different from life in the big centres of the eastern Mediterranean or the Near East.[44]

One of the best examples of this may be the huge dwelling recently investigated on the southern terrace of az-Zantur (Figure 12.9; Kolb *et al.* 1997, 1998; Kolb 1997). Its position covering the entire natural terrace, and thus offering a splendid view over the suburbs and the rows of rock-cut façades of the entire southern part of Petra, brings to mind the rich houses of Delos or Ephesus.[45] Beside its impressive architectural remains, this dwelling will become famous first of all because of its interior decoration, especially the wall paintings. Before taking a closer look at the paintings it should be mentioned that they come from the lower level of the house, that is, the ground floor. But as the house is built partially into the natural slope, the ground floor in some parts becomes the substructure for the upper floor. Therefore, most rooms of the upper floor would probably have belonged to a splendid residential area. This is supported by the finds such as parts of very fine mosaic floors belonging to the first floor (Kolb *et al.* 1998: 261 fig. 5). For the time being, we can only imagine what the upper floor may have looked like, but the finds from the ground floor more than compensate for this lack. Well-preserved wall paintings were found in room 1 (cf. the plan Figure 12.9). The paintings illustrate illusionistic architecture similar to the stucco decoration from the Qasr al-Bint (see below) and are topped off by a decoration in the form of the so-called masonry style.[46] Room 6 contained a great mass of richly decorated stucco fragments that once covered the entire area. A semi-column with floral elements and gilded painting as well as the fragment of a moulded dentil cornice with painting in the form of fine tendrils illustrate the high living standards of the villa of az-Zantur. Relative to the house's date, a fragment of painted pottery of phase 3a was found in one of the stucco fragments, thus giving a *terminus post quem* of c. AD 20 for the entire decoration (Kolb *et al.* 1997: 234; on painting of phase 3a, see Schmid 1996b: 166, fig. 700 and Figure 12.6 this chapter). This date, together with the fact that different styles of wall painting were apparently used in the building, along with the so-called masonry (see Kolb 1997: 65, fig. 69b for the painting of the so-called masonry style; Rozenberg 1996 for parallels from Jericho; in general see Andreou 1989) and second Pompeiian styles, at a time when they were both no longer in use in the main centres, may seem a problem. However, similar out-of-fashion elements were observed in such prominent buildings as the palaces of Herod the Great (Rozenberg 1996; Fittschen 1996: especially 150; see above discussion and references to Herod's palaces). According to the overall picture obtained from Nabataean art in this general period, it seems we should grant the Nabataeans enough cultural autonomy to have deliberately selected such features, rather than labelling them provincial retards.[47]

To draw conclusions about the cultural heritage of a population in general, it may not be a good idea to

Figure 12.9 Petra, plan of residential villa.

begin with their cultic buildings, because these may very well contain some special characteristics that are related to religious purposes. So far, we have seen how the general development of Nabataean material culture in the areas of coins, pottery and private architecture seems to follow some general rules or models. The case of temples is, however, somewhat special. Like the first private dwellings, the first built temples do not seem to appear before the late first century BC. There is, however, another aspect of Nabataean religion that may find its first manifestation somewhat earlier. The Nabataeans were known to worship their gods on so-called

high places that could be located on any natural elevation. In fact, their principal deity, Dusares or Dushara, "the one from Shara" owes his name to a mountainous region.[48] Especially at Petra, many structures have been found on the tops of almost every rock. This shows an active religious life and the worship of gods in a kind of natural setting (Nehmé 1997b: 1035–1036). These structures usually consist of a kind of altar, a cistern and an entire system of water basins and channels, probably related to a procedure, that is, the pouring of a liquid such as wine, water or the blood of animals offered to the deity. One of the best-preserved examples of this specific aspect of Nabataean religion is located on top of Jabal Zib Atuf (no. 27 on Figure 12.7).

Concerning the temples, as in all the other aspects of material culture investigated so far, we witness a sudden flowering. The first huge buildings seem to appear out of nowhere, that is, we do not see any small predecessors but the development seems to start directly with such large scale buildings as Qasr al-Bint at Petra (Figure 12.10.6 [right]), dating from the end of the first century BC.[49] Research on Nabataean temples is progressing but, to date, it is difficult to draw an overall picture (Tholbecq 1997, 1998; Freyberger 1998; Freyberger 1997: 71–84). At an early stage in the history of Nabataean research, temples were roughly divided into two groups, a northern and a southern one, as they are grouped in Figure 12.10. Recently, a much finer differentiation is proposed and future research may change that picture.[50]

A common feature of most typical Nabataean temples (Figure 12.10, right) is the fact that they are more square than rectangular as are, for instance, Greek and Roman ones. This is especially true for the innermost part of the building, the *cella*, that in some cases is even wider than it is long (Figure 12.10), although it is sometimes subdivided into smaller units.[51] A further non-Greek or Roman characteristic is a kind of *podium*, the so-called *motab*, in the temple (Figure 12.10). This may be connected to the preference of the Nabataeans to worship their gods on the tops of mountains, as illustrated by the so-called high places (above). The aspect of the elevated platform for religious purposes may, therefore, stand behind the *podia* in the above-mentioned temples. This aspect appears even clearer at Qasr al-Bint at Petra (Figure 12.10.6 [right]) where on both sides at the rear steps lead to real platforms. Although we do not know how the cult was practiced in Nabataean temples, the steps leading to platforms or even onto the top of the building readily recall much older Mesopotamian temples. In fact, Strabo states that the Nabataeans "worship the sun, building an altar on the top of the house, and pouring libations on it daily and burning frankincense" (Strabo, *Geogr.* 16.4.27). Such installations in private houses are yet to be found, but the practice described by Strabo is well confirmed by the structures at high places and at Qasr al-Bint. The best example for these aspects within Nabataean temples is the sanctuary of Khirbat Tannur, situated on the top of a steep hill, with related *triclinia*, a kind of built high place (Figure 12.11; see McKenzie and Gibson and Reyes 2002 with older references). Also the *motab* or kernel, that gives the characteristic aspect of a box in a box, is very prominently visible at Khirbat Tannur, showing a continuous evolution from a small and free standing altar in the time of Aretas IV to an elaborate sanctuary of the late first-/early second century AD. Finally, the strong focusing on an inner façade flanked by porticoes is a feature that we will find again within Nabataean funerary complexes discussed below.

As mentioned above, Syrian and Mesopotamian forerunners have been suggested to explain the above (Freyberger 1998: 6–12).[52] Recently, however, other possible prototypes for Nabataean temples have been discussed. Beginning with the aspect of the "shrine in a shrine," that is, a smaller structure within a larger one, as is best demonstrated—beside the example just mentioned—at Qasr Get and in Wadi Ramm (Figure 12.10.5 [right]), but elsewhere as well, Egyptian and, more specifically, Ptolemaic temples are compared to the Nabataean ones (Tholbecq 1997: 1086–1088, 1998: 248–252).[53] We may mention here that many Egyptian temples, both from Pharaonic times and the Hellenistic period, have stairs and huge ramps leading to the roof.

Before returning to the possible Egyptian influence on Nabataean temples, the other main group, that is, the so-called northern group (Figure 12.10, left) shall be mentioned. In contrast to the southern group, these temples show a much stronger long-rectangular ground plan. A further characteristic in most cases are huge courtyards with porticoes in front of the temple proper. Mainly for the latter group, prototypes from Syria have so far been cited. One may also add that the strong tendency to emphasize the building's front by huge steps (Figure 12.10) and courtyards in front of the temple is a typical Roman feature. Indeed, most of the parallels quoted from Syria already date from a time of considerable Roman influence in the Near East.[54] Since the above-mentioned theory about Ptolemaic influence on Nabataean temples seems to be presently *en vogue*, we may add a few more thoughts on the subject. The large courtyard surrounded by porticoes in front of the temple and the general installation of the temple building itself in a huge architectural complex can easily be found in almost every Egyptian temple from the Ptolemaic period, for example, the one from Edfu.[55]

Since the development of Ptolemaic temples follows a strong pharaonic tradition, it has little in common with Nabataean cult buildings. Therefore, we should be careful about pointing out too strong a connection between them. However, it is worth mentioning that all characteristics of Nabataean temples, that is, the corridor or passageway in the inner building, the steps leading to a platform or to the roof, and the courtyard in front of the temple, can be found in prototypes from Hellenistic Egypt. In general, the manifold influence from Ptolemaic Egypt, especially on the huge tomb façades of Nabataean Petra (see below), shows that a cultural interchange existed, regardless of the economic and political differences and quarrels.

Not only Egyptian, but also possible South Arabian influences have been suggested for Nabataean temples (Zayadine 1986: 248). Since then, more work on these monuments has been done and, indeed, there are common features, such as the tripartite back-

Figure 12.10 Nabataean temples.

side of the buildings, the inner courtyard, the additional shrine, and the general quadratic aspect. The problem with the South Arabian temples as possible prototypes is mainly a chronological one, since they are dated c. 700 and in the seventh century BC [56] and are therefore considerably earlier than the Nabataean ones. However, there is evidence in some cases for their use until the fourth-century BC and there are also considerably later buildings in the same tradition.

As for the dating of the Nabataean temples considered so far, in most cases the situation is far from clear. However, it seems that a significant number of these buildings were constructed at the end of the first century BC and the beginning of the first century AD. The most prominent case may be the Qasr al-Bint at Petra (Figure 12.10.6 [right]), where we have some indications for a date in the late first century BC.[57] The same date is proposed for the first construction phase of the temple in Wadi Ramm (Figure 12.10.10 [right]; Tholbecq 1997: 1076–1077, 1998: 243–245). The "temple of the winged lions" was built, according to the archaeological evidence, during the early years of Aretas IV (Figure 12.10.7 [right]; Freyberger 1998: 18–19; Hammond 1996: 5–14). The excavators dated the temple from Dhiban (Figure 12.10.4 [right])to c. AD 10. This is confirmed by the pottery analysis of the construction layers (Tushingham 1972: 32–33).[58] The re-

cently investigated "South Temple" at Petra is a somewhat special case that should be treated with caution for the time being.[59] Several problems as for the interpretation as a temple occurred. A theatron constructed precisely at the point where one would expect the motab makes any further investigation difficult. Since to the South of the "South Temple" a sophisticated *paradeisos*-like structure was discovered, one could indeed ask whether the whole area did belong to the *basileia* of the Nabataean kings, at least to the representation sector of the *basileia*.[60] This would indeed offer a good comparison for the official representation of the Nabataeans within the royal complexes of Herod the Great that were mentioned above, showing similar huge reception halls and water basins.[61]

Architectural Sculpture

Because of the available evidence, in a consideration of the development in sculpture we may focus mainly on reliefs rather than on sculpture in the round. Since the territory of the Nabataeans did not provide any marble quarries, only a very small number of marble sculptures in the round are known. Since these may well be imported, they can hardly be studied for any stylistic development in Nabataean art. On the other hand, we do possess an important number of relief slabs, made of sandstone and limestone, from different places that allow us to trace

Figure 12.11 Khirbat Tannur, Nabataean sanctuary.

their development.[62]

For the study of chronological development, two groups of sculpture are of particular interest, one from Petra and the other from Khirbat Tannur. In accordance with the organization of this chapter, these will be treated separately in two subsections. We will, however, have to compare them directly in order to work out the stylistic and chronological differences. From near the "Temenos Gate" at Petra comes a complex of relief slabs that is known, after the date of its discovery, as "the 1967 group of sculpture" (Wright 1968; McKenzie 1988: 86–87; Freyberger 1998: 15–18; Wenning and Hübner 2004). To this group belongs a series of representations of weapons and sea creatures from a triumphal procession (Figure 12.12a, b) and a series of blocks with representations of busts, mainly of gods (Figure 12.12c). To these can be added, on the basis of stylistic comparisons, a third group that shows cupids and garlands (Figure 12.12d). They have not, however, been found with the others. Before we come to the absolute date of these sculptures, some common features must be stressed. All show a very realistic style in representing humans (or human-like gods), animals and floral decoration. Particular attention is paid to small details as in the case of the cricket on the garland of Figure 12.12d. Also, the very fine cloth and hair on Figure 12.12c make the

entire group comparable to the best examples of late Hellenistic and early imperial sculpture. On the basis of such characteristics, two more pieces may be added: another slab from near the temenos gate with the representation of a winged female torso (Nike?) on Figure 12.12f, and the bust of a god (Dusares? Baalshamin?) in a medallion (Figure 12.12e) that was found near the mosque in Wadi Mousa (on this slab and its provenience, see Tarrier 1990; Wenning 1989: 250 and n. 22).

It is generally accepted that a date in the late first century BC, or at the turn of the century at the latest, would fit these reliefs. A confirmation for this dating can be found in one slab with the representation of the god Helios that reportedly was found in debris belonging to the frieze of Qasr al-Bint (Weber 1997: 118–119 fig. 130a; McKenzie 1988: 86–87 fig. 9; Zayadine 1986: 238–238 fig. 36; on the date of the Qasr al-Bint, see above). Most of these sculptures show rather fleshy faces, as can be seen, for example, on Figure 12.12b, c. This is a characteristic feature of late Hellenistic sculpture, especially of the Near East, where such fleshy forms were considered a sign of richness and wealth leading even to *epitetha* of kings such as Tryphon and Physkon.[63] On the other hand, there are some parallels to the sculptural fashion of the middle Hellenistic period. Examples include the deep set eyes and carvings of the head (Figure 12.12e), the particular naturalistic representation of the dress (Figure 12.12f) that seems to be pressed against the body by the wind of the quick moving forward Nike(?), or the "wild" hair of the Gorgo (Figure 12.12b).[64] The eclectic character of the different groups, but also within single groups, combining features of different phases, that is, high or middle Hellenistic as well as late Hellenistic elements, can be seen as further confirmation of their date. It is precisely during the very late first century BC or the beginning of the first-century AD that such features are very prominent in the centres of the ancient world, when a certain playful handling of the different styles was *en vogue*.[65] It seems, once again, that the Nabataeans were very well familiar with the international trends and features and—this being the most important aspect—willing to adopt them.

Although we do not know what was the exact context of most of these fragments, a few thoughts on their original function may be added. As seen with the bust of Helios, the panels with representation of humans or gods (Figure 12.12c) may probably come from the decoration of Qasr al-Bint. For the group with weapons, there is good evidence that they once belonged to another richly decorated monument, because one slab is the edge of a deeply broken pediment. To this piece, the one with the head of Medusa (Figure 12.12b) and a few others may also be joined (see McKenzie 1988: 86–87; Lyttelton and Blagg 1990: 97 fig. 6.7). This pediment may have been part of the front of either a predecessor of the present "Temenos Gate" (see below) or of another building. Of special inter-

Figure 12.12 Relief slabs from Petra and Khirbat Tannur.

est is the fact that with this evidence we witness the use of a *built* broken pediment such as that represented on the huge tomb façades (below) at a very early date. The Triton and the weapons point towards a political alliteration of the original monument that could have been connected to a kind of naval victory by a Nabataean king, although most scholars think that it has to be seen as a reference to the victory of Octavian, the later *princeps* Augustus, at the battle of Actium in 31 BC (Wenning 1989: 253–254).[66] Whatever the case, we see that during this period at Petra not only does the style of sculpture definitely follow international outlines, especially late Hellenistic and early imperial stylistic tendencies, but also thematic alliterations. The same is true for the slabs with cupids and garlands, as they are undoubtedly referring to a kind of golden age that supposedly flourished in the reign of a Nabataean king, probably Aretas IV (9 BC–AD 40) or his predecessor Obodas III (30–9 BC).[67] Since we know that at least some of the reliefs with representations of weapons were found near the "Temenos Gate," it may be worth to come back again to the carefully built wall discovered immediately north of the gate (Figure 12.8). While the lower part of the foundation trench of the wall contained homogenous pottery from the third quarter of the first century BC, the lower part, corresponding to the capping blocks of the stylobat, did also show some sherds of the last quarter of the first century BC, maybe indicating some changes that occurred within that structure. As becomes clear from the engaged half column base still *in situ* and the considerable length of our wall, we are dealing with an important public building situated on one of the most important spots of ancient Petra. The half column base belongs to a type that can be found at Petra for instance at the temple of the Winged Lions, the Urn Tomb and the theatre and that is virtually identical with the column bases from Machaerus (on the bases from Petra see McKenzie 1990: pl. 50 e–g; on Machaerus see discussion and references above). Hence we do obtain a colonnade, several dozen meters long, maybe doubled by an analogous structure on the other side of the—not paved—street and dating to the decades 30–10 BC. This structure could well been decorated with the reliefs mentioned above.

Tomb Façades

For the modern visitor, the most eye-catching monuments of the ancient Nabataean capital of Petra are without doubt the large tomb façades hewn out of red sandstone. They can be roughly divided into two groups: "more oriental" and "more Hellenistic-western."[68] Their attraction certainly existed in antiquity as well, maybe even in a more forceful way, because they were most probably once covered with painted stucco and, therefore, must have offered a very spectacular sight.[69]

The date of most of the tomb façades of Petra is difficult to establish. Such is only possible on the basis of stylistic comparisons since only very few are dated by inscriptions. The only other place where Nabataean tomb façades occur in important number, Hegra in Saudi Arabia, offers a much better chronological frame, as inscriptions date many of these monuments. Unfortunately, at Hegra only the simple monuments occur and, therefore, the huge two or more-storey, richly decorated monuments like the Khazna Faraoun (Figure 12.13e) or ad-Dayr (Figure 12.13h) remain somewhat enigmatic. An attempt is made here to establish a chronological sequence for the tomb façades as well as placing them in the context of Nabataean material culture.

In discussions on Nabataean tomb façades, one of the earliest monuments, the now destroyed tomb of Hamrath at Souwayda, is usually not considered, maybe because its Nabataean origin may be doubtful (Brünnow and von Domaszewski 1909: 98–101; Dentzer-Feydy 1985–86: 263–265; Fedak 1990: 86–87, 148–150). On the basis of present evidence, this rectangular monument, divided by semi-columns and adorned with weapon reliefs, should be dated to the early first century BC, and it may very well be that such monuments provide the missing link to the Hellenistic world in Nabataean sepulchral architecture. For instance, on the island of Rhodes, several monuments show similar characteristics (in general, on Rhodian funerary monuments, see Fraser 1977, mostly dealing with smaller monuments; Mette 1992: 6–60; Lauter 1972, 1988; Fedak 1990: 83–87). An example of the same rectangular construction on a stepped base, subdivided by semi-columns, is seen in the so-called Ptolemaion in the Rhodini park (Lauter 1988: 155–156; Konstantinopoulos 1986: 229–231; Lauter 1972: 55–56; Fedak 1990: 85–87; on the Rhodian "parks" with their grottoes and *triclinia*, see also Rice 1995). As the most probable reconstruction of its upper part is a stepped pyramid, it becomes clear that the "Ptolemaion" stands in the tradition of such monuments as the Mausoleum at Halikarnassos.[70] This may also be the explanation for the Tomb of Hamrath at Suwayda in Syria, and other similar constructions. They represent a mixture between traditional funeral architectural elements and a strong Greek influence (Lauter 1986: 214, 1988: 156; Fedak 1990: 86–87).[71] Another funeral monument from Rhodes even shows further parallels to the Tomb of Hamrath as it was originally decorated with weapon reliefs very similar to the ones from Souwayda (Lauter 1988: 157, fig. 1; Konstantinopoulos 1973: 116, fig. 3).

Several other monuments from Petra, although not as spectacular as the huge main façades and, therefore, not as often considered, belong to the same category of eclectic monuments, as Zayadine has pointed out (1986: 217–221 with references to similar tombs around Jerusalem; on these see Bonato 1998).[72] Recent investigations at Jarash show that such free-standing monuments—in this case a two-storied round monument in the shape of a *tholos*, quite similar to the upper part of the Khazna Faraoun, the Corinthian Tomb and ad-Dayr existed elsewhere in Jordan too (Seigne and Morin 1995).

The Khazna Faraoun (Figure 12.13e; Brünnow and von Domaszewski 1904: 179–186, 223–31 no. 62.), the "Treasury of the Pharaoh," is the façade with the richest decoration and one of the best preserved, due to its location at the end of the Siq, where it was well protected from corrosion by wind and rain over the centuries. The lower storey shows a slightly broken entablature and a pediment supported by six columns, while the upper storey represents a *tholos* surrounded on three sides by columns evoking a peristyle courtyard. As the front side had to be opened in order to offer an insight on the *tholos*, a deeply broken entablature and pediment was created. The whole monument is richly adorned with floral and figurative elements. Similar architectural comparisons to the Khazna Faraoun can be found on Roman wall paintings from Italy belonging to the so-called second Pompeiian style (Schmid 2000a; McKenzie 1990: 85–101; Weber 1990: 108–109, 220–22 cat. nn. M 7–11; Tybout 1989; Lyttelton 1974: 17–25). The question, then, is how to explain these similarities, and further, what is represented by these two categories of monuments, that is, the Khazna Faraoun on the one hand and the Roman wall

paintings on the other? Although there are still attempts to explain the architectural wall paintings of the second Pompeiian style as representations of theatrical *scenae frontes* and, therefore, as not depicting real but fanciful architecture, it can be assumed on better evidence that they actually represent real architecture, especially the luxury architecture of Hellenistic palaces (Tybout 1989: *passim*, especially 215–273, 325–352; Fittschen 1976a: 544–556; see also Schefold 1975).[73] This, and the architectural comparisons referred to below, suggests that the Khazna Faraoun also reflects real architecture in a direct way and not, as sometimes supposed, a two-dimensional transformation of architectural complexes that in fact lie behind each other.[74]

If we are looking for comparisons showing similar architectural features like the Khazna Faraoun, we have to consider first the "Palazzo delle Colonne" in Ptolemais (Cyrenaica) (Pesce 1950; Kraeling 1962: 83–89; Lauter 1971; Lyttelton 1974: 53–60; McKenzie 1990: 75–77; Nielsen 1994: 146–152, 284– 286 cat. no. 22.). Lauter has shown that the basic elements of this monument go back to late Hellenistic times. Crucial for its dating are the capitals that can profitably be compared with examples especially from Italy and Alexandria (Lauter 1971: 151–152; see also on Alexandrian capitals Pensabene 1991: 44–46, figs. 29–33; on their evolution and comparisons in

Figure 12.13 Petra, rock-cut façades.

general, see Hesberg 1978), as well as with figurative capitals from Messene, dating to the late Hellenistic period (Lyttelton 1974: 58, pl. 63; Orlandos 1976: 36–38, fig. 37). Almost all the architectural elements described above as being characteristic of the Khazna Faraoun are found at the "Palazzo delle Colonne" as well. Examples include deeply broken entablatures and pediments in the upper storey of a façade facing an inner courtyard.[75] Especially interesting is a small rounded architectural fragment that most probably can be reconstructed as part of a *tholos* (Pesce 1950: fig. 13 top left; Lauter 1971: 172 with n. 115), which could—according to its small size—very well be placed in the upper storey, as is the case at Petra. Since the works of Pesce and Lauter, several studies presenting more material from Egypt, especially from Alexandria, strengthen the hypothesis of a close connection between the "Palazzo delle Colonne" and Ptolemaic palace architecture (Pensabene 1993: 3–147, 195–216; McKenzie 1996; Schmidt-Colinet 1993; Pensabene 1991: *passim*, especially 49–55. figs. 42–62; Hesberg 1978; Lyttelton 1974: 40–52). This seems to be true as well for Qasr Abd at Iraq al-Amir, already discussed above. In this case, the affinities with the Khazna Faraoun can be seen in the general aspect of a lower, massive storey, with only a single entrance, combined with an upper storey with several windows and *intercolumnia* (on the connections with the Khazna Faraoun, see Stucky 1990: 26; Nielsen 1994: 138–146). Further, the positions of the figurative decorations show astonishing correspondences, although at Iraq al-Amir the lions are not placed on the top of the pediments.

While not much has survived from the great royal palaces of the Ptolemies and Seleucids, we possess rather well-preserved archaeological remains of the palaces of the Hasmoneans (Netzer 1999: 3–31, 1996a, 1990: 37–42; Nielsen 1994: 155–163; on Jericho see also Netzer 2001) and of Herod the Great (Netzer 1999: 32–34, 1996b, 1990: 42–50; Nielsen 1994: 181–208). Of primary interest for our purpose is the so-called Northern Palace at Masada built c. 30–20 BC (Foerster 1996: 58–63; Nielsen 1994: 189–195, 295–296 cat. no. 27; Netzer 1999: 80–87, 1991: 134–170, 575–588). This monument shows a spectacular composition of three different building structures on three terraces of the steep northern slope of the citadel. The lower terrace bears a central rectangular hall surrounded by porticoes and some adjacent rooms. A huge *tholos*, offering a great view, stood on the middle terrace, while a semicircular balcony occupied the upper terrace with additional rooms at the back. One is especially struck by the similarity of the lower and middle terraces with the composition of the Khazna Faraoun when seen from the front,[76] proving again the connection between the Khazna Faraoun and (late) Hellenistic palace architecture.

Additional information may be gained from the description of the *thalamegos*, the famous riverboat of Ptolemy IV (Athenaeus, *Deipn.* 5, 204d–206c; the basic study is still Caspari 1916; see further Grimm 1981: 17; Nielsen 1994: 136–138; Pfrommer 1996a: 177–179; Pfrommer 1996b). On the one hand, the recent discoveries in Macedonia make clear that the ship was strongly related to Macedonian luxury architecture (Pfrommer 1996b: 102–104). On the other hand, it offers a few astonishing parallels for the façade of the Khazna Faraoun. We must first mention the general aspect of the façade with its *propylon*, flanked on both sides by colonnaded two-storied porticoes, which seems to be, according to the description, almost the same (see also the drawings by Pfrommer 1996a: 178, fig. 9; Pfrommer 1996b: 98, fig. 1; Nielsen 1994: 137, fig. 71). However, the most striking point is the mention of a *tholoid* temple (*monopteros*) of Aphrodite on the upper floor, flanked by dining rooms and bearing a marble statue of the goddess, and, therefore, very similar to the statue of a goddess, probably Isis-Tyche, in the *tholos* of the Khazna Faraoun (Zayadine 1991: 300–306; Schmid 2000a). If we imagine a section through the boat at the position of the *tholos* of Aphrodite, we would have exactly the façade of the Khazna Faraoun (see also the drawings by Pfrommer 1996a: 178, fig. 10; Pfrommer 1996b: 99, fig. 2). The description of details, such as capitals decorated with ivory and gold (Athenaeus, *Deipn.* 205c) and columns inlaid with precious Indian stones (Athenaeus, *Deipn.* 205e; especially on these luxury features see Normann 1996: 153–161), may very well be realistic and representative of Hellenistic palace architecture. This may also be seen in similar representations on the wall paintings at the *triclinium* in Oplontis or at the *oecus* of the Casa del Labirinto in Pompeii (Strocka 1991: figs. 305, 308–311).

In the light of recent discoveries in the Siq at Petra, it is worth returning to the general aspect of Khazna Faraoun once again. During cleaning and excavation works in the Siq, much additional information on the water supply of ancient Petra was gained. Although not yet excavated, the square in front of the monument deserves special attention. The excavators of the Siq, Bellwald and Keller, strongly suggest that the different water supplies leading towards the city's centre formed an artificial lake or pool just in front of the Khazna Faraoun. If this hypothesis is correct, the overall aspect of the Khazna Faraoun would be almost the same as that of the luxury ship of Ptolemy IV or of the Qasr Abd, floating in an artificial lake. For the visitor stepping out of the Siq, the huge façade reflected in the lake would have created the same impression.

Thus, we have demonstrated that the Khazna Faraoun at Petra stands in a proper Hellenistic tradition, reflecting truly the palace architecture of the Hellenistic East. However, this is of no importance for a precise dating because Hellenistic elements could be conserved for quite a long time, especially in the East (on the successors of Hellenism in the East, see Schlumberger 1969; Bowersock 1990b: 29–40).

Comparisons using the ornamental motifs of the Khazna Faraoun may be more promising. The floral ornaments of the capitals of the Khazna Faraoun and the very similar capitals from the area around Qasr al-Bint are usually compared with those of the Ara Pacis in Rome.[77] However, a closer look shows that the tendrils of the Ara Pacis are finer and intertwined in a complex way (in general on the Ara Pacis, see Castriota 1995; Settis 1988 and, for the tendrils, Sauron 1988), while the floral ornaments of the Khazna Faraoun and around Qasr al-Bint are more fleshy and straight in their composition and show a deeper relief. Better comparisons are offered by the painted tendrils from *oecus* 13 in the House of Augustus on the Palatine hill and ornaments in stucco from the upper floor of the same house, dated to c. 30 BC or immediately after (Carettoni 1983: colour pl. 7, 15; on the dating 412–419).[78] In general, late republican Roman monuments come closer to the ornaments from the Khazna Faraoun, such as the ornamental decoration of a general's burial monument from the Via Appia, dating to c. 35 BC, may show (Hölscher 1988: 363–364 cat. no. 199; Kraus 1976: 463–464 and fig. 8; Sydow 1974: especially 204–210).[79] The same stylistic characteristics can be found on several tendril fragments from Pergamon, which can be dated between c. 50 BC and the very early imperial years (Börker 1973: 296–300 figs. 6–9; Rumscheid 1994: 292–294 pl. 114.5, 6 cat. no. 188.23–24). Indeed, relations between Petra and Pergamon have also been supposed on the basis of fragments of friezes from Petra that show garlands and weapons (Lyttelton and Blagg 1990: 95, 97; Fittschen 1976b: 193).[80]

We may therefore conclude that the Khazna Faraoun was built in the second half of the first century BC, that is, about the same time that most of the above-mentioned Roman walls were painted or slightly later. As the architectural decoration of the Khazna Faraoun (e.g. the capitals) have close parallels from the area around Qasr al-Bint, we again have an indication that in the late first-century BC manifold building activities took place in Petra (cf. below). In this context, it has to be stressed that decoration in stucco showing broken and rounded pediments very similar to most of the monuments referred to so far, including the Khazna Faraoun, is applied on the exterior south wall of Qasr al-Bint (Zayadine and Larché and Dentzer-Feydy 2003: 61–5; Freyberger 1997: 74–76; Zayadine 1985: 246–247, 1986, 244–47). If we bear in mind that a date in the late first century BC was convincingly proposed for that building, we would again have a good confirmation for the date of the Khazna Faraoun.[81] To this, we can add the broken pediment with figurative decoration (Figure 12.12a) and thus we have, more or less, the contemporary appearance of this particular

architectural feature in three areas: tomb façades, stucco decoration, and free-standing monuments, all dated to the late first century BC. This chronological proposal will probably be confirmed by the recent discovery of three rock cut tombs beneath the Khazna Faraoun. These have to be somewhat older than the Khazna Faraoun since one of them was covered by the huge stairs that had to build in order to give access to the Khazna Faraoun. In one of the tombs homogenous pottery of the third quarter of the first century BC was found,[82] and, therefore, giving a *terminus post quem* for the Khazna Faraoun.

Following general models of evolution, it is believed that the simpler façades, showing stronger "oriental" influences, as in Figure 12.13a, b, would be older than the richly decorated "western" ones like the Khazna Faraoun. After establishing a more or less precise date for the Khazna Faraoun, we should return to the dating of the simpler monuments. The inscriptions of the Hegra necropolis have already been mentioned. Starting with an inscription of the year 1 BC/AD, the inscriptions date a number of such "oriental" monuments to the entire first-century AD (on the Hegra tombs and their inscriptions, see McKenzie 1990: 11–31; Schmidt-Colinet 1987a, 1987b). Another chronological indication is given by the Theatre of Petra. As the theatre was built most probably in the late first century BC/early first century AD and as the installation of its *cavea* destroyed several of these simpler tombs, they were clearly cut into the rock before the construction of the theatre (on the dating of the theatre, see McKenzie 1990: 35, 143–144).[83] The result of this short *tour d'horizon* is rather sobering: there is no good reason to believe that the simpler "oriental" façades would predate such monuments as the Khazna Faraoun or the Tomb of Hamrath, at least not for a long period. Therefore, we witness again a sudden appearance of a "new" category of Nabataean material culture, clearly adopting Hellenistic elements. Especially in the case of the elaborate façades, none seems to date before approximately 30 BC. This could lead to the hypothesis that specialized craftsmen from Ptolemaic Egypt, having lost their most wealthy client, the royal family in 30 BC, were looking for new fields of occupation and found them within the Nabataean upper class.

Preliminary Conclusions

The evidence listed in the previous sections shows that towards the end of the first century BC and the very beginning of the first century AD, Nabataean material culture passed to a stage of monumentalization. Houses, temples, rock-cut tomb façades, and architectural decoration are suddenly and prominently introduced into the repertoire of Nabataean artists and craftsmen. As with the sudden beginnings of the earliest remains of Nabataean material culture, coins and pottery, around 100 BC, one is surprised by the dynamic evolution. At least for modern scholars, it seems that these milestones could be related to an overall organization, since in both cases the sudden developments seem to come out of nowhere, that is, without any preceding "test phase." Just as the first pottery and coins fit perfectly into the Hellenistic *koiné* of the Near East, the same is true for the houses, the temples, and the tomb façades. In most cases, however, it is more difficult to point out direct prototypes.

The same scenario appears again in the general development of the city of Petra. For the buildings on the colonnaded street leading along Wadi Mousa (see Figure 12.7 for location), as well as for the impressive pavement of the Siq, including the water channels and dams, a date in the late first century BC can be established (Bellwald *et al.* 2003: 52).[84] This shows that the entire city was indeed subject to a construction boom and must have been a huge building site for years, if not decades, until Qasr al-Bint, the Temple of the Winged Lions, the "South Temple," and so on were finished. The same seems to be true for smaller settlements. The first building phase of the Nabataean temple at Wadi Ramm is dated to around the turn of the eras and there, too, we see that at about the same time the entire infrastructure becomes rather monumental, including sophisticated water channels, some of them still *in situ* (Tholbecq 1998). The same observation is true for Hawara (Humayma) and Aila (Aqabah), where a remarkable building activity is attested for the same period (Oleson 1992, 1994, 2001: 570–572; Dolinka 2003: 29–30). Maybe even this factor of monumentalization of public space can be considered in relation to the adoption of a kind of Near Eastern Hellenistic *koiné* , because it is precisely this aspect that marks Hellenistic cities, especially in Asia Minor (Hoepfner *et al.* 1999: 445–446).

As indicated, there is some occasional Roman influence, for instance in the field of pottery production (Figure 12.6.13), but also most probably in the political alliterations of some of the relief-decorated monuments in the centre of Petra (Figure 12.12a–d, f). The stronger Roman influence appears with the taking over of the Seleucid empire by Pompey in 63 BC and of Ptolemaic Egypt by Octavian in 30 BC and his attempts to control directly long-distance trade in the Arabian Peninsula as reflected by the expedition of Aelius Gallus (Strabo 16.4.21–24; Raschke 1978: especially 650–676; Sidebotham 1986a: 48–71, 113–130, 1986b and 1996 for a general overview; see further Eadie 1989; Romanis 1996: 19–21). It is clear that the increasingly stronger Roman influence in the Eastern Mediterranean since Pompey's campaigns in the 60s of the first century BC led also to new cultural elements in these regions. It is also during the early Roman imperial years that historical sources report direct contacts between Nabataeans and Romans.[85] Strabo not only witnesses the presence of many Romans and other foreigners in Petra by his time (*Geogr.* 16.4.21), but also notes

houses of stone (16.4.26) as well as a plentiful supply of water and gardens in the city (16.4.21). He thus confirms entirely the picture obtained from archaeological evidence.

The Later First Century AD and the End of the Nabataean Kingdom

The Chronological Basis: Pottery and Coins

Compared to his predecessors, the portraits of Rabbel II (AD 70–106) show a continuing dissolution of the naturalistic design in favour of a stronger ornamentalization. On most coins, Rabbel's face has a somewhat "wooden" touch. This is due to the fact that only the basic lines occur in a heavily carved style. As a matter of fact, this seems to be a characteristic of several peripheral cultures of the wider Mediterranean area. The same evolution, from naturalistic to ornamental, may be traced within south and east Arabian coins, imitating Athenian and other Greek prototypes (Huth 1999; Haerinck 1998; Munro-Hay 1991, 1994: especially 192, 198–200, 1996; Arnold-Biucchi 1991; Naster 1983; in general terms, see Potts 1991), or within Celtic coins, imitating prototypes of Philip II of Macedonia and others (Keller 1996; Sasianou 1993). Moreover, the culture of the Scythians and other peoples from the Black Sea area shows a similar approach to once naturalistic prototypes, mainly from the Greek world.[86] Within these cultures in particular we can find further confirmation for the model of settlement as outlined above for the Nabataeans. In these regions, where circumstances preserved more artefacts of organic material, it can be shown that a large part of the original material culture of these "mounted" or nomadic peoples indeed consisted of carpets, wooden tools and the like (See, for instance, Schiltz 1994: 248–289, 333–415 with many figs.; see above n. 30).

In the second and third quarters of the first century AD, the output of Nabataean pottery probably reaches its peak. Nabataean potters are now producing a great quantity of many different small forms, mainly jugs, juglets and *amphoriskoi*, many of them decorated with rouletting or stamped patterns (Figure 12.6.16–26). During the entire first and the beginning of the second centuries AD, the unpainted main forms are shallow plates with prominent vertical rims (Figure 12.6.14, 15). During the same period, the most prominent painted form is a flat open bowl, without any standing device, and a small, knobby rim (Figure 12.6.27). In the second half of the first century AD, a remarkable change in the decorative patterns of painted pottery can be observed. Up to this time, the Nabataean potters and painters preferred different small elements, such as quite realistic ivy and other leaves, covering the entire vessel (Figure 12.6.10). Now they use fewer but larger motifs, offering more space between them. Also, with the exception of the pomegranate, the floral elements lose much of their realism, becoming more abstract (Figure 12.6.27). At about the same time, new, larger geometric motifs are introduced. The beginning of this new style falls almost exactly into the time of the accession to the throne of Rabbel II and can be dated to c. AD 70/80.[87] As we will see later, this development seems also to have some astonishing parallels in other categories.

Following the general evolution in the Mediterranean area, lamps found at Nabataean sites from the late first century BC and the beginning of the first century AD are either Roman imports or imitate Roman prototypes (Zanoni 1996: 316–319, nn. 10–13.). It is only towards the second quarter and, to a greater extent, in the second half of the first century AD that a characteristic Nabataean lamp type, the so-called Negev 1 type, makes its appearance (Zanoni 1996: 314–16, nn. 7–9).[88]

In general terms, one could say that until the third quarter of the first century AD there is a rather smooth development based on the previous phases as outlined above. From c. AD 70/80, a distinctive and different fashion appears.

Sculpture, Reliefs and Architectural Decoration

As noted above, there is an early group of architectural decoration, both ornamental (Figure 12.12) and figurative (Figure 12.12), that is clearly related to a stylistic background that could be called either late Hellenistic or early imperial, according to different parallels.

If we compare these sculptures and reliefs to the sculptural finds from Khirbat Dharayh and Khirbat Tannur, the latter two realized by the same workshop, we see obvious stylistic differences.[89] Their clearly less naturalistic and somewhat wooden faces and dresses reminded Glueck of Palmyrene and Parthian sculpture (Glueck 1965: 248–259 and others). Furthermore, at Khirbat Tannur, several construction phases were observed, although their date was not easy to establish. A few reliefs, such as the so-called Atargatis panel (Figure 12.12g) and a bust of Helios, could be attributed to an earlier phase, called phase II at Khirbat Tannur, while, for instance, the Nike supporting a zodiac (Figure 12.12h) belongs to an intermediate phase IIA. The pieces from phase II and IIA show clear stylistic differences from the Petra sculptures discussed above. Glueck dated this phase to the years of Aretas IV and, therefore, contemporaneous with these reliefs from Petra. If this is correct, we would need to assume a provincial kind of style in order to explain the stylistic differences from Petra. Of further interest are the reliefs from phase III at Khirbat Tannur, including the famous dolphin and grain goddesses (Figure 12.12i), which clearly show stronger stylistic differences from the earlier series of reliefs from Petra. Glueck suggested a date, without giving proof, in the early second century AD (Glueck 1965: 138; Wenning 1987: 77–81 and McKenzie 1988).[90]

As a general observation, it needs to be mentioned that all the pottery illustrated in Glueck's reports on Khirbat Tannur and thought to be evidence for dating belongs to our phase 3c and would, therefore, confirm a date in the early second century AD (Glueck 1965: pls. 73a, 74a, 75a–b).[91] A meticulous new study of the sanctuary of Khirbat Tannur led by J. McKenzie is likely to sharpen our understanding of the cult rites but also of the chronology (McKenzie 1988: throughout and especially 88–89). Already, a much clearer picture of the different phases appears: in a first phase, dating to the reign of Aretas IV, a small altar was built; the second phase, to which most of the sculptures mentioned above belongs as well as the main building activity, is dated to the late first- or early second century AD (McKenzie and Gibson and Reyes 2002).[92] Further, these results are likely to confirm an analogous date for the main building phase, including the relief sculpture, from the sanctuary at Khirbat Dharayh. One of the closest parallels to the stylistic features of the sculptures from phase IIA at Khirbat Tannur was recently found at Khirbat Dharih (Figure 12.12j; Zayadine 1997: 618 no. 9; Villeneuve and Muheisen 1994: 745–746, fig. 5). The relief slab, with the representation of Hermes/Khutbay, comes so close to the Atargatis on Figure 12.12g in the workmanship of the thick haircurls, the prominent setting of the eyebrows, the indication of the iris, the fleshy cheeks and so on, that it confirms the idea of the same workshop being active at both sites. Although not precisely dated due to its reuse in a Byzantine wall, the Hermes from Khirbat Dharih is a very good example of Nabataean sculpture of the second half of the first century AD or the early second century AD.

Rather close in style to the sculptures from phases II and IIA at Khirbat Tannur is another series of relief blocks found in Petra in the destruction debris of the above-mentioned Temenos Gate (McKenzie 1990: 133–134, pls. 58–59; McKenzie 1988: 87–89). A sample is the winged head with fleshy face and small curls that Zayadine identified as Hermes/Khutbay (Zayadine 1997: 618, no. 10; see also McKenzie 1988: 88, 91, no. 4 and fig. 12a). To this piece may be added two heads of bearded men with a so-called Phrygian hat and strongly ornamental hairstyle, maybe pointing to Syrian or Mesopotamian influence.[93] These pieces, with their somewhat stiffly carved features, are not only related to the later pieces from Khirbat Tannur but are also clearly different from the earlier series from the same area (above, cf. Figure 12.12). As this later phase of the Temenos Gate has a most probable *terminus post quem* of AD 76, this would confirm the observations made so far (McKenzie 1990: 36, 132–134, pl. 47 b–d).[94] Further, it becomes clear that the stylistic features observed on the sculptures from Khirbat Tannur and Khirbat Dharayh have nothing to do with "provincialism" but with a chronological development that is the same as in Petra.

The evolution in Nabataean sculpture follows, therefore, the same model as other categories of material culture, such as coins or pottery. It starts with a naturalistic style, clearly adopted from late Hellenistic and early imperial examples (Figure 12.12a–f), developing into more abstract and stronger ornamentalizing representation (Figures 12.12g–j). The zenith of this evolution is exemplified in the aniconic *baityloi*. Although they existed in earlier times, they too show considerable development in the latter part of the first century AD (Wenning 1993a: 86–93; Wenning 1989: 257; Hammond 1981: 137–141). On the other hand, what is depicted on Figure 12.12g, j, could belong, according to their stylistic features, to an intermediate phase, distinguishing them both from the very naturalistic earlier group and from the stiffly carved later pieces.

Exactly the same general tendencies are seen in the floral decoration of capitals and other architectural features. The capitals and leaves decorating the temenos gate at the entrance to the area of Qasr al-Bint at Petra show obvious and strong stylistic differences from the same elements of the Khazna Faraoun, from the temple of the winged lions and other earlier monuments. The capitals from the Temenos Gate are rather close to the ones from Khirbat Tannur (see, for example, the pictures in McKenzie 1988: figs. 3, 7), making clear that they must belong to about the same period. Similar floral representation from the painted decoration of the Nabataean house on the north slope of az-Zantur may underline the late date of the Temenos Gate. In this case, a coin of Rabbel II (AD 70–106) was found in the plaster. Even when considering the difficulties in comparing painted with carved decoration, it is obvious that the style of the painting comes rather close to the floral decoration from the Temenos Gate.[95] This is further confirmed by the observation that the stylistic developments pointed out so far lead to the decorative elements of monuments such as the mausoleum of Qasr Nuweijis in the vicinity of Amman. Although not precisely dated, this funeral monument certainly belongs to the middle imperial years, that is, the second or third centuries AD, and shows similar ornamental details (see Huff 1989: especially pl. 26.1, 2). Comparisons with the architectural decoration of the Hauran region from the second and third centuries AD point in the same direction (see Dentzer-Feydy 1985–86: 286–299), as do further comparisons with other Nabataean monuments.[96] As we have seen, the Temenos Gate in the city centre of Petra plays an important role for our understanding of urbanism and sculptural decoration. Unfortunately, a definite chronology, based on archaeological context and finds, for the Temenos Gate is still outstanding. Until now, all archaeological evidence with chronological implications comes from further away and is related to the paved street, or has not been published in detail.[97] The trench on Figure 12.8 can provide

some further information, although these are not directly related to the gate either. There is a general agreement that the gate is at least slightly later than the paved street to the East of it since the gate has been inset to the pavement. Immediately to the West of the gate a few slabs of the piazza that leads to the Qasr al-Bint remain *in situ* and the trench in Figure 12.8 was extended to the last two of them that were lifted in order to obtain material with chronological relevance. The slabs are set into a layer of rather hastily produced mortar, containing pieces of charcoal that measure up to three or four centimetres Setting floor slabs into mortar was very uncommon in Nabataean times when usually a foundation of clay containing earth and a layer of smaller stones were used to prepare paving. The mortar referred to did contain some clearly identifiable fragments of painted and plain Nabataean fine ware belonging to phase 3b, i.e. to the last quarter of the first century AD. Therefore, the paving of the piazza (or the wider extention of the temenos of Qasr al-Bint) can not be earlier as c. AD 100, at least in its immediate neighbourhood to the Temenos Gate. With the evidence gathered so far it can not be decided whether the gate was built before or after AD 106. Another observation shall be added here, although related to earlier phases. There were no indications of an earlier pavement, a paved street or any other built structure (beside the gravity floor channel dealt with above) beneath the level of the c. AD 100 street. In other words, if there was an earlier paved street or temenos it has to be located further to the South of the Temenos Gate. Since the different excavations along the colonnaded street did not reveal an earlier pavement either, we can conclude that at least the installation of a paved *cardo* that follows the Wadi Mousa did not take place before c. AD 100, a rather surprising result, since on both sides of the wadi (and the "street" of beaten earth) monumental public buildings such as the Temple of the Winged Lions, the *paradeisos* or the so-called "South Temple" were standing since almost one century. Another, although less likely, explanation would be to assume a meticulous and complete reuse of older slabs on the same level.

Tomb Façades

This short overview on the Nabataeans and their culture is not the place to present a large number of Nabataean tomb façades, but just a few selected ones. Quite a number of earlier monuments of this category stand in proper Hellenistic tradition. Here, a few later examples of about the second half of the first century AD are provided.

The Corinthian Tomb (Figure 12.13g) is located in a prominent place among a row of façades on the north side of the Khubtha massif. It offers a full view of the city. The tomb's façade is of interest because its upper segment is an exact replica of the Khazna Faraoun, without, however, the sculptural décor. Its lower segment has eight semi-columns supporting a broken entablature (see the drawing by Schmidt-Colinet 1981: 78, fig. 18 (right); Brünnow and von Domaszewski 1904: 168, fig. 192, 388–389, no. 766). Differences consist of two smaller entrances on the two *intercolumnia* on the left, one with a segmental pediment that is set back by two additional columns, and an architrave at the main entrance, bearing a strong resemblance to illusionistic architecture. In addition, there is a middle zone, an *attica*, with a central segmental pediment, different zones of broken miniature or dwarf entablatures, columns and a final broken pediment.

The lower and middle levels of the Corinthian Tomb have an almost exact parallel in the so-called Bab as-Siq triclinium just outside Petra (McKenzie 1990: pls. 126–127; Brünnow and von Domaszewski 1904: 172 fig. 197, 206–208 no. 34). This is important since an inscription attributed to Malichus II (AD 40/44–70) can date this tomb (McKenzie 1990: 34 and nn. 15–18 for the somewhat puzzling evidence).

The additional features of the Corinthian Tomb, such as miniature and illusionistic architecture, cannot help in dating the monument, since these features are also known from Hellenistic architecture. Some fragments of the Palazzo delle Colonne already prove the existence of miniature architecture in late Hellenistic times (see above). Illusionistic and false architectural elements, even with segmental pediments similar to those in Petra, can be found in Alexandrian architecture from the Hellenistic period onwards. These elements are usually thought to come from tombs from Alexandrian cemeteries, especially from the Mustafa Pascha necropolis (Adriani 1963–66: 107–183, especially 128–146, pls. 48–57; on the Mustafa Pascha necropolis; McKenzie 1990: 64–65). However, the same elements occur in small altars and lockers for tomb *loculi* from different cemeteries dating from the Hellenistic period onwards (see, for example, Pensabene 1993: 104–107 fig. 93 pl. 117.3; 133–135 pl. 117.7; 98 pl. XI 1 cat. no. 14 and many others).

In general, the entire relief of the Corinthian Tomb is much flatter than that of the Khazna Faraoun and the whole monument shows less three-dimensional aspects. It can, therefore, be concluded that it should be dated somewhat later. The best evidence for dating is provided by the Corinthian capitals, being very similar to those of the temenos gate, dated most probably to post-AD 76.[98] It is probably not incorrect to assume a date in the middle or in the third quarter of the first century AD for the Corinthian Tomb.

Ad-Dayr (Figure 12.13h) received its name, "the monastery," from its use as a Christian church in late antiquity (on ad-Dayr, see Schmidt-Colinet 1981: 97–98; Zayadine 1989: 158; McKenzie 1990: 159–161 with additional bibliography; Brünnow and von Domaszewski 1904: 187 fig. 220, 331–335 no. 462). As with the Cor-

inthian Tomb, ad-Dayr too portrays considerably fewer three-dimensional elements in its lower storey compared to the Khazna Faraoun. This is due mainly to the missing propylon. The upper storey is again an almost exact parallel to the Khazna Faraoun. A difference consists in the fact that on both sides additional pillars and semicolumns have been added. The strongly broken entablature shows that this new feature should be understood as running around the portico surrounding the *tholos*. Ad-Dayr has Nabataean capitals without floral ornaments and, therefore, does not offer evidence for dating (on the capitals of ad-Dayr, see McKenzie 1990: 160–161; in general on Nabataean capitals and their possible origin in Ptolemaic Egypt, see Soren 1987: 206–212; Sinos 1990: 145–156, 227–229; Laroche-Traunecker 2000). In general, besides the Doric frieze in the upper storey, there is no additional decoration. However, in antiquity there were probably statues standing in the two niches of the lower and the three niches of the upper storey.[99] The façade of ad-Dayr appears much heavier and monumental, especially when compared to the general aspect of the Khazna Faraoun.

In the case of ad-Dayr, the additional pillars and semicolumns that frame the upper storey may give a chronological indication. Such elements, without any practical function in real architecture, are a distinguishing feature of Roman architecture of the last quarter of the first century AD onwards. These elements are a result of the interchange between traditional Roman architecture and Hellenistic luxury architecture, mainly of the East, such as the above-mentioned monuments.[100] The same elements can be found at the nymphaeum in Milet (c. AD 80) or at the library of Celsus in Ephesus (c. AD 113–117) (Strocka 1988: 294–297 and nn. 10 and 16 for additional bibliography). Comparable developments may also be observed in private architecture, mainly in villas of the second century AD (Mielsch 1997: 88). Another good example is the monument of Philoppapos at Athens (Kleiner 1983). Until now, the façade of this tomb was usually considered as reflecting architectural elements of theatrical *scenae frontes* (Kleiner 1983: 78–79), as formerly suggested for second style Pompeiian wall paintings (Tybout 1989: throughout, but especially 215–273, 325–352; Fittschen 1976a: 544–556). In accordance with the evidence given above, it is much more likely that the monument of Philoppapos refers to luxury architecture as well, all the more so if one bears in mind the history of Philoppapos, being a descendant of the royal family of Commagene (on the complex history of Philoppapos' family, see Baslez 1992). The date of AD 114–116 for Philoppapos' funeral monument corresponds perfectly to the above-outlined development of middle imperial architecture in the east (for the chronology of Philoppapos' monument, see Kleiner 1983: 14–15).

It seems, therefore, that a date not earlier than the last quarter of the first century AD may be proposed for ad-Dayr. Speculation about ad-Dayr being a monument erected during the reign of Rabbel II for the cult of the deified Nabataean king Obodas I or Obodas III should be treated with caution (Zayadine 1989: 158; Zayadine 1997: 53). The hypothesis that ad-Dayr could have served as a cenotaph for the last Nabataean king, Rabbel II (AD 70–106),[101] is also speculative. Recent cleaning of the interior of ad-Dayr revealed low benches on the sides, indicating that the monument was used for banqueting, another hint to the multifunctionality of Nabtaean tomb complexes as discussed below.

As far as the more complicated façades of the Khazna Faraoun and other monuments are concerned, it has been shown that they accurately reflect the very rich architecture of their times, that is, the late Hellenistic years in the case of Khazna Faraoun or the years around AD 100 in the case of ad-Dayr (Schmid 2000a, 2001d, 2004b; McKenzie 1990: 119–20). Therefore, the Khazna Faraoun reflects the palace architecture of the Hellenistic Age, as do the rich private houses of Delos, for instance the "House of the Hermes."[102] Such characteristic features as the two (or more) storied peristyles of Hellenistic palace architecture are not only copied in the houses of the living but also in the last resting places of the dead. This can be seen in examples from the Mustafa Pascha necropolis at Alexandria or from Nea Paphos on Cyprus.[103]

It is interesting to note that quite a few of the Nabataean tombs show a strong tendency to evoke a third dimension, that is, at least the illusion of a peristyle courtyard, one of the most typical features of Hellenistic houses and palaces. The Khazna Faraoun has a sort of small courtyard incorporated into its ground floor and evokes a peristyle in its upper storey (Figure 12.13e). The Urn Tomb (Figure 12.13d) shows additional colonnaded *stoai* at its sides (McKenzie 1990: pls. 91 and 93), while in the Wadi Farasa East the "Soldier Tomb", together with the opposite Triclinium 235 and structures between them, formed an entire complex (Figure 12.14e) dating to the middle of the first century AD (on the "Soldier Tomb" and related structures see Schmid 2001c, 2004b, both with further references), which is comparable to the most spectacular Hellenistic palace architecture known, such as the Palazzo delle Colonne, the description of Ptolemy IV's *thalamegos*, or some of the Judaean palaces mentioned above. All of these are large-scale interpretations of Vitruvius' description of the Greek house (see above; on the connection between Vitruvius' description and reality as well as palace architecture, see Zoppi 1991–92; Raeder 1988; Reber 1988). It is not only such richly decorated tombs that offer comparable structures, but rather "traditional" monuments (but still with a pediment) too, like Tomb 813 (Figure 12.14b; McKenzie 1990: pls. 163–64; Zayadine 1974, 1986: 229–237; Bockisch 1991: 89–97).[104] Most probably, many more Nabataean tombs would prove to contain three-dimensional features if they had not been eroded or cov-

ered by sand and earth. Such is the case, for example, with Tomb 676 in the Wadi Mataha on the eastern boundaries of the city (Brünnow and Domaszewski 1904: 373–375 no. 676; Lindner 1978: 88; Wenning 1987: 273). So far this tomb was mentioned mostly for its façade and the inner space, showing 15 rock-cut *loculi*. Nobody so far noticed the remains of built walls in front of the façade, clearly visible especially from above. These are forming two sides of a portico apparently including other built structures. A preliminary plan and reconstruction project the general similarity with the complex of the "Soldier Tomb" in the Wadi Farasa East and other structures mentioned above (see Schmid 2004b). Without the results from the International Wadi Farasa Project one could question the contemporaneity of the rock-cut structures of Tomb 676 and the built ones in front of it, especially since no excavation has been carried out yet. However, the past campaigns in the Wadi Farasa have demonstrated that the entire complex of the "Soldier Tomb", including porticoes, courtyard, triclinium and other structures, was constructed in the second or third quarter of the first century AD and was the result of a well planned and organised building programme, taking into account the upper terrace with its water and living installations. Therefore, one can express with some confidence the planned unity of façade and built structures also in the case of Tomb 676 in the Wadi Mattaha (Figure 12.14c). This readily confirms the information gained from the Turkmaniye Tomb's inscription, which mentions dining rooms, gardens and grottoes, all belonging to one complex.[105] More of these complexes are illustrated on Figure 12.14 and, therefore, we see that much of the formerly enigmatic Nabataean funerary architecture in fact follows quite well the common shapes and forms of the Hellenized and Romanized Near East. In the extension towards a third dimension in the form of courtyards, *stoai* and peristyles, either in reality or evoked in relief, we obtain a new criterion for a classification of the Nabataean tombs. This is the case since these features clearly reflect the above-mentioned tendencies in Hellenistic palaces, houses and funeral monuments.[106] Regarding the observed tendencies in pottery and architectural decoration, we witness a comparable evolution in the tomb façades, at least when comparing some richer examples like the Khazna Faraoun (Figure 12.13e), the Corinthian Tomb (Figure 12.13g) and ad-Dayr (Figure 12.13h). The huge and probably undecorated spaces of ad-Dayr's surface as shown on Figure 12.13h would, therefore, correspond to the large-scale ornamental decoration in Nabataean pottery of phase 3b and 3c (Figure 12.6.27, 28), that is, the last quarter of the first and the beginning of the second centuries AD. Conversely, the very rich decoration of the Khazna Faraoun, covering and filling almost every available space (Figure 12.13e), could very well be paralleled by the contemporary pottery of the late first century BC, where we see the same tendency

Figure 12.14 Petra, funerary complexes.

towards a *horror vacui*, that is, the complete filling out of space available for decoration. This tendency also continues into the very early first century AD. As seen above, a good deal of the simpler tomb façades, showing stronger oriental influence in the form of steps on roofs, or evoking a rather tower-like aspect, are likely to date from the first century AD. It would, of course, fit well the general picture drawn so far, especially if we could see an increase of stronger Arabic elements for the *later* first century within the tomb façades too. This would fit perfectly with similar trends in sculpture or coin minting and even in pottery. Beside the usual stylistic arguments, there is another favourable element: logically the rich upper class of Petra would have tried to occupy topographically dominating places for their tombs. The best location for such façades is undoubtedly Khubtha north slope where the so-called Kings' Tombs, the Corinthian, Urn, and Palace, are placed (cf. the map Figure 12.7). All these tombs clearly show elements of elaborate Hellenistic architecture. Most of the orientalizing tomb façades are located in the different wadis leading away from the city centre (cf. Figure 12.7). One is tempted to posit that they were built as the city continued to grow and, therefore, not exclusively according to a social order but at least partially according to a relative chronological sequence.[107]

Renovation and Annexation

The characteristic changes in Nabataean art and culture towards the last quarter of the first century, as outlined above, have been noted previously. This, along with some historical reflections, led to the hypothesis of a cultural and religious *renovatio* under the last Nabataean king, Rabbel II (AD 70–106) (Wenning 1993a: *passim*, especially 86–93, 1989: *passim*, especially 257–58; Wenning and Merklein 1997: 110). It has been suggested that Rabbel II, who received the throne name "the one who renewed and rescued his people," was responsible for a kind of official programme leading away from the previous realistic and "western-oriented" representations of human figures towards a stronger "oriental" traditional and abstract iconography as the prominent *baityloi* illustrate. Indeed, it is quite striking to see that, at least in cases where they can be more or less dated, the aniconic *baityloi* date to the later first century. In the earlier phases of Nabataean art, however, much stronger realistic features were used in order to represent humans and gods (Figure 12.12a–f). Further evidence for a kind of struggle in Nabataean society about such features is seen in the fact that in the temple of the winged lions a kind of iconoclasm, which destroyed the earlier naturalistic decoration, seems to have taken place towards the later first century AD.[108]

It is, of course, very difficult to decide whether the observed changes in Nabataean art, as in reliefs or architectural decoration, do indeed fall together within a programme by Rabbel II. The difficulties come mainly from ignorance of the exact chronology of the first appearance of stronger ornamentalizing artistic features, for instance, in the representation of humans and gods on relief slabs (Figures 12.12g–j) or *baityloi*. However, there may be some relevant indications. As mentioned, the coins of Rabbel II do indeed show to a great extent less naturalistic features in the portrait of the king than did the coins of his predecessors. Additional information can be gained from the painted pottery, where the remarkable change from naturalistic, small-scale motifs to ornamental, large-scale decoration cannot only be paralleled with the development in other categories of Nabataean art, but has, above all, quite precise dates. Such pottery is found alongside characteristic forms of Eastern sigillata and coins of Rabbel II. In addition, Nabataean pottery on sites with a good historical chronological *terminus*—such as Masada—proves that this change happened around AD 70/80 and, therefore, precisely during the early years of Rabbel II's reign. As the conventionally applied term of *renovatio* for these new features within Nabataean culture of the later first century AD suggests, it is believed that the Nabataeans somehow returned to their indigenous roots with these new artistic expressions. This model demands two prerequisites: first, there was an earlier cultural and religious background to which they could return; and second, the intermediate-Hellenistic and Roman influenced period was only a superficial one (see Wenning 1989: 255–259 using the metaphor of (Hellenistic) masks that were temporarily superposed on the indigenous Nabataean/Arabic features). If we stick to the evidence, this model necessarily encounters problems. First of all, about the entire "pre-Hellenistic" period—not in chronological terms but in means of cultural aspects—we can only guess. This is because there is no written evidence that is peculiarly Nabataean that would enlighten us about the presedentarized Nabataeans. Moreover, the earliest material evidence already belongs to a completely Hellenized form (see above). Further, the idea about *renovatio* was related to the assumption that both the "western"-oriented programme in sculptural decoration and other elements around the turn of the eras, as well as the rather "oriental" or "traditional" programme under Rabbel II, were imposed by the ruling class, if not by the king himself (Wenning 1989; Patrich 1990: throughout, especially 165–166). As emphasized above, there may indeed be some allusions to a political programme in major categories of art, such as architectural sculpture. But what about "smaller" categories, for example, coins and pottery? As for coin minting, we can suppose a strong programmatic influence by the ruler on how to design his portrait and on what attributes to choose. But can we imagine Obodas III indicating to the Nabataean potters which forms of the Roman thin-walled pots they should produce (Figure 12.6.11)? Or did Aretas IV chose the specific sigillata forms (Figure 12.6.13) to be copied by Nabataean workshops under his rule? Most probably these rulers did not, nor did Rabbel II decide on how to change the decorative patterns on painted pottery (Figure 12.6.27). But as such "unimportant" categories of crafts and workmanship are not only the best dated but also reflect the everyday culture of the common people, we can use them as a test of the model outlined above.

If we are dealing with a programme imposed by the authorities, we would expect at least some opposition or a contradictory tendency somewhere. The contrary, however, is the case. Pottery, coins, figurative decoration, and so on always seem to form a unity. Thus, if we do not want to conclude that the Nabataean kingdom was an "Orwellian" state, we have to posit that both tendencies discussed here, that is, the "western" and the "oriental," were not imposed by the ruling class but were well based in the entire population, or at least the majority. As suggested above, the settlement towards the late second-century BC was most probably the result of economic considerations combined with the increasing vacuum of power in the region by disinterest and weakness of at least one of the former supra-regional powers, the Seleucid empire. The archaeological evidence as well as the testimony of Strabo is proof that the new lifestyle was a complete success. Around the turning of the eras, Petra was a flourishing city of monumental public buildings and lavishly decorated residences. Huge funerary monuments were constructed or were under construction everywhere. Thus, a general economic wealth and welfare can be deduced.[109] But, early on, Strabo testifies to the importation of goods (*Geogr.* 16.4.26). Although he is referring to luxury items, this could very well be a clue for understanding further developments. As nomads, the Nabataeans had been, to a great extent, self-sufficient. Now, they became increasingly dependent on imported goods and trade.[110] As long as they had a wide selection of trading partners, the Nabataeans would have been in a rather strong position and would have been able to dictate prices and trading conditions. But with the increasing Roman political overweight in the region, they necessarily came under economic pressure too. Whether or not Rabbel II, indeed, tried to move his capital from Petra to Bosra,[111] the entire picture shows that the Nabataeans were struggling not only for political, but also for economic survival. It seems that under the reign of Rabbel II agricultural activities improved considerably.[112] This shows that the Nabataeans tried to turn again towards self-sufficiency in order to balance the loss in trade. We see therefore that the former advantage, that is, the better contacts, and so on, with the sedentarized infrastructure and increasing specialization, suddenly turned into a serious disadvantage.[113] As is evident from modern parallels, it must have been such elements of social and economic pressure that led to a more "traditional" stream

within Nabataean society and culture, rather than an imposed programme.[114]

In AD 106 the Roman emperor Trajan decided to incorporate the Nabataean kingdom into the Roman Empire (see Schmid 1997a with further bibliography; Fiema 1987; Schmid 2000b: 143–146). The Roman annexation of the Nabataean kingdom and the creation of the province of Arabia is generally believed to have occurred peacefully. The movements of their forces show that the Romans were at least prepared for possible resistance. Not only had the III Cyrenaica from Egypt and probably the VI Ferrata from Syria sent considerable detachments into Arabia, but two additional *cohortes* (I Hispanorum and I Thebaeorum) were transferred to Judaea on the eve of the annexation (Bowersock 1983: 79–82; on the troops and their movements, see also Zayadine and Fiema 1986; Fiema 1987: 28 and nn. 20 and 21; Kennedy 1980). Thus, the Nabataeans were hemmed in on three sides. Two Safaitic inscriptions, unfortunately undated, mention "the year of the Nabataean war" and another one reports "the year when the Nabataeans revolted against the people of Rome" (Sartre 1982: 131–132; 1985: 63–72 especially 68–69; Bowersock 1983: 80, n.13; Wenning 1993a: 100–101; on these and other Safaitic inscriptions where Rome and Romans are mentioned, see Macdonald 1993: 328–34). These graffiti, together with the archaeological evidence, suggest that the annexation did not occur without military confrontation. According to archaeological results, it seems that places like Oboda, Moje Awad, Khirbat Dharayh, Dhiban and Sbaita were destroyed in the very early second century AD. In Petra too, evidence of a contemporary destruction was reported on several occasions (for detailed analysis as well as related bibliography, see Schmid 1997a, 2000b: 141–143).

A hostile component of the Roman takeover seems to be confirmed by a passage in Ammianus Marcellinus stating that, "It [the Nabataean kingdom] was given the name of a province, assigned a governor, and compelled to obey our laws by the emperor Trajan, who, by frequent victories crushed the arrogance of its inhabitants..." (Ammianus Marcellinus 14.8.13)[115] Furthermore, the promotion of a military tribune from the III Cyrenaica as well as the *ornamenta triumphalia* bestowed upon the commander of the annexation, A. Cornelius Palma, in AD 107, suggest military activities.[116] Bowersock observes a sort of an unofficial *damnatio memoriae* of the Nabataeans in the literary sources of the second century AD that could be very well interpreted as a reaction against their resistance to integration into the Roman Empire (Bowersock 1988).[117] This would also explain why in the contemporary sources there is, besides the scanty mention in Dio Cassius, almost no report of the annexation, only in Ammianus Marcellinus, writing in the fourth century AD.

The annexation of the Nabataean kingdom has to

be seen in a wider context within the planning of Trajan's further activities in the East. The annexation was probably not planned for AD 106 because at that time the Roman army was still involved in the war against the Dacians. The death of Rabbel II may have led to the decision in favour of immediate annexation.[118] After the annexation, the project most quickly realized in the new province was the building of the Via Nova Traiana, connecting the Gulf of Aqabah with Syria (on the Via Nova Traiana, see Graf 1992b: especially 256–259, and Freeman, this volume). It was built not simply with an economic but primarily with a military goal in mind because this road became one of the main routes for supplying the Roman army during its war against Parthia. It is generally believed that Trajan deliberately used the rich booty from Dacia and the income from the mines in Dacian territory to build new roads in the eastern provinces, especially for the planned campaign against the Parthians (see, for instance, Axioti 1980: 189–190). It seems that Trajan did not have too much trust in the loyalty of the Nabataeans and decided to integrate them into his empire, despite the not too favourable circumstances that a large part of the Roman army was tied down in Dacia.[119]

Reported contacts between the Parthians and the Nabataeans go back at least to the first century BC when in 38 BC the Romans fined the Nabataean king Malichus I for supplying the Parthian commander Pacorus during his invasion into Roman territories (41–38 BC) (Dio Cassius 48.41.5; see also Debevoise 1938: 108; Wolsky 1976: 413–414, 1993: 41, 122–124 especially n. 2). Anthony's gift of Nabataean territories to Cleopatra may also be seen in this context (Dio Cassius 49.32.5; Plutarch, *Ant.* 36.2).[120] Parthian influence on Nabataean policies can also be deduced from an episode during the Jewish throne quarrels, when Herod the Great asked Malichus I for refuge. The latter refused and argued that the Parthians had forbidden him to accept the refugees (Josephus, *Ant.* 14.14.1–2; Josephus, *War* 1.274–276).[121] Trajan could not therefore exclude the possibility of Nabataean supplies to the Parthians during his own campaign into Mesopotamia and Babylonia, for the Nabataeans would probably not have accepted the loss of their only potent trading partner in the Near East. That both events, the annexation of the Nabataean kingdom and the campaign against Parthia, were already seen as connected in antiquity may be deduced from the above-mentioned passage by Ammianus Marcellinus where he continues, "It was given the name of a province, assigned a governor, and compelled to obey our laws by the emperor Trajan who, by frequent victories, crushed the arrogance of its inhabitants when he was waging glorious war with Media and the Parthians" (Ammianus Marcellinus 14.8.13)[122]

The factor of international trade in this confrontation was not only important for the Nabataeans but for the Romans as well (on this see also Eadie 1986: 248–249). This is shown by Trajan's successful efforts to control Spasinou Charax, the most important port in Mesopotamia, as well as his statement that he would like to travel to India if only he were younger (Dio Cassius 68: 28–29; see Delbrueck 1955.56: 245).[123] The partners of the Far East trade quickly reacted to the new situation created by the provincialization of Nabataea. It is certainly no coincidence that in AD 107, immediately after the annexation, an Indian delegation made its way to Rome (Dio Cassius 68.15.1).[124]

Some Final Thoughts

When attempting to sum up the different aspects of Nabataean art, culture and history and put them in a wider context, we see a fascinating evolution during a relatively short period of time. In fact, from the first evidence of Nabataean material culture to the time of the Roman annexation, only two hundred years passed.

Thus, we see that there was in fact no continuous process of Hellenization, that is, a step-by-step adoption of what is considered Greek art and culture.[125] Indeed, the opposite was the case. The Nabataeans took over initially an almost completely Hellenized culture around 100 BC or slightly earlier. Towards the second half of the first century BC and the first half of the first century AD, they were open to stronger Roman tendencies as well as to the first steps leading towards an identifiable Nabataean "style." A distinctive Nabataean culture is only attested during the next step, that is, during the second half of the first century AD, when their potters, sculptors and coin cutters consistently freed themselves from the earlier prototypes. It is difficult to decide whether this last step in development coincides with the accession to the Nabataean throne by Rabbel II, "the one who renewed and rescued his people," or whether Rabbel was following an already existing general stream. Interestingly enough, it was only shortly before losing their political independence in AD 106 that the Nabataeans had fully developed their own material culture with the last of these phases.

When considering the evidence outlined above, one can conclude that Nabataean art and culture does show a comparable tripartite system of evolution—such can be applied to cultural development in general: a first phase of "initialization;" a second phase of *akmé*, that is, the peak of the evolution; and, finally, a third phase, already leading towards decline. However, things seem to be more difficult in the case of the Nabataeans. The easiest case may be the pottery (cf. Figure 12.6), where indeed the subdivision into three phases with some sub-phases works quite well. In a first stage, the purely Hellenistic prototypes are taken over; in a second, the first tendency to a "local" production is observed, combined with external (Roman) influence; and in the third step, the characteristic Nabataean style is achieved. Although of a similar general outline, other categories present different models of evolution. For instance, in sculpture and relief we also see a first phase of complete Hellenistic style (Figure 12.12a–f), but with a chronological difference of about 100 years compared with the first appearance of the Hellenistic pottery! Yet another illustration is provided by temple architecture (Figure 12.10), where from the beginning, that is, the end of the first century BC, there seem to be rather strong oriental elements, mixed with other influences from the Hellenized east.

This may be related to the particular case of the process of settlement as observed in the case of the Nabataeans. It may seem logical that in the first stage of settling down, people would not immediately start producing crafts, such as monumental architecture or sculpture that demanded a well-developed infrastructure and trained artists and craftsmen. But they would rather take their first steps in the field of "smaller" categories, such as coin minting or pottery production.[126] This may explain why there is an important chronological difference, although they follow the same general outline, within pottery and numismatics, on the one hand, and sculpture and architecture, on the other. As for temple architecture, the impact of specific religious goals may play an important role, as stressed above, although lacking detailed written sources this must remain rather mysterious for the moment (Wenning 1989: 244 and throughout).

Interestingly, most of the immediate geographical neighbours of the Nabataeans show a different model of cultural evolution. Most of them were settled for quite a long period, so that we find well-established local cultures that were increasingly influenced by Hellenistic and Roman features, until they became more or less completely Hellenized or Romanized and, at last, were incorporated into the Roman empire.

In a search for a parallel phenomenon to that found within the Nabataean culture, we must leave the Near East and turn towards Central Asia. There can be seen a comparable, suddenly increased input of western, that is, Hellenistic, culture that is due in these cases to the conquests of Alexander the Great (Litvinskij 1998; Harmatta (ed.) 1996; Invernizzi 1995; Errington and Cribb 1992; Arora 1991; Rapin 1990; Karttunen 1990; Holt 1988; Ozols and Thewaldt 1984, all with abundant additional references. Still not replaced is Schlumberger 1969). The Greek colonists established, within a very short time, a strongly Hellenized culture, as can be seen chiefly in coins [127] and pottery (Gardin 1990, 1985, 1984), while in the field of architecture is found a large amount of local forms and shapes beside the imported Greek elements (Pitschikjan 1996; Nielsen 1994: 124–128, 278–280 cat. no. 19; Bernard 1996: especially 110–116, 1990).[128] Already during the first 150 years or so after the founding of these Greek settlements, there are some tendencies towards a similar evolution as observed in the case

of the Nabataeans. The first coins of the Graeco-Bactrian and Indo-Greek kings show perfectly minted Greek coins with typical Hellenistic portraits of the ruler and Greek inscriptions. But around 200 BC at the latest, the first issues occur with a mixed legend, that is, in Greek on one side and in local script on the other.[129] Around the middle of the second century BC, nomads originating from regions in present-day Turkestan and China conquered the territories of most of these Greek kingdoms (Enoki *et al.* 1996; Zadneprovskiy 1996; Bernard 1987). Therefore, the surviving Greek settlements were cut off from their direct connection to Mesopotamia and the Mediterranean and in the material culture a stronger tendency towards local elements can be observed. The coins now are consequently inscribed in local alphabets on one side and show at least partially non-Greek iconographic elements. Likewise, pottery develops its own style, although there are occasionally influences from the west. The last remnants of these former Greek cultural spots in Central Asia can be seen in the arts of the Kushan and the well-known Gandhara reliefs, incorporating both local and western elements (Puri 1996; Pugachenkova *et al.* 1996; Nehru 1990.).[130]

Although in general terms quite similar to the lines of development in Nabataean material culture, there are some crucial differences, mainly of a sociopolitical nature. The first Graeco-Bactrians were in fact Greeks, simply producing their own crafts in a place far away from their homelands. The first Nabataeans who produced their own material culture, on the contrary, were already "at home" in central Jordan around 100 BC for more than two hundred years. They had, however, no preceding material culture that they could work on and, therefore, they adopted a foreign one, taking over the cultural *lingua franca* of the region. In a further development, the Graeco-Bactrians and Indo-Greeks continuously lost their former cultural roots because it became increasingly difficult for them to maintain a direct contact with the Mediterranean.[131] The Nabataeans, on the other hand, developed their own material culture in a surrounding that would have been extremely favourable to maintaining the former, that is, the Hellenistic one. Therefore, one could say that it was probably by distancing themselves from the predominant Hellenistic and later Roman cultural elements in their immediate neighbourhood that the Nabataeans became a sociocultural unity (on this see also Bouzek 1995: 115).[132]

The typical Nabataean culture did not entirely perish with the incorporation of the Nabataean kingdom into the Roman Empire. For instance, the characteristic Nabataean painting on pottery occurs at least into the fourth century AD as do the shapes of that pottery.[133] However, from AD 106 onwards no new elements can be found but rather a degeneration of the already established features. The shapes as well as the painting of the pottery could be said to be degenerated versions of the shapes and decorations as introduced in the last quarter of the first century AD. Thus, it seems that with the Roman annexation, the Nabataeans not only lost their political independence, but also their innovative spirit.[134]

Acknowledgments

The author would like to thank (in alphabetical order) the following persons for their manifold practical and intellectual help: André Barmasse (Basel), Ulrich Bellwald (Amman), Suleiman Farajat (Wadi Mousa), Zbigniew T. Fiema (Helsinki), Caroline Hugenot (Lausanne), David F. Graf (Miami); Daniel Keller (Basel), Bernhard Kolb (Basel), Judith S. McKenzie (Oxford), Martin Seyer (Vienna) and Fawzi Zayadine (Amman).

Notes

1. Literature about the Hellenistic period is legion; for mainly historical aspects one can consult Shipley 2000; Green 1990; Gehrke 1990; Walbank *et al.* 1984; Will 1982; information on culture and arts through Bengtson 1988; Pollitt 1986; Onians 1979.

2. On the Seleucid kingdom see Grainger 1997 and 1993; Sherwin-White and Kuhrt 1993; Finkbeiner 1993; on Ptolemaic Egypt see Finocchi 2002; Hölbl 2001; Vanoyeke 1998; Bowman 1986 and many more.

3. On the conflicts between the diadochs see Bosworth 2002; Bengtson 1987; for Coele Syria see Hackl and Jenni and Schneider 2003: 36–39.

4. A natural cave somewhat to the North of the temple is interpreted as belonging to a pre-Hellenistic cultic activity.

5. Seigne indicates Iron Age material from a cave that was used for cultic purposes and later incorporated into the temple of Zeus. This could be a further analogy with Gadara, where a similar installation was observed near the presumed temple of Zeus.

6. The absence so far of a synthesising publication complicates the understanding and interpretation of the different building phases. The most synoptic illustration has been published in a somewhat unexpected context: Rasson and Seigne 1989: 118 fig. 1; the same sequence of drawings in a publication for a wider audience: Seigne 1987: 58–9.

7. If indeed the proposed date is correct, one would be somewhat cautious about the strong Ptolemaic connection proposed by the authors.

8. A concise summary on Amman's history is given by Lichtenberger 2003: 244–7; see also the more detailed accounts by Hübner 1992 and MacAdam 1992.

9. See the references in MacAdam 1992: 30–2; on the Nabataeans and the cities of the Decapolis see Wenning 1992, on Amman 84–86; on the relations between Nabataeans and Seleucids see Schmid (2004c).

10. One has to bear in mind that these coins could have circulated in later periods as well.

11. For instance Zayadine 1977–78: fig. 23 bottom right (two more Nabataean sherds of the first century AD are reported from the area of the Roman forum); Nabataean coins are even of more doubtful evidence since they do not necessarily point to Nabataean presence, contrary to the pottery; on the different distribution patterns of Nabataean coins and pottery outside the Nabataean heartland (see Schmid 2004a).

12. See below on Nabataean pottery; the Hellenistic pottery from the citadel is illustrated in Zayadine (1977–78: figs. 12–15); to be sure, a review would be necessary.

13. The direct impact of the Tobiads on Amman depends on whether one accepts the interpretation that the quoted "Birta" (fortress) of the Ammanitis has to be located on the Amman citadel; see also MacAdam 1992: 28–30.

14. For Alexandrian parallels see Lauter (1971: 151–152); cf. on Alexandrian capitals Pensabene (1991: 44–46 fig. 29–33; on their evolution and comparisons in general, see Hesberg 1978. For the connection between the "Palazzo delle Colonne" and Ptolemaic palace architecture see Pensabene (1993: 3–147, 195–216); McKenzie (1996); Schmidt-Colinet (1993); Pensabene (1991: *passim*, especially 49–55. figs. 42–62); Hesberg (1978); Lyttelton (1974: 40–52).

15. More likely than Herodes Antipas; see the concise account and interpretation by Lichtenberger (1999: 40–47).

16. See also below on reflexes of Hellenistic luxury architecture within Nabataean funerary complexes.

17. While the present contribution focuses deliberately on the Herodian building complexes at Machaerus and Kallirrhoë, other sites in Transjordan, yet to be excavated, are likely to be connected to Herod as well; see the short account given by Kokkinos (2001).

18. On the stucco fragments from Kallirrhoë see Strobel and Wimmer (2003: pl. 18A); Clamer (1997: 55 fig. 91b); for parallels from the third palace at Jericho and from lower Herodion see Netzer (1999: 47 fig. 65; 104 fig. 143); Rozenberg (1996: 135–136, figs. 21–23); at Petra similar stucco decorations were found within the rich mansion at az-Zantur (see below notes 46, 47, especially Kolb and Keller (2002: 288, fig. 14); the South Temple, Egan (2002: 353 figs. 3. 4); Joukowsky (2003: 401–402 figs. 18–19) and the funerary complex of the "Soldier Tomb" in the Wadi Farasa.

19. Exhibitions (selection): Schmitt-Korte 1976; Inoubliable Pétra 1980; Nabatäen 1981; Voie royale 1986; Königsweg 1987; Lindner and Zeitler 1991; Petra und die Weihrauchstrasse 1993; Frösén and Fiema 2002; Petra Rediscovered 2003. For publications on the Nabataeans or related to them, systematic research in the catalogue entries of the German Archaeological Institute at Rome, available on Dyabola (which, especially on peripheral cultures, is far from being complete), led to the following result: 1960–69: 34 entries; 1970–79: 60 entries; 1980–89: 111 entries; 1990–99: 174 entries. In other words, since 1960 output on the Nabataeans almost doubles every decade. Wenning gives the best overview on Nabataean archaeology (1987, 1990).Wenning (1987: 307–346,

1990: 367–377) gives a detailed bibliography on the subject. Therefore, in this chapter some of the older works are not quoted as they can be found easily in the contributions of Wenning. On the other hand, recently published works are emphasized.

20. For an attempt to put the available evidence on the Nabataeans in a wider perspective, see Wenning (1989); a concise overview is given by Dijkstra (1995: 34–80); quite inspiring, although rather superficial, is the chapter "arte nabatea" in Garbini (1993: 211–219); strongly tending towards an ideological interpretation of Nabataean culture and, therefore, to be considered with caution is Patrich (1990); likewise, Mettinger (1995: 57–68).

21. For the general historical frame concerning the early Hellenistic period see the references above notes 1, 2; for comments on the historical sources cited in this chapter see Hackl and Jenny and Schneider (2003).

22. See also below; for new research on Sela, see Lindner and Zeitler (1991: 180); Hart (1986B); Hart and Falkner (1985) for an overall view of that survey. The question revolves not only on where was the stronghold of the Nabataeans, but also on "*al-Sela*" of the Edomites, mentioned in the Bible.

23. "There is evidence, in the form of Hellenistic pottery and coins of the third century BC, of settlement in Petra by that date; but so far no undisturbed levels of that period have been located." (Parr 1960: 135).

24. I owe much of the information about Poseidippos and his epigram to David F. Graf (Miami) who will soon publish some more detailed reflections about this subject; on the problem of kingship within the Nabataean society see Hackl and Jenni and Schneider (2003: 61–63).

25. The chronology of that inscription is based on the mention of M. Perperna, consul of the year 130 BC an who died in 129 BC, a summary of the chronological argumentation can be found in Rumscheid (1994: 46).

26. Since 1999 a French team is excavating the area in front of Qasr al-Bint and according to not published information Hellenistic as well as Iron Age layers were discovered. However, so far there are only the few pages published by Augé *et al.* (2002).

27. On the uncertainties about the beginning of the mint in Petra, see also Schmitt-Korte (1997: 101–102 and fig. 105).

28. The difference between the mention of "king of the Nabataeans" on coins and the reference by Poseidippos reported above is, besides the unsecure reading of Poseidippos' epigram, that the coins surely reflect the Nabataean viewpoint, while the epigram gives a view through the Greek glasses.

29. The only distinctive characteristic is the infrequent simple painting. For a possible explanation, see Schmid (1996a: 130, nn. 18–22); Schmid (2000b); see also the observations on Hellenistic pottery from Northern Jordan in note 12, above.

30. This seems to be the case in other rather parallel developments from nomadism to sedentarism too, as can be seen

for the Scythians and others; cf. below note 86. A small reflection of these "archaic" features of the pre-settlement culture of the Nabataeans may be seen in some terracotta types, for example, the frequently occurring camels and the horse riders: Bignasca (1993: figs. 133–138); Parlasca (1997: 126–131 especially 130–131); Parlasca (1990a: 164–167 pl. 31; 1990b: 91–92 figs. 26–37). The chronology of Nabataean terracottas is still rather unsatisfactory. A first indication that the camels and horses should be rather early in date may be seen by the fact that from the Late Roman layers on az-Zantur only very few fragments were ascribed to these types, while in the earlier layers they are much more prominent: Bignasca (1996: 266–288).

31. The passage, as well as the use of the monsoon winds, were known to the South Arabian people for a longer time, but they hid their knowledge from their rivals in trade; Casson (1989: 11–12, 283–291); see also Kitchen (1994: 22–25) on the date of the *Periplus*.

32. Comparable phenomena, i.e., Arab tribes pushing into gaps of power at the periphery of the Mediterranean world and creating new political factors and eventually becoming sedentarized, occurred on several occasions in antiquity (Funke 1996).

33. This trench was part of the "Hellenistic Petra Project," jointly directed by David F. Graf (Miami), Leigh-Ann Bedal (Erie) and the present author; a first preliminary report is published in the *Annual of the Department of Antiquities of Jordan* 49: 417–441, 2005.

34. However, this did not exclude the camel raiders from having houses in their home city.

35. The careful analysis in the case of Unayzah offers hope for reconstructing the process of settlement and social diversification among the Nabataeans. On this subject see Fiema (1996).

36. As is proven by the finds of Nabataean pottery at sites such as Jawf, Thaj, Hegra, Qaryat al-Fau, Gharrain, Marib, Qana and Khor Rori; on this see Schmid (2000b: 127–131, 2004a). As this pottery apparently was not used as an export good, these finds point to Nabataean presence.

37. For Nabataean Hawara see Oleson (2001: 570–572); on Nabataean Aila see Dolinka (2003: 29–30), both with further references.

38. Good pictures in Toynbee (1978: 155 figs. 307, 308); on Nabataean royal portraits see Schmid (1999, 2001e).

39. Wreath: Meshorer (1975: 92 nn. 33, 35, 37, 39); (1975: 92 no. 37) is interpreted as diademed, but as Schmitt-Korte (1990: 110 nn. 21–22) shows wears a wreath; diademed: Meshorer (1975: 92 nn. 32, 34, 36, 38); Schmitt-Korte (1990: 111 no. 24).

40. Diademed: Meshorer (1975: 94–96 nn. 46, 47, 47A, 50, 52, 55); Schmitt-Korte (1990: 116–117 nn. 52–54); wreath: Meshorer (1975: nn. 48–49A).

41. The date of "late second-/early first century BC" proposed in the preliminary report has to be slightly corrected according to personal communication by the excavator.

42. A stronger oriental influence was deduced from the not so systematic orientation of the smaller units; see Stucky (1996: 48–49); Kolb (1997: 63). Parallels from Neo-Assyrian and Neo-Babylonian Mesopotamia show that even in such cases more extensive planning usually existed; see Miglus (1999: 254). The basic types of these Mesopotamian houses, showing one (Babylonia) or even two (Assyria) inner courtyards with the different rooms for "official" and private use grouped around them, deserves special mention, see Miglus (1999: 133–175, for Assyria, 179–213 for Babylonia). As tempting as it is to consider such houses as the forerunners of the Nabataean ones, there are important chronological and geographical gaps yet to be filled.

43. See the plan by Andreae (1975: 77); in the villa at Boscoreale there is—beside the huge main peristyle—a small one (no. 15) at the periphery, showing porticoes only on three sides, while the fourth one contains only semicolumns against the wall; for Pergamon, see Pinkwart and Stamnitz (1984: 36–42, pls. 51, 52).

44. Indeed, Hellenistic houses and palaces from Nippur and Seleucia show similar features: Kose (1996: 206 fig. 4, 208 fig. 6). As these monuments show considerable Hellenistic influence too, we may conclude that the houses so far excavated at Petra simply illustrate the *interpretatio nabataea* of the common Hellenistic house type; cf. in a broader context Colledge 1987. Taking into consideration also the remarks in note 42, it seems probable that the oriental variant of the Hellenistic house generally contained some older local elements.

45. The same is true for the houses on the northern slope of az-Zantur and on Khatute. From both places, an impressive view of the city's centre is possible. On the Ephesian houses, see Lang-Auinger *et al.* (1996 with an older bibliography); similar house types are reported from other areas in Asia Minor too, for instance, from Limyra (Seyer 1993; Seyer and Rasch 1997).

46. On illusionistic paintings from Italy and built parallels from the Hellenistic world, see below note 73.

47. This is not the place to enter into detail on that subject. A detailed publication of these wall decorations, including the various interpretative aspects, is in preparation by B. Kolb (Basel).

48. On Nabataean religion see Hackl and Jenni and Schneider (2003: 76–90); Healey (2001); specifically on Dusares, see Arrian (*Anab.* 7.20.1); Wenning and Merklein (1997: especially110); Zayadine (1990a); Gawlikowski (1990: 2662–2665); Moutsopoulos (1990: *passim*, especially 53–54); Bowersock (1990a); Tran Tam Tinh (1990); Knauf (1990).

49. On Qasr al-Bint, see now Zayadine, Larché and Dentzer-Feydy (2003); Zayadine (1985); the recent excavations mentioned in note 26 may perhaps provide evidence for a predecessor of the actual Qasr al-Bint that could, therefore, belong to the third quarter of the first century BC and would confirm the early beginning of the "construction boom" discussed here.

50. As in other fields of research, at an early stage, a rather simple model is usually proposed; it is replaced at a second stage by a very detailed differentiation; and at a third stage, it is often simplified again to some general outlines.

51. In the case of the Temple of Qasr (Figure 12.10.1 [right]), it is not clear whether we have to reconstruct an inner subdivision in the form of a wall subdividing the rectangular building into a front and a rear part. If so, then al-Qasr would become an almost exact parallel to Qasr al-Bint at Petra (Figure 12.10.6 [right]); see the study of Altherr-Charon (1977) on temples with a tripartite cella.

52. Freyberger stresses that the typically eclectic putting together of different elements may be a general characteristic of the Hellenistic Near and Middle East. This seems in general the best explanation for the phenomena observed in Nabataean culture as observed in note 44 above, and discussion and references above relating to private architecture.

53. One could also refer to the famous tent of Ptolemy II as described by Kallixeinos *apud* Athenaeus (*Deipn.* 5.196–197). There, too, a central hall, surrounded on three sides by porticoes, is mentioned. This shows that such features were quite widespread in Ptolemaic Egypt; on the tent see also below.

54. On the impact of Roman architecture on Near Eastern buildings and on interchanges between them, see Strocka (1988).

55. On Ptolemaic temple building in Egypt in general, see Aufrére *et al.* (1997: 215–261); Schloz (1994); Siegler (1969); Arnold (1999, especially 137–224); for a broader view on Egyptian temples, see the contributions in Gundlach and Rochholz (1994).

56. On South Arabian temples in general, see now Schmidt (1997–98); for illustrations compared to the plans of Nabataean temples see Schmid (2001c: 381; fig. 10).

57. Zayadine, Larché and Dentzer-Feydy (2003); Freyberger (1998: 6–7); Zayadine (1985: especially 248–249, 1986: 238–248); if indeed, as Zayadine supposes, the temple of the late first century had a predecessor that could probably be dated to a generation before Obodas III (Zayadine 1985: 249), this would be the earliest cultic building known from the Nabataean area and would at least fill partially the chronological gap between their settlement and the first monumental buildings. Other possible early cult buildings are indicated by epigraphic evidence but not much is known about the architecture related to them(Wenning 1989: 249).

58. The latest element from the assemblages connected to the construction of the temple would be the painted bowl (Tushingham 1972 fig. 2, 59 of phase 2c); for a detailed analysis, see Schmid (2000b: 104–105).

59. Preliminary reports are regularly published in the *Annual of the Department of Antiquities of Jordan*, the last to date is Joukowsky (2003); see also Netzer (2003: 72–81) Freyberger (1998: 21–24); Joukowsky *et al.* (1998).

60. For the *paradeisos*-like structure see Bedal (2003, especially 176–177) for a possible interpretation of the whole area—*paradeisos* and "South Temple"—as belonging to

the Nabataean *basileia* (with further references to the thesis of E.L. Schluntz). This solution offers indeed some advantages, even if these structures can not be *the* Nabataean palace. Even when considering the so-called baths as belonging to the same overall structure, there is not enough that could be interpreted as the residential area of the Nabataean royal palace. It could be possible that representation features and the residence of the Nabataean kings were located within different building complexes.

61. The Petra *paradeisos* was constructed in the reign of Aretas IV according to the excavator (Bedal 2003: 67–72), although some of the chronological indications need verification. As for the chronology of the "South Temple", one will have to wait for a final publication. It is worth mentioning, however, that under the pavement of the temple forecourt no pottery later than phase 2b was found, giving a *terminus post quem* of 1 BC for the initial construction of the monument; on pottery of phase 2b, see Schmid (1996b: 165–168, 173–174). For the pottery from the South Temple, see Joukowsky (1998: 313, n.14). This pottery from trench 18 loci 3 and 10 (from the 1996 season) was identified by the author and the results were communicated in a letter to the excavator dated 27 January 1997. However, in 1997, in a trench parallel to trench 18 (trench 46 on fig. 1b in Joukowsky 1998: 295) apparently pottery of a much later date was found in layers below the pavement. The bowl on fig. 9 in Joukowsky (1998: 299) belongs not, as stated in the caption, to the second style, but to phase 3c, post-dating ad 100! If, indeed, the wrongly labelled pottery comes from below the pavement, this would be later than AD 100 and would, therefore, completely change the chronology of the entire building.

62. On Nabataean sculpture in general, see McKenzie (1990); Lyttelton and Blagg (1990); McKenzie (1988); all with additional references. The book by Weber (2002: 519–541) gives now an excellent summary of Nabataean freestanding sculpture; for figural reliefs from Petra see now Wenning and Hübner (2004).

63. On that, especially in connection with Nabataean sculpture, see Schmid (1999) and Smith (1991: 223–228), in a broader context. As a matter of fact, the first appearance of such classicizing features within Hellenistic sculptures goes back to the middle or even the first half of the second century bc. On the famous altar from Pergamon, the baroque style, as seen within the giants on the big frieze, already occurs together with the calm and fleshy faces on the small frieze: Smith (1991: 155–166). From then on, prominent examples like the group with Achilles and Penthesilea show that the classicizing style continues during the entire second and into the beginning of the first century BC; cf. Jaeggi and Schmid (1996: 23–24, 31–33).

64. Weber (1997: 118–119) points out that the above-mentioned bust of Helios from the Qasr al-Bint is another good example, and the fragment of a Nike (Figure 12f), despite its incomplete preservation, is of outstanding quality, both in technical terms as well as naturalistic styling.

65. This is true, for example, for such famous sculptural groups like the Laocoön or the sculptures from the Sperlonga cave (Smith 1991: figs. 143–146). While Laocoön himself is related predominantly to the baroque style of the high Hellenistic period, his sons show rather the classicistic aspect. In Sperlonga, one would compare the beautiful baroque head of Ulysses with the fleshy face of Diomedes (Conticello and Andreae 1974: pls. 14. 37). On these aspects, see Jaeggi and Schmid (1996: 26–29, 32–33) with many additional references. Since then Despinis (1996: *passim*, especially 306–314) added some new information, relevant mostly to the presumed prototypes of the rape of the Palladion; on Laocoön and the Sperlonga groups, see now Schmid(2003); Lahusen (1999) and Strocka (1999).

66. As pointed out above on the iconography of the royal coin portraits of the Nabataeans, we indeed see a stronger reference to Rome at this date. On the other hand, Thüroff (1989: 96) suggests a very interesting hypothesis: therefore, the triton on a relief slab from Petra would be holding a torch, an otherwise rather unusual attribute for a sea creature, especially in connection with the weapons on the same frieze (tritons holding torches may occur on representations of Poseidon's wedding with Amphitrite). This could be understood as a reference to the Nabataean troops burning the ships of Cleopatra VII that she had prepared at a Red Sea port in order for Octavian to flee after the battle at Actium (Dio Cassius 51.7.1; Plutarch, *Ant.* 69.3); see also Polito (1998).

67. The most prominent example, but by far not the only one, for this thematic conjecture is the lower part of the outer frieze of the Ara Pacis at Rome, also showing a richly developed flora and fauna referring to Augustus' golden age; on the Ara Pacis see note 77 below.

68. The tomb façades of the Nabataeans in general, and the ones from Petra in particular, have been treated many times in the history of research. Concise overviews are given by Netzer (2003: 13–65); McKenzie (1990); Zayadine (1989); Schmidt-Colinet (1981); see also the revised version in Weber and Wenning (1997: 87–94); Fedak (1990: 150–157); Lyttelton (1974: 61–83). The work of Matthiae (1991) gives a good introduction as well, although some interpretations, especially of the monuments treated here, seem difficult to substantiate; cf. below note 74. Special reference should be made to the seldom-used work of Qusus (1984); the basic works, especially for detailed descriptions, by Brünnow and von Domaszewski (1904: 137–428) and Bachmann *et al.* (1921: 8–28) are still irreplaceable; Schmid (2000a) gives a brief introduction. In general terms, one has to state, after more or less one century of research, that all attempts to obtain a chronological sequence by classifying these monuments in typological order, did not attempt their goal. The range of time within which the Nabataean rock-cut façades were produced is apparently too short and the diversity of mouldings and other details to heterogene for such approaches, as was probably the Nabataean society. The most promising way to obtain chronological information about these monuments is excavating their interior and the space in front of them; cf. below on Nabataean funerary complexes.

69. The covering with stucco is confirmed in most cases by the "fixing" holes still *in situ* and, in rare cases, by fragments of conserved stucco. How spectacular these decorations

could have been is shown by some gilded fragments related to the temple of Qasr al-Bint or even to a predecessor; see Zayadine (1985: 240). However, the rich fragments from private houses also confirm this general picture (cf. above).

70. The bibliography on the Mausoleum is legion; a concise summary on recent research can be found in Jeppesen (2002, see also 1998); Higgs (1997); Jenkins *et al.* (1997); Jeppesen (1997); Walker and Matthews (1997); Waywell (1997); Fedak (1990: 71–74).

71. Lauter quotes parallels from Cyrene. This would, of course, fit well the often discussed Alexandrian influence in Nabataean tomb architecture. On tombs from Cyrenaica, see Stucchi (1975: 149–192).

72. On similar monuments from Numidia, like the Nabataean funeral architecture contesting the peripheral eclecticism between local tradition and Hellenistic influence, see Coarelli and Thébert (1988); Rakob (1979, 1983); and, in a broader framework, Camps (1995). It must be mentioned that a small tomb in the Bab as-Siq outside Petra is completely hewn out of the rock, i.e., free-standing. For other "smaller" Nabataean monuments, strongly depending upon Hellenistic influence, see Weber (1997: 117–18).

73. Although Fittschen (1996) recently partially modified his theory about the cultural background of some eastern wall paintings this does not affect his and other reflections on what the architectural paintings of the second Pompeiian style represent.

74. This theory, for the Khazna Faraoun as well as for other façades is mainly represented by Matthiae (1995, 1994, especially 284–285, 1991, especially 259–265, 1989, 1988).

75. See the impressive reconstruction by Pesce (1950: pl. X; Lauter 1971: 163 fig. 15). It must be mentioned that all architectural elements used in that reconstruction were actually found, at least partially.

76. See the drawing by Netzer (1991: 583 plan 62), bearing in mind that the reconstruction of the roofs is hypothetical; cf. also Nielsen (1994: 193); Foerster (1996: 60–61).

77. On the capitals from Petra see Ronczewski (1932); comparisons with the Ara Pacis: Schmidt-Colinet (1981: 62, 90–92); see also Freyberger (1997: 72, 1998: 6–7) who, although he points out the similarities with late republican ornaments, again returns to the comparison with the Ara Pacis.

78. The paintings belong to the very late second (lower floor) and to the very early third Pompeiian style ("studiolo" in the upper floor).

79. See also the very rich comparative material by Schörner (1995: 17–46) for the third quarter of the first century BC and (1995: 46–51) for the early imperial years; see also the comparisons quoted by Freyberger (1998: 7) and Bienkowski (2002: 90).

80. Fittschen (1976b: 193) thinks that the frieze slabs from Petra with representations of weapons are rather western/Roman in their composition and discusses the possibility

of eastern influences on Augustean motifs.

81. It must be mentioned, however, that the stucco decoration could, theoretically, have been applied at a later time, although this does not seem very likely. At least the wall paintings from az-Zantur, with a well established *terminus post quem* of AD 20, show that such pediments continued to be used as decorative features into the first century AD.

82. Information kindly provided by Suleiman Farajat (Wadi Mousa).

83. Hammond (1965: 55–65), the excavator, dates the theatre in the reign of Aretas IV (9 BC–AD 40).

84. It has to be stated that the colonnaded street in the city center, at least around the "Temenos Gate," was not paved until around AD 100; see below.

85. In the sense of increasing presence of Nabataeans in Italian ports and cities (Schmid 2004a; Roche 1996: 86–95, 99).

86. In general, on Scythian and related art, see Jacobson (1995); Schiltz (1994); Zazoff (1996). The tendency towards ornamentalization can be seen in an exemplary way within the so-called "Rolltiere." It was formerly believed that the Scythians arrived in the Black Sea area without a material culture of their own and started taking over and developing foreign prototypes; see also Stucky (1976: especially 20–21 with the older references). As good as this theory is for a parallel to what can be observed in Nabataean culture, it now seems that the Scythians already had a culture of their own and the adoption of naturalistic (Greek) prototypes and their change towards ornamentalization was just one aspect within it; see Brentjes (1994: especially 159–161); on the manifold and complex aspects of Scythian culture, see also Cugunov (1998: especially 303–305); see on similar evolution and contacts within Celtic and Scythian art, Guggisberg (1998).

87. On Nabataean pottery from the later first and the early second century AD and its historical context, see Schmid (1997a); on the date of the change from sub-phase 3a to 3b c. AD 70/80, see Schmid (1996b: 168, 173, 2000b).

88. Interestingly, the Negev 1 type too seems to have close forerunners in Hellenistic types, mainly from Alexandria (Mlynarczyk 1998: 338–339, 341 fig. 12a, b).

89. On Khirbat Dharayh see Villeneuve (2002); Villeneuve and al-Muheisen (2000), both with further references; on Khirbat Tannur, see Glueck (1965). On problems related to precise chronological sequences, see Wenning (1987: 77–81) and McKenzie (1988). Kader (1996: 130–131) and especially Freyberger (1998: 34–41) insist on a date in the reign of Aretas IV for all three phases and, therefore, for the entire sculptural decoration from Khirbat Tannur that appears impossible to the present writer. See now the new study by McKenzie, Gibson and Reyes (2002).

90. Indeed, some of these sculptures bear some stylistic and technical similarities to a group of sculptures from the Hauran, dated to the second and third centuries AD (Diebner 1982; Bolelli 1985–86).

91. All the other pottery, some of it earlier in date, illustrated

in *Deities and Dolphins* comes from Petra and Amman and is not related to the temple of Khirbat Tannur. Glueck (1965: 139) refers to such pottery as being found under the pavement of phase II. Therefore, it would pre-date even the earlier sculpture. However, as Glueck himself notes, some of the pottery may have been intrusive from higher levels. Judith McKenzie recently "discovered" the pottery from Glueck's excavation at Khirbat Tannur, stored in the Semitic Museum at Harvard. Examination by the present writer revealed a few sherds from the late first century BC, but they all come from contexts with huge amounts of later pottery and are, therefore, of no direct value for dating the different building phases.

92. The arguments for the new chronology seem very convincing; only the third phase, tentatively dated to the fourth-century AD remains somewhat obscure.

93. The Department of Antiquities acquired one of the heads from the art market. It probably comes from Petra since a very close iconographic and stylistic parallel was found there; see Königsweg (1987: 224, 227 no. 210) and Weber (1997: 116–117, 2002: 534–535).

94. The dating of the Temenos Gate is connected with a trench dug a few metres away (Parr 1970: especially 369–370; Lyttelton and Blagg 1990: 92, 95).

95. In addition, it may be noted that the painted floral motifs in the az-Zantur house have convincing parallels within the painted pottery of phase 3a, dated to c. AD 20–70/80 and, therefore, indicating a later date; cf. Schmid (1996b: 168, 173); Nabatäer (1981: pl. 79).

96. For instance, the fragments with "inhabited scrolls," in this case tendrils with panthers, from the temple of al-Qasr (Wenning 1990: pl. 21.7; cf. Tholbecq 1997: 1080–1081), have good parallels within the wider region, confirming a date in the later first or early second century AD (Ovadiah and Turnheim 1994: 87–91 and others), although a chronological analysis is missing from the work of Ovadiah and Turnheim (1994).

97. New results and a concise overview of older research related to the street are given by Fiema (1998); see also Fiema (2003) for the wider frame, especially Fiema (2003: 48) for the street.

98. On the capitals from the Temenos Gate, see Ronczewski (1932: 87–89 fig. 38); McKenzie (1990: 36. 132–134 pl. 47 b–d); on the chronology of the Temenos Gate, cf. above. In a recent study, Kader (1996. 108–149) concludes that the gate and its capitals should be dated considerably earlier to the reign of Aretas IV. Kader (1996: 128–132) argues that the capitals are badly corroded and, therefore, were erroneously compared with later examples; Kader prefers comparisons with earlier parallels, such as the ones from the Khazna Faraoun, Qasr al-Bint and others (see Schmid 2001c: p. 389 figs. 11.19 and 11.20), and suggests a dating only slightly later than these, but still within the reign of Aretas IV. However, one should bear in mind that the corrosion of the capitals also reflects on the comparisons with earlier capitals and, therefore, should not be over-interpreted.

99. Also the painting of its façade may have contributed to the decoration of the monument.

100. See above on the different palaces and other luxury architecture. Strocka (1988) has considered the exchange between traditional Roman architecture and Hellenistic luxury architecture that was especially fruitful in Asia Minor (cf. Schmidt-Colinet 1993: 6–13).

101. Rabbel II may have transferred his capital from Petra to Bostra, as suggested by some scholars (Milik 1958: 233–235; Peters 1977: 272–274; Bowersock 1983: 73), although others rejected this hypothesis (Wenning 1993a: 94–95). If the hypothesis is correct, Rabbel II could have died outside Petra and ad-Dayr could have been erected as his cenotaph. For the events connected with the annexation of Nabataea by the Romans in AD 106, see Schmid (1997a) and below.

102. On the Hellenistic houses of Delos, see now Trümper (1998), on the "House of the Hermes" Trümper (1998: 234–241 cat. no. 35); Kreeb (1988: 36–40, 200–215 cat. no. 24); both with the references to the excavation reports.

103. Mustafa Pascha: (Adriani 1963–66: 128–146 pls. 48–57; McKenzie 1990: 64–65); Nea Paphos: (Mlynarczyk 1990: 87–94, 223–232, 1996: especially 200–202) points out the close similarity between such peristyle tombs and the dwellings of the rich and wealthy. On the island of Rhodes there are, beside the above mentioned free-standing monuments, quite similar *hypogaea* as the ones from Alexandria and Nea Paphos: Konstantinopoulos (1986: 226–227 fig. 253).

104. In the mean time much more of these complexes showing built structures related to the tomb façades were identified; see Schmid (2001d, 2004b).

105. CIS 2.350; McKenzie (1990: 35, n. 30); Bachmann *et al.* (1921: 89–90) noted previously the close connection between what is mentioned on the Turkmaniye inscription and what is found in the "Soldier Tomb" complex.

106. This has already been noted (Schmidt-Colinet 1987a: especially 149–150) for the Urn Tomb; in a broader sense on the same subject, see Schmidt-Colinet (1991). As interesting as is Schmidt-Colinet's hypothesis about the Urn tomb being the grave of Aretas IV, imitating the forum of Augustus at Rome, there is hardly any additional evidence supporting it since the Urn tomb can also be explained as a variation of a Hellenistic peristyle house or palace.

107. As Freyberger (1991) has pointed out, there is good evidence to date the Tomb of Sextius Florentinus earlier than the usually adopted *terminus ad quem* of AD 129 (on this see McKenzie 1990: 33, 47, 165). However, if Freyberger's proposition of an Augustean date is correct, then we would have to suppose that the Khubtha north slope was already occupied at that time. This, however, seems rather improbable. The miniature architecture of the Tomb of Sextius Florentinus shows strong similarities with the Palace Tomb, the Corinthian Tomb and the so-called Bab as-Siq triclinium. I would like therefore to propose an analogue date for all these monuments, related to the probable date of Bab as-Siq triclinium (McKenzie 1990:

34, nn. 15–18) and, therefore, around the third-quarter of the first century AD. This chronology has recently found support while excavating the so-called Renaissance Tomb in the Wadi Farasa East. The decoration of the façade is very similar to the one of the tomb of Sextius Florentinus and the objects from the tombs inside the rock-cut cavity point to a date within the third quarter of the first century AD; a first report can be found in the *Annual of the Department of Antiquities* 48, 2004.

108. Freyberger (1998: 19, n. 231); Hammond (1986: 22) tentatively dates the reconstruction to the reign of Malichus II. In his later publications he is much less precise in dating and interpreting this phase: Hammond (1996: 11–12). For the temple in Wadi Ramm, a "reorganization" of the monument including building activities was observed and tentatively dated to the time of Rabbel II (Tholbecq 1998: 245–247).

109. We can most probably see the not very flattering characterization of Obodas III (30–9 BC) as being weak and slack in the same context (Josephus, *Ant.* 16.7.6; Strabo, *Geogr.* 16.4.24). For all we know, there simply was no need to be more active or to handle the kingship more restrictively because the income from trade was more than sufficient. Most probably, Obodas' biggest mistake was to count on the fact that after the incorporation of Egypt into the Roman Empire, the Nabataean position in the area would improve, all the more as the Nabataeans stood on the side of Octavian during his conflict with Anthony and Cleopatra. It seems that he did not take into consideration the Roman striving for control of long-distance trade. This miscalculation led to a series of conflicts with Rome, the first one being the unfortunate events during the campaign of Aelius Gallus into South Arabia.

110. As pointed out above, settlement also led to a continuous specialization within Nabataean society.

111. See note 101, above.

112. Bowersock (1983: 73) refers to irrigation installations in the Negev in order to optimize agricultural activities. The same may be true for the area around Petra. During a survey related to the Finnish Jabal Haroun Project (FJHP, see the first preliminary report by Frösén *et al.* 1998) in 1998 some barrages or terracing walls related to agricultural activities were investigated. The collected pottery was studied by the author during a seminar at Helsinki University in December 1998 and it turned out to be predominantly of phase 3b and, therefore, from Rabbel II's time.

113. Interestingly, again the parallel examples from modern South Arabia seem to confirm this picture: Altorki and Cole (1989: 232–248); see above notes 34 and 35.

114. Of course, modern archaeology should be very sensitive and cautious not to over-interpret the connection between ancient and modern data in general. Some of the very tricky cases with many stimulating comments can be found in Meskel (1998).

115. "Hanc provinciae imposito nomine, rectoreque adtributo, obtemperare legibus nostris Traianus compulit imperator, incolarum tumore saepe contunso..." (after Loeb Classical Library); Wenning (1993a: 100–103, n. 97) sees in this passage a proof for a Nabataean rebellion that justified the Roman intervention. For another translation of *tumor*, see Eadie (1985).

116. The tribune's promotion is discussed by Syme (1965: 353) and was, like the *ornamenta triumphalia* for Palma, not necessarily connected to the annexation of Arabia, although it is likely; the bestowing of the *ornamenta triumphalia* upon Palma is mentioned on an honorific statue in Rome (*CIL* 6.1386); the statue is also reported by Dio Cassius (68.16.2; Wenning 1993a: 101, n. 107). There are only rare cases known where the *ornamenta triumphalia* were bestowed for non-military successes; see Zimmermann (1992: especially 295–296); Matteotti (1993: 194).

117. Bowersock suggests that this suppression of the Nabataean *ethnikon* had been instigated by (among others) the cities of the Decapolis who had suffered economically under Nabataean competition (Bowersock 1988: 51–52). It seems unlikely that writers such as Ptolemaios of Alexandria and others would have been influenced by such local animosities. It is much more probable that they followed Roman policies. For Rome, on the other hand, there would have been no reason for treating the Nabataeans differently to other subject peoples, if they had not shown considerable opposition against their integration into the empire.

118. See also Starcky (1966: 920); Bowersock (1983: 82); Sartre (1985: 70). Wenning (1993a: 97–98) has doubts, arguing that Rabbel II could not have been very old in AD 106. In any case, the dynasty of the Nabataean kings did not cease with Rabbel II since, according to one of the Babatha papyri and one inscription from Khubtha, Rabbel II had two sons (*RES* 1434; Meshorer 1975: 87–88; Bowersock 1983: 80, n. 15; Graf 1988: 177, n. 39); for additional matters about the annexation, see Fiema (1987).

119. Fiema (1987: 28–89) is somewhat sceptical, thinking that Roman planning did not go that far. On the other hand, Domitian had already made preparations for a campaign against the Parthians who were later conquered by Trajan; (cf. Wolsky 1993: 176–178). This shows that the Roman emperors had freed themselves from the earlier republican step-by-step policies towards their provinces and clients and attempted to integrate them into future planning.

120. In the case of the Ituraean king Lysanias, his execution and the donation of Ituraean territories to Cleopatra are explicitly explained by his support of Pacorus.

121. Although Josephus claims this was just a pretext, this seemed plausible to Herod for he continued his flight to Cleopatra's Egypt.

122. "Hanc provinciae imposito nomine, rectoreque adtributo, obtemperare legibus nostris Traianus compulit imperator, incolarum tumore saepe contunso, cum glorioso Marte Mediam urgeret et Parthos" (after Loeb Classical Library); see also Sartre (1985: 72).

123. The period from the conquest of Mesopotamia and Babylonia by Trajan (AD 115–117) until Hadrian abandoned them shortly thereafter is the only period in history when Rome directly controlled all starting points for the Far East trade, except the South Arabian ports.

124. The Indians were not the only delegation but they were probably the most exotic, which explains their special mention by Dio. It is, moreover, remarkable that the Chinese, who were very interested in contact with the West, withdrew completely, precisely in AD 107, from the Middle Asiatic Sea, their starting point for trade with the West; on this see Delbrueck (1955.56: 251, 264–269). It seems, therefore, that in the Middle and Far East, political and economic changes around the Mediterranean were sharply observed.

125. Such a process of Hellenization has been proposed for South Arabia by Pirenne (1965) with a first phase of a rather autochthonous culture and occasional western influence and a second phase with a strong western influence.

126. Also because, in the case of the first Nabataean coins, it seems that they simply used the well established mint of Damascus.

127. Due to the circulation and publication of many coin hoards from Central Asia without precise archaeological context, the bibliography about this subject is much richer than in the cases of pottery or architecture (Smirnova 1995; Bopearachchi 1991, 1990; Guillaume 1991, 1987; Holt 1981; Kraay 1981; all with additional references).

128. The local elements are predominantly present in palace architecture, while other buildings, such as theatres and *gymnasia*, show purely Greek features as can be seen at Aï Khanoum. In general terms, the Hellenistic rulers of the East adopted much from their oriental forerunners, mainly because the forms of royal representation were not well developed in mainland Greece. The local tradition of the Bactrian palace buildings is obvious, as well as their connections to Babylon and the Achaemenid Empire (Sarianidi 1985).

129. These are not related to stronger non-Greek influence but to the fact that new territories in India were conquered by the Greeks and the coins, therefore, had to be understood also by the new subjects.

130. As Nehru (1990) correctly points out, the western influences in Gandharan sculpture are not the result of one single period of east–west contacts but of several such interactions from the Achaemenid to the Roman periods. However, the Hellenistic input may be considered the most important one; see also Taddei (1984); see now the bibliography on Gandhara by Guenée *et al.* (1998).

131. This shall not be understood as a negative development, because, while losing their former culture, they created a new one.

132. "Es scheint also eine Regel zu sein, dass eigenständige Kunststile in der Alten Welt für ihre Herausbildung zwar den fruchtbaren Kontakt mit griechischen Vorbildern benötigten, aber gleichzeitig auch Distanz, damit die Kraft der griechischen Kunst nicht die Ausprägung der spezifischen Elemente unterdrücken konnte." (Bouzek 1995: 115).

133. On some fragments of this late painted pottery with a well-defined, late fourth and early fifth centuries AD con-

text, see Schmid (1996b: 168, nn. 614, 615); Fellmann Brogli (1996: 240 fig. 844–849).

134. The fact that no new elements are introduced into Nabataean culture after AD 106 but older features are only repeated should also caution us from an interpretation that there was a continuing Nabataean political entity into the second to fourth centuries AD. In fact, the observations made above should finally offer a possible explanation why there are still remnants of Nabataean cultural elements long after the end of the Nabataean kingdom and resolve the *aporia* observed by Dijkstra (1995: 38–40) and others: cultural remnants, therefore, could exist without political entity.

Bibliography

Adriani, A.

1963-6 *Repertorio d'arte dell'Egitto greco-romano.* Serie C 1 and 2. Palermo: Banca di Sicilia.

Altherr-Charon, A.

1977 Origine des temples à trois cellae du bassin méditerranéen est: état de la question. *L'Antiquité classique* 46: 389–440.

Altorki, S. and D.P. Cole

1989 *Arabian Oasis City: The Transformation of 'Unayzah.* Austin: University of Texas.

Andreae, B.

1975 Rekonstruktion des grossen Oecus der Villa des P. Fannius Synistor in Boscoreale. In B. Andreae and H. Kyrieleis (eds.), *Neue Forschungen in Pompeji und den anderen vom Vesuvausbruch 79 n.Chr. verschütteten Städten,* 71–92. Recklinghausen: Bongers.

Andreou, A.

1989 *Griechische Wanddekorationen.* Michelstadt: Neuthor-Verlag.

Arnold, D.

1999 *Temples of the Last Pharaohs.* Oxford: Oxford University Press.

Arnold-Biucchi, C.

1991 Arabian Alexanders. In W.E. Metcalf (ed.), *Mnemata: Papers in Memory of Nancy M. Waggoner,* 99–115. New York: American Numismatic Society.

Arora, U.P. (ed.)

1991 *Graeco-Indica: India's Cultural Contacts with the Greek World.* New Delhi: Ramanand Vidya Bhawan.

Aufrére, S., J.-C. Golvin and J.-C. Goyon

1997 *L'Egypte restituée. I. Sites, et temples de Haute Egypte.* 2nd edn. Paris: Errance.

Augé, Ch., F. Renel, L. Borel and Ch. March

1990 Sur la figure de Tyché en Nabatène et dans la province d'Arabie. In F. Zayadine (ed.), *Petra and the Caravan Cities,* 131–146. Amman: Department of Antiquities.

Augé, Ch., F. Renel, L. Borel and Ch. March

2002 New Excavations in the Qasr al-Bint Area at Petra.

Annual of the Department of Antiquities of Jordan 46: 309–313.

Axioti, K.

1980 Rōmaikoí drómoi tés Aitōloakarnanías. *Archaiologikon Deltion* (Meletes) 35: 186–205.

Bachmann, W., C. Watzinger and Th. Wiegand

1921 *Petra*. Wissenschaftliche Veröffentlichungen des deutsch-türkischen Denkmalschutz-Kommandos 3. Berlin: Springer Verlag.

Bartlett, J.

1979 From the Edomites to the Nabataeans: A Study in Continuity. *Palestine Exploration Quarterly* 111: 53–66.

1990 From Edomites to Nabataeans: The Problem of Continuity. *Aram* 2: 25–34.

Baslez, M.

1992 La famille de Philopappos de Commagène. Un prince entre deux mondes. *Dialogues d'histoire ancienne* 18(1): 89–101.

Bedal, L.-A.

2003 *The Petra Pool-Complex. A Hellenistic Paradeisos in the Nabataean Capital*. Piscataway: Gorgias Press.

Bengtson, H.

1987 *Die Diadochen. Die Nachfolger Alexanders (323–281 v.Chr.)*. Munich: C. H. Beck.

1988 *Die hellenistische Weltkultur*. Stuttgart: Franz Steiner.

Bennett, C.-M.

1979 Excavations on the Citadel (Al Qal'a), Amman, 1978 Fourth Preliminary Report. *Annual of the Department of Antiquities of Jordan* 23: 161–170.

Bernard, P.

1987 Les nomades conquérants de l'empire gréco-bactrien. Réflexions sur leur identité ethnique et culturelle. *Académie des inscriptions et belles lettres. Comptes rendus*: 758–768.

1990 L'architecture religieuse de l'Asie centrale à l'époque hellénistique. In Deutsches Archäologisches Institut (ed.), *Akten des XIII. internationalen Kongresses für klassische Archäologie, Berlin 1988*, 51–59. Mainz: von Zabern.

1996 The Greek Kingdoms in Central Asia. In J. Harmatta (ed.) *History of Civilizations of Central Asia*. II. *The Development of Sedentary and Nomadic Civilizations: 700 b.c. to ad 250*, 99–129. 2nd edn. Paris: UNESCO.

Bienkowski, P.

1990 The Chronology of Tawilan and the 'Dark Age' of Edom. *Aram* 2: 35–44.

2001 The Persian Period. In B. MacDonald, R. Adams and P. Bienkowski (eds.), *The Archaeology of Jordan*, 347–365. Sheffield: Sheffield Academic Press.

2002 *Busayra Excavations by Crystal-M. Bennett 1971–1980*. Oxford: Oxford University Press.

Bignasca, A.

1993 Die Terrakotten. In Rolf Stucky (eds.), *Petra und die Weihrauchstrasse*, 65–67. Zürich: Ausstellungskatalog Zürich.

1996 Terrakotten aus spätrömischen Befunden. In A. Bignasca, B. Kolb, S.G. Schmid, *Petra. Ez Zantur I: Ergebnisse der Schweizerisch-Liechtensteinischen Ausgrabungen 1988–1992*, 283–294. Terra Archaeologica 2. Monographien der schweizerisch-liechtensteinischen Stiftung für archäologische Forschungen im Ausland. Mainz am Rhein: Philipp von Zabern.

Bignasca, A., B. Kolb and S.G. Schmid

1996 *Petra. Ez Zantur I: Ergebnisse der schweizerisch-liechtensteinischen Ausgrabungen 1988–1992*. Terra Archaeologica 2. Monographien der schweizerisch-liechtensteinischen Stiftung für archäologische Forschungen im Ausland. Mainz am Rhein: Philipp von Zabern.

Bockisch, Ch.

1991 Das Grab 813 aus archäologischer Sicht. In M. Lindner and J.P. Zeitler (eds.), *Petra: Königin der Weihrauchstrasse*, 89–97. Fürth: UKA-Verlag.

Bolelli, G.

1985–6 La ronde bosse de caractère indigène en Syrie du Sud. In J.-M. Dentzer (ed.), *Hauran I, Recherches archéologiques sur la Syrie du Sud à l'époque hellénistique et romaine*, I, 311–372. Paris: Geuthner.

Bonato, S.

1998 Les mausolées hellénistiques de la nécropole de Jérusalem, reflets de la propagation et de l'assimilation de l'hellénisme en Judée. *Annales d'histoire de l'art et d'archéologie* 20: 23–46.

Bopearachchi, O.

1990 Graeco-Bactrian Issues of Later Indo-Greek Kings. *Numismatic Chronicle* 150: 79–103.

1991 *Monnaies gréco-bactriennes et indo-grecques: Catalogue raisonné*. Paris: Bibliothéque nationale.

Börker, Ch.

1973 Neuattisches und pergamenisches an den Ara Pacis-Ranken. *Jahrbuch des deutschen archäologischen Instituts* 88: 283–317.

Bosworth, A. B.

2002 *The Legacy of Alexander. Politics, Warfare, and Propaganda under the Successors*. Oxford: Oxford University Press.

Boucharlat, R. and P. Lombard

1985 The Oasis of Al Ain in the Iron Age. Excavations at Rumeilah 1981–1983; Survey at Hili 14. *Archaeology in the United Arab Emirates* 4, 44–43. Al-Ain: Department of Antiquity and Tourism.

1991 Datations absolues de Rumeilah et chronologie de l'âge du fer dans la peninsule d'Oman. In Klaus Schippmann, Anja Herling and Jean-François Salles (eds.), *Golf-Archäologie: Mesopotamien, Iran, Kuwait, Bahrain, Vereinigte Arabische Emirate und Oman*, 301–314. Göttingen: Leidorf.

Boucharlat, R. and M. Mouton

1993a Mleiha (3e s. avant J.-C. . 1er/2e s. aprés J.-C.). In U. Finkbeiner (ed.), *Materialien zur Archäologie der*

Seleukiden- und Partherzeit im südlichen Babylonien und im Golfgebiet, 219–249. Tübingen: Wasmuth.

1993b Importations occidentales et influence de l'hellénisme dans la péninsule d'Oman. In A. Invernizzi and J.F. Salles (eds.), *Arabia antiqua: Hellenistic Centers around Arabia*, 275–289. Rome: Istituto italiano per il Medio ed Estremo Oriente.

Bouzek, J.

1995 Griechische Kunst in den Randkulturen: Ihre Rezeption, Funktion und Umbildung. In D. Rössler and V. Stürmer (eds.), *Modus in rebus: Gedenkschrift für Wolfgang Schindler*, 114–115. Berlin: Mann.

Bowersock, G.W.

1983 *Roman Arabia*. Cambridge, MA: Harvard University Press.

1988 The Three Arabias in Ptolemy's Geography. In P.-L. Gatier, B. Helly and J.-P. Rey-Coquais (eds.), *Géographie historique au Proche-Orient (Syrie, Phénicie, Arabie, grecques, romaines, byzantines): Actes de la Table Ronde de Valbonne, 16.18 septembre 1985*, 47–53. Paris: Editions du centre nationale de la recherche.

1990a The Cult and Representation of Dusares in Roman Arabia. In F. Zayadine (ed.), *Petra and the Caravan Cities*, 31–36. Amman: Department of Antiquities.

1990b *Hellenism in Late Antiquity*. Cambridge: Cambridge University Press.

Bowman, A. K.

1986 *Egypt after the Pharaohs. 332 BC–AD 642, from Alexander to the Arab Conquest*. London: British Museum Publications.

Bowsher, J.M.C.

1990 Early Nabataean Coinage. *Aram* 2: 221–228.

Brands, G.

1996 Halle, Propylon und Peristyl. Elemente hellenistischer Palastfassaden in Makedonien. In W. Hoepfner and G. Brands (eds.) *Basileia: Die Paläste der hellenistischen Könige. Internationales Symposion in Berlin vom 16.12.1992 bis 20.12.1992*, 62–72. Mainz: von Zabern.

Brentjes, B.

1994 Ortband, Rolltier und Vielfrass. Beobachtungen zur 'skythischen' Akinakes-Zier. *Archäologische Mitteilungen aus Iran* 27: 147–64.

Brünnow, R.E. and A. von Domaszewski

1904–9 *Die Provincia Arabia auf Grund zweier in den Jahren 1897 und 1898 unternommener Reisen und der Berichte früherer Reisender*, I (1904), III (1909). Strassburg: Trübner.

Camps, G.

1995 Modèle hellénistique ou modèle punique? Les destinées culturelles de la Numidie. In *Actes du IIIe Congrés international des études phéniciennes et puniques, Tunis 11.16 novembre 1991*, 235–248. Tunis: Institut national du patrimoine.

Cardi, B. de

1984 Survey in Ras al-Khaimah, U.A.E. In R. Boucharlat and J.-F. Salles (eds.), *Arabie orientale, Mésopotamie et Iran méridional de l'âge du fer au début de la période islamique*, 201–215. Paris: Editions recherche sur les civilisations.

Carettoni, G.

1983 La decorazione pittorica della Casa di Augusto sul Palatino. *Mitteilungen des deutschen archäologischen Instituts. Römische Abteilung* 90: 373–419.

Caspari, F.

1916 Das Nilschiff Ptolemaios IV. *Jahrbuch des deutschen archäologischen Instituts* 31: 1–74.

Casson, L.

1989 *The Periplus Maris Erythraei: Text with Introduction, Translation, and Commentary*. Princeton: Princeton University Press.

Castriota, D.

1995 *The Ara Pacis Augustae and the Imagery of Abundance in Later Greek and Early Roman Imperial Art*. Princeton: Princeton University Press.

Clamer, C.

1997 *Fouilles archéologiques de 'Aïn ez-Zâra/Callirrhoë, villégiature hérodienne*. Beyrouth: l'Institut français d'archéologie du Proche-Orient .

Coarelli, F. and Y. Thébert

1988 Architecture funéraire et pouvoir: Réflexions sur l'hellénisme numide. *Mélanges de l'Ecole française de Rome. Antiquité* 100: 761–819.

Colledge, M.

1987 Greek and non-Greek Interaction in the Art and Architecture of the Hellenistic East. In A. Kuhrt and S. Sherwin-White (eds.), *Hellenism in the East: The Interactions of Greek and non-Greek Civilizations from Syria to Central Asia after Alexander*, 134–162. Berkeley: University of California Press.

Conticello, B., and B. Andreae

1974 Die Skulpturen von Sperlonga. *Antike Plastik* 14. Berlin: Mann.

Cugunov, K.V.

1998 Der skythenzeitliche Kulturwandel in Tuva. *Eurasia antiqua* 4: 273–309.

Debevoise, N.C.

1938 *A Political History of Parthia*. Chicago: University of Chicago Press.

Delbrueck, R.

1955–6 Südasiatische Seefahrt im Altertum. *Bonner Jahrbücher* 155–156: 8–58, 229–308.

Dentzer-Feydy, J.

1985–6 Décor architectural et développement du Hauran dans l'antiquité (du Ier s. av. au VIIe s. de notre ére). In J.-M. Dentzer (ed.), *Hauran I: Recherches archéologiques sur la Syrie du Sud à l'époque hellénistique et romaine*, I. 2: 261–309. Paris: Geuthner.

1992 Le décor architectural en Transjordanie de la période hellénistique à la création de la Province d'Arabie en 106. In M. Zaghloul, K. Amr, F. Zayadine, R. Nabeel and N. Rida Tawfiq (eds.), *Studies in the History and Archaeology of Jordan IV*, 227–232. Amman: Department of Antiquities.

Despinis, G.I.

1996 Studien zur hellenistischen Plastik II: Statuengruppen. *Mitteilungen des deutschen archäologischen Instituts. Abteilung Athen* 111: 299–336.

Diebner, S.

1982 Bosra: Die Skulpturen im Hof der Zitadelle. *Rivista di archaeologia* 6: 52–71.

Dijkstra, K.

1995 *Life and Loyalty: A Study in the Socio-Religious Culture of Syria and Mesopotamia in the Graeco-Roman Period Based on Epigraphical Evidence*. Leiden: E.J. Brill.

Dolinka, B. J.

2003 *Nabataean Aila (Aqaba, Jordan) from a Ceramic Perspective*. British Archaeological Reports International Series 1116. Oxford: Archaeopress.

Dorandi, T.

1995 La Villa dei papiri a Ercolano e la sua biblioteca. *Classical Philology* 90: 168–182.

Drexhage, R.

1988 *Untersuchungen zum römischen Osthandel*. Bonn: Habelt.

Eadie, J.W.

1985 Artifacts of Annexation: Trajan's Grand Strategy and Arabia. In J.W. Eadie and J. Ober (eds.), *The Craft of the Ancient Historian: Essays in Honor of Ch. G. Starr*, 407–423. Lanham, MD: University Press of America.

1986 The Evolution of the Roman Frontier in Arabia. In Ph. Freeman and D. Kennedy (eds.), *The Defence of the Roman and Byzantine East: Proceedings of a Colloquium held at the University of Sheffield in April 1986*, 243–52. British Archaeological Reports International Series 297. Oxford: British Archaeological Reports.

1989 Strategies of Economic Development in the Roman East: The Red Sea Trade Revisited. In D.H. French and C.S. Lightfoot (eds.), *The Eastern Frontier of the Roman Empire: Proceedings of a Colloquium held at Ankara in September 1988*, Vol 1, 113–120. British Archaeological Reports International Series 553. Oxford: British Archaeological Reports.

Egan, E. C.

2002 Stucco Decoration from the South Corridor of the Petra Great Temple: Discussion and Interpretation. *Annual of the Department of Antiquities of Jordan* 46: 347–361.

Enoki, K., G.A. Koshelenko and Z. Haidary

1996 The Yüeh-Chih and their Migrations. In J. Harmatta (ed.) *History of Civilizations of Central Asia*. II. *The Development of Sedentary and Nomadic Civilizations: 700 b.c. to ad 250*, 171–189. 2nd edn. Paris: UNESCO.

Errington, E. and J. Cribb (eds.)

1992 *The Crossroads of Asia: Transformation in Image and Symbol*. Cambridge: Ancient India and Iran Trust.

Fedak, F.

1990 *Monumental Tombs of the Hellenistic Age: A Study of Selected Tombs from the Pre-Classical to the Early Imperial Era*. Toronto: University of Toronto.

Fellmann Brogli, R.

1996 Die Keramik aus den spätrömischen Bauten. In A. Bignasca, Bernhard Kolb and Stephan G. Schmid, *Petra. Ez Zantur I: Ergebnisse der schweizerisch-liechtensteinischen Ausgrabungen 1988–1992*, 219–281. Terra Archaeologica 2. Monographien der schweizerisch-liechtensteinischen Stiftung für archäologische Forschungen im Ausland. Mainz am Rhein: Philipp von Zabern.

Fiema, Z.T.

1987 The Roman Annexation of Arabia: A General Perspective. *Ancient World* 15: 25–35.

1996 Nabataean and Palmyrene Commerce. The Mechanisms of Intensification. In *Palmyra and the Silk Road*. Annales archéologiques arabes syriennes 42: 189–195.

1998 The Roman Street of the Petra Project, 1997—A Preliminary Report. *Annual of the Department of Antiquities of Jordan* 42: 395–424.

2003 Roman Petra (A.D. 106–363). A Neglected Subject. *Zeitschrift des Deutschen Palästina-Vereins* 119: 38–58.

Finocchi, C.

2002 *I Tolomei. L'epopea di una dinastia macedone in Egitto*. Genova: ECIG.

Fischer, Th.

1980 *Seleukiden und Makkabäer: Beiträge zur Seleukidengeschichte und zu den politischen Ereignissen in Judäa während der 1. Hälfte des 2. Jahrhunderts v.Chr.* Bochum: In Kommission beim Studienverlag N. Brockmeyer.

1990a Hasmoneans and Seleucids: Aspects of War and Policy in the Second and First Centuries B.C.E. In G. Fuks, A. Kasher and U. Rappaport (eds.), *Greece and Rome in Eretz Israel: Collected Essays*, 3–19. Jerusalem: Yad Izhak Ben-Zvi.

Fischer, M.L.

1990b *Das korinthische Kapitell im alten Israel in der hellenistischen und römischen Periode*. Mainz: von Zabern.

Fittschen, K.

1976a Zur Herkunft und Entstehung des 2. Stils. Probleme und Argumente. In P. Zanker (ed.), *Hellenismus in Mittelitalien: Kolloquium in Göttingen vom 5. bis 9. Juni 1974*, 539–563. Abhandlungen der Akademie der Wissenschaften in Göttingen. Philologisch-Historische Klasse. Dritte Folge 97. Göttingen: Vandenhock and Ruprecht.

1976b Zur Panzerstatue in Cherchel. *Jahrbuch des deutschen archäologischen Instituts* 91: 175–210.

1996 Wall Decorations in Herod's Kingdom: Their Relationship with Wall Decorations in Greece and Italy.

In K. Fittschen and G. Foerster (eds.), *Judaea and the Greco-Roman World in the Time of Herod in the Light of Archaeological Evidence*, 139–161. Göttingen: Vandenhoeck and Ruprecht.

Fittschen, K. and G. Foerster (eds.)

1996 *Judaea and the Greco-Roman World in the Time of Herod in the Light of Archaeological Evidence*. Abhandlungen der Akademie der Wissenschaften in Göttingen. Philologisch-Historische Klasse. Dritte Folge 215. Göttingen: Vandenhoeck and Ruprecht.

Foerster, G.

1995a The Plaster Decoration. In G. Foerster, *Masada V. Art and Architecture*, 1–69. Jerusalem: Israel Exploration Society/Hebrew University.

1995b Black and White Mosaics. In G. Foerster, *Masada V. Art and Architecture*, 151–157. Jerusalem: Israel Exploration Society/Hebrew University.

1996 Hellenistic and Roman Trends in the Herodian Architecture of Masada. In K. Fittschen and G. Foerster (eds.), *Judaea and the Greco-Roman World in the Time of Herod in the Light of Archaeological Evidence*, 55–72. Göttingen: Vandenhoeck and Ruprecht.

Förtsch, R.

1996 The Residences of King Herod and their Relations to Roman Villa Architecture. In K. Fittschen and G. Foerster (eds.), *Judaea and the Greco-Roman World in the Time of Herod in the Light of Archaeological Evidence*, 74–119. Göttingen: Vandenhoeck and Ruprecht.

Fraser, P.M.

1977 *Rhodian Funerary Monuments*. Oxford: Clarendon Press.

Freyberger, K.S.

1991 Zur Datierung des Grabmals des Sextius Florentinus. *Damaszener Mitteilungen* 5: 1–8.

1997 Blattranken, Greifen und Elephanten. In Th. Weber and R. Wenning (eds.), *Petra: Antike Felsstadt zwischen arabischer Tradition und griechischer Norm*, 71–84. Antike Welt, special issue. Mainz: von Zabern.

1998 *Die frühkaiserzeitlichen Heiligtümer der Karawanenstationen im hellenisierten Osten. Zeugnisse eines kulturellen Konflikts im Spannungsfeld zweier politischer Formationen*. Mainz: von Zabern.

Frösén, J., Z.T. Fiema, H. Haggrén, K. Koistinen, M. Lavento and G.L. Peterman

1998 The Finnish Jabal Harun Project: Report on the 1997 Season. *Annual of the Department of Antiquities of Jordan* 42: 483–502.

Frösén, J. and Z.T. Fiema (eds.)

2002 *Petra. A City Forgotten and Rediscovered*. Helsinki: Amos Anderson Art Museum.

Funke, P.

1996 Die syrisch-mesopotamische Staatenwelt in vorislamischer Zeit. Zu den arabischen Macht- und Staatenbildungen an der Peripherie der antiken Grossmächte

im Hellenismus und in der römischen Kaiserzeit. In B. Funck (ed.), *Hellenismus. Beiträge zur Erforschung von Akkulturation und politischer Ordnung in den Staaten des hellenistischen Zeitalters*, 217–238. Tübingen: J.C.B. Mohr.

Gagsteiger, G.

1991 Die Architektur Petras. In M. Lindner and J.P. Zeitler (eds.), *Petra: Königin der Weihrauchstrasse*, 49–68. Fürth: UKA-Verlag.

Garbini, G.

1993 *Aramaica*. Studi semitici 10. Rome: Universita degli studi 'La Sapienza'.

Gardin, J.C

1984 Die Ursprünge der Kusana-Keramik. In J. Ozols and V. Thewaldt (eds.), *Aus dem Osten des Alexanderreiches: Völker und Kulturen zwischen Orient und Okzident. Iran, Afghanistan, Pakistan, Indien*, 110–26. Cologne: DuMont.

1985 Les relations entre la Méditerranée et la Bactriane dans l'antiquité, d'après des données céramologiques inédites. In J.-L. Huot, M. Yon and Y. Calvet (eds.), *De l'Indus aux Balkans:Recueil à la mémoire de Jean Deshayes*, 447–60. Paris: Recherche sur les civilisations.

1990 La céramique hellénistique en Asie centrale: Problèmes d'interprétation. In Deutsches archäologisches Institut (ed.), *Akten des 13. internationalen Kongresses für klassische Archäologie, Berlin 1988*, 187–93. Mainz: von Zabern.

Gatier, P.-L., B. Helly and J.-P. Rey-Coquais (eds.)

1988 *Géographie historique au Proche-Orient (Syrie, Phénicie, Arabie, grecques, romaines, byzantines): Actes de la Table Ronde de Valbonne, 16–18 septembre 1985*. Paris: Editions du centre nationale de la recherche.

Gawlikowski, M.

1990 Les dieux des Nabatéens. In H. Temporini and W. Haase (eds.), *Aufstieg und Niedergang der römischenWelt*, II. 18.4: 2659–2677. Berlin: W. de Gruyter.

Gehrke, H. J.

1990 *Geschichte des Hellenismus*. Munich: Oldenburg.

Glueck, N.

1965 *Deities and Dolphins: The Story of the Nabataeans*. London: Farrar, Straus and Giroux.

Graf, D.F.

1988 Qura Arabiyya and Provincia Arabia. In P.-L. Gatier, B. Helly and J.-P. Rey-Coquais (eds.), *Géographie historique au Proche-Orient (Syrie, Phénicie, Arabie, grecques, romaines, byzantines): Actes de la Table Ronde de Valbonne, 16.18 septembre 1985*, 171–211. Paris: Editions du centre nationale de la recherche.

1990 The Origin of the Nabataeans. *Aram* 2: 45–75.

1992a Hellenisation and the Decapolis. *Aram* 4: 1–48.

1992b Nabataean Settlements and Roman Occupation in Arabia Petraea. In M. Zaghloul, K. Amr, F. Zayadine, R. Nabeel and N. Rida Tawfiq (eds.), *Studies in the History and*

Archaeology of Jordan IV, 253–260. Amman: Department of Antiquities. Amman: Department of Antiquities.

Grainger, J. D.

1993 *The Cities of Seleukid Syria.* Oxford: Clarendon Press.

1997 *A Seleukid Prosopography and Gazetteer.* Leiden: E.J. Brill.

Green, J.A., K. 'Amr, K. Rielly, A. Betts, D. MacCreery, F. Koucky and D. Reese

1992 Deep Sounding on the Lower Terrace of the Amman Citadel: Final Report. *Annual of the Department of Antiquities of Jordan* 36: 113–144.

Green, P.

1990 *Alexander to Actium. The Hellenistic Age.* London: Thames and Hudson.

Grimm, G.

1981 Orient und Okzident in der Kunst Alexandriens: In N. Hinske (ed.), *Alexandrien: Kulturbegegnungen dreier Jahrtausende im Schmelztiegel einer mediterranen Grostadt*, 13–25. Mainz: von Zabern.

Guenée, P. , F. Tissot, P. Callieri and P. Bernard

1998 *Bibliographie analytique des ouvrages parus sur l'art du Gandhara entre 1950 et 1993.* Avec la collaboration de Francine Tissot, Pierfrancesco Callieri. Mémoires de l'Académie des inscriptions et belles-lettres 16. Paris: de Boccard.

Guggisberg, M.

1998 'Zoomorphe Junktur' und 'Inversion'. Zum Einfluss des skythischen Tierstils auf die frühe keltische Kunst. *Germania* 76: 549–572.

Guillaume, O.

1987 *L'analyse des raisonnements en archéologie: Le cas de la numismatique gréco-bactrienne et indo-grecque.* Paris: Recherche sur les civilisations.

1991 *Graeco-Bactrian and Indian Coins from Afghanistan.* New York: Oxford University Press.

Gundlach, R. and M. Rochholz (eds.)

1994 *Ägyptische Tempel: Struktur, Funktion und Programm. Akten der ägyptologischen Tempeltagungen in Gosen 1990 und Mainz 1992.* Hildesheim: Gerstenberg.

Guzzo, P. G.

1999 La Villa dei papiri. Fasti passati, novità recenti. *Cronache ercolanesi. Bollettino del Centro internazionale per lo studio dei papiri ercolanesi* 29: 39–51.

Hackl, U. and H. Jenni and Ch. Schneider

2003 *Quellen zur Geschichte der Nabatäer. Textsammlung mit Übersetzung und Kommentar.* Freiburg/Göttingen: Universitätsverlag/Vandenhoek and Ruprecht.

Haerinck, E.

1983 *La céramique en Iran pendant la période parthe (circa 250 av. J. C. à circa 225 après J. C.): Typologie, chronologie et distribution.* Iranica antiqua Supplement 2. Leuven: Imprimerie Orientaliste.

1998 More Pre-Islamic Coins from Southeastern Arabia.

Arabian Archaeology and Epigraphy 9: 278–301.

Hammond, Ph.C.

1965 *The Excavation of the Main Theater at Petra, 1961–1962: Final Report.* London: Quaritch.

1973 *The Nabataeans: Their History, Culture and Archaeology.* Studies in Mediterranean Archaeology 37. Gothenburg: Aström.

1981 Ein nabatäisches Weihrelief aus Petra. In *Die Nabatäer: Erträge einer Ausstellung im Rheinischen Landesmuseum Bonn, 24. Mai . 9. Juli 1978*, 137–141. Cologne: Rheinland-Verlag/Bonn: Habelt.

1986 Die Ausgrabung des Löwen-Greifen-Tempels in Petra (1973–1983). In M. Lindner (ed.), *Petra: Neue Ausgrabungen und Entdeckungen*, 16–30. Munich: Delp.

1996 *The Temple of the Winged Lions Petra, Jordan 1974–1990.* Arizona: Petra.

Hannestad, L.

1983 *The Hellenistic Pottery from Failaka. Ikaros. The Hellenistic Settlements 2.* Aarhus, Denmark: Jysk Arkaeologisk Selskab.

Harmatta, J. (ed.)

1996 *History of Civilizations of Central Asia. II. The Development of Sedentary and Nomadic Civilizations:* 700 b.c. to ad 250. 2nd edn. Paris: UNESCO.

Hart, S.

1985 Survey and Soundings between Tafileh and Ras en-Naqb 1985. *Liber Annuus* 35: 412–414.

1986a Some Preliminary Thoughts on Settlement in Southern Edom. *Levant* 18: 51–58.

1986b Sela': the Rock of Edom? *Palestine Exploration Quarterly* 118: 91–95.

1987 Five Soundings in Southern Jordan. *Levant* 19: 33–47.

Hart, S. and R. Falkner

1985 Preliminary Report on a Survey in Edom 1984. *Annual of the Department of Antiquities of Jordan* 29: 255–277.

Healey, J. F.

2001 *The Religion of the Nabataeans. A Conspectus.* Leiden: E.J. Brill.

Heermann, V.

1986 *Studien zur makedonischen Palastarchitektur.* Berlin: Papyrus-Druck.

Hesberg, H. von

1978 Zur Entwicklung der griechischen Architektur im ptolemäischen Reich. In H. Maehler and V.M. Strocka (eds.), *Das ptolemäische Ägypten: Akten des internationalen Symposions 27–29. September 1976 in Berlin*, 137–145. Mainz: von Zabern.

Higgs, P.

1997 A Newly Found Fragment of Free-standing Sculpture from the Mausoleum at Halicarnassus. In I. Jenkins and G.B. Waywell (eds.), *Sculptors and Sculpture of Caria and the Dodecanese*, 30–34. London: British Museum.

Hoepfner, W.

1996 Zum Typus der Basileia und der königlichen Androne. In W. Hoepfner and G. Brands (eds.) *Basileia: Die Paläste der hellenistischen Könige. Internationales Symposion in Berlin vom 16.12.1992 bis 20.12.1992,* 1–43. Mainz: von Zabern.

Hoepfner, W. and G. Brands (eds.)

1996 *Basileia: Die Paläste der hellenistischen Könige. Internationales Symposion in Berlin vom 16.20.12.1992.* Mainz: von Zabern.

Hoepfner, W.

1999 Die Epoche der Griechen. In W. Hoepfner (ed.), *Geschichte des Wohnens. I. 5000 v.Chr. – 500 n.Chr.: Vorgeschichte, Frühgeschichte, Antike,* 123–608. Stuttgart: Deutsche Verlags-Anstalt.

Hoffmann, A.

1999 Ein hellenistisches Heiligtum in Gadara. *Topoi* 9, 2: 795–831.

2001 Hellenistic Gadara. In *Studies in the History and Archaeology of Jordan VII,* 391–397. Amman: Department of Antiquities

Hoffmann, A. and C. Bührig

2000 Die Stadtmauern der hellenistisch-römischen Dekapolisstadt Gadara. Zusammenfassender Bericht über die seit 1991 durchgeführten Ausgrabungen und Untersuchungen. *Archäologischer Anzeiger,* 175–233.

Hölbl, G.

2001 *A History of the Ptolemaic Empire* (English translation of German orginal 1994). London: Routledge.

Hölscher, T.

1988 Historische Reliefs. In Antikenmuseum Berlin (ed.), *Kaiser Augustus und die verlorene Republik,* 351–400. Mainz: von Zabern.

Holt, F.L.

1981 The Euthydemid Coinage of Bactria: Further Hoard Evidence from Ai Khanoum. *Revue numismatique* 23: 7–44.

1988 *Alexander the Great and Bactria: The Formation of a Greek Frontier in Central Asia.* Leiden: E.J. Brill.

Hübner, U.

1992 *Die Ammoniter. Untersuchungen zur Geschichte, Kultur und Religion eines transjordanischen Volkes im 1. Jahrtausend v. Chr.* Wiesbaden: Harrassowitz.

Huff, D.

1989 Das Qasr Nuweijis bei Amman. *Istanbuler Mitteilungen* 39: 223–236.

Huth, M.

1999 An Important Hoard of Early South Arabian Coins from the Kingdom of Qataban. *Schweizerische numismatische Rundschau* 78: 37–51.

Inoubliable Pétra

1980 *Le royaume nabatéen aux confins du désert.* Musées royaux d'art et d'histoire, 1 mars–1 juin 1980. Brussels: Snoeck-Ducaju.

Invernizzi, A. (ed.)

1995 *In the Land of the Gryphons: Papers on Central Asian Archaeology in Antiquity.* Florence: Le lettere.

Invernizzi, A. and J.-F. Salles (eds.)

1993 *Arabia antiqua: Hellenistic Centers around Arabia.* Rome: Istituto italiano per il Medio ed Estremo Oriente.

Jacobson, E.

1995 *The Art of the Scythians: The Interpretation of Cultures at the Edge of the Hellenic World.* Handbuch der Orientalistik 8, 2. Leiden: E.J. Brill.

Jaeggi, O. and S.G. Schmid

1996 Beiträge zur Sammlung Lagunillas des Museo Nacional de Bellas Artes in Havanna (Kuba). *Antike Kunst* 39: 14–37.

Japp, S.

2000 *Die Baupolitik Herodes' des Grossen. Die Bedeutung der Architektur für die Herrschaftslegitimation eines römischen Klientelkönigs.* Rahden: Leidorf.

Jenkins, I. and G.B. Waywell (eds.)

1997 *Sculptors and Sculpture of Caria and the Dodecanese.* London: British Museum.

Jenkins, I., C. Gratziu and A.P. Middleton

1997 The Polychromy of the Mausoleum. In I. Jenkins and G.B. Waywell (eds.), *Sculptors and Sculpture of Caria and the Dodecanese,* 35–41. London: British Museum.

Jeppesen, K.

1997 The Mausoleum at Halicarnassus: Sculptural Decoration and Architectural Background. In I. Jenkins and G.B. Waywell (eds.), *Sculptors and Sculpture of Caria and the Dodecanese,* 42–48. London: British Museum.

1998 Das Maussoleion von Halikarnass, Forschungsbericht 1997. *Proceedings of the Danish Institute at Athens* 2: 161–231.

2002 *The Maussolleion at Halikarnassos. Reports of the Danish Archaeological Expedition to Bodrum, 5. The Superstructure. A Comparative Analysis of the Architectural, Sculptural, and Literary Evidence.* Aarhus: Aarhus University Press.

Joukowsky, M.S.

1998 Brown University 1997 Excavations at the Petra Great Temple. *Annual of the Department of Antiquities of Jordan* 42: 293–318.

1999 Brown University 1998 Excavations at the Petra Great Temple. *Annual of the Department of Antiquities of Jordan* 43: 195–222.

2003 More Treasures and Nabataean Traditions at the Petra Great Temple: The Brown University 10th Campaign, 2002. *Annual of the Department of Antiquities of Jordan* 47: 389–406.

Joukowsky, M. S. (ed.)

1998 *Petra: The Great Temple, 1. Brown University Excavations 1993–1997.* Providence: Johnson.

Kader, I.

1996 *Propylon und Bogentor: Untersuchungen zum Tetrapylon von Latakia und anderen frühkaiserzeitlichen Bogenmonumenten im Nahen Osten.* Damaszener Forschungen 7. Mainz: von Zabern.

Karttunen, K.

1990 Taxila: Indian City and a Stronghold of Hellenism. *Arctos* 24: 85–96.

Kehrberg, I. and J. Manley

2002 The 2001 Season of the Jarash City Walls Project: Preliminary Report. *Annual of the Department of Antiquities of Jordan* 46: 197–203.

Keller, D.

1996 Gedanken zur Datierung und Verwendung der Statere Philipps II. und ihrer keltischen Imitationen. *Schweizerische numismatische Rundschau* 75: 101–119.

Kennedy, D.L.

1980 *Legio VI Ferrata*: The Annexation and Early Garrison of Arabia. *Harvard Studies in Classical Philology* 84: 283–309.

Kenrick, Ph.

2000 Fine Wares from the City Wall Section at Bait Nawashi (Area XLII). *Archäologischer Anzeiger*: 235–265.

Kitchen, K.A.

1994 *Documentation for Ancient Arabia. I. Chronological Framework and Historical Sources.* Liverpool: Liverpool University Press.

Kleiner, D.E.E.

1983 *The Monument of Philopappos in Athens.* Rome: Bretschneider.

Knauf, E.A.

1986 Die Herkunft der Nabatäer. In M. Lindner (ed.), *Petra: Neue Ausgrabungen und Entdeckungen,* 74–86. Munich: Delp.

1990 Dushara and Shai' al-Qaum. *Aram* 2: 175–183.

1997 Der sein Volk liebt: Entwicklung des nabatäischen Handelsimperiums zwischen Stamm, Königtum und Klientel. In Th. Weber and R. Wenning (eds.), *Petra: Antike Felsstadt zwischen arabischer Tradition und griechischer Norm,* 14–24. AntikeWelt, special issue. Mainz: von Zabern.

Kokkinos, N.

1998 *The Herodian Dynasty: Origins, Role in Society and Eclipse.* Sheffield: Sheffield Academic Press.

2001 A Reconnaissance Trip to Peraea. *Annual of the Department of Antiquities of Jordan* 45: 479–482.

Kolb, B.

1997 Petra-eine Zeltstadt in Stein. In Th. Weber and R. Wenning (eds.), *Petra: Antike Felsstadt zwischen arabischer Tradition und griechischer Norm,* 62–66. AntikeWelt, special issue. Mainz: von Zabern.

Kolb, B., D. Keller and R. Fellmann Brogli

1997 Swiss-Liechtenstein Excavations at az-Zantur in Petra

1996: The Seventh Season. *Annual of the Department of Antiquities of Jordan* 41: 231–254.

Kolb, B., D. Keller and Y. Gerber

1998 Swiss-Liechtenstein Excavations at az-Zantur in Petra 1997. *Annual of the Department of Antiquities of Jordan* 42: 259–277.

Kolb, B. and D. Keller

2001 Swiss-Liechtenstein Excavation at az-Zantur/Petra: The Eleventh Season. *Annual of the Department of Antiquities of Jordan* 45: 311–324.

2002 Swiss-Liechtenstein Excavation at az-Zantur/Petra: The Twelfth Season. *Annual of the Department of Antiquities of Jordan* 46: 279–293

Königsweg

1987 *Der Königsweg: 9000 Jahre Kunst und Kultur in Jordanien und Palästina.* Exhibition Cologne, Schallaburg, Munich.

Konstantinopoulos, G.

1973 Néa eurémata ek Rhodou kai Astupalaías. *Athens Annals in Archaeology* 6: 114–24.

1986 *Archaia Rhodos: Episképésé tés istorías kai tés téchnés.* Athens: Morphotiko Hidryma Ethnikes Trapezes.

Kose, A.

1996 Zur Säulenarchitektur im parthischen Mesopotamien. In E.-L. Schwandner (ed.), *Säule und Gebälk: Zu Struktur und Wandlungsprozess griechisch-römischer Architektur,* 203–220. Mainz: von Zabern.

Kraay, C.M.

1981 Demetrius in Bactria and India. *Numismatica e antichità classiche. Quaderni ticinesi* 10: 219–233.

Kraeling, C.H.

1962 *Ptolemais, City of the Libyan Pentapolis.* Chicago: The University of Chicago.

Kraus, Th.

1976 Überlegungen zum Bauornament. In P. Zanker (ed.), *Hellenismus in Mittelitalien: Kolloquium in Göttingen vom 5. bis 9. Juni 1974,* 455–70. Abhandlungen der Akademie der Wissenschaften in Göttingen. Philologisch-Historische Klasse. Dritte Folge 97. Göttingen: Vandenhock and Ruprecht.

Krause, C.

2003 *Villa Jovis. Die Residenz des Tiberius auf Capri.* Antike Welt special issue. Mayence: von Zabern.

Kreeb, M.

1988 *Untersuchungen zur figürlichen Ausstattung delischer Privathäuser.* Chicago: Ares.

Kuhrt, A. and S. Sherwin-White (eds.)

1987 *Hellenism in the East: The Interactions of Greek and non-Greek Civilizations from Syria to Central Asia after Alexander.* Berkeley: University of California Press.

Kushnir-Stein, A. and H. Gitler

1992–3 Numismatic Evidence from Tel Beer-Sheva and the Beginning of Nabataean Coinage. *Israel Numismatic Journal* 12: 13–20.

Lahusen, G.

1999 Bemerkungen zur Laokoon-Gruppe. In *Hellenistische Gruppen: Gedenkschrift für Andreas Linfert*, 295–305. Mainz: von Zabern.

Lang-Auinger, C., G. Forstenpointner and G. Lang

1996 *Hanghaus 1 in Ephesos: Der Baubefund.* Forschungen in Ephesos 8, 3. Vienna: Verlag der Österreichischen Akademie der Wissenschaften.

Laroche-Traunecker, F.

2000 Chapiteaux 'nabatéens', 'corinthiens inachevés' ou 'simplifiés'? Nouveaux exemples en Egypte. *Ktéma* 25: 207–213.

Lauter, H.

1971 Ptolemais in Libyen: Ein Beitrag zur Baukunst Alexandrias. *Jahrbuch des deutschen archäologischen Instituts* 86: 149–178.

1972 Kunst und Landschaft-ein Beitrag zum rhodischen Hellenismus. *Antike Kunst* 15: 49–59.

1986 *Die Architektur des Hellenismus.* Darmstadt: Wissenschaftliche Buchgesellschaft.

1988 Hellenistische Sepulkralarchitektur auf Rhodos. In S. Dietz and I. Papachristodoulou (eds.), *Archaeology in the Dodecanese*, 155–163. Copenhagen: National Museum of Denmark, Department of Near Eastern and Classical Antiquities.

Lichtenberger, A.

1999 *Die Baupolitik Herodes des Großen.* Wiesbaden: Harrassowitz.

2003 *Kulte und Kultur der Dekapolis. Untersuchungen zu numismatischen, archäologischen und epigraphischen Zeugnissen.* Wiesbaden: Harrassowitz.

Lindner, M.

1978 Die 3. archäologische Expedition der Naturhistorischen Gesellschaft nach Jordanien, 19.3.78 bis 2.4.78. *Natur und Mensch. Jahresmitteilungen der Naturhistorischen Gesellschaft Nürnberg e.V.*: 81–96.

Lindner, M. (ed.)

1986 *Petra: Neue Ausgrabungen und Entdeckungen.* Munich: Delp.

1989 *Petra und das Königreich der Nabatäer: Lebensraum, Geschichte und Kultur eines arabischen Volkes der Antike.* Munich: Delp.

Lindner, M. and J.P. Zeitler (eds.)

1991 *Petra: Königin der Weihrauchstrasse.* Fürth: UKA-Verlag.

Litvinskij, B.A.

1998 *La civilisation de l'Asie centrale antique.* Archäologie in Iran und Turan 3. Rahden: Leidorf.

Lyttelton, M.

1974 *Baroque Architecture in Classical Antiquity.* London: Thames and Hudson.

Lyttelton, M. and T. Blagg

1990 Sculpture in Nabatean Petra, and the Question of Roman Influence. In M. Henig (ed.), *Architecture and Architectural Sculpture in the Roman Empire*, 91–107. Oxford: Oxford Committee for Archaeology.

MacAdam, H.I.

1992 The History of Philadelphia in the Classical Period. In A. Northedge (ed.), *Studies on Roman and Islamic 'Amman. The Excavations of Mrs C-M Bennett and Other Investigations, 1. History, Site and Architecture*, 27–45. Oxford: Oxford University Press.

MacDonald, B. and R. Adams and P. Bienkowski (eds.)

2001 *The Archaeology of Jordan.* Sheffield: Sheffield Academic Press

Macdonald, M.C.A.

1993 Nomads and the Hawran in the Late Hellenistic and Roman Periods: A Reassessment of the Epigraphic Evidence. *Syria* 70: 303–413.

MacDonald, B. and R. W. Younker

1999 *Ancient Ammon.* Leiden: E.J. Brill.

Markoe, G. (ed),

2003 *Petra Rediscovered. Lost City of the Nabataeans.* New York: Harry N. Abrams.

Matteotti, R.

1993 Zur Militärgeschichte von Augusta Rauricorum in der zweiten Hälfte des 1. Jahrhunderts n.Chr. Die Truppenziegel der 21. Legion aus Augst. *Jahresberichte aus Augst und Kaiseraugst* 14: 185–197.

Matthiae, K.

1988 Die Fassade des *Bab-es-Siq*-Trikliniums in Petra: Bemerkungen zu ihrer Gestaltung. *Zeitschrift des deutschen Palästina-Vereins* 104: 74–83.

1989 Die Fassade von Ed-Der in Petra. *Klio* 71: 257–279.

1991 Die nabatäische Felsarchitektur in Petra. *Klio* 73: 226–278.

1994 Der Platz vor der Khazne-Fassade in Petra: Beobachtungen zur Gestaltung der unteren Etage dieser Fassade. *Das Altertum* 39: 275–286.

1995 Die Tholos der *Hazne*-Fassade in Petra. *Zeitschrift des deutschen Palästina-Vereins* 111: 151–161.

Mattingly, G.L.

1990 Settlement on Jordan's Kerak Plateau from Iron Age IIC through the Early Roman Period. *Aram* 2: 309–335.

McKenzie, J.S.

1988 The Development of Nabataean Sculpture at Petra and Khirbet Tannur. *Palestine Exploration Quarterly* 120: 81–107.

1990 *The Architecture of Petra.* Oxford: Oxford University Press.

1996 Alexandria and the Origins of Baroque Architecture. In *Alexandria and Alexandrianism: Papers Delivered at a Symposium Organized by the J. Paul Getty Museum and The Getty Center for the History of Art and the Humanities and Held at the Museum April 22.25, 1993*, 109–125. Malibu: The J. Paul Getty Museum.

McKenzie, J. S. and S. Gibson and A. T. Reyes

2002 Reconstruction of the Nabataean Temple Complex at Khirbet et-Tannur. *Palestine Exploration Quarterly* 134: 44–83.

Meshorer, Y.

1975 *Nabataean Coins*. Qedem 3. Jerusalem: Institute of Archaeology, Hebrew University of Jerusalem.

Meskel, L. (ed.)

1998 *Archaeology under Fire: Nationalism, Politics and Heritage in the Eastern Mediterranean and Middle East*. London: Routledge.

Mette, B.D.

1992 Skulptur und Landschaft: Mythologische Skulpturengruppen in griechischer und römischer Aufstellung. Unpublished PhD thesis, University of Cologne.

Mettinger, T.N.D.

1995 *No Graven Image? Israelite Aniconism in Its Near Eastern Context*. Stockholm: Almquist and Wiksell.

Mielsch, H.

1997 *Die römische Villa: Architektur und Lebensform*. Munich: Beck.

Miglus, P.A.

1999 *Städtische Wohnarchitektur in Babylonien und Assyrien*. Baghdader Forschungen 22. Mainz: von Zabern.

Milik, J.T.

1958 Nouvelles inscriptions nabatéennes. *Syria* 35: 227–251.

1982 Origines des Nabatéens. In A. Hadidi (ed.), *Studies in the History and Archaeology of Jordan I*, 261–265. Amman: Department of Antiquities.

Millar, F.

1993 *The Roman Near East, 31 BC–AD 337*. Cambridge, MA: Harvard University Press.

Mlynarczyk, J.

1990 *Nea Paphos in the Hellenistic Period*. Nea Paphos 3. Warsaw: PWN-Editions scientifiques de Pologne.

1996 Palaces of Strategoi and the Ptolemies in Nea Paphos: Topographical Remarks. In W. Hoepfner and G. Brands (eds.) *Basileia: Die Paläste der hellenistischen Könige. Internationales Symposion in Berlin vom 16.12.1992 bis 20.12.1992*, 193–202. Mainz: von Zabern.

1998 Terracotta Mould-Made Lamps in Alexandria (Hellenistic to Late Roman Period). In J.-Y. Empereur (ed.), *Commerce et Artisanat dans l'Alexandrie hellénistique et romaine*, 327–352. Bulletin de correspondence hellénique Supplément 33. Athens: Ecole française d'Athens.

Moutsopoulos, N.C.

1990 Observations sur les représentations du Panthéon nabatéen. In F. Zayadine (ed.), *Petra and the Caravan Cities*, 53–75. Amman: Department of Antiquities.

Munro-Hay, S.C.

1991 The Coinage of Shabwa (Hadramawt) and other Ancient South Arabian Coinage in the National Museum, Aden. *Syria* 68: 393–418.

1994 Coins of Ancient South Arabia. *Numismatic Chronicle* 154: 191–203.

1996 Coins of Ancient South Arabia, II. *Numismatic Chronicle* 156: 33–47.

Nabatäer

1981 *Die Nabatäer: Erträge einer Ausstellung im Rheinischen Landesmuseum Bonn, 24. Mai . 9. Juli 1978*. Cologne: Rheinland-Verlag/Bonn: Habelt.

Nabateërs

1971 *De Nabateërs, een vergeten volk aan de Dode Zee, 312 v..106 n.Chr. Provincial gallo-romeins Museum, Tongeren (B), 19 februari tot 12 april 1971*. Tongeren: Provincial gallo-romeins Museum.

Naster, P.

1983 Remarques au sujet des imitations des monnaies d'Athénes dans la presqu'île arabique. In P. Naster, *Scripta Nummaria: Contributions à la méthodologique numismatique*, 141–146. Louvain-La-Neuve: Seminaire de numismatique Marcel Hoc.

Nehmé, L.

1997a L'habitat rupestre dans le bassin de Pétra à l'époque nabatéenne. In G. Bisheh, M. Zaghloul and I. Kehrberg (eds.), *Studies in the History and Archaeology of Jordan VI*, 281–288. Amman: Department of Antiquities.

1997b L'espace cultuel de Pétra à l'époque nabatéenne. *Topoi* 7: 1023–1067.

Nehru, L.

1990 Hellenism in Gandharan Sculpture. In Deutsches Archäologisches Institut (ed.), *Akten des XIII. internationalen Kongresses für klassische Archäologie, Berlin 1988*, 317–319. Deutsches Archäologisches Institut. Mainz: von Zabern.

Netzer, E.

1990 Architecture in Palaestina prior to and during the Days of Herod the Great. In Deutsches Archäologisches Institut (ed.), *Akten des XIII. internationalen Kongresses für klassische Archäologie, Berlin 1988*, 37–50. Mainz: von Zabern.

1991 *The Buildings: Stratigraphy and Architecture*. Masada 3. Jerusalem: Israel Exploration Society.

1996a The Hasmonean Palaces in Palaestina. In W. Hoepfner and G. Brands (eds.) *Basileia: Die Paläste der hellenistischen Könige. Internationales Symposion in Berlin vom 16.12.1992 bis 20.12.1992*, 203–208. Mainz: von Zabern.

1996b The Palaces Built by Herod . A Research Update. In K. Fittschen and G. Foerster (eds.), *Judaea and the Greco-Roman World in the Time of Herod in the Light of Archaeological Evidence*. Abhandlungen der Akademie der Wissenschaften in Göttingen. Philologisch-Historische Klasse. Dritte Folge 215, 27–54. Göttingen: Vandenhoeck and Ruprecht.

1999 *Die Paläste der Hasmonäer und Herodes' des Grossen*. Antike Welt, special issue. Mainz: von Zabern.

2001 *Hamonean and Herodian Palaces at Jericho. Final Reports of the 1973–1987 Excavations, 1. The Architecture.* Jerusalem: Israel Exploration Society.

2003 *Nabatäische Architektur. Insbesondere Gräber und Tempel.* Mayence: von Zabern.

Nielsen, I.

1994 *Hellenistic Palaces: Tradition and Renewal.* Aarhus, Denmark: Aarhus University.

Normann, A. von

1996 *Architekturtoreutik in der Antike.* Munich: tuduv.

Oleson, J. P.

1992 Hellenistic and Roman Elements in Nabataean Hydraulic Technology. In G. Argoud, *L. Marangou, V. Panayotopoulos and C. Villain-Gandossi* (eds.), *L'eau et les hommes en Méditerranée et en Mer Noire dans l'antiquité, de l'époque mycénienne au regne de Justinien,* 473–497. Athens: National Centre of Social Sciences.

1994 The Origins and Design of Nabataean Water-Supply Systems. In K. 'Amr and F. Zayadine and M. Zaghloul (eds.), *Studies in the History and Archaeology of Jordan V,* 707–719. Amman: Department of Antiquities.

2001 King, Emperor, Priest and Caliph: Cultural Change at Hawar (Ancient al-Humayma) in the First Milllennium AD. In *Studies in the History and Archaeology of Jordan VII,* 569–580. Amman: Department of Antiquities.

Onians, J.

1979 *Art and Thought in the Hellenistic Age. The Greek World View 350–50 B.C.* London: Thames and Hudson.

Orlandos, A.K.

1976 Neóterai éreunai en Messéné. In U. Jantzen (ed.), *Neue Forschungen in griechischen Heiligtümern: Internationales Symposion in Olympia vom 10. bis 12. Oktober 1974,* 9–38. Tübingen: Wasmuth.

Ovadiah, A.

1994 Mosaic Pavements of the Herodian Period in Israel. In P. Johnson and R.Ling and D.J. Smith (eds.), *Fifth International Colloquium on Ancient Mosaics held at Bath, England, on September 5–12, 1987,* 67–76. Ann Arbor.

Ovadiah, A. and Y. Turnheim

1994 'Peopled' Scrolls in Roman Architectural Decoration in Israel: The Roman Theatre at Beth Shean/Scythopolis. Rome: Bretschneider.

Ozols, J. and V. Thewaldt (eds.)

1984 *Aus dem Osten des Alexanderreiches: Völker und Kulturen zwischen Orient und Okzident. Iran, Afghanistan, Pakistan, Indien.* Cologne: DuMont.

Pandermalis, D.

1976 Beobachtungen zur Fassadenarchitektur und Aussichtsveranda im hellenistischen Makedonien. In P. Zanker (ed.), *Hellenismus in Mittelitalien: Kolloquium in Göttingen vom 5. bis 9. Juni 1974,* 387–397. Abhandlungen der Akademie der Wissenschaften in Göttingen. Philologisch-Historische Klasse. Dritte Folge 97. Göttingen: Vandenhock and Ruprecht.

Parlasca, I.

1990a Seltene Typen nabatäischer Terrakotten: Östliche Motive in der späteren Provincia Arabia. In Ch. Börker and M. Donderer (eds.), *Das antike Rom und der Osten:Festschrift Klaus Parlasca zum 65. Geburtstag,* 157–174. Auslieferung Universitätsbibliothek Erlangen. Erlangen: Universitätsbund Erlangen-Nürnberg.

1990b Terrakotten aus Petra: Ein neues Kapitel nabatäischer Archäologie. In F. Zayadine (ed.), *Petra and the Caravan Cities,* 87–105. Amman: Department of Antiquities.

1997 Götter und Reittiere. Religions- und kulturgeschichtliche Bedeutung nabatäischer Terrakotten. In Th. Weber and R. Wenning (eds.), *Petra: Antike Felsstadt zwischen arabischer Tradition und griechischer Norm,* 126–131. AntikeWelt, special issue. Mainz: von Zabern.

Parr, P.J.

1960 Excavations at Petra, 1958–59. *Palestine Exploration Quarterly* 92: 124–135.

1968 Découvertes récentes au sanctuaire du Qasr à Pétra, I: Comptes rendu des derniéres fouilles. *Syria* 45: 1–24.

1970 A Sequence of Pottery from Petra. In J.A. Sanders (ed.), *Near Eastern Archaeology in the Twentieth Century: Essays in Honor of Nelson Glueck,* 348–381. Garden City, NY: Doubleday.

Patrich, J.

1990 *The Formation of Nabatean Art: Prohibition of a Graven Image among the Nabateans.* Jerusalem: Magnes.

Pensabene, P.

1991 Elementi di architettura alessandrina. In S. Stucchi and M. Bonanno Aravantinos (eds.), *Giornate di studio in onore di Achille Adriani,* 29–85. Studi Miscellanei 28. Rome: 'L'Erma' di Bretschneider.

1993 *Elementi architettonici di Alessandria e di altri siti egiziani: Repertorio d'arte dell'Egitto greco-romano.* Serie C 3. Rome: Bretschneider.

Pesce, G.

1950 *Il 'Palazzo delle colonne' in Tolemaide di Cirenaica.* Rome: 'L'Erma' di Bretschneider.

Peter, M.

1993 Münzprägung und Münzumlauf im Gebiet der Nabatäer. In *Petra und die Weihrauchstrasse,* 18–20. Catalogue of an exhibition in Zurich and Basel. Zurich: Konzept Gut.

1996 Die Fundmünzen. In A. Bignasca, B. Kolb and S.G. Schmid. *Petra. Ez Zantur I: Ergebnisse der schweizerisch-liechtensteinischen Ausgrabungen 1988–1992,* 91–127. Terra Archaeologica 2. Monographien der schweizerisch-liechtensteinischen Stiftung für archäologische Forschungen im Ausland. Mainz am Rhein: Philipp von Zabern.

Peters, F.E.

1977 The Nabataeans in the Hawran. *Journal of the American Oriental Society* 97: 263–277.

Petra und die Weihrauchstrasse

1993 *Petra und die Weihrauchstrasse.* Catalogue of an exhibition in Zurich and Basel. Zurich: Konzept Gut.

Pfrommer, M.

1996a Roots and Contacts: Aspects of Alexandrian Craftmanship. In *Alexandria and Alexandrianism: Papers Delivered at a Symposium Organized by the J. Paul Getty Museum and The Getty Center for the History of Art and the Humanities and Held at the Museum April 22–25, 1993*, 171–189. Malibu: The J. Paul Getty Museum.

1996b Fassade und Heiligtum: Betrachtungen zur architektonischen Repräsentation des vierten Ptolemäers. In W. Hoepfner and G. Brands (eds.) *Basileia: Die Paläste der hellenistischen Könige. Internationales Symposion in Berlin vom 16.12.1992 bis 20.12.1992*, 97–108. Mainz: von Zabern.

Pinkwart, D. and W. Stamnitz

1984 *Peristylhäuser westlich der unteren Agora.* Altertümer von Pergamon 14. Berlin: W. de Gruyter.

Pirenne, J.

1965 Les phases de l'hellénisation dans l'art sud-arabe. In *Le rayonnement des civilisations grecque et romaine sur les cultures périphériques: Huitiéme congrès international d'archéologie classique (Paris 1963)*, 535–541. Paris: de Boccard.

Pitschikjan, I.

1996 Die Entwicklung des baktrischen Palast-Tempels. In W. Hoepfner and G. Brands (eds.) *Basileia: Die Paläste der hellenistischen Könige. Internationales Symposion in Berlin vom 16.12.1992 bis 20.12.1992*, 226–233. Mainz: von Zabern.

Polito, E.

1998 *Fulgentibus armis. Introduzione allo studio dei fregi d'armi antichi.* Rome: L'Erma di Bretschneider.

Pollitt, J.J.

1986 *Art in the Hellenistic Age.* Cambridge: Cambridge University Press.

Potts, D.T.

1991 *The Pre-Islamic Coinage of Eastern Arabia.* Copenhagen: Carsten Niebuhr Institute of Near Eastern Studies, University of Copenhagen/Museum Tusculanum.

Pugachenkova, G., S.R. Dar, R.C. Sharma and M.A. Joyenda and H. Siddiqi

1996 Kushan Art. In J. Harmatta (ed.), *History of Civilizations of Central Asia.* II. *The Development of Sedentary and Nomadic Civilizations: 700 BC to AD 250*, 331–395. 2nd edn. Paris: UNESCO.

Puri, B.N.

1996 The Kushans. In J. Harmatta (ed.), *History of Civilizations of Central Asia.* II. *The Development of Sedentary and Nomadic Civilizations: 700 b.c. to ad 250*, 247–263. 2nd edn. Paris: UNESCO.

Qusus, N.

1984 *Pétra: Ē nabataikē prōtēuousa tes iordanikēs erēmou.*

Sumbolē stēn architektonikē ka tē morfologia tōn mnēmeíon. Thessaloniki: Marrogenis.

Raeder, J.

1988 Vitruv, de architectura VI 7 (aedificia Graecorum) und die hellenistische Wohnhaus- und Palastarchitektur. *Gymnasium* 95: 316–368.

Rakob, F.

1979 Numidische Königsarchitektur in Nordafrika. In H.G. Horn and Ch.B. Rüger (eds.), *Die Numider: Reiter und Könige nördlich der Sahara*, 119–171. Cologne: Rheinland-Verlag/Bonn: Habelt.

1983 Architecture royale numide. In *Architecture et société: De l'archaïsme grec à la fin de la république romaine. Actes du Colloque international organisé par le Centre national de la recherche scientifique et l'Ecole française de Rome (Rome 2–4 décembre 1980)*, 325–348. Paris: Le Centre national de la recherche scientifique.

Rapin, C.

1990 Greeks in Afghanistan: Aï Khanoum. In J.-P. Descoeudres (ed.), *Greek Colonists and Native Populations*, 329–342. New York: Oxford University Press.

Raschke, M.G.

1978 New Studies in Roman Commerce with the East. In H. Temporini and W. Haase (eds.), *Aufstieg und Niedergang der römischen Welt*, II. 9.2: 604–1076. Berlin: W. de Gruyter.

Rasson, A.-M. and J. Seigne

1989 Une citerne byzantino-omeyyade sur le sanctuaire de Zeus. In AA.VV., *Jerash Archaeological Project 1984–1988, II*, 117–151. Paris: Geuthner (= *Syria* 66, 1989).

Reber, K.

1988 Aedificia graecorum: Zu Vitruvs Beschreibung des griechischen Hauses. *Archäologischer Anzeiger*: 653–666.

Rice, E.E.

1995 Grottoes on the Acropolis of Hellenistic Rhodes. *Annual of the British School at Athens* 90: 383–404.

Roche, M.-J.

1996 Remarques sur les Nabatéens en Méditerrané. *Semitica* 45: 73–99.

Roller, D. W.

1998 *The Building Program of Herod the Great.* Berkeley: University of California Press.

Rollin, S. and J. Streetly

1996 *Jordan.* Blue Guide. London: A and C Black.

Romanis, F. de

1996 *Cassia, cinnamomo, ossidiana: Uomini e merci tra Oceano Indiano e Mediterraneo.* Rome: 'L'Erma' di Bretschneider.

Ronczewski, K.

1932 Kapitelle des El Hasne in Petra. *Archäologischer Anzeiger* 47: 38–89.

Rozenberg, S.

1996 The Wall Paintings of the Herodian Palace at Jericho. In K. Fittschen and G. Foerster (eds.), *Judaea and the Greco-Roman World in the Time of Herod in the Light of Archaeological Evidence*. Abhandlungen der Akademie der Wissenschaften in Göttingen. Philologisch-Historische Klasse. Dritte Folge 215, 121–138. Göttingen: Vandenhoeck and Ruprecht.

Ruben, I.

2003 *The Petra Siq. Nabataean Hydrology Uncovered*. Amman: Petra National Trust.

Rumscheid, F.

1994 *Untersuchungen zur kleinasiatischen Bauornamentik des Hellenismus*. Mainz: von Zabern.

Sarianidi, V.

1985 Monumental architecture of Bactria. In J.-L. Huot, M. Yon and Y. Calvet (eds.), *De l'Indus aux Balkans: Recueil à la mémoire de Jean Deshayes*, 417–432. Paris: Recherche sur les civilisations.

Sartre, M.

1982 *Trois études sur l'Arabie romaine et byzantine*. Collection Latomus 178. Brussels: Revue d'études latines.

1985 *Bostra: Des origines à l'Islam*. Bibliothéque archéologique et historique 117. Paris: Geuthner.

Sasianou, A.

1993 Copies and Imitations of Thasian Tetradrachms. In *Proceedings of the XIth International Numismatic Congress*, I: 123–131. Louvain-La-Neuve: Association Professeur Marcel Hoc pour l'encouragement des recherches numismatiques.

Sauron, G.

1988 Le message esthétique des rinceaux de l'Ara Pacis Augustae. *Revue archéologique*: 3–40.

Schefold, K.

1975 Der zweite Stil als Zeugnis alexandrinischer Architektur. In B. Andreae and H. Kyrieleis (eds.), *Neue Forschungen in Pompeji und den anderen vom Vesuvausbruch 79 n. Chr. verschütteten Städten*, 53–59. Recklinghausen: Bongers.

Schiltz, V.

1994 *Die Skythen und andere Steppenvölker: 8. Jahrhundert v.Chr. bis 1. Jahrhundert n.Chr.* Munich: Beck.

Schloz, S.

1994 Das Tempelbauprogramm der Ptolemäer: Die Darstellung eines Rekonstruktionsproblems. In R. Gundlach and M. Rochholz (eds.), *Ägyptische Tempel: Struktur, Funktion und Programm. Akten der ägyptologischen Tempeltagungen in Gosen 1990 und Mainz 1992*, 281–286. Hildesheim: Gerstenberg.

Schlumberger, D.

1969 Nachkommen der griechischen Kunst ausserhalb des Mittelmeerraums. In F. Altheim and J. Rehork (eds.), *Der Hellenismus in Mittelasien*, 281–405. Darmstadt: Wissenschaftliche Buchgesellschaft.

Schmid, S.G.

1995 Nabataean Fine Ware from Petra. In K. 'Amr, F. Zayadine and M. Zaghloul (eds.), *Studies in the History and Archaeology of Jordan V*, 637–647. Amman: Department of Antiquities.

1996a Die Feinkeramik der Nabatäer im Spiegel ihrer kulturhistorischen Kontakte. In M. Herfort-Koch, U. Mandel and U. Schädler (eds.), *Hellenistische und kaiserzeitliche Keramik des östlichen Mittelmeergebietes. Kolloquium Frankfurt 24–25 April 1995*, 127–145. Frankfurt am Main: Arbeitskreis Frankfurt und die Antike, archäologisches Institut der Johann Wolfgang Goethe-Universität.

1996b Die Feinkeramik. In A. Bignasca, B. Kolb and S.G. Schmid. *Petra. Ez Zantur I: Ergebnisse der schweizerisch-liechtensteinischen Ausgrabungen 1988–1992*, 151–218. Terra Archaeologica 2. Monographien der schweizerisch-liechtensteinischen Stiftung für archäologische Forschungen im Ausland. Mainz am Rhein: Philipp von Zabern.

1997a Nabataean Fine Ware Pottery and the Destructions of Petra in the Late First and Early Second Century ad. In G. Bisheh, M. Zaghloul and I. Kehrberg (eds.), *Studies in the History and Archaeology of Jordan VI*, 413–420. Amman: Department of Antiquities.

1997b Eierschalendünne Tongefässe und grobe Waren. In Th. Weber and R. Wenning (eds.), *Petra: Antike Felsstadt zwischen arabischer Tradition und griechischer Norm*, 131–137. Antike Welt, special issue. Mainz: von Zabern.

1999 Un roi nabatéen à Délos? *Annual of the Department of Antiquities of Jordan* 43: 279–298.

2000a The 'Hellenistic' Tomb Façades of Nabataean Petra and their Cultural Background. In V. Christides and Th. Papadopoullos (eds.), *Proceedings of the Sixth International Congres of Graeco-Oriental and African Studies. Graeco-Arabica 7–8, 1999–2000*, 485–509. Nicosia: Archbishop Makarias III Cultural Centre.

2000b *Die Feinkeramik der Nabatäer. Typologie, Chronologie und kulturhistorische Hintergründe. Petra ez Zantur II 1. Ergebnisse der schweizerisch-liechtensteinischen Ausgrabungen* (Terra archaeologica 4). Mainz: von Zabern.

2000c The International Wadi al-Farasa Project (IWFP). Exploration Season 1999. *Annual of the Department of Antiquities of Jordan* 44: 335–354.

2001a The Impact of Pottery Production on the Sedentarisation of the Nabataeans. In J.R. Brandt and L. Karlsson (eds.), *From Huts to Houses. Transformations of Ancient Societies. Proceedings of an International Seminar Organized by the Norwegian and Swedish Institutes in Rome, 21–24 September 1997*, 427–436. Stockholm/Jonsered: Paul Aströms Förlag.

2001b The 'Hellenisation' of the Nabataeans: A New Approach. In Department of Antiquities (ed.), *Studies in the History and Archaeology of Jordan VII*, 407–420. Amman: Department of Antiquities.

2001c The Nabataeans. Travellers between Lifestyles. In B.

MacDonald, R. Adams and P. Bienkowski (eds.), *The Archaeology of Jordan*, 367–426. Sheffield: Sheffield Academic Press.

2001d The International Wadi Farasa Project (IWFP). Between Microcosm and Macroplanning—A First Synthesis. *Palestine Exploration Quarterly* 133: 159–197.

2001e König, nicht Königin. Ein nabatäisches Herrscherporträt in Paris. *Archäologischer Anzeiger*: 91–105.

2003 Wieder einmal Sperlonga. Trink- und andere Geschichten in Latium. *Numismatica e antichità classiche. Quaderni ticinesi* 32: 199–225.

2004a The Distribution of Nabataean Pottery and the Organisation of Nabataean Long Distance Trade. In F. al-Khraysheh, K. 'Amr, H. Taher and S. Khouri (eds.), *Studies in the History and Archaeology of Jordan VIII*, 415–426. Amman: Department of Antiquities.

2004b The International Wadi Farasa Project (IWFP). Progress on the Work in the Wadi Farasa East, Petra. *Palestine Exploration Quarterly* 136: 163–186.

2004c Les Nabatéens et leurs contacts avec la Mésopotamie et la région du golfe arabo-persique. In F. Duyrat and V. Chankowski (eds.), *Le roi et l'économie. Autonomies locales et structures royales dans l'économie de l'empire séleucide*. Topoi Suppl. 6, 463–484. Lyon: Topoi. Orient-Occident.

Schmidt, J.

1997–8 Tempel und Heiligtümer in Südarabien: Zu den materiellen und formalen Strukturen der Sakralbaukunst. *Nürnberger Blätter zur Archäologie* 14: 10–40.

Schmidt-Colinet, A.

1981 Nabatäische Felsarchitektur: Bemerkungen zum gegenwärtigen Forschungsstand. In *Die Nabatäer: Erträge einer Ausstellung im Rheinischen Landesmuseum Bonn, 24. Mai . 9. Juli 1978*, 61–102. Cologne: Rheinland-Verlag/Bonn: Habelt.

1987a The Mason's Workshop of Hegra, its Relation to Petra, and the Tomb of Syllaios. In A. Hadidi (ed.) *Studies in the History and Archaeology of Jordan II*, 143–150. Amman: Department of Antiquities.

1987b Zur nabatäischen Felsnekropole von Hegra, Medain Salih in Saudi-Arabien. *Antike Welt* 18, 4: 29–42.

1991 Exedra duplex: Überlegungen zum Augustusforum. *Hefte des archäologischen Seminars der Universität Bern* 14: 43–60.

1993 Der ptolemäische Eckgiebel: Ursprung und Wirkung eines Architekturmotivs. In Invernizzi and Salles 1993: 1–13.

Schmitt-Korte, K.

1990 Nabataean Coinage, Part II. New Coin Types and Variants. *Numismatic Chronicle* 150: 105–133.

1997 Das Münzsystem der Nabatäer. In Th. Weber and R. Wenning (eds.), *Petra: Antike Felsstadt zwischen arabischer Tradition und griechischer Norm*, 101–104. Antike Welt, special issue. Mainz: von Zabern.

Schmitt-Korte, K. and M. Cowell

1989 Nabataean Coinage, Part I. The Silver Content Measured by X-Ray Fluorescence Analysis. *Numismatic Chronicle* 149: 33–58.

Schmitt-Korte, K. and M. Price

1994 Nabataean Coinage, Part III. The Nabataean Monetary System. *Numismatic Chronicle* 154: 67–131.

Schneider, Ch.

1996 Die Importkeramik. In A. Bignasca, B. Kolb and S.G. Schmid. *Petra. Ez Zantur I: Ergebnisse der schweizerisch-liechtensteinischen Ausgrabungen 1988–1992*, 129–49. Terra Archaeologica 2. Monographien der schweizerisch-liechtensteinischen Stiftung für archäologische Forschungen im Ausland. Mainz am Rhein: Philipp von Zabern.

Schörner, G.

1995 *Römische Rankenfriese: Untersuchungen zur Baudekoration der späten Republik und der frühen und mittleren Kaiserzeit im Westen des Imperium Romanum*. Mainz: von Zabern.

Seigne, J.

1987 Le sanctuaire de Zeus. *Les dossiers de l'archéologie* 118: 56–61.

1992 A l'ombre de Zeus et d'Artémis: Gérasa de la Décapole. *Aram* 4: 185–195.

1993 Découvertes récentes sur le sanctuaire de Zeus à Jerash. Rapport préliminaire à la campagne de fouille de 1992. *Annual of the Department of Antiquities of Jordan* 37: 341–358.

1997a De la grotte au périptère. Le sanctuaire de Zeus Olympien à Jérash. *Topoi* 7: 993–1004.

1997b Habitat hellénistique et romain de Gerasa. In C. Castel and M. al-Maqdissi and F. Villeneuve (eds.), *Les maisons dans la Syrie antique du IIIe millénaire aux débuts de l'Islam. Pratiques et représentations de l'espace domestique*, 73–82. Beirut: l'Institut français d'archéologie du Proche-Orient.

2002 Gerasa-Jerasch – Stadt der 1000 Säulen. In A. Hoffmann and S. Kerner (eds.), *Gadara – Gerasa und die Dekapolis*, 6–22. Mayence: von Zabern.

Seigne J. and Th. Morin

1995 Preliminary Report on a Mausoleum at the Turn of the BC/AD Century at Jarash. *Annual of the Department of Antiquities of Jordan* 39: 175–191.

Settis, S.

1988 Die Ara Pacis. In *Kaiser Augustus und die verlorene Republik*. Catalogue of an exhibition, Berlin, 400–426. Mainz: von Zabern.

Seyer, M.

1993 Die Grabung in den Hanghäusern von Limyra. In J. Borchardt and G. Dobesch (eds.), *Akten des II. Internationalen Lykien-Symposions* I, 171–181. Vienna: Österreichische Akademie der Wissenschaften.

Seyer, M. and B. Rasch

1997 Die Grabung in der Nordweststadt. In J. Borchhardt (ed.), *Grabungen und Forschungen in Limyra aus den Jahren 1991–1996*, 338–348. Jahreshefte des Österreichischen archäologischen Institutes in Wien. Beiblatt 66.

Sherwin-White, S. and A. Kuhrt

1993 *From Samarkhand to Sardis: A New Approach to the Seleucid Empire*. London: Duckworth.

Shipley, G.

2000 *The Greek World after Alexander*. London: Routledge.

Sidebotham, S.E.

1986a *Roman Economic Policy in the Erythra Thalassa 30* bc–ad *217*. Mnemosyne Supplement 91. Leiden: E.J. Brill.

1986b Aelius Gallus and Arabia. *Latomus* 45: 590–602.

1996 Romans and Arabs in the Red Sea. *Topoi* 6: 785–797.

Siegler, K.G.

1969 Die Tore von Klabsha. *Mitteilungen des deutschen archäologischen Instituts. Abteilung Kairo* 25: 139–153.

Siganidou, M.

1996 Die Basileia von Pella. In W. Hoepfner and G. Brands (eds.) *Basileia: Die Paläste der hellenistischen Könige. Internationales Symposion in Berlin vom 16.12.1992 bis 20.12.1992*, 144–147. Mainz: von Zabern.

Sinos, A.

1990 *The Temple of Apollo Hylates at Kourian and the Restoration of its Southwest Corner*. Athens: Leventis Foundation.

Smirnova, N.

1995 Bactrian Coins in the Pushkin State Museum of Fine Art. *Ancient Civilisations from Scythia to Siberia* 2: 335–352.

Smith, R. H.

1990 The Southern Levant in the Hellenistic Period. *Levant* 22: 123–130.

Smith, R.R.R.

1991 *Hellenistic Sculpture*. London: Thames and Hudson.

Soren, E.

1987 *The Sanctuary of Apollo Hylates at Kourion, Cyprus*. Tucson: University of Arizona.

Starcky, J.

1966 Pétra et la Nabatène. *Dictionnaire de la Bible, Supplément* 7, 886–1017. Paris: Letouzey et Ané.

Stevens, K.G.

1994 Surface Finds from Qarn bint Sa`ud (Abu Dhabi Emirate.U.A.E.), *Mesopotamia* 29: 199–262.

Strobel, A. and S. Wimmer

2003 *Kallirrhoë (`Ên ez-Zāra). Dritte Grabungskampagne des Deutschen Evangelischen Instituts für Altertumswissenschaft des Heiligen Landes und Exkursionen in Süd-Peräa*. Wiesbaden: Harrassowitz.

Strocka, V.M.

1988 Wechselwirkungen der stadtrömischen und kleinasiatischen Architektur unter Trajan und Hadrian. *Istanbuler Mitteilungen* 38: 291–307.

1991 *Casa del Labirinto*. Häuser in Pompeji 4. Munich: Hirmer.

1999 Zur Datierung der Sperlonga-Gruppen und des Laokoon. In *Hellenistische Gruppen: Gedenkschrift für Andreas Linfert*, 307–322. Mainz: von Zabern.

Stucchi, S.

1975 *Architettura Cirenaica*. Rome: 'L'Erma' di Bretshneider.

Stucky, R.A.

1976 Achämenidische Ortbänder. *Archäologischer Anzeiger*, 13–23.

1990 Hellenistisches Syrien. In *Akten des XIII. Internationalen Kongresses für Klassische Archäologie, Berlin 1988*, 25–31. Mainz: von Zabern.

1996 Die nabatäischen Bauten. In A. Bignasca, B. Kolb and S.G. Schmid, *Petra. Ez Zantur I: Ergebnisse der Schweizerisch-Liechtensteinischen Ausgrabungen 1988–1992*, 13–50. Terra Archaeologica 2. Monographien der schweizerisch-liechtensteinischen Stiftung für archäologische Forschungen im Ausland. Mainz am Rhein: Philipp von Zabern.

Sydow, W. von

1974 Die Grabexedra eines römischen Feldherrn. *Jahrbuch des deutschen archäologischen Instituts* 89: 187–216.

Syme, R.

1965 Governors of Pannonia Inferior. *Historia* 14: 342–361.

Taddei, M.

1984 Neue Forschungsbelege zur Gandhara-Ikonographie. In J. Ozols and V. Thewaldt (eds.), *Aus dem Osten des Alexanderreiches: Völker und Kulturen zwischen Orient und Okzident. Iran, Afghanistan, Pakistan, Indien*, 154–175. Cologne: DuMont.

Tarrier, D.

1990 Baalshamin dans le monde nabatéen: A propos de découvertes récentes. *Aram* 2: 197–203.

Tholbecq, L.

1997 Les sanctuaires des nabatéens: Etat de la question à la lumiére de recherches archéologiques récentes. *Topoi* 7: 1069–1095.

1998 The Nabataeo-Roman Site of Wadi Ramm (*Iram*): A New Appraisal. *Annual of the Department of Antiquities of Jordan* 42: 241–254.

Thüroff, R.

1989 Waffenfriese im Gebiet des östlichen Mittelmeers: Zur Entwicklung eines Friestyps in hellenistischer und frührömischer Zeit. Unpublished MA thesis, University of Basel.

Toynbee, J.M.

1978 *Roman Historical Portraits*. London: Thames and Hudson.

Tran Tam Tinh, V.

1990 Remarques sur l'iconographie de Dusares. In F. Za-yadine (ed.), *Petra and the Caravan Cities*, 107–114. Amman: Department of Antiquities.

Trümper, M.

1998 *Wohnen in Delos: Eine baugeschichtliche Untersuchung zum Wandel der Wohnkultur in hellenistischer Zeit*. Rahden: Leidorf.

Tushingham, A.D.

1972 *The Excavations at Dibon (Dhibân) in Moab: The Third Campaign 1952–53*. Annual of the American School of Oriental Research 40. Cambridge, MA: American Schools of Oriental Research.

Tybout, R.A.

1989 *Aedificiorum figurae: Untersuchungen zu den Architekturdarstellungen des frühen zweiten Stils*. Amsterdam: Gieben.

Vanoyeke, V.

1998 *Les Ptolémées, derniers pharaons d'Egypte. D'Alexandre à Cléopatre*. Paris: Tallandier.

Villeneuve, F.

2002 Le sanctuaire nabatéen des IIe – IVe siècles apr. J.C. à Khirbet edh-Dharih (Jordanie du Sud). *Revue archéologique*, 189–194.

Villeneuve, F. and Z. al-Muheisen

1994 Découvertes nouvelles à Khirbet edh-Dharih (Jordanie), 1991–1994. *Académie des inscriptions et belles lettres. Comptes rendus*, 735–757.

2000 Nouvelles recherches à Khirbet edh-Dharih (Jordanie du Sud), 1996–1999. *Académie des inscriptions et belles lettres. Comptes rendus*, 1525–1563.

Voie royale

1986 *La voie royale: 9000 ans d'art au royaume de Jordanie*. Musée du Luxembourg 26 novembre 1986–25 janvier 1987. Paris: Association française d'action artistique.

Walbank, F. and A.E. Astin and M.W. Frederiksen

1984 *The Cambridge Ancient History. Second Edition, 7, 1. The Hellenistic World*. Cambridge: Cambridge University Press.

Walker, S. and K.J. Matthews

1997 The Marbles of the Mausoleum. In I. Jenkins and G.B. Waywell (eds.), *Sculptors and Sculpture of Caria and the Dodecanese*, 49–59. London: British Museum.

Waywell, G.B.

1997 The Sculptures of the Mausoleum at Halicarnassus. In I. Jenkins and G.B. Waywell (eds.), *Sculptors and Sculpture of Caria and the Dodecanese*, 60–67. London: British Museum.

Weber, M.

1990 *Baldachine und Statuenschreine*. Rome: Bretschneider.

Weber, Th.

1997 Die Bildkunst der Nabatäer. In Th. Weber and R. Wenning (eds.), *Petra: Antike Felsstadt zwischen arabischer Tradition und griechischer Norm*, 114–125. Antike Welt, special issue. Mainz: von Zabern.

1993 *Pella Decapolitana. Studien zur Geschichte, Architektur und bildenden Kunst einer hellenisierten Stadt des nördlichen Ostjordanlandes*. Wiesbaden: Harrassowitz.

2002 *Gadara–Umm Qes, I. Gadara Decapolitana. Untersuchungen zur Topographie, Geschichte und der bildenden Kunst einer "Polis Hellenis" im Ostjordanland*. Wiesbaden: Harrassowitz.

Weber, Th. and R. Wenning (eds.)

1997 *Petra: Antike Felsstadt zwischen arabischer Tradition und griechischer Norm*. Antike Welt, special issue. Mainz: von Zabern.

Weiser, W. and H.-M. Cotton

1996 'Gebt dem Kaiser, was des Kaisers ist…' Die Geldwährungen der Griechen, Juden, Nabatäer und Römer im syrisch-nabatäischen Raum unter besonderer Berücksichtigung des Kurses von Sela'/Melaina und Lepton nach der Annexion des Königreiches der Nabatäer durch Rom. *Zeitschrift für Papyrologie und Epigraphik* 114: 237–287.

Wenning, R.

1987 *Die Nabatäer. Denkmäler und Geschichte: Eine Bestandesaufnahme des archäologischen Befundes*. Novum Testamentum et Orbis Antiquus 3. Göttingen: Vandenhoeck & Ruprecht.

1989 Maskierte Götter? Anmerkungen zum Aufeinandertreffen von Ost und West am Beispiel der arabischen Nabatäer. In K. Rudolph and G. Rinschede (eds.), *Beiträge zur Religion/Umwelt-Forschung*, I: 243–260. Geographia Religionum 6. Berlin: Dietrich Reimer.

1990 Das Nabatäerreich: Seine archäologischen und historischen Hinterlassenschaften. In H.-P. Kuhnen, *Palästina in griechisch-römischer Zeit*, 367–415. Handbuch der Archäologie 2, 2 Munich: Beck.

1992 The Nabataeans in the Decapolis/Coele Syria. *Aram* 4: 79–99.

1993a Das Ende des nabatäischen Königreiches. In Invernizzi and Salles 1993: 81–103.

1993b Eine neuerstellte Liste der nabatäischen Dynastie. *Boreas* 16: 25–38.

1994 Die Dekapolis und die Nabatäer. *Zeitschrift des Deutschen Palästina-Vereins* 110: 1–35.

Wenning, R. and U. Hübner

2004 Nabatäische Büstenreliefs aus Petra – zwei Neufunde. *Zeitschrift des Deutschen Palästina-Vereins* 120: 157–181.

Wenning, R. and H. Merklein

1997 Die Götter in der Welt der Nabatäer. In Th. Weber and R. Wenning (eds.), *Petra: Antike Felsstadt zwischen arabischer Tradition und griechischer Norm*, 105–110. Antike Welt, special issue. Mainz: von Zabern.

Will, E.

1982 *Histoire politique du monde hellénistique, 323–30 av. J.-C.* Nancy: Presses universitaire de Nancy.

Will, E. and F. Larché

1991 *'Iraq al-Amir: Le château du Tobiade Hyrcan.* Paris: Geuthner.

Wolski, J.

1999 *The Seleucids: The Decline and Fall of their Empire.* Krakow: Nakladem Polskiej Akademii Umiejetnosci.

Wolsky, J.

1976 *Les Parthes et la Syrie.* Acta Iranica IIIéme série 5. Louvain: Bibliothèque Pablavi.

1993 *L'empire des Arsacides.* Acta Iranica IIIéme série 18. Louvain: Peeters.

Wright, G.R.H.

1968 Découvertes récentes au sanctuaire du Qasr à Pétra, II. Quelques aspects de l'architecture et de la sculpture. *Syria* 45: 25–40.

Zadneprovskiy, Y.A.

1996 The Nomads of Northern Central Asia after the Invasion of Alexander. In J. Harmatta (ed.) *History of Civilizations of Central Asia.* II. *The Development of Sedentary and Nomadic Civilizations:* 700 b.c. to ad 250, 457–472. 2nd edn. Paris: UNESCO.

Zanker, P.

2002 Domitian's Palace on the Palatine and the Imperial Image. In A.K. Bowman, H.M. Cotton, M. Goodman and S. Price (eds.), *Representations of Empire. Rome and the Mediterranean World*, 105–130. Oxford: Oxford University Press.

Zanker, P. (ed.)

1976 *Hellenismus in Mittelitalien: Kolloquium in Göttingen vom 5. bis 9. Juni 1974.* Abhandlungen der Akademie der Wissenschaften in Göttingen. Philologisch-Historische Klasse. Dritte Folge 97. Göttingen: Vandenhoeck and Ruprecht.

Zanoni, I.

1996 Tonlampen. In In A. Bignasca, B. Kolb and S.G. Schmid. *Petra. Ez Zantur I: Ergebnisse der schweizerisch-liechtensteinischen Ausgrabungen 1988–1992*, 311–336. Terra Archaeologica 2. Monographien der schweizerisch-liechtensteinischen Stiftung für archäologische Forschungen im Ausland. Mainz am Rhein: Philipp von Zabern.

Zayadine, F.

1973 Recent Excavations on the Citadel of Amman. A Preliminary Report. *Annual of the Department of Antiquities of Jordan* 18: 17–35.

1974 Excavations at Petra (1973–1974). *Annual of the Department of Antiquities of Jordan* 19: 142–150.

1977–8 Excavations on the Upper Citadel of Amman. Area A (1975 and 1977). *Annual of the Department of Antiquities of Jordan* 22: 20–56.

1985 Recent Excavation and Restoration at Qasr el Bint of Petra. *Annual of the Department of Antiquities of Jordan* 29: 239–249.

1986 Tempel, Gräber, Töpferöfen: Ausgrabungen des Department of Antiquities in Petra. In Lindner 1986: 214–269.

1989 Die Felsarchitektur Petras: Orientalische Traditionen und hellenistischer Einfluss. In Lindner 1989: 124–161.

1990a The Pantheon of the Nabataean Inscriptions in Egypt and the Sinai. *Aram* 2: 151–174.

1990b La campagne d'Antiochos III le Grand en 219–217 et le siège de Rabbatamana. *Revue biblique* 97: 68–84.

1991 L'iconographie d'Isis à Pétra. *Mélanges de l'Ecole française de Rome. Antiquité* 103: 283–306.

1997 Hermes/al-Kutbay Lexicon Iconographicum Mythologiae Classicae (LIMC) Supplementum, 616–619. Zurich/Düsseldorf: Artemis.

Zayadine, F. (ed.)

1990c *Petra and the Caravan Cities.* Amman: Department of Antiquities.

Zayadine, F. and Z.T. Fiema

1986 Roman Inscriptions from the Siq of Petra: Remarks on the Initial Garrison of Arabia. *Annual of the Department of Antiquities of Jordan* 30: 199–206.

Zayadine, F. and J.-B. Humbert and M. Najjar

1989 The 1988 Excavations on the Citadel of Amman. Lower Terrace, Area A. *Annual of the Department of Antiquities of Jordan* 33: 357–363.

Zayadine, F. and J. B. Humbert

1992 Trois campagnes de fouilles à Ammân, 1988–1991. Troisième terrasse de la citadelle. Mission franco-jordanienne. *Revue biblique* 99: 214–260.

Zayadine, F. and M. Najjar and J.A. Greene

1987 Recent Excavations on the Citadel of Amman (Lower Terrace). A Preliminary Report. *Annual of the Department of Antiquities of Jordan* 31: 299–311.

Zayadine, F. and F. Larché and J. Dentzer-Feydy

2003 *Le Qasr al-Bint de Pétra. L'architecture, le décor, la chronologie et les dieux.* Paris: Editions Recherche sur les Civilisations.

Zazoff, P.

1996 Bildchiffren der skytho-thrakischen Kunst. *Hamburger Beiträge zur Archäologie* 18: 167–180.

Zimmermann, B.

1992 Zur Authentizität des 'Clemensfeldzuges'. *Jahresberichte aus Augst und Kaiseraugst* 13: 289–303.

Zoppi, C.

1991–2 L'architettura abitativa in età ellenistica: Il modello vitruviano e i documenti superstiti. *Rendiconti della Accademia di archeologia, lettere e belle arti, Napoli* 63: 157–198.

13. The Roman Period

Philip Freeman

Introduction

Jordan was the province of Arabia in the Roman period. However, the northern part of the province also extended into what is today Syria and where lay the "capital" of Arabia, Bostra (modern Busra al-Sham) along with a number of adjacent towns. As such, they are omitted from this discussion. There is, however, a considerable modern literature that reports on recent work in the area (e.g. Dentzer 1986; MacAdam 1986b; Burns 1992). In contrast the "Jordanian" cities of Gadara and Pella, once members of the informal pre-province league known as the Decapolis, were transferred to the province of Syria when the Nabataean kingdom was annexed in AD 106. Although part of another province in the Roman period, these particular cities are discussed here as they are now in Jordan. Finally, I have defined the Roman period as spanning the mid-first century AD to the end of the fourth century.

Writing about the Roman period is made difficult by the way that it is sandwiched between two more strongly defined periods. In its strictest sense, the Roman era in Jordan is relatively short. On the one hand it could be said to start c. 63 BC (with Pompey's "eastern settlement") when it first came into intimate contact with Roman politics. Alternatively, it came into the full Roman sphere in AD 106 when the Nabataean monarchy was removed in preference to a full Roman province. This "period" lasted down to sometime in the early fourth century when the Byzantine period is said to commence. This periodization represents a significant problem, since the start of the period is defined by a political event even though the region had been in contact with the Roman empire for at least 150 years. The end of the era is likewise thought to have been occasioned by modifications in the existing Roman administration of the region in the late third to early fourth century, or simply because the capital of the empire was shifted in the 320s. In both cases, whatever the criteria for defining the political/administrative transitions, they had minimal if no (immediate) implications for the economic, religious, social and cultural conditions of the region. The situation is compounded by the fact that for different researchers the term Roman means different things. Broadly speaking, British scholars have tended to regard the succeeding Byzantine period as commencing in the fifth and even the sixth century. On the other hand, American scholars tend to place the divide in the early fourth century (e.g. Parker 1986). But even then more discrepancies are evident. For instance, for the (Australian) Pella project, "Early Roman" means 63 BC to AD 135 and Late Roman 135–324, a convention adopted by Khouri (1988). In contrast Homès-Fredericq and Hennessy define Early Roman as 63 BC–AD 106 and Late Roman as 106–324 (Homès-Fredericq and Hennessy 1989: 10), while, for example, the Hisban Survey saw its Early Roman period as 63 BC–AD 193, and its later equivalent spanning 193–365 (LaBianca 1989: 261–269). The start and end dates for the period as a whole are derived from historical sources. The sub-divisions owe as much to periods derived from the evidence of ceramics, and then from a limited number of excavated sites. In recent times Sauer's Hisban ceramics sequence has been extensively used to cross-date many surveys across all of Jordan (e.g. Parker 1986). In turn, it has led to the creation of the unrealistic Early Roman 1, 2, 3 and Late Roman 1, 2 and 3 subdivisions.

Moving away from the chronological issue, archaeology's great strength is its ability to look at humankind's cultural, technological and economic progress. It is less effective in exploring its political condition. But in examining Roman Arabia, we are dealing with a period that did not necessarily have an obvious cultural effect. For a political Roman Arabia does not equate with the on-going cultural situation. Irrespective of the fact that the region was part of the empire, culturally, socially and economically, Roman Arabia owes more to an earlier Hellenistic and Nabataean framework than to anything that could be described as distinctly Roman. While it would be rash to deny that changes did occur in these spheres, they came with time. That sense of cultural continuity exists in the equally arbitrarily defined Byzantine period, which owed as much to the earlier periods as it did to the consequences of the Roman presence. So, for instance, the urban framework of the province can now be shown clearly to pre-date the annexation. Where there is information, the same impression is apparent in the region's smaller communities as well as in the countryside. Likewise, in terms of material culture, there is the same clear sense of continuity from the Hellenistic period to the Roman and from the Roman to the Byzantine. In one respect, then, to talk of a specific archaeological period that is characteristically or purely Roman is misleading, if not erroneous.

Another inhibiting factor in attempting to synthesize the archaeology of Roman Jordan is the standard of fieldwork and its processing. While there are notable excep-

Figure 13.1 Roman period sites mentioned in the text.

tions, it is disappointing to note how little substantial work can be reported for certain important themes about the Roman province. Stern *et al.*'s (1993) atlas of excavations in the Holy Land is site specific. It contains useful summaries of work at individual sites but fails to synthesize that data for the wider picture of Roman Arabia. In a similar way, Homès-Fredericq and Hennessy's (1989) synthesis of the archaeology of Jordan shows that, despite so many of the sites reported producing "Roman" data (often recovered through excavation), little of that material is treated with satisfactory attention. The imbalances of treatment are frequently a consequence of the priorities that occasioned that work. A good example, but by no means unique, is the number of entries reporting work at Byzantine Christian sites. The majority of such sites have almost incidentally produced earlier Roman deposits and yet the emphasis in these entries is limited to discussions of architectural typologies and the style and the iconography of mosaics rather than consideration of the relationship of the pre-Byzantine to the Byzantine data. Another consequence of the explosion in the quantity of fieldwork, both in terms of survey and excavation, which is being undertaken in Jordan is that relatively little of that work has been written up and published as definitive statements. Instead there is a considerable literature of interim statements, results that can be easily rendered out-dated or liable to re-interpretation.

It is for these reasons that, despite the explosion in the scope and pace of research, it is surprising to find that, contrary to expectations, it is not an easy task to compose a synthesis outlining the current understanding of the archaeology and so the history of Roman Jordan. This situation is a consequence of a number of factors. Available discussions are either too dated, too limited in subject matter or paradoxically too general in scope. For instance, Bowersock's work on Roman Arabia (1983) is restricted to the period from 63 BC to the early third century and is written almost exclusively from the perspective of frontiers and Arabia as part of the wider empire. Parker's (1986) work on the province's military history is similarly restricted by its emphasis on a frontier system whose existence is debatable. Isaac's (1990) and Millar's (1993) studies on the army in the east and cultural milieu of the Roman Near East lose much in being generalized studies, and, in the case of the latter, does not employ the archaeological evidence to anything like its potential. Nor is there anything comparable to MacAdam's (1994) and Schick's (1994) surveys of the countryside in Byzantine Jordan.

Chronology and Period Parameters

The Romans first impinged politically on the region in the mid-first century BC as a consequence of Pompey's actions in Syria and then in Judaea. At this time the bulk of the region formed the kingdom of Nabataea. One of the consequences of Pompey's intervention was the creation of the league of cities known as the Decapolis. The precise form and function of this federation of Hellenistic cities remains unclear. One school of thought sees it as a cultural entity—islands of Greek culture in a Semitic ocean. More plausible is that it was a group of communities released from Seleucid, Hasmonean and Nabataean domination and made the responsibility of the Roman governor of Syria. "Member" cities, although it is clear that the "league" was never formally constituted, included Gerasa (known as Antioch Chrysorhoas in the second century ad: modern Jarash) (Figure 13.2), Pella (modern Tabaqat Fahl), Gadara (modern Umm Qays) (Figure 13.4), Abila (modern Quwayliba) (Figure 13.5), Philadelphia (= Rabbath-Ammon: modern Amman) (Figure 13.3), Capitolias (= ancient? Raphana, Arbela: modern Bayt Ras), Hippos (modern Qalat Husn/Susiya) and Dium (location unknown) and to the north, in Syria, Damascus and Canatha (modern Qanawat). It is safe to assume that the Jordanian Decapolis cities must have enjoyed at least contiguous territories.

In subsequent Roman history the Nabataean kingdom played a marginal role in the Civil Wars. In ?6 BC, Augustus initiated a campaign, led by the legate Aelius Gallus, to Arabia Felix from Egypt. Bowersock's (1983: 45) hypothesis, on a reading of Strabo (16.4.21), that Nabataea became a (temporary) Roman possession in c. 2 BC is attractive. However, for the rest of the first century AD the region is almost totally anonymous in Greek and Latin sources. We are reliant on Nabataean inscriptions, fleshed out in part by Josephus's account of events in the Jewish world, for a chronology of events and developments in the region. In AD 106 the Nabataean kingdom was annexed as the new province of Arabia (Freeman 1996). While the circumstances behind the decision on Rome's part to annex the region following the death of Rabbel II, the last Nabataean king, are obscure, a number of developments have been dated to the immediate aftermath of the action. It appears, for instance, that the Decapolis was broken up with the transfer of Gadara and Pella to the province of Syria. The majority of the other communities became the responsibility of the governor of Arabia. At this time there is also the appearance of a new era for dating in Arabia which did not use the traditional regnal convention but had as its epoch the arrival of the Roman governor in Bostra. The annexation has been seen in some circles as inevitable; elsewhere as being the result of the force of circumstances. The only certain events that can be placed in this period are the commencement of the recruiting of Nabataean units into the Roman army from c. 113 and the erection of milestones on the Via Nova Traiana running from Aila to the borders of Syria. The tendency has been to regard this road as a coherent unit, one constructed to facilitate the process of annexation. Something, however, is lost in this characterization. The road, rather than being a fresh construction, may have been the consolidation of an earlier route known in biblical sources as the King's Highway (Num 20.17; 21.22, though see Miller 1989). Dated milestones from along its length reveal that sections of it were (re-)built at different times (e.g. the southern part, Aqabah to Philadelphia in AD 111–112; the Bostra–Philadelphia section in AD 114). It is perhaps better then to see it more as a group of short stretches of roads linking communities than as a deliberate attempt to impose a strategic spine to the new province.

At about this time the city of Bostra is believed to have supplanted Petra as the "capital" of Nabataea, if that change had not already occurred under Rabbel II. It was under the emperor Trajan that Bostra was renamed, presumably in recognition of its new status, as Nea Traiane Bostra, while Petra was elevated to the status of a *metropolis*. Because the governors of the province were based in Bostra, as was the main garrison (the legion III Cyrenaica), it is commonly asserted that the city became the administrative centre of the province. It is known, however, that the governors were never bound to remain at Bostra. They were expected to tour their province on a regular basis, not least to hear legal cases, and so on in its major communities. At the same time, the epigraphy of the region shows that the cities continued to undertake the same range of administration that they had executed before Nabataea was annexed. The origins of that administrative framework go back to the Hellenistic city model. Similarly, it would seem that Bostra was not the financial capital of the province. Judging from the number of inscriptions put up by imperial financial officers, the procurators, Gerasa seems to have become the financial focus of the region, which in turn must be a reflection of its commercial pulling power over the other cities in the province. It may not be coincidental then that the emperor Hadrian wintered in Gerasa in AD 129/130, as commemorated in an inscription and arch put up in that city. As the emperor proceeded on to Jerusalem, it is highly plausible that he would have already visited Bostra, and, perhaps later on, communities such as Rabbath-Moab and Petra. The region may have enjoyed the dubious privilege of another imperial tour in AD 199 when the emperor Septimius Severus toured the eastern provinces. It is known that it was Severus who decided to enlarge the Arabian province, with the transfer to it of the Jabal Druze and the region of the Leja (e.g. the territory of Canatha). A further indication of Severus's interests in the region is the way that a number of Arabs seem to have benefited from his patronage at the imperial court in Rome. The emperor Caracalla (AD 211–218) raised Gerasa to the status of a *colonia*, with the name Aurelia Antoniniana, while the emperor Elagabalus (AD 219–222) did the same for Petra. Bostra

became a *metropolis* under Philip (AD 244–249) who also accorded privileges to his previously insignificant hometown Shabha, now renamed Philipopolis. By c. 300 an additional small legionary fortress had been constructed at Lajjun in central Jordan in order to accommodate the legio IV Martia recently transferred from western Europe, while by the early fourth century legio X Fretensis had moved from Jerusalem to a new base at Aila. Under Gallienus, in AD 262, the governorship of Arabia passed from a pro-praetorian legate to an equestrian *praeses*. Because of the problems of the Roman empire at the end of the third century, direct control of Arabia passed to the Palmyrenes, under Zenobia and Vaballuthus. Roman control was reasserted in AD 272. In or after AD 295 and the reforms of Diocletian, the old province of Arabia was partitioned as part of a broader scheme of administrative reforms. The region south of Wadi Hasa, combined with the Sinai and Negev, became the new province of Palestina Salutaris (later called Palestina Tertia) with its capital at Petra. The now smaller original province retained the old name. Both provinces were controlled by *duces*.

Roman Arabia was subject to a number of earthquakes that at various times have inflicted considerable damage to the province's communities. For instance, major earthquakes have been identified in the early second century AD, AD 306 and AD 363, with the last of these, which destroyed much of Petra, being especially destructive (Russell 1985). Numerous references and allusions to low-scale warfare involving nomads, Arabs and Saracens along with Roman responses also punctuate the history of the province. It is difficult, however, to pin down these events. They are largely undated and geographically vague coupled with a laxity in terminological precision (Bowersock 1983; Shahid 1984, 1989).

The Geography of Roman Arabia

At the time of its annexation, the northern boundary of the province would have extended into modern Syria, up to and beyond the ancient city of Bostra, the "provincial" capital. The Jordan Valley determined the western boundary of the province. With respect to the province's eastern and southern borders, this is not so much of an issue, primarily because this was desert. The boundaries of the province were probably in the first place those of the Nabataean kingdom, and would thus, in the north and west, have been determined by the boundaries of the city-states in those areas. In north and northwest Arabia, some of the cities that had been part of the Decapolis since the mid-first century BC but nominally attached to the province of Syria were now added to Arabia. The communities affected included Philadelphia, Capitolias, Abila, Pella and Gadara. The boundaries of Pella and Gadara ran along the Jordan Valley and more than likely would also have been the province's western boundaries. As there were no comparable city-states to the east and south, the boundaries here were ephemeral or non-existent, defined by tribal territories, themselves liable to be vague and disputed. Still, there has been debate about whether Roman authority extended as far south as the Hisma or even Madain Salih. There was a slight modification of the province's boundaries sometime after the early fourth century AD but by this time the region had begun to merge into its Byzantine phase.

The Sources of Evidence

As it lies in what might be called the historic era, any summary of the region under the Romans has to refer to the disparate historical sources: few, if any, originated from the region. This material tends to be written within the framework of diplomatic, military and political relations of the eastern Roman empire. There are relatively few ancient sources that write of Arabia in the Roman period *sensu stricto*. The early first century AD geographical writer Strabo in book 16 of his *Geography* reports numerous ethnographic, historical and geographical anecdotes about the region. The country appears as a marginal area in Josephus's account of Jewish history down to the late first century AD in the *Jewish Antiquities* and *Jewish War*, but he does occasionally let slip some interesting incidental details. Those later historians that discuss the region, including the fourth century Latin historian Ammianus Marcellinus, are inevitably limited in scope and subject matter. Almost an anomaly, the cities of Gadara and, to a lesser degree, Pella, are known from Greek, Latin and Jewish literary sources to have had reputations for artistic accomplishment as well as something akin to leisure resorts.

Potentially more valuable are cartographic sources (Bowersock 1983: 164–186). Ptolemy's *Geography*, composed in the mid-second century AD, is a register of place names which provides co-ordinates and lists of the significant places, regions and tribes of Arabia at the time the document was compiled. The Peutinger Table, also of the mid-second century AD, is a map that describes the road system of the Roman empire at various times. The Arabian section evidently illustrates elements of the pre-Roman and later Roman provincial network. The same applies to the Antonine Itinerary, while the early fourth century AD *Notitia Dignitatum* is a summary, often not entirely reliable, of the military dispositions, by unit and location, of the Roman army in the region. The sixth century AD Madaba Map in the Church of St George is a mosaic which depicts the Holy Land and lists 157 cities from Tyre and Sidon in the north to Egypt in the south, and from east to west the Mediterranean coast and the Syrian Desert. Close analysis of the places recorded on the mosaic suggests that it is based on the fourth century *Onomasticon* of the Church historian Eusebius, who is an important source of information for the arrival of Christianity in the region and so indirectly about life in pagan Arabia.

Society, religion and the economy of the region rarely appear directly in the ancient sources, although the province's epigraphy offers a database which some scholars have started to exploit (MacAdam 1986a, 1990; Sartre 1982; Sartre 1986; Graf 1988, 1989; Macdonald 1993). Other than individual or small groups of inscriptions published in articles, Brünnow and von Domaszewski (1904–1909), Butler (1907–1919), and Kraeling (1938) have variously published the Latin and Greek inscriptions of the region. Subsequent survey and excavation projects have published inscriptions as they discover them. The bringing together of this evidence, a difficult task, has not enjoyed the most illustrious of histories (MacAdam 1986a, 1990). Work on the *Inscriptions grecques et latines de Syrie* (*IGLS*), which would have included Transjordan, began in 1905. In recent years, with the problems of the *IGLS* programme and the creation of a separate Jordanian state, this scheme has evolved into the *Inscriptions grecques et latines de Jordanie* (*IGLJ*), since modified to *Inscriptions de la Jordanie* (*IJ*). Five volumes of inscriptions and commentaries are planned of which volume 2, edited by Gatier, on the epigraphy of Central Jordan, including Amman, has been published (1986; and Gatier 1989: 54).

Finally, in recent years there has been published a collection of papyri from the caves above En Gedi at the southern end of the Dead Sea. These papyri are invaluable for understanding the condition of the region at the end of the first and early second century AD. The documents, the property of a Jewish widow who deposited them in the aftermath of the Bar Kochba rebellion of AD 132, are better known as the Babatha Archive. It includes a mishmash of documents referring to aspects of a number of legal disputes that Babatha got into with the families of her deceased (two) husbands over the years AD 93/94–132. While not explicitly related to the province, the documents indicate aspects of life in the region around Petra at about the time of the Roman annexation of Nabataea (Lewis 1989; Isaac 1992). At the other end of the time scale, the Petra Papyri, recently excavated from a Byzantine church in the city, date to the later sixth century. Preliminary readings of these documents show that they contain indirect evidence of earlier (Roman) aspects of life in the city and countryside around Petra (Humphrey 1995).

History of Fieldwork in Roman Jordan

The variable quality of research on the archaeology of (Roman) Jordan which has been noted is in part a consequence of the way that fieldwork in the region has evolved. Before attempting to summarize what is our present understanding of Roman Jordan, it is worth outlining what has conditioned the accumulation of that knowledge. In general terms, it is possible to isolate, over the 150 years or so that fieldwork has been conducted in the region, a number of broad shifts in research mentalities.

The earliest antiquarian-cum-archaeological explorations of Roman Jordan occurred in the early nineteenth century, although in truth these were not motivated purely by the cause of historical research (Geraty and Willis 1986; Khouri 1988). Here the emphasis was on visiting and recording the architectural splendours of what might be described as monumental sites, places such as Gerasa and Petra. The earliest (western) records of the archaeology of the region were the consequence of the exploits of explorers such as Seetzen's 1806–1807 visit to Gadara, Abila, Gerasa and Pella. Other explorers at this time include Burckhardt, whose original plan was to visit Makkah. One of the results of his sojourn in the region was the discovery of Petra in 1812 and a visit to Jarash. As the nineteenth century progressed, the pace of "scientific" investigation accelerated. In this respect, research was increasingly driven by the support of institutions and academic organizations established to support exploration, especially of sites with biblical associations, as well as to promote, if not safeguard, national interests. Burckhardt operated under the auspices of the Royal Geographical Society of London. The Palestine Exploration Fund was established in 1865 to obtain and disseminate "information respecting ancient and modern Syria (e.g. Syria, Lebanon, Jordan and Israel)...and the ancient and modern inhabitants thereof...the History, Literature...Ethnology, Mineralogy, Numismatics, Topography, Geography (physical and political), Geology, Zoology, Botany, Meteorology, Natural History and the manners and customs of the same (countries)." American involvement in the region went through an even more tortuous process (MacAdam 1986a).

In addition to the part played by governments and learned societies, the support of academic institutions became increasingly significant from the late nineteenth century. In 1897–98 Brünnow and von Domaszewski traversed the northern and central parts of the country, describing, mapping and photographing the major (Classical and Byzantine) sites, forts, roads and other monuments. This phase of exploration culminated at the turn of the century in two major American expeditions, both led by Butler: the 1899–1900 American Archaeological Expedition to Syria and the 1904–1905 and 1909 Princeton Archaeological Expedition to Syria. The common feature of this period was that research continued to be city/site specific, recording architecture, monuments, inscriptions and the evidence of Christianity. Following on from the work of Brünnow and von Domaszewski and Butler *et al.* in the north, the popular perception is that systematic archaeological work on Roman and Byzantine Jordan, if not entirely drawing to a halt, then slowed to a trickle until a resumption in the late 1960s (Bowersock 1971). This impression is valid for the military dimension, although Stein and Poidebard did add much relevant and (as subsequently shown) irrelevant material to the picture by the use of air reconnaissance (Gregory and Kennedy 1985; Kennedy and Riley 1990). However, there was progress in other aspects of the Roman archaeology of the region.

As archaeology in general in the early twentieth century came to be equated with excavation, so in Transjordan the same perceptions shaped research, with the digging, often in the name of conservation and restoration, of the same types of sites that had attracted attention in the previous century. From the second decade of the twentieth century a new phase of exploration in the region becomes evident. From 1917 down to 1950 Transjordan was administered under a British Mandate. In this arrangement antiquities were the responsibility of a (British-run) Department of Antiquities, which naturally enough tended to focus research on themes of interest to British (and, by implication, European and American) scholarship. This partition meant the *de facto* exclusion of German work in the region after the First World War, as well as the effective curtailment of other European activity too. After Jordan gained its independence, the same interests and priorities continued to influence work in Jordan, not least because the earliest directors of Antiquities were Britons. From the mid-1920s various British teams, initially under the auspices of the British School at Jerusalem and then later the newly created Department of Antiquities, began programmes of clearance work and so limited excavation. Horsfield commenced such work at Gerasa in 1925. This became the route by which the Americans gained an entry to the site, culminating in the publication of Kraeling's *Gerasa* (1938). Work at the site continued with Lankester Harding clearing the "Oval Piazza" and parts of the *cardo* and in the 1950s with Kirkbride's restoration of the South Theatre. In the meantime, Horsfield had moved to Petra where he commenced clearance work in 1929, which eventually culminated with Kirkbride, Parr and Wright each clearing a large part of the heart of the city in the 1950s and 1960s. Elsewhere, less romantically, field survey continued to be undertaken and was influential by initiating a new phase of research. Notable exponents at this time include the Americans Albright and Glueck. While their work may not have been to the highest methodological standards and both were more preoccupied with the identification of late (biblical) prehistoric sites, Glueck in particular located innumerable Roman and Byzantine sites, notably in his explorations in eastern Transjordan (Glueck 1934–1951; Parker 1976; Graf 1983).

From the late 1960s to the early 1970s the direction of archaeological work again shifted, with more extensive use of field survey. The reasons for the transition are numerous. Changes in research priorities, themselves a consequence of developments in archaeology in general, and recognition of the fact that sites are merely parts of larger (archaeological) landscapes are partly responsible. Equally significant is the way that the potential of commercial aviation made the region more accessible to Westerners. There was also the fact that politically the region was relatively stable. At about the same time the potential of (international) tourism was recognized by the Jordanian government who, with relative economic prosperity, encouraged foreign teams to explore the "traditional" sites as preparatory to developing them for tourism. The major initiatives of this period were the concentrated programmes of excavation at Petra and Jarash. At the latter site was created, in 1983, the Jarash Archaeological Project, "part of a comprehensive and long range programme of restoration and conservation of Jarash and its monuments. The Jordanian Government indeed recognizes both Petra and Jarash as the country's chief tourist attractions. They are thus of enormous value to the economy and their conservation and protection are prerequisites for increasing this source of income" (Hadidi in Zayadine 1986: 6). Work at Petra and Gerasa was assisted not least because the two sites are relatively unencumbered with the over burden of subsequent reoccupation. The same cannot be said of the other major Roman-period sites. Gadara, which since the late 1970s has been largely a German monopoly under the auspices of the German Protestant Institute for Archaeology, is in part obscured by the late Ottoman settlement of Umm Qays (Weber 1990; Kerner 1994). Likewise Philadelphia is almost totally lost below Amman. In contrast Abila and Pella, while not built over, are covered by very substantial deposits of hillwash. Another of the consequences of this period of economic prosperity and the concomitant property boom was a refocusing of research priorities. With the Jordanian landscape under increased pressure from population growth, construction projects and agricultural and industrial exploitation, it was recognized by the late 1970s that part of the country's archaeological potential was diminishing before it was being identified. Field survey, now often used as a cheaper alternative to excavation, has increasingly been employed as a means of obtaining an overview of the archaeology of the region from which more intensive research might evolve. The culmination of these two tensions—academic research and the threat to Jordan's heritage—was the inception in 1987 of the Cultural Resources Management Programme (Tell *et al.* 1993). This is a joint Jordanian Department of Antiquities and American Center of Oriental Research (ACOR) initiative which is an umbrella title for a number of actions ranging from impact assessments in advance of construction work to statutory protection and exploration. The programme is also intimately linked with the JADIS (Jordan Antiquities Database and Information System), an initiative funded by the United States Agency for International Development (USAID), a computerized database for the registration and recording of archaeological sites from published information and archive files (Palumbo 1993).

The purpose of the preceding résumé is to explain the strengths and inadequacies of our understanding of Roman Jordan. Despite the massive upsurge in the range and quality of fieldwork in Jordan, there are still a number of problems which hinder efforts to synthesize the results of that work into a broader picture of the region under Roman administration. Excavation has long tended to concentrate almost exclusively on the "big" urban complexes (notably Gerasa and Petra, and more recently Pella, Abila and Gadara) and to a lesser degree, Umm Jimal, Madaba and Humayma, and even then only on aspects of these communities. It remains a fundamental issue whether it is valid to construct a history of the region based on the interpretation of developments that in the first instance pertain to those communities. The situation is not assisted by the variable degree of publication of the results of some of this work. The 1980s phase of work at Gerasa is now reasonably accessible (Zayadine 1986, 1989), as are the Amman results (Northedge 1992; Kanellopoulos 1994). Work at Pella has tended to emphasize the pre-Classical and especially prehistoric deposits (McNicoll 1982, 1992). Its Roman levels have also been covered and/or destroyed by Byzantine activity. Compounding this is the fact that the (civic) core of the city would have lain in Wadi Jirm in which the hillwash from Tall Husn has accumulated. Abila too has produced more about the Byzantine and Umayyad phases of its history than the Roman. Synthesis of the Abila and Gadara material is much less advanced, although both sites have enjoyed the prompt publication of interim, but still raw, statements (Mare 1994; Weber 1990). The fact that work at the pair is on-going has in part hindered interpretation, as it has at Humayma and Petra. The results of nearly 20 years of fieldwork at Umm Jimal are promised (de Vries 1998).

With this background, where certain "Roman" sites have attracted more attention and resources, gaps are now clearly apparent in other aspects of the region's "Roman" archaeology. One major deficiency has been at the southern terminus of the major "Roman" road through the country, ancient Aila, modern Aqaba, a site that has long lost out to its Byzantine/early Islamic successor (Zayadine 1994). The search has, however, begun for its Roman progenitor. This project involves a regional environmental and archaeological survey (the Southeast Wadi Arabah Survey) and excavation of the Roman/Byzantine city for insights into its economy (Parker 1997). Elsewhere, recent fieldwork has also indicated more of the sort of "large" towns that were often missed or ignored in the nineteenth century surveys. For instance, Tuwana (Ptolemy's Thana/Thoana, Thoruna in the Peutinger Table) is actually a series of complexes. Originating in the Nabataean period, its urbanization commenced in the first century BC and continued down to the late Byzantine period. Its evident prosperity has been linked to long-distance trade, its proximity to Petra and the Via Nova (Fiema 1993). The excavators of Tall Shuna in the Jordan Valley, while originally interested in the prehistory of the site, were struck by just how extensive were its Hellenistic, Roman and Byzantine deposits (Baird and Philip 1994). This was clearly a large site at this time, possibly as large as 25 ha, although little is currently known about the form and structure of this settlement. Unfortunately, understanding of the other communities in this hierarchy—the "small towns"—remains poor, although with the on-going exploration of the likes of Rabbathmoba, Charachmoba (modern Karak), Hisban, Humayma, Walid, Umm Rasas, Madaba and Udhruh there is potential. It is certain that more work at these sorts of sites will redress the balance in our understanding of settlements.

The greatest explosion of data has been in that amassed by field survey. Again, however, there exist problems in relating the results of even adjacent surveys, let alone those spread across the country. Survey, although able to accumulate data rapidly and cheaply, tends to be preconditioned by the strategy that determines how and what it accumulates (Banning 1996). Different approaches can also be conditioned by the terrain to be explored as well as, for want of a better expression, what might be labelled different national traditions or approaches to field survey. This is evident when trying to correlate the results of British, American and French fieldwork in the region. Likewise surveys can work on the micro-regional level (e.g. as part of just one wadi, and so tend to be intensive in their data retrieval) or a macro-regional dimension (and so are more extensive and, therefore, less concerned with detail). The situation is compounded by the way that some surveys have been one season long, while others have been conducted over a number of years and may consequently have evolved their methodologies. Surveys too have a tendency, in spite of the best efforts of the project, to be initially, at least, especially interested in specific periods or themes. The Southeast Arabah Survey is interested in the Nabataean/Roman/Byzantine settlement pattern to the north of Aqaba. The 1993 Madaba Plains Project was concerned mainly with inscriptions in a 5 km radius around Tall Umayri. The Jarash Regional Survey, despite its title, was more concerned with the Neolithic–Early Bronze Age transition. The Wadi Faynan Project involves a collection of different (British) teams looking at various aspects of the geology and archaeology of a number of environmental zones in a wadi complex due south of the Dead Sea (Barker *et al.* 1997). This sort of project, despite its attempts to integrate the various results of the constituent projects, typifies the problems involved in correlating survey data. The variable geography, topography and climate of Jordan are bound to have had an effect on settlement patterns. It is, therefore, going to be just as difficult to extrapolate a nationwide perspec-

tive from regional surveys. A final problem which complicates the issue of field survey is the unevenness in the processing and interpretation of the data that each survey has accumulated. Indicative of this particular problem is the way that Alcock (1994), while acknowledging the considerable increase in fieldwork in Jordan, still had recourse to just the Wadi Hasa survey in her summary of the Jordanian countryside in the Hellenistic period. Part of her problem is that surveys can easily become what Banning (1986) has called the creation of inventories of sites.

These factors explain that in attempting to summarize what is known of the archaeology of Roman Jordan certain aspects of it are better understood than others. In particular, certain "big" city sites predominate, where there has been considerable discussion about the form and evolution of their street plans and so the identification of building programmes (Barghouti 1982; Segal 1988, 1997). Histories of this limited sort can be constructed for Gerasa and Petra, into whose framework communities such as Pella, Gadara and Philadelphia can be reasonably accommodated. There is also scholarly attention on churches and Christianity, again because of the bias of western scholarship coupled with the fact that the evidence for them has been found in such cities.

Perhaps the greatest gap in our knowledge is what might have been occurring in the territories—the countryside—of these sorts of communities as well as in their larger counterparts. With the growth of field survey as a prospecting technique, this represents the biggest explosion of data available to the archaeologist. In its ancient sense the city was the smallest politically autonomous community, although in reality the degree of autonomy was restricted when the city was a possession of kings and empires. In this definition the city-state was the combination of the principal community (after which the city took its name) and satellite towns, villages and hamlets as well as the countryside (*chora*). The two elements, namely, of city and territory, were indivisible. And yet, for all the regional surveys that have been undertaken, it is disappointing to report just how little is known about these sorts of relationships in the Roman period. There have been undertaken a number of surveys of regions that must have lain within the territories of some of the major cities (Homès-Fredericq and Hennessy 1989: 13-97). For instance, Wadi Yabis lies between Pella and Gerasa and Wadi Arab between Irbid and Gadara. Both wadis have been surveyed recently. However, such projects are frequently hindered or limited by the research biases noted above. In contrast, despite its title, the Greater Amman Survey (Abu Dayyah *et al.* 1991) is not really a systematic attempt to explore the territory of the city at any time in its past. Instead, it is more an exercise in trying to record sites as they emerge and/or are destroyed as the modern city grows. Its links with the Cultural Resource Management Programme are obvious. As a part of the excavation of the large late Roman, Byzantine and Umayyad town at Udhruh, Killick (1983) undertook a survey of some 800 km² of its hinterland. While not a "classical" city by any stretch of the imagination, not least because very little is known of it, the Southeast Arabah Survey has been looking at the countryside around Nabataean and Roman Aqabah (Smith *et al.* 1997). More specifically, only recently has work been directed towards exploration of the territories of Gerasa and Pella (Koucky in McNicoll *et al.* 1992; Watson 1996). The potential for the exploration of the territory of Gerasa has been increased immeasurably by the discovery of a series of marker stones which appear to delimit at least the eastern fringes of the city and so provide an indication of the resources that were available within its *territorium* (Seigne 1997). This should complement earlier surveys that have been conducted in the region (Hanbury-Tenison 1987; Sapin 1987). Another aspect of the archaeology of the Roman countryside, one little explored, are the Roman deposits and architectural fragments scattered around many of the modern agricultural communities in the vicinity of Gerasa. Many of the (modern) communities in its vicinity, places such as Khirbat Qusayr southwest of the city, are generously scattered with Roman architectural fragments and other surface detritus and as such would almost certainly reward further investigation.

There is one more comment to be made about our relatively poor understanding of the archaeology of Roman Jordan. The range of field techniques has until recently been limited to a combination of traditional architectural studies, excavation and lately various forms of field survey. There has been the failure in the past, for understandable reasons, to use other forms of reconnaissance evidence. The obvious example in this respect is air photography, although the situation is beginning to change (Kennedy and Riley 1990; Kennedy 1998). Other forms of remote sensing technology, including Geographic Information Systems, are becoming increasingly used. The potential of these methods to provide a better understanding of the archaeology of Jordan as a whole is almost infinite.

A good example of the potential of new approaches to data collection with respect to the ancient countryside is to be found in the Umm Jimal report (de Vries 1998). While reporting on work in the town itself, that work concentrated mainly on excavation and survey of the main settlement. In doing so, it has identified the Nabataean antecedent to the visible Roman and early Byzantine site that attracts visitors today. However, exploration of the countryside around the site was not originally given a high profile in the project. More recently, Kennedy (1998) has used a set of aerial photographs taken in 1953 to identify sites on the swathe of land covered by the 1:50,000 K737 map of the Umm Jimal area, some 400 square kilometres. On these photographs were identified over 1050 "sites" of 22 different morphological types, making for an average site density of 2.5 per square kilometre. Of course the main problem with this sort of approach is that the air photographs fail to distinguish between different periods of activity, which could range from prehistoric to modern, but certain patterns can be identified, not least when the results are tested against ground proofing. At the very least, this particular exercise has served to provide an indication of just how intensively exploited was a region that had previously been imagined to be too desolate and desiccated to have been farmed in the past. Comparable studies of other parts of northern Jordan are promised. Assisting in the understanding of the importance of agriculture in Roman Jordan, field survey is constantly hinting at preserved ancient landscapes made up of field systems and clearance zones. Kennedy has identified what look to be extensive Hellenistic-Nabataean-Roman field systems in the Hauran region in the north of the country, while comparable systems have been seen in Wadi Faynan in the south (Kennedy, MacAdam and Riley 1986; Kennedy and Freeman 1995; Barker *et al.* 1997, 2007).

It is because of the absence of work on the relationship between town and country that what can be said of society and the economy in the Roman period is hampered. Our understanding of religion too is limited principally to urban-based cults, with some notable exceptions. However, one positive feature is that the situation with regard to the military history of the region is in some respects immeasurably better but in others similarly impaired. The evidence available is sufficient for the writing of a history of the defence of the province, but of only one dimension: namely its eastern (i.e. desert) margins. The issue of the relationship of the military to the city and towns (and so the countryside) remains neglected, if not ignored. Bearing in mind these comments, the following account is as much a summary of the current state of progress in the archaeology of Roman Jordan as a pointer to potential areas of research. Irrespective of these general comments, a number of recurring features in excavations and field surveys can be discerned.

Cities, Towns and the Countryside

As is well documented, there are a number of unmistakably Graeco-Roman cities in Jordan, namely, Gerasa (Figure 13.2), Philadelphia (Figure 13.3), Capitolias, Gadara (Figure 13.4) and Abila (Figure 13.5), as well as Petra in the south and Bostra in what is now Syria (and which is excluded from this discussion). Because of it being so far south and because of its unique location and architecture, there is a temptation to regard Petra as something of an exception to the picture in the northern cities that conversely often tend to be treated as a homogeneous group. However, in writing about all of these cities, there are a number of problems. We know next to nothing about their origins, other than that all these sites show evidence of prehistoric occupation (as far back as the Middle Pal-aeolithic), as revealed at Abila, Pella, Philadelphia, Gerasa and Petra. With the exception of Petra, they all appear to have been (re-)founded in the early Hellenistic period and to have thrived thereafter. On the other hand, little or no early Hellenistic occupation has so far been found at Petra. Indeed, there is relatively little "Roman" data from this site, and that which exists is frequently problematic (Parr 1996). Our next problem is that not much is known about the shape or form of these foundations. This is an important issue because it may have had a bearing on the development of the communities in the Roman period. Unfortunately, a combination of little work, post-Hellen-istic destruction and the re-utilization of those Hellenistic features and structures makes discerning this difficult. In the past it was common to believe that it was the Roman occupation of Arabia that provided the impetus or second wind for urbanization in Arabia. However, archaeologi-cal work is constantly demonstrating that this is not the case and that much of what has traditionally been attrib-uted to the early second century can be traced back into the first century BC/AD. For instance, the street plan of Roman Gerasa (Figure 13.2), evidently redefined in the second century AD, owed much more to a Hellenistic antecedent than was once imagined before being re-mod-elled in the mid-first century AD. The same applies to Bostra, where the framework of the city's layout is now known to have been created in the first century AD, under the Nabataeans, rather than as a consequence of the Rom-an occupation and the establishment of power there. Of Philadelphia, a Hellenistic (re-)foundation (Figure 13.3), it cannot be said if its plan was a Hellenistic or Roman adaptation. All of its extant buildings date to the second–third centuries AD, with the rest, along with its street plan, lost beneath the modern city.

The cumulative impression is that the layouts of the street plans of these cities show more than just a little care. The best example of this is Philadelphia where the city planners, whoever they were, were faced with an espe-cially difficult topographic canvas. The site lies in a deeply incised valley (Wadi Amman), joined by subsidiary wadis, all of which dissect a limestone plateau that comprises a number of peaks (e.g. Jabal Amman). The wadi has a per-ennial stream, fed by the spring Ras al-Ayn, 1 km south-west of the ancient town. Into this wadi was placed the *decumanus maximus*, probably built before AD 160, and the other civic accoutrements of a major Graeco-Roman community. The constricted location meant that it was not able to develop a full-blown street grid, which itself could be useful today for identifying the evolution of the city. It could only really spread to the southwest and the east. Unfortunately, with the way that "down town" Amman has grown up in Wadi Amman, on present evi-dence it is not possible to identify any traces of a Hel-lenistic plan.

In contrast to Philadelphia, the topography of Gerasa is much simpler. The visible remains appear, superficially, to suggest that the public buildings of the city were con-structed on the western bank of the Chrysorohas River. Admittedly, largely on negative evidence, it has been assumed by some that on the eastern side of the river, under the modern town of Jarash, would have been most of the city's domestic quarter. However, recent excava-tions have shown that private residences existed in the western sector of the site. It would also be speculative, if not foolhardy, to argue that there was ever a split between public and private organization of the city. The evidence from the western part of the city shows that much of the road network here originated in the late Hellenistic era, with minor readjustment of *insulae* in the Roman period, along with the attaching to it of new streets on largely the same alignments. Work commenced on the Temple of Zeus (Olympias) in at least AD 22/23 (although there must have been a Hellenistic foundation below it), at the South Theatre (AD 90/91) and the "Oval Piazza'. What is striking in all this work is that in the case of the former, at least, construction was funded in part by private do-nations. This sort of benefaction was common enough for citizens of such communities, but in this example the contribution was made by a Roman official at a time when the city was extra-provincial. Similar gifts from Roman officials and soldiers become increasingly com-mon throughout the first century AD.

The two principal roads of the city are still visible at Gadara (Figure 13.4). It is difficult, however, to say much about the development of the site because there are very few extant structures in the lower part of the city (e.g. to the west of the acropolis) to project the arrangement of the subsidiary roads. The city was founded by the Ptolemies as a military colony in the Yarmuk Valley. Unfortunately the heart of that and the subsequent community would have been on the natural hill that became its acropolis and has always been attractive for settlement. However, recent excavations have discovered incontrovertible evidence of (early) Hellenistic deposits (Kerner 1994). The road from the west (Tiberias) Gate to the Jordan Valley was paved in c. AD 50–100, along with the appearance of a necropolis on both sides of the street. Also constructed at this time was the Tiberiade Gate (so-called because of its similari-ties with a comparable gate excavated at nearby Tiberias; Weber 1991a). This was a pair of circular towers forming a gate some 600 m beyond the city's west walls. Its purpose, outside a set of functioning city gates, is enigmatic. The excavators' view that it represented a customs or border post on the outskirts of the city is unconvincing. Excava-tions have exposed part of the southwest corner of the city wall on the south side of the acropolis, built sometime between 100 and 50 BC. This was evidently demolished some 100 years later (Josephus, *Ant.* 4.416). That this was the case is not difficult to understand. The first century

BC/AD was, generally speaking, a period of stability, admittedly with the occasional blip. That period is reflected in the building work that has been dated to this period. Above all, it was Petra that seems to have prospered most at this time. During this time were constructed its theatre and a number of major civic temples, the *decumanus* and the temple known today as the Qasr al-Bint (McKenzie 1990; but see Parr 1996 for counter-arguments; Fiema 2000). This prosperity and a sense of public-spirited community clearly continued, perhaps even accelerated, into the second century AD.

In all of this discussion of the Decapolis cities conspicuous by their absence are Capitolias, Abila and Pella, where the evidence is so poor that it is difficult even to estimate with any confidence the alignment of their *decumani* let alone what went with them. Pella, destroyed by Alexander Jannaeus in 83 BC, was still evidently in ruins by the time that Pompey passed through the region. Its rebirth as an urban complex seems to have been delayed to the late first century AD, when a new street layout with public buildings was established over the Hellenistic ruins in Wadi Jirm. Constructed after this were the *odeon*, public baths, a public courtyard (*parvis*) and *agora*. Coins of the city also suggest that a *nymphaeum* and at least one major temple still await discovery. The fact that so little is known about Roman Pella has led one commentator to observe that "the Roman Decapolis city does not seem to have been as impressive as some of the other contemporary cities" (Smith and McNicoll 1992: 135). The failure to define Roman Pella is due to the overburden which now covers the site. It has been hypothesized that it may have also been a small community, perhaps affected by population decline at this time. The available evidence suggests that its main period of prosperity was in the fifth century AD (as it was in the other cities) although it must be noted that this may be more a reflection of the nature of the work that has been done at the site than historical fact (Smith and McNicoll 1992). Farther south, on-going excavations at Aila have found the Nabataean and Roman town and demonstrated that it was largely a creation of the first century BC. There does not appear to be a Hellenistic antecedent to the settlement (Parker 1997). The town continued into the Late Roman and Byzantine periods with its rise and success being attributed to the development of the trade route through the Gulf of Aqaba.

Although, as has been noted, the first century AD witnessed significant building work at most of the major cities of Arabia, still the second century AD is striking for the quantity and quality of construction. The bulk of the public buildings at Philadelphia date to this century, perhaps as part of a coherent scheme. Those structures built include the *agora*, theatre, public baths and portico. In addition, inscriptions from the city point to the existence of a council house and a *gymnasium*. Elsewhere, at Gadara, the *nymphaeum* adjacent to the *decumanus maximus* preserves dedications of the second century AD. It is believed that the city expanded westward in the same century, away from the (Hellenistic) *acropolis* and heart of the original city. Once the city's west wall/gate had been established, there was then constructed a hippodrome and monumental arch farther west, and so beyond the west gate, in a fashion that also occurred at Gerasa. At Gerasa the central part of the *cardo* was widened in the second century AD. The South Theatre was reconstructed in the early part of the same century, and in the period AD 161–166, at a time when the Temple of Herakles/Hercules was being completed at Philadelphia, the Temple of Zeus Olympias was embellished further. In AD 129/130, in light of Hadrian's visit, the city's Triumphal Arch was erected. Standing so far south of the city's walls, it has been suggested that its position reflected aspirations to extend the city. This work was followed by the hippodrome (c. AD 140) and in c. AD 150 by the *propylaea* of the Artemis temple, which itself necessitated changes in the vicinity of the temple. Still later, the so-called "Eastern Baths" and the North Theatre (or *odeon*) were added in AD 162–166. What is significant in this, as with the earlier building activity, is that it would have all been funded by private donations and benefactions (*euergetism*), as is reflected in the city's epigraphy.

There has been, in the past, a temptation to attribute those developments in Arabia that can be dated to the second century AD and after to direct Roman intervention, perhaps on the part of emperors or through their governors. However, the degree of imperial initiatives is debatable. Recent work is repeatedly showing that the towns and cities of the region prospered before the Roman annexation, although their success may be an indirect consequence of the relative stability that Roman suzerainty in the wider region brought. That stability and thus prosperity continued when Nabataea became a full Roman possession. In addition to this, the degree of intervention from the Roman authorities in local government was minimal. Communities appear to have retained their pre-Roman administrative frameworks and control of their resources, other than the taxation that they were expected to provide. Where the contribution of Romans to building work is preserved, this should be interpreted as a reflection of the sort of personal patronage that underscored social relations in the ancient world rather than a reflection of imperial policy. The one potential exception to this impression is Petra. Fiema (2000) has summarized the evidence for pre-Roman and Roman-period building activities in the city. Those that appear to post-date AD 106, he has tentatively linked with refurbishment following an earthquake of c. AD 113. This may have been assisted by relief from the imperial power. That said, he is as prepared to see them as the result of an influx of wealth and stability following the annexation.

The impression of prosperity in the major cities in the

second and early third centuries AD is paralleled in some of their smaller counterparts. At Umm Jimal it has been found that an earlier, possibly Nabataean, "rural" settlement was destroyed sometime in the third century AD, perhaps during the Palmyrene interlude, after which the focus of the community shifted some 300 m westwards to another site that appears to have been developing since the mid-second century AD. This settlement, the one that is visible today, prospered throughout the Byzantine period, defended by a *prae-torium/castellum* of the late third century AD, built under the emperor Diocletian. This would imply that Umm Jimal was an important part in the later Roman defence systems (de Vries 1998). As a word of caution, it has to be said that this picture might not be universal. It may be the case that the broad picture is not consistent or uniform. For instance, at Humayma (ancient Auara), where there was a sizeable pre-Roman Nabataean community founded under Aretas III and an early (e.g. second/third century) Roman fort perhaps built on

an earlier Nabataean one, there is at present little sign of the Roman period between the Nabataean and Byzantine horizons, other than a second century AD bath house. The fort was probably abandoned in the late third century, then renovated for domestic occupation in the fourth century.

It is a truism, but another aspect of city life is that people lived in them. In the past, however, this simple fact lost out to grander research schemes. As regards domestic and private accommodation, as is to be expected where there has been excavation, there is good evidence for seamless continuity from pre-Roman to Roman-period housing. For instance, Late Roman houses have been found on top of late Nabataean dwellings at Petra. Unfortunately, these were subsequently buried under or incorporated into Byzantine structures (e.g. as with the recently excavated "Petra church" constructed c. AD 363; Z. Fiema pers. comm.). Excavations by Zeitler (1990) revealed two complete buildings and part of a third in the east of the city. The earliest stone-built structure, a rec-

Figure 13.2 Gerasa of the Decapolis (Jarash).

Figure 13.3 Philadelphia of the Decapolis (Amman).

tangular unit measuring 2.8 × 2.6 m, was erected 30/20 BC and abandoned at the start of the first century AD. In AD 50, after a period of dereliction, a second larger four room building (13 × 11.5 m) with a cistern was put up on the site. The third structure was placed beside this building. These two buildings were evidently destroyed (by an earthquake?) in the fourth century AD, after which they were further modified. Data recovered from the site revealed something of the diet of the occupants. The structures had their own bread kiln. Animal bones included much sheep/goat, but considerably less pig, dog, fish and bird. These dwellings complement those that have been excavated elsewhere in the city, at az-Zantur. Here the evidence of continuity spans the first four centuries AD (e.g. Stucky 1994). Houses were also found on the pre-second century AD acropolis at Philadelphia. However, these structures were then levelled when the temple complex was prepared. At Gerasa, a group of houses has been excavated in the vicinity of the "Oval Piazza" and along the southern *decumanus*. At Gadara, evidence of housing has been located perpendicular to the westward running *decumanus maximus*, in more-or-less rectangular blocks that are believed to date back to the Hellenistic period. Houses

have also been reported under the third century AD Roman bathhouse at Humayma. On a slightly larger scale, an archaeological park has been created at Madaba that has as its focal point the Roman street system using the *decumanus* and its adjacent buildings. Visible structures are mainly Byzantine churches built atop Roman-period domestic structures.

As already explained, what was occurring in the territories of these towns and cities at this time is difficult to discern. The situation is not helped by our inability to locate with any precision the territorial boundaries of the cities, which would in turn allow some estimations of their agricultural and other resource potential. The one exception to this is Gerasa, where recent discoveries of marker stones by Seigne (1997) have delineated at least parts of the eastern and southern extent of the *chora*. Parts of the territory of Petra have been explored by various survey projects but there has been little effort at correlating the results (Lindner 1989: 83). Otherwise the results of field survey remain too general, while there have been too few site-specific excavations. Despite this negative assessment, some interesting points are beginning to emerge. Broadly speaking, it seems that the Roman–

period was one of prosperity as reflected in
settlement densities than previously had been the
survey of Wadi Ziqlab in the northern Jordan Valley
that the most intensive settlement densities lay in
the Roman–Byzantine period (Khouri 1988: 15–20). In
the survey argued that the decline in settlement in
periods can be linked with erosion and colluviation.
deterioration not only has implications for the vis-
of sites during survey, but for the success of settle-
in general over time (Banning 1996). This picture
paralleled to a certain degree in Wadi Arab, where sur-
produced data that should be relevant to Gadara (and
a lesser extent Capitolias) and the upper Jordan Valley (Hanbury-Tenison et al. 1984). Topographically, this
was a mixed region which was going to make large-scale
arable farming difficult on the slopes between the valley
but easier on the plateau upon which Gadara lies. Therefore, we might envisage an emphasis on olive and grape
production in the hilly region and tillage on the plain.
Again, field survey has created a picture of increasing settlement densities through the Iron Age, Classical and Byzantine periods in this region. The Wadi Yabis Survey found
that in the Roman (and Byzantine) period settlement and
agricultural activity reached an all-time peak (Palumbo
et al. 1990). The South Hauran Survey in north Jordan
has tentatively concluded that there was an increase in
settlement densities in the Roman period compared to
the preceding Iron Age and Hellenistic periods (Kennedy
and Freeman 1995). Farther south, beyond the Dead Sea,
exploration of the Southern Ghors region and the northeast Arabah has demonstrated that they were extensively
occupied in the Nabataean–Roman–Byzantine periods
with clear continuity from the one to the other (Mac-

Donald 1992: 83–95). The same trend was identified in
Wadi Hasa, where Nabataean, Roman and, to a lesser
degree, Byzantine sites proved to be the most common
and where most of the sites explored were isolated farmsteads and small hamlets of a few households and corrals
(MacDonald (ed.) 1988; Clark et al. 1994). Likewise, the
Hisban Survey identified a progressive rise in rural settlement densities (LaBianca 1984 in Homès-Fredericq and
Hennessy 1989: 261–269). In this particular case, there
was also detected an accelerating trend towards "urbanization" (= nucleation), a process that reached its height
in the early Byzantine period. The Northwest Ard Karak
Survey identified many hamlets, isolated farmsteads and
campsites in a region that was extensively exploited under the Roman pax. Relative to the Wadi Faynan Project,
the objectives of which have been noted above, the most
substantial visible remains appear to be Roman and Byzantine in date (Barker et al. 1997). The Southeast Arabah
Survey, looking at the southeast sector of Wadi Arabah
and up to 7 km northeast of Aila, has suggested that the
Nabataean–Early Roman periods were marked by significant occupation densities which began to fall away in the
Late Roman–Byzantine periods. The rise in settlement
density under the Romans is linked with the development
of Aila and the rise of a regional road network in the first
and second centuries AD (Smith et al. 1997).

Although there have been numerous regional field
survey projects, few Roman-period rural sites have been
excavated. Their data and interpretation, nevertheless,
remains problematic. At Tall Faysal, located a few kilometres south of Gerasa and discovered in the early 1960s,
a structure that was originally erected in the late second
century AD and used on and off down to the twelfth or

Figure 13.4 Gadara of the Decapolis (Umm Qays).

Figure 13.5 Abila of the Decapolis (Quwayliba).

fourteenth centuries AD was excavated in 1991 (Palumbo *et al.* 1993). Because of its rectilinear shape it has been interpreted as a small fort or watchtower overlooking a crossing on the Zarqa River on the road between Gerasa and Philadelphia. However, it might as easily be interpreted as a farmstead. At Khirbat Faris, survey of an area 3 × 3 km and then excavation of a specific building revealed something of a Classical (and later) agricultural settlement, which seems to have been especially prosperous in the first and second centuries AD (McQuitty and Falkner 1993). Recent excavations at Khirbat Salameh have revealed a 14-room building of the Iron Age to Hellenistic and then Late Roman to Byzantine periods. While there is as yet no firm explanation of its purpose, it looks to have been part of an agricultural complex (Bikai 1994a).

How one is to explain the rise in settlement density in the Roman period is problematic. Direct Roman (imperial) stimulus seems unlikely. More attractive is the explanation that it is an indirect consequence of a trickle-down effect of the peace and prosperity that the *pax Romana* brought to a process that is evident in parts of the country

under the Nabataeans. After the burst of building activity in the towns and cities and the intensification in the exploitation of the countryside in the province, the momentum seems to have been lost. The amount and quality of civic building activity from the third century AD onwards declines significantly. Why the curtailment? Perhaps the momentum had reached a natural conclusion, where the cities now possessed most if not all the recognized features of major communities. For all of them exhibit the range of civic buildings expected of the typical Graeco-Roman city of the eastern Mediterranean: theatres (Abila, Philadelphia and Petra, along with three each at Gerasa and Gadara), basilicas/*stoa*s (Abila and possibly Gadara), odeons (Abila, Pella and Philadelphia), agora/fora/*macella* (Gerasa, Philadelphia, Pella, Petra and Gadara), public baths (Pella and Gerasa), *nymphaea* (Pella, Philadelphia and Gadara), (extra-mural) monumental gates and arches (Gadara, Petra and Gerasa) and hippodromes (Gerasa and Gadara). The fact that at Gerasa and Gadara at least some building work seems to have been left incomplete at this time implies something more serious. Work on the hippodrome at Gerasa, itself the smallest known Roman example (at 245 m long), commenced sometime between the mid-second century and AD 209/212, although it ceased to act as a public arena for horse races some 100 years later. It was then modified solely for games at its northern end in the late third and fourth centuries AD, after which its buildings were reoccupied for industrial and domestic purposes as well as for residences and a quarry for dressed stone. Its initial decline was due to its extremely poor foundations that caused the southwestern section of the complex to collapse (Ostrasz 1989). The end of the working life of the hippodrome came in the seventh century AD following a series of earthquakes. At Gadara, construction again started in the later third century AD but, in this case, was never completed. Looking at the historical framework, the failure to complete or repair civic structures may have something to do with the problems of the wider region and the turmoil of the Roman Empire in general. This may have had a knock-on effect on the commercial prosperity of the region which could no longer fund these sorts of (privately funded) building programmes. An alternative explanation or else contributory factor may have been the proximity of these communities to one another coupled with their common (Hellenistic) origins. It is known that the rivalry between certain cities in the Greek East could be counter-productive. Pliny's (*Epistles* 10.39–40, 49–50, 70-71, 98–99) account of the mess that a number of cities in the province of Bithynia got into shows how the attempts of some to match and outstrip the facilities that neighbouring cities possessed could ruin them. It requires no stretch of the imagination to see something similar in Roman Jordan, judging from the way that most of the cities seem to possess the same array of civic buildings and that they appear to have been erected at roughly the same time.

The provision of public amenities in the cities of the region is important because, indirectly, it permits estimates about the size of their populations. Ancient city records rarely provide breakdowns of population. Where there are figures they usually relate to male citizens and exclude women, children, slaves and resident non-citizens. In trying to calculate the size of populations, the capacity of certain public amenities can provide rough indications of the potential size. Unfortunately, our knowledge of the public facilities of the cities of Arabia is limited. The best known are those at Gerasa (Figure 13.2). Here the South Theatre is thought to have been able to seat 4000 spectators. The later North Theatre could accommodate 1600. Perhaps more indicative of a minimum size of the community is the capacity of the hippodrome which could hold 15,000. What cannot be taken into account in calculating a minimum size for the population of the city is the numbers living in and on the countryside. The reasons for this inability have already been explained. As such, estimates that the population of Jarash was in

the range 17,000–20,000 represent a minimum estimate for those living in just the city and not the city-territory. Similar estimates can be attempted with even less confidence for Philadelphia and Gadara.

The Military Dimension—the Defence of the Province

The military history of Roman Arabia is in part one of fluctuating diplomatic relations with the indigenous tribes rather than having to deal with any (major) external threats and invasions. In the first instance, there was the contact with the Nabataeans. Later on, when the Romans had moved into the region, the Ruwwafa inscription of AD 166/169 implies close ties between Rome and a Thamudic tribal confederation (Graf 1978; Parker 1986: 124). In the Palmyrene period, the Tanukh, an Arab tribe originally from the northeast Arabian Peninsula, migrated northwest to avoid Sassanid control. This led them into the Hauran where they formed a tribal confederation which came to ally itself with Rome and which helped Rome in the destruction of Zenobia. In the later fourth century AD we learn more and more about the Arabs with implications for their organization. For instance, there was Mavia and her "Saracens" in the AD 360/370s and the rise of the tribe of the Salih in the late fourth century AD, led by (Roman) *phylarchs*. It was these local potentates who came, in time, to assume responsibility for the defence of Arabia: the Kindites in the late fifth century AD and ultimately the Ghassanids in the later fifth–early sixth centuries AD (Graf 1988; Shahid 1984, 1989).

In the past, almost inevitably, the military occupation of the province has been written within the framework of the historical narratives, made tangible by those fort sites discovered by earlier field expeditions, notably those of Brünnow and von Domaszewski, Stein and Glueck. Added to this was the belief that the known activities of emperors elsewhere in the empire would have been paralleled by similar developments in Arabia. The military history has, therefore, usually been written in terms of frontier history. But for this approach to be valid, it has to: (1) identify who were the (frontier's) enemy, which in turn permits identification of (2) where the frontier was and (3) how it looked and functioned. Potential enemies who might have determined where the frontier was located have included the Parthians, the Arabs (also known as the Saracens), nomads and/or internal threats.

Credit for reawakening scholarly interest in the "Roman frontier" in Arabia lies with Parker's *Limes Arabicus* Project which commenced work in 1975 and ceased in 1993 (Parker 1986, 1987). This project was a combination of field survey, test excavation at selected sites and a concerted programme of excavation at the site of the legionary fortress at Lajjun. From this work Parker was able to construct a narrative history of the frontier. For the Roman period, that history might be summarized as follows:

(1) Following the annexation of 106 the Nabataean defensive network provided the initial framework for the Roman occupation, although not all Nabataean sites were occupied. Added to this arrangement was the work on the Via Nova Traiana. That said, the second century AD occupation of most forts in the region remains largely a blank.

(2) Under Septimius Severus the province's territory expanded northwards. The evidence of military activity indicates a major strengthening of the northern sector of the frontier, especially around Wadi Sirhan that implies, in Parker's opinion, trouble with nomads. There also occurred at this time a widespread repair to the road system. These developments are related to the aggressive frontier policy of Severus and in part to help his eastern campaigns in Mesopotamia. In contrast, the central and southern sectors appear to have been relatively quiet.

(3) Repairs to the road system, which was maintained until c. 250 AD, occurred in the mid-third century AD, after which the Arabian garrison was probably denuded to bolster the frontiers to the north. This process may be detected in the archaeological record, although the system was maintained as the denuding of other garrisons continued in the Palmyrenian period.

(4) While the garrison in Arabia was restored under the emperor Aurelian, it is more likely that it was one of his successors, probably Diocletian, who was responsible for the actual building restoration of the frontier. This involved a number of elements: repair of the existing road network, new forts and repairs, especially in the central sector of the frontier's forts (including the construction of a new legionary fortress at Lajjun), and the creation of the *strata Diocletiana* to protect southern Syria and north Arabia from Persian and Arab raids. Behind the garrisons stationed on the province's frontier road system, a reserve of mobile cavalry units (*equites*) was kept in the towns.

(5) The fourth/fifth century AD represents the most heavily fortified period of the *Limes Arabicus*, although it was essentially that system created by Diocletian.

> ...a broad fortified zone in Transjordan from Bostra to Aila and a secondary zone of defence in southern Palestine from the Mediterranean to the Dead Sea. All the legions and the bulk of the *auxilia* were deployed in the outer zone. This zone was designed to contain the attacks of the Hijaz tribes and control movement through Wadi Sirhan... The inner zone was crucial for the security of Palestine (Parker 1986: 145).

(6) The late fifth century AD saw the decline of the Arabian frontier's defences, with the cessation of build-

ing activity and the abandonment of forts. This was probably occasioned by the weakening of the garrison in response to problems elsewhere. The evidence from the frontier's central sector (including that from Lajjun) is that this was abandoned in c. AD 550. Few sites remained occupied in the southern sector. Only in the north is there evidence of continued Roman military activity. This decline was matched by another in the quality of the troops in late fifth/early sixth century AD Arabia.

Despite the neatness of Parker's explanation of the form and evolution of the Roman frontier in Arabia, there are a number of problems. Nearly all aspects of his work and interpretation have been subsequently challenged. These include his survey methodology, the accuracy of the ceramics sequence he used to date his sites and the presumption that datable occupation at his forts necessarily denotes military presence. However, the most aggressive debate concerns to what extent the "frontier" was designed to halt a nomadic threat. Parker's position has long been that it was so designed. In contrast, others have challenged, with reference to other criteria, virtually every aspect of Parker's views. For instance, there was never a real nomadic threat and the frontier was never a frontier-in-depth. A central element to understanding the defence of the province has been widely seen as the Via Nova Traiana. Unfortunately, as we have already seen, the known facts about the road are actually quite slight. It was evidently constructed between c. AD 111 and 114, probably from the south northwards. In turn, there is some debate as to whether or not military sites were located with particular reference to the road. The lack of other information permits any number of hypotheses as to how the frontier might have worked. It may have functioned in any number of guises, none so far decisively identified. Parker failed to take into account the part played by urban-based garrisons (which were based far from the frontier proper). As an army of occupation, perhaps it was meant to look to internal problems. Indeed, there was a failure on the part of the project to search for new forts elsewhere (e.g. away from the frontier and along the Jordan Valley). Finally, non-military aspects of the frontier were not addressed. In conclusion then, in light of these many criticisms, perhaps Parker's most lasting achievement of his work is that it reinvigorated the subject, generating a debate, often vigorous, which is on-going (Isaac 1988, 1990; Kennedy 1992; Graf 1986, 1989, 1997; Fiema 1995 against Parker 1992).

The subject of the province's defences includes the issue of urban fortifications. While it is clear that a number of communities did possess walls and towers to defend themselves, the nature and date of these fortifications is problematic because the evidence has been so neglected. At Gerasa, for instance, the location of only four gates to the city is currently known, although there must have been more. The dating of the provision of defences is usually established by dating the gates themselves. On the available information, there seems to be no consistent explanation for when fortifications were thrown up, but if they were contemporary it would imply a common response to problems in the region. One might suggest that the erection of urban defences need not reflect a deteriorating security situation but could be another aspect of the sense of rivalry and emulation that existed between the major cities. At Gerasa the walls were 3500 m long with over 100 towers and enclosed an area of 850,000 square m. The date of their erection is difficult to establish. They seem to have been built in AD 60–70. However, the North Gate replaced an earlier example in c. AD 115, a pattern that corresponds with the South Gate. In contrast at Gadara, the third century necropolis on the west side of the city was robbed for the construction of the (west) gate and wall. The date of the monumental gate at Gadara is problematic as excavation revealed no significant stratified finds. The excavators, however, have argued for a dedication in the late third century AD, under the Severan emperors (Hoffman 1990). If the parallel with Gerasa holds, where it has been argued that the erection of the gate there was in anticipation of or to persuade the imperial authorities (e.g. Hadrian?) to patronize the extension of the city, then at Gadara one would be tempted to link it with Septimius Severus's visit to the east. Alternatively, under Philip the Arab in the mid-third century AD the region benefited from much imperial patronage. The Tiberiade Gate has been dated to the second century AD (Weber 1991a). The reasons for this fortification are unknown but they may be contemporary with developments at Gerasa. By this time the westward expansion of Gadara had ceased. There are no known fortifications around the lower city of Philadelphia, although the citadel/acropolis appears to have been fortified in the second century AD, as part of the initiative that saw the completion of the Temple of Herakles/Hercules. These walls evidently served as defences for the whole town, or so Ammianus would suggest. Other towns in Arabia were provided with fortifications but these appear to date to the Byzantine period (e.g. as at Umm Rasas). The one exception is at Umm Jimal, where it has been argued on the basis of a now lost inscription that the town was fortified as early as the reign of Caracalla in the early third century AD. One site which does not fit entirely with the province's defences is that of Machaerus, a late Hellenistic–Early Roman palace and fortress 15 km north of Wadi Mujib on the eastern side of the Dead Sea. Used by the Jewish king Herod the Great, who also used the thermal springs at nearby Kallirrhoë (modern Zarka Main or else at Ayn Zara), in the First Jewish Revolt it was besieged and sacked by the Romans, as shown by the impressive siege works that are still visible around it.

Another element of the archaeology of the province which is frequently associated with the military history of the province is the form and evolution of its road network, as emphasized by discussions about the Via Nova Traiana and the Strata Diocletiana in the north of the country. Two distinct areas of research might be highlighted: (a) in the north, the work of Bauzou (1986) on the Via Nova Traiana and Kennedy (1982, 1997) on the road system in the South Hauran region (and to a lesser degree by MacAdam 1986a); and (b) towards the south, Graf has been for a number of years exploring the network of roads which fed into the Via Nova Traiana around and south of Petra (Graf 1995, 1997).

The Economy of the Province: Trade, Production and Agriculture

Measuring the economy of Roman Jordan covers a multitude of themes, ranging from the macro-to the micro-, from the local (e.g. the household) to the regional. Unfortunately, yet again, it is difficult to extrapolate a satisfactory interpretation of this evidence, derived as it is from a largely undigested database of field survey and limited excavation. One potential indicator of the economy of the region might be its coinage. Most of the cities before the Roman annexation minted their own coins. This privilege was frequently continued under the Romans. This is in itself a reflection of the often relaxed approach that they took to imperial government. It was, however, a privilege. Rome retained the sole authority to issue precious *specie* while at the same time curtailing and often removing the rights of cities to issue low denominations in their own name. The cities of the Decapolis are known to have minted coins well into the Roman period (Spijkerman 1978), but it is a contentious issue whether coinage is a direct or reliable indicator of the vitality of an economy. At the very least, there has been little study of the rise and fall in the circulation of coinage in Arabia that might in turn say something about the general state of the region at any particular time.

The strength of the province's economy has traditionally been measured by the vibrancy and quality of building work in its cities. In turn, the ability to initiate and fund this work is linked to the vitality of the (international) caravan long-distance trade that passed through the region, from the Far East to the Mediterranean (Miller 1969; Raschke 1978; Sidebotham 1986, 1991). It was the revenues of tax and the re-distribution and processing of these materials that is believed to have been the basis for the region's wealth. In turn, it is from this sort of trade that the evident prosperity of Petra in the first century BC/AD has been predicated. There may be something in the way that caravan trade indirectly funded building work. But just as fieldwork is constantly demonstrating that the countryside around these "caravan" communities was densely occupied (and thus intensively exploited?), so the raw foundation of these communities was based on their agricultural prosperity. The relatively high cost of land transportation in antiquity is well documented, which meant that the cities had to rely on local sources for everyday items. For the caravan trade was never noted for the movement of such basics as grain and olive oil, but rather for luxuries and exotica. It may not be coincidental that the (Jordanian) Decapolis cities are to be found on the high plateau of northwest Jordan, with Pella at the western foothills. This region, although hilly and interspersed with valleys, is today agriculturally productive and must have been so in antiquity. Foodstuffs must then have had to be acquired and so transported locally.

The emphasis that has been given in the past to the part of the caravan trade is due in part to the lasting influence of Rostovtzeff's *Caravan Cities* (1932), an important work which drew extensively from the results of the sort of limited fieldwork that had been completed up until the 1930s. In addition to this, there was Rostovtzeff's (flawed) perception of the form and organization of the ancient economy, a model that consistently underplayed the importance of land. Nowadays the balance has been redressed as exploitation of land is now seen to be the basis of the ancient economy. Reflecting this change, with reference to the economy of Pella, Smith (1987) has argued that while engaged in trade at all periods of its history, it could never have maintained its viability solely on the basis of the caravan trade. It must have been dependent on other sources or activities. Such observations must have implications for other cities in the region. The same line of argument has been applied to the settlement at Umm Jimal. That the site comprises substantial and extensive standing remains today has misled scholars in the past to see the basis of the town's wealth as being derived almost exclusively from the profits from the caravans. However, the plainness of the town's architecture, coupled with appreciation of its domestic buildings (houses with enclosed courtyards and ground floor as barns and stables), implies, on modern parallels, households principally concerned with farming. This does not deny, however, that the community might have benefited from stop-over traffic passing through the region.

The two exceptions to this picture are Petra and perhaps Aila, where at the former the evidence of excavation suggests that there is little Roman data from a city that seems to have flourished in the first and second centuries AD, judging from the building work that occurred at this time. Why the city should have gone into an architectural (and thus economic?) stagnation in the third century AD has been attributed to a decline in the amount of commercial traffic that passed through it in the Roman period. This was a result of a shift in caravan routes, when the Roman occupation of ancient Syria and Arabia is supposed to have created the conditions for a better protected and more reliable route from the east than the preceding route through the Persian Gulf and the Arabian

Peninsula. The consequences of this shift were that the communities farther north, such as Gerasa, profited in turn. Parker's work at Aila is rather ambitiously trying to address the question: "What was Aila's role in international trade between the Roman Empire and its neighbours?" (1997: 25). The evidence recovered so far shows that materials from the western and eastern Mediterranean and Egypt were passing through it. Literary sources also attest to its vibrant commercial links with the Far East.

Archaeology has also revealed something of the micro-regional production of everyday objects. But this is a far from complete picture. Shops have been discovered along the main roads of most of the major cities of the region. More formal market or commercial places (*agora*, *fora* and *macella*) are known at a number of sites. Recent excavations in Gerasa of an octagonal-shaped building at the southern end of the *cardo* and just north of the Oval Piazza exposed a *macellum* which was constructed c. AD 125 but which went through a substantial refurbishment in the late second–early third century AD (Martin-Bueno 1992). Segal (1997) has made the highly attractive suggestion that a similar-shaped building currently being excavated at Gadara may also have been a *macellum*. There is also the temptation to regard any large open spaces at the heart of cities and towns as *fora*. At least two such areas have been identified at Gerasa (e.g. the Oval Piazza and one adjacent to the North Theatre). At Petra, there are three suspiciously large terraces above the *cardo*. These have been seen as *fora* for the city, an idea that has its attractions, not least because they seem to be linked to a range of shops along the *cardo*. They are known today as the Upper Market. In addition to these commercial zones, we know quite a lot about particular industries in particular cities (e.g. the Jarash Bowl industry at late Gerasa, [Watson 1989]) but have difficulty in relating them to each other or to the wider economy of the individual cities. Metalworking, glass production and pottery kilns, as well as quarries, are now common enough discoveries at the major city sites. Parker's (1997) excavations at Aqabah have exposed a second-to fourth century AD complex of bread kilns and pottery workshops.

Religious life

Most of what can be said about religious life in the Roman province is derived yet again from what was occurring in its cities. In general terms, there has been a considerable failure to explore regional cult centres like that at Si in southern Syria (Dentzer 1986). One exception is the Nabataean temple at Wadi Ramm in southern Jordan. Excavated in 1959, the complex seems to have been dedicated to the Nabataean goddess Allat in the first century BC or early first century AD. A similar complex is that at Khirbat Tannur, 23 km southwest of the Dead Sea, which was again founded in the first century BC and continued into the second century AD. This demonstrates yet another factor that has to be taken into account when considering religious life in Roman Jordan, namely, the longevity of religious sites and where the deity venerated could also evolve and/or be replaced by another. Likewise, there is the Roman propensity to adopt and manipulate regional deities to its own end. It should also be borne in mind that if the Roman occupation of Nabataean Arabia does not mark a cultural divide, we should have no problem in envisaging a continuity in indigenous religious practices. Pre-Roman deities are known to have continued in Gerasa where the Nabataean cult of Dushara (akin to the Greek Dionysius) is attested, as well as Pacides and another "Arab" god (Welles 1938: Nos. 2, 17–22, 192). The cult of Maiuma at Gerasa, which was later associated with a Graeco-Roman festival celebrating the goddess Artemis, was probably originally a Phoenician cult that was later equated with the cult of Artemis. Its cult was later converted to a Christian "harvest festival." As elsewhere in the empire, the cities of the region played a part in the imperial cult along with the associated priesthood. Furthermore, a cult of Tiberius is known in Gerasa as early as AD 42/43.

It is inscriptions that refer to the existence of specific cults of a variety of deities in most of the region's cities and so indirectly to their worship at temples and shrines. The sites of most of these cults unfortunately remain to be located. However, an interesting feature common to Philadelphia, Pella, Gerasa, Abila and perhaps Gadara (Figures 13.2–5) is the way that each appears to have had substantial temple complexes in prominent, natural positions and that these positions were enhanced architecturally. Something similar may be visible at Tall Shuna (N) (Baird and Philip 1994). They all also show evidence of long occupation sequences that might imply a continuity in function. Each of these religious complexes was dedicated to different deities, which would serve to enhance the idea that these were specialist cult centres (e.g. of Herakles/Hercules at Philadelphia and Artemis at Gerasa).

At Philadelphia there is the so-called Great Temple, more commonly known as the Temple of Herakles/Hercules, set at the southern end of the acropolis and not the highest spot (Figure 13.3). This position made the temple more visible to the lower city and must be a reflection of its importance to the community. The acropolis was unfortunately heavily re-used in the early Islamic era which has meant that much of the detail of the temple is now lost (Bowsher 1992). Measuring 43.8 x 27.5 m, it was set on an artificial platform with a courtyard at its front. The entire complex was linked to the lower city by a monumental staircase which zig-zagged its way down the southern slope of the acropolis to a monumental *propylaeum* built on the northern side of the east–west *decumanus* which lay at the base of the acropolis. Inscriptions imply that the temple was dedicated between AD 161 and 167, which in turn provides a *terminus ante quem* for the *decu-*

manus (and thus the layout of the lower city). The temple was probably placed on the site, cleared in the early second century AD, of an earlier cult centre, perhaps the Ammonite deity Milkom, who in the Hellenistic period came to be equated with Herakles. The cult had its own festival in the Roman period. The Herakles temple, however, was not the only cultic establishment built on the acropolis, but was probably part of a scheme to accommodate a number of other temples. There is evidence for at least two other temples, namely, one dedicated to Tyche and the other known today as the Northern Temple. The Herakles site has more recently been subject to consolidation and restoration work carried out by the Department of Antiquities and the American Center of Oriental Research (Kanellopoulos 1994). Recently Bikai (1994b) has published the results of excavations on a sixth-to seventh century AD church on the Jabal Luweibdeh. He has made the intriguing suggestion that this church incorporated material, if not the actual site, of an earlier Roman building, perhaps a temple. The likelihood is that the church was dedicated to St George, a saint who is known to have been equated with Herakles in the transition from paganism to Christianity.

While the Philadelphia temple is badly preserved, the best examples of cults placed on prominent sites that retained a spiritual significance over time are the Temples of Zeus (Olympias) and the Temple of Artemis and its Sanctuary at Gerasa (Figure 13.2). The Temple of Zeus, situated on a prominent rise at the south of the city, was placed on a site that shows occupation from the Middle Bronze and Iron Ages onwards. In AD 22/23 a new temple was built, although there had been a Hellenistic foundation on the site. It was further embellished, evidently under the patronage of a Roman governor, sometime between AD 161 and 167. This temple comprised a series of terraces that accommodated the hill's steep slope. It was presumably intimately linked with the South Theatre which was attached to the site. Judging by the size of the temple, the cult of Zeus at Gerasa was surpassed by another, that of Artemis, who was the community's protecting deity. The Temple of Artemis complex was an all-the-more substantial structure, deliberately and carefully planned to incorporate a number of mutually supportive elements (Kalayan 1982; Parapetti 1982). Five components can be highlighted in this scheme. From the eastern half of the city there was a *propylaeum* which entered another *propylaeum* on the western side of the *cardo*. Part of the temple complex, therefore, stretched over one of the city's principal roads. This second *propylaeum* led to the third element, an outer court before the temple court and finally the temple itself. This work involved complex engineering as it took in the slopes and hill terraces as part of the monumental approach to the temple. Work on the temple commenced in AD 79/80, with the addition of the *propylaea* in c. AD 150. This addition caused a change in the area immediately around the temple. Surprisingly, no pre-temple building is currently known at this site, although there must surely have been one. As already noted, a form of the Artemis cult, that of Maiuma, was celebrated elsewhere at Gerasa, at the Birketein complex, 1.2 km north of the city, which possessed two bathing/reservoir pools and a festival theatre. Finally, the so-called Great Cathedral at Gerasa, dedicated in c. AD 365, is believed to have re-used the impressive temple of an unnamed deity which was perhaps erected in the first century AD.

At Pella, the civic complex was positioned below Tall Husn, in Wadi Jirm. Coins of the city depict a large temple so far unlocated but presumably on the *tall*. Excavation in Wadi Jirm has revealed Roman buildings which, repaired in the fourth/fifth century AD, were possibly part of the temeno*s* or *propylaeum* of a major Classical-period sanctuary. In the case of Abila, another site sandwiched between two principal hills, Tall Abila and Khirbat Umm Amad, excavations on the former have exposed a substantial sixth century AD basilica which in turn appears to have been placed on top of an earlier temple or church. The evidence for Roman Gadara is not so strong. Again, coins of the mid-second century AD show a sitting Zeus-type figure, placed in a tetrastyle temple. However, the city also venerated Tyche and the Three Graces. At Gadara, there was a bath and theatre complex at Hammeh Gader, comparable to Birketein, north of the city.

The similarities between these sites are too much of a coincidence. There seems to have been a tradition in the region to site (major) religious buildings on prominent natural locations and to embellish them further with architectural features and monumental elements. Why there should have been this phenomenon is difficult to explain. It might be a feature of religion in this area—the utilization and adaptation of particularly venerated cults in these communities. Equally, it might be indicative of the sort of private-funded but civic-encouraged competition which is better attested in regions such as Bithynia where civic pride had as much to do with religious devotion.

With respect to other sites, Petra exhibits a number of Greek-style temples. The "South Temple" (or Great Temple) exhibits extensive Hellenistic influences (Joukowsky 1994). Its history is complex. The levelling and preparation of the site probably occurred in the mid-first century AD, with its precinct being modified sometime between the mid-second century AD and AD 330. It was then damaged by the earthquake of AD 303, 331 or 363, after which it was heavily modified but continued to function until the mid-sixth century AD, before being destroyed by an earthquake in AD 551. Another temple which has been excavated at Petra is the so-called Temple of the Winged Lions, built c. AD 25 and destroyed in the earthquake of AD 363 (see Parr 1996 for problems with the foundation date).

Traditionally, burials in the Roman period had to be placed outside the city limits. Extensive cemeteries have been reported around virtually all the major sites of Roman Jordan; there are Roman period rock-cut tombs at Petra (McKenzie 1990). The extensive collection of second-and third century tombs at Marwa, 7 km northeast of Irbid, might be associated with the Decapolis city of Capitolias. A number of tombs have been excavated at Pella (Smith and McNicoll 1992). Gadara was surrounded by a number of large cemeteries and some particularly significant graves. The Tomb of the Germani and the Tomb of Sentius Modestus, both first century AD, are to be found outside the east gate. Modestus' funerary inscription describes him as a Holy Herald of the City that indicates that he was an organizer of sacred games and festivals. In addition to these tombs there are those of Chaireos (AD 90/91) and the North Mausoleum of an unknown family but dated to AD 355/356. There is also the so-called Underground Mausoleum that was extended in the fourth century AD but which was originally built outside the city walls. It should, therefore, be earlier than the third century AD when the walls were built. At Philadelphia, there are three main concentrations of burials (at the southern end of the Jabal Hussayn, at the western end of Wadi Amman and along Jabal Ashrafiah and Jabal Jaufa to the south). There are also at least three noteworthy mausolea scattered around the city: at Quwaysma (Qasr Sab), at Qasr Nuweijis, and at Khirbat Souk, all dated on architectural criteria to the second or third century AD.

The other great theme in the archaeology of Jordan in the Roman period is the arrival of Christianity. This is manifested archaeologically by the appearance of churches, cemeteries and other iconographic representations. While the full flourishing of the religion and its archaeological evidence are features of the Byzantine period, its earliest manifestations date to the Roman period. As a generalization, it might be said that many of Jordan's Byzantine churches are actually based on earlier Roman structures, some of which were temples. For instance, at Tall Nimrin (near South Shunah in the Jordan Valley), excavations have produced a sixth-to eighth century AD church, although the site appears in fourth-and fifth century AD Christian sources as Bethnamaris (Piccirillo 1982). Likewise, Eusebius reports Christians and churches at Petra well before the dated archaeology. The earliest literary references in Arabia are to Christian refugees and later to martyrdoms under particular emperors. Refugees are reported at Pella at the end of the First Jewish Revolt (c. ad 70). Hagiographic sources imply that Christians lived in Philadelphia in the late third or early fourth century AD. At Gadara, martyrs are attested in the very early fourth century AD, while a bishop of the community is known to have attended the Council of Nicaea in AD 325. Gerasa was represented at the Council of Seleucia in AD 359. With respect to archaeological remains, at least 15 churches are known at Gerasa, although all of them date to the late fourth/fifth century AD. The Great Cathedral seems to have been dedicated as early as the mid-fourth century AD. This building can be associated with reports of a miracle at Gerasa. The Christian writer Bishop Epiphanus (c. AD 315–403) authored the *Panarion* or Medicine Chest, which offered advice for curing 80 heresies. In this work he refers to a *martyrium* and fountains at Gerasa where every year a spring ran with wine on the anniversary of the miracle of Cana, which was also the Feast of the Epiphany. The fact that there is a re-used first/second century AD fountain in the Great Cathedral has prompted the suggestion that it was the location of this event. Finally, excavations by Parker (1997) at Aila have exposed a basilica-type structure. Initial and admittedly speculative interpretation of this building proposes it as an early fourth century AD church, which, if it is, would make it one of the earliest known churches in Jordan to date. Christianity arrived in Aila by the early fourth century AD. The community there was represented by Bishop Petrus at the Council of Nicaea. Eusebius recounts that early Christians were sent to work in the copper mines at ancient Phaeno (Khirbat Faynan in Wadi Faynan in southern Jordan). The mines are known to have been worked at this time (Hauptmann and Weisgerber 1992). At least three churches are preserved at the Faynan site, although they have not yet been securely dated. In time, Phaeno was represented at a number of church councils in the fifth and sixth centuries AD.

Thanks to Josephus's account of events before the First and Second Jewish Revolts, we know that there were substantial Jewish communities in some of the Decapolis cities. The relationship between Jews and Gentiles in such cities at the outbreak of the First Revolt (AD 66–70) does not appear to have been entirely friendly. Massacres in the "Jordanian" Decapolis are specifically attested at Pella and Philadelphia. A more tolerant atmosphere is reported in Gerasa, where the population there offered protection to its Jewish community (*War* 2.458; 2.480). Architectural fragments from a synagogue there have been found in the triumphal arch built for Hadrian, while later still, one of the city's churches was built in c. AD 530 from a converted third/fourth century AD synagogue. Finally, a synagogue was constructed in the first century ad at the bath complex of Hammeh Gader at Gadara.

Technology

Understanding of the exploitation of Roman Arabia's natural resources is similarly inhibited by a relative lack of fieldwork. However, two avenues of research might be noted here. With respect to Jordan's natural metal deposits, the clearest demonstration of their exploitation is to be found in the south of the country, in the Wadi Arabah region. Here, in the Wadi Faynan complex, fieldwork has shown that the deposits were exploited from the seventh

millennium BC onwards. By the Roman period, the miners were largely reduced to reworking old deposits. Survey has also identified over 120 mines as well as over 70,000 tons of Roman-period slag (Khouri 1988: 121–127; Hauptmann and Weisgerber 1982; Hauptmann 1990). It seems that the ores from the mines scattered throughout the surrounding wadis were in the main smelted at the one site, one close to Khirbat Faynan. Extensive Roman (copper) mining activities have also been identified elsewhere in Wadi Arabah, north of Aila. More recently, complementing this industry, there is evidence of copper working in Aila itself (Parker 1997). Such was the scale of metal production and its need for charcoal and other resources, in at least the southern part of Arabia, that one can only imagine what were the environmental and floral consequences (cf. Barker *et al.* 2000: 44).

Roman-period stone quarries have been widely identified throughout the province, although the criteria for identifying them as such are often obscure. The scale of monumental building work in at least the cities and towns of the region would have ensured that this must have been a thriving industry. Unfortunately, little is known of its organization. Analysis of the marbles used for monumental architecture and funerary furniture across the province indicates that the Arabian cities imported this material from the usual centres of production in the eastern Mediterranean, Egypt and Asia Minor.

Another subject that is attracting increasing attention in the cities and towns of the country is that of the supply of water. Water-collection systems are known and have been studied at Gadara since 1992. Parts of what must have been a considerable system for the movement of water under the city have been recorded, with an upper channel of at least 380 m in length and lower one at over 360 m located directly under the city's acropolis (Weber 1991a, 1991b; Kerner 1994). Sources 3 km from the site, at Ayn Gadara, and 12 km east, at Ayn Terab, were evidently tapped. At least three (Roman) aqueducts are known at Abila: that from the Ayn Khuraybah, 2.5 km away from the city, and two underground systems, one on top of the other under Umm Amad, both certainly used in the Roman and Byzantine periods and perhaps dating back to the Hellenistic era. Gerasa too possessed a sophisticated system of water supply. The two reservoirs at the Festival complex at Birketein stored water to be piped into the city. Drawing in part on a natural spring, the pools measured 43.5 x 88.5 m and had a capacity of c. 1,500,000 litres. The flow of water into the city was regulated. It would have then fed at least the public bath houses, the nymphaea and public fountains of the city. In addition to this source of water, unpublished fieldwork to the north of the city has also discovered traces of pipe systems up to 5 km from the city that fed the Birketein pools.

With the subject of water supply comes consideration of the public and private use of the resource. In the case of the former, we are talking principally of baths and *nymphaea*. Two and perhaps three bathhouses have been identified at Gadara, with the Baths of Herakleides (third century AD) and another constructed into the very steep slope on the south side of the *decumanus maximus* in the early fourth century AD. *Nymphaea* or public fountains were located along the *decumanus* which dates to at least the late second century AD. In addition to these facilities, close to the city, some 7 km east of the Sea of Galilee in the Yarmuk Valley and 4 km north of Gadara is the bath and theatre resort of Hammeh Gader. This complex, which flourished in the second and third centuries AD, enjoyed something of a reputation (e.g. Strabo 16.2.45). Warm-water springs also existed at Pella, which likewise enjoyed something of reputation in rabbinic sources. At Gerasa, the baths were located close to the Chrysorohas River, on the eastern side of that river. They remain undated. A *nymphaeum* was built adjacent to the Artemis complex. A well-preserved structure in downtown Amman has long been interpreted as a *nymphaeum* and dated to the second century AD. Recent restoration work on this structure has led to a better understanding of its form and evolution into the Byzantine and Islamic periods (Waheeb and Zubi 1994). A *nymphaeum* of the second century AD(?) along with a public bath lies on the main road through Petra, both of which imply a sophisticated hydraulic system.

Away from the larger sites, important work has been undertaken elsewhere. For instance, the current programme of work at Humayma is the result of an earlier survey of the hydraulic systems at the site (Oleson 1986, 1992; Oleson *et al.* 1993). Kennedy (1995) has summarized the evidence for the collection and management of water resources in a number of small northeastern "Roman" villages. Utilizing a combination of survey data and air photographs, he has attempted to calculate the collection potential at a number of sites where considerable amounts of water were stored. With few if no signs that the water was for civic purposes, the conclusion has to be that it was for domestic uses as well as for animals. The results demonstrate just how sophisticated was the management of a vital resource, a skill that has been lost today. Meanwhile, the stepped dam at Wadi Jilat in northeast Jordan has recently been restudied (Politis 1993). While the date of its construction remains unknown, it has been compared to a Roman example at Merida in Spain, although it has also been concluded that the Jordanian example might equally be Nabataean with a Byzantine reconstruction.

Conclusion

In summarizing the archaeology of Roman Jordan, the overall impression is detailed knowledge in a few limited spheres, a volume of largely undigested data in others, and a number of glaring gaps in certain fundamental ar-

eas. In the first category come aspects of the public buildings in the country's cities. In the second group should be included the processing of field survey data pertinent to the period, while the third represents the creation of better databases (e.g. for environmental evidence), understanding of the less monumental aspects of urban life, more detailed exploration of a range of rural sites, and finally the marrying of these various strands of evidence to create a broad impression of what it must have been like to live in a Roman province that had a long and sophisticated cultural, economic and political history.

Irrespective of these deficiencies, what can be said of Jordan under the Romans? From the evidence summarized in the preceding pages, it seems clear that the second and early third centuries AD represented a period of considerable prosperity in Roman Jordan, if the scale and vitality of building work, settlement densities and agricultural activity are true indicators. This built on the accelerating prosperity of the first century BC and first century AD. Similarly, decline and depression are reflected in reduced building activity, as apparent in the late third and fourth centuries AD. These conditions appear to have been reversed from the late fourth century when, on the criterion of building activity (notably in the form of church building), the region seems to have enjoyed something of a renaissance, unless at least there was a general redistribution of how individuals and groups deployed their surplus resources, from work to benefit the community as whole to supporting the nascent church. This impression is derived from the towns. It does not seem to be reflected in the countryside, if settlement densities are an accurate reflection of prosperity. Indeed, increases in the distribution of what are only broadly dated Roman settlement patterns need not just be indicative of stability and success. They may in fact denote decline as farmers tried to re-establish themselves at new sites because of regional over-exploitation and/or climatic deterioration.

What explains these rises and declines? If the picture can be detected nationwide, then a single cause might be suggested. The stability Roman dominance brought to the Middle East as a whole in the first century BC/AD must surely have had positive consequences for the economy of the region. Conversely, an obvious example of the negative effects of Roman rule would be the general malaise that the political crises of the third century AD is supposed to have inflicted on most parts of the empire. The rivalry that is detectable in a number of aspects of the cities might have also burnt out their vitality. However, a nationwide interpretation may not necessarily be the only explanation. Regional aspects and factors could have had comparable consequences to the large-scale explanation. Bearing in mind how close was the relationship between town and country, environmental degradation and over-exploitation of the land in the later Roman period might have been a significant negative factor, as has been suggested in some regional case studies. Unfortunately, the quality of the evidence so far accumulated is not decisive either way. Finally, there is the possibility of localized factors, notably the effects of earthquakes and the consequent longer term dislocations.

The abiding impression of the archaeology of Roman Jordan is not so much what has been achieved as the incredible potential that remains. In spite of the long history of field work in the region and the immense threats to the surviving archaeology, the stable political conditions and climate of the region, coupled with what is still a vast untouched potential, will ensure that the region continues to contribute immeasurably to our understanding of what it must have been like to live in one of the frontier provinces of the Roman empire.

Acknowledgments

I am grateful to Graham Oliver, Zbigniew Fiema and Fiona Aiken for casting critical eyes at various stages over this text. They do not necessarily agree with the observations or conclusions made. Lorraine McEwan prepared the comparative illustration of the plans of Gerasa, Philadelphia, Gadara and Abila.

Bibliography

Abu Dayyah, A.S., JA Greene, I. Haj Hassan and E. Suleiman

1991 Archaeological Survey of Greater Amman Phase 1: Final Report. *Annual of the Department of Antiquities of Jordan* 35: 361–395.

Alcock, S.

1994 Breaking up the Hellenistic World: Survey and Society. In I. Morris (ed.), *Classical Greece: Ancient Histories and Modern Archaeologies*, 171–190. Cambridge: Cambridge University Press.

Baird, D. and G. Philip

1994 Preliminary Report on the Third Season (1993) of Excavations at Tell esh-Shuna North. *Levant* 27: 111–133.

Banning, E.B.

1986 Peasants, Pastoralists and *Pax Romana*: Mutualism in the Southern Highlands of Jordan. *Bulletin of the American Schools of Oriental Research* 261: 25–50.

1996 Highlands and Lowlands: Problems and Survey Frameworks for Rural Archaeology in the Near East. *Bulletin of the American Schools of Oriental Research* 301: 25–46.

Barghouti, A.N.

1982 Urbanization of Palestine and Jordan in Hellenistic and Roman Times. In A. Hadidi (ed.), *Studies in the History and Archaeology of Jordan I*, 209–230. Amman: Department of Antiquities.

Barker, G., O.H.Creighton, D.D. Gilbertson, C.O. Hunt, D.J. Mattingly, S.J. McLaren and D.C. Thomas, G.C. Morgan

1997 The Wadi Faynan Project, Southern Jordan: A Preliminary Report on Geomorphology and Landscape Archaeology. *Levant* 29: 19–40.

Barker, G.W., R. Adams, O.H. Creighton, P. Daly, D.D. Gilbertson, J.P. Grattan, C.O. Hunt, D.J. Mattingly, S. McLaren, P. Newson, C. Palmer, F.B. Pyatt, T.E.G. Reynolds, H. Smith, R. Tomber and A.J.Truscott

2000 Archaeology and Desertification in the Wadi Faynan: The Fourth (1999) Season of the Wadi Faynan Landscape Survey. *Levant* 32: 27–52.

Barker, G.W., D.D. Gilbertson and D. Mattingly (eds.)

2007 *Archaeology and Desertification: The Wadi Faynan Landscape Survey, Southern Jordan*. Levant Supplementary Series 2. Oxford: Oxbow Books.

Bauzou, T.

1986 Les voies de communication dans le Hauran 'al' époque romaine. In J.M. Dentzer, (ed.), *Hauran I: Recherches archéologiques sur la Syrie du 'Sud al' époque héllenistique et romaine*, 137–166. Bibliotheque archéologique 124. Paris: Libraire Orientaliste Paul Geuthner.

Bikai, P.

1994a University of Jordan Excavations at Khirbet Salameh 1993. *Annual of the Department of Antiquities of Jordan* 38: 395–399.

1994b The Byzantine Church at Darat Al-Funun. *Annual of the Department of Antiquities of Jordan* 38: 401–415.

Bowersock, G.W.

1971 Report on Provincia Arabia. *Journal of Roman Studies* 61: 219–242.

1983 *Roman Arabia*. Cambridge: Harvard University Press.

Bowsher, J.M.C.

1992 The Temple of Hercules: A Reassessment. In A. Northedge *Studies on Roman and Islamic Amman I: History, Site and Architecture*, 129–138. British Academy Monographs in Archaeology 3. Oxford: Oxford University Press.

Browning, I.

1982 *Jerash and the Decapolis*. London: Chatto and Windus.

1989 *Petra*. London: Chatto and Windus.

Brünnow, R.E. and A. von Domaszewski

1904/09 *Die Provincia Arabia auf Grund Zweier in den Jahre 1897 und 1898 unternommenen Reisen und der Berichte früherer Reisender*. 3 vols. Strassburg: Trübner.

Burns, R.

1992 *Monuments of Syria: An Historical Guide*. London: I.B. Tauris.

Butler, H.C.

1907/19 *Publications of the Princeton University Archaeological Expedition to Syria in 1904–1905 and 1909*. Leiden: E.J. Brill.

Clark, G.A., D.I. Olszewski, and J. Schuldenrein

1994 Survey and Excavation in Wadi Al-Hasa: A Preliminary Report of the 1993 Field Season. *Annual of the Department of Antiquities of Jordan* 38: 41–55.

Dentzer, J.M. (ed.)

1986 *Hauran I: Recherches archéologiques sur la Syrie du 'Sud al' époque héllenistique et romaine*. Bibliotheque archéologique 124. Paris: Libraire Orientaliste Paul Geuthner.

de Vries, B.

1998 *Umm el-Jimal: A Frontier Town and its Landscape in Northern Jordan* I. Journal of Roman Archaeology Supplementary Series 26. Portsmouth: Journal of Roman Archaeology.

Fiema, Z.

1993 Tuwaneh and the *via nova Traiana* in Southern Jordan: A Short Notice on the 1992 Season. *Annual of the Department of Antiquities of Jordan* 37: 549–550.

1995 Military Architecture and the Defense 'System' of Roman-Byzantine Southern Jordan—A Critical Appraisal of Current Interpretations. In K. 'Amr, F. Zayadine and M. Zaghloul (eds.), *Studies in the History and Archaeology of Jordan V*, 261–269. Amman: Department of Antiquities.

2000 Byzantine Petra: A Reassessment. In T.S. Burns and J.W. Eadie (eds.), *Urban and Rural in Late Antiquity*, 111–131. East Lansing, MI: Michigan State University Press.

Freeman, P.

1996 The Annexation of Arabia and Imperial Grand Strategy. In D.L. Kennedy (ed.), *The Roman Army in the East*, 91–118. Journal of Roman Archaeology Supplementary Series 18. Ann Arbor: Journal of Roman Archaeology.

Gatier, J.-P.

1986 *Inscriptions de la Jordanie*. II. *Région central*. Paris: Geuthner.

1989 Inscriptions of Jordan Survey. In D. Homès-Fredericq and J. B. Hennessy (eds.), *The Archaeology of Jordan* II/1–2, 54–55. Akkadica Supplementum 7–8. Leuven: Peeters.

Geraty, L.T. and L.A. Willis

1986 Archaeological Research in Transjordan. In L.T. Geraty and L.G. Herr (eds.), *The Archaeology of Jordan and Other Studies*, 3–75. Berrien Springs, MI: Andrews University.

Glueck, N.

1934–51 *Explorations in Eastern Palestine*. 4 vols. Annual of the American Schools of Oriental Research 14/ 15: 18–19, 25–28. New Haven, CT: American Schools of Oriental Research.

Graf, D.

1978 The Saracens and the Defense of the Arabian Frontier. *Bulletin of the American Schools of Oriental Research* 229: 1–26.

1983 The Nabateans and the Hisma: In the Footsteps of Glueck and Beyond. In C. L. Meyers and M. O'Connor (eds.), *The Word of the Lord Shall Go Forth: Essays in Honor of David Noel Freedman in Celebration of his Sixtieth Birthday*, 647–664. Winona Lake, IN: Eisenbauns.

1986 Review of "Roman and Saracens: A History of the Arabian Frontier." *Journal of Near Eastern Studies* 50: 151–153.

1988 Qura Arabiyya and Provincia Arabia. In P.-L.Gatier (ed.), *Géographie-historique au Proche-Orient: Notes et Monographies Techniques* 23: 171–222. Paris: Editions du Centre National de la Recherche Scientifique.

1989 Rome and the Saracens: Reassessing the Nomadic Menace. In T. Fahd (ed.), *L'Arabie préislamique et son environment historique et culturel: Actes du colloque Strasbourg 24–27 Juin 1987*, 341–400. Leiden: E.J. Brill.

1995 The *via nova Traiana* in Arabia Petraea. In J. Humphrey (ed.), *The Roman and Byzantine Near East: Some Recent Archaeological Research*, 241–265. Journal of Roman Archaeology Supplementary Series 14. Ann Arbor, MI: Journal of Roman Archaeology.

1997 The *via militaris* and the *limes Arabicus*. In W. Groenman-Waateringe, B.L. Beek, W.J.H. Willems and S.L. Wynia (eds.), *Roman Frontier Studies 1995*, 123–133. Oxbow Monographs 91. Oxford: Oxbow Books.

Gregory, S. and D.L. Kennedy

1985 *Sir Aurel Stein's Limes Report*. British Archaeological Reports International Series 272. Oxford: British Archaeological Reports.

Hanbury-Tenison, J.W.

1987 Jarash Region Survey. *Annual of the Department of Antiquities of Jordan* 31: 129–157.

Hanbury-Tenison, J.W., S. Hart and R.K. Falkner

1984 Wadi Arab Survey 1983. *Annual of the Department of Antiquities of Jordan* 28: 385–423.

Hauptmann, A.

1990 The Copper Deposits of Feinan, Wadi Araba: Early Mining and Metallurgy. In S. Kerner (ed.), *The Near East in Antiquity: German Contributions to the Archaeology of Jordan, Palestine, Syria, Lebanon and Egypt* I, 53–62. Amman: German Protestant Institute for Archaeology of the Holy Land/Al Kutba.

Hauptmann, A. and G. Weisgerber

1992 Periods of Ore Exploitation and Metal Production in the Area of Feinan, Wadi Araba, Jordan. In M. Zaghloul, K. Amr, F. Zayadine, R. Nabeel and N. Rida Tawfiq (eds.), *Studies in the History and Archaeology of Jordan IV*, 61–66. Amman: Department of Antiquities.

Hoffman, A.

1990 The Monumental Gate *extra muros* in Gadara. In S. Kerner (ed.), *The Near East in Antiquity: German Contributions to the Archaeology of Jordan, Palestine, Syria, Lebanon and Egypt* I, 95–103. Amman: German Protestant Institute for Archaeology of the Holy Land/Al Kutba.

Homès-Fredericq, D. and J. B. Hennessy (eds.)

1989 *The Archaeology of Jordan* II/1–2. Akkadica Supplementum 7–8. Leuven: Peeters.

Humphrey, J.H.

1995 Editor's Note (The Petra Papyri). In J.H. Humphrey (ed.), *The Roman and Byzantine Near East: Some Recent Archaeological Research.* Journal of Roman Archaeology Supplementary Series 14. Ann Arbor, MI: Journal of Roman Archaeology.

Isaac, B.

1988 Review of Parker 1986 "Roman and Saracens: A History of the Arabian Frontier." and 1987 "The Roman Frontier in Central Jordan: Interim Report on the Limes Arabicus Project 1980–1985." *Journal of Roman Studies* 78: 240–241.

1990 *The Limits of Empire: The Roman Army in the East.* Oxford: Oxford University Press.

1992 The Babatha Archive: A Review Article. *Israel Exploration Journal* 42: 62–75.

Joukowsky, M.

1994/93 Archaeological Excavations and Survey of the Southern Temple at Petra, Jordan. *Annual of the Department of Antiquities of Jordan* 38: 293–332.

Kalayan, H.

1982 The Symmetry and Harmonic Properties of the Temples of Artemis and Zeus, and the Origin of Numerals as used in the enlargement of the South Terrace in Jerash. In A. Hadidi (ed.), *Studies in the History and Archaeology of Jordan III*, 243–254. Amman: Department of Antiquities.

Kanellopoulos, C.

1994 *The Great Temple of Amman: The Architecture.* American Center of Oriental Research Publications 2. Amman: American Center of Oriental Research.

Kennedy, D.L.

1982 *Archaeological Explorations on the Roman Frontier in North-East Jordan.* British Archaeological Reports, International Series 134. Oxford: British Archaeological Reports.

1992 The Roman Frontier in Arabia (Jordanian Sector). *Journal of Roman Archaeology* 5: 473–489.

1995 Water Supply and Use in the Southern Hauran, Jordan. *Journal of Field Archaeology* 22: 75–90.

1997 Roman Roads and Routes in North-East Jordan. *Levant* 29: 71–94.

1998 The Area of Umm el-Jimal: Maps, Air Photographs and Surface Survey. In B. de Vries (ed.), *Umm el-Jimal: A Frontier Town and its Landscape in Northern Jordan I*, 39–90. Journal of Roman Archaeology Supplementary Series 26. Portsmouth: Journal of Roman Archaeology.

Kennedy, D.L., H.I. MacAdam and D.N. Riley

1986 Preliminary Report on the Southern Hauran Survey, 1985. *Annual of the Department of Antiquities of Jordan* 30: 145–153.

Kennedy, D.L. and D.N. Riley

1990 *Rome's Desert Frontier from the Air.* London: Batsfords.

Kennedy, D.L. and P.W. Freeman

1995 Southern Hauran Survey 1992. *Levant* 27: 39–73.

Kerner, S.

1994 The German Protestant Institute for Archaeology and Other German Projects in Jordan. In S. Kerner (ed.), *The Near East in Antiquity: Archaeological Work of National and International Institutions in Jordan IV*, 49–64. Amman: German Protestant Institute for Archaeology of the Holy Land/Al Kutba.

Khouri, R.G.

1988 *The Antiquities of the Jordan Rift Valley.* Amman: Al Kutba.

Killick, A.C.

1983 Udruh—1980, 1981 Seasons: A Preliminary Report. *Annual of the Department of Antiquities of Jordan* 27: 231–244.

Kraeling, C.H.

1938 *Gerasa: City of the Decapolis.* New Haven: American Schools of Oriental Research.

LaBianca, Ø.S.

1984 Objectives, Procedures and Findings of Ethnoarchaeological Research in the Vicinity of Heshbon in Jordan. *Annual of the Department of Antiquities of Jordan* 28: 269–288.

1989 Hesban. In D. Homès-Fredericq and J. B. Hennessy (eds.), *The Archaeology of Jordan* II/1–2, 261–269. Akkadica Supplementum 7–8. Leuven: Peeters.

Lewis, N. (ed.)

1989 *The Documents from the Bar Kokhba Period in the Cave of Letters: Greek.* Jerusalem: Israel Exploration Society/The Hebrew University of Jerusalem/The Shrine of the Book.

Lindner, M.

1989 Southern Jordan Survey. In D. Homès-Fredericq and J. B. Hennessy (eds.), *The Archaeology of Jordan* II/1–2, 84–90. Akkadica Supplementum 7–8. Leuven: Peeters.

MacAdam, H.I.

1986a *Studies in the History of the Roman Province of Arabia: The Northern Sector.* British Archaeological Reports International Series 295. Oxford: British Archaeological Reports.

1986b *Bostra Gloriosa. Berytus* 34: 169–192.

1990 The *IGLS* Series Then and Now (1905–1989). *Journal of Roman Archaeology* 3: 458–464.

1994 Settlements and Settlement Patterns in Northern and Central Transjordania, ca. 550–ca. 750. In G.R.D. King and A. Cameron (eds.), *The Byzantine and Early Islamic Near East*, II. *Land Use and Settlement Patterns*, 49–93. Princeton: Darwin.

MacDonald, B. (ed.)

1988 *The Wadi el Hasa Archaeological Survey 1979–82, West-Central Jordan.* Waterloo, ON: Wilfrid Laurier University.

MacDonald, B. (ed.)

1992 *The Southern Ghors and Northeast 'Arabah Archaeological Survey*. Sheffield Archaeological Monographs 5. Sheffield: J.R. Collis.

Macdonald, M.

1993 Nomads and the Hawran in the Late Hellenistic and Roman Periods. A Reassessment of the Epigraphic Evidence. *Syria* 70: 303–413.

McKenzie, J.

1990 *The Architecture of Petra*. British Academy Monographs in Archaeology 1. Oxford: Oxford University Press.

McNicoll, A.W., Basil Hennessy and R.H. Smith

1982 *Pella in Jordan I: An Interim Report on the Joint Expeditions of Sydney and the College of Wooster Excavations at Pella, 1979–1981*. Canberra: Australian National Gallery.

McNicoll, A.W., R.H. Smith, P.M. Watson and S. Gordon (eds.)

1992 *Pella in Jordan II. The Second Interim Report of the Joint University of Sydney and College of Wooster Excavations at Pella, 1982–1985*. Mediterranean Archaeology Supplement 2. Sydney: Meditarch.

McQuitty, A. and R. Falkner

1993 The Faris Project: Preliminary Report on the 1988, 1989 and 1990 Seasons. *Levant* 25: 37–61.

Mare, W.H.

1994 The 1992 Seasons of Excavations at Abila of the Decapolis. *Annual of the Department of Antiquities of Jordan* 38: 359–378.

Martin-Bueno, M.

1992 The *Macellum* in the Economy of Gerasa. In M. Zaghloul, K. Amr, F. Zayadine, R. Nabeel and N. Rida Tawfiq (eds.), *Studies in the History and Archaeology of Jordan IV*, 315–320. Amman: Department of Antiquities.

Millar, F.

1993 *The Roman Near East 31 bc–ad 337*. Cambridge: Cambridge University Press.

Miller, J.

1969 *The Spice Trade of the Roman Empire*. Oxford: Oxford University Press.

Miller, J.M.

1989 Moab and the Moabites. In J.A. Dearman (ed.), *Studies in the Mesha Inscription and Moab*, 1–40. Atlanta: Scholars Press.

Northedge, A.

1992 *Studies on Roman and Islamic Amman I: History, Site and Architecture*. British Academy Monographs in Archaeology 3. Oxford: Oxford University Press.

Oleson, J.P.

1986 The Humayma Hydraulic Survey: Preliminary Report of the 1986 Season. *Annual of the Department of Antiquities of Jordan* 30: 253–260.

1992 The Water-Supply System of Ancient Auara: Preliminary Results of the Humeima Hydraulic Survey. In M. Zaghloul, K. Amr, F. Zayadine, R. Nabeel and N. Rida Tawfiq (eds.), *Studies in the History and Archaeology of Jordan IV*, 269–275. Amman: Department of Antiquities.

Oleson, J.P., K. 'Amr, R. Schick, R.M. Foote and J. Somogyi-Csizmazia

1993 The Humeima Excavation Project: Preliminary Report of the 1991–1992 Seasons. *Annual of the Department of Antiquities of Jordan* 37: 461–502.

Ostrasz, A.

1989 The Hippodrome of Gerasa: A Report on Excavations and Research 1982–1987. In F. Zayadine, *Jerash Archaeological Project 1984–1988 2: Fouilles de Jerash 1984–1988*, 51–78. Extrait de *Syria* 66. Paris: Libraire Orientalishe Paul Geuthner.

Palumbo, G.

1993 JADIS (Jordan Antiquities Database and Information System): An Example of National Archaeological Inventory and GIS Applications. In J. Andresen, T. Madsen and I. Scollar (eds.), *Computing the Past: Computer Applications and Quantitative Methods in Archaeology*. Computer Applications in Archaeology Conference, 1992. Aarhus: Aarhus University.

Palumbo, G., J. Mabry and I. Kuijt

1990 The Wadi el-Yabis Survey: Report on the 1989 Season. *Annual of the Department of Antiquities of Jordan* 34: 95–118.

Palumbo, G., K. 'Amr, A. Musa and M. Rasson-Seigne

1993 Salvage Excavations at Tell Faysal. *Annual of the Department of Antiquities of Jordan* 37: 89–118.

Parapetti, R.

1982 The Architectural Significance of the Sanctuary of Artemis at Gerasa. In A. Hadidi (ed.), *Studies in the History and Archaeology of Jordan I*, 255–260. Amman: Department of Antiquities.

Parker, S.T.

1976 Archaeological Survey of the *Limes Arabicus. Annual of the Department of Antiquities of Jordan* 21: 19–31.

1986 *Roman and Saracens: A History of the Arabian Frontier*. Winona Lake, IN: Eisenbauns.

1987 *The Roman Frontier in Central Jordan: Interim Report on the Limes Arabicus Project 1980–1985*. British Archaeological Reports International Series 340. Oxford: British Archaeological Reports.

1992 The Nature of Rome's Arabian Frontier. In V. Maxfield and M.J. Dobson (eds.), *Roman Frontier Studies 1989*, 498–504. Proceedings of the XVth International Congress of Roman Frontier Studies. Exeter: University of Exeter.

1997 Preliminary Report on the 1994 Season of the Roman Aqaba Project. *Bulletin of the American Schools of Oriental Research* 305: 19–44.

Parr, P.

1996 The Architecture of Petra: Review Article. *Palestine Exploration Quarterly* 128: 63–70.

Piccirillo, M.

1982 A Church at Shunat Nimrin. *Annual of the Department of Antiquities of Jordan* 38: 335–342.

Politis, K.D.

1993 The Stepped Dam at Wadi el-Jilat. *Palestine Exploration Quarterly* 125: 43–49.

Raschke, M.G.

1978 New Studies in Roman Commerce with the East. In H. Temporini and W. Haase (eds.), *Aufstieg und Niedergang der römischen Welt*, II.9.2, 604–737. Berlin: W. de Gruyter.

Rostovtzeff, M.I.

1932 *Caravan Cities.* Oxford: Oxford University Press.

Russell, K.W.

1985 The Earthquake Chronology of Palestine and Northwest Arabia from the 2nd through the mid-8th Century ad. *Bulletin of the American Schools of Oriental Research* 260: 37–59.

Sapin, J.

1987 Jerash Region Survey. *Annual of the Department of Antiquities of Jordan* 21: 129–157.

Sartre, M.

1982 *Trois études sur l'Arabie romaine et byzantine.* Collection Latomus 178. Brussels: Revue d'études latins.

1986 Les peuplement et le développement du Hauran antique 'a la lumière des inscriptions grecques et latines. In Dentzer, J.M. (ed.), *Hauran I: Recherches archéologiques sur la Syrie du 'Sud al' époque héllenistique et romaine,* 189–204. Bibliotheque archéologique 124. Paris: Libraire Orientaliste Paul Geuthner.

Schick, R.

1994 The Settlement Pattern of Southern Jordan: The Nature of the Evidence. In G.R.D. King and A. Cameron (eds.), *The Byzantine and Early Islamic Near East II: Land Use and Settlement Patterns,* 133–154. Princeton: Darwin.

Segal, A.

1997 *From Function to Monument: Urban Landscapes of Roman Palestine, Syria and Provincia Arabia.* Oxbow Monograph 66. Oxford: Oxbow.

1988 *Town Planning and Architecture in Provincia Arabia.* British Archaeological Reports International Series 419. Oxford: British Archaeological Reports.

Seigne, J.

1997 Les limites orientale et meridionale du territoire de Gerasa. *Syria* 74: 121–138

Shahid, I.

1984 *Rome and the Arabs: A Prolegomenon to the Study of Byzantium and the Arabs.* Washington, DC: Research-History and Collections, Dumbarton Oaks.

1989 *Byzantium and the Arabs in the Fourth Century.* Washington: Dumbarton Oaks Research Library.

Sidebotham, S.E.

1986 *Roman Economic Policy in the Eurythra Thalassa: 30 bc–ad 277.* Leiden: E.J. Brill.

1991 Ports of the Red Sea and the Arabia–India Trade. In V. Begley and R.D. de Puma (eds.), *Rome and India: The Ancient Sea Trade,* 12–37. Madison, WI: University of Wisconsin.

Smith, A.M., M. Stevens and T.M. Niemi

1997 The South-East Araba Archaeological Survey: A Preliminary Report of the 1994 Season. *Bulletin of the American Schools of Oriental Research* 305: 45–72.

Smith, R.H.

1987 Trade in the Life of Pella of the Decapolis. In A. Hadidi (ed.), *Studies in the History and Archaeology of Jordan III,* 53–58. Amman: Department of Antiquities.

Smith, R.H. and A. McNicoll

1992 The Roman Period. In A.W. McNicoll, R.H. Smith, P.M. Watson, and S. Gordon (eds.), *Pella in Jordan II. The Second Interim Report of the Joint University of Sydney and College of Wooster Excavations at Pella, 1982–1985,* 119–144. Mediterranean Archaeology Supplement 2. Sydney: Meditarch.

Spijkerman, A.

1978 *The Coins of the Decapolis and Provincia Arabia.* Jerusalem: Franciscan Press.

Stern, E., A. Gilboa-Lewinson and B. Aviram (eds.)

1993 *The New Encyclopedia of Archaeological Excavations in the Holy Land,* I–IV. Jerusalem: Simon Schuster.

Stucky, R.A., Y. Gerber, B. Kolb and S. Schmid

1994 Swiss-Liechtenstein Excavations at Ez-Zantur in Petra 1993: The Fifth Campaign. *Annual of the Department of Antiquities of Jordan* 38: 271–292.

Tell, S., G. Palumbo, A.S. Abu Dayyeh, K. 'Amr, J.A. Greene, R. Kanaan, E. Kraczkiewicz, C. Shartzer, M. Swemat and M. Waheeb

1993 The Cultural Resources Management Project in Jordan. *Annual of the Department of Antiquities of Jordan* 37: 67–164.

Waheeb, M. and Z. Zubi

1994 The Amman Nymphaeum Excavation Report: A Short Note on the 1992–93 Seasons. *Annual of the Department of Antiquities of Jordan* 38: 507–508.

Watson, P.

1989 Jerash Bowls: Study of a Provincial Group of Byzantine Decorated Fine Ware. In F. Zayadine, *Jerash Archaeological Project 1984–1988 2: Fouilles de Jerash 1984–1988,* 223–261. Extrait de *Syria* 66. Paris: Libraire Orientalishe Paul Geuthner.

1996 Pella Hinterland Survey 1994: Preliminary Report. *Levant* 28: 63–72.

Weber, T.

1990 One Hundred Years of Jordanian–German Fieldwork at Umm Qais (1890–1990). In S. Kerner (ed.), *The Near East in Antiquity: German Contributions to the Archaeology of Jordan, Palestine, Syria, Lebanon and Egypt I*, 15–28. Amman: German Protestant Institute for Archaeology of the Holy Land/Al Kutba.

1991a Gadara of the Decapolis: Tiberiade Gate, Qanawat el-Far'oun and Bait Rusan: Achievements in Excavation and Restoration at Umm Qais 1989–1990. In S. Kerner (ed.), *The Near East in Antiquity: German Contributions to the Archaeology of Jordan, Palestine, Syria, Lebanon and Egypt II*, 123–134. Amman: German Protestant Institute for Archaeology of the Holy Land/Al Kutba.

1991b Gadara of the Decapolis. Preliminary Report on the 1990 Season at Umm Qais. *Annual of the Department of Antiquities of Jordan* 36: 223–231.

Welles, C.B.

1938 The Inscriptions. In C.H. Kraeling, *Gerasa: City of the Decapolis,* 355–494. New Haven, CT: American Schools of Oriental Research.

Zayadine, F.

1986 *Jerash Archaeological Project 1981–1983.* Amman: Department of Antiquities.

1989 *Jerash Archaeological Project 1984–1988 2: Fouilles de Jerash 1984–1988.* Extrait de *Syria* 66. Paris: Libraire Orientalishe Paul Geuthner.

1994 Ayla–'Aqaba in the Light of Recent Excavations. *Annual of the Department of Antiquities of Jordan* 38: 485–505.

Zeitler, J.P.

1990 Houses, Sherds and Bones: Aspects of Daily life in Petra. In S. Kerner (ed.), *The Near East in Antiquity: German Contributions to the Archaeology of Jordan, Palestine, Syria, Lebanon and Egypt I*, 39–52. Amman: German Protestant Institute for Archaeology of the Holy Land/Al Kutba.

14. The Byzantine Period

Pamela Watson

Terminology

The period in Western Asian history from the fourth to the mid-seventh centuries AD is variously referred to as "Roman," "Late Roman," "Late Antiquity" or "Byzantine." The term "Byzantine" is used here, following the refined period division of Levantine archaeologists to distinguish the last centuries of the eastern Roman empire before the Islamic conquest. There is no historically formal beginning for the period, the choice being one of scholarly convenience. The year AD 324, when Constantine I founded the new imperial capital of Constantinople, provides a logical marker. The eponymous site, at the junction between Asia and Europe, was the old Greek settlement of Byzantion. The focus of administration of the Roman empire moved from Rome to centre on the Balkans and the eastern Mediterranean. It is from here that a Christian and primarily Greek-speaking state evolved.

For Jordan and the general area of the Levant, the Byzantine period ended with the Muslim Conquest of 636/640, although the empire continued elsewhere until the mid-fifteenth century. Within this regional context only, there are broad chronological subdivisions into early Byzantine (fourth–fifth century) and late Byzantine (sixth–early seventh century).

"Classical" is the general term used to describe the period of Graeco-Roman political sway in the Levant, from the time of the conquest by Alexander the Great in 322 BC to the demise of the Byzantine empire in the southeast c. AD 640. It thereby encompasses the Hellenistic, Roman and Byzantine periods.

The modern state of Jordan does not coincide with state or provincial boundaries in antiquity, which were changeable. The term "Transjordan," that is, the inhabited region east of the Jordan Rift Valley (the Jordan Valley, the Dead Sea and Wadi Arabah), is used as a neutral geographical location for the area.

Origins

There is no definable boundary between the Roman and Byzantine periods. Nevertheless, within an administrative, cultural and economic continuum, changes were occurring to the empire. At the beginning of the fourth century AD, the administrative and economic reforms of Diocletian had given it a new lease of life. In the east, this institutional and administrative structure remained largely intact until the Persian and Arab invasions of the early seventh century AD. Diocletian's successor Constantine I—responding to the growing importance of the eastern half of the empire—chose to administer it from an eastern centre, Constantinople. At the same time, he gave religious preference to a hitherto minor religion, Christianity, laying the foundations for its eventual dominance of the spiritual life of the state. The shift to the east and the rise of Christianity in the early fourth century AD represent a significant change in the character of the empire. Subsequently, the administration of the West and the East was separated and the West was later lost to the barbarians. Church hierarchy and theological conflicts influenced the affairs of state, while Christian mores affected social and cultural attitudes. The central bureaucracy was reinforced, court ceremonial permeated all aspects of life, and the army was restructured, giving prominence to the defensive forces. Provincial governors and their staff replaced municipal bodies, and military and civil powers were separated. The empire had evolved into a definably different entity to its precursor centred in Rome.

Sources and Chronology

Chronological precision varies within the Byzantine period, according to the quality and availability of the sources at hand. Written sources may be biased, selective or inaccurate. The archaeological record is imperfectly preserved and its exploration through excavation and survey is uneven. The conjunction between the written and physical sources of information can be at times fortunately direct or unfortunately obscure. Written sources fall into a number of categories: ecclesiastical writers (documenting the history of the church and the lives of the saints); secular historians and panegyrics to the emperors; documentary material, for example, accounts of the church councils, the law codes of the emperors, and military and administrative lists; and regional records such as papyrus archives. Some sources, such as later Arab and Byzantine chroniclers of the early seventh century AD, are not contemporary and rely on earlier records now lost. A comprehensive list of ancient sources and their editions is found in Jones (1973: 1464). For a discussion of the sources, see also Shahid (1984, 1989) and Kaegi (1992). Inscriptions, either dedicatory, public monumental, or funerary, are of primary importance in dating structures and events, providing names, genealogies, ranks, language usage and other glimpses of society. They are numerous but often fragmentary.

Environment

Jordan is climatically marginal, and small fluctuations in rainfall and temperature make a considerable difference to agricultural productivity. The land is particularly sensitive to human-induced degradation of the natural vegetation. Population peaked in the Byzantine period and land

use was correspondingly intensive. It is not surprising to find indications of depleted natural vegetation as well as highly sophisticated land and water management strategies that were devised to maximize production from the existing resources.

There is evidence for deforestation in the highlands of northern Jordan during the Classical period (Sapin 1985:

Figure 14.1 Byzantine period sites mentioned in the text.

225, 227). The ecological equilibrium maintained by the ancient village system was superseded by the demands of an urban socio-economy generated by the expanding cities of the region, such as Gerasa, Pella, Gadara, and Capitolias. Resources of wood and stone were heavily exploited and the Byzantine period witnessed an abrupt increase in deforestation. Agriculture was expanded to meet the needs of the cities, encroaching upon traditional pastoral zones that had protected low vegetation. The resulting degradation contributed to progressive erosion in this area (Beaumont 1985: 291–296).

Archaeobotanical research at Tall Hisban on the western edge of the central plateau indicates a change in the flora of the region during humankind's occupation. This was probably due to overgrazing which altered the selective advantage of certain species over others. It was neither a process of desertification nor the result of climate change. (LaBianca and Lacelle 1986: 123–140). During the Byzantine period, when land use was most intense, land that was previously pastoral was converted to cultivation, and elaborate water management works were constructed (Geraty and LaBianca 1985: 327–328).

Evidence from Pella in the north Jordan Valley documents a progressive shift from the use of forest species for fuel and timber to that of cultivated trees or naturally occurring wadi species. A species such as hackberry gradually disappears, becoming extinct by the Byzantine period. In the Umayyad period the population was reduced to lower-grade wadi plants for fuel, such as oleander and tamarisk (McNicoll *et al.* 1992: 256). Evidence from farther down the valley at Tall Dayr Alla suggests a similar pattern of depleting resources of wood over time (Van Zeist 1985: 203).

In the southern copper mining area around Wadi Faynan in Wadi Arabah, the culling of local terrace and wadi growth provided the main source of fuel for the smelting operations. Exploitation of the southern forests had ceased by the Iron Age (Hauptmann 1986: 418; Engel 1993; Engel and Frey 1996). The extent to which progressive deforestation led to human-caused desertification in this area is still being researched (Barker *et al.* 2000; Hunt *et. al.* 2004; Grattan *et al.* 2007 (and further references therein).

The Byzantine period witnessed the climax of settlement and land use in Jordan, leading to the expansion of sedentary occupation and agriculture into marginal semi-desert areas. This is particularly apparent in the northeastern basalt area of the southern Hauran, along the steppic fringes of central Jordan, and to a lesser degree in the south. The viability of life in these marginal regions depended upon well-organized systems of water collection and distribution to support the growing of crops and to supply the needs of the villages and towns. At Umm Jimal, one of a network of towns in the Hauran, we find the remains of aqueducts bringing winter rainwater from the highlands in the north, a series of public and private reservoirs for long-term storage, and channels collecting local winter runoff. Traces of a complex hydraulic system for water diversion and storage exist in the surrounding countryside along with agricultural terracing, corrals and barns. Urban housing was designed specifically for the stabling and husbandry of animals as well as people (De Vries 1985). To the east, a network of fossilized field boundaries surround ancient villages such as Umm Quttayn (Kennedy 1982: 331–335).

In southern Jordan, the extensive ancient field systems of Wadi Faynan reveal systematic hydrological management for agricultural production. These fields continued to flourish in the Byzantine period, servicing the copper-mining communities (Barker *et al.* 1997). The urban centre of nearby Petra was sustained by the organization of sophisticated hydrological systems and the careful terracing and husbandry of all suitable wadis and plateaux within its mountainous environment (Gentelle 1984: especially 27; Ruben 2003).

Could a minor fluctuation towards a cooler/wetter climate favour and perhaps influence the unprecedented expansion of settlement in the Byzantine period? A variety of data sources for climate indicators has led to conflicting conclusions. Some analyses supported the cooler/wetter trend while others suggested that the Byzantine period was more arid than the Roman period; some of the latest evidence suggests the former trend for both the Roman and Byzantine periods (Bookman *et al.* 2004). Whatever the case, minor undetectable climatic fluctuations as well as a range of human factors may also have had considerable influence on land use and demography. The prevailing political and economic conditions probably did more than climate to encourage population and settlement expansion at this time.

Historical Background

In the late third century AD, the Emperor Diocletian instituted a major restructuring of the administration of the Roman empire. Provincial divisions were redrawn, and the military system was reorganized and strengthened. Constantine and his successors continued this process, establishing the administrative framework for the next two centuries. Jordan was divided between four Byzantine imperial provinces that also extended into Palestine/Israel and Syria (Palestine I, II, III, and Arabia; see Figure 14.2).

After a prolonged period of struggle, Constantine achieved sole power, defeating his final rival Licinius in AD 324. He relocated imperial administration to Constantinople, a position more central to the geographical realities of the empire. Initially, the empire was run by joint rule, with the emperor delegating responsibility for certain areas to a junior Augustus and sometimes subordinate Caesars (Jones 1973: 325). On the death of Theodosius in AD 395, the empire was divided between his two sons Arcadius and Honorius, into the East and West respectively. This administrative division became a permanent reality when the West, which had been progressively declining, finally succumbed to external pressures in AD 476. The continuation of the Roman empire thereafter was carried by the eastern half alone.

The Role of Christianity

Constantine's conversion to Christianity, a religion intensely persecuted by his predecessor Diocletian, marked another significant departure in the development of the empire. Christianity was legalized in AD 313, and, with a brief exception in the reign of Julian (AD 361–63), grew rapidly under the patronage of the fourth century AD emperors to become the official state religion. Constantine's energetic espousal of Christianity involved him in the doctrinal controversies of a developing church, setting a pattern of imperial involvement in ecclesiastical affairs that would continue for centuries. The provinces of Palestine, Arabia, and Syria, the geographical origin of the new religion, were affected by this favoured status.

The Role of the Arab Nomads

Economically, the provinces of Arabia and Palestine were of minor significance in the empire. They were relatively poor in resources, although the luxury trade by caravans through the area was a lucrative source of revenue. Their main strategic importance was geographical, as a land bridge between the rich provinces of Syria and Egypt. Bordered by a desert that was sparsely populated by nomads, the southeastern frontier was not considered as vulnerable to serious invasion as the frontiers with Persia and the West. Nevertheless, the nomadic Arab presence became an influential factor in the administration of the eastern provinces and Roman policy evolved to accommodate it. During Constantine's reign, a significant tribal group and its leader, Imru al-Qays, is attested in eastern Syria. The epitaph on his grave at Namara (between Busra and Damascus) describes him as "king of the Arabs" (Isaac 1990: 239–240). The use of powerful Arab tribes as allies in their continuing conflicts becomes a feature of both Roman and Persian strategy in the buffer zone of the eastern desert from the fourth century AD onwards. The Lakhmids, based on the Euphrates, served the Persian cause. By the late fourth century AD, the Salih had become the dominant tribe in southern Syria and northern Transjordan. They are attested as Roman *phylarchs* (tribal commanders under the patronage of Byzantium) from the reigns of Valens to Anastasius at the beginning of the sixth century AD.

In the last decade of the fifth century AD, disruptive nomadic incursions were reported in the eastern provinces, probably reflecting competition between the major clans (Sartre 1982: 155–156). At this time, the Kinda

tribe, moving out of central and northern Arabia, raided Palestine and southern Syria, an area hitherto dominated by the Salih. The Kindite war (AD 498–502) revealed the weakness of the Byzantine defences in Transjordan and Palestine. The Emperor Anastasius eventually concluded a treaty with Harith the Kindite in AD 502, making him a formal Byzantine ally and *phylarch* of the Kindites in the area of Palestine III (Shahid 1989: 130). Another tribe, the Ghassanids, had filtered into Transjordan through Wadi Sirhan in c. AD 300. The Salih permitted them to settle in the Balqa district south of Amman (Trimingham 1979: 178–179; Sartre 1982: 157). In AD 498, the leader of the Ghassan, Jabala, was reported to be raiding into Palestine and was curbed by the Byzantine *dux* of Pales-

Figure 14.2 Byzantine provincial divisions.

tine, Romanos. The Ghassanids proved their ascendancy over the Salih and the Byzantines gave them the *phylarchy* in the area of Arabia. Their position was enhanced in AD 529/530 when, after trouble with the Kindites and the Lakhmids, the Emperor Justinian appointed Harith the Ghassanid as supreme *phylarch*, patrician and king of all the Arab tribes allied to Byzantium (the *foederati* or federates). This co-ordinated federate force was formed in response to the effective power of the Persian Arab allies led by al-Mundhir, king of the Lakhmids. The Ghassanids thus became responsible for protection of the frontier from Palmyra to Wadi Hasa. The area of Palestine III was assigned to Harith's brother, Abu Karib. Justinian's policy was to reduce the role of the imperial frontier forces, the *limitanei*, shifting their responsibilities to the Arab federates unified under a single commander (see below, Defence).

Conflict with Persia

During the fourth century AD, several wars were fought against the Sassanian Persians to the northeast. This, however, had little impact on the southern areas. Constantine's son, Constantius, was engaged in a number of campaigns. His successor, the pagan emperor Julian, was killed on campaign in AD 363. The fifth century AD was a time of relative peace between the Persians and the Byzantines, although there were occasional lapses. Both parties were more concerned with internal problems and border pressures elsewhere.

During the reign of Justinian (AD 527–65), there were three periods of conflict with the Persians, AD 527–32, 540–45, and 549–62, all occurring in Syria and beyond (Jones 1973: 269-94). Justinian's main concern was ensuring peace and security within his borders rather than conquest in the East. The focus of his aggression was in the opposite direction, that is, attempting to regain the lost western provinces. In AD 532, Justinian and Chosroes signed a treaty of Eternal Peace but this proved to be a misnomer. A 50-year peace was finally signed in AD 562. The Arab federates played a significant role as raiders, complementary to the activities of the main army. They were mentioned specifically in the peace treaty (Isaac 1990: 240–249).

The policy of Justinian's successors was less supportive of the Ghassanids and trouble ensued. Al-Mundhir, the Ghassanid leader, had problems with Justin II and then Tiberias, culminating in Mundhir withdrawing his forces during conflict with the Persians in AD 581. He was finally betrayed and exiled. In revenge, his son ravaged Syria, Palestine and Arabia over the next two years (Whitby 1995: 91). The success of this raiding illustrates the weakness of Byzantine control in the southeast provinces, with imperial forces concentrated east of the Euphrates.

The Persian invasion and occupation of the Levant between AD 613 and 628 was far more determined and acquisitive than anything seen in previous centuries. Instead of merely seeking booty and gaining an advantageous peace on the borders, as had been the pattern in the past, Chosroes II sought to conquer and retain. Besides pushing through Asia Minor to the Bosphorus, he overran Syria and Palestine, burning and sacking Jerusalem in AD 614 and removing the relic of the Holy Cross to Ctesiphon. He took Egypt in AD 619, cutting off the corn supply to the Byzantine capital. Energetic counterattacks by the emperor Heraclius (AD 610–41) in Asia Minor and Persia eventually prevailed. Chosroes was deposed and murdered and his son sued for peace. The Persians evacuated all conquered territories in AD 628 and Heraclius returned the Holy Cross to Jerusalem in triumph in AD 630 (Schick 1992: 108–111).

The Islamic Conquest

No sooner was the land recovered than an unexpected threat emerged from the remote southern regions of Arabia. The appearance of a small religious movement seeking a larger audience had almost gone unnoticed. Yet, within the space of six years, the Byzantines were pushed out of Palestine, Transjordan and Syria forever. They were victorious in their first encounter with the invading Muslim forces in AD 629, at Mutah, south of Wadi Mujib, but their triumph was short lived. Heraclius's decision to end subsidies to certain tribes in southern Palestine prompted them to assist the Muslim forces to gain access to Gazan territory in AD 633/34. Major defeats of the Byzantines occurred at Ajnadayn and then Fihl (Tabaqat Fahl), in AD 634, and Damascus was captured in AD 635. The decisive Muslim victory came at the Battle of Yarmuk in AD 636 and by AD 640 the final pockets of Byzantine resistance were removed from the region. Thus ended almost a thousand years of Graeco-Roman rule in the Levant (Kaegi 1992: 66–146).

Settlement Patterns

Population and settlement intensity reached its peak in most of Jordan during the Byzantine period, as attested by recent excavations and surveys in many parts of the country. Numerous factors contributed to this situation, chief among them being the sense of general security that allowed settlement and food production to exist in safety. Healthy trade and economic networks encouraged an overall prosperity. An expanding religious community enjoyed the highest political support and attracted pilgrims as part of the Holy Land itinerary, albeit on the periphery.

Basic factors affecting settlement patterns are the geographical and climatic divisions of the landscape and the political organization. The following discussion is divided into natural geographical regions as they fall within the modern borders.

1. The northwest region, from the Yarmuk River to Zarqa River, including the east side of the Jordan Valley and eastwards to the Via Nova Traiana on the edge of the steppe (roughly a line from Zarqa to Khirbat Samra to Mafraq).

2. The north-central plateau and westward wadis to the Dead Sea, from Zarqa River to Wadi Mujib.

3. The south-central plateau (ancient Moab) from Wadi Mujib to Wadi Hasa, including the Southern Ghors south of the Dead Sea.

4. The southern region below Wadi Hasa to the Gulf of Aqabah.

5. The eastern steppe and desert areas, roughly eastwards from the line of the Via Nova Traiana, incorporating the southern Hauran and Azraq Oasis.

Useful syntheses of information on settlement patterns in Jordan for the Byzantine period have been made by: Piccirillo (1985) concerning rural settlements throughout Jordan; MacAdam (1994) and Kennedy (2004) concerning northern and central Jordan; Parker (1992) for central Jordan; and Schick (1994) and Fiema (1991) for the southern half of Jordan. A register of surveys and site excavations up until the mid-1980s (with some omissions) is found in Homès-Fredericq and Hennessy (1986, 1989). King has published brief preliminary accounts of his overall survey of Byzantine and Islamic sites in Jordan (1982, 1983, 1987, 1989). Graf (2001) has provided a useful overview and comparative analysis set within a wider contextual framework. The foundations for these investigations were laid by Glueck (1934–1951) in his extensive coverage of "Eastern Palestine." Primary information comes from more specific regional surveys and excavations, which vary in intensity, purpose and methodology. Consequently, there are gaps in the coverage and variation in the quality of information.

The Northwest Region and North Jordan Valley (within the Provinces of Palestine II and Arabia)

The climatically benign area of the northwestern region, with its rolling wooded hills, lush valleys and perennial springs, supported the majority of the population. It accommodated members of the former classical league of Hellenized cities known as the Decapolis, such as Gerasa (Jarash), Pella (Tabaqat Fahl), Gadara (Umm Qays), Abila (Quwayliba), Capitolias (Bayt Ras), and the unidentified Dium (also called Dion, possibly Tall Ashari). Another important urban centre existed at Arbela (Tall Irbid). These large centres were surrounded by a network of towns and villages, roads, agricultural installations, farmsteads and villas, reaching an occupational peak in the Byzantine period unsurpassed until the twentieth century. Eastwards, the land undulates more gently and rainfall decreases. Sites are more dispersed but the important

north–south communication route of the Via Nova Traiana and its offshoots ensure a zone of occupation, supporting towns such as Khirbat Samra, Rihab, and Yasileh. Survey in the eastern Wadi Zarqa has recently added to this picture (Caneva *et al.* 2001).

Excavations in the Decapolis cities have revealed concentrated and extensive occupation during the Byzantine period. Increased population and changing cultural requirements led to alterations in the metropolitan fabric. General tendencies, such as the encroachment upon public spaces and facilities by private enterprises, and the reuse or demolition of major institutional structures such as temples, theatres and hippodromes, are in evidence in these centres. New monumental architecture is dominated by the building of a multitude of churches in the fifth and sixth centuries AD. The grid-like order of Roman-town planning had been attempted at some sites such as Gerasa, and Gadara, but was not always achieved in other Hellenized cities such as Abila and Pella, where the hilly topography influenced street alignments. The Roman-period plans were often disturbed by the imposition or insertion of these new structures. A more organic approach to urban development, closer to the traditional oriental format, began to re-emerge. Archaeological evidence is detailed in numerous excavation reports from: Gerasa/Jarash (Kraeling 1938; Zayadine 1986, 1989; Kehrberg and Ostrasz 1997; Seigne 1992); Pella/Tabaqat Fahl (Smith 1973; Smith and Day 1989; McNicoll *et al.* 1982, 1992); Gadara/Umm Qays; Abila/Quwayliba; Capitolias/Bayt Ras; and Arbela/Tall Irbid (most with preliminary reports in the *Annual of the Department of Antiquities of Jordan* from the 1980s).

The North-Central Plateau and South Jordan Valley/ Dead Sea Littoral (within the Provinces of Palestine I and Arabia)

The area lies between Wadi Zarqa in the north and Wadi Mujib in the south. The heartland of this region is the rich agricultural plains of the Balqa around Madaba, and the similarly productive Baqah Valley. The northern wooded hills and watered wadis of the western edge of the plateau give way to a more open, drier landscape in the south, and the eastern steppe merges into the desert. The old Decapolis city of Philadelphia (Amman) dominated the north of this region but the agricultural lands to the south were serviced by important towns such as Hisban, Madaba, Umm Rasas and Dhiban. Modern-day Salt (another ancient Gadara) had been the Roman capital of Peraea, set deep in a valley west of Amman, surrounded by densely wooded hills. The major wadis between the plateau and the Jordan Valley operated as important link zones between the two extremes of elevation, providing access routes with monitoring facilities and pockets of agricultural settlement.

Surveys indicate the closely settled nature of this

Agricultural Centre?

region. The area around Amman/Philadelphia contains many settlements, most of them first noted because of the presence of churches, such as Jubayha, Swafiyeh, Quwaysma, Khirbat Salameh, Khilda, and Yajouz. Information on Byzantine Philadelphia and its territory is patchily known through survey and excavation (Glueck 1939; Abu-Dayyah *et al.* 1991; Northedge 1992: 39–45, 59–60, 155). The same pattern continues in the hilly region around Salt and north to the Zarqa River. Settlements tended to lie on hilltops, many now bearing modern villages. Very few of these sites continued into the Early Islamic periods.

The Baqah Valley, the rich terra rossa plain just northwest of Amman and adjacent to the above-described hills, is anomalous in showing little evidence of installations for this period. Perhaps, surrounded as it was by hilly settlements, it was devoted to large-scale agriculture. Intensive Byzantine settlement, dropping significantly in the early Islamic period, is attested in the hinterland of Iraq al-Amir in Wadi Sir, running westwards from Amman. Similarly, in the area of the Balqa south of Amman, comprising the hinterland of Hisban and the Madaba Plains, the Byzantine period was clearly the most populous, engaging in intensive food production throughout the landscape. Towns acted as thriving market centres, surrounded by scattered hamlets, farmsteads and related installations (cisterns, reservoirs, perimeter walls, terrace walls, mills, presses, roads). Settlement was not constrained by factors of defence or natural water supply, indicating a secure and highly organized environment (MacAdam 1994: 80–88, nn. 183, 184, 187 for references). Excavation has been undertaken at the town sites of Tall Hisban, Tall Umayri, Tall Jawa, Drayjat and Madaba (MacAdam 1994; also Bikai and Dailey 1996), and numerous Christian sites in the area, such as the monastery/church complex of the Memorial of Moses at Mount Nebo and its related town (Khirbat Mukhayyat) as well as hinterland chapels, monasteries and sanctuaries, at Ayoun Musa, Main, Massuh, and Abu Sarbut (Piccirillo 1993). The landscape is littered with Christian monuments and the remnants of intensive viticulture.

Connecting routes from this area down to the Jordan Valley north of the Dead Sea have been documented (e.g. Piccirillo 1987). Sites are fewer in the southern and drier half of the east Jordan Valley and mostly unexcavated. Work at Tall Nimrin near South Shuna suggests affluence in this period (Flanagan *et al.* 1994). There were more medium to small villages and farms than defensive or strategic types of sites. Many new agricultural sites on the valley floor were first settled in the Late Byzantine period. A pair of well-preserved Roman-Byzantine forts with extensive hydraulic facilities lie at the mouth of the nearby Wadi Kafrayn. They probably controlled and protected the renowned warm springs below, popular with pilgrims, as well as the rich agricultural lands of the valley floor and a route to the plateau (Prag and Barnes 1996). The mountainous eastern shores of the Dead Sea contain isolated thermal springs with lush vegetation. The Roman bathing complex of Ayn Zara (Kallirrhoë) continued to be occupied in the Byzantine period, as part of a wider fertile area divided into farms with other farmsteads and villas, a possible fort and a paved road leading to the plateau ('Amr *et al.* 1996: 445).

The plateau between Wadi Wala and Wadi Mujib reveals a similar settlement pattern to that of the Madaba Plains, with a peak of activity in Roman and Byzantine times (Ji 2000). The towns of Umm Rasas/Kastron Mefaa (Piccirillo 1989: 269–308) and Dhiban (Tushingham 1972) provided strong market and religious centres in the Byzantine period. Survey of the area between Hisban and Karak found a substantial number of Byzantine sites (just over half) but not as great as in the Roman period (Homès-Fredericq 1986: 81–100; MacAdam 1994: 80, 181). This variation in the settlement pattern, particularly for the area south of Wadi Mujib, is supported by other survey data from the Karak Plateau, see below.

The South-Central Plateau and the Southern Ghors (the Provinces of Arabia and Palestine III)

Different zones of the south-central plateau (the Karak Plateau, or Central Moab) have been surveyed over time (Glueck 1939; Canova 1954; Parker 1987: chs. 3–4; Parker 1992; MacDonald [ed.] 1988; Miller 1991), as have the Southern Ghors around the Lisan Peninsula of the Dead Sea and south to the rise into Wadi Arabah (Rast and Schaub 1974; King *et al.* 1987; MacDonald [ed.] 1992).

Byzantine settlement patterns are less homogenous here than in the northern regions. On the plateau, the greatest density of population occurred in the Nabataean/Early Roman period, slumped somewhat in the Late Roman period and revived, but not quite to the same extent, in the early Byzantine period, declining again in the sixth century AD. The eastern line of fortifications was abandoned by the beginning of the sixth century AD and the eastern area in general was sparsely occupied (Parker 1992). The two main towns of the period were Areopolis (Rabbah) and Charachmoba (Karak), although other towns and villages are known from ancient sources. These are largely unexcavated (Miller 1991: 12–13). The legionary base of Betthoro (Lajjun) reveals a functional decline from the fifth century AD (Parker 1986, 1987). Secondary Roman-Byzantine road systems have been documented through the agricultural hinterland west of the Via Nova Traiana down to the shores of the Dead Sea. They were associated with fortified isolated buildings and farms.

Byzantine settlement retains its ascendancy in the Southern Ghors of the Rift Valley, where activity was widespread on the valley floor and up the tributary wadis, utilizing all available agricultural terrain. The area straddled important communication routes between southern Palestine and the northern Negev and the Moabite Plateau. The largest concentration of settlement was around Safi, biblical Zoara, and the religious centre at Dayr Ayn Abata, the Monastery of Saint Lot (King 1987: 446–449; MacDonald [ed.] 1992: 104, 111–112; Politis 1997). The highest annual tax payment scheduled for Palestine III in the Beersheba Edict of the early sixth century AD was from Zoara, presumably an indicator of its economic standing. Both sites were depicted on the Madaba map. The monasteries and hermitages in the vicinity indicate the religious importance of this area (Holmgren and Kaliff 1997; MacDonald [ed.] 1988: 242–244, 1992: 104). Military control of east–west routes across the northern Arabah continued through the occupation of sites such as Umm Tawabin, Qasr Fayfa (the Praesidium of the *Notitia Dignitatum* and the Madaba map), Qasr Umruq and Qasr Khanazira (King 1987: 449–451; Fiema 1991: 230; MacDonald [ed.] 1992: 104–105). The tomb remains of a Roman soldier who died around the end of the fourth/early fifth century AD were found at Haditha east of the Lisan. MacDonald [ed.] conclude that the dense sherd scatters on the valley floor are the only remnants of the many Byzantine village and town sites since subsumed under later activity (1992: 111).

The Southern Plateau, the Hisma and Wadi Arabah (Palestine III)

Southern Jordan with its arid climate and remoteness from the centres of administration supported a lower population. Dry farming was possible on the western side of the plateau, but pastoralism remained the mainstay of the economy. Previously, in the time of Nabataean hegemony, the caravan trade from South Arabia was a primary source of wealth, and population and agriculture was at its height. Trade between the Hijaz and Syria continued to be important through to Islamic times. Byzantine settlement tended to cluster around a number of centres in the south, as isolated concentrations of activity rather than the integrated network that existed in Nabataean/Early Roman times.

Both textual sources and survey-excavation work in this area are limited (reviewed in Schick 1994; Fiema 1991). However recent surveys were conducted in the southern Wadi Hasa, around Busayra/Tafila, Petra, Dana, Wadi Faynan, the southern Wadi Arabah, and the Hisma (MacDonald 1996; MacDonald [ed.] 1988, 2001; 'Amr 2001; Lavento 2004; Lindner 2000, 2002; Tholbecq 2001; Ruben *et al.* 1997; Smith *et al.* 1997; Graf 1992). A few major settlement sites such as Petra (Parr 1986; Fiema 1991, 1995; Patricia Bikai 1995; Joukowsky 2001; Schmid and Kolb 2000), Udhruh (Killick 1986, 1987), Humayma (Oleson *et al.* 1992, 1994, 2002), Aila[1] (Parker 1996, 1996, 1998) and Arindela (Gharandal) (Walmsley 1998) have been excavated, and a network of secondary

road systems identified (Graf 1992, 2001).

Like the Karak Plateau, the Edomite Plateau was less populous in the Byzantine period than in the Roman period, declining in the sixth century AD towards a marked drop in early Islamic times. Byzantine activity concentrated around Arindela (Gharandal) in symbiosis with the busily populated region of the Southern Ghors and the copper-producing wadis flanking Wadi Arabah. Settlement decreases eastwards, with a clustering of sites around two routes from the south and southeast into Wadi Hasa (Wadi Ali and entrances near Qalat Hasa) but not in any other wadis. Sites were surprisingly sparse along the Via Nova Traiana itself and generally in the central plateau. This stretch of road seems little used or scarcely monitored at this time (MacDonald [ed.] 1988: 232, 246, 292–95; Fiema 1991: 223–225). Yet Khirbat Dharih (c. 5 km west of the Via Nova Traiana in Wadi Laban) has revealed Byzantine settlement that was not apparent in the original survey (MacDonald 1996: 326). Similarly Tuwana (Roman Thana/Thoana/Thornia, on the Via Nova Traiana south of Dharih) flourished until its decline towards the end of the Late Byzantine period. However, a surveyed section of the Via Nova Traiana south of Wadi Hasa found no Late Byzantine sherds in the farthest watchtowers north or south from Tuwana. The area covered by the Tafila/Busayra Survey revealed a high proportion of chronologically undifferentiated Byzantine presence.

The broad pattern of activity suggests a preferred use of the desert route for efficient north–south communications at the expense, but perhaps not the total demise, of the established central route, at least between Udhruh and Wadi Hasa. A secondary, undulating western route along the escarpment linked the more numerous western settlements (Fiema 1991: 283, Map 9; Graf 2001: 469).

Another focus of settlement was around Udhruh, attesting to the continued importance of this town. Udhruh paid the second highest amount of taxes recorded in the Beersheba Edict of the early sixth century AD (Killick 1983: 231). The Ghassanid, Jabal b. Harith, was reported to have rebuilt the town in the sixth century AD. The line of the Via Nova Traiana has been identified, along with a network of support roads, small forts, watchtowers, farmsteads, large unwalled settlements, and agricultural systems, all dated to the Byzantine period (Killick 1983, 1986).

Recent excavations have altered the perception that Byzantine Petra was in terminal decay. The pattern of urban use changed in the same way as in the Decapolis cities of the north, and new churches were built or existing structures transformed. In the early sixth century AD Petra still had a city council (inferred from an inscription found at Elji), and the latest housing found so far dates to the middle and late sixth century AD. Textual references to bishops from Petra continue up to the late sixth century AD. Papyrus scrolls dating between AD 537 and 592 provide a mine of information on the daily life of the local inhabitants, presenting an image of social and economic vitality based now on land ownership rather than international trade (Pierre Bikai 1996; Frösén 2004). Surrounding settlements and buildings are mentioned, as well as key figures in the life of Petra. From the dating formulae used, it is apparent that imperial orders were received quickly and efficiently, confirming the continued status of Petra as an important regional administrative centre in the late Byzantine period. The recently deciphered Scroll 60 indicates that c. AD 540, Petra remained the dominant city in relation to Udhruh (Augustopolis) and that the fiscal administration of the imperial house was still active there (Kaimio and Koenen 1997). Recent surveys of the immediate hinterland including the Wadi Musa and Tayyiba areas confirms the picture of active land use and settlement in the sixth century as portrayed in the scrolls ('Amr 2001).

The Nabataean town of Humayma (Auara) in the Hisma also retained its importance in Byzantine times although activity in the desert farther east was diminished. At least five churches have now been identified and the occupation area doubled. The Roman fort ceased to function by the end of the fourth century AD, reducing the military character of the settlement while the civilian population expanded significantly (Oleson 2001: 575–577). A third century AD bathhouse was modified in the fifth/sixth century AD and, presumably, the extensive hydraulic systems were maintained.

The Roman road and control systems in the south continued through the early Byzantine period. Subsidiary roads radiating from the Via Nova Traiana were identified at Petra, Basta, Sadaqa, Qana and Humayma (Graf 1992). Only the Via Nova Traiana road forts of Khirbat Khalde and Khirbat Kithara towards Aila show evidence of Late Byzantine occupation. Farther north, the sixth century AD occupation of Udhruh and Ayl may, like Humayma, represent civilian rather than military use (Parker 1986: 87–113).

The Roman-Byzantine town of Aila has recently been discovered within modern Aqabah, northwest of Islamic Aylah. The site had long functioned as the gateway for seaborne and overland trade between India, Africa, South Arabia, Egypt, the Mediterranean and Syria, and maintained its importance through the Byzantine period (see below, Foreign Relations and Trade). Militarily, it was the base for the Tenth Fretensis Legion, possibly up to the sixth century AD (see below, Defence). Bishops from Aila attended ecclesiastical councils from the fourth–century AD onwards, and it was an important halt for pilgrims on the way to Mount Sinai (see below, Religion). Aila was fortified or refortified in the late fourth century AD by a city wall with towers, which was repaired in the late sixth century AD and fell into disrepair in the early seventh

century AD. A mudbrick church, possibly the earliest known, and domestic areas of the Late Byzantine period have been exposed. Material remains attest to wide-ranging contacts in the Byzantine period (Parker 1996, 1998, 2002).

The number of sites declined in the arid hinterland of Aqabah, the southern Wadi Arabah, after the early Byzantine period. These had been small way stations and forts, such as Gharandal/Aridela, Qasr Wadi Tayyiba, Qasr Wadi Musa, and Bir Madhkur, principally serving the east–west traffic across the valley along a limited number of routes. The recent discovery of a section of stone-paved road running north–south may alter our understanding of these connections, but dating is uncertain. Evidence from the west side of the Arabah suggests that a reduced traffic tended more to the west, from Yotvata to Gaza (Smith *et al.* 1997; Fiema 1991: 233–234). Sites are relatively sparse in the northern Arabah, principally comprising forts that control water sources, such as Qasr Tilah, Qasr Fayfa, Qasr Khanazira and Qasr Umruq. Again, occupation fades away in the Late Byzantine period.

Passage between Aila and Wadi Faynan in the central Arabah must have remained feasible while it still produced and marketed copper. The extensive remains of ancient Phaeno (Khirbat Faynan) include at least five churches, attesting to the legacy of the early Christian martyrs forced to work in the mines (Figure 14.3). The latest known bishop is recorded on a building inscription, dated AD 587–88 (Ruben *et al.* 1997). Two large cemeteries, an aqueduct, reservoir and mill facilities are located nearby. Inscriptions and grave goods from the South Cemetery date its use from the fifth up to the late sixth centuries AD (Findlater *et al.* 1998). Remnants of extensive field systems dominate the broad wadi to the west (Barker *et al.* 1997). There has been detailed investigation of the ancient mines and smelting centres in the vicinity, focusing on the geology and metallurgical developments (Hauptmann and Weisgerber 1992; Hauptmann 2000). In the Roman-Byzantine period, the remaining low-grade ores were worked at least until the end of the fifth century, AD and the town flourished. There is little evidence for Early Islamic activity, and the site seems to have been in decline during the Late Byzantine period.

The Eastern Steppe and Desert (Province of Arabia)

The only fertile areas in this region are the southern Hauran with its productive volcanic soil and the Azraq Oasis. Building on the early surveys of Butler (1919), the area has recently been examined by Kennedy (1982, 1997; Kennedy and Freeman 1995) and King (1983). This is supplemented by Parker's studies of the *limes* system (1986, 1987), excavations at Umm Jimal, Qasr Burqu, and Qasr Hallabat (De Vries 1985, 1993, 1998; Betts *et al.* 1991; Bisheh 1986). Work in the Syrian Hauran informs and complements all these studies. MacAdam summarized much of the evidence for settlement patterns in the region (1994: 53–68).

The southern Hauran comprises the basalt desert region of northeastern Jordan (the *harra*) in a marginal rainfall zone. The area extends into southern Syria and the lava slopes of the Jabal Druze, with Bostra (Arabic = Busra), the capital of the province of Arabia, dominating the region. Systematic settlement on a large scale began in the Nabataean period and reached its apogee in the Byzantine period when settlements were closely scattered across the landscape. During the fourth and fifth centuries AD, a system of fortifications, watchtowers and signalling posts functioned to control and monitor these southeastern limits of the Byzantine empire, creating a wide area of civilian security. In the sixth century AD, military policy delegated this control to the Ghassanids, and the imperial garrisons disappeared. Civilian activities flourished and expanded in these times and many churches were built. At Umm Jimal, the Late Roman fort lost its military value during the fifth century AD, with its role assumed by the smaller Barracks complex. The fort was turned over to domestic (probably commercial) use. The construction of domestic housing reached its peak in the sixth century AD and 15 churches were built. Umm Jimal had become a prosperous rural Christian community within a similarly settled hinterland, a short day's journey from Bostra (Figure 14.4).

Sophisticated systems of water collection and distribution supported cereal production as well as pastoral activities. A previously unknown Roman fort has been tentatively identified at Umm Quttayn, surrounded by domestic housing, extensive traces of field boundaries, and a Roman road leading towards Bostra (Kennedy and Freeman 1995). These settlements are just two examples of the scatter of towns and villages, usually with churches or even monasteries, linked by a network of roads which facilitated communications beyond the line of the Via Nova Traiana (Kennedy 1997). Major trade routes straddled the region bringing associated economic incentives and profit to the inhabitants. Pre-and post-Islamic Arabic texts and traditions confirm the importance of the Hauran trade with the Hijaz and Makkah in the sixth and early seventh centuries AD (Sartre 1987: 160–162).

Farther east, occupation was restricted to isolated fortifications sometimes with small attached settlements. These were placed along the Strata Diocletiana, the easternmost zone of imperial control providing a communication route running north from Azraq to the Euphrates River (Parker 1986: 15-36). The fourth–fifth century AD fort of Dayr Kahf monitored the south-eastern Hauran, with a small surrounding settlement and traces of agricultural activity. Nearby is the Roman-Byzantine settlement of Dayr Qinn and an outlying watchtower overlooking Jawa (King *et al.* 1983: 415). The remote outpost of Qasr Burqu is situ-

Figure 14.3 Khirbat Faynan, ancient Phaeno. View east showing building ruins covering the foreground and the tell behind.

Figure 14.4 View across Umm Jimal.

ated at an eastern water source along a minor route from the south (Betts *et al.* 1991; Parker 1986: 21; see Figure 14.5).

The large oasis of Azraq at the outlet of Wadi Sirhan was a pivotal location in the eastern desert. Besides the large fort and reservoir, it must have supported some settlement and agriculture. Subsequent occupation has destroyed most of the early evidence. Outlying sites comprise small forts and watchtowers along established routes. There is no surface evidence of Late Byzantine occupation at these sites. Farther west, Qasr Hallabat also had traces of field and terrace walls in the vicinity but later activity has obliterated any Roman-Byzantine evidence, save for the pottery. There are some traces of Byzantine activity in the steppe south of Qasr Hallabat, near the Umayyad agricultural villa of Qasr Mushash (King *et al.* 1983: 391–92). Byzantine settlement in these arid areas was minimal, associated with military installations where conditions allowed it. The remote Nabataean-Roman fort of Bayir was abandoned by the Byzantine period. As in the south, early Byzantine control seems consolidated within a zone further westwards.

Material Culture

The abundant remains of the Byzantine period in Jordan have yielded a wealth of cultural artefacts. Pottery is the most enduring and ubiquitous survivor of ancient material culture, but other hardy classes of material such as glass, metalwork, coins, worked bone, and carved stone are found, not to mention architectural decoration such as relief sculpture, wall painting and mosaics. Limited occupation in highly arid areas has allowed survival of some organic materials such as fabrics, wood, leather and matting that normally would have disintegrated.

Pottery

Pottery vessels, from the menial to the fine, were an essential part of daily life. Sites with extensive stratified deposits of occupation from the fourth to seventh centuries AD have aided documentation of the changes in pottery through time. In the north, excavations at Pella, Jarash, Umm Jimal and Tall Hisban produced useful pottery sequences for this period (Smith 1973; Smith and Day 1989; McNicoll *et al.* 1992: 163–181; Watson 1992; Zayadine 1986, 1989: 85–97; De Vries 1998: ch. 11; Sauer 1973). The greater stability of settlement in the north, with large multi-period sites that attracted major archaeological investigations, has led to a bias in our current knowledge. The pottery sequence in the centre and south is less understood, although the situation is improving with the recent excavations at Lajjun, Humayma, Petra and Aqabah.

The local pottery of Byzantine Jordan is regional in nature, with the northern sequence being distinct from the middle and south. The intra-regional relationships reflected in the pottery distribution patterns tend to be more east–west than north–south, broadly following provincial divisions of the time, as well as geographical ease of access. A few classes of pottery, mostly imported, range more widely. They are predominantly fine-ware bowls and amphorae. Some pottery forms are popular throughout Transjordan but are reproduced locally in different fabrics. The wares or fabrics tend to be well differentiated from previous Late Roman productions in the north, although this is less evident in the south. From the paler buffs, pinks and creamy-yellows, the favoured colouring of the clay becomes more red-orange and grey, with occasional creams. The cooking wares become grittier. Combed decoration, finger impressions and pie-crust decorations occur. At the end of the period, however, the production of many of the fabrics and forms continues with little change into the Umayyad period. Not until the Abbasid period is a marked change of direction noticeable. A few Umayyad wares are distinctive, as are developments in form and decoration, particularly in the eighth century AD. But the mid-to late seventh century AD transition is difficult to identify without a large assemblage of material to evaluate (McNicoll *et al.* 1982: 100; Watson 1992).

A brief selection of some of the most common and typical Byzantine pottery types follows, as an example of the pottery of Byzantine Jordan. Of the ordinary daily wares, the so-called "Palestinian bag-shaped amphora" is the most distinctive and common container recovered, presumably because it was used not only to transport liquids such as wine, but as the standard water carrier (Figure 14.7.2). In the north, it is generally grey (occasionally red or mottled) with white-painted swirling decoration on a ribbed body and two short loop handles on the shoulder. The fabric is hard and metallic. Farther east and south, the fabric changes to a red or buff. The ware of the common ribbed or plain cooking casserole with cut rim and lid also varies regionally, but the form is relatively constant (Figure 14.6.1). The basic cooking pot with spheroid body (mostly ribbed) and wide-mouthed short-or no neck, has a variety of diagnostic rim forms that change over time (Figure 14.6.2) and occurs in the same regional wares as the casserole. Very large hand-made storage jars with hole-mouth opening and folded collar rim continue to be used from the Roman period, generally in a pink to buff, hard fabric (changing regionally). In the north, it converts to grey ware by the Early Islamic period (Figure 14.7.1). Large hand-made basins have flat bases, flaring walls, and a variety of thickened rim forms. In the north, these were manufactured in a chaff-tempered buff-brown ware (Figure 14.7.3), and, in the Late Byzantine period, in the same fine hard grey ware as the later large storage jars, continuing into the Islamic period (Figure 14.7.4). Jarash is a known production centre for the grey ware. Jugs and juglets appear in many forms. In the Jarash red

Figure 14.5 Qasr Burqu. View northeast when the seasonal lake is full (mid-ground), showing the surrounding basalt *harra*.

Figure 14.6 Byzantine pottery. 1. Cooking casserole and lid (Pella. Watson 1992: fig. 1.1, 2) 2. Cooking pot (Pella. Cat. No. 72) 3. Jug (Lajjun. Pub. No. 306) 4. Jarash lamp (Jarash. Rasson and Seigne, in Zayadine [ed.] 1989: 145, fig.13.5) 5. Jarash bowl (Jarash. Watson, in Zayadine [ed.] 1989: 244, fig.9.1) 6. "Fine Byzantine" bowl (Amman. Koutsou-kou. 1997: 107, no.172).

Figure 14.7 Byzantine pottery and glass. 1. Grey ware storage jar (Jarash. Fisher and McCown 1931: 35) 2. Palestinian bag-shaped amphora (Pella. Cat. No. 10640) 3. Hand-made basin in chaff-tempered coarse ware (Pella. Cat. No. 2153) 4. Grey ware basin (Jarash. Rasson and Seigne, in Zayadine [ed.] 1989: 133, fig. 7.7) 5. Glass bowl (Jarash. Dussart 1989: 106, fig. 2b).

ware, the appearance of simple, white-painted swirls and single stripes on handles of jugs heralds the more exaggerated use of white painted decoration in the Early Islamic examples. Plain conical cups were a feature. The repertoire of fine ware bowls and plates is dominated by imported Phoenician and African red slip wares (from Asia Minor and North Africa respectively), and some Cypriot and Egyptian imitations (Hayes 1972). These were fine red wares, slipped and sometimes decorated with rouletting and stamps. Local manufacturers tended to imitate these forms, the most spectacular series being produced at Jarash (known as "Jarash Bowls") and further embellished with pictorial decorations in white and red paint (Watson 1992: 242; Uscatescu 2001; see Figure 14.6.5). Another group of less distant imports that appeared widely is the bowls and jugs of "Fine Byzantine" ware probably manufactured in Jerusalem (Figure 14.6.6; Watson 1992: 242; "Ware K"). Common amphorae types of external origins were the "Gaza" (Figure 14.8) (Peacock and Williams Class 49), the "Antioch/Cypriot" type (Class 44), and the "Abu Mina" (Egyptian Delta, Kellia Type 186), all attesting to dynamic relations with the Mediterranean world to the west (Watson 1992: 239–240, H2, H1, H4).

Byzantine oil lamps are mould-made, evolving out of the Hellenistic-Roman tradition. They vary in type and are usually regional in their distribution, with a pronounced difference between northern and southern Jordan. Popular forms in the early Byzantine period belong to the bow-shaped nozzle family and the bilanceolate candlestick family. The former develops into the broad-nozzle type, while the latter enlarges over time into the Late Byzantine "candlestick" type, which continues into the Early Islamic period. A similar time span is observed for the "Jarash" lamps, a distinctive group with tongue handles that develop into a zoomorphic form. The general tendency in the development of shape is a thickening of the nozzle until it becomes one piece with the body. There is a coarsening and simplification of the decoration and the size of the handle increases. The same handle form can appear on several body types. The most common Byzantine motif is a shoulder decoration of radiating lines (Zayadine 1986: 163-66, 367–375; 1989: 85–97; Da Costa 2001).

Two major pottery production centres have been identified in the north and the south, namely, at Jarash and Petra. The Jarash production ranged from Roman through to Abbasid times. The Byzantine pottery manufacturing area was concentrated in the disused hippodrome where, besides kilns producing many other types, a dump of unfired Jarash bowls was found (Kehrberg and Ostrasz 1994, 1997). A sixth century potter's shop of deformed "seconds" was unearthed in the retail area by the South Gate (Zayadine 1986: 71). Jarash pottery and their distinctive lamps had a wide distribution in northern Jordan. Doubtless, other centres existed in the north, for instance, a Late Byzantine pottery kiln was discovered in a salvage

excavation in Wadi Zarqa (Palumbo *et al.* 1993). Late Roman pottery kilns of the third/fourth centuries AD have recently been identified at both Abila and Pella, lending credence to the assumption that they also produced pottery in the Byzantine period.

The kilns at Petra-Zurrabah functioned from the Nabataean period through to the sixth century AD, the latest kiln proving the continued production of the "Nabataean painted" ware into the Late Byzantine period. A predominance of cream surfaces was reported in the late phases, as well as a decline in craftsmanship generated by the requirements of mass production, leading to much coarser, poorly levigated clay ('Amr 1991, 2004). Kilns of the mid-seventh century AD at Aqabah produced a typical Byzantine corpus, including the "Ayla-Axum" amphora that appears as early as the fifth century AD. Kiln wasters and slag provide further evidence for production in the Byzantine period (Melkawi *et al.* 1994; Parker 1998: 388–389, 2002: 423–425). The corpus from the seventh century production is described as "southern Jordanian/Palestinian," with wares that are more "sandy" and less hard and metallic than their northern counterparts, no-

Figure 14.8 Petra Church mosaic detail: Man holding an amphora of "Gaza" type (cf. McNicholl *et al.* pl. 116.8).

tably lacking in painted decoration. Strong associations with Egyptian products are noted.

Glass

Ancient "Syria" was famous for its glass industry, and Syrian glass-blowers travelled far and wide. Recent excavations in Jordan suggest that some provincial centres had their own production facilities. At Jarash, numerous glass cakes were found in the "Glass Court" near the Cathedral, possibly being reused for the manufacture of glass tesserae for mosaics. A thick dump of broken glass was found nearby, but no actual kilns have been located. A Byzantine pottery kiln that was converted to a glass furnace in the Early Islamic period was found by the Gerasa–Philadelphia road, near Zarqa River (Palumbo *et al.* 1993). Glass production is postulated at Abila, where a large quantity of glass fragments and lumps of glass slag was found in the theatre *cavea*. Most of the information on glass in Jordan comes from studies of glass found at Jarash, with minor contributions from other sites (such as Meyer 1988; Kraeling 1938: 505–46).

With the invention of moulds and, later, the technique of blowing, glass objects could be industrially produced in quantity, rather than being exclusive items of luxury. Byzantine glass is relatively abundant and diverse, with many new forms appearing. The colour, however, is standardized, being light blue, blue-green or green. Vessel walls are very thin, more so than the Roman product. Forms introduced include simple conical beakers (that are rare outside the area), the double unguentaria (double kohl tubes or flasks, characteristically "Syro-Palestinian"), globular and piriform flasks with very long necks and flaring mouths, small bottles with narrow necks, and stemmed goblets. Glass lamps in the form of a goblet, with handles or stem, were introduced after the fourth–fifth centuries AD. They were especially popular in churches, eventually replacing ceramic lamps. Glass dishes and bowls were less common (Figure 14.7.5). Decorative techniques were limited to cutting, engraving and moulding, while ruffles and particularly trailed threads became characteristic decorative features of the region, commonly applied to bottles. Glass jewellery was popular, in the form of plain or twisted rings and bracelets of coloured glass.

Most of the Byzantine glass windowpanes found at Jarash and Pella are flat, and probably cast. In the early seventh century "crown" panes, which permit more rapid manufacture than cast glass, prevail. The majority of windowpanes occur in the debris of churches, where glass mosaic tesserae used for wall and hemidome decoration are also common. Glass lamps also predominate in these contexts and the quantity of glass bottles and goblets suggests that they were used in church services. Apart from the generally fragmentary material provided by stratified excavations, tombs have produced the bulk of whole vessels. The advantage of intact survival in such contexts is diminished by their generally poor precision in dating, but they serve as useful reference parallels for the fragments.

Metalwork

The survival of metal in the archaeological record is haphazard, owing to the problems of corrosion. Apart from utilitarian objects such as nails, hinges and locks, occasional fine objects are recovered. Church ritual and embellishment encouraged the production of a wide variety of metal objects such as crosses, chandeliers, lamp holders, small bells and incense burners (see, for example, Zayadine 1986: 152, 155, 338; McNicoll *et al.* 1982: pl. 150, 2). A bronze repoussée plaque, from a fourth century AD tomb at Pella, is remarkable for documentation of early Christian iconography. It apparently depicts Christ's entry into Jerusalem on one side and the twin Constantinian shrines of Golgotha and the Holy Sepulchre on the other (McNicoll *et al.* 1982: 100).

Coinage

After AD 324, a uniform monetary system was applied throughout the whole empire. It was based on a new gold unit, the solidus, valued at 72 to the pound. A gold half-solidus, the semissis, and the more obscure 1½ scripulum were also introduced. The latter was replaced by the tremissis (third-solidus) during the reign of Theodosius I in AD 383. Silver coinage was revived under Constantine, with the miliarensis (one-eighteenth solidus) and the siliqua (one-twenty-fourth solidus), becoming widely used by his successors throughout the fourth century AD. Their production ceased around 400. As silver coinage became popular, the use of debased silver for smaller denominations was gradually abandoned, replaced by copper-alloy coins in the fourth and fifth centuries AD. These varied in size and weight but generally became smaller over time, reflecting a constantly changing and unstable standard. They are referred to as nummi or, more specifically, "bronze" (Æ) 1, 2, 3, or 4, the Æ4 being the smallest and the most common by the fifth century AD. During the fifth century AD the most important coinage was gold. Very little silver was minted, and an inadequate quantity of copper coins was issued, causing a shortage of officially minted coins. The tiny base-metal coins were, therefore, imitated in large numbers by forgers. Many of them were needed to buy a commodity, hence their frequent discovery in large hoards.

The monetary reform of Anastasius in AD 498 introduced new larger copper coins. For numismatists, this marks the beginning of Byzantine, as distinct from Roman coinage. These new coins filled the awkward gap between the *tremissis* and the Æ4, where between 2400 and 4800 of the latter were needed to equal one of the former. The new copper denominations were of revolutionary design, with the most prominent feature being the use of a large Greek letter indicating the value in *num-*

mi on the reverse type: M (= 40 *nummi*) the *follis*; K(=20 *nummi*) the half-*follis*; I(=10 *nummi*) the *decanummium*; E(=5 *nummi*) the *pentanummium*. This set a pattern for the next three centuries.

The designs on coins of the fourth century AD do not change suddenly from pagan to Christian imagery, as there was no official iconography to draw upon. The Christian *chi-rho* monogram appeared initially in a minor role as a mint-mark. The image of the "hand of God" receiving the deified deceased emperor, or appointing a new emperor, was used in various forms. Such symbols became more prominent in the fifth century AD. The cross appeared as an attribute of the city of Constantinople or decorating the official sceptre. The standard design on the reverse of the eastern *solidi* from the fifth until the seventh centuries AD, was the cross with the figure of Victory. The traditional depiction of the emperor's head on the obverse, shown in profile to right, changed under Constantius II (AD 337–61) to a three-quarter facing bust, helmeted, with spear and shield. This was regularly used until the sixth century AD under Justinian I, when the face became fully frontal, the characteristic "Byzantine" representation. Later, a crown replaced the helmet. *Tremisses*, however, continued to use profile portraits. The post-reform *folli* show a transition on the obverse type from the typical Roman profile bust (standard under Anastasius) to the typical Byzantine facing bust introduced by Justinian, although the profile type lingered on occasionally until the seventh century AD. Justin II introduced the emperor and empress enthroned side-by-side, and double and even triple images became common in the seventh century AD.

After the mid-fourth century AD, the minting of gold coins was confined to the *comitatus*, the place of residence of the emperor (principally Constantinople and Thessalonica). In the east, base-metal coinage was produced separately at a number of state mints: Constantinople, Thessalonica, Heraclea, Nicomedia, Cyzicus, Antioch and Alexandria. Constantinople, Nicomedia and Cyzicus produced the bulk of the coinage. Before the Anastasian reform, most of these mints had collapsed, with only Constantinople and Thessalonica remaining in operation. After AD 498 and during the sixth century AD, they reopened, with the exception of Heraclea. Other mints were activated, such as Carthage and Constantine in Numidia. During the prosperous reign of Justinian (AD 527–65), at least 15 mints were operational. The troubled reign of Heraclius in the early seventh century AD saw another reduction of Byzantine mints and short-lived operations at various new locations such as Alexandretta, Isaura, Seleucia (in Isauria), Jerusalem and Cyprus. Copper coins generally bore recognizable mint-marks unless they were too small but, after Anastasius, silver and gold coins were rarely marked (Whitting 1973; Burnett 1987).

The most common Byzantine coinage recovered in Jordan and the Levant in general is that of Justinian I (AD 527–65). His reign was long, and he needed money to conduct prolonged wars against Persia. His successor Justin II (AD 565–78) is also well represented in finds. Apart from the *nummi*, fifth century AD coinage is less common.

Organic Remains

Textiles rarely survive in other than extremely arid climates. The carbonized remains of silks found in the Umayyad earthquake destruction of Pella are a unique find in Jordan, but the cloth was widely available in the region before this. The Persian control of the silk trade was broken in the mid-sixth century AD when silk moth eggs were brought to Constantinople. From here, under the patronage of the Byzantine emperors, the industry developed and regional workshops flourished. Syria produced silks at Tyre, Damascus, Aleppo and Antioch, and silk remains have been found in the Byzantine sites of Halabiyeh on the Syrian Euphrates as well as Avdat in the Negev (McNicoll *et al.* 1992: 257–265). Scythopolis (Bayt Shan), in the northwest Jordan Valley, was renowned for its manufacture of fine linen from the Late Roman period onwards. Remnants of shrouds have survived in Roman and Byzantine tombs in arid areas south of the Dead Sea (Politis 1998; Findlater *et al.* 1998). On the Lisan Peninsula of the Dead Sea, fragments of clothing, including wool and linen, ropes and plaited work were recovered from the excavation of the monastery of Dayr Qattar (Holmgren and Kaliff 1997: 324).

Leather, usually sandals, and wood also survive in such conditions, for example, at Wadi Faynan, in the form of small objects such as a spindle, a wooden kohl tube, jewellery (ring and bracelet), and a comb, as well as coffins (Findlater *et al.* 1998). Peculiar thermal conditions emanating through the bedrock and sealed within some tombs at Pella allowed coffins and even laurel leaves to survive in a much more humid climate (McNicoll *et al.* 1992: 141, 143).

Wall Painting

Very little art in this genre has survived in Jordan, and for the Byzantine period, virtually none. For the Roman period, painted tombs have been found at Abila and Bayt Ras, and domestic wall painting at Petra. The renowned wall paintings of Qusayr Amra are Umayyad. Fragmentary remnants were found in the East Church at Pella, probably from the upper wall. Wealthier churches tended to be decorated with marble panels and mural mosaics, while the poorer churches would use plaster and paint, a far more fragile medium.

Sculpture

Monumental, free-standing sculpture was popular in the classical Greek and Roman artistic context. During the

Byzantine period many of the significant religious and public buildings of the earlier era were abandoned, reused, altered and plundered for their useful components. Most Byzantine churches re-used columns, capitals, carved architraves and lintels from their pagan predecessors. More often than not, archaeologists have found major items of classical sculpture in the dump and fill deposits relating to the process of dismantling and reconstruction. Provincial sculptural expression during the Byzantine period was limited to relief carvings on tomb and building lintels, sarcophagi, church furniture such as chancel screens and altars, and small-scale figurines.

Architectural and furniture reliefs continue the design motifs of previous centuries with an additional overlay of Christian symbolism. The cross in its numerous manifestations was a dominant image, as well as the vine, the wreath, animals from paradise, the tree of life, the chalice, and others in common with the iconography found on the mosaics. Newly made column capitals break away from the traditional classical Corinthian form and depict a variety of the above images, including human figures (Piccirillo 1993: ills. 316, 321, 326–329, 727–730). They vary from simple elegant designs, recalling the format of their foliate predecessors, to busy overall patterning of details and images charged with meaning.

Production of pottery figurines continued from the Roman period, employing Christian iconography that easily transferred meaning from pagan imagery. For instance, the popular image of the "Madonna and Child" grew from traditional Egyptian images of Isis with Horus and the Semitic figurines of Astarte (Bienkowski 1991: pl. 66). An interesting class of "mirror plaques" in clay or plaster has been found in Byzantine tombs from the south to the north. They can be anthropomorphic or in the shape of fish, with painted details, and carry the inset for a small glass mirror or reflector. Possibly, they have a symbolic and prophylactic function (Bienkowski 1991: pl. 65; Humbert 1997: 55).

Social and Political Organization

Administrative Structure

By the late fourth century AD, the area covered by modern Jordan was included in four Roman provinces: Palestine I (*Palaestina Prima*), Palestine II (*Palaestina Secunda*), Palestine III (*Palaestina Salutaris*, later *Palaestina Tertia*) and Arabia. They formed part of a diocese within the Prefecture of Oriens. The organizational details of this structure are unclear, but for the beginning of the fifth century AD we have the *Notitia Dignitatum*, an official "List of Offices," which records the provinces, military placements and offices.

Starting from the northwest of Jordan, each province covered the following area (Figure 14.2): Palestine II extended from the west across the north Jordan Valley onto the western side of the plateau, including the cities of Pella, Capitolias (Bayt Ras), Arbela (Irbid), Abila (Quwayliba) and Gadara (Umm Qays). Scythopolis (Bayt Shan) was the capital.

Palestine I extended from the west across the south Jordan Valley to the plateau, including Livias (Shunat Nimrin), Gadara (Salt), Amathus, and Bacatha(?). The capital was on the coast at Caesarea Maritima.

Palestine III initially extended south of Wadi Hasa to the Gulf of Aqabah, with its capital at Petra. Sometime between AD 451 and 535 the northern boundary was moved north to Wadi Mujib.

The province of Arabia extended from the Hauran south to Wadi Hasa (later retracted to Wadi Mujib) and included Gerasa (Jarash), Philadelphia (Amman), Esbus (Tall Hisban), and Madaba. The capital was Bostra (Busra), today in southern Syria. The southern and eastern boundaries fade into the adjacent deserts. Negative evidence suggests that earlier Roman penetration into the northern Hijaz was withdrawn in the Byzantine period (Fiema 1991: 128–133; Sartre 1982: 133).

A governor who was responsible for civil jurisdiction administered each province, while overall military authority was in the hands of the *dux* or military commander. In Arabia, the military performed civil functions as well, but inefficiently and for its own profit, prompting reorganization in the sixth century AD. Distribution of the military forces changed over the centuries, diminishing from the fifth to seventh centuries AD (see below, Defence). Ecclesiastical divisions seem to have followed the imperial administrative units. Jordan contained about 18 bishoprics, as attested by inscriptions in church mosaics (see below, Religion).

Society

The cities in northwestern Jordan had been under a strong Hellenizing influence since the conquests of Alexander the Great. Nevertheless, even here, the population retained its indigenous ties. Inscriptions and artefacts reveal personal names recorded in Semitic, Greek and Latin script. The proportion of Semitic to Graeco-Roman personal names increases in towns to the east such as Umm Jimal and Khirbat Samra, where the mix of cultures sees the same name inscribed in both Greek and Aramaean (Sartre 1985: 199). The strength of the local Aramaean communities is evident in the emergence of an Aramaean Christian scripture in a church dominated by Greek as the official language (Humbert and Desreumaux 1989: 121; MacAdam 1994: 74). The language of the Petra scrolls is overwhelmingly Greek, yet the Semitic character of the area is clearly evident in the transcription of personal names, toponyms and descriptive or designatory terms taken from Nabataean, Aramaic and Arabic. The papyri are economic and legal documents dealing with issues of real estate, inheritance, marriage, contracts, disputes, loans and sales. As well as ordinary people, administrators in the ecclesiastical, civilian, and military ranks are mentioned. The backbone of Petra society had shifted from engagement in long-distance trade to land-ownership and the maintenance of vineyards, orchards, sown lands, slaves and housing complexes (Bikai 1996; Kaimio and Koenen 1997; Frösén 2004).

Regional surveys show that the countryside in the watered areas was dotted with farmsteads in the Byzantine period. Their frequency and relatively unfortified nature suggests a peaceful and productive agricultural economy, as depicted in mosaics of the period. The hinterlands of towns in the more arid regions such as Umm Jimal, Phaeno, Petra or Humayma contain vestiges of careful water collection, storage and distribution for intensively worked fields (aqueducts, channels, cisterns, reservoirs and networks of field walls). The environment to the east was hostile in many ways, as the desert settlements, especially in the northeast, were fortified with continuous walls, towers and military posts. Farm workers and landholders must have formed a significant section of society, supporting the burgeoning towns and their economies.

Urban shopkeepers and artisans were organized into guilds (*collegia*), useful for tax collection, pricing, civic contributions and compulsory services of various kinds. Petra Scroll 60 refers to a *collegium* of tax collectors situated in Petra. One assumes that the potter's guild at Gerasa (attested in a third century AD inscription) was maintained, as ceramic production continued as a major industry for the city. Slaves were integral to ordinary life, as personal servants, industrial and agricultural workers, and objects of commerce. The harsh copper mining centre of Phaeno in the foothills of Wadi Arabah was infamous for the exploitation of condemned Christians during the persecutions of Diocletian and later. They were the seed for a thriving Christian community as the mines continued working throughout the fourth and fifth centuries AD.

Changes to urban civic life reflect fundamental religious and philosophic shifts during these centuries. Major public buildings such as temples, theatres and hippodromes fell into disuse when their functions were no longer relevant or favoured. By the fourth century AD, drama had given way to mime, a kind of ballet with themes drawn from Greek mythology. This exacerbated Christian dislike of the theatre. Actors may have been popular idols but they were despised by Christians and excluded from the church. The hippodrome at Gerasa was poorly built and, therefore, had a short working life, while the hippodrome at Gadara was never finished. The changes at Gerasa are probably representative of the other Decapolis cities. The city was re-walled in the early fourth century AD and the abandoned hippodrome outside became an industrial centre for pottery and lime for the next three centuries. In the late fourth century AD, a "cathedral" was built directly over a pagan temple. The sanctuary of the Temple of Artemis came to house a Christian complex in one area and another pottery production centre, operating from the fifth to eighth centuries AD. The North Theatre was out of use by the fifth century AD and Byzantine buildings encroached upon it. The main streets became encumbered by shop extensions within the colonnades, reducing their width and the original aesthetic of the streetscape. Nevertheless, the integrity of the basic urban structure survived. Churches were erected all over the city, often plundering the temples for their architectural elements. Attention was lavished on the interiors, with rich mosaics and marble panels (Kraeling 1938; Zayadine 1986, 1989; Seigne 1992; Kehrberg and Ostrasz 1997). Similar patterns of urban change have been recorded at Abila, Gadara, Pella, Amman and Petra. However, changes were incremental rather than absolute, and survival of the pagan ethos is noted at Gerasa, with the sporadic continuation of the controversial nautical festivals of Maiuma into the sixth century AD (Jones 1973: 1021). Bishops and their priests grew to have an important role in the community, reaching into the countryside with numerous village churches and monastic settlements. A strong sense of village solidarity and ecclesiastical involvement is gained from the acknowledgments in village church inscriptions on the Jordanian plateau.

Natural catastrophes affected the social and economic life of the Byzantine East during the fifth and sixth centuries AD. Numerous earthquakes left many urban centres in ruins, some with inadequate means of recovery. The bubonic plague appeared in AD 541 and recurred in a series of devastating epidemics lasting more than 200 years. The depopulation described by Procopius and John of Ephesus affected social and economic activities in the countryside and towns. Local Ghassanid poetry of the pre-Islamic *Jahiliya* expresses the fear it inspired. Archaeological evidence for hurried mass burials at sites such as Umm Jimal, Gerasa and Pella has been explained as the result of the plague (Conrad 1986; Cheyney 1995; Kehrberg and Ostrasz 1994; McNicoll *et al.* 1992: 218-19). The plague may have contributed to the decline of Byzantine society in this region in the late sixth and early seventh centuries AD.

Economy

Agriculture

The proliferation of towns and villages in the Byzantine period was sustained by intensive husbandry of precious food and water resources (see Environment). In the north, the rich plains of the western plateau continued to be important for cereals such as wheat and barley. As rainfall diminished towards the east, the settlements of the southern Hauran carefully tended their water resources to enable irrigated cultivation where today there is desert. The moister western plateau and the spring-fed wadis leading down to the Jordan Valley permitted cultivation of a variety of products, particularly vines, olives, fruit and nut trees (such as fig and almond) and a range of horticultural products. Wine from the region of Capitolias and Gadara (Umm Qays) was praised in the sixth century AD poetry of the pre-Islamic Arabs (Lenzen and Knauf 1987: 35–37).

The recent survey around Pella has found hillsides full of small wine presses and occasional larger complexes, attesting to a thriving local industry. The size and distribution of these presses suggests that this industry was predominantly small-scale, processed *in situ* as it was harvested, for local consumption rather than trade (Watson and O'Hea 1996). Surveys elsewhere in the northern hilly regions reveal a similar pattern for these installations. A number of large presses have been recorded in the Amman region (Khalil and Nammari 2004). Fewer olive presses were found but they formed larger complexes. The more arid southern regions also produced cereals in the marginal rainfall zones. Irrigated agricultural activity was concentrated in spring-fed wadis, with the same dedication to water husbandry. Every town and village had its associated gardens. The ancient field and water systems recorded around Udhruh, Petra and Khirbat Faynan are visible reminders of successful production in a harsh environment (Killick 1986; Gentelle 1984; Lindner 2000, 2002; Lavento *et al.* 2004; Barker *et al.* 1997).

Pastoralism

Architectural remains attest to the herding of animals. The better-preserved basalt towns and villages in the Hauran have many examples of stables for larger animals such as cows and horses (Figure 14.9). Similar stabling facilities were excavated at Pella and Jarash (Figure 14.10) (see Architecture). Sheep and goats tend to be corralled rather than stabled, and remains of these are found in the countryside of the Hauran. Analysis of faunal remains from excavated sites of the period shows that sheep and goat formed a major part of the diet, followed by cattle, pig, camel, and other domestic animals, and hunted animals such as partridge and gazelle. Bucolic pastoral scenes on contemporary mosaics provide vivid depictions of such activities.

Industry

Knowledge of local industry in the Byzantine period is patchy. Study of the distribution pattern of pottery forms and wares reveals a strong regional pattern of domestic production overlaid by more widely travelled imported products linking the regions. Major centres of production were found in Jarash, Petra and Aila, with defined industrial areas and distribution markets beyond their immediate vicinity. The movement of goods tended to be more east–west rather than north–south, facilitated by the arrangement of administrative units. It is assumed, from the patterns of ware distribution, that there were many other centres (undiscovered) catering for local demand. The Hauran produced a distinctive ware, probably at Bostra, where Islamic kilns have been identified. The Byzantine glazed pottery from Dayr Ayn Abata south of the Dead Sea (an accidental technological development that led nowhere) was another local production (Freestone *et al.* 2001). Late Roman pottery kilns found at Abila and Pella reinforce the impression of small-scale production at numerous sites, despite the close proximity of a dominant industrial centre such as Scythopolis (Bayt Shan)was to Pella.

Evidence for the production of glass is sparse, with possible activity at Jarash and Abila (see Material Culture). The *macellum* (market place) at Jarash contained a tannery and dye works probably from the late Byzantine period, and limekilns were found in the area west of St Theodore's, and in the hippodrome. A limekiln has been identified in the domestic quarters at Gadara. Such industry represents localized production for local consumption.

Copper continued to be mined and smelted at Phaeno until the end of the fifth century AD when the ore bodies seem to have been exhausted. Until this time, the area of Wadi Faynan had been the major copper-production centre in the southern Levant. (Hauptmann and Weisgerber 1992). The trading port of Aila seems to have processed some of this ore, as metal slag was found in the recent excavations. Aila may have sustained a valuable fishing industry, as *garum* (fish sauce) from the Red Sea has been identified in the residue of a ceramic vessel found in a fifth century AD context at Petra (Parker 1998: 11).

Pilgrimage

The local economy was enhanced by a small amount of pilgrim traffic and the facilities to service it. While the majority of holy sites were located in western Palestine, pilgrims also travelled into Transjordan (see Religion). The main interest lay east and south of Jericho, at sites such as Sapsafas (commemorating St John the Baptist, on the east bank of the Jordan River), Mount Nebo and the hot springs of Baaru (modern Hammamat Main). Established routes crossed the Jordan and also went around the Dead Sea. The monastery of St. Lot near Zoara at the south end of the Dead Sea was famous. The complex at Jabal Harun near Petra has proved to be the monastery and pilgrimage centre venerating St. Aaron mentioned in one of the Petra scrolls. Moving even further south, Aila was an important staging post on the way to St Catherine's Monastery in the Sinai (Politis 2001; Fiema 2004; Frösen 2004; Waheeb 2004).

Architecture

Churches

With the acceptance of Christianity, the construction

of churches proliferated in the towns and countryside, reaching a peak in the sixth century AD. The dominant form was the basilica, consisting of a nave and two side aisles, sometimes expanded to four side aisles. They terminated in the east as a central apse flanked by two rooms, or three apses, with a larger central apse. The triapsidal type was more favoured in the sixth century AD. At the western end of the church was a square or rectangular colonnaded courtyard, the atrium. An antechamber or narthex sometimes separated the church from the atrium. The main altar was placed on a low dais in front of the central apse, separated from the body of the church by a chancel screen of decorated marble slabs set between marble posts. Chapels, baptisteries, sacristies and complexes for the clergy were often attached to the side of the main structure. Sometimes churches were built in clusters, as seen at Gadara and Gerasa.

Centralized churches were less common, but varied in form. The church at Gadara, for example, was planned as an octagon within a square (Figure 14.11), while the Church of St. John the Baptist at Gerasa was based on a circle within a square. The now-destroyed Church of the Prophets, Apostles and Martyrs at Gerasa was a cross within a square, with a small projecting apse, while the Church of the Virgin Mary at Madaba has a round nave

with an elongated apsed presbyterium (Piccirillo 1993).

The exterior of these churches was quite austere, with simple ornament restricted to doorjambs, lintels and cornices. Many of the architectural elements such as columns, capitals, and architraves were reused from earlier temples. However, the interiors were lavishly decorated with mosaics on the floors and walls, painted plaster walls, carved marble chancel screens and posts, marble facing, and patterned pavements.

Town Planning

Life in most towns continued within the framework of Roman-period urban planning and buildings. Adaptations were made as requirements changed. The Byzantine approach was more pragmatic than aesthetic, filling in and modifying open public spaces and monumental buildings to suit commercial and social requirements. Damage by intermittent earthquakes such as that of AD 363 must have aided this process of transformation. These changes are evident from excavations at Gerasa, Philadelphia, Pella, Gadara, Madaba and Petra. The colonnaded streets of Gerasa and Petra became cluttered with shops between the columns, as did the oval piazza in Gerasa. Some public buildings (temples, theatres and hippodromes) were re-used as industrial, commercial and religious centres, as

Figure 14.9 Umm Jimal. Mangers with stone troughs in a stable (house complex 49). Blocking of fenestrations is from later use.

Figure 14.10 Pella, Tall Husn. Mangers with flat sills in a domestic context (XXXIVE). The bench behind belongs to a later phase of re-use.

well as "quarries" for useful architectural elements. Pagan festivals and theatrical performances were progressively abolished from the fourth century AD onwards, and the process of transformation was well advanced by the fifth century AD. In Philadelphia, the vestibule of the Umayyad Palace based its cruciform plan on earlier Byzantine foundations dating no earlier than the fifth century AD. This plan closely resembles the praetorium or audience hall of the Ghassanids at Resafa in north Syria. However, the presence of the north and south doorways in the Amman structure suggests it may have been a monumental gate to the civic area (Almagro 1994).

In some parts of the east, where Hellenization had little impact, towns were not planned in the orthogonal system. They developed more organically, influenced by topography, existing structures, privately owned land and other practical considerations. Umm Jimal and associated settlements in the Hauran are good examples of this phenomenon. They have narrow winding streets, irregular open spaces, domestic and public agglomerations that are closed to the exterior but open internally onto courtyards, and an exterior circumference defensively closed by continuous walling between adjoining buildings. Their predominantly Arab population retained the traditional urban patterns documented from the earliest periods

of urbanization in the Middle East, reflecting a social organization based on family and tribal authority rather than a civic municipal authority.

Domestic Architecture

Our knowledge of domestic architecture of the period is relatively comprehensive due to the preservation of the Hauran settlements and to extensive excavations of domestic structures at Gerasa, Pella, and Amman. The availability of resources naturally led to regional differences in structural materials and solutions. The inhabitants of the Hauran, where wood was scarce, resorted to ingenious methods of roofing using stone corbels and arches. This enabled the construction of sturdy multi-storey buildings, which have survived some 1500 years (Figure 14.4). Basalt was also used for doors, window grills and shutters. The wooded western hills, predominantly limestone country, facilitated the construction of stone buildings with wooden-framed roofs, either pitched or tiled, or flat with rush and pisé. Housing at Pella had ground floors of stone with an upper floor of mudbrick and pisé. As the snecked-stone construction was set in clay mortar that could erode in wet weather, the walls were probably plastered seasonally with pisé. This method of construction continued in use to the twentieth century. Finer buildings, such as the churches, used ashlar masonry, carefully fitted with no mortar or pebbles between the stones. Much of the domestic housing at Aila was mudbrick and stone.

A common element in most houses was the internal courtyard, generally with an opening direct to the street, sometimes embellished by a vestibule. Classical houses have an atrium or peristyle, which have the formality of an interior room open to the sky, whereas this interior space functioned as a working yard. It was the place for domestic activities such as cooking, drawing water, the thoroughfare of animals and access to the upper stories or the roof. Native eastern traditions held sway over introduced western models. Many houses, particularly in the Hauran, have fenestrated internal walls on the ground floor, comprising a row of "windows" with a flat sill or a sunken stone trough, resembling mangers in a stable (Figures 14.9 and 14.10). Cows and equids were caught in such rooms in the AD 749 earthquake at Pella. It seems likely that people and animals coexisted in many of these houses, with people inhabiting the upper floors (De Vries 1985; McNicoll *et al.* 1982: 136).

Military Architecture

Most of the forts in Jordan were built in the late third or fourth centuries AD and continued in use through the early Byzantine period (Figure 14.12). Their plans fall into three main types: the quadriburgia (small forts with four projecting corner towers, such as Qasr Bshir, Qasr Thuraiya), forts with projecting square interval and angle towers (Dayr Kahf, Qasr Azraq, Khirbat Zona, Khirbat Fityan, Dajaniya, Umm Jimal, Khirbat Samra), and forts with U-shaped and semi-circular external towers (Lajjun and probably Udhruh). Sometimes internal rooms were built against the curtain wall, but the larger forts tend to have independent structures within the enclosure. Few forts are known to be constructed in the Byzantine period. The fifth century AD barracks at Umm Jimal and Qasr Baiq have no projecting towers but were protected by internal towers. It seems that several different types of forts were built in the same period and region, perhaps motivated by different conditions or purposes (Parker 1995).

Foreign Relations and Trade

Byzantine Jordan was connected on three sides with imperial provinces, easing relations and trade with the immediate north, west and southwest. The arrangement of the three Palestinian provinces facilitated movement between Transjordan and the Mediterranean. Thus, the ceramic corpora from Transjordanian sites contain imports from North Africa, Egypt, coastal Palestine, Cyprus and coastal Anatolia (see Material Culture). At this time, the region was truly part of a Mediterranean culture.

While tensions fluctuated with the Persians to the northeast, interaction between the two great powers occurred well beyond the borders of Jordan and the

Figure 14.11 Umm Qays. Columns (basalt) of the Octagonal Church with rectangular collonaded atrium (in limestone) behind. View north towards Wadi Yarmuk and the Golan Plateau.

effects were felt indirectly. This changed in the early seventh century with the Persian invasion of AD 613, although their 15-year occupation has left little or no trace in the archaeological record. The desert to the east and southeast was the domain of Arab tribes whose emergence during these centuries played a significant role in social and political developments (see History). The Salih, the Kinda and the Ghassanids were tribes who had migrated westwards into imperial territory. They were utilized and controlled by the Byzantines through alliances, subsidies and delegated military roles (see Defence).

The commercial significance of the region in Roman imperial times had been primarily as a transit route for trade between the Far East, India and the West, and between the more economically significant regions of Egypt and Syria. However, trading routes varied through the centuries according to political factors, changing the fortunes of towns along the way. By the sixth century AD, Petra was no longer an entrepôt for the caravan trade from South Arabia and beyond, as routes shifted north through the Persian Gulf and Syria, or south via the Red Sea. Some activity may have continued. Chinese annals, such as those of Liu-Sung (written c. AD 500, referring to the period AD 420–478) and the Wei Dynasty (written before AD 572, covering the period AD 386–556), may record a silk trade between China and Petra (even-

tually leading to Antioch). The sea route was longer but easier than the overland northern route, time was not so important, and the profits were high. The Sassanian Persian policy in the northeast was to hinder Byzantine access to the overland route as much as possible and they controlled the traffic in silk through that area (Miller 1969: 132–139).

Byzantine Aila continued to be commercially significant as a port of sea trade with India, Egypt, Africa and the Arabian Gulf. It was the terminus for the major trunk road linking Syria to the Red Sea, and the nexus for important caravan land routes to the Mediterranean across the Negev Desert and to Egypt across the Sinai. The desert route from the Hijaz to Syria helped sustain the settlements in the southern Hauran. Excavations have revealed evidence for widespread contacts with the western Mediterranean, southern Arabia and beyond, throughout the Byzantine period (Parker 1998, 2002). Fine-ware pottery, oil, glass and metals passed through the port. The presence of Egyptian and Gaza amphorae implies the importation of wine and other agricultural products from Egypt and Palestine, and the importation of African red slip pottery is well attested. By the early fifth century AD, Aila seems to have been producing its own amphorae as transport containers (the "Ayla-Axum" amphorae) that percolated the length of the Red Sea. Literary sources reveal the far-flung

Figure 14.12 Qasr Bshir. View of the western (entrance) façade.

connections of the port. Eusebius in c. AD 290 notes that commercial traffic from India and Egypt passed through Aila (*Onomasticon* 6.17–21). The discovery of a freshly minted Byzantine-Sassanian hoard of coins and jewellery near Humayma attests to a significant Arabian–Persian trade coming through Aila in the early fifth century AD (Oleson, 'Amr and Schick 1992). In the late fifth century AD, Timotheus of Gaza mentioned that a native of Aila and a trader in Indian goods passed through Gaza bringing two giraffes and an elephant as gifts for the Emperor Anastasius. The importance of Red Sea commerce in c. AD 500 is reflected in the campaigns by Romanus, the *dux* of Palestine, to re-establish control of the Red Sea island of Iotabe where tariffs were levied on cargoes (see below). The identification of Iotabe is controversial, but it is more likely to be Jezirat Farun, an island c. 40 minutes sailing from Aila where Byzantine sherds are well represented and there is suitable anchorage (Glueck 1939: 11; Rothenberg 1970: 22; Fiema 1991: 175). Procopius of Caesarea, in the late sixth century AD, states that Roman vessels sailed from Aila into the Red Sea. Around AD 570, the Piacenza pilgrim records that it was eight staging posts from Mount Sinai to Aila and that shipping from India comes into port at Aila, bringing a variety of spices. Another text recounts an anecdote from an Egyptian monk Joseph, where a man from Aila offered to pay Joseph to pray for the successful return of a trading ship he had sent to Ethiopia (Parker 1996: 234–235; Schick 1994: 151).

The lands of Axum (Ethiopia) and Himyar (Yemen) flanked the gateway to the Red Sea. Byzantine diplomacy secured influence with these natural intermediaries for further trade to East Africa, India, Ceylon and China, thereby avoiding Persian customs duties. The principal source on eastern trade is Cosmas Indicopleustes, a sixth century AD Egyptian merchant turned monk who describes the role of Ceylon (Taprobane) as a great emporium for trade between East and West. Silk, aloes, cloves, sandalwood, pepper, copper, musk and castor were traded (Bury 1958: II, 320–333). The Ethiopians acted as intermediaries for the Byzantines (although they did not carry silk), while the Persians traded directly, having their own commercial colony in Ceylon. Maritime traffic up the Red Sea headed for Clysma at the head of the Gulf of Suez, and Aila at the head of the Gulf of Aqabah. When the Himyarite Dhu Nuwas attempted to disrupt this trade and to persecute Christians, the Byzantines supported the Ethiopian conquest of South Arabia in AD 525. Fifteen ships were sent from Aila. Fifty years later, South Arabia came under the control of the Sassanians and commercial and political power shifted to North Arabia.

Arabic sources record details of the terms of surrender of Aila to Muhammad in AD 630, where it was agreed to pay one dinar poll tax per adult, a total of 300 dinars. This indicates a considerable drop in population from the ear-

lier Byzantine period when the legion was stationed there. Possibly, the legion was removed c. AD 530 when Justinian transferred the primary responsibility for defence of the frontier from the *limitanei* (the Roman frontier forces) to the allied Arab federates, the Ghassanids. Evidence for defortification in Arabia in the sixth century AD is widespread (Parker 1986: 149–152; see Defence). The number of sites in the hinterland of Aila and elsewhere in Wadi Arabah declined in the late Byzantine period, as did the facilities along the southern Via Nova Traiana. Goods from Aila were channelled through the Negev to Gaza and the Mediterranean, rather than through southern Transjordan (see Settlement Patterns).

There is increasing evidence that desert routes from the south, through Tabuk and Tayma to Bayir, Jafr and Maan, were developed in the sixth and early seventh centuries AD. Pre-Umayyad occupation of the "desert castles" at Qasr Mushash and Qasr Hallabat, east of Amman, has been established. In the northern Hijaz, a Byzantine/early Islamic monastic hermitage existed at Kilwa, and a Byzantine presence continued at Qurayya until AD 600. The southern Via Nova Traiana was no longer important as a protected route, with most of its forts and caravanserais being abandoned by the late sixth century AD, yet the marginal land between Maan and Udhruh witnessed a substantial expansion of population in the late Byzantine period. Sites such as Mutrab, Hammam, Jabal Tahuna and Jarba had no previous occupation phases (Killick 1986: 236; Parker 1986: 100–102; Fiema 1991: 185). The commercial use of the caravan track from the northern Hijaz through Qurayya and Mudawwara to Maan may have been the sustaining factor behind these settlements.

At the same time, the more easterly connections were utilized between the Hijaz and Syria/Palestine through Wadi Sirhan and further east through Qasr Burqu (Sartre 1987; Fiema 1991: 178–191; Figure 14.5). Qasr Burqu commands a lesser route between north Arabia and central Syria, running east of the *harra* from Wadi Sirhan via Wadi Muqat and Qa Abu Hussayn, where there is a small strategic site with Safaitic inscriptions and Roman-Byzantine sherds (King *et al.* 1983: 416). Historical information and material remains suggest Byzantine commercial presence in the northern Hijaz. Byzantine pottery occurs at sites in the central and northern Wadi Sirhan. Marginal settlements between Azraq and Bostra expanded and flourished in this period, servicing the trade route and secured by forts and garrisons. Bostra was renowned in the pre-Islamic Arabic sources as an artisanal and agricultural centre, and a redistribution market for trade with the Arabs and Persians. The trade south was not dependent on luxuries but on essentials such as cereals, wine, raisins, hides, leather products, arms and coarse cloths. During the sixth century AD Makkah rose to prominence as a dynamic trading centre, facilitated by the incessant wars in Mesopotamia between Sassanid Persia, Rome and their

Arab clients, the Lakhmids and the Ghassanids. The Sassanian take-over of South Arabia in the late sixth century AD and the eclipse of Axum reinforced this process. Substantial caravans of 2500 camels were regularly organized from Makkah, bringing the spices and aromatics procured in South Arabia to Bostra, where they were redistributed to the west and north. As yet, we have no evidence for the terms of this exchange. Thus, the Hauran flourished in the late Byzantine period, a time, for example, of unprecedented building and renovation of public structures and churches. Continuing trade with the south, combined with an ethnic affinity between the Arab populations of the Hauran and the Hijaz, reduced the impact of the Persian occupation and ultimately smoothed the transition from Byzantine to Islamic control. Surrounding areas of the empire, however, were unravelling under the strain of religious crises, military disorganization, the incursions of the Persians, earthquakes and recurrent plague.

Defence

The Transjordanian region formed the south-eastern borders of the Byzantine Empire, protected farther east and southeast by hostile deserts. Security was more concerned with controlling the nomadic Arab tribes (called the *saraceni* by the Roman historians) who roamed these deserts and interacted with the sedentary agricultural population on the desert fringe. Constant friction with the Persians to the northeast was a less immediate problem, but was brought closer by the use on both sides of the nomadic tribes as allies, operating in a strategic buffer position between the two powers.

The Saracens existed both in conflict and symbiosis with Persia and Byzantium, who utilized their skills for reconnaissance, skirmishing and harassing an enemy army on the march. In return, they were paid subsidies in money or commodities in kind, and their leaders received titles and dignities. They were termed the *foederati* (federates) in the Byzantine system, serving as allies under their tribal leaders, headed by a *phylarch* (Parker 1986: 143–147; Mayerson 1989).

Early Byzantine Defensive Systems

During the late third and early fourth centuries AD, the Emperor Diocletian, followed by Constantine, reorganized the military structure of the empire, especially in the frontier zones. A system of forts, fortlets, watchtowers and roads was consolidated into a chain of military installations stretching from Egypt to the Euphrates River. As part of this system, legionary bases were established or strengthened in the Transjordan at Udhruh, Lajjun (Betthoro), in southern Syria at Bostra, and perhaps at Aila. Apart from Lajjun, these were all situated in towns on the major north–south road, the Via Nova Traiana. Lajjun was sited to the east, at the primary water source for the area. With its associated watchtowers and fortlets,

this fort covered the access routes from the east into Wadi Mujib. The Strata Diocletiana was established as a fortified road running from Azraq in northeast Transjordan, along the eastern slopes of the Jabal Druze, to the Euphrates River. Construction of the fort at Dayr Kahf is dated to c. AD 306 by an inscription, and the fort at Umm Jimal is dated to c. AD 300. The contemporary fort at Azraq seems to have been repaired in AD 326–33. In the south, there is no evidence of any military occupation in the Hisma east of the Via Nova Traiana and Wadi Ramm, or in the northern Hijaz, reflecting a retreat of influence beyond the marginal zone in this area. Attention to the frontier zone is matched by a withdrawal of legions from near the coast. No garrisons were posted on the road network within the populous agricultural heartlands or in their large urban centres, such as the cities of the Decapolis. Evidence from milestones along the Via Nova Traiana shows that the roads continued to be maintained in the fourth century AD (Parker 1986).

Early Byzantine occupation of the larger military sites in Wadi Arabah continued at sites such as Gharandal/Aridela and Bir Madhkur. The abandonment of smaller defensive posts in this period may be due to the added security provided by the Tenth Fretensis Legion in Aila. A fourth century AD road and milestones were identified in the western Arabah north of the fort at Yotvata (Smith *et al.* 1997: 67). The route from Aila up Wadi Arabah continued to be fully functional at this time, branching west and northwest across the Negev to the Mediterranean and the rest of Palestine. Like eastern Transjordan, the Negev was a monitored zone studded with forts and garrisons.

A number of Saracen attacks in the late fourth century AD underlines the need for this system of security. In AD 378 Mavia, queen of the Saracens, attacked the towns of the *limes* (frontier zone) of Palestine and Arabia and plundered the neighbouring provinces. Peace was restored through diplomacy. Around AD 383, another Saracen revolt is recorded, resulting in the Salih replacing the Tanukh as the dominant tribe (Parker 1987: 817–818). Attention has also been drawn to a significant economic motivation behind this security system, in the protection and facilitation of important trade routes (Leadbetter 2004).

In the fourth and fifth centuries AD, there were two basic categories of Roman troops: the mobile field army or *comitatenses*, elite troops under the direct command of the emperor or the *magistri militum*, and the regional garrisons or *limitanei*, under the command of the regional *duces*. Most auxiliary units were stationed in forts or towns between the legionary bases. The pattern is visible in the plateau area east of the Dead Sea where the hinterland of Lajjun has been extensively surveyed. A chain of forts spreads north and south of the legionary fortress, typically 10–15 km apart. From their size they must have held garrisons of c. 150 troops. The legion at Lajjun is estimated to have numbered 1000–2000 men. Fourth century AD legions were smaller than their predecessors, which, in the second century AD, numbered around 6000 men. Numerous watchtowers were placed between the forts. Towers and forts cluster around the shallow eastern entrances to the wadis, which were the preferred routes of travel for the nomadic tribes. Within this secure system, settlement expanded significantly in the marginal areas. Survey of the Edomite Plateau to the south has revealed a lattice of minor roads servicing an expanded population in the Byzantine period (Graf 1992: 259).

Use of the terms *limes* and *limitanei* has generated considerable debate. A reasonable consensus refers to the *limes* as a frontier district or zone rather than a defended border. It was under the military command of a *dux limitis*, and comprised a variety of military installations (forts, fortlets, police posts, watchtowers), protected water sources (such as the spring at Lajjun, or the reservoirs at Azraq), and communication routes. These bases served to contain and monitor tribal movements and behaviour, secure the passage of caravans and travellers, and protect the settled populations in the marginal lands.

In general, the *limitanei* were units under the regional command of a *dux limitis*, as distinguished from the field army or *comitatenses*. They were given tax-free land for their own cultivation and profit and received a salary (Parker 1987: 814). At the time of Justinian, Procopius reports that the pay fell into serious arrears, was later revoked, and eventually the *limitanei* were disbanded (*Secret History* 24.12–14). The accuracy of this account has been questioned, as elsewhere the *limitanei* are mentioned as operating throughout Justinian's reign. Payment arrangements, however, may have altered significantly (Isaac 1990: 210–211; Whitby 1995: 112–113). It should not be assumed that they were militarily less competent, being "soldier-farmers," given that land ownership does not require farming in person.

Late Byzantine Defensive System

In the early fifth century AD, Saracen incursions into Palestine and Syria (as recorded by Jerome in Epistle 126) may have encouraged a number of defensive measures. The barracks at Umm Jimal were built in AD 412/413, and the nearby fort of Qasr Baiq in AD 412. An inscription from the fort at Ziza, south of Amman, indicates some building activity in AD 410. The two forts east of Maan in Edom, Hammam and Mutrab, possibly date to the early fifth century AD (Parker 1986: 146). Inscriptions from Bostra and Gerasa refer to refortification of the city walls in AD 440–41. However, the barracks complex at Umm Jimal represents a reduced military capacity as it replaced a large fourth century AD fort that was converted into a market place in the early fifth century AD. Similarly, the fort at Humayma went out of use at the end of the fourth century AD (De Vries 1993: 452; Oleson

et al. 1995: 324). It is apparent that fourth century solutions were being revised in the fifth century AD, evolving a more decentralized imperial military authority.

In the reign of Leo (Ad 457–74), a tribal leader Amorkesus seized the island of Iotabe in the Gulf of Aqabah. He levied tolls on the passing trade and applied successfully to Leo to be appointed *phylarch* of the "Saracens around Petra." Leo's acquiescence illustrates the weakness of Byzantine control in the area, but also his pragmatism in converting an outlaw into a law enforcement officer. It was not until AD 498 that this lucrative position was restored to the Byzantines. In the later fifth century AD, there is evidence for a decline in the quality of the *limitanei* and a continued depletion of military installations along the eastern frontier. The Theodosian law of AD 443 confirming the agricultural and land rights of the *limitanei* seems motivated by a need to redress a problem. The excavations at Lajjun suggest that life at the fort had run down, and the soldiers' families were now living within the precinct. A metalworking industry in the barracks, presumably maintaining weapons and equipment, ceased by the end of the century. The shoddy architectural restoration of the structure after the AD 502 earthquake implies a lack of resources. A number of military sites in the region were peacefully abandoned by c. AD 500: Khirbat Fityan, Rujm Beni Yasser and Qasr Bshir. No new forts were built after the early fifth century AD (Parker 1987: 818–820).

The continuity of the fortified zone was disrupted by the widespread abandonment of forts. Some concern is shown in the north, where an edict of Anastasius, found in fragments at Qasr Hallabat and elsewhere, declares that fines for illegal treatment of the *limitanei* should be used for restoration of the forts. Another inscription of AD 529 records the restoration of the fort at Qasr Hallabat. This is the last imperial military building inscription from Arabia (Parker 1987: 821). Nevertheless, the only other forts in the northern sector with sixth century AD pottery are Baiq (near Umm Jimal) and Qasr Asaykin (near Azraq). The evidence for Azraq is unclear, and the barracks at Umm Jimal may have been converted from military to monastic use. In the central sector, only three forts appear occupied after the early sixth century AD: Muhattat Haj (monitoring a crossing of Wadi Mujib), Khirbat Zona (monitoring the caravan route east along the edge of the desert) and Lajjun. Most military sites in Edom were abandoned by the mid-sixth century AD, other than Udhruh and Aila which may have been civilian by then. The fortlets of Khirbat Khalde and Qasr Kithara in the Hisma continued in use, but the remaining watchtowers were unoccupied. Weakened imperial protection probably led to the refortification of town walls recorded at Scythopolis (Bayt Shan) in the AD 520s, Bostra in AD 540, and Umm Jimal sometime in the sixth century AD.

The reduced commitment of imperial troops in the southeast frontier zone is associated with the increasing importance of the Arab federates, led in the sixth century AD by the Ghassanids (see History). Anastasius confirmed their leading role after the Kindite wars of c. AD 502/503, conferring the *phylarchy* of Palestine on the Kinda, and that of Arabia on the Ghassanids. Around AD 530, Justinian appointed the Ghassanid leader Harith as supreme *phylarch* of all the allied Arab tribes, responsible for protecting the eastern frontier from Palmyra to Wadi Hasa. They opposed in kind the Persian Arab allies united under the Lakhmid king Mundhir. Byzantine defence policy shifted from a network of imperial troops garrisoned in forts, to mobile troops of subsidized allies drawn from the local power base. It derived from a pragmatic assessment of the physical and economic realities of the time. Maintenance of the old fortified system was costly at a time when funds were needed to counter the Persians in Syria and Mesopotamia, and to reconquer the lost western provinces.

The reformed strategy worked well for the next half century. However, emperors in the late sixth century AD progressively weakened the Ghassanids without taking any compensatory measures along the frontier. Justin II (AD 565–78) cut off subsidies to some of the tribes. A major dispute erupted in AD 580–81 between the Byzantines and the Ghassanids, inflamed by intrigue and treachery on the part of the emperor Maurice. He was intensely hostile to the Monophysite creed followed by the Christian Ghassanids. After the capture and exile of the Ghassanid *phylarch* Mundhir, his sons defeated the *dux* of Arabia, laid siege to Bostra, and for two years ravaged Syria, Palestine and Arabia. Eventually the Ghassanid confederation disintegrated into its constituent tribal elements (Sartre 1982: 189).

The Eve of the Muslim Conquest

Following another peace with Persia in AD 591, many of the eastern troops were transferred to Europe to counter the Avars and the Slavs. Little is known about the Byzantine army in the southeast in the early seventh century AD. The paucity of historical sources reflects the declining economic and political significance of the area to the Byzantine state. Palestine and Arabia had not been invaded by regular armies since the time of Zenobia in the third century AD, and their experience was limited to local security. In AD 613–14, the Persians under Chosroes II swept easily through Syria to Arabia and Palestine. Few details are known, but Arabia was probably overtaken prior to the siege and pillage of Jerusalem in AD 614. Bostra and Adraha (Dara) were reportedly taken by assault. There is no clear evidence in the archaeological record of destruction of towns east of the Jordan, or of the following 14 years of occupation. The implied lack of resistance by local authorities foreshadows a similar reaction in two decades time. Trade between Bostra and the Hijaz and Makkah continued without interruption, while inscriptions show that churches at Rihab and Samah were renovated and embellished (Schick 1992: 110–111).

The emperor Heraclius marshalled the imperial resources against the Persians and, after prolonged battles and the eventual murder of Chosroes, regained the region in AD 628. He had little time to re-establish control in the southeast or to reorganize the system of security. He seems to have continued parts of the previous administrative system, and old military units reappear (Kaegi 1992: 73–74).

The Byzantines were not expecting any concerted Arab invasion from the south, treating the initial conflicts as more of the same nomadic raids they had endured through recent centuries. They defeated the first Muslim advance at Muta in AD 629. The tribal allies of the Byzantines initially opposed the Muslim invaders and a number of hostile encounters are recorded (Schick 1992: 113; Kaegi 1992: 66–111). Nevertheless, on the way to Muta the raiders were able to stay two nights at Maan without any opposition. The fact that Mohammed in AD 630 accepted the surrender of Udhruh, Jarba or Aila, negotiated with the local bishop, implies that there were no regular garrisons stationed in the south or any imperial administration. The move to re-establish Byzantine control could not immediately cover the whole area and they may have set up an initial defensive line east of the Dead Sea (Parker 1986: 154). The concerted Muslim conquest of Syria had begun by early AD 634, with the capture of Areopolis (modern Rabbah) on the plateau south of Wadi Mujib. The Muslims then advanced across Wadi Arabah to western Palestine. Byzantine reliance on Arab allies was inevitable, and the decision to end subsidies to some of the tribes was a disaster. Disgruntled tribesmen aided the Muslims in defeating the Byzantines at Dathin near Gaza in early AD 634. As there were no garrisons in southern Palestine, a unit had to be dispatched from as far away as Caesarea Maritima. The battle of Ajnadayn, southwest of Jerusalem, was a more decisive victory, followed by Fihl (Tabaqat Fahl), near Pella. Finally, the Byzantine army was annihilated at the Battle of Yarmuk in AD 636. Their commanders lacked unity and were ultimately outmanoeuvred. Syria was rapidly overtaken and by AD 640 the last of the opposition surviving behind the walls of Ashkelon, Gaza, Jerusalem and Caesarea Maritima had been removed (Kaegi 1992: 112–146). Most towns submitted peacefully, perhaps mindful of the terms that had been offered to towns such as Aila, Tiberias and Pella, where security of life and property were guaranteed in return for payment of a poll tax (Schick 1995: 72–73). The conjunction of the Muslim invasion with the poorly re-established and vulnerable Byzantine recovery of Arabia and Palestine had proved disastrous for the Byzantines and opportune for the Muslims (Kaegi 1992: 236–287).

Burial Customs

Burial practices in the fourth–seventh centuries AD continued in the traditions of the Roman period, with some minor adaptations for Christian sensibilities in decoration (the addition of crosses) and preferred orientation. Major towns were surrounded by cemeteries, often lining access routes or located in the rocky slopes of adjacent wadis. Interments inside sanctified structures were common. Mausolea and graves beneath the floors of churches have been documented at many sites. The sites of Abila, Gadara (Umm Qays), Yasileh, Umm Jimal, Pella, Jarash, Amman, Hisban and many others have all revealed tombs re-used over the centuries from the Roman period through the Byzantine period.

There were a variety of grave types, from the elaborate to the simple. The socio-economic position of the interred and geographical context seem to be the principal determinants of type. Elaborate monumental built tombs are found near urban centres such as Gadara, Jarash and Amman. The "North Mausoleum" at Gadara is dated by inscription to the mid-fourth century AD. It was built in the form of a small temple, on a square podium with a staircase, and a crypt in the centre of the podium. The architect's name, "Arabios," indicates his indigenous origins (De Vries 1973). The finely constructed subterranean Roman hypogaeum at the same site was expanded and altered in the Byzantine period to accommodate important burials associated with the Christian basilica built above it. Stone-lined shaft tombs (cists) were cut through the floor of the vaulted entrance hall to the west of the domed main chamber. The lead sarcophagus of a deaconess was placed in front of the barrel-vaulted passageway that girdled the main chamber. Two adjacent built tombs at Jarash, south of the Hadrianic Gate, were Roman constructions re-used in the Byzantine period (Zayadine 1986: 12–16, 1989: 201–218). They comprised vaulted chambers with a monumental superstructure (now destroyed), containing stone-lined cist graves as well as free-standing sarcophagi.

Most of these Transjordanian towns lie in rocky areas, suitable for rock-cut features and favouring cave formations. A popular tomb type of relatively high status is the chamber tomb with radiating loculi. The latter may be flat or have rectangular shafts cut into them. This type is common at Pella, for example, where there is no evidence for cremation or grave burials in the Roman/Byzantine period. Another type of chamber tomb contains *arcosolia*, arched openings off the main chamber. Both chamber types generally have an entrance passage (*dromos*), often approached by steps from above. The more elaborate façades have architraves, decorated lintels and stone doors with elaborate lock mechanisms. The remains of wooden coffins have been found in some of the loculi and chambers. Some chambers contain stone sarcophagi (McNicoll *et al.* 1992: 141–144). These types occur throughout the country, for instance, at Abila where single trough (cist) graves in chambers are also recorded. Two private tomb

precincts with temenos walls are dated to the Byzantine period (Mare 1984). All these tombs contained multiple interments, of mixed gender and ages. When undisturbed, the skeletons are found supine, with legs outstretched and arms either by their side or laid across the chest. There is evidence for shrouds wrapping the bodies, and sometimes a suggestion of clothing and leather sandals. The peculiar thermal conditions at Pella have enabled the survival of laurel leaves in one tomb, presumable used to sweeten the air. Grave goods consisted of personal jewellery, glass vessels including unguentaria (for the dispensing of aromatics), spatulae and spoons, pottery lamps and vessels, plaster mirrors and make-up palettes. These can be found with the bodies or scattered around the chamber. Items peculiar to the interred may be included, such as the surgical tools of a medical practitioner recovered at Abila.

Significant cemeteries have been excavated in the east at Umm Jimal and Khirbat Samra (Brashler 1995; Nabulsi and Humbert 1996). They revealed simpler tomb types presumably for people of lower or poorer status. The seventh century AD cemetery at Khirbat Samra consisted of trenches dug in the soil, with a shelf left c. 30–60 cm from the bottom, bearing the covering slabs of basalt flagstones. These were predominantly children's graves. Umm Jimal cemetery AA contained unlined pits with or without grave objects, well-constructed stone-lined cists for single occupants, and simple pits with coffins. Cemetery Z contained a number of types: loculi, cist and coffin-lined tombs, representing a range of socio-economic levels.

At Dhiban on the Moabite Plateau, a late fourth century AD cemetery revealed two types: a cist with earth floor, containing multiple burials, with head placed to the west; and simple inhumations. Early seventh century AD cist graves were found inserted in the pavement of the disused Nabataean temple (Tushingham 1972: 86, 107–115).

In the large Byzantine cemetery at Khirbat Faynan (Phaeno) in Wadi Arabah, the standard grave consists of a rectangular cut with rounded ends, oriented east–west, with a groove cut into the vertical sides (occasionally a ledge) to bear the covering slabs of roughly cut ovoid sandstone. These were laid perpendicular to the length of the grave, and sealed by a mixture of pebbles and mud. The grave contained a single body, laid supine with head to the west. Over 50% had remnants of shrouds. Generally, there were no grave goods other than personal jewellery. The majority of graves were marked with an orthostat stone at the western end, sometimes inscribed with a cross of varying design. One hundred and eighty out of 1200 orthostats have inscribed Christian crosses, but names are rare. The cemetery was well organized into rows of graves (Findlater *et al.* 1998).

A more rare and elaborate type of grave had a built stone superstructure. It comprised either cut and dressed sandstone blocks or more roughly cut blocks, laid on the ground surface or within a shallow foundation trench, forming a rectangular plan which was filled with rubble. Only one course is extant but the amount of rubble suggests that they may have stood up to 1 m high. While this type is not found elsewhere in Jordan, it has parallels with Coptic burials in North Saqqara of the late fourth and early fifth centuries AD, where the superstructure is of mudbrick. Another unusual type is represented by three examples, marked by a line of medium to large rocks following the outline of the grave cut. This is the standard type found in the Byzantine cemetery at Rehovot in the Negev. These links with Egypt and southern Palestine accord with textual information, which reports that many of the early Christian martyrs forced to work in the mines of Phaeno came from Egypt and Gaza.

Vast Byzantine cemeteries in the Southern Ghor around Safi have come to light through extensive plundering activities. Attempts to rescue the remaining information have recorded more than 300 funerary stelae, 90% of which are inscribed in Greek, the remainder in Aramaic (Politis 1999). The Monastery of St. Lot at Dayr Ayn Abata overlooks the area. Disarticulated secondary burials were found in the venerated cave behind the church, and in one of the cisterns that was re-used as a communal burial chamber. Such burial customs are well known in early Christian monastic orders.

Examination of certain burials at Umm Jimal, Jarash and Pella has independently prompted speculation on the great plague which ravaged the region from the sixth to the eighth centuries AD (Conrad 1986: 146). Many of the Late Byzantine tombs at Pella had single loculi and sarcophagi containing up to five multiple interments of all ages and sexes. One coffin showed clear evidence of rapid multiple interment: cloth was laid over a body that had not yet decomposed, then plaster was poured over it to make a base for the next body. The jar in which the plaster was mixed was left nearby, suggesting carelessness and haste. Scant respect was often shown to the earlier occupants whose bones were simply scattered around the chamber (McNicoll *et al.* 1992: 143, 218–220). At Umm Jimal, a common-class cist grave was dug to hold a minimum of four individuals with a wide range of ages, buried close in time or contemporaneously with each other. The effort in digging such a grave is negligible and, therefore, the need to place them together is considered unusual (Cheyney 1995). More telling is the evidence from the hippodrome at Jarash. Two chambers were re-used for mass burial around the mid-seventh century AD, containing more than 100 bodies dumped without ceremony on top of mounds of discarded pottery. Prior to disintegration of the flesh, the stone-vaulted roof collapsed onto the bodies, probably due to the earthquake of AD 659 (Kehrberg and Ostrasz 1994).

Religion and Ritual

The Rise of Christianity

The fourth century AD is marked by the rapid rise of Christianity to a position of power and influence in the empire (see above, Historical Background). While Constantine I became an enthusiastic Christian he remained tolerant in his beliefs. On the one hand, he confiscated the treasures and endowments of the temples and banned pagan sacrifice; on the other, he founded two new pagan temples in Constantinople. There was a short interlude of pagan resurgence under the emperor Julian (AD 361–63), but his early death prevented its consolidation. In AD 380, Christianity became the formal religion of the state. In AD 391, Theodosius I issued the first of a series of laws that progressively banned all pagan ceremonies. The privileges of the priestly class were withdrawn in AD 396. Temples were closed and many were demolished, their materials re-used for the repair of roads, bridges and aqueducts. Unauthorized attacks on temples and their conversion into churches had been tolerated for some time. In Jordan, disorders were recorded at Petra and Areopolis, where the strongly pagan local population had vigorously defended their temples. However, pagan beliefs were not banned outright, and the cult survived into the sixth century AD. Finally, Justinian forbade pagans to hold professorial chairs, to receive inheritances or bequests, or to testify in court. In AD 529, he ordered all pagans to accept baptism under penalty of confiscation and exile (Jones 1973: 167–169, 938–943; Trimingham 1979: 82).

Conversion of the Nomads

The Arabs of the Syrian Desert began to be converted in the mid-fourth century AD, apparently through their encounters with priests who dwelt among them and the monks in retreat in the deserts. These ascetics, who eschewed urban forms of Christianity, were admired for their healing powers and ability to expel possessive spirits. Early in the reign of Valens, an Arab leader called Zokomos was able to beget a son through the intercession of a hermit and, in gratitude, he and his whole tribe became Christians. Barochius "bishop of the Arabs" (nomads) is mentioned at the Council of Seleucia in AD 359, while Theotimus of the Arabs was present at the Synod of Antioch in AD 363. Bishops solely associated with nomads were not given town or territorial titles. Those based in towns, such as Germanus of Petra and Arabion of Adraha, as well as the bishops of Palestine III, also had relationships with the nomads. In the early fifth century AD, Aspebetos was the leader of a tribe that relocated from Persian to Roman territory. The monk Euthymius cured Aspebetos's son of paralysis and the whole tribe converted. They established an encampment (*parembole*) near Euthymius, west of the Dead Sea, and Aspebetos was made Bishop of the Encampments in AD 427 (Trimingham 1979: 94–120).

Christian Administration and Hierarchy

Bishoprics were established in centres of population, mostly in cities. However, in the province of Arabia, where the village was the normal unit of government, village bishoprics were common. In Palestine, the four regions of the Jordan Valley were independent bishoprics (Jericho, Amathus, Livias and Gadara/Salt).

The bishop of a metropolis or capital city of a province had the position of Metropolitan, with authority over the other bishops within his province. The boundaries of a bishopric or ecclesiastical province generally coincided with the civil administrative province. The bishoprics or episcopal sees of Madaba, Esbus, Philadelphia and Gerasa were within the province of Arabia under the Metropolitan of Bostra. Palestine I, with Caesarea Maritima as its metropolis, incorporated the bishoprics of Livias, Gadara (Salt), Bacatha and Amathus. Palestine II, with Scythopolis (Bayt Shan) as its metropolis, contained the bishoprics of Pella, Gadara (Umm Qays), Capitolias and Abila. In the south, Palestine III contained Areopolis (Rabbah), Charachmoba (Karak), Aila (Quwayliba), Zoara (Safi), Phaeno (Khirbat Faynan), Arindela (Gharandal) and Augustopolis (Udhruh), under the metropolitan city of Petra. The bishops of Arabia answered to the patriarch of Antioch, who had primacy over the area by tradition. In AD 431 the three provinces of Palestine came under the jurisdiction of the patriarch of Jerusalem. Mosaic inscriptions from the many churches in Jordan confirm or clarify these divisions, allegiances and hierarchical structure. Priests, deacons, deaconesses, lectors and others assisted the bishops in the towns, while an archpresbyter might assist in a village (Jones 1973: 873–894; Piccirillo 1993: 43–45).

A rich ecclesiastical geography had developed by the sixth century AD in Jordan. Churches and monasteries dotted the countryside, revealing the penetration of the new faith beyond the cities into the rural and nomadic communities. This was encouraged by the Emperor Justinian's promotion of an ecclesiastical building programme and the sympathetic security provided by the Christian Ghassanids.

Christian Interpretation and Schisms

Christianity was an evolving religion in this period, seeking consensus on interpretation and organization throughout the empire. Argument and division characterized its development as the faith of the establishment. A series of church councils attempted to deal with the variety of viewpoints on doctrinal issues and matters of order and authority. The Arian controversy, over the relationship of God the Son to God the Father, dominated the fourth century AD. During the fifth century AD,

controversies concerning the nature of Christ reached a climax. The Nestorian doctrine was condemned, followed by the Monophysite interpretation of the single nature of Christ. A diophysite (dual nature) interpretation was promoted as the orthodox "Chalcedonian" doctrine. These doctrinal conflicts and resolutions were as much an expression of political struggle as disputes over theology. Because of imperial support and the institutionalization of the Church, disagreements came to be heresies and liable to punishment by the state. Moreover, imperial religious policy tended to change with individual emperors, making it indecisive and inconsistent.

Syro-Palestinian Christians were divided into opposing communions. Antioch, the metropolis of orthodox Greek Christianity, was alien to the majority of Aramaean congregations in the region. The gap in communication was filled through the medium of the monastic movement that was predominantly Monophysite. Most of the people followed the monks rather than the bishops and clergy. However, Euthymius, the moulder of the Dead Sea monastic movement in the early fifth century AD, and his protégé the Bishop of Jerusalem, supported the Orthodox creed, creating conflict within the monastic movement. Eventually the Aramaean Monophysite element within the Palestinian monks was eliminated. In the province of Arabia, the Ghassanids became staunch Monophysites. It is impossible to determine, from the remains of its architecture or decoration, which rite an ancient church might have used. Thus, the affiliation of specific churches and, therefore, the pattern of affiliation, is still unknown (Trimingham 1979: 80–188; Jones 1973: 232–235, 929–942, 967).

In the early seventh century AD, Heraclius introduced an alternative interpretation to the religious debate, Monotheletism, in an attempt to resolve the doctrinal split. More controversy ensued and the effort was notably unsuccessful. At the time of the Muslim invasions, the eastern provinces were divided in their Christian allegiances, but the schism does not seem a decisive factor in determining loyalties. Many moderate Monophysites were prepared to unite with the Orthodox Christians, and later Monophysite writers under Arab rule were not demonstrably anti-Byzantine (Schick 1995).

Monasticism and Pilgrimage

The founder of the eremitic and monastic movements was the Egyptian Antony, who retired into the desert in the AD 270s. During the Great Persecution at the beginning of the fourth century AD, he organized the numerous disciples who had followed him into a loose-knit community. Such groups of hermits, who lived in separate cells and met only for common worship, were later known as *laurae*. A few decades later, another Egyptian, Pachomius, founded the first *coenobium*, where the monks led a communal life under strict discipline. Both forms of monasti-

Figure 14.13 Umm Rasas. View of the tower east of the town.

cism caught on rapidly in Egypt and soon spread to Palestine. In the late AD 350s, the movement spread to Syria (Jones 1973: 929–933; Trimingham 1979: 107–116, 183–184).

A number of monasteries, *laurae* and hermitages have been identified in Transjordan. In the north, the monastery at Fadayn, near Mafraq, is known from texts and excavation (Humbert 1989: 126). The "barracks" complex at Umm Jimal was possibly converted into a religious institution in the sixth century AD (De Vries 1985: 251), and one interpretation of Qasr Burqu is that it functioned as a reclusive refuge for a hermit, later expanded to a monastery (Betts *et al.* 1991: 15–16). An eremitic function is proposed for the isolated tower at Umm Rasas (Figures 14.5 and 14.13). A partial list of the Monophysite monasteries in the province of Arabia, dating to c. AD 575, survives in the "Letter of the Archimandrites." There were 137 signatories, all heads of monasteries in the province (MacAdam 1994: 59).

Many of the monasteries in the fertile zones were working agricultural establishments: Zay Gharbi, west of Amman, Munyah, Mount Nebo, the nearby smaller monastery of Keniseh, and another near Ayn Keniseh. An inscription at Mukhayyat provides the first epigraphic

evidence for a "stylite" (an ascetic who lives on top of a pillar) in the Madaba region. The Memorial of Moses at Mount Nebo was a prominent sanctuary, servicing pilgrims. The remains of at least three small monastic complexes were found in the adjacent valley of Ayoun Musa (Springs of Moses), and a hermitage at Ayn Jammalah. A rock-cut *laura* has been identified at Muallaqah, in the desolate Wadi Jebara to the west of Iraq al-Amir (MacAdam 1994: 81 n. 185).

Mount Nebo was the main destination for most of the pilgrims venturing east of the Jordan, and the nearby desert area attracted monks and hermits. On the east bank of the Jordan River lies Sapsafas, connected with the baptism of Jesus and John the Baptist. A *laura*, known from historical records, has been identified at Wadi Kharrar in caves in the marl cliffs, as well as remains of a monastic-pilgrimage centre (Waheeb 2004). The pilgrim road continues via Livias (Tall Rama) towards Esbus (Tall Hisban) on the plateau, turning off to the Springs of Moses (Ayoun Musa) and Mount Nebo. Main lies further south, with its monastery of Khirbat Dayr and remains of an inn and baths. The nearby hot springs of Baaru were a therapeutic destination. A hermitage has been found in the vicinity at Ayn Qattara (Piccirillo 1987).

Isolation in a desert environment was the desirable context for an ascetic lifestyle. A number of remote hermitages have been identified in Wadi Mujib and Wadi Hasa, for example, at Hammam Afra (MacDonald 1980), and near the outlet to the Southern Ghor near Safi. The southern end of the Dead Sea contains a cluster of hermitages and monasteries that link geographically with the Judaean desert and its monastic society. A "bridge" is provided by a ford to the Lisan Peninsula, which contains a number of hermitages and a monastery. The major hermitage of Qasr Tuba was possibly the centre of a *laura*. The monastery of Dayr Qattar dates from the fourth century and became the focus for a large monastic community in the area into the seventh century AD and beyond (Holmgren and Kaliff 1997; Politis 2001). The location of these monasteries may have been determined by the Byzantine tradition concerning the destroyed "cities of the Plain" (Gen. 13.12), Sodom and Gomorrah. In the Southern Ghor, overlooking ancient Zoara, the Sanctuary of Lot at Dayr Ayn Abata comprised monastic and pilgrim facilities (Politis 1997; 2001). Many of these holy sites are depicted on the sixth century AD mosaic floor known as the Madaba Map (see Mosaics).

Jabal Harun, southwest of Petra, was thought to be the burial site of Aaron, the brother of Moses. Recent survey and excavations suggest a monastic pilgrimage centre operated here from the fifth to eighth centuries AD, succeeding an earlier Nabatean (possibly sacral) presence (Peterman and Schick 1996; Fiema 2004). An allusion to the monastery is found in one of the Petra scrolls dated to 573 (Frösén 2004). A well-known hermitage lies above the processional route from Petra to ad-Dayr. The latter pagan monument was re-used as a Christian shrine, probably in the Byzantine period. A monastery called Dayr Qunfudh is reported at Aila. The monastic movement penetrated the northern Hijaz with a monastic hermitage identified at Kilwa (Fiema 1991: 185).

Churches

Eusebius states that churches had been built in many large cities before the Great Persecution at the end of the third century AD (*HE* 8.1.5), but none has survived. Church construction revived in the fourth century AD but most of these were replaced in the fifth and sixth centuries AD. Excavations at Aila have found a mudbrick basilica, tentatively believed to be a church, dated to the end of the third/beginning of the fourth century AD, and destroyed by an earthquake, probably that of AD 363 (Parker 1998; 2002). This would make it the earliest known purpose-built church in the world.

Many towns, particularly in the north, had multiple churches, curiously more than adequate for their population base. Umm Jimal had 15, Rihab and Khirbat Samra had 8 each, Umm Rasas 16, Madaba 11, Humayma 5, and so on. Schick has collated a useful summary of identified Christian churches and material remains for southern Jordan (2001). Church design gives no indication of differing tribal or doctrinal affiliations. Mosaic inscriptions reveal that many of the church donors in Jordan were individuals or groups of individuals, sometimes from one family. Sometimes a village was a donor. Donors possibly sought divine favour through such bequests, encouraging this proliferation. Vriezen suggests that the accumulation of churches may reflect the development of commemorative liturgy and the erection of "stational" churches dedicated to different saints and relics (2004).

Writing

Our knowledge of the written language for this period comes mainly from inscriptions and, to a lesser extent, literary references. A small proportion of the population was ethnically Greek, yet Greek was the primary language of written communication. It was the formal language of the Byzantine administration, of power and prestige and flourished particularly in the Hellenized northwest of Jordan. Latin, the other language of Roman administration, never dominated in the East and ceased to be used in inscriptions after the fourth century AD. The majority of the population was Semitic, speaking Arabic or Aramaic, despite any imposed cultural veneer (but see Politis 2004, for a persistent Hellenic component in the multi-ethnic society around the Dead Sea). Syriac (eastern Aramaean) is mentioned as the language of the urban centres of Palestine I and II (Shahid 1984: 291). Many of the personal names found in Greek inscriptions from the Hauran and Moab are Arabic (Sartre 1985: 198–202; Canova 1954).

Greek was the official language of the church used in dedicatory inscriptions, nevertheless, Syro-Palestinian Aramaic inscriptions are found in churches at Mount Nebo, Ayoun Musa, Quwaysma, and Khirbat Kursi. A cemetery at Khirbat Samra contained 46 funerary stelae with inscriptions in Greek and 65 stelae inscribed in Aramaean. The same names could appear in either script, attesting to the mixed cultural milieu. Arabic inscriptions, rare at this time, are found at the church of St. George at Mukhayyat and the double church at Umm Jimal (Piccirillo 1993: 45; De Vries 1993: 448, 454; Humbert and Desreumaux 1989).

Further evidence for the use of Arabic as spoken language is found in the sixth century AD papyrus scrolls from Petra. Roll 10, for example, reveals names used for places, districts, fields, orchards, buildings, houses, and even parts of houses, in Arabic or Aramaic, transcribed in Greek. It is clear that there was a scribal tradition in Petra in the sixth century AD that included knowledge of Arab philology (Pierre Bikai 1996; Frösén 2004). A few earlier inscriptions and references provide evidence for Arabic as the language of everyday life in the eastern and southern areas in the Byzantine period. The earliest dated inscription is the Namara text of AD 328, written in Arabic using the Nabataean Aramaic alphabet. Epiphanius, writing in the later fourth century AD, says that the language of the pagan liturgical celebrations of the feast of Venus in Petra was Arabic. Sozomen attests to the use of Arabic in the composition of poetry celebrating the victories of Queen Mavia in the later fourth century AD (Shahid 1984: 292). The Arabic script, the direct representation of the spoken language, developed out of Aramaic, the traditional lingua franca of the Semitic Middle East. The earliest dated inscription in this new script comes from Zabad (near Chalcis in northern Syria) c. AD 512, suggesting that the process of differentiation occurred during the fifth century AD (Shahid 1989: 409–419).

Writing and language at this time reflect a complex linguistic history. The public written language differed from the spoken languages, which themselves varied according to area. It is difficult to determine from the sources how closely the written language matched the language that was spoken, and we cannot assess the relative proportion of speakers of Greek, the different dialects of Aramaean, and Arabic.

Conclusion

The Byzantine period in Jordan marks a high point in the occupational history of the land, as abundantly attested by the archaeological record. A seasoned system of law and administration, from municipal to military and imperial levels, provided the security for the population to expand and flourish throughout the countryside. A healthy economy, utilizing the available resources and capitalizing on established trade routes that covered the region, supported this population and prospered within the zone of imperial security. A religion that had a local genesis became a prominent social and cultural force within the Byzantine empire, endowing the region with status and attention. The continuity of this society was undermined in later years by a number of factors. Administrative changes, determined by a variety of considerations and miscalculations, diluted imperial control. Christological controversies linked with political struggles affected regional cohesion. Natural catastrophes such as earthquakes and endemic plague made life more difficult and uncertain for ordinary people. When faced with a close sequence of external threats, first from Persia and then from northern Arabia, the region was ill-equipped to defend its physical territory or the status quo. Centuries of western dominance of the eastern Mediterranean were replaced with astounding rapidity by a focused political and religious force emerging from indigenous Arab society.

Note

1.   This spelling of "Aila" follows Parker's spelling and reasoning (1996: 232). A variety of spellings are attested in the sources, and "Aila" for the Nabataean/Roman/Byzantine period distinguishes it from Islamic "Aylah" which was at a different adjacent location.

Bibliography

'Amr, K.

1991   Preliminary Report on the 1991 Season at Zurrabah. *Annual of the Department of Antiquities of Jordan* 35: 313–323.

2004   Beyond the Roman Annexation: the Continuity of the Nabataean Pottery Tradition. In *Studies in the History and Archaeology of Jordan VIII*, 237–245. Amman: Department of Antiquities of Jordan.

'Amr, K., K. Hamdan, S. Helms and L. Mohamadieh

1996   Archaeological Survey of the East Coast of the Dead Sea, Phase 1: Suwayma, az-Zara and Umm Sidra. *Annual of the Department of Antiquities of Jordan* 40: 429–449.

'Amr, K., and A. al-Momani

2001   Preliminary Report on the Archaeological Component of the Wadi Musa Water Supply and Wastewater Project (1998–2000). *Annual of the Department of Antiquities of Jordan* 45: 253–285.

Almagro, A.

1994   A Byzantine Building with a Cruciform Plan in the Citadel of Amman. *Annual of the Department of Antiquities of Jordan* 38: 417–427.

Barker, G.W., O.H. Creighton, D.D. Gilbertson, C.O. Hunt, D.J. Mattingly, S.J. McLaren, D.C. Thomas and G.C. Morgan

1997   The Wadi Faynan Project, Southern Jordan: A Preliminary Report on Geomorphology and Landscape Archaeology. *Levant* 29: 19–40.

Barker, G.W., R. Adams, O.H. Creighton, P. Daly, D.D. Gilbertson, J.P. Grattan, C.O. Hunt, D.J. Mattingly, S. McLaren, P. Newson, C. Palmer, F.B. Pyatt, T.E. Reynolds, H. Smith, R. Tomber and A.J. Truscott

2000   Archaeological and desertification in Wadi Faynan : The fourth (1999) season of the Wadi Faynan Landscape Survey. *Levant* 32: 27–52.

Beaumont, P.

1985   Man-induced Erosion in Northern Jordan. In A. Hadidi (ed.), *Studies in the History and Archaeology of Jordan II*, 291–296. Amman: Department of Antiquities of Jordan.

Betts, A., S. Helms, W. and F. Lancaster

1991   The Burqu'/Ruweishid Project: Preliminary Report on the 1989 Field Season. *Levant* 23: 7–28.

Bienkowski, P.

1991   *Treasures from an Ancient Land: The Art of Jordan.* Stroud: Alan Sutton.

Bikai, Pierre

1996   Petra Church Project, Petra Papyri. *Annual of the Department of Antiquities of Jordan* 40: 487–489.

Bikai, Patricia

1995   Petra Ridge Church Project. *American Journal of Archaeology* 99: 530–531.

Bikai, Patricia, and T.A. Dailey

1996   *Madaba Cultural Heritage.* Amman: American Center of Oriental Research.

Bisheh, G.

1986   Qasr al-Hallabat: A Summary of the 1984 and 1985 Excavations. *Archiv für Orientforschung* 33: 158–162.

Bookman, R., Y. Enzel, A. Agnon, and M. Stein

2004   Late Holocene lake levels of the Dead Sea. *Geological Society of America Bulletin* 116: 555–571.

Brashler, J.

1995   The 1994 Umm al-Jimal Cemetery Excavations: AREA AA and Z. *Annual of the Department of Antiquities of Jordan* 39: 457–469.

Burnett, A.

1987   *Coinage in the Roman World.* London: Seaby.

Bury, J.B.

1958   *History of the Later Roman Empire.* 2 vols. New York: Dover.

Butler, H.C.

1919   *Division II, Architecture: Section A, Southern Syria. Syria: Publications of the Princeton University Archaeological Expeditions to Syria in 1904–5 and 1909.* Leiden: E.J. Brill.

Caneva, I., M. Hatamleh, Z. Kafafi, M. Munzi, G. Palumbo, F. Parenti, A.H. al-Shiyab, M. Wilson, B. Bianchi, P. Conti and N. Qadi

2001   The Wadi az-Zarqa'/Wadi ad-Dulayl Archaeological Project. Report on the 1997 and 1999 Fieldwork Seasons. *Annual of the Department of Antiquities of Jordan* 45: 83–117.

Canova, R.

1954 *Iscrizioni e monumenti protocristiani del Paese di Moab.* Rome: Vatican City.

Cheyney, M.

1995 Umm al-Jimal 1993: A Cist Burial. *Annual of the Department of Antiquities of Jordan* 39: 447–455.

Conrad, L.I.

1986 The Plague in Bilad al-Sham in Pre-Islamic Times. In M.A. Bakhit and M. Asfour (eds.), *Proceedings of the Symposium on Bilad al-Sham during the Byzantine Period II (English)*, 143–163. Amman: University of Jordan.

Da Costa, K.

2001 Byzantine and Early Islamic Lamps: Typology and Distribution. In E. Villeneuve and P. Watson (eds.), *Byzantine and Early Islamic Ceramics in Syria-Jordan (IVth–VIIIth Centuries)*. International Colloquium, Amman 1993. Beirut: Institut Français d'archéologie du Proche-Orient.

De Vries, B.

1973 The North Mausoleum at Umm Qeis. *Annual of the Department of Antiquities of Jordan* 18: 77.

1985 Urbanization in the Basalt Region of North Jordan in Late Antiquity: The Case of Umm el-Jimal. In A. Hadidi (ed.), *Studies in the History and Archaeology of Jordan II*, 249–256. Amman: Department of Antiquities of Jordan.

1993 The Umm al-Jimal Project, 1981–1992. *Annual of the Department of Antiquities of Jordan* 37: 433–456.

De Vries, B. (ed.)

1998 *Umm el-Jimal: A Frontier Town and its Landscape in Northern Jordan*, I. Journal of Roman Archaeology Supplementary Series 26. Portsmouth: Journal of Roman Archaeology.

Dussart, O.

1989 Recherche sur le verre antique en Jordanie et Syrie du Sud. *Contribution française à l'archéologie jordanienne*, 105–108.

Engel, T

1993 Charcoal Remains From an Iron Age Copper Smelting Slag Heap at Feinan, Wadi Arabah (Jordan). *Vegetation History and Archaeobotany* 2: 205–11.

Engel, T. and W. Frey

1996 Fuel Resources for Copper Smelting in Antiquity in Selected Woodlands in the Edom Highlands to the Wadi Arabah/Jordan. *Flora* 191: 29–39.

Fiema, Z.

1991 Economics, Administration and Demography of Late Roman and Byzantine Southern Transjordan. Unpublished PhD dissertation, Department of Anthropology, University of Utah.

1995 Culture History of the Byzantine Ecclesiastical Complex

at Petra. *American Center of Oriental Research Newsletter* 7: 1–3.

2001 Remarks on the Urbanistic Development of Petra's Center in the Nabataean and Roman Periods. In *Studies in the History and Archaeology of Jordan VII*, 433–436. Amman: Department of Antiquities of Jordan.

2004 St Aaron Revisited—The Finnish excavations at Jabal Harun near Petra. In *Studies in the History and Archaeology of Jordan VIII*, 129–139. Amman: Department of Antiquities of Jordan.

Fiema, Z.T., C. Kanellopoulos, T. Waliszewski and R. Schick

2001 *The Petra Church.* Amman: American Center for Oriental Research.

Findlater, G.

1998 The Wadi Faynan Project: The South Cemetery Excavation, Jordan 1996: A Preliminary Report. *Levant* 30: 69–83.

Fisher, C.S. and C.G. McCown

1931 Jerash-Gerasa 1930. *Annual of the American School of Oriental Research* 11: 1–62.

Flanagan, J., D. McCreery and K. Yassine

1994 Tell Nimrin: Preliminary Report on the 1993 Season. *Annual of the Department of Antiquities of Jordan* 38: 205–244.

Freestone, I.C., K.D. Politis and C.P. Stapleton

2001 The Byzantine Glazed Pottery from Deir 'Ain 'Abata, Jordan. In E. Villeneuve and P. Watson (eds.), *Byzantine and Early Islamic Ceramics in Syria-Jordan (IVth–VIIIth Centuries)*. International Colloquium, Amman 1993. Beirut: Institut Français d'archéologie du Proche-Orient.

Frösén, J.

2004 Archaeological Information from the Petra Papyri. In *Studies in the History and Archaeology of Jordan VIII*, 141–144. Amman: Department of Antiquities of Jordan.

Gentelle, P.

1984 Traces de champs autour de Petra. In F. Villeneuve (ed.), *Contribution française à l'archéologie jordanienne*, 24–27. Amman: Institut Français d'archéologie du Proche-Orient.

Geraty, L.T. and Ø.S. LaBianca

1985 The Local Environment and Human Food-Procuring Strategies in Jordan: The Case of Tell Hesban and its Surrounding Region. In A. Hadidi (ed.), *Studies in the History and Archaeology of Jordan II*, 323–330. Amman: Department of Antiquities of Jordan.

Glueck, N.

1934 *Explorations in Eastern Palestine* I. Annual of theAmerican Schools of Oriental Research 14. New Haven, CT: American Schools of Oriental Research.

1935 *Explorations in Eastern Palestine* II. Annual of theAmerican Schools of Oriental Research 15. New Haven, CT: American Schools of Oriental Research.

1939 *Explorations in Eastern Palestine* III. Annual of theAmerican Schools of Oriental Research 18–19. New Haven, CT: American Schools of Oriental Research.

1951 *Explorations in Eastern Palestine* IV. Annual of theAmerican Schools of Oriental Research 25–28. New Haven, CT: American Schools of Oriental Research.

Graf, D.

1992 Nabataean Settlements and Roman Occupation in Arabia Petraea. In M. Zaghloul, K. 'Amr, F. Zayadine, R. Nabeel and N. Rida Tawfiq (eds.), *Studies in the History and Archaeology of Jordan IV*, 253–260. Amman: Department of Antiquities of Jordan.

2001 First Millennium AD: Roman and Byzantine Periods Landscape Archaeology and Settlement Patters. In *Studies in the History and Archaeology of Jordan VII*, 469–480. Amman: Department of Antiquities of Jordan.

Grattan, J.P., D.D. Gilbertson, C.O. Hunt

2007 The local and global dimensions of metaliferrous air pollution derived from a reconstruction of an 8 thousand year record of copper smelting and mining at a desert-mountain frontier in southern Jordan. *Journal of Archaeological Science* 34: 83–110

Hauptmann, A.

1986 Archaeometallurgical and Mining-Archaeological Studies in the Eastern 'Arabah, Feinan Area, 2nd Season. *Annual of the Department of Antiquities of Jordan* 30: 415–419.

2000 *Zur Frühen Metallurgie des Kupfers in Fenan/Jordanien.* Der Anschnitt Supplement 11. Bochum: Deustches Bergbau-Museum.

Hauptmann, A. and G. Weisgerber

1992 Periods of Ore Exploitation and Metal Production in Feinan. In M. Zaghloul, K. Amr, F. Zayadine, R. Nabeel and N. Rida Tawfiq (eds.), *Studies in the History and Archaeology of Jordan IV*, 61–66. Amman: Department of Antiquities of Jordan.

Hayes, J.W.

1972 *Late Roman Pottery.* London: British School at Rome.

Holmgren, R. and A. Kaliff

1997 The 1995/96 Excavation of Dayr al-Qattar al-Byzanti: A Preliminary Report. *Annual of the Department of Antiquities of Jordan* 41: 321–340.

Homès-Fredericq, D. and J.B. Hennessy (eds.)

1986 *Archaeology of Jordan* I. Leuven: Peeters.

1989 *Archaeology of Jordan* II. Leuven: Peeters.

Humbert, J.-B.

1997 Les figurines byzantines du cimetière de Samra. *Le Monde de la Bible* 104: 55.

1989 El-Fedein/Mafraq. In F. Villeneuve (ed.), *Contribution française à l'archéologie jordanienne*, 125–131. Amman: Institut Français d'archéologie du Proche-Orient.

Humbert, J.-B. and A. Desreumaux

1989 Khirbet es-Samra. In F. Villeneuve (ed.), *Contribution française à l'archéologie jordanienne*, 113–121. Amman:

Institut Français d'archéologie du Proche-Orient.

Hunt, C.O., H.A. Mohamed, D.D. Gilbertson, J. Grattan, S. McLaren, F.B. Pyatt, G. Rushworth and G.W. Barker

2004 Early Holocene alluviation and environment in the Wadi Faynan, Jordan. *The Holocene* 14(6): 921–930.

Isaac, B.

1990 *The Limits of Empire: The Roman Army in the East.* Oxford: Clarendon Press.

Ji, C.C., and J.K. Lee

2000 A Preliminary Report on the Dhiban Plateau Survey Project, 1999: The Versacare Expedition. *Annual of the Department of Antiquities of Jordan* 44: 493–506.

Jones, A.H.M.

1973 *The Later Roman Empire 284–602: A Social, Economic and Administrative Survey.* Oxford: Blackwell.

Joukowksy, M.S.

2001 More Pieces in the Petra Great Temple Puzzle. *Bulletin of the American Society for Oriental Research* 324: 43–58.

Kaegi, W.E.

1992 *Byzantium and the Early Islamic Conquests.* Cambridge: Cambridge University Press.

Kaimio, M. and L. Koenen

1997 Reports on Deciperment of Petra Papyri (1996/7). *Annual of the Department of Antiquities of Jordan* 41: 449–462.

Kehrberg, I. and A. Ostrasz

1994 Gerasa, Hippodrome. *American Journal of Archaeology* 98: 546–547.

1997 A History of Occupational Changes at the Site of the Hippodrome of Gerasa. In M. Zaghloul, K. Amr, F. Zayadine, R. Nabeel and N. Rida Tawfiq (eds.), *Studies in the History and Archaeology of Jordan IV*, 167–173. Amman: Department of Antiquities of Jordan.

Kennedy, D.L.

1982 *Archaeological Explorations on the Roman Frontier in North-East Jordan.* British Archaeological Reports International Series. Oxford: British Archaeological Reports.

1997 Roman Roads and Routes in North-East Jordan. *Levant* 29: 71–93.

2004 Settlement in the Jarash Basin and its Wider Context: A Proposal for Fieldwork and a Research Project to Interpret and Explain Settlement and Landuse in North-West Jordan. In *Studies in the History and Archaeology of Jordan VIII*, 197–215. Amman: Department of Antiquities of Jordan.

Kennedy, D.L. and P. Freeman

1995 Southern Hauran Survey 1992. *Levant* 27: 39–73.

Khalil, L.A., and F.M. Al-Nammari

2000 Two Large Wine Presses at Khirbet Yajuz, Jordan. *Bulletin of the American Schools of Oriental Research* 318: 41–57.

Killick, A.C.

1983 Udhruh, 1980, 1981, 1982 Seasons: A Preliminary Report. *Annual of the Department of Antiquities of Jordan* 27: 231–244.

1986 Udhruh and the Southern Frontier. In P. Freeman and D. Kennedy (eds.), *The Defence of the Roman and Byzantine East*, 431–446. British Archaeological Reports International Series. Oxford: British Archaeological Reports.

King, G.R.D.

1982 Survey of Byzantine and Islamic Sites in Jordan. *Annual of the Department of Antiquities of Jordan* 26: 85–95.

King, G.R.D., C.J. Lenzen and G.O. Rollefson

1983 Survey of Byzantine and Islamic Sites in Jordan. *Annual of the Department of Antiquities of Jordan* 27: 385–436.

King, G.R.D., C.J. Lenzen, A. Newhall, J.L. King and J.D. Deemer

1987 Survey of Byzantine and Islamic Sites in Jordan. *Annual of the Department of Antiquities of Jordan* 31: 439–460.

King, G.R.D., C.J. Lenzen, A. Newhall, J.L. King, J.D. Deemer and G.O. Rollefson

1989 Survey of Byzantine and Islamic Sites in Jordan. *Annual of the Department of Antiquities of Jordan* 33: 199–217.

Kraeling, C.H.

1938 *Gerasa, City of the Decapolis*. New Haven, CT: American Schools of Oriental Research.

LaBianca, Ø.S. and L. Lacelle (eds.)

1986 *Environmental Foundations: Studies of Climatological, Geological, Hydrological, and Phytological Conditions in Hesban and Vicinity*. Berrien Springs, MI: Andrews University.

Lavento, M., A. Siiriäinen, H. Jansson, P. Kouki, A. Mukkala, S. Silvonen and T. Tenhunen

2004 The Jabal Harun Survey—Settlement History and Land Use in the Area, In *Studies in the History and Archaeology of Jordan VIII*, 225–235. Amman: Department of Antiquities of Jordan.

Leadbetter, B.

2004 Trade, Frontier and the Limes Palestinae. In *Studies in the History and Archaeology of Jordan VIII*, 247–251. Amman: Department of Antiquities of Jordan.

Lenzen, C.J., and E.A. Knauf

1987 Beit Ras/Capitolias. A Preliminary Evaluation of the Archaeological and Textual Evidence. *Syria* 64: 21–46.

Lindner, M., U. Hübner and J. Hübl

2000 Nabataean and Roman Presence between Petra and Wadi 'Arabah. survey Expedition 1997/98: Umm Ratam. *Annual of the Department of Antiquities of Jordan* 44: 535–567.

Lindner, M., and E. Gunsam

2002 A Fortified Suburb of Ancient Petra: Shammasa.

Annual of the Department of Antiquities of Jordan, 46: 225–241.

MacAdam, H.I.

1994 Settlements and Settlement Patterns in Northern and Central Transjordania, ca 550.ca 750. In G. King and A. Cameron (eds.), *The Byzantine and Early Islamic Near East II: Land Use and Settlement Patterns*. Princeton: Darwin.

MacDonald, B.

1980 The Hermitage of John the Abbot at Hammam 'Afra, Southern Jordan. *Liber Annuus* 30: 351–364.

1996 Survey and Excavation: A Comparison of Survey and Excavation Results from Sites of the Wadi Hasa and the Southern al-Aghwar and Northeast 'Arabah Archaeological Surveys. *Annual of the Department of Antiquities of Jordan* 40: 323–337.

MacDonald, B. (ed.)

1988 *The Wadi Hasa Archaeological Survey 1979–1983, West-Central Jordan*. Waterloo, ON: Wilfrid Laurier University Press.

1992 *The Southern Ghors and Northeast 'Arabah Archaeological Survey*. Sheffield Archaeological Monographs 5. Sheffield: J.R. Collis.

MacDonald, B., L. Herr, M.P. Neeley, S. Quaintance and A. Bradshaw

2001 The Tafila-Busayra Archaeological Survey: Phase 2 2000. *Annual of the Department of Antiquities of Jordan* 45: 395–411.

Mare, W.H.

1984 The 1982 Season at Abila of the Decapolis. *Annual of the Department of Antiquities of Jordan* 28: 39–54.

Mayerson, P.

1989 Saracens and Romans: Micro-Macro Relationships. *Bulletin of the American Schools of Oriental Research* 274: 71–79.

McNicoll, A.W., R.H. Smith and J.B. Hennessy

1982 *Pella in Jordan* I. Canberra: Australian National Gallery.

McNicoll, A.W., R.H. Smith, P.M. Watson, and S. Gordon

1992 *Pella in Jordan* II. Sydney: Meditarch.

Melkawi, A., K. 'Amr and D. Whitcomb

1994 The Excavations of Two Seventh Century Pottery Kilns at Aqaba. *Annual of the Department of Antiquities of Jordan* 38: 447–468.

Meyer, C.

1988 Glass from the North Theatre Byzantine Church, and Soundings at Jerash, 1982–1983. In W.E. Rast (ed.), *Bulletin of the American Schools of Oriental Research Supplement* 25, 175–222. Baltimore, MD: American Schools of Oriental Research.

Miller, J.I.

1969 *The Spice Trade of the Roman Empire, 29 BC–AD 641*. Oxford: Clarendon Press.

Miller, J.M.

1991 *Archaeological Survey of the Kerak Plateau*. Atlanta, GA: Scholars Press.

Nabulsi, A.J. and J.-B. Humbert

1996 Excavations in the Byzantine Cemetery at Khirbet as-Samra, Site B 1995. *Annual of the Department of Antiquities of Jordan* 40: 491–493.

Northedge, A. (ed.)

1992 *Studies on Roman and Islamic Amman* I. Oxford: Oxford University Press.

Oleson, J.P., K. 'Amr and R. Schick

1992 The Humeima Excavation Project: Preliminary Report of the 1991 Season. *Echos du monde classique/Classical Views* 36, ns 11: 137–169.

Oleson, J.P., K. 'Amr, R.M. Foote and R. Schick

1995 Preliminary Report on the Humeima Excavation Project1993. *Annual of the Department of Antiquities of Jordan* 39: 317–354.

Palumbo, G., K. 'Amr, A. Musa and M. Rasson-Seigne

1993 The Cultural Resources Management Project in Jordan: Salvage Excavations at Tell Faysal, Jarash. *Annual of the Department of Antiquities of Jordan* 37: 89–117.

Parker, S.T.

1986 *Romans and Saracens: A History of the Arabian Frontier*. Winona Lake, IN: Eisenbrauns.

1992 The Limes and Settlement Patterns in Central Jordan in the Roman and Byzantine Periods. In M. Zaghloul, K. 'Amr, F. Zayadine, R. Nabeel and N. Rida Tawfiq (eds.), *Studies on the History and Archaeology of Jordan IV*, 321–325. Amman: Department of Antiquities of Jordan.

1995 The Typology of Roman and Byzantine Forts and Fortresses in Jordan. In K. 'Amr, F. Zayadine and M. Zaghloul (eds.), *Studies in the History and Archaeology of Jordan V*, 251–260. Amman: Department of Antiquities of Jordan.

1996 The Roman Aqaba Project: The 1994 Campaign. *Annual of the Department of Antiquities of Jordan* 40: 231–257.

1998 The Roman 'Aqaba Project: The 1996 Campaign. *Annual of the Department of Antiquities of Jordan* 42: 375–394.

Parker, S.T.

2002 The Roman 'Aqaba Project: The 2000 Campaign. *Annual of the Department of Antiquities of Jordan* 46: 409–427.

Parker S.T. (ed.).

1987 *The Roman Frontier in Central Jordan: Interim Report on the Limes Arabicus Project 1980–1985*. British Archaeological Reports International Series. Oxford: British Archaeological Report.

Parr, P.J.

1986 The Last Days of Petra. In M. Bakhit and M. Asfour (eds.), *Proceedings of the Symposium on Bilad al-Sham during the Byzantine Period II (English Section)*, 192–

205. Amman: University of Jordan.

Peterman, G. and R. Schick

1996 The Monastery of Saint Aaron. *Annual of the Department of Antiquities of Jordan* 40: 473–480.

Piccirillo, M.

1985 Rural Settlements in Byzantine Jordan. In A. Hadidi (ed.), *Studies in the History and Archaeology of Jordan II*, 257–261. Amman: Department of Antiquities of Jordan.

1987 The Jerusalem-Esbus Road and its Sanctuaries in Transjordan. In A. Hadidi (ed.), *Studies in the History and Archaeology of Jordan III*, 165–172. Amman: Department of Antiquities of Jordan.

1989 Chiese e i mosaici di Um er-Rasas-Kastron Mefaa. In M. Piccirillo (ed.) *Chiese e mosaici di Madaba*, 269–308. Jerusalem: Franciscan Printing Press.

1993 *The Mosaics of Jordan*. Amman: American Center of Oriental Research.

Politis, K.D.

1997 Excavations and Restorations at Dayr 'Ayn 'Abata 1995. *Annual of the Department of Antiquities of Jordan* 41: 341–350.

1998 Survey and Rescue Collections in the Ghor as-Safi. *Annual of the Department of Antiquities of Jordan* 42: 627–634.

2001 Early Byzantine Monasticism in Southern Jordan. In Department of Antiquities of Jordan (ed.), In *Studies in the History and Archaeology of Jordan VII*, 585–589. Amman: Department of Antiquities of Jordan.

2004 Ancient Arabs, Jews and Greeks on the Shores of the Dead Sea. In *Studies in the History and Archaeology of Jordan VIII*, 361–370. Amman: Department of Antiquities of Jordan.

Prag, K., and H. Barnes

1996 Three Fortresses on the Wadi Kafrain, Jordan. *Levant* 28: 41–61.

Rast, W. and T. Schaub

1974 Survey of the Southeastern Plain of the Dead Sea, 1973. *Annual of the Department of Antiquities of Jordan* 19: 5–53.

Rothenberg, B.

1970 An Archaeological Survey of South Sinai: First Season 1967/1968. *Palestine Exploration Quarterly* 102: 4–28.

Ruben, I., R.H. Barnes and R. Kana'an

1997 Mapping and Preliminary Survey in Wadi Faynan South Jordan. *Annual of the Department of Antiquities of Jordan* 41: 433–452.

Ruben, I. (ed.)

2003 *The Petra Siq: Nabataean Hydrology Uncovered*. Amman: Petra National Trust.

Sapin, J.

1985 Prospection géo-archéologique de l'Ajlûn 1981–82: Example de recherche intégrante. In A. Hadidi (ed.),

Studies in the History and Archaeology of Jordan II, 217–227. Amman: Department of Antiquities of Jordan.

Sartre, M.

1982 *Trois études sur l'Arabie romaine et byzantine*. Revue des études latines. Brussels: Latomus.

1985 Le peuplement et la développement du Hauran antique à la lumiere des inscriptions grècques et latines. In J.-M. Dentzer (ed.), *Hauran* I, 189–202. Paris: Geuthner.

1987 Le Hawran byzantin à la veille de la conquête musulmane. In M.A. Bakhit (ed.), *Proceedings of the Second Symposium on the History of Bilad al-Sham during the Early Islamic Period up to 40 A.H./640 AD* I, 155–167. Amman: University of Jordan.

Sauer, J.A.

1973 *Heshbon Pottery 1971*. Berrien Springs, MI: Andrews University.

Schick, R.

1992 Jordan on the Eve of the Muslim Conquest AD 602–634. In P. Canivet and J.-P. Rey-Coquais (eds.), *La Syrie de Byzance à l'Islam, VII–VIII siècles: Actes du colloque international, Lyon, Paris, 1990*, 107–119. Damascus: IFAPO.

1994 The Settlement Pattern of Southern Jordan: The Natureof the Evidence. In G. King and A. Cameron (eds.), *The Byzantine and Early Islamic Near East* II: *Land Use and Settlement Patterns*, 133–154. Princeton: Darwin.

1995 *The Christian Communities of Palestine from Byzantine to Islamic Rule: A Historical and Archaeological Study*. Princeton: Darwin.

Schick, R.

2001 Christianity in Southern Jordan in the Byzantine and Early Islamic Periods. In *Studies in the History and Archaeology of Jordan VII*, 581–584. Amman: Department of Antiquities of Jordan.

Schmid, S. G. and Kolb, B.

2000 *Petra Ez Zantur, 2: Ergebnisse der schweizerisch-liechtensteinischen Ausgrabungen 1*. Mainz: Philipp Von Zabern.

Seigne, J.

1992 Jérash romaine et byzantine: Développement urbain d'une ville provinciale orientale. In M. Zaghloul, K. Amr, F. Zayadine, R. Nabeel and N. Rida Tawfiq (eds.), *Studies in the History and Archeology of Jordan IV*, 331–341. Amman: Department of Antiquities of Jordan.

Shahid, I.

1984 *Byzantium and the Arabs in the Fourth Century*. Washington: Dumbarton Oaks.

1989 *Byzantium and the Arabs in the Fifth Century*. Washington: Dumbarton Oaks.

Smith, A.M., M. Stevens and T.M. Niemi

1997 The Southeast Araba Archaeological Survey: A Preliminary Report of the 1994 Season. *Bulletin of the American Schools of Oriental Research* 305: 45–71.

Smith, R.H.

1973 *Pella of the Decapolis* I. Wooster, OH: The College of Wooster.

Smith, R.H. and L.P. Day

1989 *Pella of the Decapolis* II. Wooster, OH: The College of Wooster.

Tholbecq, L.

2001 The Hinterland of Petra from the Edomite to the Islamic Periods: The Jabal ash-Sharah Survey (1996–1997). In *Studies in the History and Archaeology of Jordan VII*, 399–405. Amman: Department of Antiquities of Jordan.

Trimingham, J.S.

1979 *Christianity among the Arabs in Pre-Islamic Times*. London: Longman.

Tushingham, A.D.

1972 *The Excavations at Dibon (Dhibân) in Moab: The Third Campaign 1952–53*. Cambridge: American Schools of Oriental Research.

Vriezen, K.J.

2004 Churches in Urban Context in the Fifth–Eighth Centuries in Jordan and Palestine. In *Studies in the History and Archaeology of Jordan VIII*, 469–476. Amman: Department of Antiquities of Jordan.

Walmsley, A.G.

1998 Gharandal in Jibal: First Season Report. *Annual of the Department of Antiquities of Jordan* 42: 433–441.

Waheeb, M.

2004 The Hermit Caves in Bethany Beyond the Jordan (Baptism Site). In *Studies in the History and Archaeology of Jordan VIII*, 477–484. Amman: Department of Antiquities of Jordan.

Watson, P.M.

1992 Change in Foreign and Regional Economic Links with Pella in the Seventh Century: The Ceramic Evidence. In P. Canivet and J.-P. Rey-Coquais (eds.), *La Syrie de Byzance à l'Islam, VII–VIII siècles: Actes du colloque international, Lyon-Paris 1990*, 233–247. Damascus: Institut français de Damas.

Watson, P.M. and M. O'Hea

1996 The Pella Hinterland Survey 1994: Preliminary Report. *Levant* 28: 63–76.

Whitby, M.

1995 Recruitment in Roman Armies from Justinian to Heraclius (ca. 565–615). In A. Cameron (ed.), *The Byzantine and Early Islamic Near East*, III. *States, Resources and Armies*, 61–124. Princeton: Darwin.

Whitting, P.D.

1973 *Byzantine Coins*. New York: G.P. Putnam's Sons.

Zayadine, F. (ed.)

1986 *Jerash Archaeological Project 1981–1983*, I. Amman: Department of Antiquities of Jordan.

1989 *Jerash Archaeological Project 1984–1988*, II. Paris: Department of Antiquities of Jordan.

Zeist, W. van

1985 Past and Present Environments in the Jordan Valley. In A. Hadidi (ed.), *Studies in the History and Archaeology of Jordan II*, 199–204. Amman: Department of Antiquities of Jordan.

15. The Umayyad and Abbasid Periods

Donald Whitcomb

The End of Antiquity?

In a volume such as this on the archaeology of Jordan, it would not have been surprising in years past to find the articles ending with the "coming of Islam." The dominating model was that this momentous event sealed the past and began a new, fully historical Mediaeval period. This somehow implied that full historical documentation (would that such a thing existed) somehow obviated the need for archaeology. For scholars studying the period after this defining event, archaeological methodology was seen as subsidiary to historical, a scholarly tendency commonly encountered in the study of any society that left written sources. Although written records may provide details, thoughts, reasoning, and the like, broader trends, both temporal and spatial, frequently may be clarified only through the archaeological record.

In the past several decades the archaeology of Jordan in the early Islamic period (c. 600–1000 CE) (Figure 15.2) has witnessed a concentration of research, both conceptual and in the field, unparalleled in previous years or in the experience of other countries of the Levant. Archaeologists working in the field have amassed an evidential base unrivaled in neighbouring regions of the Middle East (Figure 15.1). These excavations, combined with interpretative analysis relating this data to historical contexts, have made major advances illustrating, for example, the urban system of this region during the transition from Late Antiquity to early Islam.

Increased attention has been paid in recent decades to the concept of Late Antiquity as a research focus, often in combination with early Islam. They have been defined in various chronological periodizations (Figure 15.2). What is clear and significant is the abandonment of the assumption of the Fall of Rome in 476 as a pivotal turning point; as Cameron notes, no significant economic or social change seems to be associated with this event or date (1993: 33). Likewise, the idea that 636 CE was a turning point has given way to an appreciation of the continuity of material culture reflected in the cumulative value of archaeological research on individual sites and survey patterns (e.g. MacAdam 1994, and other articles in the second volume of *The Byzantine and Early Islamic Near East*, King and Cameron [eds.]).

A central facet of recent studies on Late Antiquity has been settlement patterns and in particular the study of urban systems. The fate of the Classical city has been explored, and it is widely recognized at this point that those cities had, in the immediately pre-Islamic Near East, developed into a type that was no longer "classical." Again, this realization is the result of careful analysis, the combination of textual and archaeological resources; the doctoral study of Schick, with its very useful gazetteer, is an exemplar of this trend (1995). His volume benefits from the intensive fieldwork undertaken in Jordan, usually reported in the *Annual of the Department of Antiquities of Jordan*. If one chronicles the occurrence of articles pertaining to Islamic archaeology, one observes only a rare report until the late 1970s and a curve of activity in the late 1980s; since the hiatus of the Gulf War, Islamic archaeology represents a fairly substantial portion of the archaeology of Jordan.

Jordan has in effect become a leading venue for re-evaluating historical assumptions and testing new ideas concerning the cultural ramifications of early Islam, a crucial period in the history of the Islamic world. Work now focuses on interpretations and historical synthesis; the next and subtler campaign needs to be directed toward delineation of cultural changes and their explanations. As current research in early Islamic history questions accepted perceptions of historical sources, it becomes more and more important to consider archaeological evidence in the framing and answering of historical questions. An example of archaeological applications to the investigation of the formation of early Islam, though somewhat controversial, is found in revisionism of evidence from the Negev (Whitcomb 1995: 500–501). The Negev and much of Jordan are peripheral regions where contemporary documentation is minimal (though one may note that anepigraphic sites such as Qasr Mushatta and Qasr Kharrana, discovered almost 100 years ago, have recently revealed inscriptions: Imbert 1995 and Imbert and Bacquey 1989; cf. Urice 1987). However, such remote sites frequently reflect an intimate relationship with broader cultural changes.

The Umayyad State and Arab *Qusur*

The political structure of early Islamic Bilad ash-Sham (Greater Syria or the four modern Levantine states) was conceived in terms of *junds*, a term that is unusual and ambiguous. Following the lead of Shahid (1986), these political regions stretching "from the sea to the desert" may be associated with the late Classical term "theme" as indicative of a military district. These may further be associated, as is the word itself, with Persian toponymy, imposed during the reorganization of the Persian occupation (614 to 628 CE; Whitcomb 1994a). The modern state of Jordan coincides with portions of three *junds*: Filastin, al-Urdunn, and Dimashq, with corresponding capitals in Ramlah, Tabariya, and Damascus. Jordan, or rather the Transjordanian segment of these *junds*, lay to the east and south of these political centres.

The structure of the *junds* has importance for our understanding of the role of archaeological sites in modern Jordan during the formative era of Islamic culture. Careful examination of Byzantine towns and monasteries shows, with increasing clarity, a continuation, often without apparent change, well into the Abbasid period (e.g. Madaba, Umm Rasas, Zughar, and others). Like-

Figure 15.1 Sites mentioned in the text.

Political Periods	Pella 1992	Pella	Amman Northidge	Hesban 1978	Humayma F102	Aqaba	Archaeological Periods	Revised Periods
Fatimid			IIa Fat.	VA	2	D Fat.	middle Islamic I	11th century
Ikhshidid Tulunid			III	969		C late Abb.	early Islamic III	early Islamic III
	III Abb.			VB Abb.	3			early Islamic II
Abbasid			IVb Abb.		4	B Abb.	early Islamic II	early Islamic I
Umayyad	VII	IV Um.	Va	VI Um.	5	A Um.	early Islamic I	7th century
	VI		Vb	661				
Rashidun	V	V Byz.	VI	VII 614			late Byzantine	
	IV			late Byz.				late Byzantine
Byzantine	IIIa, b II		VII	VIII				

1050 — 1000
950
850 — 900
750 — 800
650 — 700
550 — 600
— 500

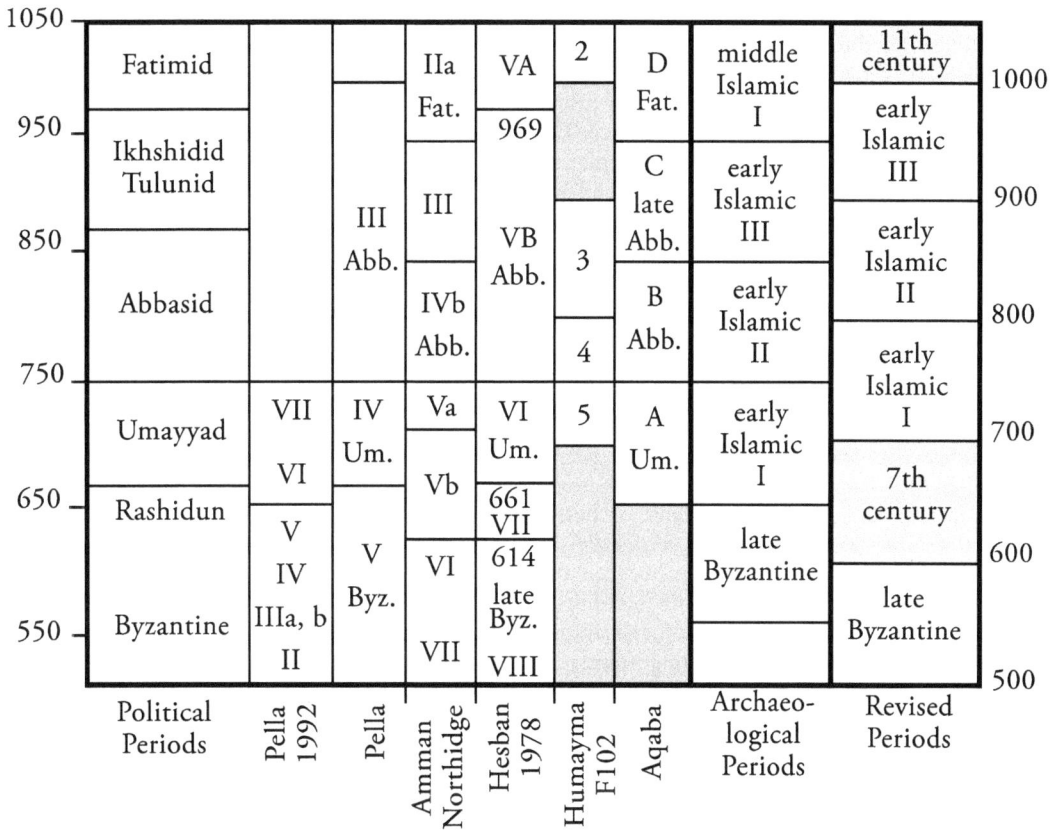

Figure 15.2 Chronological periodization of the early Islamic priods in Jordan.

wise, cities such as Amman, Jarash, Pella, and Gadara also continued, although their structural organization and their relation to their dependencies bear some examination. The apparent innovations seem to lie on the eastern periphery of the *junds*, where extant settlements of earlier periods became the loci for new social relations (see Figure 15.1).

The desert had been crossed by roads and was the locus of settlements and fortifications in pre-Islamic times (usually, during the Classical period, under the rubric of the *limes*, however one may define the concept; Parker 1986). Such remains dating to Classical times must be seen in light of the Nabataean and Ghassanid political achievements which, while hardly confined to this periphery, indicate a strong role of Arab tribes in the pre-Islamic period (MacAdam 1994). An appreciation of this focus on the desert may begin with the remarkable but largely neglected study of Helms (1990). He begins with a study of Qasr Burqu, an apparently typical *qasr* (or "desert castle," see below) of the Umayyad period; he expanded this field research by investigating the atypical site of ancient Risha, a collection of minimally preserved structures, individual buildings arranged in parallel lines with a mosque and large formal building. The settlement of Risha seems to be a sedentarized camp, but at least one of its buildings, Structure C, is parallel to the enclosures that are the core element for most of the *qusur* (as implied in the name, see Conrad 1981). Perhaps a better example of a settlement complex involves the well-excavated *qasr* at Umm Walid (Bujard and Haldimann 1997); the pattern of settlement, involving three *qusur*, seems to indicate a tension between unifying enclosure and social privacy dramatized in the subsidiary walls subdividing the common court.

Helms uses the morphology of Risha to reconstruct a crucial aspect of social organization, the process of sedentarization in the early Islamic period (a process important for many periods; Finkelstein 1995). He makes a strong case from ethnoarchaeological models of the bedouin camp for the *parembole nomadon* or *hadir* as developmental stages toward the *amsar* of the early Islamic period (Helms 1990: 39–41; Whitcomb 1994a). This model might be stronger with the term "arab" rather than "bedouin," since the later ethnic ramifications of "arab" are crucial as this society develops beyond a socio-economic definition limited to the desert. Just as the architectural elements and ceramics of Risha come from urban sources, so the familiarity of Arab societies with urban society facilitated formation of the early Islamic state. The desert became the scene for a pastoral peasantry, that is, the affective regions of cities increased in a new or perhaps more intensive manner. Understanding "this remarkable breakthrough in social organization" (Donner 1981: 269) has proven elusive from documentary sources. Donner's focus on nomads, or better, the tribal foundations of Arab Muslims, has been salutary but marred by neglect of the archaeological resources that might bear upon the subject (see now Whitcomb 2006).

Renewed archaeological research on the *qusur* has concentrated on broader contexts. In past decades, interpretations have shifted the balance from romantic explanations to economic factors (as caravanserai systems or desert exploitation, the latter close to Sauvaget's *latifundia*) or social organization (as interactive facilities between the settled and nomad/tribal, rather like *majlis* buildings). Thus Ghazi Bisheh excavated Qasr Hallabat for its stratigraphy and construction details and, more importantly, as a complex of mosque, agricultural enclosures, and quarries (1985, 1993; see also his work at Qasr Mushash 1989). On the contrary, the potential of Muwaqqar has not been realized in spite of important epigraphic and ceramic evidence (Hamilton 1946; Najjar 1989). Likewise, the efforts to record Qastal include a broader perspective, studying not only the *qasr* and mosque, but a bath (Bisheh 2000), an agricultural barrage, and a cemetery (Carlier and Morin 1989; Qusayr Amra is a similar potential complex, Almagro *et al.* 1975). Another complex is the estate of the Abbasid family at Humayma (Foote 1994).

Consideration of function brings one back to more traditional approaches, including art historical analysis, for which one may note the new perspectives provided by Bacharach (1996). His construction of Marwanid political patronage relies heavily on traditional sources yet recognizes the importance of structural patterns, notably locational relationship of the palace, bath, and *dar al-imara* (aspects he develops more fully in broader contexts, 1991). The monuments concerned are recognized as set in a context of tents, that is, camps; further, the locations where they were constructed almost always had pre-Islamic structures, often ruins, psychological magnets for renewed occupation. The structural patterns of the *qusur* lead to the inescapable conclusion that these were intended to be urban, or, better, to bring an urban pattern to new regions. Further, the few decades of building occurred some 50 years after the conquest; like the Islamic urban pattern imposed on Jerusalem, this seems likely to have begun during the long rule of Mu'awiya (as governor and caliph, 640–80; Whitcomb 1995).

Abbasid Revolution or Devolution?

Study of archaeological sites in Jordan demonstrates how, until the mid-eighth century, this region played the role of an influential margin in the development of an imperial state. More clearly than in any other region of the early Islamic world, except potentially Arabia itself, one may observe the material remains of a new civilization that would dominate the entire Middle East for many centuries. The Abbasid revolution, and more precisely the period of changes directly following this political upheaval, produced instability expressed in material changes in the archaeological record in Jordan. It is still deceptively easy to see cultural discontinuities as regional devolution. Thus Kennedy may observe that "there is no significant surviving architectural monument in Bilad ash-Sham from the period between the abandonment of the last Umayyad palace construction and the restoration of the al-Aqsa mosque by the Fatimids" (1992: 106; LaBianca 1990: 241, more dramatically, sees no settlement remains for the same period).

Oleg Grabar, who has made many fundamental contributions to the study of the *qusur*, discovered a historical fragment concerning the *qasr* or fort of Tall Hisban (see below) and its role as a centre of Umayyad partisans during the al-Faddayni revolt of 813 CE (1964; discussed in Cobb 1997). This historical fragment may reflect a richer settlement pattern than heretofore acknowledged for the earlier Abbasid period. The necessity to control viable Arab settlements in Jordan may have led the Abbasids to focus their attention on Amman and to establish this city as a regional capital and seat of a provincial governor. Following Umayyad attentions to the Balqa region, the Abbasids appointed three known governors (including Salih ibn Sulayman in 796 CE, who may have restored the palace and citadel of Amman; see below). The Tulunid interim of 878–905 CE was followed by Abbasid restoration about 918 CE, when the governor of Amman was Muhammad ibn Tughj (who later founded the Ikhshidid dynasty of Egypt in 935 CE; Northedge 1992: 53).

To begin to understand Amman, one must consider the lower town, where Northedge has plausibly reconstructed a *jami* or congregational mosque (1989). This mosque may be taken together with a putative *hammam* and *dar al-imara* to configure an early Islamic city within the remnants of Philadelphia (Whitcomb 2000: fig. 3); this urban complex was no doubt an Umayyad foundation, as Northedge suggests. Construction on the citadel is another matter; using stratigraphic elements presented by Northedge (1992; see Whitcomb 2000) and the structural elements excavated by Almagro, one may find an interpretation diametrically opposed to their Umayyad identification (Harding 1951). The focus of the Amman

Citadel is the northern palace complex, which shows an axial orientation beginning with the Entrance Hall or "*iwan*," then a court and street with nine residential units, and finally a court and Throne Room flanked again by four residential units. While the formation of the citadel is unlike most of the *qusur*, there is a striking resemblance to Qasr Mushatta. A careful comparison of Almagro's justified plan of Amman Citadel (1987: fig. 14) with Qasr Mushatta clearly shows striking parallels in size, orientation, and hierarchical arrangement of architectural elements (Figure 15.3). It may be significant that the only carved stone decoration in these structures is the façade panel at Qasr Mushatta and the analogous entrance pavilion at Amman. Grabar has argued a very plausible case on formal and stylistic grounds for the Abbasid foundation of Qasr Mushatta (1987).

The Entrance Hall may be seen reflexively as the north gate of the upper city, with a *hammam* to its east, transiting the palace into an urban complex. This is the startling result of Almagro and Arce's new excavations: a large court flanked by shops, more vernacular residences and streets (Northedge 1991) and, south of the court, a broad esplanade and arcade fronting a large *jami* mosque. The combination of urban and palatial elements in a hierarchical arrangement clearly reflects the palace-city typical of Late Antiquity, as clearly described by Curčić (1993). This second *jami* mosque (Acre, in press), and indeed occupation of the citadel itself, are problematic for the Umayyad period but, along with the parallels with Qasr Mushatta, these features suggest that the entire Amman Citadel should be dated to the Abbasid period. The socio-cultural correlate of this architectural phenomenon

Figure 15.3 Comparison of plans of Qasr Mushatta (left) and Amman Citadel (right) (justified, after Almagro 1987: fig.14).

may be found in the gathering of Umayyad estates in the hands of the Banu Salih, a family that Kennedy describes as a sub-dynasty maintaining the wealth and prosperity of Abbasid Bilad ash-Sham (1981: 74–75).

Both Qasr Mushatta and Amman Citadel have been considered in light of the so-called "desert castles," but their more palatial character suggests they should also be studied with reference to contemporary urban entities. This leads to the necessity of examining the continuities of late Byzantine cities, particularly those of the Decapolis in modern Jordan which were typical of the Classical urban tradition and, more importantly, of transformations in Late Antiquity (Kennedy 1985). Jarash represents an important example of this phenomenon, where the temples, theatres, and baths of the Classical city had been transformed under Christian urban values exemplified in the construction of at least 15 churches, mainly in the sixth century. An early excavation, that of the bath of Placcus, noted later restorations which seem associated with numbers of Arabic coins (Kraeling 1938: 265–269). In a similar manner, the intensive archaeological research in the 1980s concentrated on reconstruction of the Classical city, recording, but not utilizing, the evidence of later Islamic occupations (Zayadine 1986, 1989).

Virtually everywhere in the city, the uppermost layers contained abundant evidence of kilns, indicating a ceramic industry and suggesting that the town was a regional production centre (Schaefer and Falkner 1986). Excavators consistently suggest that the apparently sudden cessation of production was linked with the 747/748 CE earthquake. An important exception to this interpretation is found in the study by Gawlikowski of a residential area near the North Decumanus that continued well into the Abbasid period, when it likewise began ceramic production. He boldly states that "there is no evidence for the earthquake of 746–47 ad that destroyed Pella and which supposedly marked the end of Jerash as well" (1986: 115). The location of innumerable kilns, a notoriously undesirable industry, in theatres, temples, and other central locations indicates a metamorphosis in the urban structure of Jarash. The mosque found near the Cardo is not only small but also rather doubtful (Naghaweh 1982). The early Islamic city of Jarash may require examination of the wider cityscape, such as advanced by Parapetti (1993: fig. 35). Alternatively it is easy to forget how much of Jarash remains insufficiently explored. Recent Danish excavations by Walmsley have discovered the *jami* mosque near the southern tetrakionion (2003, Figure 15.4) This is near the residential area identified by Gawlikowski and suggests that further excavations to the west of the Cardo may reveal other institutions of the Umayyad city of Jarash.

Pella (Fihl) is another Classical city with a complex history (and archaeology) stretching into the early Islamic period. The excavations of Smith produced ample ceram-ic evidence of this continuity (1973), while detailing residential and civic institutions of the city. The excavations of the University of Sydney added a specific concern with the Islamic periods in 1979, investigating the residential sectors III, IV, VIII, and IX of the Umayyad period. Though other earthquake events are periodically cited (e.g. 659/660 CE; note Russell's caveats on earthquakes, 1985), the destruction caused by the 747/748 CE catastrophe seems clear in the residential areas and in the Civic Complex. The Civic Complex is a particularly interesting urban centre with religious and commercial aspects, the latter dependent on the identification of a northern caravanserai (Smith and Day 1989; Walmsley 1992). Neither here nor in the Tall Husn complex (Watson 1992) is there clear evidence of major changes or the introduction of new "Islamic" elements during the Umayyad period: nor was there an obvious continuation into the Abbasid period, as Walmsley noted:

The delayed recognition of Abbasid settlement levels at Fihl is attributable to a number of factors. In particular there is a marked reluctance to acknowledge any permanent occupation of the site after the late Umayyad earthquake, a view that continues to find support from Smith. Furthermore both Sydney and Wooster have overlooked the remains of the successive Islamic settlements in the centre of the tell by concentrating on the east and west ends of the mound. Finally as the Abbasid houses were probably demolished to make way for the Ayyubid/Mamluk village—the remains of this settlement are obscured by later human activity on the tell (Walmsley 1987: 114–115).

More recent research has uncovered expanded settlement, literally a suburb to the north of the main mound, Tabaqat Fahl (Walmsley 1991). This settlement seems to be a new foundation associated with Abbasid period ceramics, an important key for defining this corpus (see below). While the function of these structures is not completely clear, the orthogonal plans with streets suggest an expansion of urban planning typical of other Abbasid foundations (Whitcomb 1995). Similar histories might be generated for Umm Qays (Gadara; Nielsen *et al.* 1993), Abila (Quwayliba; Fuller 1987), Umm Jimal (Knauf 1984), and Bayt Ras (Capitolias; Lenzen and Knauf 1987) in the north of Jordan (see Figure 15.1). In each case, one finds a provincial city of Late Antiquity continuing as a regional centre; structural and architectural changes began before the arrival of Islam, gradually unfolding into a still poorly defined Islamic city. The apparent absence of an Abbasid chapter in their urban histories may be a matter of self-fulfilling prophecy demanding renewed archaeological attention.

The definition of this urban tradition in the early Islamic period for other sites along the western edge of Jordan (Figure 15.1) must await further research and synthesis; though these sites are manifestly complex, the progress in understanding them has been significant.

Figure 15.4 Preliminary outline plan of the Umayyad mosque in Jarash (plan by Ian Simpson, permission A. Walmsley).

Within this context, the study of ceramic evidence was a fundamental technique for advances in chronological and cultural understandings. Perhaps the most important single accomplishment in this field was the contribution by Sauer (1973), which attempted a synthesis of ceramic diagnostics for the Islamic as well as earlier periods. His formulation of Islamic ceramics stood for a decade or longer, until evidence amassed from Tall Hisban and other sites in Jordan led to necessary revisions in this first consensus. The heritage of earlier archaeological practices in Palestine, specifically the reliance on a pottery "reader," has meant often-discarded evidence and hence unverifi-

able conclusions and idiosyncratic interpretations. Many of the excavations discussed here consciously addressed this problem, for example, Jarash, Pella, and Aqabah (Aylah, see below). For the Umayyad and Abbasid periods, changes were connected with the problem of distinguishing Byzantine and earliest Islamic production, and secondly, the problem of identification of Abbasid wares. In both cases, misidentifications led to accentuation of the earlier period (i.e., Byzantine, Umayyad) and underestimation of settlement during the Abbasid and later periods for the large number of intensive regional surveys available in Jordan.

Research on the Pella ceramics has produced one of the clearest patterns for early Islamic ceramic changes. Walmsley builds upon the perceptive studies of Byzantine ceramics by Watson (1992) and acknowledges the termination of a number of types at the end of the sixth or early seventh centuries (1995: Wares 1–5). During the period 660 to 900 CE, there are four stylistic phenomena:

1. Dark grey, metallic wares (Wares 11–14), some with white paint, continue throughout, associated with cooking pots and basins. These may be related to contemporary wares from Khirbat Mafjar (Whitcomb 1988b) as well as the manufactures of Jarash (Schaefer and Falkner 1986).
2. Cream wares appear around the mid-eighth century and may be an innovation of the Abbasid period (Wares 7 and 9); the Mahesh wares of the south (Whitcomb 1989c) may have influenced this introduction.
3. Red-painted wares (Ware 8) appear at about the same time as a regional Abbasid type; its apparent abundance at Jarash signals that site as a major production center. Fine painted "palace wares" and the "fine Byzantine" cups (Ware 10) seem later elements within this tradition.
4. By the ninth century one sees the introduction of Abbasid ceramics, an early Syrian tradition of glazed ware, fine cream wares, and steatite imitations (Wares 15–19); these types form the classic definition of "Mefjer wares," though the term needs to be used with caution. One may note that this understanding of Abbasid ceramics stands separate from the Samarra ceramic tradition, in part antecedent and in part a contemporary regional tradition of some enterprise.

The Seljuq/Fatimid Epilogue

The archaeological story of Pella ends abruptly in the Abbasid period, only to pick up with the Mamluk mosque and village. Recognition of Abbasid settlement and sherds has significantly narrowed the divide between the Umayyad and the Ayyubid; as has been noted, "there is more than enough [remaining] pottery to fill the gap..." (Whitcomb 1992). Within the past decade, the acceptance of Abbasid occupation layers and settlement achievements has resulted in the transfer of the gap, decline, abandonment or abatement to the late ninth and tenth centuries. As in the earlier periods, one cannot divorce the history of Transjordan from Palestine. This period marks the beginning of a new regional phenomenon, the hegemonic sequence of Egyptian dynasties; these are the Tulunids, Ikhshidids and Fatimids of the Early Islamic 3 and Middle Islamic 1 archaeological traditions (Figure 15.2). These are followed by the Ayyubids and Mamluks, after the brief interruption. Given the strength of these mature Islamic cultures, it is tempting to let peripheries decline to invisibility.

Aqabah (or Aylah, as it was known in this period) was by its very nature on this periphery but in a way that documents the interactions of Bilad ash-Sham, Egypt and Arabia. The excavations at Aylah have contributed to understanding aspects of the *misr* type of early Islamic urban development and early Islamic artifacts (Melkawi *et al.* 1994; Whitcomb 1989a). Aylah continued and indeed was revived during the Abbasid period; the latest periods (Phases C and D) document the late Abbasid and Fatimid occupations (Whitcomb 1994b). The Fatimid residence is an example of architectural transformation, where the crossing of the axial streets was marked by a tetrapylon that was converted into a large house (Whitcomb 1988a). The ceramics in this area and elsewhere duplicate Abbasid types outlined at Pella (although with clear regional variations, particularly the Mahesh and Coptic glazed wares; Whitcomb 1989b, 1989c). Since Aylah was a port, a number of Samarra ceramic wares are also present. The late Abbasid (period C, or the Ikhshidid and Tulunid periods) features ceramics of an interregional style, only recently being isolated at Alexandria, Ashkelon, and Caesarea Maritima. The glazed wares reflect commercial relationships and, on the other hand, the development of regional styles in Palestine (Whitcomb 1990–91). By the eleventh century, luxury trade in Chinese ceramics and Fatimid lustre wares are balanced with hand-made "Tupper wares" in contexts of trash accumulation, suggesting a mixture of prosperity and decline.

The late ninth and tenth centuries witnessed transformations in religion and culture not unlike those seen in the sixth and early seventh centuries (this may suggest a revised periodization, one reflecting transitional periods of the seventh and eleventh centuries; Figure 15.2). As in the early transition, efforts at periodization are often misleading with no clear historical date. In general terms, by the beginning of the eleventh century, categories of material culture have changed enough to justify the beginning of a middle Islamic archaeological period. In terms of Aylah, the Qarmati revolt from 901–906 CE resulted in a battle fought near Aqabah. Then the Qarmatians, allied with Jarrahids, captured and administered the southern region from Ramlah in 968 CE, and again they defeated a Fatimid army at Aqabah in 982 CE. Finally, the Jarrahids attacked and sacked Aylah in 1024 CE, an action that may have caused the deposition of a hoard of Sijilmasa dinars (Whitcomb 1994b). This last example is perhaps clear archaeological evidence of events reflecting a broader political and economic instability. Once again, the spectre of thundering hoards of nomads may be overdrawn and suggestions of decline and collapse mask complex social and religious movements. The Qarmatians were apparently much more than successful desert warriors and the Jarrahids may have been tribal but not necessarily Bedouins. Once again, the history of Jordan may become an illuminating peripheral region through contributions of archaeological interpretation.

Bibliography

Amalgro, A.

1987 Origins and Repercussions of the Architecture of the Umayyad Palace in Amman. In A. Hadidi (ed.), *Studies in the History and Archaeology of Jordan III*, 181–191. Amman: Department of Antiquities.

Amalgro, A. and P. Jiménez

2000 The Umayyad mosque of the citadel of Amman. *Annual of the Department of Antiquities of Jordan* 44: 459–475.

Almagro, M. *et al.*

1975 *Qusayr 'Amra: Residencia y banos Omeyad en el Desierto de Jordania.* Madrid: Ministerio de Asuntos Exteriores.

Bacharach, J.L.

1991 Administrative Complexes, Palaces, and Citadels: Changes in the Loci of Medieval Muslim Rule. In I. Bierman, *R. Ali Abou-El-Haj and Donald Preziosi* (eds.), *The Ottoman City and Its Parts: Urban Structure and Social Order*, 105–122. New Rochelle: Caratzas.

1996 Marwanid Umayyad Building Activities: Speculations on Patronage. *Muqarnas* 13: 27–44.

Arce, I.

in press The Umayyad Congregational Mosque and the Souq Square Complex at Amman Citadel. Architectural Features and Urban Significance. In I. Thuesen (ed.), *Proceedings of the Second International Congress on the Archaeology of the Ancient Near East, Copenhagen 2000.* Winona Lake: Eisenbrauns.

Bisheh, G.

1985 Qasr al-Hallabat: An Umayyad Desert Retreat or Farmland. In A. Hadidi (ed.), *Studies in the History and Archaeology of Jordan II*, 263–265. Amman: Department of Antiquities.

1989 Qasr Mshash and Qasr 'Ayn al-Sil: Two Umayyad Sites in Jordan. In M.A. Bakhit and R. Schick (eds.), *The Fourth International Conference on the History of Bilad al-Sham during the Umayyad Period* II, 81–103. Amman: University of Jordan.

1993 From Castellum to Palatium: Umayyad Mosaic Pavements from Qasr al-Hallabat in Jordan. *Muqarnas* 10: 49–56.

2000 Two Umayyad mosaic floors from Qastal, *Liber Annus* 50: 431–438.

Bujard, J. and M.-A. Haldimann

1997 Umm al-Walid et Khan az-Zabib, cinq qusur omeyyades et leurs mosquées revisités. *Annual of the Department of Antiquities of Jordan* 41: 351–374.

Cameron, A.

1993 *The Mediterranean World in Late Antiquity,* ad *395– 600.* London: Routledge.

Carlier, P. and F. Morin

1989 Qastal al-Balqa': An Umayyad Site in Jordan. In M.A. Bakhit and R. Schick (eds.), *The Fourth International Conference on the History of Bilad al-Sham during the Umayyad Period* II, 104–139. Amman: University of Jordan.

Cobb, P.M.

1997 White Banners: Contention in 'Abbasid Syria, 750–877. Unpublished PhD dissertation, The University of Chicago.

Conrad, L.I.

1981 The Qusur of Medieval Islam: Some Implications for the Social History of the Near East. *al-Abhath* 29: 7–23.

Curčić, S.

1993 Late-Antique Palaces: The Meaning of Urban Context. *Ars orientalis* 23: 67–90.

Donner, F. McG.

1981 *The Early Islamic Conquests.* Princeton: Princeton University Press.

Finkelstein, I.

1995 *Living on the Fringe: The Archaeology and History of the Negev, Sinai and Neighboring Regions in the Bronze and Iron Ages.* Sheffield: Sheffield Academic Press.

Foote, R.

1994 The 'Abbasids and their Residence in Humeima. *al-'Usur al-Wusta* 6(1): 1–3.

Fuller, M.J.

1987 Abila of the Decapolis: A Roman-Byzantine City in Transjordan. Unpublished PhD dissertation, Washington University, St. Louis.

Gawlikowski, M.

1986 A Residential Area by the South Decumanus. In F. Zayadine (ed.), *Jerash Archaeological Project 1981–1983* I, 107–136. Amman: Department of Antiquities.

Grabar, O.

1964 A Small Episode of Early 'Abbasid Times and Some Consequences. *Eretz-Israel* 7: 44–47 .

1987 The Date and Meaning of Mshatta. *Dumbarton Oaks Papers* 41: 243–247.

Hamilton, R.W.

1946 An Eighth century Water-Gauge at al Muwaqqar. *Quarterly of the Department of Antiquities of Palestine* 12: 70–72.

Harding, G.L.

1951 Excavations on the Citadel, Amman. *Annual of the Department of Antiquities of Jordan* 1: 7–16.

Helms, S.

1990 *Early Islamic Architecture of the Desert: A Bedouin Station in Eastern Jordan.* Edinburgh: Edinburgh University Press.

Humbert, J.-B.

1989 El-Fedein/Mafraq. In F. Villeneuve (ed.), *Contribution française à l'archéologie jordanienne 1989*, 124–131. Amman: Institut Français d'archéologie du Proche-Orient .

Imbert, F.

1995 Inscriptions et espaces d' écriture au Palais d'al-Kharrana en Jordanie.In K. 'Amr, F. Zayadine, and M. Zaghloul (eds.), *Studies in the History and Archaeology of Jordan V*, 403–416. Amman: Department of Antiquities.

Imbert, F. and S. Bacquey

1989 Sept graffiti arabes au palais de Musatta. *Annual of the Department of Antiquities of Jordan* 33: 259–267.

Kennedy, H.

1981 *The Early Abbasid Caliphate: A Political History*. London: Croom Helm.

1985 From Polis to Madina: Urban Change in Late Antique and Early Islamic Syria. *Past and Present* 106: 3–27.

1992 Nomads and Settled People in Bilad al-Sham in the Fourth/Ninth and Fifth/Tenth Centuries. In M.A. Bakhit and R. Schick (eds.), *Bilad al-Sham during the Abbasid Period*, 105–113. Amman: University of Jordan.

Knauf, E.A.

1984 Umm el-Jimal: An Arab Town in Late Antiquity. *Revue Biblique* 91: 578–586.

Kraeling, C.H. (ed.)

1938 *Gerasa, City of the Decapolis*. New Haven, CT: American Schools of Oriental Research.

LaBianca, Ø.S.

1990 *Sedentarization and Nomadization: Food System Cycles at Hesban and Vicinity in Transjordan*. Hesban I. Waltham, MA: Brandeis University.

Lenzen, C.J. and E.A. Knauf

1987 Beit Ras/Capitolias: A Preliminary Evaluation of the Archaeological and Textual Evidence. *Syria* 64: 21–46.

MacAdam, H.I.

1994 Settlements and Settlement Patterns in Northern and Central Transjordania, ca 550–ca 750. In G.R.D. King and A. Cameron (eds.), *The Byzantine and Early Islamic Near East II: Land Use and Settlement Patterns*, 49–94. Princeton: Darwin.

Melkawi, A., K. 'Amr and D. Whitcomb

1994 The Excavation of Two Seventh Century Pottery Kilns at Aqaba. *Annual of the Department of Antiquities of Jordan* 38: 447–468.

Naghaweh, A.

1982 An Umayyad Mosque at Jerash. *Annual of the Department of Antiquities of Jordan* 26: 20–22.

Najjar, M.

1989 Abbasid Pottery from el-Muwaqqar. *Annual of the Department of Antiquities of Jordan* 33: 305–322.

Nielsen, I. *et al.*

1993 *Gadara-Umm Qes*. III. *Die byzantinischen Thermen*. Wiesbaden: Otto Harrassowitz.

Northedge, A.

1989 The Umayyad Mosque of Amman. In M.A. Bakhit and R. Schick (eds.), *The Fourth International Conference on the History of Bilad al-Sham during the Umayyad Period* II, 140–163. Amman: University of Jordan.

1991 The Citadel of 'Amman in the Abbasid Period. In M.A. Bakhit and R. Schick (eds.), *The Fifth International Conference on the History of Bilad al-Sham during the Abbasid Period*, 179–194. Amman: University of Jordan.

1992 *Studies on Roman and Islamic Amman I: History, Site and Architecture*. Oxford: Oxford University Press.

Parapetti, R.

1993 Gerasa, Town Plan. *American Journal of Archaeology* 97: 500–501.

Parker, S.T.

1986 *Romans and Saracens: A History of the Arabian Frontier*. American Schools of Oriental Research Dissertation Series 6. Winona Lake, IN: Eisenbrauns.

Russell, K.W.

1985 The Earthquake Chronology of Palestine and Northwest Arabia from the 2nd through the mid-8th Century ad *Bulletin of the American Schools of Oriental Research* 260: 37–59.

Sauer, J.A.

1973 *Heshbon Pottery, 1971*. Berrien Springs, MI: Andrews University.

Schaefer, J. and R.K. Falkner

1986 An Umayyad Potters' Complex in the North Theater, Jerash. In F. Zayadine (ed.), *Jerash Archaeological Project 1981–1983* I, 411–459. Amman: Department of Antiquities.

Schick, R.

1995 *The Christian Communities of Palestine from Byzantine to Islamic Rule: A Historical and Archaeological Story*. Princeton: Darwin.

Shahid, I.

1986 The Jund System in Bilad al-Sham: Its Origin. In M.A. Bakhit and M. Asfour (eds.), *Proceedings of the Symposium on Bilad al-Sham during the Byzantine Period* II, 45–52. Amman: University of Jordan.

Smith, R.H.

1973 *Pella of the Decapolis*.I. *The 1967 Season of the College of Wooster Expedition to Pella*. Wooster, OH: The College of Wooster.

Smith, R.H. and L.P. Day

1989 *Pella of the Decapolis*. II. *Final Report on the College of Wooster Excavations in Area IX, the Civic Complex, 1979–1985*. Wooster, OH: The College of Wooster.

Urice, S.

1987 *Qasr Kharana in the Transjordan*. Durham, NC: American Schools of Oriental Research.

Walmsley, A.G.

1987 The Administrative Structure and Urban Geography of the Jund of Filastin and the Jund of al-Urdunn: The

Cities and Districts of Palestine and East Jordan during the Early Islamic, 'Abbasid and Early Fatimid Periods. Unpublished PhD dissertation, University of Sydney.

1991 Architecture and Artifacts from 'Abbasid Fihl: Implications for the Cultural History of Jordan. In M.A. al-Bakhit and R. Schick (eds.), *The Fifth International Conference on the History of Bilad al-Sham during the Abbasid Period*, 135–159. Amman: University of Jordan.

1992 The Social and Economic Regime at Fihl (Pella) between the 7th and 9th Centuries. In P. Canivet and J.-P. Rey-Coquais (eds.), *La Syrie de Byzance à l'Islam VIIe–VIIIe siècles*, 249–261. Damascus: Institut Français de Damas.

1995 Tradition, Innovation, and Imitation in the Material Culture of Islamic Jordan: The First Four Centuries. In K. 'Amr, F. Zayadine, and M. Zaghloul (eds.), *Studies in the History and Archaeology of Jordan V*, 657–668. Amman: Department of Antiquities.

2003 The newly-discovered congregational mosque of Jarash in Jordan. *Al-'Usural Wusta: The Bulletin of Middle East Medievalists* 15(2): 17–24.

Watson, P.M.

1992 Change in Foreign and Regional Economic Links with Pella in the Seventh Century ad: The Ceramic Evidence. In P. Canivet and J.-P. Rey-Coquais (eds.), *La Syrie de Byzance à l'Islam VIIe–VIIIe siècles,* 23–34. Damascus: Institut Français de Damas.

Whitcomb, D.

1988a A Fatimid Residence in Aqaba, Jordan. *Annual of the Department of Antiquities of Jordan* 32: 207–224.

1988b Khirbet al-Mafjar Reconsidered: The Ceramic Evidence. *Bulletin of the American Schools of Oriental Research* 271: 51–67.

1989a Evidence of the Umayyad Period from the Aqaba Excavations. In M.A. Bakhit and R. Schick (eds.), *The Fourth International Conference on the History of Bilad al-Sham during the Umayyad Period* II, 164–184. Amman: University of Jordan.

1989b Coptic Glazed Ceramics from the Excavations at Aqaba, Jordan. *Journal of the American Research Center in Egypt* 26: 167–182.

1989c Mahesh Ware: Evidence of Early Abbasid Occupation from Southern Jordan. *Annual of the Department of Antiquities of Jordan* 33: 269–285.

1990–1 Glazed Ceramics of the Abbasid Period from the Aqaba Excavations. *Transactions of the Oriental Ceramic Society* 55: 43–65.

1992 Reassessing the Archaeology of Jordan of the Abbasid Period. In S. Tell, G. Bisheh, F. Zayadine, K. 'Amr, and M. Zaghloul (eds.), *Studies in the History and Archaeology of Jordan* IV, 385–390. Amman: Department of Antiquities.

1994a Amsar in Syria? Syrian Cities after the Conquest. *ARAM* 6: 13–33.

1994b *Ayla: Art and Industry in the Islamic Port of Aqaba.* Chicago: The Oriental Institute.

1994c The Ayla mosque: Early Islamic remains in Aqaba, Jordan. *Fondation Max van Berchem Bulletin* 8: 3–6.

1995 Islam and the Socio-Cultural Transition of Palestine, Early Islamic Period (638–1099 C.E.). In T. Levy (ed.), *The Archaeology of Society in the Holy Land*, 488–501. London: Leicester University.

2000 Hesban, Amman, and Abbasid Archaeology in Jordan. In L.E. Stager, J.A. Greene, and M.D. Coogan (eds.), *The Archaeology of Jordan and Beyond: Essays in Honor of James A. Sauer*, 505–515. Winona Lake, IN: Eisenbrauns.

2001 Archaeological evidence of the early mosque in Arabia. In J. Neusner and J.F. Strange (eds.), *Religious texts and material contexts*, 185–197. Lanham: University Press of America.

2006 Archaeological Evidence of sedentarization: Bilad al-Sham in the Early Islamic Period. In S.R. Hauser (ed.), *Die Sichtbarkeit on Nomaden on saisonaler Besiedlung in der Archäologie*, 27–45. Halle, Orientwissenschaftlicher hefte 21.

Zayadine, F. (ed.)

1986 *Jerash Archaeological Project 1981–1983*, I. Amman: Department of Antiquities.

1989 *Jerash Archaeological Project 1984–1988*, II. Amman: Department of Antiquities (= *Syria* 66: 1-260).

16. The Middle Islamic and Crusader Periods

Alan Walmsley

No Longer Hidden: A New Archaeological View of Middle Islamic Jordan

During much of the twentieth century, archaeologists commonly assumed that Jordan played only a marginal role in the history of the Levant in the middle Islamic period (roughly mid-ninth to fifteenth centuries CE). To one of Jordan's pioneer archaeologists, G.L. Harding, these were inconsequential centuries characterised by economic gloom and social decline.

> In the ninth century AD the conquering Abbasides transferred the capital to Baghdad, and Jordan began to be forgotten; not being on any trade route, or producing any natural wealth, the country was left to fall into decay. But it was still of sufficient importance for the Crusaders in the twelfth (sic) century to occupy part of it and build castles there, the chief of which were Shobak and Karak. After that its prosperity declined still further, and it was a country of small, poor villages, scraping a bare existence among the ruins of past splendour (Harding 1967: 52).

The archaeological view of Harding, as with other archaeologists at that time, was based upon an understanding—or rather misunderstanding—of the available material evidence, especially architecture. Apart from a few castles, which were generally perceived as Crusader inspired, there were few monuments to be observed and no major settlements that could compete visually with those from earlier periods or were of the same intellectual interest, for instance Biblical Dhiban, Nabataean Petra, Roman Jarash, or the Umayyad "Desert Castles."

Based more on unsubstantiated Eurocentric perceptions than any concrete evidence, this interpretation of the past grew out of biased and unchallenged nineteenth century attitudes: a belief in the true magnificence of Roman and early Christian civilisation and the "desolation of Islam." Writing of the Hauran, the American explorer Selah Merrill lamented the decimation of an early Christian society in a historical reconstruction sounding more like an imaginative Hollywood script than impartial scholarship.

> The crosses and other Christian symbols which exist on the buildings here indicate that the houses remain as they were left in the early centuries, when the Moslems swept away the inhabitants of this region, leaving the cities and the land in desolation (Merrill 1881 [1986]: 22).

The theme of social and urban devastation in the wake of an Arab/Muslim/Bedouin invasion, embraced with enthusiasm by Merrill apparently after reading De Vogüé (Merrill 1881 [1986]: 60–70), dominates much nineteenth century writing (Johns 1994: 1). Few explorers, it seems, could resist its attention-grabbing appeal; and likewise neither could many archaeologists of the early twentieth century. The publication of the Yale Joint Mission to Jarash, edited by C. Kraeling (1938), only in passing mentions an Islamic presence at the site, even though there was overwhelming archaeological evidence—architectural, numismatic and ceramic—to the contrary. With dissenting voices subdued, a belief in the collapse of civilization with the "Arab conquest" effortlessly entered Western popular literature, for instance the frequently reprinted *Pleasure of Ruins* by Rose Macaulay. In a chapter headed "The Ruinous Paradise," she writes:

> Entering some Arab village of squalid hovels, we are in a Roman colony, among temple columns, triumphal arches, traces of theatres and baths which no one has had the intellect or the cleanliness to use since the Arabs expelled the civilized Graeco-Roman-Syrian inhabitants and squatted among their broken monuments, stabling their horse in the nave of a Christian basilica, their camels in a richly carved pagan temple, their families in mud huts clustering about the proscenium of a theatre: the broken heirlooms of the race that ruled stand like desolate ghosts among the squalor. (Macaulay and Beny 1977: 44).

Publications like that of Macaulay and Beny, with their smoothly seductive words and evocative images, were—and still are—substantial obstacles to refuting a biased, and indeed bigoted, point of view. Only with the discrediting of such value-laden judgements will it be possible to initiate a fresh re-evaluation of social and economic life in middle Islamic Jordan.

The concept of Muslim "thundering hoards" (see Silberman 2001) was gradually superseded in the academic world (but still not in popular belief, unfortunately) in the third quarter of the twentieth century by a new and more reasoned theory on socio-urban decline in late antique and early Islamic Jordan. That thesis argued for the continuation of urban communities (mostly Christian) after the Islamic expansion, but their dispersion in the mid to late eighth century due to a combination of natural factors (notably earthquakes) and human events, especially growing social pressure on Christianity and the relocation of the capital of the Islamic empire from Damascus to Iraq. This was the chronology for the devolution of urban society in Jordan presented in brief by Harding in his seminal *Antiquities of Jordan*. Rather than the arrival of Islam, the political and cultural marginalization of Jordan was attributed to the fall of the Umayyad dynasty and

the subsequent anti-Umayyad policies of the Iraqi-based Abbasids.

At about the same time, there was a growing recognition of extensive rural developments under the Egyptian-based Mamluk sultanate (mid-thirteenth to early sixteenth centuries CE) resulting from the active market economy of Egypt, land tenure systems and the sugar industry. This

Figure 16.1 Sites mentioned in the text.

view, however, postulated a mid-to-late fourteenth century collapse resulting in widespread abandonment of the land, and did not explain the complexity of settlement profiles in Mamluk Jordan, especially the dynamics of socio-economic interaction between the countryside and major settlement points such as Karak or Salt.

Given the orthodoxy attained by the devolutionary post-conquest theory formulized by Harding, it is not surprising that archaeological research in the 1960s and 1970s largely bypassed the middle Islamic periods, with only a few notable exceptions. As a result there was a scarcity of information and little motive to question prevailing ideas, and this explanation for the supposed social and urban disintegration of early Islamic Jordan developed, by default, into a three-stage model. It presented a most gloomy scenario.

1) Urban collapse and rural depopulation
   It was widely accepted that by the Fatimid period the absence of strong central government after the fall of the Umayyads had brought about growing political chaos and precipitated the rapid collapse of urban infrastructure. Without organized resistance, the region lay open to predatory Bedouin incursions, resulting in rural depopulation and economic recession, especially in the south. The "desert" had won at the expense of the "sown."

2) Crusader reassertion
   Then in the twelfth century, it was asserted, the Crusaders re-imposed centralized authority over south Jordan, constructing imposing castles at Shawbak, Wadi Musa and, later, Karak in particular. The resultant stability led to an improvement in levels of rural settlement. The north, however, as a zone of conflict was sparsely populated except for military outposts of both sides, notably the castles at Ajlun and Salt.

3) Mamluk revival
   It was further argued that the expulsion of the Crusaders after the Battle of Hattin (1187 CE) and the eventual reunification of the Levant with Egypt under the Mamluks in the late thirteenth century heralded a new era of moderate prosperity based on a rejuvenated rural economy, especially a flourishing sugar industry in the tropical climate of the Jordan Valley. The widespread occurrence of brightly coloured glazed pottery on the surface of many sites in Jordan indicated a growing population until the destructive invasions of Timur-Leng, political disintegration and economic impoverishment at the onset of the fifteenth century.

The apparent authenticity and intellectual convenience of this three-stage model ensured its rapid acceptance, especially as it explained away a bothersome period of little concern to many archaeologists whose primary interest, and that of their funding bodies, was Biblical, Roman

and early Christian Jordan. The repetition of an urban devolutionary model was to emerge repeatedly, unwittingly or otherwise, in overviews of the settlement history of many sites, such as for Pella (Smith 1973: 164–166; Smith and Day 1989: 8–9, 92–94) and Hisban (LaBianca 1990; critically reviewed by McQuitty 1993), and surfaced in more general accounts of Islamic history as well.

Few contemporary archaeologists would be comfortable with such a simplistic scenario for explaining change in middle Islamic Jordan, especially as single-cause explanations for social transformations have been effectively discarded in archaeology during the last few years. A major concern of this work is to evaluate and challenge the three-stage devolutionary model outlined above by a comparative analysis of the available textual and archaeological data. In the last two decades, new archaeological work has reassessed the character and extent of settlement in Fatimid, Saljuq, Crusader, Ayyubid and Mamluk Jordan, and sought new understandings of cultural, political and economic change in the period. While these periods remain grossly underrepresented in current research, significant contributions have been made by a number of individuals including R.M. Brown (Brown 1992; 2000), J. Johns (Johns 1994), J. Kareem (Kareem 2000), C.L. Lenzen (Lenzen 1995a; 2000; Lenzen and Knauf 1987), R. Schick (Schick 1995; 1998), B. Walker (Walker 1999; 2003c) and D. Whitcomb (Whitcomb 1994; 1997; 2000), with work on Fatimid to Mamluk Jordan by this writer (Walmsley 1992b; 1998; Walmsley and Grey 2001; Walmsley, Karsgaard, *et al.* 1999).

The objective of this current study is present in outline the main cultural and economic transformations that affected the region of modern Jordan, events which brought its people and their society into growing contact with the vicissitudes faced by the wider Arab-Muslim world and resulted in a society that it was almost imperceptible to archaeological practice until recent times. Yet as the last two decades have shown, it is now possible to identify the major centres and rural populations—agricultural and pastoral—through a growing body of source material resulting from textual and archaeological research. The assumed hiatus in the settlement history of middle Islamic Jordan can now be sufficiently filled so as to seriously question any period of abandonment, and to reject permanently the eighteenth and nineteenth century European romantic tragedy of a Muslim/Bedouin influx at the expense of urban and settled life.

Between History and Archaeology: The Contribution of Written Sources

The Failure of Past Scholarship

Past scholarship has, with only rare exceptions, shown scant interest in promoting the archaeological study of the post-antique world in the east Mediterranean (Northedge 1999; Walker 2003c; Walmsley 2004). Archaeology had nothing useful to contribute after the Islamic expansion, or even earlier with the foundation of Constantine's empire; the study of the Middle Ages belonged to historical studies and art history. One major reason for the poor showing of Islamic archaeology in Jordan was the obvious discrepancy between the few archaeological reports available and written sources—historical, biographical and geographical. While the sources mentioned central places and an active rural sector, archaeologists reported urban abandonment and a depopulated countryside. Not surprisingly, historians of Islam have been frustrated by and tended to ignore the obviously flawed archaeological results, thereby creating an almost impermeable barrier to comparative historical-archaeological studies until recent

Figure 16.2 The geopolitical features of tenth century Jordan, based on the account of the Arab geographer al-Maqdisi

times. In the last couple of decades, the emergence of an archaeology dedicated to an understanding of the Islamic world through the implementation of new approaches and attitudes has encouraged a collaborative approach to archaeological and historical sources. It would now be simply inconceivable to undertake archaeological research into Fatimid, Saljuq, Crusader, Ayyubid and Mamluk Jordan without reference to written material, such as the detailed works of geographers and travellers or, as Walker has recently demonstrated, *waqf* (endowment) manuscripts for later periods (Walker 2004). The information preserved in these sources will serve as a starting point, and offers an informative parallel to the available archaeological studies.

The Historical View

Since the time of Ahmad Ibn Tulun (d. 884 CE), if not long before, much of the southern Levant rested within the political and cultural orbit of Egypt, and the extension of Fatimid control over the area in 970 represented a straightforward historical continuation of that arrangement. Control extended to the region east of the Jordan Rift Valley through garrisons and tribal alliances, and it seems as though the region played a continuous role in the social and economic life of Fatimid Palestine-Jordan. This is particularly apparent from the detailed account of the geographer al-Maqdisi (al-Muqaddasi, d. 1000 CE), a native of Jerusalem (Bayt al-Maqdis) who wrote in about 985 (for a translation see: Muqaddasi (al-Maqdisi) 1994). According to al-Maqdisi, the area of Jordan north of the Wadi Zarqa, then known as Jabal Jarash, was included in the district of al-Urdunn and had Adhriat (Deraa) as its chief town (Figure 16.2). The area was populated with many villages and produced olives, various fruits including grapes, and honey. This agricultural productivity was such, noted al-Maqdisi, that it contributed to the wealth of Tabariyah (Tiberias), al-Urdunn's capital. Between the Wadi Zarqa and Wadi Mujib was the Balqa area, which belonged to the district of Filastin (Palestine). Around its principal town of Amman were villages, farms, grainfields, mills and flocks, and nearby was Kahf al-Raqim where pilgrims could visit the Cave of the Sleepers. Perhaps the most interesting aspect of al-Maqdisi's account is his identification of a separate district south of the Wadi Mujib called Sharah. The leading centre was located at Sughar (Zughar, Zoara) in the Southern Ghor, south of the Dead Sea, and had six other townships including Maab (Rabbah, Areopolis), Muan (Maan), Udhruh and Waylah (Aylah, Aela). Maab, the principal town in the mountains, had many productive villages and the holy site of Mutah with the tombs of the Prophet's companions. Aylah and Zughar, strategically located at either end of the Wadi Arabah, were thriving commercial centres. The well-populated Red Sea port of Aylah served Filastin and the Hijaz, with roads heading northwards to Ramlah (six marches) and Zughar (four marches). From Zughar roads continued onto Jerusalem, Nablus, and Amman. Another important road described by al-Maqdisi was the Hajj or pilgrimage route from Damascus. This passed through Adhriat and Zarqa to Amman, which was a major assembly place for pilgrims from Palestine, and continued south by way of two watering stops to Muan then Tabuk, three stops later.

From al-Maqdisi's description it is difficult to avoid the conclusion that Fatimid Jordan supported a minimum of eight major population centres (and probably more; Maqdisi's account appears incomplete, especially for north Jordan) through an active rural economy and considerable inter- and intra-regional trade. In particular, south Jordan came to benefit from the revival of the Red Sea trade routes under the Fatimid caliphs of Egypt, which found expression in the political events of the later tenth and early eleventh centuries. In this period, the tribal shaykhs of south Palestine and Jordan played an active, and sometimes counter-productive, role in the affairs of Filastin, either as allies of or rivals to Fatimid domination (Kennedy 1986: 307, 320–329, 335–340). Facing often formidable opposition, the Jarrahid's strength lay in a stable and prosperous base in Sharah and the northern Hijaz, held through a number of strongholds including Karak (Schick 1997).

Following the imposition of Saljuq control over the Levant (1071–1079 CE), the Arabic sources continued to refer to the old districts of Balqa, Maab, Jibal and Sharah, but within these districts political power had already shifted to other population centres particularly Wadi Musa (for Sharah) and Karak (for Maab). Accordingly, Crusader sources identify Wadi Musa, ancient Petra (McKenzie 1991), as the principal object of military activity south of the Dead Sea during the first quarter of the twelfth century (Schick 1997). The first expedition took place in 1100 CE when Baldwin I (r. 1100–1118 CE) lead a campaign across the Jordan, reaching Wadi Musa by way of Zughar south of the Dead Sea, causing the (Muslim) inhabitants of both localities to flee. After staying three days and visiting the monastery of St. Aaron on Jabal Harun, Baldwin returned to Jerusalem by the same route (Fulcher of Chartres 1969: 145–147; William of Tyre 1941a [1976]: 427). In 1105 CE, Baldwin campaigned in the Sawad (Crusader Terre de Suete, essentially the fertile plains and valleys of north-west Jordan), but failed to secure control. Wadi Musa was the object of another campaign in 1106–1107 CE, successfully evicting a Saljuq force sent from Damascus under the leadership of al-Ispahbad and regaining Crusader control over Sharah, Jibal, Maab and Balqa. Following his success, Baldwin returned to Jerusalem by a route north of the Dead Sea. Together al-Ispahbad's mission, Baldwin's response and his return route indicate the considerable spread of Crusader control as far north as Balqa. Also in

the same year the Crusaders campaigned in the Sawad and Jabal Awf (the Ajlun district), resulting in a greater measure of control over north Jordan. This de facto situation was soon formalized by the signing of share agreements with Tughtigin, Atabeg of Damascus, in 1109 and 1111 CE. The agreements covered nearly all Jordan, from the Sawad to Sharah in the south, although the status of Amman and Balqa in the centre is unclear (Ibn al-Qalanisi 1932 [1967]: 74–75, 81–82, 92, 113; William of Tyre 1941a [1976]: 429–430; William of Tyre 1941b [1976]: 470). These agreements show that with the arrival of the Crusaders (and presumably before) Jordan was under the jurisdiction of the Atabeg of Damascus, but that by 1111 CE the Crusaders under Baldwin had deeply penetrated this territory and established a permanent presence, although the extent to which these moves were supported by the local Christian population is unclear.

The Latin kings of Jerusalem now set about consolidating their control over the Jordan River, and were particularly successful in the south away from Damascus close to the lucrative resources of the Dead and Red seas. In 1115 CE, Baldwin initiated the construction of a large castle at Shawbak, which he named Krak de Montréal (Fulcher of Chartres 1969: 215; William of Tyre 1941a [1976]: 506–507; for this castle see: Kennedy 1994: 23–25). By this action, Crusader domination over Sharah (the *Syria Sobal* and *Arabia Tertia* of the Crusader sources) was ensured. In the following year Baldwin extended control as far as Aylah (Aqabah) on the Red Sea (Fulcher of Chartres 1969: 215–216; William of Tyre 1941a [1976]: 513), possibly building a fortress there. At about this time Christians from other, presumably less controlled regions (perhaps Balqa and the Jarash areas) were encouraged to migrate and settle in Jerusalem (William of Tyre 1941a [1976]: 507–508). Shortly after, in 1120 CE, Tughtigin built a castle at Jarash to enforce his interests in Jabal Awf, but this was destroyed in the following year by a Crusader raid under Baldwin II (r. 1118–1131 CE). Fulcher (d. 1127 CE) is the principal source on the castle.

> The inhabitants of the area called this fortress Jarash. It was inside a city wondrously and gloriously built in ancient times on a strong site. The castle was built of large squared stones. But when the king considered that he had taken the place with difficulty and that it would be hard to provide it with the necessary men and provisions, he ordered the castle destroyed and all his men to return home. (Fulcher of Chartres 1969: 235; see also William of Tyre 1941a [1976]: 538–539).

In the south, control of the strategically located settlement of Wadi Musa was not without its problems for the Latin kings. Baldwin II suppressed a revolt there in 1127 CE (Ibn al-Qalanisi 1932 [1967]: 182), and although fortified and garrisoned with a formidable castle (Li Vaux Moise, Wuayrah, built by 1115–1116 CE) the town again rebelled against Crusader domination in 1144 CE. The townsfolk managed to capture the castle with the help of a small Saljuq force (William of Tyre 1941b [1976]: 144–145), but the youthful Baldwin III (r. 1143–1162 CE) besieged and eventually captured the fortress through brutal economic warfare. Perhaps at this time the Crusader outpost at Habis in the heart of ancient Petra was erected to monitor the activities of the cave-dwellers and the Wadi Arabah routes. To boost Crusader domination over south Jordan another castle, this time on a massive scale, was constructed in 1142 CE in Maab at Karak, Crusader Arabia Secunda (William of Tyre 1941b [1976]: 127). This site, the former Jarrahid stronghold, was endowed with formidable natural defences and controlled the profitable Dead Sea routes. The move completed Crusader domination over the fertile wheat-growing and pastoral lands south of the strategic Wadi Mujib and heralded the establishment of the great Lordship of Oultrejourdain based at Karak.

While providing a clear outline of Crusader activity in Jordan, the Latin sources also preserve a valuable glimpse of socio-economic conditions in the early twelfth century. Dates grew at Zughar, villages lined the route to Wadi Musa, itself a valley "very rich in the fruits of the earth" with "luxuriant olive groves which shaded the surface of the land like a dense forest" and mills on its streams, while around Shawbak was "fertile soil, which produces abundant supplies of grain, wine, and oil." In other areas were "many Christians living in villages' who left for Jerusalem with their 'flocks and herds," while camels and asses were common booty from raids (Fulcher of Chartres 1969: 146–147; William of Tyre 1941a [1976]: 506–508; William of Tyre 1941b [1976]: 145). Although only incidental references, nevertheless Fulcher and William depict Jordan as having a mixed settled and nomadic population actively engaged in agricultural and pastoral pursuits.

The Crusader presence east of the Jordan was short-lived, for Oultrejourdain including the still disputed lands in the north were all lost in second half of the twelfth century through the actions of Nur al-Din (d. 1174 CE) and the famous Salah al-Din b. Ayyub, known in the West as Saladin (d. 1193 CE). Unlike the fortified south, Crusader claims over north Jordan were always weak, consisting of an agreement to share the crops (wine, grain, olives) and revenues with the rulers of Damascus. This could only last as long as the Damascus atabegs agreed, and Nur al-Din—who gained control of Damascus in 1154 CE—clearly did not. Continuing the *jihad* against the Franks begun by his father Zangi, Atabeg of Aleppo and Mosul (d. 1146 CE), Nur al-Din besieged the Crusader outpost of Habis Jaldak on the south bank of the Wadi Yarmuk, but after battle with Baldwin III retreated to Damascus (1158 CE). Towards the end of his rule Nur al-Din, with the ambiguous support of Salah al-Din (at

this point governor of Egypt), penetrated Oultrejourdain with the intention to take Karak and Shawbak, but without success (on these events and those of the following Ayyubid period, see recently Milwright 2006: 3–9). Salah al-Din returned in 1173 CE, causing "everything found outside the fortresses to be burned, bushes and vines to be cut down, and villages to be destroyed" (William of Tyre 1941b [1976]: 272–273, 387–390, 470).

The real losses, however, came with the rise of Salah al-Din, culminating in the decisive Muslim victory at Hattin immediately west of Tabariyah (Tiberias) in northern Palestine (1187). Although it took Salah al-Din twelve years after the death of Nur al-Din to effect the political unification of Syria and Egypt, he was most active in this period. In 1182 CE he encamped at Jarba and conducted raids around Shawbak before continuing to Damascus, while other Muslim forces took Habis Jaldak, only to lose it a few months later. In 1183 and 1184 CE, Karak was besieged for months on end, and although the castle withstood Salah al-Din's armies the lower town was looted with great loss of property: "all their household possessions, all their furniture and utensils of every description, were seized by the enemy" (Ibn Jubayr 1952: 301, 311, 313–314; William of Tyre 1941b [1976]: 301, 311, 313–314). The brutish and rash Lord of Oultrejourdain, Reynald de Châtillon (r. 1177–1187 CE), attracted Salah al-Din's unrelenting rage by raiding the pilgrimage routes from Damascus and Cairo, his threatening behaviour towards the Holy Cities of Makkah and Madinah, and his barbarous treatment of prisoners (Maalouf 1984: 186-88). Once Salah al-Din had brought Syria and Egypt under his control (1183 CE), he was able to draw on vast resources to oppose the Latin Kingdom. In the following year he entered Crusader territory north of Tabariyah (Tiberias) and took the town. The Crusaders responded and, as was their practice, brought together all available manpower to repel the Muslim force. In the resulting battle (July 1187 CE) the Crusader force was totally defeated with great loss of life. Of the captured leaders, Salah al-Din's greatest wrath was reserved for "the most malicious, evil and treacherous" Reynald, who was promptly executed (al-Safadi in Holt 1986; Maalouf 1984: 190–194). The Crusader disaster at Hattin left Oultrejourdain, as with the whole Latin Kingdom, largely undefended, so in 1188 CE Karak and Shawbak capitulated with little resistance to al-Adil (d. 1218 CE), Salah al-Din's brother and his vicegerent in Egypt. By 1193 CE, the year of Salah al-Din's death, the Arabic sources reveal that Jordan was divided between two administrations. The area south of the Wadi Zarqa, including Salt and Balqa, was governed from Egypt by al-'Aziz Uthman, one of Salah al-Din's sons, while Jabal Awf (Ajlun district) and the Sawad in north Jordan belonged to al-Afdal Ali, Salah al-Din's eldest son based in Damascus (Humphreys 1977: 63–64, 75–77, 83).

For the remainder of the Ayyubid period (to 1263 CE in Jordan) and in the subsequent Mamluk period (1263–1517 CE), the Jordan region and its castles of both Crusader and Muslim origin continued to play a leading role in the political and social history of Egypt and the Levant. In addition to the existing Crusader constructs in south Jordan, Muslim castles were built at Ajlun (between 1188 and 1192 CE), Azraq (1236–1237 CE) and Salt (1220 CE), which had become the chief town of Balqa in place of Amman. These were intended to oversee communication routes and monitor the local population, being built after the Crusader threat to Jordan had been largely neutralized. Most frequently mentioned in the Ayyubid-Mamluk historical sources was the immensely strong and strategically located castle of Karak (Humphreys 1977; Irwin 1986; Thorau 1987 [1992]: 134–141). As in earlier times, the castle at Karak controlled the Red Sea and Wadi Arabah trade routes to the west and the Hajj (pilgrimage) road from Damascus located to the east, but most significantly it oversaw movement between Cairo and Damascus while the Crusaders continued to hold sections of coastal Palestine. For a while in the mid-thirteenth century, Karak remained independent of Damascus and Cairo, becoming particularly active in political affairs under the Ayyubid prince al-Mughith 'Umar (d. c. 1264 CE), the great grandson of al-'Adil. Although al-Mughith backed Baybars during the turbulent first decade of the Mamluk sultanate (1250–1260 CE), soon the essentially centralized nature of the Syro-Egyptian Mamluk administration as constituted by Baybars (r. 1260–1277 CE) could not allow an independent-acting Karak and al-Mughith was treacherously deposed by his former confederate in 1263 CE. Karak, with Shawbak, now became one of six Syrian provinces, but it often served as a distant outpost of Egypt, a place of refuge, exile and sometimes rebellion. The castle's most celebrated residents, willing or not, were:

- *al-Sa'id Muhammad Baraka Khan* (d. 1280 CE), the deposed son of Baybars, his brothers and the queen-mother (in Karak 1279–1296 CE);
- *al-Nasir Muhammad* (d. 1341 CE) on two occasions, firstly as a child (1297–1299 CE) then in 1309–1310 CE in a successful ploy to regain the sultanate;
- *al-Nasir Ahmad* (d. 1344 CE), son of al-Nasir Muhammad who grew up in Karak and, after becoming sultan, removed himself and much of the treasury back there before being deposed (1342 CE); seven campaigns were required before Karak was taken and al-Nasir Ahmad captured;
- *Barkuk* (d. 1399 CE), the first of the Circassian Mamluk sultans, who gained support while exiled in Karak during 1389–1390 CE to reclaim the sultanate.

Geographical works and the journals of travellers offer a particularly valuable source of information on socio-economic conditions in Ayyubid and Mamluk Jordan. There is much material from the thirteenth to fifteenth centuries: the encyclopaedic work of Yaqut (d. 1229 CE) with numerous and often extensive entries on places and regions arranged alphabetically, the geography of Dimashqi (d. c. 1327 CE) a sometimes confusing mixture of brief first hand and copied accounts, also that of Abu'l-Fida (d. 1331 CE) extensively drawn from personal observations, the travelogue of Ibn Battuta (d. 1377 CE) and al-Qalqashandi's authoritative encyclopaedic work (d. 1418 CE), although incorporating earlier material. In these works are described the administrative divisions, places and localities in Jordan, although the quality and detail of the accounts vary considerably. The mostly original fourteenth and fifteenth century works emphasize the castle towns (especially Karak, Shawbak and Ajlun), holy sites (Mutah/Mazar, Amata, and Kahf al-Raqim) and the stopping points along the pilgrimage route between Damascus and the Hijaz. The evidence from the written sources suggests that these three settlement types dominated Mamluk Jordan. The sources also pay attention to the vibrant rural economy in which pastoral industries and agriculture, both subsistence and cash crops, played an equally important role.

In general terms, Jordan in the Mamluk period was divided between two broad administrative divisions called *mamlakah* (self-controlling provinces headed by an *amir*). The south was included in the province of Karak while the north fell within Damascus, although the structure was quite fluid over time (referenced summary in Walker 2003b). The Mamlakat al-Karak included the major castle-towns of Karak and Shawbak, and extended northwards to the strategic settlement at Ziza (Jiza, south of Amman), westwards to include Zughar, the Wadi Arabah and the Sinai Peninsula, and into the northern Hijaz (Figure 16.3). Other places mentioned in the province include Maan, Mutah, Lajjun, Hisa and Wadi Musa, plus the districts of Jibal and Sharah. Dimashqi also placed Amman, Salt, Zarqa, Azraq and the Balqa in the Mamlakat al-Karak, and on occasions these districts may have been transferred to the control of Karak, perhaps to provide provisions for troops. He lists, for a second time, the Balqa and the towns of Salt, Amman and Zarqa as part of the Mamlakat Dimashq to which he adds Hisban, for a time the capital of the Balqa according to Abu'l-Fida. Undoubtedly included in Mamlakah Dimashq were Jabal Awf, the district of Jarash with its castle-town of Ajlun, the Sawad, the town-districts of Bayt Ras and Fihl, and the upper and middle Jordan Valley and their respective towns of Qusayr (North Shunah) and Amata (Abu Ubaydah). The fourteenth and fifteenth century sources show that the east-west boundary between Mamluk Karak and Dimashq was located somewhat north of the Wadi Mujib/Wadi Wala, continuing southwards on the west

Figure 16.3 Major centres, provincial divisions and the pilgrimage route in Mamluk Jordan.

along the Dead Sea and the Wadi Arabah. This division continued a long established politico-cultural boundary seen in ancient and Roman times that reappeared during the Fatimid period (compare Figures 16.2 and 16.3).

Also given major treatment in the thirteenth to fifteenth century works were a number of holy sites. Leading these were: Mutah/Mazar with the tombs of three Companions of the Prophet including Ja'afar b. Abi Talib, the brother of Ali, slain by a Byzantine force in 629 at the Battle of Mutah; Amata, burial place of Abu Ubaydah (d. 639 CE), conqueror and first governor of Bilad al-Sham (Syria-Palestine); Kahf al-Raqim, the reputed site of the Cave of the Sleepers; Wadi Musa and its spring (Quran 2.60); Jabal Harun, burial place of the prophet Aaron, brother of Moses; and Irbid with the tombs of Moses' mother and four sons of Jacob (on these see further below). Even the major commercial centres of the

Southern Ghor, namely Qusayr Muin (South Shunah) and Zughar, were credited with religious traditions (Gibb 1958: 82–83; Le Strange 1890 [1965]: 73–74, 274–292, 393, 457–458, 548–549). A third important group of settlements was those positioned on the Darb al-Hajj, the pilgrimage route from Damascus to the Hijaz (Figure 16.3). After Busra, Ibn Battuta lists these as Ziza, Lajjun, Karak and Maan, the latter being "the last town in Syria" (Gibb 1958: 159–160). Amman was bypassed, for it was in a state of ruin (*dimnah*) according to Dimashqi. The pilgrimage route probably also passed through Zarqa and Hisa, both mentioned by Dimashqi in his description of the mamlakah.

The entries in Dimashqi, Abu'l-Fida, Ibn Battuta and al-Qalqashandi leave little doubt that living conditions in the towns and countryside had largely recovered from the military and political upheavals of the twelfth and thirteenth centuries, although the relative importance of individual sites had changed considerably. The north was dominated by Ajlun, with its strong castle and fruit-bearing lands being repeatedly mentioned in the sources (see in Le Strange 1890 [1965]: 388–389). Also important was populous Salt, then as now renowned for its pomegranates, and also Hisban with (as Abu'l-Fida relates) mills and fields lining the wadi to the Jordan Valley (Le Strange 1890 [1965]: 456, 529–30). In the south, the sources emphasize the castle-towns of Karak and Shawbak, both at the centre of a thriving arboricultural industry (apricots, pears, pomegranates) and largely populated with Christians (Ibn Battuta 1958; Le Strange 1890 [1965]: 479–480, 536).

More recently, the detailed reading of local Syrian-based thirteenth to fifteenth century geographical and administrative accounts has uncovered further detailed material on towns, villages and agricultural practices in Mamluk Jordan (see, in particular, Walker 2004). To these can now be added select *waqfiyat* (religious endowment documents) studied by Walker which contain astonishing details about investment, cropping and revenues from farms in Jordan, especially the north and central regions. One example concerns the village of Malka, near Umm Qays in north Jordan, which features in a *waqfiyah* of 1393 (796 H) granted by the Sultan Barquq to support his renowned *madrasah* built between 1384 and 1386 CE in central Islamic Cairo. This document reveals that the area was densely settled, producing olives and grapes and supporting presses to process the agricultural products for the market (Walker 2004: 130–131). As Walker notes, the significance of this and similar documents is the rebuttal they contain for a supposed widespread decline in the rural economy at the end of the fourteenth century. Rather, the sources, backed by new archaeological evidence (see below), argue for considerable continuity into Ottoman times, especially in the north of Jordan. While the agricultural regime clearly faced difficulties in the fifteenth century, the absence of complete socio-economic collapse is confirmed by the Ottoman *defters* (tax registers) of the sixteenth century, which document an active rural society of major villages and satellite settlements supported through subsistence agriculture and cash cropping.

Texts and documents provide a valuable source of information on socio-economic conditions in Jordan from the Fatimid to the Mamluk period, and offer a useful outline to which detailed archaeological work can bring fresh understanding and new perspectives. The written sources reveal a number of major developments, which together had a major impact on the social history of middle Islamic Jordan. In essence these were as follows.

1. The political and probably social distinctness of Jordan south of the Wadi Mujib, perhaps of long standing but first very apparent in the Fatimid period.
2. The dynamic economy of Fatimid-Saljuq Jordan, embracing agriculture and arboriculture, pastoral industries, and trade and commerce.
3. The geographical extent of Crusader control over much of Jordan, which was achieved by treaty (for the north) or direct rule (the lordship of Oultrejourdain) south of the Wadi Mujib/Wadi Wala catchment.
4. A permanent shift in settlement from sites along the badiyah fringe (e.g. Amman, Maab) to a line of defensive sites (e.g. Karak, Ajlun) on high points along the Jordan Valley scarp. This development first appeared in the Fatimid period but intensified in Crusader and Ayyubid times. A parallel development is the greater importance of Holy Places (e.g. Mutah, Kahf al-Raqim, Abu Ubaydah), again beginning in the Fatimid period but increasing in Ayyubid and Mamluk times.
5. The social and economic reconstruction of Jordan after the Crusader experience, concentrating on enhancing holy places with shrines and mosques, and investment in the rural sector especially arboriculture and commercial cropping such as sugar.

Site Settlement: An Archaeological Survey

The archaeology of tenth to sixteenth century Jordan is beset with difficulties, and even more so than is usual in archaeology, for the general paucity and poverty of research means that there is no established starting point and the quality of data is patchy. Few excavations have been undertaken with the specific purpose of investigating the nature and extent of site occupation, and there has been little attention to determining the range, characteristics and development of material culture in middle Islamic Jordan. Likewise, regional surveys have frequently cursorily, sometimes recklessly, treated the usually abundant architectural and ceramic evidence for the occupation of sites in the Islamic periods, and a disinterested attitude to the middle Islamic periods has introduced considerable distortion to settlement profiles as a result. Archaeologically, Fatimid and Saljuq Jordan are almost invisible, the twelfth century solely evidenced by Crusader and Muslim castles, while Ayyubid and Mamluk Jordan (the two periods, covering 250 years, are commonly but misleadingly clumped together) is typified by the many small village sites identified in regional surveys through their ceramic assemblages.

Due to this haphazard approach, it becomes exceedingly difficult to build up an archaeological profile that faithfully represents the full extent of social and economic life in the formative middle Islamic period. Inevitably, then, given the current state of research, this study ends up concentrating on the architectural features of surviving monuments—predominantly castles, mosques and shrines—and on the distribution of mostly poorly recorded village and hamlet sites located by regional surveys. Only a scattering of middle Islamic sites, large and small, has been competently excavated (and then usually unintentionally) and little research has been done on urban sites, many of which are overlain by the major towns of modern Jordan. The absence of reliable, well-contextualized and sufficiently extensive archaeological data imposes considerable limitations on its usefulness in accurately detailing the form and development of socio-economic structures and the emergence of modern Jordan out of the middle ages into a key player in the Middle East today.

Sites of the Fatimid and Saljuq Periods (Tenth and Eleventh Centuries)

Archaeological evidence for settlement during the tenth and eleventh centuries is particularly sparse, which is at variance with al-Maqdisi's positive account of urban and rural conditions in the late tenth century. Only a few sites—Amman and Aylah (Aqabah) are the important examples—have clearly identified Fatimid and Saljuq occupation levels, and then usually associated with structures of an earlier Islamic date. Other major sites with reported firmly-attested Fatimid occupation include: Pella, Tall Abu Qadan, Tall Nimrin and Khirbat Shaykh Isa in the Jordan Valley; and Tall Hisban, Dhiban, Bayt Ras, Khirbat Faris and Qam in the mountains.

At Amman, excavations between 1975 and 1979 by C. M. Bennett and A. Northedge for the Department of Antiquities produced clear evidence for settlement on the citadel in the Fatimid period (eleventh century). Occupation was identified within the former Umayyad Palace complex and in adjacent domestic structures (Northedge 1992: 159). Stratum III of the excavations, dated to the eleventh century, was the last major period of occupation on the Amman Citadel, and represented an unbroken continuation of the previous stratum (IVb, ninth–tenth century). In Area C, two parallel lines of squares sectioned the west slope to the Umayyad fortification wall, revealing two streets and four building complexes. Although probably constructed in the Abbasid period, these buildings were substantially modified in Fatimid times. Their sudden and simultaneous destruction was perhaps due to the earthquake of 1068. Dating is provided by two coins, a dinar of al-Hakim (407 H/1016–1017 CE) and a worn dirham of al-Zahir (411–427 H/1021–1036 CE), the latter found embedded in the terminal floor surface of Building 3. A similar sequence is found in Areas B and D, where Umayyad-period houses were continuously utilized and modified until the Stratum III destruction. In Area B five buildings and a street were excavated, although one unit (Building C) produced some evidence of Ayyubid-period reuse. The palace also continued to be occupied into Fatimid times, but was subdivided into smaller units; these were residential according to Northedge, indicating a reduced or non-official role for the palatial complex by the eleventh century. Most notably the reception hall was converted into a self-contained building, which required the insertion of a wooden roof over the open central court (Northedge 1992: 78, 81, 83–84, 88). The fortification wall surrounding the upper terrace of the citadel had fallen out of use long before the eleventh century, as it had been built over by Abbasid-Fatimid domestic structures in Areas C and D (Wood 1992: 124–125).

The archaeological evidence on the nature of Fatimid and Saljuq settlement at Amman is paralleled by the discoveries at Islamic Aylah, although the role of Aylah, which was primarily commercial, was quite different from the administrative and military functions served by Amman. At Aylah, the Fatimid and Saljuq periods coincide with the end of the early Islamic II and the first half of the middle Islamic I periods, as defined by Whitcomb. In this last phase of occupation, ending with the Crusader conquest of 1116 CE, the original Umayyad and Abbasid structures continued in use but with structural modifications, although construction standards were inferior. Whitcomb's excavations of the town gates and wall towers, the Central Pavilion building in the middle of the town, the Egyptian street (one of four axial roadways that led from the gates to the Central Pavilion), the beach-side suq along the south wall, and the congregational mosque have detailed an uninterrupted sequence from later Abbasid into Fatimid times. Particularly revealing is the later occupation of the Pavilion Building, excavated in 1986 and 1987 (Whitcomb 1988a; 1988b). Originally set up as a public monument at the junction of Aylah's intersecting axial streets, the structure in its last manifestation was a well-appointed residence of eight rooms around a central courtyard, onto which opened a deep *iwan* (porch). The courtyard, iwan and adjacent rooms formed the domestic nucleus of the house. In a 4.2 m square corner room, entered from a doorway in the west wall of the *iwan*, a polychrome fresco-decorated wall was uncovered. This room and another on the east produced an astounding collection of luxury and everyday ceramics as well as other objects, including a dirham of al-Hakim

(996–1020 CE). A bath, latrine and kitchen were exposed to the north of the courtyard, while to the east the piers of staircase to the roof or a second storey were identified. Entrance to the house was from so-called Egyptian Street to the west through an anteroom, with doorways positioned off-axis to protect the privacy of the household. Whitcomb's excavations at Aylah have revealed dramatic evidence for a major urban dislocation in the mid-eleventh century, involving "slumping and possibly massive subsidence of walls and buildings of the city" and due to, in all likelihood, the powerful earthquake of 1068 CE (Whitcomb 1995: 505). There is no archaeological evidence for a comprehensive rebuilding program after the earthquake, suggesting that the town never recovered from this major setback and hence presented an easy target for Baldwin's Crusader forces.

The archaeological work at Amman and Aylah reveals a shared trend in their urban history: a severe reduction if not end to their political and administrative functions, probably in the second half of the tenth century but no later than the early eleventh century. The clearest evidence for the change is the usurpation and conversion of public buildings into private dwellings, notably the palace on the Amman Citadel and the Central Pavilion at Aylah. While construction techniques were generally mediocre, levels of personal wealth were still good as illustrated by the quality and quantity of objects recovered from these structures. A similar downgrading of urban functions can be documented for the towns of north Jordan, although the evidence from Fihl/Pella, Bayt Ras and Jadar (Umm Qays) suggests that this transformation happened a century earlier or more, about the middle of the ninth century (Walmsley 1992a).

The evidence for Fatimid and Saljuq occupation at other major sites in Jordan is patchy and undistinguished when compared with Amman and Aylah, but nevertheless suggests a settlement profile similar to what probably were the two major towns in tenth to eleventh century Jordan. At Bayt Ras, Phase IVb, dated 900–1100 CE, saw the continued utilization of urban structures including a line of vaults in Area A, thought to have been a market place of the Byzantine and early Islamic town (Lenzen 1995b; Lenzen and Knauf 1987). During Phase IVb the original Byzantine-period tessellated pavement of Phase VI (300–600 CE) was substituted with flagstones, however a continuing public role for the vaults appears unlikely especially as the church opposite the vaults had seemingly fallen out of use in the preceding Phase V (600–900 CE). Elsewhere at Bayt Ras, eleventh century ceramics attest continued occupation during the Fatimid period. In the Jordan Valley at Pella, the Abbasid town centre has revealed domestic and industrial occupation continuing, it would appear, into the early Fatimid period (Walmsley 1995). Continuity of occupation throughout the Fatimid and Saljuq periods at Zughar, modern Khirbat Shaykh

Isa, has been established by two surveys of the site (Whitcomb 1992a) and recent archaeological investigations.

A continuing use of existing stone buildings and ambiguous ceramic typologies for Fatimid and Saljuq Jordan could well account for the absence of reported tenth and eleventh century occupation at other major archaeological sites in Jordan. Any major hiatus in occupation at historically important sites such as Tall Hisban and Dhiban is difficult to accept. Sauer correctly recognizes early Fatimid pottery at both sites (Sauer 1982: 333), but the architectural evidence from the Dhiban excavations for Fatimid and Saljuq occupation on the tell, while tantalizing, is impossibly confused (Tushingham 1972: 77–83). Also contributing to the shortage of data is the lack of excavation or publication of sites including some of the major centres mentioned in Maqdisi, notably Maan, Maab and Udhruh. In other cases the substantial redevelopment of leading eleventh century centres in later times would have largely destroyed the evidence for Fatimid and Saljuq period settlement. Karak is the obvious example, where the Jarrahid stronghold would have been demolished or incorporated in the Crusader edifice, while at Tall Hisban earlier Islamic structures were demolished to their foundations with the construction of a Mamluk-period citadel (see the comments in Walker 2003a: 452–453). Admittedly this reasoning relies in part on negative evidence, but then neither does the absence of available evidence demonstrate site abandonment. The material from Amman, Aylah, Bayt Ras, Pella and Zughar suggests a continuing settlement history into Fatimid times for many of the major towns of Jordan, although their politico-administrative and hence part of their urban role was considerably diminished or even terminated during the ninth and tenth centuries.

Fatimid and Saljuq occupation at other sites is not widely reported although there are some notable exceptions, especially in the Jordan Valley. Soundings at Tall Abu Qadan (Gourdan), next to Tall Dayr Alla in the middle valley, produced nineteen phases (A to T, omitting I), all of Islamic date (Franken and Kalsbeek 1975). The soundings exposed a long sequence of courtyard surfaces laid over mudbrick collapse, but few other features. Unlike the other sites considered so far, the buildings at Tall Abu Qadan were of mudbrick, and as they had a much shorter life a more representative early to middle Islamic sequence has been preserved. However, chronology is a problem as dating the finds (mostly ceramics) was not the purpose of the excavations and no firm dating evidence (namely coins) was found. A reinterpretation of the pottery indicates that, while Phase A is possibly eighth century Umayyad, the sequence properly begins with the early Abbasid period (B–C = ninth century) and continues with late Abbasid and early Fatimid occupation (Phases D–G = tenth–eleventh centuries). The stratigraphic and pottery evidence very strongly suggests

that the major "destruction" at the end of Phase E can be equated with the end of the Abbasid town centre at Pella, maybe early in the Fatimid period. If so, Phases F and G would be of Fatimid date, and specifically in the eleventh century. Phases H to T continue the sequence into the Ayyubid and Mamluk periods, making eight centuries of settlement that, contrary to the view of Franken and Kalsbeek, would not allow for any significant gap in site occupation. A similar picture emerges from the important excavations at Tall Qudsiyah, 15 km south of North Shunah in the north Jordan Valley (Kareem 1987: 92–123). Again the main building material was mudbrick, and by trimming bulldozer cuttings and excavating soundings J. Kareem identified a major unbroken sequence extending from late antiquity to the Ottoman period. The Fatimid levels, consisting of ash, soil and mudbrick layers (courtyards?), were dated by lustre and other glazed wares and decorated cream wares.

In the mountains the use of stone as the primary building material has resulted in evanescent Fatimid remains, yet the identification of eleventh and twelfth century levels has not been an impossible obstacle for problem-driven projects such as that at Khirbat Faris (Johns and McQuitty, *et al.* 1989; McQuitty and Falkner 1993). Excavations within and around House 2 have recorded the continuous use of this stone structure from its construction in the first century CE until today with Stage 3, made up of a series of surfaces 60–70 cm deep, ranging across the ninth–tenth to twelfth centuries. Interestingly, this time span was barely recognized in the surface sherding survey, with only five out of the 246 squares surveyed producing material identified as ninth–twelfth centuries. The lesson is obvious, often stated, but bears repeating: surface collections, even when correctly read, do not accurately represent either the periods of settlement or extent of occupation of a site.

The Faris project demonstrates unequivocally that little weight can be given to the results of regional surveys based upon surface collection (note the comments of Johns 1994: 3–9). Thus the low representation of Fatimid and Saljuq occupation in many surveys, in both the north and south of the country, reflects neither the nature nor extent of urban and rural settlement and land use in the tenth to twelfth centuries. Clearly there were important differences with the situation in the Byzantine and Umayyad periods, but simply to stipulate a settlement "gap" or total site abandonment in the Fatimid and Saljuq periods based simply on the "presence/absence" of very imperfectly-known ceramic types (especially those of the middle Islamic period) avoids a fuller consideration of a more complex series of human land-use issues (Brown 1991: 229–232; Johns 1994; Miller 1991: 19–20). A number of related reasons can be postulated to explain the poor showing of Fatimid and Saljuq sites in surveys: the imperfect and cursory nature of survey techniques; the substantial refurbishment of towns, villages and holy sites after the expulsion of the Crusaders and hence the virtual absence of major structures such as shrines and mosques; different exploitation strategies; and, as already noted, a very poor understanding of the material culture of the period, especially ceramics. Where middle Islamic ceramics are better known, for instance the north Jordan Valley, survey results have been considerably more successful in identifying widespread settlement (e.g. Kareem 1987: 450–452).

While it is probably unfair to single out any one survey, for the error is widespread, the high-profile Hisban Survey offers a clear example of unrepresentative survey results and their skewed interpretation. From a Byzantine peak of 126 inhabited sites, only 33 Umayyad and seven Abbasid period sites were identified in the Hisban region; no Fatimid and Crusader site-occupation was recorded. From these figures it has been proposed that the population plunged from an all-time high of 70,000+ in 635 CE (the Islamic conquest) to as few as 1,200 in 900 CE. Concurrently intensive land use strategies based on cereals, gardens and orchards were replaced by extensive, pastoral/nomadic strategies until there was no sedentary occupation at or around Tall Hisban during the three centuries of Fatimid, Saljuq and Crusader domination (Geraty and LaBianca 1985; LaBianca 1990). As McQuitty (1993: 168–169) points out:

> La Bianca does not offer any different interpretations of the settlement history of Jordan. He fits the food-system concept into the conventional models of the last fifty years despite tantalizingly touching on the necessity of discussing the *type* of land-use and settlement if the complexity of each period is to be characterized.

Johns (1994: 8–9) precisely summarizes the problem plaguing many surveys: often early Islamic wares, originating in a Byzantine tradition, are misassigned to the earlier period, while the origin of many Ayyubid-Mamluk types (especially hand made wares) in the Fatimid and Saljuq periods has yet to be recognized, leading to similar mistakes in periodization; and the situation is probably worse south of the Wadi Mujib. As Whitcomb (1992b: 388) remarks "there are more than enough ceramics published as Umayyad and Ayyubid/Mamluk to fill in the Abbasid/Fatimid period and make it quite a respectable occupation in Jordan's history."

Not surprisingly, given the differences of approach and interpretation, we seem to be in completely different worlds when reading LaBianca on Hisban and Johns on the Ard Karak during the early to middle Islamic periods.

Sites of the Crusader Period (Twelfth Century)

The archaeology of Crusader-period Jordan (1100–1188 CE) suffers from all the problems associated with Fatimid and Saljuq period archaeology. Apart from the few monu-mental castles at Shawbak, Karak and Petra, where later Ayyubid and Mamluk additions have often obscured the original Crusader structures, the twelfth century is virtually invisible in archaeological terms. The castle at Ajlun, now thought to date from between 1188 and 1192, is an Ayyubid construct and will be considered with the castles of the thirteenth century at Salt and Azraq in the Architecture section below.

Few excavated sites have produced identifiable twelfth century occupation, but one major exception is Wuayrah, the Crusader castle of Li Vaux Moise that dominated the entrance to Petra (Brown 1987; Kennedy 1994: 25–27; Vannini and Tonghini 1997). Excavations by R. Brown during 1987 in two areas of the castle identified two distinct architectural and depositional phases. Phase I was Crusader and dated 1108/1116–1188 CE, while Phase II was early Ayyubid and dated to the late twelfth to early thirteenth centuries. In Square 4, set in front of the Northeast Corner tower, a ceramic-rich sequence of occupational levels was excavated. The earliest was Phase IA, a series of courtyard levels, above which came Phase IB characterized by a floor and domestic occupation levels, and finally Phase II when a secondary enclosure was erected for domestic occupation. At the East Tower, Phase II was also identified by the erection of secondary structures, again for domestic purposes. More recent work at Wuayrah has expanded Brown's original conclusions (Vannini and Tonghini 1997; Vannini and Vanni Desideri 1995). Phase I represents the original Crusader castle, built between 1107 and 1116 CE, Phase II the substantial remodelling of the castle defences in the 1140s CE, Phase III Crusader occupation levels, Phases IIIa and IV a short span of non-military use in the Ayyubid period (roughly equivalent to Brown's Phase II), and four major collapse levels (V–VIII). Crusader to early Ayyubid material, similar to the Wuayrah finds, was also recovered by Brown from Phase I of the Ayyubid Palace at Shawbak (Brown 1988: 230-32). The work at Wuayrah and Shawbak, by successfully isolating twelfth to early thirteenth century occupational strata, carries major implications for other middle Islamic sites with reputedly "Ayyubid-Mamluk" levels, for instance Dhiban where the Ayyubid-period material includes ceramics of the previous century; hence twelfth century occupation at Dhiban should be suspected.

Other evidence for twelfth to early thirteenth century settlement in Jordan comes from Jarash, where two occupation levels were identified in the vaulted passages of the Zeus complex, terminating with a 1202 CE destruction level containing copious amounts of pottery. Considering the degree of occupation around the Zeus temple and the absence of comparable material at the Temple of Artemis, J. Seigne has suggested that Tughtigin's stronghold was located in the Zeus area, perhaps at the south theatre (Seigne 1989: 322–323, cf. the Saljuq-Ayyubid fortress at Busra in the Hauran). One site which seems to have experienced a considerable erosion of its position at this time was Amman, as the excavations on the citadel, unwalled since the Abbasid-Fatimid period, produced no significant occupation between the 1068 CE earthquake and the late twelfth century at the earliest (Northedge 1992: 161). Similarly, Whitcomb suggests the early Islamic town of Aylah, badly damaged in the earthquake of 1068 CE, was abandoned with Baldwin's expedition of 1116 CE (Whitcomb 1997). Recent archaeological work at the Mamluk fort to the southeast has not located an earlier Crusader stronghold, and any evidence for twelfth century Aylah/Aqabah has yet to be found. Perhaps an outpost on Jazirat Farun in the north Gulf of Aqabah served to secure the region, although Kennedy (1994: 30) rejects a Crusader date for the existing structure, arguing that a twelfth century Muslim attribution is much more probable.

Regional surveys make scant mention of the twelfth century as this period is equally, if not more, invisible as the Fatimid and Saljuq centuries. Of particular hindrance has been the perceived amorphous nature of Hand Made Geometrically Painted Ware (HMGPW), generally but inaccurately identified as a hallmark of a generalized "Ayyubid-Mamluk" phase of occupation. However current understanding of HMGPW does not recognize any differentiation within a three hundred year plus period nor, until recently, a pre-Ayyubid (i.e. late Fatimid-Crusader) variety of the hand made pottery (on HMGPW see more below). Furthermore Ayyubid-Mamluk redevelopment of settlements after the Crusader occupation would have also obscured the twelfth century, and as with the Fatimid and Saljuq periods few reliable conclusions can be drawn from survey data on settlement density in the twelfth century.

Sites of the Ayyubid and Mamluk Periods (Thirteenth to Sixteenth Centuries)

The range of Ayyubid and Mamluk period sites in Jordan is extensive, and includes examples with significant architectural features. The major categories range from holy sites adorned with mosques or shrines to fortified localities, typically town-based castles and forts/khans, and from agricultural and industrial establishments to innumerable villages sometimes with identified cemeteries. The contrast with the earlier Islamic periods, between the Abbasid and Fatimid-Saljuq, is immediately apparent: this was an age of reconstruction and building after the Crusader debacle and has left, in the archaeological record, a more tangible and high-profile presence. Consequently the number of excavated and surveyed sites with identifiable Ayyubid-Mamluk occupation is considerably greater, although the period is often poorly reported particularly when the recovery of Islamic remains is not the primary intention of a project.

Important work on sites with major architectural remains includes the controlled excavations at Karak and Shawbak by Brown (Brown 1988; 1989a; 1989b; 1989c; 1989d); a study of the castle at Ajlun (Johns 1932; Minnis and Bader 1988); ongoing work at Hisban with a citadel complex with bathhouse and other structures (de Vries 1986; 1994; Walker 1999; 2003a; 2003b), the survey of Mamluk forts at Zarqa, Ziza and Aqabah (Glidden 1952; Petersen 1991); soundings in a Mamluk khan at Dhra al-Khan (Kareem 1997; Kareem 2000); and the excavation of village mosques at Pella and Lahun (Whitcomb in Homès-Fredericq 1989; Walmsley 1992b; 1998). The architectural component of these and other sites will be considered in the next section. The intentional (compared to accidental) excavation of settlements with Ayyubid-Mamluk occupation include Khirbat Faris, Bayt Ras, Khirbat Ayn Janin (Hart 1987: 45), Khirbat Shaykh Isa (Photos-Jones, Politis, *et al.* 2002), Nakhal (Schick, Mahasneh, *et al.* 1994), Tall Abu Qadan and Tall Abu Sarbut (Haas, LaGro, *et al.* 1989; 1992), Tall Qudsiyah and Pella (Bourke and Hendrix 2001: 85–86; McPhillips 2001). The renewed excavations at Hisban by Walker, focusing on the Islamic heritage of this important site up until modern times, are producing exciting results with great promise for more.

Sites with evidence (usually ceramic) for an Ayyubid-Mamluk presence figure prominently in large scale regional surveys. Usually the sites are multi-period with evidence for earlier settlement periods but in other instances sites appear to have only an Ayyubid-Mamluk presence, perhaps an indication of settlement expansion to some degree in the thirteenth to fourteenth centuries. By the mid-1990s, excavations and surveys in Jordan had identified Ayyubid and Mamluk occupation at 795 out of a total of 3843 historical sites (i.e. excluding prehistoric and unknown-period sites), or 20.69 percent, with 442 of these sites (55.6 percent) also recording Umayyad to Fatimid occupation (Palumbo 1994). While this latter figure is almost certainly too low for the reasons already elucidated, these figures do suggest two aspects of Ayyubid-Mamluk settlement in Jordan: a reasonably high proportion of site occupation and considerable and largely unbroken continuity from the earlier Islamic periods. However the JADIS figures, when treated by individual sector (see Table 16.1), also indicate that the density of site occupation was much higher in the north of the country (range 20–40%, average 28.19%) while south of Karak the density abruptly fell to within a low 3–12% range (average 4.84%). As far as it is possible to tell the figures show greater uniformity across the different environmental zones of the Jordan Valley, the elevated mountains and plains and *badiyah*.

While this rather severe dichotomy between the north and south of Jordan may be a product of both a poor understanding of regional ceramic traditions in the thirteenth to sixteenth centuries and the research objectives of survey teams, it could nevertheless indicate a relatively lower density of sedentary population in the south due to the greater resources of the north with the intensification of a village-based cash crop economy. Unfortunately, developments during the three centuries of Ayyubid-Mamluk hegemony in Jordan can not be chronologically isolated due to an elementary knowledge of the pottery. Similarly as it is impossible to isolate early Ottoman ceramics, the number of northern sites attributed to the Ayyubid-Mamluk period could have been inflated by the inclusion of sites with late sixteenth–seventeenth century occupation (again, see the comments in Johns 1994: 19–22). Thus any settlement processes that produced this differential can not be identified based on these figures alone, although they raise tantalizing issues of variable site density, changing land use and divergent economies.

A relatively good record of regional surveys and excavations in the Karak district has permitted an unusually reliable and particularly illuminating survey of Ayyubid-Mamluk occupation in the towns and the countryside of the Ard Karak (Brown 1984; 1992; Johns 1994: 20–22; Miller 1991; Milwright 2006: 15–20). The pioneering excavations by Brown at Karak and Shawbak castles have been particularly decisive in identifying Ayyubid and Mamluk phases in a continuous site history from the Crusader period to the recent past. At Shawbak, Brown (1988; 1989c) conducted excavations in the Ayyubid Palace complex, concentrating on the Reception Hall, the North Palace and the East Palace. Four major phases were identified:

I   Ayyubid, the construction of the Palace complex;

II Later Ayyubid, represented by additions and rebuilds in the North Palace;

III Mamluk, perhaps fourteenth–fifteenth century, which saw major spatial changes with the abandonment of the Reception Hall and alterations to the North and East palaces; and

IV Ottoman.

The phases were determined by demonstrable architectural changes. Few chronological indicators were recovered except a limited number of ceramics; unfortunately their broad dating makes them particularly unsuitable for the task. Interestingly, however, HMGPW was largely absent from the otherwise overwhelming Mamluk assemblage of Phase III, and was seen by Brown as a reflection of the higher social status of the castle occupants. A small scale excavation at Karak also concentrated on the Islamic Palace, which is a large building complex on the upper court originally interpreted as Crusader private apartments (Brown 1989a; 1989b). A sounding in the south *iwan* (recess) of the Palace Reception Hall identified two major occupational phases: Phase I (Mamluk),

JADIS sector	Ayyubid-Mamluk	total no. historic sites	% of total	JADIS zone
1	187	531	35.22	Irbid/N. Jordan Valley
2	176	525	33.52	Ajlun/Jarash
3	29	135	21.48	Mafraq
4	121	530	22.83	Amman/S. Jordan Valley
5	38	111	34.23	Kharraneh
6	28	178	15.73	Dhiban
7	11	44	25.00	Qasr Tuba
8	8	20	40.00	Azraq/Ruweished
9	93	362	25.69	Karak
10	29	298	9.73	Ader
11	16	306	5.23	Tafilah
12	49	439	11.16	Wadi Hasa
13	0	2	0	Bayir
14	10	340	2.95	Aqabah/Petra
15	0	22	0	Maan/Jafr

Table 16.1   Total number of Ayyubid-Mamluk sites and percentage of total number of historical-period sites by JADIS sectors.

which produced ceramic and numismatic evidence for a fourteenth century construction date (indicating that this complex should be equated with the Palace of Sultan Nasr Muhammad, built in 1311 CE); and Phase II, Ottoman. As at Shawbak, HMGPW and local monochrome glazed wares were scarce in the Mamluk levels whereas imported glazed and wheel-made cream wares dominated the corpus. Again, this was seen as evidence for the bifurcated nature of Mamluk society in Jordan, divided between the urban ruling elite and the rural peasantry.

Stemming from a detailed analysis of the results of Miller's Karak Plateau Survey, Brown (1992) has argued for a major demographic shift on the Ard Karak from the highly productive arable plains in the centre of the plateau to the more broken and isolated terrain located on the south and south-west. As a zone of perennial springs but limited cultivable land, food production became more intensive, revolving around irrigated fields and orchards. Brown suggests that this shift took place after the fifteenth century as a result of competition for resources with nomadic groups (the Bedouin), but Johns (1994: 22) has firmly and convincingly argued for a seventeenth or eighteenth century date for this change and rejected the theory of competition for land with pastoral groups.

Recent survey work has revealed similarly high levels of socially complex settlement based upon a productive rural economy for much of Ayyubid and Mamluk Jordan. The work of MacKenzie (2002) focusing on Ajlun has brought together information on towns, villages, mills and industrial sites, thereby revealing the richness of Islamic settlement in this area. Correlating written sources with field work, still in its early stages, Walker (2004) has begun to systematically locate and identify settlement profiles in the different regions of Jordan proposing, in general terms, significant continuity in north Jordan, some variability in levels of settlement in central Jordan with Hisban as an example of site reduction and abandonment in the fifteenth century, contraction in the Jordan Valley following the plague and the collapse of the sugar industry, and widespread settlement retrenchment in the south by the sixteenth century. Overall, Walker reveals settlement dynamics to be complex between the thirteenth and fifteenth centuries and continuing into Ottoman times, related to a number of interacting factors including levels of organized Mamluk investment in the countryside. No single economic model is valid for the entire region, and certainly not one that proposes a precipitous decline at the end of the fourteenth century.

Architecture: Religious and Secular, Public and Private

The architectural heritage of Middle Islamic Jordan is modest and almost exclusively Crusader, Ayyubid and Mamluk in date. This is not to say that nothing was built in the Fatimid period. Very possibly the Shi'ite Fatimids enlarged or embellished the shrine at Mazar to commemorate the three companions of the Prophet including Jaafar ibn Abi Talib, brother of the Orthodox Caliph Ali most favoured by the Shi'ites. Tombstones and other finds certainly attest a strong Fatimid interest in Mazar. The burial places of other Companions, for instance the tomb of Abu Ubaydah in the Jordan Valley, could have received similar attention. However these and any other possible Fatimid structures have not survived due to the extent of Ayyubid-Mamluk reconstruction. The holy sites of Palestine and Jordan generally attracted a higher profile in the ninth and especially tenth centuries, and quite probably the erection of a new Ayyubid-Mamluk mosque or shrine was undertaken at the expense of an existing (but perhaps derelict) Fatimid, or Fatimid augmented, structure.

Castles, Forts and other Fortifications

One of the most tangible expressions of the Crusader presence in south Jordan is the presence of impressive, if ruined (to varying degrees), castles at Karak, Shawbak and Petra. The Ayyubid and, after them, Mamluk elites that replaced the Crusader lords at Karak and Shawbak repaired and extended the fortifications of both castles, building towers and walls (Figure 16.4). At Shawbak, the Ayyubids inserted a palace in an Islamic style, and at Karak the Mamluks did likewise; these palaces parallel examples at Raqqa, Cairo and Jerusalem (Brown 1988; 1989a; 1989b; 1989c).

The Ayyubid princes similarly secured their domination over north Jordan following the Crusader defeat at Hattin in 1187 CE by constructing castles at Ajlun (between 1188–1192) and Salt (1220), a watch tower over Amman, a fortlet at Zarqa, and a more substantial fort at Azraq (by

Izz al-Din Aybeg, Lord of Salkhad in 1236–1237).

The watch tower at Amman was built on the south edge of the Citadel, overlooking the lower town where the Ayyubid and Mamluk settlement would have been located. Its plan is a 9.45 x 7.55 m rectangle, with a single internal chamber measuring 4.8 x 3.1 m and entered through a doorway in the north wall (Ostrasz 1997; Wood 1992: 113–114, 125). The tower, as with other Ayyubid towers, would have been vaulted. Arrow slits in rectangular recesses penetrate the west, south and east walls, while a staircase within the north wall once lead to the roof. The tower was constructed out of large limestone blocks, many reused from the nearby Roman-period Temple of Hercules. Of particular note are two column drums laid horizontally in the south wall and wedged in place with triangular-shaped stones. Horizontally-laid column drums were a feature of Ayyubid military architecture (cf. the theatre/fort at Busra, with towers dated 1202–1228 CE), and the discovery of an Ayyubid *fals* from Damascus sandwiched between two floor levels confirms an Ayyubid date (late twelfth or early thirteenth century) for the tower at Amman.

Figure 16.4 Shawbak castle: the square tower constructed by the Mamluk Sultan Husam al-Din Lajin (r. 1296–1299). View to the north-west (photo: Walmsley).

Of probable similar date, based on architectural comparisons, is the small fort at Zarqa named Qasr Shabib (Petersen 1991). The fort sits on an elevated wadi spur above the Zarqa River, and is an uncomplicated structure. Made of large limestone blocks, some of which are clearly reused, the plan is a straightforward 13.75 m square with walls about three metres thick. The single entrance is located in the north wall, and consists of a pointed-arch doorway set back within a 3.4 m high double-voussoired arch similarly pointed. A recess above the doorway once held an inscription (see the Azraq castle, below), while behind the outer arch and above the doorway was a concealed machicoulis (see the outer gateway at Ajlun,

below). The doorway leads into a barrel-vaulted chamber and a single room, from the north-east corner of which a staircase leads to the roof. Arrow slits, now blocked, in pointed-arch recesses are visible in the west, south and east walls. The building once stood much higher than its surviving eight meters, but the upper storey is considerably ruined. Nevertheless its plan and architectural features (doorway, arrow slits) suggest a thirteenth century date for Qasr Shabib.

The Ayyubid castle at Salt, now largely destroyed, was built on a hill top to the north of the town, and boasted stout towers of undressed stone and rock-cut dry moats. That Salt was equipped with a castle and Amman, it

Figure 16.5 Ajlun castle: plan showing the original structure (1188–1192) with gateway at (A), and early thirteenth century additions with an inner (B) and outer (C) gateway (based on C.N. Johns 1931, plate 21).

seems, only with a watch tower represents the changing fortunes of these two centres in the twelfth and thirteenth centuries, for by this date Salt, as already noted, had replaced Amman as the chief town of the Balqa.

Likewise benefiting from its strategic position was the village of Ajlun in the Jabal Awf, above which, perched on a hilltop, was erected a small but stout castle that looked out over the central Jordan Valley and the Wadi Kafrinji, a major route into the Jordanian highlands from the valley. Constructed by the amir Izz al-Din Usama between 1188–1192 CE (and probably not the commonly accepted date of 1184, see Humphreys 1977: 77), the castle formed an unevenly shaped quadrilateral, determined by the shape of the hilltop, with four square towers at each corner with a single entrance in the east wall (Figure 16.5). An outer gate was positioned between the northeast and south-east towers, and while seemingly part of the original structure (it bonds with the south-east tower) the doorway proper might be a later reconstruction. At a lower level on the east and south sides were two baileys, of which the eastern was the larger and better-equipped, having a tower at either end. All the towers and intervening walls were periodically pierced by plain arrow slits. Water was provided by five rock-cut cisterns under the castle. In the early thirteenth century, after the castle was captured from Izz al-Din Usama, the defences were strengthened by the construction of a massive tower on the south side and the original structure given added height to match the new tower. To accommodate these changes two new gates were added, the inner one of which was decorated with birds and provided with a *machicoulis* accessed from the first floor (Figure 16.6). An inscription on the south tower dates these additions to 1214–1215, and were undertaken by Izz al-Din Aybeg, Lord of Salkhad, for the Ayyubid prince al-Muazzam (d. 1227), son of al-'Adil and his father's successor in Damascus (1218). The dry moat that surrounds the castle must have been cut, or at least completed, as part of these additions, for it makes allowance for the projection of the south tower. Today the castle at Ajlun, named Qalat Rabad, shows evidence of later repairs but the plan is as Izz al-Din Aybeg left it, and hence it is a fully Ayyubid structure.

The Azraq fort was also constructed by Izz al-Din Aybeg but after Ajlun, in 1236–1237, as recorded in an inscription over the entrance (Figure 16.7). Perhaps originally Diocletianic in date, the solely basalt structure approaches a square (c. 79 x 72 m) with projecting rectangular corner towers and intervening towers of irregular spacing and number (Kennedy 1982: 75–96). The basic plan conforms to a late Roman type, and the original masonry is identifiable in places especially the outer walls. Differing construction styles indicates that the thirteenth century work involved considerable reconstruction of the towers, walls and internal features, even taking into account Druze additions in this century. Entry to the cen-

tral courtyard of the Ayyubid fort was through a projecting tower set off-centre in the south wall. The tower defended a right-angled entrance with a doorway set back under a slightly pointing arch and equipped with heavy basalt door leaves, the left of which is a recent restoration. Above the arch is the inscription, an arrow slit (one of four in the room above the entrance, each set in pointed arches) and a *machicoulis*. The tower once had a third storey, now largely destroyed. Inside the fort are rooms of varying dimensions opening out onto a spacious courtyard. The originally three-storeyed group in the middle of the west wall had three large windows in the courtyard wall of the second storey, and has been appropriately named called the "praetorium" for it was clearly the nucleus of the fort. Large rectangular arched rooms along the north wall probably functioned as stables. Water could be accessed through a subterranean room on the east wall. Very possibly these parts of the fort served similar functions in both the late Roman and the Ayyubid periods, as the structures appear to form part of the original fort, yet retained their essential architectural integrity with Izz al-Din Aybeg's

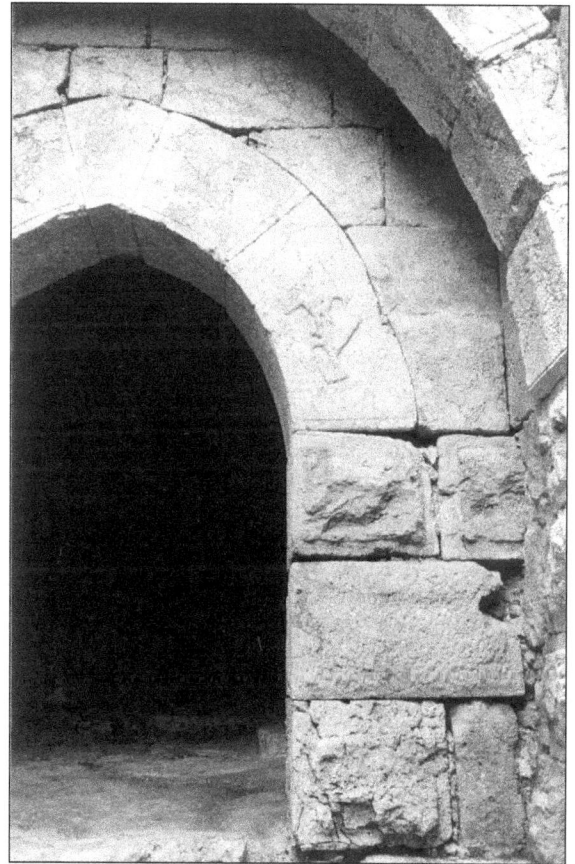

Figure 16.6 Ajlun castle: the inner gateway to the additions of 1214–1215 (at 'B' on the plan), featuring a broad *machicoulis* and an arch decorated with two birds. View to the north-west (photo: Walmsley).

Figure 16.7 Azraq: entrance to the fort, 1236–1237. View to the north (photo: Walmsley).

rebuild. In the north-east quadrant of the courtyard is a small free-standing mosque, which probably dates to the Ayyubid garrisoning of the fort (see below).

The extent of military building in the later twelfth and thirteenth century reveals that the Ayyubid princes and their governors paid particular attention to securing the regions of north and south Jordan. The Crusaders, although critically weakened by the loss at Hattin, still remained firmly entrenched on coastal Palestine, which ensured the continued prominence of the inland Jordanian routes between Cairo and Damascus. Existing Crusader castles in the south were restored and improved while new strongholds were built in the north to defend the main routes and monitor the local population, some of whom had spent nearly three generations under Crusader influence if not rule.

In the following Mamluk period, especially after the final expulsion of the Crusaders from Palestine, attention shifted to improving security on the main roads especially those that passed between Damascus, the Hijaz and Egypt. On the *Darb al-Hajj* (Pilgrimage route) from Damascus to Makkah (Mecca) a small but solid fort was built at the strategic site of Ziza (Jiza) where a large reservoir provided water for travellers, especially pilgrims and armies (Petersen 1991). Although modified in more

recent times by the addition of second-storey windows, the plan is original and consists of a main rectangular structure 21.5 m (N–S) x 12.2 m and a smaller square annex on the east side which continues the line of the southern facade of the fort. Walls of large squared limestone blocks average 2.5 m thick, and were originally perforated by slit windows. The doorway, positioned flush with the south facade, has a flat lintel and is surmounted by a slit window then a graceful triple-arched window. Inside are two storeys. The ground floor is a large chamber with a slightly pointed barrel vault, from which a staircase leads to the upper floor in the thickness of the east wall. Upstairs is a complex of four rooms around a courtyard, all of later (probably nineteenth century) construction. The doorways have charming rosette-decorated flat lintels surmounted by a relieving arch and a circular vent in the spandrels. Other structures once existed near the fort, including a mosque, but these are no longer extant.

To the west of Ziza at Hisban, new investigations into the Islamic settlement have identified a citadel on the summit of the site, probably a residence belonging to the Mamluk governor of the Balqa region (Walker 2003a; Walker 2003b: 250–261). The complex is square in shape, with heavy masonry walls and corner towers that incorporated earlier structures. Internally, the complex revolved around a sunken paved courtyard flanked by an *iwan*-type throne room, a small bathhouse and barrel-vaulted rooms. Access to the citadel was through an arched gateway on the south side. In plan the Hisban citadel resembled the Mamluk palace at Karak. Damaged caused by earthquakes in the fourteenth century may to have ended the official function of the Hisban citadel, with thick destruction levels being excavated in areas.

Abundant fresh water and the reinstitution of the Pilgrimage route around the north shore of the Red Sea ensured the continuing importance of Aqabah throughout the Mamluk period. To secure the area, a small fortified khan was constructed on the northeast shore of the gulf, which although substantially modified inside has a well-preserved gateway dated to the late Mamluk period (Glidden 1952). The fort is constructed of small squared blocks laid in even courses of alternating colours. It was equipped with stout round corner towers and an unpretentious gateway, consisting of an arched entrance between two half-round towers, mid-point in the north wall. An inscription spanning both sides of the doorway declares that the fort was constructed in the time of Sultan Qansawh al-Ghawri (1501–1516), the penultimate Mamluk sultan and a great builder. The doorway, which was reduced in size at a later date, leads into a passageway roofed with a pointed barrel vault. Beyond stands a large open courtyard, which once was flanked with stables, storehouses and sleeping quarters for travellers and pilgrims. The style and construction of the Aqabah fort confirms a late Mamluk date, however al-Ghawri's contribution may have been a substantial refurbishment around the gateway rather that a complete rebuilding of the fort (cf. the Citadel of Aleppo). The fort played a key role during the Arab Revolt, in which modern Jordan was released from the Ottoman Empire, as celebrated by the Hashemite coat of arms above the fort entrance.

Road stations were also constructed on the route known as the Darb Quful that passed from Damascus into Palestine through Irbid and the north Jordan Valley in the Mamluk period. At Dhra al-Khan in the Jordan Valley, at the foot of the pass to Irbid, excavations have exposed a major caravanserai, rectangular in plan (64 x 54 m) with 1.2 m thick buttressed walls constructed from large limestone blocks (Kareem 1997; Kareem 2000). Rooms were arranged around a central courtyard, entered by a gateway in the middle of the northern wall. Coins suggest a construction date under the Mamluk sultan Qalawun (1280–1290) or shortly after, and a major reconstruction during the third reign of al-Nasr Muhammad (1310–1341). Occupation continued into the Ottoman period. To support these developments Baybars, Barquq and other Mamluk sultans had bridges built or rebuilt over the Jordan River at a number of locations between Damiya (in 1265 CE under Baybars) and Jisr Majamia to connect north Jordan with Baysan, Tabariyah and Nablus.

Mosques and Shrines

The Ayyubid and Mamluk reconstruction of social life in Jordan following the Crusader interregnum was especially directed towards restoring and improving the religious infrastructure of the region. Two categories of mosque were built: commemorative mosques (*mashhad*) at holy sites usually constructed at state expense, and congregational mosques (*masjid*) in towns and villages financed by the local community. At the Muslim holy sites new mosques replaced earlier and, especially in the former Crusader regions, probably neglected structures, including Mazar and Mutah south of Karak, at the tombs of Abu Ubaydah at Amata and Muadh bin Jabal near North Shunah in the Jordan Valley, and at Kahf al-Raqim near Amman. Most notably a shrine was built atop Jabal Harun near Wadi Musa (Petra), for seemingly the Christian monastery encountered by Baldwin I in 1100 did not continue after the mid-thirteenth century. Numerous mosques were also built to meet the needs of towns and villages, and these are known from the modest specimens from Lahun, Tabaqat Fahl, Azraq and the Ajlun area.

The commemorative shrine on the summit of Jabal Harun was constructed over the reputed tomb of Aaron, the brother of Moses (Musa) and also a prophet in Islam (Quran 19.53 "Miriam"). Later Muslim traditions recount the death of Aaron in a cave after he and his brother were attracted to enter by a bright light and seeing there a golden throne, Aaron was drawn to sit upon

it at which moment the Angel of Death struck. Moses was subsequently accused by the Israelites of killing his brother, but miraculously his innocence was proven. The present structure, which at c. 1350 m above sea level is visible from a great distance, is dated by an inscription to the year 1338–1339 in the time of the third reign of the Sultan Nasr Muhammad. Constructed from local stone, much of it reused, the shrine measures 12.5 (N–S) x 9 m and has a flat stone roof with a prominent dome in the south-east corner. The single chamber, roofed with low vaults resting on a central pier, is entered by an arched doorway located at the south end of the west wall. Inside by the south wall stands the cloth-draped cenotaph of Aaron, positioned midway between the doorway and a *mihrab*. Above the *mihrab* stands the dome. At the opposite (northern) end of the chamber in the west corner a descending staircase leads to the sepulchre of Aaron, a rock-cut chamber with 19 loculi and clearly a tomb of much earlier date (Nabataean or Roman?). The mid-fourteenth century Muslim shrine partially rests on the foundations of an earlier and larger memorial, almost certainly a Byzantine-period church which in 1217 CE was still inhabited by two Greek monks. That only fragments of the church were incorporated in the Muslim shrine, including marble screen and column pieces, suggests the summit church was abandoned for a period before the construction of the current structure. On a plateau to the west of the summit are the remains of a large monastic complex some 60 (N–S) x 50 m in area, consisting of rooms, a chapel/church, courtyards and cisterns (see recently, Frösén, Fiema, *et al.* 2003). Conceivably this was the monastery "joyously found" by Baldwin I, although the excavations have not been able to identify occupation within the monastery after the eighth century, so this reference may refer to the summit church.

Another holy site to receive renewed attention in the Mamluk period was the Cave of the Sleepers at Kahf al-Raqim, located a short distance from the Hajj route south-east of Amman. Although the Christian legend of the sleepers locates the cave near Ephesus in Turkey, the Balqa cave named Kahf al-Raqim is specifically linked to the Quranic version of the story, for instance by two tenth century geographical sources (Istakhri, al-Maqdisi) and al-Yaqut in the thirteenth century. In the Quran (18: 9–26; the whole chapter is named al-Kahf after the tale) the youths, variously understood to have been three, five or seven in number, with their dog Qitmir hide in a cave to preserve their faith in One God, for others had taken to believing in other gods. They sleep for 309 years, the youths turning occasionally (as one does in sleep), and their dog, forelegs outstretched (as dogs can sleep, yet remain alert, with their heads resting on their forelegs) at the doorway. Upon waking, they reckon that they have been asleep no more than one day. It is a miraculous story, conveying the promise of resurrection and extolling the virtues of Islamic monotheism in the face of persecution and rejecting compromise—precisely the challenges facing the fledgling Muslim community in Makkah at the time this chapter was revealed to Muhammad.

The inspiration to build a mosque over the cave would have come directly from the Quran (18: 21):

> Thus did We make their case known to the people, that they might know that the promise of God is true, and that there can be no doubt about the Hour of Judgement. Behold, they dispute among themselves as to their affair. (Some) said, 'Construct a building over them': Their Lord knows best about them: those who prevailed over their affair said, 'Let us surely build a place of worship over them.' (Yusufali translation).

There are, however, two mosques at Kahf al-Raqim, a near-square structure with a courtyard and minaret above the cave and rectangular building with a long east–west axis in front of the cave (Figure 16.8). The latter mosque conforms to a Mamluk style in Jordan and in all probability is thirteenth or fourteenth century; architecturally the mosque above the cave appears earlier, as one would expect from the Quranic account. The walls of the upper mosque survive to 1.5 m or less in height, and are made from large limestone blocks up to one metre in length. A deep *mihrab* in the south wall confirms that this building functioned as a mosque, but the large blocks suggest the conversion of an existing Roman or Byzantine structure (if in situ) or are reused. Two rows of columns and wall pilasters suggest that the mosque roof was originally supported by arches. A doorway in the east wall opened out onto a portico as evidenced by two columns, and was flanked on the north by a minaret and staircase, of which four steps remain. The date of this mosque is uncertain, but the square plan, side entrance and deep *mihrab* complies with the small mosque style of Umm Walid, Khan Zabib and Jabal Usays, usually attributed to the Umayyad period by association with larger adjacent complexes (King and Lenzen *et al.* 1983: 399–405). Interestingly as with the mosque at Umm Walid, the upper structure at al-Kahf was once mistakenly interpreted as a temple (Brünnow and Domaszewski 1905: 195–206). The lower mosque sits immediately in front of the cave entrance and, as side walls butt up to the rock face, access to the cave entrance was only through two doorways, one later blocked, in the west wall. The open doorway gave entry into an irregular courtyard positioned between the mosque and the rock face. From here entry to the mosque, measuring c. 19.6 (E–W) x 4.65 m, was through three broad (2.37 m) doorways in the north wall, probably originally arched and permanently open. In the centre of the south wall was a two metre deep *mihrab* and, to its right (west), a minbar built of stone blocks with four steps remaining. As the layout of this mosque is very

similar to the village mosques of the thirteenth and fourteenth century at Tabaqat Fahl and Azraq (below), a late Ayyubid or early Mamluk date is very likely. The cave, the centre of all this activity, is a much earlier (late Roman or Byzantine) construct. A doorway in the decorative facade leads down into a rock-cut chamber flanked with three deep *arcosolia*, the two lateral *arcosolia* having three graves apiece. Apart from its legendary associations the tomb has no exceptional features.

As already discussed, particular attention was paid to embellishing the burial places of the Companions of the Prophet in the Ayyubid and Mamluk periods, notably Abu Ubaydah in the Jordan Valley and the tombs of Jaafar ibn Abi Talib, Zayd ibn al-Harithah and Abd Allah bin Rawahah at Mazar. Accordingly, these sites figure prominently in the sources of the thirteenth–fifteenth centuries. Accompanying these developments was the recognition of many burial places belonging to a local "saint" or *wali*. One example is the shrine of Abu Sulayman Dirani near Shawbak (Khammash 1986: 81–83). Of probable Mamluk date, the shrine is rectangular in shape (17 x 8.2 m) with a dome emphasising the burial place at the west end. A single doorway in the north wall gives entry to a rectangular, tunnel-vaulted room with a recessed, pointed-arched *mihrab* in the south wall, opposite the entrance. To the west the tomb is marked by a headstone and foot stone of marble within an oval of stones, above which is the partly collapsed dome. The tomb chamber is a modest but elegant structure with a second, plain *mihrab* in the centre of the south wall. The remains of the dome rest on an octagon supported by four low-slung pointed arches which spring from piers in each corner of the room. The octagon, with four corner decorative squinches and four small windows at the apex of the arches, cleverly and decoratively acts as a transition between the square room and the circular base of the dome. Khammash (1986: 83) records an interesting account of the ceremonies at the shrine.

> In weekly ceremonies at the gravesite, the villages would pay tribute by drumming and lighting oil lamps or candles. They would bring new fabric to cover the grave and would tear off small pieces of the old fabric to keep for good fortune. Prayers for the sick and other supplications were addressed to the wali. Women dyed their hands and their hair with henna which was also applied to the walls as an offering. "They bring incense, henna and sacrifices. Women walk about the shrine. Before, it was said that there used to be ostrich eggs hanging in the dome in a net. There were lamps, some of glass and some of clay," explained the old caretaker.

Similar, if not the same, ceremonies have probably been enacted at this shrine, and many others like it, since Ayyubid and Mamluk times (and possibly long before), as

Figure 16.8 Kahf al-Raqim: general view of the site, with the Mamluk mosque in lower foreground with cave (obscured) and upper mosque behind (photo: Walmsley).

local holy figures served an important function, especially in rural communities. Country women in particular were attracted to local shrines as access to the congregational mosque of the town proved geographically and socially difficult.

The restoration of the social infrastructure of Jordan after the expulsion of the Crusaders also required the erection of community mosques in towns and villages. Serving both a social and political purpose, this activity was widespread with numerous examples known and many more being identified as archaeological and anthropological work intensifies in Jordan. At Tibneh near Irbid, Khammash has documented the "old mosque" (*al-jamia al-qadim*) of the village which he suggests is of Ottoman date (eighteenth century). Built over a cave, the mosque is "simply and powerfully proportioned, … a perfect square, 12.5 x 12.5 meters, approximately 5 meters high" (Khammash 1986: 60). Walls are solidly built in even courses of roughly dressed stone blocks averaging 24 x 34 cm, with a double-arched doorway offset to the east in the north wall. Inside is a single chamber with a *mihrab* opposite the doorway in the south wall and a central pier to support the roof, cross-vaulted except for the south-east

quadrant where a dome once stood over the *mihrab*. The similarities with the Shrine of Harun are clear (vaulted chamber, dome over *mihrab*, cave underneath), suggesting a Mamluk date for the Tibneh mosque (conversely, it could be argued that the Harun shrine is an Ottoman rebuild and the inscriptions date an earlier structure, but this seems less likely).

Recent excavations at Tabaqat Fahl and Lahun have firmly identified the Mamluk-period village mosques for these two centres. Two categories of mosques, one Ayyubid to early Mamluk and the other later Mamluk, can be tentatively recognized.

The mosque at Tabaqat Fahl (Figure 16.9) was excavated by Ghazi Bisheh as part of the University of Sydney Excavations at Pella in 1982 (Walmsley 1992b: 188–192; Walmsley 1998: 131–136). The plan is very similar to the later mosque at Kahf al-Raqim, in that it consists of a plain rectangle measuring 15.8 (N–S) x 6.85 m formed by two-faced, rubble core stone walls with a deep *mihrab* midpoint in the south (*qiblah*) wall. Engaged columns, clearly reused, were built into the internal face of the *qiblah* wall either side of the *mihrab*. Immediately to the right (west) of the *mihrab* the lower section of a *minbar*

Figure 16.9 Tabaqat Fahl: view of the Mamluk mosque after excavation and consolidation. View to the north-east (photo: Walmsley/
    Pella Excavations).

was uncovered with three stone steps remaining. Oppo-site the *mihrab* in the north wall was the only doorway into the mosque, although three elongated windows either side of the entrance would have admitted plenty of light. The roof of the mosque, probably of perishable materials, was supported by two rows of evenly spaced columns from which, at about a metre above the floor level, once sprung high-pointed arches, the voussoirs of which were found fallen on the packed earth floor of the mosque. Floor to ceiling height would have been around 3.85 m. Short buttresses carried the thrust of the arches on the end columns to the outside walls, the resultant alcoves being hidden by the construction of thin dividing walls. Some care was taken in the building of the mosque, with re-used squared blocks being used to strengthen the corners of the building. All but the south wall were built in 35 cm deep foundation trenches, while the load-bearing columns were sunken below ground level to between 50 and 75 cm. Ceramics and coins suggest a fourteenth to fifteenth century date for the construction and use of this mosque. Village houses contemporary with the mosque have been located to the north, and excavations in this area, while limited in extent, have uncovered a well-stratified sequence of Mamluk ceramics (McPhillips and Walmsley 2007).

The similarities in overall plan between the mosques of Tabaqat Fahl and Azraq are immediately apparent. The Azraq mosque is a free standing structure of local basalt in the courtyard of the fort, one imagines built as part of Izz al-Din Aybeg's reconstruction in the mid-thirteenth century. Essentially rectangular in plan, the long axis of the mosque runs parallel to the *qiblah* wall, as does a double line of high pointed arches that rest on deeply buried columns. However the Azraq mosque is not as wide as the example at Tabaqat Fahl with two, not three, arches per row, while the arches terminate on pilasters, not engaged pillars. Also different is the location of the doorway, which at Azraq is in the short east wall, and the inclusion of only two elevated windows in the *qiblah* wall, which makes the mosque interior very dark. In spite of these differences, the two mosques clearly belong to a common tradition—the arch spans are within five centimetres of each other—that can be dated to the late Ayyubid and early Mamluk period (thirteenth–fourteenth century) in Jordan. Similar long-room mosques with a deep horseshoe-shaped *mihrab* have been identified, and some excavated, in the *Ajlun* area (Ghawânmah 1986; MacKenzie 2002).

The small mosque at Lahun, investigated by Whitcomb

as part of the Belgium Committee of Excavations in Jordan (D. Homès-Fredericq, Director), is rectangular in shape with walls of rough field stones. In the short south wall is a deep *mihrab* with an opposing doorway in the north wall. Thus the long axis of the mosque is orientated north–south. No windows or a *minbar* are present. Pottery and a coin recovered from within the building suggest a later Mamluk date, c. fifteenth century. Houses belonging to a small village have been identified nearby. Although the evidence is preliminary, the Lahun mosque could represent a later Mamluk long-room tradition distinguishable from the late Ayyubid and early Mamluk broad-room style found at Tabaqat Fahl, Kahf al-Raqim and Azraq. However, the difference may also be regional.

Other Secular Architecture: Urban and Rural, Domestic and Industrial

Evidence for secular architecture in the Fatimid and Saljuq periods is meagre due, in part, to the extensive building programs of the Crusader, Ayyubid and Mamluk elites. From the eleventh century the emphasis in secular architecture is on military or quasi-military architecture (castles, forts and khans as described above). Furthermore, in the highlands stone-built domestic structures, often of Roman date, show continuity of use from earlier periods, with superimposed floors and internal modifications to the structures the only evidence for ongoing occupation. Better preserved is the domestic and industrial architecture of the Jordan Valley. Construction was widespread due to a prosperous agricultural economy, while at village sites the use of unbaked brick and the frequency of earthquakes have resulted in the preservation of superimposed levels of domestic architecture.

The few sites with reported Fatimid–Saljuq domestic occupation indicate smooth continuity from the Abbasid period; structures were modified or rebuilt, depending on requirements. As described earlier in this chapter, the central monument of Islamic Aylah was redesigned in the Fatimid period as an aristocratic residence, featuring a central courtyard with a porch and eight rooms (Whitcomb 1988b). Similarly on the Amman Citadel the Umayyad Palace, including the Reception Hall, was extensively converted into dwellings and the nearby stone houses of Umayyad and Abbasid construction were substantially modified before their destruction in the mid-eleventh century (Northedge 1992: 159 and above).

The improved economic environment after the expulsion of the Crusaders had a deep but varied impact on a new generation of domestic architecture in the Ayyubid and Mamluk periods. In many places, especially in the uplands, the erection of completely new houses was unnecessary, as existing stone structures simply continued to be used and, when required, were altered to meet domestic requirements. The reutilization of architectural resources is clear from work at Khirbat Faris. Structures

excavated in the House 2 area show an unbroken sequence of occupation, represented by a series of surfaces, through the twelfth–thirteenth centuries until perhaps as late as the sixteenth century (McQuitty and Falkner 1993). This sequence continued seamlessly from earlier Fatimid and Saljuq levels. Yet between about the eighth and nineteenth centuries no major construction work was undertaken as existing structures, when re-roofed and given new floors, made perfectly adequate quarters. While investigations at other upland sites do not match the fine detail characteristic of the Khirbat Faris work, instances of existing architecture being continuously used or reutilized in the Ayyubid and Mamluk periods were recorded at Bayt Ras, Amman, Umm Quttayn (after a proposed hiatus from the mid-eighth century), Umm Dananir, Qastal and Udhruh. Of particular interest are the reoccupied sites of Balua, Lahun and Arair in middle Jordan, where Mamluk villages were constructed within, and by reusing elements from, the derelict Iron Age houses.

Surveys and excavations have turned up evidence for new Ayyubid and Mamluk domestic architecture at a number of sites, for instance Gharandal, Nakhal, Hisban, Dhiban and Khirbat Ayn Janin. However, detailed information is scarce as sites with thick Islamic deposits have been assiduously avoided in the past, and most discoveries have been incidental to wider research programs. Consequently, the archaeological evidence may favour sites with continuous or resettled histories, and overlook developments and innovations in the domestic architecture of new establishments. At Dhiban, part of a large house and other structures were uncovered (Tushingham 1972: 83–84). The house, made from reused stone, comprised a courtyard and large rooms (c. 6 x 7 m), each spanned with closely spaced transverse arches. Bins, ovens and a cistern were found in associated occupation levels. However elsewhere at Dhiban, pre-existing structures, obviously still extant at the time, were converted into dwellings. New work has revealed more evidence for Mamluk occupation at Dhiban, confirming that the site was an important settlement in the period. At the multi-period sites of Gharandal and Nakhal, domestic structures were built within the remains of Byzantine churches as well as in other areas. The Gharandal structures, part of a larger settlement, incorporated existing walls built in a continuous sequence from the ninth century when the ecclesiastical function of the church had apparently ceased. Well reported are the thick Mamluk strata at Hisban (Str. 3, 1260–1400 CE; Str. 2, 1400–1456 CE. A housing quarter was excavated to the west of the acropolis complex (de Vries 1994: 161–165), revealing stone structures, haphazardly built on a freshly cut terrace, with each unit typically consisting of a number of originally vaulted rooms around a court. Excavation of the Islamic-period structures below the citadel has been recommenced by Walker as part of the new work at the site. Many outlying sites with Ayyubid and Mamluk occupation (52, or 35% of all sites) were located as part of the Hisban regional survey, identifying a distinctive village architecture characterized by arches, vaulted buildings semi-subterranean rooms and caves (Ibach 1987: 191–194), similar to that at Khirbat Faris.

Differences in domestic architectural styles to those in the uplands can be observed in the Jordan Valley. A major variation was in the building materials utilized, with most houses on the valley floor being made of sun-dried mud brick, not stone (which is scarce in the valley), during the middle Islamic period. Where necessary, houses were replaced as they became derelict or collapsed, resulting in deep, stratigraphically-distinct sites made up of a long sequence of surfaces and mud brick collapse, as uncovered at Tall Abu Qadan and Tall Abu Sarbut, both village sites near Tall Dayr Alla (Franken and Kalsbeek 1975; Haas, LaGro, *et al.* 1992). At Tall Abu Sarbut, walls of mud bricks were built on foundations of field stones before both the walls and floor were covered with a yellowish plaster.

Overall, domestic constructions of the Ayyubid and Mamluk periods were basic and practical, representing personal undertakings rather than state or community projects. Houses were generally one to three adjacent single-storeyed rooms with independent doorways to a common walled courtyard. In stone-built houses transverse arches were employed in larger rooms to support the roof. Mud brick rooms were generally small enough to be bridged by wood beams, and while domes could have been employed, the surviving walls do not appear thick enough.

Surviving public architecture in an urban context is rare for middle Islamic Jordan as most of the important sites, being major centres in modern Jordan (e.g. Salt, Karak), have undergone considerable urban renewal especially in the last half century, and the evidence is lost or hidden. The written sources record the construction of a mosque, bath, khan, hospital and *madrasah* (school) at Karak besides the palace (Brown 1989b). Similarly at Hisban, the capital of the Balqa region for a time in the Mamluk period, the urban accruements of a palace, mosque khan and bath are attested (de Vries 1986; Walker 2003a; 2003b; 2004). The bath, excavated in 1973 by Van Eldreren, is a modest 14.5 x 4.0 to 5.5 m, constructed of stone and originally roofed with barrel vaults. The layout consisted of an entry hall, a dressing room with storage niches and two elevated platforms where bathers could rest, a lateral transitional corridor to the bath room with a rest bench, and the bathing room with a water tank, benches either side and a heated floor. Beyond and not accessible from the bath were the water tanks above a furnace, reached by way of a service room. The Hisban bath is very similar in layout to the Hammam al-Ayn in Jerusalem, although on a smaller scale. The Hammam al-Ayn, a typi-

cal Mamluk public bathhouse (*hammam*), forms part of the large *Suq al-Qattanin* (Market of the Cotton Merchants) complex west of the Haram al-Sharif, which was built in 1336–1337 CE during the sultanate of Nasir Muhammad (Burgoyne 1987: 273–298). However, the bath itself appears to have been built a little earlier, as it was in existence by 1330 CE. The Hammam al-Ayn begins with an architecturally appealing change-room featuring a domed roof, central octagonal fountain and raised platforms in pointed-arched recesses, very similar to (although grander than) the dressing room at Hisban. A doorway, as at Hisban, gives entrance to a transverse corridor but (properly) with a small cold room at the far end, not simply a bench. From the corridor a doorway leads directly into the warm and then hot rooms, unusually six in number; at Hisban the functions of these rooms were condensed into a single hot room. While considerably smaller than Hammam al-Ayn, the Hisban bathhouse conforms to a standard early Mamluk type and probably dates to sometime in the fourteenth century.

One significant architectural legacy of the economic restructuring of rural post-Crusader Jordan was the erection of water mills for sugar cane crushing and the grinding of grain. In the face of declining agricultural production in fourteenth and fifteenth century Egypt, the Mamluk elite directly invested in developing the resources of the Jordan Valley including the general utilization of water energy through the construction of mills (Abu Dalu 1995; Greene 1995; McQuitty 1995; Rogan 1995; Walker 2004). Along the edge of the many *wadi*s (valleys) that open out into the east bank of the Jordan Valley stand the ruins of numerous stone-built mills, but their construction dates are problematic. While a Mamluk date can be (and often is) plausibly offered for the widespread construction of water-driven mills in the Jordan Valley, many of the mills as they exist today appear to be substantially mid-nineteenth to early twentieth century, in some (perhaps many) instances the result of major restorations of derelict Mamluk-period mills. For instance, ten water mills were identified along the upper Wadi Hisban during the Hesban Regional Survey, but Ayyubid/Mamluk pottery was found at only one of these (Ibach 1987: 194). Numerous mills were located during the East Jordan Valley Survey in 1975, "often with millstones *in situ* and often associated with large quantities of "sugar pots" (Ibrahim, Sauer, *et al.* 1976: 182–183, 202–203). However, the excavation of a horizontal-wheel flour mill in the fast-flowing Wadi Jirm near Tabaqat Fahl produced a firm late Ottoman date with no evidence of an earlier Mamluk-period structure or occupation. Nevertheless, mills are widely reported in the written sources for the Mamluk period and earlier, specifically Fatimid, times. The earlier Islamic mills were, perhaps, mostly of the vertical wheel variety, for at Tabaqat Fahl a heavy pottery vase, although recovered from the mid-eighth century deposits, was originally intended for roping to a vertical water wheel (Walmsley 1982: 149, pl. 145.4).

The Economy, Trade, Pilgrimage and Routes

The dearth of archaeological data on the Fatimid and Saljuq periods in Jordan is especially apparent when attempting to describe economic activity in the tenth and eleventh centuries. The prevailing view for the highlands, typified by the conclusions of the Heshbon Expedition (LaBianca 1990: 218), is for a shift to "low intensity configuration" of land use in the Abbasid period—that is, from plow agriculture to pastoral activities—and a "retreat" from a sedentary lifestyle to nomadism by the Fatimid and Saljuq periods. However, this view does not rest comfortably with the textual evidence, particularly as the tenth century geographers Ibn Hawqal and al-Maqdisi depict Jordan as agriculturally productive. North Jordan was populated with villages producing olives, honey and fruits especially grapes, the Balqa was an area of villages, fields and water mills with grain, fruit and honey as the main produce, the Maab region was renowned for its grapes and especially almonds, while Jibal and Sharah in the south were also prosperous. These sources further remark upon the cultivation of tropical crops, specifically dates, indigo, rice and bananas, in the Jordan Valley. Both writers also note that around Amman and further south the herding of sheep and goats played a significant role in the economy. As mentioned earlier, the Crusader sources of the early twelfth century likewise describe Jordan as widely settled with villages. The crops are unchanged: grain, grapes (for wine), dates, olives and oil, again with sheep and goat herding. Just before the Muslim reconquest of south Jordan Ibn Jubayr (1952: 301) could still describe the Karak region as "the choicest part of the land… it being said that the number of villages reaches four hundred." Together, the tenth century Islamic geographies and the twelfth century Crusader-period sources depict Jordan as inhabited by a mixed settled and nomadic population engaged in mutually beneficial agricultural and pastoral activities.

The rise of the Fatimid dynasty in Egypt stimulated the Indian Ocean trade, with ships reaching as far as China, Sumatra and Java (Chaudhuri 1985: 34–62; Chaudhuri 1990). Ceramic evidence from Fustat indicates that the volume of Red Sea trade to China increased markedly after about 1000 CE (Scanlon 1970). At this time Aylah, strategically positioned at the eastern head of the Red Sea, was described by al-Maqdisi as Palestine's port on the "Chinese Sea," and the excavations of Donald Whitcomb have vividly illustrated the international outlook of the town in the Fatimid period. Of particular note is the glazed pottery from the Pavilion Building (Whitcomb 1988b). Two large blue-green jars with barbotine decoration seemingly originated from Basra in southern Iraq (Figure 16.11.5), lustre wares came from Iraq and perhaps Egypt, while fine celadons and porcelains originated in China. A hoard of 32 gold *dinars* of the early eleventh century and a collection of glass and bronze weights further attest the importance of the Indian Ocean and Far East trade to Fatimid Aylah. In addition to Palestine, land routes from Aylah linked Udhruh, Muan, Maab and Amman to the Red Sea trade networks.

In part, the Crusader occupation of Wadi Musa and Aylah was an attempt by Baldwin I to gain some control over the Red Sea trade, simultaneously restricting Fatimid domination and weakening the economic benefits to Egypt. Under Reynald, Lord of Karak, raiding reached the Holy Cities of the Hijaz, but in general Crusader activity in the Red Sea was limited and ended altogether with the recovery of south Jordan by Salah al-Din in 1188 CE. However, within the Crusader realms there was a flourishing trade in agricultural produce and minerals. Wheat, oil, wine, dates, sugar, bitumen and salt in particular were shipped in boats across the Dead Sea from the Southern Ghor and the highlands of Oultrejourdain to Jericho and Jerusalem (Johns 1994: 10–14). Annual fairs were held in the Sawad and Karak, while shipping and caravan traffic was subject to taxes.

The return of all Jordan to Islamic hegemony and its economic reintegration into the market systems of Damascus and Cairo revived the many traditional agricultural practices temporarily disrupted, but clearly not completely destroyed, by the political and social partitioning of Jordan in the Crusader period. The main destructive factor was the protracted period of warfare between Salah al-Din and Reynald, which appears to have inflicted considerable damage on the village economy of south Jordan (Johns 1994: 12–13). Conditions did not improve substantially until well into the thirteenth century. In the rural context, the return to normality resulted in the restoration of a village-based economy, founded upon conventional agricultural pursuits (grain, legumes and aboriculture), pastoral activities and a revival of cash crops, especially sugar and indigo. The produce was destined for the large urban markets such as Damascus, Cairo, and Ramlah, but also locally important centres for instance Karak, Salt, Hisban as well as other places, and for export to more distant locations.

Sugar cane cultivation was introduced to the Jordan Valley and coastal Palestine perhaps as early as the seventh century, and had become a major crop by the tenth century (Galloway 1989: 23–47; Watson 1983). Arab-Islamic society of the seventh and eighth centuries provided a favourable political and economic environment for the growth of the sugar industry. Irrigation technology, a requisite for water-thirsty cane, was improved and diffused throughout the Islamic realm, enforceable legal frameworks controlled the distribution of water, investment capital was plentiful to finance the expensive cane processing factories, and a burgeoning urban population—increasingly wealthy and sophisticated—was keen to adopt new tastes in food. After the expulsion of the Crusaders these factors re-emerged to promote a revival of the sugar industry, which flourished until the mid to late fourteenth century. Arabic sources and travel accounts concur that cane was cultivated in the Jordan Valley wherever water was available in copious quantities, including east and south of the Dead Sea (Ashtor 1981: 92–93). Karaki sugar was highly regarded in Europe. The availability of labour was a critical factor, as the process of obtaining sugar from the cane was laborious, inefficient and costly (Galloway 1989: 37–40). The juice was extracted by milling and pressing, usually through a combination of both techniques, which required the cane to be cut into short lengths. Mill technology differed little from that used to grind wheat or extract liquids from olives or grapes. Two types of mills were used in Palestine and Jordan: the upper rotating stone variety with either a flat or conical millstone, and the "edge-runner" in which a vertically fixed round stone was rolled on a pivot in a circle over the cane. They were powered by flowing water, animals or humans. Once extracted, the juice was boiled to thicken it, and then poured into thick pottery cones to crystallize. The cones were set upon bag-shaped jars to collect molasses. Repeated boiling improved the quality of the sugar, but consumed great quantities of fuel. Olive waste, used in earlier times for firing pottery kilns, was an obvious source.

Archaeological evidence for the sugar industry in the Southern Ghor has been identified through regional surveys and site excavations (reviewed in Kareem 2000: 13–16; see also Photos-Jones, Politis, *et al.* 2002). Sherds from sugar cones and jars, made in a distinctly heavy ceramic, are common discoveries at the numerous Mamluk-period sites in the Southern Ghor. The jars frequently turn up on sites in the highlands of Jordan, and provide evidence of the movement of agricultural produce from the Southern Ghor to places in the uplands such as Hisban (Walker 2003a: 447–451). As mentioned earlier, numerous stone-built mills have been identified along the east bank extending south of the Dead Sea, although the problems surrounding the precise dating of these mills have not yet been resolved.

The decline of the Mamluk sugar industry in the Jordan Valley and the rest of Syria-Palestine was just as sudden and complex as its thirteenth century resurgence (Ashtor 1981; Walker 2003b: 248–449; Walker 2004). A fall off in cultivation can be detected in the later fourteenth century, but by the sixteenth century the sugar industry had disappeared. The principal factors behind the failure were economic and technological. The industry was labour and energy intensive and became increasingly expensive to operate following a major decline in the population, perhaps by a third, due to a series of plagues and warfare during the fourteenth and fifteenth centuries. In addi-

tion, the policies of the Mamluk elite perpetuated inefficiencies and corruption, while mills were not maintained nor technologies improved due to the prohibitive costs involved (Rogan 1995). The arrival of cheap and better sugar from the Americas in the sixteenth century precipitated the final collapse.

Other primary and secondary industries in Jordan flourished under the direct or indirect patronage of the Mamluk elites. The horses, camels and sheep of the Karak region were highly prized in Cairo for transport, wool and meat (Irwin 1986: 185–186). Iron was mined and smelted at Mugharat Wardah in the Ajlun Mountains throughout the Ayyubid and Mamluk periods. Alongside the mine smelting furnaces, an ore roasting oven, slag and ash were identified and dateable by the associated pottery (Coughenour 1989). Copper and perhaps iron mining and smelting was resumed at Wadi Faynan in the Arabah, and copper finger and earrings were commonly worn for personal adornment. Many local industries flourished at a village level. For instance glass may have been manufactured into bracelets and other items at Tall Dayr Alla in the Jordan Valley and cottage potting industries, producing the ubiquitous Hand Made Geometric Painted Ware (see below), must have been a feature of every village of note. Unquestionably, other village industries such as weaving, woodworking, basketry and mat making would have equally prospered, but these are rarely recorded as they are archaeologically "invisible" and were of no great interest to scholars or travellers.

A major boost to the local economy would have been the passage of the annual pilgrimage to the Holy City of Makkah in the Hijaz. The pilgrimage route changed a number of times during the period under consideration, mostly in response to the Crusader occupation of south Jordan in the eleventh century, hence different centres benefited at different times. During the Fatimid period, the path followed a set route through the *badiyah* (eastern steppe lands) of Jordan, and is described in some detail in the geographical accounts especially al-Maqdisi (described in Musil 1926: 326–331, Appendix 15; Musil 1927: 516–520). Going southwards from Adhriat (Deraa in Syria), Zarqa was reached after a day, then another day lead to the major assembly point of Amman, where pilgrims from surrounding districts could join the caravan. After Amman, two unspecified watering places (most likely Qatranah and Hisa) were passed to reach Muan (Maan) where provisions could be obtained, after which the route continued south to Tabuk and the Hijaz.

The *badiyah* route continued in use during the Crusader occupation of Jordan, but while this route avoided Crusader territory it still left the caravans liable to attack. In 1180 CE a caravan of merchants was looted on its way to Makkah by Reynald de Châtillon, Lord of Karak. More seriously, in 1186 CE merchants and pilgrims were attacked and summarily executed or captured in blatant violation of a truce with Salah al-Din. All protestations were ignored, leading Salah al-Din to revive the *jihad* against the Crusaders, and which saw victory—and the immediate execution of Reynald—within the year (Maalouf 1984: 186–194).

The prolonged struggle between the Crusaders and Muslims of Syria and Egypt brought to prominence the fortress towns of Jordan, especially Karak. By the Mamluk period Karak served as a major stop for the Damascene pilgrimage before entering the more physically challenging and desertous territory to the south. Two sources of the fourteenth century present a comparatively detailed picture of the route and conditions on the journey (Abu'l-Fida 1983; Ibn Battuta 1958; Peters 1994: 79–86). Ibn Battuta gives a full account of the route he followed in 1326 CE (Figure 16.3). From Damascus the caravan made two stops before reaching Busra in the Hauran, where a stop of four nights allowed late comers to catch up and the pilgrims to buy provisions. From Busra the caravan travelled to the pool at Ziza. The most likely route for the caravan was through Zarqa, as suggested by the construction of a small fort in the thirteenth century (described above). Amman, seemingly not repopulated to any major extent since Crusader times, held no attraction so was bypassed. From Ziza, where there was also a Mamluk fort (above), the caravan continued to Lajjun, where water was plentiful, and then reached Karak. After a stop of four days at Karak, the pilgrims set out for Maan, almost certainly by way of Hisa where there was a toll station, and then Tabuk. The brief account of Abu'l-Fida shows that the wealthy travelled by horseback to Karak, sending their baggage and servants in advance, and from there went by camel (Abu'l-Fida 1983: 65). The Mamluk caravans were always large. In 1432 CE some 3,000 camels returned to Damascus; in 1503 CE, 35,000 camels, 40,000 people and a guard of 60 Mamluks set out from the same city (Peters 1994: 80–85). The figures would seem to be inaccurate guesses, but nevertheless reveal the considerable size of the annual pilgrimage.

Other roads transversed Jordan, linking the settlements on the Hajj route to places to the west and south. In the Fatimid period a major road joined Amman with Jerusalem by way of Hisban, Bayt Ram and Jericho. A second route from Amman ran down the highland range to Maab, probably by way of Hisban, and then to Zughar in the Wadi Arabah. From here the road travelled down the Wadi Arabah through Ghamr (where another road left to Ramlah), Ayn Gharandal and Ghadhian to Aylah. From Zughar, a second road ascended the scarp to Udhruh and Muan, probably by way of Wadi Musa. As Ibn Jubayr (1952: 300–301) makes clear, roads remained open despite warfare between the Muslims and Crusaders, with taxes being widely imposed on travellers by both sides. An important route ran from Busra and Adhriat to Tiberias and Safad by way of Bayt Ras and Jadar (Umm Qays), and both Crusader and Muslim armies marched along this road in the battle for Tiberias and the north Jordan Valley (Mershen and Knauf 1988: 132–136). Later, a toll station was placed in the village of Jadar, resulting in a name change to *mkis* (from which originates the Umm Qays of today).

The Ayyubid and especially Mamluk road system was extensive in its coverage, consisting of the official *barid* (postal service) roads, which doubled as trade routes and were usually well maintained, and a network of connecting routes. The Darb Quful, mentioned earlier, crossed into north Jordan from Baysan at Jisr Majamia, and continued eastwards through Qusayr (North Shunah) before ascending the scarp to Irbid. As an official state road the Darb Quful remained popular until the late fifteenth century, when Safad rose to prominence and the northern crossing at Jisr Binat Yaqub gained greater popularity. Another important road was the southern route from Cairo to Shawbak and Karak, transversed by Baybars in June, 1276 CE in only eleven days (Zayadine 1985). The first five days were spent crossing the Sinai to Wadi Musa (Petra), entering from the Wadi Arabah. Once watered, he continued onto Shawbak and Karak, where a rebellion was suppressed. From Karak, the link to Damascus followed the Hajj route through Ziza and Zarqa, while another route crossed at Zughar to Khalil (Hebron) and Jerusalem. A third route ran up the mountain range between Dhiban, Hisban (link to Jericho and Jerusalem), Salt, Ajlun (link to Nablus) and Irbid, finally joining the Darb Quful at Umm Qays. Further east a circuit route through the *badiyah* joined Petra and Aqabah with Maan, then to Bayir and Azraq (link to Zarqa), and northwards to the Hauran. As already mentioned, most of these strategically placed nodules in the communications network were progressively fortified in Ayyubid and Mamluk times. Other roads crossed between the major routes and centres and very possibly many were restored in the Mamluk period and marked out with edging stones. Frequently, one suspects, these roads are mistakenly classified as Roman constructs, especially as many would have traced old Roman routes

Material Culture

At first glance, the more than five hundred years between the late tenth century and the start of sixteenth century coincided with significant changes in the material culture of Jordan, in keeping with neighbouring Palestine and Syria. These changes have often been seen as indicative of, and explained by, broader trends in the socio-economic regime of Islamic Jordan. The view has been largely negative: the collapse of urban life, political disintegration, external domination, the end of specialized manufacturing industries (wheel-thrown pottery, for instance), a short rural boom especially in the Jordan Valley, and a rustication of the population. Many of these judgements were ostensibly supported by an assessment of the relative worth of wheel-made and hand-made ceramics, based on the assumption that the latter—of coarser fabric and soft firing—were definitely inferior. The hand made wares were interpreted as representative of small, isolated communities surviving at little more than a subsistence level, an easy if misleading imagining. Likewise, the large and heavy bowls and jars used in the sugar industry came to portray equally disadvantaged migrant labour in the cane fields of the Jordan Valley.

The material culture of middle Islamic Jordan clearly did experience major shifts in the tenth to sixteenth centuries, including a rise in the popularity of hand made wares, especially hand made geometrically painted wares (or HMGPW), and the ubiquitous appearance of sugar pots in the Jordan Valley, but also the proliferation of local and imported glazed wares. A re-evaluation of all the material, not simply ceramics (or one class of ceramics), presents a more complicated scenario based on the exploration of new economic opportunities, the prescription of socio-political identities, and the status of elites in middle Islamic Jordan.

The repertoire of surviving material finds from middle Islamic sites in Jordan is standard for a historical period, and includes ceramics, glass, metals (including coins), stone artefacts including architectural decoration, and ivory or bone. The characteristics of each group will be summarized before entering into discussion on the socio-economic implications of the material.

Ceramics

As numerous authors have already observed, pottery traditions are mostly unaffected by political events and dynastic changes. Other factors, social and economic, promoted change, and thus ceramics can be a valuable tool for the historian as they reflect developments over a wide cross-section of society, especially the otherwise invisible lower socio-economic groups (Walmsley 1997). In this necessarily brief treatment of middle Islamic pottery from Jordan, the material will be classified by type: plain and decorated wheel made, mould made, glazed (wheel and mould made), and hand made wares including HMGPW. The development of each type will be traced over time with the intention of avoiding dynastic labels for particularly distinctive ceramic types. The treatment will largely concentrate on Jordanian material, and the referenced reports should be consulted if further information is required on dates and parallels from Palestine and Syria.

Pottery Dated to the Eleventh to Early Twelfth Century

A reliable starting point for eleventh century pottery can be found in the excavations at Amman Citadel and Aqabah. On the Citadel of Amman, excavations by C.-M. Bennett of two buildings in Area C recovered a limited range of ceramics from an eleventh century destruction at the end of Stratum III, while in a house in Area B an abandonment deposit, also of Phase III date, and a pit produced further eleventh century material (Northedge 1984: 275–281; Northedge 1992: 143–147, figs 137, 141, 150–151). The pottery is largely utilitarian, and features:

- cooking jars in a red fabric with broad strap handles, often with applied clay lugs to body and a glazed interior (Figure 16.10.1);
- moulded "arcade" lamps with bunched grape decoration (Figure 16.10.2).
- glazed bowls, slipped with yellow, blue and green glaze (Figure 16.10.3);
- plain "earthenwares," a general grouping of wheel made jars and bowls in a reddish-yellow to light brown fabric, mostly undecorated although one example has white painted wavy lines (Figure 16.10.4);
- large hand-made, thick-rimmed basins and storage jars with loop handles, fired light-brown to reddish-yellow and sometimes decorated with combing and thumb impressions (Figure 16.10.5);
- "bag-shaped" jars (*zirs*), light-brown fabric with body-combing (Figure 16.10.6);
- thin-bodied, cream-ware jars featuring flaring necks and turban handles (for this ware in Palestine and Jordan see: Magness 1997; Walmsley 2001);
- *Kerbschnitt* (engraved) bowls;
- coarse handmade ware of coil manufacture.

As Northedge observes, the corpus shows considerable continuity from the preceding Stratum IVb (Abbasid); similarly, it represents a development of the tenth century material recovered at Pella (Walmsley 1991; 1995). Noticeably different are the glazed cooking pots and the first appearance of a course handmade ware. Northedge dates this corpus to the end of Stratum III, which he suggests was caused by the earthquake of 1068 CE, although elements of the corpus may suggest a date at the start of the twelfth century. Hence, rather than an earthquake destruction, the end of this phase may represent the evacuation of Saljuq forces from Amman under Crusader pressure.

The pottery from the Pavilion Building at Aqabah ranges from plain to glazed wares of local and imported origin (Whitcomb 1988b). Like the Amman Citadel material, the Pavilion Building corpus may spill over into the early twelfth century, but the absence of distinctive twelfth century Chinese imports suggests a mostly eleventh century date, with possibly some tenth century material persisting. Major varieties include:

- glazed monochrome and polychrome lustre ware bowls of Iraqi or Egyptian manufacture (Figures 16.11.1, 16.11.3);

Figure 16.10 Amman Citadel: pottery of the second half of the eleventh century. 1: red ware cooking jar; 2: moulded lamp with grape decoration; 3: white-slipped bowl with blue-green glaze; 4: red fabric jar with white paint; 5: pale brown storage jar; 6: light brown bag jar (based on Northedge 1992, figures 137, 141, 150).

- monochrome, splash-decorated, Fayyumi and sgraffiato glazed bowls of Iraqi, Egyptian north Syrian and local manufacture (Figure 16.11.2);

- Chinese celadons and porcelains, most commonly fine Qingbai porcelains including comb decorated variety (Figure 16.11.4);

- large "Arab-Sasanid" jars, with incised and applied decoration and a heavy blue-green glaze (Figure 16.11.5);

- common earthenwares, including jars, juglets and bowls in red to orange-red and tan fabric and with instances of combed and incised decoration (Figures 16.11.6, 16.11.8–11);

- handmade bowls, basins, cups and jars with sand temper (no chaff), fired buff, orange to grey and sometimes decorated with red paint (Figure 16.11.7);

- large storage jars with fattened rims and loop handles in a red to red-orange gritty fabric, sometimes with applied decoration below neck (similar to the Citadel types);

It needs to be noted that most of the recovered pottery was common earthenwares (around 60% of the count). Glazed wares were always rarer (about 10%), while the coarse handmade wares only become common in the last period.

Another significant change at Aqabah in the eleventh century was the advent of two quite different types of lamps. Islamic ceramic lamps in Jordan were traditionally almond-shaped with moulded decoration of arcades, vine tendrils, grape bunches, animals and palmettes, as with the Amman Citadel example (Figure 16.10.2). Glazed examples are also known (Figure 16.12.1). Clearly different in both shape and manufacture are the two new eleventh century forms at Aqabah. The first had a wheel-made enclosed bowl with a deep channel spout, raised loop handle and a green or yellow glaze (Figure 16.12.2). The form was most likely of Egyptian origin, with parallels at Fustat. The second type, first attested in the later eleventh century, was the saucer lamp, also wheel made with a loop handle and central reservoir (Figure 16.12.3). Both types were to develop further in the following centuries; most notably, the central reservoir of the saucer lamp diminished in size to almost vestigial proportions by the fifteenth century.

The excavations on the Amman Citadel and at Aqabah have produced a reliable ceramic horizon for Jordan datable to the eleventh century with, perhaps, elements from the start of the twelfth century. The material recovered ranged from imported and local glazed wares to utilitarian storage vessels and gritty-fabric cookers. At Aqabah new lamp types, conventionally considered Ayyubid-Mamluk in date, were in circulation, while at both sites coarse handmade wares had made an appearance. Some of the handmade pottery was decorated with paint, and may have been precursors for the ubiquitous Hand Made Geometric Painted Wares of the thirteenth to fourteenth centuries and later. Fortunately, a twelfth century link has now been recognized that confirms this suggestion.

Pottery Dated to the Twelfth and Early Thirteenth Century

Excavations in the Crusader castles of Wuayrah and Shawbak have identified a limited corpus of twelfth to early thirteenth century pottery for Jordan, but overall this period is poorly represented. In a preliminary treatment of the ceramics from the 1987 excavations at Wuayrah, Brown (1987) noted the preponderance of handmade wares with only a few wheel-thrown *zirs* and glazed bowls. In the earlier (Crusader, twelfth century) phase the handmade coarse wares were decorated with linear designs and dots in red paint, while in Phase II (Ayyubid, late twelfth to early thirteenth century) the linear-painted ware persisted but geometric painting in red to grey was more prevalent. Wheel-made bowls glazed in yellow and green, common in later assemblages (below), first appeared in Brown's Phase II. More recent excavations at Wuayrah by Vannini and Tonghini (1997) confirmed the predominance of handmade wares, but without being able to duplicate the sequence from linear to geometric painted. However, they did observe that a monopoly of north Syrian frit-wares in Phase III (Crusader occupation levels of the later twelfth century) gave way to monochrome glazed slipped-wares by Phase IV (Ayyubid). Overall, glazed wares constituted a small percentage of recovered pottery. Unglazed pottery made on a wheel was also attested, including a cream ware with stamped decoration from Phase IV. One interesting feature of the twelfth century pottery from Wuayrah is its overwhelmingly local character. According to Brown (1987: 284), there was "absolutely nothing specifically Crusader" about the pottery corpus recovered at Wuayrah, whereas Vannini and Tonghini (1997: 382) recognized a Crusader presence in the Phase III fritwares, which they believed were of north Syrian origin.

At Shawbak castle, Brown (1988) was again able to identify a discrete twelfth to early thirteenth century date for early handmade coarse-wares in the constructional Phase I of the Ayyubid Palace complex. The coarse-wares included linear-painted types, often with criss-cross patterns (Figure 16.12.4–13). The assemblage also contained a few examples of HMGPW and monochrome glazed, as would be expected of a corpus that ran into the thirteenth century. By Phase III (Mamluk, fourteenth to fifteenth centuries) monochrome glazed bowls, underglazed painted, celadons, wheel-thrown cream wares and HMGPW had become typical (see below).

Admittedly, the twelfth and early thirteenth century pottery groups from Wuayrah and Shawbak are limited in size, and caution must be exercised in their use. However, support for Brown's thesis of an early series of hand made

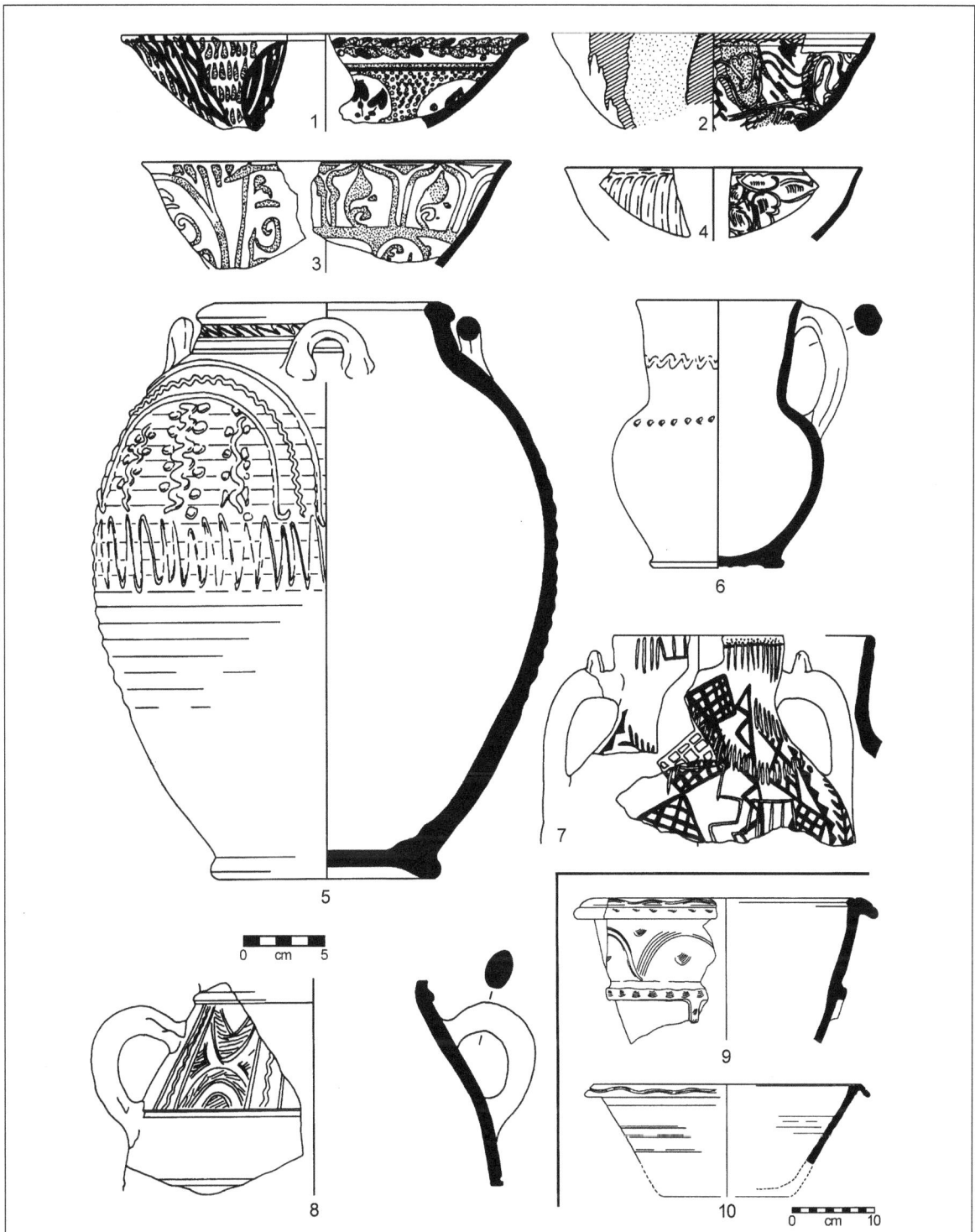

Figure 16.11 Aylah: pottery of the eleventh century from the Pavilion Building. 1, 3: glazed polychrome lustre ware bowls; 2: polychrome glazed sgraffiato bowl; 4: Qingbai porcelain bowl; 5: blue-green glazed jar with applied and incised decoration; 6: buff-coloured incised juglet; 7: black painted and incised handmade jar; 8: red to buff-coloured jar with incised decoration; 9–10: buff-orange to cream incised bowls, 10 with dark green glaze on interior (based on Whitcomb 1988b).

coarse wares including linear red painting comes from the excavations at Khirbat Faris, where a similar handmade pottery painted in red line and dot patterns was recovered in a ninth to twelfth century context (Falkner in McQuitty and Falkner 1993: 53–54). Similarly, an analysis of the middle Islamic pottery from excavations at Gharandal, near Tafilah, has identified painted and unpainted precursors for HMGPW (Walmsley and Grey 2001). The Gharandal material is low-fired, thin-walled and heavily tempered with chaff, unlike that from Aqabah where no chaff but much sand was used. The Gharandal painted examples were decorated with straight, wavy and zigzag red lines. These initial impressions suggest the first handmade wares exhibited considerable local variability in fabric and decoration between the eleventh and early thirteenth century, whereas by the fourteenth century HMGPW had, in relative terms, attained a much greater degree of regional standardization. Generally, the extent of ceramic variability in the eleventh–thirteenth centuries, and hence the absence of an easily identified corpus, would account for the poor showing of these centuries in regional surveys. Understandably the tendency has been to lump the early coarse wares into the Mamluk, or even Ottoman, periods, thereby greatly under-representing over two centuries of settlement in Jordan. The extent of the error is demonstrated by a reconsideration of the stratigraphy and pottery from a number of sites in Jordan, for instance Dhiban and Tall Abu Qadan, in which strata and material of the eleventh–thirteenth centuries can be successfully identified.

Farther north at Tall Hisban, a discrete Ayyubid (c. 1174–1263 CE) corpus was identified and dated through coin evidence by J. Sauer (1994: 268–270). HMGPW was "abundant" and decorated with set designs in dark purplish red and brown paint. Glazed wares were rarer, and included glazed cookers. No earlier twelfth century coarse handmade wares could be identified, and both the Tall Hisban coins and the Wuayrah and Shawbak pottery would suggest that Sauer's Ayyubid corpus is, rather, mostly mid-thirteenth century and after. Finally, excavations at Rujm Kursi have produced three early thirteenth century lamps from a coin-dated context. They were handmade in two parts from a coarse gritty fabric, and feature a central filling hole, handle and pierced wick hole.

Pottery Dated Between the Later Thirteenth and Fifteenth centuries

The equation between certain pottery types and Mamluk-period occupation in Jordan has almost exclusively concentrated on two distinct varieties: slipped wheel-made bowls supporting a yellow or green glaze and, more usually, HMGPW. They have the advantage of being easily identified during surveys and are a relatively common feature of the archaeological landscape in Jordan, in that

they represent the last major pre-modern phase in the occupation of many sites. As with earlier periods the material is generally poorly published and dating imprecise, and similarly this assessment of pottery from the later thirteenth to fifteenth centuries relies upon the more reliable reports.

The excavation of the mosque on the main mound at Tabaqat Fahl (Pella) produced a representative range of ceramics that can be dated, substantially on coin evidence, to the second half of the fourteenth and early fifteenth centuries (McPhillips 2001; Walmsley 1992b; 1998). The major pottery varieties identified were:

- Handmade geometric painted ware (HMGPW), slipped and sometimes burnished and liberally decorated with painted monochrome or bichrome geometric designs in dark red, purple and black. Jars, jugs, bowls and basins were the common shapes (Figure 16.12.14–18; Figure 16.13.1–2).
- Under-slipped glazed ware bowls, internally slipped or decorated with brush strokes and over-glazed with brilliant yellow or green glazes over a wheel-made bowl (Figure 16.13.3, 5–7).
- Sgraffiato ware, white slipped and incised with a yellow to green glaze (Figure 16.13.4).
- Under-glaze painted ware with very fine bichrome and polychrome painted designs under a clear glaze (Figure 16.13.8–9).
- Plain ware, wheel-made elongated jars and straight sided bowls in a soft, light yellow-brown to reddish-yellow ware and linked with the sugar industry (Figure 16.13.10–13).
- "Cooking pot" ware; coarse with numerous inclusions and used in the hand manufacture of large, splayed-necked cooking jars with solid handles in the shape of a pointed-ear (Figure 16.13.15–16).
- Thin-walled, painted ware, wheel-made and reddish-yellow to pink in colour with limestone grits, freely painted in reddish-brown to brown-black on the rim, handles and body.
- "Silhouette" ware, with black paint under turquoise blue or green glaze.

HMGPW, sugar pot ware and under-slipped glazed ware bowls, all seen as local products, formed the largest groups in the corpus. Only a few sherds of the last three glazed varieties, most likely imports from north Syria, were recovered. They are conventionally dated to the fourteenth and fifteenth century, which neatly complies with the numismatic evidence.

Also in the Jordan Valley, the neighbouring sites of Tall Abu Qadan and Tall Abu Sarbut produced large quantities of pottery of about the same date as the material from Tabaqat Fahl. At Tall Abu Qadan a long sequence

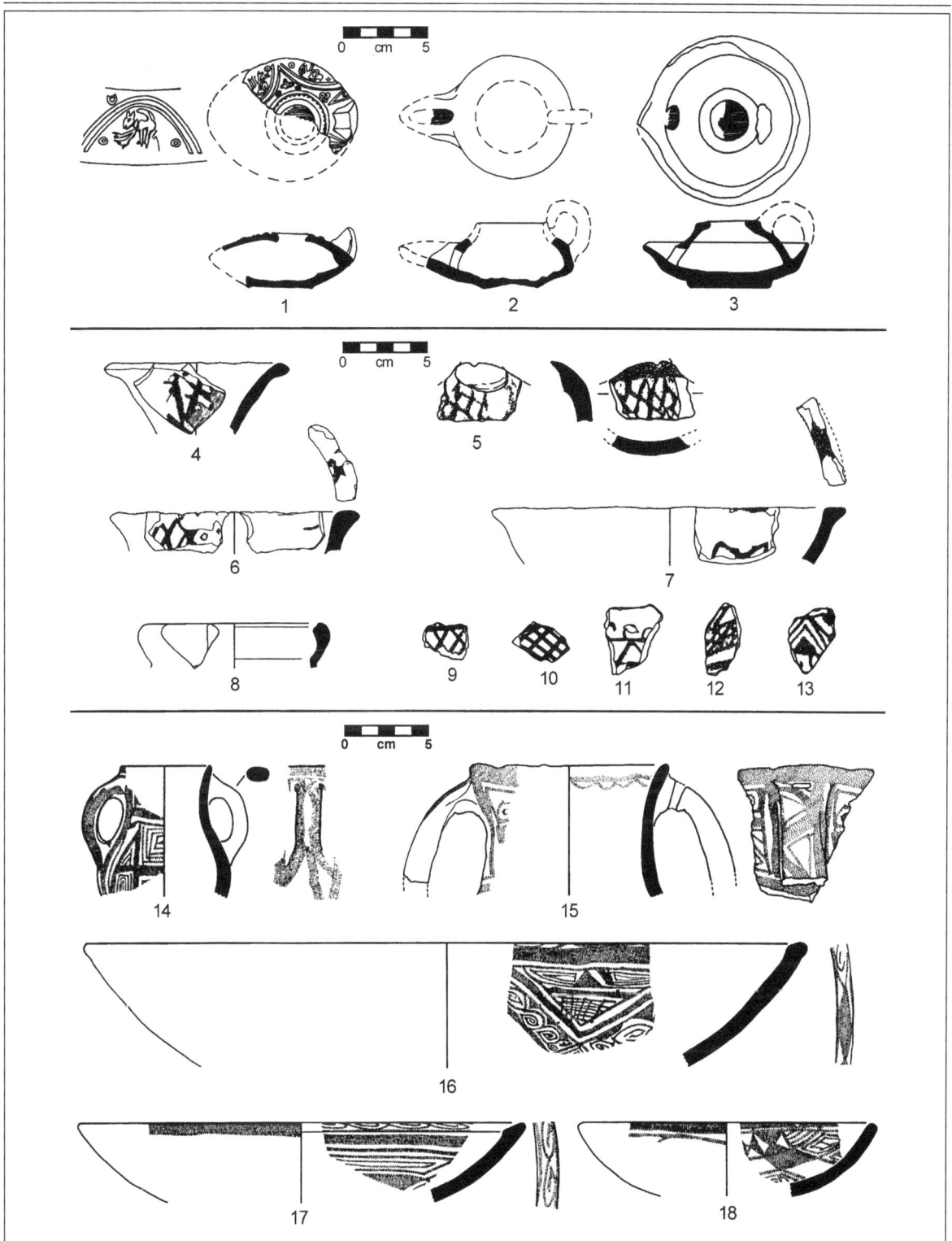

Figure 16.12 1–3: Aylah, lamps of the eleventh century (Whitcomb 1994); 4–13: Shawbak, handmade, red-painted coarse wares of the twelfth–early thirteenth century (Brown 1988); 14–18: Tabaqat Fahl (Pella), dark red to purplish painted jars and bowls in Hand Made Geometric Painted Ware of the second half of the fourteenth to fifteenth century (Walmsley 1992b).

Figure 16.13 Tabaqat Fahl, pottery of the second half of the fourteenth to fifteenth century: 1–2: HMGPW bowls; 3–7: green and yellow glazed bowls with brushed (3, 5) or full slip (6–7) and some sgraffiato (4); 8–9: bichrome and polychrome under-glaze painted wares; 10–13: light brown to reddish-yellow sugar pots; 14–16 heavy hand made coarse wares including cooking jars (Walmsley 1992b, supplemented with unpublished examples).

of thirteenth to fifteenth century pottery was recovered, although there are considerable problems with stratigraphy and dating (Franken and Kalsbeek 1975: 107–203; note the important review of Sauer 1976). The different pottery types as identified by Franken and Kalsbeek were as follows.

- HMGPW, found in profusion. It appeared in a developed form, typically with a burnished surface and decorated with care at first. Later forms were slipped and the decoration poorer.

- Glazed wares, predominantly slipped wheel-made bowls and including sgraffiato decoration. A major change in firing technology occurred in the fourteenth century when bowls were stacked right-side up (previously up-side down) in the kiln.

- Faience bowls decorated in blue and black.

- Hand-made cooking pots with large pierced handles.

- Sugar pots, both jars and bowls, mass produced in large kilns roughly five metres in height. This type of pottery was completely absent before Period 2.

- Red-firing wheel-made pottery, often with a salt bloom, used in the manufacture of cooking pots, bowls, jars and jugs, some of the latter with coarse and fine sieve necks and spouts.

- Light red, hard firing jars (equivalent to thin-walled, painted ware at Tabaqat Fahl).

- White wares, but very scarce (and perhaps remnants from earlier levels).

Franken considered HMGPW unrelated to the prevailing ceramic traditions in Islamic Jordan and Palestine, and decided upon a North African inspiration for the ware (Franken and Kalsbeek 1975: 213–222; Homès-Fredericq and Franken 1986: 239–244). His reasoning has not meet with wide acceptance, and the subsequent identification of eleventh and twelfth century precursors with linear decoration would argue that HMGPW was a local development. The volume of wheel made wares at Tall Abu Qadan were much less frequent than HMGPW, and were mostly confined to Phase 2 (which is more satisfactorily dated to the later thirteenth and fourteenth century). Franken also saw these thrown wares as sufficiently different as to indicate an independent tradition, but this view is likewise difficult to accept.

Few sites in the highlands have produced distinct later thirteenth to fifteenth century ceramics from stratigraphically sound and coin-datable levels. The most accessible material has come from Tall Hisban, Rujm Kursi, Khirbat Faris, the Karak Plateau Survey, Shawbak and, most interestingly from a socio-economic aspect, Karak. Based on the coin evidence, Sauer has differentiated two pottery groups dating to the later thirteenth and fourteenth century at Tall Hisban. These were labelled "Early Mamluk I" (EM I), dated c. 1263–1300 CE, and "Early Mamluk II" (EM II), c. 1300–1401 CE, and mostly originate from a well-stratified cistern (Sauer 1994: 270–273). In EM I, brown became the preferred paint colour on HMGPW, while glazed wares were more common. In EM II the paint had become darker brown or black and the pot surface lighter (light yellowish to greenish); glazed wares continued. Sauer also suggested that a "Late Mamluk" (c. 1401–1516 CE) stratum was distinguishable in which HMGPW, featuring a darker paint and narrower lines, was present but glazed wares were scarce. In a combined study of all HMGPW groups at Tall Hisban, Sauer (Sauer 1973: 55–56) identified 13 major designs: squares, waves, single and double zigzags, hourglass, diamond nets, semi-spirals, interlocking triangles, dotted lines, fine-lined lozenges, lined dots, nets and wavy lines. One vessel often was decorated with a combination of designs, which currently do not appear to have a chronological significance. At Rujm Kursi the mid-thirteenth century corpus of HMGPW, dated by coins, was slipped and decorated with reddish-brown paint in ten design categories (Khadija 1992). In addition to seven of Sauer's thirteen groups, Khadija identified three new categories of motifs: diamonds, triangles and stars. A selection of HMGPW has also been published from Khirbat Faris, although no firm dates are offered. However, the comment is made that some doubt still exists as to a terminal date of HMGPW, and a post sixteenth to seventeenth century date is not unreasonable as HMGPW sometimes appears with tobacco pipes, which are usually not dated before the seventeenth century.

A very valuable assessment of thirteenth to fifteenth century pottery in Jordan was undertaken by Brown as part of an archaeological survey of the Karak Plateau directed by Miller (Brown 1991: 232–241). The study was based on pottery picked up during the survey which, from this period, was mostly HMGPW with some monochrome glazed wheel-thrown bowls. Very rare were:

- unglazed wheel-thrown wares, both household vessels (e.g. strainer jugs) and industrial (sugar pots), and ranging in colour from buff to pink and red; glazed bowls with sgraffiato decoration;

- glazed moulded vessels of pink, white and red fabric;

- a hard, metallic grey ware used in the production of small moulded conical vessels, probably containers for mercury or other precious liquids;

- imported glazed wares.

Brown provides a full evaluation of each category, referencing widely published and unpublished material from sites in Jordan, neighbouring Syria and Palestine, and beyond. While the range of sites with comparative material is extensive, no new conclusions on the chronology of forms and decoration were possible as all the sherds came from unprovenanced surface collections.

Based upon her investigation of Karak castle, Brown has been able to drawn a sharp distinction between the ceramic profile in the countryside, as identified by the Karak Plateau Survey, and the pottery recovered from within the castle confines (Brown 1992). Unlike the countryside, where monochrome glazed wares and especially HMGPW predominated, the castle ceramics included many fine imported wares and, in proliferation, wheel-made pale-bodied glazed bowls and many types of plain vessels. Imported glazed wares included Chinese celadons and imitation celadons, polyglaze sgraffiato, underglazed painted in blue and black, and Rusafa ware. Apart from the celadons, these glazed varieties demonstrate wide interregional contacts between Karak, north Syria and Egypt in the period. HMGPW, by way of contrast, was uncommon even though it was readily available locally. Brown argues convincingly that the contrast between the rural and urban assemblages at Karak reflected the deep socio-economic gap that existed between the town of Karak and the surrounding countryside. The Mamluk elite of Karak, which (as has been seen) included high-profile exiles from the ruling class of Cairo, enjoyed a lifestyle considerably better than that in rural areas, where fine and imported wares—indicative of a wider consumption of luxury goods—were exceedingly rare. In Brown's analysis the ceramics reveal that urban Karak and rural Ard Karak were located at the opposite ends of the socio-economic scale under Mamluk rule.

Non-Ceramic Finds

Non-ceramic finds manufactured from materials including stone, glass, ivory, bone and metals have only been sporadically mentioned and erratically described, as most writers with any interest in middle Islamic Jordan have concentrated on pottery in an attempt to establish a basic ceramic chronology for the eleventh to fifteenth century. Accordingly, no general survey can be offered at this time. However, specific mention should be made of select categories of non-ceramic finds, especially in the few instances where these are reported in sufficient detail.

A significant collection of stone, glass, metal and ivory artefacts, dating to the later tenth and eleventh centuries, was recovered from the upper levels at Aylah (Whitcomb 1994). Outstanding in quality and significance were the many ivory decorative plaques, probably furniture inlays, depicting enigmatic scenes military and heroic in tone, some seemingly of quite ancient inspiration. Other Fatimid-period objects from Aqabah included steatite bowls from northwestern Arabia (also popular in earlier periods), and a collection of eleventh century glass and bronze weights used to measure precious-metal coins. The weights are testimony to the expanding commercial role of Aqabah in the Fatimid period, a development further supported by the discovery of a hoard of 32 *dinars* just inside the north gate. All but three, which are standard

Fatimid issues, originated far to the west in Morocco, and were minted under the authority of the Spanish Umayyad Caliph Hisham II of Cordoba (r. 976–1009 CE). They travelled as a group, probably with a merchant, until their concealment near the mosque of Aylah. Also dateable to the Fatimid period is a group of engraved stone tombstones at Mazar, including a refined marble panel in decorative Kufic from the tomb of Jaafar ibn Abi Talib, brother of Ali and a favourite of the Fatimid Caliphs. The tenth and eleventh century finds from south Jordan, while still extremely limited in scope, are further evidence for the prevailing influence of Egypt, the Hijaz and south Arabia on the cultural matrix of the region under Fatimid hegemony.

The non-ceramic finds from the twelfth to fifteenth centuries reveal the richness of the period, but little has been adequately reported. At Tall Hisban, a wide range of finds were recovered, mostly domestic, commercial and personal objects manufactured from stone, clay, bone, ivory, metals and glass. Likewise at Tabaqat Fahl the partial excavation of a fourteenth and fifteenth century settlement and cemetery has produced a corpus of copper finger rings, earrings and bangles for arms and ankles. Also present were bangles of glass, mostly made by twisting and joining multi-coloured canes. Similar glass bracelets were recovered at Tall Abu Sarbut and the cemetery on Tall Dayr Alla, with some evidence for a local manufacturing centre. Copper coins struck under the Ayyubids and Mamluks are a relatively common discovery at larger sites, although no Ayyubid or Mamluk mints operated in Jordan. At Tabaqat Fahl eleven Mamluk copper coins were found, all of fourteenth century date and spanning the reigns of al-Mansur Abu Bakr (1341) to al-Zahir Barquq (second reign, 1390–1399 CE). The positively identified mints were Damascus and Cairo, with others possibly originating in Hamah, Alexandria and Tarablus. The geographical spread of mints reveals long distance contacts with districts in Egypt and *al-Sham*. From Tall Hisban a total of 39 copper and one silver Ayyubid-period coins were recovered, increasing to 65 copper and 71 silver coins in the Mamluk period. Most of the Mamluk silver coins were found as a hoard of 66 concealed in a lamp. A larger hoard of 2,244 early Mamluk silver coins was found at Karak in a ceramic pot (Sari 1986). All were struck in the short period between 1257–1296, but as many were worn they were probably concealed after the end of the thirteenth century.

While the evidence is tantalizing for an abundant and varied cultural horizon in Ayyubid and Mamluk Jordan, the available evidence continues to be patchy and incomplete. Until large scale, systematic excavations are undertaken on a series of major Ayyubid and Mamluk sites in Jordan (which would probably require working in currently occupied towns in some instances), and while existing excavations remain unpublished, the prevailing narrow view of "Ayyubid-Mamluk Jordan equals only rough hand made pottery" will persist unchallenged. The diversity of finds emanating from the earlier and recent projects at Tall Hisban, when coupled with material recovered at Karak, Dhiban, Pella and other sites, indicates that archaeology has failed to adequately investigate and explain the Ayyubid and Mamluk periods, with only few exceptions.

Settlement Patterns and Population: Towards a Social History of Middle Islamic Jordan

The Arabic and Crusader written sources, archaeological results (what exists) and, most critically, the activities of the Crusaders east of the Jordan Rift Valley point to a sustained level of socio-economic activity in the eleventh and twelfth centuries. There were at least eight major population centres reliant on Jordan, supported by a vibrant rural sector, trade and commerce. The importance of trade, especially in the eleventh century, is demonstrated by the finds at Aylah (Aqabah), but the benefits would have spread along the main communication routes. There is growing evidence, at Khirbat Faris and Dhiban for instance, that many sites with easily recognized Ayyubid and Mamluk occupation were also settled in Fatimid, Saljuq and perhaps Crusader times, the later material often disguising earlier evidence (a problem especially apparent in surveys). If so, the supposed "settlement gap" between the early Abbasid and Mamluk periods quickly disappears. Settlement levels were probably not significantly less than those in the Ayyubid and Mamluk periods

The emergence of new local power nodules, notably the Jarrahids, in eleventh century Jordan had a profound impact on urban and rural settlement, especially the relative importance of the major population centres. In the mountains of south Jordan, where the trend is very clear, the traditional political and social functions of Maab were taken over by Karak, strategically placed on major communication routes and easier to defend. Likewise Wadi Musa, astride routes leading into the Wadi Arabah, took the place Udhruh. In the north a similar trend can be recognized, although the evidence is more circumstantial. Probably during the eleventh century the traditional socio-political roles of Amman and Jarash were transferred to Salt and Ajlun, for both sites were easier to defend while straddling main routes into the Jordan Valley. Equally, the ascendancy of Irbid at the expense of Bayt Ras probably began at this time. Geographically, the overall shift was westwards, away from the open *badiyah* to strategic, defensible locations on high points along the east Jordan Rift. Put another way, citadel-settlements became the norm during the eleventh century. In the gestation of these strongholds, three important points need emphasizing.

1. The rise of citadels was in response to the political uncertainties of the eleventh and twelfth centuries, and represented the political aspirations of local shaykhdoms, usually of Bedouin origin, and their opposition to expanding Fatimid domination.

2. They did not originate in a "desert and sown" conflict. Indeed many of the shaykhdoms gained powerful backing from settled populations.

3. This movement marked the final phase in the urban eclipse of many of the once dominant Classical-period centres, for instance Udhruh, Maab, Amman, Jarash and Bayt Ras. They were still occupied, obviously, but served no major politico-military role.

The changes appear to have happened quite rapidly and may have been accompanied by a severe, if relatively brief, impact on overall occupation levels. Hence the rise of citadels in Jordan as strong points for the ruling elite was well underway before the arrival of the Crusaders in the early twelfth century.

Seen in this light, the Crusader occupation of south Jordan and their attempts in the north represent an intensification of a process already underway. Major castles were built at Shawbak and Wadi Musa in 1115–1116 CE, and Karak in 1142 CE (replacing the Jarrahid stronghold). In the north the Muslims built a fort at Jarash in 1120 CE, but it was soon destroyed. The Crusader-Muslim struggle brought fortified towns to the fore in the twelfth century, a process that continued into the Ayyubid period. Further castles were built by the Ayyubids at Ajlun (1188–1192 CE), Salt (1220 CE) and Azraq (1236–1137 CE). In addition, Karak and its ancillary but equally impregnable castle of Shawbak were substantially renovated under the Ayyubids and early Mamluks. Walls were strengthened, towers added and palaces built to accommodate the elite in suitable style, although all this activity essentially ceased after the rise of the Circassian Mamluks in 1382 CE. In general, the Mamluks were more interested in securing the major roads, especially the Darb al-Hajj and the postal routes between major centres. A number of forts and caravanserais were erected at major passage points, especially where there was water, and toll stations were established. The Mamluks also directed their attention to the Muslim holy sites of Jordan, for instance Mutah-Mazar, Amata, Jabal Harun and Kahf al-Raqim. The Fatimids had taken particular interest in developing these holy sites, notably Mazar, and in part the Mamluk intention was to reduce the Fatimid-Shiite presence by reasserting Muslim orthodoxy. The holy sites represent another important example of social continuity from the Fatimid period into Mamluk times.

In the fields of settlement, society and culture the threads of continuity are demonstrably very strong between the Fatimid and Mamluk periods although, as has been seen, change is undeniably apparent. The ceramics further reflect this dichotomy. Hand made geometric painted wares were clearly present in the later eleventh to twelfth century, but in these early stages it displayed considerable regional variation in fabric and manufacture. By the thirteenth century there was greater standardization across Jordan, Palestine and Syria, with the wares continuing into the fifteenth century and probably beyond. The rise of HMGPW took place at the expense of wheel-made utilitarian pottery, although it was still to be found in urban contexts. The ceramics at Karak, especially the fine glazed and wheel-made wares, argue for a high degree of social bifurcation in the Mamluk period, the final outcome of more than 300 years of socio-cultural development in south Jordan.

The tone of this offering has been deliberately "upbeat." It has tried to redress the unduly negative view of Jordan under Fatimid, Saljuq, Crusader, Ayyubid and Mamluk hegemony. The available historical and archaeological information has been interpreted within a positive and assertive framework, using the limited data at hand to develop an image of Islamic Jordanian society in the throws of deep and permanent political, cultural and economic change in the immediately pre-modern age. Only when middle Islamic Jordan is evaluated in this manner, freed of irrelevant concepts of state and society devised within the context of Classical and Biblical archaeology, will a more honest assessment become possible, and the modern Middle East more accessible to the Western mind.

Bibliography

Abu Dalu, R.

1995 The Technology of Sugar Mills in the Jordan Valley during the Islamic Periods. In K. 'Amr, F. Zayadine, and M. Zaghloul (eds.), *Studies in the History and Archaeology of Jordan V*, 37–48 (Arabic). Amman: Department of Antiquities.

Abu'l-Fida

1983 *The Memoirs of a Syrian Prince.* Wiesbaden: Steiner.

Ashtor, E.

1981 Levantine Sugar Industry in the Late Middle Ages: a Case of Technological Decline. In A.L. Udovitch (ed.), *The Islamic Middle East, 700–1900*, 91–132. Princeton: Darwin Press.

Bourke, S. and K. Hendrix

2001 Twenty Years of Australian Physical Anthropology in Jordan: Retrospects and Prospects. In A. Walmsley (ed.), *Australians Uncovering Ancient Jordan. Fifty Years of Middle Eastern Archaeology*, 77–88. Sydney/Amman: Research Institute for Humanities and Social Sciences/ Department of Antiquities.

Brown, R.M.

1984 Late Islamic Settlement Patterns on the Kerak Plateau, Trans-Jordan. Unpublished MA Thesis, State University of New York.

1987 A 12th century A.D. sequence from southern TransJordan: Crusader and Ayyubid Occupation at el-Wu'eira. *Annual of the Department of Antiquities of Jordan* 31: 267–288.

1988 Summary Report of the 1986 Excavations: Late Islamic Shobak. *Annual of the Department of Antiquities of Jordan* 32: 225–245.

1989a Excavations in the 14th century A.D. Mamluk Palace at Kerak. *Annual of the Department of Antiquities of Jordan* 33: 287–304.

1989b Kerak Castle. In D. Homès-Fredericq and J.B. Hennessy (eds.), *Archaeology of Jordan II.1. Field Reports, sites A–K*, 341–347. Leuven: Peeters.

1989c Shaubak. In D. Homès-Fredericq and J.B. Hennessy (eds.), *Archaeology of Jordan II.2. Field reports, sites L–Z*, 559–566. Leuven: Peeters.

1989d Wueira. In D. Homès-Fredericq and J.B. Hennessy (eds.), *Archaeology of Jordan II.2. Field reports, sites L–Z*, 625–630. Leuven: Peeters.

1991 Ceramics from the Kerak Plateau. In J.M. Miller (ed.), *Archaeological Survey of the Kerak Plateau*, vol. 1, 168–279. Atlanta, GA: Scholars Press.

1992 Late Islamic Ceramic Production and Distribution in the Southern Levant: a socio-economic and political interpretation. Unpublished Ph.D Thesis, State University of New York at Binghamton.

2000 The Distribution of Thirteenth to Fifteenth century Glazed Wares in Transjordan: a Case Study from the Kerak Plateau. In L.E. Stager, J.A. Greene, and M.D. Coogan (eds.), *The Archaeology of Jordan and Beyond. Essays in Honor of James A. Sauer*, 84–99. Winona Lake, IN: Eisenbrauns.

Brünnow, R.E. and A.V. Domaszewski

1905 *Die Provincia Arabia.* Strassburg: Trübner.

Burgoyne, M.H.

1987 *Mamluk Jerusalem. An architectural study.* London: British School of Archaeology in Jerusalem/World of Islam Festival Trust.

Chaudhuri, K.N.

1985 *Trade and Civilisation in the Indian Ocean: an economic history from the rise of Islam to 1750.* Cambridge: Cambridge University Press.

1990 *Asia before Europe: economy and civilisation in the Indian Ocean from the rise of Islam to 1750.* Cambridge: Cambridge University Press.

Coughenour, R.A.

1989 Mugharat el Wardeh. In D. Homès-Fredericq and J.B. Hennessy (eds.), *Archaeology of Jordan II.2. Field Reports, sites L–Z*, 386–390. Leuven: Peeters.

Franken, H.J. and J. Kalsbeek

1975 *Potters of a Medieval Village in the Jordan Valley.* Amsterdam: North Holland.

Frösén, J., Z.T. Fiema, M. Lavento, C. Danielli, R. Holmgren, J. Latikka, A. Rajala, N. Gheiska and A. Lahelma

2003 The 2002 Finish Jabal Harun Project: Peliminary Report. *Annual of the Department of Antiquities of Jordan* 47: 295–320.

Fulcher of Chartres

1969 *A History of the Expedition to Jerusalem 1095–1127.* Trans. F.R. Ryan. Knoxville, TN: University of Tennessee Press.

Galloway, J.H.

1989 *The Sugar Cane Industry. An historical geography from its origins to 1914.* Cambridge: Cambridge University Press.

Geraty, L.T. and Ø.S. LaBianca

1985 The Local Environment and Human Food-procuring Strategies in Jordan: the case of Tell Hesban and its surrounding region. In A. Hadidi (ed.), *Studies in the History and Archaeology of Jordan II,* 323–330. Amman: Department of Antiquities of Jordan.

Ghawânmah, Y.

1986 *al-Masâjid al-Islâmiyah al-Qadîmah fî Mintiqat Àjlûn.* Irbid: Jâmiàt al-Yarmûk, Markaz al-Dirâsât al-Urdunniyah.

Gibb, H.A.R.

1958 *The Travels of Ibn Battuta.* Cambridge: Cambridge University Press/The Hakluyt Society.

Glidden, H.W.

1952 The Mamluk Origin of the Fortified Khan at al-ʿAqabah, Jordan. In G.C. Miles (ed.), *Archaeologica Orientalia. In Memoriam Ernst Herzfeld,* 116–118. New York: J.J. Augustin.

Greene, J.A.

1995 The water mills of the ʿAjlun-Kufranja Valley: the relationship of technology, society and settlement. In K. ʿAmr, F. Zayadine and M. Zaghloul (eds.), *Studies in the History and Archaeology of Jordan V,* 757–765.

Haas, H.d., H.E. LaGro and M. Steiner

1989 First Season of Excavations at Tell Abu Sarbut, 1988: a Preliminary Report. *Annual of the Department of Antiquities of Jordan* 33: 323–326.

1992 Second and Third Season of Excavations at Tell Abu Sarbut, Jordan Valley (Preliminary Report). *Annual of the Department of Antiquities of Jordan* 36: 333–343.

Harding, G.L.

1967 *The Antiquities of Jordan.* New York: Praeger.

Hart, S.

1987 Five soundings in southern Jordan. *Levant* 19: 33–47.

Holt, P.M.

1986 *The Age of the Crusades: the Near East from the eleventh century to 1517.* London: Longman.

Homès-Fredericq, D.

1989 Lehun. In D. Homès-Fredericq and J.B. Hennessy (eds.), *Archaeology of Jordan II.2: field reports, sites L–Z,* 349–359. Leuven: Peeters.

Homès-Fredericq, D. and H.J. Franken

1986 *Pottery and Potters — Past and Present. 7000 years of ceramic art in Jordan.* Tübingen: Attempto.

Humphreys, R.S.

1977 *From Saladin to the Mongols: the Ayyubids of Damascus, 1193–1260.* New York: State University of New York Press.

Ibach, R.D.

1987 *Archaeological Survey of the Hesban Region: catalogue of sites and characterisation of periods.* Berrien Springs, MI: Andrews University Press.

Ibn al-Qalanisi

1932 *The Damascus Chronicle of the Crusades.* Trans. H.A.R. Gibb. London: Luzac. Reprint 1967.

Ibn Battuta

1958 *The Travels of Ibn Battuta, A.D. 132 –1354.* Trans. H.A.R. Gibb. Cambridge: Cambridge University Press.

Ibn Jubayr, M.i.A.

1952 *The Travels of Ibn Jubayr.* Trans. R.J.C. Broadhurst. London: Jonathan Cape.

Ibrahim, M., J.A. Sauer, and K. Yassine

1976 The East Jordan Valley Survey, 1975. *Bulletin of the American Schools of Oriental Research* 222: 41–66.

Irwin, R.

1986 *The Middle East in the Middle Ages: the early mamluk Sultanate 1250–1382.* London: Croom Helm.

Johns, C.N.

1932 Medieval ʿAjlun. *Quarterly of the Department of Antiquities of Palestine* 1: 21–33.

Johns, J.

1994 The *Longue Durée:* State and settlement strategies in Southern Transjordan Across the Islamic Centuries. In E.L. Rogan and T. Tell (eds.), *Village, Steppe and State. The social origins of modern Jordan,* 1–31. London: British Academic Press.

Johns, J., A. McQuitty, and R.K. Falkner

1989 The Faris Project: preliminary report upon the 1986 and 1988 seasons. *Levant* 21: 63–95.

Kareem, J.M.H.

1987 Evidence of the Umayyad occupation in the Jordan Valley as seen in the Jisr Sheikh Hussein region. Unpublished MA Thesis, Yarmouk University.

1997 The site of Dhraʿ al-Khân: a main caravanserai on Darb al-Qufûl. In G. Bisheh, M. Zaghloul, and I. Kehrberg (eds.), *Studies in the History and Archaeology of Jordan, VI: Landscape Resources and Human Occupation in Jordan throughout the Ages,* 365–369. Amman: Department of Antiquities of Jordan.

2000 *The Settlement Patterns in the Jordan Valley in the Mid- to Late Islamic period.* Oxford: Archaeopress.

Kennedy, D.L.

1982 *Archaeological Explorations on the Roman Frontier in North East Jordan.* Oxford: British Archaeological Reports.

Kennedy, H.

1986 *The Prophet and the Age of the Caliphates: The Islamic Near East from the Sixth to the Eleventh Century.* London: Longman.

1994 *Crusader Castles.* Cambridge: Cambridge University Press.

Khadija, L.

1992 Designs on Painted Ayyubid/Mamluk Pottery from Rujm al-Kursi, 1990 season. *Annual of the Department of Antiquities of Jordan* 36: 345–356.

Khammash, A.

1986 *Notes on Village Architecture in Jordan.* Layfayette, LA: University of Southwestern Louisiana.

King, G., C.J. Lenzen, and G.O. Rollefson

1983 Survey of Byzantine and Islamic Sites in Jordan. Second Season Report, 1981. *Annual of the Department of Antiquities of Jordan* 27: 385–436.

Kraeling, C.H. (ed.)

1938 *Gerasa, City of the Decapolis.* New Haven, CT: American Schools of Oriental Research.

LaBianca, Ø.S.

1990 *Sedentarization and Nomadization: Food System Cycles at Hesban and Vicinity in TransJordan.* Berrien Springs, MI: Andrews University Press.

Le Strange, G.

1890 *Palestine under the Moslems.* Beirut: Khayats. Reprint 1965.

Lenzen, C.J.

1995a Continuity or discontinuity: urban change or demise? In S. Bourke and J.-P. Descoeudres (eds.), *Trade, contact, and the movement of peoples in the eastern Mediterranean. Studies in honour of J. Basil Hennessy,* 325–331. Sydney: Mediterranean Archaeology.

1995b From Public to Private Space: changes in the urban plan of Bayt Ras/Capitolias. In K. 'Amr, F. Zayadine, and M. Zaghloul (eds.), *Studies in the History and Archaeology of Jordan V,* 235–239. Amman: Department of Antiquities.

2000 Seeking Contextual Definitions for Places: the case of north-western Jordan. *Mediterranean Archaeology* 13: 11–24.

Lenzen, C.J. and E.A. Knauf

1987 Beit Ras/Capitolias. A Preliminary Evaluation of the Archaeological and Textual Evidence. *Syria* 64: 21–46.

Maalouf, A.

1984 *The Crusades Through Arab Eyes.* Trans. J. Rothschild. London: Al Saqi Books/American University in Cairo Press.

Macaulay, R. and R. Beny

1977 *Pleasure of Ruins.* London: Thames and Hudson.

MacKenzie, N.D.

2002 Ayyubid/Mamluk Archaeology of the 'Ajlun Area. A Preliminary Typology. *Annual of the Department of Antiquities of Jordan* 46: 615–620.

Magness, J.

1997 The Chronology of Capernaum in the Early Islamic period. *Journal of the American Oriental Society* 117: 481–486.

McKenzie, J.

1991 The Beduin at Petra: the historical sources. *Levant* 23: 139–145.

McPhillips, S.

2001 Ceramics from Middle Islamic Fahl. In A. Walmsley (ed.), *Australians Uncovering Ancient Jordan. Fifty Years of Middle Eastern Archaeology,* 271–278. Sydney/Amman: Research Institute for Humanities and Social Sciences/Department of Antiquities.

McPhillips, S. and A. Walmsley

2007 Fahl during the Early Mamluk Period: archaeological perspectives. *Mamluk Studies Review* 11(1): 119–156.

McQuitty, A.

1993 Review of O.S. LaBianca, *Sedentarization and Nomadization, Hesban I. Palestine Exploration Quarterly* 125: 167–169.

1995 Water-mills in Jordan: technology, typology dating and development. In K. 'Amr, F. Zayadine, and M. Zaghloul (eds.), *Studies in the History and Archaeology of Jordan V,* 745–751. Amman: Department of Antiquities of Jordan.

McQuitty, A. and R.K. Falkner

1993 The Faris Project: preliminary report on the 1989, 1990 and 1991 seasons. *Levant* 25: 37–61.

Merrill, S.

1881 *East of the Jordan: a record of travel and observation in the countries of Moab, Gilead, and Bashan.* London: Darf. Reprint 1986.

Mershen, B. and E.A. Knauf

1988 From *Gadar* to *Umm Qais. Zeitschrift des Deutschen Palästina-Vereins* 104: 128–145.

Miller, J.M. (ed.)

1991 *Archaeological Survey of the Kerak Plateau.* Atlanta, GA: Scholar's Press.

Milwright, M.

2006 Central and Southern Jordan in the Ayyubid Period: Historical and Archaeological Perspectives. *Journal of the Royal Asiatic Society* 16(1): 1–28.

Minnis, D. and Y. Bader

1988 A Comparative Analysis of Belvoir (Kawkab al-Hawa) and Qal'at al-Rabad ('Ajlun Castle). *Annual of the Department of Antiquities of Jordan* 32: 255–263.

Muqaddasi (al-Maqdisi)

1994 *The Best Divisions for the Knowledge of the Regions (Ahsan al-Taqasim fi maʿrifat al-Aqalim).* Trans. B. Collins and M. al-Tai. Reading: Garnet.

Musil, A.

1926 *The Northern Hegaz. A Topographical Itinerary.* New York: American Geographical Society.

1927 *Arabia Deserta.* New York: American Geographical Society.

Northedge, A.

1984 Qalʿat ʿAmman in the Early Islamic Period. Unpublished Ph.D thesis, University of London.

1992 *Studies on Roman and Islamic ʿAmman, Volume 1. The Excavations of Mrs C-M Bennett and Other Investigations.* Oxford: British Institute at Amman for Archaeology and History/Oxford University Press.

1999 Archaeology and Islam. In G. Barker (ed.), *Companion Encyclopedia of Archaeology,* 1077–1106. London: Routledge.

Ostrasz, A.

1997 The Citadel of Amman. The Conservation and Restoration of the Ayyubid Tower. *Annual of the Department of Antiquities of Jordan* 41: 395–402.

Palumbo, G. (ed.)

1994 *JADIS The Jordanian Antiquities database and information system: a summary of the data.* Amman: Department of Antiquities of Jordan/American Centre of Oriental Research.

Peters, F.E.

1994 *The Hajj. The Muslim pilgrimage to Mecca and the Holy Places.* Princeton: Princeton University Press.

Petersen, A.

1991 Two forts on the Medieval Hajj route in Jordan. *Annual of the Department of Antiquities of Jordan* 35: 347–359.

Photos-Jones, E., K. Politis, H.F. James, A.J. Hall, R.E. Jones, and J. Hamer

2002 The Sugar Industry in the Southern Jordan Valley: an interim report on the pilot season of excavations, geophysical and geological surveys at Tawahin as-Sukkar and Khirbat ash-Shaykh ʿIsa, in Ghawr as-Safi. *Annual of the Department of Antiquities of Jordan* 46: 591–614.

Rogan, E.L.

1995 Reconstructing Water Mills in Late Ottoman Transjordan. In K. ʿAmr, F. Zayadine, and M. Zaghloul (eds.), *Studies in the History and Archaeology of Jordan V,* 753–756. Amman: Department of Antiquities of Jordan.

Sari, S.K.

1986 A Critical Analysis of a Mamluk Hoard from Karak. Unpublished PhD Thesis, University of Michigan.

Sauer, J.A.

1973 *Hesbon Pottery 1971. A preliminary report on the pottery from the 1971 excavations at Tell Hesban.* Berrien Springs, MI: Andrews University Press.

1976 Pottery Techniques at Tell Deir ʿAlla (review article). *Bulletin of the American Schools of Oriental Research* 224: 91–94.

1982 The Pottery of Jordan in the Early Islamic Period. In A. Hadidi (ed.), *Studies in the History and Archaeology of Jordan I,* 329–337. Amman: Department of Antiquities of Jordan.

1994 The Pottery at Hesban and its Relationship to the History of Jordan: An Interim Hesban Pottery Report, 1993. In D. Merling and L.T. Geraty (eds.), *Hesban After 25 Years,* 225–281. Berrien Springs, MI: Andrews University Press.

Scanlon, G.T.

1970 Egypt and China: Trade and Imitation. In D.S. Richards (ed.), *Islam and the Trade of Asia. A Colloquium,* 81–95. Oxford: Bruno Cassirer.

Schick, R.

1995 *The Christian Communities of Palestine from Byzantine to Islamic Rule.* Princeton: Darwin Press.

1997 Southern Jordan in the Fatimid and Seljuq periods. *Bulletin of the American Schools of Oriental Research* 305: 73–85.

1998 Palestine in the Early Islamic Period: Luxuriant Legacy. *Near Eastern Archaeology* 61: 74–108.

Schick, R., H. Mahasneh, and S. Maʿani

1994 Nakhal. *American Journal of Archaeology* 98: 553–554.

Seigne, J.

1989 Jerash—The Sanctuary of Zeus. In D. Homès-Fredericq and J.B. Hennessy (eds.), *Archaeology of Jordan II.1. Field Reports: Surveys & Sites A–K,* 319–323. Leuven: Peeters.

Silberman, N.A.

2001 Thundering Hordes: the Image of the Persian and Muslim Conquests in Palestinian Archaeology. In S.R. Wolff (ed.), *Studies in the Archaeology of Israel and Neighboring Lands in Memory of Douglas L. Esse,* 611–623. Chicago/Atlanta: Oriental Institute/American Schools of Oriental Research.

Smith, R.H.

1973 *Pella of the Decapolis Volume 1. The 1967 Season of the College of Wooster Expedition to Pella.* Wooster, OH: College of Wooster.

Smith, R.H. and L.P. Day

1989 *Pella of the Decapolis Volume 2. Final Report on the College of Wooster Excavations in Area IX, the Civic Complex, 1979–1985.* Wooster, OH: College of Wooster.

Thorau, P.

1987 *The Lion of Egypt: Sultan Baybars I and the Near East in the Thirteenth Century.* Trans. P.M. Holt. London: Longman. 1992 Edition.

Tushingham, A.D.

1972 *The Excavations at Dibon (Dhiban) in Moab. The third campaign 1952–53.* Cambridge: American Schools of Oriental Research.

Vannini, G. and C. Tonghini

1997 Medieval Petra. The stratigraphic evidence from recent archaeological excavations at al-Wuʿayra. In G. Bisheh, M. Zaghloul, and I. Kehrberg (eds.), *Studies in the History and Archaeology of Jordan VI: Landscape Resources and Human Occupation in Jordan throughout the Ages*, 371–384. Amman: Department of Antiquities of Jordan.

Vannini, G. and A. Vanni Desideri

1995 Archaeological research on Medieval Petra: a preliminary report. *Annual of the Department of Antiquities of Jordan* 39: 509–540.

de Vries, B.

1986 The Islamic Bath at Tell Hesban. In L.T. Geraty and L.G. Herr (eds.), *The Archaeology of Jordan and other studies presented to Siegfried H. Horn*, 223–235. Berrien Springs, MI: Andrews University Press.

1994 Hesban in the Ayyubid and Mamluk periods. In D. Merling and L.T. Geraty (eds.), *Hesban after 25 years*, 151–166. Berrien Springs, MI: Andrews University Press.

Walker, B.J.

1999 Militarization to Nomadization: The Middle to Late Islamic Periods. *Near Eastern Archaeology* 62: 202–232.

2003a The Islamic *Qusur* of Tall Hisban: Preliminary Report on the 1998 and 2001 Seasons. *Annual of the Department of Antiquities of Jordan* 47: 443–471.

2003b Mamluk Investment in Southern Bilad al-Sham in the Eighth/Fourteenth Century: the Case of Hisban. *Journal of Near Eastern Studies* 62: 241–261.

2003c Southern Syria in the Islamic Period: Political Periphery or Nexus? In D. Clark (ed.), *One Hundred Years of American Archaeology in the Levant: Proceedings of the ASOR Centennial Celebration, Washington DC April 2000*, 385–409. Boston, MA: American Schools of Oriental Research.

2004 Mamluk Investment in Transjordan: a "Boom and Bust" Economy. *Mamluk Studies Review* 8: 119–147.

Walmsley, A.

1982 The Umayyad pottery and its antecedents. In A. McNicoll, R.H. Smith, and B. Hennessy (eds.), *Pella in Jordan 1. An interim report on the joint University of Sydney and The College of Wooster Excavations at Pella 1979–1981*, 143–157. Canberra: Australian National Gallery.

1991 Architecture and Artefacts from Abbasid Fihl: Implications for the Cultural History of Jordan. In M.A. Bakhit and R. Schick (eds.), *Proceedings of the Fifth International Conference on the History of Bilad al-Sham. Bilad al-Sham during the Abbasid Period (English and French Section)*, 135–159. Amman: History of Bilad al-Sham Committee.

1992a Fihl (Pella) and the Cities of North Jordan during the Umayyad and Abbasid Periods. In S. Tell, G. Bisheh, F. Zayadine, K. ʿAmr, and M. Zaghloul (eds.), *Studies in the History and Archaeology of Jordan IV*, 377–384. Amman: Department of Antiquities.

1992b The Islamic Period: the later Islamic periods. In A.W. McNicoll, J. Hanbury-Tenison, J.B. Hennessy, T.F. Potts, R.H. Smith, A. Walmsley, and P. Watson (eds.), *Pella in Jordan 2. The Second Interim Report of the Joint University of Sydney and College of Wooster Excavations at Pella 1982–1985*, 188–198. Sydney: Mediterranean Archaeology.

1995 Tradition, Innovation, and Imitation in the material Culture of Islamic Jordan: the first four centuries. In K. ʿAmr, F. Zayadine, and M. Zaghloul (eds.), *Studies in the History and Archaeology of Jordan V*, 657–668. Amman: Department of Antiquities.

1997 Ceramics and the Social History of Early Islamic Jordan: the example of Pella (Tabaqat Fahl). *Al-ʾUsur al-Wusta* 9: 1–3, 12.

1998 Settled Life in Mamlûk Jordan: views of the Jordan Valley from Fahl (Pella). *ARAM* 10: 1–15.

2001 Turning East. The appearance of Islamic Cream Wares in Jordan—the end of antiquity? In E. Villeneuve and P.M. Watson (eds.), *La céramique byzantine et proto-islamique en Syrie-Jordanie (IVe–VIIIe siècles)*, 305–313. Beyrouth: Institut Français d'Etudes Arabes.

2004 Archaeology and Islamic Studies: the development of a relationship. In K.V. Folsach, H. Thrane, and I. Thuesen (eds.), *From Handaxe to Khan: essays presented to Peder Mortensen on the occasion of his 70th birthday*, 317–329. Århus: Aarhus University Press.

Walmsley, A. and A. Grey

2001 An Interim Report on the Pottery from Gharandal (Arindela), Jordan. *Levant* 33: 139–164.

Walmsley, A., P. Karsgaard, and A. Grey

1999 Town and Village: Site Transformations in South Jordan (The Gharandal Archaeological Project, Second Season Report). *Annual of the Department of Antiquities of Jordan* 43: 459–478.

Watson, A.M.

1983 *Agricultural Innovation in the Early Islamic World: the diffusion of crops and farming techniques, 700–1000*. Cambridge: Cambridge University Press.

Whitcomb, D.

1988a *Aqaba "port of Palestine on the China Sea"*. Chicago, IL: Al Kutba.

1988b A Fatimid Residence at Aqaba, Jordan. *Annual of the Department of Antiquities of Jordan* 32: 207–223.

1992a The Islamic Period as seen from selected sites. In B. MacDonald (ed.), *The Southern Ghors and Northeast ʿArabah Archaeological Survey*, 113–118. Sheffield: J.R. Collis.

1992b Reassessing the Archaeology of Jordan of the Abbasid Period. In S. Tell, G. Bisheh, F. Zayadine, K. ʿAmr, and M. Zaghloul (eds.), *Studies in the History and Archaeology of Jordan IV*, 385–390. Amman: Department of Antiquities of Jordan.

1994 *Ayla: art and history in the Islamic port of Aqaba*. Chicago: Oriental Institute, Chicago.

1995 A Street and the Beach at Ayla: the fall season of excavations at 'Aqaba, 1992. *Annual of the Department of Antiquities of Jordan* 39: 499–507.

1997 The Town and Name of Aqaba: An Inquiry into the Settlement History from an Archaeological Perspective, *Studies in the History and Archaeology of Jordan VI: Landscape Resources and Human Occupation in Jordan throughout the Ages*, 359–363. Amman: Department of Antiquities of Jordan.

2000 Hesban, Amman, and Abbasid Archaeology in Jordan. In L.E. Stager, J.A. Greene, and M.D. Coogan (eds.), *The Archaeology of Jordan and Beyond: Essays in honor of James A. Sauer*, 505–515. Winona Lake, IN: Eisenbrauns.

William of Tyre

1941a *A History of Deeds Done Beyond the Sea, Volume 1*. Trans. E.A. Babcock and A.C. Krey. New York: Octagon Books. Reprint 1976.

1941b *A History of Deeds Done Beyond the Sea, Volume 2*. Trans. E.A. Babcock and A.C. Krey. New York: Octagon Books. Reprint 1976.

Wood, J.

1992 The Fortifications. In A. Northedge (ed.), *Studies on Roman and Islamic 'Amman* 1, 105–127. Oxford: British Institute at Amman for Archaeology and History/ Oxford University Press.

Zayadine, F.

1985 Caravan routes between Egypt and Nabataea and the Voyage of Sultan Baibars to Petra in 1276. In. A. Hadidi (ed.), *Studies in the History and Archaeology of Jordan* II, 159–174. Amman: Department of Antiquities of Jordan.

17. The Ottoman Period

Alison McQuitty

Introduction

For much of the span of Ottoman rule in Jordan (A.D. 1516–1918) the archaeological evidence for settlement, society and economy within the country is patchy. Apart from the Hajj forts and associated sherd dumps, a sprinkling of tobacco pipes, railway stations and a few mid-to-late nineteenth century buildings, there is little material culture to indicate the Ottoman imperial nature of the country. Jordan was an area of rural settlement, predominantly ahistorical, certainly tribal and definitely "the Other" as far as the authors of the historical documentation available were concerned, that is, the Ottoman administration and nineteenth century European travellers. This distinction between "the archaeology of an Empire and the archaeology of a time period" (LaBianca 2000: 213) runs throughout but the purely archaeological evidence is very much that of a specific time period and of the rural landscape.

Practical and ideological factors have also contributed to this patchy impression. It is only very recently that sites of the latter half of this period have been protected by the law. In 2004 the Antiquities Law was amended to re-define antiquities as "Any movable or immovable object which was made, written, inscribed, built, discovered or modified by a human being before the year AD 1750." In 2005 a new Law of Urban and Architectural Heritage was introduced which aims at protecting buildings and sites of cultural value post-AD 1750. Contemporary perception has played its role in the archaeological ignorance surrounding the Ottoman centuries. As Baram and Carroll point out, "Archaeology in this region has a long tradition of being the search for a distant, romantic past….. Few consider the Ottoman period to be a golden age worthy of sustained research" (2000: 4). Clearly, until recently, these late periods have not aroused much interest or attention from archaeologists and legislators (Palumbo *et al.* 1993: 69–84; Silberman 1989). This situation is gradually changing with the publication of "A Historical Archaeology of the Ottoman Empire" (Baram and Carroll 2000). However, various strands of evidence are already available which can be used to weave a more complete impression of the period: historical (official, tribal, and oral), archaeological, architectural (official and vernacular), and the material culture (Table 17.1).

History

Ottoman Administration (terms in Turkish/Arabic)

For the sake of simplicity the terminology given below relates to the nineteenth century. Different units and terms could be used in previous centuries. At the head of the provincial administrative hierarchy was the *vilayet/wilayah* (province) where the *vali/wali* (governor) resided. The new territories of the province were divided into *sancaks/liwa*s (sub-provinces), which again were sub-divided into *kazas/qada*s (districts). The leader of the *sancak/liwa* was the *mutasarrif* and of the *kaza/qada* the *kaymakam* (district governor). The smallest unit of administration, several of which comprised the *kaza*, was the *nahiye* headed by a *mudir* (Hütteroth and Abdulfattah 1977: 17–20; Rogan 1994: 37). The *nahiye* was made up of a collection of villages and nomads/tribes. These administrative units were both military and fiscal in purpose, and they served as recruiting areas for the provision of troops for the Ottoman army and taxes were levied according to the economic potential of the *nahiye*. It is the description at the *nahiye* level that offers the greatest information to the archaeologist.

Historical Sources and Their Use

Archaeologists fortunate enough to work in historical periods often rely too heavily on interpretations based on documents that were not primarily compiled to describe the nature of settlements, their interaction with each other, their burial customs and their material culture. They try to "fit" their data to the historical overview. As Davis summarizes it: "historians have tended to focus on the big pictures, while archaeological investigations by their very nature are more likely to generate information that pertains to little pictures of the past" (1991: 133). What are the historical "big pictures" in our time-frame that can contribute to the archaeological "little pictures" and *vice versa*?

The treasury of sixteenth century Ottoman tax records, so comprehensively studied and analysed by Hütteroth and Abdulfattah (1977), was compiled by Ottoman officials as a fiscal register facilitating the tax and control of the peoples of the Empire. The records give an insight into the way in which the Ottoman administration collected taxes, provide a terminology for the settlement hierarchy, and pinpoint the geographical position of some types of settlements. They aid population estimates (although see Faroqhi 1999: 89ff. for *caveats*) and give the scholar a checklist of the agricultural produce from each area. The records do not reveal the material culture correlates, for example, what a *qarya* (village) or *mazraa* (farm with no permanent settlement) looks like and if they can be distinguished archaeologically. Nomads are recorded but no light is shed (or can be shed from this collection of documents) on their interaction with more sedentary populations. Above all, the flexibility and variety of human adaptation to the environment is not conveyed by the static categorization that bureaucracies such as the Ottoman tax collectors demand. Nineteenth century land records or *tapu* documents reveal much about the relationship of the administration to its "subjects" although there is debate about whether the regional diversity shown can be explained by the lack of registration by the Ottoman authorities or regional diversity *per se* (Mundy 1996). For the archaeologist, the value of these documents lies in

Figure 17.1 Sites mentioned in the text.

Historical Source	Related Bibliography	Date
defter i mufassal	Hutteroth and Abdulfattah 1977	16th century
tapu (land) registers and court records	Mandaville 1966; Mundy 1996; Rogan 1991, 1994, 1995	19th and 20th centuries
Papers of Church Missionary Society	Held at University of Birmingham (UK) library	19th and 20th centuries
Archives of the Latin Patriarchate of Jerusalem		19th and 20th centuries
Ethnography and tribal/oral history	Abu Jaber 1989; Lewis 1987 and all European travellers' accounts	17th 20th centuries
Various photographic archives only UK locations mentioned	Palestine Exploration Fund, Gertrude Bell Archive, University of Newcastle St Antony's College, Oxford	19th and 20th centuries

Table 17.1 Historical sources for the Ottoman period in Jordan.

background information that can be added about population centres and the agricultural diversity that existed in the country as a whole.

Tribal and oral history give a vivid view of the way-of-life and world view of bygone years that is not written down. Coupled with the accounts of nineteenth century European travellers this casts invaluable light and detail on the lives, interactions and material culture of peoples history usually forgets. Three *caveats* in using this information are:

1. Tribal histories are as much about justifying the present as recording the past;
2. European travellers were often motivated by a desire to see traces of biblical pastoral scenes or classical ruins which certainly coloured what they reported (Silberman 1982: 242);
3. There is a real danger of extrapolating back from the nineteenth century to characterize the seventeenth and eighteenth centuries which are largely missing from the historical record.

Historical Evidence for Jordan in the Ottoman Period

In the control of its provinces, the Ottoman empire, after a glorious and firm beginning, exerted less and less control which, by the eighteenth century, had become nominal in several cases. In many areas, the history of government was the history of inter-tribal conflicts and the local *shaykh* or tribal leader was the link between the Ottoman administration and the province (Findley 1986: 4). One of the most important tasks of the "link-man" was tax collection. Tax registers were no longer compiled or updated by central government. This is one reason for the dearth of historical documents comparable to the *defters* during these later centuries. As an imperial authority, the Ottomans were notable for their ability to incorporate local realities and translate them into the Ottoman administrative system. Jordan became Ottoman in AD 1516 after

the Ottomans had defeated the local Mamluk governor of Aleppo. By early AD 1517, the Ottomans had proceeded through Bilad ash-Sham to Cairo and the local chiefs had all paid homage to their new rulers (Pitcher 1972: 104–106). Throughout the history of Ottoman hegemony in Jordan, the priority always lay with keeping open the Hajj route from Damascus to the Holy Places of Makkah (Mecca) and Madinah. It is here that imperial Ottoman architecture and material culture is seen as opposed to architecture and material culture of the Ottoman period.

The country lay within the *vilayet/wilayah* (province) of Damascus. At the *sancak/liwa* (sub-province) level, Jordan consisted of the *Qada Hawran* and *Liwa Ajlun*, itself sub-divided, as far as the destination of tax revenues were concerned, between Ajlun and Karak, Jabal Karak and Shawbak (Hütteroth and Abdulfattah 1977: 18). The sixteenth century *defter-i mufassal* was arranged according to this framework but probably reflected the countryside, administrative divisions and agricultural products of the preceding Mamluk administration (Hütteroth and Abdulfattah 1977: 18).

The *defter* is a detailed register of the villages within each *nahiye* compiled for taxation purposes. It contains: the village names and number of households in each village; the names of the tribes that occupy land; the types, value and proportions of agricultural produce within the various environmental zones of Jordan; the types of settlement varying from *mazraa* (an agricultural area with no permanent settlement, see below) to small town; non-agricultural activities carried out in the *nahiye*; and the destinations of the taxation. A fiscal landscape can be drawn which also gives valuable insight into the agricultural landscape of Jordan. Models for the type of agriculture practised can be suggested on the basis of this *defter*. What cannot be revealed is whether *mazraa* and *qaraya* (often translated as village or hamlet) are materially distinguishable; whether areas registered as under the unit of the *ashira* or *jamaa* (tribe), and yet producing agricultural products, were necessarily barren of settlement; and how long this snapshot of late sixteenth century rural life continued. It is not until the 1930s, under the British Mandate, that a comparative exercise was carried out throughout Jordan (Fishbach 1994). However, land registration had been proceeding since the mid-nineteenth century, and nineteenth century travellers' accounts, the 1881 Palestine Exploration Fund map of a portion of Jordan, the 1899 Schumacher map of Ajlun and the 1889 Conder map of Moab do give some comparison.

The sixteenth century *defter* demonstrates variation in economic strategies within Jordan; nineteenth century land registration documents and court records show variation in the relationships between region and government. No variation in material culture can be shown by these documents and here one must turn to archaeology.

Environment

Climate, Vegetation and Wildlife

While the climate in Jordan has not dramatically changed for the last 4000 years, there have been long-term wet and dry cycles which can have major effects on the rural economy and settlement. It has been suggested that one such cool, wet cycle affected the Middle East in the seventeenth–nineteenth centuries, bringing more favourable conditions for agriculture (Koucky 1987: 19: Faroqhi 1994: 467). More evidence on the micro-level (e.g. dendrochronology) is needed before such a conclusion can be sustained or rejected. It is ironic that, if correct, such an optimum period for the agricultural economy seems to equate with a period of low settlement figures. Certainly the local variability in climatic conditions is not in doubt and this has had an impact on the type of economic strategy followed.

By the Ottoman period, it seems from historical accounts that most of the natural vegetation cover had been removed in the course of agriculture, grazing and for the collection of firewood and building material. The increased demand for wood during the building and running of the Hijaz railway is inevitably cited as the reason behind the denuding of Jordan's forests. Traces of the branch railway line extending into the previously wooded area around Shawbak in south Jordan can still be seen on the ground. Nineteenth century travellers' accounts mention the wide-open pastures on the plateau, the fields of corn and thickets in the wadis but not great stands of woodland. The analysis of faunal remains from archaeological sites gives a checklist of the kinds of wild animals found in a localized area. At Khirbat Faris, faunal remains attest to the presence and/or hunting of (possibly) wild boar, gazelle, oryx, fox, large felid (Persian lion, leopard or cheetah) porcupine and Egyptian vulture (Rielly 1989;

Yeomans 2003). At Tall Hisban the wild animals included gazelle, wild boar, ibex, hare, fox and hyena (LaBianca and Lacelle 1986: 68).

Natural Disasters: Plague, Drought and Earthquakes

The cycle of natural disasters that affected Jordan throughout this and preceding periods has often been used as an explanation for the comparative paucity of rural settlement. Along with general insecurity, plague, drought and earthquakes are taken to account for "the flight of the peasant from the land," the decline in sedentary agriculture and permanent settlement (Brown 1984; Lewis 1987: 13). While all these natural disasters are the backdrop against which the period should be understood, they are not always phenomena detectable in the archaeological record.

The plague epidemic that struck Egypt and Syria in the preceding Mamluk Period was undoubtedly the devastating pneumonic plague which led to a definite demographic decline (Dols 1979). However, the strain of plague affecting this area in the sixteenth–nineteenth centuries is not identified in the historical literature and its impact on population figures cannot be assessed. Pneumonic plague is almost always fatal. Bubonic plague is "one of the least contagious epidemic diseases and causes few deaths" (Dols 1979: 169). Added to this is the question of the extent to which the plague would have spread rapidly in rural and often remote districts. Rogan suggests that while the plague may not have spread rapidly in rural districts, it would have caused depopulation of the countryside as the population migrated into the plague-ravaged towns of Jerusalem and Damascus (pers. comm.).

Throughout the Ottoman period, agriculture in Jordan was largely dependent on rainfall. In years of no rain, the impact on agriculture is devastating. In a more recent period, the droughts of the 1940s–50s in central Jordan led to far-reaching changes as the village of Qasr was more permanently occupied to take advantage of the government water and food-distribution centre while the cattle of the nearby Beni Hamaida tribe were slaughtered (Kana'an and McQuitty 1994; Lancaster and Lancaster 1995: 116). Such periods are not recorded in history on this local level but their occurrence may account for radical shifts in local settlement type and pattern as well as economic strategy. The effect of droughts on pastoralism is equally dramatic as herds are slaughtered or die for want of food and water, and nomads and their herds move farther into cultivated lands in search of water and grazing.

Archaeologists tend to have a rather selective attitude towards earthquakes and use them conveniently for explaining destruction or abandonment episodes within settlements. The information comprising earthquake tables is usually obtained from historical information derived from chronicles often several decades and geographically distant from the chronicler who may exaggerate or underestimate damage and casulties for their own purpose. In addition, effected areas miss out on being recorded if they are remote from urban centres. Poirier and Taher, when considering the lack of information on earthquakes of the fifteenth–eighteenth centuries mentioned in Arab chronicles, conclude it is "probable that earthquakes ceased being recorded due to the low level of cultural life in Damascus under Mamluk and Ottoman rule" (1980: 2186). However, one major earthquake, in AD 1588, is historically attested for this period with its epicentre in the Northern Hijaz (Ambraseys and Melville 1989: 1279). There were regular smaller and localized shocks and tremors throughout the Ottoman Period (Ghawanmeh 1992: 53–60:) but the effects of the earthquakes are not known outside urban areas.

Land-use and Economy

Throughout history, the main land-use and economic strategy followed in Jordan has been mixed farming with pockets of specialization. Rather than seeing a dichotomy between nomadic pastoralism and settled agriculture, it is considered more useful to conceive of a continuum with specialized nomadic pastoralism at one end and intensive sedentary agriculture at the other (Johns *et al.* 1989). The proportion of pastoralism and agriculture to each other varies between communities exploiting the same environmental zone and through time. There are additional variations in the type of agriculture practised, whether intensive or extensive (Davis 1991: 138–139). Mixed farming can be practised from a permanently built settlement or a cave or a tent or a combination of the three, that is, the population can be sedentary or semi-nomadic and the archaeologist cannot always be certain that lack of permanent settlement means nomadic pastoralism. In short, the simple term "mixed farming economy" conceals a wealth of complexity.

The *defter*s give a fine overview of the type of rural economy extant in the sixteenth century and reveal the economic variation in the country with its balance of agriculture and pastoralism (Figure 17.2). In the northern hills, a concentration of mixed-farming villages is found. Olives, fruit-trees and pulses were cultivated on terraces with extensive cultivation of wheat and barley taking place on flatter land. To the east, in the southern reaches of the Hauran, the concentration of agricultural production is on wheat, with summer-crops and barley providing a sizeable fraction. The area to the south of Wadi Zarqa is recorded in the *defter*s as nomadic with a large number of *mazraa* producing a fixed amount of taxes, but what the balance of produce is not clear. On the Karak Plateau the balance is also characteristic of a mixed-farming economy, although different from that farther north, with wheat/barley/summer crops and livestock being in almost

equal quantity. This balance remains true for the hilly area of Shawbak where fruit trees including vines and olives replace summer crops. Livestock form part of the produce proportion of all areas but do show concentrations on the Karak Plateau and on the eastern edge of the Jordan Valley. They are almost entirely absent from the southern Hauran Plain. Singer notes that in the *defter* for Palestine the term "goat" may well include sheep as well (1994: 51). The area south of Shawbak lay in the *vilayat* of *Misr* (Egypt) and the taxable produce for these areas is not recorded in this *defter*. The archaeological information to compare with this situation is simply not available: archaeology can provide the localized view but rarely the grand sweep. Two sites that have produced adequate data for suggesting the economic regime that was practised are Khirbat Faris (Rielly 1989; Yeomans 2003) and Tall Hisban (LaBianca and von den Driesch 1995: 72). In the early Ottoman period at Khirbat Faris, the environmental evidence shows a mixed-farming community herding overwhelmingly sheep/goat, with cattle being raised as a significant minority (for an account of this practice in the same area in

Figure 17.2 Map showing economic variety in the sixteenth century. Based on Hütteroth and Abdulfattah (1977).

recent times see Lancaster and Lancaster 1999: 202–203). The slaughter pattern of the cattle shows that the animals were not kept to beyond four years: this suggests that they were kept mainly for their meat. Camel-meat was also a significant part of the diet. Over time, the proportion of sheep to goats changes, with goats becoming more numerous. Sheep exist better with cultivation and goats fare better in degraded conditions (Köhler-Rollefson 1989: 91). Other domesticated animals included donkey, horse, dog, cat, dove and chicken. Salt-water fish are present, suggesting trade with the Red Sea. Botanical evidence from the same period suggests the cultivation of barley, wheat, millet, oat and possibly sorghum with other legume crops, for example, lentil, bitter vetch and common pea being grown alongside. Stones of cultivated fruit/nut trees were also found on the site, including grape, date, fig, pistachio and olive. The botanical remains analysed in detail seem to be crop by-products that have ultimately been used as fuel for clay ovens/*tawabeen*, whether directly or as animal fodder which, in dung form, was used as fuel (Charles 1992; Charles and Hoppé 1997–1998). The faunal evidence from Tall Hisban is interpreted as belonging to a later period, namely, 1870–1976. The range of domesticated species is similar to that at Khirbat Faris: sheep, goat, cattle, pig, camel, ass, horse, dog and cat. There is a slight preponderance of goat and the cattle bones have butcher-marks, indicating that they were used for meat (LaBianca and von den Driesch 1995: 103). The botanical information is based on a few samples and shows cultivation of wheat and barley with legumes and a few olive stones (Gichon and Linden 1986: 125).

Trade

The provisioning of the Hajj caravan with its demand for transport and baggage animals, grain and fresh meat provided a major annual market for the Jordanian countryside (Landau 1971: 59). The traffic in grain was also carried on westwards to Palestine and the markets in Jerusalem and Khalil/Hebron. The Bedouin also sent plant-ash to Nablus for the soap industry (Lancaster and Lancaster 1995: 118) while bitumen was collected from the Dead Sea for use as fuel and in veterinary remedies. Indigo and sulphur were traded from the Jordan Valley (Hütteroth and Abdulfattah 1977: 83). Urban merchants from the towns of Palestine and Syria came to Jordan to trade manufactured goods such as pottery, textiles, tobacco pipes and glass but for the most part the economy was subsistence-based where barter rather than money-exchange was the rule. The trade was between the raw materials of Jordan and the manufactured goods of Syria and Palestine. Exchange undoubtedly took place between the various life-style groups, that is, pastoralists exchanging animals and dairy products with the grain of agriculturists. Such things, however, are not recorded in history or visible to archaeologists.

Archaeological Framework

There are methodological issues to be taken into account when considering the data used for reconstructing an Ottoman settlement hierarchy. As discussed below there are real problems in distinguishing the material culture of the Ottoman period. Most of the evidence relating to settlement patterns is derived from survey data that is itself reliant on well-dated artefacts. In the past this often led to a complete ignoring of the Ottoman period. Surveys themselves can be misleading: the surface ceramic data from Khirbat Faris bore little relation to the excavated remains beneath. The type of survey (e.g. purposive, intensive) influences the outcome. Taken together, these factors result in a patchy and undoubtedly inaccurate picture of the settlement pattern. Once the data has been retrieved there is the issue of its categorization. Commonly, in the Islamic centuries, dynastic terms, meaningful only for political periodization, have been used to describe material culture. The pitfalls and illogicality of this approach have been discussed elsewhere and increasingly archaeologists are using more appropriate terminology that can still be linked to political periodization and more regional circumstances (McQuitty 2005: 4; Walker and LaBianca 2003: 448; Whitcomb 1992: 386). For the purposes of this volume, organized in dynastic terms, this writer prefers the solution adopted by MacDonald *et al* (1992: 75) who refer to two main periods: Mamluk/Ottoman (thirteenth–end of the sixteenth centuries) and Ottoman/Modern (mid-nineteenth–early twentieth centuries). The archaeologically elusive seventeenth–early nineteenth centuries, termed Middle Ottoman by Walker and LaBianca, remain the great *lacuna*.

Survey coverage in Jordan has increased over the past ten years so that the centre and south of the country is reasonably well-covered. Surveys in the north of the country concentrate on the east–west wadi systems. These more recent surveys have on the whole been more intensive so that no longer is the presence or absence of a particular chronological period the sole fact recovered. Sites are no longer just considered as a dot on the map: their context is explored (e.g. the Pella Hinterland Survey, Watson and O'Hea 1996). This contributes to off-site information, which presents itself as scatters of material culture, usually ceramics, that may indicate complementary activities e.g. animal shelters, rural cemeteries, field terraces and manuring, which enable interpretations of *how* the landscape was used rather than just *when*.

However patchy, the survey information shows that by the Ottoman period settlement in Jordan was overwhelmingly rural. Coupled with historical evidence, broad statements regarding the pattern of this settlement can be proposed. In general it seems that areas of more intensive agriculture where olives and fruit-trees were part of the farming-cycle, retained their permanent village settlement into the nineteenth century. Although there has been no archaeological excavation in these villages, hints from the standing architecture support this statement. In the village of Hubras and the Ajlun Hills, there is evidence that the Ayyubid/Mamluk village mosques continued in use into the Ottoman period (MacKenzie 2002; Walker 2005). In contrast, by the seventeenth century, areas of grain and summer-crop production (Irbid Plains, Madaba plains, Karak Plateau) show nuclei of permanent settlement, e.g. Karak, and in their hinterland, seasonally—but regularly—used buildings and land. Here, the use of the land was permanent while the settlements were both seasonal and permanent. For these areas, the settlements permanently occupied after the sixteenth century seem to be concentrated along the western plateau edge where access was eastwards to a hinterland of grain-growing land and westwards down the *wadis* to the Jordan Valley/Wadi Arabah. Irrigated agriculture producing both grain and summer-crops was a feature of *wadi* cultivation (Charles and Hoppé 2003).

Ottoman Imperial Settlement and Architecture

The prime concern of the Ottoman sultans was to maintain and protect the Islamic pilgrimage route through their newly acquired territory of Bilad al-Sham (*Darb al-Hajj al-Shami*). During the reign of Suleyman the Magnificent (AD 1520–1566), the route was shifted eastwards from the King's Highway to the present-day Desert Highway. Within Jordan, five forts were established in the sixteenth century (Mafraq, Dabaah, Qalat Qatrana, Qalat Unayza, Qalat Maan) and four in the eighteenth (Ziza, Qalat Hasa, Qalat Fassua, Qalat Mudawwara). All the forts have the same basic square plan with a central courtyard opening onto stables and storage-rooms. The upper floor usually contained accommodation for the garrison, a *mihrab* (mosque) and sometimes a stairway leading to an upper parapet. The Hajj caravan would camp outside the fort. The sixteenth century examples show more architectural decoration while the details of the military architecture vary with the development in military technology. One of these forts, Qalat Unayza, has been excavated but unfortunately little material culture was found *in situ* (Petersen 2003).

The major function of these garrisons was to provide protection to the water-supplies, i.e. cisterns and water-management systems in nearby *wadis*, on which the caravan depended. Besides the large cisterns, related installations that still survive include the road itself and bridges. During these periods, fortified sites further west, such as Ajlun, Karak and Shawbak castles were also used for guarding resources (Brown 1988: 240), and it may be that sites such as Khirbat Dusaq,[2] near Shawbak, should be considered as part of Ottoman guardianship of communication routes. Brünnow and von Domaszewski recorded Khirbat Dusaq as "eine Karawanserai aus saraze-

nische Zeit" (1904: 98; Glueck 1934: 76) and produced a plan showing three structures built on an enclosing courtyard wall. Wallin (cited in Brünnow and von Domaszewski 1904: 463) had visited the site earlier in 1854 when it was abandoned. His Bedouin guide told him that the site, known as "Khan Alzebib," was a Hajj route station built by Sultan Suleiman. Now all that remains are two parallel barrel-vaulted galleries with no evidence for connecting walls. The construction is of stone with simple stone surround to the windows. Udhruh fort also seems to be another candidate for imperial military architecture. It guards both a communication route and water source. The construction date is unknown but it is similar in form to the sixteenth century fort at Qasr Qatrana. The elevation and *khanat* plan show several phases of rebuilding. The façade is plain with a machicolation over the doorway and arrow-slits along the top storeys (Killick 1983: 115). The fort at Aqaba housed a garrison and was used by Egyptian pilgrims in the same manner as those on the *Darb al-Hajj al-Shami*. Its visible form dates from the early sixteenth century but was refurbished by Sultan Murad III in AD 1587–1588. The fort featured prominently in the First World War/Great Arab Revolt when its walls and internal building ranges were partly destroyed (De Meulemeester and Pringle 2003). While not strictly speaking architecture but dating from the same period, the trenches and machine-gun emplacements linked with the Turkish defence of Maan are still visible in aerial photographs (Kennedy and Bewley 2004: 271).

It is the Hajj route, not surprisingly, which again provides a good example of nineteenth century Ottoman imperial architecture, standardized throughout the empire. The Hijaz railway, running from Istanbul to Makkah (Mecca), was completed in 1908. Railway stations took the place of Hajj forts and were standardized in design from north to south. The simple rectangular two-storey structures were roofed with a pitched, tiled roof supported by iron I-beams and represent a typically Ottoman implant into the local architectural tradition (Daher 1995: 341–49, Figure 17.3). Of similar style is the complex at Maan where the Railway Hotel was used as a residence by Emir (later King) Abdullah (Kennedy and Bewley 2004: 269).

As the Ottomans reasserted their control over the province south of Damascus, a school was built at Karak. After the Ottoman Education Law of 1869, which tried to regulate more efficiently the organization of education, a number of state schools were set up, mainly for the Muslim population (Landau 1975: 499). Ottoman education was free; the schools were supported by *waqf* endowments. Turkish was the language of instruction for a curriculum that included religious instruction. The foundation of these schools was a direct case of instilling Ottoman values in previously excluded tribal populations and thus "incorporating the periphery" (Rogan 1996;

Figure 17.3 Qatrana railway station (A. McQuitty).

1999). The Kerak school was built in 1893 on the orders of Sultan Abdul Hamid II and is a two-storey building arranged around a central courtyard. It is still in use today as the Karak Boys' Secondary School. One other government building that is still in use is the *serai* in Irbid, converted from the *kaymakam* residence to the town's prison to the town's museum. This building was constructed in the mid-nineteenth century and is very similar in detail to the urban architecture of that period. Its plan is akin to the earlier Hajj forts and caravanserai being square surrounding a central courtyard. The entrance, which would have contained the *kaymakam* residence, consists of two storeys and is located opposite an *iwan* wing.

Towns

In the *defters*, size was no criterion for determining whether a settlement was a town (Hütteroth and Abdulfattah 1977: 23). The term "town" applied to settlements that included non-agricultural activities and that were subject to different taxes, that is, its function not its form. Until the mid-nineteenth century, little is known about the physical aspect of settlements that in the sixteenth century Ottoman tax-records are called towns. Hubras, near Irbid, is mentioned in the *defters* as a town and is now the focus of a multi-disciplinary project (Walker 2005). At present, it is a large village and there are few

traces of pre-nineteenth century buildings. With few exceptions, it was not until the mid-nineteenth century that settlements with the recognizable form of towns or urban centres, for example, Salt and Irbid, started to appear in Jordan. Until that time the urban centres lay north and west in Damascus, Jerusalem and Khalil, while seasonal markets were regularly provided by the Hajj pilgrimage. Karak, which, due to its strategic situation, is an exception, commanded both the routes north–south and westwards to the Jordan Valley and the fertile hinterland of the Karak Plateau. It is a natural central place and was both a garrison and a market centre, a role it played in the preceding Mamluk period. Maan, with its position on the Hajj route and location around permanent springs, was also an exception.

The architecture of the town of Salt stands out in Jordan; the revival of Salt and its transformation from a small rural centre to an urban settlement started in 1867 when the *vali* of Damascus re-established order and Ottoman control. New styles and building materials were introduced and a large number of trading families moved east from Nablus bringing new ideas and architects with them. A Middle Eastern regional style, recognizable from Jaffa to Nablus to Alexandria, developed and is evident in the façades of the merchants' buildings. In 1907 the Small Mosque, a building that with its pitched tile roof and large windows would not look out of place in any Anatolian town, was erected in Salt (Khatib and al-Asir 1995). The town of Madaba is another excellent example of a settlement that includes buildings of regional urban style (Denton and St. Laurent 1996) and even Irbid boasted houses with intricate façades.

Vernacular Settlement and Architecture

Rural Settlement

From historical sources, primarily the *defter i-mufassal*, it is known that the rural settlement of sixteenth century Jordan encompassed both permanent and seasonal settlement. The framework for reconstruction of the settlement hierarchy exists: the challenge lies in detailing its physical attributes. The *defter* identifies *qarya*, *mazraa* and *khirbah* (Hütteroth and Abdulfattah 1977: 22–56). *Qarya* refers to a permanently inhabited rural settlement of any size. The normal translation of *mazraa* is "an agricultural area with no permanent settlement" i.e. seasonal settlement that is defined by the activity carried out rather than the physical nature of the settlement. Put another way, based on work in Syria, Rafeq (1984) and Schilcher (1991: 186) have suggested that the term should be interpreted as defining the type of agricultural produce, that is, grain, rather than the type of occupation. *Khirbah* (Khirbat) is generally translated as "ruins" but the term may stay in use as part of a populated settlement name. These fiscal categories are not distinguishable archaeologically. In the survey of the Karak Plateau, Miller (1991: 171–172) records 77 "deserted village" settlements of the Middle/Late Islamic period. This can be compared with the 23 villages recorded in the *defter* for the same area, Nahiya Karak. In addition, for the same area, 20 percent of the taxation revenue is indicated as coming from *mazraa*: it seems reasonable to assume that some of the 77 sites that Miller recorded represent *mazraa* (Hütteroth and Abdulfattah 1977: 96, 172).

In many regions of Jordan there is evidence of continuous village occupation, particularly in the northern part of the country. These villages have been the subject of study by archaeologists, architects, anthropologists, historians and developers (Biewers 1992, 1997; Biewers and Kana'an 1993; Fakhoury and Sweiss 1995; Kana'an and al-Rifai 1988; Kana'an and McQuitty 1994; Khammash 1986; Merschen 1992; Noca 1985). In the centre and south of Jordan the majority of settlements, based on ethno-historical sources, seem to have been refounded during Ottoman/Modern times after a period of abandonment or use as a seasonal settlement by semi-nomadic tribes. Often the buildings of these settlements incorporated caves or there are examples of caves themselves forming nucleated "cave-villages." LaBianca has quite rightly emphasized the importance of the cave as a dwelling house and its importance in the site hierarchy.

Failure to take caves into account leads to a significant under-estimation of settlement figures. Habitation caves typically had a masonry entrance and smoke-blackened ceilings from the use of domestic fires (LaBianca 1991: 227–228; MacDonald (ed.) 1988: 272; Walker and LaBianca 2003: 461). Perhaps the best-known example of caves being used for habitation comes from Petra where, until recently, the Bedul occupied both Nabataean tombs and caves (Bienkowski and Chlebik 1991).

Specific to the Ottoman period, purely archaeological evidence is more patchy. Several abandoned late Ottoman villages have been recorded on survey (MacKenzie 2002) and in the Wadi Ziqlab Banning *et al.* excavated a nearly complete barrel-vaulted structure at Ras Qabub that contained Late Ottoman material (1989: 54). At Khirbat Faris in central Jordan, a complex of barrel-vaulted units and oven-houses clustered around a courtyard suggest a *qaraya* in the Late Mamluk/Early Ottoman period that by the nineteenth century had been replaced by a *mazraa*. Two standing and one unexcavated "arch-and-grain-bin"[3] houses date from the last years of the nineteenth century and were part of a farming complex used during the production and storage of grain by a semi-nomadic population: the *mazraa*. At Tall Hisban, also in central Jordan, a Mamluk barrel-vaulted complex makes way for a nineteenth century cemetery and an earlier building is converted into a "transverse-arch house," (Walker and LaBianca 2003: 454). In southern Jordan, north of Petra, Lindner and his team have identified a series of small settlements near springs and agricultural land that the team date to the Mamluk and Ottoman period (1999). The dating evidence is provided by ceramics that from the illustrations and description appear to this author to date from much later in the Ottoman period. The architecture is of individual stone-built units opening onto courtyards or alleys and with roofs supported by posts or re-used columns. In the same area similar architecture is reported from Baja I (Bienert *et al* 2000: 135). Several of these settlements have been used seasonally in the last twenty years by a semi-nomadic population.

Seasonal use of rock-shelters in the Ottoman period has been archaeologically recorded at Tur Imdai (Russell and Simms 1987). Several surveys record sites that are almost certainly related to nomadic and semi-nomadic pastoralist populations (MacDonald (ed.) 1988: 255–280; Miller 1991). These sites not only include caves but also tent sites and animal pens. Modern studies of tent sites have shown that the same location is used repeatedly for seasonal exploitation of the area and that the traces of tent emplacements and their hearths can be easily distinguished (Banning and Köhler-Rollefson 1992; Palmer 2000). These sites are difficult to date but they must be considered as part of the settlement hierarchy if the complexity of Ottoman land-use is to be realized. It is much easier to detect these sites on the fringes of cultivated land

Figure 17.4 Reconstruction drawing of a "transverse-arch house" (S. Pressey).

but that does not mean that their occupants were confined to these fringes: all trace of these ephemeral sites on land now cultivated will have been erased over time.

This disparate evidence leads to one main conclusion —that the chronological shift in settlement patterns varies considerably regionally and is not necessarily a shift between occupation and abandonment but between characters of occupation, i.e. between seasonal and permanent.

Vernacular Architecture

Almost without exception the rural houses of Ottoman Jordan are single storey and single-unit opening directly onto the courtyard rather than interconnecting with each other. Various types of building that span the whole period and geographical area are known from excavations and extant villages.

Stone-built barrel-vaulted houses are known from earlier Mamluk contexts but continued to be constructed until the recent past. They are small (average dimension 4.5 x 3.00 m) and of sturdy but haphazard construction. The massive side-walls, often one metre thick, support a vault of stone, rubble and large amounts of mud mortar. The vault was constructed over a form of heaped-up sacks filled with soil or chaff that was removed once the vault was complete. The end-walls are almost incidental being narrow and non-load-bearing, often only one-course wide. The usual position of

the door was in the end-wall. These barrel-vaulted rooms varied between being free-standing or part of a courtyard complex. Khammash comments that such barrel-vaulted houses were a common sight in Jordanian villages of the recent past when they were used as animal stables or oven-houses (1986: 43). A twentieth century example at Hmoud was used for both dwelling and storage.

The "transverse arch house" plans show variation from north to south but are based on a similar construction method (McQuitty 2005, Figure 17.4). They are the core of the nucleated "traditional" villages of mid-nineteenth–early twentieth century Jordan. Apart from the Jordan Valley, all construction is in stone. Most of the houses measure c. 9.5 x 10.5 m with a roofed area ranging from 64–100 m². The house is a simple rectangular shape with minimal openings with the front door always in the wall parallel to the arches. The house-walls are not built in foundation-trenches. Arches support a flat roof of beams, brushwood and earth. The arches spring from arch-walls that are built perpendicular to the house-wall or from the base of the house-wall rather than being bonded to the house-wall. The space between the arch-walls is often taken up with *rawiyat* (grain bins) or used for free-standing storage bins used for *qawair* (free-standing storage bins). Particularly in the south of Jordan storage facilities seem to have been provided by a separate and semi-secret room

(Biewers 1990: 112 construction no. 158). In the Ajlun Hills, examples can be found that closely mirror those houses common in Palestine. Here, humans, agricultural stores and animals are all housed under one roof and the division in use of space is marked by differences in height. The animals are stabled on the lower level, near the door; while the main sleeping and entertainment space is on an upper level. Below that is a storage area. Elsewhere the houses do not show the same height divisions. Examples of this type of construction are known from the late twelfth century at Khirbat Faris (McQuitty 2005: 7), the fourteenth century in northern Syria (Fuller and Fuller 1987–1988: 279) and the eighteenth century, also in Syria (Aurenche 1990:46).

Cross-vaulted houses are far less common in villages and where they do occur, seem to be concentrated in northern and central Jordan where they date predominantly from the mid-nineteenth century onwards. Umm Qays is the best-known example—here many of the houses were domed and cross-vaulted using the skill of professional masons brought from Palestine (Shami 1989). Examples are also known from Bayt Ras (McQuitty f.c.), Hartha (McQuitty 2004), Tall Hisban (Walker and LaBianca 2003), Irbid (McQuitty 1989), Main (Ma'in) (Khammash 1986) Madaba (Denton and St. Laurent 1996), Muhei, Karak and Tibneh (Khammash 1986). In general, vaulting is used in buildings that variously had a specialist use such as the motorized grain-mill in Irbid or were part of housing complexes owned by wealthier sections of society as at Umm Qays and Tibneh or were part of

urban architecture as in Madaba and Karak. By the end of the nineteenth century urban style was definitely making incursions into rural architecture. In the village of Hartha, the house of Hajj Guweida Suleiman Obeidat, a member of the dominant tribe in the district, shows ornate treatment of the entrance façade which would be more in place in towns such as Salt or Irbid (McQuitty 2004b, Figure 17.5). This phenomenon was obviously linked to wealth accumulation and is also a graphic reminder of the tribalism that had by then in some places replaced and in others supplemented Ottoman central government as the main power in the land. Many of the complexes including vaulted rooms decorated with fine masonry were tribal strongholds designed not just as farmsteads but also to impress the surrounding population. Examples include eighteenth century Tibneh that was the power-base of the Shraydeh tribe. The family's traditional residence, *al-Alali*, crowns the hill on which the village is situated. It is a two-storey cross-vaulted construction that stands out from the surrounding village of flat-roofed and arched houses. A large pointed arch distinguishes the entrance and there is ribbed stone decoration around the windows. A prayer-room is included in the upper floor. It is further distinguished from the surrounding village houses of agriculturalists since no courtyard is attached (Khammash 1986: 62–66). Other examples are provided by the nineteenth century residental/agricultural complex at Tall Hisban that was a centre for either the Nabulsi family or Adwan tribe (Walker and LaBianca 2003: 456) and the eighteenth century Adwan *qasr* (see discussion

Figure 17.5 Nineteenth century house of Haj Guweida Suleiman Obeidat in Hartha (A. McQuitty).

Figure 17.6 Interior of nineteenth century "arch-and-grain-bin" house at Qasr (A. McQuitty).

below) located near Ayn Hisban (LaBianca 2000: 204).

The "arch-and-grain-bin" houses employ the same construction technique as used for the "transverse arch house" but on a much larger scale. The roofed area falls within the range 135–225 m² and the average internal height is five metres. The sensation of standing inside an intact example is one of being in a dark and lofty cavern (Figure 17.6). The spaces between the arch-walls were closed-off, plastered and used as *rawiyatm*, as general storage rooms or as private areas for sleeping (although such houses were not routinely used for dwelling). The *rawiyat* was filled through a hole in the roof and a common sight in such buildings is the ramp up which the sacks of grain were dragged or carried by donkeys to be poured into the bin. Apart from the grain-bins there are generally few built-in features, mainly various shaped-niches recessed into the thick walls. The exterior is severe and fortress-like with no windows. Such houses were essentially store-houses and indicative of an extensive agricultural/generalized (as opposed to specialized) pastoral regime. Prior to and at the same time as grain-storage in such houses, grain was stored and hidden in cisterns. They were used as a complement to the tents in which the household's dwelling and socializing took place. The "arch-and-grain-bin" house is distinguished by standing in isolation or as part of a small farmstead rather than clustering around a courtyard. Mitqal Pasha, from the Beni-Sakhr tribe, while continuing to live in his tent, constructed one such house to be part store-house, part family and tribal headquarters, at the centre of his territory in Umm Amad near Amman (Lewis 1987). Nineteenth century examples have been recorded at Khirbat Faris and Qasr (Kana'an and McQuitty 1994; McQuitty 2005). In general the "arch-and-grain-bin" houses share a distribution with the zones where the cultivation of grain is predominant. The local term for these buildings is *qasr* and LaBianca has suggested that these buildings can develop into "*qusur* villages," being clusters of fortified farms/substantial agricultural compounds (LaBianca 1990: 201–232), or, as above at Khirbat Faris, *mazraa*.

Water-Mills

Water-mills (McQuitty 2004a) for grinding grain were an integral part of the Jordanian rural economy and are commonly attributed to the Ottoman period although they continued in use until the middle of the twentieth century and undoubtedly had earlier antecedents (Abu Delu 1995; McQuitty 1995). Dating from the start of the Ottoman period, there are many historical references to the taxation of mills in the sixteenth century *defter*. Nineteenth century European travellers also comment frequently on their occurrence. Conder reports: "At

Sumieh and below Ain Hesban are the mills, which were erected by Dhiab of the Adwan in the year 1191 of the Hejirah (ad 1777)" (1889: 129). Ottoman land registers of the late nineteenth century record their registration, sale and restoration (Rogan 1995). Archaeological evidence also suggests this span of construction and use. Excavation by Malkawi (1994) of five mill-houses in the Wadi Kufranjah produced Late Mamluk–Early Ottoman ceramics. By calculating the rate of tufa accumulation in the water-channel leading to the penstock, Gardiner and McQuitty suggest an eighteenth century date for mills in the Wadi Arab in north Jordan (1987: 28).

All these mills are of the *arubah* penstock/horizontal-wheeled type and usually comprise a single tower attached to what would have been a mill-house (Figure 17.7). The mills are often part of a chain of mills fed by a water-channel taken from higher up in the wadi. The masonry of the tower, the chute and its immediate channel were of good quality. The techniques required for building the *arubah* penstock and the wheel-chamber were specific and it seems likely that there were groups of masons specializing in building the mechanisms of water-mills. The only exception to this horizontal-wheeled type mill are the five vertical undershot and possible overshot mills at *Lajjun*. These mills relate to the early twentieth century stationing of a Turkish garrison at the spring of *Lajjun* and are a totally alien import into Jordanian mill technology (de Vries pers. comm.). Both types were used for milling grain although the horizontal-wheeled type was used in earlier periods for crushing sugar-cane (see Walmsley this volume, Chapter 16).

From historical evidence, it appears that the mill-owners of the eighteenth and nineteenth centuries were individuals or tribes, not necessarily local, who were responsible for the maintenance and refurbishment of the equipment (Conder 1889: 129; Rogan 1995: 754–755). The owners were "paid" in kind with a proportion of the grain to be milled (Palmer 1998: 155). Mills were an integral part of the subsistence rather than market economy. The farmers and Bedouin alike brought their own grain to be milled. If cereals were sold to markets outside the region, they were traded as grain which keeps better than flour.

Material Culture

Identifying Ottoman material culture remains the major challenge for archaeologists working in this period. To date, our knowledge of Ottoman ceramics in Jordan is based on rural assemblages, apart from Milwright's study of the corpus from Karak castle (2000). This has inevitably introduced an element of bias into the discourse about the nature of settlement and market networks that only future research can redress. Distinctions within material culture are traditionally used in Near Eastern archaeology as the main interpretative tool for survey and excavation results but the material culture may not

itself be well dated. Too often the distinctions become the basis for identifying chronological divisions when differences may be reflecting social divisions, for example, between pastoral and village sites, and between urban and village sites. In addition, scant attention has been paid to "late" levels that are often cleared rather than being stratigraphically excavated. The sites within Jordan that most reliably produce stratified Ottoman material are Tall Hisban and Khirbat Faris: both rural sites. In almost all of the major urban sites of earlier periods, for example, Umm Qays, Jarash, Pella, Humayma, and the continuously occupied villages throughout the country, ceramics have been found that are probably Ottoman but that have no context. However, the stratigraphic context is vital in establishing the chronology of Ottoman ceramics. Apart from the fine ware, much of the pottery may never be recognizable standing on its own.

Ceramics

There were several trends that continued into Ottoman and Early Modern times from the preceding periods and they are worth highlighting here.

1. An increasing division in terms of material culture assemblages between site types within regions, that is, a rural material assemblage as opposed to an urban material assemblage. Excavations of Mamluk/Early Ottoman Khirbat Faris, a rural site, have produced a handful of glazed sherds. Karak castle, a major site of the Mamluk Sultanate and only 20 km away, produced large amounts of glazed and unglazed wheel-made ware that continued into the Early Ottoman period (Milwright 2000: 194, fig. 2).

2. An increasing tendency for the production of hand-made rather than wheel-made coarse ware. By the Ottoman period, the overwhelming bulk of ceramics were hand-made and their chronological position is largely distinguished by stratigraphic means, that is, their date is not readily identified on survey. This fact too is subject to variation within site types and between regions: excavations at Tall Ti'innik (Taanach) in Palestine include a far greater percentage of wheel-made wares in the assemblages of later periods than those recognized in Jordan (Ziadeh 1995). This is also possibly part of a pattern that can be more generally identified in eighteenth–nineteenth century ceramic repertoires from Palestine: hand-made ceramics were gradually replaced by wheel made coarse wares (Milwright 2000:195).

3. Regional variation even within the hand-made coarse ware tradition. This trait had already been evident within Mamluk assemblages: a Hand-Made Geometrically Painted Ware (HMGPW) jar from southern Jordan differed in quality of fabric and decoration from one found in northern Palestine although they were both of the same broad type.

Figure 17.7 Diagram to show watermill technology (A. McQuitty).

Fine-Wares

Greater emphasis has been laid, in all periods, on the identification of fine-wares. This category includes lead-glazed ware, Chinese and European porcelain. The time period and place of manufacture of these ceramics is usually known and therefore they have great potential for illuminating chronological divisions and trading patterns. But in Jordan Ottoman fine-ware is largely confined to museum collections and heirlooms and is almost always

unprovenanced. Few sites that might produce imported fine-ware have been excavated. One exception is the Hajj fort of Qalat Unayza. Here "glazed and unglazed wheel-made pottery, tabun, fritware, porcelain and tobacco pipes" were part of a rubbish tip associated with the Ottoman fort were excavated by Petersen *et al* (2003: 65). Until now one has had to look beyond the modern borders for information on such ceramics (Gilmors *et al.* 1984; Pringle 1986; Miles 1985; Milwright 2000).

Equally, candidate sites for producing fine-wares have

been extensively re-used and successively cleared so that the material culture of recent centuries has no chance of surviving *in situ*. Karak castle was used by the locally pre-eminent tribes as a seat of "government" and by the Ottomans to garrison their troops until the beginning of the last century. Brown excavated in the Mamluk Palace which, according to the elders of the town, had been used in the early twentieth century as a prison (1989: 295). Since that time most of the vaults have been cleared out for various purposes, most recently to become part of the museum.

Coarse Wares

Hand-made as opposed to wheel-made coarse wares constitute the overwhelming majority of ceramics found both on survey and on excavation in late levels. For the Mamluk period, the best-known and ubiquitous hand-made ware is vividly painted with close geometric decoration (HMGPW, Johns 1998). However, pottery, like site-types, does not change with dynasty. It is almost certain that these ceramics continued into the sixteenth century. Indeed, there is good evidence to suppose, as the later discussion on tobacco-pipes shows, that many assemblages interpreted by excavators as Mamluk may in fact be later. Subsequent to the Mamluk period, relative to excavated sites in Jordan, there seems to be a trend for painted decoration to continue for some time, although on more crudely made fabric. Eventually the tradition of painting intricate geometric designs disappears or itself becomes crude. Brown reports, from Shawbak, decorated jar/jug forms with painted geometric decoration on crudely fashioned bodies with heavily chaff-pocked surfaces. Cooking-pots of hard grey ware with impressed raised bands on the exterior for decoration come from the same context. A base with a chaff-pocked, red slipped surface was also found (Brown 1988: 240, and Figure 17.8). It is this feature of a chaff-pocked, red-slipped surface that Sauer focuses on as distinguishing Ottoman ceramics from Tall Hisban (1993: 273). A number of "village" sites, e.g. Khirbat Muallaq, have been reported from the area north of Petra that have produced surface pottery including hand-made storage jars and cooking-pots, (Lindner 1999). Lindner suggests that these ceramics should be dated **pre-** the rise of HMPGW, i.e. pre-thirteenth century. However, some of the illustrated forms with their "swollen tongue" ledge handles and crudely applied decoration are suggestive of a later date. A very distinctive grey/black wheel-made coarse ware starts to appear in the eighteenth century. Such ceramics seem to have had an initial distribution in Jordan and north Palestine but by the Mamluk/Ottoman period this had spread to central and southern Palestine (Schaeffer 1989: 43). These vessels are commonly known as "Gaza" ware because numerous workshops for their manufacture were found there but it is likely that other production centres sprang

up in Palestine, (Milwright 2000: 196). At Tur Imdai, a seasonally occupied cave site in southern Jordan, a total of 16 pots were found, all but two of them hand-made. The wheel-made vessels were storage jars with a very dark grey exterior and dark brown core, probably Gaza Ware. All of these ceramics are dated on the basis of radiocarbon to the eighteenth century (Russell and Simms 1987). The excavators of the ceramics at Tur Imdai report that they could easily be mistaken for prehistoric examples were it not for the fact that their dating is fixed by radiocarbon. The functions suggested by the forms are that ceramics were used for cooking, food containers and storage.

The continuation of hand-made ceramic production in Jordan has been extensively documented in the last few years (Franken and Kalsbeek 1975; London and Sinclair 1991; Merschen 1985). In these ethnographic studies, the potters are always women producing hand-made pottery as part of the agricultural year, that is, seasonally. The forms are usually jars and jugs as well as large storage and water vessels that are decorated with applications of "Tree of Life" motifs or simulated rope bands, sherds of glazed pottery, fragments of mirror (Figure 17.9). The decoration does not include paint or slip. The pots are fired in a clamp or bonfire fuelled by dung. This twentieth century pottery fits well with the Late Ottoman/Modern tradition.

Lamps

Lamp-types, traditionally called Mamluk but found in Ottoman contexts, are variations of the saucer lamp, very similar to Bronze/Iron Age examples. Some were made with a loop handle reaching from the middle of a small saucer formed at the centre of the reservoir to the rim of the lamp and many were glazed (Kareem 1993: 220). Gichon and Linden suggest, based on stratigraphic evidence from an excavated bath-house/shrine in Palestine, that these open saucer lamps (without the handle) date from the eighteenth century (1984: 166). These lamps are not glazed: Gichon and Linden consider glaze and decorated closed shapes to be an indication of a Mamluk date. Little is known in Jordan of post-Mamluk lamps. Suggestions for examples of later Ottoman lamps are usually based on value judgments and the view that the poorer quality the manufacture is the later the date of the object. A lamp was found in abandonment rubble of the latest occupation phase at Khirbat Faris. It is hand-made from two pieces of clay. The height of the top section is more decorative than functional and the oil reservoir is exceptionally small (Figure 17.10).

Tobacco-Pipes

In Jordan, tobacco pipes are the most reliable chronological indicator of Ottoman material culture. Tobacco smoking was first introduced into the Ottoman empire in the early seventeenth century and became widespread

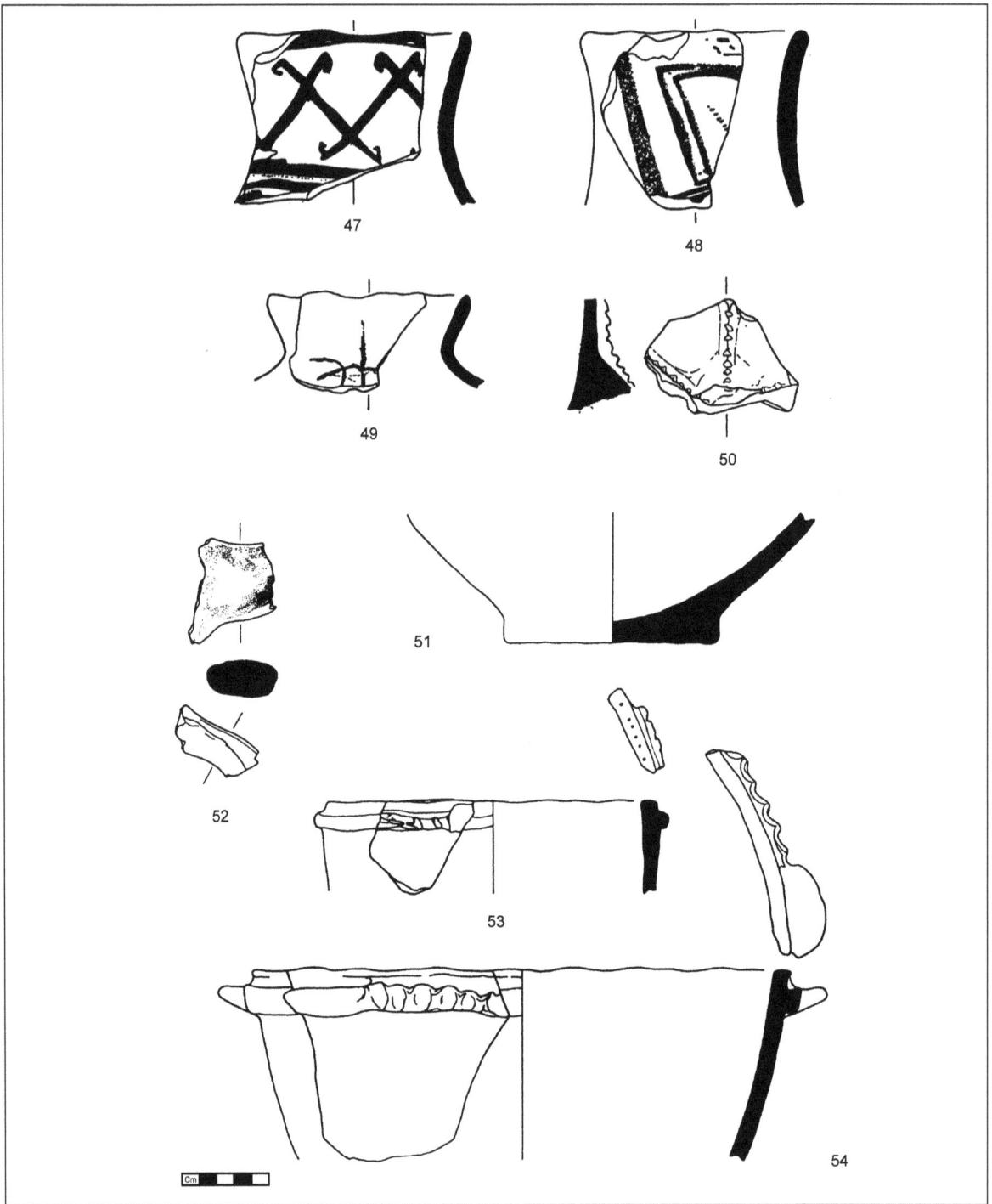

Figure 17.8 Ottoman pottery from Shawbak. Reproduced from Brown (1988: fig. 14): (47) Jug/Jar:Ware (W)=5YR 6/4 Light Reddish Brown; Exterior Slip (ES) 10R 5/6 Red; Exterior Paint (EP) = 10R 3/1 Dark Reddish Gray; Handmade (H). (48) Jug/Jar: W = 2.5YR 6/6 Light Red; ES = 10R 5YR 8/4 Pink; EP = 10R 5/4 Weak Red, 5YR 3/1 Dark Gray H. (49) Jug/Jar: W = 5YR 8/4 Pink; Self Slip; H. (50) Handle:W= 5YR 7/4 Pink; ES = 10YR 8/3 Very Pale Brown; H. (51) Base:W= 5YR 7/4 Pink; ES = 10R 5/4 Weak Red; H. (52) Handle: W = 2.5YR 6/6 Light Red; ES = 10R 5/6 Red; EP = 10R 4/1 Dark Reddish Gray; H. (53) Cooking Pot: W = 5YR 5/1 Gray; H. (54) Cooking Pot: W = 5YR 5/1 Gray; H.

in the latter part of the century. Smoking was part of the relaxation to be enjoyed in the increasing number of cafés that sprang up in the urban centres, e.g. Cairo and Jerusalem. Tobacco-smoking obviously quickly spread to more domestic surroundings and it was in the houses and rubbish-tips of Jordanian villages that the examples described below were found. Tobacco was grown in Anatolia, Lebanon, Palestine, Persia and arguably, Jordan (Baram 2000). For the archaeologist the significance of this is that any contexts containing pipe fragments are automatically dated to the seventeenth century and later. Many previous excavations have erroneously reported assemblages containing pipes as being Mamluk (e.g., Riis 1957).

Istanbul, Diyabaker and Luleburgaz near Edirne in Turkey, as well as Assiut in Egypt, are known to have been centres of pipe production (Robinson 1985: 152; Simpson 1990) and, closer to Jordan, Beirut, Nazareth, Jaffa and Jerusalem. Robinson comments that "Probably every town of any size had at least one pipe-maker. In lesser villages perhaps the potter would turn out a few pipes; he may have made his own moulds from a pipe or pipes brought from a major center" (1985: 153).

The Eastern or Turkish pipe consisted of a ceramic bowl, the most frequent find on survey and excavation, into which the stem was inserted. The bowls were made of specially washed and filtered fine clay in two-part moulds of stone or metal (Robinson 1985: 157). The earliest pipes were of white/grey clay, probably imitating European examples, but by the nineteenth century the most popular fabric was red clay which could be obtained in Egypt, the Lake Van area of Anatolia, and Bulgaria. When this red clay was not available, the alternatives would often be covered with a red slip (Robinson 1983: 266). Early pipe-bowls were small because of the high price and luxury nature of tobacco but by the end of the century the pipe bowls and stem opening were becoming larger. Their chronology, distribution and development have been well illustrated and analysed for urban sites in the Western Ottoman empire: the Sarachane, Istanbul (Hayes 1980), Corinth and the Athenian Agora (Robinson 1985), and the more rural Kerameikos, near Athens (Robinson 1983). An increasing number of sites in the Eastern Ottoman Empire, more particularly Bilad al-Sham, are producing single examples or small groups (for distribution see Baram 2000; Milwright 2000:203-5; Simpson 2000: 169–170). Recently, the excavation and analysis of a large assemblage of well-stratified pipes from a village site located within the structures of an earlier Crusader castle (Belmont Castle), in the Jerusalem area has enabled more sophisticated conclusions regarding their use within a site (Simpson 2000). Most of the pipe fragments were found in the central courtyard and Simpson suggests that this was due to pipe-smoking being a social activity carried out in the communal area where the men of the village gathered after a hard day's work to relax and smoke

Figure 17.9 Twentieth century *habia* from north Jordan (A. McQuitty).

tobacco. No evidence for imports from Europe, the urban centres of the Western Ottoman Empire or even Egypt were found which suggests that the production was very much a local affair.

In Jordan, pipes have been published from Jarash, Tall Hisban, Dhra al-Khan, Ras Qabub, Tawilan and Udhruh. In Jarash, four bowl fragments from the upper levels of the re-occupation in the northern Roman Theatre are recorded (Clark *et al.* 1986: 266). At Tall Hisban pipes "may have been near the surface in the village part of the site" (Sauer 1993: 273; Wimmer 1978: 150). At Dhra al-Khan, stratified tobacco pipes were found in levels dated by the excavator to the fourteenth–fifteenth centuries according to the ceramic type. Clearly the ceramics were all residual or there needs to be some re-interpretation. These fragments of pipe were "dusky-red" (Kareem 1993: 216, 259–260). At Ras Qabub, fragments of small pipe bowls were found in association with wheel-made pottery in a barrel-vaulted structure (Banning *et al.* 1989: 52). At Tawilan, a pipe fragment was found apparently out of context, associated with Nabataean/Roman pottery (Bennett and Bienkowski 1995: 92 and fig. 9.41.7). At Udhruh, pipe fragments appear to come from the southwest corner tower of the Roman fort (Killick 1983: 129). At Khirbat Faris, only four of the 11 fragments are stratified and these all come from upper abandonment levels. All the fragments illustrated come from the surface (Figure 17.10).

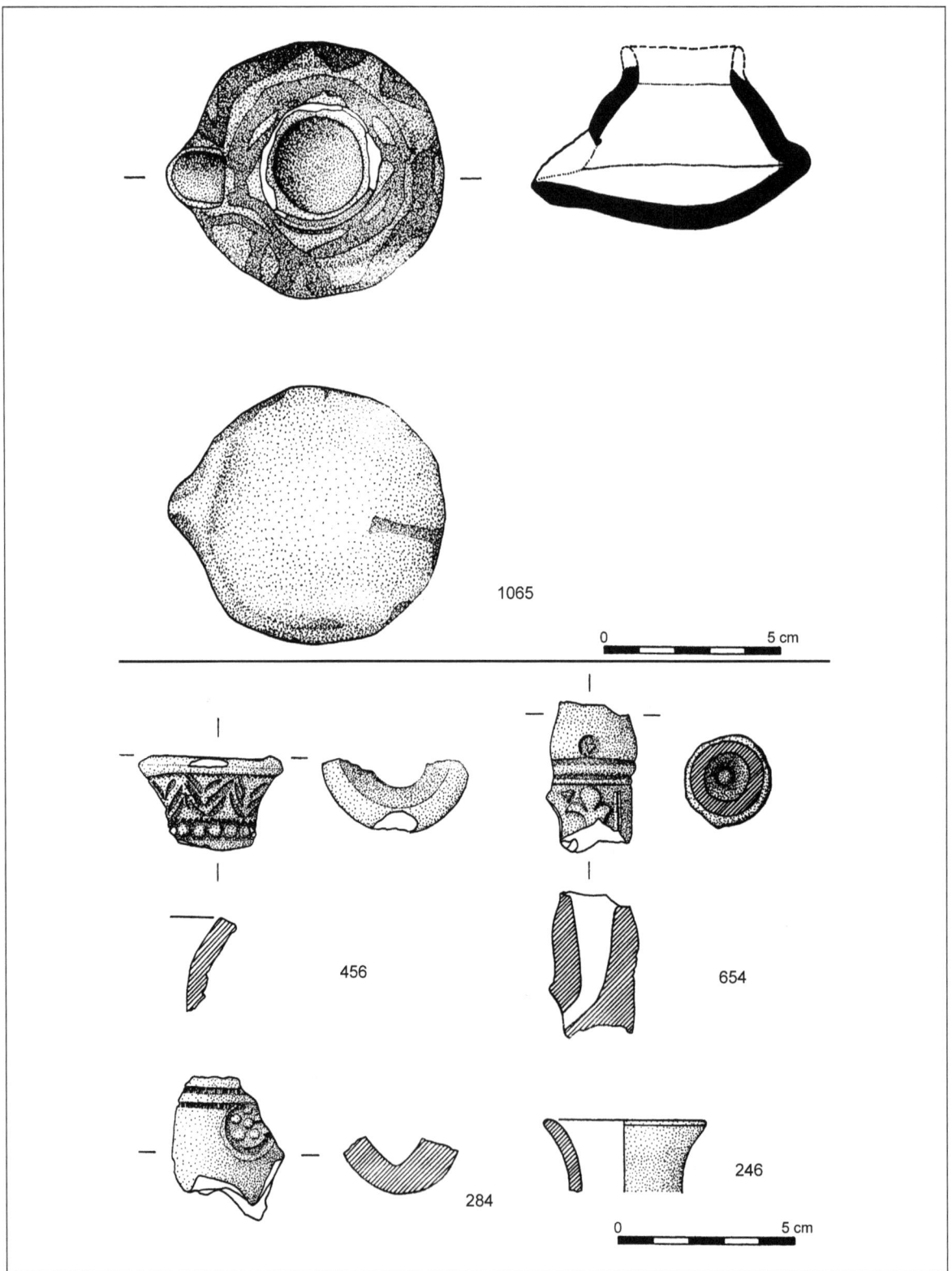

1065

0   5 cm

456

654

284

246

0   5 cm

Figure 17.10a Ottoman lamp and tobacco pipe fragments from Khirbat Faris (M. Sarley-Pontin).

Figure 17.10b Lamp and Pipe Description (descriptions by Madeline Sarley-Pontin).

(1065) Lamp: Core = 10R 6/6 Light Red; Exterior Surface slipped = 5YR 7/6 Pink and much effected by lime concretions. Interior Surface=10YR 7/1 Light Grey. Oxidized, hard, even firing. Plaster, basalt, shell and mica inclusions. Decoration = Weak Red 10R 4/4 paint unsteadily applied with wide zig-zag pattern. Context 194.

(246) Tobacco Pipe bowl rim and body. Core = 10R 6/8 Light Red; Exterior and Interior = 10R 5/1 Reddish Grey. Exterior Surface highly burnished, 10R 4/3 Weak Red. Interior Surface 10R 4/3 Weak Red, with no burnishing. Reduced firing, very hard, very smooth. Plaster, grog and basalt inclusions. Bell shaped bowl with everted rim. No decoration present. Ceramic spot date: c. 1850 onwards. Parallels: Hayes VIII. Surface.

(284) Tobacco Pipe-stem. Core=10YR 6/1 Light Brownish Grey; Exterior Surface burnished (10R 4/4) Weak Red. Oxidized, very hard, very smooth. Dense fabric. Flint inclusions and voids. Decoration: moulded then stamped; moulded serrated double lines around the stem, over-stamped by a rosette in a circle. Ceramic spot date: c. 1850 onwards. Parallels: form like #654. Surface.

(456) Tobacco Pipe bowl rim and body. Core = 10YR 7/1 Light Grey; Exterior Surface highly burnished = 10R 3/6 Dark Red; Interior Surface = 10R 4/3 Weak Red. Oxidized, very hard, very smooth. Shale (?) inclusions and voids. Bell shaped bowl. Decoration: moulded then cut. Plain rim, with a moulded serrated line below. Under the serrated line is a wide area left plain by the moulding, which has had wedges cut from it to create a tulip leaf pattern. Lastly, a heavily moulded line of pearls, high-lighted along their top edge by three knife point incisions. Ceramic spot date: c. 1850 onwards. Parallels: Hayes XV. Surface.

(654) Tobacco Pipe stem and socket. Core = 10YR 8/1 White; Exterior Surface highly burnished = 7.5YR N3/0 Very Dark Grey. Oxidized, very hard, very smooth. No added inclusions to the dense, fine fabric. Decorated by moulding and then stamping. Stem: Base has a wide, plain band decorated with parallel lines, one each side, running from the socket. Around the stem side of the socket are two parallel lines, the first thick and serrated, the second is plain. On each side of the stem, are moulded, stylized leaves. The left is a fleur de lis and on the right, acanthus leaves. Socket: Plain, except for a stamp towards the stem, on the left. This is faint and could be a backwards looking deer. Ceramic spot date: c. 1850 onwards. Parallels: Form is like Hayes XVI, but no mention of black burnishing. Surface.

Ovens

Another form of material culture frequently found on settlement sites and in modern villages is the clay oven, which is used for many forms of baking, not just bread. Like the pottery of the recent past, the women of the village make these ovens as part of the agricultural year. Most of the ovens found in late contexts on excavations and in use today are of the *tabun/tawabeen* type, (Figure 17.11). Their form varies in detail from the north to the south of Jordan but the basic method of manufacture and use is the same. The ovens are made of locally collected clay to which grit temper, animal hair and occasionally calcite is added. The ovens are coil-made and highly burnished before being left to dry in the sun. They are then fired in position in the oven house, which may be a purpose-built structure, an abandoned house or cave, but this type of oven is never used in the open in a courtyard. The oven is heated up for baking by lighting a fast, hot fire. The heat is retained when the oven is not in use by covering the mouth and then clamping the whole with animal dung, straw and/or the remains of olive pressing (*jift*). Several of the ceramic finds from archaeological sites in this late period seem to be clay oven covers (McQuitty 1993–1994: 56; Lindner *et al.* 1996: 124–125). A curved line of stones to contain the ash heap when it is cleared out is a frequent feature near the oven house.

Glass

Little to nothing is known from excavation about Ottoman vessel glass. It seems probable that fifteenth century Mamluk glass continued into the Ottoman period. By the nineteenth century, ethnographic accounts by European travellers take up the story and known glass-production centres, for example, Hebron/Kahlil, are well documented. One of the features of glass, namely, its recyclability, may also account for its apparent absence in the archaeological record. In addition, as with ceramics, the type of site excavated is extremely significant for the type of assemblage that will be found.

Glass bracelets, in contrast, are an extremely common find on surveys and on both rural settlement and cemetery sites. They are known from the Roman period but later examples are of different manufacture. These bracelets are almost exclusively of the seamless type, that is, a small piece of molten glass was pierced by a metal rod after which a larger ring was formed by rotating it on the rod with the help of a second tool (Steiner 1995: 537). They were used in conjunction with metal bracelets at the cemetery of Tall Dayr Alla, in which many examples were found in female graves dating from the past 500 years (Steiner 1995: 538). Eight seventeenth–eighteenth century female graves excavated at Umm Qays contained glass, metal and studded leather bracelets (Merschen 1991: 137). Walker reports examples from a nineteenth century cemetery at

Figure 17.11 Tabun oven (A. McQuitty).

Tall Hisban (2001) and Saller describes examples found in "late tombs" at Mount Nebo (1941: 314). At Khirbat Faris fragments were found amongst barrel-vaulted houses dating to the later occupation of the site. Despite being used throughout the Islamic centuries, based on increasing numbers of excavated examples and museum collections, it appears possible to isolate types that are Ottoman (Boulogne n.d.; Spaer 1992: 44–62).[4] Later examples are multi-coloured, with opaque blue, green, yellow, red and white glass being used. The bracelets are also decorated in a myriad of patterns including spots, stripes and bands. It is this increased flamboyancy with a greater range of colours and decoration that is characteristic of Ottoman examples. The cross-section of the bracelet is semi-circular, flat, evenly pointed or obliquely pointed. Spaer (1992) comments that the latter type, the obliquely pointed bracelet, is unlikely to have been used before the Mamluk period and some variations are of the Late Ottoman period. Boulogne considers that these bracelets required specialist manufacture and until the late Ottoman period, Hebron/Khalil appears to have been the main location in Bilad al-Sham for bracelet workshops. They were probably distributed through regular markets often located at pilgrimage sites or along pilgrimage routes, e.g. the Hajj route, but also by itinerant salesmen.

Beads and Jewellery

As well as glass and metal bracelets, the excavations of the Abu Naml cemetery in Umm Qays produced large numbers of beads and perforated coins that had been sewn onto textile to compose headdresses, bead necklaces, rings, an earring, cosmetic utensils and rosaries from bone-beads (Merschen 1991: 137). Most useful for dating purposes are the easily recognizable trade-glass beads that were produced in industrial centres in Italy, the Netherlands, Czechoslovakia and elsewhere and distributed all over the world. Based on this evidence and that from the perforated coins used in the jewellery, Merschen was able to date this cemetery to the seventeenth–eighteenth century. A similar range of material was found at the nineteenth century cemetery excavated at Tall Hisban (Walker 2001). Many of the beads are recognizable from ethnographic contexts and are still in use today for particular medicinal or magical properties. The materials used range from stone, bone, amber, shell and coral to glass. Neither the choice of colour or material was purely accidental. Blue and black beads are usually to ward off the evil eye and clear or white are worn by women when breast-feeding. Orange and red agates and amber are for love (Mershen 1991: 140). Simpson notes that it is not just the colour but also the material and shape of the bead that carries a specific meaning. For example, stone and cowries are also effective against the "evil eye." Dark green stone can ward off post-natal diseases and help menstrual problems whilst coral signifies "kindness and good fortune." Red agate, amber and carnelian also have a healing property specifically "preventing ear/throat inflammation, abortion, internal bleeding and other dangers". Regarding shape, circular and triangular beads are seen as giving "powerful magic" (Simpson 1995: 246). Although the beads discussed by these two authors have been found within a mortuary context, the significance of their colour, material and shape is equally relevant in daily life.

Coinage and Money

The most distinctive feature of Ottoman coinage is the *tughra*, or Ottoman sultan's name, which appears on the coins as well as the information relating to the denomination, year of minting and mint. Each sultan had his own *tughra* which is often unreadable but always recognizable as each *tughra* is distinct. The *tughra* was included "as a sign of common allegiance to the Sunni Muslim state and its leader, the Sultan" (Darley-Doran 1988: 90).

When considering Ottoman coinage and money-exchange, the key words are variability and regionality, both chronologically and geographically. The two main points to take into account are:

1. The extent to which Ottoman coinage was *produced* for the provinces; and

2. The extent to which Ottoman coinage was *used* in the provinces.

Just as Ottoman administration incorporated local realities into its execution, so too did the coinage. When the Arab provinces were conquered in the sixteenth century, there were already well established local Muslim currencies in use. Mamluk coinage was not immediately supplanted by Ottoman coinage, as Darley-Doran (1988: 89–90) comments:

> ...the Ottomans made no concerted effort to displace them because they wished to avoid economic disruption and popular unrest... In Egypt and Mamluk Syria the standard silver coin continued to be the *medin*, which originally began as a half dirham under the Burji Mamluks.

In the seventeenth and early eighteenth centuries, Ottoman coinage started disappearing and the use of earlier coinage was supplemented by the use of foreign coinage. In addition, the actual mint activity declined (Pamuk 1994: 962). A new monetary unit, the *kurus* (piaster), was introduced at the end of the seventeenth century as an attempt by the Ottoman government to reassert control over the economy. This coinage was, however, not minted anywhere in Syria while the mint in Baghdad was used only occasionally (Pamuk 1994: 966). The examples found in Jordan probably came either from Istanbul or Cairo. It was not until the mid-nineteenth century that the Ottomans were able to gain more control over the production of their coinage. It was also at this time that imitation coins started to be produced for jewellery purposes, to adorn female head-dresses and necklaces. The imitations often bore a countermark or included an incorrect date in order to differentiate them from genuine coins. Prior to this, it seems that old coins were hammered and perforated for jewellery purposes.

It is no easy matter to determine the use of coinage in Jordan throughout the Ottoman period. The agricultural taxation referred to in the *defters* was presumably gathered in kind (Hütteroth and Abdulfattah 1977: 89), although at some point this would have been converted into money if the taxation destination was far from the point of production, that is, Istanbul rather than Damascus. In Palestine, it appears to have been given in cash form (Singer 1994: 56). Surplus agricultural produce would have been sold at local or Hajj markets. However, it seems likely that much local exchange was carried out on a barter basis and that the rural Ottoman economy in Jordan was *not* a monetary economy. The absence of Ottoman coins on archaeological excavations does not reflect the absence of an Ottoman population per se: coins were not part of the rural material culture assemblage. However, there have been a few stratified surface finds of Ottoman coins. Some of these are imitations of gold coinage ("sequins")that were commonly produced in the late Ottoman period and used as jewellery items. The "sequins" were pierced and sown onto women's veils (J. Johns pers. comm.; Granquist 1965: 62).

Ethnography and Material Culture

One of the most useful aspects of the nineteenth century European travellers' and ethnographers' accounts is the insight that they give into the everyday life and material culture of the inhabitants of Jordan and their material culture. Engravings and early photographs from the period give hints of the way things were used and the general environment of the nineteenth century. In the twentieth century, Ottoman material culture became the focus of collections and catalogues: in particular, the jewellery and dress of that period, although the everyday and agricultural items have also been collected, for example, cooking vessels, animal harnesses, threshing sleds, Circassian carts (Volger *et al.* 1987). In addition, very important studies of the "Way of Life" and the technology of both urban and rural populations have been carried out, mainly in Palestine (Canaan 1933, 1934; Dalman 1932–33; Granquist 1965). There is a treasury of information about material culture of the recent past in Jordan and it should not be divorced from the information gained from archaeology.

Religion and Ritual

Throughout the Ottoman period, Jordan was overwhelmingly Sunni Muslim with a minority of Orthodox Christians (Hütteroth and Abdulfattah 1977: 40), who began to convert to Catholicism and Protestantism in small numbers during the late nineteenth century.

Mosques and Churches

There are no remains of mosques dating definitely from the sixteenth–nineteenth centuries found on excavation although examples dated as Mamluk may have continued into the sixteenth century, for example, Lahun and Pella. Many mosques that are in use today have incorporated earlier structures into their fabric, for example, Karak Congregational Mosque which was built in the late nineteenth century (Dowling 1896: 330), but a few standing examples of early mosques survive. The Hajj forts each included a mosque for use by the garrison. In Tibneh, there are three mosques: one is a simple rectangular structure with an exterior staircase leading to part of the roof which was used by the muezzin for the call to prayer; another was on the first floor of the *al-Alali* referred to above; and the third, the largest, constructed of different stone from the houses, rendering it very distinctive within the village. The main Tibneh mosque is a perfect square, 12.5 x 12.5 m. It comprised three cross-vaulted units supporting a flat roof while a fourth, in front of the *mihrab*, probably supported a dome (Khammash 1986: 60). The stone façades of the mosque are simple and undecorated although a symbolic *mihrab* protrudes from the *qibla* wall and the east wall. A staircase is built into the thickness of the west wall giving access to the roof from which the muezzin made the call to prayer. Khammash concludes that this mosque is undoubtedly Ottoman and may be eighteenth century (1986: 61). The plan and proportions are certainly different from the examples known to be earlier and more akin to eighteenth century examples from Palestine (Petersen 1996). Later but of similar plan is the mosque at Hubras that was constructed inside the earlier fourteenth century example (Walker 2005). This has been dated by architectural style to the late nineteenth/early twentieth century. Many of the villages and towns of the Ajlun Hills and northern Jordan include similar simple structures that have been cleared by the Ministry of Awqaf, (Ghawanmah 1988). Ghawanmah dates most of the original foundation of these by inscription to the earlier Ayyubid/Mamluk period but, as at Hubras, many were altered but still used during the later Ottoman periods. As mentioned previously, the Small Mosque in Salt, dating to 1907, is an excellent example of Ottoman architecture that owes little to regional tradition. However, the style of classic Ottoman minarets became that which was followed throughout Jordan in the early-mid twentieth century.

A common but practically un-datable type of mosque found on survey is "the desert mosque" or *musalla*. This type comprises the outline of a mosque and *mihrab* traced with a rough stone wall about two courses high. These mosques usually measure c. 4m east–west and only 1.2 m north–south. Inscriptions, both of Arabic and earlier scripts, for example, Safaitic, often distinguish the stones of the *mihrab*. These structures are referred to as "desert mosques" because they are easily recognized within desert environments, although they occur anywhere where there is temporary occupation of a site and a group of Muslims who require a facility for communal worship: the author saw a "desert mosque" that had just been constructed in the proximity of a group of tents before the Holy Month of Ramadan. As mosques are associated with built shrines (see discussion below), these "desert mosques" are associated with Bedouin tombs (Lancaster and Lancaster 1993: 153; 1999: 251–252).

Although Christianity survived in Jordan throughout the Mamluk and Ottoman centuries, practically nothing is known of the associated buildings, burial practices and rituals until the influx of Christian missionaries in the mid-nineteenth century. It is not until this time that the building of churches is reported. The most famous example is St. George's Church in Madaba, constructed in 1898 on the foundation of a sixth century basilica that included the Madaba Map. The church was built as part of the re-settlement of Madaba. In a similar but slightly later re-settlement, the villagers of Hmoud (near Karak) built their church in the vernacular style in 1910 (Khammash 1986: 25). The Orthodox Christians of Karak worshipped in the Church of St. George, built in 1849 (Dowling 1896: 330) while a church "building-boom" took place in Salt as the town expanded.

Shrines

There are numerous shrines, both Islamic and Christian, in Jordan: shrines for the Companions of the Prophet, for prophets mentioned in the Quran as in the Old Testament, and for local wise and holy men (MacKenzie 2002: 617–619; Turab 1996). These shrines are still visited by pilgrims, both local and from afar, for example, Mazar, Arasat Suleiman ibn Daud near Sirfe (Lancaster and Lancaster 1999:274). Often the shrines become the nucleus for cemeteries and focus for seasonal markets. The *defter i mufassal* does not mention these shrines specifically nor did *waqf* payments go towards their upkeep. In most cases, the construction of the shrines, usually over a grave and with a small mosque or at least a *mihrab* associated, is undated although those in the Ajlun Hills are accompanied by inscriptions (Ghawanmeh 1988).

Graves, Tombs and Cemeteries

The stipulations for Islamic burial are well known and documented.

> Burial itself is in a grave deep enough to conceal odor and prevent abuse of the body by animals. Within the grave a niche is dug on the *qiblah* side of the grave or else a smaller trench is dug on the floor of the grave. Into this the body is placed without a coffin, lying on its right side, facing the *qiblah*. The cheek is bared and placed on a stone. The niche or trench is then sealed with bricks or stones, and earth is replaced in the grave and rounded slightly above ground level (Reinhart 1995: 34–35).

Simplicity is the keyword: "a simple headstone may mark the grave, but anything more elaborate is to be avoided" (Denny 1995: 35–37). These are the stipulations: what is the practice?

Again, nineteenth century travellers and twentieth century ethnographers give an insight into the ritual surrounding burial, including the construction of graves (Granquist 1965: 55–56; Walker 2001: 57–59). Most archaeological surveys record graves, obviously Islamic because of their orientation, which stand out as a heap of raised earth and stones surrounded by a kerb of small stones. Often these graves are within a cemetery group and the location determines whether these are recorded as belonging to a sedentary or nomadic/semi-nomadic (Bedouin) population. From a simple visual examination, the precise dating is problematic. One type of individual and very distinctive grave, associated with Bedouin, is the stone tomb/cairn that is a common sight on the prominent headlands of the basalt desert, the *harra*. One group of these, recently built by the Ahl al-Gabal group of tribes, has been extensively described by Lancaster (1993: 151–169). These elaborate tombs consist of a cairn, marking the tomb itself, flanked by two "wings" or stone walls about 1m high. Near the tomb is a stone platform on which the body was washed prior to burial and occasionally a "desert mosque," usually south of the tomb, is found. The symbolism of these structures is considered to be the representation of a tent (the "wings"). From the interviews conducted by Lancaster and Lancaster with the Ahl al-Gabal, it appears that "none of these elaborate tombs were built for politically influential figures in the conventional sense" (1993: 157). Some were built for healers who "were (are?) important for the political health of the community." While the particular tombs recorded by Lancaster and Lancaster are modern, this type of distinctive "desert tomb" undoubtedly had predecessors in the *harra* and can certainly be seen closer to areas of permanent agriculture. The grave-marker shown in Figure 17.12 was erected at the end of the nineteenth century and marks the grave of one of the Adwan: a powerful semi-nomadic tribe with seasonal lands near Amman. This grave is located in a small cemetery northeast of Amman which is not associated with any permanent settlement of comparable date. The headstone obviously dates from the Ottoman era as the familiar symbol of crescent moon and star shows.

Intentional excavation of Muslim cemeteries in Jordan is not common. Many projects, however, come across Muslim graves in the course of their work since archaeological "ruins" are frequently re-used as burial sites, particularly by nomadic and semi-nomadic tribes. Two cemeteries have been partially excavated in the northern town of Umm Qays. In 1987, Andersen and Strange reported 16 disturbed graves located within an earlier outdoor structure, possibly a courtyard. Some of the graves were dated to the Mamluk period and all were of the stone-cist type, that is, the dug grave was lined with stones and the body was covered with flat cap-stones. Two graves included glass and iron bangles (1987: 78–100). This grave-type was repeated, also in Umm Qays, at the cemetery of Abu Naml that appears to have clustered around the shrine of Abu Naml, which has since disappeared. Merschen dates these 15 graves to the seventeenth–eighteenth century (see discussion under "beads and jewellery"). Steiner reports similar burials from Tall Dayr Alla (1995: 537). These cemeteries are composed of individual graves. A major contrast is provided by the recently excavated burials at Tall Hisban, (Walker 2001). Here 100 individuals were buried in a cist-grave located in the ruined "storeroom of the Mamluk governor's residence." The communal grave has been dated, on the basis of grave-goods, to the end of

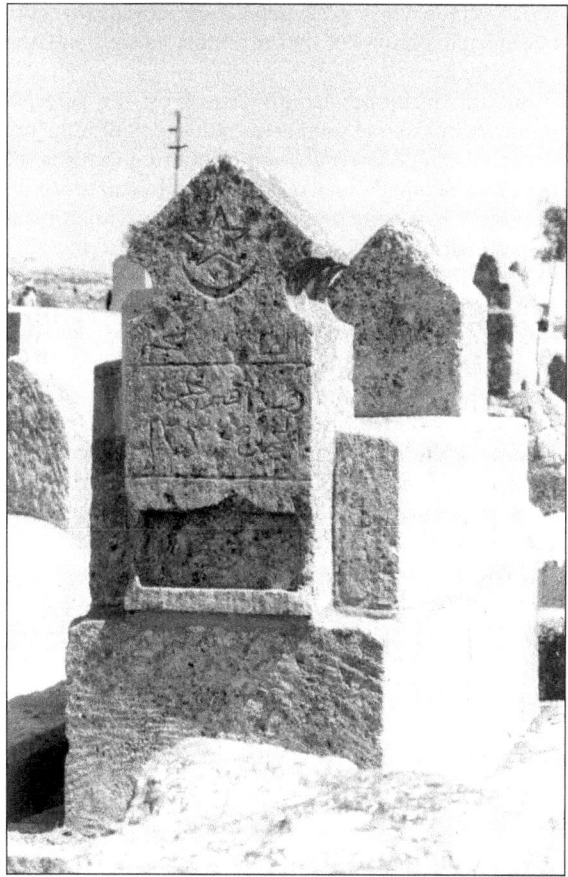

Figure 17.12 Nineteenth century grave-marker (A. McQuitty).

the nineteenth century and is very likely to be linked with the Adwan. Parker reports a communal Bedouin grave, re-using one of the towers, from his excavations at the Roman fort of Lajjun (1987: 260). It is tempting to see in this contrast between individual and communal graves a difference between village and semi-nomadic/nomadic cemeteries. Walker suggests that the difference may also relate to "differences in funerary ritual" (2001:57).

Conclusions

Perhaps more than most periods, our impression of Ottoman rural settlement within Jordan suffers from preconceptions. The Ottoman centuries are characterized as a time of decline and devastation: of lawlessness when wild Bedouin preyed on defenceless peasants, savaged the crops and converted arable land into pastures for their flocks. Continuing on these lines, the argument goes that by the seventeenth century central Ottoman control had waned and, in the face of this lack of security, villages and agricultural life retreated to the security of the mountains or were totally abandoned in favour of nomadism and pastoral life or flight to the cities of Syria and Palestine. To be sure, there are elements of truth in this: historical and tribal records report great population movements, tribal raiding and a retreat of the area under cultivation (Abu-Jaber 1989; Lewis 1987).

But this historical narrative based on the perceived influence of external powers (or rather lack of influence) is not the whole story. The more enduring factor is that the overwhelmingly rural population of Jordan continued to practise its mainly subsistence economy with elements of pastoralism and agriculture. In physical terms, there was both continuity and discontinuity. Continuity is seen in the vernacular architecture. Some building types, e.g. the "transverse-arch house," have antecedents in the twelfth century yet continued to be built until the 1950s. Watermills, whose technology was used in the tenth century sugar industry, also continued in use for grinding grain until the 1960s. Elements of rural architecture and technology demonstrably exhibit an inherent conservatism. The settlement patterns changed on a regional basis but probably not as drastically as previous research has suggested. Based on present evidence, the underlying themes of rural life e.g. the prevalence of seasonal and permanent settlement, tribalism as exhibited in the *qasr* phenomenon, seem to represent Middle-Ottoman/Modern phenomena. However, like vernacular architecture, they too may have earlier antecedents. Conclusions simply await further research, both in terms of excavation and detailed landscape study.

By contrast and with the *caveat* that our current state of knowledge is woefully incomplete, the character of the rural artefact assemblages suggests a break between the Mamluk/Ottoman periods and the Middle Ottoman period that changes again with the advent of the Modern period. Discontinuity is seen in the constituent parts of artefact assemblages e.g. ceramics, although this is not true across the board, e.g. glass bracelets. This break between the Middle Ottoman and Ottoman/Modern also marks the point at which new elements of settlement type and architecture are introduced and in some areas permanent settlement is re-established on previously seasonally occupied lands. To a certain extent, Jordan's entry into the "modern" world during the mid-nineteenth century, marked the most distinctive changes in material culture and settlement type but the underlying thread of rural continuity that did not effectively change until the 1940s is a fact that should not be ignored. Until the Ottoman/Modern period life in Jordan carried on in the countryside not the towns. Archaeology is well-suited to telling this story: the challenge is to examine the evidence for settlement, society and economy during those centuries objectively and to characterize the Ottoman period on that basis.

Notes

1. I am extremely grateful to Dr. Eugene Rogan (Middle East Centre, Oxford University) for commenting on the original draft of this contribution. His suggestions were invaluable but any errors remain my own. I would like to acknowledge and thank those who assisted in the completion of illustrations: Madeleine Sarley-Pontin and Simon Pressey. The original research for and writing up of this contribution was completed while the author was Amman Director for the Council for British Research in the Levant.

2. Brünnow and von Domaszewski and Glueck spelled the toponym Khirbat ed-Doshak. The spelling used here is that of Palumbo (1995), site 2099024.

3. For the use of this terminology "arch-and-grain-bin house" and "transverse arch house" see discussion below.

4. This view is not universally shared—see Scanlon (2002: 176–180) for an alternative and earlier date attribution that seems to be largely based on value-judgements.

5. *Waqf* refers to the practice of endowing religious institutions with the proceeds from taxation on property, that is, rather than the taxation going to the Ottoman government in Istanbul it went towards the upkeep of a religious institution. *Waqf* were often established by rulers or provincial officials.

Bibliography

Abu Dalu, R.

1995 The Technology of Sugar Mills in the Jordan Valley during the Islamic Periods (in Arabic). In K. 'Amr, F. Zayadine and M. Zaghloul (eds.), *Studies in the History and Archaeology of Jordan V*, 37–48. Amman: Department of Antiquities.

Abujaber, R.S.

1989 *Pioneers over the Jordan: The Frontier of Settlement of Transjordan 1850–1914*. London: I.B. Tauris.

Ambraseys, N.N. and C.P. Melville

1989 Evidence for Intraplate Earthquakes in Northwest Arabia. *Bulletin of the Seismological Society of America* 79: 1279–1281.

Andersen, F.G. and J. Strange

1987 Bericht über drei Sondagen in Umm Qes, Jordanien, im Herbst 1983. *Zeitschrift des deutschen Palästina-Vereins* 103: 78–100.

Aurenche, O.

1990 Habitat de nomades et habitat de sédentaires en Syrie et en Jordanie: Etude de cas. In H.F. Frankfort (ed.), *Nomades et sédentaires en Asie centrale*, 31–48. Paris: Centre National de la Recherche Scientifique.

Banning, E.B., R. Dods, J.J. Field, S.L. Maltby, J. McCorriston, S. Monckton, R. Rubenstein and P. Shepherd

1989 Wadi Ziqlab Project 1987: A Preliminary Report. *Annual of the Department of Antiquities of Jordan* 33: 43–58.

Banning, E.B. and I. Köhler-Rollefson

1992 Ethnographic Lessons for the Pastoral Past: Camp Locations and Material Remains Near Beidha, Southern

Jordan. In O. Bar-Yosef and A. Khazanov (eds.), *Pastoralism in the Levant*, 181–204. Monographs in World Archaeology 10. Madison, WI: Prehistory Press.

Baram, U.

2000 Entangled Images from the Palestinian Past. In U. Baram and L. Carroll (eds.), *A Historical Archaeology of the Ottoman Empire,* 137–159. New York: Kluwer Academic/Plenum Publishers.

Baram, U. and L. Carroll (eds.)

2000 *A Historical Archaeology of the Ottoman Empire.* New York:Kluwer Academic/Plenum Publishers.

Bennett, C.-M. and P. Bienkowski

1995 *Excavations at Tawilan in Southern Jordan.* Oxford: Oxford University Press.

Bienert, H-D., R. Lamprichs and D. Vieweger

2000 Ba'ja—the archaeology of a landscape. 9000 years of human occupation: a preliminary report on the 1999 field season. *Annual of the Department of Antiquities* 44: 119–148.

Bienkowski, P. and B. Chlebik

1991 Changing Places: Architecture and Spatial Organisation of the Bedul in Petra. *Levant* 23: 147–180.

Biewers, M.

1990 L'habitat traditionnel à 'Aima. *Unpublished doctoral thesis. Université Lumière Lyon 2.*

1992 Occupation de l'espace dans le village traditionnel de 'Aima: Approche ethnoarchéologique. In S. Tell, G. Bisheh, F. Zayadine, K. 'Amr, and M. Zaghloul (eds.), *Studies in the History and Archaeology of Jordan IV,* 397–402. Amman: Department of Antiquities.

1997 *L 'habitat traditionnel à 'Aima: Enquête ethnoarchéeologique dans un village jordanien.* Maison de l'orient méditerranéen/British Archaeological Reports International Series 662. Oxford: Archaeopress.

Biewers, M. and R. Kana'an

1993 Vernacular Architecture Survey of Kurkuma. In G. Palumbo, J. Mabry, M. Abu Abileh, E. Avellino, M. Biewers, C. Conati, R. Kana'an and S. Mammi, The Wadi el-Yabis Survey and Excavations Project: Report on the 1992 Season, 316–319. *Annual of the Department of Antiquities of Jordan* 37: 307–324.

Brown, R.M.

1984 Late Islamic Settlement on the Kerak Plateau, Trans-Jordan. Unpublished MA dissertation, State University of New York at Binghamton.

1988 Summary Report of the 1986 Excavations: Late Islamic Shobak. *Annual of the Department of Antiquities of Jordan* 32: 225–245.

1989 Excavations in the 14th Century ad Mamluk Palace at Kerak. *Annual of the Department of Antiquities of Jordan* 33: 287–304.

1992 Late Islamic Ceramic Production and Distribution in the Southern Levant: A Socio-Economic and Political Interpretation. Unpublished PhD dissertation, State University of New York at Binghamton.

Boulogne, S.

in press Le Verre au Bilad al-Sham Mamelouk (1260–1517) et Ottoman (1517–1840): Hypotheses de Production Regionale et d'Exportations, Le Cas des bracelets de Verre Colore. *Bulletin d'Études Oriéntales*

Brünnow , R.E. and A. von Domaszewski

1904 *Die Provincia Arabia,* I. Strassburg: Trübner.

Burkhardt, J.L.

1992 *Notes on the Bedouins and Wahabis.* London: Garnet Publishing.

Canaan, T.

1932 The Palestinian Arab House. *Journal of the Palestine Oriental Society* 12: 223–247.

1933 The Palestinian Arab House. *Journal of the Palestine Oriental Society* 3: 183.

Charles, M.

1992 *Charred Plant Remains: Khirbat Faris.* Unpublished archive report.

Charles, M. and Hoppé. C.

1997 The Archaeobotanical Remains in A. McQuitty, M. Sarley-Pontin, M. Khoury, M. Charles and C.F. Hoppé. Mamluk Khirbat Faris. *Aram* 9: 194–198.

2003 The Effects of Irrigation on the Weed Floras of Winter Cereal Crops in Wadi Ibn Hammad (Southern Jordan). *Levant* 35: 213–230.

Clark, V.A., J.M.C. Bowsher and J.D. Stewart

1986 The Jerash North Theatre. In F. Zayadine (ed.), *Jerash Archaeological Project* I, 205–202. Amman: Department of Antiquities.

Conder, C.R.

1889 *The Survey of Eastern Palestine.* London: Palestine Exploration Fund.

Daher, R.

1995 The Resurrection of the Hijaz Railroad Line. In K. 'Amr, F. Zayadine andM. Zaghloul (eds.), *Studies in the History and Archaeology of Jordan V,* 341–350. Amman: Department of Antiquities.

Dalman, G.

1932–3 *Arbeit und Sitte in Palästina.* Gütersloh: Bertelsmann.

Darley-Doran, R.E.

1988 An Alternative Approach to the Study of Ottoman Numismatics. In *A Festschrift Presented to Ibrahim Arturk on the Occasion of the 20th Anniversary of the Turk Numismatik Dernagi,* 8/–90. Istanbul: Turk Numismatik Dernegi Yayinlari.

Davis, J.L.

1991 Contributions to a Mediterranean Rural Archaeology: Historical Case Studies from the Ottoman Cyclades. *Journal of Mediterranean Archaeology* 4: 131–216.

Denny, F.M.

1995 Modern Practice. In J.L. Esposito (ed.), *The Oxford*

Encyclopedia of the Modern Islamic World, 35–37. New York: Oxford University Press.

Denton, B. and B. St. Laurent

1996   Early Twentieth Century Architecture. In P.M. Bikai and T.A. Dailey (eds.), *Madaba: Cultural Heritage*, 47–89. Amman: American Center for Oriental Research.

Dols, M.W.

1979   The Second Plague Pandemic and its Recurrences in the Middle East: 1347–1894. *Journal of the Economic and Social History of the Orient* 22: 162–189.

Dowling, T.E.

1896   Kerak in 1896. *Palestine Exploration Fund Quarterly Statement*, 327–332.

Fakhoury, L. and R. Sweiss

1995   Tayyiba 'A Thriving Village'. In K. 'Amr, F. Zayadine and M. Zaghloul (eds.), *Studies in the History and Archaeology of Jordan V*, 361–374. Amman: Department of Antiquities.

Faroqhi, S.

1999   *Approaching Ottoman History.* Cambridge: Cambridge University Press

1994   Crisis and Change. In H. Inalcik and D. Quataert (eds.), *An Economic and Social History of the Ottoman Empire*, 411–636. Cambridge: Cambridge University Press.

Findley, C.F.

1986   The Evolution of the System of Provincial Administration as Viewed from the Center. In D. Kushner (ed.), *Palestine in the Late Ottoman Period*, 3–29. Leiden: E.J. Brill.

Fishbach, M.R.

1994   British Land Policy in Transjordan. In E.L. Rogan and T. Tell (eds.), *Village, Steppe and State: The Social Origins of Modern Jordan*, 58–79. New York: British Academic Press.

Franken, H.J. and J. Kalsbeek

1975   *Potters of a Medieval Village in the Jordan Valley.* North-Holland Ceramics Studies in Archaeology 3. Amsterdam: North-Holland.

Fuller, M. and N. Fuller

1988   Tell Tuneir on the Khabur: Preliminary Report on Three Seasons. *Les Annales archéologiques arabes syriennes* 37: 279–290.

Gardiner, M. and A. McQuitty

1987   A Water Mill in Wadi el-Arab, North Jordan and Water Mill Development. *Palestine Exploration Quarterly* 119: 24–32.

Ghawanmeh, Y.

1988   *Al-masajid al-islamiyah al-qadimah fi mintiqat 'Ajlun.* Amman.

1992   Earthquake Effects on Bilad ash-Sham Settlements. In S. Tell, G. Bisheh, F. Zayadine, K. 'Amr, and M. Zaghloul (eds.), *Studies in the History and Archaeology of Jordan IV*, 53–59. Amman: Department of Antiquities.

Gichon, M. and R. Linden

1984   Muslim Oil Lamps From Emmaus. *Israel Exploration Journal* 34: 156–169.

Gilliland, D.R.

1986   Palaeoethnobotany and Palaeoenvironment. In Ø.S. LaBianca and L. Lacelle (eds.), *Environmental Foundations: Hesban 2*, 123–142. Berrien Springs, MI: Andrews University.

Gilmors, M., S. al-Hiwah and I. Resseeni

1984   Dhrub al Hajj Architectural Documentation Program: Preliminary Report on the Architectural Survey of the Northern Pilgrimage Routes. *Atlal* 8: 143–161.

Glueck, N.

1934   Explorations in Eastern Palestine I. *Annual of the American Schools of Oriental Research* 14: 1–113.

Granquist, H.

1965   *Muslim Death and Burial: Arab Customs and Traditions Studied in a Village in Jordan.* Commentationes Humano rum Litterarum. Helsinki.

Hayes, J.W.

1980   Turkish Clay Pipes: A Provisional Typology. In P. Davey (ed.), *The Archaeology of the Clay Tobacco Pipe* IV, 3–10. British Archaeological Reports International Series 92. Oxford: British Archaeological Reports.

Hütteroth, W.-D. and K. Abdulfattah

1977   *Historical Geography of Palestine, Transjordan and Southern Syria in the Late 16th Century.* Erlangen: Frankischen geographischen Gesellschaft.

Johns, J.

1998   The Rise of Middle Islamic Hand-Made Geometrically Painted Ware in Bilad al-Sham (11th–13th Centuries AD). In R.-P. Gayraud (ed.), *Colloque international d'archéologie islamique*, 65–93. Textes arabes et études islamiques 36: Institut française d'archéologie orientale.

Johns, J., A. McQuitty and R. Falkner

1989   The Faris Project: Preliminary Report upon the 1986 and 1988 Seasons. *Levant* 21: 63–95.

Kana'an, R. and T. al-Rifai

1988   *'Iraq al-Amir wa al-Bardon.* Amman: University of Jordan.

Kana'an, R. and A. McQuitty

1994   The Architecture of al-Qasr on the Kerak Plateau: An Essay in the Chronology of Vernacular Architecture. *Palestine Exploration Quarterly* 126: 127–151.

Kareem, J.

1993   The Settlement Patterns in the Jordan Valley in the Mid to Late-Islamic Period. Unpublished PhD dissertation, Freie Universität, Berlin.

2000   *The Settlement Patterns in the Jordan Valley in the Mid to Late-Islamic Period.* Oxford: Archaeopress.

Kennedy, D. and Bewley, R.

2004 *Ancient Jordan from the Air* London: Council for British Research in the Levant.

Khammash, A.

1986 *Notes on Village Architecture in Jordan.* Lafayette: University Art Museum.

Khatib, R.Y. and H.S. al-Asir

1995 The Golden Era of as-Salt (1870–1950): Urban and Architectural Development. In K. 'Amr, F. Zayadine and M. Zaghloul (eds.), *Studies in the History and Archaeology of Jordan V*, 351–360. Amman: Department of Antiquities.

Killick, A.

1983 Udhruh: The Frontier of an Empire: 1980 and 1981 Seasons, A Preliminary Report. *Levant* 15: 110–31.

Köhler-Rollefson, I.

1987 Ethnoarchaeological Research into the Origins of Pastoralism. *Annual of the Department of Antiquities of Jordan* 31: 535–539.

Koucky, F.L.

1987 The Regional Environment. In T.S. Parker (ed.), *The Roman Frontier in Central Jordan*, 11–40. British Archaeological Reports International Series 340. Oxford: British Archaeological Reports.

LaBianca, Ø.S.

1990 *Hesban I: Sedentarization and Nomadization, Food System Cycles at Hesban and Vicinity in Transjordan.* Berrien Springs, MI: Andrews University Press.

1991 A Note on Seasonally Occupied Cave Villages. In L.G. Herr, L.T. Geraty, Ø.S. LaBianca and R.W. Younker (eds.), *Madaba Plains Project 2*, 353–355. Berrien Springs, MI: Andrews University.

2000 Daily Life in the Shadow of Empire in Baram, U. and Carroll, L. (eds.) *A Historical Archaeology of the Ottoman Empire:* 203–217. New York:Kluwer Academic/Plenum Publishers.

LaBianca, Ø.S. and A. von den Driesch (eds.)

1995 *Faunal Remains: Hesban 13.* Berrien Springs, MI: Andrews University.

LaBianca, Ø. S. and L. Lacelle (eds.)

1986 *Environmental Foundations: Hesban 2.* Berrien Springs, MI: Andrews University.

Lancaster, W. and F. Lancaster

1993 Graves and Funerary Monuments of the Ahl al-Gabal, Jordan. *Arabian Archaeology and Epigraphy* 4: 151–169.

1995 Land Use and Population in the Area North of Karak. *Levant* 27: 103–124.

1999 *People, Land and Water in the Arab Middle East*, II. Studies in Environmental Anthropology. Amsterdam: Harwood Academic.

Landau, J.M.

1971 *The Hejaz Railway and the Muslim Pilgrimage: A Case*

of Ottoman Political Propaganda. Detroit, MI: Wayne State University Press.

Lewis, N.N.

1987 *Nomads and Settlers in Syria and Jordan 1800–1980.* Cambridge: Cambridge University Press.

Lindner, M.

1999 Late Islamic Villages in the Greater Petra Region and Medieval 'Hormuz'. *Annual of the Department of Antiquities of Jordan* 43: 479–497.

Lindner, M., E.A. Knauf and J.P. Zeitler

1996 An Edomite Fortress and a Late Islamic Village Near Petra (Jordan): Khirbat al-Mu'allaq. *Annual of the Department of Antiquities of Jordan* 40: 111–135.

London, G.A. and M. Sinclair

1991 An Ethnoarchaeological Survey of Potters in Jordan. In L.G. Herr, L.T. Geraty, Ø.S. LaBianca and R.W. Younker (eds.), *Madaba Plains Project 2*, 420–428. Berrien Springs, MI: Andrews University.

MacDonald, B. (ed.)

1988 *The Wadi el Hasa Archaeological Survey 1979–1983, West-Central Jordan.* Waterloo, ON: Wilfrid Laurier University.

1992 *The Southern Ghors and Northeast 'Arabah Archaeological Survey.* Sheffield Archaeological Monographs 5. Sheffield: J.R. Collis.

MacKenzie, N.D.

2002 Ayyubid/Mamluk Archaeology of the 'Ajlun Area: A Preliminary Typology. *Annual of the Department of Antiquities of Jordan* 46: 615–620.

Malkawi, M.S.

1994 *The Watermills of Wadi Kufranjeh during the period between the late Mamluk and early Ottoman: a technological study.* Unpublished M.A. thesis. Yarmouk University, Irbid, Jordan (Arabic).

McQuitty, A.

1993/4 Ovens in Town and Country. *Berytus* 41: 53–76.

2004a Harnessing the Power of Water: Watermills in Jordan. In H-D Bienert and Jutta Häser (eds.) *Men of Dikes and Canals*, 261–272. Orient Archäologie Band 13. Rahden: Verlag Marie Leidorf.

2004b The Architecture of Hospitality. In K. van Folsach, H. Thrane and I. Thuesen (eds.) *From Handaxe to Khan*, 255–264. Aarhus: Aarhus University Press.

2005 The rural landscape of Jordan in the seventh–nineteenth centuries A.D.: the Kerak Plateau. *Antiquity* 79: 1–12.

in prep. The Vocabulary of Rural Settlement: Beit Ras.

McQuitty, A. and R. Falkner

1993 A Preliminary Report on the Khirbat Faris Project: The 1989, 1990 and 1991 Seasons. *Levant* 25: 37–62.

McQuitty, A.M. and C.J. Lenzen

1989 An Architectural Study of the Irbid Region with Particular Reference to a Building in Irbid. *Levant* 21: 119–128.

Merschen, B.

1985 Recent Hand-Made Pottery from Northern Jordan. *Berytus* 33: 75–87.

1990 The Islamic Cemetery of Abu an-Naml. In T. Weber and A. Hoffman (eds.), Gadara of the Decapolis: Preliminary Report of the 1989 Season at Umm Qeis. *Annual of the Department of Antiquities of Jordan* 34: 331–333.

1991 The Islamic Cemetery of Abu en-Niml. In S. Kerner (ed.), *The Near East in Antiquity* 2, 135–141. Amman: Al Kutba.

1992 Settlement History and Village Space in Late Ottoman Northern Jordan. In S. Tell, G. Bisheh, F. Zayadine, K. 'Amr, and M. Zaghloul (eds.), *Studies in the History and Archaeology of Jordan IV*, 409–416. Amman: Department of Antiquities.

De Meulemeester, J. and D. Pringle

2001 The Archaeological Investigation of 'Aqaba Castle. *Council for British Research in the Levant Newsletter* 19–21. London: Council for British Research in the Levant.

Miles, G.C. (ed.)

1985 The Coins from the Armenian Garden. In A.D. Tushingham (ed.), *Excavations in Jerusalem 1961–67*, 156–177. Toronto, ON: Royal Ontario Museum.

Miller, J.M.

1991 *Archaeological Survey of the Kerak Plateau*. Atlanta, GA: Scholars Press.

Milwright, M.

2000 Pottery of Bilad al-Sham in the Ottoman Period: a Review of the Published Archaeological Evidence. *Levant* 32: 189–208.

Mundy, M.

1996 Qada' 'Ajlun in the Late Nineteenth Century: Interpreting a Region from Ottoman Land Registers. *Levant* 28: 77–95.

Noca, L.

1985 *Smakieh: Un village de Jordanie*. Ecole d'architecture de Lyon: Travail personnel de troisième cycle, Lyon.

Palmer, C.

1998 'Following the Plough': The Agricultural Environment of Northern Jordan. *Levant* 30: 129–166.

2000 "Ethnoarchaeology." In G.W. Barker, R. Adams, O.H Creighton, P. Daly, D.D. Gilbertson, J.P. Grattan, C.O. Hunt, D.J. Mattingly, S.J. McLaren, P. Newson, C. Palmer, F.B. Pyatt, T.E.G. Reynolds, H. Smith, R. Tomber and A.J. Truscott. Archaeology and Desertification in the Wadi Faynan: the Fourth (1999) Season of the Wadi Faynan Landscape Survey. *Levant* 32: 27–52.

Palumbo, G., A.S. Abu Dayyeh, K. 'Amr, J.A. Greene, R. Kana'an, E. Kraczkiewicz, C. Shartzer, M. Shwemat and M. Waheeb

1993 Cultural Resources Management in Jordan. *Annual of the Department of Antiquities of Jordan* 37: 69–84.

Palumbo, G. (ed.)

1995 *The Jordan Antiquities Database and Information System*. Amman: Department of Antiquities and the American Center of Oriental Research.

Pamuk, S.

1994 Money in the Ottoman Empire, 1326–1914. In H. Inalcik and D. Quataert (eds.), *An Economic and Social History of the Ottoman Empire*, 947–985. Cambridge: Cambridge University Press.

Parker, S.T. (ed.)

1987 *The Roman Frontier in Central Jordan*. British Archaeological Reports International Series 340. Oxford: British Archaeological Reports.

Petersen, A.

1996 A Preliminary Report on Three Muslim Shrines in Palestine. *Levant* 28: 97–113.

2001 Ottoman Haj Forts. In B. MacDonald, R. Adams and P. Bienkowski (eds.), *The Archaeology of Jordan*, 685–691. Sheffield: Sheffield Academic Press.

Petersen, A., P. Brun and A. Shurma

2003 A Preliminary Report on Excavations and Survey at Qal'at 'Unaiza, Jordan. *Levant* 35: 49–70.

Pitcher, D.E.

1972 *An Historical Geography of the Ottoman Empire from Earliest Times to the End of the Sixteenth Century*. Leiden: E.J. Brill.

Pourier, J.P. and Taher, M.A.

1980 Historical Seismicity in the Near and Middle East, North Africa and Spain from Arabic Documents (VIIth–XVIIIth Century). *Bulletin of the Seismological Society of America* 70: 2185–2201.

Pringle, D.

1986 *The Red Tower*. British School of Archaeology in Jerusalem Monographs 1. London: British School of Archaeology in Jerusalem.

Rafeq, A.-K.

1984 Land Tenure Problems and Their Social Impact in Syria around the Middle of the Nineteenth Century. In T. Khalidi (ed.), *Land Tenure and Social Transformation in the Middle East*, 371–396. Beirut: American University.

Reinhart, A.K.

1995 Legal Foundations. In J.L. Esposito (ed.), *The Oxford Encyclopedia of the Modern Islamic World*, 34–35. New York: Oxford University Press.

Rielly, K.

1989 Khirbat Faris 1989 Excavation Season: Interim Animal Bone Report. Unpublished archive report.

Riis, P.J. and V. Poulsen

1957 *Hama. Fouilles et recherches de la Fondation Carlsberg 1931–1938. IV. 2. Les verreries et poteries médiévales*. Copenhagen: Danish National Museum.

Robinson, R.

1983 Clay Tobacco Pipes from the Kerameikos. *Mitteilungen des deutschen archäologischen Instituts* 98: 265–284.

1985 Tobacco Pipes of Corinth and of the Athenian Agora. *Hesperia* 14: 147–203.

Rogan, E.L.

1994 Bringing the State Back: The Limits of Ottoman Rule in Jordan, 1840–1910. In E.L. Rogan and T. Tell (eds.), *Village, Steppe and State: The Social Origins of Modern Jordan*, 32–57. New York: British Academic Press.

1995 Reconstructing Water Mills in Late Ottoman Transjordan. In K. 'Amr, F. Zayadine and M. Zaghloul (eds.), *Studies in the History and Archaeology of Jordan V*, 753–756. Amman: Department of Antiquities.

1996 Asiret Mektebi: Abdülhamid II's School for Tribes (1892-1907). *International Journal of Middle Eastern Studies* 28: 83–107.

1999 *Frontiers of the State in the late Ottoman Empire: Transjordan 1850–1921*. Cambridge: Cambridge University Press.

Rogan, E.L. and T. Tell (eds.)

1994 *Village, Steppe and State: The Social Origins of Modern Jordan*. New York: British Academic Press.

Russell, K.W. and S.R. Simms

1997 Tur Imdai Rockshelter: Archaeology of Recent Pastoralism in Jordan. *Journal of Field Archaeology* 24: 459–472.

Saller, S.J.

1941 *The Memorial of Moses on Mount Nebo*. Jerusalem: Studium Biblicum Franciscum.

Sauer, J.A.

1993 The Pottery at Hesban and its Relationship to the History of Jordan: An Interim Hesban Pottery Report, 1993. In D. Merling and L.T. Geraty (eds.), *Hesban after 25 Years*, 225–281. Berrien Springs, MI: Andrews University.

Scanlon, G.

2002 Islamic Glass Bracelets: Some Hints from Fustat. In W. Ball and L. Harrow (eds), *Cairo to Kabul: Afghan and Islamic Studies presented to Ralph Pinder-Wilson*, 176–180. London: Melisende.

Schaeffer, J.

1989 Archaeological Remains from the Medieval Islamic Occupation of the Northwest Negev Desert. *Bulletin of the American Schools of Oriental Research* 274: 33–60.

Schilcher, L.

1991 The Grain Economy of Late Ottoman Syria and the Issue of Large-Scale Commercialization. In C. Keyder and F. Tabak (eds.), *Landholding and Commercial Agriculture in the Middle East*, 173–228. Albany: State University of New York.

Shami, S.

1989 Settlement and Resettlement in Umm Qeis: Spatial Organisation and Social Dynamics in a Village in North Jordan. In J.P. Bourdier and N.A. Sayyad (eds.), *Dwellings, Settlements and Tradition*, 451–476. New York: American Universities.

Silberman, N.A.

1982 *Digging for God and Country: Exploration, Archaeology and the Secret Struggle for the Holy Land 1799–1917*. New York: Knopf.

1989 *Between Past and Present: Archaeology, Ideology and Nationalism in the Modern Middle East*. New York: Holt, Reinhart and Winston.

Simpson, St. John

1990 Ottoman Clay Pipes from Jerusalem and the Levant: A Critical View of the Published Evidence. *Society for Clay Pipe Research Newsletter* 28: 6–16.

1995 Death and Burial in the Late Islamic Near East: Some Insights from Archaeology and Ethnography. In S. Campbell and A. Green (eds), *The Archaeology of Death in the Ancient Near East*, 240–251. Oxford Monographs 51. Oxford: Oxbow Books.

2000 The Clay Pipes. In R. Harper and D. Pringle (eds.), *Belmont Castle: the Excavation of a Crusader Stronghold in the Kingdom of Jerusalem*, 147–171. British Academy Monographs in Archaeology 10. Oxford: Oxford University Press.

Singer, A.

1994 *Palestinian Peasants and Ottoman Officials*. Cambridge: Cambridge University Press.

Spaer, M.

1992 The Islamic Glass Bracelets of Palestine: Preliminary Findings. *Journal of Glass Studies* 34: 44–62.

Steiner, M.

1995 Glass Bracelets from Tell Abu Sarbut. In K. 'Amr, F. Zayadine and M. Zaghloul (eds.), *Studies in the History and Archaeology of Jordan V*, 537–540. Amman: Department of Antiquities.

Turab

1996 *The Holy Sites of Jordan*. Amman: Turab.

Tushingham, A.D.

1985 *Excavations in Jerusalem 1961–67*. Toronto, ON: Royal Ontario Museum.

Volger, G., K. von Welck and K. Hackstein (eds.)

1987 *Pracht und Geheimnis*. Cologne: Rautenstrauch Joest-Museum.

Walker, B. J.

2001 The Late Ottoman Cemetery in Field L, Tall Hisban. *Bulletin of American Schools of Oriental Research* 322: 47–65.

2005 The Northern Jordan Survey 2003. Agriculture in Late Islamic Malka and Hubras Villages: A Preliminary Report of the First Season. *Bulletin of American Schools of Oriental Research* 339: 67–111.

Walker, B.J. and Ø. S. LaBianca

2003 The Islamic *Qusur* of Tall Hisban: Preliminary Report on the 1998 and 2001 seasons. *Annual of the Department of Antiquities of Jordan* 47: 443–471.

Walmsley, A.

1992 Fihl (Pella) and the Cities of North Jordan during the Umayyad and Abbasid Periods. In S. Tell, G. Bisheh, F. Zayadine, K. 'Amr, and M. Zaghloul (eds.), *Studies in the History and Archaeology of Jordan IV*, 377–384. Amman: Department of Antiquities.

Watson, P. and M. O'Hea

1996 Pella Hinterland Survey 1994:Preliminary Report. *Levant* 28: 63–72.

Whitcomb, D.

1992 Reassessing the Archaeology of Jordan of the Abbasid Period. In S. Tell, G. Bisheh, F. Zayadine, K. 'Amr, and M. Zaghloul (eds.), *Studies in the History and Archaeology of Jordan IV*, 385–390. Amman: Department of Antiquities.

Wimmer, D.H.

1978 Area G.4, 13, 15. In R.S. Boraas and L.T. Geraty (eds.), *Heshbon 1976*, 149–156. Andrews University Monographs 10. Berrien Springs: Andrews University.

Yeomans, L.

2003 The Mammalian and Bird Bone from Khirbat Faris. Unpublished archive report.

Ziadeh, G.

1995 Ottoman Ceramics From Ti'innik, Palestine. *Levant* 27: 209–245.

Sites and Places Mentioned in the Text **577**

Lightning Source UK Ltd.
Milton Keynes UK
UKHW051808050219

336792UK00004B/209/P

9 781845 530372